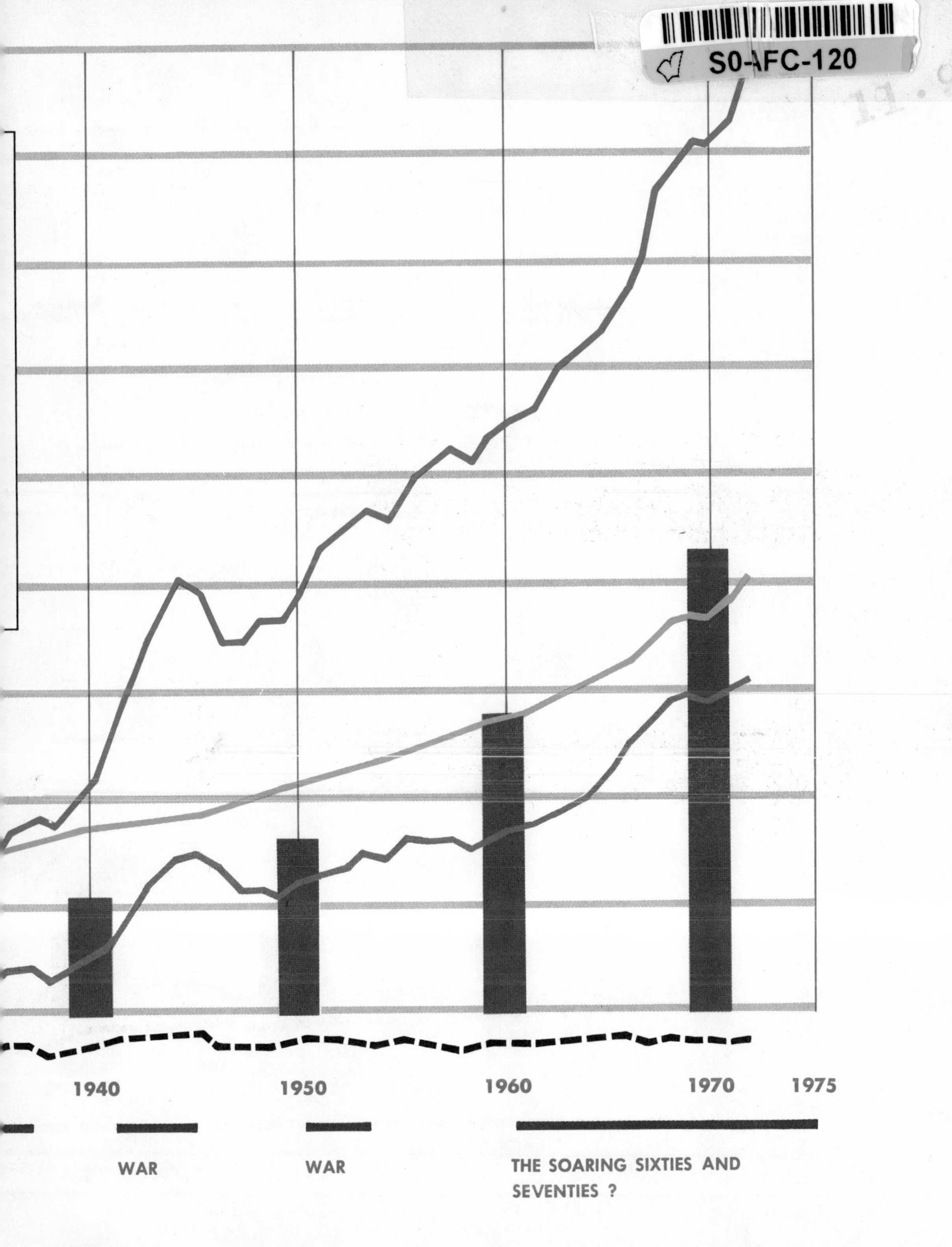
1940
1950
1960
1970
1975
WAR
WAR
THE SOARING SIXTIES AND
SEVENTIES ?

ECONOMICS

An Introduction to Analysis and Policy

ECO

PRENTICE-HALL, INC.

ENGLEWOOD CLIFFS, NEW JERSEY

NOMICS

An Introduction to Analysis and Policy

EIGHTH EDITION

GEORGE LELAND BACH

Frank E. Buck Professor of Economics and Public Policy, Stanford University

Library of Congress Cataloging in Publication Data

Bach, George Leland
Economics; an introduction to analysis and policy.

Includes bibliographical references.
1. Economic policy. 2. Economics.
HB171.B13 1974 330.1 73-17051
ISBN 0-13-227363-2

EIGHTH EDITION

ECONOMICS

An Introduction to Analysis and Policy

GEORGE LELAND BACH

Printed in the United States of America.

10 9 8 7 6 5 4 3 2 1

PRENTICE-HALL INTERNATIONAL, INC., *London*
PRENTICE-HALL OF AUSTRALIA, PTY. LTD., *Sydney*
PRENTICE-HALL OF CANADA, LTD., *Toronto*
PRENTICE-HALL OF INDIA PRIVATE LIMITED, *New Delhi*
PRENTICE-HALL OF JAPAN, INC., *Tokyo*

Contents

PART TWO

National Income, Employment, and Prices

PART THREE

Markets, The Price System, and The Allocation of Resources

PART EIGHT

The Changing Economic World

LIST OF CASES

SUGGESTED OUTLINES FOR ALTERNATIVE COURSES

course A / One Semester / Emphasizing MICROECONOMICS

(about 380 pages)

course B / One Semester / Emphasizing MACROECONOMICS

(about 390 pages)

course C / One Year or Two Quarters / MACRO FIRST

First Semester

(about 320 pages)

part	
I	Some Foundations
II	National Income, Employment, and Prices
VII	Economic Growth

Second Semester

(about 345 pages)

III	Markets, the Price System, and the Allocation of Resources
IV	Incomes, Economic Power, and Public Policy
V	Public Goods, Externalities, and the Public Sector
VI	The International Economy
VIII	The Changing Economic World

Course D / One Year or Two Quarters / MICRO FIRST

First Semester

(about 335 pages)

part

I	Some Foundations
III	Markets, The Price System, and the Allocation of Resources
IV	Incomes, Economic Power, and Public Policy
V	Public Goods, Externalities, and the Public Sector

Second Semester

(about 330 pages)

II	National Income, Employment, and Prices
VI	The International Economy
VII	Economic Growth
VIII	The Changing Economic World

Preface

Every teacher and every student deserves to know what the author of a text is trying to accomplish. This is a book focused on what the **student** does—written for students, not for teachers. The evidence is overwhelming that students retain little of what they learn in college economics courses unless they become interested enough to continue to use it as they read the newspaper and vote in elections, after they leave the classroom. If the text and the class do not kindle a real interest in economics and give them concepts and methods that they can use **for themselves** after the course is over, the student will retain little.

Thus the emphasis here is on:

- **A few key concepts, principles, and models—the core, no more, of essential theory; and**
- **How students themselves can apply these analytical tools to big and little, real-world, "relevant" problems.**

This is a good-sized book, not because its goal is to cram students full of information, but to provide teachers a variety of lively applications from which they can choose to fit the interests of their students. It is designed for either a full year or a one-semester course, especially reorganized for instructors who wish to introduce either macro or micro first.

The edition not only looks new. It is new, with the following innovations.

1. **Twenty-seven new, real-world cases, each attached to a chapter where it shows the student how to apply the concepts and principles developed in that chapter.** In addition, **Suggestions for Analysis** for each case, segregated at the end of the book, so that students can check their own reasoning and understanding of the concepts and principles involved. Some of the cases are simple applications; others involve more complex decisions on public policy or managerial issues; still others raise broad issues for analysis and discussion, where answers hinge on value judgments and the weighting of goals as well as on economic analysis.

The complete cases are listed in the Table of Contents. A sample:

- **How Much for Auto Safety?**
- **Cash or Food Stamps for the Poor?**
- **Does Capitalism Need War for Prosperity?**
- **Airline Takes the Marginal Route**
- **Advertising and Consumerism**
- **Battle of the Supermarkets**
- **Poverty and Inequality**
- **Marx, "Radical Economics," and Profits**
- **Black Economic Development**
- **The Urban Crisis**
- **Up or Out for Gold?**
- **The $66 Billion Mistake**
- **The Energy Crisis**

2. **A major new section (four chapters) on The Public Sector, which now accounts for about 30 percent of all economic activity.** This incorporates the new literature on collective choice, and emphasizes comparison between the private and public sectors as means of allocating resources.

3. **An exceptionally thorough treatment of two major macro issues: (a) inflation and unemployment,** including the latest theoretical and empirical material on the Phillips-curve issue; and (b) **money and monetarism,** with a thorough synthesis of monetary and fiscal analysis.

4. **Stress on the new "national priorities" (the environment, urban reconstruction, health, and so on) and means of compromising them with millions of divergent private wants.**

5. **A light, bright look, to make the book interesting and inviting to students.** A little help from Peanuts and a few New Yorker cartoons

to liven things up and to drive some key points home.

Beyond these innovations, the book is built throughout on new developments in learning theory and research:

Student motivation—cases and big and little applications to involve students.

Clear focus on objectives—what the student should learn and retain; see Chapter Previews and end-of-chapter lists of key concepts.

Learning retention—through repeated, explicit use of concepts and principles.

And it offers a varied selection of new, up-to-the-minute teaching aids:

Instructors Manual and Test Bank—2000 easy-to-grade objective and discussion questions; plus suggested examinations and suggestions on how to use the new cases. Free on adoption.

A delightful new *Study Guide* (by Michael Block and Henry Demmert), including programmed review materials, objective questions, cases, and dozens of imaginative new problems and crossword puzzles for all chapters. Answers included for student self-teaching and self-grading.

Economic Analysis and Policy—a new, up-to-date edition (with Myron Joseph and Norton Seeber) of the experience-tested readings volume, presenting conflicting viewpoints on key policy issues and problems.

Microeconomics and Macroeconomics—new editions (with Richard Attiyeh and Keith Lumsden) of leading programmed books to supplement the text if desired.

Black and white transparency masters—for all charts and major tables. Free on adoption.

Suggested divisions of the text for year-long courses putting macro or micro first, and for different one-semester courses, are included immediately following the Table of Contents.

Over successive editions, my indebtedness to colleagues and friends has become so vast that it is patently impossible to list all those who deserve credit. For this eighth edition, however, a number of economists at different institutions were kind enough to do major reviews leading to perceptive suggestions for improvements. I must thank especially Kenneth Alexander (Michigan Technical University), Michael Boskin (Stanford), Conrad Caligaris (Northeastern), Richard Cooke (University of Cincinnati), William Dunkelberg (Stanford), Sonia Gold (John Carroll), William Gunther (Alabama), James Gwartney (Florida State), Eric Herr (Indiana), Lewis E. Hill (Texas Tech University), Myron Joseph (Carnegie-Mellon), Sanford Kahn (University of Cincinnati), L. E. Kreider (Beloit), Stewart Lee (Geneva), Keith Lumsden (Stanford), John Megan (Milwaukee Area Technical College), John Pencavel (Stanford), Stephen Renas (Wright State), Phillip Saunders (Indiana), John Scadding (Stanford), Richard Sherman (Ohio State), and Nancy Spillman (Los Angeles Technical College). Professor Michael Lovell of Wesleyan University continues to share authorship of the mathematical appendixes. The usual warning that only I am responsible for the final outcome needs to be added, however, for I have accepted only some of the suggestions advanced. Lastly, I want to add my appreciation to Colette Conboy and Marvin R. Warshaw, of Prentice-Hall for their most valuable help in making the book more readable and attractive throughout, to Hildegard Shaffer for her many patient hours of typing, and to Perry Quick for preparing the index.

ECONOMICS

An Introduction to Analysis and Policy

SOME FOUNDATIONS

PART ONE

Economics: Theory, Facts, and Fantasy[1]

CHAPTER PREVIEW

CHAPTER ONE

How is it that we in America are, by and large, well-fed, well-clothed, and well-housed, while over two-thirds of the world's population is desperately poor—over two billion people living on per capita incomes of less than $20 per month? What explains the incomes we receive—$300,000 for Wilt Chamberlain, $20,000 for a master plumber, $2,000 for an itinerant fruit-picker? Why has big business boomed in some sectors of the economy (for example, autos), while in others small businesses seem to thrive (for example, dry cleaning)? Why do we have air and water pollution when almost everyone agrees that we need a cleaner environment? How can we have a better life for all, in the United States, and in the rest of the world?

These are questions of economics, these and many others like them. There are no simple answers to most of the questions. Indeed, most of this book is aimed at analyzing them. But although economics can't give simple answers to complex questions, it can go a long way in helping you understand the complex economic world in which you live and the issues on which you have to take positions and vote.

WHAT IS ECONOMICS?

Economics is the study of how the goods and services we want get produced, and how they

[1] Some instructors may prefer to assign Chapter 2 first, reversing the order of Chapters 1 and 2. They are written to be usable in either order.

are distributed among us. This part we call **economic analysis.** Economics is also the study of how we can make the system of production and distribution work better. This part we call **economic policy.** Economic analysis is the necessary foundation for sound economic policy, and this book is about both economic analysis and policy.

Another, slightly different, definition of economics, favored by many economists, is this: Economics is the study of how our scarce productive resources are used to satisfy human wants. This definition emphasizes two central points. First, productive resources are scarce, in the sense that we are not able to produce all of everything that everyone wants free; thus we must "economize" our resources, or use them as efficiently as possible. Second, human wants, if not infinite, go so far beyond the ability of our productive resources to satisfy them, that we face a major problem in trying to make the best possible use of our productive resources so as to satisfy the largest possible number of these wants. Indeed, most major economic problems arise from this fact of scarcity, and the need to make effective use of our resources to satisfy our wants. If there were plenty of everything for everyone to have without working or paying for it, there would be no economic problem. But, alas, this is not the state of the world, even in the affluent American society, and certainly not in the poorer economies that hold most of the world's people.

STRAIGHT THINKING IN ECONOMICS

Straight thinking is hard work. Few of us have acquired the careful, orderly mental habits and disciplines demanded by straight thinking.

For many people straight thinking is especially difficult in economics. Not that economics is inherently more difficult or more complex than many other fields. But economics is so mixed up with our everyday lives that, without realizing it, we have accumulated a mass of opinions, ideas, hearsay, and half-truths that subtly dominate our minds when economic questions arise.

It's not surprising then that most people have views on the economic questions stated in the first paragraph. They are in the newspapers every day, and in every election campaign. Moreover, the tendency for every man to be his own economist is strengthened by the fact that economics is close to the pocketbook. It is especially hard to be objective about things that affect us intimately. But merely living in the economic world doesn't make us experts on how the economy operates, any more than having teeth makes us experts on dental health and how to fill cavities. Few people consider themselves experts on bridge building just because they drive across a bridge every day going to work, or on physics just because they live in the physical world. Yet many people, especially if they've "met a payroll," somehow feel they are experts on economics simply because they are successfully living in the economic world. Alas, it ain't necessarily so!

Facts and Theory in Economics

The social scientist, unfortunately, can seldom run controlled experiments to validate his theories. We can't get everything else in the economy to stand still while we lower income taxes 10 percent to see just what would happen. Nor can we get reliable results by putting a sample of a few people in a closed room and lowering their income tax 10 percent. So how can economists be sure their theories are right—for example, that people do buy more of any product at a lower price than a higher one, other things equal?

The answer is that when we state a theory we then go out into the real world to see how well it works. What, for example, will happen to aggregate consumer spending in the economy, other things equal, if the government cuts consumers' income taxes by $1 billion? This is a very important question if we want the government to help get the economy out of a recession.

Suppose we theorize ("hypothesize") that the

amount people spend on goods and services in any year will depend stably on the after-tax, or disposable, income they have in that year. We hypothesize that consumer spending is a "function of" disposable income—that consumer spending depends on, or is predictably related to, the disposable (after-tax) income consumers receive. Economists write this functional relationship:

$$C = f(DI)$$

where C stands for consumption, f for "a function of," and DI for disposable income. To say that C is a "function of" DI means it "depends on" DI.

Suppose now that we get records showing the disposable incomes and consumption spending of a large number of families over the past ten years. Looking at these records, we find that most families have spent about 90–95 percent of their disposable incomes on consumption in most years, but there are many exceptions. For example, young families seem consistently to spend more, families in their fifties spend less, and retired families spend more. (These differences make sense if you think about it; young families are just starting out, buying new durable goods and raising babies, so they are able to save little; older families, once their homes are established and their children raised, find it easier to save out of their incomes; while retired families have reduced incomes and spend down past savings.) We also find that in years when incomes have risen rapidly, the percentage spent on consumption falls below .9. (Again, this seems reasonable, because it takes time for people to adjust their spending to new higher incomes.) And so we might find other special forces at work. But over all, for the average of all families in periods of reasonably stable, prosperous times, consumption hovers around 92–94 percent of disposable income. The value of f in the equation above will be .92 to .94.

From this statistical analysis we could not safely predict the behavior of any particular family without knowing a lot about that family. But on the hypothetical evidence cited we would be increasingly comfortable in saying that, *other things equal,* in reasonably stable, prosperous periods consumers *as a group* will spend about 93 percent of their disposable income on goods and services, given a reasonable amount of time to adjust to the new income.

This is an oversimplified theory, but it suggests the way in which we must go about building up reliable empirical evidence on economic behavior. Actually, as we shall see later, consumer behavior is more complex than this, and we need a more elaborate theory to explain and predict it satisfactorily. Indeed, even if we found that consumers, on the average, had *always* spent just 93 percent of their disposable income on consumption in the past, we still couldn't be *sure* they would do so in the future because they *might* change their spending-saving patterns. But through intensive empirical analysis of consumer behavior in the past, we can greatly increase our confidence in the predictions we make. And modern statistical techniques make it increasingly possible for us to use past information as a basis for predicting the future. Economics, like any other empirical science, must continually develop new theories, test them out against the real world, and reformulate them in the light of empirical evidence.

Facts and Fantasy in Economics

Robert Malthus, one of the first economists, saw economics as a dismal science. He predicted that population growth would persistently outrun the earth's capacity to feed it, so that man's standard of living would seldom rise much above the subsistence level. Malthus has proved to be spectacularly wrong in America and the Western world, but much more nearly right in many of the less-developed nations. Why did his theory largely square with the facts in some places, but turn out to be fantasy in others? Indeed, fantasy seems as common as fact in economics as we read it in the newspapers and hear it in everyday conversation. Consider some simple examples.

Even in rich America, between 10 and 15

percent of the population are "poor," with incomes below the government's officially-established poverty level of about $4,300 (in 1972) for a four-person urban family. Clearly, it would be desirable to get rid of poverty. Fantasy: If Congress would only pass a law requiring that everybody receive a minimum wage of $2.50 an hour, poverty could be abolished in one fell swoop. Taking about 2,000 hours as a standard full-time annual job, this would provide each worker with an income of about $5,000 per year, above the poverty level. Fact: It sounds great, but alas, it's in considerable part fantasy. Congress could pass such a law, but Congress could not make businesses keep on hiring everyone who now has a job, much less hire others looking for jobs, at the $2.50 hourly wage, which is much above the wage currently paid many workers. Indeed, we would predict quite the contrary from the fact that most businessmen are in business to try to make a profit. It would pay them to hire fewer workers at the higher wage per worker, and to substitute machinery for labor. Workers who kept their jobs at $2.50 per hour would, indeed, be above the poverty level, but unemployment would probably rise, other things equal. Moreover, of the approximately twenty-four million people living in poverty in the United States in 1972, some 60 percent were children, women with small children, elderly people, and others who could not take a job. Thus even paying a minimum wage of $2.50 per hour to all workers looking for jobs would leave a large portion of the poverty problem unsolved.

Second example. Nowadays, just about everybody agrees that we need to clean up the environment—cleaner air and cleaner water. Fantasy: If only greedy, profit-seeking businesses would become socially minded and stop polluting the air and water, the problem would be solved. Fact: Alas, pollution is a very complex problem. The government's Council on Environmental Quality estimated in 1972 that for the decade ending in 1980 it would take a minimum of $287 billion to clean up the environment enough to meet the minimum standards contemplated by government requirements at that time. All corporation profits after taxes in 1972 were only about $50 billion, of which about half was paid out in dividends to stockholders. Total dividends paid by all businesses in the ten years ending in 1972 were less than $200 billion. Thus it's clear that expecting "greedy" businesses to simply clean up all pollution runs up against some serious problems. For businesses to absorb all the costs would put many businesses out of business. There is little reason to suppose that profit-seeking businesses will simply absorb pollution-control costs. On the contrary, they will mainly pass the costs on to consumers, that is, to all of us, which is where the burden of cleaning up the environment is going to have to rest for the most part.

Moreover, businesses account for only a fraction of the total pollution in our system. Municipal sewage, primarily handled through government agencies, does more to pollute the waterways of our nation than do industrial firms. Farmers using fertilizers and pesticides on their crops, which help to produce low-cost food for all of us, did more to make Lake Erie a "dead lake" than all the businesses pouring waste into the lake, as the residues of the fertilizers ran off farmland into the lake. Alas, it's the old story. Total productive resources are scarce relative to our many wants. Cleaning up the air and water will be expensive. With cleaner air we will have more expensive food, steel, and automobiles, and we will have less of other things we would like.

But sometimes the fact is a happy one when the fantasy is a false black cloud. Fantasy: Communists and other radical critics often claim that the American economy cannot provide jobs for American workers except by waging wars like that in Vietnam—that the prosperity of America depends fundamentally on our involvement in military activities. Consider the Vietnam case. Fact: At its peak, the Vietnam war cost about $28 billion per year, of which about $8 billion would have been spent anyhow, leaving a net expenditure of about $20 billion. (By 1972 this figure had dropped to about $5 billion.) During these same years, total national production in the United States (the gross national product) averaged about $1 trillion per year. About 2 percent of total employment in the United

States depended on Vietnam war spending at its peak. It is highly implausible that the entire prosperity of the country should depend upon government expenditure on Vietnam equalling about 2 percent of total national production and providing only 2 percent of total employment. Similarly, of the approximately $90 billion of total U.S. corporate profits before taxes in 1970, about $250 million, or less than one-third of 1 percent, came from private investments in all of Southeast Asia.

On the theoretical side, as we shall see later, *if* government spending is essential to maintain total demand for goods and services so as to give jobs to all seeking them, the government can equally well spend on civilian-type activities (education, health, highways, and the like) and support total demand in that way. Military spending, in Vietnam or elsewhere, is not essential to maintaining prosperity in the American capitalist economy.

Consider last the speeches and newspaper stories one encounters on the public debt. Fantasy: A rising public debt means inevitable economic collapse and disaster, or at least inevitable runaway inflation. Fact: At the simple factual level, this fantasy has been persistently refuted for the last half century. The public debt has risen from less than $20 billion in the 1920s to nearly $500 billion in the 1970s, yet the American standard of living has risen persistently over the period. Total output is about five times what it was in 1929 and per capita real income (that is, income adjusted for inflation) is about three times what it was in 1929. The number of Americans holding jobs has risen from forty-eight million to eighty million over the same period. The growing national debt in the United States has been associated with rising total economic activity, and the debt today is less than 50 percent of total gross national product, about the same level as in the 1920s. Moreover, virtually all the government bonds are held by Americans, so, from the point of view of the public as a whole, the debt represents a transfer among Americans when we pay interest on it or when we pay off parts of it. In a growing economy both private and public debt can grow apace with total jobs and production without causing severe economic problems. This is not to say that there are no difficulties with the rising national debt; there are some. But it is to say, as in the other cases above, that the sweeping statements of doom here are fantasy, just as the sweeping statements of an easy road to a clean environment and the end of poverty are fantasy on the other side.

Conclusion: Economics is a field where it is easy to be led astray by the daily news and casual conversation. A major purpose of this book is to give you some tools so you can avoid such everyday fantasies. Economics can give you the analytical concepts and theories, as well as the facts, to see through a lot of the fantasies that you will encounter in the years ahead.

Economics as an Empirical Science

It is important at the outset to know something about how economists go about analyzing the complex economic world. Fundamentally, as the preceding sections suggested, economics is an empirical science. Like other sciences, it has to develop theories about the complex world in which we live; and these theories, if they are to be useful, must rest on validated facts and relationships about the world they are analyzing. The consumer-spending case above is an example. Consider in more detail how economics goes about this task.

The most apparent fact about economic reality is its complexity. There are millions of businesses, over 200 million consumers, hundreds of thousands of different products, multiple stages in the production of nearly every product. Faced with this overwhelming complexity, we obviously have to find some way of simplifying things to manageable proportions. Thus, the first job is to simplify.

Use of Simplified Models: Theory

In order to simplify, the economist, like other scientists, begins by developing an analytical framework, or model, of the reality he wants to analyze. This model focuses on the main elements and the main relationships he is studying. Such simplified models are often called "theories." They make no pretense of being accurate descriptions of the economy. If they were completely accurate, they would defeat their own purpose by getting back to all the detail. Instead, they are intended as highly simplified abstractions of the main elements of the reality to which they apply.

The notion of a model or theory can be illustrated by a noneconomic example. Suppose you want to understand how a bicycle works—a theory of its operation. You could study every detail of a single bicycle, or a large number of them, examining the tires, the handlebars, the sprocket, the paint, and so on. But if you could instead get a simple diagram, or a stripped-down working model of a bicycle, you'd get to the essentials quicker. This diagram wouldn't be concerned with all the details of paint, style, quality of steel, and so on. Instead, it would show the fundamental parts of the bicycle—wheels, frame, sprockets, driving chain, brake—and the basic relationships among these parts.[2] People have used such a model of a bicycle many times, and its predictions have been thoroughly validated by empirical evidence. The theory, or model, is thus a good one in that it helps us to understand the way a bicycle works and to predict the consequences of changing the main variables—for example, the sizes of the two sprocket wheels. The theory "works."

So it is in economics. A model is a simplified diagram indicating the main elements in any situation, and the main interactions among these elements. The more firmly validated these relationships are by empirical observation of many cases, the safer we feel in using them in our model. Some models are very sketchy, merely identifying the main elements and loosely stating their interrelationships. Others are more detailed.

An economic model may be stated as a diagram, and many graphs are used in the pages ahead. It may be stated in words, as in the bicycle case above. Or it may be stated in mathematical terms, but except for some simple algebra and geometry used in the diagrams, we shall use little mathematics.[3] Most economic models can be stated in any of these three ways.

Last, it is important to emphasize that the economist doesn't apologize for the fact that his theories don't describe the real world precisely and in detail. On the contrary, like any other scientist, he says that any theory is a skeleton, a framework, to help simplify the intricate complexity he is attempting to understand and predict.

"Other Things Equal" and "Equilibrium"

The real world is far too complex to analyze everything in it at once. Thus, in common with many other scientists, economists use the concept of holding "other things equal" in order to analyze the effects of one thing at a time.

In the chemistry laboratory, we hold "other things equal" through controlled experiments. We put two elements (say hydrogen and oxygen) together in a test tube **under controlled conditions,** and get water if the proportions are two to one. In the bicycle example above, we hold friction, gravity, air pressure, and various other factors constant as a first approximation (or assume them away altogether) in analyzing the way the bicycle works.

So it is in economics. One of the simplest, and most fundamental, theories in economics is that people will, other things equal, buy more of any good or service at a lower price than at a higher one. If the price of T-bone steak goes up, con-

[2]In terms of basic physics, it might help to have explanatory notes on the diagram indicating that the principles of mechanical advantage are used, with the pedal being a second-class lever and the relative sizes of the gear wheels being crucial in determining the speed and power resulting from any given foot pressure on the pedals.

[3]However, there is a set of special mathematical appendixes at the end of the book for students familiar with calculus. References are indicated in the chapters to which these appendixes apply.

sumers will buy less steak. Housewives complain bitterly, blame the greedy supermarket or farmer, and switch to lower-priced alternatives. But note that this is a safe prediction only if other things are equal. Suppose at the same time you get a big raise. Then you may well buy more T-bones even at the higher price. Or suppose the prices of pork, veal, and fish all go up even more than steak. Obviously the "other things equal" assumption is critical. In the real world, other factors may not stay constant; but by assuming temporarily that they do, we can analytically isolate the effects of the higher price for steak.

This idea is closely related to the concept of **equilibrium**, which is also widely used by other scientists. In chemistry, for instance, after we've combined hydrogen and oxygen to form water, this equilibrium state is maintained until something disturbs it. In the same way, economists generally think of the economic system as tending to move toward a new equilibrium whenever some disturbing change occurs. In talking about equilibrium, scientists are nearly always holding many other things constant to focus on the equilibrium of some part of the total system.

Consider a simple example. In economics, we generally theorize that people spend their incomes to get the greatest possible satisfaction from their expenditures. (Any other assumption obviously raises difficult questions as to why they don't switch to a satisfaction-maximizing spending pattern.) If people are allocating their incomes to maximize their satisfaction, given their incomes, we say they are "in equilibrium." Now suppose the government cuts taxes, so everyone's after-tax income rises. Consumers will now be out of equilibrium. With larger spendable incomes they will start spending more, and probably saving more as well, until their new spending pattern again maximizes their satisfactions, given their new higher incomes—that is, they adjust their spending and saving until they are again in equilibrium. Similarly, suppose you are in equilibrium, buying four pizzas per week, and the price of pizzas goes up sharply. You are thrown out of equilibrium and will presumably cut back your weekly pizza consumption, substituting some other stable-priced goody to restore your equilibrium. **By equilibrium we mean a situation in which those involved are satisfied to keep on doing what they are doing. In economic equilibrium, there's nothing at work to change the economic behavior under consideration.**

To repeat, "equilibrium" and "other things equal" are purely analytical concepts. No one believes that in the real world "other things" do always stay equal when we are trying to analyze the behavior of the economy, or that economic units are always in equilibrium. Use of these concepts simply helps us to trace through what *would* happen *if* all "other things" in the economic system remained unchanged until the new factor under consideration (such as the higher price for steak) had fully worked itself out. But don't think that this makes economic analysis just an intellectual game. Such analysis can give us powerful conclusions as to the *direction* that consumers, businesses, and the economy will move in response to different private actions or government policies, even if it can't always tell us precisely what the end result will be in the complex real world.

ECONOMICS IN A DEMOCRACY

These are the problems of economics. They, and many others like them—big and little, national and local, public and personal—are the problems of this book. Throughout your life, economics will play a major role in determining what you do and how happy you are doing it. If there are depressions or inflations, you will not be able to escape them. Your income will depend largely on how effectively you participate in the economic process. Thus, from a purely selfish point of view, it will pay you to understand how your economic system works.

But the main reason citizens in a democracy need to understand the economic system is that they are voters as well as active participants in the economy. Not long ago governments didn't interfere much in economic life, but that time has passed. Today, almost everyone agrees that the government should provide national defense, social security, education, and a score of other services not forthcoming through the private-enterprise economy; that it should regulate the supply of money; that it should protect consumers against the excesses of monopoly; that it should prevent depressions and inflations. Many people believe the government should do much more—provide medical protection for the poor, support the prices of farm products, legislate minimum wages, even guarantee full employment.

This is a book on "political economy." It is concerned with using economic analysis to find answers to the problems above and to many more. The goal is to understand how our economy works now and how to make it work better. The political economist doesn't sit on the sidelines. He is interested in what to do about the big and little problems we face.

But if you expect to find the answers in this book to what you or the government should and should not do, you're in for a disappointment. **The job of a course in economic analysis is to give you the tools and the background for making up your own mind on the important economic issues of the day, and to teach you how to think about economic problems—not to tell you what to think.** Better understanding of how the system works will go a long way toward making you a more intelligent citizen. But you should recognize from the outset that even with a thorough understanding of economics, not everyone will come out with the same answers on problems of public policy. This is because we have different ideas on where the nation ought to be headed. Some people, for example, think that avoiding inflation is the most important thing. Others believe that assuring everyone a reasonable minimum income should have first priority. Any respectable economist will advise the government to do different things, depending on which of these objectives is placed first. Such conflicts among the goals of different individuals and groups are an inescapable part of today's economic problems.

OBJECTIVES OF THE BOOK

If you're going to spend several months or a year studying a book, you deserve to know what the author is trying to accomplish. A good deal of the flavor of this book has been given in the preceding pages. It's a mixture of analysis and policy. But specifically, the book is aimed at these objectives.

1. **To provide an overview of the way our individualistic, largely private-enterprise but mixed, economic system works.**
2. **To focus attention on the big problems faced by our economic system, and to arouse an interest in these problems that will last after you leave college.** If your use of the concepts in this book ends with the final exam, the book will have failed. Its real goal is to help you read the newspaper, argue understandingly with your neighbor, and vote intelligently on economic issues over the years ahead.
3. **To provide a few fundamental analytical concepts and principles that will stick with you and help you in thinking about economic problems for yourself.** You need an economic tool kit.
4. **To help develop an orderly, systematic way of thinking through economic problems—of applying the concepts and theories in your economic tool kit.** There's nothing unique about straight thinking in economics. But the preceding pages have suggested that straight thinking here takes some real mental discipline.
5. **To provide enough descriptive material on the present economic system to give you a foundation for understanding what the problems are.** Without understanding a problem in its whole setting, there's little chance of solving it effectively. And knowing the crucial facts is a first step. But the book takes the position that your main job is to learn how to think straight for yourself, not to cram your head full of facts. A mind cluttered with transient details seldom sees the major issues. And few things will be deader ten years from now than many of today's facts. In any case, the evidence is clear that we

don't remember most of the facts we memorize anyway. So learn the main outlines of the economic system and the facts you need to understand each problem that you study. But don't make a fetish of facts.

SOME SUGGESTIONS ON HOW TO USE THE BOOK

The most important suggestions on how to use this book are contained in the preceding sections. But there are some tricks in using a book like this that may help you do a better job than just plowing through each assignment.

1. **Know Where You're Going Before You Start Reading.** Before you start a chapter, look at the "Chapter Preview" on the first page. Then skim through the chapter itself. Every chapter is organized so that the major headings mark off the main parts. These headings are designed to give a summary picture of what is covered, and to provide an outline of the chapter to help you keep the main points in focus. With this framework in mind, then study the chapter thoroughly.

2. **As You Read, Keep Asking Yourself, "What Is the Main Point of this Paragraph and of this Section?"** Try to put the ideas in your own words. Some sections are largely descriptive. Some are full of tightly reasoned analysis, usually supplemented by an example of how the analysis might apply. It's important to remember that the analysis is the main point; don't let the example become the center of your attention except as an example. To help you, main ideas are set in blue type so they will stand out. In addition, the old-fashioned devices of underscoring main points in the text and making notations in the margins can help in studying and reviewing throughout the book.

3. **Much of Economics Is Cumulative.** So if you don't understand a paragraph or a section the first time you read it, don't kid yourself. **Be sure you understand as you go along.** Otherwise, as the course goes on, things are likely to get progressively foggier, not clearer.

4. **When You've Finished Reading, Review to See What You've Really Learned.** A tough but very useful test is to shut the book, put aside any notes you have taken, and then write down in a few sentences the fundamental points of the chapter. If you can do this, you've read the right way—concentrating on the fundamentals and using the rest of the chapter as a setting for understanding them. If it takes you more than a page, you may have read the chapter well, but you had better recheck to be sure you have the central points clearly in mind.

REVIEW

For Analysis and Discussion

Throughout the text, these end-of-chapter questions are designed as a basis for class and out-of-class analysis and discussion. They are "think" questions. Drill and self-test questions and problems, to test whether you understand the mechanics of the theory presented and its use, are available in Michael Block and Henry Demmert, *Workbook in Economics,* (Englewood Cliffs, N.J.: Prentice-Hall, Inc., 1974), designed specifically for use with this text.

1. Why are we in America generally so well-off (per capita annual income nearly $5,000) while some two billion people in the less-developed nations are so poor (per capita incomes under $200)? Is your answer based largely on theory or facts? Or fantasy?
2. Why does the typical master plumber earn nearly $20,000 per year while the typical itinerant fruitpicker earns less than $2,000? Same questions as above on the basis for your answer.
3. Why do we have widespread air and water pollution when nearly everyone agrees we should have a cleaner environment? Same questions as in (1) on the basis for your answer.
4. What is a "theory?" A "model?"
5. Why should we assume "other things equal" in economics when we know they aren't that way in the real world?
6. We suspect that ten-year-olds' demand for ice cream cones depends on the temperature, their allowances, and the price of ice cream cones. Can you write an equation showing the demand for cones (D_c) as a function of these three explanatory variables? How might we go about determining the relative importance of the explanatory variables for ten-year-olds in a particular community?
7. According to the "laws" of probability, if you toss an unbiased penny 100 times, it will come down heads and tails about 50 times each. How does this compare with an economic "law"—for example, that, other things equal, people will buy less of any product at a higher than at a lower price?
8. "Theory is all right for college professors, but not for me. I'm a practical man. Give me the facts and they'll speak for themselves." Do you agree or disagree with this sentiment? Why? How do facts speak for themselves?
9. (*Based on the appendix*) Analyze the validity of the following statements. In each case, explain carefully why you accept or reject the statement.
    a. What goes up must come down. (True about prices?)
    b. Human beings are all different so you can't generalize about them. Just look at any five of your friends.
    c. In the past, booms have always been followed by depressions, so we can look forward to a real depression in the next few years.
    d. The way for farmers to get higher incomes is to raise larger crops. (Consider the position of the individual farmer and all farmers combined.)

APPENDIX

Some Common Fallacies

The preceding sections have outlined the positive job of straight thinking in economics. But the buzzing, booming, confusing world of economics seems to produce controversy everywhere. This appendix is intended to point up some of the common fallacies lying in wait for the unwary. Many of these fallacies, incidentally, show up everywhere you go, not merely in economics.

WISHING IT WERE SO. One of the most common of human frailties is to believe the things we want to believe. The boss believes his employee-education program is opening the worker's eyes to the necessity of large profits for continued prosperity—and he may be a surprised man the next time the wage contract comes up for renewal if he's just been wishing it were so. Remember the wishful thoughts on poverty and pollution control in the text above.

This is one of the most insidious fallacies. We tend to talk to people who agree with us, to read the newspaper that reports things the way we like, and to run away from information and conclusions that are painful to us. Confronted with two interpretations of an event, one favorable and the other unfavorable, most of us will choose the favorable one. The union members believe the company could pay lots higher wages if only it would. Top management believes that all right-thinking people see that management is right and labor wrong in most wage disputes. Just wishing it were so?

POST HOC, PROPTER HOC. Suppose there's a bad depression. The government pays out large sums on public-works projects. Six months later we're on the way up. Was the government spending the cause of the recovery?

Many people would say "yes." The government spent, and recovery came. What could be clearer? But maybe the recovery was on its way anyhow, and the government spending did no good at all. The observed evidence tells us that government spending *may* have caused the recovery. But the mere fact that one event precedes another doesn't necessarily mean the first caused the second. They both may have been caused by some third factor. To assume that causation can be determined so simply is the fallacy of **post hoc, propter hoc**—"after this, therefore because of it." Keep your ears open and notice how often people rely on this sort of reasoning, especially in discussing economic problems.

THE FALLACY OF COMPOSITION. Next, perhaps the most dangerous fallacy of all in economics—the fallacy of composition. Suppose one rancher increases his cattle production. He can reasonably expect that the increase will bring him more money when marketing time comes around. But suppose that all ranchers decide to raise more beef cattle this year. Will they get more money for the cattle in total? Quite possibly not. More cattle coming to market will, other things equal, push down the price of cattle. If prices fall a long way because of the increased production, the total revenue to all cattle farmers may be less for the larger output of cattle. Clearly what is true for one rancher alone is not necessarily true for all ranchers taken together.

Consider another example. Saving is obviously a sensible procedure for most families. But suppose that in a depression everyone decides to increase his savings. What this will mean, other things equal, is that everyone cuts down on his consumption expenditures. Unless someone else spends more, merchants' sales will fall off. People may lose their jobs. Incomes fall, and with lower incomes people may actually find they are able to save *less* than before.

There are examples elsewhere too. Suppose you're in a crowded hall and can't see the stage very well. So you stand on your chair and can see beautifully. But now suppose everyone else stands on his chair too. As a result, no one is better off. You can't conclude that what worked for you will work for the whole crowd.

To assume that what is true of one part will necessarily be true of the whole is the fallacy of composition. It may not seem reasonable that when we aggregate everybody together, everything may go topsy-turvy from the way it looked when we considered one person alone. But it does in economics, in a surprising number of cases. It's easy but fallacious to assume that what you know about the individual family or business is necessarily true for the whole economy.

REASONING BY ANALOGY. One of the most effective ways to explain something is to use an analogy. For example, in trying to explain the effect of continued repression on human behavior you may say, "Not letting someone express his feelings is like building up steam in a boiler." This conveys a vivid impression; if those feelings aren't let out, the person is going to burst like an overheated boiler.

Is the analogy a fallacy, or a useful means of communication? It may be either, depending on how closely a human being with repressions actually corresponds to a steam boiler. It would be difficult to communicate without using analogies, but don't let the analogies lead you farther than can be justified by careful analysis. Analogies are everywhere. For example, are big businessmen in economic life robber barons?

GENERALIZING FROM SMALL SAMPLES. "I know that businessmen are greedy; my grocer is always trying to palm off wilted vegetables and overripe fruit, and look at the huge profits big businesses make." Or, "I know that dogs like bones, because I've seen lots of dogs and they all like bones!" Such statements are a favorite way of backing up your position that you "know for a fact."

To generalize about all businessmen or about all dogs on your personal small sample is extremely dangerous, unless you have some convincing reason to suppose that this tiny sample is representative of the whole universe of grocers or dogs. There is probably no commoner fallacy than that of generalizing unthinkingly from small samples. We are continually learning from what we see and do; this is the commonest way of extending our knowledge. Thus we inevitably build up tentative generalizations about the world from our everyday experience. But anyone's limited experience may or may not be typical. The safest generalizations have been established by careful, systematic observation of a large number of cases. When is a fact a fact?

BLACK, OR WHITE, OR GRAY? There is another related fallacy. If you are not wary, you can go astray by (explicitly or implicitly) assuming that there is no middle ground between two extremes. On a foggy day, someone asks, "Is it raining?" You reply, "No." "Then," he may retort, "you mean it is sunny." But of course it may just be cloudy. Often there is a perfectly logical middle ground between what appear at first glance to be two mutually exclusive alternatives; the alternatives stated may not exhaust the possible situations. The wise observer of the economic scene is the one who sees the grays in their proper shadings—not the one who sees everything as black or white, true or false.

Private Wants and National Priorities

CHAPTER PREVIEW

CHAPTER TWO

The United States, it is said, is an affluent society. We are, indeed, rich by comparison with other nations. In 1972, the prodigiously productive American economy turned out nearly $1.2 trillion of goods and services, about 35 percent of the total production in the entire world, although only about 6 percent of the world's people live in the United States. Table 2–1 shows per capita output of goods and services in the United States as compared with a dozen other nations. We lead the Swedes and the Canadians, the next most affluent nations, by over $1,000 per person in total output, and we have roughly double the output per capita of Western Europe. Our lead over the so-called developing countries is enormous. (Such international comparisons are very rough, but they suffice to suggest orders of magnitude. We will examine them in detail later.)

In 1972, the median family income in the United States was about $11,100; half of all families received more and half less than this amount. (This is considerably less than output per family, because a large amount of total production goes into building factories, replacing worn out productive machinery and housing, and the like that are not directly income to families.) But not all Americans are affluent. Figure 2–1 shows the distribution of income in America in 1972. About 12 percent of all families were classified as "poor" by official government statistics; a typical four-person family liv-

TABLE 2–1
World Output per Capita, 1972[a]

COUNTRY	DOLLARS	COUNTRY	DOLLARS
United States	$5,500	Italy	$1,800
Sweden	4,400	Mexico	750
Canada	4,200	Brazil	400
West Germany	3,600	Egypt	200
France	3,300	China	150
Japan	2,500	India	100
United Kingdom	2,500	Ethiopia	70
USSR	1,900	Yemen	55

[a]Converted into U.S. dollars 1972 exchange rates.

For sources, more complete data, and an explanation of what is included, see Table 45–1.

ing in a city was considered poor if its income was $4,275 or less. By contrast, the median per capita income of over two-thirds of the world's population, over two billion people, was less than $200.

Figure 2–1

The United States has a wide range of family incomes. Each bar represents one-fifth of all families. Three-fifths of all families had incomes between $5,600 and $19,800, but the 20 percent with higher incomes received 40 percent of the national total. Half got more than $11,100, half less. (Source: U.S. Census Bureau; preliminary data.)

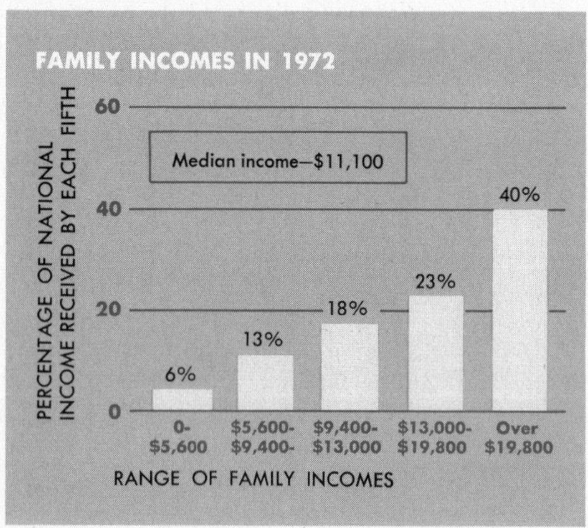

What did our huge gross national product of $1.2 trillion in 1972 include? We produced nearly one-half billion loaves of bread and 150 billion passenger-miles of air travel; about $3 billion worth of books, $3 billion worth of frozen fruits and vegetables, $2 billion worth of toys and games, over $60 billion worth of health services, and about $60 billion worth of educational services. The auto industry turned out about 10 million cars, bringing the total on the road to nearly 100 million. We built over 2 million new housing units, and over 95 percent of all existing housing had inside plumbing, a rarity among the world's nations. The economy provided jobs for over 80 million people, an increasing proportion of them in retail and wholesale trade, government, and other service occupations, in contrast to agriculture and manufacturing which had earlier provided most of the nation's jobs. Figure 2–2 presents a summary picture of what has happened to the composition of jobs in the American economy over the past century; the total number of jobs over the same period has risen by more than 400 percent from about 18 million in 1869.

With all this productivity, the American economy has also produced some of the world's largest slums in our great central cities, a growing amount of air and water pollution that threatens our health and the natural beauty of

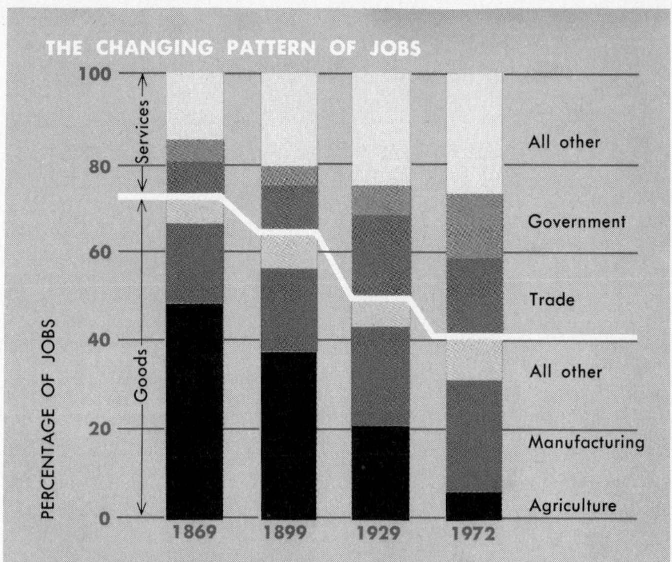

Figure 2–2

The past century has seen a dramatic change in the way Americans earn their livings. Today over 60 percent of all jobs are in service industries; only about 30 percent work at producing physical goods. Note the decline in agriculture. (Sources: National Resources Committee and U.S. Department of Commerce.)

the land, some wide discrepancies in the quality of education provided to students of different races and different locations, and substantially different opportunities for different people in our society. The average income of blacks was only about 60 percent of that of whites, although blacks' incomes have risen more rapidly since World War II than those of whites. Defense spending in 1972 totalled about $80 billion, enough to eliminate poverty and provide drastically improved education and health services for the American people if those resources could have been allocated to peaceful purposes.

Looking at these shortcomings, many Americans, including many college students, have recently called for a redirection of our national priorities. They say we are using our resources for the wrong purposes. They have challenged the traditional American emphasis on more production and more growth, calling for less emphasis on the "quantity" of GNP and more on the "quality" of life. Some radicals in the "New Left" argue that modern American society is a mess, characterized by inequality of income and opportunity, alienation, capitalist imperialism internationally, and a topsy-turvy set of values. Although most Americans find these criticisms grossly overdrawn, there is a widespread feeling that we need to reassess our national priorities, without giving up the demonstrated virtues of the American mixed-capitalist type of economy.

WHAT ARE OUR NATIONAL GOALS?

What are our national goals? Do we have our priorities straight? Are we producing the right things with our productive resources?

Unless we have at least a rough idea of what we want the economy to achieve for us, it is impossible to judge meaningfully whether it is doing a satisfactory job or not, and how we might improve it. Different people have different goals for the economy; this is one thing that makes it very difficult indeed in our individual-oriented system to agree on how well we are doing and what, if anything, ought to be done to improve matters. Economists often list a set of goals something like the following, focusing primarily on the economic aspects of life, as one useful way of stating the problem:

1. Progress: a rising average standard of living for the people.
2. Production in accordance with individual (consumer) preferences.
3. Equitable distribution of income.

4. Economic security.
5. Individual freedom and opportunity.

In the late 1960s a group of distinguished Americans prepared for the U.S. Department of Health, Education, and Welfare a thoughtful document, *Toward A Social Report*[1]. This commission chose seven major goals, or sets of goals, for emphasis:

1. Health and illness—Are we becoming healthier at a satisfactory rate?
2. Social mobility—Do we have enough equality of opportunity?
3. Income and poverty—How fast are we as a nation, and particular groups within the nation, becoming better off economically?
4. Physical environment—Is the environment improving or worsening?
5. Public order and safety—Does our society provide a safe, orderly environment for living?
6. Learning, science, and art—Are they enriching society as they should?
7. Participation and alienation—Is our system increasingly leaning toward participation and away from alienation for significant groups?

Other groups, for example President Eisenhower's Commission on Goals for America in 1960, have laid out their sets of national goals. But the two above will suffice to suggest what they are like. Clearly, one of the questions is how much stress should be placed on improving the standard of living of the American people and how much on other priorities that are only partially economic—for example, social mobility, reducing alienation, health, and the like. Moreover, it is clear that there may be conflicts between some of the goals listed, and in such cases we can obviously have more of one only by having less of another. For example, provision of complete economic security and more equality in the distribution of income for all might well reduce the incentive of many people to work hard and hence slow down the progress toward a higher average standard of living, or even reduce it.

There is a further problem—such goals have very different meanings to different people. For example, what is "individual freedom"? You and your roommate may have quite different ideas. What is an "equitable distribution of income"? The answer of an activist member of a minority group is likely to be very different from that of a comfortably situated white lawyer or businessman. Does "economic security" mean a guaranteed job, a guaranteed above-poverty standard of living, protection against the loss of a job because of ill health? Setting out an agreed list of overriding national goals is a far more difficult task than it seems at first glance. Everyone is in favor of a better life. But just what that means is highly debatable. The stylish statement that we need to redefine our national priorities sounds good, but the problem, again, is far more difficult than it may seem at first glance.

[1]Department of Health, Education, and Welfare, *Toward a Social Report* (Washington, D.C.: U.S. Government Printing Office, 1969).

PERSONAL WANTS, NATIONAL GOALS, AND PRIORITIES

If nature somehow provided free everything each of us wants, there would be no need to economize—no need to choose among alternative uses of resources. But alas, this is not the case. Affluent though we are by historical and comparative standards, our resources are far short of assuring that each of us can have all he wants without working for it. In this fundamental sense, our resources are scarce—limited in relation to our vast wants. **Given limited resources, we must choose what to have and what to forego. We must establish priorities.**

Consider housing, for example. America still has vast slums. Nearly everyone agrees that there should be decent housing for all. We might set as a national goal a modest $25,000 house or apartment for each family in the United States, a pleasant but certainly not luxurious home. But to achieve merely this one national goal would require about $1 trillion worth of new housing—the equivalent of over thirty years of our total housing production at peak construction rates. To achieve this goal in only one year or in a few years is obviously impossible, even if we gave it a top priority. We have neither the materials and labor, nor the manufacturing capacity for the components that it would take to meet such a goal. Nor is it clear how we could find the land on which to build all these houses in areas that would be pleasant and also reasonably close to the jobs of all the people concerned. It would mean dispersing and reconstructing virtually every one of the great urban centers that now mass people together in congested areas, and moving the jobs that go with them.

Consider another goal that seems less far-fetched. One thing the typical American wants is lots of electricity. He has a passion for gadgets that freeze, defrost, mix, blend, toast, roast, iron, sew, wash, dry, open garage doors, trim hedges, entertain with sound and picture, heat his house in winter, and cool it in summer. Residential use of electricity has been growing at some 12–15 percent per year, to which must be added the large increases for industrial and commercial use. The whole northeastern section of the country was shut down for hours in the great electric blackout of 1965, and temporary brownouts now threaten every summer in New York City and the entire Northeast.

To increase electric generating capacity to meet these soaring demands will require huge outlays—resources that cannot then be used for something else. Unfortunately, electric generating plants can be unsightly and often pollute the air and water around them. Electric transmission lines cut great scars across the countryside. Nuclear and fossil-fuel plants occupy scenic sights along the rivers and shores because their condensers require huge amounts of cooling water. The growth in private demand for electricity alone will, by 1980, mean that an amount equal to one-sixth of all fresh flowing water in the United States will pass through, and be heated by, the condensers of generating plants. How many new plants shall we build? Who shall be told no, when he wants to buy more electricity, and by whom? If we must choose, shall we have enough electricity to fulfill our wants, or landscapes and rivers free of the pollution and unsightliness of generating plants? Actually, at a high enough cost we can have both, all the electricity people want to buy and clean air and water around the plants, but the resources diverted from other uses would be huge.

So it is with myriads of other things some or all of us want. Rich as this nation is, we can't have them all. We must choose.

How Shall We Set Our Priorities?

Most of our individual wants are registered by purchases in the marketplace. We set our personal priorities when we decide how much we will spend on the different goods and services we buy. In earning our incomes, if we prefer money to leisure we set our own priorities by taking jobs where the pay is high even though the hours are long. When one adds together the actions of over 200 million individuals in the United States today, he gets the priority-setting mechanism for most of our economic activity and the machinery that satisfies the wants expressed in those priorities. To go back to the examples at the beginning of the chapter, who decided in 1972 that we should produce nearly a half billion loaves of bread? Answer: Millions of individual housewives voted with their dollars at the local grocery. And so it is for most of the things we produce in our economy. Over three-fourths of all the goods and services produced are in response to private demands expressed through the marketplace. Less than a quarter is in response to spending by federal, state, and local governments.

With over 200 million consumers, no one person has much individual market power over what gets produced. Indeed, one of the virtues of the market system is that each dollar spent counts as much as every other. The "little men" who each have only a few dollars can still register their own priorities in spending those dollars, and those priorities will be met by the market if the price they are willing to pay is higher than the cost of producing what they want to buy—

Upper-middle-class homes in Maryland. (M.E. Warren—Photo Researchers, Inc.)

not precisely nor in every case but by and large. Conversely, if consumers decide, for whatever reason, that they don't want to buy something, say cigarettes, profits in the cigarette industry will fall and fewer resources will be devoted to cigarette production. Thus in the private sector of the economy, how much is produced of different goods and services depends directly on the priorities of millions of consumers—on how many dollars consumers spend on that good or service. And the process automatically provides direct representation of majority and minority views. There is no formal ranking of national goals, no formal ranking of alternatives, but the result seems to many observers an impressively effective one in meeting individual priorities.

The other main approach to determining priorities is through the political process. We vote for representatives who will support those goals we consider most important. If your senator or representative votes to spend too much on national defense and not enough on urban reconstruction, you can vote for his opponent in the next election. (You can also use the political process to regulate how the private sector does its job, but we shall skip over that for the moment.) You, plus eighty million or so other voters, hold the ultimate power in determining what the government should or should not do, how much of the national output shall be devoted to priorities determined through the government and how much left in private hands. For when the government taxes income away from all of us and uses the money to buy highways, education, and moon shots, it is in that way determining national priorities.

These examples make it clear that defining national goals and priorities is far from simple. Arguments that we should alter our national priorities—for example, devote fewer resources

Lower-income homes in Baltimore. (Bradley Smith—Photo Researchers, Inc.)

Living standards vary enormously around the world and in the United States. Housing is a striking example.

Indian village. (Phillipa Scott—Photo Researchers, Inc.)

to the military budget and overpowered autos, and more to urban reconstruction and better diets for children—touch a responsive chord in many American hearts. Polluting the streams and the air, many argue, doesn't make sense. But, if so, what decision shall we make in the electricity-generating pollution case above? Who shall decide how much the cost of electricity should be increased to provide clean streams and unmarred scenery, and who should be shut out from the use of electricity?

Once in a while, the president will establish a major national objective and mass support behind it—for example, President Kennedy's statement in 1961 that we would send a man to the moon before 1970. But mainly the political process operates through adjustments at the margin—more for educational benefits next year, less for dams and highways, an increase in the income tax on high-income groups, a decrease on low-income groups. Unfortunately, it provides no simple process for reflecting minority votes on particular issues. You vote for *A* or *B* as your senator, and you have to take the bundle of preferences that is the winner, even though you like some and dislike others.

These descriptions of the market and political processes make both sound more effectively democratic than they are. In the marketplace, big corporations and big unions exert market power that sometimes overrides the wishes of consumers. The power of a billion-dollar corporation or a million-member union is constrained by competition in the market, but is by no means eliminated. Thus, the market process reflects individuals' priorities and wants only imperfectly. Advertising can sway and shape consumer preferences. Big business and big labor unions sometimes grab off for themselves more of the increase in consumer spending than is justified by the working of competitive markets. The market process doesn't work satisfactorily when big "externalities" exist—for example, where the production of some good (say steel) involves social cost (dirt and smoke in the surrounding neighborhood) not included in economic costs paid by the producers and hence not included in the price of steel to consumers. In such cases, people buying steel products don't pay the full cost and the burden is borne by those who have to live with the dirt and grime. In all these cases, people tend to turn to the government to express their new priorities—a better deal for consumers, controls on big business and big labor, regulations to control pollution put out by steel mills and other polluters.

Similarly, governments, and the bureaucracies that often control them, also have a power of their own. "The public" is vast but generally unorganized. The political process is *ad hoc,* pragmatic. Those who are most concerned over issues take steps to get their viewpoints across to Congress and the administration, and to state and local governments. Those who feel helpless or who don't care so much are apt to be silent. Minorities who feel strongly enough can sometimes get their wishes heeded—indeed, they can override the majority. The net result is very uneven; sometimes it seems as if the administration in power, and the lobbyists, can get anything through, however contrary it may be to the "public interest." The American democratic political system is a far-from-perfect instrument for finetuning national policy, though it generally works, albeit slowly sometimes, on the big issues. Most Americans feel there is no obviously superior political process that might replace it, but the practical results of government are far from the theoretical one-man–one-vote democratic model.

Clearly, our political and economic processes do not represent neat, orderly ways of establishing and implementing our private and national goals and priorities. Both the American economy and the American political system are pragmatic, adaptive mechanisms. With over 200 million people, they both disperse power widely among many individuals and groups—though in the eyes of some, not widely enough. In the market, Madison Avenue is said to have too much power to mold consumer preferences. In the political process, legislators and bureaucrats seem inadequately responsive to what the people want.

Nonetheless, the marketplace and the political process are the two big mechanisms we have in America for reflecting and compromising individual and group wants, individual and national priorities. Parts Three and Four examine the marketplace as a mechanism for meeting consumer wants and priorities, and some of the government interventions and controls that we have established to make the system work better. Part Five then looks in detail at how well the political process (the "public sector") reflects individuals' wants and priorities.

CONCLUSION

As you read, formulate your own personal priorities and what you think our national goals and priorities should be. One view, emphasizing the private marketplace, denies that it is meaningful to formally list "national goals" at all in a nation of 200 million individuals where individual freedom is the overriding goal. If individual freedom is dominant, the only meaningful national goals are those that arise out of the combined free actions of individuals acting in accord with their own wishes. But a lot of other people reply that somehow this doesn't get a lot of the most important things done very well—rebuilding the cities, protecting the environment, eliminating poverty, and so on—and that we need to rely on government more. Either approach we take, it is essential to remember that the fundamental problem is one of choice. Since we don't have enough resources to produce all of everything everyone wants, somehow we have to establish priorities as to what shall be done with our productive resources. And the more efficiently we use them, the better off we will all be.

REVIEW

For Analysis and Discussion

1. Do you believe the uses of our productive resources (bread, autos, and so on) in 1972 described at the beginning of the chapter were optimal? Who decided these were the right things to produce? What should we have produced?
2. What is your list of major national goals?
3. Can you establish priorities among those goals? If so, what are they?
4. What are your personal economic priorities? Are they different from the national priorities you list? If so, why are they different?
5. How should we as a nation set our national goals and establish operational priorities among them? Who should determine the goals and priorities? Should we use the market or the political process?
6. Are you more likely to achieve your personal economic goals if we rely on the market or the political process to establish our national priorities—for example, on the issue of equalizing incomes and abolishing poverty?

CASE 1

How Much for Auto Safety?

In 1973, over 50,000 persons were killed in automobile accidents. Over 2 million were injured. On the other hand, of the over 150 million Americans who rode in autos that year, over 98 percent went through the year with no auto accident injury. Until 1972, Americans were free to decide for themselves whether or not to invest in such auto passenger safety equipment as seat belts, which have been available as optional equipment on all new U.S.-made cars since the 1950s, and the vast majority decided not to. But in 1972, Congress made seat belts, padded dashboards and visors, and safety glass windshields mandatory equipment on all new cars; and by 1976, automatically inflatable air bags will also be required in all new cars unless Congress modifies its new legislation in the meantime. Together, all the required passenger safety features will probably raise total cost and, hence, the price, by perhaps $100 per car. Congressional action to require this safety equipment reflected widespread demands from consumer safety advocates that we "do something to end this needless slaughter on the highways." The result was a requirement that new car buyers each year spend about $1 billion on seat belts, air bags, and other safety features that, by the test of the pre-legislation market, most would not buy voluntarily. (New car sales are over 10 million annually.)

Is the new auto safety legislation desirable? Should Congress have decided for all new car buyers that they must spend $1 billion annually to protect themselves against injury in possible auto accidents, or should each citizen be free to decide for himself how much he wants to spend to protect himself?

Stop and analyze the issue for yourself before you go further. To help you, there are at the end of the book, for this and for each case, suggestions to help you with your analysis. But this case and all the others that follow are primarily designed to get you to use independently the concepts and principles in the chapter each follows. You will learn most if you work the cases through yourself, possibly in discussion with others, before you check your solution against the suggestions for analysis.

Private Enterprise, Government, and the Price System: An Overview

CHAPTER PREVIEW

CHAPTER THREE

The purpose of this chapter is to provide a brief overview of the way our largely private-enterprise system works. It begins by presenting the foundations of production in any economic system and the fundamental problem of economizing. It then briefly outlines the way our system solves the four big economic problems. The purpose of the overview is to provide a road map for the more detailed chapters to come, so you can see the forest while you are busily studying some of the trees of the economy. It concludes with a look at the role of government in the system. Ours is a mixed system, fundamentally capitalist and market-directed, but with a large amount of government intervention.

THE FOUNDATIONS OF ECONOMIC PROGRESS

Our standard of living depends on the resources at our disposal and the effectiveness with which we use them. The United States is rich in natural resources; it is rich in produced resources, such as factories, houses, and machinery; and it is rich in human resources, the most important of all. We have the world's most advanced technology, and vast research expenditures generate a steady stream of new products and new methods. The American businessman, continually watched over by the government and consumers, somehow manages to keep the whole combination going in a way that excites the mixed envy, dismay, and sometimes disdain of his less aggressive counterparts in the rest of the world. These resources and this technology are the real foundations of the American standard of living—of our sweeping growth over the centuries.

In addition, we have developed a high degree of economic specialization and a complex exchange system. How many people do you depend on to get your everyday economic wants satisfied? You may say, not many. But think a minute. Who built the house you live in, and who provided all the materials to build it? How about the car that you drove to school, or the shoes if you walked? Where did your breakfast come from? Suppose you take in a movie tonight or watch TV. How many people have had a hand in making this possible?

To produce all the things we want takes many people, each specializing in what he can do best. Charlie Chaplin immortalized the forlorn worker on the assembly line, day after day screwing his single bolt onto the cars as they went by. But specialization goes far deeper than this. The engineer who designs the plant is a specialist. So is the banker who lends money for its construction. So are the accountant who keeps the records and the secretary who does the typing. Only by dividing up tasks and developing highly specialized human skills and equipment can the economy obtain the benefits of "mass production."

But specialization and division of labor would be fruitless without a system for exchanging the goods and services produced by the specialists. The lawyer, the banker, the truck driver, the engineer—all would starve if the intricate system of exchange we take for granted didn't enable them to buy the food they need with the incomes they earn. Even the farmer who might eat his own carrots and potatoes would be in desperate straits if he were really cast on his own—without electricity, new clothing, gas for his car, mail delivery, and the thousand things he gets from other specialists. Every minute of our daily lives we depend on the specialization and exchange all of us take for granted. None of us would dare specialize if we couldn't count on being able to exchange our services and products for the wide range of things we want.

(1) Productive resources, (2) technology, (3) specialization, and (4) exchange. These are the four foundation stones of the productive power of the American economy—and of every other highly developed modern economy, communist or capitalist. These four basic factors make the difference between poverty and plenty. Many of the most common economic fallacies are rooted in the neglect of these simple truths.

THE NEED TO ECONOMIZE

As Chapter 2 emphasized, because resources are scarce relative to what we want from them, we must "economize" them. That is, we must choose among alternative ways of using our resources to satisfy the largest possible share of human wants with them. We need to economize time, money, and productive resources, anything that is scarce, if we are to best fulfill our private wants and achieve our national goals.

For most of the world, economic scarcity is painfully evident; hundreds of millions live on the edge of starvation. Even in the United States we must choose between alternatives when we would like to have both. At the individual level, few of us have all the money we want. If you buy a car, you can't afford a new stereo set too. Time is a scarce resource. It would be nice this afternoon to play golf, to go to the movies, to study, and to pick up some spare cash by working, but you can't do them all at the same time. If we use land for a shopping center, we can't use it for a school. If we use steel for autos, we can't use it for refrigerators. If we use engineers to design missiles, they can't work on pollution control devices.

For the nation as a whole, the heavy hand of war points up vividly this fundamental dilemma of scarcity. In 1973 we spent over $80 billion—about 7 percent of our total national production—on "national defense." If the government had merely left this money in the hands of taxpayers, on the average every American family would have had nearly $1,500 more to spend on clothes, housing, recreation, and the like.

Unemployment and Depression: An Exception?

Few deny the basic fact of economic scarcity in the world today. Yet in America the newspaper headlines sometimes tell of millions unemployed, of auto factories idle because the public doesn't buy enough cars, of massive waste of men and machines because there isn't enough demand to buy the goods and services that could be produced with everyone at work. How can this be reconciled with the proposition that limited resources and scarcity are the basic economic problem?

Widespread unemployment of men and factories reflects a breakdown in our economic machinery. Resources are still limited relative to the vast unsatisfied human wants they might help to fulfill. People still desire better houses, more food, more of almost everything. The unemployed want jobs. Businessmen want to increase production and give them jobs—if only they could sell their products. A million men involuntarily unemployed for a year means between $5 billion and $10 billion worth of potential output lost forever. In depression, we mistakenly and involuntarily allocate part of our scarce productive resources into unemployment and waste. Part Two examines the reasons in detail.

CHOOSING AMONG ALTERNATIVES

Economists are fond of illustrating the problem of economizing with an economy that must choose between guns and butter, between bombers and bungalows. These symbolize any two competing groups of commodities for which we might use our resources.

The Production-Possibilities Curve

Assume that our economy has a fixed stock of productive resources (land, labor, machines, and the like) and of technological knowledge about how to use these resources in producing the things we want. With these resources and this technological know-how, we can produce guns or butter—military or civilian goods—or a combination of the two. To simplify, assume that only those two commodities (or groups) can be produced.

Table 3–1 shows the hypothetical range of possibilities open to us. If we use all our resources to produce houses, we can have 1 million bungalows a year. Or if we use all our resources to produce bombers, we can have 50,000 bombers. In between, various combinations are possible—for example, .8 million bungalows and 15,000 bombers, or .6 million bungalows and 28,000 bombers, and so on.

The point of this table is to show the production possibilities open to us. Of course, bombers and bungalows are merely arbitrary examples. We might have used highways (a public good) and refrigerators (a private good), or any other pair of products to illustrate the same point. The important thing to see is that there is a **tradeoff** between the two commodities. We can get more of one only by giving up some of the other.

It is convenient for many purposes to put the

TABLE 3–1
Production Possibilities for Bungalows and Bombers

ALTERNATIVES	BUNGALOWS (IN MILLIONS)	BOMBERS (IN THOUSANDS)
1	1.0	0
2	.8	15
3	.6	28
4	.4	38
5	.2	45
6	0	50

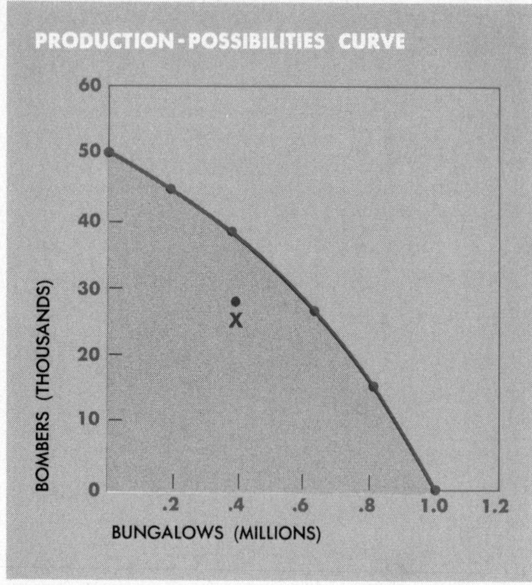

Figure 3–1

The curve shows how many bombers, how many bungalows, or what combination of the two we could produce with our limited resources.

production-possibilities table in the form of a curve, or graph. This is done in Figure 3–1.

Economists use graphs a great deal, so it is important to understand how to read them. In Figure 3–1, we show millions of bungalows along the horizontal axis and thousands of bombers along the vertical axis. Each heavy dot plots one of the production-possibility combinations from Table 3–1. For example, the top dot shows that we can produce 50,000 bombers and no bungalows (alternative 6 in Table 3–1). The next dot shows we can produce 45,000 bombers and .2 million bungalows, and so on for the other dots. The figure is merely a graphical representation of the table, with a curve connecting the dots.

Some Applications

The production-possibilities curve can help illuminate a variety of economic problems. Suppose that, perhaps because of a depression, the economy only produces 28,000 bombers and .4 million bungalows, as shown by the dot labeled *x* to the left of the production-possibilities curve. This dot shows that the economy is not fully utilizing its productive capacity, as in fact happens during depressions. To operate at point *x* is clearly to waste productive resources. We could have had an additional .2 million bungalows and the same number of bombers, or an additional 10,000 bombers and the same number of bungalows, if we had employed all our resources. Point *x* shows the economy operating *inside the production-possibilities frontier*. We are inside the frontier when for some reason we don't fully utilize our productive capacity.

Now suppose that immigration occurs, so that we have more workers than before, or that scientists improve technology, so we can obtain more output from the same amount of resources. Then

Figure 3–2

If a nation's resources expand or its technology improves, its production-possibilities curve moves out to the right. This expansion of productive capacity is the essence of economic growth.

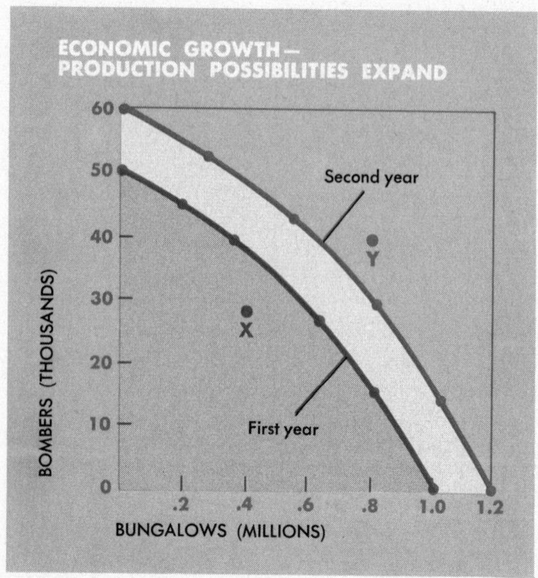

there will be a new production-possibilities curve to the right of the first-year curve. This is illustrated in Figure 3-2. The curve labeled "first year" is the same as in Figure 3-1. The curve labelled "second year" is farther out, to the right. This new curve for the second year shows economic growth. The economy can now produce a larger total output—more houses and the same number of bombers, or vice versa, or a combination involving more of both.

Suppose the economy tries to produce 40,000 bombers and .8 million houses (shown by point *y*). Clearly this is impossible. Production will fall short of one target or the other, or both. The economy cannot produce more than its production-possibilities curve permits.

COOPERATION AND COMPETITION IN A PRIVATE-ENTERPRISE ECONOMY

Let us focus first on the private, market-directed sector of the economy. How does it allocate our scarce production resources?

Consider New York City, teeming with eight million people crowded into a few square miles. As Bastiat, a famous economist, remarked about the Paris of a hundred years ago, here are millions of human beings who would all starve in a short time without a constant flow of provisions into the metropolis. Hardly one could support himself for more than a few days without help from the far corners of the nation. "Imagination is baffled," Bastiat wrote, "when it tries to appreciate the vast multiplicity of commodities which must enter tomorrow in order to preserve the inhabitants from falling prey to the convulsions of famine, rebellion, and pillage. Yet all sleep, and their slumbers are not disturbed for a single minute by the prospect of such a frightful catastrophe."

Every day, New York City gets hundreds of tons of meat, huge amounts of fresh vegetables, coal, oil, furniture. Every year, it gets millions of shirts, automobiles, rugs, hairnets, movies, and more other goods and services than you can think of. Yet no individual, business, or government agency plans it that way. The same is true, on a smaller scale, of every city and village throughout the country.

Man lives by cooperating with his fellow men. In all economics there is no more basic truth. And in the modern American economy this cooperation is indescribably broad and complex. Yet this vast cooperative system, as a system, has not been consciously designed by man. No human director tells the eighty million workers in the United States where to work, what to do, or how to do it. Somehow the system seems to organize itself, with a minimum of central planning or direction. Viewed from above, Adam Smith wrote 200 years ago, it is as if a beneficent invisible hand were guiding the competitive, private-enterprise system to allocate our scarce productive resources to produce the most of what we want at the lowest possible costs.

Man can organize, and indeed he has organized much. Tens of thousands of workers are employed in some large industrial plants. Often many of these huge plants are joined together in a single organization. The General Motors Corporation, for example, spreads over the entire world, with over 750,000 employees, and annual sales of $30 billion. But in spite of the immense power of such huge aggregations, each business concern plays a tiny part in the total picture of organizing economic resources to satisfy human wants in our $1.2 trillion economy. And in spite of the great expansion of government controls, the private enterprise economy still does the bulk of the job in its long-established, unplanned way—in contrast to the central plans that control our biggest rival, the Soviet economy.

HOW A PRIVATE-ENTERPRISE SYSTEM SOLVES THE BASIC ECONOMIC PROBLEMS

Even though you may be swallowing hard on the beneficent invisible hand, patience! We shall examine the problems in due course. It is useful first to summarize in a systematic way how a private-enterprise system allocates resources to solve four basic economic problems, continuing to disregard government intervention.

How It Decides What to Produce

Under a private-enterprise competitive, free-price system, consumers control what is produced. Consumers register their preferences by the amount of money they spend on various goods and services. The more you want something, the more you will spend on it and the higher price you will be willing to pay for it. This is how the price system decides which are the most important goods and services to produce. The price consumers will pay for each good is a signal of how much of it they want produced.

But one point is vital. In order to count, consumer demands have to be backed up with dollars. The price mechanism is hard-boiled, impersonal. It produces Cadillacs for millionaires when poor youngsters have no toys. Prices reflect not how much consumers "need" goods and services, but how much they are willing and able to pay for them.

How It Gets the Goods Produced

The goods and services consumers want get produced by businessmen in search of profits. They will make the largest profits by producing

The high American standard of living rests on mass production and modern technology, in assembling Chevrolets and in picking cotton.
(Courtesy of General Motors—Chevrolet Division)

(Joe Monroe—Photo Researchers, Inc.)

things whose prices most exceed their costs of production. Profit-seeking businessmen thus have an incentive to produce more when consumer demand bids up the price of anything. They equally have an incentive to reduce their costs of production because that too will increase their profit margins. In producing more, businessmen will offer more jobs in those industries, and workers will be pulled into the production of the most-wanted goods because that is where they will be able to earn the largest incomes.

But, alas for the businessman! If competition prevails, whenever he finds a high-profit venture those high profits will lure other profit seekers into the same industry. Thus, although he may temporarily make big profits by meeting new consumer demands or reducing costs without cutting prices, the competition of rivals will soon increase output and force prices down to a level where they just cover costs and a normal profit. Why does the businessman keep trying if he knows competition will eat away his excess profits? Because many businessmen are optimists, and he may make handsome profits while he leads his rivals.

Thus, the businessman is essentially a link between consumers and productive resources. His private goal is to make profits, but his social function is to organize productive activity in the most efficient (lowest-cost) way possible and to channel productive resources toward industries where consumer demand is strongest. Profits are the mainspring of the system—the carrot in front of the profit seeker. In seeking profits, the businessman performs a vital social function. And prices play a key role in allocating resources to where consumers want them most.

How It Distributes Products

Who gets the goods that are produced? The market system allocates them to those who have the desire and the income to buy them. There are two steps in this process.

The first is the distribution of money incomes. We earn our incomes primarily by working for businessmen, helping to produce the goods and services consumers want. The prices we get for our services depend on how much we are worth to the businesses we work for. Competition forces the businessman to pay each of us about what he contributes to the sale value of what he is producing. **The incomes we receive in this way largely determine what we can afford to buy.**

The second step is the distribution of goods and services to those with money income to pay for them. The price of each commodity is bid up until the buyers least able and willing to pay for it are eliminated. This does not necessarily mean that low-income buyers are eliminated completely. Often it means that they can afford only a few units at the price established, while higher-income groups can afford more. Poor people buy steaks, but not many. In other cases, such as mink coats and country estates, the poor are eliminated from the market. **Here again prices play a vital role; they ration final products among consumers.**

How It Decides Between Present and Future: Economic Growth

We can use our productive resources either for current consumption or for capital accumulation. By building new factories and other productive facilities, we can shift the economy's productive-possibilities curve out. In the same way, we can send our children to school rather than putting them directly to work, thereby investing in "human capital" and increasing the nation's future productive potential at the cost of lower present output. Here again, the private-enterprise system largely depends on the free decisions of consumers and profit seekers to allocate resources between present and future.

In money terms, to grow we must save some of our incomes and invest some in building new factories and the like, rather than spending everything on consumption. In our individualistic economy, each person and each businessman decides how much of his income to save. If these savings are a large proportion of our total income, investment in factories and people can be large relative to current consumption and the economy will grow rapidly. If we save only a small proportion of our total income and investment is correspondingly small, the growth in productive capacity will be slow.

Solving All the Problems Simultaneously

These four major decisions are not made separately. The economic system is a huge, interconnected set of markets, each with many buyers and sellers. All four big decisions are simultaneously the outcome of millions of free, individual choices by people largely concerned with their own private welfare. How all these complex decisions are simultaneously and continuously made and how they interact in our economic system is the core of the study of economics.[1]

The Organizers: Self-Interest and Competition

If you look back, you will see that we rely chiefly on private initiative, in search of wages and profits, to get the job done. Self-interest is a powerful incentive for consumers, laborers, businessmen. Indeed, labelled "greed" it might well lead to chaos if it were not constrained and directed to the common good by the force of competition, which Smith properly stressed as absolutely essential to the working of the "invisible hand." With competition and effective markets, Smith and his followers argue, in a private-enterprise economy absence of planning and control does not mean chaos, but rather order in an economy so complex few human minds can comprehend it.

Suppose, for example, that instead of relying on private initiative and the market, you were made Grand Economic Planner for the nation. How, for example, would you decide whether Joe Jones ought to spend his time grinding fine edges on a machine tool later to be used in manufacturing tractors later to be used in producing corn later to be fed to hogs later to be eaten as pork; or whether he ought to spend his time making TV cabinets, or flying an airplane, or operating a corner grocery store? What would you do about the minor problem of how many sheep to raise, when each sheep yields both wool and mutton, the demands for which are almost completely independent? Wool is used for clothing, blankets, rugs; mutton is used for dinner. How are you going to make them come out

[1]In mathematical terms, it may be helpful to think of all these interdependent markets and decisions as a large system of simultaneous equations. In fact, one of the first clear perceptions of the entire process was by Leon Walras, one of the first mathematical economists, who saw it just that way about a century ago.

even? How would you decide who is to have the tractors and corn and cabinets and mutton and wool once they are produced? This is the merest suggestion of the problems faced—and it matters not whether the economic system is capitalist, communist, Fascist, or what not. Somehow these decisions have to be made.

The Incredible American Economy

It's easy to find things wrong with a largely private-enterprise, "unplanned" economy, like ours. Today's world is different from that of Adam Smith, and a lot of people feel that Smith was way too optimistic, that any market-type economy will fall short on many scores. But thoughtful observers, even including such critics as Karl Marx, have long been impressed by its remarkable efficiency in producing the infinite variety of goods and services consumers want.

Understanding how a market-directed economy solves the basic economic problems is a number one task in studying economics. But this is a lesson that must not be overlearned. We can understand and admire the way the private-enterprise, market-directed system ticks on year after year, impersonally solving its millions of intertwined problems, and still not shut our eyes to its failings. For failings there are—drastic ones, some people think. The invisible hand must have slipped up, they say, to produce those continuing huge profits for billion-dollar corporations, all that smog outside the window, filthy streets and decaying slums.

THE IMPORTANT ROLE OF GOVERNMENT

We have left government out of this overview so far. But it is time now to turn to the important role government plays in the modern American economy. There are a lot of doubters about that invisible hand. A little history can help provide perspective.

The British, French, and American revolutions that gave us political democracy provided the ideological framework for economic individualism. Political democracy and modern private-enterprise economics arose in the same historical setting, part of the same broad sweep of history. Individual freedom and self-interest were at the core of this revolution of the eighteenth and nineteenth centuries. In politics, every man should be free to vote as he pleases—to look out for his own interests at the ballot box. In economic life, every man should be free to seek his own self-interest—to work where he wished, and to spend his money on whatever he wanted most. Self-interest and individual initiative were the driving forces for the common good. The ballot box in politics and the market in economics were the ultimate, impartial arbiters of differences of opinion.

This philosophy assigned to government only a small role. The less government interfered with individual freedom, the better. This was the laissez-faire philosophy of the nineteenth century. To be sure, individualism never went so far as to exclude government intervention altogether. True freedom necessarily involves some restrictions on freedom. A society that gave you freedom to murder your neighbor whenever you felt like it would be anarchy.

So it was in the economic sphere. Clearly the government needed to establish and enforce a few "rules of the game." One basic rule was the guarantee that no one should be deprived of life, liberty, or property without due process of law. Another was the long-standing rules against fraud and against default on contracts. But the rules should be simple, and government had no business in economic life outside these rules.

As time passed, mass production and the modern corporation swept away the possibility of an economy of tiny, highly competitive firms. Powerful unions replaced the individual worker in bargaining with big business. Throughout the economy, concentration of economic power and reliance on group activity spread steadily. Many new products brought objectionable side effects, such as smoke from factory chimneys and polluted rivers.

Moreover, with a wealthier, more complex

society, people wanted more things that couldn't be readily provided through private profit-incentive in the marketplace—schools for all, highways, national defense, and the like. Thus, besides setting the rules of the private-enterprise game, governments were called on to do more and more things directly. At the same time, common concern grew for the individual who couldn't take care of himself. Government "welfare" and social security largely replaced private poor relief. Willingness to abide by the impersonal income allocations of the market steadily diminished. Desire to "do something" about booms and depressions became widespread. A subtle shift in the meaning attached to the words "individual freedom" marked the changing tenor of the times. The rules of the game have grown into an intricate mass of law and administrative controls. The government has become a major participant as well as the umpire in the economic game. Today, federal, state, and local government taxes and expenditures total nearly one-third of the gross national product.

The Mixed Economy

Today, ours is a mixed economy—still basically private-enterprise but with large areas of government control and direct participation. It's up to you to decide whether you like what's been going on—whether you want to move back toward the traditional private-enterprise system, or on toward a more administered, planned economy, or in some other direction.

This is no ivory tower, academic issue, dreamed up for college classrooms. It is a basic issue of public economic policy today. Clearly the government must step in to provide national defense and highways, but how about slum clearance and public housing? How heavily should government tax upper-income families to guarantee minimum incomes for all, whether they work or not? Everyone agrees that the government must act to minimize inflationary booms and depressions, but how far should it regulate private decisions on wages and prices in the process? These are big national policy issues of the 1970s and 1980s. You will have to answer them if you are to vote intelligently. The issue of how much private enterprise, how much government, is everywhere.

CAPITALISM TODAY

"Capitalism" is a term often used but seldom defined. Words so used often generate more heat than light, and over the years "capitalism" has become a fighting word for many who advocate and oppose it. Recourse to dictionaries and learned treatises of economists and historians unfortunately does not resolve the dilemma of just what we should mean when we say capitalism, for these authorities are far from agreement.

So, instead of talking about capitalism, this book uses such less colorful but more descriptive terms as the "private-enterprise, free-price system" and "market system" in referring to the big private sector of the modern American economy. But, though we shall generally eschew the emotionally colored term, a brief note on "capitalism" may be useful. Many writers agree that a "capitalist" economy is marked by at least these major characteristics:

1. Private ownership of property prevails.
2. Property has been accumulated by individuals and businesses, and this accumulated "capital" provides incomes to its owners.
3. Individuals and businesses are free to seek their own economic gain; the profit motive plays a central role in economic life.
4. Some writers add to this list a highly developed banking and credit system.

This list gives the basic flavor of such a system. But once we look at the points in detail, the trouble begins. How free must individuals be to own and use property if a system is to be termed "capitalism"? Is an income tax that takes away part of your income each year, depending on how much you earn, consistent with capitalism? Does a federal law that limits the monopoly power you can attain violate the essential freedoms of capitalism?

We shall be concerned with all these questions and others like them. But there is little to be gained by debating just which measures are and which are not consistent with "capitalism" when there is so little agreement on what the term means. Instead, we will concentrate on trying to decide whether proposed policy measures are good or bad on their merits, taking into account the different social goals held by different groups in America today. In talking about a "basically private-enterprise, market-directed system" throughout most of the book, we will be talking about the system many writers call "modern capitalism." If you like the term, use it. But don't let your emotional attachment or antagonism toward it get in the way of thinking objectively about the issues.

REVIEW

Concepts to Remember

This chapter has introduced some important concepts that will be reused many times throughout the book. Recheck especially the following to be sure you have them firmly in mind:

- productive resources
- technology
- specialization
- exchange
- scarcity
- economizing
- production-possibilities curve
- production-possibilities frontier
- private-enterprise, free-price economy
- market system
- economic growth
- laissez-faire
- capitalism

For Analysis and Discussion

1. Does this chapter help explain the wide differences in per capita outputs shown in Table 2–1? Explain how.
2. "Man lives by cooperating with his fellow men. In all economics there is no more fundamental truth than this." "The core of the competitive, free-market system is the driving urge of most men to get ahead in the world, to rise above their fellow men."

   Are these two statements about the American economic system consistent or contradictory? If they are consistent, how do you reconcile their apparent contradiction?
3. The price system allocates resources where consumers spend their dollars. Thus the rich man has far more influence than the poor man. Is this consistent with the democratic presumption that every man is equal?
4. In a market-directed system, who decides how many jobs there will be in each industry? Who should make the decision?

5. What reasons can you think of explaining why there will be poor people in a market-directed economy, even if the average income level is high?
6. "The economics of scarcity is obsolete in our affluent society. There's plenty for everybody." True or false? Define "scarcity," "plenty," and "everybody" in answering. Do we still face the need to economize?
7. Does the present level of government spending tend to raise or lower our standard of living? Use a production-possibilities curve in explaining your answer.
8. Suppose American college students were to develop a craze for pork-chop sandwiches, instead of hamburgers. Trace through as carefully as you can the impact of this craze on the allocation of the economy's productive resources. Would such a shift be good or bad?
9. Leading TV stars receive annual salaries in the hundreds of thousands of dollars. Many baseball players receive $50,000 to $100,000 for the eight-month season. Yet an intelligent, skilled, hardworking nurse or farmer will ordinarily earn no more than $10,000 or so per year.
    a. Are such differences predictable results of the free-market system, or do they reflect breakdowns in the functioning of the system?
    b. Do you approve of such inequalities in the distribution of income? Why or why not?

Business Firms and Market Supply

CHAPTER PREVIEW

CHAPTER FOUR

In a private-enterprise economy, profit-seeking business firms produce most of the goods and services that consumers want. The business firm is at the center of the economic process. The businessman decides what will be produced in response to market demand, and how much of it. In the process, he decides how many employees to hire and how much he is willing to pay them. Within the rules established by society, his decisions most directly determine how effectively the private-enterprise economy utilizes its resources.

Anybody can see that business firms in the modern economy are a long way from the myriad of small competitors envisaged by Adam Smith two centuries ago. Not only General Motors, Ford, General Electric, AT&T, and other such well-known firms are industrial giants, but hundreds of other firms like them have sales of hundreds of millions or even billions of dollars per year. They employ thousands of people, and obviously have some degree of market power in deciding what market prices shall be. At the same time, small firms, not unlike those envisaged by Smith, number in the millions—especially in agriculture, retail trade, and the service industries (for example, dry cleaners, doctors, lawyers, and so on). Over the last century, there has been some tendency for very large firms to grab off a bigger share of the total economy's activity, but only a modest increase. Moreover, this increase has come almost entirely in manufacturing, which now provides only about 25 percent of all the jobs in the country. In the services, including the most rapidly growing sectors of the economy, small businesses have prospered and the dominance of the giants is far less widespread. But be they large or small, businesses have the job of responding to consumer demands and using our resources effectively to produce what consumers want.

It is the purpose of this chapter to describe briefly the major forms of business enterprise in the modern American economy, with some attention to small businesses but more to the huge corporations that dominate the news headlines. If you want to understand the role of big business in America and how much economic power it really has, you need to know something about what corporations are and how they operate. Especially if you sympathize with the modern radical criticisms of big business—that it holds vast power over both economic and political life—you need to know something of how such businesses are organized, how they are managed, and how you can understand their financial statements.

ENTREPRENEURS, PLANTS, FIRMS, AND INDUSTRIES

Business enterprises are called "firms." John Brown and his family run a farm; the farm is a firm. United States Steel is a firm, with steel mills in many cities, with iron and coal mines, with ore ships on the Great Lakes. The important characteristic of the firm is that it is owned and controlled essentially as a unit, however diverse its parts.

The function of making fundamental policy decisions in a firm is generally called "entrepreneurship." The entrepreneur decides when to establish a firm, what goods to produce, how the concern will be financed, what price policies to follow, when to expand or contract, and so on. A firm is thus a business unit under one coordinated "entrepreneurship."

In the independent corner grocery store, the proprietor is the entrepreneur. He decides whether to borrow funds to remodel his store, what prices to set on his merchandise. In bigger businesses, it is harder to pick out the entrepreneur. For example, who is the entrepreneur of AT&T? The three million stockholders? The board of directors? The finance committee of the board? The president? Here it is impossible to pick out any person or group of persons as the entrepreneur; the functions of the entrepreneur are performed in a coordinated way by the various individuals and groups concerned.

A "plant" is a building or a group of buildings, along with other more or less fixed physical equipment, that are used together in producing something—such as a shoe-manufacturing plant or an auto-assembly plant. The Ford Motor Company is a firm with plants in Dearborn, St. Louis, Kansas City, and so forth. John Brown's farm, on the other hand, is a firm with only one plant.

An "industry" is harder to define. Usually we use the word to mean all the producers of any "commodity." Farmer Brown is part of the wheat industry if he produces wheat, part of the corn industry if he produces corn; he may be in both simultaneously. General Motors is part of many industries; it produces a wide range of autos, trucks, diesel engines, refrigerators, and hundreds of other products. The trouble comes when we try to be precise. Shall we consider a "motor-vehicle industry," or an "auto industry," or a "low-priced auto industry"? For many purposes, how finely we divide up commodities is not a major problem. You will seldom get in trouble if you let common sense be your guide and if you stick to the same definition of "commodity" and the associated "industry" in analyzing any problem.

The Shifting Legal Organization of Firms

The legal forms of business firms have changed with the times. When small-scale business was the rule, the individual proprietorship was dominant. This is a simple arrangement in which an individual puts up the money, starts his own business, runs it himself, and has the profits and losses to himself. There are still more individual proprietorships in the United States than any other form of business organization—some nine million in all. Of these, three million are in agriculture, and most of the rest are small-scale retail concerns and service enterprises, such as cleaning establishments, filling stations, doctors, lawyers, and so on. Ninety-nine percent of all farms are still single-proprietorships, but the 1 percent that are corporations do about 20 percent of all the business. In wholesale and retail trade, the 82 percent of all firms that are single proprietorships do only about 25 percent of the business; remember Sears and the big grocery chains.

As the need for larger capital funds increased, partnerships became popular. In these, two or more people become joint proprietors—usually with joint provision of funds, joint management, and joint financial responsibility. This arrangement has substantial advantages over the single-proprietorship, but it still falls short of providing enough capital for really large-scale business operations. And it shares one serious drawback with the single proprietorship: The partners are personally liable for all the debts of the business. Thus, in most cases, each partner is personally liable to an **unlimited** amount for the deeds of the other partners—a somewhat precarious position at best, and definitely not suited to drawing in funds from absentee investors. Partnerships are not very important in the United States today, though there are some 900,000 in existence. About half of them are in retailing; the rest are widely scattered.

THE MODERN CORPORATION

The modern corporation, which was conceived to meet the needs of large-scale business organizations and to avoid the drawbacks of partnerships, has become the dominant form of American business enterprise. Although there are only about 1.5 million business corporations, they do the bulk of the nation's business, employ over 50 percent of the workers, account for about two-thirds of the nation's privately produced income, and pay out over 50 percent of the total national income. They do virtually all the business in public utilities, manufacturing, transportation, and finance; around half in trade and construction; but less than a quarter in services and agriculture.

The biggest modern corporations are Goliaths. In 1972, for example, the assets of the American Telephone and Telegraph Company (the world's largest business) were $61 billion. Those of Exxon (formerly Standard Oil of New Jersey) and of General Motors were $18 and $22 billion, respectively. GM's 1972 sales of $30 billion were larger than the entire gross national product of most of the world's nations. In all, in 1972 there were 140 nonfinancial corporations with sales over a billion dollars.

Many financial corporations (banks and insurance companies) are as large, though most of their assets consist mainly of investments in corporate and government securities and of direct loans to businesses and individuals. In 1972, the total assets of the Prudential Life Insurance Company, the largest insurance company, approached $34 billion. Those of the Bank of America, the biggest bank, were $41 billion.

Modern finance and industry are heavily concentrated in the hands of large firms (more details in Chapters 25–27) and critics complain bitterly about the great power this gives them. Nevertheless, there are still many more small firms than large ones. Only about one American worker in four works for a large corporation. If we include government and other nonprofit service industries (for example, health and education), the share of the total national income produced by all private corporations has declined gradually since hitting a peak of 55 percent in the mid-1950s. The market share of the giants in manufacturing has grown gradually since World War II, but their profits haven't grown as fast as their sales. Keep an open mind; big business is very big, but there may be more life left in competition and the invisible hand than meets the eye.

What Are Corporations?

A corporation is an organization that exists as a "legal person" apart from the individuals who own and control it. A corporation may carry on business in its own name, enter into contracts, sue and be sued, own property, borrow and lend money. In general, it may as a business unit do all the things that any individual person may legally do in business.

The main advantages of the corporate form of organization center around its financial arrangements. Briefly, they are the following:

1. Stockholders who invest money in corporations have no liability for the debts of the corporation; at worst, they can lose their original investment. Thus, corporations can obtain funds by selling "stocks" and "bonds" to many investors who merely want to earn a return on their investments without further financial involvement. These advantages are spelled out below.
2. In a corporation, management is delegated to a board of directors elected by the stockholders. The directors in turn supervise the salaried officials who actually run the business. Thus, the individual stockholder need not concern himself with the details of managing the concern unless he wishes to—quite another story from the continuous attention required in a single-proprietorship or partnership. Freedom to delegate power and responsibility to expert "managers" is essential to the operation of today's mammoth business enterprises.
3. Corporate securities are readily transferrable. No matter how many individual stockholders die or lose interest in the corporation, the business can go on unaffected.

Financing Corporate Enterprise—Stocks and Bonds

Corporations obtain funds by selling "stocks" and "bonds" to savers. Individual investors who buy these securities may be part owners of the corporation, or they may simply lend money to the business. Stocks represent ownership in the corporation. Bonds represent money lent to the corporation by bondholders. There are many variations within each class, and at the margin they run together. The most important differences are: (1) the priority of the security-owner's claim on the income of the enterprise; and (2) the owner's right to vote on personnel and corporate policy, and hence his power to control the corporation.

Common stockholders are the owners of a corporation. They own the company's stock. They have the right to elect the board of directors and hence to control the policies of the corporation. They are entitled to any income remaining after prior claims of creditors have been met. If the corporation is dissolved, they get all that remains (if anything) after everyone else has been paid. The common stockholders are the "residual claimants" to the corporation's income and property. They gain the most when income is high, and they are the first to lose when things go badly.

Profits paid out to stockholders are called "dividends." Although the profits of the business "belong" to the stockholders, often the corporation does not pay them all out, but instead reinvests part in the business. This is called "plowing back" earnings. Whether the profits are paid out or reinvested, however, they accrue to the benefit of stockholders, since reinvested earnings increase the value of the business.

Bondholders are creditors of the corporation. When corporations want to borrow large sums for long periods, they commonly issue bonds that are sold to people or institutions with funds to invest. Bonds are promises by the corporation to repay the funds to bondholders, at some specified future date with a set rate of interest.

If you own a bond, you are merely a creditor. You ordinarily have no voting power to elect directors and control the corporation's policies. You take less risk than the stockholders, since the interest on your bonds must be paid before they get any dividends. On the other hand, you will receive only your set rate of interest no matter how big profits are. Bondholders also have a prior claim on the assets of the corporation in case of liquidation.

Preferred stockholders have a position intermediate between common stockholders and bondholders. Preferred stock sometimes carries a vote; more often it does not. Typically, it has a set rate of dividends, say $6 per share, that must be paid before any dividends can be paid on the common stock. It also has priority over common stock in case of liquidation. But preferred stock stands behind bonds in priority of claim on income and assets.

Who Controls the Corporations?

Suppose you own one hundred shares of General Electric stock. How much control do you have over how General Electric is run?

The answer is, for practical purposes, none. Not because anyone is cheating or hoodwinking you—least of all the GE management, which makes a continuous effort to keep stockholders informed and to get them interested in company affairs. It is because of a combination of factors. In the first place, you own only a tiny fraction of 1 percent of the company's stock. Moreover, you don't and can't know much about the operations and internal policies of GE, a $10 billion corporation producing thousands of products, most of them involving complex scientific processes and know-how. Besides, GE pays good dividends on your one hundred shares, and that's what you bought them for. You haven't the slightest intention of spending a lot of money and time on an obviously fruitless trip all the way to Schenectady, New York, to try to tell the management how to run GE, or to throw them out for a new management.

Even if you don't go to the annual stockholders' meeting, you are entitled to send a "proxy," a person of your choice whom you designate to vote for you. Before each annual meeting, you will receive from the management a proxy form, suggesting that you designate someone to vote for you in case you don't plan to be present. You may throw the proxy in the wastebasket. If you do send it back, the chances are you'll designate the person suggested—partly because you don't know anyone else to designate—thereby giving the present management the votes to reelect themselves.

Surprisingly enough, you will be acting like the typical stockholder when you do this, even though you may assume there are many other interested "big" stockholders who are keeping a sharp eye on the operating management from a stockholder viewpoint. AT&T now has 3 million stockholders, no one of whom owns as much as 1 percent of its stock. U.S. Steel has over 300,000 stockholders, Westinghouse over 175,000. Many big corporations now have more stockholders than employees. On the other hand, a few well-to-do people and large investment institutions (like pension and trust funds) own large blocks of stock in many well-known companies.

This widespread dispersion of stock ownership, coupled with the lethargy of most stockholders, goes far to explain the substantial control over most large corporations exercised by small groups of active stockholders, and often by the operating management "insiders" who may themselves own very little stock. This divorce of active control from ownership is a major development of modern business enterprise. It is probably inevitable in the large corporation. It certainly does not provide a "democratic" government of corporation affairs in most cases, however good the intentions of the management on this score.

Of course, stockholder lethargy does not always exist. In some smaller companies, stockholders take an active interest in the conduct of the business. Even in large corporations, conflicts and sharp struggles for proxies sometimes occur, with control of the corporation at stake. But for the most part, management or other minorities retain effective control without holding more than a small fraction of the voting stock. They are on the scene; most of the stockholders are far away and little interested. Less than 10 percent of the voting stock is enough to assure working control of most major corporations.

A 1966 study of the 200 largest nonfinancial corporations in the United States found that in 85 percent of the companies, control was exercised by the management without material stock ownership. None of the corporations was directly controlled by a private family through ownership of over 50 percent of the stock; and in only 12 percent was direction exercised by a particular family or other special group of stockholders with a substantial share of the stock—say 20 to 50 percent. By contrast, in 1929 only 44 percent of the top 200 companies were management-controlled, while 50 percent were controlled by families or other special groups through substantial blocks of stock holdings. Clearly, there has been a change in the way our major corporations are controlled.[1]

What proportion of the public owns corporation stock? There are now over thirty million individual stockholders in "publicly owned" corporations, plus probably one to two million more in "privately owned" companies whose stock was held entirely by family or private control groups. The comparable total for 1955 was only six or seven million. Thus, perhaps 25 percent of all adults now own stock in business corporations, but remember that most of them own only a few shares.

Financial Control Groups in the Modern Economy

By means of large investments, mergers, interlocking directorates, and "insider" control, a few major financial groups exercise substantial control over groups of large corporations. Grouping the 50 largest financial corporations with the 200 largest nonfinancial, the National Resources Committee found in the late 1930s that out of total assets of $115 billion for the whole lot, the J.P. Morgan-First National Bank of New York group controlled over $30 billion, and that the Kuhn-Loeb investment banking interests controlled over $10 billion, primarily railroads. Of the purely family groups, the Rockefellers controlled over $6 billion; the Mellons over $3 billion, and the DuPonts over $2.5 billion.

Although their form has changed, such financial control groups continue. Often they operate through interlocking directorates, which include directors of banks and nonfinancial businesses. Today the dollar amounts are much larger, though the total economy has grown so fast that the proportion controlled by such groups is probably smaller than a half century ago. Modern tightly knit control groups tend to center in major cities—New York, Chicago, Pittsburgh, and so on—where large corporations are headquartered.[2]

An even bigger and rapidly growing share of all corporate stock is held by financial institutions—pension funds, bank trust departments, mutual funds, insurance companies, and the like. They probably now hold about a third of all stock. To date, such financial institutions have seldom intervened directly in corporate management. But as savings pile up in such institutions, their potential power becomes enormous, far exceeding that of the wealthiest families. Even corporations' and unions' own pension funds, amounting to billions of dollars, are now being invested in corporation stocks, posing intriguing problems of future corporate control. Who should watch over the managers of these vast accumulations of funds?

CONCLUSION

Critics of modern capitalism and big business argue that the U.S. economy is dominated by corporate giants and a few powerful, greedy capitalists who control them. Concentration of power is alleged to be the dominant characteristic of America today; they say there is no resemblance between this reality and the competitive forces on which Smith's invisible hand relied to regulate the avarice of businessmen.

The facts of business size are reasonably clear; we shall return to them in detail in Chapters

[1]The data are from R. J. Larner, "Ownership and Control in the 200 Largest Nonfinancial Corporations," *American Economic Review,* September 1966. See also R.A. Gordon, *Business Leadership in the Large Corporation* (Washington, D.C.: The Brookings Institution, 1964), Chap. 2.

[2]See P.C. Dooley, "The Interlocking Directorate," *American Economic Review,* June 1969.

25–27. There are, indeed, many huge corporations on which we rely for a wide variety of products. There are also many markets supplied by multitudes of smaller firms. The American trillion-dollar economy is so vast that even corporate giants are tiny by comparison, and often find themselves competing vigorously with other giants. As we shall see, absolute size confers some types of economic power, but it is the intensity of competition that matters most for getting consumer demands met efficiently. If large firms must compete actively with others, their economic power is greatly constrained. The degree of competition in different markets will be a recurring, central question in the chapters ahead.

This is not to say that corporate size per se does not confer other types of power on managerial and financial control groups. It does. But again, we shall need to look with care. It is by no means clear that most "insiders" are using their power to the disadvantage of either other stockholders or consumers. On the contrary, many big business concerns are now managed both more efficiently and with a greater view to social welfare than they were under the direct control of owner-operators. If you have $5,000 invested in General Motors, it is doubtful that your interests would be better protected were Messrs. R.C. Gerstenberg and Edward Cole (the top executives of GM) larger stockholders than they in fact are, or if you could personally participate in the management of the business. Similarly, today's growing group of professional managers seems more concerned with serving the public well than was the typical captain of industry a half century ago. Nor is there much evidence that most dominant large stockholders use their positions to exploit other stockholders. Indeed, many investors prefer such companies as DuPont and Alcoa partly because they want the watchful guidance given these companies by the DuPont and Mellon families.

There is little likelihood that the modern corporation, with its vast accumulations of capital and its professional management divorced from most stockholders, will soon disappear from the American scene. Its advantages are too great. The problem is how to make such businesses effective suppliers of wanted goods and services, with effective controls on excessive concentrations of economic power where they exist.

REVIEW

Concepts to Remember

The concepts in this chapter deal largely with institutions and legal forms. Be particularly sure that you understand the following:

entrepreneur	corporation
plant	common stock
firm	"plowed-back" earnings
industry	preferred stock
individual proprietorship	bond
partnership	dividends

For Analysis and Discussion

1. Explain the difference between stocks and bonds.
2. Suppose you are planning to set up a small dry-cleaning shop. Will you be better off with a single proprietorship, a partnership, or a corporation as your legal form of business? What are the main considerations involved in choosing?
3. Single proprietorships and partnerships predominate in retailing and agriculture, while corporations dominate the manufacturing industries. How do you account for these differences? How can you reconcile the above statement with the great success of such retail corporate giants as Sears, Roebuck and J.C. Penny?
4. Public-opinion polls repeatedly indicate that the majority of the public view common stocks as a speculative and somewhat uncertain investment. How do you account for this fact, in view of the great growth in the aggregate value and earnings of American corporations over the past century?
5. If you are a stockholder in General Motors, would you prefer to have earnings paid out to you as dividends or directly reinvested by the management? Why?
6. Should individual stockholders in business concerns take a more active part in the management of the concerns involved? Why or why not?
7. (*Based on the appendix*) Construct the profit-and-loss statement of the Amalgamated Widget Company for 1974 from the following data.

Wages and salaries paid	$ 500,000
Interest paid on bonds	40,000
Materials used	500,000
Net sales	3,000,000
Selling costs	250,000
Dividends on common stock	50,000
Provision for income taxes	200,000
Real estate taxes	60,000
Dividends on preferred stock	20,000
Maintenance and repairs	250,000
Administration costs	400,000
Depreciation	150,000

8. (*Based on the appendix*) XYZ Corporation reports the following data on its position as of December 31, 1974. Construct its balance sheet. Note that the figure for surplus is missing and must be computed.

Accounts payable	$300,000
Common stock	400,000
Accounts receivable	500,000
Buildings and equipment	500,000
Inventories on hand	250,000
Bonds outstanding	300,000
Cash	250,000
Goodwill	10,000
Surplus	—
U.S. Government bonds	50,000
Reserve for taxes	70,000
Loan from bank	300,000

APPENDIX

The Elements of Business Accounting

In order to understand the workings of modern business, you need to know something about the elements of business accounting. Although the details of accounting are complex, its fundamentals are simple. Only a knowledge of these fundamentals is essential for our purposes.

THE BALANCE SHEET. A balance sheet is a cross-section picture of the financial position of a firm at some given point of time. It is an instantaneous snapshot. A second sort of picture, discussed below, is an "income" or "profit-and-loss" statement that summarizes the firm's operations over some period of time, say a month or a year.

The balance sheet of any business rests on a fundamental equation. One side of the balance sheet shows what the business owns—its assets. Exactly corresponding to the value of these assets must be their ownership, which goes on the other side of the balance sheet. Obviously the two are always equal—the balance sheet always balances.

It is not easy to say just *who* "owns" the assets of the business. At the one extreme, the common stockholders are considered the "residual owners"—that is, the ones who would receive all the cash left over if the business were liquidated and its debts paid off. But this statement makes it clear that the various creditors of the business (for example, the bank that has loaned it funds or the supplier from whom it has bought on credit) also have a claim on the assets. Such "creditors," to whom the business owes money, are at the other extreme of the claimants on the business' assets—they get their funds first. Bondholders, whose interest is contingent on satisfactory earnings, have a less preferred claim on the assets; preferred stockholders are still further down the list. Plainly the line between "creditors" and "owners" is indistinct. The two groups shade into one another as a continuum of claimants on the business' assets.

Fundamentally, the balance sheet reflects the basic accounting equation (or identity) that assets = liabilities + net worth; or put the other way round, that net worth = assets − liabilities. That is, the business is worth to the stockholders what assets they would have left over if all the liabilities were paid off.

Table A is the balance sheet of a hypothetical Gadget Manufacturing Company, as of December 31, 1973. The left-hand side lists all the assets of the company—everything of value that it owns. The right-hand side lists all claims against these assets, broken down into two groups: first, its liabilities (what it owes); and second, its capital and surplus accounts (sometimes called its "net worth" or "proprietorship") on this date.

ASSETS. Once you see the basic equation underlying the balance sheet, most of its items are self-explanatory. For convenience, assets are often arranged beginning with the most liquid (the most readily convertible into cash) and ending with the least liquid.

The last asset calls for special explanation. Two hundred thousand dollars is the value attached, for accounting purposes, to the patents and goodwill accumulated by the company. Obviously this is an estimated figure, a more or less arbitrary valuation determined by the company's officials and accountants. The item is so obviously intangible, albeit of tremendous importance for such well-established products as Coca-Cola and Lucky Strike, that it has become accepted conservative business practice to place a very low value on it.[3]

Actually, this is only the most conspicuously estimated item; others are estimated too. The current value placed on plant and equipment, as we shall see, is particularly susceptible to the vagaries of managerial and accounting judgment, because the "current value" shown is generally nothing but the original cost of the assets less an estimated amount of depreciation.[4] Some assets can be valued somewhat

[3]United States Steel and American Tobacco (Lucky Strike), for example, carry "goodwill and patents" at $1. Coca-Cola, on the other hand, carried goodwill, trademarks, formulae, and so on, at their cost—$56 million in 1972.

[4]See the discussion of "depreciation" charges in the following section.

TABLE A
Gadget Manufacturing Company

Balance Sheet, December 31, 1973

ASSETS		
Current assets:		
Cash	$2,000,000	
U.S. government securities	1,000,000	
Accounts receivable	2,000,000	
Inventories on hand	2,000,000	
Total current assets		$ 7,000,000
Fixed assets:		
Investment in affiliated company		300,000
Plant and equipment		3,000,000
Patents and goodwill		200,000
Total		$10,500,000

LIABILITIES AND PROPRIETORSHIP		
Current liabilities:		
Accounts payable	$ 500,000	
Accrued taxes	900,000	
Total current liabilities		$ 1,400,000
Bonds outstanding		3,000,000
Capital and surplus:		
Preferred stock outstanding	$1,000,000	
Common stock outstanding	2,000,000	
Surplus	3,100,000	
Total capital and surplus		6,100,000
Total		$10,500,000

more precisely; but only cash is clearly and inevitably "worth" exactly the figure at which it is carried.

Liabilities and Net Worth. The liability side seems a little more tricky at first glance. "Accounts payable" is easy—these are debts owed to suppliers. "Accrued taxes" represent tax liabilities that have been incurred but have not yet been paid. Bonds outstanding are liabilities that may not come due for a much longer time.

"Capital and surplus" (net worth) consists of three items in this particular balance sheet. Part of the company's funds were obtained by sale of preferred, part by sale of common stock. The amounts shown for each are the "par," or "face," value of the stock outstanding. This value is presumably the amount for which the stock was originally sold, though this is not always so.[5] Surplus reflects profits of the company that have not been paid out as dividends to stockholders.

Surplus is a peculiarly misleading word. It seems to connote an extra fund of cash lying around somewhere, but such is far from the case. Surplus is nothing but a formal accounting subitem as part of the general capital and surplus (net worth) category. Total "capital and surplus" is nothing but a derived figure that follows from the values placed on assets, less the company's "liabilities," which may also be partly estimated. The fact that capital plus surplus on December 31,1973, was $3,100,000 more than the paid-in value of the stock reflects that amount of past earnings not paid out in dividends.

There is no reason to suppose that these past profits now repose in the cash account. More likely, as part of the firm's regular operations, they have been "reinvested" or "plowed back" into inventory, plant and equipment, or some other assets. Or they may be reflected in a reduced level of the firm's

[5] In the 1800s, it was common practice to set a fictitiously high value on the capital stock. Part of this stock was issued to original founders who provided not money but goods and services that were overvalued. The term "stock watering" in reference to this practice came from the then common practice of inducing cattle to drink as much water as possible just before being marketed in order to temporarily increase their weight. Although supervisory control now exercised by the U.S. government Securities and Exchange Commission has made such watering very difficult for stocks "listed" on the major exchanges, it still can be done with unlisted stocks.

liabilities. It is essential to understand that there is no direct correspondence between individual items on the two sides of the balance sheet. Any attempt to link up individual items directly will lead to fallacious conclusions.[6]

THE INCOME (PROFIT-AND-LOSS) STATEMENT. The income, or profit-and-loss, statement is the accountant's summary view of a firm's operation over some period of time, say a year.

Table B shows a hypothetical income statement for the Gadget Manufacturing Company during the year ending December 31, 1974, the year following the balance sheet shown in Table A. This is a straightforward account of the income received during the year and what was done with it. The first part of the statement summarizes the income from[7] and expenses of operations; then separate items are included for other income and expenses; then federal income tax liability is deducted, which gives net profit after taxes for 1974.

The last part of the statement shows how the corporation allocates this profit. Only $500,000 is paid out as dividends. The other $600,000 is reinvested in the company. Capital and surplus (net worth) will now be $600,000 higher than if all the profits had been distributed to the stockholders. Common stockholders—the corporation's "owners"—may thus be as well off one way as the other. In one case, they get cash dividends; in the other, the value of their investment accumulates. Such plowing back of earnings has long been commonplace in American industry, and many industrial giants such as Eastman Kodak and Ford have grown almost entirely through reinvestment of earnings.

One warning about the profit-and-loss statement: The income and costs shown are not necessarily cash receipts and outlays; the profits are not necessarily cash profits. The distinction between cash transactions and accounting records is illustrated by the "materials" item. The materials used may have been purchased long before and already have been in inventory at the year's beginning. Or materials pur-

[6]The common argument that higher wages should be paid out of surpluses is an example of such an inadequate understanding of the elements of accounting.

[7]The "net sales" item corresponds to the revenue from sales shown by the "demand curves" in the following chapters.

TABLE B
Gadget Manufacturing Company

Income Statement for Year Ended December 31, 1974

Net sales		$10,000,000
Manufacturing and selling costs:		
Materials	$2,000,000	
Labor cost	3,000,000	
Depreciation	500,000	
Maintenance and repairs	400,000	
Administrative and selling costs	1,400,000	
Taxes (other than income taxes)	600,000	7,900,000
Net profit from operations		2,100,000
Other income—interest and dividends		150,000
Less interest charges on own bonds outstanding		50,000
Net income before federal income taxes		2,200,000
Provision for federal income taxes		1,100,000
Net income (or profit)		$ 1,100,000
Allocation of net income:		
Dividends on preferred stock		$ 100,000
Dividends on common stock		400,000
Increase in surplus		600,000

chased during the year might have been double the $2,000,000 shown, if the firm had chosen to build up its inventories during the year. The $2,000,000 materials cost is the accounting figure for materials **used**, not for materials **bought** during the year.

The same point is illustrated by the cost item "depreciation." Every engineer and accountant knows that plant and equipment depreciate. If a truck bought in 1970 is expected to last five years, after each year it has one year less life. At the end of five years it has only scrap value if the original estimates were accurate. The concern will not have to buy another truck until 1975, but if it does not figure the using up of the truck as a current expense it is obviously understating its costs and overstating its profits in the intervening years. If no current depreciation is charged, in 1975 the entire cost of the new truck would have to be charged against 1975 income. Hence, accountants "charge" depreciation annually, even though no cash outlay is involved. Thus, one-fifth of the value of the truck might be charged off as a current cost each year, or some more complicated depreciation formula might be used. There need be no cash expenditure that matches the depreciation shown.

Since cost and income items are accounting entries rather than cash transactions, obviously there is no necessary cash accumulation at the year's end equal to net profit earned during the year. The firm's cash may be higher or lower, depending on what has seemed to the managers the best use of available funds. Managers need only be sure they have cash on hand to meet their obligations, one of which is dividends when dividends are to be paid. In fact, dividends may be paid in years when no profits have been made. AT&T, for example, paid its regular cash dividend of $9 per year straight through the depression of the 1930s, even though annual profits fell well below $9. Capital and surplus, of course, then declined by the excess of dividend payments over net profits.

RELATION BETWEEN INCOME STATEMENT AND BALANCE SHEET. These observations tell us a good deal about the relation between the income statement and the balance sheet. Suppose now we draw up a balance sheet for the Gadget Company at the end of 1974—another spot picture, linked to the earlier one by our income statement.

During the year, assets have been continually used up in the production of current output; sales or other sources of funds have continually rebuilt the firm's assets. Since a net profit of $1,100,000 after taxes was made during 1974, total capital and surplus (net

TABLE C
Gadget Manufacturing Company

Balance Sheet, December 31, 1974

ASSETS		
Current assets:		
Cash	$2,100,000	
U.S. government securities	1,200,000	
Accounts receivable	2,600,000	
Inventories on hand	2,000,000	
Total current assets		$ 7,900,000
Fixed assets:		
Investment in affiliated company		300,000
Plant and equipment		2,500,000
Patents and goodwill		200,000
Total		$10,900,000

LIABILITIES AND PROPRIETORSHIP		
Current liabilities:		
Accounts payable	$ 400,000	
Accrued taxes	800,000	
Total current liabilities		$ 1,200,000
Bonds outstanding		3,000,000
Capital and surplus:		
Preferred stock	$1,000,000	
Common stock	2,000,000	
Surplus	3,700,000	
Total proprietorship		6,700,000
Total		$10,900,000

worth) was up by this amount at year-end before payment of dividends. As was emphasized above, the increase in assets over the year may have come in cash, inventories, accounts receivable, or any other item—or there may have been a decrease in liabilities. All we know from the income statement is that, on balance, assets less liabilities are up $1,100,000.

This $1,100,000 is reduced to $600,000 by the payment of dividends. On the asset side the reduction is in the cash item when cash is paid out; in the capital and surplus accounts it is in the surplus item, which would have shown a steady increase through the year if monthly balance sheets had been made. This leaves the surplus account up $600,000 over December 31, 1973. Together, the income statement and balance sheets provide an overall accounting of the firm's financial operations and status for the period.

Corporate Profits and the Stock Market. Throughout this appendix, we have been primarily concerned with the mechanics of business accounting. Stop now and look for a moment at what this all means economically. During 1973, the Gadget Manufacturing Company had a good year. It made $1.1 million of profits on its total net worth (capital and surplus) of $6.1 million at the beginning of the year. This is around a 17 percent return on net investment, even after paying taxes. Before taxes, the return was more than twice as high. If you compare this rate of return with that of many leading American corporations, you will find that it looks very good.

How did this good year show up for the common stockholders? They collected $400,000 of dividends on $5.7 million stated net worth to the common stockholders. This would be a return of 7 percent on money invested in the stock at that price, a high rate. We can safely assume that the price of the stock has been bid up in the market by investors to reflect this high rate of return. Although market prices of common stock fluctuate widely, depending on many circumstances, an effective dividend yield of 4 or 5 percent on good small companies would have been reasonable in 1974; this would imply a market price for the company's shares totaling $8–10 million, on which the $400,000 dividends would amount to 4–5 percent return. The price per share would depend on the number of shares into which the company's capital stock had been divided. Suppose there were 200,000 shares (giving an original-issue, or "par," value of $10 per share). At current market prices we might expect these shares to be selling for perhaps $40–50 apiece ($8 million or $10 million total value divided by the 200,000 shares).

The stockholders also gained from the $600,000 of profits plowed back into the business, which show up on the December 31,1974, balance sheet as $600,000 additional surplus in the "Capital and Surplus" section. It means that the company now has either that many more dollars' worth of assets, or that much less debt, or some combination of both. This condition should make it a more profitable company in the future, with larger total profit figures in the years ahead. And generally this fact would be reflected in a correspondingly high value for the company's stock on the market.

REVIEW

Concepts to Remember

This appendix has introduced several important new concepts. You will meet many of the following terms not only throughout the course but in the newspaper as well:

balance sheet	profit-and-loss statement
assets	income statement
liabilities	dividends
proprietorship	depreciation
capital	reinvested earnings
surplus	net worth

Consumers and Market Demand[1]

CHAPTER PREVIEW

CHAPTER FIVE

By and large, businesses can make profits only by producing goods and services that people want to buy—autos, houses, dry cleaning, air travel, dogfood. If there is no consumer who is willing and able to buy, the businessman is out of luck. Maybe the government will temporarily come to his rescue with a subsidy, or maybe he can keep going by using up his own invested capital. *But over the long pull, it is customers who are willing and able to buy who direct production in a private-enterprise economy.*

[1]Note to instructors: This chapter has a mathematical appendix at the end of the book, for those who want to assign it.

THE SOVEREIGN CONSUMER?

Consumers direct production by the way they spend their money—the way they allocate their incomes among different goods and services. If consumers demand yellow refrigerators, the chances are good that businesses will produce yellow refrigerators. If consumers want to rent cars at airports, the rent-a-car agencies will prosper. If consumers develop a taste for artichokes, enterprising farmers will soon be raising artichokes to gain a profit by meeting that demand.

Consumer demand is the mainspring of economic activity. But never forget—it is the consumer with money to spend who counts! Many of us would like to have a Cadillac, and T-bone steak for dinner. But unless we have the money and are willing to spend it on these objects, our desires have little significance for General Motors or for the local supermarket.

Thus, your "vote" on what gets produced in a private-enterprise economy is largely determined by your income, unless you have accumulated funds to supplement your income. The mill hand has a lot less influence than the rich man, even though the former may be a virtuous, hardworking father of five needy children and the latter a ne'er-do-well who has inherited his money through no effort of his own. This is not to imply that virtue resides in poor rather than rich souls, but merely to emphasize that the private-enterprise economy responds to what people have to spend, not to who they are.

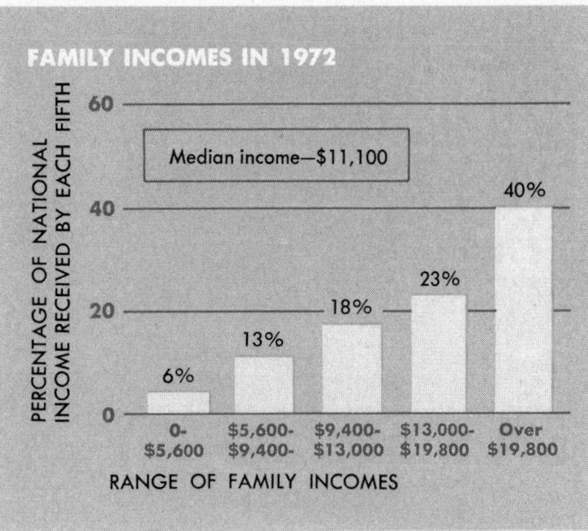

Figure 5–1

In 1972, three-fifths of all families fell in the $5,600–19,800 income range, and they received 54 percent of the national income. But the top fifth, receiving income of roughly $20,000 and up, had a big chunk of the total spending power. (Source: Preliminary estimates based on Census Bureau data.)

Figure 5–1 shows who has the buying power in America. It emphasizes the huge buying power of the "middle class." Two-thirds of all families fell in the $5,000–20,000 income group in 1972, and the average income of this group is steadily moving up.

But Figure 5–1 points up the extremes too. Ten million families, one family out of five, had an income below $5,600. These families received only 6 percent of total personal income—far less than their proportionate say over what gets produced for the market. At the other extreme, about one million families (2 percent of the total) received incomes over $40,000, giving them a larger leverage over what the system produces.

The consumer is a powerful, and sometimes capricious, monarch. Table 5–1 shows what he spends on some major categories in the American economy. He still spends the biggest chunk of his income on food, housing, and clothing. But the proportion spent on food and clothing has dropped sharply since 1929 (to only 31 percent as against 42). Spending on services (medicine, transportation, recreation, and the like) has grown rapidly as we have become richer and able to devote more of our incomes to "nonessentials." The bottom three items show what kind of living consumers now like.

Most of us are not coldly calculating "economic men." Still, most of us face a real problem of how to allocate our incomes among far more goods and services than we are able to pay for. Perhaps the Aga Khan buys everything he wants without concern for what it costs. But most of us have to calculate how to divide up our incomes among the things we want to buy. You may devote most of your income to nourishing foods, college tuition, and durable clothes; I may spend most of mine on books, stereo albums, and

TABLE 5–1

Percentage Breakdown of Consumer Spending

SPENDING CATEGORY	1929	1972
Food and drink	28	21
Housing	14	15
Clothing	12	10
Household furnishings	6	6
Medical services	4	8
Recreation	3	7
Autos and operations	3	13

airplane trips; our neighbor may prefer a dissolute life of wine, women, and song. Though none of us is a human calculating machine, all of us face the need to allocate our limited incomes to maximize our satisfactions from spending them.

The economist does not pass judgment on which pattern of expenditure is the proper one. Nor does he pretend to tell you how you should spend your income to lead a happier, healthier, more learned, or other kind of life. What he does do is assume that normally you spend your money on the things you want most. Thus, if you spent a dollar on the movies this afternoon, he takes that as evidence that you preferred going to the movies over buying a new necktie or paperback at the same price. If you stop and think about it, any other assumption leads to very strange results, as long as we assume freedom of individual action in spending incomes.

These rather obvious observations become important later on when we try to evaluate how well the economic system works. Unless we can assume that consumers' expenditures generally reflect what they want most, we will be at a loss for any measure of how well the system does in fact allocate its scarce productive resources to satisfying consumer wants. So we shall generally assume that people spend their money on the goods and services they want most, wisely or not.

Advertising and the Management of Demand

"Consumer sovereignty" is just establishment rhetoric, say some critics of the U.S. economy. Reality is just the opposite, they argue. Businesses decide what they can make the most profit producing; then they convince consumers through advertising and other high-pressure selling, that that's what they want to buy. Businesses, helped by Madison Avenue, are the sovereigns; consumers' wants are managed, manipulated, indeed created outright.

Insofar as the critics are right, the basic argument for an individual-oriented, free-market economy is undermined, since the whole system rests on the notion of consumer wants directing the use of society's resources. Does big business in fact dictate your wants, as a consumer? Clearly, modern advertising influences what a lot of people buy. In 1972 businesses spent over $20 billion on advertising—on TV and billboards, in newspapers, magazines, stores, and by direct mail. Procter and Gamble was the nation's largest advertiser, on soaps, detergents, and a myriad of household products. General Foods was second; each spending about 8 percent of its sales income on advertising. Sears Roebuck was third, with less than 2 percent of its sales, followed by General Motors, with seven-tenths of 1 percent of sales. Twenty billion dollars is a very large amount, but it's less than 2 percent of the gross national product. Most observers can't see how that percentage can dominate all our "wants," and clearly a lot of the advertising is primarily informational, not merely want-manipulating. Nearly a third of the total is newspaper advertising, with huge ads by supermarkets on weekend grocery prices and the like, presumably useful information for the housewife. Some advertising is seriously misleading, or dishonest; some is illegal, and not all of it is caught.

Obviously, advertising is a complicated problem, and there's a major section on it in Chapter

24, including both factual data and analysis of the major issues. There is surely some truth to the critics' charges, and the recent upsurge of "consumerism" shows that a lot of people are concerned. At the same time, the charges are easy to blow up into emotional overstatements; the facts just don't support some of the wilder ones. So remember that for the next few chapters we're oversimplifying by assuming that consumers decide for themselves what they want and freely express these preferences in the market. But it's a useful first approximation, and there'll be plenty of opportunity to alter it in Chapters 24–27.

INDIVIDUAL DEMAND

Since consumer demand largely directs production in a private-enterprise system, it is important to define "demand" accurately at the outset. **"Demand" is the schedule of amounts of any product that buyers will purchase at different prices during some stated time period.** This definition takes some explaining, since it obviously isn't quite what the word means in everyday conversation.

What is your demand for pizzas? A little thought will tell you that this is a meaningless question until you ask, "At what price and over how long a time?" You'll surely buy more at fifty cents than at $1.00 each; and obviously you'll buy more in a year than in a week. Recognizing this need to specify prices and a time period, we might construct a hypothetical "schedule" of the numbers of pizzas you would buy at different prices during a week, as in Table 5–2. The table shows how many pizzas you will buy during the week at each price shown, **assuming that other things (especially your income and the prices of other commodities) remain unchanged.**

When we speak of your "demand" for pizza, we mean this entire schedule of amounts that you would buy at various prices, other things equal. It is meaningless to say that your demand is one or three pizzas a week. By "demand" we mean instead your entire state of mind as to how many pizzas you would buy at different prices, other things remaining unchanged. In principle, we might list every possible price from zero to infinity. Table 5–2 pictures your demand only over the price range shown.

TABLE 5–2

Individual Demand for Pizzas

PRICE PER PIZZA	PIZZAS BOUGHT PER WEEK
$1.20	0
1.00	1
.80	2
.60	3
.40	4
.20	5

This state of mind (your demand) can be shown graphically, as in Figure 5–2. If we plot price on the vertical axis and pizzas bought on the horizontal axis and connect the points, we can read off the resulting curve how many pizzas you will buy during the week at any price shown, continuing the assumption of other

Figure 5–2

The demand curve shows how many pizzas this individual will buy in a week at different prices. He will buy more at lower than at higher prices.

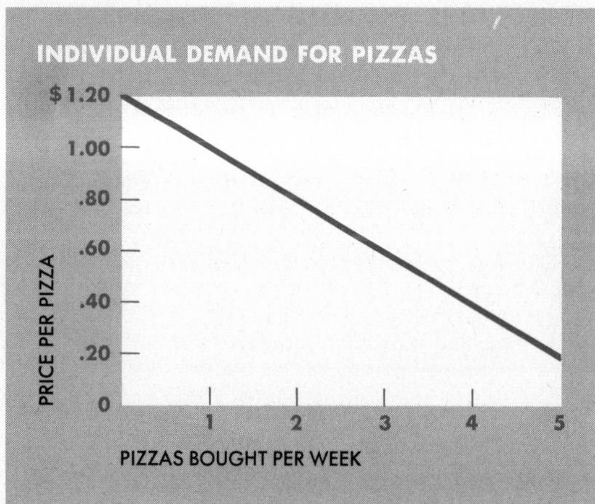

things equal. Thus, at $1.20 you will buy none, at $1.00 you will buy one, and so on down the curve. If you haven't had much experience with graphs, it may be useful to practice plotting and reading off a number of such points. Whether we use the schedule or plot the points graphically is a matter of convenience.

But watch out for one tricky point, whether you use schedules or graphs! Going back to your demand for pizzas, suppose the price is $1.00 and you are buying one per week. Now the local pizza parlor lowers the price to eighty cents and you step up your weekly purchases to two. This is not a change in demand. Your demand (your state of mind toward pizza) has not changed. You have merely moved to a different point on your demand schedule, or curve, as a result of the lower price, as the original demand schedule or curve says you would do. Your increased purchase at a lower price is merely a reflection of the downward slope of your demand curve.

Why Demand Curves Slope Downward

It seems obvious that you will buy more of anything at a low price than at a high one. Thus, on the kind of graph we have drawn, the demand curve will slope down, from northwest to southeast. Why? First, at a lower price for anything you can afford to buy more of it out of any given income. Second, at a lower price you are likely to want to buy more of it because it becomes relatively more attractive compared with other things you might spend your money on, given unchanged prices of other things. You will want to substitute pizza for hamburger another night each week as pizzas become cheaper.[2]

Many economists associate downward-sloping demand curves with the "law of diminishing marginal utility." The additional, or marginal, utility (satisfaction) you obtain per unit falls as you consume more units within the stated time period. Marginal utility is the want-satisfaction obtained from having one additional unit of some commodity per unit of time. Try applying the law to yourself—for oranges, movies, airplane trips home.

Changes in Demand

Remember that your "demand" for pizzas is your entire set of intentions about buying pizzas. These depend on how much income you have, your taste for pizza compared with other things, and the prices of alternatives. Now suppose that you get tired of pizza and develop a taste for seafood. You will now buy fewer pizzas than before at each of the prices shown. This change in attitude is a change in demand. Your demand for pizzas has decreased.

A change in demand is easily illustrated by using demand curves. Begin with curve *AA* in Figure 5–3. Your *lower* demand for pizzas would be reflected in a new demand curve, to the left of, or below, the old curve. You will now buy only one per week at eighty cents, and none at any higher price; only two at sixty cents; and so on. This new, *lower* demand curve is shown in Figure 5–3 as curve *BB*. If something increases your demand for pizzas, say a fatter paycheck to finance such delicacies, the new *higher* demand might be indicated by *CC*. A change in demand is shown by a move to another demand curve.

Why would your demand for pizzas, or Porsches, or neckties change? There are three major reasons. First, your tastes may change. You simply decide you don't like pizza, or that you now prefer Porsches to other cars. Second, your income may change. As a beginning office

[2]Three exceptions should be mentioned: (1) "Prestige goods," such as mink coats and exotic perfume, may be bought largely because their price is high. A decline in price might lead some people to buy less as the goods come down into a price range open to the less wealthy. (2) Some goods, called "inferior," are bought by poor people simply because they are cheap and useful. Potatoes in Ireland are the classic example. If the price of the food staple, potatoes, goes up, the Irish peasants may have to buy even more potatoes, which are still the cheapest food, because they have even less left than before to buy other more expensive foods. (3) When price drops, people may buy less because they expect the price to decline still further. But this is a dynamic effect that depends not on whether price is high or low but on the way it is changing.

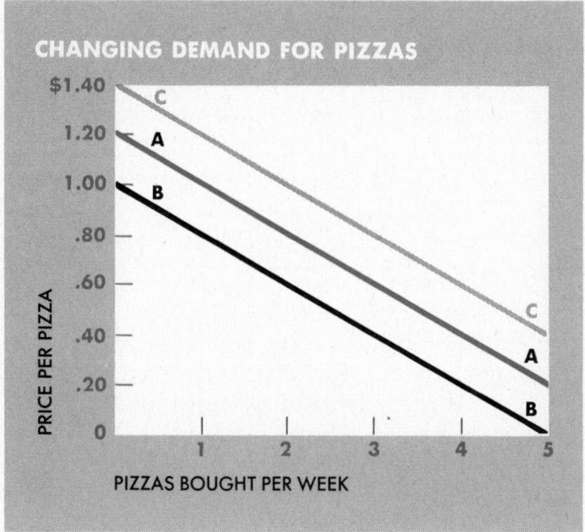

Figure 5–3

Curve CC shows an increase in demand from AA, curve BB shows a decrease. How many pizzas would consumers buy at $1.00 per pizza in each case?

clerk, you may have to be satisfied with a secondhand Volkswagon. With a doubled paycheck you may be in the Camaro class. **Third, changes in the availability and prices of other commodities may change your demand.** If hamburger prices soar, your demand for pizzas may rise because you'll buy more pizzas than before now that the alternatives cost more.

It is important to distinguish between movements along the same demand curve and shifts in the curve itself. Many economic fallacies are perpetrated through slippery use of the concept of "demand." Try checking your own grasp with these questions: (1) Production of sheep rises, prices fall, and consumers buy more mutton. Is there an increase in the demand for mutton? (Hint: Does the demand curve itself shift, or do customers merely buy more mutton on the same demand curve at lower prices?) (2) Chrysler comes out with a new, more powerful engine and Buick sales decline. Is there a drop in the demand for Buicks? (3) Philco raises the price of its TV sets and sales drop off. Is there a drop in demand? (4) Congress puts a new tax on movie admissions and movie attendance drops. Is there a drop in demand?[3]

EQUILIBRIUM OF THE CONSUMER

If we assume that consumers (households) generally try to maximize the utility (or satisfaction) they get by spending their incomes, two important propositions follow.

1. **First, each consumer will change the pattern of goods and services he buys whenever he can get more utility by spending an extra dollar on item *A* rather than on item *B*. He will maximize his total utility when he allocates his income so that the marginal utility he receives from the last dollar spent on each item he buys is identical. When he so allocates his income, the consumer is "in equilibrium," in the sense that he is maximizing the satisfaction he can obtain by spending his income. He has no incentive to change to another spending pattern.**

This is only common sense. If you can get a larger marginal utility by spending a dollar on *A* than on *B*, obviously you should spend it on *A*. Whenever the marginal utility of the last dollar spent on different commodities is unequal, you can increase your total utility by switching from the lower to the higher marginal utility commodities. If, to simplify, we assume that the price of every commodity is the same, you should so allocate your income as to obtain the same marginal utility from every commodity you buy. We could write this in equation form as follows: $MU_x = MU_y = MU_z$, and so on, where x, y, and z are the commodities bought.

If the prices of different commodities differ, the consumer in equilibrium would not expect to get the same marginal utility from each commodity, but only from the last dollar spent on each commodity. It would be nonsense to think of so allocating your income as to obtain the same marginal utility from a movie and an automobile. But if we divide the marginal utility

[3] Answers: (1), no; (2), yes; (3), no; (4), no.

from each by the price of each, then we have made them comparable. Then we can state our central proposition again: For the consumer to be in equilibrium, the marginal utility of the last dollar spent on each commodity must be equal. In equation form, the equilibrium condition is,

TWO APPLICATIONS

Advertising and Consumerism

Each consumer will maximize his utility by spending his income so that his marginal utility is the same from the last dollar spent on each product he buys. Does advertising improve or lessen his chances of reaching this equilibrium?

Clearly, insofar as advertising provides information on available products and their prices, it helps. You can optimally allocate your income only if you know what your alternatives are—new products, characteristics of existing products, prices. But insofar as advertising provides misleading or inaccurate information, it lessens your chances of maximizing your utility. Modern consumerism is right to push for meaningful, accurate advertising.

The hardest problem arises on another issue. Suppose advertising convinces you that you want a new 10-speed bike, when previously you had been content with your older model. You buy the new bike, using the principle of equating marginal utilities. Is your utility being maximized? Given your new (post-advertising) preferences, the answer is clearly yes. But having now spent $80 for a new bike, you have that much less to spend on other goods and services. Are you better off now, with the new bike but without $80, or with your old model but the $80 in your pocket? If you say, the latter, would you favor a law that forbids advertising new products?

Figure 5-4

The consumer pays only fifty cents (gray rectangle) for his five bananas, but his demand curve shows he would have been willing to pay more than ten cents for each of the first four. Thus the light blue triangle measures how much more he would have been willing to pay to get the total utility provided by five bananas, and hence measures the "consumer's surplus" he obtains free.

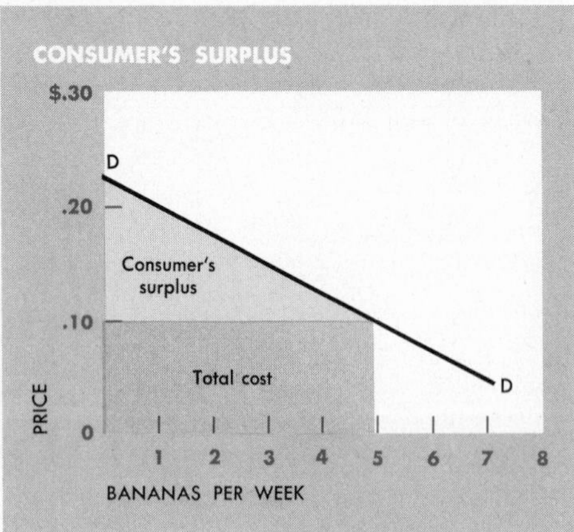

Consumer's Surplus

When a consumer is in equilibrium he is usually receiving a "consumer surplus" on the commodities he buys. Figure 5-4 shows a typical downward-sloping demand curve, say for bananas. The market price is ten cents, and you buy five per week. But your demand curve shows that you would have been willing to pay twenty cents for the first banana, seventeen cents for the second, and so on. The price you would have paid for each banana indicates the marginal utility you expect to receive from that banana. Thus, you get a "consumer's surplus" of utility on each of the first four bananas, since you have to pay only ten cents for each. The light blue area provides a measure of this consumer's surplus.

(Brainteaser: How much consumer's surplus do you get on each gallon of water you drink? On each cubic foot of air you breathe? Hint: The answer depends on the difference between total utility and marginal utility.)

therefore:

$$\frac{MU_x}{P_x} = \frac{MU_y}{P_y} = \frac{MU_z}{P_z}, \text{ etc.,}$$

where P is the price of each commodity.[4]

We can extend this reasoning to other uses of households' incomes. You may save part of your disposable income rather than spending it. To be in equilibrium, you must so allocate your income between saving and spending that the marginal utility obtained from a dollar saved is equal to that obtained from a dollar spent on each item you buy. Equating marginal utilities works for all uses of the dollars we have to spend or to save.

2. When consumers spend their incomes this way, their demand curves for different products accurately reflect the relative marginal utilities they think they will obtain from different products they might buy. If you spend a dollar for a necktie rather than for a movie ticket, we assume you prefer the tie to the movie. Your preferences are reflected in your demand curves for the two products, and your demands will reflect to producers the relative values you place on neckties and movies. This is an extremely important point, since in our system we rely largely on consumer demand to give signals to producers on what should be produced and in what quantities.

[4] Wouldn't this lead the consumer to allocate all his income to x instead of y or z, if x has the highest marginal utility? No, because of the law of diminishing marginal utility. Remember that the marginal utility obtained from an additional unit of each commodity declines as the consumer gets more of it in any time period. Thus, spending more dollars on x will produce diminishing marginal utility for x, and will generally keep the consumer from switching all his expenditures to x (that is, to any one commodity).

MARKET DEMANDS—SIGNALS TO PRODUCERS

Millions of consumers, each allocating his income to provide the greatest satisfaction to himself, provide the basic signals to producers telling what consumers want produced. The local department store isn't much concerned with your personal demand for shirts. But it is very much concerned with the aggregate market demand for shirts in its market territory. Aggregate, or market, demand is the sum of all the individual demands in each market. Such market demand provides the main signal to producers as to what they should supply to meet consumers' wants. The market demand schedule provides an effective signal to the local grocer of the relative importance attached by its customers to getting more pounds of sugar at different prices (given their incomes and the prices of other products).

Consider the market demand for sugar at the crossroads store of an isolated village with only three families. The demand schedules of the three families, and total demand, might look something like Table 5-3. The market demand

TABLE 5-3
Crossroads Demand for Sugar

PRICE PER POUND	PURCHASES PER WEEK BY: A	B	C	ALL THREE	EXPENDITURES	DEMAND
20 cents	3 lb	1 lb	2 lb	6 lb	$1.20	
						Elastic
15 cents	4 lb	2 lb	4 lb	10 lb	1.50	
						Unitary
10 cents	6 lb	3 lb	6 lb	15 lb	1.50	
						Inelastic
5 cents	6 lb	4 lb	7 lb	17 lb	.85	

schedule for sugar, as seen by the crossroads grocer, is the sum of the individual demands of his customers. It could be plotted on a graph just like the individual's demand schedule. The total expenditures column shows the grocer's total weekly sales of sugar at different prices. (For the moment, disregard the right-hand column.)

ELASTICITY OF DEMAND[5]

The preceding sections say the most important things about individual and market demands as signals from consumers to producers. But demands for individual products vary widely, and it is useful to be able to describe some of these differences precisely in analyzing how well the economic system responds to changing consumer demands.

Consider salt. Suppose ordinary table salt sells for ten cents a pound and you use about a pound a month. If the price goes up to fifteen cents, how much less salt will you use? Probably no less at all. Unsalted beans and potatoes don't taste very good, and the fraction of a cent saved each day by not salting your food is trivial compared with the better taste of flavored cooking.

This is a case where quantity bought responds very little, or not at all, to price changes. Plotted on a graph, the demand curve for table salt at the local grocery store would be substantially vertical over the ten-to-fifteen cent price range. We say that the demand for table salt is very "inelastic" over this price range. Quantity bought changes very little in response to a change in price.

At the other extreme, take your demand for steak at the local A&P if you are substantially indifferent about whether you eat beef or pork. Suppose the price of beef jumps 10 percent. The chances are you will cut back your steak purchases sharply and substitute pork. Here your demand for steak would be highly "elastic." You would cut your purchases a lot in response to an increase in price.

"Elasticity" is a measure that tells how much the quantity bought will change in response to a change in price. Thus, elasticity of demand is a measure of the responsiveness of quantity bought to changes in price. (A more precise definition will be given on page 60.) Elasticity is one characteristic of **any given demand curve or schedule.** To say a given demand is elastic or inelastic is merely to describe it, just as you might describe your next-door neighbor as tall or short.[6]

Total Revenue and Elasticity of Demand

The concept of demand elasticity helps us to predict what effect price changes will have on total expenditure for a commodity. Look now at the last column of Table 5–3. Suppose the grocer cuts the price of sugar 25 percent, from twenty to fifteen cents a pound. Sales jump from six to ten pounds per week, a 67 percent increase, and his total revenue from sugar goes up from $1.20 to $1.50 per week. The increase in quantity sold more than offsets the decrease in price per pound. Looking at what happens to total expenditures (revenue) gives us a precise measure of elasticity. **If demand is elastic, total expenditures will change in the opposite direction from a change in price. If demand is inelastic, total expenditures on a commodity will change in the same direction as a change in price.** Examine the reasoning.

1. Elastic Demand—Total Revenue Moves in the Opposite Direction from Price. This is the case just described. Although the storekeeper gets 25 percent less per pound, he sells

[5]Mathematical Appendix I at the end of the book provides a precise mathematical statement of demand elasticity, which may be helpful to students who think readily in mathematical terms. Ordinarily, the appendix will be most useful *after* you have read the remainder of the chapter.

[6]Strictly, we should call this concept "price elasticity of demand." There is a related concept, "income elasticity of demand," that measures the response of quantity bought to a change in income received. However, throughout this book we shall use "elasticity" to mean "price elasticity." At a more advanced level, we can also speak of "cross-elasticity" of demand. This is the percentage change in the amount of product *A* that will be bought in response to a given percentage change in the price of product *B*.

67 percent more pounds and total revenue increases. Demand is elastic. Reverse the process over the same price range and you will see again that total revenue moves in the opposite direction from price.

2. **Inelastic Demand—Total Revenue Moves in the Same Direction as Price.** Now observe what happens when the grocer cuts the price from ten to five cents. He gets 50 percent less for each pound of sugar, but he sells only 13 percent more pounds. The volume increase, with such inelastic demand, is not great enough to offset the lower price per pound sold. Total revenue drops with a cut in price. Demand is inelastic. Now reverse the process over the same price range. Total revenue will rise if he raises the price from five to ten cents.[7]

3. **Unit Elasticity—Total Revenue Is Unaffected by Price Changes.** The borderline case between elastic and inelastic demand is called "unit" elasticity. This occurs where an upward or downward shift of price is just offset by a proportional change in quantity bought, so that total revenue remains unchanged. The crossroads demand for sugar between ten and fifteen cents is a case in point. Total expenditure on sugar is identical at either price, since the shift in amount bought just offsets the change in price.

A warning: Note that the same demand curve may be elastic in some price ranges and inelastic in others. In most cases, it is not correct to speak of a demand curve as elastic or inelastic as a whole. You need to specify at what price.

The Real-World Importance of Elasticity

The elasticity of demand for his product is a prime concern of every businessman, whether or not he uses that technical term. Consider two important real-world examples that will show why.

First, the farmer. Modern econometric studies show that the demand for most basic farm products is inelastic over the relevant price ranges. What does this mean if farmers all work hard, the weather cooperates, and a bumper crop rolls out? It means that the *total revenue* farmers get from selling their crops will be *lower* as a result of this bonanza, because the bigger crop can be sold only by cutting prices more than proportionately. This simple fact goes far to explain the continuing stream of government-sponsored crop-reduction plans, beginning with the New Deal AAA program, all aimed at raising total farm income. With inelastic demand, even a small crop restriction may induce a substantially higher price and more total revenue from crop sales.

Contrast this with the depression-period attempts of the railroads to increase their total revenues by raising passenger fares in the 1930s. Unfortunately for the railroads, the customers stayed away in droves. Either they stayed at home, or they traveled by bus or car. Demand turned out to be elastic and total revenue moved down, not up. Only when fares were *cut* did total revenue actually rise. The impossibility of filling the coffers by raising price in an elastic-demand market is plain to see, once you understand the concept of elasticity.[8]

[7]Notice that the percentage change in price from ten to five cents is different than that from five to ten cents—50 percent compared with 100 percent. This is because the base with which we compared the five-cent change varies with the direction in which we calculate. The difference really doesn't matter for our purposes, since the effect on total revenue will always give the right answer. (If you always take the percentage change on the bigger price or quantity figure you'll get around this directional problem.) Obviously, the discrepancy between the two ways of figuring percentage change will gradually vanish as we take smaller and smaller price intervals—for example, a price change between ninety-nine cents and $1.00. There is a more precise formula in the mathematical appendix.

[8]What makes demand elastic or inelastic? Demand is likely to be inelastic when (1) your outlay on the object is small, (2) your want for it is urgent, (3) good substitutes are unavailable, and (4) it is wanted jointly with some complementary item. Conversely, demand is likely to be elastic where (1) the outlay involved bulks large in your total expenditures, (2) your want is not urgent, (3) close substitutes are available, (4) the commodity is durable or repairable, and (5) the commodity has multiple uses. The availability of satisfactory substitutes is crucial. For example, nobody's want for Exxon gasoline is likely to be terribly urgent as long as a similar grade of Gulf can be had for the same price across the street.

A Quantitative Measure of Elasticity

For some purposes it is useful to be able to say just how elastic or inelastic demand is. A ready measure can be worked out from the previous reasoning. Elasticity depends on the relative changes in quantity and price. If the percentage change in quantity bought (Q) is more than the percentage change in price (P), total revenue moves in the opposite direction from price; demand is elastic. Thus, we can easily get a numerical value for elasticity by the formula:

$$\text{Elasticity} = \frac{\%\text{ change in } Q}{\%\text{ change in } P}$$

For example, if a cut in the price of steel ingots from \$80 to \$76 per ton (5 percent) leads to an increase in sales from 100 million to 101 million tons (1 percent), by inserting the 5 percent and 1 percent in the formula we get an elasticity of demand of .2. Any value less than 1 (unity) is called inelastic demand. Any value of more than 1 is called elastic demand. Unitary elasticity of demand means exactly offsetting changes in quantity and price.[9]

[9]Since price and quantity move in opposite directions, elasticity will always be a negative figure. The minus sign is customarily dropped in using elasticity measures. Strictly, our formula needs to be applied only to very small changes in price and quantity. For a more precise statement, see the mathematical appendix.

TABLE 5–4

Estimated Elasticities of Demand

Furs	2.6
Autos	1.5
Refrigerators	1.1
Local phone calls	1.0
Luggage	.8
Movie tickets	.4
Electric light bulbs	.3
Matches	0

Source: Treasury estimates presented before House Ways and Means Committee, 1960.

Econometric estimates have been made of the elasticity of demand for many products, although many of these are very rough. Table 5–4 gives estimates for several common products (for price variations near their then prices). The preceding footnote on what makes demand elastic or inelastic should help you explain the elasticities of the different products. Another study recently found the present demand elasticity for butter to be about 1.3, compared to a pre-World War II estimate of about .6. Can you explain the difference? (Hint: Consider possible substitutes then and now. Margarine came into general use in the 1940s.)

Elasticity in Graphical Presentations

A perfectly inelastic demand curve would obviously be vertical; the same quantity would be bought at every price. An example might be your demand for insulin over a wide price range if you needed the insulin to stay alive. Highly elastic demand would be a nearly horizontal demand curve. Very small changes in price would lead to very large changes in the quantity bought. But in between these extremes, trying to read elasticity by the slope of a plotted demand curve is dangerous business. Look, for example, at the two charts in Figure 5–5. Both show the demand schedule seen by our old friend the crossroads grocer, but they use different horizontal and vertical scales. Exactly the same demand is shown on both.

Because the left-hand graph uses an extended horizontal scale, the demand curve is relatively flat throughout. Yet it is exactly the same demand as in the right-hand graph, and the elasticity at every point along it is identical with the corresponding points on the right-hand graph. Both curves are marked to show the elastic and inelastic areas. This example emphasizes the danger in trying to generalize that flat demand curves are elastic, whereas steep ones are inelastic. You have to remember that elasticity is a matter of relative (percentage) changes in price and quantity. Elasticity changes continuously along a straight, diagonal demand curve.

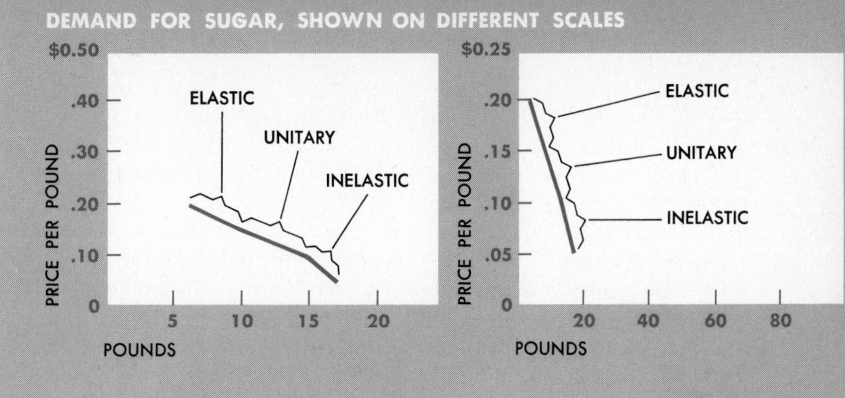

Figure 5–5

Trying to judge elasticity of demand by looking at the slope of a demand curve is tricky. These two curves show identical demands, plotted on different scales.

Check it for yourself if, as is likely, this statement seems to you intuitively wrong.[10]

INTERACTING DEMANDS

If you buy a car, your demand for gasoline is pretty sure to increase. But, assuming that your total income stays unchanged, your demand for some other things (say bus rides) will drop. This example illustrates the two main kinds of interrelationships among demands for different things: (1) complementary, or joint, and (2) substitutive, or competitive. When you buy a car, you take on a "complementary" demand for gasoline to run it. But now you don't need to ride the bus. Bus rides are "competitive" with cars in your demand pattern.

In the broadest sense, if your income is a given amount, every expenditure is competitive with every other. More of anything means less of something else. But in many instances this effect is quite remote; for example, your car purchase may have little effect on your demand for potatoes. By contrast, the substitution of car rides for bus rides is very direct. Thus, in many cases it is important to recognize complementary demands, even though in the broader sense all are competitive, given the budget constraints nearly all of us face.

[10]For mathematicians: The curve which shows unitary elasticity at all points is a rectangular hyperbola. The equation is $xy = \text{constant}$.

REVIEW

Concepts to Remember

This chapter has presented a string of important new analytical concepts that will be used repeatedly. Check to be sure you have them clearly in mind:

demand	elasticity of demand
individual and aggregate demand	elastic demand
marginal utility	inelastic demand
total utility	unit elasticity
law of diminishing utility	competitive demands
equilibrium of the consumer	complementary demands

For Analysis and Discussion

1. Is price a good measure of the marginal utility of a good to each buyer? Explain.
2. Do you act like the mythical "economic man" in allocating your income among alternative uses to maximize your satisfaction from it? If your answer is "no," are you saying that you are irrational?
3. Calculate roughly how big a voice people in your own family's income groups have in the allocation of the economy's resources. Does it seem to you to be a fair share? (Check the income data in Figure 5-1.)
4. Explain the concept of "equilibrium of the consumer." How useful does this concept seem to you in understanding consumer behavior? If you don't think it is useful, can you suggest a better model?
5. "Every individual is different. Thus it makes no sense for economists to lump them all together in talking about aggregate market demand." True or false?
6. "Since consumers' demand signals what is to be produced in America, it follows that consumers are responsible if our economy produces "wasteful" products like elaborate chrome trim on automobiles." Do you agree or disagree?
7. How elastic is your demand for the following, at the present price for each?
   a. Beer
   b. Stereos
   c. Porsche roadsters
   d. Required textbooks
   e. Gasoline
   f. Airplane tickets home

   In each case, see if you can isolate the factors that make the elasticity what it is.
8. If the demand for wheat is inelastic, would a bumper crop raise or lower wheat farmers' total income?
9. What effect would a successful advertising campaign by the Gulf Oil Company have on the elasticity of consumer demand for Gulf gas? Explain your answer.
10. Suppose unsold stocks of gasoline are piling up in the storage tanks of the major refineries. If you were regional sales director of one of the major companies, would you recommend a marked reduction in the filling-station price? How would you go about deciding?

CASE 2

Cash or Food Stamps for the Poor?

One controversial part of the government's overall program to aid the poor has been the food stamp program, which cost nearly $2 billion in 1972. Under this program, a poor family of four could receive up to $106 monthly in free food stamps. Less needy families or individuals could receive food stamps by paying part of their value, for example, thirty-five cents for each dollar stamp. The government then redeems the stamps from the grocers.

The purpose of the program is to assure that poor families, especially those with children, receive a reasonably adequate diet. By giving the poor food stamps instead of money, proponents argue, we can be sure the aid will be used for food rather than liquor, gasoline, drugs, paying off old debts, or other less urgent needs. But others, including some of the poor themselves, disagree. It is insulting and inefficient, they say, to give food stamps rather than money, restricting the recipients' freedom to judge for themselves what is best for them. It is inefficient, this counterargument runs, because if the government gave the poor the same amount of money, the poor could not possibly be worse off, and might well be better off. The poor recipient could buy all food if that is what he wants and needs most, or he could use the funds for something else if other needs are more urgent. The plan is insulting because it implies that the poor cannot be trusted to know and to do what is best for themselves and their children.

Who is right? Should we scrap the food stamp plan and go to a system of cash-grants-only for the poor? The question is an important one because the same basic issue arises with many other types of government assistance—for example, rent supplements to provide better housing, free public education, and subsidized public health benefits.

Supply, Demand, and Market Prices

CHAPTER SIX

Chapter 3 provided a bird's-eye view of how producers respond to consumer demands in a private-enterprise, free-market economy. Chapters 4 and 5 looked briefly at businesses and households, the main suppliers and demanders in the economy. This chapter will examine in more detail the role of the market and market prices in connecting consumers and producers. If you thought economics was going to be about "supply and demand," this is it.

THE ROLE OF MARKETS AND MARKET PRICES

In a loose way, it is easy to see how consumer demands get the goods and services produced that consumers want. If consumers buy more paint, the immediate result is increased retail sales, and paint stores order more paint from wholesalers to replenish their stocks. The wholesalers in turn order more paint from the manufacturers. And the manufacturers, with joyous hearts, produce more paint, because their profits depend on producing and selling paint. The linkage may be jerky and imperfect, but each participant has an incentive to do his part—the profit incentive.

Sometimes the linkage between consumer and producer is direct. An example is the barber who cuts your hair. More often, consumer demand has to pass through several links before it hits the ultimate producer. An example is consumer demand for steel nails, which goes through the local hardware store and a wholesaler before it gets to, say, Bethlehem Steel, which makes nails.

But Bethlehem in turn has to obtain iron ore, coal, and other ingredients of steel, to say nothing of steel-making machinery, buildings for its operations, adding machines for its cost clerks, and stationery for its typists. Yet nails are a relatively simple commodity. Try autos, or new houses, or air travel. If you chart the branching-out relationships that start with consumer demand, you will soon find yourself rapidly running out of sheets of paper.

What ties all these myriad links together is a structure of markets and market prices. The grocer knows you want sugar when you walk into his store and buy ten pounds at the prevailing price. Similarly, there is a market that links grocers to wholesalers; one that links wholesalers and sugar refiners; one that links sugar refiners and sugar growers.

In each market, price acts as the adjuster between demand and supply. When you demand more, price tends to move up. When price rises, there is an increased incentive to produce more. **It is this interaction between demand, supply, and price that is the core of the self-adjusting mechanism of the private-enterprise system. A good understanding of the much-cited "law of supply and demand" is a powerful tool indeed for understanding how the modern economy works.**

SUPPLY

Businesses are the main suppliers of goods and services in our economy. But to understand more precisely how they respond to consumer demands, we need to define "supply" more carefully.

Supply is a schedule of amounts that will be offered for sale at different prices during some time period, other factors remaining unchanged. Like demand, supply can also be plotted on a curve with amounts on the horizontal axis and prices on the vertical one. But it differs from demand when it is plotted, since the supply curve ordinarily slopes uphill whereas the demand curve ordinarily slopes downhill. The upward slope of the supply curve reflects that fact that more units will usually be offered for sale at high than at low prices, in contrast to the reverse demand relationship.

Upward sloping supply curves may seem obvious to you. The higher the price, the greater will be the profit inducement to produce and to sell more. Or they may seem anything but obvious. You may think of the economies of mass production and suspect that more units will be produced when demand increases, without any rise in price. This may, of course, be true under some circumstances, and sometimes —for example, in the auto industry—to a significant extent.

The relation between firms' costs and the supply curves for their products is analyzed in detail in Chapters 19–21. For the moment, take it on faith that most supply curves are flat or upward sloping. And even if supply curves should turn out to be downward sloping in some cases, the type of interaction between supply, demand, and price described in the following pages will still be useful.

Individual and Market Supply

Individual consumers and households are the basic economic decision makers underlying market demand curves. Similarly, individual suppliers are the basic decision makers underlying market supply curves. For consumer goods and services, business firms are the main suppliers; for labor and other productive resources, individuals are the main suppliers.

We aggregate individual supplies to obtain market supply curves. Suppose there are three dairy farms. At various milk prices each will produce and offer different amounts for sale, as in Table 6–1. This is the market supply schedule for milk in this area.[1]

This supply schedule can be plotted on a graph just as the demand schedule was. Again putting price on the vertical axis and quantity on the horizontal one, we get the market supply curve shown in Figure 6–1.

[1]Farmer *C* is what some economists call a "marginal producer." He comes into the market only if the price rises to a relatively high level.

TABLE 6–1

Supply Schedule for Milk

PRICE PER QUART	NUMBER OF QUARTS SUPPLIED PER WEEK BY:			
	A	B	C	ALL
20 cents	50	50	20	120
15 cents	40	50	20	110
10 cents	40	40	0	80
5 cents	30	35	0	65

It is important to remember some of the same warnings on supply that apply to demand: (1) Supply is a schedule, not a single amount. Thus, more output at a higher price may merely be a movement to a new point on the supply schedule, not an increase in supply. A change in supply is a change in the schedule (a shift of the curve). (2) Supply has meaning only with reference to some time period. The period should always be specified. (3) A supply schedule or curve is always drawn on the assumption of "other things equal"—for example, costs of labor and raw materials, technology, and the like. Just what "other things" we hold constant will vary from case to case, depending partly on the time period involved. For a one-day period, the number of cows and the amount of mechanical equipment the farmer has must be taken as constants. If we're talking about supply per year, obviously such matters become variables. This would lead you to suspect that the supply curve per year might look quite different from the supply curve per day—and it does, as we shall see next.

Figure 6–1

The supply curve shows how many quarts will be supplied each week at different prices.

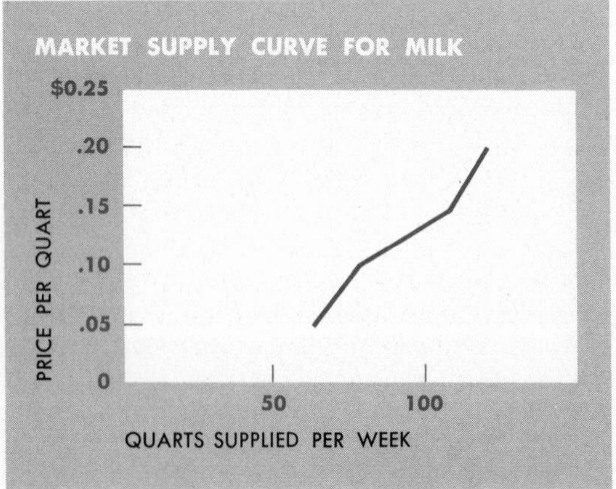

Elasticity of Supply

Supply can be elastic or inelastic, just like demand. This is true of both individual producers' and market supplies. If the amount put on the market is highly responsive to price changes, the supply is elastic. If the amount offered is little affected by price variations, the supply is inelastic. Except that the amount supplied and the price ordinarily move in the same, rather than in opposite directions, the concepts of demand and supply elasticity are similar.

Elasticity of supply varies with the time period involved. Take an extreme case of inelastic supply first. Suppose you have a strawberry patch and a roadside stand, but no overnight refrigeration. If you picked twenty quarts this morning, you must sell them today at whatever price you can get or let them spoil (neglecting the possibilities that you may eat them fresh yourself or preserve them). Thus your supply curve *for the day* may be completely inelastic—a vertical line at twenty quarts of strawberries. By the end of the day, if you have them left you're willing to sell your twenty quarts at any price from zero up—the higher the better, of course. Figure 6–2 pictures this simple assumption, in which cost of production appears to play no role in determining your supply curve.

Now take a case at the other extreme. Suppose some simple commodity like lead pencils can be produced almost without limit at a cer-

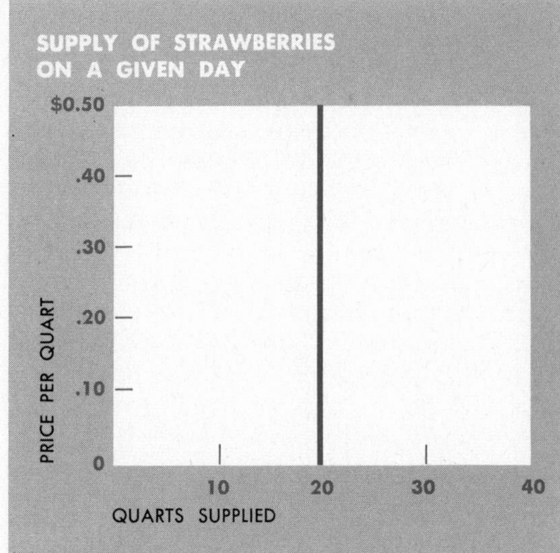

Figure 6–2

This chart shows completely inelastic supply. The same number of quarts is offered at any price shown.

Figure 6–3

This chart shows infinitely elastic supply. Given a long time to adjust, any number of pencils can be produced for sale at three cents a pencil.

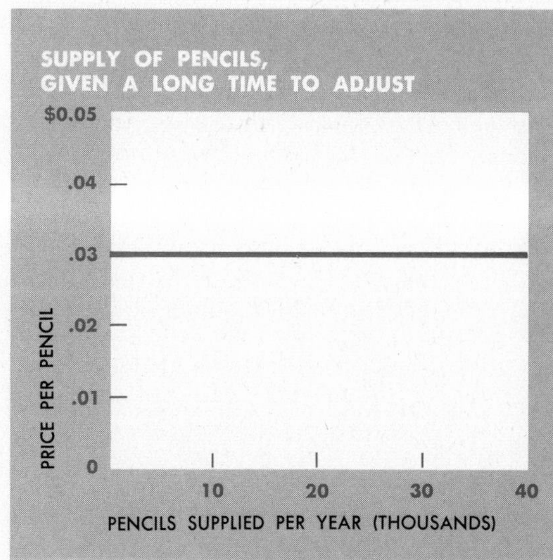

tain cost, say three cents per pencil, merely by duplicating existing manufacturing facilities, materials, and workers. Given enough time to build new facilities, almost any given number of pencils will be produced for sale at a price of three cents or above. Thus, the supply curve might be completely elastic—a horizontal line, at three cents per pencil, as in Figure 6–3.

This case, like that of strawberries, is oversimplified; cost per pencil may not be quite constant in the real world, and the resulting supply curve may not be perfectly flat. Most cases and most time periods, of course, fall somewhere between these two extremes.

SUPPLY, DEMAND, AND MARKET PRICE

You may have visited the "wheat pit" at the Board of Trade in Chicago, which is one of the world's major wheat-trading markets. Here millions of bushels of wheat are bought and sold daily by a relatively small number of men, acting largely as dealers and agents for others. Suppose the supply and demand for wheat in the pit on some particular day are as shown in Table 6–2, and that these schedules are constant for the entire day.

In effect, each of these men acts as an agent for people wanting to sell or buy wheat. Imagine that each seller tries to auction his wheat off at the highest possible price. Suppose that the first bid on this day is $1.50 a bushel for 1,000 bushels. It is readily filled, but it's clear that at this price there's going to be trouble, because buyers will demand 17 million bushels, whereas sellers are willing to offer only 12 million bushels. Table 6–2 shows that a lot of buyers are willing to pay more than $1.50 if they have to. And most of them soon discover they have to, because offerings are 5 million bushels short of demand at $1.50. We say there is an "excess demand" of 5 million bushels at $1.50. As buyers bid higher prices to get the wheat they want, the price will move up toward $2.00. As the price rises, those unwilling to pay the higher price will drop out and new sellers will come in, until at

TABLE 6–2

Supply and Demand for Wheat, Chicago, on a Given Day

BUSHELS OFFERED (IN MILLIONS)	PRICE	BUSHELS DEMANDED (IN MILLIONS)
18	$3.00	8
16	2.50	11
14	2.00	14
12	1.50	17
10	1.00	20

$2.00 the amount offered for sale just matches the amount demanded. There is no reason to suppose that the price will be bid higher this day, because everyone who is willing to pay $2.00 is getting his wheat and everyone who has wheat for sale at $2.00 sells it.

Try starting with a price of $3.00 to see whether that price could last long in this market. Where does the price stabilize?

Figure 6–4

With these supply and demand curves, the equilibrium price will be $2.00, with 14 million bushels exchanged.

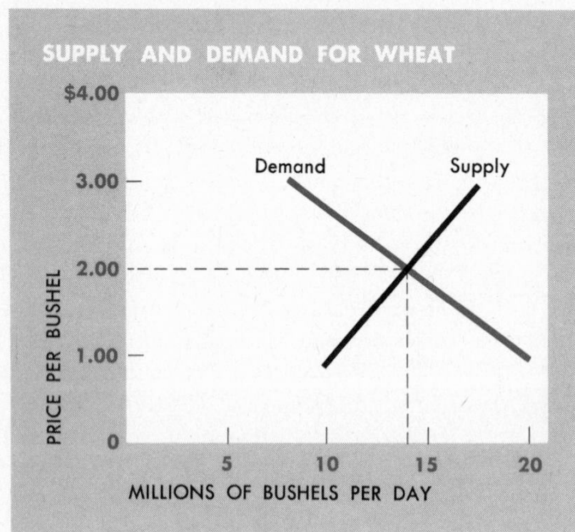

This same analysis can be done graphically just as well. Figure 6–4 graphs these same demand and supply schedules. The curves intersect at a price of $2.00 with 14 million bushels traded. This is the only price at which the amount demanded just matches the amount supplied, and it is the price that will be reached through bargaining in the market. The reasoning is the same as with the schedules. Try any higher price, say $3.00, and you can see from Figure 6–4 that it can't last. At $3.00, 18 million bushels will be offered but only 8 million bushels demanded; there is an "excess supply" of 10 million bushels. Competition among sellers will push the price down. At any price higher than $2.00, there is excess supply. There will be too many sellers for the buyers, and sellers will shade their prices in order to find buyers. At any lower price, buyers won't be able to get the wheat they demand and will shade up the prices they offer.

Equilibrium Price and Market Equilibrium

When a price is established that just clears the market, economists call it an "equilibrium price." The amount offered just equals the amount demanded at that price. Price is in equilibrium when, with given demand and supply curves, it stays put at that level. At any other level, price will not be in equilibrium, because there will be excess supply or excess demand, that will drive price up or down toward a level that will eliminate the excess supply or excess demand.

When an equilibrium price has been reached, with given demand and supply curves, we say the market is in equilibrium. At the prevailing price, there is neither excess supply nor excess demand. Unless either demand or supply changes, price will remain unchanged, as will the amount bought and sold each time period.

Consumer demands and producers' responses to those demands are thus meshed together through market adjustments toward equilibrium. Once a market has reached equilibrium, it has impersonally and automatically:

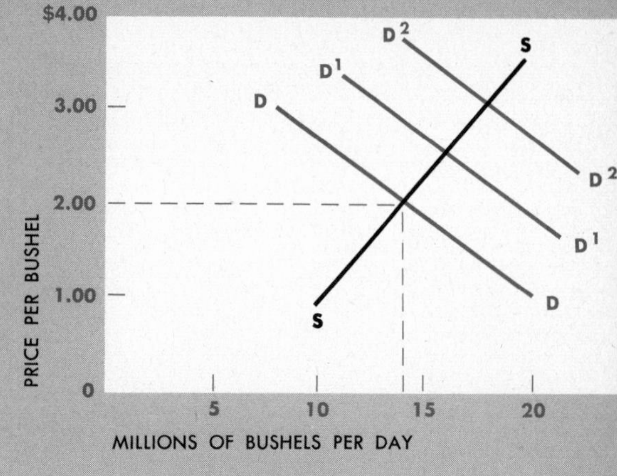

Figure 6–5

Increases in demand to D^1D^1 and D^2D^2 cause increases in both price and quantity traded. The new equilibrium with D^2D^2 involves a price of $3.00 and 18 million bushels exchanged daily.

1. Reflected the wants of all consumers willing to spend their dollars in that market, weighting each want by the number of dollars that particular consumer will spend at different prices. If each consumer's demand schedule truly reflects the marginal utilities of different amounts of the product to him, the market has given him the largest utility obtainable for his dollars.

2. Led firms to produce as much of the product as consumers will buy, taking into account the costs of producing the commodity. These costs are reflected in the supply curve; the higher costs of production are, the less will be produced at each price offered by consumers.

And we can be reasonably sure this equilibrium accurately reflects the preferences of all parties concerned, buyers and sellers, because the exchanges are voluntary. If any individual saw the purchase or sale as against his best interests, he would not have bought or sold at that price.

Changes in Demand and Supply

Suppose that on the following day the demand for wheat increases, to D^1D^1 on Figure 6–5. The supply curve remains unchanged. Common sense tells you that with constant supply and increased demand, the price will be bid up—and it is. With increased demand D^1D^1, the price is bid up to $2.50 with 16 million bushels bought. Although the supply curve is constant, more wheat is supplied at the higher price. The result of the increased demand is *both* a higher price and more wheat traded. Suppose now that on the third day demand rises again to D^2D^2. The price is then bid still higher—up to $3.00 with 18 million bushels bought. The demand curve slides up the fixed supply curve.

Now try holding a demand curve constant and increasing or decreasing supply. Figure out the effect on price and sales of each shift in supply.

Last, consider a case in which both demand and supply shift simultaneously. Suppose the price of turnips is ten cents a pound and 2,000 pounds are being sold daily, with curves *SS* and *DD* in Figure 6–6. Now both supply and demand increase, to S^1S^1 and D^1D^1. The result is a big increase in sales, to 4,000 pounds, and a rise in price to twelve cents. Try shifting the curves to other positions, and with steeper and flatter slopes.

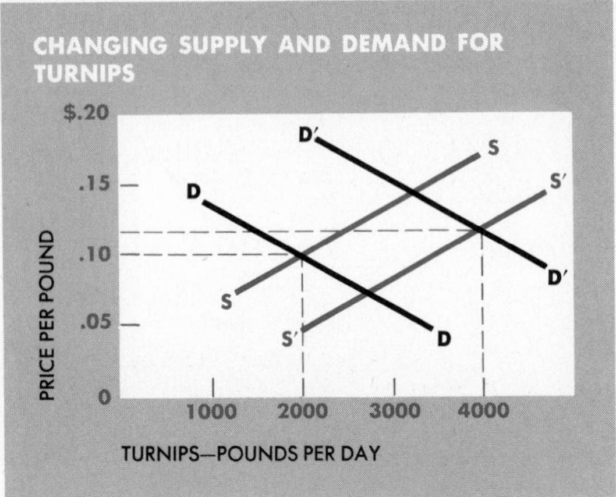

Figure 6–6

When both demand and supply shift simultaneously, as shown by the dashed lines, sales rise to 4,000 pounds and price rises to twelve cents. Try shifting the curves to other positions.

Supply and Demand: Some Special Cases

Completely Inelastic Supply. Some extreme cases may help to clarify what is involved in market adjustments to different demand-and-supply relationships. First take a case in which the amount supplied is absolutely fixed. A favorite economists' example is that there are only four corners at State and Madison Streets in Chicago, sometimes called the busiest corner in the world. The supply curve for building space on this corner is thus completely inelastic—there's no more land available on the corner no matter how high land prices or rents may go. Suppose we graph the supply of land on this corner in square feet, and the demand (*DD*) for it on either a purchase or rental basis. The picture might look roughly like Figure 6–7, with annual rents in equilibrium at $1,000 per square foot.

Now suppose the demand for space on the corner increases. The demand curve moves up to D^1D^1. Property owners can now charge $1,100 per square foot. The amount of land rented is identical before and after the increase in demand. This outcome is very nice for the landowner, not so good for the consumer. But if demand falls, the full burden falls on the landowner. The price (rent) going to the supplier (landowner) is determined solely by the demand. Supply in this extreme case, and only in this case, has no active role in determining the price.

Completely Elastic Supply with "Constant Costs." Now take the other extreme—the pencil industry described before where the amount supplied could be increased at a constant cost by merely duplicating productive facilities. Given a long enough time period, the supply curve here would look perfectly flat, as in Figure 6–8. If *DD* is the demand, the price of pencils will be three cents and 10,000 per day will be made and sold. If demand increases to D^1D^1, the price remains unchanged while production and sales rise to 12,000 daily. This is a case of "constant costs." Since more pencils can be produced at the same cost per pencil, increased demand will simply call forth more pencils without bidding up the price.

Most real-world cases lie between the land and pencil extremes—though many commodities approximate the pencil case, given a long

Figure 6–7

With completely inelastic supply, increased demand means merely a higher price.

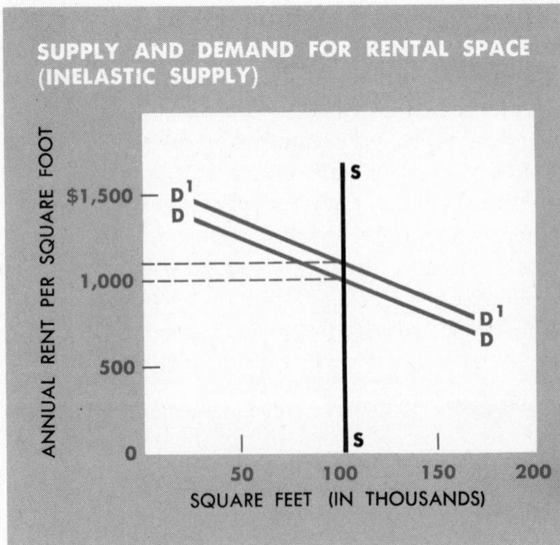

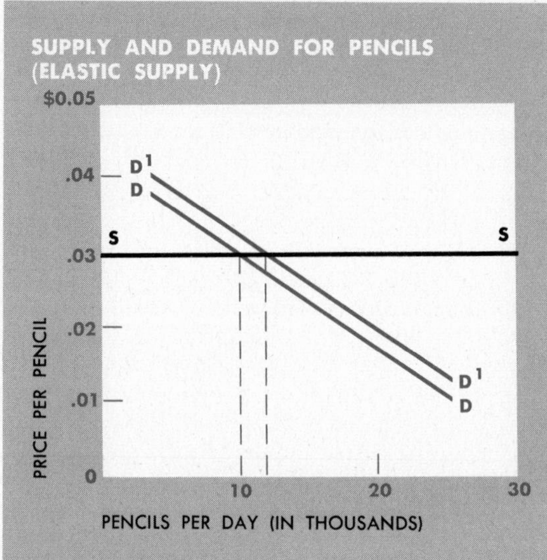

Figure 6–8

With infinitely elastic supply, increased demand leads to more output with no increase in price.

time period for adjustment. If increased output can be obtained only by constructing more expensive factories, or by paying higher prices for raw materials and labor, the supply curve will slope upward. This is the case that economists call "increasing costs," and it is a common one.

Try working out graphically the results of increased demand in constant and increasing cost cases. You will see that it makes a good deal of difference to you, the consumer, which kind of product you want more of. In one case, you get more at the same price; in the other, you get more only at a higher price. (With decreasing costs and a downward sloping supply curve, which we have temporarily ruled out, you could be happier still, since then increased demand could mean more goods at a lower price.)

THE ECONOMICS OF PRICE FIXING

The law of supply and demand states that market price and quantity sold are determined by supply and demand under competitive conditions, such as in the wheat-market case above. But lots of times, people—labor unions, farmers, businessmen, congressmen—don't like the prices and quantities set by market demand and supply. And they want to do something about it. What then?

Price Ceilings

Most people don't like to pay high prices. When prices rise, the pressures mount on Congress and the president to hold them down. "How can I pay $1.00 a pound for butter and $200 a month rent for a poor apartment when my income is only $4,000 a year?" asks the mill hand. And he's not going to be very happy about getting an answer from the politicians in Washington that the law of supply and demand says it has to be that way. He wants something done, or he's easy picking for the other party next election.

So sometimes Congress passes a law to keep prices down. Suppose it slaps an eighty cent price ceiling on butter, below the equilibrium level. The demand for and supply of butter are shown in Figure 6–10. The equilibrium price would be $1.00 a pound.

At the legal price ceiling, clearly there is excess demand of about 600 pounds; people want a lot more butter than there is to buy. The amount demanded daily is 2,200 pounds; that offered is only 1,600.

Who gets the butter? The price system is tied down—it can't allocate the butter by equilibrating supply and demand through a higher price.

"First come, first served" may be the answer. Housewives get the children off to school early and head for the grocer's. They stand in lines in the grocery store. This solution is not calculated to make anyone very happy, least of all the grocer who fast loses his friends when there isn't enough to go around, and the working wives who can't do their shopping till evening.

In frustration, grocers may set up informal rationing systems of their own—say, only a half pound to a customer. Or they may decide to protect their regular customers, so they put away

Who Really Pays the Taxes?

Suppose the government imposes an additional $1.00 tax on each fifth of whiskey distilled for sale. Assume that the long-run supply curve before the new tax is *SS* in Figure 6–9 (same in both halves). The left-hand diagram shows a highly elastic demand curve for whiskey, the right-hand diagram a highly inelastic one. Before the new tax the price is $5.00 per fifth, and 100,000 fifths are being sold weekly in both diagrams.

The new tax raises the effective cost of producing whiskey by $1.00 per fifth; hence the supply curve moves up (to the left) by $1.00 at each level of output. Less will be produced at each price. S^1S^1 represents the new supply curve (after tax) in both halves of the diagram. But as supply is restricted, the results are very different with the two demand curves.

With highly inelastic demand (right-hand diagram), as price moves up consumers continue to buy nearly as much whiskey; the new equilibrium shows nearly as much whiskey produced and sold as before the tax, with the price to the consumer higher by nearly the full amount of the tax. Nearly the whole $1 tax has been shifted onto consumers. With highly elastic demand (left-hand diagram) the amount bought drops rapidly as price rises. The new after-tax equilibrium shows mainly a reduction in production and purchases, with the new price (including tax) only a little above the old $5.00 level. The main result is that consumers get less whiskey, while producers share $1 of the $5+ price with the government. Simple supply-and-demand analysis can produce illuminating results if we use it to examine particular markets.

"Free Goods."

How is it that air, without which we should all die, is free, whereas most other things, which are much less essential, command a price? The answer is obvious, once you try a demand-and-supply analysis. What is the supply of air? It is substantially unlimited at zero cost. The supply curve would rise above the zero-cost line only at some very high quantity figure for most real-world situations. Thus, even though we might be willing, if necessary, to pay a very high price for air, it just isn't necessary. Draw a demand curve, probably highly inelastic, wherever you wish and it will still intersect the zero-cost supply curve at a price of zero.

But now suppose pollution threatens to reduce breathable air below healthy standards. Then the supply of acceptable air is no longer infinite at a zero cost. The supply curve will slope up, reflecting the cost of providing enough clean air, and we shall have to pay a price to get the acceptable air we need.

Figure 6–9

A new tax on whiskey is largely passed on to consumers if demand is inelastic (right-hand portion), but results mainly in reduced output and purchase if demand is elastic (left-hand portion).

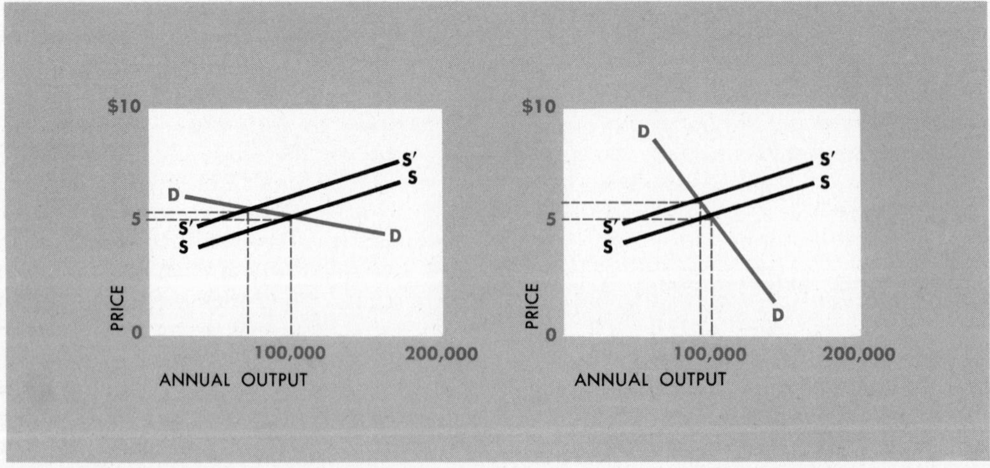

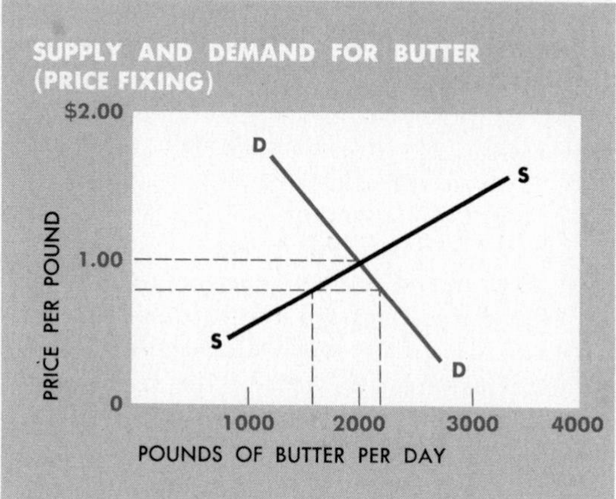

Figure 6–10

When the government sets a legal maximum price below the market equilibrium price, there's trouble. There is excess demand for butter at the artificially low price.

a few cases of butter for them. This is hard on wives who shop around, and disastrous for families that move to new neighborhoods.

If enough people become unhappy enough, the government may have to step in with a formal rationing plan, whereby the customer has to have a government ration ticket as well as money to buy a pound of butter. Nobody is very happy about being rationed, and everybody complains about the red tape. Unless the government officials are both skillful and lucky, the number of ration tickets issued won't exactly match the supplies available, and mixups can be counted on.

Lastly, the price system may sneak in the backdoor again and take over part of the equilibrating job outside the law. "Black markets" may develop. It's pretty hard for well-to-do consumers not to offer the corner grocer a little extra for an extra pound of butter. And it's pretty hard for the grocer, pinched between rising costs and fixed price ceilings, to refuse. Short of a regimented system like Hitler's Germany, it's hard to see how rigid price ceilings can be tightly enforced when excess demand is large. In World War II, such ceilings worked reasonably well in the United States, partly because of intense patriotic pressures and partly because the government gradually raised ceilings as pressures built up on various commodities. The surprising thing to most economists was not that black markets developed, but that the public's basic sense of fair play was so strong that the price-control system didn't blow apart faster than it did.

Whether the job is done by informal seller rationing, government rationing, or black-market price increases, someone or something has to decide who is to get the butter when a price ceiling is imposed below the equilibrium market price. A price ceiling works no magic. It just transfers the equilibrating job to some other channel. You can't get rid of the basic supply-and-demand forces at work by passing a law.

Price Floors and Income Supports

Some people—usually sellers—worry because prices aren't high enough. Labor unions often try to set wages above free-market levels. Some business firms do the same thing with their prices. The government is a large-scale participant in the game of putting floors under prices above the free-market level; parity farm-support prices and minimum-wage legislation are big examples.

Suppose the government decrees that wheat shall not sell for less than $3.00 a bushel when the free-market price would be only $2.00, as pictured in Figure 6–11. It's clear that there is going to be a lot of unsold wheat around—excess supply at the $3.00 price is about 30 million bushels.

Suppose the government price floor is enforced and nobody undercuts the stated $3.00 price. Are wheat farmers better or worse off as a result? First, only about 80 million bushels will be bought. Another 30 million bushels are offered, and either the government will have to buy them up or strong price-cutting pressures will develop among the farmers with the unsold wheat. Second, our old friend elasticity of demand reenters. If demand is inelastic (as in Figure 6–11) total expenditures on wheat are larger at the higher price and total farm income is up (even though consumers get less wheat to eat). But if demand is elastic, the higher price leaves everyone worse off; then farmers get less total income from their wheat, and consumers get less wheat.

But even if demand is inelastic over the price range involved, this simple form of government price edict won't prove very satisfactory. If you are one of the farmers with the millions of bushels of wheat that nobody bought, the higher total income of wheat farmers is small solace to you when you have no income at all. You want the government to help you, too.

So the government program will probably take one of two basic courses. (1) The government may support the legal price through buying up the extra 30 million bushels of wheat. This would in effect move the total (private plus government) demand curve to the right, so the equilibrium price is \$3.00 with 110 million bushels sold. Or (2) the government may restrict wheat production (maybe through a "soil-conservation" program) to reduce supply to a point where the new market price is \$3.00 with sales of 80 million bushels. This policy would bring supply and demand into equilibrium by shifting the supply curve to the left.

Figure 6–11

When the government sets a minimum price higher than the market equilibrium price, there's also trouble. At \$3.00 there is an excess supply of 30 million bushels. D'D' shows the new demand curve if the government buys up the excess; S'S' the new supply curve if the government induces farmers to restrict their output.

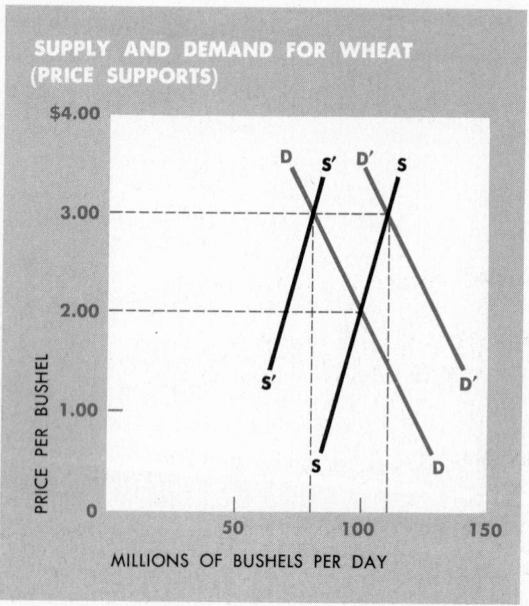

In approach (1), the government ends up buying the 30 million bushels of wheat at \$3.00 a bushel—at a cost of \$90 million to the taxpayers. This result is nice for the farmers but not so nice for the taxpayers. The consumer ends up with less wheat and a higher price for what he buys. Moreover, unless something changes, the government will keep on piling up wheat indefinitely.

In approach (2), this continuing "surplus" situation is avoided by requiring that 30 million fewer bushels of wheat are produced. If the government merely required everybody to cut production by the required percentage, this would be the end of the matter. But actually, the government pays farmers for not producing. Here again the taxpayer picks up the bill for the subsidy paid to farmers for not producing the 30 million bushels of wheat. And as under approach (1), consumers pay more and get fewer bushels of wheat.

The government can keep the price up—if it's willing to eliminate excess supply by buying it up or by restricting output. But laws that fix prices above or below market-equilibrium levels without dealing with excess demand or supply soon face painful problems of which simple supply and demand analysis can give ample warning.

CONCLUSION: SUPPLY, DEMAND, AND MARKET EQUILIBRIUM

A surefire way to sound like an expert in economics is to observe sagely, "You can't repeal the law of supply and demand!" This remark is especially good if the argument is running against you, or you need a clincher when your own position is shaky.

The preceding pages should help to clarify both how meaningless such a statement is until it is carefully applied to the problem at hand, and how powerful an analytical tool supply-and-demand analysis can be. Obviously the government and private groups can control market prices—they do it every day. But unless they recognize that they must do it ultimately through controlling either supply or demand, they're headed for some unhappy surprises.

Supply-and-demand analysis provides a powerful tool in thinking through a wide range of economic problems. It is a simple tool you can use for yourself in thinking through many everyday problems. Over and over in the chapters ahead we shall be asking: What determines demand and supply in this market, how do they interact, and what is the equilibrium outcome toward which they move? These questions are the core of analytical economics.

REVIEW

Concepts to Remember

Recheck your understanding of the important new concepts introduced in this chapter. They are:

equilibrium price	market equilibrium
supply	excess demand
supply curve	excess supply
elasticity of supply	constant costs
market price	increasing costs

For Analysis and Discussion

1. Define supply carefully. What is a change in supply?
2. Is it demand or supply that primarily determines price? If your answer is, "different in different cases," give an example in which you would expect each to be the dominant force.
3. Explain carefully what is meant by saying that an equilibrium price "clears the market."
4. When demand is large, we can be sure the price of the commodity will be high. True or false? Why?
5. Why are diamonds so high-priced, when they serve for the most part only as decoration, while air is free?
6. Are the factors determining the price of a Picasso painting the same as those determining the price of potatoes? Explain your answer.
7. Go back to Figure 6–10, and assume the demand for butter increases. Explain what will happen.
8. Suppose that the demand for cigarettes is very inelastic and a new tax is imposed on cigarettes. Would the tax be passed on to consumers through higher prices? Compare this with a product for which the demand is highly elastic.
9. How does elasticity of demand help to explain why historically governments often imposed a salt tax when they wanted to obtain more revenue?

CASE 3

Consumer Credit and Usury Laws

Throughout the Middle Ages, to charge interest for the use of money was improper under Catholic Church doctrines (most lending was done by Jews) and was prohibited by law in many kingdoms—with violation sometimes punishable by death. Such laws were commonly evaded by borrowers and lenders because of the obvious benefits to both of borrowing and lending, and, with the Protestant Reformation and the commercial and industrial revolution, official antagonism to lending at interest faded rapidly. Yet today, most states still have laws limiting the interest rates that can legally be charged on loans, presumably to safeguard borrowers against greedy lenders.

State laws have varied widely, but most have had a general ceiling (say 10 percent or so on business loans) with an escape provision permitting higher rates where (as on small loans to consumers) extra costs or risks of lending can be shown. In such cases, upper limits of 30–42 percent are not uncommon.

The volume of such lending is large—over $100 billion of consumer credit was outstanding in 1972 on department store installment credit, credit cards, bank loans, auto purchase loans, and the like.

In response to the recent wave of "consumerism," the National Uniform Credit Act was passed to limit to 1.5 percent per month (18 percent per annum) the interest rate that department stores, credit card companies, auto dealers, banks, and others can charge borrowers. This was well below the going rate for many borrowers, especially high-risk, low-income individuals and families. Moreover, by 1972, four states had gone still further and reduced the legal ceiling rate to 10 (Arkansas) or 12 percent (Minnesota, Washington, and Wisconsin). Consumer protection groups are pushing such legislation in other states.

Should your state pass such a law? What do you predict will be the results of these new consumer protection laws? Who will gain and who will lose?

NATIONAL INCOME, EMPLOYMENT, AND PRICES

PART TWO

The Macroeconomy: An Overview[1]

CHAPTER PREVIEW

CHAPTER SEVEN

We now have, from Chapters 1 through 6, an overview of the way a basically market-directed economy handles the big economic problems. This analysis is often called "microeconomics," because it focuses on the way individual households and businesses behave, and the way their interactions govern the uses society makes of its productive resources.

We turn now in Part Two to examine the "macroeconomy"—the totals of output, employment, income, and prices, when we add together all the individual economic units in the economy. Where microeconomics looks at the output of shoes or pizzas, macroeconomics looks at the total national output of all goods and services added together, at the total national income earned by everyone in the economy, at the average price level for all goods and services. Clearly, macroeconomics must build on the foundation of microeconomics, for the national totals are nothing but the sum of the individual parts. And we shall find that the concepts of aggregate demand and aggregate supply (when we add together all households and businesses) help in understanding the outcome of excess supply and demand at the national level, much as supply and demand do for individual products and services.

[1]Some instructors may prefer to use Parts Three and Four on microeconomics and the distribution of income before Part Two on macroeconomics. These parts are written to be equally usable in either order.

THE CIRCULAR FLOW OF SPENDING AND PRODUCTION

In a market-directed economy, goods and services are produced only when there is a market demand for them. If businesses produce more than customers buy (that is, if there is excess aggregate supply), unsold inventories pile up, prices fall, and businessmen cut back on production, laying off workers. Conversely, if customers try to buy more than is being produced (that is, if there is excess aggregate demand), prices are bid up (there is inflation), and businesses increase output and employment.

From an overview, money spending provides the flow that controls the level of aggregate output, employment, and prices. Businesses pay wages, interest, and other income to the public. The public, as consumers, channels the income back to businesses in payment for finished goods and services. This demand, in turn, leads businessmen to hire workers to produce more goods and services for consumers.

Figure 7–1 shows this circular flow of income. The inner circle shows consumers' spending to businesses for goods and services (top half) and businesses' spending back to the public through wages and interest (bottom half). The outer circle shows the corresponding reverse flow of productive services and final products. On the bottom half, labor and other productive services are being hired by businesses from the public. On the top half, finished goods are moving from businesses to consumers.

Which comes first, business hiring and wage payments or consumer spending? This is a chicken-and-egg question. The main point is that neither can go on for long without the other. Economic activity in a private-enterprise system is a continuous flow of productive services and finished products, called forth by a matching counterflow of money spending and guided by the price system into thousands of different product channels within the main streams shown in the diagram.

You can readily see that this picture is oversimplified. Again the government has been left out. And the diagram omits savings and production of capital goods that aren't sold to consumers. But the simple picture points up the central role of the circular-flow process. Unless there is a continuous flow of money-spending by businesses to the public and by the public to

THE CIRCULAR FLOW OF ECONOMIC ACTIVITY

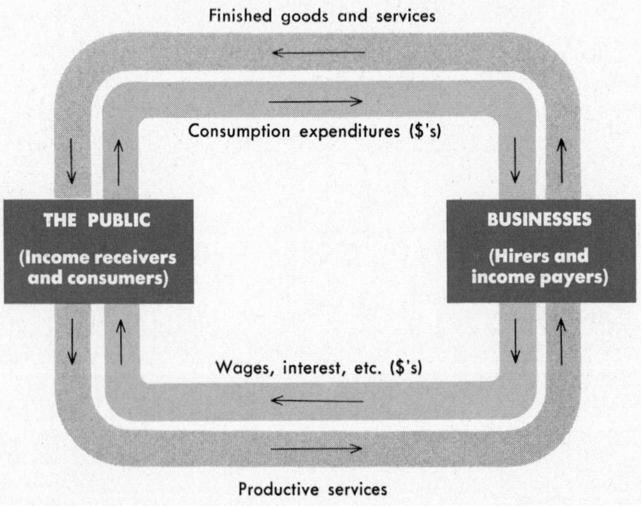

Finished goods and services

Consumption expenditures ($'s)

THE PUBLIC

(Income receivers and consumers)

BUSINESSES

(Hirers and income payers)

Wages, interest, etc. ($'s)

Productive services

Figure 7–1

Dollars flow from consumers to businesses and back in a continuous circle, in payment for final goods and productive services, respectively.

businesses, we're in trouble. If something dams up the flow of spending (say, either households or businesses don't respend the incomes they receive), there is excess total supply; depression and unemployment result, and the economy wastefully operates inside its production frontier. Conversely, if households and businesses spend more than the economy is producing (say, by drawing on past savings or borrowing new money from banks), there is excess demand.

Thus, in macroeconomics, the levels of both aggregate demand (total spending) and aggregate supply (total capacity of the economy to produce goods and services) are very important. In the short run, the potential full-employment output of an economy is roughly fixed, set by its production possibilities frontier. Thus, in the short run, the major focus of macroeconomics is on aggregate demand, for that largely determines the level of current production, employment, incomes, and prices. But in the long run, we can increase the economy's capacity to produce—by saving and investing in new machines and factories, by training workers to produce more efficiently, and the like. Thus, in the long run, the major focus is on expanding potential aggregate supply, for that determines the rate at which society's output and standard of living can rise.

GROWTH AND FLUCTUATIONS IN THE AMERICAN ECONOMY

Viewed macroeconomically, how well has the American economy performed? The answer can be summed up in three statements:

1. Total national output has grown rapidly and vigorously, more so than in any other country over the past two centuries.
2. Output has grown far more rapidly than the number of people at work—that is, output per person has also risen rapidly.
3. Real growth has been spasmodic and uneven, interrupted by intermittent recessions and inflations.

Growth in Total Output

Figure 7–2 shows the growth in national output over the past century. National output (often called gross national product, or GNP) in actual prices rose from $7 billion to over $1 trillion. If you take out the price inflation, the growth is less, but it's still phenomenal—from about $25 billion to about $950 billion in constant dollars (at 1964 prices). This is a more-

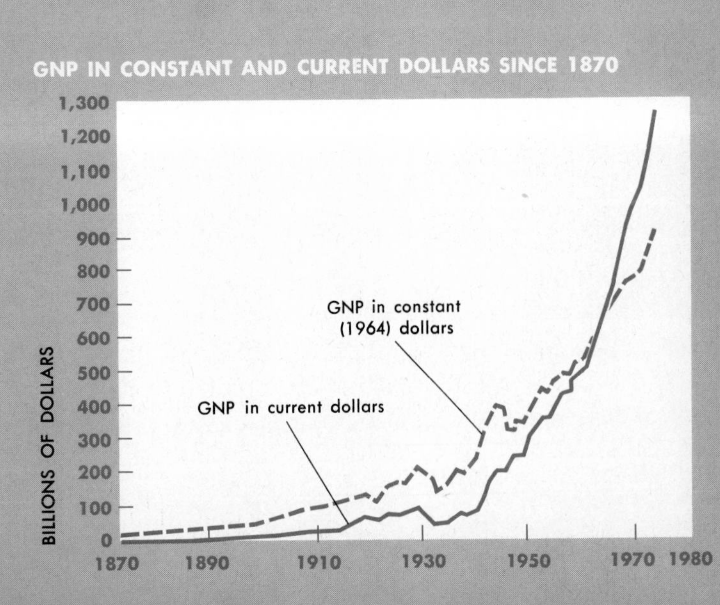

Figure 7–2

Total national output has grown rapidly, but in spurts, over the past century. The solid line shows GNP in current dollars, while the dashed line shows GNP in dollars of constant (1964) purchasing power. The latter thus shows the growth in real output. (Sources: National Bureau of Economic Research and U.S. Department of Commerce.)

than-thirtyfold increase. Total real output grew between 3 and $3\frac{1}{2}$ percent per annum. This rate doesn't sound like much in a single year, but it compounds fast as the decades go by. An annual growth rate of $3\frac{1}{3}$ percent will more than double GNP every two decades.

Growth Rates—A Digression

Figure 7–3, which takes an even longer look at American economic history, emphasizes the importance of considering annual growth *rates*—that is, about the percentage increase per year. The left-hand portion shows real national income—in constant prices—from 1800 to 1973. This chart makes it look as if the growth rate had speeded up enormously in the last half century. The line goes almost straight up, with an increase of over $500 billion in the last fifty years.

But look at the right-hand portion. This shows exactly the same data (national income since 1800, in constant prices) on a "ratio," or "logarithmic," scale. In contrast to regular charts, which give equal vertical distance to equal absolute increases, this ratio scale on the vertical axis gives equal distance to equal percentage increases. Thus, on the ratio scale an increase from five to ten takes about a third of an inch vertically, and an increase from 100 to 200, or from 500 to 1,000, takes exactly the same distance.

A ratio scale permits easy comparison of annual growth rates over a long period. A constant percentage increase—say 3 percent per year—will show as an equal vertical increase each year—a steadily rising straight line. If the growth rate is 4 percent, the line will be steeper. If it is only 2 percent, the line will be flatter.

Thus when we look at the right-hand section of Figure 7–3, we see the past in different perspective. What looks on the regular-interval scale like a big increase in the recent growth rate turns out on the ratio scale to be just about the same annual growth rate as over most of our history.

Growth in Output per Worker and per Capita

This growth in national output in part reflects the steady increase in the number of people working. But over the past century, only somewhat over 1 percent of the 3+ percent annual growth in real output has come from more workers. The other 2+ percent a year

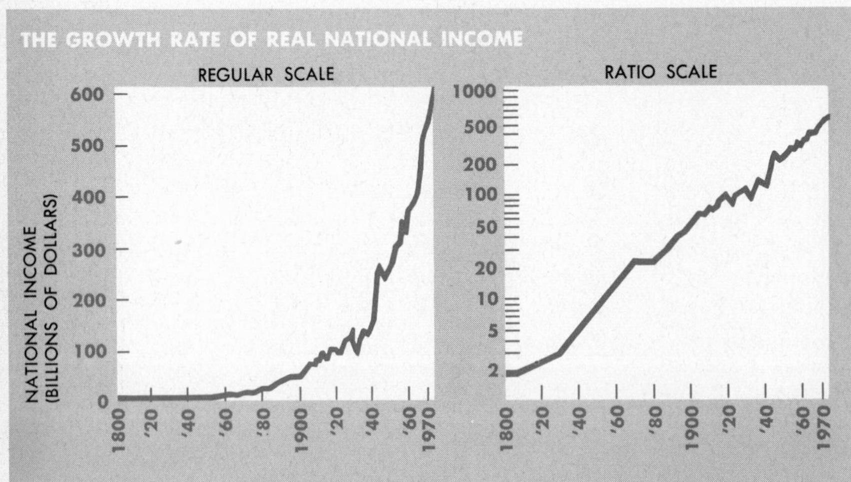

Figure 7–3

Both halves of the chart show the same data—national income since 1800 in constant (1956) dollars. But the ratio scale shows that the annual growth rate has been quite stable over the past century, not rising sharply as the regular scale suggests. (Sources: National Industrial Conference Board and U.S. Department of Commerce.)

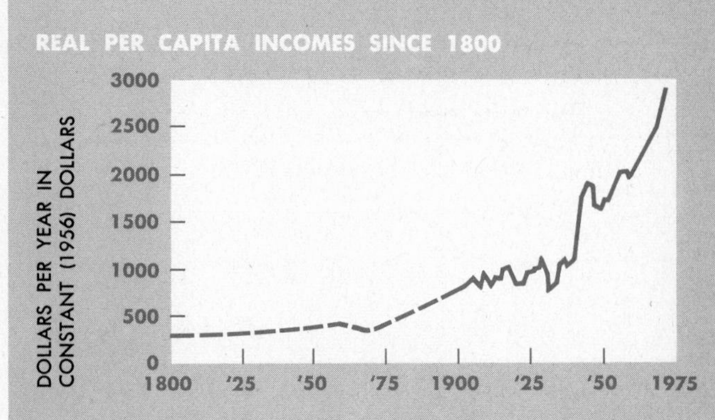

Figure 7–4

Per capita real income has grown rapidly but erratically over the past century, apparently less rapidly during the early 1800s. Note the big recent spurts, but remember that this is not a ratio scale. (Data from Figure 7–3 divided by population.)

represents increased output per worker, which in turn reflects more capital, improved technology, and better management, as well as improved worker skills and education.

Figure 7–4 shows the growth in real output (and income) *per capita* since 1800. As in the other charts, data before the present century are rough, and are plotted only once each decade to give a picture of major trends. Note the big increase in recent decades—but remember that this is a regular-interval, not a ratio, scale. On a ratio scale, the speedup has been moderate, between ½ and 1 percent per annum.

Unemployment and Inflation—Two Big Problems

Over the long run, growth in output, employment, and incomes dominates the macroeconomic picture. But in the short run, unemployment and inflation are often the problems that fill the headlines. Although over the long run the economy has grown impressively, growth has come in surges (inflationary booms) followed by recessions and unemployment. At their worst these recessions develop into major depressions, with massive unemployment of men and machines.

Figure 7–5 shows our intermittent booms and recessions since World War I, superimposed on the strong growth trend in total output. The dashed lines roughly connect the peaks of the booms and the troughs of the recessions.[2] The vertical shaded areas are periods officially labeled recessions, when output was actually falling or at least growing so slowly that unemployment was piling up. Clearly, periods of recovery and prosperity exceed those of recession. But if we think of the top dashed line as roughly the growing full-employment productive capacity of the economy, it is equally clear that much of the time we have wasted potential output by operating inside the economy's production-possibilities frontier. How far the actual output curve falls short of the top dashed line gives a rough picture of the potential output wasted by operating below full employment.

Growth, booms, and depressions are thus part and parcel of the same economic process. However, it is convenient to consider them separately, and the remainder of Part Two primarily focuses on the determinants of output, employment, income, and prices in the *short run,* postponing until later the *long-run* problems of economic growth. Let us first look briefly at the two big

[2]The top of the World War II boom (1942–45) is shown above the dashed line because the economy was then clearly operating beyond its normal capacity level. Housewives, old people, and children were temporarily pulled into the labor force, and workers were called on for vast amounts of overtime to meet wartime production goals.

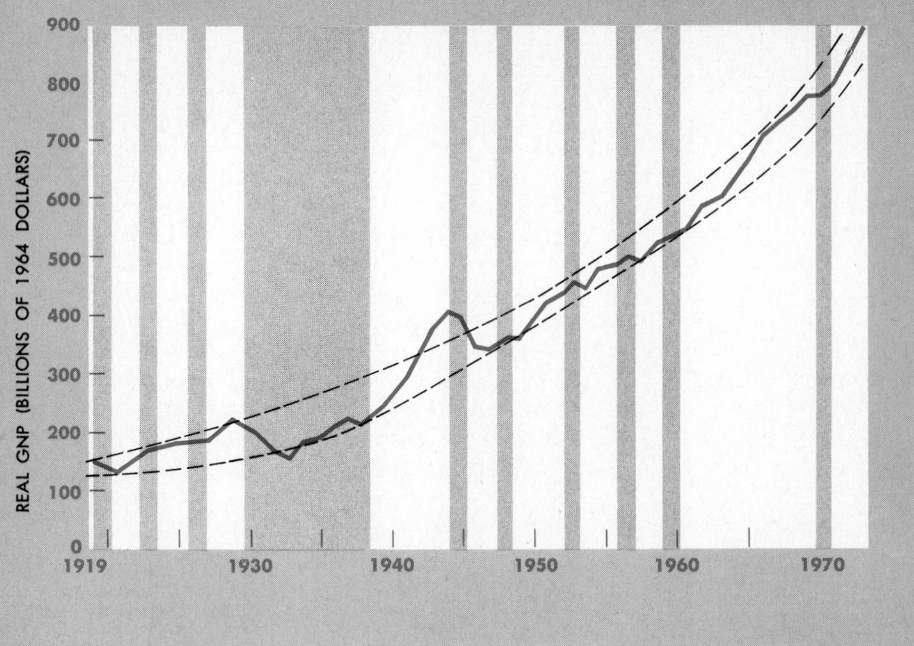

Figure 7–5

The shaded areas show the recessions and depressions since 1919. Recessions since World War II have been mild, hardly more than a flattening out of the growth in real GNP, though quarterly data would show sharper fluctuations. (Sources: U.S. Department of Commerce and National Bureau of Economic Research.)

problems that short-run economic instability has frequently posed—unemployment and inflation—as a backdrop for our analysis of the short-run macroeconomy.

UNEMPLOYMENT

The case for high-level employment of men and machines is clear. Involuntary unemployment wastes productive capacity. It means less housing, fewer refrigerators, highways, and factories than we could otherwise have. It means human misery, decay of skills, degrading deprivation for the unemployed and their families. It means a lower average standard of living for the nation today and in the future. In 1970, our last recession year, total output was about $75 billion short of the economy's high-employment capacity.

What is Unemployment?

Unemployment is defined in the official U.S. statistics to include all those in the labor force who are not employed or self-employed. The labor force includes all those sixteen years old or over who have a job, are self-employed, or are looking for a job; in essence the unemployed are those who don't have a job and are looking for one.

How do we decide who is unemployed? We ask. A scientific sample of the entire population in the relevant age group is asked: Do you have a job? If the answer is no, the respondent is asked: Are you looking for a job? If the answer is no, the respondent is not in the labor force and is not considered unemployed. If the answer is yes, he is in the labor force and is unemployed. The interview probes somewhat further, but this is the core of the matter. A person may be in the labor force, and unemployed, even though he is only looking for a part-time job; large movements of students into and out of the labor force often account for big swings in the unemployment totals during the summer and other vacation periods.

How Low Can Unemployment Be?

Back in the Great Depression of the 1930s, unemployment exceeded 25 percent of the labor force, and millions of others held only part-time or makeshift jobs. National output in 1932 and 1933 wasn't much over half of potential, an enormous human and economic waste. During the 1955–65 decade, which saw two mild recessions, unemployment varied from 4–7 percent. Even these modest unemployment figures meant that we wasted some $300–500 billion in potential real output (at current prices)—or in terms of wasted manpower, the equivalent of some 20–30 million man-years of work.

Clearly, there is some unavoidable minimum of unemployment. In a large, free economy like ours, millions of people are always on the move. In 1972, for example, some 18 million people changed jobs. It takes time for people to move from one job to another; such unemployment is often called "frictional." Moreover, there are always some essentially "unemployable" people looking for jobs—individuals with very poor health, very low mental capacities, no training, and the like. Still others are potentially employable, but their skills and locations are badly out of line with job openings, or their wage demands are unrealistically high for what they can offer; these are the "structurally" unemployed.

How large is unavoidable minimum unemployment? There is no precise answer. With enough pressure of aggregate demand (as in World War II) unemployment can be reduced to almost zero, and indeed millions of new workers can be drawn into the labor force by high wages—if we are willing to accept the accompanying inflation. Careful empirical studies suggest that perhaps 2–3 percent of the labor force may be taken as a reasonable approximation of frictional unemployment plus job seekers who are, for practical purposes, unemployable under normal conditions.[3] As a practical matter, many observers consider 4 percent or so a reasonable high-employment target for an economy such as ours, and this figure is often used in assessing the economy's performance relative to its "high-employment" potential. Others say 3, or 5, percent. Our aspirations on the minimum unemployment level vary with recent experiences.

Other nations set us as a goal to shoot at. In Western Europe since World War II, unemployment rates have generally been much lower than ours, in most cases varying between 1 and 3 percent of the labor force over the past decade. But these results have generally been achieved at the cost of somewhat higher inflation than in the United States.

The Human Costs of Unemployment

Fewer than 15 percent of today's 200 million people were adults at the onset of the Great Depression of the 1930s. Thus, most of today's Americans have no memory of that period and its devastating impact on human morale and well-being, as well as on the aggregate production of the economy.

Figure 7–6 presents the cold statistics. Unemployment reached a peak of over 25 percent of the labor force in 1933, and it averaged between 15 and 20 percent for the entire decade of the thirties. Moreover, many of the people employed were on a part-time basis at drastically reduced rates of pay, and there were millions of "hidden unemployed" barely eking out an existence in agriculture. At the bottom of the depression not more than two-thirds of the total labor force had regular full-time jobs, and some estimates put the figure nearer one-half.

But statistics are bloodless things. Listen to the testimony given by an economist before a

[3] See, for example, *The Extent and Nature of Frictional Unemployment,* published by the Joint Economic Committee of Congress in 1959, and *Economic Report of the President,* January 1970, pp. 147–56.

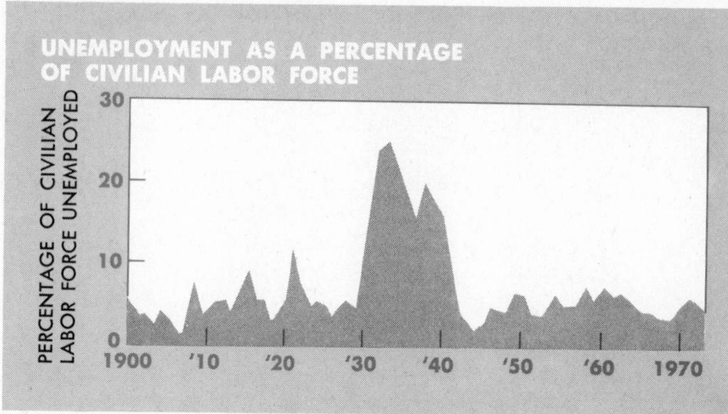

Figure 7–6

Unemployment soars in depression, and even in recessions. What is a reasonable minimum unemployment level for us to shoot at? (Source: U.S. Department of Labor.)

Senate subcommittee investigating unemployment in 1932:[4]

Mr. deSchweinitz: When I appeared before the subcommittee last December, I stated that there were 233,000 persons out of work in Philadelphia. . . . There are now 298,000 persons out of work. . . . In December I told you that 43,000 families were receiving relief, today 55,000 families are receiving relief.

In December, our per family grant was $4.39 per week per family. It is now $4.23 per family. Of this $4.23 per family, about $3.93 is an allowance for food. . . .

I want to tell you about an experience we had here in Philadelphia when our private funds were exhausted and before public funds became available. . . . There was a period of about eleven days when many families received nothing from us. We have received reports from workers as to how these families managed. The material I am about to give you is typical, although it is based on a small sample.

One woman said she borrowed 50 cents from a friend and bought stale bread for $3\frac{1}{2}$ cents per loaf, and that is all they had for eleven days except for one or two meals.

One woman went along the docks and picked

[4] *Federal Cooperation in Unemployment Relief,* Hearings before Senate Committee on Manufactures, 72nd Cong., 1st sess., 1932, pp. 20–26. This testimony and that which follows is reproduced more completely in D.A. Shannon, *The Great Depression* (Englewood Cliffs, N.J.: Prentice-Hall, Inc., 1960).

Unemployed men during depression. (Bonnie Freer—Photo Researchers, Inc.)

up vegetables that fell from the wagons. Sometimes the fish vendors gave her fish at the end of the day. On two different occasions this family was without food for a day and a half.

The gas company was careful not to turn off gas in the homes of a great many of these families, so in some instances food could be cooked.

Another family did not have food for two days. Then the husband went out and gathered dandelions and the family lived on them.

I should also like to say that when we talk to people to ask about unemployment, they say, "Well, people manage to get along somehow or other, don't they? You do not have very many people who really drop dead of starvation." That is true. Actually, death from starvation is not a frequent occurrence. . . . They live on inadequacies, and because they live on inadequacies the thing does not become dramatic, and we do not hear about it. Yet the cost in human suffering is just as great as if they starved to death overnight.

Now listen to the testimony of another witness, given before a House subcommittee at about the same time.[5]

Mr. Ameringer: The last thing I saw on the night I left Seattle was numbers of women searching for scraps of food in the refuse piles of the principal markets of that city. A number of Montana citizens told me of thousands of bushels of wheat left in the field uncut on account of its low price that hardly paid for the harvesting. In Oregon I saw thousands of bushels of apples rotting in the orchards. Only absolutely flawless apples were still salable, at from 40–50 cents a box containing 200 apples. At the same time, there are millions of children who, on account of the poverty of their parents, will not eat one apple this winter.

While I was in Oregon, the *Portland Oregonian* bemoaned the fact that thousands of ewes were killed by the sheep raisers because they did not bring enough in the market to pay the freight on them. And while Oregon sheep raisers fed mutton to the buzzards, I saw men picking meat scraps in the garbage cans in the cities of New York and Chicago. I talked to one man in a restaurant in Chicago. He told me of his experience in raising sheep. He said that he had killed 3,000 sheep this fall and thrown them down the canyon because it cost $1.10 to ship a sheep, and then he would get less than a dollar for it. He said he could not afford to feed the sheep, and he would not let them starve, so he just cut their throats and threw them down the canyon.

The roads of the West and Southwest teem with hungry hitchhikers. The campfires of homeless are seen along every railroad track. . . .

Most American families were not in such desperate straits. But fear was everywhere. Many fought to maintain respectability. For many others, long-continued failure wiped out self-respect and the will to try. Parks were sprinkled with desolate men in shabby clothes, merely sitting. Many more stayed home.

Is such evidence on the human cost of unemployment relevant today? Today, unemployment is far more modest even at the depths of our postwar recessions. Nationwide unemployment insurance provides temporary financial support for regular workers who have been laid off. Government relief payments help others. Many unions have obtained private unemployment-compensation plans. Thus, modern unemployment is far less devastating than during the desperate days of the 1930s.

But these unemployment-insurance plans provide only a fraction of regular wage incomes, and all have time limits, some as short as thirteen weeks. Moreover, to receive unemployment-insurance benefits, one must have held a regular job, and many unemployed persons fail to qualify on this test. In depressed areas—for example, the soft-coal fields of the Appalachians—many workers have been jobless for years. Discouragement, and then despair, take over when no job is available month after month.

Who are the unemployed today? Table 7–1 gives the answer for 1971, the latest year with a relatively high unemployment level. Unemployment was 5.9 percent of the labor force—five million people.

Note that a quarter of all the unemployed were teenagers. This total rose sharply during the summer months, although many teenagers were only seeking part-time jobs. They had by far the highest unemployment rate of any age group, 16.9 percent compared to 3.5 percent for

[5] *Unemployment in the United States,* Hearings before House Committee on Labor, 72nd Cong., 1st sess., 1932, pp. 98–99.

TABLE 7–1
Unemployment, 1971

	NUMBER UNEMPLOYED (IN THOUSANDS)	RATE (PERCENT)
Total unemployment[a]	4,993	5.9
Age:		
Teenagers, 16–19	1,258	16.9
Adults, 20 and over	3,736	3.5
Race:		
White	4,074	5.4
Black and others	919	9.9
Type of worker:		
Blue-collar	3,654	7.4
White-collar	1,339	3.5
Sex:		
Male	2,776	5.3
Female	2,217	6.9
Marital Status:		
Married men	1,520	3.2
Other	3,473	7.1

[a] Data will not necessarily add to totals because of rounding.
Source: U.S. Department of Labor.

TABLE 7–2
Reasons for Unemployment, 1971

REASON	NUMBER UNEMPLOYED (IN THOUSANDS)	PERCENTAGE DISTRIBUTION
Total unemployment	4,993	100
Lost last job	2,197	44
Voluntarily left last job	649	13
Reentered labor force	1,498	30
Entered labor force, first time	650	13

Source: U.S. Department of Labor

adults. Minority groups (mainly blacks) consistently showed unemployment rates about twice those for whites; unemployment averaged 32 percent for minority-group teenagers.

Why were the unemployed out of work? Table 7-2 provides one set of answers. Nearly twenty million people were unemployed at some time during the year, though the average at any given time was only five million. Rapid technological change, shifting consumer demands, and seasonal patterns in some industries all lead to continually shifting job patterns. But note that less than half had actually lost their last job; all the rest had either quit voluntarily or had just recently begun looking for a job, and in prosperous years, such as 1972 and 1973, quits far exceeded layoffs even though average unemployment was over 4.5 percent. Many of the unemployed, especially younger people, quit jobs frequently to look for better positions. Many quit jobs that they find unsatisfactory or consider dead-end. The data are not consistent with the common impression of a large hard core of continuing unemployed, who are unable to find any job.

Variations in unemployment are thus closely linked to variations in its duration. As Table 7–3 shows, nearly half of all the unemployed were out of work only one to four weeks. Only 517,000 (10 percent of the total) were out of work for as long as six months. But if unemployment worsens and depression comes, mounting unemployment usually reflects longer out-of-work periods as much as newly unemployed workers, as new jobs become harder to find.

These data show that unemployment is relatively short-lived for most workers; so long as major depressions are avoided, for most it reflects preferences for quitting to look for a better

TABLE 7–3
Duration of Unemployment, 1971

WEEKS	NUMBER (IN THOUSANDS)	PERCENTAGE OF UNEMPLOYED
Less than 5	2,234	44.7
5 to 14	1,578	31.6
15 to 26	664	13.3
27 and over	517	10.4

Source: U.S. Department of Labor

job elsewhere or the need to adjust to a constantly shifting economic scene. A five million unemployment figure does not mean that five million people were out of work for the year; very few were. But this fact is of little solace to those unemployed workers who have no job and little hope of finding one.

INFLATION[6]

Nearly everyone agrees that most involuntary unemployment is bad. But the case against inflation is less obvious.

What Is Inflation?

When you use the word inflation to mean a rise in the price level and your neighbor uses it to mean more money printed by those irresponsible fellows in Washington, it's no wonder you don't succeed in talking sensibly about it—especially if neither of you bothers to make clear how you are defining inflation. Socrates said, "If you want to argue with me, first define your terms." And he was right. There are several common definitions of inflation, so one must be clear about which he is using.

"Inflation," in this book, means a rise in the average price of all currently produced goods and services. Note that this definition does not include higher prices of existing assets, such as houses or stocks and bonds. It does not include rising wages or money and credit. All these are usually found when inflation, as we define it, occurs; but inflation per se is merely a rise in the price level of currently produced goods and services. Figure 7–7 presents the evidence on inflation over the past century.

Hyperinflation

When inflation runs away and reaches astronomical proportions, it is often called "hyperinflation." Every American schoolboy learns about the great hyperinflation in Germany following World War I. The government had to make huge expenditures (including heavy reparation payments to the victorious Allies), and it financed its expenditures by printing paper money rather than by drastically increasing taxes. This new money increased total spending and sped the price spiral upward, for the war-torn German economy could not rapidly increase its output of goods. As prices spiraled, so did government costs, requiring further recourse to the printing presses. People receiving

[6]For a more complete analysis of the causes and effects of inflation, see G.L. Bach, *The New Inflation* (Prentice-Hall, Inc., 1973).

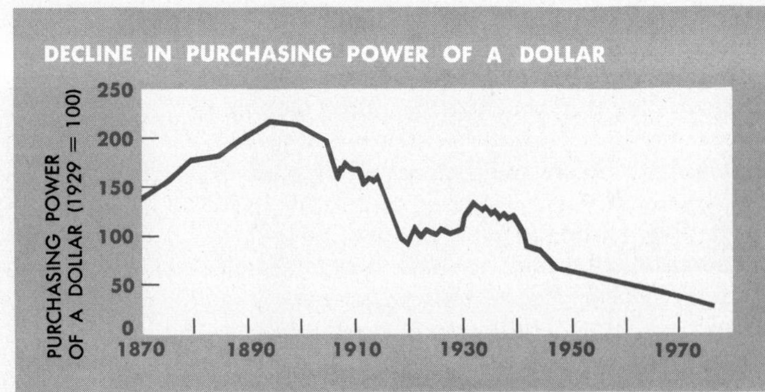

Figure 7–7

Inflation has repeatedly eroded the value of a dollar, with the biggest increases coming during and after wars. (Source: U.S. Department of Labor.)

money spent it as fast as they could, to convert it into goods before it fell further in value. Prices, government spending, and new money soared to fantastic levels.

Near the peak of the inflation in 1923, a box of matches sold for more than 6 billion marks, the total amount of German marks in circulation ten years before. Before the war all mortgages in Germany totaled 40 billion marks; at the peak of the inflation 40 billion marks were worth only a few cents. Things happened as in a feverish dream. Life insurance policies, when paid out, would not buy a handkerchief. No one wanted to lend, everyone wanted to borrow, because it would soon be so easy to pay off today's debts as the value of money fell. Interest rates rose to 900 percent, and even then lenders were not protected. Wages, as well as prices, came to be adjusted daily, sometimes several times a day. Savings invested in fixed-income securities were completely wiped out, and many of the middle class became paupers while skillful speculators became fabulously wealthy. Prices rose so fast that productive activity was disrupted and real output was reduced. The distribution of income and wealth was cruelly and arbitrarily altered.

Inflation can be a terrible thing. Happily, there have not been many hyperinflations, and interestingly two common elements have linked them all. They were associated with war or its aftermath, especially in defeated countries; and, they were financed by great issues of new money to cover huge government expenditures.

One other introductory fact. You often hear the statement that we can't have "just a little" inflation, that inflation, once started, inevitably builds up and runs away. This assertion is just wrong on the evidence of history. Both here and in other nations, there have been many periods of moderate or creeping inflation followed by stable or moderately declining prices; few inflations have turned into hyperinflations. Most economists agree that inflation has some self-feeding elements, mainly the expectation that price increases will accelerate. But they need not do so.[7]

THE EFFECTS OF MODERATE INFLATION

What are the effects of moderate (creeping) inflation of only a few percent a year, the kind most major industrialized nations have faced since World War II? Who gains and who loses? Does such inflation rob everyone except big business and a few sly profiteers?

Everyone complains about having to pay higher prices in inflation. But clearly, this is too narrow a view of the situation, because incomes (the prices of productive services) rise in inflation along with the prices we all have to pay. If your dollar buys less but you have a lot more dollars of income, you will be better off in terms of real buying power, not worse.

Because it is the public's real buying power that matters, what happens to our total output of goods and services is the best single measure of whether the nation as a whole is better or worse off in a period of inflation. We need to peer through the veil of money and prices to real output and real buying power. Second, because each of us is concerned with his individual welfare, total national output provides only part of the answer. To see what inflation does to each individual or group, we need to know what happens to his **share** of total output—whether his individual income rises faster or slower than the prices he has to pay. So we need to ask two basic questions: (1) Does moderate inflation increase or decrease total national output? (2) How does it affect the distribution of real incomes and wealth?

Effects on National Output

In principle, inflation can increase or decrease national production. **In the short run,** inflation clearly cannot increase real output unless there are unemployed resources; if we are already fully utilizing our productive resources, more spending can only mean more inflation. If there is unemployment, more spending may

[7] Many of the less-developed countries have had repeated periods of rapid, though not hyper-, inflation. Brazil, for example, has had inflation varying between 20 and 100 percent annually over many decades.

lead businessmen to hire more workers and increase output—if in the inflation their selling prices rise faster than wages and their other costs of production. In that case, they have an incentive to increase output. But if wages and other costs rise faster than selling prices, profits are cut and businessmen will reduce employment and output. Do wages lead or lag selling prices in moderate inflations? Sometimes one, sometimes the other. There is no consistent relationship over history, but since World War II the wage-lag that characterized many earlier inflations appears to have generally given way to a wage-lead in this country.

Inflation can also decrease output in the short run if prices rise so fast they disrupt business and individual economic planning and operations. As noted above, this clearly happened in the great German hyperinflation. But there is not much evidence of such disruption from the moderate inflations in the United States in recent years, although inflation may trigger speculative price rises that increasingly set the stage for a collapse.

Conclusion: In the short run, moderate inflation may help to stimulate more output in times of unemployment, but this effect is uncertain. In full-employment periods, it can do little good and may do harm by helping to precipitate a recession. Either way, remember it's the impact on the employment of real resources—on jobs and real output—that counts.

In the long run, we can increase the economy's productive capacity by saving and investing more in factories, machinery, and human beings (through education and training), by spending on research and development, and the like. If inflation induces people to save and invest more, it will speed the rate of economic growth; if it reduces saving and investment, the opposite will occur.

What is the evidence? Mixed, and subject to lots of argument. But the data seem reasonably clear on three points: First, hyperinflation cuts down on saving and productive investment. Second, moderate, or creeping, inflation has little effect one way or the other on the level of saving and investment. Third, again the critical relationship in determining the effect of moderate inflation on growth is that between selling prices and wages, because wage-lag tends to stimulate profits and investment. More details on this problem in later chapters.

Effects on the Distribution of Income

In a full-employment economy, inflation cannot increase total output. But it can change who receives the output. Think of total national output as a big pie. With full employment, inflation cannot increase the size of the pie (except possibly over a long period through speeding growth), but it can affect the size of the pieces that different people get.

First, a very fundamental fact. **Given the size of the real pie, inflation does not make people in the aggregate either better or worse off economically. If someone gets a smaller piece, someone else is bound to get a bigger one.** Moving up from a $900 billion to a trillion dollar GNP merely through higher prices does not make the economy either better or worse off in terms of real output and income if the same level of employment prevails before and after.

The central principle about how inflation affects the distribution of income for a given real GNP is this: Those whose incomes rise faster than the average get bigger pieces of the real GNP, and those whose incomes rise slower or not at all get smaller pieces. In a full-employment economy, inflation usually means that prices rise at about the same rate as money GNP. The man whose income just keeps pace with rising prices will keep about the same-sized piece of pie. The man whose income lags behind rising prices will get a smaller piece. Those whose incomes rise faster than prices will get bigger shares.[8] Remember, however, that in an underemployed economy, real GNP may expand with inflation.

[8]To be strictly accurate, the principle must be modified to recognize that different people buy different things whose prices may rise faster or slower than the average. So how an individual is affected depends on the increase in his income relative to the increase in the prices of the goods he buys, not relative to some general price index. But the simple proposition in the text provides a good first approximation in a full-employment economy.

"My client would like to point out, Your Honor, that he would only be charged with petty larceny were it not for spiralling inflation." (Drawing by Modell; © 1973. The New Yorker Magazine, Inc.)

The Importance of Anticipations. Whose income lags and whose leads depends heavily on how accurately different people anticipate the amount of inflation ahead. If everyone expected prices to rise 10 percent annually, everyone would presumably try to build this anticipation into his actions. Unions would demand 10 percent higher wages to avoid losing real purchasing power. So would lenders on interest rates they charged on loans. So would businessmen pricing their products, recognizing that costs would rise that much. At the same time, businesses would be more willing to give big wage boosts, borrowers would pay higher interest rates, and the like, because they would expect their earnings to be 10 percent higher due to the inflation. In principle, if there were no market barriers (such as long-term wage or interest-rate agreements) and everyone were equally able to adjust, all prices would be adjusted upward by 10 percent in accordance with inflation anticipations. Real incomes and relative income shares would remain unchanged. By the same reasoning, inflation would have no effect on real output and employment, since all prices, costs, and asset values would increase proportionately.

In fact, of course, inflation anticipations are far from perfect, and abilities to adjust vary greatly. The uneducated, the poor, the unsophisticated are likely to be badly informed and unable to adjust effectively, compared to the educated and well-to-do. But others also face difficulties in adjusting. Bondholders are stuck with a real loss on their fixed-interest bonds. So are workers with long-term wage contracts and others with fixed committments.

Shifts in Income Shares. It used to be said that interest receivers and wage and salaried workers had lagging incomes and were hurt by inflation, while businessmen and stockholders gained. But even if this was once so, the recent picture of leads and lags is more complex. Consider 1950–71, a period of nearly continuous inflation, beginning after the special forces of World War II had worked themselves out.

Just about everyone's real income went up.

Total output in the economy more than doubled. Table 7–4 shows what happened to different income shares. Within the rapidly growing total, the wage and salary share rose by a whopping 6.6 percent (from 61 to over 67 percent of the total) between 1950 and 1971, while the corporate profits share fell by 6.2 percent (from 15.7 percent to only 9.5 percent of the total). Farmers and other unincorporated businesses (retail shops, legal and medical practices, and the like) fared no better than corporations. Interest receivers were the only other substantial gainers, but the interest increase is partly explained by the fact that government policy held interest rates down through World War II until 1951, and the interest rise since then reflects in substantial part simply a return to a freer play of market forces. Moreover, the big income shifts to wages and salaries against corporate profits were concentrated in the three surges of inflation: 1950–52, 1955–57, 1965–71. In fact, labor's share grew by 7.9 percent in these three inflation surges but by only 6.6 percent in the total 1950–71 period. Thus the labor share eroded in 1953–54 and 1958–64, the substantially noninflationary years in the 1950–71 period. Conversely, the corporate profits squeeze was concentrated in the inflationary surges. Similar results prevailed during the persistent inflation of 1939–49, although the shift toward wages and salaries was somewhat less pronounced.

The bottom line of Table 7–4 bears special attention, in addition to these regular income-share shifts. Transfer payments to persons are largely government social security and welfare benefits. These transfer payments further augmented the big increase in the wage and salary share going to individuals rather than businesses; the biggest increase was social security payments concentrated in the 1965–71 inflation surge. Thus, the mass of wage and salary recipients appear to have protected their incomes well against inflation; the much smaller number of corporation owners lost position badly.

The fact that income shares changed in favor of wage and salary workers and against corporate profits during the past two decades of inflation does not, of course, prove that this shift was due to the inflation. Nor does it prove that a similar shift will be extended in any future inflation. But the facts do emphasize that the widely held wage-lag hypothesis is not applicable to modern America, nor the presumption that businesses generally gain from inflation.

TABLE 7–4

Changes In Percentage Shares of National Income, 1950–71

	1950–71	1950–52	1955–57	1965–71
Wages and salaries	+6.6	+2.6	+1.4	+3.9
Unincorporated business profits:				
Farm	−3.7	−0.5	−0.4	−0.7
Nonfarm	−3.8	−0.7	−0.2	−1.4
Corporate profits[a]	−6.2	−2.0	−1.7	−4.0
Rents	−1.0	+0.1	−0.2	−0.5
Interest	+3.4	+0.1	+0.3	+1.0
Transfer payments to persons[b]	+4.7	−1.8	+0.6	+4.1

[a] After inventory adjustment, before corporation income taxes.
[b] Not a part of national income.
Source: U.S. Department of Commerce.

There are other distributional effects of inflation. Except for those on social security, older persons are hard hit, because they are retired, with no wages to raise in order to offset the higher prices they must pay. So are others without marketable services to sell or other means of raising their incomes. Inflation's effects vary widely among different individuals.

Effects on Distribution of Wealth

Inflation also affects the ownership of existing wealth. It transfers real purchasing power from creditors to debtors.[9] If you borrow $1,000 for a year and an unexpected inflation of 10 percent occurs, although you repay the full $1,000 in fact you have only repaid $900 of real purchasing power for the $1,000 you received. As a debtor you have gained from inflation; the lender has lost part of his principal to you.

The same effect occurs if you hold money during an inflation. If you hold $1,000 in your safe deposit box while prices rise 5 percent, you have effectively lost 5 percent of your $1,000. Even if you have invested in a safe security, such as a government bond, which pays you interest, inflation erodes the real buying power of both the interest and principal you receive when the bond comes due.

Don't be tricked into thinking that the loss doesn't amount to much as long as inflation only creeps. Table 7–5 shows how long it takes for a dollar to lose half its purchasing power at different small rates of inflation. At only 5 percent inflation a year, half its purchasing power is gone in fourteen years.

TABLE 7–5

Half-Life of a Dollar with Inflation

ANNUAL RATE OF INFLATION	YEARS TO LOSE HALF ITS PURCHASING POWER
1 percent	70
2 percent	35
3 percent	23
4 percent	18
5 percent	14

Table 7–6 shows the main net debtors and net creditors in America. Households are the main net creditors exposed to inflation, and governments (mainly the federal government) are the biggest net debtors, followed by business firms. Of course, we need to peer through both governments and business firms to the people behind them, but crudely we can say that unanticipated inflation transfers wealth from households to taxpayers and owners of business firms.

Although households are clearly the main net creditors, they vary widely. Some are heavily in debt, others have few debts and many monetary assets susceptible to inflation's erosion. Table 7–7 shows which families are most likely to lose, and which to gain, from inflation on wealth account. Families with a high proportion of their assets in money and other such fixed-money-value assets as bonds (monetary assets) are vulnerable to inflation; those with high ratios of debt to total assets tend to gain from inflation. Loosely speaking, very low- and very high-income families appear most vulnerable to inflation because of their relatively high monetary-asset and relatively low debt ratios; while middle-income

TABLE 7–6

Net Debtor and Net Creditor Groups, 1970[a] (In billions of dollars)

Households	+658
Unincorporated businesses	− 90
Nonfinancial corporations	−187
Financial corporations	− 63
Governments	−326

[a] + shows net creditor; − shows net debtor.

For details see Bach, *The New Inflation*, p. 25.

[9] More accurately, we must calculate the net debtor or creditor position of each economic unit. For example, if Family *A* has $10,000 of money and bonds but owes $6,000, it is a "net creditor" by $4,000.

TABLE 7–7
Assets and Debts of Households, 1969

INCOME LEVEL:	PERCENTAGE OF ALL HOUSEHOLDS	PERCENTAGE OF TOTAL ASSETS: MONETARY ASSETS	DEBTS
Under $3,000	17	20	8
3,000–4,999	14	20	15
5,000–9,999	33	18	23
10,000–14,999	24	14	29
15,000–24,999	9	12	21
25,000–49,999	2	14	18
$50,000 and over	0.4	18	10
AGE OF HEAD OF HOUSEHOLD:			
18–24	10	14	49
25–34	21	8	48
35–44	18	9	37
45–54	17	13	22
55–64	15	21	9
65 and over	19	23	3

Source: G. Katona et al, *1969 Survey of Consumer Finances* (Ann Arbor, University of Michigan, 1970), p. 310.

families tend to be gainers because of the reverse situation. More clearly, inflation helps the young at the expense of the aged. Young people are heavily in debt and hold relatively few monetary assets, while old people have virtually no debts and a big proportion of their assets in monetary forms.

As was emphasized above, if everyone anticipated inflation correctly, bargains between borrowers and lenders would reflect those anticipations and interest rates would rise to take expected inflation into account. If the noninflationary interest rate was 4 percent and a 5 percent inflation was expected by both parties, the interest rate would be raised to 9 percent to allow for the inflation. Thus, neither party would gain or lose from the inflation. In periods of continuing inflation, some such adjustment clearly takes place, but much past inflation has not been fully anticipated by many borrowers and lenders. One recent estimate suggests that inflation has transferred half a trillion dollars of real purchasing power from creditors to debtors since World War II. About $3.5 trillion of monetary assets are now in existence, susceptible to erosion by inflation. A 1 percent unanticipated inflation would thus transfer $35 billion from creditors to debtors. Of course, this huge transfer of purchasing power did not represent a loss of real wealth to society as a whole. But it was a capricious and inequitable redistribution of real wealth that is hard to justify.[10]

International Effects of Inflation

If costs and prices in one country rise faster than elsewhere, that country will have increasing trouble meeting competition in international markets. Conversely, as its own incomes rise, its people will import more from abroad. Thus, it will end up with an international "balance-of-

[10] See Bach, *The New Inflation*, pp. 23–27.

payments deficit"—it will owe more abroad than it has to collect from foreigners. For any nation heavily dependent on foreign trade (for example, most of Western Europe and many of the less-developed countries), this fact constitutes a major barrier against accepting more rapid inflation than other countries with which it trades. We postpone detailed consideration of the international aspects of inflation to Part Six, but it is important to recognize that inflation may involve major international costs to any country whose prices rise faster than those abroad.

How Bad is Inflation?

How bad is inflation, putting all the above effects together? Try the following exercise to test your understanding. Evaluate this statement by a well-known senator: "Inflation reduces the buying power of every dollar, and impoverishes the American people. It is a national disaster!"

The first half of the first sentence is true by definition. Inflation is rising prices, and higher prices do reduce the purchasing power of any dollar. But it does not necessarily follow from this that inflation impoverishes the American people.

Consider the decade of the 1960s. The price level rose from 100 to 130, using 1960 as the base year, or by 30 percent. In 1960, total national income was $415 billion; in 1970, it was about $800 billion. If we adjust the 1970 national-income figure downward to eliminate the effect of inflation, we get a 1970 real income of $615 billion in constant (1960) prices. This was an increase of $200 billion (almost 50 percent) over the 1960 real income. Even allowing for possible error in the price index, it is hard to see how this inflation impoverished the American people as a whole. Although one dollar would buy less in 1970 than in 1960, the increase in money incomes received far outdistanced the loss caused by rising prices. Real output rose, not fell.

However, this historical evidence doesn't prove that inflation *caused* the increase in output, so we are not justified in giving inflation credit for the extra goods and services produced. Moreover, even though the public as a whole had 50 percent more real income in 1970 than in 1960, some people were absolutely harmed by the inflation—people whose money incomes were relatively fixed and who were net monetary creditors—and others saw their relative income positions worsen. Inflation was certainly no national disaster in the 1960s, but it's easy to understand why a lot of people object to it strongly.

CONCLUSION

Whether we have prosperity or depression will go far to determine what kind of job you have and how well you live when you graduate—indeed, perhaps whether you have any job at all. With this overview of the macroeconomy and its problems, we turn now to a detailed examination of what determines the levels of national production, employment, incomes, and prices, and of why we sometimes have good times, sometimes bad. Equally important, we shall consider what can be done to reduce the amount of both unemployment and inflation. Some economists feel that we will probably have to choose between high employment and stable prices—that we can have one or the other, but not both. But others deny this dilemma and argue that proper policies will permit both simultaneously. This issue runs through the following chapters, as does the implicit issue of which goal should have precedence if, indeed, we must choose between them. On the basis of this preliminary overview, how would you weigh high employment and avoiding inflation as goals of national macroeconomic policy?

REVIEW

Concepts to Remember

The following important new concepts were introduced in this chapter:

macroeconomics
circular flow of spending
growth rate–ratio scale
unemployment
frictional unemployment
structural unemployment
inflation
hyperinflation
redistributional effects of inflation

For Analysis and Discussion

1. Looking at Figures 7–2 and 7–5, how well would you say the American economy has performed over the past century? How do you rate it on the two criteria of growth and stability?
2. In setting goals for the economy, is it more important to avoid unemployment or inflation, if we must choose?
3. Who are the main sufferers from "moderate" unemployment like we have had in recent years? Use Tables 7–1, 7–2, and 7–3 in answering.
4. Should students looking for part-time jobs be counted as unemployed? (They are.) Discouraged workers who have given up looking? (They are not.)
5. In 1973, unemployment averaged just over four million people. Of these, only about 300,000 were out of work for as long as half a year; over half were out of work for a month or less; and the unemployment rate was below 3 percent for married males. Would you consider this a satisfactory approximation to full employment? Look back at Table 7–1.
6. Who are the main sufferers from "moderate" inflation like we have had in recent years? Use Tables 7–4, 7–6, and 7–7 in answering.
7. Explain why anticipations play a crucial role in determining who is hurt and who helped by inflation.
8. If unemployment wastes real output while moderate inflation mainly just redistributes income and wealth, how can you explain why the general public seems to consider inflation the major problem in periods like 1972–73 when inflation and unemployment both averaged 4–5 percent? (Consider both the number of people affected and the importance of the impact on each in answering.)

The National Income Accounts and Economic Welfare

CHAPTER PREVIEW

CHAPTER EIGHT

Modern economics is an empirical science. To understand and regulate the behavior of an enormously complex economy, we need measures of its performance—just as a business needs accounts to measure its performance. We need a measure of the nation's total output of goods and services, and a measure of the total income received by all its people. We also need more detailed measures—of how much people have left to spend after paying their taxes, of corporate profits, of family and business savings, and so on.

Over the past half century, the United States and most other economically developed nations have evolved detailed sets of "national income accounts" to provide such measures. They are the topic of this chapter. For our elementary purposes it is not important to know all the details of these accounts. But the major items, such as gross national product (GNP), national income (NI), and the consumer price index (CPI) are not only vital in analyzing how the macroeconomy works, but they have also become part of America's standard newspaper and TV news vocabularies. Many people use these figures as measures of general economic welfare, though their use for this purpose is sharply debated. Be sure you understand the basic GNP accounts.

MEASURES OF NATIONAL PRODUCTION AND INCOME

Economic Production Defined

To begin, a basic question: What do economists mean by "production"?

To the economist, production is the creation of any good or service that people are willing to pay for. Raising wheat is production, and so is making the wheat into flour, and the flour into bread. It is also production for the local grocer to have the bread on his shelf when you want it, or to deliver it to your door. The agricultural, manufacturing, and marketing services all satisfy human wants, and people are willing to pay for them.

In fact, over half the people employed in the United States today render services rather than manufacture or raise anything. Over half of what you pay goes for middlemen's services—the retailer, the wholesaler, the banker, the trucker, and many others. Lots of people object to this situation. "There are too many middlemen!" they say. Maybe there are. But if you stop to think about it you'll run head-on into this question: Are there too many manufacturers, or too many farmers? The real economic test for all producers of goods or services is whether they satisfy a consumer demand—not how many pounds of physical stuff they produce.

Production as the economist defines it is thus not a moral or ethical concept. Making and selling cigarettes is production, just like raising and selling food. The test of the private-enterprise economy is the test of the market. If an act helps satisfy a want that someone is willing to pay for, that act is production.

Gross National Product

Gross national product is the nation's total production of goods and services (usually for a year) valued in terms of the market prices of the goods and services produced. This concept goes directly back to the definition of production above: Production is whatever people will pay for, and what they pay is an economic valuation of the worth of the product or service. GNP includes all the economic production in the country in any given time period. It can also be thought of as all the current production that provides jobs in any time period.

Gross national product is stated in money terms, because this is the only meaningful way of adding together the output of such diverse goods and services as carrots, machine tools, maid service, air travel, and Fords. Strictly, then, GNP is the money value of total national production for any time period.

GNP is also the nation's total expenditures on goods and services produced during the year. Each unit produced is matched by an expenditure on that unit. Most goods and services produced are bought outright. But how about the ones produced but not sold? Economists regard these as having been bought by the producers who hold them, as inventories. Then it is clear that the production and expenditure totals are identical. Viewed as total expenditure, GNP is the very important concept "aggregate demand," which we shall use repeatedly in the chapters ahead.

GNP is also the total income received by all sellers of goods and services. What someone spends on current output, someone else receives as income. This is GNP seen from the receipts side.

Thus, national output = national expenditure = national (gross) income. We get the same total each way we calculate GNP.

Estimating GNP. There are two ways to calculate GNP, each designed to avoid the danger of double-counting in a complex economy. One way is to sum up all expenditures on *final* products sold to consumers or to businesses for final use as producers' goods—all spending on potatoes, factories, missiles, legal services, and so on. Note the word "final"; we must be careful not to double-count. Miners dig iron ore out of the ground and sell it to U.S. Steel. The latter makes the ore into steel and sells the steel to Westinghouse. Westinghouse makes refrigerators and sells them to us. We don't count the value of the iron ore, plus the value of the steel, plus the value of the refrigerator. That would involve counting the iron ore three times. Instead, everything that is used in another product during the year shows up and is counted only in the *final* product (in this case, refrigerators), since the value of the final product will reflect the value of all the raw materials, labor, and other productive services included in it.

Producers' goods, like machinery, which are bought by businesses, pose an obvious problem, because they are not directly incorporated into the final consumers' goods the way raw materials are. We count machinery and other producers' goods once, when they reach *their* final buyer—for example, when Westinghouse buys a new machine tool. This process of summing up all final purchases is called the "final-products approach" to estimating GNP.

GNP can also be estimated in another (equivalent) way, by the "value-added" method. Here the estimators establish the value added by each producer at each stage of production, then sum up all these values. For example, in converting the iron ore to steel, U.S. Steel adds value to the product it passes along. This added value is the difference between what it pays for the ore, coal, and other products that it uses and the price at which it sells the steel to Westinghouse; roughly, it is the wages, interest, and rents paid by U.S. Steel plus the profit it earns. Similarly, we can compute the value added by Westinghouse. And so on for each productive unit in the economy. By summing up all the values added, we come out with the gross national product, again avoiding double-counting.

TABLE 8–1
U.S. Gross National Product, 1972

COMPONENTS	(IN BILLIONS)
Consumer purchases	$ 721
Private investment expenditures (including foreign)	176
Government purchases	255
Total	$1,152

Source: U.S. Department of Commerce.

Composition of GNP. Table 8–1 shows who buys the goods and services in the GNP, a useful breakdown in a market-directed economy. Buyers are divided into three big groups: consumers, businesses (buying "investment," or "producers," goods), and governments. To provide historical perspective, Figure 8–1 then presents the same data from 1929 through 1972. Take a look at the three major segments.

1. The biggest part of total production is goods and services for consumers—turnips, stoves, dresses, movies, medical services, hats, and all the other things that consumers buy.

2. The next group is "producers'" or "capital" goods, in which businesses invest. These are buildings, machinery, equipment, and other capital goods used in the production of further goods or services. Such producers' goods are purchased primarily by businesses. But houses are also included in the investment-goods category, on the ground that they are so durable that in effect they represent investment goods owned directly by consumers.[1] Business investment also includes—as inventories—any increase in unsold goods in process or final form.

Three important warnings about the private-investment category.

First, "investment" means the purchase of investment goods (buildings, machinery, and so on) produced during the year. For example, if someone buys a ten-year-old factory, this is not investment; the factory was included in the gross national product ten years ago, when it was built.

Second, investment does not include mere financial transfers, such as the purchase of stocks and bonds. For example, if you buy a share of General Motors stock from GM or me, this is

[1]Although it is reasonable to treat new private housing as investment, note that houses differ only in degree from such durable consumer goods as autos, refrigerators, and vacuum cleaners, which are treated as consumption goods.

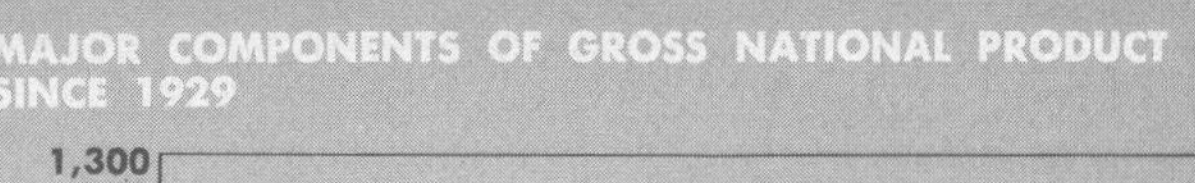

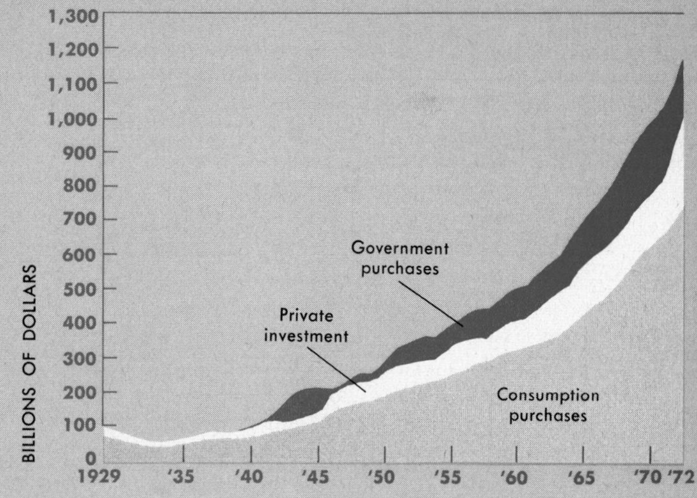

Figure 8–1
Consumers buy most (two-thirds) of the GNP. The other third is divided between private investment and government purchases. (Source: U.S. Department of Commerce.)

not investment for purposes of the national income accounts, because it does not pay for any new production.

Third, note that investment includes gross purchases of investment goods. It includes production that merely replaces depreciating buildings, machinery, and equipment, as well as production that represents a net increase in society's stock of capital goods. We come to the net increase in the nation's capital goods in the section on "net national product" below.

3. Government purchases of goods and services include both consumption and investment goods. Federal, state, and local governments buy food, police services, and other current consumption items, as well as investment goods such as roads, buildings, and parks. But note that government purchases of goods and services do not include all government expenditures. Governments also spend large sums on "transfer payments" (such as unemployment insurance and social security payments) that are not payments for currently produced goods and services and are hence not included in gross national product.

4. We have included "foreign investment," or "net exports," in private investment here, although it is often shown as a separate item. If, for example, the United States exports more than it imports, we include this net production in GNP. It provides jobs in the U.S. economy though it does not increase U.S. consumption or investment goods. Conversely, a net excess of imports over exports is deducted in computing GNP. We will take a more thorough look at this item in Part Six on The International Economy.

To summarize, GNP is made up of: (1) consumer goods and services bought by individuals and households, (2) investment goods bought mainly by businesses, and (3) both consumer and investment goods and services bought by federal, state, and local governments. **In all three categories, remember that only goods and services produced during the current year count; transfers of existing assets are excluded. GNP may be thought of as the total national pie for each year, with the big slices going to consumers, businesses, and governments.**

Net National Product

GNP includes some producers' goods that just replace already existing producers' goods that are "depreciating," or wearing out. As we saw in looking at the individual corporation (in Chapter 4), if a truck lasts ten years we might say that one-tenth of it is used up every year, and the business that owns it would consider this tenth as an annual cost that year.[2] So it is with all other producers' goods; they wear out. Thus, before a firm or the economy as a whole adds anything *net* to its stock of producers' goods, part of each year's production must go to replacing depreciated capital goods.

Net national product (NNP) is the net national production of goods and services. It is GNP, less those goods that merely replace depreciating buildings and machines. In 1972, for example, GNP was $1,152 billion. Depreciation (sometimes called "capital consumption allowances") was estimated at $104 billion. Thus, *net* national product was $1,048 billion, about 9 percent less than gross national product, because 9 percent of our total output went to replace depreciating producers' goods and houses. Net national product measures the total production of goods and services available for current consumption and for adding to our stock of producers' equipment, including housing.

National Income

National income is the total of all income earned by the "factors of production"—land, labor, capital, and management. The national income is basically the net national product viewed from the income side, but with one difference. The factors of production (laborers, managers, machinery, and so forth) do not actually receive as income the full value of their output, because businesses that hire them must pay indirect taxes (sales taxes, excises, and property taxes) to the government, which cut down on the income left to pay to the factors of production. If we subtract indirect business taxes from NNP, we have left the national income that goes to all factors of production. In 1972, indirect taxes were $110 billion. Deducting this from net national product, we get a national income of $935 billion.[3]

[2] Accountants have more complicated depreciation plans, which recognize the fact that buildings and machines do not necessarily wear out at constant rates.

Table 8–2 shows the share of the national income earned by each major factor of production. Note the large share of wages and salaries—75 percent in 1972. This percentage has risen substantially since World War II, although the shares have generally been quite stable.

Personal Income and Disposable Personal Income

For many purposes, we need to know how much income households (individuals) have to spend on consumer goods. For this, we need "personal income" and "disposable personal income." **"Personal income" is the total income received by all individuals in the country—what individuals actually have to spend, save, or pay taxes with.** It differs from national income mainly because national income includes total corporation profits whereas individuals receive only part of these profits in dividends, and because personal income includes large transfer payments (especially social security and other

[3] This omits some minor items that explain the apparent discrepancy in subtraction.

TABLE 8–2
U.S. National Income, 1972

SOURCE OF INCOME	(IN BILLIONS)
Total	$935
Wages and salaries	705
Net income of unincorporated business[a]	75
Corporation profits	88
Interest	41
Rental income	26

[a] Mainly farmers and professional men in business for themselves.

[b] Of which $41 billion was paid out in income taxes and $26 billion was plowed back as reinvested earnings. Dividends paid out to stockholders were $26 billion.

Source: U.S. Department of Commerce.

TABLE 8–3
U.S. Personal Income, 1972

		(IN BILLIONS)
Total personal income		$936
Less: Personal income taxes	$141	
Equals: Disposable personal income		795
Of which:		
Consumer outlays		740
Personal saving		55

[a]Consumer outlays include $18 billion of consumer interest payments, which are excluded from the "consumer purchases" shown in Table 8–1. The Department of Commerce defines "consumers expenditures" to include only consumer payments for goods and services.
Source: U.S. Department of Commerce.

government benefits) that are not payments for productive services. As the footnote to Table 8–2 indicates, nearly half of corporation profits go to Uncle Sam as corporation income taxes, and half of what's left is plowed back into businesses rather than paid out to stockholders. We must subtract these amounts from national income to get income actually paid out to individuals. On the other hand, "transfer payments" to individuals (social security, interest on the national debt, and so forth) now roughly offset the corporate profits not paid out to individuals. By chance, national and personal income were almost identical in 1972, though they usually differ. (Table 8–4 shows the comparison in detail for 1972.)

Table 8–3 shows what people did with their total personal income in 1972. First, they paid their income taxes. What they had left we call "disposable personal income." Most of this they spent on consumption and the rest they saved. **The concept of "disposable personal income" (what people have left after they pay their taxes) will be important later on in analyzing consumer spending and saving behavior.**

The Integrated National Income Accounts[4]

Table 8–4 summarizes the complete set of interconnections for 1972 just explained, beginning with the gross national product total. Figure 8–2 shows the same set of interconnections as a flow diagram, tracing the entire income-and-payments flow. This figure ties the circular flow of gross national product back to the simple, fundamental circular-flow diagram in Figure 7–1. (A few minor items are omitted, which explains the apparent discrepancies.)

In Figure 8–2, begin with the gross national product of $1,152 billion, as in Table 8–4. Then $104 billion of capital consumption (depreciation) allowances drains off as a form of private saving, leaving $1,048 billion of net national product. From NNP another $110 billion drains off to the government through indirect business taxes, leaving national income of $935 billion. From this, corporate income taxes, social security taxes, and corporate saving (undistributed profits) are drained off, while interest on the government debt and other transfer payments are added back into the income stream, to make up $936 billion of personal income. The resulting personal income total is reduced to personal disposable income by the payment of personal income taxes, and then part of disposable income drains off into personal savings while the bulk flows on into consumption expenditures and into GNP.

Now add back the private-investment and government-spending flows out of private savings and government tax receipts. Together these three types of spending make up GNP, the three big components of aggregate demand for currently produced goods and services—consumption, investment, and government spending.

[4]Within the last few years, a new set of social accounts has been released by the Federal Reserve System. These are called the "flow of funds accounts." They include all financial transactions in the economy, including payments in the stock market, for other financial transfers, for existing assets, and for a variety of other purposes not included in the national income accounts. These new money-flows accounts can be integrated with the national income accounts, and now provide a complete picture of money payments throughout the economy.

TABLE 8–4
National Income Accounts for 1972[a]

		(IN BILLIONS)
Gross national product		$1,152
Deduct: Capital consumption allowances (mainly business depreciation allowances)	$104	
Net national product		1,048
Deduct: Indirect business taxes	110	
National income		935
Deduct: Corporation profits taxes	41	
Corporate savings (undistributed profits)	26	
Social security taxes	74	
Add: Transfer and interest payments	136	
Personal income		936
Deduct: Personal taxes	141	
Disposable personal income		795
Of which: Consumer outlays[b]		740
Personal saving		55

[a] A few minor items are omitted, which explain the apparent discrepancies in the table.

[b] Includes $18 billion of interest paid by consumers not considered an expenditure on goods and services.

Remember these, for they are at the center of the analysis of Chapters 10 and 11.[5]

CHANGING PRICE LEVELS AND PRICE INDEXES

When prices change, GNP expressed in terms of dollars is no longer an adequate measure of the real goods and services produced. A 100 percent increase in real national output would mean a great rise in the national standard of living. But doubling GNP merely through doubling prices is no real economic gain at all. In order to separate "real" from merely "dollar" changes in individual and national incomes, we have to make an adjustment for price-level changes.

[5] Note that private investment need not equal the private saving flow in the bottom loop nor need government spending equal tax collections in the top loop. Either sector may run a surplus or a deficit, as will be explained in Chapter 10.

Figure 8–3 indicates the big fluctuations in prices in the United States over the last two centuries. The problem of price-level changes is no minor one.

What Is a Price Index?

In 1929, a family income of $1,300 would have bought a group of goods and services called a "subsistence standard of living." In 1933, you could have bought the same collection of goods and services for about $900. By 1970, you would have needed about $2,800.

If all prices changed in the same proportion in the same direction at the same time, measuring price-level changes would be simple. But the world of real prices is not simple and orderly. Even in the big price rises shown in Figure 8–3,

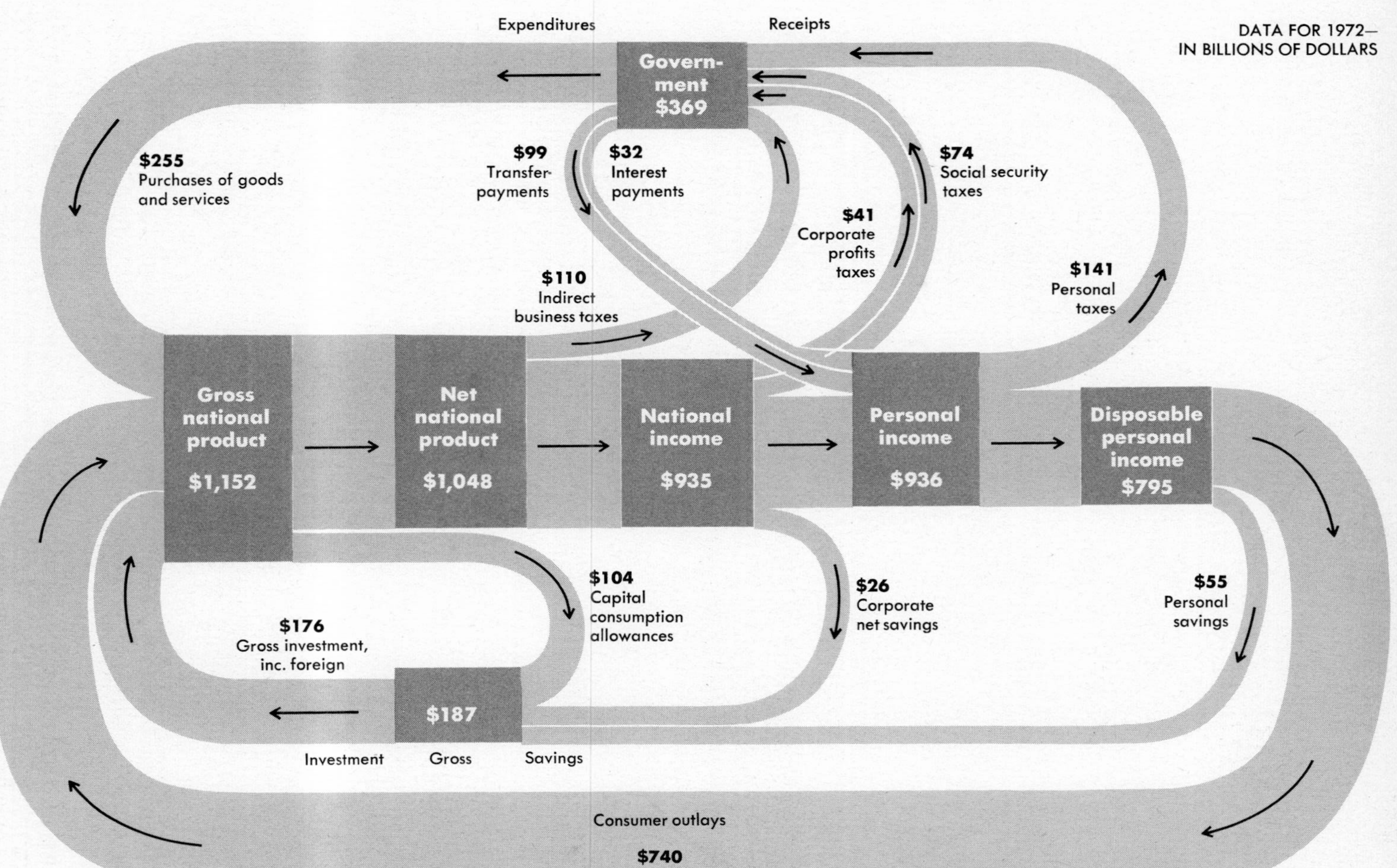

Figure 8–2

National income and expenditure make essentially a circular flow, with many side loops. This is a more complete version of the simple circular money flow illustrated in Figure 7–1. Some minor items are omitted and "consumer outlays" include $18 billion of consumer interest payments generally excluded from "consumer expenditures" and GNP, so figures will not add exactly to GNP and some subtotals. Note that government spending exceeds tax receipts, and private saving exceeds private investment.

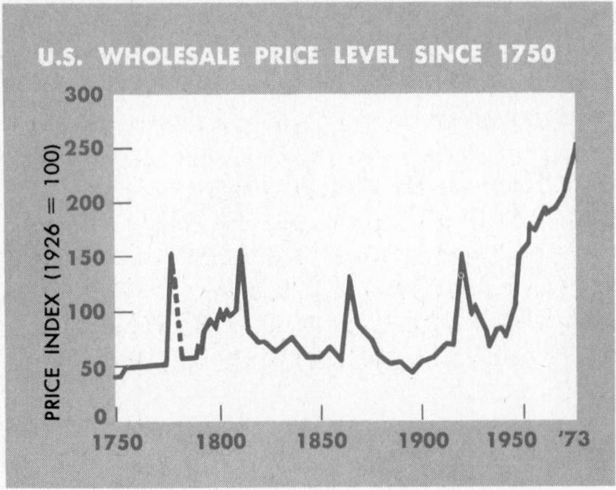

Figure 8–3

Prices have fluctuated sharply throughout our history. The big peaks have come during or after major wars. So far, there has been no price slump since World War II. (Source: U.S. Department of Labor.)

some prices declined and others rose at very different rates. Yet, even though not all prices rose, we say that the "price level" rose because the average of all prices rose. The price of the same market basket of goods was higher than before.

Table 8–5 shows how to calculate a simple "price index" for a market basket of four commodities, to show whether their price level went up or down between 1960 and 1970. A price index is a measure of price-level changes.

With 1960 as the "base year," the price of each item in that year is 100 percent of itself. This is what people mean when they say, "Take 1960 as 100." Then we compute what percentage each 1970 price is of the 1960 price. For example, eggs at six cents each are 120 percent of the 1960 price. This 120 percent is the 1970 "price relative" for eggs, since it shows the 1970 price relative to that in 1960. To find the change in the price level (the average of all four prices), we simply take the average of the four 1970 price relatives, which gives us 108 percent for the 1970 price level. (The percentage sign is usually omitted for convenience.) Of course, most price indexes include more commodities, but they are made in a generally similar way.[6]

This simple method of calculating price-level changes may give misleading results, however. It tacitly assumes that eggs, hamburger, turnips, and apples are equally important. A 10 percent change in the price of hamburger influences the index exactly as much as a 10 percent change in the price of turnips. Actually, hamburger is more important than turnips in most budgets, and it seems logical that the price of hamburger should affect the index more.

Thus, in most price indexes, each price is

[6]The final index numbers merely indicate relative average prices in the two years. We could just as well have taken 1970 as 100, in which case the 1960 index would have been 93. Although the actual index numbers would have been different, either set shows equally well the relative price levels in the two years: 93/100 = 100/108. Thus the year chosen as 100 has little significance.

TABLE 8–5

Price Index for 1970 with 1960 as Base Year

PRODUCT	1960	1970	
Eggs, each	5¢ = 100%	6¢ = 120%	of the 1960 price
Hamburger, per lb	40¢ = 100%	50¢ = 125%	of the 1960 price
Turnips, per lb	9¢ = 100%	6¢ = 67%	of the 1960 price
Apples, per lb	10¢ = 100%	12¢ = 120%	of the 1960 price
	4)400%	4)432%	
	100% = price level in 1960	108% = price level in 1970	

"weighted" according to its importance. For example, the U.S. Bureau of Labor Statistics weights the prices in its widely used consumers' price index (CPI) as follows: The statisticians take a "market basket" of the goods and services bought during the 1960s by typical urban wage earners' families. Choosing some 400 of the most important prices, they weight each roughly in accordance with the proportion of the families' total expenditure for that commodity. If the families bought lots of potatoes, potatoes make up a sizable part of the weekly market basket; rent is a big item in the basket. In effect, the market-basket approach weights the price of each commodity according to the weekly amount spent on that commodity.

Having decided on the contents of the hypothetical market basket, the B.L.S. gets its price index by comparing the cost of the basket from one week to the next. If the index uses 1957–59 as a base period (100), a weekly index reading of 120 means that the cost of the market basket is up 20 percent from the 1957–59 price level for those goods and services.

Price Indexes for Different Price Levels

A price level is merely an average of some group of prices, so we can speak of many different price levels. One may reflect the prices paid by a group of consumers; another, the level of wages in manufacturing.

Figure 8–4 shows the movements of four important price indexes from 1929 through 1972. What price level is most significant depends on what you are talking about. If you want to measure changes in the cost of living for a particular group, the logical choice is an index of the prices of the goods and services the group buys. Given the wide diversity of price movements, it is hard to devise a single price index that will be a significant measure for the whole economy. The closest approach is an index developed by the Department of Commerce to eliminate the effects of price-level movements from the gross national product. This adjustment is spoken of as "deflating" the GNP. In it, first special indexes are determined for the different major sectors of GNP, and then these are combined to obtain a "GNP deflator." The result is a price index for all goods and services in the gross national product.

If we had a price index for *all* prices, including all those not included in GNP, we would have an index of the changing purchasing power of the dollar. Clearly, the value of money (the purchasing power of one dollar) varies just inversely with the general price level. If all prices double, one dollar will buy just half as much. But remember the warning at the end of Chapter 7 against confusing the purchasing

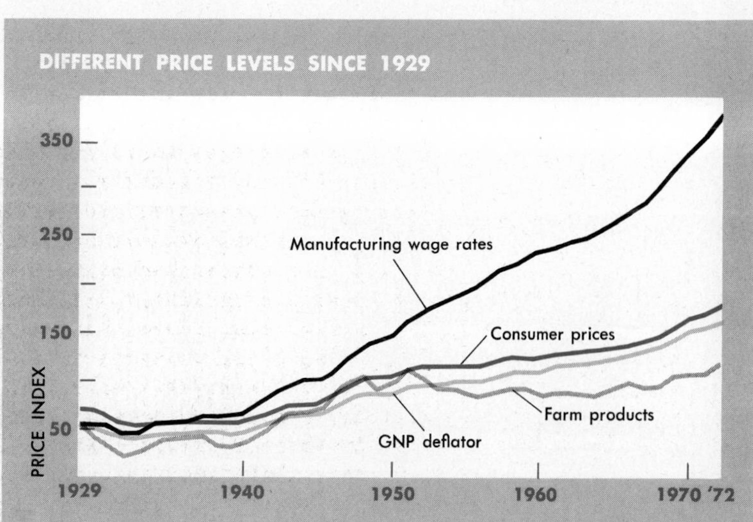

Figure 8–4

Different prices move diversely in the American economy. The GNP deflator comes closest to showing price changes for all currently produced goods and services. Note the rapid rise of the wage-rate index. (Sources: U.S. Departments of Labor and Commerce.)

power of one dollar with that of all dollars in the economy.

Figure 7–2 compared GNP since 1870 in the actual (current) prices that prevailed each year with GNP in constant (1964) prices.[7] We often speak of the constant-price GNP as "real" GNP, because with the elimination of price-level changes the GNP index measures real changes in output of goods and services. In periods of rapidly changing prices, the money GNP figures give a seriously misleading picture of what is happening to real GNP.

How Good Are the Price Indexes?

How accurately do the well-known price indexes mirror the price changes they are intended to summarize? The most widely used indexes are prepared by the government—the consumers' price index, the wholesale price index, and the GNP deflator. These are the product of years of hard work and millions of dollars, and they're as good as the experts can make them. Many privately-made indexes fall short of these standards of excellence, even though they may serve useful purposes. Others are extremely accurate, though they measure only a few prices—for example, the well-known Dow Jones index of a small group of leading stock prices.

How good the price indexes are is no mere academic question. Millions of workers' wages are adjusted periodically under their union contracts for changes in the "cost of living," which are usually measured by the CPI. Other indexes are used daily in business and government decision making. In 1959 President Eisenhower appointed a group of the country's leading economists and statisticians to restudy the CPI. Their report gave the index high marks but pointed to a number of tough statistical problems yet to be solved. For example, they found that the index probably doesn't recognize quality improvements as effectively as it should. Suppose Ford ups the horsepower in next year's models and adds a new type carburetor, but doesn't change the price. The index should not show the price of Fords unchanged; it shows them as lower (because you get more car for your money). But if lower, how much? Many economists believe the CPI shows prices rising perhaps 1 percent a year too fast because of the difficulty of promptly reflecting such changes due to new products and quality improvements, but this is a debatable issue. Moreover, the price indexes are largely based on prices formally quoted by sellers and fail to reflect many cases in which actual prices are shaded below list prices to get business, especially in recessions.

[7] Remember from above that we could have chosen some year other than 1964 as the "base" year for calculating constant-price GNP over the years. Another base year would give different absolute levels for the constant-price GNP but would not change the relative movements in the two curves.

GNP AND ECONOMIC WELFARE

GNP was devised as a measure of economic output. It is, however, often used as a measure of economic welfare; more GNP means we are better off. More real GNP per capita does indeed suggest that, on the average, we are economically better off, but GNP has some serious weaknesses as a measure of economic well-being. Indeed, modern supporters of "zero economic growth" (ZEG) argue that growth in GNP worsens, not improves, the nation's economic well-being, because growth in production destroys the quality of life, even though it means more quantity of output.

This controversy is an important one, and we shall look into it in detail presently. First, however, eight warnings on the use of GNP as a measure of economic welfare.

1. Be sure the figures used are *real,* that is, price-level-adjusted, GNP. Changes in GNP merely because of changes in prices obviously do not reflect changes in real output.

2. GNP per capita or per family is generally more useful as a welfare measure than the national totals. Ultimately, economic welfare must refer to the situation of individuals. A big nation

like China is poor with a large GNP; a small one like Switzerland is well off with a tiny GNP.

3. GNP places no value on leisure. Over the past century, in the United States the average workweek has been cut in half—from 75 to 39 hours; vacations have lengthened greatly; people start working later in life and retire earlier. Although it is difficult to value this great increase in leisure, to say that it has made no contribution to our economic well-being would obviously be foolish.

4. GNP includes for the most part only production that passes through a market transaction. It takes no account of such important items as nonpaid housewives' services and home labor, such as painting, gardening, and the like. If a bachelor marries his maid, GNP is reduced. If Mrs. *A* and Mrs. *B* simply did each other's housework and paid each other $5,000, GNP would be $10,000 higher with no change in real activity. In only a few cases, such as the estimated value of services from owner-occupied homes, has it proved practicable to include real production that is not sold in the marketplace.

5. GNP counts durable consumers' goods like autos when they are produced, although their actual services are consumed over their entire lives. If production and consumption run at even rates, this causes no problem. But in depressions when few new durables are produced, GNP understates real consumption, because consumers continue to use the services of existing durables. Conversely, GNP overstates real consumption in booms when consumers' durables are produced faster than they are used.

6. GNP says nothing about *what* goods and services are produced. A dollar spent on one thing counts the same as a dollar spent on anything else. Many critics argue that in fact some kinds of output are more valuable to our well-being than others, dollar for dollar. For example, they say that a dollar spent on nourishing food is more valuable than one spent on whiskey or bombs. But this is far from obvious; think back to Chapter 5 on consumer behavior. If GNP production is in response to free consumer choices, presumably the marginal dollar spent by each consumer on each thing he buys gives roughly equal satisfaction; otherwise he would spend his dollars so that they do.

The biggest problem comes with goods and services provided by the government. If we presume that democracy works well, the government presumably provides public services and requires people to pay for them through taxes in accordance with the public's wishes. But in this case, the individual can only vote for his representative; then he must go along with the particular taxes and expenditures Congress votes, whether he likes them or not. Clearly, the public sector provides only a rough response to individual wishes, but to handle government taxes and spending in any other way in the GNP accounts would seem even less satisfactory. So GNP says that a dollar spent on anything by individuals or governments counts the same as any other dollar. Ask yourself: Should a dollar spent on schools or national defense be considered more or less important to our economic welfare than one spent on steak or cigarettes?

A further problem arises as modern life becomes more complex. Now we build elaborate subway, elevated, and highway systems in our cities. They provide incomes to thousands and serve millions daily, contributing billions to the annual GNP. Do these billions reflect increased well-being for our city dwellers, or do they reflect instead a huge amount of resources devoted to the painful necessity of getting around in crowded cities? Some economists call them "regrettables," and argue that our larger GNP gives a misleading picture of how much better off we actually are than, for example, a rural nation with no complex transportation system.

7. GNP gives no *negative* weight to those side effects of GNP that do harm rather than good. Air and water pollution is a vivid case. Factories that spew out smoke and dirty water as well as wanted products get overcounted. Their products increase GNP dollar for dollar, but there is no negative charge for all the damage done by pollutants. Such side effects (called "externalities" by economists) are common in our modern, crowded, high-technology society.

Nor does GNP give any negative weight to the sheer disamenities of living in dirty, noisy, crowded cities and slums, compared to more open, pleasant surroundings.

8. GNP measures only *economic* production, which is only one part of what makes us happy or unhappy, contented or alienated. Critics of modern life point to high suicide rates, alienation, and what they see as the dull monotonony and broad discontent of middle-class American life. But defenders counter that comfortable homes, modern plumbing, healthy children, an automobile, modern mass education, and a well-paying office or factory job look very good compared to the lives of our grandfathers—and that the alienated critics had better be careful not to throw out the baby with the bath water. Clearly, GNP doesn't measure everything that contributes to human happiness—peace, health, friendships, and so on. But focusing on the economic issues, are we happier—better off—with our high GNP per capita than if we were poorer? This controversy will seldom be far from the surface through the chapters to come.[8]

TABLE 8–6
GNP and Net Economic Welfare, 1929 and 1965 (In Billions, 1958 prices)

	1929	1965
GNP	$204	$618
NNP	184	563
Add:		
Leisure	340	630
Nonmarket activities	86	295
Other services of private & gov't capital	30	79
Deduct:		
Regrettables	−17	−94
Disamenities	−13	−35
Other capital consumption and growth requirement	−65	−195
Net economic welfare	544	1,241

Source: W. Nordhaus and J. Tobin, *Economic Growth* (New York: National Bureau of Economic Research, 1972), p. 12.

GNP, Growth, and Net Economic Welfare

To introduce more reason into the somewhat feverish rhetoric of debate on economic growth and the quality of life, Yale's James Tobin and William Nordhaus have attempted rough estimates to convert the GNP accounts into a usable measure of economic welfare. Table 8–6 summarizes their attempt to make some order-of-magnitude judgments for 1929 and 1965 about what has really been happening to economic welfare in American economic growth.

Beginning with the regular GNP figures, they estimated the value of leisure and nonmarket activities in both years, and added them, plus services of capital not usually included in GNP, to the GNP totals. They then subtracted from the total, "regrettables" (such as national defense, police, and other resource uses that really don't add to our well-being even though they may be necessary) and "disamenities" (dirt, smoke, noise, and other externalities, mainly associated with urban life). They also subtracted a large amount of capital use each year devoted mainly to keeping the economy growing in per capita income at about the rate it is used to; large additions to our capital stock are needed each year just to keep per capita incomes growing, or even from declining as population grows. The result is a rough dollar measure of net economic welfare (NEW) in the two years.

The results, though very rough, are striking. The dollar measure of economic welfare each year is far larger than GNP. The estimated dollar value of leisure and of nonmarket activities exceeds the entire GNP. Although the estimated costs of regrettables and disamenities, plus the heavy use of capital just to keep total output growing, are large, they are far less than the additions from valuing leisure and nonmarket activities. In total, the measure of economic welfare in 1929 was nearly three times GNP, in 1965 more than twice GNP. And total U.S. economic welfare in 1965 was more than double that in

[8]For an interesting study concluding that the answer is "yes" for improvements in each individual's income, but not necessarily so if all incomes go up together, see R. Easterlin, "Does Money Bring Happiness?", *The Public Interest,* Winter 1973.

1929, in spite of the costs of economic growth stressed by its critics—although economic welfare did grow at a slower rate than GNP, which tripled over the same period. We shall return to these issues on growth in Part Seven.

Tobin and Nordhaus emphasize that different underlying assumptions can greatly change the results of such calculations. For example, how leisure time and nonmarket labor are valued obviously makes a huge difference to the results. And valuation of the disamenities of modern life is clearly arbitrary. So use the estimates only as suggestions. But they do indicate something of the extent to which the national income accounts can reasonably be used as indicators of economic welfare.

REVIEW

Concepts to Remember

This chapter introduces some of the most important concepts in economics. The following checklist is to help you make sure that you have them firmly in mind:

production	disposable personal income
gross national product	personal consumption
"real" GNP	personal saving
"value-added approach"	private investment
"final-products approach"	producer's, or capital, goods
net national product	per capita income and output
capital consumption allowance	price level
depreciation allowance	price index
national income	net economic welfare
personal income	

For Analysis and Discussion

1. Define production. Which of the following are production, as defined by the economist?
   a. Delivering milk.
   b. Making steel.
   c. Selling cigarettes to minors.
   d. Playing golf.
2. In the national income accounts, production is measured by what people pay for it. Is it therefore true that a dollar spent on liquor, on bombs, and on bread are all equally important?
3. Using Figure 8–2, explain each diversion from the main circular flow of income, and trace through the way in which it returns to the main stream. Did government add to or deduct from the flow of spending in 1972?
4. A recent congressional investigation found that over half the consumer price

of many food products went to middlemen at different levels—retailers, wholesalers, and so on; in some cases, as little as 20 percent to the farmer. Farm and consumer groups testifying before the committee urged action to rectify this situation.

a. Do you agree that Congress should take some action? Why or why not?
b. If Congress should act, what should it do?

5. Is gross national product, net national product, or disposable personal income after taxes the best measure of the overall performance of the economy? Why?
6. Should we substitute the Tobin-Nordhaus measure of net economic welfare for gross national product in our official government statistics? Why or why not?
7. The steady growth in service workers is a sign of weakness in our economy, because they produce no *real* goods output comparable to farm output of food and raw materials. (True or false? Why?)
8. From the following data on disposable personal income and the consumer price index, compute disposable personal income for the years shown in constant (1947–49) dollars. Did "real" disposable income fluctuate more or less than money disposable income?

	CURRENT DISPOSABLE PERSONAL INCOME (IN BILLIONS)	CONSUMER PRICE INDEX (1947–49 = 100)	DPI IN 1947–49 DOLLARS
1929	$ 83	73	______
1933	46	55	______
1939	70	60	______
1959	337	126	______
1972	795	178	______

9. Suppose that prices for certain products in 1960 and 1970 were as follows:

	1960	1970
Round steak (per pound)	$ .70	$ 1.00
Butter (per pound)	.90	.75
Men's suits (each)	40.00	60.00
Ford sedans (each)	1,600.00	2,800.00
Student notebooks (each)	1.00	1.00

a. Construct a price index showing the change in the price level of these commodities from 1960 to 1970. If you feel you need further data, explain why, make a reasonable assumption on the data, and then construct the index.
b. Does this index give a reasonably good picture of the change in the cost of living between 1960 and 1970? Why or why not?

Should GNP Measure Social Welfare?

In 1971, the *Survey of Current Business,* which publishes the government's official national income accounts, was fifty years old. To celebrate the occasion, a number of distinguished economists wrote evaluative reviews of the accounts. One of the most interesting was addressed to the producers of the national income accounts by Arthur Okun, former Chairman of President Johnson's Council of Economic Advisors. Okun argued strongly against trying to convert the nation's economic accounts into a measure of economic welfare. Evaluate his arguments as you read them. What is your conclusion: Should GNP be revised to try to measure social welfare?

"The national accounts system is a great accomplishment of modern quantitative economics; it supplies an intelligible, integrated, and invaluable body of information about the functioning of the nation's economy. Its big summary number—the gross national product—has become a household word and has even been enshrined in a clock in the lobby of the Department of Commerce.

"Yet, even as your numbers are receiving greater use and attention than ever before, they also are receiving more criticism. Put simply (perhaps caricatured), the fundamental criticism is that, even after correction for price and population change, the gross national product does not yield an unambiguous measure of national welfare; a rise in real GNP per capita does not necessarily mean that the nation has become better off. This diagnosis may be followed by either of two prescriptions: (1) ignore GNP, or (2) fix GNP so that it does measure social welfare.

"I know you will not ignore the GNP. I urge you to bear the criticism with pride as a symbol of your success. I urge that you not try to "fix" it—to convert GNP into a purported measure of social welfare. You are doing your job so well that people are asking you to take on a different and bigger job. Resist at all costs, for you can't do that job; indeed, nobody can. Producing a summary measure of social welfare is a job for a philosopher-king, and there is no room for a philosopher-king in the federal government. . . .

"Obviously, any number of things would make the nation better off without raising its real GNP as measured today. We might start the list with peace, equality of opportunity, the elimination of injustice and violence, greater brotherhood among Americans of different racial and ethnic backgrounds, better understanding between parents and children and between husbands and wives, and we could go on endlessly. To suggest that GNP could become *the* indicator of social welfare is to imply that an appropriate price tag could be put on changes in all of these social factors from one year to the next. This would hardly be a minor modification of the national accounts. As I have suggested, it would be asking the national income statistician to play the role of philosopher-king, quantifying and evaluating all changes in the human condition. And it is absurd to suggest that if the national income statistician can't do that job, the figure he writes for GNP is not interesting.

. . .

"What you can and do measure as national income statisticians is the output resulting from market-oriented activity. The key to market-oriented activity is the presence of price tags—the essential ingredient in an objective standard of measurement. Price tags enable you to sum up physicians' prescriptions and phonograph records and pounds of steak and packages of beans, or all the things that money can buy. But if you were to be seduced by your critics into inventing price tags that neither exist nor can be reasonably approximated for things that money can't buy, you would have sacrificed the objective yardstick.

". . . . Let me run through some examples of changes you should *not* make.

"Imputation of The Value of Housewives' Services and of Leisure. For good reasons, you violate the normal institutional boundary between business and consumers when you include in GNP the imputed rental value of owner-occupied housing. You do this because the owner-occupant is short-circuiting the market that tenants go through. You do the same for the food farmers produce and consume within their own households rather than sending to market. Why, so the argument goes, should you not similarly treat the housewife as short-circuiting the market by providing services that other families obtain by hiring domestic workers? I find it a compelling argument

that a housewife is not a maid—and that this difference is of a higher order than the difference between the title to a house and a lease. The valuation of the housewife's hourly services by the wage rate of maids, or any multiple thereof, would not really translate her activity into dollars and cents.

"I have never been disturbed by the well-known paradox that when the bachelor marries his cook, the national product goes down. The GNP measures the output of market-oriented activity, and the market-oriented activity is reduced by the cook's marriage. Why is this any more paradoxical than the fact that the national product will go down if I take a month's unpaid vacation in order to travel around the world? In both cases, the nation's marketable output is reduced, but that doesn't mean that welfare is reduced.

"The vacation example brings us to the largest element of what might conceivably be viewed as potentially marketable services that do not show up in the national accounts—that is, time allocated to everything but work. . . . Leisure is a good thing, but it is one of many good things that do not bear a reasonably determinate price tag. It is an important subject for analysis and research, but it does not belong in GNP.

"'*Regrettable Necessities.*' It is obvious that many of the things consumers buy are not intended for pure enjoyment, but are rather a means of avoiding discomfort or preventing deterioration of physical and human capital. Yet you count them all as final product. You have been urged to try to eliminate "regrettable necessities" from final product and thus to classify them as a cost of living rather than a source of satisfaction. Don't start down that path. If you should do so (regrettably and unnecessarily), you would find that it winds along forever. Costs of physicians' services and other medical care are obviously regrettable necessities. So are the services of lawyers, policemen, firemen, sanitation workers, and economists (including national income statisticians). So are heating and air-conditioning outlays. Except for the few people who live to eat rather than eating to live, food is a regrettable necessity. Indeed, it is hard to imagine any output that clearly serves the purpose of pure, unmitigated enjoyment. But even if you could invent some arbitrary definition that kept final-product consumption from falling to zero, the exclusion of regrettable necessities would make no sense. . . .

"*Imputations for Externalities.* It is obvious that the producer does not incur all the costs of producing certain types of output, nor does the consumer get all the benefits. The producer whose factory belches smoke or sends effluents into the river is imposing a cost on society that is not reflected in private costs of production. On the other hand, draining a swamp or building a park may create benefits that are equally absent in your measure of the gross national product. Why, then, should you not try to estimate the net deterioration (or improvement) of the environment as a cost of productive activity, netting it out of GNP?

"Again, I must ask how such a valuation could be made, if the market and the democratic process didn't provide price tags. Following your present rules, you will report the costs and benefits that society recognizes and responds to. If a ban is placed on activity that is inherently dangerous, or fees and taxes are imposed, you will follow the signals and properly reflect them in your valuation of output. If society changes its mind, you will make some rather puzzling changes in your definition and coverage of outputs. But any puzzles that arise concern the volatility of the nation's collective judgment, not of your practices. Your principle of excluding the output of illegal activity from the national product abides by the social judgment that some activities have such important negative externalities that they subtract from society's output even though somebody is willing to pay for them as an ultimate consumer. However sensible or foolish it was for the nation to decide that the sale of alcoholic beverages was illegal and then that it was legal again, it was completely sensible for the national income accountant to follow those verdicts.

. . .

"In short, the GNP is not the whole story of our society or even of our economy, and no conceivable redefinition can turn it into the whole story. You can help in many ways to put together some of the other pieces required to develop the whole story about social performance. But you would not assist by compromising on the proposition that GNP is *not* a measure of total social welfare. The beauty of your present practice is that no sensible person could mistake it for such."[9]

[9]Arthur Okun, "Should GNP Measure Social Welfare?" *Survey of Current Business,* Part II, July 1971.

Aggregate Supply and Aggregate Demand

CHAPTER PREVIEW

CHAPTER NINE

Why do we have booms, depressions, inflations, and unemployment? What determines how fast an economy grows? For over a century economists have examined these problems. Today, we have a reasonably good understanding, though some important unanswered questions remain.

The next five chapters present the basic theory of income, employment, and prices—the general analytical model that has proved most useful in understanding what determines the overall level of income, employment, and prices in the American economy. No section of the book is more important to understand thoroughly. Chapters 15–18 then turn to the question of stabilization policy—how to avoid unemployment and inflation, and how to have a prosperous, stably-growing economy.

A SIMPLE MODEL

To understand the complex real economic world, it is useful to begin with a very simple model. You will recall from Chapter 1 that the essence of a model is that it focuses on a few critical variables and the relationships among them, abstracting from many details in order to highlight these essentials. We want to understand the determinants of real GNP, of aggregate employment, and of price level. Let us begin by focusing on two major variables—aggregate demand and aggregate supply.

Aggregate demand is the combined expenditures of consumers, businesses, and governments that make up GNP. Aggregate supply is the total amount of goods and services that will be produced (supplied) in response to different levels of aggregate demand. In our private-enterprise economy (leaving government aside for the moment), goods and services are produced only when they can be sold at a profit. If there is no market demand, businesses will soon stop producing. Thus, we think of supply as a schedule of different amounts that will be produced in response to different levels of aggregate demand.

Obviously, as we look back on any time period, aggregate demand (the amount bought) and aggregate supply (the amount produced) will be the same. What is produced (measured in dollars) is identical with what is spent on it. This is simply GNP looked at from the production and expenditure sides. But whether the two sides are equal at a high or low level of GNP—whether at full employment or depression—is the vital question.

AGGREGATE SUPPLY AND AGGREGATE DEMAND

What determines the economy's aggregate supply schedule? The "real" productive capacity of any economic system sets the upper limit to its real GNP at any time. This productive capacity—the economy's production-possibilities curve for total output from Chapter 3—depends on its underlying real productive resources, its technology, and its economic organization.[1] But an economy may not achieve this full-production potential. History shows that nations often fall short of obtaining the maximum production possible from their economies, for example in the Great Depression of the 1930s. This failure primarily reflects a shortage of aggregate demand. There is not enough total spending by consumers and businesses to buy all the goods that could be produced at full employment.

Conversely, aggregate spending may exceed the productive capacity of the economy at existing prices. If that occurs, prices are bid up and there is inflation, because no more can be produced as demand rises.

The Short-Run Supply Schedule and Supply Curve

At any given time, the production-possibilities curve for an economy is given. Keeping this fact in mind, let us construct an aggregate-supply schedule for the economy, assuming that the full-employment production limit is $400 billion. Column 1 in Table 9–1 simply shows different assumed levels of aggregate demand; column 2 shows the amount that will be produced in response to each level of demand. As long as the economy is below its capacity limit, rising demand calls forth more output, dollar for dollar. But after full capacity is reached, more demand cannot increase output further. The result will be inflation, but this doesn't show in Table 9–1, because the aggregate-supply schedule there is in real (constant price) terms. Above $400 billion of aggregate demand, total real output is unchanged at $400 billion, although money GNP rises with inflation.

It is useful to represent this aggregate-supply schedule graphically as an aggregate "supply curve" for the economy. This curve will show how much will be produced (supplied) in re-

TABLE 9–1
Aggregate Demand and Aggregate Supply

AGGREGATE DEMAND (IN BILLIONS)	AGGREGATE SUPPLY (IN REAL TERMS, IN BILLIONS)
$100	$100
200	200
300	300
400	400
500	400
600	400

[1]Over time, some economies have been able to increase their productive capacity rapidly, while others seem to get nowhere. But for the moment we take the nation's production-possibilities curve as given. This is reasonable, because we want to begin by analyzing the behavior of the economy at a given point in time.

sponse to different levels of aggregate demand.[2]

In Figure 9–1, we show on the horizontal axis the amount supplied—that is, real GNP (in initial prices). On the vertical axis we show aggregate demand—total spending by all those who buy goods and services in the economy in this period. Equal distances show equal amounts on both axes.

At one extreme, if there is no demand, nothing will be produced in our profit-motivated economy. If demand is OD_1, businessmen will produce OQ_1, and so on for different levels of demand. If demand is OD_3, output is OQ_3, the maximum real output possible for the economy in this period. Output OQ_3 corresponds to $400 billion in Table 9–1. No matter how much people spend, more than this cannot be produced.

Thus, if we imagine the output levels called forth by all possible levels of aggregate demand from zero to OD_3, we would have the line OA, rising at a 45° angle from the zero point. It rises at a forty-five-degree angle because for each level of OD, real output on the horizontal axis is an identical amount. **We call this line *OA* the economy's aggregate-supply curve; it shows how much the economy would produce at each different level of aggregate demand.**

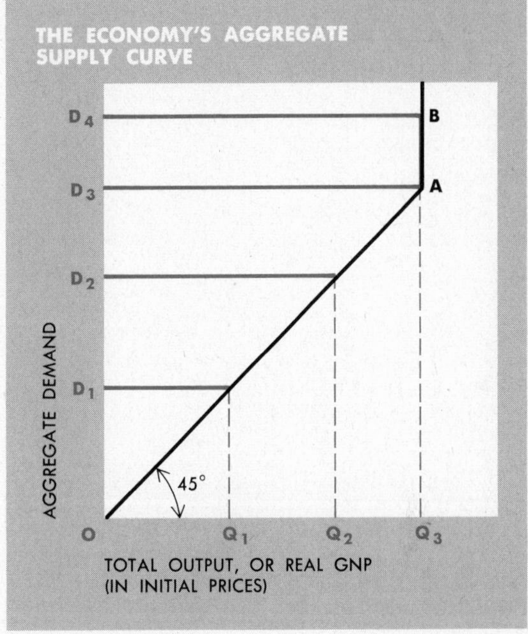

Figure 9–1

Curve OA suggests that as aggregate demand rises, output will be increased proportionately without any price increase (inflation) up to full-employment output OQ_3. If demand increases further, however, the result will be purely rising prices since output cannot be expanded further in the short run.

But once the economy has reached its full-employment GNP (here OQ_3), it cannot increase output further. Thus, the aggregate-supply curve OA becomes perpendicular at that point; it becomes OAB. Further increases in demand, say aggregate demand of OD_4, will simply bid up prices rather than call forth more output.

It is important to recognize that by the same reasoning, if aggregate demand falls, the results are exactly the reverse. Given the aggregate supply curve OAB, when aggregate demand falls from OD_4 to OD_3 the result is purely lower prices. But when demand falls from OD_3 to OD_2 or to OD_1, the result is purely reduced real GNP, not falling prices. **That is, we assume temporarily that below full-employment output, rising or falling aggregate demand will alter only real GNP, while after full employment has been reached changes in demand will affect only the price level.** We shall see later that this is not strictly true, but it is a useful temporary assumption.

[2]We shall see the terms "supply schedule" and "supply curve" are used somewhat differently here from Parts Three and Four, in which they apply to individual business firms and markets. Here, the supply schedule shows the aggregate amounts that will be produced in response to different levels of aggregate demand. Later, supply schedules for individual firms will show the amounts produced in response to different prices for the product concerned.

AGGREGATE DEMAND, UNEMPLOYMENT, AND INFLATION

Our model is of course a highly oversimplified representation of the real world. Let us now make it a little more realistic, to analyze more

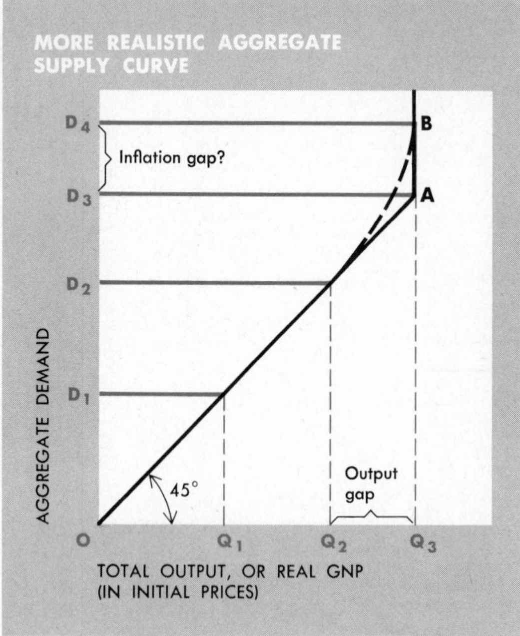

Figure 9–2

As the dashed section of OB shows, when an economy approaches full employment prices ordinarily begin to rise before full-capacity output is reached. Here full-employment output, OQ_3, can be achieved only with aggregate demand, OD_4, which would imply substantial inflation.

fully when rising demand will call forth additional output, when inflation, and when a mixture of both.

In the real world, it is not true that rising aggregate demand will always call forth solely dollar-for-dollar increases in real GNP up to full employment, and pure inflation thereafter. Actually, we would expect some prices to begin to rise before full employment is reached, because increases in demand might cause production bottlenecks and shortages in some sectors of the economy before full employment occurred in others. Demand would normally rise faster for some products than for others.

To show this situation, Figure 9–2 reproduces the aggregate-supply curve from Figure 9–1, as solid line OAB. But it adds a dashed segment that rounds off the corner where solid OAB has a sharp kink at A. This dashed segment shows that prices will begin to rise before we reach full employment. Put otherwise, it shows that we can reach full-employment output OQ_3 only with aggregate demand OD_4 and the considerable inflation that implies.

Try using Figure 9–2 to predict the consequences of different levels of demand. If demand rises from OD_1 to OD_2, the result is still purely rising output and employment as before. But if demand moves on up to OD_3, now some of the growth in demand will induce more output but some will go into higher prices. To push the economy all the way to its full-employment output of OQ_3, we must now have aggregate demand of OD_4, and with it a lot of inflation. Demand OD_3 won't do the job any more.

This situation can pose a difficult dilemma for economic policy makers. As we approach OQ_3, should the government expand aggregate demand further in order to reduce unemployment to a bare minimum, even though this brings on some inflation? Or is it better to keep aggregate demand at a lower level, accepting some unemployment but also avoiding inflation? This will be a central issue in Chapters 15–18.[3]

The Output Gap and the Inflation Gap

If aggregate demand falls short of the economy's full-employment capacity level, unemployment of men and factories will result. For example, if aggregate demand is only OD_2 in Figure 9–2, output will be only OQ_2 and there will be an "output gap" of $Q_2 - Q_3$ by which output falls short of full capacity. Sometimes this is called the "employment gap." In a depression this gap is large.

[3]A second modification of this Figure 9–1 model is in order if we want more realism. In the real world, full-employment GNP (OQ_3) is never as rigid a limit as is shown in the diagram. As prices rise, housewives, students, and older people enter the labor force. Workers put in longer hours. Production managers push plants beyond their quoted capacities. The full-employment ceiling on output is a mushy one. To reflect this accurately, the vertical segment of OAB should bend over a little to the right.

If, on the other hand, aggregate demand exceeds full-employment capacity output at existing prices, there will be an "inflation gap." If demand is D_4, for example, prices will rise. Thus, the inflation gap would be $D_3 - D_4$, showing the rise in prices as a result of excess aggregate demand. Actually, as Figure 9–2 suggests, the concept of the inflation gap is a slippery one. Because prices would begin to rise once demand exceeded D_2, we might call $D_2 - D_4$ the inflation gap even though output Q_2 is far short of full employment. But usually $D_3 - D_4$ is called the inflation gap.

GROWTH IN PRODUCTIVE CAPACITY

The aggregate-supply curves in Figures 9–1 and 9–2 are for a given time period—say a year. They are what economists often call short-run supply curves. Over longer periods, of course, the productive capacity of an economy can grow—for example, through investment in new factories, increases in the labor force, and technological progress. In that event, full-employment output each year is larger than the year before; the production-possibilities frontier moves out. It is important to note that if productive capacity grows this way, what is full-employment aggregate demand for one year will be inadequate to call forth full-employment output the next year.

We can readily show this in Figure 9–3. It reproduces supply curve OAB from Figure 9–1, and adds on extended segments ACC and ADD to show how potential real GNP moves out year after year with new investment, more labor, and advancing technology. By the same token, Figure 9–3 shows that larger aggregate demand will be needed each year to call forth full-employment GNP.

Thus, the aggregate-supply curve for year 2 is OCC. Potential real GNP has moved out to OQ_4, and demand OD_4 is required to assure full employment. In year 3 the aggregate-supply curve becomes ODD, and aggregate demand OD_5 is needed for full employment. In terms of Chapter 2, the economy's production frontier moves out.

Chapters 9–18 are primarily concerned with the short-run behavior of the economy. They generally take the productive capacity of the economy as substantially fixed, even though this is not quite accurate, and focus on aggregate demand as the major determinant of the level of output and prices. Part Seven later focuses on long-term economic growth, and there the expansion of capacity will be the center of attention.

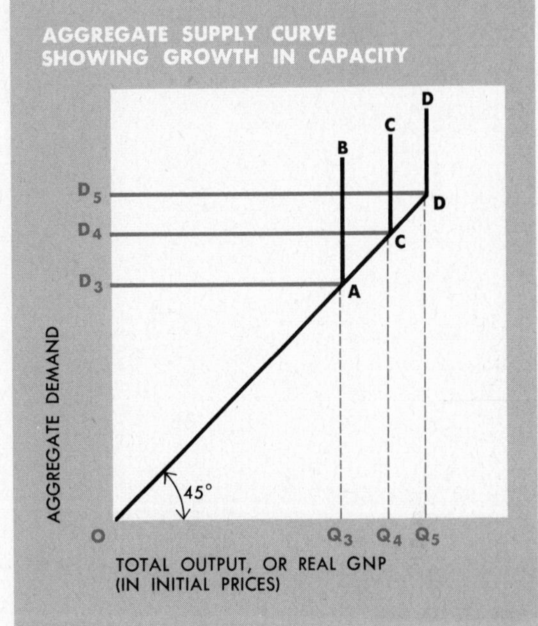

Figure 9–3

With more productive resources and improved technology, an economy's productive capacity increases. With increased capacity, more aggregate demand is required to call forth full-employment output. In years 2 and 3, full-employment capacity has risen to OQ_4 and OQ_5 respectively.

REVIEW

Concepts to Remember

This chapter introduces new basic concepts that will be used over and over. Be sure you understand:

aggregate supply	inflationary gap
aggregate demand	output gap

For Analysis and Discussion

1. Why does the economy's aggregate supply curve slope upward as demand rises.
2. Explain the relationship between an economy's production-possibilities curve and its aggregate-supply curve.
3. Does the aggregate-supply curve in Figure 9–1 or that in Figure 9–2 make it easier for the economy to achieve full employment without inflation? Explain.
4. In a private-enterprise, profit-motivated economy, why is it reasonable to say that aggregate production will depend on the level of aggregate demand?
5. After an economy reaches full employment, raising aggregate expenditure must always cause inflation. (True or false? Does the time period involved influence your answer?)
6. What are the main ways by which a nation can move its production-possibilities curve out (to the right)?

The Modern Theory of Aggregate Income, Employment, and Fiscal Policy

CHAPTER TEN

In the short run, whether we have depression, stable prosperity, or inflation depends largely on the level of aggregate demand. Chapter 9 examined the short-run supply curve for the economy. Chapters 10–13 now examine the factors that determine the level of aggregate demand that calls forth the aggregate supply described in Chapter 9.

Two general approaches have been stressed. One, often called the income-expenditures, or neo-Keynesian, approach, emphasizes that spending depends largely on the incomes people and businesses receive.[1] This approach, which focuses on consumption, investment, and government spending from Chapter 8, is explained in Chapters 10 and 11. The other, often called the "monetarist," or neo-classical, approach, emphasizes the stock of money as the dominant force determining total spending. It is explained in Chapters 12 and 13, and Chapter 13 also integrates the two approaches. (We shall con-

[1] This general approach was first popularized by a noted economist, John Maynard Keynes, during the depression of the 1930s. Keynes achieved wide fame because he was one of the earliest advocates of fighting depressions with deficit spending. Whatever you think about that issue—it's central to Chapter 15—you should understand that the present chapter deals only with neutral analytic tools that can help you understand the determinants of aggregate demand, but they don't necessarily tell you what is the best way to fight depressions and inflations.

tinue to ignore temporarily international considerations, postponing their discussion to Part Six).

SIMPLE STATIC GNP MODEL[2]

To simplify, first temporarily assume that there is no government spending or taxation. Thus, aggregate demand is the sum of consumption (C) plus investment spending (I). Because aggregate demand is also equal to gross national product, we can say that GNP equals $C + I$. (Economists typically use Y to represent national income or GNP, and so will we. Thus $Y = C + I$.)

Second, assume (what many economists consider a crude first approximation to reality) that consumption spending depends entirely on the incomes that people receive. Moreover, the portion of their income households don't spend on consumption, they save. Because saving is defined as simply that income received that is not spent on consumption, saving also depends on the amount of income people receive. Obviously, saving equals income minus consumption ($S = Y - C$). Thus, both consumption spending and saving are "induced" by the level of consumer income.

Third, assume that business investment spending is autonomously determined. That is, businessmen decide how much to invest on the basis of considerations other than consumer spending and saving. The independently determined, "autonomous" nature of investment thus contrasts with the dependent, induced nature of consumption and saving.

This contrast between autonomous and induced expenditure is a critical one for the analysis that follows. Be sure you understand the difference. Autonomous expenditure is determined by forces outside our system, or model; induced expenditure is determined by the forces at work inside the model.[3]

Given these assumptions, we can readily show how consumption and investment spending interact to produce an equilibrium level of aggregate demand (and, hence, real GNP) each year. The reasoning can be presented verbally, graphically, or algebraically. It's done all three ways below, because different people find different approaches most helpful. Note, therefore, that the following three sections repeat substantially the *same* analysis in these different forms.

Algebraic Presentation

We have defined aggregate demand as identical with GNP, which is equal to consumption plus investment spending. Let Y stand for aggregate demand and GNP. Then:

$$Y = C + I$$

Now assume that consumption spending is always just .75 of income (that is, people spend three-fourths of their incomes on consumption and save one-fourth), so that:

$$C = .75 \cdot Y$$

Saving (S) is the portion of their income that people don't spend on consumption. Thus,

$$S = .25Y$$

Remember that investment (I) is autonomous; it is independently determined. Suppose that business investment spending is 100 this year, so:

$$I = 100$$

Now, substitute the values for C and I in our original equation, $Y = C + I$. We get:

$$Y = .75Y + 100$$

[2]Section II of the Mathematical Appendix, at the end of this text, presents the central argument of this chapter in mathematical terms. Students who know calculus and find mathematical formulations helpful may find the appendix a useful aid, but it is recommended for use only *after* the following text sections have been read.

[3]As we move later to more complex models, we shall see that actually both consumption and investment are partly autonomous and partly induced, and must then be broken down into these separate parts for analysis.

Using the rules of elementary algebra, move the $.75Y$ to the left side of the equation. This changes the sign from plus to minus, and we have:

$$Y - .75Y = 100, \text{ or}$$
$$.25Y = 100, \text{ or}$$
$$Y = \frac{100}{.25}, \text{ and}$$
$$Y = 400$$

Equilibrium aggregate demand, or GNP, will be 400 if investment is 100 and people spend three-fourths of all the income they receive on consumption. Households will be spending 300 each year on consumption, and saving 100.

This is the "equilibrium" level of aggregate demand and GNP, given our assumptions. That is, it is the level to which aggregate demand and GNP will move, and the level at which they will stay once they get there, unless something new comes along to change them.

Verbal Presentation

Put the reasoning in words. Given our assumptions, clearly when GNP is 400 everyone is content to keep on doing what he is doing. With total income of 400, people are consuming .75 of the income they receive, and saving 100, just enough to match the investment that businesses are spending on investment.

But wouldn't some other GNP be equally good? The answer is no. Try 500, for example. This means that businesses are producing 500 each year. But on the demand side buyers would purchase only 475, that is, 375 of consumption goods (three-fourths of 500) plus 100 of investment goods. Unsold inventories would pile up, and businesses would reduce production (GNP). And so it would be for any other GNP above 400. Conversely, if we assume a GNP less than 400, then demand ($C + I$) would be larger than production. For example, suppose GNP (production) were 300. Then demand would be 325—100 of investment plus the 225 people would consume if their incomes were 300. Businesses would have to increase production to meet the larger demand. GNP would thus rise toward 400.

Work out as many examples as you like and you'll always get one and only one equilibrium value of aggregate demand and GNP; with our assumptions it is 400. Equilibrium requires that the public decide to save just the amount businesses have decided to invest; the withdrawals from the income stream through saving just offset the autonomous investment spending.

Of course, the particular numbers in our example are arbitrary. If business investment is higher, say 150, the equilibrium GNP is higher. If consumers spend 80 instead of 75 percent of their income on consumption, equilibrium GNP will be higher. Try it and see. But the reasoning—the underlying economic adjustment process—is unchanged.

Graphic Presentation

The same reasoning can be presented in graphical terms. But in doing so, let us change the numbers and make the model more realistic by introducing a more realistic "consumption function," which is what economists call the relation between people's income and their consumption spending. The only difference from the preceding example is that people now consume a lower percentage of their incomes at high than at low incomes, instead of always just three-fourths. This shift will, of course, change the equilibrium level of GNP. Again, consumption and saving depend entirely on GNP and investment is autonomously fixed at 100.

The Consumption and Saving Schedules

Figure 10–1 shows these new consumption and saving functions. On the left-hand chart, line *CC* shows consumption spending at different levels of GNP; for example, consumption spending (vertical axis) would be about 200 if GNP were 300 (horizontal axis).

In addition, the chart has a 45° line, every

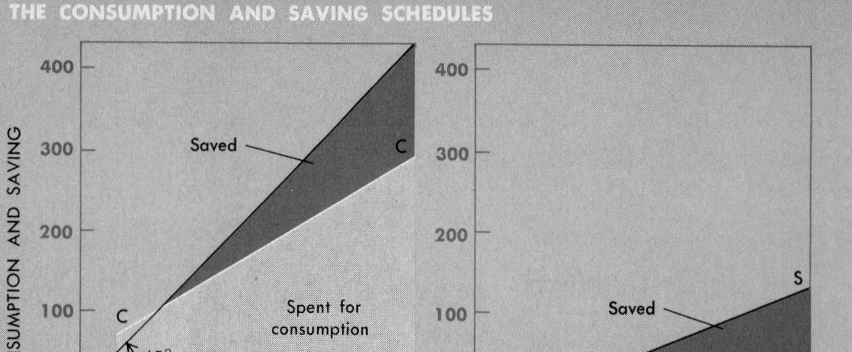

Figure 10–1

The left-hand portion of this figure shows that people will spend a smaller proportion of their income on consumption as income rises, and will save a larger proportion. The right-hand portion shows the same saving behavior by itself.

point on which is equidistant from the two axes. Thus, if line *CC* coincided with the 45° line, consumers would spend all their income (GNP) on consumption; there would be no saving. Whenever the consumption curve (*CC*) is below the 45° line, part of GNP is being saved. For example, at a GNP of 200, the economy would spend 160 on consumption and save 40. Note that if GNP were as low as 50, people would spend more than their full incomes on consumption; they would "dissave" by borrowing or drawing on past savings.[4]

The right-hand part of Figure 10–1 shows the corresponding saving schedule (*SS*). This is drawn simply by taking the amount saved at each level of GNP from the left-hand portion. Saving will be negative at low income levels when *CC* exceeds total GNP, and will be positive at higher income levels. The *SS* curve will, of course, cross the zero line at the same income level as the *CC* curve cuts the 45° line, where all GNP is spent on consumption—at 100 on Figure 10–1.

We can show graphically how equilibrium is determined in two ways. First, plot the saving curve (*SS*) in Figure 10–2, from the right-hand portion of Figure 10–1. Now add investment (*II*). It is a horizontal line at 100, because we have assumed that investment is fixed at that

[4]For readers who like mathematics, the equation of this consumption function is: $C = a + b(Y)$, where a and b are constants with $a = 40$ and $b = .6$. Therefore, $C = 40 + .6Y$. That is, consumption is always 40 plus .6 of the amount of income received. The basic $Y = C + I$ equation can be solved just as before by making the new substitution for C. Thus:

$$\begin{aligned} Y &= (40 + .6Y) + 100, \text{ or} \\ Y - .6Y &= 40 + 100 \\ .4Y &= 140, \text{ so} \\ Y &= 350 \end{aligned}$$

The Mathematical Appendix at the end of the book and the appendix to this chapter on "Econometric Models" show more fully how simple mathematical systems can be used to determine equilibrium GNP levels under more complicated conditions.

Figure 10–2

Equilibrium GNP is established where the public wishes to save just enough to match the amount being invested.

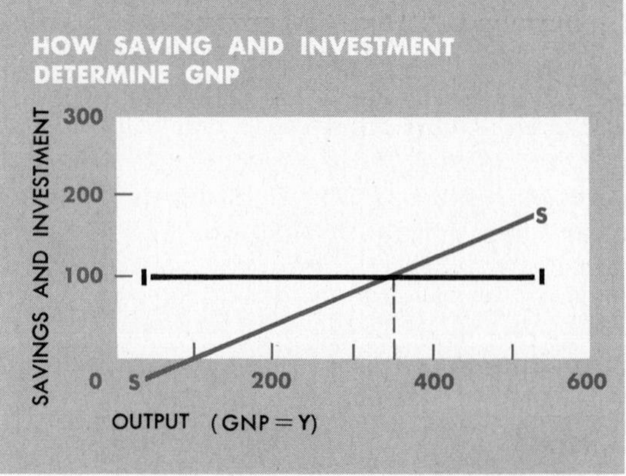

level. *II* intersects *SS* at a GNP of 350, and this is the equilibrium level. Note that equilibrium GNP here is different from the preceding example, because we have assumed a different consumption function. People no longer spend just 75 percent of their incomes on consumption.

Why is 350 the equilibrium level? The reasoning is the same as before: Because at this level of GNP the amount businessmen invest is exactly offset by the amount people want to save. Thus, the circular flow of income will be complete and stable. Consumers will receive 350 of income each year from producing the 350 GNP, and (reading from the left-hand portion of Figure 10–1) they will save 100 and spend 250 on consumption. Each year, businesses will invest 100, just equal to the amount people save; and so on indefinitely.

There is a second way of showing the same results graphically. Figure 10–3 shows the consumption and investment functions on the same graph. It adds to consumption spending (the *CC* curve of Figure 10–1) 100 of investment spending at each income level each year. Thus, $C + I$ is the amount that households and businesses will spend on consumption plus investment at each level of GNP (total output and income). Now, because consumption and investment spending are on the vertical axis, and total GNP is on the horizontal axis, the 45° line shows all the points at which aggregate demand ($C + I$) will just equal total production (GNP).

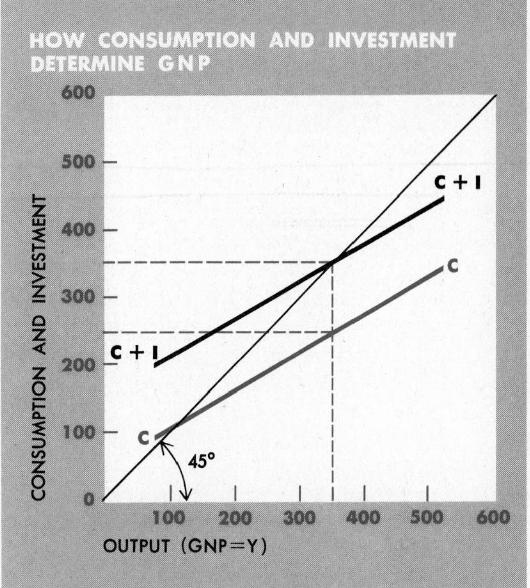

Figure 10–3

Equilibrium GNP is established where the sum of consumption- and investment-spending (on the vertical axis) just equals GNP (on the horizontal axis). This gives the same equilibrium level as Figure 10–2.

In Figure 10–3, aggregate demand ($C + I$) just equals GNP (cuts the 45° line) at 350, the equilibrium GNP for these investment and consumption assumptions. At 350, and only at 350, does the sum of consumption and investment demand just equal GNP (output).

Test the result. As before, assume any GNP lower than 350 (say 300), and you will see that it can't last. At a GNP of 300, consumption plus investment spending, shown by $C + I$, would be above the 45° line. Thus, demand would exceed production and businesses would increase production. GNP would rise toward 350. The opposite is true if we assume GNP is anything higher than 350, say 400. At a GNP of 400, $C + I$ would be less than 400; people would not buy all the goods being produced; unsold inventories would pile up; and production would fall toward 350.

A crucial reminder: All the above analysis assumes that consumption and saving are functions solely of income received. If consumption spending changes for any other (autonomous) reason, the equilibrium level of income will be changed. In the model, such a change would be shown as a shift in the consumption function (on the chart, a shift of the *CC* line to the right or left).

Equilibrium Not Necessarily Full Employment

It is important to recognize that an equilibrium GNP does not necessarily imply that there is full employment. Look back at the short-run aggregate-supply curve in Figure 9–1. It shows that if equilibrium GNP is less than OD_3 and OQ_3, there will be unemployment and the economy will be operating inside its production-possibilities frontier; there will be an output gap. If equilibrium GNP is above OD_3, the result will be inflation; there will be an inflation gap. "Equilibrium" GNP as we have defined it is thus a neutral analytical concept. It does not imply anything, either good or bad, about the level of employment or how well the economic system is performing. The aggregate supply curve shows what the economy's equilibrium response will be to different levels of aggregate demand.

CHANGING INVESTMENT—THE MULTIPLIER

Suppose now that businessmen decide to increase their investment spending, perhaps because of a new invention. This decision will raise the *II* curve in Figure 10–2 and the $C + I$ curve in Figure 10–3. The result, common sense tells you, will be a higher equilibrium level of GNP after the increase in investment. Conversely, a decrease in investment spending will lead to a lower equilibrium level.

But one additional fact may not be equally obvious: **Each dollar of increase in autonomous spending will increase aggregate demand and GNP by a larger, or multiplied, amount.** This is because each new dollar of investment, as it is spent, becomes income to a consumer who saves part but respends the rest on consumption. This induced consumption spending constitutes income to someone else, who in turn saves part but respends the rest. And so on. The number of times the final increase in income (GNP) exceeds the new investment is called the "multiplier." For example, if one additional dollar of investment spending generates four additional dollars of GNP, the multiplier is four.

Marginal Propensity to Consume (MPC)

To explore this process more fully, we now need to distinguish between the "average" and the "marginal" propensity to consume. Suppose that total income (GNP) is 100 and people are spending 75 on consumption and saving 25 each period. Then the **average** propensity to consume is .75. However, it does not necessarily follow that if they receive additional income they would maintain this same consumption-income ratio. Suppose their incomes now rise to 110 but they only consume .5 of this additional 10 of income. Then the **marginal** propensity to consume is .5. **The marginal propensity to consume (MPC) is the proportion of additional, or marginal, income that is spent on consumption.** It is the marginal propensity on which we need to focus our attention when we are analyzing *changes* in the level of GNP.

The Multiplier

Begin with an equilibrium GNP of 350 and assume that the *marginal* propensity to consume is .75. Suppose now that businessmen increase their investment spending by 10. When the 10 is spent on new investment (say, building a new plant), it becomes income to the recipients, who then spend 7.5 on consumption and save 2.5. The 7.5 of consumption spending becomes income to someone else who in turn respends 75 percent (5.6) on consumption and saves 25 percent (1.9). The 5.6 becomes income to someone else, and so the process goes. Remember that savings are withdrawn from the income stream and are *not* respent in this model; nor do they induce more investment, because investment is autonomous. We get a table like the following.[5]

	NEW INCOME	NEW CONSUMPTION	NEW SAVING
Initiating New Investment	10.0	7.5	2.5
On Round 2	7.5	5.6	1.9
On Round 3	5.6	4.2	1.4
On Round 4	4.2	3.2	1.0
	.	.	.
	.	.	.
	40	30	10

The table shows only the first four rounds, but it gives the general picture. The 10 of new investment generates a chain of respending on consumption, the "multiplier" effect. Each round makes a smaller net addition to income than its predecessor, because part of the new income is drained off into saving by each recipient. If you carry the arithmetic to its conclusion, you will find that the total new GNP generated is 40 (including the 10 of new investment). Of this total, 30 is spent on consumption and 10 is saved, in accordance with our marginal propensity to consume of .75. The expansion has continued until the amount people want to save of their higher income just offsets the 10 of new investment. Adding these increments to the original equilibrium values, we get a new equilibrium GNP of 390. **The multiplier is 4, since GNP has risen by 40 in response to 10 of autonomous investment.**

This result is shown graphically in Figure 10–4. The *CC* and $C + I$ curves before the increase in investment are reproduced directly from Figure 10–3. Now we add 10 more of investment at each level of income, so the new $(C + I)'$ now represents consumption plus 110, instead of plus 100. The *CC* line is unchanged because the consumption function is unchanged. The new equilibrium level of GNP is 390, up 40, where the new $C + I'$ curve cuts the 45° line.

If this looks like graphical trickery, consider the economic reasoning. Under what conditions will the multiplier be large, and when small? There are four important points:

1. The multiplier effect hinges on the fact that people respend on consumption part of each increment of income they receive. If at any point they save all their new income, the respending spiral stops short.

2. The larger the proportion of its additional income that the public respends each round, the larger will be the multiplier.

[5]Assume for this example that the businesses get the funds for the extra 10 of investment by borrowing newly created funds from the banks, rather than by saving out of their own current incomes.

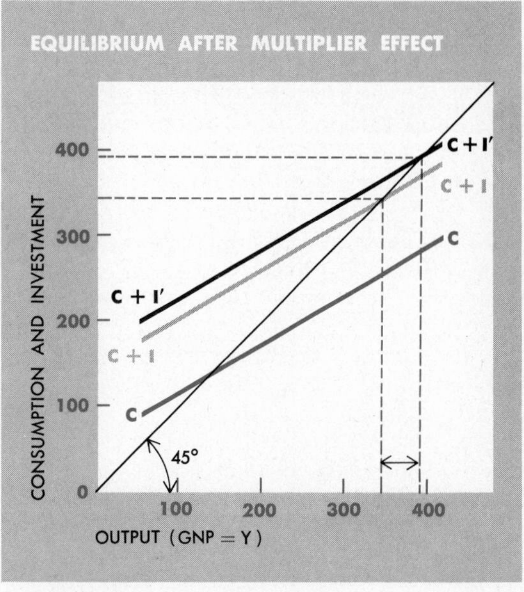

Figure 10–4

An additional 10 of investment raises the C + I curve to C' + I' and brings a new equilibrium level of GNP of 390, up 40 from the previous equilibrium. The investment multiplier is 4.

3. The size of the multiplier is given precisely by the formula:

$$M = \frac{1}{1 - \text{Marginal propensity to consume}}$$

Thus, if the marginal propensity to consume is .75, the multiplier will be:

$$M = \frac{1}{1 - .75} = \frac{1}{.25} = 4.$$

If the economy's marginal propensity to consume out of GNP were .90, the multiplier would be 10. (Work out the .90 case in the equation for yourself.) An easy way to look at it is this: The multiplier is the reciprocal of the marginal propensity to save, *given our simple assumptions.* Thus, if consumers save one-fourth of their new income, the multiplier is 4. If one-tenth, the multiplier is 10. And so on.

4. Last, review again the economic reasoning

behind this formula. **A dollar of autonomous spending will set off an induced spending spiral that will continue until the public's income is such that it wants to save just enough to offset the amount of autonomous investment. Only if these two just match will the circular flow of income be continuous and stable.**

This is the basic multiplier process. But a warning is needed. In the real world, with government taxes and spending and with business as well as consumer saving, the picture becomes more complex. To calculate real-world multipliers, see the box, "The Multiplier in the Real World."[6]

[6]This multiplier reasoning suggests a curious paradox, sometimes called the "paradox of thrift." If consumers decide to save a larger percentage of their incomes, other things equal this increased propensity to save will lead to a lower multiplier, lower consumption, a lower GNP, and

THE MULTIPLIER IN THE REAL WORLD

Suppose the economy is in recession, with widespread unemployment. The preceding pages on the multiplier suggest something the government can do about it—increase expenditures without raising taxes. Suppose it increases expenditures by $10 billion to fight unemployment this year. What will the multiplier be? How much will GNP rise?

Your first question presumably will be, what is the consumption function? Looking ahead to the next chapter, you can find that households have quite consistently spent about .9 of their disposable personal income on consumption and saved about .1. So the multiplier would be a powerful 10, raising GNP by $100 billion. Right? Wrong! The real-world multiplier would probably be far less, more like 2 or less. Why?

1. First, the multiplier depends on the *marginal,* not the average, propensity to consume, and experience suggests that consumers are generally slow to adjust to sharp increases in income. Thus, their marginal propensity to consume this year out of the new income is likely to be nearer .5 or .6 than .9.

2. Even if households were to consume .9 of each dollar of disposable personal income, there are numerous other leakages from the $10 billion of autonomous government spending. First, corporations also save, by retaining part of their profits and their depreciation accounts. More important, government tax collections will rise with rising incomes, even though tax *rates* are kept unchanged. Part of the income will drain off to the government through corporate and personal income taxes and through indirect taxes such as sales taxes. Look back at Table 8–4 and trace the $10 billion down the table from GNP to disposable personal income. Taxes and corporate saving are likely to drain off a quarter to a third of the $10 billion before it gets to disposable personal income. So, even if the marginal propensity to consume were .9, it would apply to only, say, $6 or $7 billion, not $10 billion. Another way to look at it is, the marginal propensity to consume *out of GNP* is likely to be more like .5 than .9, so the multiplier on GNP will be more like 2 than 10.

3. This chapter has omitted money and interest rates from the analysis. As we shall see in Chapter 13, government borrowing to get the money to spend may well bid up interest rates, thereby discouraging private investment and inducing a negative multiplier effect that partly offsets the positive multiplier effect of the government spending.

All this is not to say that government fiscal policy can't help fight depressions. It certainly can. But to apply multiplier analysis reliably to the real world requires that we take all the complications into account. And the result is a much smaller multiplier than a casual application of the .9 average propensity to consume out of disposable personal income would suggest.

INDUCED INVESTMENT AND DYNAMIC PROCESSES

Thus far, we have assumed that investment decisions are autonomous—that is, determined independently of the level of consumption and GNP. But actually, the level of sales (consumer expenditures) is an important determinant of business investment plans. If we say that business investment is induced—dependent on consumer spending in the preceding period—we get what economists call "dynamic" analysis. In that case, the new equilibrium level in Figure 10–4 would not be a lasting equilibrium, since the higher consumer spending would in turn induce more business investment. The new induced investment in turn would lead to a further multiplier effect on consumption and GNP. Intuitively, you might expect such a process to spiral upward indefinitely—and under some conditions it would. But under others, the spiral will die out, or even reverse itself and start downward.

Such dynamic processes are the essence of booms and depressions (business cycles). An upswing started by new investment will raise income through the multiplier. More income leads to more consumption, and that improves business sales, which leads to more investment. But it is better to postpone such dynamic analysis until we have equilibrium analysis firmly in hand. We shall return to dynamic processes in detail in Chapter 14.

---

a *lower* level of aggregate saving in the new equilibrium. Here is an example of the fallacy of composition. More saving out of any given level of income may be a very good thing for the individual household, but a simultaneous attempt by many households to save more out of their incomes may throw the economy into a recession that makes us all worse off, and in which we actually save less because of our lower incomes.

But note that an increase in the economy's propensity to save *need* not throw us into recession. If the increased thriftiness comes in a period of inflation, it can help reduce inflationary pressure. And even in noninflationary periods, the increased propensity to save may be offset by higher private investment or government spending.

GOVERNMENT TAXES AND EXPENDITURES (FISCAL POLICY)

Now let us put government taxes and spending into our model, to bring it into closer correspondence with the real world. Government taxes take away part of the spendable income of households and businesses, and governments spend on current output. Thus, we need to add government on both the spending and saving sides of the picture.

We can treat government spending on goods and services as similar to autonomous private-investment spending, determined by forces other than the current level of GNP. Government spending constitutes effective demand for goods and services. We can treat government tax collections as similar to private savings; they constitute a leakage out of the respending stream, with their amount determined (induced) by the level of GNP, given any set of tax rates.

We now have a slightly more complex model in which both private investment and government spending are autonomous, whereas consumption spending is an induced expenditure; and on the other side both private savings and government tax receipts are withdrawals from the income stream. Thus, the new equation is:

$$C + I + GE = C + S + GR$$

where *GE* is government expenditure and *GR* is government tax receipts. That is, if the sum of private investment plus government expenditures (autonomous spending) exceeds the "leakages" from the spending stream through private savings and tax receipts, GNP will rise. Conversely, GNP will fall if investment plus government spending is less than the leakages through saving and tax receipts.

Fiscal Policy

This suggests a way the government can raise aggregate demand in a depression or reduce it in an inflation. The government can increase aggregate demand by spending more than it collects in taxes, or reduce it by spending less than it collects in taxes. Either way, the change in (autonomous) government spending induces a multiplier effect, positive or negative.

Look back at the circular-flow diagram of Figure 8–2. The government may spend back more into the income stream than it currently withdraws from it, thus swelling the total. Or it may spend back less, thus reducing the flow of total spending. Obviously, the net impact on GNP depends on the expansionary effect of government spending offset against the depressive effect of tax collections.

An autonomous increase in government expenditures raises GNP, other things equal. The increase per dollar of government spending is determined by the multiplier. Each additional dollar of government spending on goods and services adds directly to GNP and becomes income to an individual or a business, thereby inducing more consumption spending, just as private investment does. If the multiplier for the economy is three, for example, each dollar of additional government spending will generate a $3 increase in GNP.

An autonomous increase in tax collections reduces GNP. The decrease per dollar of tax collections again depends on the multiplier. When individuals or businesses pay taxes out of their incomes, they reduce their disposable incomes and their spending on goods and services. This reduction has a negative multiplier effect, the reverse of the positive multiplier associated with government expenditures.

The net multiplier effect of the government budget on the economy depends on the net result of these plus and minus factors. The larger the excess of government expenditures over tax receipts (that is, the larger the deficit), the larger will be the effect of government fiscal policy on total GNP, other things equal. Conversely, the larger the excess of tax receipts over expenditures (that is, the larger the government surplus), the lower GNP will be, other things equal. Such government tax and expenditure changes to influence aggregate demand are called fiscal policy. These propositions will need to be qualified somewhat presently, but they provide a powerful first approximation. When we want the government to exert strong expansionary pressure on GNP, a larger government deficit is desirable.

Figure 10–5 presents the analysis graphically. Let the *CC* and $C + I$ lines be identical with the lines in Figure 10–3, back on page 125. Equilibrium income would then be 350, where $C + I$ cuts the 45° line. Now suppose the government enters the picture and begins to spend 10 each year without collecting any taxes (perhaps borrowing at the banks). We can thus draw a new government spending layer (*GE*) on top of the $C + I$ curve. This new $C + I + GE$ curve is 10 higher at every point. The autonomous government spending becomes income to the private economy and has a multiplier effect through inducing new private consumption, just as private investment does. If the marginal propensity to consume is .75, the new equilibrium level of GNP in Figure 10–5 will be 390, as the multi-

Figure 10–5

Net new government spending of 10 increases autonomous spending by 10 and, with a multiplier of 4, raises GNP by 40—up to a new equilibrium of 390. This is identical with the multiplier effect of 10 of new private investment in Figure 10–4.

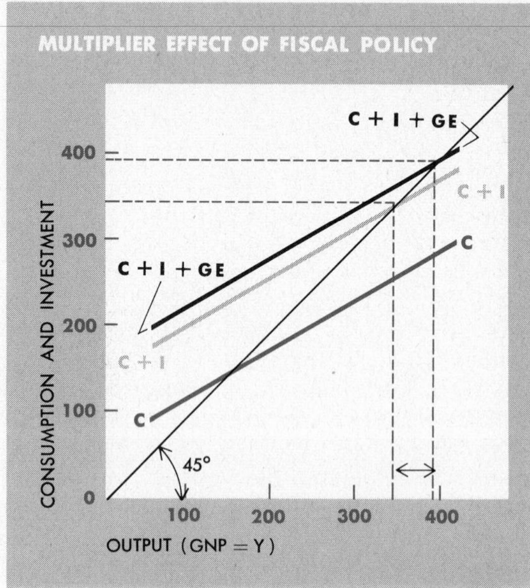

plier raises total income by four times the original government spending. Note that this new equilibrium income is identical to that in Figure 10–4, in which the additional autonomous spending of 10 was private rather than government.

The Balanced-Budget Multiplier

It may appear intuitively that a balanced government budget (that is, tax collections just equal to government spending) will always be neutral with respect to GNP. But this is not quite correct. An increase in government spending matched by an identical increase in tax collections provides some net expansionary multiplier effect, and conversely for a decrease in government expenditures exactly matched by a tax reduction. This is called the **balanced-budget multiplier.** It works this way:

Assume that the government increases its spending by $10 million, and that the public's marginal propensity to consume is .5. The $10 million of new government spending immediately constitutes $10 million of new GNP, to which the multiplier adds another $10 million through respending. This gives a total increase in GNP of $20 million in the new equilibrium level of GNP.

Now trace through the deflationary impact of an identical $10 million tax increase to finance the expenditures. With a marginal propensity to consume of .5, private spending will fall by $5 million in the first round, $2.5 million in the second, $1.25 million in the third, and so on as in the preceding example. The total sequence of induced spending cuts ($5 million plus $2.5 million plus $1.25 million plus. . . .) adds up to a total reduction of $10 million in spending from the tax increase.

Note that this negative tax multiplier is just $10 million less than the positive expenditure multiplier, just the amount of the budget increase. The respending effects after the first impact of the new government spending and of the new government taxes are the same, but the $10 million increase in government purchases of goods and services become a direct part of GNP, whereas the tax payment by the private economy to the government was simply a transfer of purchasing power that is not part of GNP. The "balanced-budget multiplier" is thus just 1 in this example; GNP rises by precisely the amount of the increase in government spending financed by an identical increase in government tax receipts.[7]

Most economists agree that a balanced-budget multiplier effect of this sort occurs. But this precise result of 1 depends on three assumptions: That the government spending is on goods and services rather than on transfer payments; that the propensity to consume out of disposable personal income is the same for taxpayers and recipients of government spending; and that neither government spending nor taxes induce any change in private investment. In any event, the balanced-budget multiplier is, at most, only 1. Most economists believe that deficit-financed government spending is a far surer road to a higher GNP.

Surpluses and Deficits—Public and Private

There is no reason, of course, why government taxes and spending must exactly balance in each time period. Neither, once we introduce government into our model, is there any reason why private saving and private investment must exactly balance in each time period. Our basic equation is now:

$$C + I + GE = C + S + GR.$$

Thus, the private part of the economy may be investing more than it saves at equilibrium GNP, while the government is collecting more taxes than it spends. In that case, the private economy is running a "deficit" and the government a "surplus." Conversely, the private economy may run a surplus by saving more than it invests while the government runs a deficit by spending more than it collects in taxes.

[7]It follows from this reasoning that the tax multiplier will always be smaller than the expenditure multiplier per dollar of tax reduction or expenditure increase. Can you explain why?

It should be clear then that it is total autonomous spending (here $I + GE$) that is the base for the multiplier effect. And the equilibrium condition now is: GNP must be such that private savings plus government tax collections just offset autonomous expenditure (here private investment plus government spending).

Three Warnings

Fiscal policy is a powerful tool for the government against unemployment and inflation, and the preceding simple model provides the essential analysis. But you may suspect there must be some problems or we would already have eliminated unemployment and inflation. And there are. Three major warnings are in order.

1. Remember that the real-world multiplier is far smaller than in the preceding examples. (See the box on "The Multiplier in the Real World.")

2. We have assumed that consumption is completely induced, a known function of income, and that private investment is autonomous, independent of government spending and taxes. But as the next chapter emphasizes, consumption is often partly autonomous, and fluctuates in its relationship to income. Moreover, higher government taxes or government borrowing to finance deficit spending may reduce private investment, thereby partly or completely offsetting the autonomous government spending.

3. We have said nothing about the role of money in determining aggregate demand. Many economists believe that the stock of money plays *a*, perhaps even *the*, dominant role in determining total private spending, overriding the effects discussed above. Nearly everyone agrees that we need to add money to the model to understand the real world. So keep an open mind on the effectiveness of fiscal policy until Chapters 12 and 13 on money.

REVIEW

Concepts to Remember

This is a major chapter. Its analytical concepts and models are used throughout the rest of the book. Be sure you understand the basic reasoning in the chapter and the following new concepts:

income-expenditure approach
autonomous and induced expenditure
consumption function
average and marginal propensities to consume
saving function
equilibrium GNP
average and marginal propensities to save
underemployment equilibrium
fiscal policy
the multiplier
balanced-budget multiplier
paradox of thrift

For Analysis and Discussion

1. Assume that gross national product is $1,100 billion. Investment is $200 billion. Consumption expenditures are $900 billion. Assume no government participation in the income stream:

a. If investment rises to $225 billion, with the marginal propensity to consume = .8, what will be the new equilibrium level of GNP?
b. Explain why this will be an equilibrium level.

2. Would you expect that decisions to save for the year ahead in the economy would ordinarily be about the same as decisions to invest? Why or why not?
3. What is the multiplier? Explain why the real-world multiplier will always be smaller than

$$\frac{1}{1 - \text{MPC out of disposable personal income}}.$$

4. What is the "paradox of thrift"? Explain why its strange result occurs.
5. Suppose that in a hypothetical economy, GNP is running at an annual rate of $1,200 billion. Other major items in the national income accounts are as follows:

Consumption	$800 billion
Investment	140
Savings	200
Government expenditures	260
Taxes	200

The marginal propensity to consume is three-fourths. (For purposes of this problem, take the three-fourths marginal propensity to consume against income before taxes.)

Suppose that the government now balances its budget through a reduction in government expenditures while maintaining taxes at the level of $200 billion. Private investment remains unchanged. What will be the effect on the levels of (a) GNP, (b) consumption, and (c) savings? Explain.

6. Assume the following conditions in an economy that includes a government sector:

Government spending	$100 billion
Government tax receipts (obtained from a tax that is independent of the level of GNP)	100
Consumption expenditure = $30 billion plus .8 of the GNP remaining after payment of taxes	
Investment expenditure	50
GNP = $C + I + G$	

a. Calculate the equilibrium levels of GNP, consumption, and savings.
b. Investment increases to an annual rate of $75 billion and remains constant at that level. Calculate the new equilibrium levels of GNP, consumption, and savings.
c. Under the conditions described in (a), government spending increases to an annual rate of $200 billion and annual tax receipts are raised to $200 billion. Both figures then remain constant. Calculate new equilibrium levels of GNP, consumption, and savings.
d. What is the balanced budget multiplier in (c)?

7. Explain why, if the private sector runs a "deficit" (that is, invests more than it saves), the public sector must run an exactly offsetting "surplus" (that is, collect more in taxes than it spends).

Answers: (1) = 1,225; (5a) = −240, (5b) = −180, (5c) = −60; (6a) = 500, 350 and 50; (6b) = 625, 450 and 75; (6c) = 600, 350 and 50; (6d) = 1.

CASE 5

Does Capitalism Need War for Prosperity?

Radical (Marxist) critics assert that without war spending modern capitalism would collapse into disastrous depression. Without massive defense spending ($80 billion in 1973) aggregate demand would collapse because consumers receive incomes too small to buy all the goods capitalism produces.

Are the radicals right? Leaving aside the details of their argument, suppose that peace breaks out tomorrow and, happy day, we can cut our defense spending immediately by $40 billion. Would the result be disaster—massive unemployment and depression?

Your congressman, no economist, asks your advice on the problem. In early 1973, there were 2.5 million persons in the armed services, so a 50 percent cut might throw perhaps 1.3 million people onto the job market. Apparently 6–7 million civilian jobs are dependent on the government's defense spending. He is understandably concerned about growing unemployment if the big cut in government spending is actually carried out. What do you advise him?

"I knew something like this would happen if we switched to a peacetime economy." (*Drawing by Oldden; © 1972. The New Yorker Magazine, Inc.*)

APPENDIX

Econometric Models

Modern economics, like other sciences, has increasingly come to use precisely stated analytical models, which are often most conveniently put in mathematical form. Modern economics also has become increasingly empirical—that is, concerned with measuring its variables in the real world, as distinguished from merely theorizing about them. Thus, "econometrics" has become an increasingly important branch of economics.

Econometrics deals with the science of economic measurement, as is obvious from its components, "econo" and "metrics." Broadly, econometrics involves setting up precise models of economic phenomena in mathematical form; then measuring in the real world the variables and relationships included in the model; and then solving the model to see how closely it conforms to or can predict actual economic behavior.

Simple Income-Determination Models.[8] The simple model back on page 123 provides an example. We specify a model:

$Y = C + I$, and
$C = f(Y)$, where f stands for "function."

This equation says that C is a function of (or depends on) Y. The model is obviously too simple to represent the real world precisely, but assume for the moment that it does. Next we have to measure in the real world the crucial variables and relationships specified by the model. Suppose we find that I is always 100 and is independent of Y and C; and estimate that C is always just .75 of Y. Then we can insert these values in $Y = C + I$, as on page 123, and get our final equation: $400 = 300 + 100$.

But note that our model, if it is a true model of the real world, can tell us other things. If I rises to 125, we can predict that, other things remaining unchanged, GNP will rise to 500; this follows directly by inserting the new value for I in the model—since we know from empirical evidence that C is always .75 of Y, I must always be .25 of Y. So an econometric model is in effect a forecasting device, which says that *if* we know the values of some of the crucial variables and relationships, *then* we can predict others—in this model, GNP and consumption.

More Complex Simultaneous-Equation Models.[9] More complex econometric models involve precisely the same basic steps: specification of the model, measurement of the relationships and variables, and solution of the model (system of equations). Some years ago, *Business Week,* while poking a little fun at econometricians, summed up the method of econometrics effectively in the sketch on page 136.

Note that the basic model is stated in the system of multiple equations in #3. Equations 1, 2, and 3 are "behavioral" equations; that is, they describe the behavior of units in the economy. Equations 4 and 5 are "identities"; that is, they merely state what we have defined as being identical. For example, we define GNP as the sum of consumption plus investment plus government spending. Obviously, equations 1 through 3 are the critical ones. The solution of the model (that is, the value of GNP) depends on solving the set of five equations simultaneously, just as in the real world all the factors are interacting simultaneously to determine GNP.

This a more complex model than was used in Chapter 10, though it is still too simple to represent the real world effectively. The government is added, and investment is made a function of profits in the proceding time period. (P_{-1} means profits in the preceding time period; most econometricians label all their variables with time subscripts, since time is so important in most economic relationships.) This model will predict this year's national income and consumption if we know last year's profits (to predict I in equation #2) and government expenditures. These two—last year's profits, and government

[8]These are technically called "single-equation" models, since, although they begin with more than one equation, they reduce to one equation for statistical fitting to the real-world situation they represent.

[9]These are called "simultaneous equation" models, since several equations must be fitted statistically on a simultaneous basis.

The Junior Econometrician's Work Kit.

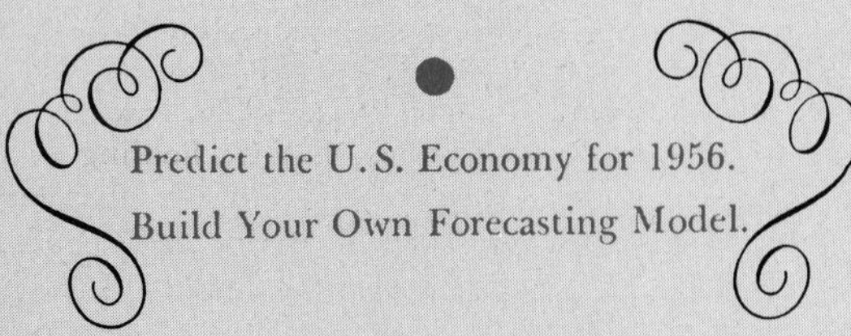

DIRECTIONS:

1. Make up a theory. You might theorize, for instance, that (1) next year's consumption will depend on next year's national income; (2) next year's investment will depend on this year's profits; (3) tax receipts will depend on future Gross National Product. (4) GNP is the sum of consumption, investment, and government expenditures. (5) National income equals GNP minus taxes.

2. Use symbols for words. Call consumption, C; national income, Y; investment, I; preceding year's profits, P_{-1}; tax receipts, T; Gross National Product, G; government expenditures, E.

3. Translate your theories into mathematical equations:

(1) $C = aY + b$　　(4) $G = C + I + E$

(2) $I = cP_{-1} + d$　　(5) $Y = G - T$

(3) $T = eG$

This is your forecasting model. The small letters, a, b, c, d, e, are the constants that make things come out even. For instance, if horses (H) have four legs (L), then $L = aH$; or $L = 4H$. This can be important in the blacksmith business.

4. Calculate the constants. Look up past years' statistics on consumption, income, and so on. From these find values for a, b, c, d, and e that make your equation come out fairly correct.

5. Now you're ready to forecast. Start by forecasting investment from this year's profits. Look up the current rate of corporate profits — it's around $42-billion. The model won't tell what federal, state, and local governments will spend next year — that's politics. But we can estimate it from present budget information — it looks like around $75-billion.

6. Put all available figures into your model. (We've put in the constants for you.)

(1) $C = .7Y + 40$　　(4) $G = C + I + 75$

(2) $I = .9 \times 42 + 20$　　(5) $Y = G - T$

(3) $T = .2G$

7. Solve the equations. You want values of C, I, T, G, Y. Hints: Do them in this order — (2), (1), (4), (3), (5). In solving (1), remember that I and E are both part of G, $Y = G - T$, and $T = .2G$.

8. Results. (See if yours are the same.) For 1956, consumption will be $260.0-billion; investment, $57.8-billion; GNP, $392.8-billion; tax receipts, $78.6-billion; national income, $314.2-billion. These results are guaranteed — provided that the theories on which they're based are valid.

Reprinted with permission from *Business Week*, September 24, 1955 spending—turn out to be the crucial "independent variables" that control the predicted level of national income, given the relationships specified in the model. In fact, if we want to predict more than one year ahead we need a more complex model, since profits this year will obviously depend partly on the levels of C, I, and G this year (as well as on other variables). Thus, a more complete model would need a behavioral equation to integrate the determinants of profits into the system. Then, only government spending would remain a truly autonomous variable; and even that might turn out to depend on some of the other variables, such as tax receipts of the government. If so, the model would then require another behavioral equation to specify government spending.

All this may begin to sound complex, and it is. There are now several working econometric models of the economy involving 20 to 200 equations.[10]

[10]A substantial econometric model of the economy is described in nontechnical language in "A Quarterly Econometric Model of the United States," *Survey of Current Business,* May 1966.

Problems of Statistical Estimation. Building an econometric model requires an underlying theory. But equally it requires careful statistical estimation of the variables and relationships in the equations. A good econometrician is thus as much a statistician as an economist. Statistical estimation of complex economic relationships is a difficult job indeed. Interactions among important variables in our economy—for example, among personal consumption, disposable income, the money stock, holdings of liquid assets, and the like—are complex and sometimes shifting. Although most of the preceding discussion is about constructing models, the bulk of econometricians' work is studying the empirical behavior summarized in the individual equations that make up the models.

Modern statisticians are gradually developing methods to handle such complex interrelationships and forecasting problems. They are too intricate to consider here. But remember that progress in understanding what determines what in the economy depends heavily on this kind of behind-the-scenes interacting theoretical and empirical work.

The Determinants of Consumption and Investment

CHAPTER PREVIEW

CHAPTER ELEVEN

In the simple income-expenditures model of Chapter 10, consumption was entirely induced—a function of the level of income—and investment was entirely autonomous—unaffected by the level of income and consumption spending. In fact, the determinants of both consumption and investment are more complex. While consumption depends heavily on income, people sometimes change their consumption spending for quite different reasons. And business investment depends importantly on recent and expected sales, as well as on autonomous forces influencing profit expectations. Thus both consumption and investment are partly induced, partly autonomous. This chapter examines in more detail the determinants of both consumption and investment.

CONSUMPTION EXPENDITURES

The Consumption Function

It seems intuitively reasonable that consumption expenditures depend heavily on people's disposable incomes, and they do. As far back as our data go, they show consumption rising and falling with aggregate disposable personal income. Figure 11-1 plots this relationship since the 1920s. For example, in 1970 disposable personal income was $690 billion and consumption expenditures $630 billion. For 1933, the lowest year, DPI was only $45 billion while personal consumption expenditures were $46 billion, actually more than disposable personal income. People used accumulated savings and went into debt to keep themselves fed and housed when incomes fell in the depression.

The line running from southwest to northeast on the chart is drawn to "fit" the dots plotted. The fact that most years fall about on the straight line shows that the relationship between disposable income and consumption spending has been a rather stable one. But the fact that some years are substantially off the line shows equally that the stable relationship has not always held. During World War II, for example, consumption spending fell far below what would normally have been expected for the high incomes received during those years.

Figure 11–1

During the depression people spent nearly all their disposable income on consumption; during World War II they saved a large proportion. Since then their spending and saving behavior has been quite stable. Note that the trend line leans over a little, showing how much consumption spending is less than disposable income. (Source: U.S. Department of Commerce.)

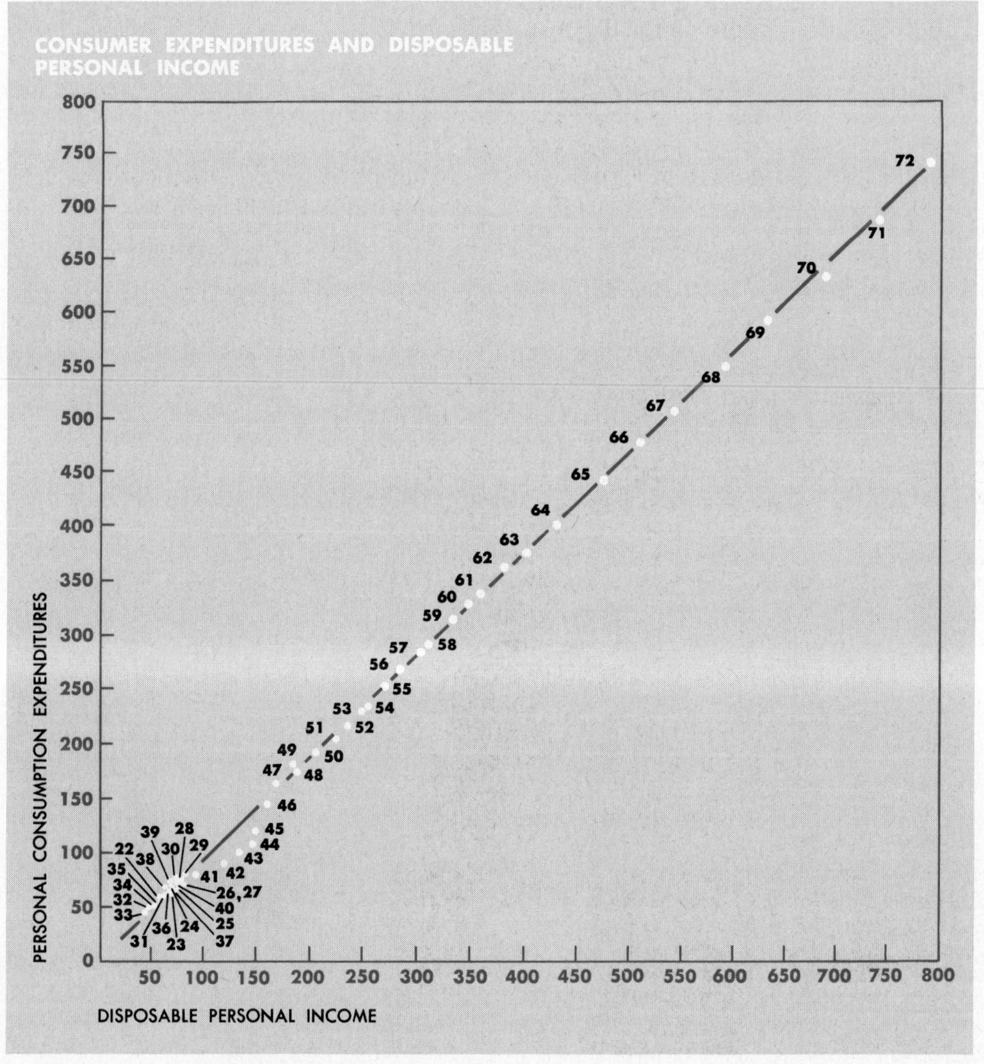

Put in common-sense language, this evidence says that the percentage of DPI spent on consumption rose as incomes fell in the depression; people tried hard not to cut back their living standards as much as their incomes fell. Conversely, in generally prosperous periods (for example, most years since 1950) the percentage spent on consumption has hovered around 92–94 percent. And under special circumstances such as World War II, when many goods were unavailable and the government urged everyone to save more to avoid inflation, the consumption percentage fell sharply—down to about 75 percent in 1943 and 1944. The fact that the "fitted" line leans over toward the right shows that the percentage relationship is not a constant one, like $C = .9$ DPI. Such an equation would give us a line that shows zero consumption at zero DPI. But we see that households in fact raised their consumption to over 100 percent of DPI in 1932, when income was well above zero. Try fitting a shorter straight line to the years through 1945 only, and you will see that it leans over much more to the right, reflecting experience in a more sharply cyclical period.[1]

[1]The equation that approximately fits the solid line is $C = a + b(Y)$, where a and b are constants that show the relationship between consumption (C) and disposable income (Y). This is the consumption function used on page 124.

The Saving Function

By definition, consumers save that portion of their disposable income that they do not spend on consumption. The relationship between consumer saving and disposable personal income is shown in Figure 11–2, which gives the percentage of DPI *saved* each year. The underlying data are the same as those for Figure 11–1. The percentage saved is of course one minus the percentage consumed for each year.

Figure 11–2 indicates vividly the high percentage of DPI saved in the war years, and the negative savings in the years 1932 and 1933 at the bottom of the Great Depression. But more significantly it stresses the quite stable percentage saved (about 6–8 percent) during the reasonably stable, prosperous times since 1950.

What Determines Consumption Expenditures?

The preceding data reinforce our intuitive presumption that consumption spending depends mainly on DPI. But they also warn us that other forces may shift the consumption function, slightly or dramatically. We need now to take a more detailed look at the forces that have influenced consumption spending over the past half century.

Figure 11–2

Personal saving has been a quite stable percentage of disposable personal income in peacetime prosperity, but has fluctuated sharply in depressions and wars. (Source: U.S. Department of Commerce.)

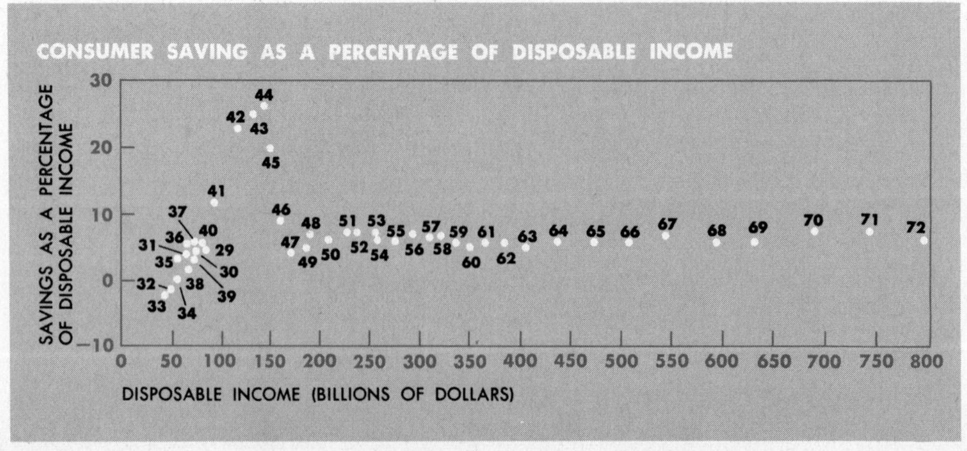

Income—Present, Past, and Future. The generally close relationship between present income and current consumer spending is obvious. But sophisticated statistical work over the past decade has suggested that adding past income and income expectations gives a better explanation of consumer spending than does present income alone.

The influence of past income is persistent. Once families have become used to any real consumption level, they are reluctant to slide back down to a lower level, even if their income drops. Rather than reduce their standard of living as income falls, they will (at least temporarily) reduce their saving levels to well below the amount they would have saved at that income on the way up. Similarly, when incomes rise sharply, consumption spending rises more slowly. That is, with rising incomes the marginal propensity to consume is lower in the short run than in the long run.

Recently, some research workers have advanced a more sophisticated hypothesis. They suggest that consumption spending is a substantially constant and similar proportion of DPI for average families at all income levels—if we exclude major disruptions like war and mass depression, if we include consumer durables (especially houses, autos, and household furnishings) with saving (investment),[2] **and if we consider their "permanent" or "life-span" incomes rather than the particular income of any given year, which may be distorted by special factors.**

One version of this approach (the life-cycle hypothesis) holds that families, consciously or subconsciously, estimate their long-range income over the years ahead (over their entire life cycle), and adjust their current consumption spending to their expectations for the entire period. During their early married years most couples spend most of their income and even go into debt to start families and to set up households. A little later, as income rises and these special expenses have passed, they begin to save more, for retirement, to send their children to college, and so on. After their houses are well furnished and their children are educated, they commonly save at a much higher rate. Late in life, after they retire, the saving ratio drops again and often becomes negative. Averaged over this life span, the ratio of consumption to income is, if the investigations of this group stand up under further scrutiny, surprisingly similar for typical families at different income levels. By the same token, this suggests that consumption is a quite stable function of income for the population as a whole.

[2]That is, families consume only the current services rendered by durable goods, just as businesses use each year only the current services of their factories and machinery.

The "permanent income" hypothesis is similar. It holds that families base their consumption on what they expect their "permanent" income to be. Temporary deviations in income up or down from this permanent expectation will usually not affect consumption much. Rather, if income falls temporarily, the family will cut back its savings, use up its liquid assets, or go into debt to maintain consumption. If income bulges temporarily, the bulge is likely to go mainly into saving and investment (including purchases of consumer durables).

What is the evidence on the life-span and permanent-income models? Good statistical evidence is hard to get, and interpretation of the data in relation to these models is tricky. There is some evidence that supports the models, but enough contradictory data to require a suspended judgment as far as practical use of the models is concerned.

Money and Wealth. Other things equal, a family with large wealth (ownership of economic assets such as money, stocks, bonds, and houses) will spend more on consumption than will a low-wealth family with the same income. For example, suppose a family receives an annual income of $10,000 and has accumulated wealth of $25,000. Now imagine that a wealthy relative dies and leaves the family another $25,000, or the stock market soars so its wealth doubles. We would expect its level of consumption to rise even if the father's salary stayed at $10,000. Note, incidentally, that this effect is closely related to the "permanent" income hypothesis above. With more wealth, the family's permanent, or lifetime average, income has increased, because the family's income now includes the interest, dividends, or other yield on the additional $25,000 of wealth. But it also faces the permanent income test if it's the stock market that increases wealth; will stock prices stay up?

Money is one form of wealth, and more money, other things equal, will surely lead households to spend more on consumption (and possibly on other things as well). But money is a special form of wealth—the only one that can be freely used to buy other goods and services. Some economists (the "monetarists") argue that this special quality of money makes it an especially powerful determinant of consumer spending. They contend that the stock of money in the economy is the main determinant of consumption, and indeed of total aggregate demand.

This alternative approach to explaining aggregate demand is examined in detail in Chapters 12 and 13. In the meantime, remember that money may be a very important variable, which is being temporarily set aside here.

Consumer Credit. One way of getting around the limitation of income is to borrow money or to buy on credit. A net increase in consumer credit correspondingly increases consumer spending power, beyond that provided by current income. Until the last few decades, consumers did little credit buying except in purchasing homes. But since World War II a huge volume of houses and consumer durables (especially automobiles) has been bought on credit. By 1973, households were over half a trillion dollars in debt on houses and durables.

But there is a counterforce at work here too. The deeper you are in debt, the bigger are the interest and debt repayments you must meet before current income can be devoted to new consumption expenditures. In 1973, the proportion of current disposable income committed in this way exceeded 15 percent.

Consumer Stocks and Availability of Durables. Sometimes, as during World War II, you just can't buy lots of "hard goods" like refrigerators and automobiles because they are unavailable. Thus, in 1943–44 the economy's consumption ratio dropped to below 75 percent of DPI. By 1946, consumers had accumulated an enormous backlog of demand for such consumer durables, which undoubtedly helps explain the big postwar buying surge.

The converse effect occurs when consumers have built up unusually large stocks of durable goods. Consumer spending on nondurables and services is relatively stable, but spending on durables (autos, refrigerators, TVs, and so on) fluctuates sharply with fluctuations in income. Thus, after consumers engage in a big buying spree on durables (for example, twelve million autos in 1973), they are likely to slack off their buying until the new durables are at least a few years old, even though consumer income holds up.

Price Expectations. If you expect prices to rise, the time to buy is now, before they go up. If you expect deflation, you had better hold off postponable purchases until prices go down. Changing expectations of future prices can thus bring violent shifts in the consumption-income relationship. Immediately after the outbreak of the Korean War in 1950, for example, current consumer saving dropped almost to zero as consumers rushed to stock up before prices skyrocketed and goods vanished from the market. Such drastic shifts in price expectations are rare, but when they do occur, they can dominate the more stable consumption-income relationships that generally prevail. Unfortunately, there is no one simple expectations-spending relationship. Some consumers reduce buying of nonessentials when they expect inflation, to conserve their funds for the most urgent needs.

Modern Econometric Evidence

Although the above generalizations give us some guides to consumption behavior, they are too rough to be satisfactory for national forecasting purposes—for example, when we want to predict the probable effects of a tax cut or tax increase. Thus, modern econometricians have devoted a great deal of attention to analyzing precisely the empirical relationships between the various causes listed above and consumption spending in the past.

One approach is to break down consumer spending into a number of major components—spending on services, on nondurable goods, on automobiles, on other durable goods, and the like. One well-known econometric model, for example, relates changes in spending on nondurable goods to disposable income, the level of spending on nondurables in the preceding period, and holdings of liquid assets in the preceding period, plus a "catch-all" factor for other variables. In fitting this equation to the real world, the following results were obtained:

$$\Delta ND = .224\Delta Y + .205\Delta ND_{-1} + .143\Delta L_{-1} - .149.$$

In this equation, Δ means change from the last quarter to this one; ND is spending on nondurables; Y is disposable personal income; L is liquid asset holdings; the subscript $_{-1}$ means in the quarter preceding this one; and no subscript means in the present quarter, or the one being predicted. Thus ΔND in any quarter is .244 of the change in income, plus .205 of the change in spending on nondurables over the preceding quarter, plus .143 of the change in liquid assets over the past quarter, minus .149. Similar equations have been worked out in this and other models for consumer spending on automobiles, other durables, services, and housing, and for other major variables.[3]

Where do all these considerations leave us on the determinants of consumer spending? At the risk of oversimplification, we can say that the long-run ratio of consumption to disposable personal income has been quite stable. At high-employment levels, it has seldom varied from the 92–94 percent range, moving outside that range for long only in response to identifiable special forces. The short-run marginal propensity to consume is much more variable. But in spite of short-run fluctuations in business cycles, consumers as a whole appear to adjust their consumption upward roughly in proportion to rising incomes. Will this tendency persist over the years ahead? Nobody knows. But the historical relationship has prevailed long enough to make it a reasonably good bet.

[3]See D.B. Suits, "Forecasting with an Econometric Model," *American Economic Review,* March 1962, p. 113. For students who know mathematics, the entire article may be interesting. It includes comparable forecasting equations for all major sectors of the economy and for many of the subsectors in those major groupings. See especially the last section of the article, which lists all the forecasting equations. A more complex set of equations is presented in the study cited in the Appendix to Chapter 10.

INVESTMENT EXPENDITURES

Private investment has been the most dynamic and unstable major component of the gross national product. Most economists think it plays a central role in explaining both economic growth and fluctuations. Figure 11-3 shows the fluctuation in private-investment spending since 1929. The top line is gross, or total, investment, as in the GNP accounts. The lower line is net investment, which subtracts the allowance to replace capital goods worn out (depreciated) during that year.

Private investment expenditure is partly autonomous, but it also depends partly on the level of consumer spending. That is, rising consumption may induce more investment, as well as the other way around. Thus, a more thorough look at the system will require us to complete the circle: Investment spending $\rightarrow$ more consumption $\rightarrow$ more private investment $\rightarrow$ more consumption. . . and so on. To do so, we need to ask specifically, what controls businessmen's decisions to invest?

As with consumer expenditure, the answer is gradually being clarified through both theoretical and empirical work. Begin again with a simplified theoretical model of a profit-maximizing business. Then we shall look at some of the modern empirical evidence.

Fundamentally, expected profit determines

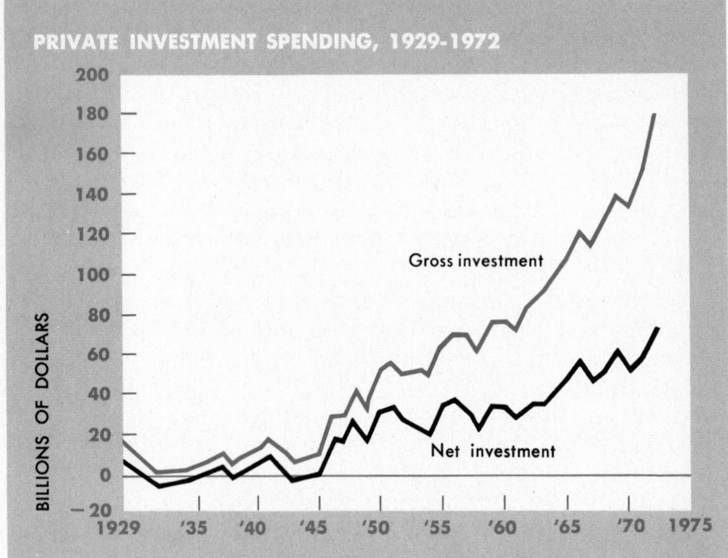

Figure 11–3

Private investment fluctuates sharply. It is now higher than ever before, but is a lower percentage of GNP than in other prosperous periods. (Source: U.S. Department of Commerce.)

how much a business will spend on investment in any given year. When a businessman thinks he can invest in a new machine and get back over the life of the machine what it costs, plus running expenses, plus interest on the money invested, plus some extra return (profit), he will make the investment. **He will invest when the expected rate of return on his invested capital exceeds the going rate of interest (cost of capital) he must pay for funds to make the investment.**

The Marginal Efficiency of Investment

Economists call the expected rate of return on investment the "marginal efficiency of investment" (MEI). Suppose, for example, a businessman is thinking of buying a new milling machine for his plant. He knows the machine will cost $10,000 and his engineers estimate that it will increase the annual output of the plant by about $2,000, with unchanged costs for labor and materials. To maintain the machine, however, will cost about $500 a year. (To make the example easy, assume the machine lasts indefinitely.) Thus, the expected annual net return on the $10,000 investment in the machine will be $1,500. The marginal efficiency of investment would thus be 15 percent (that is, $15 return annually on every $100 invested). If he could borrow money at, say, 5 percent to buy the machine, it looks like a good investment.[4]

The businessman's estimate of MEI (the expected rate of return) obviously plays a central role in his decision. What factors determine the marginal efficiency of investment in typical cases? Some of the major ones are:

Expected Product Demand. The dominant consideration is the expected demand for the firm's product. Note that it is **expected** return on investment that matters. Thus, whenever a businessman **expects** the demand for his product to rise, this anticipation increases the **expected** rate of return he can get by investing in new plant and equipment that will increase his output or improve the quality of his product.

[4]For a more complex and precise analysis of how to compute the net rate of return on investments and how businessmen look at the investment problem, see Chapter 31.

The fact that expectations govern the marginal efficiency of investment makes it subject to wide fluctuations, depending on how things look to the businessman. If the world looks black, down goes the marginal efficiency of investment. Note the tie back to consumer spending. One of the big forces influencing the expected return on new investment is consumer spending—the demand for business' products.

Technology and Innovation. Research and development push the marginal efficiency of investment up. If a new machine promises to lower costs or to improve product quality, this promise will be reflected in a larger expected net return on the investment. Technological advance is the foundation of most present-day investment in plant and equipment.

Taxes. Businessmen are primarily concerned with the expected rate of return on investment after taxes. Corporations pay income taxes of about 50 percent on their profits. (If we take this factor into account, the milling-machine investment above loses a lot of its glamor.) An increase in corporation tax rates, other things equal, will lower MEI; a decrease will raise it.

General Outlook. A businessman can never estimate precisely all the factors involved over the life of a major investment. Will demand for the final product really be what he expects? Will the government step in and regulate his business? Will a new machine come along that will make this one obsolete? With all this uncertainty, the general outlook of the businessman often plays a big role in his final decision on whether or not to invest.

Interest Rates—"The Cost of Money"

The other side of the picture is the interest rate—the cost of the money needed to make the investment under consideration. If the businessman has to borrow the funds needed, we can get a direct figure for the cost of money—maybe it's 5 percent. But even if he has the money already, possibly in retained earnings from previous profits, he must still figure "implicit" interest on the funds used, since when he ties them up here he will be foregoing interest he could earn by investing them elsewhere. Then the proper interest rate to charge is harder to estimate, but he must settle on some figure for his calculation. We'll look at the details presently.

The Investment Schedule and Investment Decisions

At any time, many alternative investment opportunities are open to any business, some promising high rates of return, some low. We can graph these investment opportunities as in Figure 11–4. Suppose we list all the possible investment opportunities that the firm foresees for next year, beginning with the most profitable. A few projects will promise a high rate of return; more will promise at least a medium rate; many will be available that promise at least a very low rate. Plot these in curve *II*. A few investments (about $140,000) promise 5 percent or more; about $300,000 promise 4 percent or more; and so on. Note that the $300,000 includes all that

Figure 11–4

The curve II shows the amount of investment it will pay to undertake at each level of the interest rate.

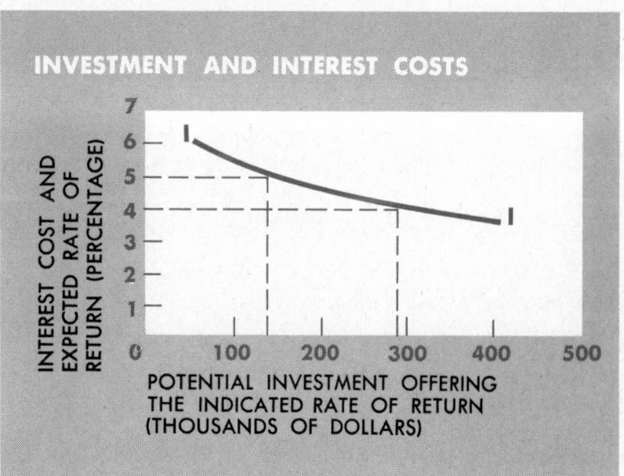

promise 4 percent *or higher;* it includes the $140,000 that promise 5 percent or more.

Now we can easily see how much a rational, profit-seeking businessman will invest. Suppose the interest rate he must pay or charge himself is 4 percent. Then any investment opportunity on his investment schedule that will yield above 4 percent is profitable. Figure 11–4 shows that this business should invest $300,000 if the interest cost is 4 percent, taking on all the projects promising to yield 4 percent or higher. If the interest cost is 5 percent, it will only pay to invest $140,000 this year—only in those projects above where the 5 percent line intersects *II*. Each point on *II* shows how much will be invested at that interest rate. It shows investment as a function of the interest rate ($I = f(i)$).[5]

To summarize: Business investment spending in any given time period is determined by the marginal efficiency of investment in relation to the interest rate (cost of capital). Many business firms consciously go through the type of analysis outlined above for each major investment considered. Others make their calculations much more roughly. Some operate by hunch and intuition. For present purposes, assume that our model gives a rough approximation for the economy as a whole.

Business Investment in Inventories

The above analysis of business investment applies basically to business investment in plant and equipment—buildings, machinery, and the like. Business investment in inventories (raw materials, goods in process, and finished goods still on hand) raises other special problems, which become especially important when we consider booms and depressions—short-run economic fluctuations. For the moment, only a warning that inventory investment is a special problem, one we will examine in more detail in Chapter 14 on business cycles.[6]

[5]Many businessmen introduce a "safety factor." They require an expected return of 15 or 20 percent on new investment before taking action, even though they can go to banks or the open market and borrow at 6 or 7 percent. Why?

Taxes are part of the story. They take about half of most business profits. A second answer is uncertainty; businessmen say they never know whether things will turn out as well as expected. Third, some businessmen are reluctant to go into debt, even when it is directly profitable to do so. Fourth, many businessmen calculate the effective cost of money to themselves as much higher than current market interest rates, especially if they must issue new stock to get funds. These facts do not change the general principle in the text, but they do reduce the number of investment opportunities that many businessmen will consider attractive at any given time.

MONEY IN THE INCOME-EXPENDITURES MODEL

Money has entered the analysis of the last two chapters only peripherally. In conclusion, it is important to clarify the role of money in the income-expenditures (neo-Keynesian) model.

In this model, changes in the stock of money influence the interest rate, and through the interest rate the level of investment. An increased supply of money lowers its price (the interest rate), and a decreased supply raises the interest rate, other things equal. A higher or lower interest rate in turn decreases or increases investment.

The way money fits into the income-expenditures model can be seen easily from the following causal chain. If the government adds more money to the system, it affects GNP as follows:

$$+M \rightarrow -i \rightarrow +I \rightarrow +\text{GNP}$$

where M stands for money, i stands for interest rate, and I stands for investment. Note that in this approach more money does not directly stimulate consumption spending; its only effect is to lower the interest rate, thereby stimulating investment.

Moreover, Keynes argued, often changes in M won't affect interest rates very much, espe-

[6]Net foreign investment has also been neglected throughout this chapter, even though it may have a multiplier effect on GNP similar to that of domestic private investment. Net foreign investment has been relatively small since World War II, and it is more convenient to consider it in Part Six on The International Economy.

cially in depressions (for reasons to be explored in the next chapters). Besides, he argued that fluctuations in interest rates are generally smaller than variations in the marginal efficiency of investment, which depends on expectations of profits and other factors in the future—and these may swing widely. Thus, moderate changes in the stock of money, bringing about only moderate changes in interest rates, generally have a limited influence on investment spending. But the sensitivity of investment to interest rate changes is a factual issue, on which the evidence is mixed. Some of the relevant information is presented in Chapters 14 and 17. Many economists argue that changes in *M* affect investment powerfully and directly.

REVIEW

Concepts to Remember

Be sure you understand the following new analytical concepts introduced in this chapter.

"permanent income"
"life-cycle income"
marginal efficiency of investment
interest rate
implicit interest
"cost of capital"
investment schedule

For Analysis and Discussion

1. What are the main factors that determine your personal consumption expenditure? What forces would you expect to shift your consumption function over the next ten years?
2. How would you expect the marginal propensity to consume to compare for families at the same income level (say, $15,000 per year) at the following ages for the head of the family: 25, 40, 60, 75? Explain your answer. How does it relate to the permanent-income hypothesis?
3. Consumer surveys have found that when people expect inflation, some raise their MPC, others lower it. Which seems to you rational behavior? Which would you do if you expected a higher rate of inflation over the next five years?
4. Investment spending has often fluctuated sharply during booms and depressions. Using the model of business-investment decision making in the chapter, can you explain why this is likely?
5. Explain how you would decide whether to invest in a new set of store furnishings if you were the owner of an ice cream parlor.
6. Would you expect higher interest rates to stimulate or retard business investment? Explain why, using a graph like Figure 11–4.

CASE 6

Interest Rates, Investment, and Inflation

For many years, Congressman Wright Patman of Texas, now Chairman of the House Banking and Currency Committee and senior member of the House in years of service, has argued that high interest rates damage the nation's economy and impose a needless burden on taxpayers when the government borrows at higher than nominal interest rates. He believes the government, which has the power to create money, should hold interest rates low, presumably through creating enough money to achieve this result. Then it could borrow at low interest rates, avoiding the heavy interest burdens it has faced since World War II and holding the national debt far below present levels.

Many economists who have testified before Mr. Patman have disagreed with this position, pointing out that plentiful money to hold interest rates low in periods of high employment would stimulate more investment and consumption spending, and hence more inflation. Thus, the apparent saving in interest costs to the government would be illusory, because its total expenses would rise by far more than the interest savings as inflation pushed up the prices of everything it buys.

In reply, Congressman Patman says that higher interest rates raise prices, not hold them down. Interest is a cost to businessmen, and they just pass the higher costs on to consumers if the Federal Reserve attempts to restrain business investment through tight money and high interest rates.

The issue is posed by the following interchange at hearings before Representative Patman's Committee in 1964:[7]

CHAIRMAN PATMAN: It should be mentioned that if the (2½ percent) interest rates that prevailed after the war had been continued and had not increased, we would have a national debt . . . $40 billion less than it is today. . . . Did you look with favor upon those higher interest rates, Dr. Bach?

DR. BACH: It seems to me that there is a good case for higher interest rates when one wishes to restrain the level of economic activity. . . .

CONGRESSMAN BROCK: On the question of interest rates . . . what would have happened if we had kept that (2½ percent) ceiling on interest rates from 1951 until this time?

DR. BACH: If we had continued to peg the long rate at 2½ percent . . . we would have had a lot more inflation between 1951 and now. . . .

I do not think that low interest rates or high interest rates per se are good. The interest rate is a . . . very important price because it (greatly influences) the level of total borrowing, investment, and consumer spending in the economy. . . .

Who was right, Congressman Patman or Dr. Bach?

---

[7] *The Federal Reserve System After Fifty Years,* Hearings before Subcommittee on Domestic Finance, House Banking and Currency Committee, March 11, 1964, pp. 1402 ff.

Money and the Price Level: The Classical View

CHAPTER TWELVE

Chapters 10 and 11 explained aggregate demand with little mention of money. There, spending depended largely on incomes received. But we receive our incomes in the form of money, and somehow it seems that money must be more than peripheral. It is! Chapters 12 and 13 now focus on money and the important role it plays in determining aggregate demand, real output, and the price level. This chapter presents a simple, "classical" analysis of the role of money.[1]

[1]Teachers who want their students to understand monetary mechanics (the operations of the banking system) before considering money in relation to aggregate demand should assign Chapter 16, before Chapter 12.

THE FACTS

What is money? What controls its supply? What are the facts about money in relation to aggregate demand, real output, and the price level?

What is Money and Who Controls It?

In today's economy, money is composed of bank demand deposits (which we spend by writing checks) and currency (coins and paper money). Together, as of early 1973 they totalled about $250 billion. Contrary to the common impression, bank deposits make up the bulk of our money (nearly 80 percent); currency plays only a minor role.

It is important to distinguish between money and income. A man with an *income* of, say, $10,000 annually may possess only a few hundred dollars of *money* at any given time. Money is a form of wealth, an asset; income is a flow or stream of payments made by exchanging money. Each dollar of money may thus be spent many or a few times a year, creating "income" each time it is spent on transactions that enter the national income accounts.

For example, in 1972 the average amount of money outstanding (currency and checking deposits) was about $240 billion, while GNP was $1.15 trillion. Thus, on the average, people and businesses held money equal to only about one-fifth of their total incomes at any given time. Put another way, on the average each dollar of money was spent on a GNP transaction about five times during the year.

The Constitution gives Congress the power to create money and regulate the value thereof. Congress has delegated this power, under certain restrictions, to the U.S. Treasury and to the Federal Reserve System, the nation's "central bank." The Treasury mints coins, a routine function. The Federal Reserve issues paper currency, and, more important, regulates the supply of bank deposits by controlling the "reserves" that commercial banks must hold behind their deposits.

Broadly speaking, therefore, the government (including the Federal Reserve) controls the supply of money. This is not entirely accurate, as we shall see, but it will do as a first approximation until Chapter 16.

Some Historical Facts

Figure 12–1 summarizes some important relationships among money, aggregate demand, real output, and prices since 1900. The bottom line shows the growth in the stock of money, averaging $5\frac{1}{2}$ percent per annum since 1900. The next two lines show that "real" gross national product (that is, GNP in constant prices) rose at about $3\frac{3}{4}$ percent per annum over the same period, while money GNP rose at about $6\frac{1}{4}$ percent annually. The top line shows that the price level rose by an average of about $2\frac{1}{2}$ percent annually, the difference between money gross national product and real gross national product.

It is clear that on the average the growth in *money* GNP paralleled closely the increase in the money stock; and that about two-thirds of the growth in money GNP was growth in real output, while about one-third was inflation.

Deviations from these average (trend) growth lines are as interesting as the trends themselves. The big inflation of World War I is clearly visible. The money stock shot up from 1915 to 1920 as new money was created to finance the war, and prices soared roughly apace. About 1927, the money stock began to fall below the economy's 3+ percent real long-term growth rate, and the long depression of the 1930s began two years later. The great collapse (in both output and prices) came between 1929 and 1933, when the money supply was contracting severely.

World War II was financed by newly created money, and both money GNP and prices rose rapidly. After World War II the growth rate of the money stock slowed down, as did money GNP and prices, but with the Vietnam War of the late 1960s all again rose more rapidly.

Some economists infer from these facts that the money supply exercises a powerful effect on the level of both real output and prices. When the money supply rises much faster than the growth in the economy's real output potential, inflation results. Growth in the money supply parallel to growth in potential real GNP (about 3+ percent per annum over the past half century) would go far to ensure stable economic growth. Slower growth in money means recession. But others say that this is too simple an analysis of a highly complex problem, and that it overstates the role of money. We now turn to the monetary theory developed by the classical economists to explain how money affects aggregate demand and prices.

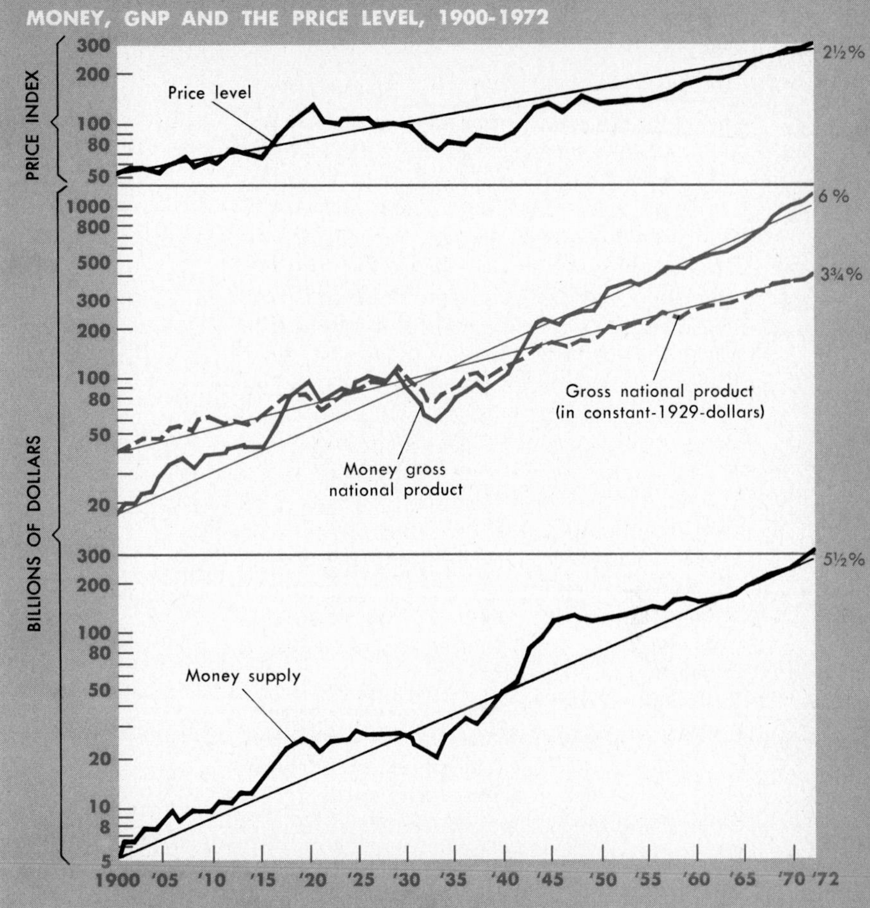

Figure 12–1

The money stock has risen about $5\frac{1}{2}$ percent annually and money GNP a little faster. GNP in constant prices has grown only about $3\frac{3}{4}$ percent annually, however, and a price rise of about $2\frac{1}{2}$ percent per annum accounts for the difference. Has the excess of money supply over the growth in real GNP caused the inflation? (Sources: Federal Reserve Board, U.S. Department of Commerce, and National Bureau of Economic Research.)

MONEY AND PRICES—THE CLASSICAL VIEW

The classical economists—the long tradition from Adam Smith through David Ricardo and Alfred Marshall, up to the decade of the 1920s—gave money a central role in explaining aggregate spending and prices. They had two main points. First, the amount of money will determine aggregate money spending; and second, variations in aggregate money spending will generally affect the price level but not real GNP and employment, except for temporary aberrations.

First, if people have more or less money, they will generally spend proportionately more or less. In general, the rate at which people spend the money they receive will be stable, or change only gradually. Thus, changes in the amount of money will generally lead to proportional changes in total spending. **This analysis is called the quantity theory of money, because in it the quantity of money determines aggregate spending, and, as we shall see, generally the price level as well.**

Second, these variations in total spending will mainly just bid the price level up or down, without changing the level of real output and employment. The classical economists argued that a free-market economic system would ordinarily tend to be self-equilibrating at approximately full employment. They reasoned that whenever resources are unemployed or unsold, their market price will move down until it falls low enough so that everything offered is hired or sold—just as will the price of wheat or coal. There may be temporary deviations from full employment and, indeed, these deviations may involve booms and depressions. But they will be aberrations, explained largely by special external factors such as wars or famines; by cumulative, herdlike sweeps of expectations that lead to gluts of overproduction and depression; and especially by the erratic behavior of the monetary system. Over the long pull, the economic system will always tend toward full employment. More or less money will change spending proportionately, and thus lead to a correspondingly higher or lower price level, not to a change in real output.

In terms of our earlier diagrams, this classical position can be put as follows. The economy will always tend to operate on its production possibilities frontier—at full employment. Thus, in Figure 9-1 the economy's short-run aggregate-supply curve is, as a practical matter, not *OAB* but instead a vertical line rising from the horizontal axis at OQ_3. This is because the economy will tend to operate at full employment whatever the level of aggregate demand is. If aggregate demand falls, prices will fall but output and employment (real GNP) will be unchanged; if aggregate demand rises, prices will rise but real GNP will remain unchanged. It is important to see that the classical proportionality of changes in the price level to changes in money depends on the special aggregate supply assumptions made. If supply conditions instead are as in Figure 9-1, full employment will not always prevail and more money will lead to higher prices only when there is full employment. But the quantity theory could still be correct in explaining aggregate demand.[2]

Money, Velocity, Output, and Prices

Just how do changes in money lead to changes in aggregate demand (money GNP)? To explain, the classical economists asked (1) how much money do people have, and (2) how fast do they spend it? A simple "equation of exchange" (proposed by Professor Irving Fisher a half century ago) points up the relationships involved in this approach. The equation is:

$$MV = PT = \text{GNP}$$

M stands for the amount of money in the hands of the public; *V* for the average "velocity of circulation," or the number of times each dollar is spent per time period; *P* for the price level, or average price per unit sold; and *T* for the number of units sold during each time period. If we think of *T* as the real goods and services produced in any year, it becomes the real GNP of the economy; and *P* can be thought of as the "GNP deflator" from Chapter 8. Then *V* is called "income velocity" because it shows the average number of times a dollar is spent each year on income-creating transactions in the GNP accounts.[3]

For example, in a very simple hypothetical economy, suppose *M* is $1,000. Suppose further that during some year 2,000 units of physical goods are sold, and that their average price is $2. The *T* (real GNP) in our equation would then be 2,000, and the *P* would be $2; *PT* equals $4,000, the total amount paid for the goods sold. The *V*, the average number of times per year

[2]These remarks do less than justice to the classical economists, but the purpose here is merely to give some background on their view of money's role, not to paint a complete picture of what different economists thought. In particular, they realized that severe booms or depressions could occur while these long-run forces were gradually moving the economy back toward full-employment equilibrium, and that "sticky" prices (because of monopoly or other market imperfections) could keep the equilibrating price adjustments from occurring.

[3]Obviously we could include in *T*, *all* transactions during the period, adding in purchases of stocks and bonds, of existing houses, of secondhand autos, and so on. Then *MV* and *PT* would be equal to a much larger total that would include sales of existing assets as well. In 1972, GNP was about $1.15 trillion, whereas total expenditures on all transactions were estimated roughly at over $10 trillion—perhaps ten times GNP. If we use this broader approach, *V* reflects spending on all transactions, and is called "transactions velocity."

each dollar is spent, is then obviously 4, since total expenditures were $4,000 so each of the 1,000 dollars must have been spent four times during the year on the average. The whole equation is then:

$$MV = PT, \text{ or}$$
$$\$1{,}000 \times 4 = \$2 \times 2{,}000$$

The two sides of the equation are defined so that they will always be equal. MV is simply the total amount *spent* on goods and services during the time period—the total number of dollars multiplied by the average number of times each dollar is spent in the period. PT is the total amount *received* for goods and services during the period—the number of units sold multiplied by the average price per unit. The two are identical; what someone spends, someone else receives.

The equation of exchange is obviously a truism. Why, then, is it a useful analytical tool? The answer is, because it sets out four important variables for analyzing booms and depressions, inflations and deflations. The equation certainly doesn't provide any answers, but it is a framework for looking at the complex real world. It skips over the whole detailed analysis of consumer and business spending decisions in Chapters 10 and 11. But it suggests that behind the scenes, the quantity of money may be the basic factor controlling the level of spending.

M and V in History

Assume that the receipts (PT) side is by and large passive, as the classical economists did. Then the equation says that an increase in the amount of money will lead to a higher volume of expenditures, unless it is offset by a decrease in the velocity at which the money is spent.

World War II provides an historical example. The money stock increased from about $36 billion to $110 billion, as we financed the war in considerable part by creating new money. The equation of exchange suggests that with such a big increase in the money supply, GNP should have risen in the same proportion unless income velocity increased or decreased during the war.

What did happen? Money GNP rose rapidly. But V declined substantially over the war period, and total spending rose much less than in proportion to the money supply. On the average, people held more dollars in relation to their incomes. This was partly because many goods were unavailable, partly because there was a lot of patriotic pressure against spending, and partly because of price controls. As a result, money GNP (MV) rose only from $91 billion to $211 billion, as indicated in the lines for 1939 and 1946 in the table:

1929: M ($ 26 billion) × V (4.0) = GNP ($104 billion)
1939: M ($ 36 billion) × V (2.5) = GNP ($ 90 billion)
1946: M ($110 billion) × V (1.9) = GNP ($211 billion)
1972: M ($240 billion) × V (4.8) = GNP ($1.15 trillion)

The 1929 and 1972 lines of the table provide some historical perspective. Back at the peak of the boom in the 1920s, V was high. People were spending their money fast, holding their idle money balances to a minimum. Then came the big drop of the depression and war years, as billions were piled up in temporarily idle balances. After World War II, people began to spend down their accumulated balances, and V rose persistently. Higher interest rates provided an inducement to put idle money into securities and other assets, and as money became "tighter" both businesses and individuals were again forced to "economize" their cash balances, cutting them back to the minimum consistent with their needs. V has shown a persistent uptrend since the 1930s.

If V were stable, changes in M would be a good predictor of GNP. Indeed, by controlling M we could control GNP. Professor Fisher argued that by and large his V (which was a little different from ours) was relatively stable over long periods, so that changes in M would have roughly proportionate effects on PT.[4]

[4] In fact, Fisher went further and argued that changes in M would generally lead to corresponding changes in P, since T as well as V would be roughly stable—a simple version of the "quantity theory of money." But he recognized that V might fluctuate substantially in the short run.

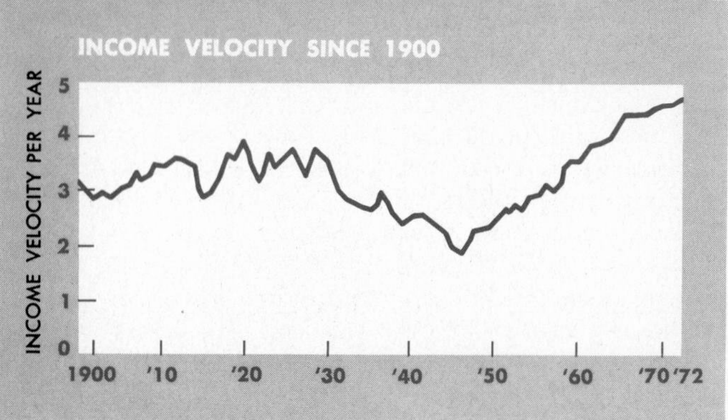

Figure 12–2

Income velocity has shown a gradual updrift over the long run. It rises and falls sharply in booms and depressions, and sometimes falls dramatically for special reasons—note the World War II period. (Calculated by dividing M into money GNP for each year.)

Has the evidence borne Fisher out? Yes and no. The preceding table makes V look highly unstable. But over the long pull, if we eliminate the long dip from 1930 to the early 1960s, V has been reasonably stable with a gradual upward trend that may reflect increasing efficiency in our payments mechanism (for example, use of credit cards and computers). Figure 12–2 provides the data since 1900. Both M and V have dropped sharply in depressions and have increased in booms, in spite of the more stable long-term trend.

Equilibrium and the Demand for "Real-Money" Balances

Obviously, a crucial question for the classical economists was what determines V—the amount of M people decide to hold rather than spend. This is a central question in the next chapter, on the modern monetarists. But before going on to that, an exercise to show the usefulness of the traditional monetary analysis in understanding the effects of money and money-holding habits on output and prices.

Suppose that we all decide to build up our real-money balances by decreasing our expenditures relative to our incomes; as a group we want to hold more purchasing power in the form of money balances. We want to increase our real buying power over goods and services.

Will the result be higher money balances all around? If your inclination is to say yes, stop and think again. With any given stock of money, there can be no change in the total amount of nominal money balances held, because there isn't any more money for the public to hold and every existing dollar must be held by someone. Thus, the result of a general attempt to build up money balances is a decrease in total expenditures as V decreases, not an increase in total balances, as long as the total amount of money is unchanged. (Remember the fallacy of composition.)

Will this concerted attempt to accumulate buying power over goods and services be completely thwarted? The answer is no. By reducing total expenditures, the public's desire to build up its real balances will ultimately decrease prices (and probably production and employment as well). As prices fall, the existing amount of money will command more real goods and services. Thus, even though the total stock of money remains unchanged, the public will succeed in increasing its "real balances." People don't plan it that way, but they increase the real value of their money balances by bringing on deflation. When prices have fallen enough to give existing money balances the desired amount of real purchasing power in relation to incomes and other assets, the public's demand for money balances will again be in equilibrium. People (households, businesses, and others) will again be satisfied to hold just the amount of money that exists.[5]

This can be put in equilibrium terms. Suppose there is some fixed amount of nominal money (M). If people have more money than they want to hold, M^s will exceed M^d. That is, there will be an excess supply of money, which people will spend on goods, bonds, or whatnot. They will continue to try to spend down their money balances. Spending and prices will thus rise until $M^s = M^d$, that is, until the amounts of money demanded and supplied are equal. Only then is there monetary equilibrium.

Conversely, if M^d exceeds M^s, people will try to build up their real balances. They will reduce their spending and prices will decrease until at the lower prices M^d just equals M^s.

CONCLUSION—POLICY IMPLICATIONS

This classical monetary analysis led to two main policy conclusions, one reassuring, the other discouraging. First, the quantity theory said that aggregate money demand could be roughly stabilized by maintaining a stable quantity of money. We can avoid both big fluctuations in aggregate demand if only we keep the money stock growing at a stable rate. Since population and the productive capacity of the economy grow over time, it will be desirable to increase the money stock gradually, roughly apace with the growing full-employment-output capacity of the economy; otherwise prices will fall steadily as output increases. If inflation prevails, slow the growth in M. If deflation is the problem, increase M faster.

The second, discouraging, policy implication was that monetary policy can't do much to eliminate unemployment if we get into a depression, if we accept completely the classical analysis stated above. Note that this conclusion follows from the classicists' assumption about the economy's aggregate supply curve, not from the quantity theory per se. Fundamentally, the analysis says that unemployment occurs because it does not pay employers to hire all workers at existing wage rates, and for some reason wage rates don't fall to absorb unemployed workers. Thus the level of employment is not determined by aggregate demand. More M to raise aggregate spending will mainly increase prices rather than provide more jobs.

But few classical economists were such purists as to accept the theory in the extreme form stated above. Mainly, they shifted their views on the aggregate supply function. Many believed that increases in M in depressions could help raise employment by pushing up aggregate demand and prices, since generally prices would rise faster than wages, thereby reducing real wages and inducing businessmen to hire more workers. As the long depression of the 1930s wore on, fewer and fewer economists were content to wait for the promised long-run forces to restore high employment. It was this concern with the short-run "transitory" problem of massive unemployment that led to both the neo-Keynesian revolution proposing active fiscal policy and modernized versions of monetary analysis that accord money a much more potent role in avoiding unemployment as well as inflation. They are the topic of Chapter 13.

[5]It is important to note that if prices are flexible downward as spending falls, the attempt to increase real balances will succeed without any decrease in real output and employment. But if prices and costs are inflexible downward, the result is likely to be a big decline in output and employment before prices fall far enough to satisfy the increased demand for real balances.

REVIEW

Concepts to Remember

The following new concepts in this chapter are worth careful review:

- money
- difference between money and income
- velocity of circulation
- equation of exchange
- nominal money
- real money balances
- demand for money
- quantity theory of money

For Analysis and Discussion

1. Figure 12–1 shows that growth in money GNP closely parallels that in money. Does this demonstrate that the monetarists are right—changes in *M* are the main causes of changes in money GNP? Is the possibility that changes in GNP cause changes in *M* also consistent with the evidence? Do you need a theory to decide between the hypotheses?
2. By and large, would you expect prices to rise in proportion to any major increase in the supply of money? Explain.
3. Suppose the government holds the stock of money roughly constant over the next decade. Would you expect constant, rising, or falling price and income levels? Explain.
4. Is your own spending rate primarily a function of your recent income, your cash balance, or other factors?
5. Suppose the 1980 full-employment potential GNP is $2 trillion. How big a money supply do you estimate will be needed to finance this GNP?
6. Suppose the public's demand for money balances increases because of fear and uncertainty at the beginning of a recession. If the government wants to keep prices and employment stable, what should it do about the stock of money?
7. "In depression, an increase in the money supply leads to more jobs; in prosperity to inflation." Is this quotation correct? Does the equation of exchange help in analyzing it?

Money and Aggregate Demand: The Modern Synthesis

CHAPTER THIRTEEN

The monetarists focus on two major factors in explaining aggregate demand—the supply of money and the public's demand for money. We understand reasonably well what controls the supply of money (see Chapter 16), but the classical economists never explained changes in V (that is, changes in the demand for money) very satisfactorily. You can't eat money, drink it, or use it directly for anything. Thus, we need to explain why people ever hold money, instead of spending it immediately on consumption or on some kind of investment that yields a return, like houses, bonds, or factories. Modern monetarists have concentrated on explaining the demand for money, because if they can explain that and the supply of money, they can explain aggregate demand.

WHY DO PEOPLE HOLD MONEY?

Fundamentally, people hold money because of the buying power it gives them over goods and services, now and in the future. If John Doe decides he doesn't need to hold as much money as he has on hand, he will spend it. But if he feels that he needs a larger money balance, he will hold down his expenditures relative to his income to build up his money balance. Thus, changes in the desired level of money balances will have a direct impact on V and current spending.

Modern economists have tried to explain the public's demand for money balances through empirical research. Presumably, people are primarily interested in the real buying power of their money, and research has focused on the demand for *real* money balances. Theorizing suggests that the larger an individual's income or the more wealthy he is, the more money he will usually hold for normal transactions purposes, as well as just to have some spare funds (liquidity) on hand. But why does he hold money instead of maintaining that liquidity by holding bonds or other interest-yielding securities? The answer is that securities aren't as liquid as money—they involve some risk that you can't convert them into cash on short notice without loss, and in any event there is often a transactions cost (in time and money) in converting them into cash when you need it. So people will hold some money, even though it yields no interest return. But the higher the interest rate available on securities (close money substitutes), the more reluctant people will be to hold money and forego that interest.

Thus, it seems plausible that the demand for money is a function of two variables, the public's income or wealth and the interest rate on close money substitutes (say, U.S. government securities). And empirical research confirms that this is generally so. The demand for real money balances is:

$$m^d = f(Y, i),$$

where Y is real income and i is the interest rate. Total wealth (W) can be substituted for Y with about equally good results. These results suggest that if we know the public's income and the interest rate, we can predict its demand for money (or V), assuming that people behave in the future as they have in the past. They also say that, other things equal, if incomes rise so will the demand for money, and that the demand for money to hold will vary inversely with the interest rate.[1]

These are powerful findings. But the public's behavior varies somewhat from time to time, and the empirical results are not consistent enough to permit us to predict precisely what V will be for any period ahead. The equation gives us a first working approximation for estimating the effects on aggregate demand of changes in M under different income and interest rate conditions, but only an approximation because we never know just how the public will behave in the future, especially if circumstances are out of the ordinary.

[1]If we take Y to stand for "permanent," or average lifelong, income, the accuracy of the equation improves appreciably, because people's demand for money apparently does not vary with all short-run fluctuations in incomes received.

MONEY, PORTFOLIO BALANCING, AND AGGREGATE DEMAND

We can now spell out more precisely the theory that underlies the preceding empirical findings about the public's demand for money (V). The reasoning is precisely parallel to the model in Chapter 5, where consumers maximized their utility by allocating their incomes so the marginal utility obtained from the last dollar spent on each product was identical. Just so, they will maximize their utility from their total assets, or wealth, by allocating their wealth (their "portfolios") among assets so that the utility obtained from the last dollar invested in each asset is identical. Each household and business will be in equilibrium when it has allocated its total wealth (assets) among money, other liquid assets (bonds, savings accounts, and so on), and real assets (houses, durable goods, and so on) so that the marginal return from the last dollar invested in each asset is the same. If this were not so, it would pay to shift out of the low-yield assets into higher-yield assets.

For example, suppose a family receives an unexpected gift of $10,000 cash from a forgotten aunt. It now has more money than it wants to hold and will use this "excess" money to acquire other assets, such as an auto, clothes, or bonds. It will spend down its money balance until the marginal satisfaction obtained from the last dollar held in money just equals that received from the last dollar invested in bonds, housing, and any other asset the family wants. Then its asset portfolio would be in equilibrium. If MU is the marginal utility, or satisfaction, obtained from the last dollar invested, then equilibrium is obtained when:

$$MU\,(\text{money}) = MU\,(\text{bonds}) = MU\,(\text{clothing}) = MU\,(\text{autos})\ \ldots \text{ and so on}$$

for all assets held.

Note that this implies that holding money provides utility (a return) even if the money yields no money interest return. Clearly, this is correct. Money provides generalized, riskless, immediately available buying power. Other assets provide different returns. Securities provide interest or dividends and possibly the expectation of capital gains, although they also involve some risk. Capital goods (like machinery) provide a direct contribution to business profits. Consumers' durable goods provide current services to their users. All these assets are in the portfolio that must be balanced to maximize the total utility obtained. And the same portfolio-balancing model holds for business firms as well as households.

It should now be easy to see how putting more or less M in the system will increase or decrease spending on other assets. Your aunt's $10,000 gift leads you to buy a $1,000 government bond, ten shares of AT&T stock, and a new car, as well as to increase your checking balance at the local bank (that is, to hold more money). Note that an increase or decrease in the stock of *any* asset, or a change in its yield, will logically lead to a reshuffling of portfolios. Whenever individuals or businesses find that the marginal returns on different assets are different, they will always move toward equilibrium by shifting out of assets with lower marginal yields into higher-yielding ones. And this will lead them to spend more or less on different assets.

It is important to note also that increased spending induced by more M may or may not directly increase aggregate demand (money GNP). If you reduce your money balance by buying General Motors stock, U.S. bonds, or an existing house, this is merely an exchange of existing assets. Your expenditure does not directly increase GNP. But if you buy a new coat, or have your car repaired, your money expenditure does directly increase GNP. Similarly, a business may shift out of money into new plant and equipment, thus directly increasing the investment component of GNP; or it might simply invest its excess money in bonds. **It is this portfolio balancing that provides the linkage between money stocks on the one hand and the flows of consumption and investment spending in the GNP accounts on the other.**

THE MODERN SYNTHESIS

Both the income-expenditures model of Chapters 10 and 11 and the monetarist model of this chapter provide plausible explanations of how aggregate demand is determined. Both have something to contribute; we now need to merge them.

The income-expenditures model says that equilibrium can be attained **only** when households are consuming and saving in relation to their incomes at the rates they prefer, and **only** when businessmen are investing at the rate they judge will maximize their profits. This is an analysis in terms of income flows—through consumption and investment expenditures—not in terms of equilibria between supplies and demands of assets held. Money (an asset) is ignored or introduced only indirectly through its effect on the interest rate.

The monetarist (portfolio-balancing) model says that the system will be in equilibrium **only** when households and businesses are content to hold just the existing stock of money and other assets. This equilibrium will occur when each household and business has allocated its total wealth so it is maximizing its total yield, and so that all economic units together are content to hold just the existing stock of every asset, including money. In this approach, the emphasis is on assets, with spending flows derived from people's decisions about what assets to hold.

Thus, for equilibrium to be obtained in the economy, both the "flows" of the income-expenditures model and the "stocks" of the portfolio-balancing model must be in equilibrium. Unless all economic units are in equilibrium on both accounts—that is, unless they are content to keep on doing what they are doing—they will change their behavior and bring about a movement in spending, output, and prices toward the desired equilibrium state.

M Increases Wealth and Aggregate Demand: An Example

Consider now two experiments. First, suppose the government simply prints up some new money and gives it to the public, say in the form of unemployment relief. This increases the money and total assets (wealth) of the public and simultaneously increases disposable personal income. Let us trace through the effects of this increase in *M*.

Consider the monetarist analysis. The public now has more money than previously. If it was previously satisfied with its money holdings (that is, its asset portfolios were balanced), it now has too much money compared to other assets, such as consumers' goods and securities. The marginal satisfaction from holding money has fallen relative to that on other assets, because the public has more money but no more of other things. It therefore will spend some of the new money for other assets. This will bid up prices of other things and thus gradually decrease the satisfaction obtainable by spending an additional dollar on them. (Note that the total stock of *M* does not change; what *A* spends *B* receives.) The public will continue to spend its new money balances until rising prices restore an equilibrium in the rates of return provided by a marginal dollar held in money and in all other assets. Thus, on the asset side, more *M* leads to more spending, as people act to rebalance their portfolios.[2]

In income-flows analysis, the increase in disposable income will lead to more consumption, and through the multiplier to a higher GNP. Equilibrium is reestablished when GNP rises to a new level where consumers are at their desired consumption-income ratios and businesses are at their desired investment levels relative to their receipts and profit expectations given their larger income.

Thus, households and businesses throughout the economy adjust both their asset portfolios and their current spending patterns until they are content with new equilibria attained on both fronts. Both adjustments go on simultaneously.

But note an important difference between the monetarist and Keynesian conclusions. The monetarists predict a *continuing* higher level of GNP, consistent with the new permanently higher level of *M*. But the Keynesians predict that there will be only a *temporary* increase in GNP, unless the higher autonomous relief payments are repeated in succeeding periods. The increased aggregate demand is based on the increased autonomous spending in their theory, not on the increased *M*. Thus, the higher GNP will continue only as long as its autonomous spending base is continued; the increase in *M* is only incidental, except insofar as it may directly stimulate more investment.

Clearly, which theory is right is a matter of great importance for national policy. The question is obviously an empirical one in large part. Both theories look plausible; we need to look at the evidence to see which is right.

M Increases Without Increasing Wealth

Now, a second experiment. Suppose the government increases *M* by buying up bonds

[2]To see why a rise in the price of a security or other asset is the same thing as a decline in the yield on it, consider the following. Suppose the security is a \$100 government bond paying 3 percent (that is, \$3 a year) and is due in ten years. If the price is bid up to \$110, the annual real yield falls to about 2 percent. This is because, offset against the annual interest payment of \$3, the bond buyer must consider the \$10 he will lose when he gets back in ten years only \$100 instead of the \$110 he paid. Spreading this "capital loss" evenly over the ten years takes away \$1 return per year, lowering the effective annual yield to \$2, which is an effective interest rate of 2 percent. (Actually, it is a little less than 2 percent, since you get \$2 per year on an investment of \$110.) This same type of effect holds for other assets that provide a given yield.

owned by the public. This increases the public's money balances and reduces the interest rate through bidding up the price of bonds, but it does not increase the public's total wealth. Does this lead to more spending, via either the portfolio-balancing or income-flows route?

The neo-Keynesians would say no, or at least only indirectly. It would have no effect on disposable income and hence no effect on consumption. It might indirectly increase GNP by stimulating investment through the lower interest rate, though this effect is problematical. The monetarists disagree. They concur that the stimulus to money GNP would be less than in the preceding increased-wealth case. But they argue that the new money will spill over at least in part to other assets, like consumer goods, investment goods, and securities. This difference of opinion is again an important one for governmental monetary-policy makers who must determine how much money we should have and how to introduce it.

THE MODERN SYNTHESIS AND STABILIZATION POLICY

Nearly everyone agrees that both money and the income-flow factors of Chapters 10 and 11 are important determinants of aggregate demand, and that we must take both into account. But which is more powerful, and which relationship is more stable, so we can rely upon it in predicting the future behavior of the system? Suppose, for example, there is unemployment and we want to raise aggregate demand by $10 billion. One approach: We might print up $2–2½ billion of new money and give it out in the form of relief payments, on the reasoning that income velocity recently has been about 4.8, so the new money would raise GNP by about $10 billion. Another approach: We might not change *M* at all but instead reduce personal income taxes by $4–5 billion without correspondingly reducing government expenditures. This increase in DPI should increase consumer spending by nearly as much, and neo-Keynesians suggest that the multiplier on autonomous spending is about 2–2½, given stable interest rates. Thus, the result should be an increase of about $10 billion in GNP. Which approach is better? Is the figure for income velocity (4.8 in this example) more reliable than the figure for the multiplier (2–2½ in this example) in predicting the new GNP?

The answer from econometric studies is mixed. Neither income velocity nor the multiplier is as predictably stable as their advocates would like. As a practical matter, if we want an increase of $10 billion in aggregate demand, to use either increased *M* or decreased taxes alone risks partial success. For example, the tax reduction may increase GNP, but if *M* is unchanged, rising income will increase the demand for money and interest rates, which will partially check the upswing by reducing businesses' incentive to invest. Moreover, the government will have to borrow money to finance its new deficit, which will further increase interest rates. On the other hand, to increase *M* alone (say, by buying up outstanding bonds with new money) does not increase anyone's disposable income or assets, and the income-expenditure advocates say the policy will do little more than slightly reduce the interest yield on bonds. Depending on the particular circumstances, either the tax or the monetary approach may be the more appropriate one if we must choose. **But most experts agree that it is safer to use them both simultaneously if this is feasible.**

In the meantime, more research is needed to clarify the quantitative importance of the income and money factors in household and business behavior. The simple income-expenditures model of Chapter 10 (before money was introduced) implicitly assumed that either the stock of *M* or *V* (that is, the demand for money) would passively adjust to permit the equilibrium level of GNP predicted by the income-expenditures model. If, for example, we cut taxes by $1 billion but did not change the money stock, a multiplier of, say, 2 would necessarily imply that *V* automatically rises to permit the $2 billion increase in GNP. Conversely, the monetary approach implicitly assumes a passive adjustment in MPC to permit GNP to follow changes in *M*. Suppose, for example, we increase the money stock by $1 billion but make no change in taxes, government expenditures, or the other income-flow variables. The monetary approach tells us that, if V is stable at, say, 4, GNP will rise by $4 billion. But this increase necessarily implies a corresponding upward adjustment in the public's marginal propensity to consume or in businesses' marginal propensity to invest. To decide whether tax or monetary policy is a more powerful device to regulate aggregate demand, we need to know more about the relative stabilities of the demand for money and the economy's propensity to spend out of disposable income. The evidence is simply not yet conclusive. Clearly, both the income and asset adjustment processes are important in many cases.[3]

[3]Modern econometricians are working hard to determine the relative influence on GNP of changes in M and in autonomous expenditure (often roughly defined as private investment plus most government spending). For example, to oversimplify, they say: Suppose we statistically relate changes in GNP to changes in M, and then separately relate changes in GNP to changes in A (autonomous expenditure). The results look like this for the decade of the sixties. (In the equations, t stands for time period, so t is this quarter, t^{-1} is one quarter back, and so on; and Δ stands for "change in.")

$$(1)\quad \Delta GNP_t = 5.61b. + 3.94\,(\Delta M)_{t-3} \qquad r^2 = .553$$
$$(2)\quad \Delta GNP_t = 4.94b. + 1.08\,(\Delta A)_{t-1} \qquad r^2 = .400$$

Equation (1) says that the quarterly change in GNP equaled $5.61 billion plus $3.94 for each $1 increase in M three quarters previously. Put otherwise, a $1 increase in M was associated with a $3.94 increase in GNP three quarters later. Equation (2) says that a $1 increase in A was associated with a $1.08 increase in GNP one quarter later. The r^2 in each case is called the "coefficient of determination." It shows how much of the total actual change in GNP each quarter is explained by the M or A, respectively. Thus, ΔM in the simple test explained a little more of ΔGNP than did ΔA.

But actually, of course, both M and A exert influence on GNP simultaneously. If we put both variables in the same equation, we get:

$$(3)\quad \Delta GNP = 4.00b. + 2.52\,(\Delta M)_{t-3} + .670\,(\Delta A)_{t-1} \qquad r^2 = .658$$

This equation shows that ΔM and ΔA together explain appreciably more (65.8 percent) of ΔGNP than does either alone. Quarterly changes in GNP (annual rates) over the ten years were $4 billion plus $2.52 for each $1 increase in M and 67 cents for each $1 increase in A, with the time lags shown.

This example suggests how econometricians go about using historical evidence to judge how much different factors influence GNP. But the example is greatly oversimplified, and it is important to remember that the figures shown do not provide a satisfactory answer on the relative importance of M and A for real-world use. Different time periods and different definitions of M and A give significantly different results. And a dispute rages among the experts as to whether more meaningful answers are obtained from relatively simple models like this one or complex models including many more variables.

For references to more complex models, see the appendix to Chapter 10. For contradictory analyses of the results of simple ("reduced form") models, see Leonell Anderson, "Money and Economic Forecasting" and Edward Gramlich, "The Role of Money in Economic Activity," *Business Economics,* September 1969.

Money, Interest Rates, and Expectations: Dynamics

One further complication must be added. In fact, interest rates often seem to rise when M is increased rapidly, rather than fall. Everyone agrees that the **first** direct effect of introducing more money into the economy will, other things equal, be to reduce the interest rate—directly if the government introduces the money by buying up bonds, or indirectly through portfolio balancing if the money is inserted some other way. But one of the main lessons of economics is: Don't stop with the first effect, second and third effects may also be important! And so they may be here.

More M will almost certainly raise money incomes. This, in turn, will increase the demand for money, and this **second** effect will tend to **raise** the interest rate, partially offsetting the original downward pressure of more M. This is called the "income effect." But there may be a still further, **third** effect—the "inflation effect." If the rising income comes at a time of full employment, it will stimulate further inflation. If this leads the public to expect more inflation, it will lead lenders to demand higher interest rates to offset the expected inflation. It will also increase the demand of borrowers for loans because they can repay in dollars of reduced buying power; borrowers will be willing to pay a higher interest rate if they anticipate inflation. The third effect of more M may, therefore, be **higher** interest rates, not lower ones, as both lenders and borrowers include an inflation allowance in their bargains. The final combined effect will depend on the relative size of the three effects.

In fact, rapid increases in M have generally been associated with rising, not falling, interest rates. The 1965–73 period is an example. M, commodity prices, and interest rates all rose rapidly, apparently reflecting strong expectations that more M created by the government would lead to more inflation and hence to substantial inflation allowances by both lenders and borrowers in interest-rate bargains. This direct relationship between changes in M and interest rates is often called the "Gibson paradox"; M and interest rates move together rather than in opposite directions.

MONEY IN PERSPECTIVE

So how important is money? Clearly money matters—and matters a lot. Money has played a vital role in all the big inflations. Runaway increases in the money stock have invariably been associated with soaring prices, usually in a dog-chasing-his-own-tail upward spiral where more money leads to higher prices, which leads the government to print more money to pay its bills, which leads to still higher prices, and so on. The expected yield on M becomes negative because people expect inflation to erode its value. People reduce their holdings of M to the barest minima needed for transactions and precautionary purposes.

Just how important changes in M are in explaining smaller business fluctuations is less clear. Although changes in M and in GNP are closely correlated, it is not always clear which causes which. But one historical fact stands out: Real GNP has grown stably in this country only when the money supply was growing at least roughly at the same rate as the productive capacity of the economy. Nearly everyone agrees that a growing money supply is a necessary condition for a growing real GNP. Some believe that it is a sufficient condition to induce stable growth in our economy. The implications of the two conclusions for long-run monetary policy are, happily, similar. But until we have clearer evidence, most economists are not prepared to rely solely on stable growth in M to provide stable growth in aggregate demand and real output.

REVIEW

Concepts to Remember

The following new concepts in this chapter are worth careful review:

portfolio balancing
income vs. asset adjustments
interest yields and security prices
Gibson paradox

For Analysis and Discussion

1. Explain why the public's demand for real money depends largely on its real income (or wealth) and on the interest rate of money substitutes (like government securities)—that is, $m^d = f(Y, i)$.

2. Explain how the portfolio-balancing analysis links changes in the stock of money with changes in money GNP.
3. Monetarists argue that the government can control the nominal stock of money but not the stock of *real* money, since the public will increase or decrease its spending if it receives more or less real purchasing power than it wants to hold when the government changes M. Thus, the public determines the real money stock by altering its spending rate and prices, although the government determines the nominal money stock. If this monetarist analysis is correct, does the government have any power through changing M to influence either employment or prices? Explain.
4. Suppose the public considers money and bonds to be very close substitutes, but money and goods to be distant substitutes. Would this tend to support the monetarists or the advocates of the income-expenditures model? Explain.
5. Explain why an equilibrium level GNP requires equilibrium in *both* the "flow" decisions that consumers and businesses make about their spending *and* their "stock" decisions as to the form in which consumers and businesses hold their assets.
6. In a period of inflation, would you expect an increase in the money stock to lower or raise interest rates? Would your answer be different in a recession period? Explain.

How To Fight Unemployment?

A severe recession has hit the economy. Unemployment has risen to 7 percent and profits are sagging. Just about everyone agrees that we need more aggregate demand.

Your congressman, no economist, is home, sounding out public opinion. He says that, as usual, the experts can't seem to agree on what to do. They agree that another $40–50 billion of aggregate demand is needed quickly to get unemployment back down below 5 percent, but propose at least three different aproaches to getting it. One group says, increase government spending on urban renewal, the environment, public health, and the like. They're all high-priority social goals, and another $20 billion of government spending with a multiplier of 2 should just about do the job, helping everyone and hurting no one, since, of course, taxes should not be raised.

A second group says, no way! The government is spending too much already. The thing to do is cut taxes by $20 billion or so. With the same multiplier of 2, this will give the desired increase in aggregate demand, and will give back to the people the freedom to spend their incomes on what they want most, rather than having the government tell them what they ought to want.

A third group has a different angle. Let monetary policy do the job, they say. Let the Federal Reserve increase the money stock by $10 billion or so. Given the nation's income velocity of nearly 5 for the last several years, this will increase aggregate demand by nearly $50 billion. The Fed can either put the money in circulation by buying up bonds from the public, or the money can be lent to the government (the Treasury) and given out in the form of unemployment relief—or, indeed, in any other way you like, since the basic objective is to get the money into the public's hands.

What is your advice to your congressman? What policy, or combination of policies, do you propose? Be specific in your proposal, as to the amount of any action to be taken and your reasons for believing it will do the job better than the other approaches.

Business Cycles: Unemployment and Inflation

CHAPTER PREVIEW

CHAPTER FOURTEEN

The long pull of American economic growth is impressive. But that growth has come spasmodically, in spurts separated by recessions and sometimes major depressions. In perspective, the booms and depressions of American history are fluctuations around a long-term growth trend. And this is the right way to look at them. For seldom has the trough of a recession been lower than the peak of the boom before last. Growth dominates fluctuations in our history. But this doesn't mean that repeated booms and depressions have been unimportant. Far from it!

We turn now to look at business cycles—at the twin problems of unemployment and inflationary booms which have long plagued the industrialized nations.

GROWTH AND FLUCTUATIONS IN AMERICA

The long sweep of growth in America, interrupted by repeated recessions, is shown by the top lines of the graph inside the front cover. Figure 7–5, in the introductory overview of macroeconomics, pointed up both characteristics another way; look back at it. The fluctuations of real GNP around its growth rate of some 3–4 percent per year are bounded on the top and bottom by two trend lines, roughly connecting the peaks of the booms and the troughs of the depressions. Growth is the basic process, with the economy pushing up toward the bounds of productive capacity in boom periods and slumping in recessions. The vertical shaded areas are recession periods. Note that the upswing periods are substantially longer than the shaded (recession) areas.[1]

One way of studying economic fluctuations is to separate the fluctuations from the long-term upward trend, or growth. Figure 14–1 does this for industrial production, a volatile sector of the modern American economy. To construct Figure 14–1, we first draw a "trend" line through the actual monthly data for industrial production (per capita) over the period, a rapidly but irregularly rising series. A trend line is a line drawn roughly through the middle of the fluctuating series—so the readings on the industrial-production curve above the trend line about equal those below it.[2] If, then, we lay the trend line out flat, it becomes the zero line in Figure 14–1. Thus, periods when industrial production was above the trend line are shown above zero, and conversely for those below.

All the data are shown as percentage deviations from trend. Thus, moderately prosperous 1964 runs about 10 percent above "normal," as do the similar years 1905–07. In absolute terms, of course, industrial production in 1964 was many times more than in 1905–07. The vast area below normal in the 1930s and that above normal in the 1960s on the chart are thus far smaller in comparison with earlier cycles than they would be plotted in terms of absolute, rather than percentage, deviations.

The Anatomy of Economic Fluctuations

The big booms and depressions in America have all involved major swings in real GNP, employment, and money income. The great depressions, like that of the 1930s, have meant massive unemployment, vast grey idle factories, financial disaster for millions, endless days of desperate job hunting, hunger, and malnutrition. Most college students today cannot remember a great depression, for you have never seen one.[3] Perhaps there will never be another, but we cannot be sure. The big booms have been the opposite—more jobs than workers, soaring wages and prices, big profits, speculation on the

[1] The top of the World War II boom (1942–45) is shown above the dashed line because the economy was then clearly operating beyond its normal capacity level. Housewives, old people, and children were temporarily pulled into the labor force, and workers were called on for vast amounts of overtime to meet wartime production goals.

[2] Any elementary statistics book provides information on the statistical techniques used in "fitting" trend lines to data. There are several techniques, which may be considered substantially equivalent for our purposes.

[3] Some "feel" of the Great Depression is provided by "Black Depression" from Frederick L. Allen's *Only Yesterday* (New York: Harper & Row, Publishers, 1939) and the dreary, desparate saga "Job Hunters" from E.W. Bakke's *The Unemployed Worker* (New Haven: Yale University Press, 1940) both reprinted in M.L. Joseph, N.C. Seeber, and G.L. Bach's *Economic Analysis and Policy: Background Readings for Current Issues* 4th Ed. (Englewood Cliffs, N.J.: Prentice-Hall, Inc., 1974).

Figure 14–1

The curve shows percentage deviations from the long-term upward trend of U.S. industrial production. Areas above the zero line are above trend and conversely for areas below it. (Source: Cleveland Trust Company.)

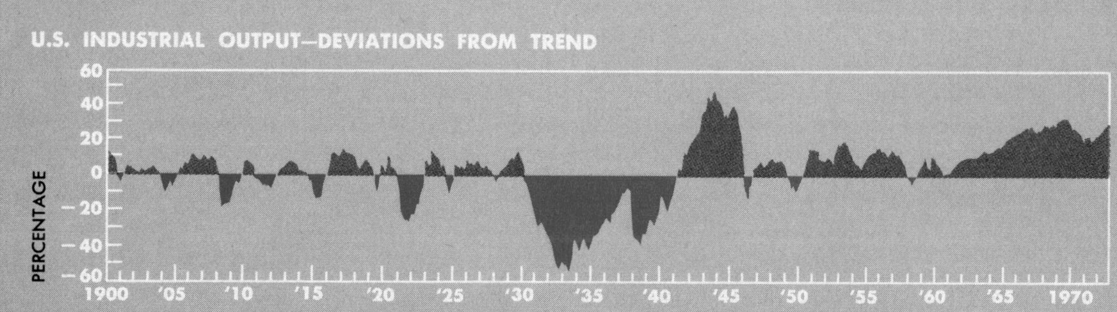

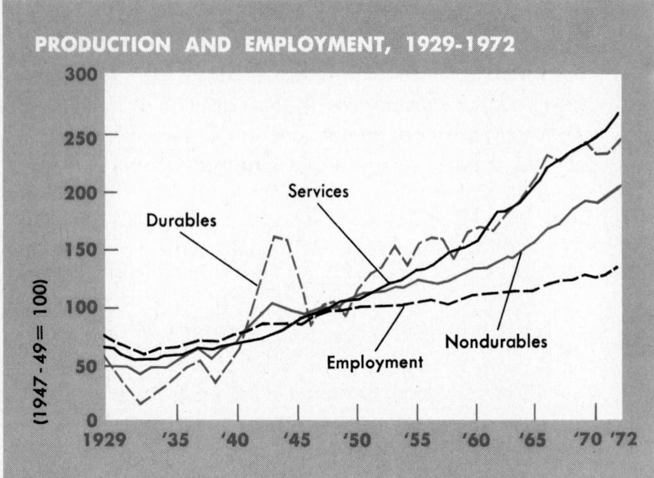

Figure 14–2

The major components of production and employment fluctuate roughly together, but with very different amplitudes. All curves except "Employment" show actual production, with 1947–49 = 100. Note the big fluctuations in the production of durables. (Source: U.S. Department of Commerce.)

stock market, good times for nearly everyone, but uncertainty about how long it all will last.

Figure 14–2 shows unemployment and three major components of real GNP in the United States over the past half century. Production of durable goods (steel, electrical machinery, automobiles, refrigerators) fluctuates far more than the other series. Fluctuations are much milder in shoes, clothing, food, and other nondurable consumer goods. And the stability of spending on services is remarkable; the growth curve hardly wobbles since the 1930s. This does not mean that services and nondurable consumer-goods industries are unaffected by cyclical fluctuations, but the heart of the problem lies in the durable goods industries.

If this were a more advanced text on economic fluctuations, we would need to look at hundreds of series rather than only a few major ones. The National Bureau of Economic Research, the leading private research organization on business cycles, has plotted hundreds of economic series and found that there is a wide spectrum of movements up and down. Some series normally lead the economy, some lag behind. Most economists prefer to focus on a few big, critical measures, like real GNP, employment, industrial production, investment, and the like; but it is important never to forget the great complexity of the real world.

Are There Business Cycles? Are there business cycles—regularly recurring booms and recessions? By now the answer should be clear. It is "no," if you stress the "regularly." Some upswings are long and strong, others short and weak. Some recessions are mild, others become massive depressions. But the answer is "yes," if you mean only that there are intermittent periods of prosperity and recession. Given these facts, some economists have dropped the words "business cycles" in favor of the term "fluctuations," which doesn't connote such regularity.

BUSINESS-CYCLE THEORY

Ever since booms and depressions began, people have been trying to figure out why they occur. Different writers have emphasized everything from sunspots to Wall Street as the primary cause of booms and depressions. A theory that seems to explain all business cycles simply and neatly is heady stuff. But alas, no one has come up with one simple theory that does the job. However, there is substantial agreement among many economists on an analytical framework for looking at the dynamically interacting variables.

This is the framework provided by Chapters

10–13. It tells us to focus on changes in aggregate demand relative to the economy's growing productive capacity. Aggregate demand is made up of consumption and investment spending (if we temporarily ignore government spending), and these in turn are influenced by the supply of money and interest rates. Booms are dynamic, cumulative, interacting processes in which increased investment stimulates more consumption, which in turn raises business sales and profits and stimulates more investment. Similarly, depressions are cumulative downward processes in which the dynamic interaction between contracting consumption and contracting investment is the core of the downswing. In both, money and interest rates generally play important roles.

We shall, therefore, focus on these three major variables (consumption, investment, and money) and on their dynamic interactions—both because this approach provides a relatively simple framework and because it is the way most economists themselves go about explaining complex real-world economic fluctuations. It is the dynamic interaction among these three, sometimes strongly affected by government policy and by random shocks such as wars, that is the essence of "business cycles."

The above model leaves the government out, since we want to consider government policy separately in the following chapters. But don't forget that government purchases and transfer payments total over 30 percent of GNP, and taxes withdraw a comparable amount from the payments stream. Moreover, government control of the money supply exerts a major influence on the economy. And, as we shall see, sometimes the government's fiscal and monetary policies can be destabilizing as well as stabilizing.

THE CUMULATIVE UPSWING

The essence of the business cycle is a cumulative, interacting, multiplier-accelerator process, supplemented by monetary forces and influenced by a number of special factors. Let us begin with an economy recovering from a recession and trace its upward progress. Assume that something happens to start an upswing. In examining the upswing, note how each expansive factor gradually develops self-limiting tendencies, which increasingly act to put a ceiling on the prosperity and to turn the economy down into recession.

Rising Consumption

Rising incomes are the main foundation for rising consumption spending in the upswing. Consumption spending rises primarily because incomes rise; consumption plays a relatively passive role. If we assume that investment spending increases, perhaps because a new product is developed, this new investment spending will generate more income and consumer spending through the multiplier. Just how much consumption rises for each dollar of new investment depends, of course, on the "leakages" through saving in each round of spending. Apparently a multiplier of two or so is not uncommon for the American economy; remember, it's the relation of consumption spending to GNP, not to disposable personal income, that provides the relevant multiplier for explaining GNP.

The ratio of consumption to disposable income tends to be high in depressions; people are able to save very little. If the *marginal* propensity to consume is high, the multiplier will be relatively large. As incomes rise into prosperity, though, the marginal propensity to save typically rises, reducing the multiplier on each additional investment dollar.

As the economy comes out of a depression, more spendable income is the only thing likely to give a major boost to consumption spending. But consumption is not completely induced. If the revival takes hold, at least three special factors may increase the marginal propensity to consume, pushing toward a larger multiplier.

First, consumers may have a backlog demand for consumer durables—refrigerators, stoves, autos, and radios—piled up from the depression. You can use the same refrigerator a long time if you're good at minor repairs and don't mind foregoing the latest improvements. But try as you will to avoid it, the day will come when you have to buy another refrigerator or have the food spoil in hot weather. The postponement of purchases of durable goods is one reason why recessions last. Catching up on these postponed purchases is one of the big lifts in revival.

Second, as prices begin to rise in revival, consumers may begin to expect still higher prices ahead. Expectations of rising prices can speed consumer buying, but this is a boost we can't count on with any confidence until the upswing is well under way.

Third, as times improve, consumer credit may become more readily available to marginal borrowers. Such credit permits consumers to spend more in relation to current income than they otherwise might.

But remember: Rising consumption in the upswing depends largely on rising incomes, and thus indirectly on rising investment or government spending.

Rising Investment

THE "ACCELERATOR." Rising consumer spending means rising sales for businesses. This will deplete inventories and push firms toward capacity limits in factories and stores. Thus, rising sales sooner or later will stimulate more investment. This effect of more consumption spending in inducing more investment is called the "accelerator." **It provides the link to complete the cumulative interaction in the upswing: more investment → more income → more consumption → more investment, and so on. In summary, the upswing is a cumulative multiplier-accelerator process.**[4]

Unless the original burst of investment and its multiplied effect on consumption in turn induce more investment, there will be no cumulative upswing—only a hump on the floor of the depression. But if the rise in consumer spending does produce a substantial accelerator effect, then the revival is on. The further induced investment in turn produces its multiplier effect, which in its turn induces further investment. If both the multiplier and the accelerator are large, any revival that gets started will be an explosive one, with consumption and investment interacting vigorously. If either is zero, that's the end of the upswing.

How strong will the accelerator in fact be? The answer is, different at different times. Rising incomes and sales will induce new investment whenever they make the **desired** amount of plant and equipment larger than the **actual** amount on hand. Thus, if sales rise and the producer has no excess productive capacity, his desired stock of plant and equipment will clearly exceed his present stock, because without more capacity he can't meet the expanding demand. But if he begins with excess capacity, he has more plant and equipment than he currently needs, so even increased sales won't necessarily raise his desired stock above what he has.

Pragmatically, when the economy is just emerging from a serious recession, the outlook for a larger accelerator effect from rising sales is bad, for two reasons.

(1) Idle capacity is widespread during depression, and moderate increases in demand can often be met by using existing idle equipment.

(2) Businessmen, whatever the capacity situation is, may cautiously wait to see whether the increased demand is permanent. If they do, no acceleration effect will occur. Their desired stock of capital depends on the permanence they attach to the increased demand.

But if revival progresses and idle capacity vanishes, further increases in consumer spending are more and more likely to stimulate new investment. History and theory both suggest that the acceleration effect can be powerful.[5]

The acceleration effect can account for a substantial part of changes in investment as con-

[4]Appendix B to this chapter presents a formal model of the cumulative multiplier-accelerator process that shows that under certain (not unrealistic) conditions, the combination of accelerator and multiplier effects can induce cyclical fluctuations in GNP even when the original stimulus of investment does not fluctuate.

[5]In some cases, as more advanced texts explain, an increase in consumer demand may stimulate a much more than proportional increase in investment spending on plant and equipment.

sumption rises. But not for all of them. Some other determinants of the cyclical behavior of investment may be at least as important.

Shifting Cost-Price Relationships. **Early in the upswing, profit margins expand as selling prices rise faster than costs, but as the upswing continues this relationship reverses. Thus, shifting cost-price relationships first stimulate business investment, but later discourage it.**

When a revival is just beginning, businessmen can increase output and build new plants without incurring higher construction or unit operating costs—because there is still a lot of unemployed plant capacity and manpower in the economy. Costs stay low as demand and prices rise in the upswing; unemployment tends to hold wage rates down, and higher plant operating rates tend to reduce costs per unit of output in existing plants. Profit margins widen, increasing the marginal efficiency of capital and providing more funds to finance new investment.

But as the boom sweeps upward, excess capacity and unemployment vanish. Increasingly, both operating costs (for example, wages and materials) and the cost of money (interest rates) rise as demands for funds increase. Thus, the return on investment is often squeezed by rising costs as the boom progresses. Businessmen complain about the "profit squeeze," and about the shortage of profits to finance new plant and equipment.

Rising labor costs in prosperity also stimulate businessmen to invest in labor-saving equipment. This fact helps account for large business investments sometimes even when there is substantial excess manufacturing capacity. Such investment does not contradict the comments about the acceleration principle above; it merely indicates that there are many different factors that influence investment decisions.

Innovation and the Development of New Industries. **Historically, most big booms have centered around the development of a few important new industries.** For example, during the 1800s railroad building, with the resultant demand for iron and steel products, was especially important. The boom of the 1920s centered around the auto and electrical industries. Actually, the inventions underlying these industries had been made years before. It was the utilization of these inventions on a large scale through developmental investment that produced the booms they dominated. And when the investment opportunities surrounding these new industries were temporarily exploited, the central thrust of the boom was gone.

Was the development of new industries at those particular times induced by the revivals then beginning, or were the revivals created by new industries? Both. Whether such innovations actually set off a revival or not, they play an important role in most major booms. Once a few entrepreneurs have successfully braved the uncertain paths by introducing new products and new methods, others are eager to follow. With big new industries, booms are long and lusty. Without them, prosperities are weaker and growth slows down.

Inventory Investment and the Inventory Cycle. **Many business cycles are predominantly inventory cycles.** When inventories become scarce relative to rising sales, businessmen try to build inventories back up to desired levels. Businesses tend to overbuy in building them up, and thus overshoot what they consider desirable inventories. Trying to unload these excess inventories, they generally overshoot again, plummeting themselves into a position where inventories are short—and they're all ready to start up again.

When businesses are accumulating inventories, production is running ahead of consumption. Obviously this can go on only for so long; the day of reckoning must come. Conversely, when business inventories are declining, consumption is running ahead of production. Obviously this too can go on for only so long. Over the long pull inventories can be expected to rise roughly with the growth in total sales—perhaps 4 percent a year assuming no inflation. You can be pretty sure that inventory accumulation a lot faster than that won't last for long. And you can

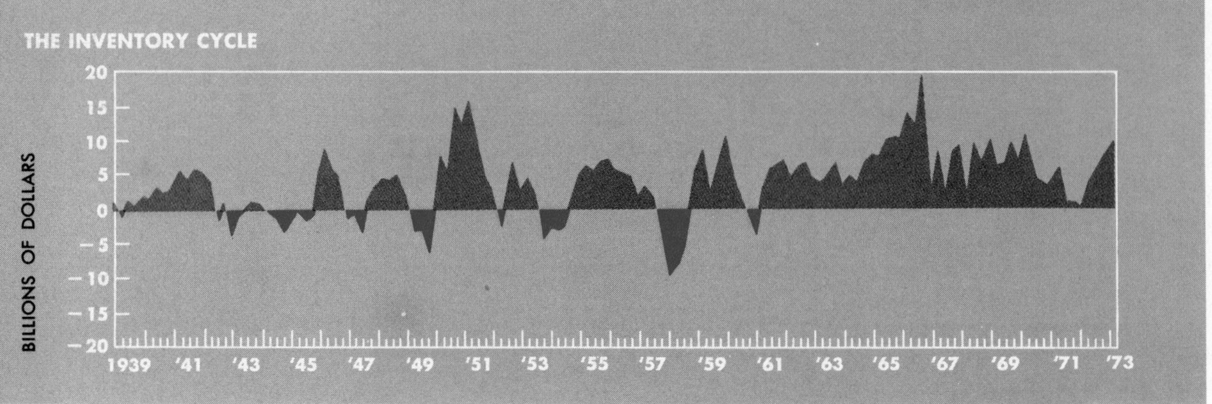

Figure 14–3

The inventory cycle shows large, sharp fluctuations in inventory investment, which are a major factor in many of the smaller swings in aggregate economic activity. (Source: U.S. Department of Commerce.)

be equally sure that if inventory falls far short of that rate, there's going to be an upswing in inventory investment.

Figure 14–3 shows the persistence and vigor of these inventory fluctuations. Note that the chart shows changes in *net* inventory investment, in accordance with the national income accounts. Thus, any figure above the zero line shows inventories building up; any figure below zero shows inventories being depleted. If you compare Figure 14–3 with the earlier data on total investment and GNP, you'll see that net inventory investment changes alone account for much of the recession drops of 1949, 1954, 1958, 1960, and 1970, and for the upswings in 1950, 1955, 1958, and 1961. If, as some argue, we are beginning to get major cyclical fluctuations under control, the inventory cycle may be our stickiest remaining cyclical problem.

Money in the Upswing

The cumulative upswing in production, employment, and income may be financed by the existing money supply for a while, as businesses and consumers draw on "idle" balances and V rises. But before long, new money is needed to finance the growing volume of business. Businesses need more working capital to expand operations and longer-term funds to finance new investment in plant and equipment. With higher incomes, consumers want to hold larger money balances. On all sides, the demand for money rises.

Will the rising demand for money be met by more M, or will it result in higher interest rates and a growing drag on the upswing process? The commercial banks, and behind them the government (through the Federal Reserve), are the only source of new money for the system as a whole, as we shall see in Chapter 16. Early in the upswing, as demands for loans increase and as better times lessen the apparent risks in lending, bankers are glad to expand loans. But as revival progresses and banks' excess reserves are used up, interest rates rise and bankers begin to "ration" their remaining credit to preferred borrowers. Unless the Federal Reserve provides more money for the system, credit stringency will gradually impose a ceiling on the upswing as businesses cannot borrow the money they need to expand.

The ceiling is not a firm one. As money tightens and interest rates rise, businesses and families increasingly economize on the money balances they hold. When working capital is scarce, corporate treasurers squeeze their idle cash down to the lowest possible levels. Households put their unneeded money to work in securities or other ways when interest rates offered on such investments rise. Thus V rises and partially offsets the credit ceiling imposed by a shortage of money. But there are limits on how small cash balances can be and still meet the needs of expanding businesses. Only provision of more money by the Federal Reserve can keep the boom going. **Every major upswing has been marked by a substantial increase in the volume of bank credit and money.**

UPPER TURNING POINTS: CAN PROSPERITY CONTINUE FOREVER?

Prosperity is wonderful. Why can't it go on forever? Maybe it can, and there are good reasons for believing our chances now are a lot better than ever before. But history warns us against too much optimism.

The cumulative upswing is many-sided and interacting. Early in the rise, everything seems to work together toward prosperity. But as the boom continues, the economic system becomes increasingly vulnerable to shocks that may precipitate a downturn, especially if the upswing is a rapid one. Inflationary booms in particular typically produce distorted patterns of activity that are difficult to maintain indefinitely.

What actually turns economic activity downward? Sometimes there is a spectacular financial crisis, as in 1907 and 1929. But economic change is complex, and often some phases of economic activity turn down while others are still moving strongly upward. Sometimes it is hard to say whether the economy is still moving up or has turned down; it depends on where you look.

So the experts are wary of predicting just what particular factor is likely to spark the downturn. Rather, a series of developments gradually set the stage for a downswing, and in such a setting it becomes increasingly likely that something will give the push that turns the economy down, even though we may not recognize it until months later.

The main limiting factors on the upswing appear to be:

1. Piling up of business inventories.
2. Accumulation of large stocks of new durables in consumers' hands.
3. Consumer resistance to rising prices.
4. End of the upward "acceleration" effect, and resulting slowdown in investment spending.[6]
5. Rising costs and profit squeeze.
6. Accumulation of new productive capacity.
7. Utilization of available new technological developments, and growing scarcity of promising large-scale investment outlets.
8. Exhaustion of excess bank reserves.
9. Weakening of confidence and expectations.

Sometimes a boom keeps going until it faces all these hurdles simultaneously. Sometimes the downturn comes when only two or three seem to present serious problems. Basically, the boom ends when the entire conjuncture gradually shifts over from favorable to unfavorable—when the driving forces of the upswing (especially spending on investment and consumer durables) give way to disappointed expectations in the face of increasingly saturated markets.

All this has left the government out of the picture. Yet increasingly, government action is a critical consideration in turning points. Government spending and tax policies and Federal Reserve monetary policy may be used to avoid the downturn and recession. Such government action is the focus of attention in the next five chapters. If we are to achieve stable high employment without inflation, it's clear we will often need positive government assistance to turn the trick.

[6]In the multiplier-accelerator model in Appendix B to this chapter, the accelerator alone is sufficient to generate upper and lower turning points in GNP.

"And so, extrapolating from the best figures available, we see that current trends, unless dramatically reversed, will inevitably lead to a situation in which the sky will fall." (*Drawing by Torenz; © 1972. The New Yorker Magazine, Inc.*)

THE DOWNSWING

A recession looks much like a boom in reverse. The multiplier and accelerator work downward instead of upward. Decreasing investment pulls out the support for a multiplied amount of income. Falling incomes mean falling consumption expenditures, which in turn reduce the incentive to invest. The upward spiral that made hearts glad seems diabolically designed as it races downward into depression.

Once a downswing gets under way, the path toward depression may be direct and cumulative. Businessmen, somewhat disappointed in sales and profits as prosperity levels off, are uneasy. Under such conditions, it takes only a downturn in expectations to undermine investment and production plans. Attempts to unload inventories and to obtain cash lead to the very price declines that sellers are trying to "beat" and to still worse expectations for the future. Banks call in their loans and the money stock declines or grows more slowly.

On the other hand, not all downturns turn into major depressions, just as not all recoveries soar into full-fledged booms. Since World War II, sustained consumer spending on nondurables and services has proved a massive block against a downward spiral. Business investment in plant and equipment has been more resistant to panic cutbacks than in earlier decades. Government spending now provides a big stable block of demand, and government tax and expenditure systems automatically lead to quick tax-liability reductions when incomes fall and to increased unemployment-compensation transfer payments. Private unemployment-insurance plans supplement this support. And the Federal Reserve has learned to keep the money stock growing to avoid financial collapse.

SOME SPECIAL FACTORS

The Role of the Stock Market

In spite of its prominent position in the public eye, the stock market has generally played a relatively minor role in business cycles. Rising security prices do help to speed the upswing, and a collapse of prices on the stock market may help set off or intensify a downswing. But usually these events bring more newspaper headlines than they justify on the basis of their importance in determining real output and employment.

The stock market has four main channels of impact. First, the biggest effect is probably psychological—a symbol of better or worse times for businessmen and the general public. Second, rising stock prices mean paper profits (increased wealth) for stockholders. With more wealth, at least on paper, stockholders may spend more out of their incomes or out of capital gains. Third, from the point of view of corporations higher stock prices mean a lower cost of capital for expansion. If a firm needs long-term funds, it can sell new stock at a higher price; that is, it can obtain new funds at a lower cost for the money obtained. Fourth, if rising stock prices have been heavily financed by borrowed money, a downturn in the market may precipitate a major collapse in stock prices as lenders call for cash, and may place serious financial pressure on banks and other lenders. A high market based on credit is thus far more vulnerable than a "cash" market, and is more likely to be a cyclically destabilizing force.

Stock prices have usually led cyclical movements in general business, though by no definite lead. As boom psychology spreads, speculative activity increases on the stock exchange. This was most spectacular in the boom of 1928–29, when speculative activity reached heights completely out of touch with the actual profit possibilities or the general level of business activity. Such a speculative boom carried within itself the seeds of its own destruction.[7]

Once the bubble was pricked in late 1929, security prices nosedived, pushed downward by calls of the New York bankers for repayment of loans that had financed most of the purchases. The result was a mass destruction of paper profits. The break in the market provided the psychological turning point of the boom—people found their airy dreams ruined, their financial security vanished, their confidence in permanent prosperity turned to utter uncertainty. Financial crisis has often characterized the upper turning point of the cycle. But with reforms in our financial system since the crash of 1929, financial crises seem likely to play a less prominent role in the future. For example, severe stock market breaks in 1962 and 1970 failed to trigger depressions.

[7]For a lively, popular account of the crash of 1929, see J.K. Galbraith, *The Great Crash* (Boston: Houghton Mifflin Company, 1955).

International Aspects of Business Fluctuations

One component of gross investment omitted above is net foreign investment. Current excess of exports over imports represents a net demand for U.S. output. It represents goods produced in this country that do not move into current U.S. consumption, just as inventories accumulated by domestic businesses are not currently consumed. Such a net export balance provides employment and incomes in the United States, just as does domestic investment; its multiplier effect is similar. The main difference is that with foreign investment the goods produced go abroad rather than being used domestically, and, as we shall see later, there are some special forces limiting the foreign-trade multiplier.

How important is the foreign-trade multiplier? Not very, most of the time. The U.S. net export surplus has seldom exceeded $5 billion, and sometimes there has been a deficit. Our foreign trade has seldom exceeded 5 percent of total GNP. But this is a far from trivial amount, and foreign trade is far more important for most other nations. In Brazil, for example, domestic income, jobs, and prices depend heavily on the international demand for coffee, lumber, and a few other main exports, and on the prices Brazil has to pay for her imports. We shall return to the whole problem of international interactions in detail in Part Six.

FLUCTUATIONS AND STABILIZATION POLICY

Can we have rapid, stable growth without booms and depressions in our basically private-enterprise, profit-motivated economy? Look back at Figure 14–1. History warns against overoptimism, unless we've learned how to turn the trick through government monetary and fiscal policy. Some economists think we have.

In principle, there's no reason investment has to come in surges that overbuild. But as long as we rely on the private-profit motive to induce investments, the likelihood is high that investments will cumulate when times are good and slump when times are bad—even though the long-term trend is strongly upward. Increasingly therefore, we have turned to government monetary and fiscal policy for help in offsetting big swings in private aggregate demand. If government stabilization policy can actually produce stable economic growth without depressions, unemployment, or inflation, the gain to mankind will be measured in hundreds of billions of dollars. The time has come to look in detail at the prospects and the problems of stabilization policy.

REVIEW

Concepts to Remember

This chapter reuses most of the important concepts introduced in Chapters 9–13. In addition to those, be sure you have a firm understanding of the following:

business cycle
boom
recession and depression
deviations from trend
accelerator
inventory cycle
innovation
cycle turning points
foreign-trade multiplier

For Analysis and Discussion

1. Explain how consumption and investment interact in an upswing, and also at upper turning points of business cycles.
2. What is the accelerator? What, if any, is its relationship to the multiplier?
3. Why do businesses often face a "profit squeeze" as full employment is reached in strong booms?
4. Why can't a boom go on forever? Or can it? If your answer is "yes," what change promises to make the future different from the past?
5. One group of business-cycle analysts argues that booms and depressions are caused by expansions and contractions in the quantity of money. Can you see any important weaknesses in this argument? If so, what are they?
6. "The bigger the boom, the bigger the bust." Is this often-heard statement true or false? Support your answer by a careful analysis of reasons why or why not.

7. The following factors are generally agreed to play important roles in cyclical upswings. Analyze how the force of each changes as national income rises from depression levels to prosperity, and how each gradually helps set the stage for the upper turning point:
   a. The banking system.
   b. The public's propensity to consume.
   c. Consumer and business price expectations.
   d. Induced investment (the acceleration effect).
   e. Cost-price relationships as they affect investment.
   f. Inventory levels.
   g. Consumer and business "psychology."
8. How many factors can you list that might reasonably be expected to provide a strong impetus to an upswing from a long, deep depression? Evaluate the likely force of each.
9. (*Based on the appendix*) Try forecasting GNP for next year, using the analytical framework provided by this chapter. (See the Business Roundup section of *Fortune* each January for an example.)

APPENDIX A

Economic Forecasting

All economic policy, public or private, involves making forecasts about the future. If the government is to help stabilize the economy, it must know whether next year promises unemployment or a boom. The businessman must forecast his sales for months ahead to plan purchases of materials, inventory levels, and sales quotas for his marketing department. He must forecast years ahead if he is to make his long-range plans soundly—when to expand plant and equipment, when the firm will need to obtain additional capital funds, what his needs will be for managers, engineers, and the like. And in most cases, the company's outlook is closely tied to the general level of business conditions. Thus, both the government and the businessman have to make economic forecasts, like it or not.

How Well Can We Forecast? How well can we forecast, using the models of the preceding chapters or other approaches as a foundation? First, no one can forecast **precisely** very far into the future, no matter how glibly he talks or how much he charges for his services. Second, real experts, using the latest tools and the mass of statistical data now available, can do a reasonably reliable job for perhaps six months to a year ahead for overall activity (say, GNP), but the reliability goes down rapidly as the distance into the future increases. Third, especially for longer-term forecasts it is realistic to recognize that ranges (say, a GNP between $200 and $210 billion higher for two years hence) are more reliable forecasts than those that pick a specific figure.

Short-Range Forecasting. Suppose you are a congressman, voting on a proposal to cut taxes. Or you are a businessman, manufacturing sewing machines and now facing production decisions on machines to be sold in the winter sales season six months hence. In each case, you'd face a similar forecasting problem. How could you go about it?

Maybe you'd want to spend your time reading the predictions of others—government economists, professional forecasting services, business magazines, academicians. But even if you rely on these, you need some criteria for judging among the conflicting predictions you're likely to find.

First, your economics should tell you that economic fluctuations are complex, ever changing phenomena, and that there is no foolproof way to predict aggregate business activity, even six months ahead. Beware of the man who has the surefire answer!

Inertia Models. Economics also suggests that there is a large amount of inertia in such a huge, diverse economy as ours. Allow for gradual growth, and disposable personal income (or any other of the major aggregates) is unlikely to be enormously different next autumn from this spring, unless some big special development is in the offing. So one simple type of short-run forecast, which has a higher batting average than many, is just to assume the next half year will be about the same as the past one, plus allowance for a 4 percent real growth trend, unless there is a strong reason to modify this prediction. Another "inertia" approach is to extend the rate of change of the present six months out a half year; this assumes that the present direction will continue at about the same rate. Neither of these is very elegant, and obviously they give only rough approximations. But each recognizes the basic fact of inertia for short-run forecasting, and they don't miss because of mistaken judgments of forecasters based on hunches, waves of hearsay, and the like, which are common in newspapers and magazines.

GNP Models. If you want a more careful, thorough forecast, most leading economists (in industry, government, and universities) now use the gross national product accounts as a framework, and try to estimate each major component separately. Then they fit the parts together to see whether they are consistent, and check for likely interactions that may have been missed in studying the individual parts. Chapter 8 provides the breakdown commonly used (though many forecasters look in considerably more detail); and Chapters 10–14 indicate most of the interrelationships among the major variables that forecasters typically work with.

For example, nearly everyone forecasts separately private investment, consumer expenditures, and government expenditures to get gross national product. Then they need separate estimates on government taxes and depreciation accounts to get to national income, and estimates of transfer payments and personal income taxes to get to disposable personal income.

How, for example, can we forecast that volatile item, business investment? For plant and equipment spending, we now have businessmen's own forecasts of their investment spending a year ahead, collected and published regularly by the U.S. Department of Commerce. These figures give a fairly good short-run bench mark. We can check them to see whether projected spending is way out of line with historical relationships to, say, consumer buying of final goods. We know that investment seldom booms when there is substantial unused capacity. And we know that businessmen typically underestimate their reactions to upturns or downturns in aggregate demand.

For investment in inventories, we also have the published plans of businessmen from time to time. But these forecasts have proved less reliable. We need to look at the ratio of inventories to sales in relation to historical standards, and to whether purchasers are facing full-capacity production conditions that may force them to wait for deliveries. We need to look at how fast businesses have been accumulating or using up inventories over the past year or two. Over the long pull, businesses won't continue to produce large inventories they don't sell. Nor will they be willing to deplete their inventories below what they consider sound business levels. On the average, we can expect that total inventories will grow at somewhere near the same rate as total sales in the economy.

To finish forecasting private investment, we'd need a separate analysis of home construction, of foreign investment, and so on in detail for all investment categories.

Similarly, we can estimate consumer spending from different sides, and thus cross check. The University of Michigan's Survey Research Center examines consumer buying attitudes and intentions quarterly and publishes the results. These give some clues. But consumer spending mainly depends on the disposable income consumers receive, plus the special factors noted in Chapter 11.

Then we need to look at the government—at tax and expenditure rates, at monetary policy expectations, at special government activities in any field that might affect economic activity. The federal budget calls for careful attention, because federal spending and tax receipts exercise such a big effect on the economy. Happily, the government publishes detailed estimates semiannually.

Put this analysis of the individual categories together in the national income accounts, cross check to see whether the individual estimates appear consistent with one another, and you should have a substantial improvement on the simpler inertia type of forecast we began with.[8]

[8]The "Business Roundup" in *Fortune* each January provides a simple example of this approach.

Econometric Models. The fastest growing modern forecasting method evolves out of the preceding one. It is the use of formal econometric models. It uses the same variables and relationships as those in the preceding paragraphs, but bases the relationships on statistical studies of past experience, and then obtains final estimates of the end variables (say, GNP) by using a computer to solve the set of equations in the econometric model, which, in essence, assumes that the statistically validated relationships of the past will hold in the future.

This approach is for the experts, even more than the preceding one. But the essentials are presented nontechnically in the appendix to Chapter 10 on econometric models. If you are seriously interested in how modern economists forecast, see the references there and in the following three chapters. Only hard empirical testing of the relationships among the key variables can give us a reliable basis for making forecasts in our complex economic system.

Leading Indicators. A last approach emphasizes leads and lags. The National Bureau of Economic Research has studied the behavior of hundreds of economic series in business fluctuations since the middle 1800s, and has found that some economic series usually lead others. Typically leading series include construction contracts, new orders for producers' durables, new business incorporations, length of the workweek in manufacturing, common stock prices, and business failures (inverted). No one alone is reliable, but if most or all of the so-called leading indicators are moving up or down together, this suggests that other parts of the economy will follow. Since most of the leading series exhibit irregular jags from month to month, it's often hard to separate out the false signals from the real ones they may be giving about turning points. For very short-range forecasts the leading indicators now provide valuable forecasting evidence, especially when interpreted by the experts. But don't be misled by the newspaper accounts; the leading indicators fall far short of providing a layman's guide to the future.[9]

It should be clear by now that short-run economic forecasting is a tough job. But substantial progress has been made in the last quarter century, both through improved methods and vastly more data. How close do the experts come? The President's Council of Economic Advisers produces the most widely used regular forecasts, at the beginning of each year. They are sophisticated experts, with the full statistical resources of the government to draw on, and they use a combination of methods, cross checking each against the other. By and large, in recent years they have done well, only once missing by more than $15 billion for the year ahead.

A miss of only $15 billion or so in a trillion dollar economy seems good to many observers. But $15 billion is a big percentage of a $100 billion annual change, and the Council is dissatisfied unless it comes closer. Some private forecasters do about as well, sometimes better, often worse.[10]

[9]The leading, coincident, and lagging series are now published monthly by the U.S. Department of Commerce in *Business Conditions Digest,* together with a substantial amount of related information.

Input–Output Models. Economists now have elaborate "input–output" models of the economy that show for past U.S. census years the interactions among the sales, materials, and labor utilization of hundreds of different industries. These interrelations are shown as matrices, listing the industries involved across the top and down the side of the matrix. One cell then shows, for example, how much steel the auto industry would buy from the steel industry to produce $1 million worth of autos. The relevant steel industry cell shows how much coal the steel industry would buy to produce that steel, and so on for thousands of other interlinkages in the economy.

While the statistical work involved in making such an input–output matrix is enormous, the principle is simple. If such matrices are accurate, they provide an unprecedented wealth of information on the ties among different industries. Moreover, if the relationships are reasonably stable over time, the effects of a billion dollars of new government spending on arms next year on all the affected industries in the country can readily be forecast from the matrix. The same is true for any other change in demand.

Note that the input–output matrix does nothing to help in forecasting the aggregates like GNP. But given a GNP forecast, it helps to spell out the implications of that forecast for individual industries. Input–output economics provides a path toward relating aggregate forecasts to forecasts for individual industries.

[10]The bookstores are full of books on forecasting, especially on forecasting the stock market. Measured scientifically by tests of what their success would have been had they been used in the past, many of them, alas, aren't much good. A recent basic text, with stress on modern quantitative and econometric approaches, is W. Butler, R. Kavesh, and R. Platt, eds., *Methods and Techniques of Business Forecasting* (Englewood Cliffs, N.J.: Prentice-Hall, Inc., 1974); see especially Part One.

How reliable are existing input–output matrices for individual industry forecasting? Experience suggests that they can be helpful, but that they're far from foolproof yet. The two main problems are (1) the accuracy of the relationships based on the census data, and (2) the question of how fixed these interindustry relationships are over time. The census data are available only infrequently, so the base information is always several years out of date. With rapid technological change and shifting economic relationships, it would be surprising if the interindustry relations did not shift substantially over a decade or so. But input–output, or interindustry, economics is one of the exciting new frontiers of economic forecasting.[11]

[11]For further information, see W. Leontief, "Structure of the American Economy," *The Scientific American,* April 1965.

APPENDIX B

A Formal Multiplier-Accelerator Model

This appendix presents a simple formal model to illustrate the types of dynamic interaction that may occur between the multiplier and the accelerator. It will be most interesting to those who like precise, theoretical reasoning, and especially to those who know some mathematics.

Suppose, in Table 14–1, that we begin with national income at 1,000. Now (say because there is a temporary war scare), businesses increase their investment rate by 100 in periods 1 and 2. The war scare then vanishes, and businessmen are prepared to drop their investment spending back to the original level. What will be the impact of this temporary surge of new investment?

Assume, for this example, that the marginal propensity to consume is .8 out of the income of the **preceding** period (perhaps a more reasonable assumption than that consumption is related to **current** income). Assume also that businessmen are led to make new investments in inventories, plant, and equipment when sales improve, and that such new induced, accelerator-type investment is just equal to the rise in consumption during the preceding time period.

On the basis of these **illustrative** assumptions, now trace through the dynamic results of this original surge of assumed autonomous business investment.

In Table 14–1, the 100 of new autonomous investment in period 1 becomes income to its recipients in that period, raising the period 1 total-income level to 1,100. The rise in income increases consumption in period 2 by 80, which is .8 of the new income in period 1. The burst of autonomous business investment continues in period 2, by assumption. Adding together the new investment and new consumption in period 2, we get new income 180 above the original level; this gives a total income of 1,180 for period 2. The higher income in period 2 in turn raises consumption in period 3; in addition, the preceding rise in consumption induces 80 of new business investment, raising total income to 1,224. And so the process goes.

This cumulative upward expansion arises out of the interacting multiplier and accelerator effects. Common sense tells us that if we increase the strength of either the multiplier or accelerator we will get a more rapid income expansion. If we weaken either, the rise in income will be slower. And these results can be checked readily by substituting a different propensity to consume or a different accelerator in the table.

This dynamic model provides a simple framework that may help you understand the cumulative upswing of the boom and the downswing of depression. But, once it's started, why does national income ever stop going up or down? Notice that income rises ever more slowly from period 1 through period 4. Since induced investment depends on the **change** in consumption, induced investment gradually falls and the acceleration effect gradually weakens, in spite of the continued upward multiplier effect of whatever new investment there is. By period 5, new investment has dropped off substantially and the drop in investment is enough to more than offset the continued rise in

TABLE 14–1
Dynamic Income-Expenditure Model

	TOTAL INCOME (1)	CHANGE FROM ORIGINAL LEVEL IN: INVESTMENT (2)	CONSUMPTION (3)	INCOME (4)
Original level	1,000			
Period 1	1,100	+100		+100
Period 2	1,180	+100	+ 80	+180
Period 3	1,224	+ 80	+144	+224
Period 4	1,243	+ 64	+179	+243
Period 5	1,229	+ 35	+194	+229
Period 6	1,198	+ 15	+183	+198
Period 7	1,147	− 11	+158	+147
↓	↓	↓	↓	↓

Assume: Original autonomous investment of 100 in periods 1 and 2 (in Col. 2).

Thereafter: To obtain change from original level: Consumption equals .8 of income during preceding period.
Investment equals the increase (+ or −) in consumption (that is, business sales) in preceding period over the next preceding period. For example, investment in period 3 is +80, because consumption was 80 higher in period 2 than in period 1.

Thus: Col. 1 equals 1,000 (original income) plus Col. 4 (change in income).
Col. 2 equals 100 in periods 1 and 2 (new assumed investment), and changes in Col. 3 in preceding period for all succeeding periods (since induced investment equals the preceding change in consumption).
Col. 3 equals .8 of Col. 4 during preceding period (since consumption is always .8 of the national income of the preceding period).
Col. 4 equals Col. 2 plus Col. 3 (since national income equals investment plus consumption).

The same model in equations (as explained in appendix to Chapter 10, on Econometric Models):

$$C_t = .8Y_{t-1}$$
$$I_t = C_{t-1} - C_{t-2}$$
$$Y_t = C_t + I_t$$

where C = consumption, I = investment, Y = income, and the subscript shows the time period. Thus $_t$ is any time period, $_{t-1}$ the preceding period, and so on.

consumption. Thus, total income falls slightly in period 5, and the expansion has passed its upper turning point. Moreover, once consumption begins to fall, investment becomes a negative figure (by our accelerator assumption). This sets off a negative multiplier effect, and the downswing is under way. Moreover, if you trace the process further, you'll see that it also reverses the downswing a few periods later.

If you think easily in mathematical terms, putting the model in the simple system of equations shown under Table 14–1 may be helpful. These are "difference equations," and the solution of the system mathematically gives the pattern of changes in income worked out arithmetically in Table 14–1.

This dynamic model gives some idea of the possible results of interacting multiplier and acceleration effects. But don't be too impressed with it. Changing the values of the accelerator and multiplier can substantially change the pattern you get for national income over a series of time periods. If you increase both—the multiplier to a very high marginal propensity to consume, and the accelerator to 3 or 4—you will find that national income "explodes" upward once anything starts it up. If you trace out the model given in Table 14–1 for about fifteen periods, you will find that income "damps" back down toward the original income level of 1,000. If you use lower values for the multiplier and accelerator, national income will return to the 1,000 level faster.

Moreover, if you make induced investment a function of the **level** of national income in the preceding period, rather than of the **change** in national income, you will get a still different pattern of interaction.[12]

Thus, the purpose of this simple dynamic model is not to show how business fluctuations really work. Rather, it is to show how simple mathematics can be used to analyze economic problems.

[12]For *constant* values of the multiplier and accelerator, an autonomous rise in investment to a new higher level will induce (a) an explosive, continued rise in income when both the multiplier and accelerator are large, (b) no cumulative upward process when either the multiplier or accelerator is zero, and (c) cyclical fluctuations around the new income level if one is weak and the other strong. In some cases under (c), the fluctuations will be damped—that is, they will gradually die out. In others, they may be constant or expanding in amplitude. For a precise statement of these cases, given different constant values for the multiplier and accelerator, see P. A. Samuelson, "Interactions between the Multiplier Analysis and the Principle of Acceleration," in *Readings in Business Cycle Theory* (New York: McGraw-Hill Book Company, 1944).

Fiscal Policy and the National Debt[1]

CHAPTER PREVIEW

CHAPTER FIFTEEN

We turn now to fiscal policy—what the government can do through its expenditures and taxes to maintain a stably growing economy without unemployment or inflation. All the Western democratic societies now take it for granted that when the economy gets off a prosperous growth path, the government should step in to help provide more income and jobs if the problem is depression, or to check rising prices if the problem is inflation. Indeed, Congress, in the Employment Act of 1946, declared that "it is the continuing responsibility of the federal government . . . to promote maximum employment, production, and purchasing power," and this statement has been the keystone of the government's economic policy ever since.

It is important to remember how new active fiscal policy is. Back in the pre-1930 days, government expenditures and taxes were only about 10 percent of the national income, and there was widespread agreement that little government was the best government. Almost no one questioned the wisdom of balancing the federal budget every year. Sometimes the government didn't manage to do it, but everyone was apologetic about the failure. But as the depression deepened in the 1930s, the federal government just couldn't balance the budget, try as both

[1]Some instructors may prefer to assign Chapter 34, which presents a summary of government taxes and expenditures, before Chapter 15, to provide further background for the discussion of fiscal policy. Monetary policy (Chapters 16 and 17) can equally well be assigned before fiscal policy by instructors who prefer that order.

Presidents Hoover and Roosevelt would. We had federal deficit financing because we couldn't avoid it. However, an increasing number of people, led by economist John Maynard Keynes, began to argue that government deficit spending was actually a good thing during depression. Modern fiscal policy was a child of the Great Depression only four decades ago. Little wonder that, as we shall see, we are still learning how to use it effectively!

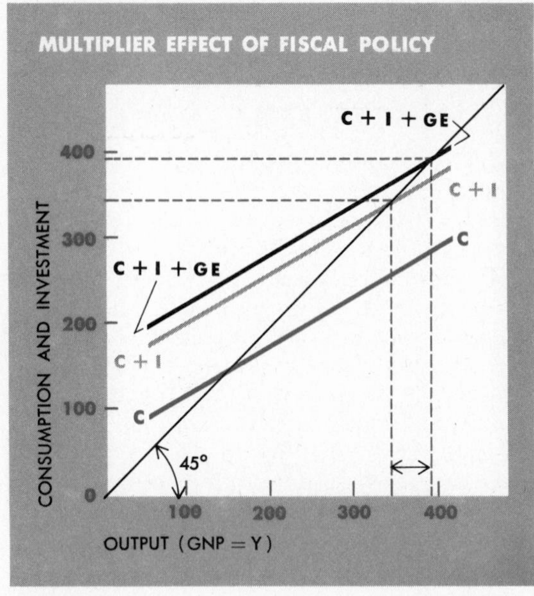

Figure 15–1

Net new government spending of 10 increases autonomous spending by 10 and, with a multiplier of 4, raises GNP by 40—up to a new equilibrium of 390.

THE THEORY OF FISCAL POLICY

The basic theory of fiscal policy was laid out in Chapter 10. In the short run, aggregate demand largely determines national production, incomes, and prices. Private spending on consumption and investment fluctuates substantially around a stable growth path, but government spending is also part of aggregate demand (GNP $= C + I + G$). To keep aggregate demand growing roughly along the economy's full-employment growth path, the government can increase or decrease its own spending, and influence private spending by raising or lowering taxes. Fundamentally, the government can increase total expenditures by spending more than it reduces private spending by collecting taxes. Conversely, the government can reduce GNP by taxing away more than it spends. Either way, the net change in autonomous spending triggers a multiplier effect.

This potential of fiscal policy was shown visually in the circular GNP flow diagram in Figure 8–2. The government may spend back into the income stream either more or less than it withdraws in taxes. A more complete and sophisticated theory of fiscal policy is shown in Figure 15–1, reproduced from Figure 10–5. Let the *CC* and $C + I$ lines be identical with the lines in Figure 10–4, back on page 127. Equilibrium income would then be 350, where $C + I$ cuts the 45° line. Now suppose the government enters the picture and begins to spend 10 each year without collecting any taxes. We can then draw a new government spending layer (*GE*) on top of the $C + I$ curve. This new $C + I + GE$ curve is 10 higher at every point. The new government spending is income to its recipients and has a multiplier effect just like private investment. If the marginal propensity to consume is .75, the new equilibrium level of GNP in Figure 15–1 will be 390, as the multiplier raises total income by four times the original government spending. The result is the same as if the 10 of new autonomous spending had been private investment or consumption spending.

To this basic theory of fiscal policy we must add four provisoes, which may be important in applying the theory in particular cases. First, remember that it is only *net* autonomous government spending that has a multiplier effect. If the new government spending reduces private investment (say because private investors are alarmed by the government deficit), this reduction of private spending must be subtracted from the government expenditure in calculating the stimulative effect. Second, the fiscal policy effect in Figure 15-1 assumes a supportive monetary policy that keeps interest rates stable. Unless the central bank increases the money stock, both rising incomes and government borrowing to finance the deficit will drive interest rates up, partially or completely offsetting the expansionary fiscal stimulus. Third, remember that expansionary fiscal policy increases money GNP; there is no guarantee that it will produce more jobs and output rather than inflation. Fourth, although government spending financed by increased taxes will normally produce a balanced budget multiplier as Chapter 10 suggests, this multiplier will normally not exceed 1. The major expansionary effect of new government spending is likely to depend on its being financed by a government deficit, preferably through new money creation so the government does not have to compete with private borrowers for available funds in credit markets (see the second point above).

AUTOMATIC FISCAL STABILIZERS

Although we normally think of fiscal policy as discretionary changes in taxes and government spending to stabilize the economy, some of the most powerful fiscal stabilizers work automatically, calling for no special action by either the president or Congress. There are two big built-in automatic fiscal stabilizers in the modern fiscal system, plus a variety of smaller ones.

1. **Automatic Changes in Tax Receipts.** If national income falls, unchanged tax rates (especially on personal and corporation income taxes) will bring lower tax receipts to the government. With present tax rates, each drop of $100 in national income reduces tax receipts by about $35. Thus, if Congress maintains government spending unchanged, falling tax receipts will automatically produce an expansionary budget deficit. Conversely, if national income rises, so will tax receipts, automatically damping the rising income. The government budget will automatically run a surplus, collecting more in taxes from the public than it spends.

Note that this built-in stabilizer works both ways. It automatically protects the economy against recession, but it also checks economic expansion, whether or not we have already reached full employment.

2. **Unemployment Compensation.** Since the Great Depression, we have developed a nationwide government unemployment insurance system, under which workers automatically draw unemployment benefits if they lose their jobs. Thus, government expenditures rise automatically when recession strikes and unemployment rises. When workers get jobs again, these benefits stop. Because the payments only go to unemployed workers, this automatic stabilizer is much less powerful than the economy-wide automatic changes in tax receipts noted above, but it does work automatically with no reliance on Congress or the administration to do the right thing at the right time. The special payroll taxes to finance unemployment benefits, incidentally, also work in a stabilizing way. Because they are a fixed percent of workers' wages, tax collections rise with increasing employment in good times and fall when unemployment strikes.

Figure 15-2 shows unemployment insurance at work as an automatic fiscal stabilizer. Benefit payments rise sharply in each recession (shown by the shaded vertical areas), while tax collections are much more stable, rising gradually in good times and falling in recessions. The system thus produces automatic deficit spending in each recession and a drag on the economy when it is moving up.[2]

A number of other special government pro-

[2]Unemployment insurance has some special weaknesses. For example, if unemployment rises through new additions to the labor force there is no automatic countercyclical effect because the new entrants have built up no claims for unemployment-insurance payments. Also, as we shall see in Chapter 18, unemployment benefits plus related tax advantages are big enough in many instances to reduce the cost of unemployment almost to zero and thereby lessen the inducement to look for another job promptly.

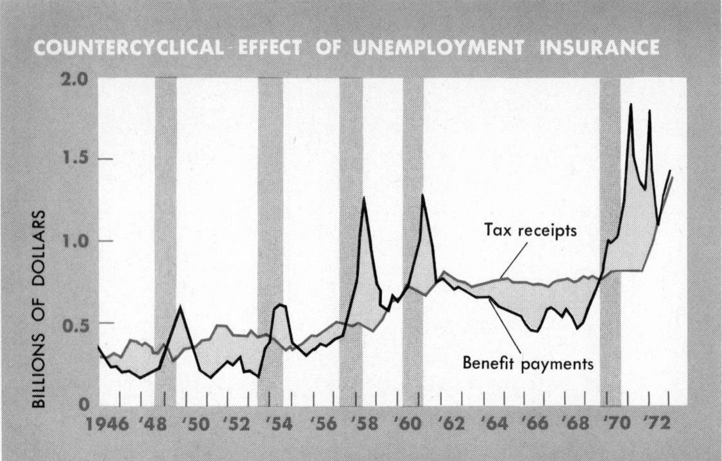

Figure 15–2

Unemployment insurance provides a strong, automatic countercyclical force. While payroll tax collections are fairly stable, benefit payments build up rapidly in recessions and fall rapidly as recovery develops. Data plotted quarterly. (Source: U.S. Department of Labor.)

grams work as built-in stabilizers. The farm aid program increases benefit payments to farmers when farm prices and incomes fall, and reduces them when the incomes and prices rise. "Welfare" and relief payments to poor families have an element of automatic countercyclical stabilization policy. So do other government expenditures that are automatically geared to increases and decreases of the recipients' incomes or prices.

Limitations of Built-in Fiscal Stabilizers. The automatic fiscal stabilizers provide a powerful first line of defense against major swings in the economy. Together, they now offset somewhere between a third and half of swings either way in national income. Against minor destabilizing forces, alone they may be enough to keep the economy near an even keel.

But against major destabilizing forces, there is no guarantee the automatic stabilizers will be enough to prevent a major depression or major inflation. To fight such disturbances, we clearly need to turn to discretionary policy—to congressional and administration policy decisions to vary tax and expenditure rates enough to slow or reverse unwanted swings in output, employment, and prices.

DISCRETIONARY FISCAL POLICY

When it wants to regulate aggregate demand, the government can change either its expenditures or tax rates. Remember that the expenditure multiplier is generally larger than the tax multiplier, but changes in tax rates have important offsetting advantages.

Public Works and Transfer Payments

Back in the 1930s, when discretionary fiscal policy was introduced, spending on public works seemed the sensible way to "prime the pump" of private spending, as the problem was first seen. Highways, parks, post offices, and the like were obviously useful in their own right, and they provided new jobs in their construction. Thus they not only gave us "something to show for our money," but also helped to maintain the morale, self-respect, and skills of otherwise unemployed workers.

But experience taught some bitter lessons. Many of the public works projects were ill-designed and wasteful (make-work jobs such as leaf-raking were prominent). More important, flexibility in public-works spending is hard to achieve. Bridges, apartment houses, highways, and the like are slow to get started—they need years of planning, blueprints, land acquisition, and so on before actual construction begins. And they are hard to stop promptly when the need is past; a bridge halfway across a river or a schoolhouse half built must be completed to avoid flagrant waste, even if recession has turned to a roaring boom. Because most recent business cycle recessions have lasted only a year or two, there is a good chance that public works planned to fight unemployment will start too late to do much good and will be carried out mainly in the boom phase of the cycle, though advance planning of a "shelf" of public works can help some.

A further objection to public works is that they may compete with private investment. This objection is advanced most strongly against low-cost housing projects, public power plants, and the like, which might have been built by private capital. But this objection can be met fairly easily. There is a wide range of available investment outlets, such as schools, highways, parks, and resource conservation, which is clearly noncompetitive with private investment.

Although public works per se are, in many people's eyes, a valuable use of society's resources, the problem of achieving countercyclical flexibility has turned many economists against them *for stabilization purposes.* Direct government transfer payments to the unemployed are generally easier to get started fast and to shut off when the need is past. Moreover, they are guaranteed to help the unemployed directly—rather than construction companies and already-employed workers, as public works projects often do.

The built-in unemployment insurance plans noted above provide a big block of countercyclical transfer payments, but transfer payments can be used on a discretionary basis as well. Special manpower training programs to help the unemployed have been popular in recent years, as well as food stamps, rent supplements, and other cash and in-kind grants to poor and unemployed people. The federal government has sometimes provided cash grants to the states to extend the periods for which unemployment benefits are provided when the regular state funds run out. Such discretionary transfer payments programs run into political problems too; they are sometimes slow to start and almost always hard to stop. But they are more flexible than public works.

Note that the transfer-payments multiplier will normally be smaller than that for government expenditures on goods and services. The latter directly increase GNP and jobs; transfer payments increase recipients' incomes, but don't raise GNP or provide jobs until the money is respent, and, of course, part of the transfer payments may be saved or used to pay off debts.

Changes in Tax Rates

Many economists favor change in tax rates over variations in spending on grounds of flexibility. Compared to public works, which may take years to get started, tax rates affect disposable income almost immediately once Congress acts. Most income taxes are withheld from wages and salaries each payroll period, usually every week or month, so the impact of tax changes is quick. Moreover, tax cuts leave households and businesses free to spend their new disposable income as they wish, in contrast to government control over resource allocation implied by increased government spending.

What are the drawbacks to relying on tax changes? First, the tax multiplier is smaller than the government expenditure multiplier. Second, if people see tax changes to fight inflation or recession as temporary and if the permanent income hypothesis is right, the public may primarily vary its saving rate rather than its consumption expenditure. This pretty clearly happened to some extent with the Johnson 10 percent income surtax in 1968, which was designed to check inflationary consumption spending. The saving rate dropped temporarily but there was little evident restraint on consumer spending. Third, those who generally favor a larger government budget are reluctant to see taxes cut to fight recessions, because they believe it will be difficult to get Congress to raise taxes again when prosperity returns with the need for increased public services.

Politics, Lags, and Fiscal Flexibility

Finetuning the economy for stable economic growth depends on accurate timing of fiscal policy: Knowing when to do what, and then doing it. For discretionary fiscal policy to work well, the administration must recognize promptly what fiscal policy is needed. Then Congress must act promptly to change expenditures or tax rates, whichever it chooses. Although there have been some cases of successful, prompt action (for example, the excise-tax cut of 1965), these have been the exception rather than the rule. The two big income tax bills of the 1960s were both based on modern fiscal theory. But it took nearly three years, first to convince President Kennedy and then to get the widely-applauded big tax cut of 1964 through Congress. The Johnson antiinflation surtax of 1968 was nearly as slow in coming. Variations in government expenditures to combat economic fluctuations have also lagged notoriously behind the apparent need for them.

Thus, the lag in using fiscal policy effectively is largely an "inside lag"—inside the government. Once the Administration and Congress act, the impact of tax or expenditure changes on income and expenditure is prompt. (By contrast, we shall see in Chapter 17, with monetary policy the problem is more an "outside lag"; the Federal Reserve can act promptly, but the effects of changes in *M* on income and employment are lagged and may spread out over a long period.)

Part of the fiscal policy problem lies in our hazy crystal ball about the future. Any honest economist will admit a lot of uncertainty about just what policy measure should be adopted and when. Economic forecasting, though improving rapidly, is still far short of complete reliability. And even when we're sure what lies ahead, we're not sure about the exact timing and size of the impact of different fiscal actions. But a lot of the problem is political, too. Both the administration and Congress have to be convinced of the need to change taxes and spending to fight the boom or recession, and then they must act. It's a slow total process, especially if the need is to damp an overheating boom. Prosperity is nice. And the prospect of being blamed for a depression strikes horror to the heart of any elected official.

The record in using fiscal policy for stabilization has thus been a mixed one. All too often, fiscal policy has been *destabilizing*. Fiscal policy, determined by a slow-moving, bickering Congress, is part of the stabilization problem as well as of its solution. It is important to remember that the ultimate fiscal authority lies with Congress, not with the president. The president proposes, but Congress disposes.

One way to reduce these lags would be for Congress to delegate limited power to the president to cut or raise tax rates temporarily in case of rising unemployment or inflation. Recent presidents have asked Congress for this power, to be exercised for a six-month period, subject to congressional veto at any time. But Congress has shown no interest in giving away its exclusive power to set tax rates.

The most fundamental reform would be to persuade Congress to consider stabilization budget proposals promptly as such, and not to let them get bogged down in the usual tax and expenditure legislation procedures. The typical tax bill is subject to long hearings before House and Senate committees, with enormous pressures from lobbies and special-interest groups, each understandably out to protect its own interests. On the expenditure side, appropriations are largely controlled by some twenty-five powerful subcommittees, each dominant over its section of the budget, and often controlled by a congressman of long seniority who rules his domain almost as a private fiefdom. Little wonder that prompt overall budget swings to offset economic instability have proved difficult to obtain!

Perhaps Congress might be persuaded to consider separately as a stabilization proposal annual presidential recommendations for a flat percentage surtax (positive, negative, or zero) on personal and corporate income taxes, avoiding the issues of relative burdens and "inequities." Or conceivably Congress might be persuaded to adopt at the beginning of each year a total expenditure ceiling based on stabilization grounds, within which individual spending decisions would have to fit. Dissatisfaction with present cumbersome congressional procedures that block effective stabilization policy is grow-

"Hold on to your hat! Here's where Nixon tightened the purse strings." (Drawing by Alan Dunn; © 1969. The New Yorker Magazine, Inc.)

ing, and change may come to facilitate more effective fiscal policy.[3]

DOES FISCAL POLICY WORK?

Some critics of modern fiscal policy argue that, however logical it all may sound, it just doesn't work, even aside from the political lags. They cite the 1930s, when there were large government deficits but massive unemployment continued; the 1954–64 decade, when the government ran persistent deficits but unemployment stayed above acceptable levels; and 1968, when the Johnson antiinflation surtax apparently had little effect on consumption. Advocates of modern fiscal policy counter these accusations, and further point with pride to the big tax cut of 1964, when the predicted stimulus to the economy worked out exactly according to plan. Who is right?

First, note the evidence. During the 1930s, unemployment rose to a peak of about thirteen

[3]For a more detailed analysis with recommendations for change, see G.L. Bach, *Making Monetary and Fiscal Policy* (Washington, D.C.: The Brookings Institution, 1971), Chaps. 7 and 8.

million people by 1933, over 25 percent of the total labor force. During the decade unemployment averaged over 18 percent of the total work force. The federal government ran a deficit in each year from 1931–40, averaging about $3 billion annually—although the government clearly tried to avoid deficits until the last three or four years of the decade. The unemployment rate fell rapidly only after 1939, when aggregate demand (and government deficits) rose with the onset of World War II. And more recently, the temporary 10 percent 1968 surtax on all personal and corporate income taxes mainly led consumers to reduce their savings to pay the temporary tax, rather than cutting back their spending as the inflationary boom surged on.

On the other hand, in the early 1960s President Kennedy's advisers urged a large tax cut to raise aggregate demand to fight persistent slack and unemployment in the economy—in spite of the already substantial federal deficit. The economists predicted that the $10 billion tax cut would raise GNP by $20–25 billion, through a combined multiplier-accelerator effect. And in fact almost exactly the result predicted by the economists occurred following the 1964 tax cut.

How shall we assess this evidence? Defenders of fiscal policy contend that the 1930s were not a fair test of their proposals. First, what deficits did occur were the result of haphazard, unplanned actions. Indeed, government expenditures were **cut** and tax rates **increased** during the first three years of the decade when the depression was spiraling downward. Moreover, state and local governments were actually running surpluses big enough to offset the complete federal deficits until the mid-1930s. Even during the latter part of the decade, when President Roosevelt and the New Dealers finally became convinced that deficit financing was a sensible thing, deficits were still small, only 2 or 3 percent of GNP. With such a massive unemployment problem, they understandably didn't eliminate unemployment.

Again in the 1950s and early 1960s, government deficits were not part of a planned attack on unemployment. Rather, they came about haltingly, as the result of haphazard governmental fiscal measures on both tax and expenditure sides. And the temporary surtax of 1968 was both too late to halt a roaring boom and limited in effectiveness because it was announced as temporary.

The Full-Employment Budget

But the main argument of the fiscal policy supporters is this—that government fiscal policy in the 1930s, 1950s, and early 1960s was **not** expansionary, in spite of the deficits. They argue that the deficits during these years were mainly the **involuntary** results of a depressed GNP that pulled tax receipts below government spending levels. Tax rates were too **high** in spite of the deficit. Each time GNP rose, rising tax receipts would have swung the budget to a surplus long before full employment was reached, given those tax rates.

To understand what really happened in those years, we need a new concept—the **"full-employment surplus."** This is the surplus (or deficit) that would have occurred with existing tax rates and government spending **if the economy had been operating at full employment.** Although actual federal deficits occurred in most of the years noted above, in all of them there was a large full-employment surplus. The federal budget on balance exerted a drag on the economy before it could reach full employment, because with existing tax rates receipts would have exceeded government spending before full employment was achieved.

In 1962, for example, the realized government deficit was $4 billion.[4] Yet, then-existing tax rates would have produced a federal budget **surplus** of $10 billion, had the economy been at full employment. That is, existing tax rates put a heavy "fiscal drag" on the upswing long before it reached full-employment levels.

Figure 15–3 shows this effect. The dark bars

[4]Data here and in Figure 15–3 for "actual" budgets are for the "national income and products account," rather than the "unified," budget.

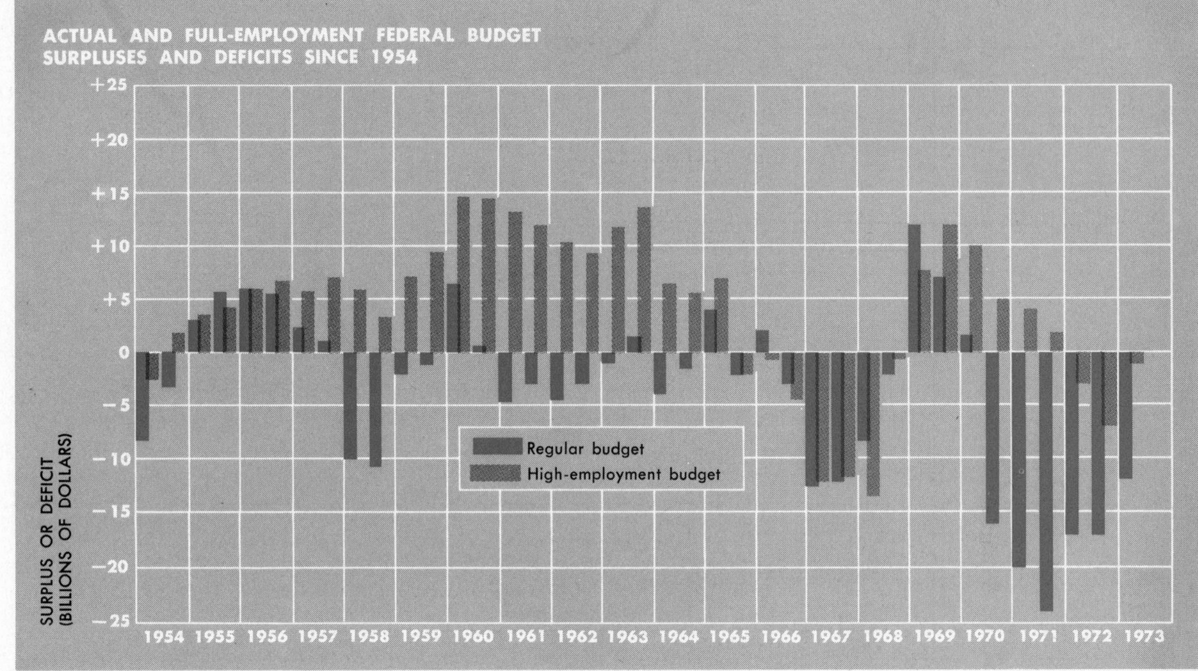

Figure 15–3

The "full-employment" and actual budgets give very different pictures of the impact of the budget on the economy. Most economists believe the former gives a better indication of the net fiscal stimulation or drag on the economy. Data are seasonally adjusted annual rates. (Source: Council of Economic Advisers.)

show the actual recorded federal deficits and surpluses over the last two decades—deficits for most years. The light bars show what the budget situation would have been had the economy been at full employment each year. In every year except 1966–68 and 1972, the federal budget would have shown a substantial surplus at full employment.[5]

It is important to recognize that the full-employment surplus is a more meaningful measure of government fiscal policy than is the actual reported surplus or deficit. But it is also important to see that a balanced full-employment budget is not necessarily desirable. If at full employment private investment would exceed private saving, then the ideal government full-employment surplus would be just large enough to offset the private-investment excess. Conversely, if at full employment private saving would exceed private investment, ideally the government full-employment budget should show an offsetting deficit.

Lastly, with both the actual and the full-employment surplus (or deficit), it is important to see that it is only changes in the level of the surplus that will induce changes in GNP. A large government surplus will mean a lower GNP, other things equal, than would a smaller surplus or a deficit. But if we want to *raise* aggregate demand, it is necessary to *increase* the government's deficit or *decrease* its surplus, and conversely to move the budget toward surplus if we want to lower GNP.

[5]Many economists now think of the federal budget as "neutral" when the full-employment surplus is zero.

THE "FISCAL DRAG" AND THE "FISCAL DIVIDEND"

Critics and advocates of modern fiscal policy alike agree on one major point: With our rapidly growing economy, if we keep any given level of government spending and set of tax rates, the federal budget will rapidly move toward surpluses as GNP increases. With a 4 percent annual increase in GNP (about our real growth potential), federal tax receipts rise by about $15 billion annually. Thus, a budget in balance one year will show a $15 billion surplus only a year later if federal spending stays unchanged. To avoid this "fiscal drag" resulting merely from the growth of the economy, we must cut federal tax receipts by $15 billion annually, increase federal expenditures by this amount, or some combination of the two. Actually, with inflation added to real growth, the fiscal drag over the years ahead will substantially exceed $15 billion annually.

Looked at another way, this fiscal drag can be seen as a huge "fiscal dividend" we can obtain by merely holding tax rates and government spending constant as the economy grows. Holding federal tax rates stable over the next decade would generate an annual surplus of over $100 billion by 1980, assuming continued growth, unchanged government spending, 4 percent unemployment, and no inflation. This potential surplus could finance a vast increase in federal spending on education, urban renewal, health, and the like. Alternatively, it would permit large tax cuts if we maintain an unchanged level of federal spending. But the fiscal-drag analysis above warns us that we will build up massive deflationary pressure over the decade if we neither cut tax rates nor increase federal spending, and the expected dividend will not materialize.

Actually, Congress' and successive administrations' spending plans seem to have already used up the anticipated fiscal dividend (wiped out the potential fiscal drag) for several years to come. They have already committed the government to large, growing expenditure programs, like social security, military pensions, and the like, that will use all the dividend at least until the last half of the decade.[6]

ALTERNATIVE BUDGET POLICIES

This reasoning suggests that government deficits and surpluses are powerful tools in fighting unemployment and inflation. Yet until the 1930s scarcely anyone questioned the proposition that the government's budget should be balanced every year. And today many people still believe a balanced budget is the best thing. Are they all wrong?

Annual Budget Balance

A balanced-budget policy is, in one sense, a "neutral" government policy. The government feeds back into the income stream just what it withdraws—no more and no less. Thus, a balanced budget seems appropriate when we are satisfied with the existing level of GNP—roughly, in periods of full employment without inflation.

But suppose recession appears. What does the annually-balanced-budget policy call for? With falling GNP and unchanged tax rates, the government's tax receipts will fall. A deficit will automatically be created unless offsetting steps are taken. To avoid the deficit, the annual-budget balancers say: Raise tax rates to get more money, or reduce spending. If you believe that the government ought to try to **expand** total spending in order to check the recession, the balanced-budget prescription is clearly wrong. To **reduce** tax rates and **increase** government spending would help raise the level of total spending, but the balanced-budget policy calls for exactly the opposite actions under recession conditions.

[6] See, for example, C. Schultze et al., *Setting National Priorities: The 1973 Budget* (Washington, D.C.: The Brookings Institution, 1973), Chap. 12, and corresponding volumes for later years.

Similarly, inflation would generate a budget surplus, calling for tax reductions and increased spending to avoid this surplus, under an annually-balanced-budget policy. Again, this clearly seems the wrong prescription for stabilization purposes. It would speed the inflation, rather than check it.

If an annually-balanced-budget fiscal policy is likely to give the wrong answer so often, why did it take so long to discover its weakness? There are probably two main answers: (1) a belief that budget deficits always lead to inflation; and (2) an analogy that if private individuals should balance their own budgets, the government should do likewise. You should be able to form your own judgment on (1) by now; government deficits do tend to raise aggregate demand, but whether this leads to inflation depends heavily on how near the economy is to full employment. On (2), we shall have more to say in the next section. For the moment, keep an open mind.

A Cyclically-Balanced Budget

The obvious difficulties of annual budget balancing led, during the 1930s, to the proposal that the budget should be balanced not annually but over the length of the business cycle. There seemed no great virtue in one year as an arbitrary accounting period. A cyclically-balanced budget would permit government fiscal policy to play a positive stabilizing role, running a deficit in depression and a counterbalancing surplus in the following boom—and at the same time maintain the basic character of a balanced budget.

But history suggests one major problem. What if the government runs a big deficit fighting a long, severe depression, and then the following boom turns out to be a weak affair that never gets up to full employment? Should the government then try to collect a large surplus to offset the preceding deficit, even though to do so would depress the economy again? The advocate of a cyclically-balanced-budget policy would presumably say "yes," but common sense rebels at the idea of a big government surplus when the problem is to get out of a recession.

If inflationary booms just offset depressions, a cyclically-balanced budget could work out precisely right. But if the two needs for fiscal policy turn out not to balance at all, the cyclically-balanced-budget philosophy exposes us to the same false prescriptions as annual budget balancing.

Functional Finance

"Functional finance" is the logical outcome of the new fiscal economics. The "functional finance" advocates say: Forget about balancing the budget as a separate goal. Use the government budget as needed to help provide full employment without inflation. If the private economy stagnates, more federal deficits than surpluses are appropriate: If the private economy is too buoyant, we need continued government surpluses. This approach is called "functional finance" because it views the federal budget functionally, as a means toward the goal of stable economic growth. If aggregate demand at present tax rates is too small to provide prosperity, to paraphrase Admiral Farragut, "Damn the deficits, full speed ahead!"

High-Employment Budget Balance Plus Built-in Flexibility

One last middle-of-the-road budget proposal is worth attention. It proposes that we should first determine federal spending (on nonstabilization grounds); then set tax rates to cover those expenditures at roughly full employment; and then, foregoing discretionary countercyclical fiscal policy, rely on built-in flexibility to keep the economy from swinging to either unemployment or inflation.

For example, suppose federal spending is set at $300 billion because that's the volume of public services we want the government to provide on the assumption we must pay for them through taxes. Then tax rates would be set to yield \$300 billion when GNP is at roughly full employment. With stable tax rates, tax yields would vary directly with any fluctuations in GNP. Stabilizing deficits and surpluses would automatically result from holding government expenditures constant. The plan would thus combine "built-in budgetary flexibility" with the basic virtue of making Congress face up to the need to balance expenditures with taxes—at full employment.

Proponents of this plan claim that they are facing political and economic realities that other approaches gloss over. The built-in flexibility plan would require no action on the part of Congress or the administration in forecasting business developments and in changing tax and expenditure policies to counter changing economic conditions. There would be no need to delegate congressional power over tax rates or spending to get quick action. Congress would need only to establish annually the basic level of government spending and set tax rates to cover those expenditures at high-level employment. The rest would be automatic; just don't try to change tax rates or expenditures to stabilize the economy, because, as a practical matter, you'll probably do as much harm as good.

But this plan has weaknesses too. First, there's no guarantee that the automatically created deficits and surpluses would be big enough to keep small swings from developing into big booms or depressions. Second, if the private economy is basically stagnant or overbuoyant, a federal full-employment budget balance won't compensate for this private under- or overspending. In those cases, the economy needs positive federal stimulus or response, not the federal neutrality of full-employment budget balance.

FISCAL POLICY AND THE PUBLIC DEBT

Much of the controversy over fiscal policy arises because people fear the rising public debt that comes with deficit financing. Since the 1920s, the public debt has risen to nearly \$500 billion. Should we view this debt with alarm? The answer is, not with as much alarm as most people have, but with some. The first step toward an objective assessment of the problem is to look at the facts.

The Facts about the Public Debt

Figure 15–4 shows the public debt (the heavy black line), and the debt as a percentage of the GNP (dashed blue line), since 1920. It is clear that much of our present \$500 billion federal debt came from World War II. It's also clear

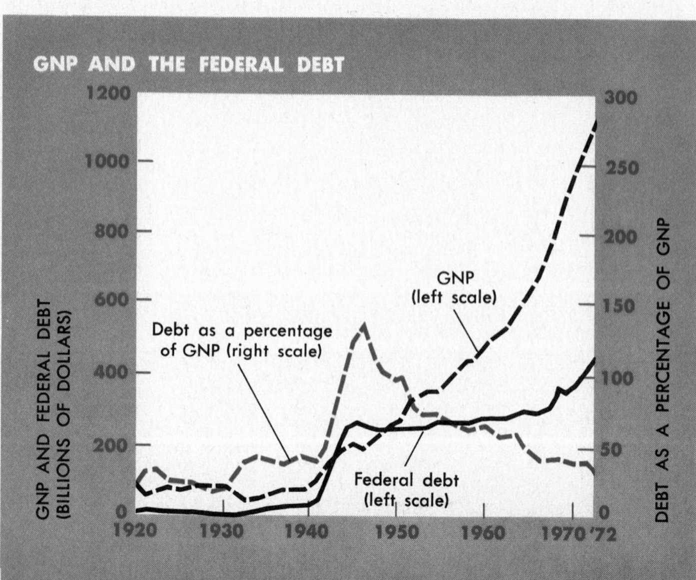

Figure 15–4

The federal debt has spurted upward in war periods, but has declined steadily relative to GNP since World War II. (Source: U.S. Treasury and Commerce Departments.)

that as a percentage of GNP the federal debt has steadily drifted downhill from a peak of about 130 percent at the end of World War II to below 40 percent now.[7]

Another useful way of looking at the federal debt is in terms of the interest charges it involves. Figure 15–5 shows annual interest payments on the federal debt since 1920, and again those payments as a percentage of GNP. Interest rates have risen persistently since World War II, and the annual interest payments on the debt have grown to $23 billion. This growth has roughly matched the steadily growing GNP, so that interest payments have run about 1.5–2 percent of GNP over most of the last decade.

It is also instructive to compare public and private debt. Figure 15–6 shows dramatically that private (corporate, household, and farm) debt accounts for most of the massive growth in total debt since 1929, and far exceeds the public debt in size. Of the private-debt increase, about half is corporate debt and the other half is debt of individuals and unincorporated businesses. The biggest single item is real-estate mortgages, which now exceed the federal debt. There's far more private than public debt to worry about.

Against these facts consider eight common objections to a large federal debt.

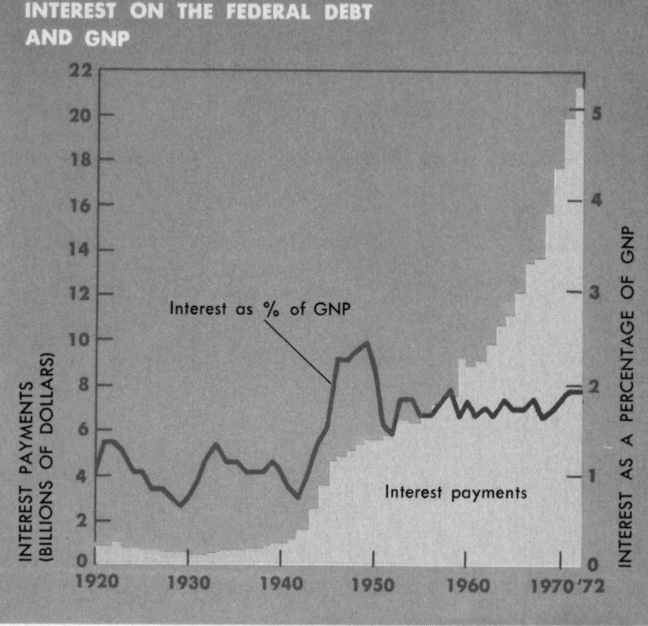

Figure 15–5

Annual interest on the federal debt now exceeds $20 billion, but it is less than 2 percent of GNP, and only a slightly higher percentage than during the 1920s. (Source: U.S. Treasury Department.)

Figure 15–6

Net public and private debt combined are now over $2 trillion, but private debt accounts for three-fourths of the total and nearly all the huge increase since World War II. (Source: U.S. Department of Commerce.)

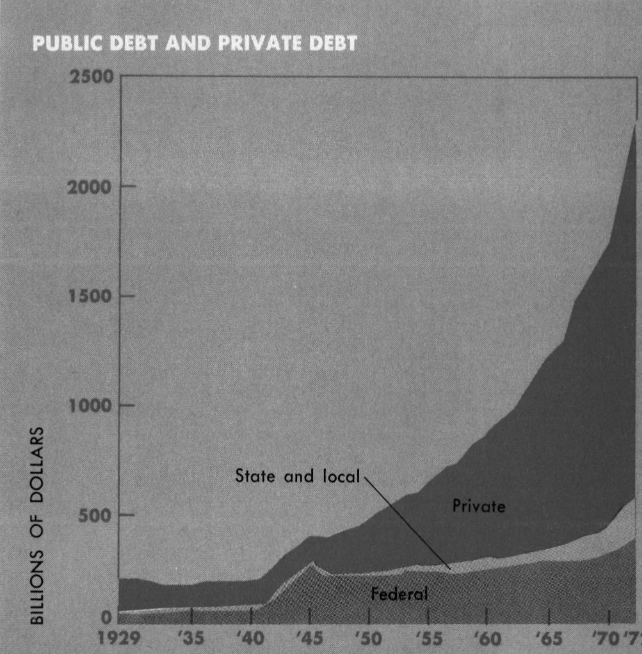

The Danger of Bankruptcy and Economic Collapse

May a big government debt bankrupt the government and lead to economic collapse? "Bankruptcy," as the word is generally used, means inability to pay one's debts when they are due. In this sense, the federal government can never go bankrupt, because it always has the power to tax, and the economic capacity of the entire economy to produce provides fundamental ability to pay taxes. Beyond this, the

[7]Over $125 billion of the national debt is held by the government's own trust funds (for example, in pension funds) and by the Federal Reserve. Thus, the national debt held by the public in 1973 was only about $375 billion, or about 29 percent of GNP.

federal government has the power to create money to service or repay the debt. It never needs to default.

But can a big public debt bankrupt "the economy"? Extremely unlikely, is the answer. Payment of interest and principal essentially involves a redistribution of income and assets within the economy, so long as the debt is domestically held, as ours is.[8] It is conceivable, of course, that the government debt might be so large as to lower drastically the credit standing of the government among investors. But U.S. government bonds are still the world's ultimate giltedged investment. Even with its huge debt, the government obtains funds in competitive markets at the lowest interest rates of any borrower. And whatever interest rate the government must pay to borrow, there is nothing involved that will "bankrupt the economy," whatever this vague term actually means.

In looking at the problems raised by a large government debt, most economists emphasize the need to look at the debt relative to current GNP. As the preceding section indicates, on this score the burden of the debt has steadily declined since World War II, while interest payments have remained a roughly constant percentage of GNP. If GNP grows at only 4 percent annually over the years ahead, the increase will be over $50 billion annually. Thus the public debt could increase by $20 billion a year and still merely maintain the present ratio of the debt to GNP.

Surely the dire predictions of economic collapse because of the public debt are overdone. But there are more worries to consider.

A Big Public Debt Must Cause Inflation

Closely related to the economic-collapse argument is the assertion that a big public debt must necessarily cause inflation, sooner or later.

A government deficit, other things equal, has an expansionary effect on aggregate demand because government spending adds more to the income stream then taxes subtract. But the result may or may not be inflation, depending largely on how near the economy is to full employment. In any case, it is important to recognize that any inflationary effect arises from the *current* expansion of total spending generated by the government's deficit spending, not from the existence of public debt per se.

But the "public debt causes inflation" claimants often argue that the larger debt will cause inflation sometime in the future, even if it doesn't now. This argument too is a dubious one. The expansionary pressure of the deficit occurs when the government spending occurs, as was indicated above. The mere existence of the resulting debt a decade later has little or no expansionary effect on total spending. Indeed, the transfer burden involved in interest charges may well be somewhat deflationary, because the transfer is generally from lower- to higher-income groups.

Is there no validity to the "inflation-in-the-future" fear? Another argument is advanced. The government, saddled with the public debt, will someday create new money to pay it off, and the newly created money will then create inflationary pressures. Obviously this second argument is difficult to rebut or support. How much weight you give it will depend heavily on your faith in governmental processes to produce responsible fiscal behavior. Certainly history shows that there need not be repudiation of a large debt through inflation, though some government debts have been eliminated this way.

It Just Passes the Burden on to Future Generations

Many people say that borrowing to pay our government bills just passes the cost on to future generations. But this concern is largely fallacious, as a little careful reasoning will show.

Suppose we are fighting a war. The real economic cost of war consists of the resources used up. If we use steel to produce jet engines and missiles, we can't use it for autos and refrigerators. A further real economic cost is the war-

[8] If the debt is held by foreigners, then payments on interest and principal involve actual costs to the domestic economy rather than merely a redistribution.

time disruption and destruction. However the war is financed—by taxation, by borrowing, or by just printing new money—these real costs are substantially the same. They are borne by the war generation. They cannot be passed on to future generations except insofar as wartime destruction may impoverish future generations because we pass on less real capital to them. If the new debt is accumulated through anti-depression deficits that succeed in putting unemployed resources to work, there is little real burden of any sort on the generation involved.

But may not borrowing impose a special burden on future generations,[9] even if it cannot remove the basic burden from the present generation? The answer is that payment of interest and principal by any future generation is just a transfer or redistribution of income within that generation. If the debt is paid off, the future generation is taxing itself to pay itself. If the debt is refunded, the result again is a redistributional one. Although the redistributional effects may be important, the crucial factors determining the economic well-being of the future generation are its accumulated real capital and its current real output. Having a money debt from earlier generations does not reduce either, and hence imposes no aggregate real burden on the future generation.[10]

There is one way that borrowing instead of taxing can pass a real burden on to future generations, even with an internal debt. This is on the assumption that people who buy bonds consider them as wealth, and base their lifetime consumption levels on the higher wealth they now hold. Thus, holding bonds from war financing, after the war the present generation would consume more than if it had been taxed, and would accumulate correspondingly less capital to be passed on to following generations. In this way, borrowing rather than taxing might burden future generations and lessen the real consumption given up by the present generation because of the war. Some economists believe this is the way people behave; many others are doubtful. In any event, the main real costs of government spending and use of resources are as indicated above.

[9]To simplify matters, a "future generation" is assumed to be one that does not overlap with the present generation. The basic reasoning is similar if the generations overlap, but the results are more complicated because then we need to consider the relative positions of working and retired people in the two generations.

[10]If the war generation borrows outside the United States, and the future generation has to pay foreign bondholders, then it may be justifiable to speak of a burden of payment being placed on the future generation in the United States.

The Transfer Burden of Interest Payments

Large annual interest costs on a big public debt may impose a real burden, even though these are only transfer payments within the economy—from one of our pockets to the other, considering the nation as a whole. The taxpayer and the interest receiver may be different people. To the individual taxpayer, higher taxes to finance interest payments on the debt seem a very real cost.

Heavy taxation tends to distort people's behavior. If the government takes a big chunk of each additional dollar earned, your incentive to work may diminish. Taxes on particular items raise their cost relative to other items and shift demand away from the taxed goods. Nobody knows just how important such distortions are, but they look substantial. And they surely increase as the tax share of the national income goes up.

Lastly, given our present tax system, taxing to pay interest on the debt tends to shift income from active earners to rentiers, and (to a smaller extent) from the poor to the rich. Taxing the workers and the poor to pay bondholders sounds unjust to many people.

Psychological Deterrents to Private Investment

Many writers allege that concern over the government debt deters private investment. Direct facts on the issue are hard to come by, but most evidence suggests that the danger is easy to overstress. Business investment depends far more on consumer demand relative to productive capacity and on expected profits than on the size of the public debt.

The business community and the general public adjust surprisingly quickly to changes in the economic environment. One of the writer's first memories of economics is the bitter controversy that raged during the 1930s over whether a public debt as huge as $50 billion could conceivably be borne without utterly destroying organized economic activity. No one seriously dreamed the debt would ever go so high—the argument concerned a hypothetical ultimate upper limit. By the 1940s, the debt of $50 billion was forgotten in the mad scramble for materials, labor, sales, and profits as government and private spending soared with the war. Soon the question, no longer an issue of burning interest, was: What about a $200 billion debt?—or $300 billion?

With the present national debt near $500 billion, per capita income at new highs each year, and the economy growing persistently, public concern over the debt is far less than it was a generation ago. Conservative financial circles still complain that the debt is too big. But there is little reason to believe that we will not adjust "psychologically" to further increases as we have in the past. The businessman who foregoes otherwise profitable investments because of the debt item on the Treasury daily statement is hard to find.

Debt Management and Monetary Policy

A big federal debt may increase the difficulty of using monetary policy effectively, as we shall see in the next chapters. This may be a serious problem, but it is not an insuperable one.

Encouragement of Government Waste

As a matter of practical politics, too easy reliance on borrowing invites easy spending. Experience has shown that when Congress doesn't feel obliged to raise taxes to pay the bills, waste and inefficiency are likely. This is a homely but important argument against too easy reliance on continued deficit financing.

How Big Can the Public Debt Be?

How big can the public debt be? There is no simple answer to this question. **The most important principle is that changes in the level of public debt—either increases or decreases—ordinarily exercise a much more direct effect on the level of current GNP than does any given level of existing debt.**

Current fiscal policy (which may increase or decrease the public debt) is thus generally more crucial than the level of existing debt. If our major aim is to maintain high-level output, the level of public debt becomes a residual effect of stabilizing fiscal policy. Paying off the debt, viewed in this fundamental fashion, is a secondary reason for running a budget surplus. Whether a budget deficit or surplus is desirable depends predominantly on whether a deflationary or expansionary effect on current GNP is needed. Once we have the public debt, its major effect has been felt. Similarly, the effect of paying off the debt will be largely through the impact of the current budget surplus. The national debt has played a much bigger role in the public's worries than is justified by the facts and careful analysis.

REVIEW

For Analysis and Discussion

1. You are asked to speak before a local voter's group on whether federal taxes should be increased, lowered, or left unchanged for the next year. Outline the talk you would give, indicating briefly how you would develop each of your major points.
2. If GNP is $50 billion short of a full-employment level and the public's marginal propensity to consume is .8, about how much additional government investment, financed by borrowing, would be necessary to raise GNP to a full-employment level? Explain, indicating clearly any assumptions you make.
3. "Since government officials can't forecast accurately what fiscal policy will be needed and when, we are better off to rely entirely on built-in fiscal stabilizers." Do you agree? Can you suggest any ways to increase Congress' flexibility in dealing with fiscal policy issues?
4. Does the "full-employment-budget surplus" analysis convince you that federal fiscal policy can work effectively, in spite of the coexistence of large deficits and unemployment in the past?
5. State carefully all the advantages and disadvantages you can think of in balancing the federal budget (a) weekly; (b) annually; (c) over the cycle; (d) over a fifty-year period; (e) only when business conditions are at the desired level, regardless of how often this occurs. Which alternative is best on the basis of your analysis?
6. Assume that international tensions require a $50 billion increase in military expenditures over the next two years. Would you recommend that the federal government raise the $50 billion by borrowing, or by increasing tax rates? Why? Does the balanced-budget multiplier affect your answer?
7. The National Association of Manufacturers has stated: "A government cannot continue indefinitely to run at a deficit without creating a serious inflationary trend." Do you agree or disagree with this statement? Why? To what extent does your answer depend on your expectation of persistent stagnation or inflationary pressures in the private sector?
8. You are asked to give an hour's talk before a businessman's club on the subject, "What Should We Do About Our National Debt?" Outline your talk, indicating briefly under each point how you would develop it. Bear in mind the backgrounds and opinions of the group in planning your talk.
9. Is public debt more dangerous than private debt, or vice versa? Why?

CASE 8

Are We Going Broke?

Reproduced here is the substance of a recent broadcast by a well-known TV commentator (name omitted to avoid prejudicing you for or against his argument). Is his analysis convincing? What should Congress and the Administration do about it?

"Today the Administration announced that before the end of this year the public debt will exceed $500 billion. That's half a trillion, in case you have trouble with how many zeros to add on big numbers. The Administration says this is nothing to worry about, that the economy's in good shape—prosperity, low unemployment, inflation under control, highest standard of living in our history.

"How long are we going to go on kidding ourselves this way? If you divide up half a trillion dollars of debt, that's about $10,000 of debt for every family in the United States, on top of what you already owe the local banker or moneylender. We're in debt up to our necks, and you know perfectly well what happens when you go on a binge by buying more on credit than you can afford to pay for. You feel great while you're enjoying the high life—but it's a painful time when the bill collector comes around. And he comes, never doubt. That's one of the sure things about life, like death and taxes!

"We're not living in the greatest era of prosperity known to mankind. We're living in one of the biggest counterfeit jobs the world has seen—living high by keeping one step ahead of the bill collector. Every time the debt comes due, borrow some more to pay it off plus a bigger and bigger interest burden. $10,000—some bag of stones to carry around on your back, if we're willing to face up to reality and admit that it's there."

Money and the Federal Reserve

CHAPTER SIXTEEN

The purpose of this chapter is to explain the operation of the American monetary and banking system, as a foundation for further analysis of the use of monetary policy to stabilize the economy.

Without financial intermediaries like banks and savings and loan associations to link savers and investors, the circular flow of income would stagnate. Without money, our complex exchange economy would grind to a halt. Think for a minute about what life would be like under a barter economy. Suppose you have a pig. But what you really want is a spool of thread, two new shirts, a movie, and a newspaper. You hear that *B* down the road has made some shirts. But unless *B* happens to want some pork chops, you're still out of luck. Your neighbor, *C*, wants a pig, but he has only lumber to trade. If you're lucky, you may be able to get lumber from *C* and swap that to *B* for shirts. But it's going to take some fancy haggling to work out a fair trade with such indivisible products, even if you all have a basic desire to swap. With money as a medium of exchange and as a standard unit for quoting exchange prices, it's easy to avoid this kind of difficulty. Money is a universally accepted unit of purchasing power, freely spendable, and easy to store if you want to postpone spending your income.

When you hear the word money, you think of coins and paper bills. But many other objects (oxen, wampum, beads) have served as money, and today we have largely substituted bank checks for currency. Computer entries will almost certainly be next.

A useful definition of money thus must be based on what money does, not on what it looks like. Actually, over 80 percent of all payments in the United States today are made by bank checks, less than 20 percent by currency (that is, coins and paper money). We have become so accustomed to using bank checks as money that for practical purposes payment by check is the equivalent of payment by currency, even though the check is a "credit" instrument that is good only if the bank will pay the sum indicated.

Money, therefore, is defined here as the total of currency and bank checking deposits, because these two constitute the nation's generally acceptable media of payment. The top part of Table 16–1 shows the amount of these two major types of money in existence in 1973.

TABLE 16–1
Money and Near-Monies in the United States[a]

		(IN BILLIONS)
Money		$261
Currency	$ 57	
Checking deposits	204	
Important near-monies		798
Savings deposits	313	
Savings and loan shares	297	
Liquid U.S. government securities	188	

[a] As of January 1, 1973. Currency shown is that held by the public outside banks. Only government securities redeemable on demand or due within one year are included.

Source: *Federal Reserve Bulletin.*

Only a thin line separates actual money from a variety of "near-monies," shown in the bottom half of the table, which are readily convertible into currency or checking deposits. Bank savings deposits, savings and loan shares, and U.S. government securities redeemable within a year are the most important of these near-monies. But there are many more that are only a little less-easily convertible, including a great mass of longer-term government bonds.

Any of these near-monies serves one function of money reasonably well—that of a store of value. In one way, they are better than money, for the holder receives interest on most near-monies and none on money itself. Balanced against this, the near-money must be converted into actual money before it can be spent. This always involves some inconvenience or delay, and sometimes a risk that the near-money can be converted only at a loss—for example, when government securities must be sold before maturity. The factors that induce people and businesses to shift back and forth between money and near-monies sometimes play an important role in determining aggregate demand.

PART A

PRIVATE FINANCIAL INSTITUTIONS AND THE MONEY SUPPLY

Many kinds of private financial institutions have developed over the years to meet people's changing needs. Some of these, such as savings and loan associations and insurance companies, receive long-term savings and channel them on into real investment in buildings, equipment, and the like. Others, such as the ordinary ("commercial") banks, serve as depositories for both currently-used funds and longer-term savings.

Banks

There are now about 14,000 "commercial" banks in the United States, which accept both "savings" (or time) accounts and "checking" (or demand) accounts. The presumption is that savings accounts represent funds put in the bank for relatively long periods of time, while checking deposits are funds that you may want to use promptly. Thus banks generally feel freer to make long-term loans when their savings deposits go up than when their checking accounts increase. Technically, the banks can require depositors to give thirty or sixty days' notice before withdrawing savings deposits, but they almost never do. Actually, the dividing line between savings and checking deposits is not very sharp once the funds have been deposited in the bank. **But there is one fundamental difference: Checking deposits are spendable money, since depositors can write checks on them. Depositors cannot write checks on savings deposits. A savings deposit can be spent only by withdrawing it in the form of hand-to-hand currency or by transferring it to a checking account.**

Other Financial Intermediaries

Financial middlemen have grown up to accommodate about every imaginable type of saver and borrower. Savings and loan associations are much like the savings departments of commercial banks; they draw mainly the savings of lower- and middle-income individuals, make loans mainly for home construction, and have grown enormously since World War II. Life insurance companies, consumer finance, and sales finance companies are other important intermediaries. So are federal, state, and local governments, though they're out of place in this section on private institutions. Whenever governments borrow from private savers to finance their expenditures, they're behaving much like private financial middlemen in linking savers with investment.

In everyday conversation, the term "investment" sometimes means *financial* investment—that is, the process of taking funds and "investing" them in stocks, bonds, or the like. Sometimes it also means "investing" in real assets, like houses, as when you buy a new or used house. Each usage is justified by the dictionary, but it is important to remember that in the national income accounts the term investment means *real* investment in *currently produced* capital goods—factories, machinery, housing, and the like. Thus, if you buy a government bond, this is often considered investment in the newspapers and everyday conversation, but it is not investment as the economist defines the term. In economics, if I use my savings to build a new house, that's real investment. But if I buy General Motors stock, that's only a financial transfer which passes my savings on to the man who sells me the stock, or to General Motors if it's new stock issue.

THE SUPPLY OF CURRENCY (GOVERNMENT-ISSUED MONEY)

Currency (government-issued coins and paper money) makes up only about one-fifth of our money supply, and it is used primarily to finance small transactions. As a practical matter, whenever you have a bank deposit account, you can readily get currency, merely by writing a check on your account. Indeed, this is the way currency is placed in the hands of the public. Although it is formally issued by the government (mainly the Federal Reserve Banks, to be explained presently), new currency is made available to the general public through providing it to the banks which in turn pay it out to depositors on demand. In essence, the Federal Reserve always stands ready to print up enough currency to permit the public to get currency in exchange for any deposits it has.

Thus, it is the public's demand for currency that determines how many coins are minted and how much paper money is printed. The Federal Reserve always prints enough paper money to give bank depositors all they want in exchange for their deposits. Once the public has deposits, it can obtain more currency at will. If for some reason the public has more currency than it wants to hold, it simply puts the currency back in the bank and receives a deposit in exchange.

People ordinarily keep about one-fifth of their total money holdings in the form of currency, and about four-fifths in demand deposits. Although this ratio varies from time to time, as a general rule the monetary authorities can predict that if households and businesses receive $100 of additional deposits, they will withdraw about $20 of it in the form of new currency.

THE SUPPLY OF BANK MONEY: CHECKING DEPOSITS

The great bulk of our money is created by the commercial banks in their day-to-day business of making loans and "investments."[1] The distinguishing feature of modern commercial banking is its ability, through making loans and investments, to "monetize" the debts of others, and thereby in effect to create demand deposits (checking accounts) which serve as money.

Thus, the commercial banks (that is, the banks we all know and deal with) in good times generally lend out more than customers have previously deposited. In bad times, they may insist on repayment of the same loans, wiping out the deposits created when the loans were made. Far from being a passive link in the savings-investment process, commercial banks may drastically affect the flow of funds from savers into real investment.

To understand this rather startling statement that commercial banks "create" checking deposits, you need to know something about how a commercial bank works. The easiest way to get this picture is to look at a simplified balance sheet of a bank, and then to trace through a few transactions. This will give you an understanding of the nature of deposits and how they get created.

The Bank's Balance Sheet

Banks, like other business institutions, keep a running financial record of what they own and what they owe to other people. What they own and what is owed to them are their assets. What they owe to other people are their liabilities. The difference between the two is the net worth of the business to its owners, its capital and surplus, just as with any other business.

A typical bank balance sheet looks like the one below, except that we have omitted a lot of minor items to make the essential categories stand out.

What this balance sheet says is that on June 30, 1974, the bank owned cash of $400,000, bonds valued at $800,000, and a building and

[1]When banks make "investments," these are financial investments in government bonds or other securities. Banks make very few direct *real* investments.

REPORT OF CONDITION

Local Bank and Trust Company

June 30, 1974

ASSETS		LIABILITIES AND NET WORTH	
Cash	$ 400,000	Demand deposits	$ 900,000
Bonds	800,000	Savings deposits	600,000
Loans outstanding	400,000	Capital and surplus	150,000
Building and fixtures	50,000		
	$1,650,000		$1,650,000

fixtures valued at $50,000. In addition, it had loaned out $400,000 to customers, who owed the money back to the bank. These are its assets.

Offsetting these assets, the bank had deposits of $1,500,000, partly demand and partly time deposits. These deposits are liabilities, because they are sums the bank promises to pay to the depositors on demand or on due notice. The difference between the assets and liabilities is $150,000, which is the estimated net worth of the bank, partly originally paid in by the stockholders as capital and partly surplus (undivided profits).

POTENTIAL CREATION OF CREDIT BY AN INDIVIDUAL BANK

If we make some highly simplified assumptions, the basic operations of the Local Bank are laid bare. Assume for the moment that: (1) the bank is on an isolated island where there are no other banks and no communications with other countries; (2) all payments on the island are made by bank check, and no currency is used by the public (the "cash" item on the balance sheet may, for example, be gold); and (3) there are no laws to control the volume of loans the bank can make.

Suppose now that you, a substantial businessman on the island, go to the banker and ask to borrow $1,000. Your credit is good, and he agrees to make the loan. What happens to the bank's balance sheet?

On the assets side "Loans Outstanding" go up $1,000, and on the liabilities side "Demand Deposits" go up the same amount. Remember that all payments are made by check, so you will simply take your loan as an addition to your checking deposit at the bank. Instead of giving you currency, the banker gives you a checking account. The balance sheet still balances, as it always must. But now there is $1,000 more spendable money (checking deposits) in existence merely as a result of the bank's making a loan to you. There is no change at all in the amount of "cash" in existence. The bank has taken your promise to pay (which could not serve as money) and has given you its promise to pay on the order of your check (which is widely acceptable money). It has "monetized" your debt.[2]

This result is shown readily by a simplified bank balance sheet (sometimes called a T-account), listing only the changes that take place in this transaction. It shows that loans increase $1,000 on the assets side and that deposits increase $1,000 on the liabilities side of the balance sheet.

ASSETS		LIABILITIES	
Loans	+$1,000	Deposits	+$1,000

Chances are you've borrowed the money because you want to spend it. What happens when you do spend it? Say you buy some machinery from John Jones and write him a check for $1,000. When Jones presents the check at the bank for payment, $1,000 is taken out of your account and put in his. Since all payments are made by check, he will not want any currency. The new $1,000 of checking deposits has been spent once and is now available for Jones to spend again.

A few days later, Jones buys a new roof for his house, and pays for it with the $1,000. Then the $1,000 is transferred again, from Jones's to the roofer's account. Now the $1,000 has financed $2,000 of transactions, and the money is as ready for spending again as if the bank had printed up a thousand one-dollar bills and lent them to you. Obviously the new deposit can be spent over and over as long as it is in existence.

In the meantime, what has been happening

[2] Banks ordinarily deduct interest on loans in advance. Thus the bank would give you perhaps $970 and keep the other $30 for interest; you would repay the full $1,000. This process of deducting interest in advance is called "discount" rather than charging "interest." Suppose for simplicity, however, that the bank gives you the full $1,000.

on the bank's balance sheet? Nothing. The $1,000 checking deposit has been moving from one account to another, but the overall totals on the balance sheet remain unchanged. The additional deposit created by the loan to you remains outstanding until the loan is paid off, and may be spent (transferred) any number of times in the meantime.

Some day your loan will come due. If you're a sound businessman, you will have built up your own checking account in preparation for the day by holding on to receipts you get from your customers. On the due date, you go in to see the banker and write him a check for $1,000 on your own account. He returns your promissory note to you, and the loan is paid off. But look at what this does to the bank's balance sheet.

Loans are down by $1,000, since the loan to you is paid off. And deposits are down by $1,000, since you have written a $1,000 check against your account payable to the bank, and this check is not transferred to any other depositor. Repayment of the loan just reverses the original entries that were made when you borrowed the money. The whole transaction has been perfectly businesslike. It has thousands of counterparts every day in the United States. Yet, in effect, the bank has acted like a little mint, monetizing your debt and creating the checking deposit it lends you, and wiping the deposit out when you repay the loan.

Look at the T-account now. Before you repay, it still shows the +$1,000 in loans and deposits from the initial loan. But now we add a −$1,000 for both deposits and loans. The balance sheet is back to its original position, but the economy had an extra $1,000 of money while the loan was outstanding.

ASSETS		LIABILITIES	
Loans	+$1,000 − 1,000	Deposits	+$1,000 − 1,000

How many other loans can the banker make simultaneously? Obviously, there is no reason why he has to stop with you. Because the public does all its business by check, and because there is no other bank on the island, he need not worry about currency withdrawals or loss of deposits to another bank. It is hard to see what will put a ceiling on the volume of loans the banker can extend. And he could just as well extend credit by buying bonds. Suppose that instead of lending $1,000 to you he buys a new $1,000 bond issued by the island government. The bank enters a $1,000 checking account for the government, which the government can spend when it pleases. The checking deposit is created in exactly the same way, and it stays in existence (however often it is spent) until the bank is repaid for the bond. Since the bank collects interest on every loan or investment made, this looks like a very good thing indeed for the banker and his stockholders.

But it all sounds a little like never-never land. You probably suspect there's a catch in it some place. If people could draw out currency, you say, the banker couldn't go around creating money like that just by writing down entries on his books. And you'd be right—partly right. We need to explore what happens when people can withdraw currency. But before you throw out this simplified example, remember that over 80 percent of all transactions in the United States today are made by bank check. The example is not far off on that score after all.

LIMITS TO CREDIT CREATION BY AN INDIVIDUAL BANK

Why don't banks keep on expanding their loans and earning more interest indefinitely, if all they have to do is create new checking accounts by making entries on their books? Now remove the simplifying assumptions of our island economy, one by one, to get a real-world situation like the one that exists in the United States today. But still assume there is no Federal Reserve to regulate the banks and to provide more currency;

the amount is fixed. Keep the other assumptions unchanged but assume now that the island's money-using habits are like those in the United States today. The people want to hold about a fifth of their total money supply in the form of currency, and the bank's "cash" account consists of currency.

Currency Withdrawals

Now the banker has to be more careful. His balance sheet shows $400,000 of cash (currency). If he is reasonably sure that the 4 to 1 ratio between deposits and currency wanted by the public will continue, he can calculate roughly how far he can safely go in extending new credit. Every time he adds $5 to his deposits the public will withdraw $1 of it in currency. Thus, he might be safe in expanding his deposits by nearly $2,000,000, of which he would expect to lose about $400,000 in currency, if he didn't mind seeing his cash account go down to almost zero.

Actually, the banker wouldn't want to run that close on his currency lest the bank be unable to meet unexpected depositors' demands and "go broke." Bankers are traditionally conservative people. Nevertheless, the basic relationship of currency to potential credit expansion is clear. Whenever there is a chance of a currency withdrawal, the bank must be sure it has enough currency to meet the requests of depositors.

What if people lose confidence in the bank and all want their money in currency right now? The answer is painfully clear. The depositors who demand the first $400,000 can be paid off, but the rest are out of luck. In a fractional-reserve banking system—that is, one where the total cash reserves are only a fraction of the system's deposits—the banks cannot pay off all their depositors in currency, for the simple reason that they don't have that much currency. This fact was faced with painful regularity during past financial crises and depressions in the United States up through the 1930s.

This situation reemphasizes the basic fact: Bank deposits largely represent credit extended through the making of loans and investments by banks, not the deposit of currency in banks. This is obviously true in the Local Bank, since it has only $400,000 in cash but deposits of $1,500,000. It is equally true in the United States today, where the total "cash" reserves of all commercial banks are about $100 billion and total deposits (demand plus savings) are over $500 billion.

Legal Reserve Requirements

Suppose now that the islanders get to worrying about whether their bank is sound (or maybe they hear about the way things are done in the United States), and pass a law requiring the bank to hold cash reserves equal to at least 20 percent of its deposits.

This legal requirement (like the one imposed by the Federal Reserve in the United States) puts a limit on the bank's expansion possibilities. With $400,000 of cash, the bank can have only $2,000,000 of deposits. It already has $1,500,000, so the limit of its new deposits (credit extension) is $500,000. The actual working limit is less, because the banker needs to worry about likely currency withdrawals as well as about the legal reserve requirement. **Thus, a legal cash-reserve requirement against deposits puts an upper limit on the amount of credit (deposits) the bank can extend, since new loans or investments mean new deposits.**

How many deposits can be supported on any given cash reserve depends on the level of the reserve requirement. With a 20 percent reserve requirement, the bank legally can have five times as many deposits as it has reserves. If the reserve requirement is 10 percent, deposits can be ten times reserves. The actual legal reserve requirement now averages about 15 percent for banks in the United States.[3]

[3]Only "cash" is counted in computing banks' legal reserves. Government securities and other assets may be nearly as liquid as cash, but they are not part of a bank's legal reserve.

The real function of bank reserve requirements is, thus, to limit the total volume of bank credit that can be extended. In other words, it is to limit the amount of money banks can create. Although bank reserve requirements do serve the purpose of protecting the security of customers' deposits to some extent, it should be clear by now that nothing short of 100 percent reserves would guarantee the continuous availability of cash for all depositors. With much smaller cash reserves, the thing that really keeps the banking system solvent is the confidence of the public in each other's checks. So long as nobody wants much more currency than usual, the banks get along fine. But if everyone tried to get currency for his deposits at the same time, the legal reserve requirement would be of only minor help in paying off the depositors.

When a bank has more cash reserves than the law requires, the excess is termed "*excess reserves*." Whenever a bank has excess reserves, it feels pressure to expand its loans and investments. Reserves earn no interest. Thus, the banker generally tries to keep his reserves at the lowest level that is consistent with his liquidity needs and the availability of safe loans and investments.

Adverse Clearing Balances

Now drop the last special assumption—that there is only one bank—and put the Local Bank in the United States. Here there are lots of other banks in operation, and the Local Bank needs to take this fact into account. If the bank makes loans to its customers, there is a good chance that they will write checks to people who do business elsewhere. And when this happens, Local Bank has to pay cash to the other bank. This is a most important change in the bank's position.

In a many-bank system, the most important limitation on the power of an individual bank to expand credit to the legal limit permitted by its reserves is the fear that it will lose reserves to other banks. If bank *A* has to pay cash to bank *B* when they settle up the checks written back and forth between their customers, we say that bank *A* has an "adverse clearing balance." And to bank *A* an adverse clearing balance is just like a currency drain—it takes away cash reserves.

Ordinarily, the checks written against any bank and the checks it has to collect against other banks roughly balance off. You send $500 to Philadelphia to pay a bill, and your neighbor gets a payment from Philadelphia. But if one bank expands its credit more rapidly than other banks do, it's likely to lose reserves on balance. Recognizing this fact, few bankers would make new loans and investments amounting to anything like $5,000 on $1,000 of excess reserves (assuming a 20 percent reserve requirement). Indeed, bankers ordinarily hesitate to extend new credit much beyond the excess reserves they have on hand.

To summarize what we have said so far about banks and the supply of money: (1) One function of financial institutions is to channel savings to borrowers. This activity has no direct effect on the volume of money. (2) Commercial banks are distinguished from other savings institutions in that they do not simply lend out the money that people have deposited. They actually "create" money by giving borrowers current spending power in exchange for future promises to repay the bank. (3) The power of an individual commercial bank to expand credit on its reserves is limited by (a) legal reserve requirements, (b) the dangers of currency withdrawals by customers, and (c) adverse clearing balances.

CREDIT CREATION AND CONTRACTION BY THE BANKING SYSTEM

Any one bank that expands loans when other banks are not expanding is checked by adverse clearing balances. But when we view the banking system as a whole, the limitation imposed by adverse clearing balances disappears. This is because the reserves one bank loses another gains. Since the banking system as a whole loses no reserves through adverse clearing balances, it can create deposits through lending up to the multiple permitted by the legal reserve-requirement ratio, just as could the island bank above. If, for example, the legal reserve requirement against deposits is 20 percent, the banking system can expand deposits up to five times its reserves.

Of course, the banking system faces limitations from the withdrawal of currency by depositors and from increases in reserve requirements, just as did the Local Bank above. For currency withdrawals reduce the volume of total reserves in the banking system. And higher legal reserve requirements reduce the multiple by which deposits can exceed reserves. But the apparent check of adverse clearing balances vanishes when we consider all banks together.[4]

It is easy to see that adverse clearing balances don't limit the expansion power of the banking system. But since individual banks normally do not lend much beyond their excess reserves, the banking system normally only gradually expands deposits to the legal limit on new reserves.[5]

The money-creation process works in reverse too. If one dollar of reserves is the basis for five dollars of outstanding bank deposits created by loans and investments, the loss of each dollar of reserves can force contraction of five dollars in deposits. Indeed, if banks are fully "loaned up" to their legal required-reserve limit, loss of reserves must cause a contraction of deposits, and hence of loans and investments. Such a contraction is brought about when banks reduce their loans or investments; remember the $1,000 reduction in deposits when your Local Bank loan was paid off above.

Sometimes, as with credit expansion, credit contraction snowballs in a massive way. In the Great Depression of the early 1930s, for example, nearly one-third of the nation's money supply (mainly demand deposits) was wiped out through the contraction of bank loans and investments. Banks lost reserves as the public withdrew currency in a scare wave, and this forced them to call for payment of loans and sell off their government bonds. Bank deposits plus currency fell from $46 billion to $30 billion between 1929 and 1933. Remember that each dollar of currency withdrawn removes the reserve base for several dollars of deposits and loans and investments.

[4]Because the Federal Reserve imposes higher legal reserve requirements against demand deposits than against savings deposits, the power of the banking system to expand credit depends to some extent on whether the public chooses to hold its deposits in demand or saving accounts.

[5]For doubters, the appendix to this chapter explains in detail how the banking system can expand deposits fivefold on new reserves, assuming a 20 percent reserve requirement, even though no individual bank ever lends out more than its excess reserves.

MONEY AND THE CREATION OF NEAR-MONIES

Only commercial banks can "create" money by monetizing others' debts because by law only banks can hold demand (checking) deposits. But savings deposits, savings and loan shares, and other near-monies are close substitutes for money as a store of purchasing power. And other financial institutions can "create" near-monies, as banks "create" demand deposits. Moreover, by shifting their savings between checking deposits and time deposits at banks and savings and loan associations, the public can change the amount of checking deposits and near-monies in existence.

Suppose John Doe, seeing an ad promising 6 percent interest at a savings and loan association, saves part of his paycheck and buys a $100 savings and loan share, which is much the same thing as putting a $100 savings deposit in the savings and loan association. Or he may just withdraw $100 from his own checking account and transfer it to the S. and L. Either way, he transfers $100 from a commercial-bank demand deposit to the savings and loan association. Demand deposits are down, S. and L. time deposits are up correspondingly. But the S. and L. association will probably soon redeposit the $100 in its own checking account at a commercial bank so that it can spend or lend the money itself.

Look now at the results: First, commercial bank reserves and demand deposits are unchanged in total; the S. and L. has returned John Doe's deposit to the commercial bank. But second, John has a fine $100 money substitute in his savings and loan account; this will presumably decrease the amount of actual money (currency and checking deposits) he needs at any given time to have an adequate margin of liquidity. It thus frees a bigger share of demand deposits for "active" use in making payments for goods and services. Third, the savings and loan association has $100, most of which it will now feel free to lend out to new borrowers. John's decision to substitute a near-money for actual money in his own financial position has both increased the nation's total supply of money plus near-monies, and increased the total lending power of all financial institutions, since the commercial banks have lost no reserves and the savings and loan association has gained $100 in additional lending power (less whatever part of the total it feels it must hold as a ready cash reserve).

Thus, we must add to the money-creating powers of the commercial banks a similar power of other financial intermediaries to "create" near-monies, as individuals and businesses transfer money holdings into near-monies. In total, therefore, the power of the financial system to generate money plus near-monies far exceeds its power to create money alone. Moreover, the money stock is, therefore, not entirely under the control of the government, although it is clear that by regulating the volume of reserves the government can generally control the volume of deposits that banks create.

In 1973 President Nixon, following the recommendations of a special commission, recommended that S. and L.s be given lending powers similar to banks', and that they be permitted to hold checking deposits. The proposals are far-reaching, and Congress will undoubtedly debate them at length before acting on them.

PART B
THE FEDERAL RESERVE SYSTEM AND THE MONEY SUPPLY

The Constitution gives to Congress the power to "coin money and regulate the value thereof." Congress has since delegated most of this power to the Federal Reserve system, which was established in 1914 after years of painful experience with repeated financial crises. The following pages first describe the Federal Reserve system and indicate briefly how it carries out its day-to-day activities. Then we analyze more fully how the Federal Reserve influences interest rates and the supply of money, the "Fed's" main channels for regulating the level of aggregate demand.

THE FEDERAL RESERVE SYSTEM

The Federal Reserve is the major agency established by Congress to provide currency for the nation; to furnish a wide variety of financial services to the government and to the economy; and, most important, to regulate the total amount of money and to maintain "monetary and credit conditions favorable to sound business activity in all fields—agricultural, industrial, commercial."[6]

Organization and Service Functions

The Federal Reserve system is made up of the following:

1. The Board of Governors.

[6] *The Federal Reserve System: Its Purposes and Functions* (Board of Governors of the Federal Reserve System), p. 23. This booklet provides an authoritative statement of the aims and operations of the Federal Reserve System.

2. The twelve Federal Reserve banks.
3. The Federal Open Market Committee.
4. The member banks.

1. The Board of Governors is composed of seven members, appointed by the president and confirmed by the Senate. Members are appointed for fourteen years. One term expires every two years, an effort to safeguard the board as far as possible from political pressure groups. In most matters, the Board of Governors is ultimately responsible for the major policies of the twelve Federal Reserve banks; and, since the Federal Reserve banks in turn supervise and regulate the member banks, ultimate responsibility for the entire system is largely centralized in the Board.

2. Each of the twelve Federal Reserve banks serves a certain district in the United States. The banks are located in Boston, New York, Philadelphia, Cleveland, Richmond, Atlanta, Chicago, St. Louis, Minneapolis, Kansas City, Dallas, and San Francisco. Each Federal Reserve bank was founded by the sale of stock to member banks, which are required to buy stock. Though technically they are thus privately owned, the Federal Reserve banks are operated in the public interest, not for profit.

3. The Federal Open Market Committee consists of the seven members of the Board of Governors, plus five of the presidents of the Federal Reserve banks. This twelve-member committee determines the system's policy on open-market operations—that is, the purchase and sale of government securities in the open market. These operations, explained below, are the primary means by which the Federal Reserve authorities attempt to control the volume of bank credit. Although the Board of Governors does not determine open-market policy independently, its seven members constitute a majority of the Open Market Committee.

4. The member banks include all national banks (chartered by the federal government) in the United States and those state banks that agree to conform to the requirements set up for member banks. In 1973, about 5,700 of the 14,000 commercial banks in the United States were member banks, but the nonmember banks were almost all small ones, holding only about 10 percent of the total deposits of the banking system.

In addition to its major policy functions, the Fed has important, though routine, service functions.

Holding Member-Bank Reserves. Each member bank must by law keep its legally required reserves on deposit at its Federal Reserve bank.[7] These reserve balances at the Reserve banks are essentially checking accounts that the member banks maintain with the Federal Reserve, just as an individual has a checking account with a commercial bank. A member bank must always keep the reserve required by law, but beyond this requirement it is free to draw on, or add to, its reserve account as it wishes.

Furnishing Currency for Circulation. All currency in the United States is issued either by the Treasury or by the Federal Reserve banks. Treasury currency—mainly coins—makes up about 10 percent of the total. The Reserve banks themselves issue our paper money, Federal Reserve notes. These are liabilities of the issuing Federal Reserve bank, and also of the federal government. Each Federal Reserve note must be fully backed by collateral—gold, government bonds, or other designated acceptable security—but in essence the Fed has virtually unlimited power to issue new Federal Reserve notes.

Currency in circulation grows gradually as the economy grows, and increases temporarily at certain periods of the year, such as Christmas and the Fourth of July, when people and businesses want more hand-to-hand money. The banks get currency by drawing on their reserve accounts at the Reserve banks and pay out the currency to customers who make withdrawals from their deposit accounts. If the public has more currency than it wants, it simply redeposits

[7]Except for the "vault cash" (currency), which it keeps in its own vaults.

the currency in commercial banks, which in turn redeposit the excess in their reserve accounts at the Federal Reserve banks.

Clearing and Collecting Checks. Most payments in the United States are made by means of bank checks. And most bank checks drawn on out-of-town banks are "cleared" through the Federal Reserve system to avoid shipping currency. Suppose Jones in Chicago sells a $100 bill of goods to Smith in Detroit, and Smith pays by a check on his Detroit bank. Jones deposits the check at his bank in Chicago. Since both banks keep their reserves with the Chicago Federal Reserve bank, the check is cleared simply by increasing the reserve account of the Chicago bank and decreasing the account of the Detroit bank. No currency has to be shipped around the country. When Jones and Smith are in different Federal Reserve districts (say Chicago and New York), the process is identical except that the New York and Chicago Federal Reserve banks must settle their accounts. They offset the checks due to each other through an "Interdistrict Settlement Fund."

To give some idea of the magnitude of this clearing function, in 1972 the Federal Reserve system handled nine billion checks. Total payments by check were $17 trillion.

Supervising Member Banks. Banks in this country are supervised by several authorities. The Federal Reserve supervises all member banks. Its examiners make detailed reports on the management, the loans and investments, and the general condition of each member bank. If any member bank refuses to conform to the standards of sound banking practice specified by the Federal Reserve, the Board of Governors may remove its officers and directors or take away its right to make use of Federal Reserve credit facilities. However, these sanctions are seldom used.

Fiscal Agent for the Federal Government. The Federal Reserve banks are bankers for the federal government. They carry most of the government's checking accounts, handle the issue and redemption of government securities, and act as fiscal agent for the government in numerous other ways. These activities are a major part of the Federal Reserve's operating responsibilities.

THE FEDERAL RESERVE, INTEREST RATES, AND THE SUPPLY OF MONEY

In the United States, the Federal Reserve is the "central bank." Its major job is to maintain monetary conditions that will help achieve a stably growing, prosperous economy.

Federal Reserve control over the supply of money and interest rates is exercised largely by controlling the volume and use of member-bank reserves. Without excess reserves, commercial banks cannot extend more credit. Excess reserves make possible (but do not assure) expansion of bank earning assets and deposits. Thus, Federal Reserve powers are designed largely to provide or reduce excess reserves.

The Fundamental Nature of Central Banking

A Federal Reserve bank is a central bank —a banker's bank. Member-bank reserves are member-bank deposits at the Reserve banks. Thus, Federal Reserve control over the volume of member-bank reserves is, in fact, control over the volume of its own deposits. And the Fed can create or destroy the reserves that underlie commercial banks' powers to lend and invest.

Before the establishment of the Federal Reserve as a central bank in 1914, the nation's commercial banks faced periodic crises. Mass currency withdrawals by depositors in times of panic exhausted reserves and forced widespread bank failures, because there was no way to convert good but illiquid loans into currency on short notice. The Federal Reserve was established largely to remedy this situation. The Reserve authorities were given power to provide new reserves for member banks in times of need.

The ability to create new bank reserves and

to provide liquidity to commercial-bank assets is the distinguishing feature of a true central bank. The Federal Reserve can create new reserves (member-bank deposits) by buying bonds or making loans to member banks, just as member banks create deposits by buying bonds or making loans to businesses and individuals. It gives deposits (new reserves) to member banks in exchange for bonds or the banks' promises to repay at a later date. Thus, if a member bank wants more reserves (that is, deposits at the Fed), it can borrow at the Fed, giving its own promise to repay. Or it can sell some of its government bonds to the Fed, receiving reserves (deposits at the Fed) in payment. In either case, the Fed "creates" the new reserves by giving the member bank a new deposit (reserve) in exchange for the assets it receives from the member bank.

The Fed authorities attempt to control the volume and direction of commercial-bank lending and investing, and hence the volume of bank deposits, through the following seven major channels. The first three (open-market operations, reserve requirements, and the rediscount rate) are aimed largely at controlling the total supply of credit and deposits, through regulating the commercial banks' excess reserves. The others are aimed more at controlling the flow of credit to particular uses, such as speculation. These latter are thus called "selective," or "qualitative," credit controls. In regulating the supply of credit, the Fed also influences interest rates—the "cost" of credit.

Open-Market Operations

Purchase and sale of U.S. government securities in the open market is the major device used by the Fed to control the volume of member-bank reserves. By buying "Governments," the Fed increases member-bank reserves; by selling Governments, it reduces member-bank reserves. To understand how this works, consider first the combined balance sheet of the Federal Reserve banks, shown at the bottom of this page.

This shows the two big assets of the Federal Reserve banks, gold and government securities. The offsetting major liabilities are member-bank deposits and Federal Reserve notes. It is essential to remember that the "cash reserves" shown on commercial-bank statements are mainly not actual currency but are instead deposits held at the Federal Reserve banks.

1. The Federal Reserve can create new reserves for the commercial banks by buying government bonds in the open market—thereby stimulating the commercial banks to make new loans and investments. If the Fed wants to encourage more bank loans, it buys $1,000 worth of U.S. government bonds, say from a commercial bank.[8] To pay for these bonds, it simply gives the bank a $1,000 deposit credit (new reserve balance) at the Federal Reserve. The commercial bank has $1,000 of new

[8] Remember that the Fed does not issue any bonds itself, but merely buys and sells government bonds that have been issued previously by the Treasury.

Federal Reserve Banks
January 1, 1973
(IN BILLIONS)

Assets		Liabilities	
Gold	$10	Member-bank deposits	$22
U.S. securities	68	Federal Reserve notes	59
	$78[a]		$81[a]

[a] Does not balance because other items are omitted.

reserves, and they are all excess reserves, since its deposits have not been changed by the transaction. The Federal Reserve has created a $1,000 member-bank deposit (reserve account) against the government bond. Because the commercial banks now have $1,000 of new excess reserves, they are in a position to expand their loans by four or five times that amount, depending on legal reserve requirements.[9]

Consider the T-accounts for the commercial and the Federal Reserve bank. They show the $1,000 addition to excess reserves on the books of both the Fed and the commercial bank.

Commercial Bank	
Cash +$1,000 Bonds − 1,000	

Federal Reserve Bank	
Bonds +$1,000	Member-bank deposits +$1,000

Does all this seem a little like black magic—new commercial-bank reserves created out of nowhere by the Federal Reserve banks, reserves which in turn can provide the basis for a much larger amount of commercial-bank deposits, also created out of nowhere? In a sense, it is. But each dollar of new member-bank reserves at the Fed is matched by a newly acquired government bond, and each new deposit at the commercial bank will be matched by a borrower's promise to repay. There is no magic. But through this process the Fed is able to "create" new member-bank reserves, which are often called "high-powered money," because they can in turn serve as the reserves behind a larger volume of newly-created deposits at commercial banks.

Is there a limitation on how many new reserves the Federal Reserve can create in this way? No direct limit. Until 1968 the Fed was required to have a specified gold reserve against member-bank deposits and Federal Reserve notes respectively, but now there is no such requirement. Fundamentally, the reserve-creating powers of the Fed are now limited only by the good judgment of the Federal Reserve authorities, and by the discretion of Congress, which can repeal or alter the Fed's powers anytime it wishes. Thus, control over the nation's money supply is ultimately subject to the control of the democratic process, just as are other government powers.[10]

How effective is the Federal Reserve in lowering interest rates and stimulating new commercial-bank loans when it provides new reserves? More reserves push a banker to extend new credit, for no banker likes to lose the interest he might earn on idle reserves. In those rare cases where excess reserves are already large because bankers don't see any "sound" borrowers looking for loans, still more excess reserves may not help much. But banks can also increase the volume of deposits by buying up government bonds. Bankers do vary the amount of excess reserves they wish to hold under different circumstances, but with rare exceptions commercial bankers have increased their loans and investments about as far as their excess reserves permit. The big exception was the depression of the 1930s, when the commercial banks held billions of dollars of excess reserves for nearly a decade.

Note that the Fed's open-market purchases also directly push down interest rates on government securities. Fed purchases will bid up the prices of bonds, which is equivalent to forcing down the interest yield on the bonds. (See the footnote on page 160 if you don't remember why.) Since lower interest rates also help to stimulate the economy, open-market purchases

[9]There is substantially, but not quite, the same effect if the Fed buys the bond from a business or individual. Trace through the effect for yourself. The following section suggests the analysis if you need help.

[10]As a practical matter, international balance-of-payments problems may also constrain the Fed's use of its powers, as we shall see in Part Six.

are a two-pronged weapon against recession.

2. **When the Open Market Committee wants to decrease member-bank reserves, it sells government securities in the open market to whoever bids for them—individuals, businesses, or banks. This reduces commercial-bank reserves when the Federal Reserve is paid for the bonds.** Consider how.

If a member bank buys the bond, it pays by giving $1,000 of its reserves to the Federal Reserve; on the member bank's balance sheet, "cash" goes down and "bonds" go up by $1,000. Thus, the bank loses a full $1,000 of excess reserves, since its deposits remain unchanged. If a business or individual buys the bond from the Reserve, the effect is almost the same. He pays by a check on his bank. His bank's reserves are reduced by $1,000 when the Federal Reserve presents the check for collection. The member bank's deposits also drop by the $1,000 transferred from the bond buyer's account to the Federal Reserve. Since the bank loses $1,000 in both deposits and reserves, its required reserves are $200 lower but its excess reserves drop by $800. Excess reserves contract a little less than in the bank-purchase case, but the general effect is similar.

If the bank buys the bond, the T-account entries at the commercial bank are as shown above the dotted line. If an individual buys it, the entries are as shown below the dotted line.[11]

Assets		Liabilities	
Cash	−$1,000		
Bonds	+ 1,000		
....	....	....	....
Cash	−$1,000	Deposits	−$1,000

Rediscount Rate Changes

When a member bank runs short of reserves, it may borrow from its Federal Reserve bank, just as you and I borrow at a commercial bank. In such a case the member bank could "rediscount" notes. The member bank has made loans to customers against customers' promises to repay, called "notes," or "commercial paper." It can "rediscount" these notes with its Federal Reserve bank—that is, it can use the note as collateral to borrow additional reserves. The rate of interest, or discount, charged by the Federal Reserve to member banks is called the "rediscount rate." Or member banks may borrow using government securities as collateral. In discounting, the initiative is in the hands of the commercial banker to increase his reserves, while open-market operations are at the discretion of the Fed.

The Fed raises the rediscount rate to discourage member-bank borrowing and lowers the rate to encourage it. But the Fed discourages member-bank borrowing except on a temporary basis. Thus, the rediscount rate is of relatively minor direct importance. But changes in the rediscount rate have an important psychological effect on the banking and business communities because they are viewed as evidence of the Fed's general position on monetary expansion or restraint.[12]

Changes in Member-Bank Reserve Requirements

In 1933, a drastic new power was given to the Board of Governors—the power to raise and lower legal reserve requirements for member banks. By raising reserve requirements, the Board wipes out member banks' excess reserves and directly restricts credit expansion. Suppose a member bank has $1,000,000 deposits and $200,000 reserves, and the required legal reserve ratio is 16 percent. It has a comfortable $40,000 of excess reserves. If the Board raises the legal

[11] If the buyer pays in currency, he reduces the amount of currency in circulation, also a reduction in the money stock. But payment in currency is very unusual.

[12] Sometimes you see the term "free reserves." These are excess reserves *less* commercial-bank borrowing from the Fed. Because each commercial bank must repay its borrowing promptly, many experts believe that free reserves are better than excess reserves as an indication of commercial banks' ability to extend new credit. When free reserves are negative, they are called "net borrowed reserves."

requirement to 20 percent, the bank's excess reserve is wiped out. Conversely, lowering legal reserve requirements increases excess reserves.

Changing reserve requirements is a relatively blunt tool of credit control, compared with the gradual, flexible way open-market operations can be used. Thus, the Reserve authorities change reserve requirements only infrequently, depending instead primarily on open-market operations.

"Selective" Credit Controls

The preceding general controls over bank reserves control the total volume of bank lending, the level of interest rates, and the stock of money, but they leave the private banker free to allocate his funds as he wishes among different borrowers. In addition, the Fed has smaller "selective" controls over particular bank loans and uses to which bank credit is put. These permit the Fed to influence directly the uses of bank credit. Many economists question the effectiveness of such controls, because money, once created, flows freely from one sector of the economy to the other, and it is very difficult to control any one sector by limiting lending directly to it. But such selective controls may have important temporary effects.

Maximum Interest Rates Paid on Deposits. The Fed has the power to set maximum interest rates on different classes of deposits, and other regulatory agencies have similar powers over other financial intermediaries, such as the savings and loan associations. By setting different ceilings on interest rates at different institutions, the bank supervisors can influence their relative competitive positions, and thus indirectly influence where savers' funds go.

For example, in the 1960s, the S. and L.s bid many deposits away from the commercial banks by offering higher interest rates, and channeled these funds into mortgages to finance home building, especially in the West. Originally, there were no government ceilings on the rates that S. and L.s could pay their depositors, but commercial banks had maximum rates on their savings deposits. In the mid-1960s, the Fed raised the maximum rates that commercial banks might pay, and thus permitted them to compete deposits back away from the S. and L.s. This channeled funds away from the housing industry toward the more diverse borrowers from commercial banks. Rate ceilings were also used to affect the competitive power of big U.S. commercial banks vis-à-vis European capital markets.

Once detailed direct controls are instituted that influence the competitive position of different financial institutions, difficult questions of equity arise, and there is an unfortunate tendency for such direct controls to proliferate. We shall return to this issue in the next chapter. The Nixon 1973 reform proposals would gradually eliminate all such differential rate ceilings.

Control of Stock-Market Credit: Margin Requirements. Often customers buy stocks and bonds "on margin." That is, they pay the broker a cash "margin" (down payment) and borrow the rest of the purchase price from the broker, leaving the newly purchased securities as collateral for the loan. The broker, in turn, typically borrows from commercial banks what the security buyer does not put up as margin (cash). The smaller the margin required, the more the buyer can borrow of the purchase price. If margin requirements are raised, therefore, the use of bank credit for purchasing securities is restricted. If margin requirements are lowered, it becomes easier to buy securities on credit.

The Fed has power to set minimum margin requirements for dealings on the major securities exchanges, ranging up to 100 percent cash payments. In the wild stock-market speculation of the late 1920s, most stock was bought on margins of 10 percent or less, so speculators found it easy to bid up prices on borrowed money. Now margin requirements are generally set between 50 and 100 percent. Most economists believe that Federal Reserve margin requirements exercise a healthy restraint on speculative stock purchases under boom conditions.

"Direct Pressure" or "Jawboning." When the Fed wants to discourage bank lending, it may use "direct pressure," or "jawboning," on the bankers. Bank examiners may be instructed to tighten up their requirements for "good" loans and investments. Reserve officials may frown when member banks come to the discount window for temporary loans. They may also make public statements warning against inflation and overexpansion of credit. In extreme cases, the Reserve banks may simply refuse to lend to offending member banks. There is not much evidence that such moral suasion is very effective. There is even less hope that it can do anything to persuade bankers to make more loans in hard times.

Consumer-Credit Controls. During World War II and in the Korean War, the Fed was temporarily given power to regulate consumer credit (on installment purchases and charge accounts) and real-estate credit. On both housing and consumer credit, the Fed imposed minimum down payments and maximum repayment periods. Raising down payments made it hard to buy without cash in hand; shortening the total payment period increased the monthly payment required. These were controversial controls, and they have found little support in the peacetime economy. Although they were powerful, they mainly restrained the purchases of lower- and middle-income families, who needed to buy on credit.

CONCLUSION

In perspective, the Fed has enormous powers to check any credit expansion—indeed, to force mass contraction—if it chooses to use them. By dumping all its $68 billion of government securities on the market and by raising reserve requirements to their legal limits, the Fed could bring on a massive deflation sure to send the entire economic system into chaos. Of course, the Federal Reserve officials would never consider such a foolish action. But this points up the great power inherent in the Federal Reserve's restrictive measures.

The Fed's ability to stimulate bank lending is also great and it has substantially unlimited power to create new reserves through open-market operations. But success on the expansion side is less sure. Banks need not necessarily make new loans in recession merely because they receive new excess reserves, although they are almost certain to increase the money stock by buying more bonds if they don't expand their loans. How effectively this will stimulate aggregate spending depends on the issues outlined in Chapter 13.

Even with these limitations, the Fed's powers are great. The real issue is how to use these powers most effectively to achieve a stably growing, high-employment economy without inflation. How to do this is the subject of Chapter 17.

REVIEW

Concepts and Institutions to Remember

This chapter has introduced several important concepts and institutions. Be especially sure you understand the following:

money
currency
demand (checking) deposits
savings and time deposits
near-monies
bank credit
commercial bank
financial intermediary
credit creation
bank reserves
excess reserves
reserve requirements
adverse clearing balance
credit contraction
Board of Governors
Open Market Committee
Federal Reserve banks
member banks
"creation" of bank reserves
open-market operations
rediscount rate
selective credit controls
interest-rate ceilings
margin requirements

For Analysis and Discussion

1. Why is currency worth more than its value as paper and ink?
2. Get a copy of a recent balance sheet from one of your local banks. What main types of credit does this bank extend? Which of these types of credit would you expect to be most liquid (most readily convertible into cash) in case of a business recession?
3. If banks hold "reserves" equal to only a small fraction of their deposits, are you safe in depositing your money in a bank? Explain why or why not.
4. If you were a banker, would you hold excess reserves? Why or why not?
5. In a small, isolated economy (that is, no foreign trade) with money-using habits comparable to those of the United States, there are five identical banks. Each bank's balance sheet is as shown below. The law prescribes that banks must hold a 20 percent cash reserve against deposits. There is no central bank.

Cash	$ 7,000,000	Deposits	$30,000,000
Loans	14,000,000	Capital and Surplus	4,000,000
Government Securities	13,000,000		
	$34,000,000		$34,000,000

a. A customer of bank *A* mines $1 million of gold (considered as cash for reserve purposes) and deposits it in his bank. Trace through any *likely* expansion of the money supply by bank *A* and by the entire banking system. What would be the *maximum* reexpansion possible? Specify clearly any assumptions that you make and state your reasoning carefully and precisely.

b. Is the banking system in a more or less *sound* position as a result of the gold deposit and the consequences you have predicted above? Explain?

6. Explain how the transfer of your $100 deposit from a commercial bank to a savings and loan association can increase society's stock of liquid assets (money plus near-monies).
7. In what ways are the objectives of a central bank (like the Federal Reserve) different from those of a commercial bank?
8. Explain the main weapons the Fed has to check an inflationary boom.
9. Suppose the Federal Reserve takes the following actions. In each case, explain what will be the likely effect on the total money stock:
   a. It sells $1 billion of government securities to the banks.
   b. It raises reserve requirements from 10 to 15 percent for all member banks.
   c. It buys $1 billion of government securities from individuals and business concerns.
   d. It buys directly from the U.S. Treasury $1 billion of newly issued government securities.
   e. It raises the rediscount rate by 1 percent.
10. Suppose the economy is in a recession. The commercial banks have substantial excess reserves. What steps would you advocate that the Federal Reserve take to help stimulate lending and recovery?

APPENDIX

The Individual Bank and the Banking System

If no individual bank lends more than its excess reserves, how can the banking **system** expand credit fivefold on its excess reserves (assuming a 20 percent reserve requirement)? An example can show how it works.

Assume, first, that the Local Bank has $1,000 excess reserves, and that all other banks are loaned up to their legal limits. As the Local Bank makes new loans and investments, its reserves are gradually drawn away to other banks, and its credit-expansion possibilities are limited. But the reserves the Local Bank loses, some other bank gains.

Suppose Local makes a new loan of $1,000, just the amount of its excess reserves. The T-account then looks like Stage 1, including the original $1,000 of excess reserves but excluding the rest of the original

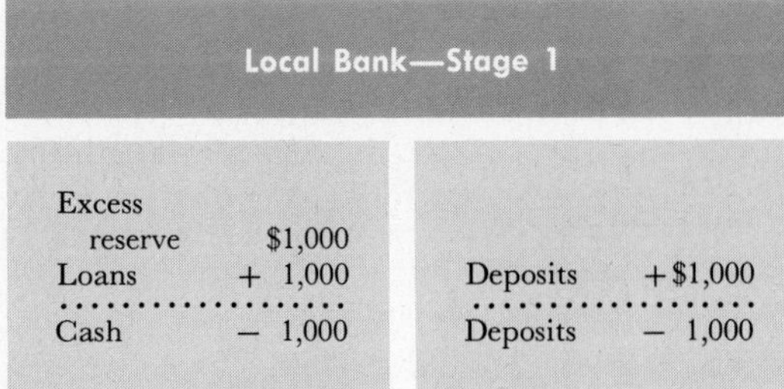

Local Bank—Stage 1

Excess reserve	$1,000		
Loans	+ 1,000	Deposits	+$1,000
Cash	− 1,000	Deposits	− 1,000

balance sheet. Consider first only the entries above the dotted line.

Soon the borrower writes a check for the entire $1,000, and the check is deposited in bank *B*. This action transfers both the $1,000 deposit and the matching $1,000 cash reserve from the Local Bank to *B*. On the Local Bank T-account, deduct $1,000 from cash and from deposits, as shown below the

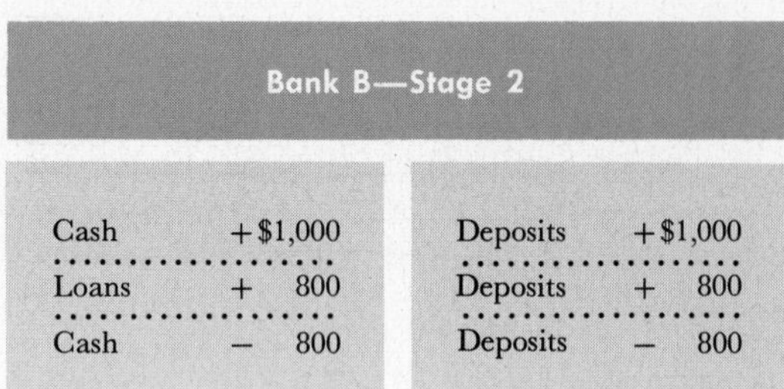

Bank B—Stage 2

Assets		Liabilities	
Cash	+$1,000	Deposits	+$1,000
Loans	+ 800	Deposits	+ 800
Cash	− 800	Deposits	− 800

dotted line, to see the bank's new position. Local is left with $1,000 of increased loans, on which it happily earns interest.

Bank *B* now has $1,000 of new reserves and $1,000 of new deposits. We can set up a T-account for bank *B*, showing (Stage 2) + $1,000 for both the new cash and deposits, above the first dotted line. Of the new reserves, only $200 is required to back the new $1,000 deposit, so $800 is excess. Obviously, *B* is now safe in extending at least $800 of new loans, since it has that much excess reserves.

So *B* makes a new $800 loan, creating $800 of additional deposits. This is shown on *B*'s T-account, below the first dotted line.

Now the borrower spends the money to a customer of bank *C*. Bank *B* loses the $800 of deposits and reserves to bank *C*. The loss is shown below the second dotted line on *B*'s accounts. Note that on the liability side, *B* still has the $1,000 original deposit created by Local bank; on the asset side, it still has a matching $200 of new reserves from Local, plus $800 of its own new loans. It is earning interest on its new $800 loan.

But *C* now has $800 of new deposits and the $800 of new reserves from *B* (Stage 3). This is shown in a new T-account, set up for *C*; the items are shown above the dotted line in Stage 3.

The total of new deposits has now risen to $1,800 ($1,000 in *B* and $800 in *C*), matched by $1,800 of new loans, even though no bank has lent a penny beyond its available excess reserves. Bank *C*, moreover, now has $640 of excess reserves ($800 new reserves, of which only $160 is required to back its $800 of new deposits). On these excess reserves it can safely make at least $640 of new loans, shown below the dotted line on its T-account. This will raise the total of new deposits to $2,440 against the original $1,000 of excess reserves. (The $2,440 total includes $1,000 in bank *B* and $1,440 in bank *C* at this stage.) And the expansion process can obviously continue. Trace it another stage for yourself, assuming that *C*'s borrower spends his deposit to someone who banks with *D*; or the effect is the same if the reserves go back to Local Bank, or to any other. The expansion can continue until total deposits have risen to $5,000 against the $1,000 of excess reserves. Each individual bank rightly hesitates to lend out more than its excess reserves, but the reserves it loses go to some other bank.

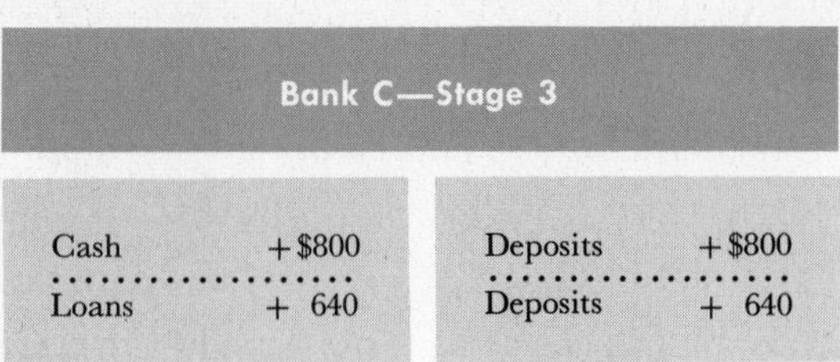

Bank C—Stage 3

Assets		Liabilities	
Cash	+$800	Deposits	+$800
Loans	+ 640	Deposits	+ 640

This process of cumulative deposit expansion is diagramed in Figure 16–1. Assume that bank *A* receives $1,000 of new reserves, say because $1,000 of newly mined gold is deposited. This $1,000 deposit requires only $200 of new reserves, so bank *A* is entirely safe in expanding its loans and investments by $800, as shown in the dark-colored bar for bank *A*. (Note that the bank letters don't match those in the preceding example.)

Now bank *A*'s new borrower writes a check to a customer of bank *B*, and the $800 is transferred to bank *B*. Bank *B* now has $800 of new deposits and $800 of new reserves, which means that it has excess reserves of $640, since required reserves increase by only $160. It is perfectly safe in lending out an additional $640, and does so, as shown in the diagram. This $640 may now be transferred to a customer of some other bank (*C*), which then has new deposits and excess reserves on which to expand its loans. At each stage, the deposits created by previous transactions are piled on top, in the dotted sections, to show the cumulative increase.

As the diagram shows, this process can continue, piling up new deposits that arise from new loans, until a total of $5,000 of new deposits is reached (the tall dark-colored bar at the right), including the original $1,000 deposit produced by the gold deposit.

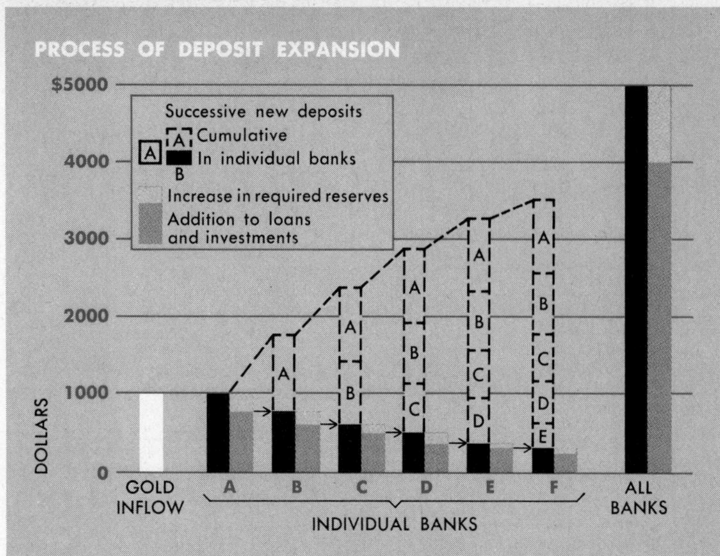

Figure 16–1

One thousand dollars of new reserves (gold) ultimately serves as the foundation for $5,000 of new deposits, as banks make new loans and investments—even though no bank ever lends out more than its own excess reserves.

This is just what we would expect: $1,000 of new reserves has been able to support $5,000 of new deposits, given a 20 percent legal reserve requirement against deposits and no currency drain. The tall light bar at the right shows the $4,000 of new loans and the $1,000 of new required reserves, just using up the original $1,000 of new gold reserves, so the growth must now stop. Moreover, this expansion has taken place even though no individual bank has ever lent out more than the excess reserves it actually has on hand. So when your banker tells you that he would never lend out more money than he has in excess reserves, he may be quite correct. Yet the banking system as a whole creates deposits equal to many times its cash reserves—in this case, equal to five times its new reserves.

The critical point is that the banking system is not limited by adverse clearing balances. For the banking system as a whole, the only overall drain on reserves comes from currency withdrawals, from international gold flows, or from Federal Reserve or Treasury policies.

Monetary Policy

CHAPTER PREVIEW

CHAPTER SEVENTEEN

Monetary policy is the second big gun in the government's arsenal against economic instability. As effective fiscal policy often depends on the cooperation of monetary policy, so effective monetary policy is often difficult without the joint use of fiscal policy. This chapter examines the theory and practical operations of monetary policy, and concludes with a look at the optimal mix of the two major policy tools.

THE THEORY OF MONETARY POLICY

Under the "gold standard" that prevailed in the Western world during most of the century preceding World War II, the stock of money was loosely controlled by an impersonal mechanism. The money supply increased and decreased when gold flowed in or out of a nation. But increasingly, economists argued against leaving the supply of money solely to this mechanism. Instead, they argued, the government or a "central bank" should be responsible for controlling the money stock in order to minimize inflations and depressions. The United States was one of the last major nations to establish a central bank. Our Federal Reserve was set up in 1914. But over the decades since, we have come to rely heavily on Federal Reserve policy in the continuing war against both unemployment and inflation.

Monetary Policy, Interest Rates, and the Money Stock

Chapters 12 and 13 provided the analytical foundation for monetary policy. If we want to increase or decrease aggregate demand, the central bank should increase or decrease M. Remember the main channels of effect.

The neo-Keynesian model suggests that more M will act only by increasing investment spending through reducing the rate of interest. Then the chain of effects runs like this:

$$+M \rightarrow -r \rightarrow +I \rightarrow +\text{GNP}$$

That is, an increase in M leads to a lower interest rate, which in turn leads to more investment, which in turn leads to a higher GNP directly and through the multiplier.

The monetarists argue that money has a broader and more direct effect. More M may lead not only to more investment through lower interest rates but also directly to more consumption and investment spending. This occurs because an increase in M will lower the marginal return on money relative to other assets and will lead consumers and businesses to spend down their real money balances, acquiring other assets (including both consumer and investment goods) instead.

What Is the Right Amount of Money?

If GNP were a constant multiple of the stock of money, then the task of monetary policy would be relatively simple. Determine the desired level of GNP, and then move the stock of money up or down to obtain that desired level. But even if M causes changes in money GNP, we know that the public's demand for money balances also varies, and that the V in $MV = PT$ varies. Thus, to determine the right M to produce any desired level of aggregate money spending, we must take into account changes in the public's demand for money balances. Figure 12–2 pictured the fluctuations in income velocity since 1900. Moreover, we know that changes in spending sometimes raise or lower prices rather than real output.

The public's demand for money balances depends on its level of income (or wealth) and on interest rates on money substitutes. The higher the income (or wealth) of the public, the larger, other things equal, will be the money balances it wishes to hold. The higher the interest rate on money substitutes, the less money it will want to hold because higher interest rates will lead people to shift their assets out of money (which yields no interest) into securities or other assets. Thus, for any level of aggregate demand we want to achieve, the right amount of M is that amount that the public desires to hold at that desired level of GNP and at existing interest rates. More M than this amount will lead to higher spending than we want; less M will lead to lower spending.

In a growing economy, the amount of money needed will gradually rise. Prima facie, we might expect the need for more money to grow apace with the growth in real-output potential—say about 4 percent a year. But just how fast M needs to grow will depend on how fast the public's demand for money balances rises at full-employment levels.

Even if the Fed could keep total spending growing at exactly the desired rate, this would not guarantee full employment without inflation. Sometimes, especially in the upsweep of a boom, more spending leads to rising prices when substantial unemployment remains. But we shall focus attention here on the control of *money* GNP, leaving to Chapter 18 the difficult problem that arises when high employment and stable prices appear to be incompatible.

Summary: The right amount of money depends both on the desired level of real GNP and on the public's demand for money balances at that level of GNP and of interest rates. A rising GNP without an increase in M will tend to raise interest rates and limit the growth in GNP. Thus, it is important that M grow gradually over the long pull—at roughly the growth rate of the economy's productive capacity, but probably with variations to offset short-run disturbances.

Should the Fed Watch *M* or Interest Rates?

Monetary theory provides no decisive answer as to whether the Fed should focus on *M* or on interest rates in attempting to control aggregate spending. The monetarist says *M*, since *V* will normally be relatively stable. The neo-Keynesians say interest rates, since interest rates influence the rate of investment, which in turn dominates GNP.

If the public's demand for money varies, the Fed can fix the stock of money, or interest rates—but not both. It must choose. Suppose the economy is growing satisfactorily at 4 percent along a high-employment growth path, and the money stock is growing at the same rate. Now interest rates begin to rise. The Keynesians say, increase *M* faster to check the rise in interest rates before they reduce investment and bring recession. But the monetarists say, just keep on increasing *M* at 4 percent per annum, since to speed that rate would increase the growth rate of GNP and generate inflation. Which is right?

The answer is, it depends on the cause of the increase in interest rates. If the cause is an increase in the public's liquidity demand for money, then *V* will fall and there will be a recession unless more *M* is provided to offset the lower *V;* the Keynesians are right. But if the cause is a rise in the transactions demand for money (for example, because businesses want more bank credit to expand their inventories and make new investments), to provide more *M* will permit this faster rise in aggregate demand and inflation will result; the monetarists are right. In principle, both can agree on the proper monetary policy *if* we know what is causing the higher interest rates—but often we don't know. The monetarists generally presume that the public's demand for *M* is stable (that is, *V* is stable), so the Fed should concentrate on providing the right growth in *M*, letting interest rates move as they will. The Keynesians presume that interest rates influence investment spending so the Fed should keep interest rates stable when the level of investment and GNP are satisfactory, varying *M* as need be to achieve this result. In any given situation the Fed must choose, and which presumption is right is no idle question.

Often no dilemma exists. For example, in depressions everyone agrees that both more *M* and lower interest rates are needed; conversely, to fight inflation both tighter *M* and higher interest rates are appropriate. But sometimes the dilemma does arise—be guided by interest rates or the money stock. The late 1960s were a painful case in point when, in retrospect, the Fed probably watched interest rates too much and the result was too much *M* and too much inflation. Today, the Fed watches both *M* and interest rates—and, until the dispute is resolved, tries to analyze each case on its own merits when the two indicators conflict.

POLICIES TO REGULATE AGGREGATE DEMAND

Monetary Restriction

If the Fed wants to restrain aggregate demand, it can sell bonds in the open market or raise reserve requirements to reduce excess reserves. Since commercial banks typically operate with small excess reserves, either action can have a direct and powerful restrictive effect on the extension of bank credit. The Fed can also raise the rediscount rate, which makes it more expensive for commercial banks to borrow additional reserves when they run tight. This is a less-powerful restraint, since banks are still able to borrow additional reserves if they are willing to pay the higher rate. But the rediscount rate is widely viewed as an indicator of the Fed's attitude on credit conditions, and thus has an important symbolic, psychological impact. The Fed has plenty of powers to restrain aggregate demand if it wants to use them.

When the economy is expanding, businesses need more money for "working capital" to finance larger inventories, to meet higher payrolls, to buy more materials, and to finance new factories and equipment. Consumers' demand for money also rises with their incomes. **In an expanding economy, therefore, if the Fed merely does nothing to provide additional reserves, this policy of inaction implies a gradual tightening** of the money markets and a rise in interest rates, since demand for M rises but its supply does not.

What do the banks do when their excess reserves are squeezed? They often raise their interest rates—the prices they charge on credit. Banks also often "ration" credit to their customers. Instead of using higher rates to eliminate the customers least willing to pay more for loans, they allocate their scarce credit to their oldest and best customers. They consider this sound long-run policy, just as many businesses don't try to squeeze the last penny out of good customers in periods of temporary shortages. Either way, tight money tends to check the upswing.

On their side, businesses and consumers try to avoid the pinch by economizing on money balances—that is, by reducing their money balances to the barest minimum needed to carry on their transactions and meet precautionary needs. The same amount of money thus does more work; V is speeded up, and the restraint of tighter money is partially avoided. The higher interest rates are forced by the credit squeeze, the greater the inducement is to put "idle" money to work.

Figure 17–1 shows this effect clearly. The dot for each year shows the average interest rate on "prime" short-term loans and the average turnover (or velocity) of demand deposits at some 400 city banks outside New York City (which is eliminated to avoid the huge volume of stock-market transactions there). Velocity varies directly with interest rates. For example, note the low interest rates and velocity during the depression years. These velocity figures include many transactions not contained in the GNP accounts and thus are only a very imperfect approximation to changes in income velocity. But in some respects they are more interesting, because they show what happens to the total use of demand deposits when interest rates rise or fall. If we plot income velocity against interest rates for the same years, the same general relationship is revealed.

But there are limits on how far working cash balances can be reduced. The public and the banks can avoid the pressure of Federal Reserve restraint temporarily, but only temporarily if the Fed keeps the pressure on. Ultimately the Fed can have as strong an impact as it wishes, by raising reserve requirements sharply and by selling a large enough volume of government securities.

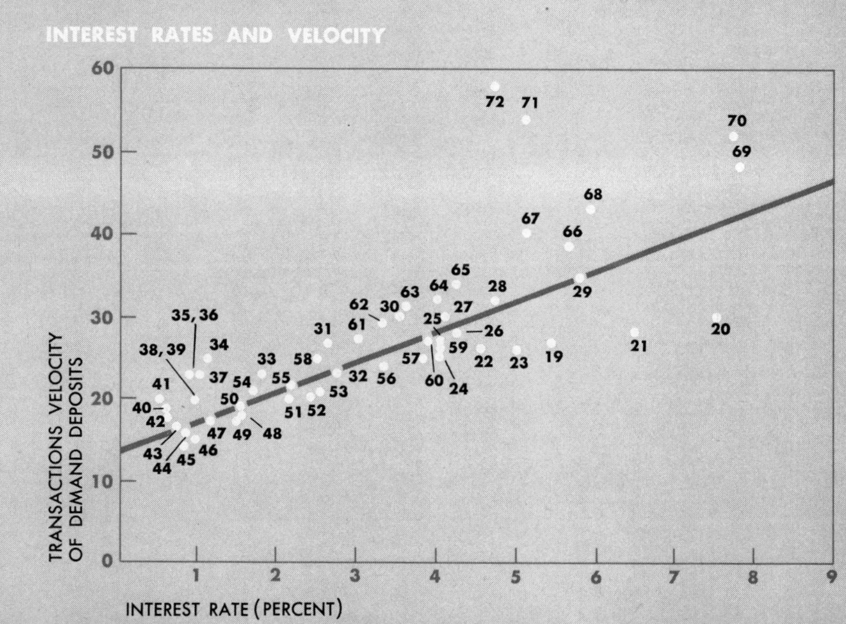

Figure 17–1

As interest rates rise, the turnover of demand deposits goes up. It pays people to economize on the use of money and to reduce their idle balances. (Source: Federal Reserve Board.)

But the Fed's job is not easy. Overly drastic action may throw the baby out with the bath water. Its task is to check the inflation and level off the boom, not to plunge the economy into depression. Tightening up credit just enough to keep consumption and investment growing at exactly the right rate is a difficult and delicate task.

The Differential Effects of Tight Money

The job is even tougher for another reason. When money tightens, some borrowers are squeezed more than others. Banks naturally tend to allocate their scarce funds to established customers. Conversely, new small firms and individuals tend to be squeezed out, especially when their credit rating is not high. Tight money especially squeezes home construction, because high interest rates bulk large in total monthly mortgage payments and because many banks rank such loans below those to businesses that they see as long-run customers. Bitter claims of inequity can be expected from potential borrowers who are shut out when interest rates rise and there aren't enough loans to go around. There is no way to restrict aggregate demand without turning away somebody, and the big, grade-A borrowers aren't likely to be the ones turned away.

A further complication arises when the monetary authorities use direct controls (interest-rate ceilings) to regulate the flow of savings to different financial institutions. Savings and loan associations, for example, lend almost entirely to builders and home buyers. Thus, if they are permitted to pay high rates to their depositors while commercial banks are limited to lower rates, both S. and L.s and the housing industry are favored relative to commercial banks and industries that borrow from the banks. But normally in tight money periods, interest rates obtainable elsewhere by savers rise above the rates S. and L.s can pay, and funds are channeled away from the housing market. Housing is thus a prime victim of tight money in most cases.

Government use of direct controls to favor some sectors over others is questioned by some, defended by others. The former say the free market should govern the allocation of credit. The latter say the government should see to it that vital areas like housing should get the funds when money is scarce. Either way, tight money must shut out someone from credit if it is to do its job. There is no way it can avoid restraining some potential borrowers more than others.

Monetary Expansion

If aggregate demand is inadequate, the Fed's first job is to be sure that banks have plenty of reserves. It can reduce reserve requirements and buy government securities in the open market, providing new bank reserves in paying for its purchases. In addition, it can lower the rediscount rate. It can guarantee liquidity to the banking system and eliminate the possibility of another debacle like that of the years 1929–33 when mass liquidation of bank loans occurred as the banks lost reserves through currency withdrawals, and forced the downward spiral ever deeper.

If the Fed provides generous excess reserves, what will the bankers do? They will want to lend, because idle reserves earn no interest. If times are reasonably good, bankers will usually increase their loans promptly. But in depression, acceptable borrowers are scarce.

Even in this case, however, bankers can put their reserves to work by buying government securities on the open market. These are always substantially safe, and they pay interest. And buying government securities increases the money stock, just as making new loans does. So flooding the banks with reserves will increase M, bidding up the price of bonds and (what is the same thing) bidding down interest rates.

History presents one big counterexample. After 1933, in the Great Depression, the inflow of gold plus Federal Reserve policy built up large excess reserves at the commercial banks. Although bank credit in fact expanded rapidly as reserves built up, it did not expand nearly as rapidly as did reserves. Thus, for the first time in history, the banking system held a huge volume of excess reserves over an extended period of years. Some economists suggest that this indicates a "liquidity trap" that we can expect to face again if we get into another serious depression. More excess reserves or more *M* will simply pile up in the idle balances, so monetary policy is a very weak stimulant to expansion under such conditions. But monetarists reply that the large excess reserves of the 1930s were the exception to the rule. More important, they stress that pumping reserves into the banking system did in fact increase *M* rapidly, and that in turn both money and real GNP rose rapidly, once the great contraction of both reserves and *M* in the period from 1929–33 was reversed.

Everyone agrees that easy money is a good thing in recessions, even though there is disagreement over its precise effects. The evidence suggests that lower interest rates are more likely to stimulate long- than short-term investment. On a long loan, like a thirty-year mortgage, a small reduction in the interest rate makes a big difference in the monthly payment. Thus, lower interest rates may be a substantial stimulus to long-term projects like houses, public utilities, factories, and the like. Low short-term interest rates are less likely to stimulate investment. Cheaper money lowers the cost of borrowing for working-capital purposes—to meet payrolls, carry inventories, and so on. But here interest is a tiny part of the relevant costs. And the short-run marginal efficiency of investment depends heavily on volatile customer demand and profit expectations.

Since everyone agrees that easy money may help some to expand aggregate demand, why not just flood the banks with reserves to get whatever stimulus more *M* can produce? The answer is that here, as in fighting inflation, there may be danger of too much as well as too little. If the Fed pours excessive *M* into the economy, given the lags of policy it may be very hard to check the ensuing boom without very strong restrictive measures if the economy "overheats." The timing problems faced in fighting recession are roughly comparable to those in fighting an inflationary boom. Just right is what's needed, neither too much nor too little!

The Problem of Timing and Lags

The Federal Reserve's problem is deciding what is the right thing to do at the right time. In large part, it's the same problem faced by the fiscal authorities, but with some important differences. The problem breaks down into two big questions: First, what is the state of the economy now, and where is it going in the absence of further monetary policy action? Second, what shall we do to mold this pattern into one of stable economic growth without inflation? Look at Figure 17–2, which provides a very rough picture of a business cycle, and put yourself in the position of a Federal Reserve Board member.

First, you have to decide where you are now. At *A*, *B*, *C*, or *D*? You don't know for sure, and neither does anybody else. Suppose you think we're probably well along in a strong business upswing—say at about *B*. Then the problem is, how near the top? Is the boom weakening, with a downturn just around the corner? Or does the upswing have months or years of booming prosperity left in it? If only you knew![1]

[1]For a discussion of how government and other economists forecast, look back at the Appendix to Chapter 14.

Figure 17–2

The Federal Reserve authorities seldom know where we are in the cycle, or just how long it will take their actions to exercise their full effects. What is the correct monetary policy if you think we're probably at B, but there's a good chance it may be C instead?

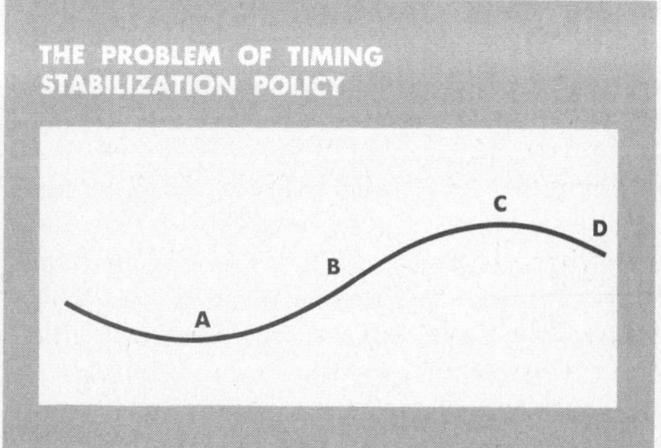

Second, given your best decision as to where we are and where we're headed, you have to decide what the Fed should do now. Suppose that you suspect we're at *B*, and that inflation poses a serious problem. Should you raise reserve requirements? Sell bonds in the open market to tighten reserves? Or is the safe thing just to wait till we're clearly at *D* if that comes, and then fight the recession, on the ground that it's better not to risk killing off prosperity by mistaken stabilization policy?

Note that here you have two subproblems. One is *how much* effect will any Federal Reserve action have on business activity? If you sell $1 billion of government bonds, will this drastically check bank lending, or only slow it slightly? The second problem is *lags*. Even if you know what the effect will be, *how long* will it take for the full impact of tighter money to be felt? If you sell bonds tomorrow, this may only gradually shut off lending and that in turn may reduce *C* and *I* still later. Thus, the full effects of your action will be spread over months, probably over a year or two. By that time the boom may have turned down. Then the lagged effect of tight money would be to speed the downturn into recession, rather than to help check an excessive boom.

The lags and uncertainties between Federal Reserve actions and their final impact on total spending are substantial. How long will it take the banks to react to tighter reserves? How fast will businesses react to tighter credit and higher interest rates? Will the Fed's action have a strong psychological effect that reduces business investment? Most economists estimate the total lag between Federal Reserve action on reserves and the ultimate major effect on GNP as long as twelve to twenty-four months and suggest that the lag varies depending on prevailing conditions. Part of the effect is felt immediately and the rest spreads over six to thirty months. Researchers are hard at work on the problem, but the Fed doesn't know for sure. And it has to act, or let things go their way without control. Question: Suppose the average lag in the effect of monetary policy is a year. Is a policy of acting to offset current booms and recessions a sound one at all times?

THE DANGERS OF DESTABILIZING POLICY

Given the uncertainties outlined above, it is not surprising that the monetary authorities sometimes make mistakes. The monetarists, who generally support reasonably stable growth in *M*, criticize the Fed for overreacting to short-run disturbances with big swings in *M* as it tries to keep interest rates and money-market conditions stable. The neo-Keynesians, on the other hand, have recently criticized the Fed for letting interest rates swing too widely in misguided attempts to keep *M* growing reasonably stably.

The 1967–70 period provides two lively case studies. By 1967, inflation had clearly become the economy's number one problem. The demand for credit soared with war spending and boom times. The Fed, seeing interest rates climbing toward historic highs, increased *M* rapidly (at over 7 percent per annum) to keep rates from soaring even faster. Nevertheless, borrowers complained of scarce and expensive credit, and by 1968, long-term interest rates, which were only 2–3 percent during the 1930s, passed 8 percent on newly issued business bonds as the inflationary boom continued.

Monetarists bitterly attacked the Fed. They argued that the rapid growth in *M* was feeding the inflation and was indeed the cause of the high interest rates because it led both lenders and borrowers to add a big inflation allowance to their interest-rate bargains (remember the concluding sections of Chapter 13). They claimed that in fact *real* interest rates were relatively low, and that actually money was "easy," since perhaps 5 percent of the quoted 8 percent rate was inflation allowance. The only way to stop the inflation and lower interest rates was to *reduce* the rapid increase in *M*, just the opposite of the neo-Keynesian prescription for attaining lower interest rates. In retrospect, the monetarists look substantially right in their criticism of the Fed in the 1967–68 period. The rapid growth in *M* was destabilizing.

But consider now the case of 1970. Very tight money (zero growth in *M* and very high interest rates) had checked the upswing in 1969 and unemployment was rising, though inflation continued. To keep the downturn from becoming a major recession, the Fed in early 1970 expanded M at a rate that temporarily exceeded 10 percent. Again the battle was on. Monetarists warned against stimulating the inflation even further. Neo-Keynesians, pointing to still high interest rates, pleaded for easier money and lower rates to avoid the danger of serious recession. They urged that the Fed not make a fetish of the growth rate of M but pour in more reserves.

Policy turned around the recession by late 1970, but rising unemployment did not check the inflation. To get interest rates down, would you have recommended that the Fed *increase or decrease* the growth rate in M? Or wouldn't you have paid any attention to interest rates, per se? Whatever your answer, such monetary disputes suggest that well-intentioned monetary policy *may* be destabilizing—that monetary, like fiscal, policy, however well meant, may be part of the problem as well as part of its solution.

STABLE GROWTH IN THE MONEY STOCK?

Some monetarists, led by Chicago's Milton Friedman, suggest a simple rule for monetary policy. Just increase M about 4 percent a year through thick and thin. (The 4 percent is based on the assumption that this is about the rate of growth in the full-employment capacity of the economy. If the growth rate of the economy is more or less, the growth rate of the money stock could be adjusted accordingly.) These economists argue that, even with the best intentions in the world, the Fed cannot forecast business conditions effectively. Moreover, the lag in effect of monetary policy is uncertain, and the Fed generally pays too much attention to short-term interest-rate fluctuations. Thus, Federal Reserve discretionary action has been destabilizing on many occasions in the past. A major example is the collapse of 1929–33 when the Fed permitted the money stock to shrink by nearly one-third; another is too much M in the inflationary boom of 1967–68.

Suppose we automatically increase M at about the full-employment growth rate of the economy, eschewing all attempts to forecast and to offset every real or imagined fluctuation. To be sure, this might not keep the economy exactly on a stable growth path. But the policy would avoid big booms and big depressions. Whenever the economy began to fall into serious recession, continued increase in the money stock at the annual 4 percent rate would provide a massive support against collapse. Conversely, if inflation began, limitation of the growth in M to 4 percent annually would be a powerful restraint on the inflation. A constant-growth-in-M rule is not a counsel of perfection; it is advanced as a sensible precept of action that would give by-and-large good results and would avoid the danger of serious errors due to fallible monetary authorities.

Few economists or laymen take the proposal to abolish the Federal Reserve and to substitute a completely inflexible rule of a stably growing money stock seriously. But many economists who have studied the evidence believe that the reasoning behind the rule has much to offer the Federal Reserve authorities. Whenever M is growing much faster or slower than the full-employment growth rate of the economy, that's a warning flag, and there ought to be a good reason for the divergence.

THE MIX OF MONETARY AND FISCAL POLICY

Fiscal and monetary policy must be effectively coordinated for optimum results. Unless they are, one may offset the other.

The 1964 experience shows the importance of such cooperation. The big tax cut led to rising incomes, to rising demands for money balances as transaction needs increased, and to upward pressures on interest rates from direct federal borrowing to finance the deficit. But simultaneously the Fed provided new bank reserves that permitted the money stock to grow about 5 percent during the year, which kept interest rates roughly stable and helped induce more spending. Whether monetary or fiscal policy deserves more credit is not the main issue here; we needed both.

The late 1960s demonstrated the problems that arise if we rely too heavily on one policy instrument without help from the other. From 1965 through 1968, fiscal policy was highly expansionary, reflecting big increases in both Vietnam and domestic spending. The Fed had to undertake single-handed the job of slowing the inflationary boom. In 1966 the Fed halted the expansion of *M*. The result was big increases in interest rates and a "credit crunch." In particular, new credit for home construction nearly vanished as lenders channeled funds to more attractive borrowers. Similarly, rising interest rates made it very difficult for local governments to borrow; many were forbidden by law to pay more than stated rates, which were below soaring market rates. New and small businesses also found funds very hard to obtain. Exclusive reliance on tight money threw the brunt of restriction on particular sectors of the economy. A more balanced stabilization program, including restrictive fiscal policy, would have permitted a broader, more equitable spreading of the burden.

The policy mix also influences the rate of economic growth. Suppose we want to stimulate faster growth when we already have high-level employment. We can do so by an easy-money policy, because low interest rates will stimulate investment. But this policy would unfortunately also produce excess aggregate demand and inflation. However, if we simultaneously raise taxes to generate a budget surplus, we can restrain demand and counteract the undesired inflationary pressure. Thus, an easy-money policy of low interest rates combined with a budget surplus could stimulate growth while maintaining high-level employment without inflation.

The need to mesh international and domestic consideration raises different problems of determining the right policy mix. During the early 1960s, for example, our international position called for high interest rates to pull funds here instead of abroad, while at home unemployment called for increased aggregate demand. Thus, many economists urged tighter money to raise interest rates in order to solve our international problem, combined with an expansionary fiscal policy to stimulate the domestic economy.

Meshing multiple policy goals calls for imaginative, flexible use of our policy tools. Moreover, history shows that the world has an unpleasant way of throwing up new problems every time we think we have the old ones well under control. Prudent economic policy will require a flexible, changing mix of monetary and fiscal policies to cope with new situations as they arise.

GOLD AND MONETARY POLICY[2]

We have said little about the fact that the United States lives in an increasingly interdependent economic world. During some periods, for example the quarter-century following the mid-1930s, Federal Reserve policy needed to pay little attention to our international position. We had a lion's share of the world's gold reserves, and monetary policy could be focused almost entirely on domestic goals.

But over much of our history it has not been so. And since the 1960s our concern over gold and the international balance of payments has again played a major role in constraining our domestic monetary policy actions. Although you can only understand the importance of gold and the balance of payments through a detailed analysis of international economic relations (in Part Six), it is important in concluding this chapter on monetary policy to recognize briefly the role gold has played.

What Was the "Gold Standard"?

The "gold standard" prevailed in the United States and most major European nations over a good share of the century preceding the 1930s. Although it varied from country to country and from period to period, it had two major characteristics. First, changes in the total amount of money in each country were to be

[2]This section can be omitted by those who will study Part Six.

roughly proportional to changes in its gold holdings. Gold itself was not the only kind of money. But as new gold was received by a country, it would serve as the basis for additional money issued in the form of currency or deposits. On $1 worth of new gold, $2, $10, or some other number of dollars of new money might be issued. Conversely, an outflow of gold would reduce the nation's money supply.

Second, each unit of money was "worth" (freely convertible into) a certain number of grains of gold. Until 1934, for example, each U.S. dollar "contained" 23.22 grains of fine gold; that is, the price of gold was fixed so that 23.22 grains of gold could always be obtained at the Treasury for $1, and vice versa.

Thus, the gold standard in its pure form was essentially an automatic regulator of the supply of money. *M* would be largely dependent on the stock of gold in each nation. Actually, the gold standard was never as automatic in operation as in theory. But it did provide a strong constraining framework for almost all monetary-policy thinking and action over a long period of years.

The Gold Standard as a Safeguard against Inflation

The main argument for the gold standard in most people's minds was that it would safeguard the economy against overissue of money and inflation. Because the government must have gold to back each dollar, gold sets a limit to how much money can be created and provides value for the money issued.

But U.S. history shows clearly that as a practical matter the gold standard was no guarantee against sharp price-level changes. Figure 7–3 shows the big inflation that took place during and following World War I, the precipitous drop following that inflation, and the sharp drop from 1929 to 1933—all while we were on the gold standard.

On the other hand, it *is* true that adherence to the gold standard would insure against any such runaway inflation as occurred in Germany after World War I, *if* sticking to the gold standard were politically and economically possible under such circumstances. Then the limited stock of gold would prevent a vast overissue of money. However, under such drastic circumstances it is hard to imagine that any country would remain on a gold standard. The drastic monetary disturbances of that period were as much a symptom as a cause of the difficulties of the German economy.

Most economists today deny that gold flows provide the best guide to how much money the economy needs. There is no reason to suppose that the optimal supply of money will correspond to how much gold is mined each year and how much goes into or out of speculators' hoards. Moreover, rigid adherence to a gold standard would tie the monetary authorities' hands against monetary action to combat unemployment and depression.

Abandonment of the Gold Standard

It was the desire to "do something" about the depression that largely explains the worldwide abandonment of the gold standard in the 1930s. Countries were increasingly loath to accept deflation as they lost gold. Getting men back to work became the major national goal. European countries faced huge gold drains into private hoards and to the United States. In 1931, England, long the financial center of the world, went off the gold standard. Remaining on gold meant intensified deflation as gold was withdrawn. Off gold, England could expand her money supply to check the depression and falling price level, regardless of gold flows.

Britain's abandonment of the gold standard was a terrific blow to the confidence of the financial world in those troubled times. Gold hoarding developed in the other major Western nations, and within a few years all, including the United States, had gone off gold. The price of contracting domestic money supplies as gold was lost was too high. Avoiding unemployment by expansionary monetary policy was more important in the dark days of worldwide depression.

Gold Today

Gold flows no longer control monetary policy in the world's major nations. But gold has not vanished from the monetary scene. It is still used as international money among governments and central banks to a limited extent, and in many nations individual citizens hold gold in coins or other forms. International monetary arrangements have been in a state of flux since the late 1960s, and we shall postpone to Part Six more detailed analysis of the international role of gold today. In the United States, at least, you will not go far wrong by omitting gold from the analysis of domestic monetary policy, as we have done.

REVIEW

For Analysis and Discussion

1. How would you rate the following for quick action to fight a recession: (a) monetary policy, (b) tax reductions, and (c) increased government spending?
2. Suppose you were a banker with a balance sheet like that of the Local Bank in Chapter 16. The Federal Reserve raises reserve requirements to tighten credit just when the demand for loans from your long-standing business customers is rising. What would you do?
3. Suppose that prices are rising, 5 percent of the labor force is still unemployed, and a recovery in process seems to be running out of steam but you can't be sure. As a member of the Federal Reserve Board, what would you do?
4. When inflation and unemployment coincide, sensible Federal Reserve action would be to raise reserve requirements while buying bonds in the open market. True or false? Explain.
5. If the Treasury must borrow to finance a federal budget deficit designed to stimulate the economy, what should the Federal Reserve do? Suppose it holds the stock of bank reserves constant; what would you expect to happen to interest rates and credit conditions?
6. Suppose an inflationary boom is under way but Congress and the administration do not raise taxes to check it, as in early 1973. Should the Fed assume the full burden by drastically tightening money, even recognizing that monetary restraint alone can probably check inflation only by precipitating a "credit crunch" that may lead to a recession? What if it does not act?
7. If the Fed wishes to encourage stable growth in real GNP and employment, can you see any serious objections to merely increasing the money stock about 4 percent each year?
8. When tight money is needed to check inflation, should the Fed provide special loopholes for housing borrowers, to avoid limiting home construction? If so, why? How should they accomplish this goal?
9. Explain the gold standard and how it was supposed to guard against inflation.

The Lessons of Monetary Experience

History presents an unending series of cases that illustrate the problems faced in monetary policymaking. In each of the following historical vignettes, ask yourself what would you have done if you had been a policymaker?

The 1920s—Boom and Bust. Following World War I, by 1922 the economy had begun a long upward pull—almost a decade of good times and substantially full employment. In 1924 and again in 1927, prosperity was broken by hesitations. And as the boom continued, some observers questioned whether times were not too good. But the stock market soared as the public proclaimed permanent prosperity. The man in the street, the businessman, and the financier became speculators "in the market." Easy profits were available for the taking, especially since stocks could be bought on margin for only a tiny fraction of their price.

In the midst of this speculative fever, industrial production leveled off in 1928 and construction activity slumped. The general price level was stable. Federal Reserve authorities were divided among themselves on what was the best policy. Finally in 1929, they took mild deflationary action, in spite of widespread criticism, raising rediscount rates and speaking out against the excessive use of bank credit for speculative purposes. In late 1929 came the stock-market crash, triggering the worst deflation and depression of America's history.

Lesson: When times are good it's hard to know what's the right policy vis-à-vis speculation and minor fluctuations. And when the boom gets roaring, steps to check it are generally unpopular. What would you have done in 1928–29?

The 1930s—Crash and Stagnation. As the economy spiraled downward, it was far from clear whether this was a major depression or merely a temporary setback after a long period of rapid economic growth. The Fed reduced discount rates to ease credit in the deflation and by early 1931 there was considerable evidence that the worst was over.

But European financial crises in mid-1931 set off worldwide gold hoarding. Facing this gold loss, the Reserve authorities adopted a tight-money, high-interest policy to keep our gold from flowing abroad. The spiral of financial liquidation resumed. Unemployment soared. Runs on banks developed everywhere. On his inauguration day, Franklin Roosevelt's first major act was to declare a nationwide "bank holiday," closing all banks until the panic could be calmed and arrangements could be made to keep the financial system from complete collapse.

Following 1933, with Roosevelt's new appointees running the system, the Federal Reserve adopted easy money and low interest rates to fight the depression. Excess reserves were pushed up rapidly, and then, as prices began to rise, pulled back down to $1 billion in 1937. Soon after, the boomlet of 1936–37 crashed precipitously back to mass unemployment in early 1938. Again there was widespread criticism of the Federal Reserve increases in reserve requirements to restrain rising prices in spite of continued heavy unemployment.

From then on, the banks were flooded with reserves. Total bank credit and the money stock rose in response to these added reserves. But by 1939, GNP was still only back up to the level of 1929; eight or nine million people were unemployed; net private investment for the entire decade was a negative figure.

Lessons: (1) When mass deflation sets in, don't hesitate to flood the economy with liquidity. Hindsight makes it clear that the Reserve authorities made a fatal error in moving so slowly. (2) When times are bad, it's still hard to know what is the best policy vis-à-vis minor fluctuations. (3) In a major depression, flooding the economy with liquidity at least checks further financial liquidation and helps to stimulate total spending; but bankers and the public may pile up idle cash rather than lending and spending. The life of a central banker is not easy!

Monetary Policy and the National Debt—1946–51. At the end of World War II, over $275 billion of government debt was outstanding, nearly $100 billion of it held by the banking system. Between $50 and $75 billion of this debt came due for refunding each year. The Federal Reserve faced a dilemma. (1) If it tightened bank reserves and raised interest rates to check the postwar inflation, the squeeze would induce banks to dump their low-yield government securities on the market to get new reserves in order to make higher-yield business loans. This would force down the price of government bonds, with cries of anguish from the Treasury and the public. (2) On the other hand, if the Fed continued to provide plentiful reserves to finance bank loans to private borrowers, it could ease the Treasury's job of refinancing the national debt by keeping bond prices up and interest rates down; but then it would be lying down on its job as the nation's monetary spearhead against inflation.

At first, the Fed chose the latter path. It stood ready to buy all government bonds from the commercial banks at par, maintaining their price against decline. This meant that the banks' huge holdings of government securities were as good as excess reserves, since they could be converted into money with no loss at any time.

The Treasury, anxious to maintain confidence in the government's credit, liked this policy. If government bond prices fell, present holders might dump their bonds and refuse to buy others except at much higher interest rates. Political repercussions from government-bond holders could be very unpleasant for the administration in power if bond prices slumped. Many economists and others argued, however, that higher interest costs and sagging bond prices were a proper price to pay for the restoration of effective monetary restraint against inflation. The Fed increasingly took this view. If monetary policy was to check inflation, it argued, the Fed must tighten the overall credit supply, including a rise in interest rates to the federal government itself.

Thus, the Federal Reserve authorities gradually tightened up the money markets. Finally, in 1951, in an open break with the Treasury, the Fed withdrew its support for government bond prices. Bond prices fell below par, but bank credit was tightened and Federal Reserve control over the money supply was partially restored.

But even then, the Federal Reserve officials made it clear they would continue to work closely with the Treasury. Why? In spite of their "nonpolitical" status, Federal Reserve Board members are appointed by the president and are responsible to Congress. They recognize fully their primary role as part of the government. Their job is to work with other government agencies to produce a stably growing economy. With a major portion of the nation's money supply outstanding against Treasury bonds, it is clear that Federal Reserve monetary policy and Treasury policy in handling the federal debt must be made cooperatively.

Lesson: There are many considerations that must be weighed in forming wise monetary policy. One of the most difficult problems is the weight to be given to Treasury financing needs when they conflict with other stabilization objectives. The life of a central banker is not easy!

The Soaring or Sagging Sixties and Seventies. During the first half of the sixties, growth was slow and unemployment persisted until after the big tax cut of 1964 and the easy money that accompanied it. But with the Vietnam War and bulging spending on civilian programs, the problem soon became inflation. In 1966, with rising employment and inflation, the Fed hauled the growth rate in M down to zero for a six-month period. The result, as noted above, was soaring interest rates and a temporary credit crunch, as many borrowers were unable to obtain the loans they had expected. The boom was slowed, and the Fed quickly released the reins on M to avoid a slide-off into recession.

But victory was short, and before long the inflationary boom was on again. With soaring government spending and no tax increase, the whole burden of slowing the boom fell on the Fed, already smarting from criticism that it had dangerously risked precipitating collapse in the crunch of 1966. But by 1968 the problem was obvious to everybody, and monetary and fiscal policy cooperated to slow the inflation. Nevertheless, again the problem was, "how much?" The income surtax of 1968 apparently had little effect, and the Fed again slowed the growth rate of M to zero in 1969–70. Again, the medicine worked, and again there were anguished cries of credit crunch from the opponents of the restrictive action.[3] Again, the Fed relaxed the reins as soon as the slowdown was obvious. And again the inflation persisted through the credit crunch.

What would you have done as the economy again soared toward a boom in 1972? Inflation had slowed, with the help of President Nixon's Phase I and II, and unemployment eased back down below 5 percent. But victory over inflation was uncertain, as prices spurted upward in 1973, and unemployment stayed stubbornly above previous prosperity levels.

Lesson: Managing aggregate demand is very difficult when the economy is in the high-employment area. Tight money can check a boom; but if the dose is too strong, a credit crisis and recession may be the result. And if inflationary expectations are deepseated, monetary restraint is likely to slow real growth and employment before it makes much headway against rising prices. The old refrain: The life. . . !

[3]Every time the Fed tightens money to restrain economic expansion, the critics complain that the Fed is too "independent" and that it should be made directly subservient to the president.

Can We Have High Employment Without Inflation?

CHAPTER PREVIEW

CHAPTER EIGHTEEN

Reducing both unemployment and inflation to a sustainable minimum is the main task of monetary and fiscal policy. Either unemployment or inflation alone can be attacked readily. The former calls for easy money and an expansionary budget, the latter for the reverse actions. But when unemployment and inflation occur at the same time, there's trouble. And since World War II they have occurred simultaneously a large share of the time in most of the Western industrialized nations. How to maintain high employment and a stable price level simultaneously looks to be the big unsolved problem of macroeconomic policy, and the problem seems to be getting worse, not better, in most of the Western world.

THE UNEMPLOYMENT-INFLATION DILEMMA

In a perfectly competitive economy, increasing aggregate demand would generally lead to more output and employment whenever unemployment existed, and to inflation only after full employment was reached, as in the simple model of Chapter 9. As long as unemployed workers competed for jobs, wage rates would stay down and no firms could raise prices without losing sales to competitors. To be sure, as Chapter 9 pointed out, even in such an economy some inflation would occur before full employment was reached, because demand rises faster for some products than for others, and bottlenecks would be reached in some industries and areas while excess capacity remained in others. But these bottlenecks would be local and temporary, and could be alleviated by approaching full employment gradually, to give resources time to shift in accordance with consumer demand patterns. One lesson for monetary-fiscal policy is clear: Don't be greedy and try to eliminate unemployment too fast when the economy is approaching high-level employment.

But we do not live in a purely competitive world, and the unemployment-inflation dilemma is more basic than just the speed of increasing demand. Recently, inflation has developed and persisted even when unemployment is widespread. For example, the recession of 1970 scarcely slowed the rapid inflation inherited from the preceding years; prices rose at 6 percent annually in the face of rising unemployment, and inflation slowed only moderately in 1971 as unemployment stayed near 6 percent. Although President Nixon's Phase I and II wage-price freeze in late 1971 did slow inflation, even then prices continued to rise, and inflation was checked only temporarily, even with continuing substantial unemployment.

The Short-Run Unemployment-Inflation Tradeoff

When unemployment exists, pouring aggregate demand into the economy is almost sure to increase employment—if we don't care how much inflation we generate. If unemployment is widespread, inflation may be minor. At the extreme, in a major depression jobs may increase with no rise in prices at all. But the nearer we are to full employment, the bigger share of rising GNP will be higher prices rather than real output. And, as noted above, the faster the growth in aggregate demand, the less time there will be for markets to adjust and the more inflation is likely. In general, the more inflation we are willing to accept with rising aggregate demand, the more unemployment can be reduced through expansionary monetary-fiscal policy—at least temporarily. This is generally called the unemployment-inflation tradeoff. We can have more employment if we will accept more inflation.

These predictions rest on the theory of the firm, which will be considered in detail in Part Three. To maximize profits, a business firm will hire more workers to increase output if demand increases so it can sell more at the same or a higher price—unless its costs of production rise. If costs rise, then the firm will increase output only if selling prices can be increased at least enough to cover the higher costs. Thus, whether wages (the biggest cost item for most firms) rise faster or slower than selling prices is a crucial question.

As long as unemployment is widespread, wages are likely to lag behind rising prices. But the stronger unions are, the shorter such lags are likely to be. And, a very important consideration in a world of inflation, the more generally inflation is expected, the more workers will insist on bigger wage increases to offset rising prices. Then the wage-lag that makes it profitable for firms to hire more workers with rising prices vanishes, and the growth in aggregate demand generated by monetary-fiscal policy turns out to generate merely inflation with higher wages and higher prices, but no growth in jobs and real output. **Fundamentally, the tradeoff between inflation and unemployment rests on this wage-lag: If prices rise faster than wage costs, real wages will be reduced and it will pay to hire more workers. If wage costs rise faster than prices, inflation provides no incentive to hire more workers; indeed, the number of jobs may be reduced if real wages rise.**[1]

Thus, acceptance of inflation as a price of expansionary aggregate demand policy does not guarantee a lower level of unemployment. In the short run, a rapid increase in aggregate demand will usually increase employment; wages will generally lag temporarily, or at least not rise faster than prices. But whether the increase will be lasting or only temporary is less certain. If

[1]This is only a rough statement of the theory involved, but it presents the central issue. A more rigorous statement is provided in Parts Three and Four.

the wage-lag is only temporary, the new inflation-induced jobs will presumably be eliminated when wage costs catch up with the higher prices, and the result will be only inflation with no lasting increase in employment.

Is There a Long-Run Unemployment-Inflation Tradeoff?

A pioneering study by A.W. Phillips of the London School of Economics in the 1950s showed that in England over the past century, whenever unemployment fell below about 5 percent wage rates rose faster than was consistent with stable prices. Some American economists believed they found the same general relationship in our economy. This apparent tradeoff between unemployment and inflation, when shown graphically, is often called a "Phillips curve." Figure 18–1 plots the rate of inflation against unemployment for the United States since 1950. A curve is roughly fitted to the points for the 1960s, which suggests the unemployment-inflation tradeoff noted by Phillips.[2]

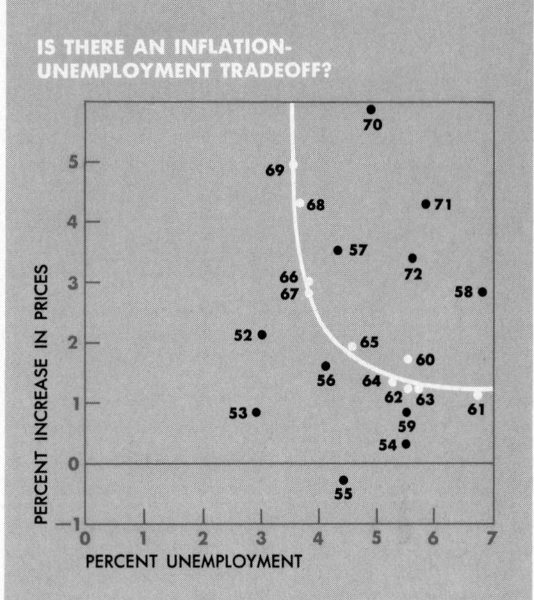

Figure 18–1

During the 1960s, prices generally rose fastest when unemployment was low, as is indicated by the curve fitted to data for the 1960s. But when data for the 1950s and 1970s are included this simple relationship no longer holds. (Source: U.S. Department of Labor.)

But economists have increasingly questioned this apparent long-run tradeoff for at least three reasons. (1) If you look at the dots for the 1950s and 1970s as well as the 1960s, it is obvious that there is no simple Phillips curve fit. The dots look almost like a random scatter; there are numerous cases of high inflation and high unemployment and the converse. (2) Look back at Table 7–4, on page 93, showing wages and profits since 1952. The wages-salaries share of national income *rose* during every inflation period, while profits were squeezed. Although these figures show wage incomes, not wage costs, they certainly don't support the hypothesis that wages have lagged during recent inflations. (3) In a world where inflation is increasingly expected, theory tells us that wage-lag will tend to vanish. As both workers and businesses come to expect inflation, workers include an inflation allowance in their wage demands, and businessmen are increasingly willing to grant such inflation allowances to buy labor peace. As inflation is built into anticipations, the wage-lag vanishes and with it businesses' incentive to hire more workers. Thus, a steady rate of inflation, once it has become anticipated, will not increase employment. Only an ever-increasing rate of inflation that continually runs ahead of anticipations can further reduce unemployment. It's hard to fool most of the people all the time that yesterday's inflation will be the last. Indeed, this reasoning suggests not only that monetary-fiscal policy cannot guarantee full employment without inflation, but that it is more likely to guarantee inflation without full employment.

How much of a long-run tradeoff actually exists between inflation and unemployment is a

[2]Actually, Phillips plotted the increase in wage rates against unemployment. But since wages are a big element in costs, many economists plot prices directly against unemployment, though logically this slides over a complex relationship between wage rates and prices.

complex, unsettled issue, on both empirical and theoretical grounds. Clearly, expectations adjust, but how fast and how completely is uncertain. Certainly we are unsafe in counting on more inflation to buy a continuing increase in employment. Two distinguished experts on the problem have summarized the situation as follows: "Authors of Phillips curves would do well to label them conspicuously: '*Unstable. Apply with extreme care.*'"[3]

Aggregate Demand and the Structure of Unemployment

Aggregate demand policy produced somewhat discouraging results during the early 1970s. Restrictive policy in 1969–70 stopped the boom and produced heavy unemployment, but it scarcely slowed the inflation. Rapidly growing aggregate demand thereafter got the economy moving again, but inflation continued while unemployment stubbornly hung around 6 percent and then only gradually fell below 5 percent in 1973, three years later. Part of the answer lay in the big increase in the labor force as prosperity returned, partly from people who had been discouraged in the recession and had temporarily stopped looking for jobs, but mainly from a huge increase in the number of teenagers and women entering the labor force for the first time.

It is useful to look behind the total unemployment figures. While total unemployment only fell to 5 percent by early 1973, unemployment of married prime-age males (25–55) was down to about 2 percent, comparable to other periods of prosperity. The high total unemployment figure reflected largely big increases in the numbers of unemployed young people, and to a lesser extent of women. Teenage unemployment was over 15 percent. A third of those were students seeking part-time jobs, and the turnover rate for other teenagers was high. During 1972, their average period of unemployment was only about eight weeks, against twelve for adults. Teenagers got jobs and left them more frequently than adults, reflecting partly frequent transitions between student and worker status and partly weak job attachment, probably because they found many of the available jobs uninteresting and dead-ends. Nearly half of all unemployed were below twenty-five.

Modern econometric models of the economy suggest that a large increase in aggregate demand which would reduce adult unemployment further and generate substantial inflation, would still leave high teenage unemployment rates, given these patterns of job behavior. If this conclusion is correct, it suggests the need for special labor-market policies to deal with the problem of teenage unemployment, rather than relying merely on aggregate demand policy—although perhaps this teenage problem will prove to be a transient one as the age structure of the population and education-job habits change.

To a lesser extent, the stubbornly high recent unemployment rate has reflected other subgroups with especially high rates. Minority unemployment has consistently averaged about twice that for whites, but there has been no huge increase of minority job-seekers comparable to that of teenagers, and the relative unemployment position of minorities has improved slightly. The unemployment rate for women has consistently been somewhat higher than that for men (6.6 against 4.9 in 1972) and there has been a huge influx of women into the labor force. Today, 44 percent of all working-age women are in the labor force, compared to only 25 percent in 1940, and women comprise nearly 40 percent of the labor force. Thus, unemployed women make up a much larger part of the total than in earlier prosperity periods, but unlike teenagers their relative unemployment rate has not worsened.[4] More aggregate demand would pre-

[3] A. Rees and M. Hamilton, "The Wage-Price-Productivity Perplex," *Journal of Political Economy,* February 1967, p. 70. For a good nontechnical summary of the controversy, see "The Relation Between Prices and Employment: Two Views," *Federal Reserve Bank of St. Louis Monthly Review,* March 1969 (and reprinted in the Joseph, Seeber, Bach *Reader*), which also includes references to more detailed studies on both sides.

[4] For a fuller account, see "The Economic Role of Women," *Economic Report of the President,* January 1973.

sumably reduce the unemployment rates of both minorities and women more rapidly than that of teenagers, though special manpower policies would seem appropriate for these two groups as well if we expect to get their unemployment rates near those for white males.

WAGE-PRICE (INCOMES) POLICIES

Monetary-fiscal policy alone is clearly not enough to guarantee full employment without inflation. Thus, nearly every major Western nation has sought other means to supplement aggregate-demand policy. One approach is direct controls to hold down wages and prices while expansionary monetary-fiscal policy generates full employment. If expansionary monetary-fiscal policy is thwarted by unions and businesses that raise their wages and prices, the answer of the man-in-the-street is simple: Pass a law forbidding inflationary wage and price increases. And nearly every major government has tried it at one time or another—but not with very much success in most cases. The other approach is manpower policies to increase the employability and employment of the unemployed, especially teenagers, minority groups, and others who lack marketable skills. Both are designed to reduce the level of inflation and increase the level of employment related to any given level of aggregate demand—to shift the Phillips curve to the left. Let us consider them in order.

The Kennedy Wage-Price Guideposts

In 1962, President Kennedy's Council of Economic Advisers suggested a set of wage-price "guideposts" for unions and businessmen, to keep wages and prices in line so aggregate-demand policy could be used to bring full employment without inflation. The Council didn't suggest government action to force unions and businesses to adhere to the guideposts, but it did urge them as useful guides to private behavior.[5]

[5]See *Economic Report of the President,* January 1962, Chap. 4.

In essence, the guideposts suggested that annual wage increases in all industries should roughly equal the average increase in output per man-hour in the economy.[6] With such wage increases, prices of final products should be kept stable. Bigger wage increases would be inflationary, while smaller ones would give an undue share of the benefits of increasing productivity to profits. The guideposts were based on the general position that wage rates should behave about as they would in a highly competitive market where supply and demand would tend to produce wage increases equal to increases in "productivity."

Consider a simple example. Assume a stable population and an economy where all income goes to wages and profits. Total output is $300, of which wages are two-thirds and profits one-third. Now suppose the total output increases by 3 percent (that is, $9), and that wages are increased by 3 percent, as suggested by the productivity guidepost. Wages will now rise by $6 (that is, 3 percent of $200), leaving $3 for increased profits (that is, 3 percent of $100). Thus, the average productivity increase guide would increase both wages and profits by the same percentage, maintaining whatever distribution

[6]Three details may help spell out the implications of the guideposts:

1. Wages in particular industries *should not* be directly related to productivity changes in that industry. Thus, if productivity in the automobile industry increases 5 percent per year, but only 3 percent for the economy as a whole, this does not justify a 5 percent wage increase in the auto industry. Rather, it calls for a decline in the price of automobiles.

2. Prices should remain approximately stable in industries that have an average rate of productivity increase. Where productivity increases faster than the national average (that is, where per-unit costs fall faster than the average), selling prices should decline. Prices should rise where productivity increases more slowly than the average.

3. Some exceptions are justified. Wages should rise less than the national average in industries where unemployment persists, to discourage additional workers from entering the industry and to encourage employers to use more labor in that industry. Wages should rise faster than the average where labor is especially scarce. (Again, these are the results to be expected from highly competitive markets.) Moreover, individual wages could rise more or less than the national average where deviation is needed to correct major inequities.

of income prevailed before. Don't make the common mistake of assuming that increasing wage rates in proportion to productivity increase would give all the increase to labor.

Critics of the guideposts made three points: First, if you don't think the present income distribution between wages and profits is fair, preserving it won't be very attractive. Many union members believe that profits are already exorbitant. Many businessmen believe profits are already too low. And at any time individual wage rates in particular firms or industries may be unfairly out of line, too high or too low.

Second, some economists said that government price- and wage-setting would lead to distortions and inefficiencies. By restricting the free play of market prices, the guideposts would block the proper responses of resources to market demands.

Third, the critics said guideposts just won't work. Both unions and businessmen told the government to keep its nose out. They wanted no government control over wages and prices. If productivity rises 5 percent annually in the auto industry, the auto workers are understandably reluctant to settle for only a 3 percent wage increase, just because productivity elsewhere has increased less than theirs. If you were head of the auto union, would you agree to a 3 percent increase when by hard bargaining you could get 5 percent? If you were president of General Motors, would you reduce prices just because the guideposts say to, when you could make bigger profits by keeping prices up? Would you take a costly strike to hold wages down to help the nation fight inflation, when the customers will pay higher prices and wages are rising in other industries? Without government sanctions, some unions and businesses will go along, but compliance is almost sure to be uneven and to erode the longer the guideposts are kept.

In retrospect, both the advocates and critics appear to have been right. Most studies conclude that the guideposts did help modestly to hold down wages and prices during their early years. But their impact was uneven and, in spite of extensive "jawboning" against violators by President Johnson and his Council of Economic Advisors, they became increasingly futile as aggregate demand soared in 1965–66, when they were abandoned.

The Nixon Wage-Price Programs

President Nixon's "game plan" on taking office in 1969 was first to halt the inflationary boom with restrictive monetary and fiscal policy, and then gradually to expand aggregate demand to restore high employment without inflationary excesses. The plan worked against the boom; real GNP levelled off and unemployment quickly shot up to 6 percent. But inflation didn't follow the scenario; prices kept right on rising, to 6 percent per annum in 1970, reflecting the preceding years of spiralling wages and prices during the Vietnam War boom. Monetary and fiscal policy were nevertheless reversed to fight unemployment, and money GNP resumed its growth, according to the game plan. But alas, the growth was over half price increases, while unemployment hung stubbornly near 6 percent.

By August 1971, the Administration couldn't tolerate the mixture of inflation and unemployment any longer, though both were gradually improving. Nixon froze virtually all wages and prices for two months, in Phase I of a new direct controls program, and then extended a less sweeping set of wage-price controls indefinitely, in Phase II.[7] A Pay Board and a Price Commission were established to administer the wage and price controls. Briefly, the Pay Board said wages should not rise more than 5½ percent annually,

[7]The President had power to impose such controls under the 1971 Amendments to the Economic Stabilization Act. For a fuller description of both Phase I and Phase II, see *Economic Report of the President,* January 1973, Chap. 2. Although their underlying philosophy was similar to that of the guideposts, the Phase II controls were applied to individual wages and prices, and differed in numerous details from the broad guidepost policies. One important difference was that the Price Commission imposed controls over business profit margins, in addition to price ceilings. If you were a businessman facing such a regulation, how much incentive would you have to increase efficiency and to reduce costs?

well below the rates of 1969 and 1970. The reasoning was that this would allow for a 3 percent growth in productivity plus a cost-of-living growth allowance of about half the existing inflation rate, thus slowing inflation down. The Price Commission said prices had to remain stable except that firms could pass along permissible wage and other cost increases. With a 3 percent annual improvement in productivity and a total $5\frac{1}{2}$ percent wage increase, labor costs per unit of output should increase only $2\frac{1}{2}$ percent or so per annum, and the 1972 inflation rate could be cut roughly in half. Then, presumably the pace could be slowed further the following year. In the meantime, aggregate demand could be expanded gradually while inflation was slowed by the direct controls.

Unlike the Kennedy guideposts, the Nixon controls had the force of law. But short of a massive new bureaucracy, it was clear there was no way to enforce ceilings on every wage and price in the United States, and the Nixon Administration had little taste for such a massive intervention. Phase I was designed to break the spiral of inflationary expectations that had developed in 1965–71. Then Phase II focused on wages and prices in large firms and pattern-setting industries where the forces of competition could not be counted on to do the job. All farm prices, interest rates, and other highly competitive markets were excluded at the outset, and the Pay Board and Price Commission soon exempted all small firms and wage bargains in other industries as well, using their limited enforcement powers against big unions and big businesses.

How well did the experiment work? We are still too near it for a definitive answer, but some facts are clear. Phase I was successful in breaking the inflation-expectations spiral at least temporarily, and inflation was completely checked for the moment. Under Phase II, the momentum of wage and price increases resumed, but the pace of inflation in both wages and prices gradually slowed; the consumer price index rose only 3 percent in 1972, down from 6 percent two years earlier, and simultaneously employment and real output soared with rising aggregate demand. Employment rose by 2.5 million in 1972, the largest peacetime increase in history. Unemployment fell below 5 percent in early 1973, for the first time since 1970.

The record was impressive. But many observers give only limited credit to the wage-price controls. They say that inflation was slowing before the controls, reflecting restrictive aggregate-demand policy in 1969–70 with the lags to be expected, and that the big improvement in real output and employment similarly reflected renewed expansionary aggregate-demand policy in 1971–72. And as the boom picked up speed in late 1972 and 1973, prices began to creep upward again in spite of controls, as aggregate-demand forces would predict.

Phase III was announced by President Nixon in January 1973. It eliminated mandatory direct controls over wages and prices while keeping a "big stick" in the closet to reimpose controls over big firms and unions that violated the Phase II criteria for wage and price increases, even though those criteria were no longer actively being enforced. Phase III, while clinging to a partial guidepost strategy, was a large step back toward free markets and reliance on monetary-fiscal policy to achieve high employment with minimal inflation. But in retrospect, the Phase II controls were relaxed too soon. Prices shot upward in early 1973, led by farm prices but followed by a wide range of industrial prices as well. Phase IV was hastily improvised to re-establish many of the Phase II controls. By the time you read this, the results will be observable. There is little evidence that the fundamental problem of the inflation-unemployment dilemma has been solved.

European Incomes Policies

Since World War II, the unemployment-inflation dilemma has been everywhere. Every major European nation has experimented with some form of wage-price, or "incomes," policy, some with several, in attempts to reconcile low unemployment with low inflation. Some countries have tried nationwide formal legal controls over all wages and prices, for example, the Netherlands and the United Kingdom. Others have tried "voluntary" plans, more like the Kennedy wage-price guideposts. Most have been somewhere in between.

Most European incomes policies have differed from the two major U.S. experiments in one major respect. In most European moves, the wage-price guidelines or rules have been developed with extensive consultation among all the major parties concerned—business, union, agricultural, and government leaders. This reflects two major facts of life in democratic nations. First, any sweeping wage-price control plan necessarily involves setting the relative income shares that will go to the major groups in the economy—hence the name "incomes policies." Second, no plan affecting such a vital economic interest of everyone involved can succeed for long without the working agreement of the major parties, whether the program is "voluntary" or legally mandatory. Unless the unions are willing to moderate their wage demands, the plan will blow up. If millions of workers strike, as they did in the United Kingdom in 1972, no democratic government can make them go back to work for long at what they consider unacceptable wages. Involving all the major interests in devising the guidelines has thus seemed to most governments essential to obtaining a national consensus with which labor, business, agriculture, and other major groups will go along.[8]

How well have European incomes policies worked? Results have varied, but two conclusions seem merited. First, they have generally helped to hold down wages and prices temporarily, for a matter of months or even years in some cases, especially where a good consensus was reached in their establishment. Second, in all cases they have failed to restrain wages and prices for long where large excess aggregate demand was permitted to develop. The force of the market and the self-interest of the millions of individuals in it are very strong, and no country has found a way to keep most workers, farmers, and businessmen indefinitely content with less income than they think they ought to have when the market invites them to raise their wages and prices. There are fewer businessmen than workers, and some nations have had better success holding down prices than wages. But the problem of acceptance cuts across all economic groups.

These European results closely parallel those in the United States. Although European incomes policies have generally involved more consultative planning, they face the same basic dilemma as the two American plans. In the showdown, most people want more, and long-continued control over millions of individual wage and price transactions is almost impossible through either legal enforcement or "voluntary" compliance if the controlled prices and wages are substantially below market levels. Incomes policies can help temporarily when there is little or no excess demand. And they can help to dramatize to everyone concerned the fact that self-defeating inflation can be avoided only if all parties keep their income demands roughly consistent with the total real GNP producible at existing prices. Thus, incomes policies may play an important educational political role. But on the evidence to date, they cannot take over from aggregate-demand policy the main job of avoiding inflation.[9]

MANPOWER AND LABOR-MARKET POLICIES

Because neither aggregate demand nor incomes policies alone seem able to assure high employment without inflation, policy makers have

[8]For an authoritative account of the European experiences, see L. Ulman and R. Flanagan, *A Study of Incomes Policies in Western Europe* (Berkeley: University of California Press, 1971).

[9]During World War II, mandatory general wage and price controls were used, complete with rationing of consumer goods and allocation of materials and labor. Even with such extensive government controls and wartime patriotic pressures for cooperation, inflation could not be eliminated. Many black markets developed, controls were widely evaded, and the authorities were forced to adjust legal wage and price ceilings upwards repeatedly during the war. Moreover, much of the inflation that was suppressed during the war materialized when controls were removed after 1945.

sought other ways to move the Phillips curve to the left—to decrease the level of unemployment associated with any given level of aggregate demand. Better job-information exchanges, training programs for the unemployed, government emergency employment, and reduced monopolistic barriers to entry by unions are examples of such measures. All are aimed at improving the efficiency of labor markets; all whittle away the core of unemployed for any level of aggregate demand; all are complementary, not competitive, with aggregate-demand policies for high-level employment.

Aggregate Demand and Structural Unemployment

Unemployment that seems impossible, or very difficult, to eliminate through more aggregate demand is often called structural unemployment. Workers whose skills are obsolete (for example, uneducated, poor, middle-aged displaced coal miners in West Virginia), whose IQs are very low, who have little education or marketable skills, or who have physical disabilities are examples of the structurally unemployed. The preceding analysis in this chapter suggests that many teenagers may also be almost structurally unemployed now, given their attitudes about the jobs they are willing to take and keep. There is some level of aggregate demand that will pull the structurally unemployed into jobs, but it may be very high and would produce rapid inflation before such unemployment was eliminated. More demand primarily bids up the wages of employed and readily employable workers, rather than providing jobs for the structurally unemployed. The obvious answer seems to be to retrain, educate, and move these unemployed to fit the jobs available.

But a warning is in order. It is easy to underestimate the power of prosperity to provide jobs. The experience of Pittsburgh in the 1960s is a good example. In 1961 the unemployment rate in Pittsburgh was over 11 percent, compared to a national average of about 6 percent. Employment in the steel mills had been declining persistently since World War II. The steel companies could produce one-third more steel than ten years previously, with fewer men. Pittsburgh was cited as a classic case of structural unemployment—unemployed steelworkers whose jobs were gone forever and who were ill equipped to take on other jobs and unwilling or unable to move to other areas.

But after the strong economic expansion of 1964, Pittsburgh unemployment at year-end was only 3.7 percent, compared to over 5 percent for the nation. Rapidly growing aggregate demand boomed needs for steel in the economy. Mills called displaced workers back to their jobs. Even more important, over the years 1960 to 1964 more than 100,000 people emigrated from the Pittsburgh industrial area as more jobs opened up elsewhere in the United States. The "hard core" of unemployed workers is of ice, not of iron. We can melt much of it away under the sun of strong aggregate demand. When private employers need labor, they usually manage to provide the training needed to fit unemployed workers to the jobs, better than special government training programs can do.

Government Manpower and Labor-Market Programs

The Kennedy and Johnson Administrations developed numerous programs to fit unemployed workers to jobs. Better employment exchanges, government job training centers, subsidies to private firms to train workers, special help for minorities, and a wide variety of educational programs were all aimed at improving the fit between the unemployed and the jobs available. At their peak in 1972, federal manpower and employment program expenditures totalled nearly $4 billion annually; this was nearly $1,000 per unemployed person, and did not include either education programs or additional manpower expenditures by state governments.

Results of these manpower programs have been discouraging. Many affected workers have not found jobs, or have not kept them if they were placed. Only training programs leading directly to known permanent jobs in private industry appear to have been generally successful. Government emergency jobs have led to only a few permanent private jobs. Many workers who were placed complained that their jobs were low-level and dead-end, which partially accounts for their high quit rates.

In the 1970s, the Nixon Administration sharply reduced federal expenditures on such programs, allocating about half the previous funds to the states and localities through revenue-sharing, on the ground that federal manpower programs were of dubious value and that local programs would have a better chance of matching workers to jobs. Above all, the Nixon Administration appeared impressed that the most efficient way to provide job training is through assuring adequate demand that will induce private firms to train the unemployed for jobs that open up.

Studies of manpower programs have suggested other problems and approaches. Given the special problems of teenagers in recent years, a special Youth Employment Service similar to that in the United Kingdom, to counsel high school graduates and help move them into suitable jobs, has been urged by many. High school programs directed toward developing vocational skills could help. Modification of the minimum wage law to permit employers to pay lower beginning rates to teenagers would remove an important barrier for many young people, who are not at the outset worth to employers the $1.60 per hour minimum they must be paid under existing law (in 1973). Some have suggested special federal subsidies to employers hiring such youths to lower the effective wage costs under the minimum wage law.

For adult workers, innovations in manpower and labor-market policies have also been suggested. For example, present unemployment insurance arrangements generally pay unemployment benefits equivalent to about half the worker's regular wage for lower-income workers. Recent studies suggest that effective unemployment benefits may approach the worker's regular wage when other taxes and benefits are added in. An employed worker earning $500 a month, for example, must pay federal income tax, social security tax, workmen's compensation tax, and state income tax in many states, all bringing his effective take-home pay down to, say $375. If he is unemployed, he gets unemployment insurance of $250, which is completely nontaxable. In addition, he is eligible for special children's benefits in most states, and for food stamps and public housing under the federal programs. For a family with two children his net income, while unemployed, is thus likely to be over $300 per month, so it only costs him $15–20 a week to be unemployed. If he has more children or if his wife works, the net cost will be even smaller, and in some cases he may receive more money unemployed than working.[10]

While unemployment insurance is an important built-in fiscal-policy stabilizer and provides major benefits for the unemployed, it obviously can substantially reduce the incentive to find another job promptly and thus increase the unemployment rate. In 1971, the average duration of unemployment was 14 weeks for those on unemployment insurance, compared to 10 weeks for others. This does not necessarily mean that unemployment insurance induces loafing; it may merely give the worker more time to look around carefully for another job. But it clearly increases the level of unemployment at any given time. The answer, most economists would argue, lies not in eliminating unemployment insurance, but in changing the total benefit system to increase the incentive to find a new job promptly.[11]

Most Western European nations, especially in Scandinavia, have government manpower and labor-market programs that go far beyond ours, and they have generally managed somewhat lower unemployment rates than ours, though

[10] Reflecting this situation, some union contracts (for example, in the auto industry) now contain "inverse seniority" provisions, giving workers with the longest seniority the right to be laid off first in seasonal cutbacks and the like.

[11] A related reform would be to alter the way in which employers are taxed to support unemployment insurance payments, so as to increase the employer's inducement to minimize seasonal and cyclical unemployment. The present employer "experience rating" system provides a very weak inducement.

generally with higher inflation rates. Sweden, for example, provides complete job retraining at full pay plus full moving allowances for workers who the government thinks will need to move to other jobs a year or more hence. Most European educational systems place more stress on occupational training, and job turnover is generally much lower in Europe than here, especially among young people. European manpower and labor-market programs are expensive, but most observers feel they have generally worked well. American manpower policy will be a source of both experimentation and controversy over the years ahead.

MORE DRASTIC (FUNDAMENTAL?) MEASURES

In a perfectly competitive economy, neither workers nor businesses would have any market power to set wages or product prices. In such a world, therefore, the unemployment-inflation dilemma would vanish, except for short-run problems when demand approached full-employment levels too fast to permit unemployed resources to adjust to shifting patterns of demand. The solution to the unemployment-inflation dilemma, therefore, some economists argue, is simple but drastic: Eliminate monopoly in the American economy! Outlaw all unions and firms large enough to have any appreciable individual market power. Goodbye to both General Motors and the United Auto Workers, to General Electric and the Electrical Workers, indeed to nearly every business firm and union we know, beyond small local establishments.

Not many Americans take such a dramatic remedy seriously. It would, in most people's eyes, involve throwing out the baby with the bathwater. But the underlying analysis suggests that less draconian measures toward more effectively competitive markets could help. Not least, abolition of such government-imposed barriers to competition as import quotas and tariffs that protect domestic producers against lower-price foreign competition, and provisions that all government-sponsored construction projects must pay prevailing peak union wage rates, could help significantly to obtain the price-reducing effects of competition.

Many steps have been suggested to lessen the unemployment-inflation dilemma. Some of them would surely help. But alas, the fact seems to be that the Western democratic economies have not yet found a real solution to this nagging problem of macroeconomics. Here, as so often, the problem is not one of economics alone, but of economics and politics together. And solutions to such problems cannot be found in economic analysis alone.

CONCLUSION ON STABILIZATION POLICY

At the end of this long analysis of stabilization policy, where do we stand? What are our chances of avoiding major depressions and inflations in the future?

The history of the last quarter century is encouraging. We weathered three wars, three reconversions to peace, and a wide variety of other economic shocks, without a major bust, albeit with a good deal of war-influenced inflation. The post-World War II growth in real GNP has been quite steady compared to its earlier roller-coaster performance. And we surely know a lot more than we did about what makes business cycles tick and how to damp them down. The optimists list the following specific factors, in roughly ascending order of importance.

1. Businessmen now plan their investment on a longer range basis. Thus, investment plans are less susceptible to short-term swings in expectations. Long-run growth is widely recognized as a dominant factor in business planning, and this factor reduces the likelihood of serious short-run collapses in investment.

2. Consumers have become adjusted to a high and rising standard of living, and they will not be panicked into cutting back their spending even though business conditions weaken. If in-

comes slide, they draw on liquid assets and borrow to protect their living standards, looking to a resumption of better times in the near future. This fact has been demonstrated repeatedly during the postwar years.

3. Federal, state, and local government spending of over $400 billion annually provides a massive, stable component of demand. Never before has there been such a huge, stable block of spending.

4. Federal tax and spending arrangements now have a large element of built-in countercyclical flexibility. All things considered, built-in federal fiscal flexibility will automatically absorb maybe a third of the shock of any drop in national income.

5. The banking and financial system has been greatly strengthened since the crash of 1929. We need never again have the enormous credit contraction that was the core of the 1929–33 collapse and of every other great depression. Federal insurance of bank deposits has substantially removed the danger of runs on banks, and the Federal Reserve now stands ready to convert bank assets into cash reserves in case of any major banking crisis, so a general financial collapse like that of 1929–33 is no longer thinkable.

6. We have learned how to fight depression through government-fiscal policy. We now understand business slumps far better than in 1929, and there is now general recognition that government deficit spending can provide massive buying power if private spending slumps. This was the lesson of World War II, when huge government spending rapidly bailed us out of unemployment into peak production and employment.

How convincing are these arguments? We're surely in better shape than ever before to avoid major depressions. But although we have powerful cannon to wheel up against big depressions, our small artillery to fight minor fluctuations merits less confidence. The inventory cycle alone is big enough to give us some nasty bumps, and we have yet to demonstrate our ability to fine-tune the economy effectively. The preceding discussion of the unemployment-inflation dilemma suggests a world of uneasy swings between the two when times are reasonably prosperous.

Yet to end on a negative note would be mistaken. Combined monetary and fiscal policy, plus improvements in our institutional arrangements, provide a powerful arsenal against instability that should eliminate massive depressions and help substantially to smooth out smaller fluctuations.[12]

[12]More thorough support for this analysis is presented in G.L. Bach, "The Search for Stability—What Have We Learned," in *Public Policy and Economic Understanding* (Washington, D.C.: American Bankers' Association, 1970).

REVIEW

For Analysis and Discussion

1. As a practical matter, is the present level of unemployment as low as we can expect without substantial inflation? Do you agree? Explain.
2. Look back at Figure 18–1. Using all the data plotted, can you see a Phillips curve tradeoff in the United States since 1950?
3. Explain how there could be a Phillips curve tradeoff in the short run but not in the long run. Why are inflation anticipations central to the analysis?
4. In the last four decades, labor unions have become much more powerful. Under these circumstances, according to some economists, government assurance that total spending will be kept up to high-employment levels would be, in effect, a guarantee of continued inflation. Why, if at all, would this be so?
5. Do the Kennedy wage-price guideposts or Nixon's Phase II and IV rules provide an equitable solution to the persistent quarrel between management and labor over income shares? Do they provide an effective means of solving the dilemma of high employment without inflation? Do they represent a dangerous intrusion of government into the private economy?
6. If neither monetary-fiscal policy nor incomes policies can assure high employment without inflation, what should we do?
7. Are big depressions and big inflationary booms obsolete? How would you rate the six arguments at the end of Chapter 18?

Stabilization Policymaking

The time is early 1973. The President has asked a number of his advisers (including you) what combination of specific monetary policy, fiscal policy, direct controls, manpower, and other measures appear most promising for the year ahead. What do you propose, and why?

The major facts are as follows:

The economy is moving up solidly from the slack levels of 1970 and 1971. Real GNP is rising at an annual rate of 7–8 percent per annum, over twice that of 1971. Employment has risen by nearly two and a half million in 1972, the largest peacetime increase in history; and, in spite of a huge increase in the labor force (mainly women and young people), the unemployment rate has at last begun to fall—to 5 percent, from 5.9 at the beginning of 1972.

However, the present unemployment rate is still far above other prosperity periods, when rates between 3 and 4 percent have been common. (The make-up of unemployment is similar to that shown in Tables 7-1, 7-2, and 7-3, but somewhat lower for all groups.) Manufacturing output is only about 85 percent of capacity. Real GNP is probably $30–50 billion below its full-employment level.

The pace of inflation has clearly slowed. Compared to a peak rate of about 6 percent per annum in 1970, the GNP deflator is now rising about 3 percent per annum. Industrial prices, especially, have slowed, although farm prices, lumber, medical care, and raw materials have begun to rise more rapidly again. New union wage settlements are running a percent or two below those of the preceding year, and few settlements are far out of line with the Pay Board Phase II ceiling of 6–6½ percent including fringe benefits. However, the big improvement in industrial prices has clearly come from the large improvement in productivity, which increased nearly 5 percent in 1972 as the economy has moved up from recession to fuller utilization of plant and equipment. Thus, labor costs per unit of industrial output in 1972 rose less than 2 percent, compared to 6 percent in 1969 and 1970.

How much of the inflation slowdown is due to the President's Phase I and II programs is unclear; coverage of the controls has been narrowed to big businesses and big union contracts only, but the government has enforced the ceilings actively against offenders in these classes. Some economists, businessmen, and labor leaders complain about inequities and distortions, and the administrative problems of enforcement are rising; but there still appears to be widespread public support for the controls over both wages and prices.

On the monetary and fiscal fronts, short-term interest rates have risen substantially, from about 3½ to over 5 percent during the year, although long-term and mortgage rates have shown little change. The money stock is rising about 8 percent per annum, well above the long-term growth rate of the economy, and money GNP is rising even faster (over 10 percent per annum); thus, velocity is rising substantially. The federal budget is heavily in deficit—nearly $20 billion for 1972—although the full-employment budget deficit is only about $5 billion.

The United States also has a large balance of international payments deficit—by far the largest in our history. Currently, imports are exceeding exports by about $6 billion annually and large amounts of capital have recently moved from this country to Europe and other nations.

The President is under pressure from both sides—to take more expansionary action to reduce unemployment faster, and to protect against a renewal of the inflation spiral. The expansionists agree that progress has been made, but point to the huge human and economic waste remaining when the economy operates so far under capacity. Inflation is substantially under control, they say, and even if prices rise a little faster, that is a small price to pay for more jobs and more output.

But the conservatives counter that the economy has a strong upward momentum, and that we are already well on the way toward a new unsustainable inflationary boom; further stimulation could be disastrous. Union wage contracts expire in crucial industries in 1973, and unless we can reduce inflation further, the workers are going to insist on new inflationary wage settlements. A realistic look at the price situation shows farm and raw material prices still out of control, and many services' prices rising at 4–5 percent and more. Recent success in slowing inflation has been due largely to huge productivity increases; these always come in business cycle upswings, and they always end when full employment is approached—to wit, during the year ahead. We are approaching full employment as fast as is consistent with avoiding a new inflationary boom and bust. Besides, unemployment today is much less serious than earlier because of its heavy teenage component and the short average duration of unemployment. Moreover, our fiscal and monetary policies are already inflationary. We have a huge government budget deficit, and the 8 percent growth rate in M is far above the sustainable growth in real output of around 4 percent annually. Lastly, our international balance-of-payments situation is desperate. The only way we can restore strength to the dollar internationally is to reduce our domestic rate of inflation and show the world we can put our own economy and monetary-fiscal policies in order. (A more complete description of the situation is available in the *Economic Report of the President,* January 1973, Chaps. 1–3.)

What do you recommend?

APPENDIX TO PART TWO

Current Research

The main job of an elementary economics textbook is to stir an interest in economic problems, to present the central analytical tools of economics, and to provide some guided experience in using them to reach independent judgments on current economic developments and public-policy issues. I hope that the preceding pages have conveyed some sense of the lively urgency of the problems with which economics deals, and some sense of the manner in which modern economics helps to solve them.

Economists spend much of their time using the tools presented here and helping to devise public policies that will make our economic system work better. But one of the further things that makes economics exciting is research—the fascination of probing for new knowledge and new insights into how the economic system works. Economics is far from a dead, stable body of theory and knowledge. It is the research of today that will make the better textbooks and the better world of tomorrow.

It is the purpose of these brief appendixes at the end of each Part to convey a brief impression of the kinds of research currently under way in economics. Some of the research cited is readily understandable by a good student at the elementary level; other parts are more difficult. But the purpose is not to provide references that all beginning students should read. Rather it is to suggest some samples of economic research that may be intriguing to students who want to look beyond the text and who want to know more about what economics is and what economists do. Pick out two or three and look at them. If they don't hit the spot, try another. The goal is to interest you and make you want to read further.

The following paragraphs briefly report a small sample of research on some major problems covered by Part Two. There is no intention to imply that they represent the best, or the most important, research under way on the problems covered. They are merely samples of research that one economist thinks might be interesting to curious students getting acquainted with economics. A . ajor criterion in selection has been variety. A half dozen other comparable lists could readily be provided—and, indeed, your instructor may be happy to provide one he feels is superior.[1]

Inflation and Unemployment. A good start on the "Phillips curve" controversy is provided by "The Relation Between Prices and Employment: Two Views," (Federal Reserve Bank of St. Louis *Review,* March 1969), (in JSB Readings). Barbara Bergmann presents a penetrating analysis of the difficulties of attaining full employment through aggregate-demand policy, with stress on the problems of minorities and women, in "Curing High Unemployment Rates among Blacks and Women," Joint Economic Committee, U.S. Congress, *Reducing Unemployment to 2 Percent,* October 17, 1972. The Brookings Institution *Papers on Economic Activity* (published three times annually) presents a series of research analyses of macroeconomic policy, at a relatively nontechnical level; see, for example, G.L. Perry, "Unemployment Flows in the U.S. Labor Market" (1972:2) and R.E. Hall, "Proposals for Shifting the Phillips Curve Through Manpower Policy" (1971:3). A broader approach, which combines economic, social, and political factors, is G.L. Bach's *The New Inflation* (Providence, R.I.: Brown University Press, 1973). Chapter 2 analyzes the effects of recent inflation on different groups. Gardner Ackley's *Stemming World Inflation* (The Atlantic Institute, 1971) stresses the international aspects of inflation. Finally, California's L. Ulman and R. Flanagan provide an authoritative, but discouraging, analysis of incomes policies in *A Study of Incomes Policies in Western Europe* (Berkeley: University of California Press, 1971).

Monetary and Fiscal Policy. The great debate between the monetarists and neo-Keynesians has

[1]A number of the following references, in this and other appendixes on current research, have been reprinted in M.L. Joseph, N.C. Seeber, and G.L. Bach, eds., *Economic Analysis and Policy,* 4th edition (Englewood Cliffs, N.J.: Prentice-Hall, Inc., 1974). These cases are marked, "In JSB Readings."

spawned a huge literature. For a starter, try "Two Views of the Role of Money," by Yale's James Tobin and Carnegie-Mellon's Allan Meltzer, in *Controlling Monetary Aggregates* (Federal Reserve Bank of Boston, 1969), (partly in JSB Readings). Milton Friedman's *A Program for Monetary Stability* (New York: Fordham University Press, 1969) is an authoritative statement of the monetarist viewpoint. Arthur Okun provides two excellent examples of applying modern fiscal analysis to recent situations in "Measuring the Impact of the 1964 Tax Reduction," in W.W. Heller, ed., *Perspectives on Economic Growth* (New York: Random House, Inc., 1968), and "The Personal Tax Surcharge and Consumer Demand" (Brookings *Papers,* 1971:1). Herbert Stein provides a fascinating account of the development of modern fiscal policy, with some surprises, in *The Fiscal Revolution in America* (Chicago: University of Chicago Press, 1969). G.L. Bach's *Making Monetary and Fiscal Policy* (The Brookings Institution, 1971) is a study of the political and economic interactions which occur in real-world policy making; see especially Chapters 5–8.

Forecasting. If you're interested in some of the newer developments in economic forecasting and know a little mathematics, any of three recent studies will give you a good introduction; "A Quarterly Econometric Model of the United States," (*Survey of Current Business,* May 1966); "Forecasting with an Econometric Model," by Daniel Suits (*American Economic Review,* March 1962); and "A Short-Term Forecasting Model," by Pennsylvania's I. Friend and P. Taubman (*Review of Economics and Statistics,* August 1964). W.W. Leontief's "The Structure of the U.S. Economy," (*The Scientific American,* April 1965), describes "input-output analysis." A survey of modern forecasting techniques is provided by Part One of W. Butler, R. Kavesh, and R. Platt, eds., *Methods and Techniques of Business Forecasting* (Englewood Cliffs, N.J.: Prentice-Hall, Inc., 1974).

MARKETS, THE PRICE SYSTEM, AND THE ALLOCATION OF RESOURCES

PART THREE

The Business Firm and Its Costs

CHAPTER PREVIEW

CHAPTER NINETEEN

Chapters 1–6 presented an overview of the way a market economy solves the big economic problems—how it allocates society's limited economic resources to meet consumers' wants. Consumers spend their money on what they want most. Businessmen, in search of profits, have an incentive to produce the goods and services consumers want most because that is how they will generally make the biggest profits. In Part Three we now want to examine in detail how, and how well, this process works, building on the simple demand and supply analysis of Part One. How far can we rely on the market process to use our limited resources efficiently? Is big business now so powerful that it diverts consumer dollars into its own pockets, and through advertising manipulates consumers so they buy what yields the biggest business profits rather than what they really want? Where and how, if at all, should we turn to government to decide what to produce, how to produce it, and who should get it?

It is useful to begin by looking carefully at the way business firms respond to consumer demands—at the supply side of the demand-supply interaction. This chapter analyzes business' costs in producing the things consumers want. Chapter 20 then explains how these costs influence businessmen's production and pricing decisions.

WHY WORRY ABOUT COSTS?

Why worry about costs? Because a businessman's costs largely determine how much he will produce in response to different demands, and the lowest price at which he can sell and stay in business. If customers won't pay more than $1 for a widget and the minimum cost of producing widgets is $1.25, you don't need to be an expert economist to see it won't pay to produce widgets. How far any business will go in producing what consumers want will depend on how much that article costs to produce relative to how much buyers will pay for it.

Business costs are important for another reason. Looked at as wages, salaries, rent, and interest payments, business costs are the incomes of workers and of resource owners. In explaining business costs, therefore, we are simultaneously explaining why most people receive the incomes they do.

But most important, in an economy with scarce resources the cost of producing anything provides a measure of the alternative uses foregone. The basic fact of scarcity (limited resources) means that the "real" cost of producing anything is the alternatives foregone that might have been produced with those resources. For example, the *real* cost of producing an auto is the other commodities given up that might otherwise have been produced with the same steel, glass, rubber, and labor. The real cost is an "alternative cost"—the alternative uses of the resources that are given up when the resources are used in producing autos. Sometimes alternative cost is called "opportunity" cost.

This concept of alternative, or opportunity, cost can be put into money terms. Thus, the cost of producing one TV is the amount of money necessary to get the factors of production needed for the set away from alternative uses. The TV manufacturer has to pay enough to mechanics to get them away from auto and radar plants. He has to pay enough for copper wire to bid it away from telephone companies. And so it is for every resource he uses. In economic terms, the total cost of the TV is the amount necessary to bid all the required resources away from the strongest competing uses.

Accounting and Economic Costs

Business money costs of production include wages, materials, rent, interest, and all the other items listed in the profit-and-loss statement in the Appendix to Chapter 4. But use of an alternative-cost concept leads economists to somewhat different cost figures from the ones that businessmen and their accountants work with. These differences arise primarily because the economist includes several items that the accountant ordinarily doesn't consider as costs when he draws up his profit-and-loss statements.

A simple example is the independent corner grocer, who has bought a store with his own money and runs it himself. In addition to the regular business costs in the profit-and-loss statement, the economist would say:

> How about a return on your own investment and a salary for yourself? If you didn't have your money tied up in the store, you could be earning 5 percent on it in another investment. If you weren't working in the store, you could earn $10,000 a year working for Krogers. You ought to account as costs a 5 percent return on your investment and a $10,000 salary for yourself before you compute your profit for the year, because these reflect real alternatives that you're giving up when you stay in your business.

If the grocer does not include these costs and finds he's making a $9,000 annual "profit," he may think he's doing well—but actually he's kidding himself. The $9,000 doesn't even give him the salary he could earn working for someone else, much less the return he could get by doing that and investing his money somewhere else. If his investment was, say, $20,000, his interest foregone elsewhere at 5 percent would be $1,000 annually. His accounting "profit" would have to be $11,000 on the store ($10,000 salary plus $1,000 interest) just to break even.

A similar, though less obvious, situation is found in business corporations. Corporations pay salaries to their officers and employees, so there's no problem there. And they pay interest to their bondholders, which is considered a cost in computing profits. But what about the interest on the owners' (stockholders') investment, just as on the corner grocer's investment?

The usual accounting calculation of corporation profits omits the alternative cost of using the stockholders' capital in this firm rather than elsewhere. Accounting profit is calculated before any dividends are paid to stockholders. **The economist, however, includes in the firm's costs a reasonable rate of return on stockholders' investment (measuring the alternative return that is foregone elsewhere). He therefore considers as "economic profit" only the excess income over and above this basic alternative cost, because a reasonable rate of return is part of the cost required to keep funds invested in any business. Thus, part of dividends to stockholders should be counted as costs.**[1]

Throughout the rest of this book, we shall use the alternative-cost concept. Thus, costs of production will include the reasonable ("normal") rate of return (profit) on investment necessary to keep the funds invested in any given concern rather than elsewhere. Costs will include the entrepreneur's salary if he is self-employed, and dividends equal to a normal return on capital invested by stockholders. Broadly, they will include all costs required to get and keep resources in the occupation under consideration. Most costs will be the same as those used by the accountant, but the differences noted above must be kept in mind. **Especially, remember that the production-cost data and curves used here include a "normal" return, or profit, on investment, if you want to avoid some dangerous pitfalls later on.**

[1]In economics, costs that show up in the usual accounting procedures are often called "explicit" costs, while alternative costs (such as a return on stockholders' investment) that are not usually recorded in modern accounting are called "implicit" costs.

CASH VERSUS ECONOMIC PROFITS: A MANAGERIAL APPLICATION

A simple managerial example may help show the importance of these distinctions, as well as give you an impression of how basic economic analysis can help in day-to-day business. Suppose you're in business for yourself, doing miscellaneous repairs (carpentering, electrical wiring, and so on) at a minimum charge of $10 per call and $4 per hour additional after the first hour. Your only equipment is your family station wagon; you have converted the back to carry your working tools. You are prepared to answer calls anywhere in your general area. You've spent $20 for an ad in the local paper and for a supply of mimeographed postcards mailed at random to names from the phone book.

After a month, you've collected a large amount of experience, considerable boredom waiting for the phone to ring, and $620. Have you made a profit? Should you stay in business?

The answer to the profit question hinges on what your costs have been. If you deduct the original $20 outlay, you have $600 left. Not bad for a summer month. But look again. There is clearly gas and oil for the station wagon. And wear and tear on the same, which may be appreciable from this use. Then, aside from any materials (for which you may have charged extra), there's the question of your own time.

Suppose gas and oil allocable to this work have cost $80. And you make a rough estimate of $50 a month extra depreciation on the car. That still leaves you $470. Is that more or less than a reasonable wage for your own full time and energy for the month? Here the concept of opportunity cost provides a guide to the answer. What could you hope to make elsewhere, doing work you consider about equally interesting, difficult, and convenient? If the answer is above $470, you've made a loss, even with $520 in the bank. If it's less than $470, you've made a profit, though maybe a very small one. Central concepts from economic analysis: the distinction between cash and income, and opportunity cost. Without them you're apt to pull a real business boner.

COST OF PRODUCTION AND THE RATE OF OUTPUT[2]

How do a business firm's costs vary with the amount it produces? Imagine a small company that produces a single product—say it assembles luxury-level stereos. Suppose the company's only costs are raw materials, labor, depreciation on plant and equipment, maintenance, and return on stockholders' investment. Suppose further that, if we look at costs over the period ahead, we find that depreciation and a normal (implicit) return on stockholders' investment are "fixed" for the next year—they go on whether the company operates at full capacity or partial capacity, or shuts down. The other costs are "variable," depending on the company's rate of output.

Assume that the "fixed" costs amount to $1,000 per month, and that the "variable" costs vary with changes in output as in Table 19–1. Total cost is simply the sum of fixed and variable costs.

These same costs are plotted in Figure 19–1. Cost is shown on the vertical axis, output on the horizontal one. The fixed cost totals $1,000, the same no matter what output is produced. On top of this, we need to put total variable cost—zero at zero output, $2,000 for one set, $2,500 for two, and so on. The total-cost curve (top line) thus shows the sum of total fixed and total variable cost at each level of output.

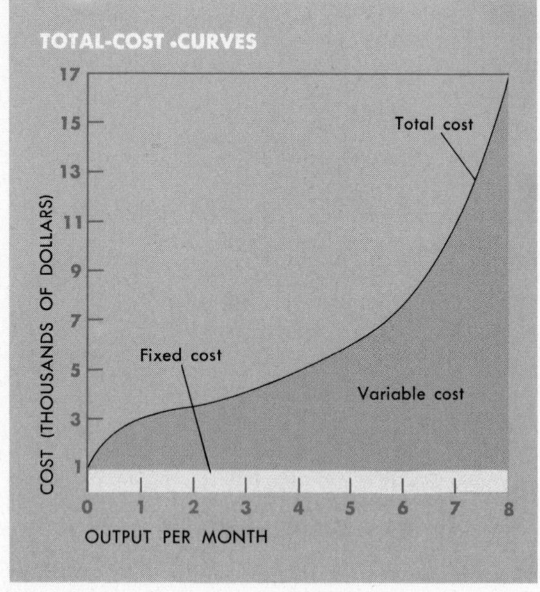

Figure 19–1

Total fixed cost is $1,000 at all outputs. Total variable cost rises as output increases. Total cost for any output is the sum of fixed and variable costs; it rises rapidly once the "capacity" of the plant is reached.

[2]The appendix to this chapter, "Physical Production Relationships Underlying Cost Curves," provides the logical foundation for this cost analysis. It should be assigned here by those instructors who wish a rigorous analytical foundation for this and the following chapter, but students can grasp the central issues in the text without it.

TABLE 19–1
Fixed, Variable, and Total Costs

OUTPUT PER WEEK	TOTAL FIXED COST	TOTAL VARIABLE COST	TOTAL COST
1	$1,000	$ 2,000	$ 3,000
2	1,000	2,500	3,500
3	1,000	3,100	4,100
4	1,000	4,000	5,000
5	1,000	5,000	6,000
6	1,000	6,600	7,600
7	1,000	10,000	11,000
8	1,000	16,000	17,000

It is easy to see that total cost does not rise at an even rate. It doesn't cost much more in total to produce two sets than one, or three than two. But as the firm gets up to six or seven sets per month, total cost begins to rise much more rapidly. It is obviously total variable cost that begins to shoot up. The reason may be that the company was set up with a capacity of only five or six sets a month, and to exceed this capacity involves expensive readjustments in equipment, hiring more workers, or overtime labor, and other such special problems. Nearly all firms see their variable costs shoot up if they try to produce beyond their plant's planned capacity.

TABLE 19–2
Total and Marginal Costs

OUTPUT	TOTAL COST	MARGINAL COST
1	$ 3,000	
2	3,500	$ 500
3	4,100	600
4	5,000	900
5	6,000	1,000
6	7,600	1,600
7	11,000	3,400
8	17,000	6,000

Marginal Cost

Marginal cost is the addition, or increment, to total cost involved in expanding output by one unit. For example, if the total cost of producing three sets per month is $4,100 and that of producing four sets $5,000, the marginal cost of expanding production from three to four units is $900. That's how much *extra* it costs us to get the fourth set produced. This calculation is shown in Table 19–2, using the cost data from Table 19–1.[3]

Marginal cost will be a very important concept in the chapters ahead. Most business decisions involve choices "at the margin"—to produce a little more of this or a little less of that. In making such choices, the logical procedure is to compare the marginal cost of the change with the marginal income, or benefit, from it, to see whether the net result is positive or negative. Be sure you understand marginal cost before going on.

Costs per Unit of Output

Except for marginal cost, the preceding data don't show costs per set produced, and you probably think of business output in terms of cost and selling price per unit. You may already have divided the total-cost figures by the number of stereos produced to see what the cost per set is at different levels of output. If you haven't, it's a sensible thing to do. The result is shown in Table 19–3.

Fixed cost per unit will always be a steadily decreasing series, because the constant total-fixed-cost figure (here $1,000) is divided by a steadily rising volume of output. This is what is commonly known as "spreading the overhead." The drop in fixed cost per unit is very rapid at first, but as volume grows the additional cost reduction per unit steadily decreases in importance.

Variable cost per unit will generally fall at the outset, then flatten out somewhat, and then rise again as plant "capacity" is approached. To produce one set, the company has to have labor and materials of all the types needed for the set. On the labor side, it will clearly be inefficient to try to call each type of skilled labor in just long enough to work on one set. If we try to use two or three jacks-of-all-trades, we get less efficient work. Similarly, it may be cheaper to buy materials in larger quantities, and so on. It's not efficient to produce only one or two sets a month.

At the other extreme, once the "capacity" for which the plant was planned has been reached,

[3]For students who study the Appendix to this chapter: Marginal cost is the cost counterpart of marginal productivity. Other things equal, marginal cost will be lowest when marginal productivity is highest.

TABLE 19-3
Fixed, Variable, and Total Costs per Unit

OUTPUT	FIXED COST PER UNIT	VARIABLE COST PER UNIT	TOTAL COST PER UNIT
1	$1,000	$2,000	$3,000
2	500	1,250	1,750
3	333	1,000	1,333
4	250	1,000	1,250
5	200	1,000	1,200
6	167	1,100	1,267
7	143	1,430	1,573
8	125	2,000	2,125

costs will shoot up if we try to produce still more sets per month. "Capacity" is seldom an absolute limit in a plant. For example, steel plants may operate above 100 percent of capacity; rated capacity allows for an average amount of shut-down time for maintenance and repairs, which can be postponed temporarily. But expansion of output beyond plant "capacity" often means expensive overtime work, hiring of lower-skilled workers, more spoilage under pressure of speed-up, and a variety of other such factors.

Thus, without going into details at the moment, it seems reasonable that with any given plant (which we have assumed) variable costs per unit will rise rapidly at some point beyond "capacity" output. Just when this point is reached depends, of course, on the individual firm. In many industries, variable costs per unit are apparently flat over wide ranges of output. In others, where small-scale operations are advantageous, increase in output beyond low levels leads quickly to rising unit costs.

Total cost per unit is simply the sum of fixed and variable costs per unit. It can also be obtained by dividing total cost by the number of units produced. The decreasing fixed cost per unit will always pull down on total unit cost as output rises. At first, as long as both fixed and variable costs per unit are declining, clearly the total cost per unit is declining. But at some point total unit costs will begin to rise, often after a long flat area in which the fixed cost per unit declines slightly and the variable cost per unit is substantially constant or slightly rising. The rise in total unit cost will begin when variable cost per unit turns up more than enough to offset the downward pull of declining fixed costs per unit. This point is at the sixth unit in our stereo plant. Total unit cost is relatively stable over the output range of three to six units, with the minimum cost per unit at an output of five sets per month.

This simple stereo example should warn you against one common fallacy—the idea that each firm has a cost of production for its product. In every firm, cost of production per unit varies with output. This is certain at the extremes of very low and above-capacity output. It often also occurs over the range of normal variation in operations.[4]

All these per-unit-cost data can readily be plotted on graphs as cost curves. Figure 19-2 shows the per-unit cost data for our stereo firm.

[4]Many firms now use what they call "standard costs" in pricing their products. A "standard cost" for our stereo would be an estimate of how much it should cost to produce one set at a normal, or typical, rate of output. If we think of four sets weekly as about normal operation, our standard-cost figure would be $1,250 per set. It is important, however, to remember that "standard cost" is only an estimate of unit cost at some selected level of output, not necessarily the minimum unit-cost level.

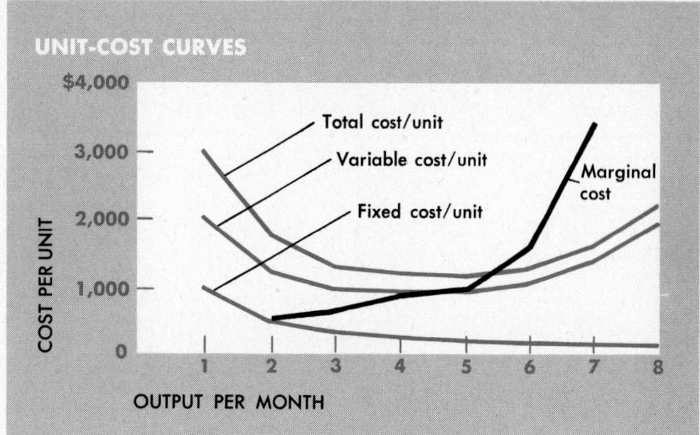

Figure 19–2

Unit-cost curves are derived by dividing the corresponding total-cost curves by total output. Here fixed unit cost slopes continuously downward as the constant total cost is spread over more units of output. The variable and total unit cost curves are U-shaped, and are cut by the marginal cost curve at their lowest points.

Fixed cost per unit falls steadily as the constant total cost is spread over more and more units. Variable cost per unit and total cost per unit are both U-shaped, for the reasons explained above. In most firms, the *TUC* (total-unit-cost) curve is probably flatter than in this hypothetical case. That is, there is a wider range of output over which total cost per unit is substantially constant, between the low-output inefficiencies shown at the left of the graph and the above-capacity inefficiencies at the right. (For a large, real-world plant producing hundreds of sets weekly, the cost curves would be smooth and continuous, without the corners shown in the curves for our very small firm.)

Be sure you know just what the graph means. For example, at an output of five sets, the fixed cost per set will be $200 and the variable cost per unit $1,000, for a total of $1,200. This happens to be the lowest point on the total-unit-cost curve. It is called the "least-cost combination." It is the lowest cost at which these stereos can be made, given the existing plant and the firm's other commitments. This is the lowest price at which we can get resources away from alternative uses and still cover all costs.

Reading the marginal cost curve takes special care, since it shows the *extra* cost involved in increasing output from one level to another. For example, the marginal cost of increasing output from two to three sets per week is $600. Read the marginal cost curve at $1,600; this point shows how much *extra* it would cost to raise output from five to six sets.

"SHORT-RUN" AND "LONG-RUN" VIEWS OF COSTS

Economists speak of the "short run" and the "long run." Time is an extremely important variable in the analysis of economic problems, and this distinction is an attempt to clarify the assumptions being made about the time period involved in any case. We mean by the "short run" any time period in which some costs (such as rent and interest on borrowed funds) are fixed and do not vary with changes in the firm's output. We mean by "long run" a time period long enough so that all costs become variable with changes in output. Thus, the distinction is an analytical one. In calendar time, the short run for one firm may be longer than a long run for another, depending on how long the cost commitments run in different cases.

Some examples will clarify this distinction. For our firm, next month is clearly a "short run." During that month certain costs are fixed no matter how many stereos we produce—depreciation on the factory building, for example. Given a longer time period, the existing plant will depreciate away or it may be sold, so the capital tied up in the plant becomes available for other uses. Similarly, the manager's salary is a fixed cost for the next month, but over some longer time period his contract will expire and his salary will become a variable cost. If a firm has commitments for fixed costs extending for years ahead, the "short run" for that firm will be a long time. The most common way to think of the "short run" is the time period over which a firm has a fixed plant and equipment to which variable agents such as labor and materials are added to achieve different output levels.

In the "long run," by contrast, all the firm's costs become variable. The entrepreneur can decide to build a new plant of different size if he likes. He can transfer his investment to another industry. He has complete freedom to move.

The Optimum Scale of Enterprise

The "long run" is thus a planning period, free from the short-run limitations imposed by fixed plant and other commitments. The big long-run planning problem is: What is the "optimum scale of enterprise" for the firm? How big a fixed plant, how big a labor force, how much equipment? The question involves everything related to planning the enterprise's scale of operations in the future.

Businesses seldom find themselves in a position to make all these decisions on future scale at one time. But they are continually making changes, so that in essence they may replan their overall scale of enterprise much more frequently than would appear from a superficial glance.

A set of five possible planning curves, showing expected costs for five different scales of enterprise, is given in Figure 19–3. Each *TUC* curve corresponds to a given scale of enterprise—a plant of certain size, equipment of certain sorts, and so on. The scale of enterprise at the extreme left is obviously too small to be advantageous except for a very small market. In this figure, the scale corresponding to the fourth cost curve gives the lowest possible least-cost point. A firm of this size is the "optimum scale of enterprise," in the sense that it provides the possibility of the lowest cost per unit of output of any possible scale of enterprise. Note, however, that, if total market demand is small, it may still not be economical to build and operate a firm of this scale.

How Big Is "Optimal"?

The optimal scale of enterprise varies widely from industry to industry. It is clear that very large plants and firms are required in some industries to obtain peak efficiency—for example, in autos, cigarettes, petroleum, and steel. But the evidence is also clear that in many industries medium-sized or even small firms manage to achieve costs as low as the giants. Rates of return on invested capital do not appear to

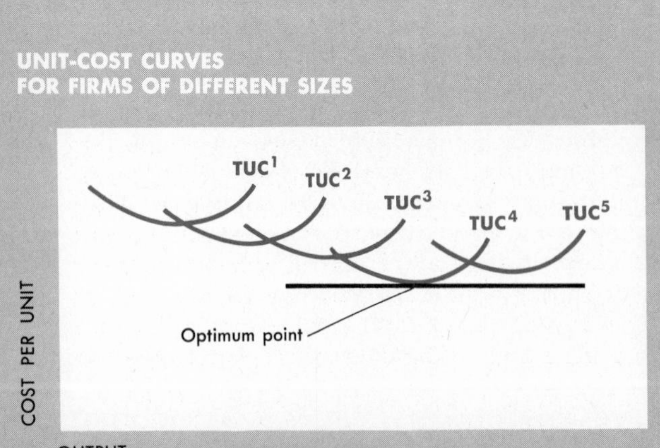

Figure 19–3

Larger firms have lower minimum total-unit-cost points until the optimal scale of firm is reached. Then still larger firms face higher minimum TUCs.

be consistently larger for huge than for medium-sized firms, though some of the giants are among the most profitable firms. An indirect test of the optimal scale of firm is provided by the size of firm that grows fastest. Here again the evidence is mixed. For the economy as a whole, the share of market obtained by the largest firms is growing, but only slowly—though nearly all firms are getting bigger as the economy grows. In only a few industries are the giants clearly increasing their dominance. In steel, for example, the share of the market held by U.S. Steel, the biggest firm, has fallen substantially over the last several decades. The empirical evidence shows clearly that there is no single, pat answer to the question: How big is optimal?

Do Businesses Operate at Optimal Scale?

If we look at all the firms in any particular industry, we will probably find a wide divergence in size. Why aren't all the firms the "optimal" size? There are many reasons. But a summary might look like this:

1. In some cases, the market isn't big enough to permit all firms to operate at optimal scale. In such industries, a firm may operate at lower costs per unit with a small plant than it would with a large plant that was used at only partial capacity.
2. Some firms just want to be big. Firms may become overexpanded as part of a drive to attain dominance in their industry. Men with dreams of industrial empire may expand beyond optimal scale in their drive for bigness and prestige. It is hard to measure this factor, but the last century of U.S. history has produced many cases where this motive appears to have been important.
3. Sometimes fear of government action holds firms back from profitable expansion. This is true when a firm fears that further growth may bring government action to break it up, under the Sherman Antitrust Act or other antimonopoly legislation. It is often alleged that this fear is what keeps General Motors from taking a still larger share of the auto market.
4. Probably most important of all, errors and delays in adjusting to changed conditions mean that at any time most firms will not be at optimal scale. Plans in establishing a new plant are inevitably imprecise on many factors: new technology, future wage rates and prices, scale of market available, and so on. And even if the estimates could be precise, change is inescapable in economic life. Before long, new situations will arise, new technological changes will appear. Replanning optimal scale is a continuous process for the well-managed firm.

SOCIAL COSTS AND PRIVATE COSTS

Large profits in an industry are a signal that resources can profitably be moved into that industry from elsewhere. Losses are a signal that resources can earn more elsewhere and should be moved away. Profits and losses are thus crucial signals in the working of a free-market economy.

If the signals are to be correct, costs of producing goods should reflect fully the alternatives foregone. Generally, the private costs incurred by the firm in obtaining resources (wages, rents, raw materials, and so on) are a good measure of what it takes to get resources away from other industries. But in some cases "social costs" are involved in the production of a good or service in addition to the private costs paid by the firm. If, for example, a steel mill produces steel for $100 per ton, but also spews out smoke and soot that cover the surrounding neighborhood, the $100 is not a complete measure of the real cost of producing the steel. The extra social cost involved in grimy windowsills and curtains, discolored paint, and smoke-filled lungs are all real costs for the people in that community. They are social costs, even though they are not included in the money costs that the steel company must pay to produce steel at $100 per ton.

In such a case, total real costs (social plus private costs) exceed the private costs seen by the producer. Thus, the full social cost of producing steel is not reflected to consumers in the price charged for steel. Only if the price fully reflects both social and private costs will profit or loss in the steel industry be an accurate guide to when resources should move into or out of the industry.

Often social costs are called "externalities." Thus, the smoke-and-dirt side effects of producing steel are "externalities," or "external diseconomies." They represent a real cost above and beyond the private costs that the steel producer pays. There are many such examples.

There may be external economies as well as diseconomies; that is, production may involve side benefits to the community instead of side costs. For example, if a lumbering company replants after it has cut the trees, the real benefits from this act may exceed the expected monetary benefits to the company. The company knows that to stay in business over the long pull it must replenish its stock of trees. Society benefits from the replanted forest for the future, through better scenery, prevention of water runoff, and the like, above and beyond the lumber future consumers will be able to buy. In such cases, special government payments to the lumber company that will encourage replanting beyond the test of the private marketplace are desirable to obtain a socially optimal allocation of resources. Social policy vis-à-vis externalities will be examined in detail in Part Five.

REVIEW

Concepts to Remember

This is another chapter of important concepts that will be used throughout the analysis of business-firm behavior. Be sure you understand the following:

alternative cost
opportunity cost
real costs
accounting costs
money costs
fixed costs
variable costs
total costs
fixed cost per unit
variable cost per unit
total cost per unit
marginal cost
least-cost combination
short run
long run
optimal scale of enterprise
social costs
externalities

For Analysis and Discussion

1. Define opportunity, or alternative, cost. Explain why the dollar-cost of producing an auto is a measure of the alternative uses of the resources foregone.
2. If you were operating a grocery store, would there be any significant difference between your cash outlays per month and your costs per month? If so, what items would account for the difference?
3. You are considering the possibility of setting up a pizza parlor near the campus. Make a list of all the costs you ought to have in mind in estimating whether

the expected demand will produce a profit. Which of the costs would be fixed regardless of how many pizzas you sold, and which would vary from week to week with sales volume?

4. The ABC company has the following costs. From this information prepare a table showing the following: fixed cost per unit, variable cost per unit, total cost per unit, and marginal costs. Then plot your data on a graph.

Total fixed cost per month $1,000
Total variable costs:

UNITS PRODUCED	VARIABLE COST
10	$ 500
11	1,000
12	1,400
13	1,750
14	2,000
15	2,400

5. Make a list of the reasons why manufacturing concerns are typically bigger than dry-cleaning establishments. Can you reconcile your list with the observed fact that some dry-cleaning establishments are bigger than some manufacturing companies?
6. "By and large, the competitive system sees to it that every firm is near the optimal size for producing its product." Do you agree with this statement? Explain carefully why or why not.
7. List three cases of external diseconomies of business firms. Do such diseconomies seem to you rare or pervasive?

APPENDIX

Physical-Production Relationships Underlying Cost Curves[5]

This appendix provides a brief statement of part of the "theory of production," which underlies the cost of production in a firm and provides a foundation for understanding the distribution of income to different factors of production. Its purpose is to examine rigorously the physical and technological relationships involved as the businessman combines the various factors of production in turning out his product.

[5]This appendix is intended for those who want a rigorous physical-output foundation for the previous and following sections on business costs. It can be omitted by others.

The simplest case arises when one variable factor of production (say, labor) is applied to a fixed amount of some other factor (say, land). Consider the results of applying an increasing number of units of labor to a fixed plot of land, abstracting from any other factors of production, such as fertilizer and tools. Table 19–4 shows what might happen in such a case. The physical outputs obtainable from various combinations of productive factors are what economists call a "production function."

Column 1 shows the number of laborers used. Column 2 shows the total production—say, bushels

TABLE 19–4

Variable Output with Increasing Inputs

UNITS OF INPUT (LABOR)	TOTAL OUTPUT (BUSHELS)	AVERAGE OUTPUT PER UNIT OF LABOR (BUSHELS)	MARGINAL OUTPUT OF LABOR (BUSHELS)
1	100	100	100
2	350	175	250
3	702	234	352
4	1152	288	450
5	1700	340	548[a]
6	2190	365	490
7	2604	372[a]	414
8	2908	364	304
9	3114	346	206
10	3240	324	126
11	3300[a]	300	60
12	3300	375	0
13	3250	250	−50
14	3080	220	−170

[a]Denotes highest point for each output series.

of wheat—obtained as more workers are added. Total product rises until at some point (twelve workers with 3,300 bushels of output in this example) so many laborers are being used on this small plot of land that they get in each other's way and thereafter there is an actual **decrease** in the total output of wheat. Obviously, no intelligent farmer would ever carry production of wheat beyond this point, because by hiring more laborers he would actually decrease the total crop he obtained.

Column 3 shows the average product (bushels of wheat) per worker on the land. This average product rises at first, because total product rises faster than in proportion to the number of workers used. But the average output per worker reaches a peak (at seven workers and 2,604 bushels in this example, which gives the maximum output per worker of 372 bushels). Thereafter, even though total product continues to rise for a while, the average output per worker falls.

Column 4 shows the "marginal product" as more workers are used. This column shows the **additional,** or *marginal,* output obtained by adding each extra worker. Thus, adding the first worker increases total product by 100 bushels. For the second worker the marginal product is 250 bushels, as total product rises from 100 to 350. Marginal product reaches its peak at five workers. After this, adding workers (up to eleven) continues to increase total product, but not as rapidly as before; so the increment per additional worker falls.

These relationships can be seen readily in Figures 19–4 and 19–5. Figure 19–4 shows total product as additional workers are hired. It rises rapidly at first as production becomes more efficient, then gradually levels off, and finally (after twelve workers and 3,300 bushels) turns down, for there are just too many workers to avoid getting in each other's way.

Figure 19–5 plots average product and marginal product from Table 19–4. Marginal product reaches its peak first and then turns down as the rate of growth of total product begins to slow. Average output per worker shows a similar inverted U, but the peak is reached with more workers, as Table 19–4 shows.

Note that the marginal-product curve cuts the average-product curve at the latter's highest point. This is necessarily true because as long as marginal product is higher than average product, each additional worker is adding more to total product than the average of all workers up to that point. As soon as the marginal worker adds less to total product than the average up to that point, the marginal-product curve will be below the average-product curve. Thus,

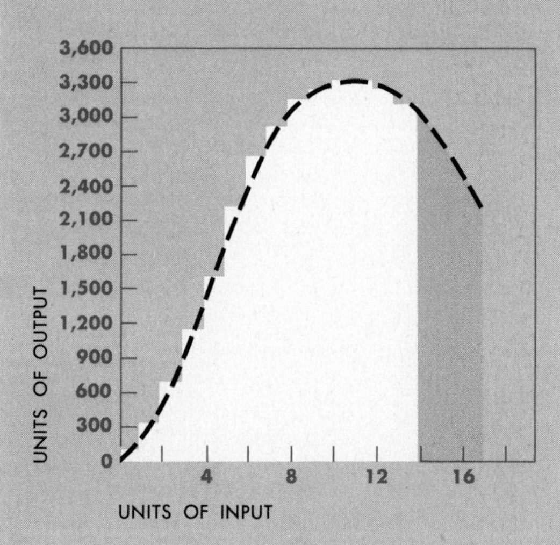

Figure 19–4

Total output rises fast at first as variable factors are added to a fixed factor, then levels off, and eventually turns down.

it will always cut the average-product curve at the latter's highest point.

The other significant point is when marginal product becomes zero. Comparing the two figures, we see that this is at twelve workers, **which is just the point where total product turns down.** This clearly must be so, because marginal product is merely the amount by which total product increases as additional workers are added. Thus, when adding another worker decreases total product, marginal product becomes negative.

The Law of Diminishing Returns, or Variable Proportions. The preceding paragraphs provide a statement of Ricardo's famous "law of diminishing returns." They show just what happens when additional units of one factor of production are combined with a fixed stock of some other factor or factors.

Modern economists have come to a more general statement of these relationships, which they call the "law of variable proportions." **As the proportion of one factor of production to other fixed factors increases, the average product of the increasing factor will first rise and then fall persistently; and the marginal product of the increasing factor will also first rise and then fall, cutting the average-product curve at its highest point.**

Thus, if all factors increase in proportion, there is no reason to expect Ricardo's law of diminishing returns to set in. This is a critical fact, for it says that neither an individual firm nor an economy need face diminishing returns just because it gets bigger.

Production Foundations of Cost Curves. These production relationships underlie the cost data for the firm. Assume that the market prices of all factors of production are fixed—labor and land in our case. Then the total-fixed-cost curve (as in Figure 19-1) is obtained directly by multiplying the fixed amount of land used (fixed factor) by its rent per acre. The total-variable-cost curve is obtained by

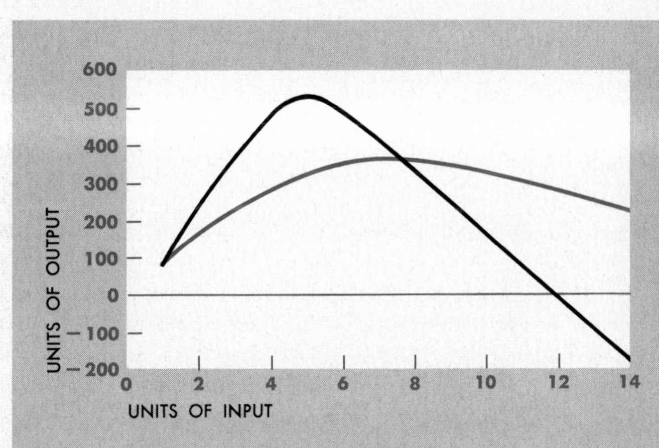

Figure 19–5

Marginal product shoots up rapidly as total output grows fast when the first variable factors are added. It turns down as the growth in total output slows, and becomes negative when total output turns down. Check it against Figure 19–4.

multiplying the number of workers (variable factors) by the wage per worker.

These total costs can readily be converted to the per-unit cost curves of Figure 19-2 by dividing through by the number of units produced. Thus, the variable-unit-cost curve will be the inverse of the average-product-per-worker curve, because wage per worker is constant. When average product per worker is rising, variable cost per unit of output falls (we continue to assume that workers are the only variable cost involved). When average product per worker begins to fall, variable cost per unit of output begins to rise. Fixed cost per unit (rent on the land in the example above) steadily falls as more bushels are produced with the same total fixed cost for land.

The combination of the persistently declining fixed-cost-per-unit curve with the U-shaped variable-unit-cost curve gives the (flatter) U-shaped total-unit-cost curve. Thus, given the prices of the factors of production, the physical production relationships determine the shape of the fixed-cost-per-unit, the variable-cost-per-unit, and the total-cost-per-unit curves in any situation. The unit-cost curves are the inverses of the physical-production curves in Figure 19-5. The marginal-product curve is the basis for the marginal-cost curve.

The Business Firm: Competitive Output and Price in the Short Run[1]

CHAPTER PREVIEW

CHAPTER TWENTY

This chapter examines how business firms, given their costs, respond to consumer demand in competitive markets. We postpone until later a look at the partially monopolized sectors of the economy.

[1]Note to instructors: Section III of the Mathematical Appendix at the end of the text provides a concise mathematical statement (for students who know calculus) of the cost relationships of the preceding chapter and of the profit-maximizing behavior of the firm in the short run, as stated in this chapter.

Some instructors prefer to concentrate on the long-run behavior of the firm and the economy, omitting the traditional marginal-cost–marginal-revenue apparatus in establishing short-run price and output. For them the text is written so that Chapter 20 can be omitted.

THE THEORY OF THE FIRM

Let us assume, as a first approximation, that firms in highly competitive industries try to maximize their profits. Profits are the difference between total cost and total revenue. Hence the firm does what it can (within the legal rules and mores of society) to maximize this difference. It tries to sell more of its own product when the price is high enough to cover costs, and it tries to keep its costs as low as possible. That is, it tries to produce its output as efficiently as possible. Whenever the firm can increase its profits by increasing its revenues or by reducing its costs, it will do so. When it is maximizing its profits to the best of its ability, the firm will be in "equilibrium"—in the sense that it will not change its own actions unless conditions change. Actually, external conditions (for example, consumer demand and wage rates) do change frequently, so business firms seldom reach equilibrium and stay in it for long. But we assume that the firm will always be aiming at this maximum-profit position in conducting its day-to-day affairs and in its long-run planning.

We know, of course, that not all firms behave this way. But for the moment, assume that firms in our highly competitive industry have the single goal of maximizing profit.

THE COMPETITIVE FIRM IN THE SHORT RUN

The individual firm in a highly competitive industry (for example, one wheat farmer or our small stereo maker) is so small it has no appreciable influence over the price of its product or the prices it pays for its inputs (labor, materials, and the like). Our small firm must take the market price as given—fixed in the market by total demand-and-supply conditions over which we have no significant control. Under this assumption, we can't charge a higher price than the one prevailing in the market. If we do, we won't sell any goods, because consumers can get all they want at the prevailing price from other sellers. In sum, our firm is a "price taker," not a "price maker."

This means that the firm sees the demand curve as a horizontal line at the prevailing market price. This assumption may seem to you extreme, and it is the limiting case of what economists call perfect competition. But it is an instructive case with which to begin. We will modify the assumption later.

Comparison of Total Costs and Total Revenue

If our stereo firm from Chapter 19 wants to maximize profits, it can compare its total cost with total revenue at each level of output, and thus determine the most profitable number of sets to produce. This is done in Table 20–1, assuming that the market price is $1,800. (Obviously the estimated total revenue will be different if the price is different, since total revenue is merely output multiplied by the price.) The table shows that the maximum-profit output is six sets per month. At only one set per month, total revenue doesn't cover costs. When the plant gets up to eight sets a month, costs shoot up so fast that they exceed even the big sales income. In between, any output is profitable, but some more so than others. Profit is the largest if we produce and sell six sets.

This same comparison can be shown graphically, as in Figure 20–1. *TC* is total cost, plotted from the second column of Table 20–1. *TR* is

TABLE 20–1
Total Cost, Total Revenue, and Profit When Price is $1,800

OUTPUT	TOTAL COST	TOTAL REVENUE	PROFIT
1	$ 3,000	$ 1,800	–$1,200
2	3,500	3,600	100
3	4,000	5,400	1,400
4	5,000	7,200	2,200
5	6,000	9,000	3,000
6	7,600	10,800	3,200
7	11,000	12,600	1,600
8	17,000	14,400	–2,600

total revenue, plotted from the third column. Everywhere *TR* is above *TC*, the firm makes a profit. The profit is largest where *TR* is farthest above *TC*—here at an output of six units monthly, just as in the table. The light grey area between the two curves shows the range over which a profit is possible. The same area is shown separately at the bottom of the chart, where it is easy to see where the vertical distance (height of area) is greatest. Note that if the price were higher than $1,800 per set, the *TR* curve would rise faster and there would be more profit opportunities. If price were lower, *TR* would be lower and so would profit opportunities.

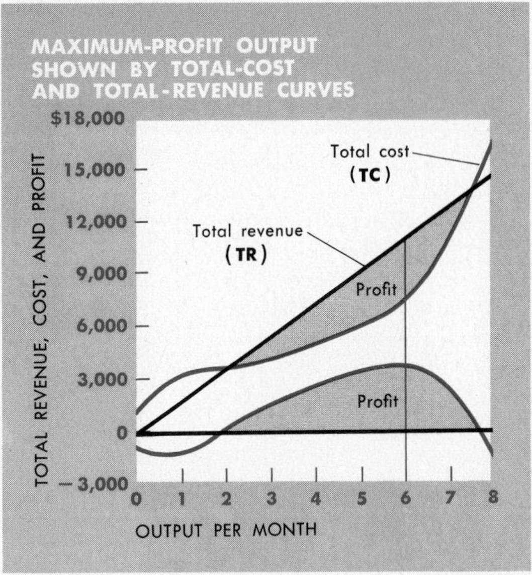

Figure 20–1

Maximum profit is where the total-revenue curve is farthest above (in vertical distance) the total-cost curve. Potential profit range is from 2–7 sets per month.

Maximizing Profits by Marginal Analysis

We can make the same maximum-profit calculation by using marginal analysis, which is simpler than calculating all possible profit positions. We already know that marginal cost is the addition to total cost in producing one more unit. We also know that for each additional unit we sell, we add $1,800 to total revenue. This addition to revenue we call marginal revenue, the counterpart of marginal cost.

As long as producing more units adds more to total revenue than to total costs, it clearly pays to keep increasing output. This is the same as saying that it pays to keep on increasing output as long as marginal revenue is larger than marginal cost. But clearly we will reduce total profits if we produce more when marginal cost is higher than marginal revenue. The principle is: Profit will be maximized by carrying production up to the point where marginal cost equals marginal revenue (here $1,800), and no further.

Check this by referring back to Table 19–2, which shows marginal costs for our stereo firm. If the price is $1,800, clearly we will add more to revenues than to costs (that is, our profits will increase) by producing each set up to and including the sixth. But to produce the seventh set would add $3,400 to costs but only $1,800 to revenue. Our profit would thereby be reduced by $1,600, the amount by which *MC* exceeds *MR*. As Table 20–1 shows, we would still be making a profit with output at seven sets monthly, but a smaller profit than by producing only six sets.

Graphical Analysis Using Marginalism

This analysis can readily be put graphically with, of course, the same answers. The cost curves in Figure 20–2 are the same as in Figure 19–2 except for the omission of the fixed-cost-per-unit curve. The marginal-cost curve shows the increment to total cost involved in increasing output by one unit at each stage. For example, the marginal cost involved in stepping up output from four to five units is $1,000; in going from five units to six it is $1,600.[2]

On Figure 20–2, line *DD* shows the demand curve as seen by our firm when the market price is $1,800, and the demand curve is the marginal

[2]For mathematically inclined readers: Marginal cost is the first derivative of total cost (not of total cost per unit). The marginal-cost curve will always cut the *TUC* curve at its minimum point. In nontechnical terms, this is so because

revenue curve. It is a horizontal line; we can sell all we make at $1,800 a set, but none if we ask a higher price. (Think of the firm as one small wheat farmer if the stereo case seems unreal to you. The farmer can sell all the wheat he produces at the going market price, but none if he asks more since his wheat is identical with millions of other bushels offered at the going price.)

The principle in using the graph is the same. To maximize profit, increase output as long as marginal revenue is above marginal cost. With *DD* (marginal revenue) at $1,800, the maximum profit output is clear. Through six units, the marginal-cost curve is below $1,800, so each additional set adds more to revenue than to cost. But the seventh unit adds more to cost than to revenue, because the marginal-cost curve is above *DD*. Therefore, six is the maximum-profit output.

Ask yourself one more question, to be sure you understand. Wouldn't we be better off to produce seven units instead of six, getting the profit on the seventh, since the $1,800 price exceeds the total unit cost of $1,573 at seven units of output? The marginal-cost–marginal-revenue comparison gives the answer. The seventh set adds $3,400 to total cost and only $1,800 to total revenue. The fact that price is above total-unit cost tells us that we can make a profit at that output level, but not that we will make our maximum profit at that level. Trying to pick up the profit on a seventh set would be a mistake, because it would actually involve adding more to cost than to revenue; average total cost per unit would be higher on all seven units if we increase output to seven. Compute the total profit at seven units and you'll see that it's only about $1,600 ($12,600 revenue less cost of about $11,000), less than at six units.

the marginal cost is the increment to total cost. Whenever this increment to total cost is less than the existing cost per unit, the average cost per unit must be falling. Whenever the increment is larger than the existing cost per unit, the average cost per unit must be rising. The same reasoning holds for the relationship of the marginal-cost and variable-unit-cost curves. For more details, see the Mathematical Appendix.

Minimizing Losses in the Short Run

With the market price at $1,800 we're in clover. But suppose consumer demand for stereo sets nosedives, and the market price falls to $1,100, shown by *D′D′*. A quick look at Figure 20–2 shows that we're going to lose money at this price, no matter what we do. The lowest total cost per unit at which we can produce is $1,200, at an output of five units.

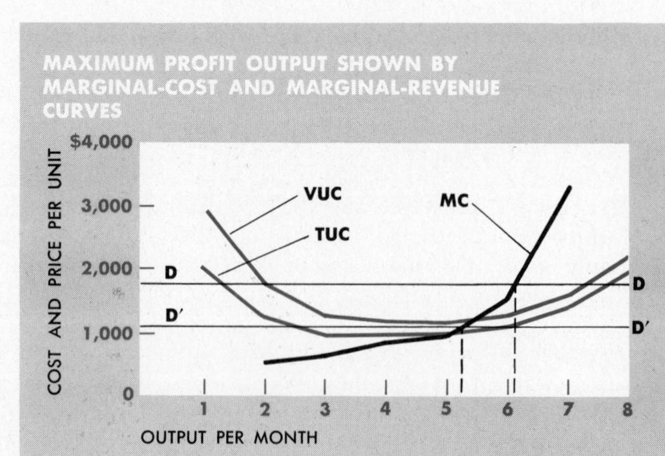

Figure 20–2

Profit is maximized by carrying production up to the intersection of the marginal-cost and marginal-revenue curves—if you operate at all. Horizontal price lines are also marginal-revenue curves for this producer under perfect competition.

What should we do to minimize our losses? One possibility would be to shut down. This way we'd lose $1,000 a month, the amount of our fixed costs, which continue whether we operate or not. But if we operate, producing three, four, or five units, we'll be getting $1,100 per set produced and only having to spend $1,000 per set in variable (out-of-pocket) costs. This income will provide $100 per set left over to apply on our $1,000 of fixed costs, which we have to pay in any case. So we'd better operate as long as we're stuck with the fixed costs, even though we lose money. By operating, we lose less than by shutting down.

The marginal-cost–marginal-revenue principle still tells us how many units to produce. The answer is five. Producing every unit up to and including the fifth adds more to revenue than it does to costs. Marginal revenue for the fifth unit is $1,100; marginal cost is only $1,000. But marginal cost for the sixth set is $1,600, above marginal revenue. The principle for minimizing loss is the same as for maximizing profit: **If you operate at all, carry production up to the point where marginal costs equal marginal revenue, and no further.**

The Decision To Shut Down in the Short Run

Would it ever pay us to shut down in the short run? Obviously, yes. If price falls below $1,000, which is the lowest variable unit cost we can manage at any output level, we'd better close up shop. Suppose price falls to $900. No matter how many units we produce, our income is not even enough to cover our variable costs, much less provide anything to help cover the $1,000 of fixed costs. Suppose we produce three units. They will cost $4,000 but will bring in only $2,700, leaving a loss of $1,300 compared with only $1,000 if we just shut down. **At any price below the lowest variable-cost-unit point, we will minimize losses by shutting down altogether.** This rule does not contradict the marginal-cost–marginal-revenue principle for maximizing profits, since that principle tells us only what to do *if* we operate at all.

Short-Run Equilibrium of the Firm

When will the business firm be in short-run equilibrium? When it is maximizing its profit or minimizing its loss, given consumer demand and given its fixed costs which it cannot alter in the short run. It will then be in short-run equilibrium when it is producing just up to the point where marginal cost is equal to marginal revenue (price).

This concept of the equilibrium of the firm parallels the concept of the equilibrium of the household (or consumer) developed in Chapter 5. Both tell us the situation toward which an economic unit will move in trying to improve its economic position. In a real world of constant change, we would seldom expect to find firms actually in equilibrium for long. But whenever a household or firm is out of equilibrium, we can expect it to move to maximize its satisfaction or profit.

PROFIT MAXIMIZING IN THE SHORT AND LONG RUNS

A firm may be in short-run equilibrium and still be making substantial profits or losses. But such a situation will not continue indefinitely. If there are large profits, other firms are likely to invade the industry, increasing supply and forcing down prices. If there are losses, the losing firm must do better or ultimately go broke. Hence, short-run losses lead firms to move resources to greener pastures unless demand rises or costs can be reduced in the long run. Short-run equilibrium in such cases is clearly only a temporary equilibrium.

In the short run managers may be inefficient; they may over- or under-adjust to change; they may guess wrong about consumer wants and production costs. But not in the long run, when there is time for new competitors to enter the industry and for firms to go broke. Adam Smith's invisible hand will be at work, and other profit-seekers will enter to produce more cheaply and (efficiently) if existing firms have high costs. If losses prevail, better profit prospects elsewhere will lure resources away from the loss-ridden industry. In the long run, excess profits and losses will tend to be eliminated by competition, and prices will tend to be just high enough to cover all costs, including a normal profit. Chapter 21 examines these long-run adjustments in detail.

SHORT-RUN COST CURVES AND SUPPLY CURVES

If firms try to maximize profits in the short run, we can tell from a given firm's cost curves what output it will produce at any given price. **The firm's marginal-cost curve will be its short-run supply curve anywhere above the minimum point on the variable-unit-cost curve.** Thus, at any price below $1,000 our firm will supply zero units. At prices from $1,000 to $1,599, it will supply five units. At prices from $1,600 to $3,399, it will supply six units. And so on up the marginal-cost curve. **The short-run marginal-cost curve is the firm's short-run supply curve.**

If this is true for all firms, it is easy to get a short-run market supply curve for any industry, by adding together the short-term supply curves (or schedules) of all the individual firms. Suppose there were 1,000 identical firms in the stereo industry. Then the short-run industry supply schedule would look like Table 20–2. At each price the supply offered would be 1,000 times the supply offered by our own little firm.

TABLE 20–2
Short-Run Industry Supply Schedule

PRICE	OUTPUT OF TYPICAL FIRM	INDUSTRY OUTPUT
Under $1,000	0	0
1,000–1,599	5	5,000
1,600–3,399	6	6,000
3,400–5,999	7	7,000
Over $6,000	8	8,000

THE FIRM AS A BUYER OF PRODUCTIVE SERVICES

Before ending this chapter, it is important to look at the short-run output policies of the firm from a different angle. Whenever businessmen decide to produce 1, 10, or 1,000 units of output, they simultaneously decide to buy or hire the "inputs" of productive services needed to produce those units—labor, raw materials, machinery, and so on.

We can, therefore, analyze the most profitable level of output in terms of units of productive inputs used, as well as in terms of units of output. For example, assume that our plant needs only labor and raw materials, and that these are conveniently hired in units costing $100 per unit—perhaps one worker per week plus the material he uses. For each number of units of input, there will be some corresponding output of stereo sets. Thus, our cost schedules above could have been stated in terms of costs to hire varying amounts of labor-plus-materials input rather than in terms of producing one, two, three, or more sets per week as output.

How many units of labor-materials input should we hire each month at $100 per unit? The marginal-cost–marginal-revenue principle holds here as before. Whenever adding one more unit of input adds more to revenue than to cost (that is, when it adds more than $100), it pays to increase inputs and hence output. As soon as marginal cost exceeds marginal revenue, stop expanding, because you have reached your best profit level. The same marginal-revenue–marginal-cost principle here again tells you what the maximum-profit or minimum-loss production level is.[3]

In explaining the firm's output decisions, we have thus explained simultaneously its demand for inputs (labor, capital, and so on). Because workers' wages depend on supply and demand forces, just like other prices, the theory of the firm here gives us for labor, half the demand the determinant of wages, as we shall see when we come to explaining in Part Four the incomes that people receive.

[3]The marginal revenue from hiring an additional unit of variable input is based directly on its "marginal product," as described in the appendix to Chapter 19, although, of course, the marginal product needs to be converted to dollar terms to become marginal revenue.

REVIEW

Concepts to Remember

The essence of this chapter is the way a profit-seeking firm would try to maximize profits in the short run by carrying production up to the point where marginal cost equals marginal revenue, and no further, if it operates at all. Check your understanding of the following concepts:

profit maximization	equilibrium of the firm
marginal revenue	price taker

For Analysis and Discussion

1. Fixed costs are often substantial and real. Why then do economists assert that businessmen should disregard them in short-run decisions on setting price and output?
2. A competitive firm will always maximize profits by producing at the lowest possible total-unit cost. True or false? Explain.
3. Explain carefully why a firm will maximize its profits by carrying production up to the point where marginal cost just equals marginal revenue. If there are any exceptions to this rule, specify them.
4. You operate a roadside fruit stand. You have been selling raspberries at $1 a quart; they cost you forty cents to produce. It is now midafternoon and raining. With customers scarce, you now estimate your demand schedule for the rest of the afternoon as follows:

PRICE	QUARTS
60¢	30
50	40
40	50
30	70
20	80

   You have eighty quarts on hand and no storage facilities to avoid spoilage before tomorrow. What price should you charge to maximize profits? Explain. What is the importance of your costs in this case?
5. You are managing the stereo plant shown in Figure 20–2 and are currently producing four sets a month. You have an order for one additional set a month, but the customer will only pay $1,050 a set, less than your minimum total cost per set. Should you accept the order? Show both graphically and through arithmetical calculations why your answer is sound.
6. Explain why the firm's short-run marginal cost curve is its short-run supply curve. Is this always true?

Airline Takes the Marginal Route[4]

Continental Air Lines, Inc., last year filled only half the available seats on its Boeing 707 jet flights, a record some 15 percentage points worse than the national average.

By eliminating just a few runs—less than 5 percent—Continental could have raised its average load considerably. Some of its flights frequently carry as few as 30 passengers on the 120-seat plane. But the improved load factor would have meant reduced profits.

For Continental bolsters its corporate profits by deliberately running extra flights that aren't expected to do more than return their out-of-pocket costs—plus a little profit. Such marginal flights are an integral part of the overall operating philosophy that has brought small, Denver-based Continental—tenth among the eleven trunk carriers—through the bumpy postwar period with only one loss year.

This philosophy leans heavily on marginal analysis. And the line leans heavily on Chris F. Whelan, vice-president in charge of economic planning, to translate marginalism into hard, dollars-and-cents decisions.

Getting management to accept and apply the marginal concept probably is the chief contribution any economist can make to his company. Put most simply, marginalists maintain that a company should undertake any activity that adds more to revenues than it does to costs—and not limit itself to those activities whose returns equal average or "fully allocated" costs. . . .

Whelan's work is a concrete example of the truth in a crack by Prof. Sidney Alexander of MIT—formerly economist for Columbia Broadcasting System—that the economist who understands marginal analysis has a "full-time job in undoing the work of the accountant." This is so, Alexander holds, because the practices of accountants—and of most businesses—are permeated with cost allocation directed at average, rather than marginal, costs.

In any complex business, there's likely to be a big difference between the costs of each company activity as it's carried on the accounting books and the marginal or "true" costs that can determine whether or not the activity should be undertaken.

The difficulty comes in applying the simple "textbook" marginal concept to specific decisions. If the economist is unwilling to make some bold simplifications, the job of determining "true" marginal costs may be highly complex, time-wasting, and too expensive. But even a rough application of marginal principles may come closer to the right answer for business decision-makers than an analysis based on precise average-cost data.

Marginal analysis in a nutshell:

Problem:	Shall Continental run an extra daily flight from City X to City Y?	
The facts:	Fully-allocated costs of the flight	$4,500
	Out-of-pocket costs of this flight	$2,000
	Flight should gross	$3,100
Decision:	Run the flight. It will add $1,100 to net profit—because it will add $3,100 to revenues and only $2,000 to costs. Overhead and other costs, total $2,500 [$4,500 minus $2,000], would be incurred whether the flight is run or not. Therefore, fully-allocated or "average" costs of $4,500 are not relevant to this business decision. It's the out-of-pocket or "marginal" costs that count.	

Proving that this is so demands economists who can break the crust of corporate habits and show concretely why the typical manager's response—that nobody ever made a profit without meeting all costs—is misleading and can reduce profits. To be sure, the whole business cannot make a profit unless average costs are met; but covering average costs should not determine whether any particular activity should be undertaken. For this would unduly restrict corporate decisions and cause managements to forgo opportunities for extra gains.

Whelan's approach is this: He considers that the

[4]Reprinted from *Business Week,* April 20, 1963, with permission of the publisher, © 1963, McGraw-Hill Book Company.

insurance are very real expenses and must be covered. The out-of-pocket approach comes into play, says Whelan, only after the line's basic schedule has been set.

"Then you go a step farther," he says, and see if adding more flights will contribute to the corporate net. Similarly, if he's thinking of dropping a flight with a disappointing record, he puts it under the marginal microscope: "If your revenues are going to be more than your out-of-pocket costs, you should keep the flight on."

By "out-of-pocket costs" Whelan means just that: the actual dollars that Continental has to pay out to run a flight. He gets the figure not by applying hypothetical equations but by circulating a proposed schedule to every operating department concerned and finding out just what extra expenses it will entail. If a ground crew already on duty can service the plane, the flight isn't charged a penny of their salary expense. There may even be some costs eliminated in running the flight; they won't need men to roll the plane to a hangar, for instance, if it flies on to another stop.

Most of these extra flights, of course, are run at off-beat hours, mainly late at night. At times, though, Continental discovers that the hours aren't so unpopular after all. A pair of night coach flights on the Houston-San Antonio-El Paso-Phoenix-Los Angeles leg, added on a marginal basis, have turned out to be so successful that they are now more than covering fully allocated costs. . . .

Continental's data handling system produces weekly reports on each flight, with revenues measured against both out-of-pocket and fully allocated costs. Whelan uses these to give each flight a careful analysis at least once a quarter. But those added on a marginal basis get the fine-tooth-comb treatment monthly.

Is Continental Airlines right in using marginal analysis to decide whether to add flights? What if each flight, looked at individually, more than covers marginal cost, but added together they don't cover the firm's total costs? Would this latter case invalidate the marginal principle?

Long-Run Competitive Equilibrium and Economic Efficiency

CHAPTER PREVIEW

CHAPTER TWENTY-ONE

Building on our detailed analysis of individual households, firms, and markets in the short run, we need now to see how they all fit together in a big picture of how a highly competitive economy would work in the long run. How efficiently would such an economy allocate society's scarce productive resources to satisfy consumers' demands? The main purpose of this chapter, thus, is to analyze how a purely competitive economy would work *in the long run*—how well the long-run competitive pressures of Adam Smith's invisible hand would guide the economy. On the basis of this examination you can judge for yourself whether Smith set economists off on the right track with his talk about the "invisible hand"—or gave us a bad steer.

But first we need to be clear on two important points that have been glossed over so far. Precisely what do we mean by "pure competition" and by "long-run equilibrium"?

COMPETITION IN THE MODERN ECONOMY

No business firm is free from competition. Even AT&T, which is often cited as a complete monopoly in the field of telephone communication, faces some competition from other forms of communication. There are only six major firms that produce aluminum today. But quite aside from the competition among the six, steel, copper, and other metals are potential substitutes for aluminum. Alcoa and the other aluminum companies are acutely aware of this fact. Competition is inescapable in business.

Nevertheless, it is obvious that competition is a lot more active in some industries than it is in others. At the competitive extreme, we find the individual farmer producing such standardized products as wheat, corn, and hogs. He has thousands of competitors, and his product is so standardized that the buyer has no interest in who the producer is. If Farmer Jones prices his No. 2 hard northern wheat one cent a bushel more than other farmers, he just won't sell any.

There is a whole spectrum of market positions between the protected monopoly position of the public utility and the extreme competition of farmers. Most of the real world lies somewhere between these two extremes, and we will look at the less-competitive sectors later. Here we want to examine how the economy would function under "pure competition"—roughly the situation of the wheat farmer above, without government intervention.

The same conditions define pure competition on the buyers' side of any market.

When there are many sellers of identical products, and when no one of them acting alone can exert a significant influence on the market price, each producer must adjust his activities to the market price. The individual firm is a "price taker," not a price setter or price maker. It takes the market price as given, and considering its costs of production decides how much to produce in order to maximize its profit.

But although no one firm alone can significantly influence market price, the summation of all the individual producers' actions can and does. If prevailing costs and market price lead each individual firm to restrict output, the summation of all the thousands of individual cutbacks will reduce market supply and, other things equal, raise the price. Thus, quantity produced and sold along with market price are "automatically" determined by the impersonal mechanism of the competitive market as it responds to consumer demand. No one has to plan how much cabbage should be produced. The profit motive and the competitive market together determine how much, as farmers respond to what consumers buy in the market.

Pure Competition

The essence of pure competition is that no single seller is important enough to have any appreciable influence over market price. Specifically, pure competition is characterized by:

1. Many sellers, each acting independently and each so small relative to the market as to have no appreciable effect on market price.
2. An identical product, so that the consumer is indifferent about the seller from whom he buys.[1]
3. Freedom of entry for new sellers who wish to enter the market. (This assumption is not logically necessary where (1) and (2) hold, but most economists include it in analyzing pure competition.)

[1]The added assumption is also usually made that all buyers and sellers have full knowledge of prices being quoted over the entire market.

Why Study Pure Competition?

There aren't many purely competitive industries in the modern American economy. Even agriculture, which has long been the standard example, doesn't quite represent pure competition any more, since the government has increasingly intervened to set prices and output levels. Why study pure competition, then? There are two main reasons:

1. Economics is concerned with the overall performance of the economic system, and with the allocation of society's resources among alternative uses. To get at these problems, we must have some overall picture of the way the various parts of the economy fit together. The purely competitive model, with all competitive markets, has the great virtue of providing a reasonably simple and predictable picture of the way mar-

kets signal consumer demands to producers, and the way producers respond to those demands. Many economists believe that this picture also provides a rough approximation of the "ideal" way in which a private-enterprise system ought to work. They thus use the model as a standard of comparison to ferret out those areas of the actual economy that aren't operating as well as they ought to.

2. Pure competition, though almost nonexistent, does provide a rough approximation to the behavior of major sectors of the modern economy. Most of agriculture, broad areas of retailing, wholesaling and service establishments, and important sectors of manufacturing where a moderate scale of plant is big enough for efficient production—all come reasonably close to the pure-competition model. To be sure, their products are not quite identical, and each producer has some control over the price at which he sells his product. But the pressures of competition are strong, and if he gets far out of competitive line the individual producer finds himself steadily losing out in the market.

Long-Run Equilibrium

Long-run equilibrium is a situation that would be reached and maintained indefinitely unless some external force came along to disturb it. Suppose we want to know how a purely competitive system, beginning from some equilibrium position, would respond to an increased consumer demand for strawberries. Assume we can hold everything else constant—the supply of productive resources, consumers' other wants, society's technological know-how, all legal and social factors. The new position to which the system would move in response to the changed demand would be its new long-run equilibrium position.

To be complete, we should consider all the millions of interrelated effects throughout the economic system. But once we get far from the strawberry industry, these effects are likely to be negligible. When, for example, the demand for strawberries rises, people may also buy more cream to put on their desserts and fewer paperback books because they have less disposable income left for other products. If we took all these effects into account, we would be looking at the **general equilibrium** of the whole economy. But most of these effects are small and distant, and we shall generally concentrate our analysis on the strawberry industry and others closely related to it. For this purpose, it is useful to look mainly at the long-run **equilibrium of firms** involved and at the long-run **equilibrium of the industries** they comprise.

Of course, in the real world there is no way to hold "other things constant," and the real world seldom reaches a state of long-run economic equilibrium. Yet this analytical device of isolating the effects of a particular event is the best way we have for getting at those effects in a real world so complex, interrelated, and ever-changing as ours is.

When we talk about long-run equilibrium, therefore, we are talking about the new situation **toward which** industry is moving and would ultimately reach if no other forces interfered. Long-run analysis provides guides to the **ultimate** effects of particular changes.

LONG-RUN EQUILIBRIUM: THE CONTINUOUS SEARCH FOR PROFITS

The mainspring of the private-enterprise economy is the businessman's continuous search for profits. This does not imply that the proprietor of the local grocery spends every waking hour worrying about how to squeeze the last nickel out of his business; or that the farmer doesn't decide to visit his friends some afternoons when he could be working. But it does imply that, by and large, the desire to earn profits is a dominant one, and business concerns adopt those policies that they think will produce the largest profits for the company.[2]

[2]To assert that most businesses try to maximize profits each day, or month, or even each year, would be naïve indeed. Any alert businessman will tell you that it is the long pull that matters. The businesses that last and pay good dividends to their shareholders year after year are seldom out to "turn a fast buck." They are the ones that

In the long run, all costs become variable. Existing plant and equipment wear out. Wage and salary contracts come up for renewal. Long-term contracts for supplies and materials expire. With all costs variable, the entrepreneur is completely free in making his output decisions. He can expand, contract, change the nature of his productive processes, or go out of business altogether.

Thus, in the long run, firms will move into or drop out of any purely competitive industry until expectations of profits or losses have been substantially eliminated—until it is no longer possible for anyone to better his position by moving into or out of the industry.[3] Thus, as long as the expected market price is above the expected minimum cost of producing a commodity, firms will move into the industry and present firms may expand. Output will increase, and the price will gradually be forced down to about the minimum-cost point. But if the expected market price is below the minimum expected cost of production, firms will drop out of the industry, output will decline, and price will gradually rise toward the minimum-cost level. **Under pure competition, with firms free to enter and leave the industry, market price cannot in the long run stay higher or lower than the minimum total cost per unit of producing the commodity. This is the long-run equilibrium price and output level toward which the industry will move.**

Long-Run Competitive Equilibrium—The Firm and the Industry

Consumer demand provides the signals to which businessmen respond. Given the pattern of consumer demands, when will firms be in equilibrium in adjusting to those demands?

The firm is in long-run equilibrium when there is no advantage in increasing or decreasing its output, either by varying utilization of existing plant or by changing the scale of plant. This equilibrium will be reached when (1) the firm is producing in the most efficient way available (otherwise there would be an advantage in shifting to more efficient operations), and (2) market price is equal to the least-cost point on the cost curve for that scale of enterprise. In this equilibrium position, profits have been eliminated by competition (remember that costs include a "normal" return on investment), and the firm will continue using just the same amount of all productive resources as it now uses.

It is important to notice further that in this equilibrium marginal cost just equals price for each firm. Remember that the marginal-cost curve necessarily cuts the average-unit-cost curve at the latter's minimum point,[4] which is also equal to price in long-run equilibrium. Thus, $MC = TUC = P$ is a critical result of the competitive adjustment.

The entire industry is in long-run equilibrium when each firm is in equilibrium and there is no incentive for firms either to enter or leave the industry. We can thus define long-run equilibrium either in terms of movement of firms or of movement of productive resources. In long-run equilibrium, there is no incentive for either firms or productive resources to enter or leave the industry. There is no incentive for entrepreneurs to hire more or fewer resources in the industry.

Survival of the Fittest and Pressures toward Cost Minimization

The competitive market is an impersonal arbiter of who survives and who vanishes from the business scene. With a standard product, such as oats, the buyer is indifferent to who the producer is. Any farmer whose production cost is above the market price simply makes a loss, and in due course will vanish from the scene

hold back new products until they have worked out the bugs, even though short-run profits are foregone. They are the ones who say that the customer is right, even when they're burned up at his unreasonable demand on return privileges. But this is not to say that the search for profits is not pervasive in the long run.

[3] Remember that a "normal," or "going," rate of return (or profit) on investment is included in the costs of each firm.

[4] For proof, see Mathematical Appendix III.

unless he improves his efficiency or receives a subsidy from someone. The fact that he may be a hard-working farmer with a good wife and six small children is irrelevant in the market. If his neighbor is thoroughly unpleasant, throws stones at small children, and refuses to contribute to the Community Chest but nonetheless produces oats at ten cents less per bushel, his neighbor will prosper in the market. In long-run equilibrium, only those who can produce at a cost as low as market price will survive, and this price will be no higher than the least-cost point on the cost curve of firms using the most efficient methods.

At any time, every industry includes firms of varying efficiency, with different levels of profits and losses. This is partly because in the dynamic economic world some firms are on the way up, some on the way down. Partly it is because many industries are far from purely competitive; some markets are not open to new firms. **But if a purely competitive long-run equilibrium position were actually attained, the lowest total-unit-cost points of all firms would be the same.**

It is easy to see that in the long run inefficient firms will be eliminated by competition. But it would be unreasonable to assume that all remaining firms become identical. Some entrepreneurs are more efficient than others. Some firms are located near good markets and pay high rents, whereas others are more distant but pay lower rents. Some firms are small and obtain efficiency through close personal supervision; others are large and count on mass-production methods to provide low costs. It is not necessary that all firms be identical or have identical cost curves. It is only necessary that the method of production used by each permit it to produce at a total unit cost as low as its competitors.

For example, suppose that one manager of a textile firm is more effective in organizing production than anyone else in the industry. Won't his firm continue to make a juicy profit even in the long run? The answer is "no." When the manager is hired, his firm will have to pay him a higher salary than other managers receive in order to keep him away from other firms. Assuming active competition among firms, his salary will be bid up until it is higher than that of a less efficient manager by roughly the differential advantage of his services. If the entrepreneur himself is the efficient manager, he must charge as a cost a salary for himself equal to what he would be able to get in alternative opportunities; this "implicit" or opportunity cost would be the compensating factor.

Illustration of Response to an Increase in Demand

Suppose that the purely competitive desk-blotter industry is in long-run equilibrium and that consumer demand for blotters increases. How will the industry respond?

The **immediate** effect will be (1) a higher price for blotters, with improved profits. (2) Then each firm will increase its output, because with a higher price it is now profitable to produce more blotters. (This is a move upward along the industry short-run supply curve, before there is time for new firms to move in.) (3) In the new **short-run** equilibrium, price will be higher, output larger, and profits in the industry greater than before the increase in demand.

This **short-run** adjustment is pictured in Figure 21–1. The left-hand portion shows the short-run industry supply of desk blotters (S^1S^1). D^1D^1 is the original demand for blotters, while D^2D^2 shows the new increased demand. The result of the increased demand is to raise the price from six to eight cents. At this higher price, each firm can increase its profits by increasing its output from 400 to 500 units, as indicated on the right-hand portion of the graph. That is, each firm increases output to the point at which marginal cost (the *SS* curve) again equals the new higher price of eight cents.

The right-hand portion shows the happy result for each firm; it is now producing more and making a profit indicated by the shaded area. The summation of all these increases is shown in S^1S^1 on the left, which indicates the total increase in blotters supplied at the higher price of eight cents. Consumers are now getting 62,500 blotters instead of the original 50,000, but they

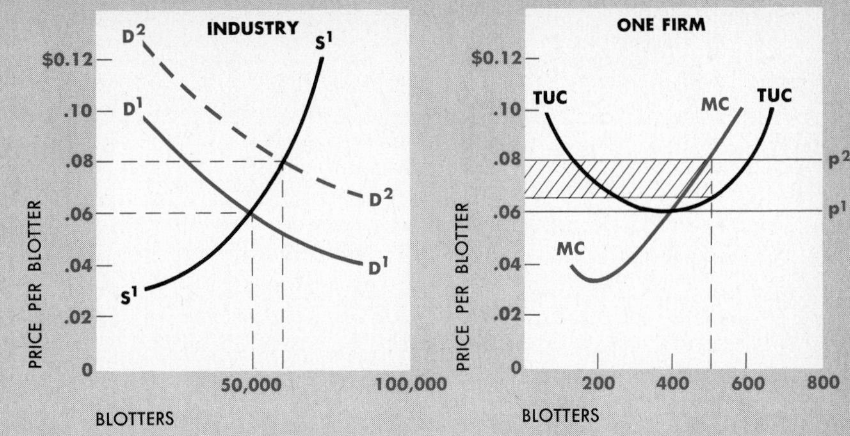

Figure 21–1

New increased demand (D^2D^2) raises the market price and makes increased output profitable for the individual firms.

have to pay eight instead of six cents per blotter. This increase results automatically from the independent actions of hundreds of purely competitive firms producing blotters.

But this situation is obviously unstable. New resources will be attracted to the industry by the generous profits. As new firms enter and productive capacity is expanded, the industry supply curve (S^1S^1) will gradually move to the right; more will be produced as more resources move into the blotter industry **in the long run.**

With more blotters produced, the price will gradually fall back toward its original level. If unlimited productive resources can be attracted without having to pay more for them (that is, if new firms can enter without bidding up costs in the blotter industry), the new long-run equilibrium will be back at the original price but with more blotters being produced. This would be a case of long-run "**constant costs**" for the industry. If, however, the entrance of new firms raises costs for all firms, because higher payments are necessary to attract labor, materials, and other resources from other industries, we have the case of "**increasing costs.**" Either way, as the price of the product falls back and costs rise, profits are gradually squeezed out. When the price is again equal to the lowest total unit cost, there will be no further inducement for new firms to enter. The new long-run equilibrium will probably be at somewhat higher costs and price than originally, with a larger industry output because the industry will probably face long-run increasing costs.

These long-run adjustments are shown in Figure 21–2. S^2S^2 is the new short-run aggregate-supply curve after new firms have had time to come into the industry; it has shifted to the right. Under these new conditions, supply and demand are equal at a price of seven cents per blotter, with an output of 70,000 blotters in the industry as a whole. This is the new long-run industry equilibrium; price is now just equal to the new higher *TUC* curve at its minimum point, shown in the right-hand portion of Figure 21–2. Thus, there is no longer any incentive for resources to move into or out of the industry. Note that the cost curves of the typical firm have risen, because the increased production of blotters has bid up the price of labor and raw materials. On the demand side, price first rose from six to eight cents, and then fell back to seven cents, the lowest point on the *TUC* curve. In the new long-run equilibrium, the typical firm is again producing about the same amount as before, again at just its lowest total-unit-cost point.[5] But since there are more firms than be-

[5]Figure 21–2 shows the new equilibrium output of the firm identical with the old—that is, the new average-cost curve is merely raised by one cent for each level of output. This will be the result if the costs of all factors of production rise in the same proportion. This need not, of course, be the case, and the particular type of cost increase shown is not important for the basic analysis of the industry's response to an increase in demand.

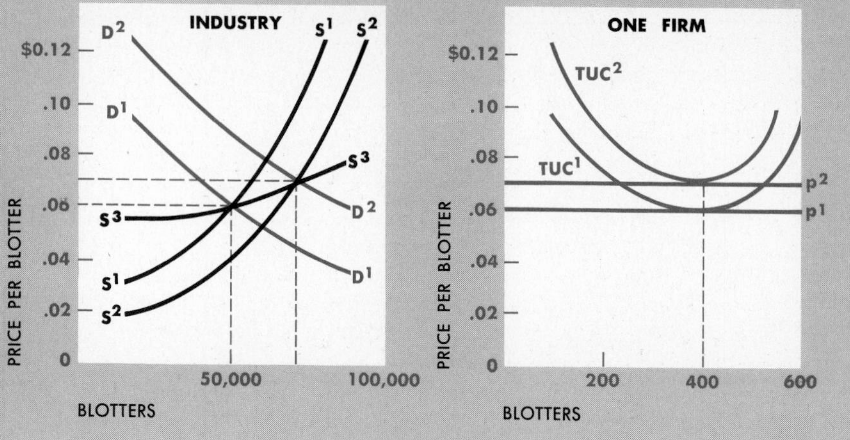

Figure 21–2

Increased demand draws new firms into the industry and produces new equilibrium for the firms and the industry at a price of seven cents. S^3S^3 is the long-run industry supply curve.

fore, the aggregate output of the industry is greater than it was initially. In response to their increased demand, consumers are getting 20,000 more blotters, and are getting them at the lowest price that will cover costs. But they have to pay one cent more per blotter because that much more was necessary to attract more productive resources from other uses into blotter making.

Long-Run Industry Supply Curves

S^3S^3 in Figure 21–2 is the long-run supply curve for the blotter industry. It joins the points at which the demand and supply curves intersect before and after the increase in demand. More fundamentally, it joins the lowest points on the typical firm's average-total-unit-cost curves as more firms enter the industry.

This is shown in Figure 21–3, which is patterned after Figure 19–3, which considered the optimal scale of enterprise for firms. The little *TUC* curves show the average-total-unit-cost curves for the typical firm as more firms enter the industry. The *SS* curve in this figure corresponds to the S^3S^3 curve in Figure 21–2. The industry is one of constant costs between 20,000 and 40,000 blotters, and one of gradually increasing costs above 40,000 blotters.

THE DEMAND FOR PRODUCTIVE SERVICES: WAGES AND OTHER INCOMES

When a business expands output to meet consumer demand, it hires more workers, rents more land, and uses more capital as long as marginal cost is less than price. Looked at from the input of productive resources such as labor, the business hires more workers as long as the marginal cost of labor is less than its marginal revenue.

Figure 21–3

This figure shows the relationship between typical individual firm average cost curves and long-run industry supply curves over a wide range of outputs.

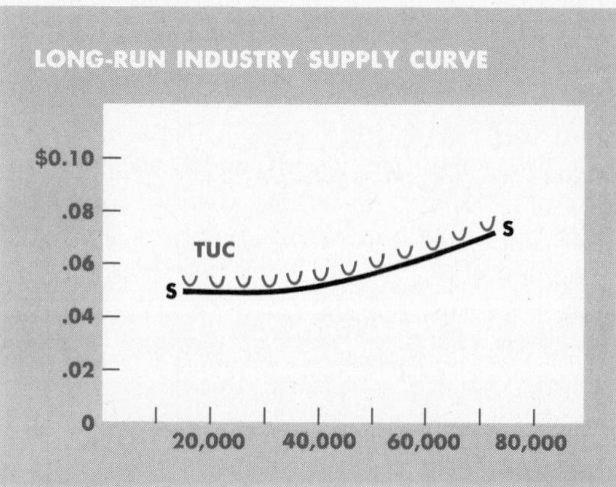

Competition among businessmen for productive resources will bid up the return (wage, rent, and so on) on each productive resource to roughly its marginal revenue, or "marginal product," and no higher.[6] Whenever the price of any productive service (say, the wage of a particular grade of labor) is lower than its marginal product, businessmen can increase their profits by hiring more of that factor, and this competition will bid the wage up. Whenever the price of a productive service is higher than its marginal product, businessmen will cut back on hiring that factor, and its price will fall until it just equals its marginal product. **In the long-run equilibrium, each worker's wage will be equal to his marginal product (or marginal revenue).**

Moreover, each productive resource will have its highest marginal product when it is in the industry where its contribution is greatest in producing the products consumers want. Thus, each productive factor will earn the most when it is contributing most to satisfying consumer demands. And each resource will be drawn to the use where its marginal product is highest if it wishes to maximize its income. The invisible hand again!

GENERAL EQUILIBRIUM OF A COMPETITIVE ECONOMY

Now an overview of the entire economy. Suppose the entire pattern of consumer demands for the economy is frozen, and a full "general equilibrium" adjustment to these demands has worked itself out in a purely competitive economy. What would be the main characteristics of the resulting long-run general equilibrium?

1. **Each consumer (household) is in equilibrium, maximizing its utility.** Each household spends its income on the different goods and services it wants most, given the prices it must pay. Thus, each household buys different products until their prices are proportional to the marginal utilities they yield. **Hence, consumer demand in the marketplace provides an accurate measure of how much satisfaction each commodity yields, and an accurate signal to producers as to how much of each commodity consumers want produced at different prices. The price paid is a measure of the marginal utility of the product to consumers who buy it.**

2. **Each business firm is in equilibrium, maximizing profits.** Each business firm, to achieve this position, carries its output up to the point where marginal cost equals price. The price is set by overall market conditions—by consumer demand and by the prices it must pay for the resources it uses. Given these prices, each firm does the best it can to maximize its profits.

3. **Each industry is in equilibrium.** The price of every commodity has been forced down by competition to the lowest point on the average unit-cost curve—to the lowest total cost of production that is consistent with known technology, with the prices of productive resources used in the industry, and with the size of consumer demands. There is no longer any incentive for firms and resources to move into or out of the industry, because economic profit has been eliminated in every industry. (Remenber that a normal return on investment is included in economic costs, so that accounting profits would remain in equilibrium in each industry.) **Put in other words, each businessman is producing his output in the most efficient way possible, so the minimum possible amount of society's scarce resources is being used in producing each commodity demanded by consumers.**

In equilibrium, thus, price equals marginal cost equals minimum average cost ($P = MC = TUC$). This is so because marginal cost equals the minimum total cost per unit for each firm, and each firm must be producing at its minimum-cost level.

4. **Each market is in equilibrium.** In each market the amount being supplied is equal to the amount being demanded at the existing

[6]Remember that marginal product is the addition to total output made by using one more unit of labor or capital.

price. There is no unsatisfied demand or excess supply in any market.

5. How can we be sure that in general competitive equilibrium, the economy is (a) producing that combination of products that consumers want most, as measured by the prices they are willing to pay; and (b) using society's resources most efficiently in producing those products?

First, how much consumers buy at any price mirrors their preferences for different products. These purchases provide signals to producers. Price paid is a measure of the product's marginal utility to buyers.

Second, marginal cost provides a measure of the additional cost it would take to produce one more unit of that output in responding to consumer signals. If marginal cost is below price, we know that too few resources are being used in that industry to satisfy consumer demand effectively. If marginal cost is higher than price, too many resources are being used in the industry in response to consumer demand. In equilibrium, more of each commodity is being produced wherever the satisfaction yielded exceeds the marginal cost of production—but none is produced where the marginal cost exceeds the marginal utility yielded. When $MC = P$, no change in resource allocation could increase the total satisfaction gained by all consumers. (See the Appendix on p. 290 for a rigorous proof.)

Put broadly, therefore, the combination of each consumer spending to maximize his own utility plus each businessman trying to maximize his own profits plus the force of competition in all markets has automatically:

(a) Forced each businessman to behave in the most "efficient" way if he is to remain in business;

(b) Led businessmen as a group to produce just as much of each product as consumers want to buy, at a price that just covers the cost necessary to attract the resources needed to produce that amount; and

(c) Obtained the maximum total output of wanted products from society's scarce productive resources.

6. The income received by each resource owner (laborers, capitalists, and the like) is equal to its marginal product and is the largest possible, given the productive powers of each and consumer demands. Each owner of productive resources is thus also in equilibrium.

In such a general equilibrium situation, could we say that consumers first demand certain goods and services, then businessmen respond to those demands, then competition forces their prices down to minimum costs, then wages and rents are set, then incomes are paid out to workers, landowners, and capitalists? Obviously the answer is "no." All these steps—millions of them each day—are being carried out simultaneously in the economy. The prices of all final goods and all factors of production are being set and adjusted continuously and simultaneously. Each depends on all the others.[7]

The Invisible Hand

Such is the case for pure competition. Everyone looks out for his own interests. The result is an organization of society's scarce resources that looks amazingly as if it has been guided by some invisible hand for the welfare of society as a whole. Each individual, as consumer, laborer, or businessman, looks out for his own self-interest. No individual consumer or resource owner has any appreciable influence over what gets produced and how much of it, but in the mass they determine the allocation of society's resources among all possible alternative uses. Individual incomes, outputs, and prices are simultaneously determined. And at the center of the process, trying to buy cheap and sell dear, is the businessman, continually searching for

[7]Some economists describe general equilibrium conditions in mathematical terms. Because general equilibrium involves considering a vast number of demands, costs, markets, prices, and productive factors simultaneously, we can view the system as a large set of simultaneous equations and investigate the effects of different changes mathematically. Leon Walras, a French economist, was one of the first, a century ago, to use mathematics in analyzing economic problems and apparently the first to state the essential general equilibrium conditions for such a competitive economy.

profits and thereby (perhaps unwittingly) providing the organizing service that merges and compromises all these millions of different interests.

PURELY COMPETITIVE ECONOMY—EVALUATION

The case for an individual-initiative, market-directed, purely-competitive economy is an impressive one. If we want to avoid authoritarian control over what gets produced and where we work, the purely-competitive private-enterprise system offers a nonpolitical, individualistic way of making the millions of interrelated compromises required among the different interests involved.

But there are problems. Such an economy, for all its virtues, would face some serious difficulties and would fall short of satisfying at least some people's personal and social goals on three major fronts. We will look at them in detail in the following chapters. Here they are merely indicated to round out this evaluative overview of an individualistic, market-directed, purely-competitive economy.

Problems in Making Competitive Markets Work Effectively

1. **Resource Allocation When Social Costs Exceed Private Costs.** To get the optimal allocation of resources among different products, the price of each product to the consumer should cover the total cost of producing it. In some cases, there are hidden costs ("externalities") that are not paid by the producer and hence do not enter into the commodity's price but nevertheless are borne involuntarily by the rest of society. In such cases, price is lower than it should be and output is larger than is socially justifiable.

Air and water pollution is a leading example. Smoke and dirt produced by many industrial plants represent real costs to residents of the vicinity. Yet these real costs don't enter into the firm's accounting costs of producing its product, and a market price that covers only the firm's private accounting costs won't cover the full social costs of producing the product.

Conversely, there may be positive externalities, where a private firm produces helpful side-effects for which it can't charge in pricing its products. An example is the flood control benefits produced when a lumber company replants areas that have been cut, in order to assure itself a stock of trees in the future.

Where "private" and "social" costs and returns diverge (where there are externalities), a market system fails to produce an "ideal" pattern of resource allocation. Most economists believe that in such cases we should take collective (government) action to bring results nearer to the competitive ideal.

2. **Imperfect Information, Immobility, and Demand Manipulation.** For a competitive system to work well, consumers must be well informed about the goods and services available at different prices, and resource owners must be well informed about employment opportunities that are open to them. If farm workers in Montana know nothing of a shortage of labor in Detroit's auto assembly plants, or secretaries in Chicago don't know about better jobs in St. Louis, the optimal allocation of resources is blocked. Perhaps the Montana worker would prefer to stay out on the range even if he knew about the higher-paying Detroit jobs, but we can't be sure unless he knows about them.

A similar malallocation may result if resources are immobile, even though information is freely available. If our farmer has a big family and no savings, he may be unable to take the better Detroit job, no matter how badly he wants it. Both the farmer and society would be better off if he could somehow get over the hump into the new industrial job.

Both imperfect information and immobility are widespread in the modern economy, especially among lower-income groups. Both block the economy from carrying out the wishes of consumers and resource owners.

Another problem is perhaps even more serious, if we temporarily drop the assumption of a perfectly competitive economy. In the modern world, advertising influences, and sometimes even determines, what consumers want. Some people say, therefore, that the basic assumption of free consumer choice is unacceptable. They say that producers tell us what we should want, rather than responding to our own wants. This is an important and complex issue, which will come to center stage in Chapter 24.

3. **The Problem of Minimum Size for Efficient Production.** Pure competition requires that no one seller be large enough to have appreciable influence over market price. If he gets very big, there is a danger that he may respond to increased consumer demand by raising price and trying to shut out new competitors, rather than by expanding output. For pure competition, there have to be lots of firms in every industry.

But in many industries, for example, autos and steel, firms have to be big in order to produce efficiently. In such industries, we face a difficult choice. We can insist on many small firms to assure competition, but this will mean higher production costs than a smaller number of large firms would involve. Or we can tolerate some degree of monopoly, but lose some of the pressures of competition obtainable with large numbers of producers. More on this dilemma in Chapters 24 and 25.

Public Goods and the Public Sector

There are some public, or collective, wants that most people feel cannot be satisfactorily provided through the marketplace. National defense and the court system are examples. We agree that they are essential, and through the political process legislate taxes (compulsory payments) to hire resources to provide them. There is no practical way to leave it up to each individual to buy in the marketplace the amount and kind of national defense or general law and order he wants. The special characteristics of public goods are that they are widely agreed to be essential, and if provided cannot practically be withheld from any citizen just because he doesn't pay.

What we do directly through government action, we often call the "public sector" of the economy. This now totals over $400 billion annually, nearly a third of the total gross national product. Just how far we should go in using compulsory taxes to "buy" public goods and services is a highly debatable issue. The lines defining public goods are sometimes far from clear. Is slum clearance a "public good," not salable through the market? For true public goods, there is no practical alternative to turning to the political process for making decisions, but lots of cases are marginal.

We will take a detailed look at how big the public sector should be—at what the government should do—in Part Five.

Equity and the Distribution of Income

Many observers believe that the distribution of income (wages, interest, profits, and the like) produced by a purely competitive economy would be inequitable, however "efficiently" the market might allocate resources in response to consumer demands. In a purely competitive economy, every man's income would rest on his own or his property's economic contribution. And this would mean an unequal distribution of incomes. Some individuals inherit large fortunes, from which they obtain large incomes in the form of interest and dividends. Some people have higher intellectual abilities than others, which tend to produce larger incomes for them. Some people are born into higher-income families, which means they get better educations and broader opportunities to develop earning power. Some people work harder and longer than others. A purely competitive economy would have rich and poor, and many Americans believe we should reduce these inequalities through government action.

On the other hand, some people argue that such an income distribution, based on "economic contribution," would be eminently just as well as efficient. It would provide both incentives and equity for all. Whether you agree or not, you can decide for yourself. What is equity in the distribution of income and buying power is a highly debatable issue and is a main topic of Parts Four and Five.

REVIEW

Concepts to Remember

Be sure you have a firm grasp of the new analytical concepts introduced in this chapter:

pure competition
long-run equilibrium
equilibrium of the firm
equilibrium of the industry
general equilibrium
equilibrium tendencies
economic efficiency
constant-cost industry
increasing-cost industry
long-run supply curves
price taker
social costs
private costs
externalities
public goods

For Analysis and Discussion

1. Explain briefly but concisely how individuals and businesses, each pursuing his own self-interest, interact to produce a widely beneficial outcome under competitive market conditions.
2. "Under pure competition, the consumer is king. The price of what he wants to buy can never stay for long above the minimum cost of producing any article." Is this quotation sound?
3. Under a purely competitive system, what incentive, if any, would remain for businessmen to do an efficient job, since competition would eliminate profits?
4. Pure competition, strictly speaking, does not prevail in any part of the economy. Then why study it?
5. "A purely competitive economic system would be ideal." Do you agree? Why or why not?
6. Suppose a tax of one cent per blotter has been included in the costs of all blotter producers. Now the tax is removed. Beginning from the situation in Figure 21–1, with the price at six cents and demand D^1D^1, trace through the adjustment to a new equilibrium.
7. As a consumer of widgets, would you prefer that the industry be one of constant or increasing long-run costs? Why?
8. "Most people would agree that a dollar means more to a poor man than to a rich man. Since this is so, an economic system that merely reacts to the

number of dollars spent is a grossly unfair system in the way it allocates resources." Do you agree or disagree? Why? If you agree, how should we modify the system to get around the problem?

9. What would be the main weaknesses, if any, of a purely competitive system? Should we use public policies to move further toward such a system?

APPENDIX

General Equilibrium and Economic Efficiency

A purely competitive system of the sort described above would provide the most efficient possible allocation of resources in the sense described in the text of the chapter. More precisely, we can show that such a purely competitive system would allocate resources most efficiently, in the sense that no possible reallocation would increase the welfare of anyone in the system without harming someone else. This condition, which economists call "Pareto optimality" (after the famous French economist who first stated it precisely) seems to some observers a weak claim for an optimal system. But it is a major claim indeed, if you stop to think about it. For if Pareto optimality does not prevail, we could make someone better off without harming anyone else, thus unambiguously increasing the public's total utility. Any system that does not provide Pareto optimality is producing a socially inefficient allocation of resources that holds total utility for the economy below what it could otherwise be.

It is possible to demonstrate precisely that Pareto optimality will prevail under competitive general equilibrium (that is, no one can be made better off without injuring someone else); while under other market arrangements (for example, with some degree of monopoly) it is generally possible to increase the welfare of someone without injuring anyone else. For simplicity, consider only two goods, x and y, although the argument can be generalized to many goods.

Assume that competitive general equilibrium prevails. We know then (from Chapter 5) that when a consumer is in equilibrium, maximizing his utility, he spends his income so that the marginal utility obtained from the last dollar spent on x is the same as that obtained from the last dollar spent on y. Alternatively, we can say that the marginal utilities of the two products must be proportional to their prices. In equation form:

$$\frac{MU_x}{MU_y} = \frac{P_x}{P_y} \qquad (1)$$

We also know (from Chapters 20 and 21) that in long-run competitive equilibrium, each producer in each industry maximizes profits by producing up to the point where marginal cost equals price. Thus:

$$P_x = MC_x \text{ (for industry } x\text{)} \qquad (2a)$$

$$P_y = MC_y \text{ (for industry } y\text{)} \qquad (2b)$$

Combining equations (1) and (2), we can then write:

$$\frac{MU_x}{MU_y} = \frac{P_x}{P_y} = \frac{MC_x}{MC_y} \qquad (3)$$

Equations (1), (2), and (3) state the conditions under which, with the competitive prices P_x and P_y, every consumer and business firm is in the best position it can achieve. No one can increase his utility or profits by changing his behavior. Equation (3) also emphasizes that prices provide the basic equilibrating link between consumers (expressing their preferences through expenditures) and businesses (maximizing their profits by hiring resources up to the point where marginal cost equals price).

Now, consider any situation where perfect competition does not prevail—for example, where a monopolist is restricting output and raising price to enlarge profits so that he holds his selling price above marginal cost. (We will demonstrate rigorously in Chapter 23 why he will do so in order to maximize his profits, once he is free from competitive pressure.) Suppose, for example, that monopoly prevails in industry y, so marginal cost in y is less than price. Then equation (2b) will not hold, and hence neither will equation (3).

Suppose, for example, that

$$\frac{MU_x}{MU_y} = 2$$

but that

$$\frac{MC_x}{MC_y} = 3$$

because marginal cost is below price in industry y while MC equals price in industry x. Thus the marginal utility of one unit of x is twice that of one unit of y, but the marginal cost of producing one more y is only one-third that for x. This means that in terms of costs, producers could make three additional units of y by giving up one of x. By so shifting resources to produce one less x and three more y we can make consumers better off, by giving them more than the two units of y they view as equivalent to one unit of x in their utility functions. Similarly, for any other condition than the (competitive) one specified in equation (3), it will be possible to make someone better off without injuring anyone else. When equation (3) is satisfied, Pareto optimality will prevail.

Competitive equilibrium provides Pareto optimality, and monopolistic equilibrium does not except in some unlikely hypothetical cases that need not concern us here. Thus, economists presume that a monopolistic situation that holds price above marginal cost will generally lead to a less-efficient allocation of resources than would a competitive system.

But remember that a Pareto optimal competitive system would not necessarily be the best system, even though it provided the most "efficient" allocation of resources in response to consumer demands. You might still object to its failure to take into account externalities, to provide enough public goods, or to produce an "equitable" distribution of income. The substantial benefits from purely competitive markets do not necessarily imply that economically no government is the best government.

Agriculture: A Case Study in Competition

CHAPTER PREVIEW

CHAPTER TWENTY-TWO

Agriculture is the area of the American economy that comes closest to the model of pure competition. For most major farm products—wheat, cotton, hogs, and many others—the conditions of pure competition substantially prevail except insofar as the government has stepped in to alter them. How well has substantially pure competition worked in agriculture? Has agriculture responded efficiently to shifting consumer demands over the years? What accounts for the far-reaching government intervention to help solve "the farm problem"? In fact, is there any "farm problem" that the forces of competition would not resolve adequately if left alone to work themselves out? Agriculture provides a fascinating case study of competition at work.

RESPONSES TO CHANGING DEMANDS

Table 22–1 presents data on spending for, and production of, food in the United States since 1929. How well has agriculture responded to changing consumer demand over the past half century? Using Table 22–1 and what you have learned about competitive markets thus far, try to answer this question for yourself before reading on.

Suggestions for Analysis

Although Table 22–1 provides only a small subset of the data for a complete answer, it has

TABLE 22–1
Food in the United States, 1929–72

	1929	1947	1972
1. Consumer expenditures on food (billions of 1967 dollars)	$ 38	$ 72	$125
2. Food as percentage of total consumption	29	28	22
3. Number of farms (millions)	6.2	5.5	2.9
4. Number of farm workers (millions)	13	10	3.5
5. Farmers as percentage of total population	25	16	4.5
6. Output per farm worker (1967 = 100)	17	33	123
7. Investment per farm worker (1967 = 100)	34	71	110
8. Acres devoted to farming (millions)	974	1155	980
9. Per capita farm income as percentage of nonfarm[a]	29	37	31

[a]Farm income excludes government payments and nonfarm earnings.

the crucial information on most of the important points.

First, what has happened to consumer demand for food since 1929? Line 1 shows that consumers bought about three times as much food in 1972 as 1929. (Total spending on food rose more, but a part of the increase was merely higher prices, and this inflation has been eliminated by converting all years to the same [1967] prices.) Thus, the line shows both growing consumer demand (mainly more people) and farmers' increased production in response to that demand. But line 2 shows an equally important fact about demand. Demand for food grew much less rapidly than demand for other goods and services: Food's share of total consumer spending fell from 29 to 22 percent as the American people became more affluent.

How did agriculture respond? We know from line 1 that production grew to meet growing demand. Lines 3 through 8 tell us more, that people have persistently moved out of farming to the rest of the economy where consumer demand has grown more rapidly, as the competitive model predicts—but that fewer and fewer farms and farmers nonetheless managed to produce the increase in food demanded. Lines 3 through 5 show the big exodus from farming to the rest of the economy, and line 9 suggests why. Average incomes from farming have persistently been far below those in nonfarm occupations. Millions of farm proprietors and workers have moved out of low-profit and low-income farming to other industries where income prospects are higher, just as economic theory says they will. A half century ago, a quarter of the labor force was in farming. Now it is less than 5 percent.

Lines 6 through 8 tell how the farm industry managed the big increase in food production. Land devoted to farming remained virtually unchanged, but farmers invested large sums in tractors, chemicals, and other modern capital equipment that dramatically raised output per worker and per acre. And modern technology has been spectacular on the farm. New fertilizers, hybrid seeds, plant-disease control, and modern farm machinery have revolutionized food production. A century ago one farmer fed five people; today he feeds nearly fifty. Output per man has grown about 6 percent per year, about twice as fast as in manufacturing. As part of this revolution the average farm nearly tripled in size; increasingly only very large farms can produce at the lowest costs per unit. Today about half of all farm products come from the largest 6 percent of farms, with over $50,000 of annual sales and utilizing advanced modern machinery

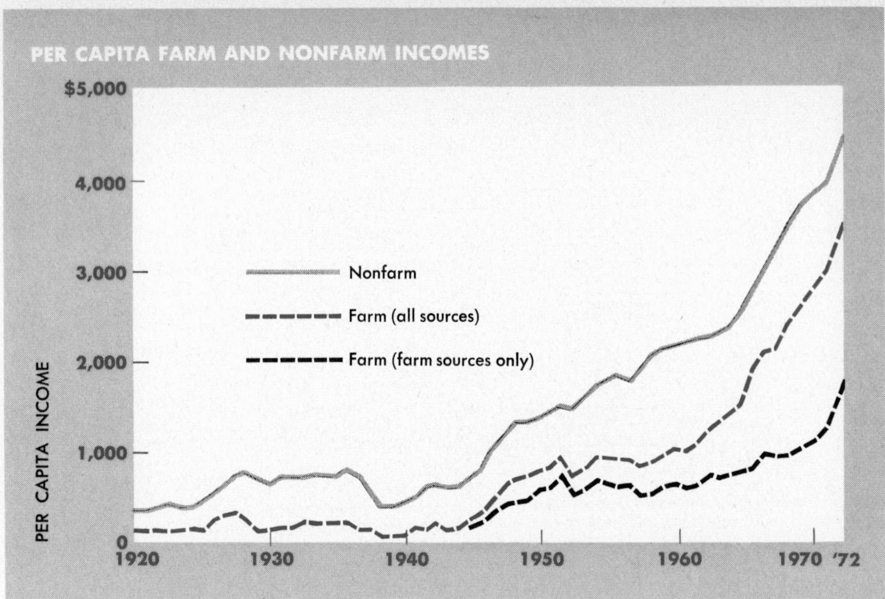

Figure 22–1

Per capita farm incomes have long been under nonfarm incomes. Recently a substantial part of total farm income has come from nonfarm sources. (Source: U.S. Department of Agriculture.)

and technology. But although farm experts estimate that it is a rare farmer selling $10,000 or less annually who can cover his costs in basic crops, over 40 percent of all farms still have total sales (not profits) of less than $2,500 annually—clearly far too small to produce efficiently with modern methods.

Line 9 is perhaps the most striking of all. In spite of a large, continuing exodus of young people from farming, per capita income from farming (excluding government subsidies) remains only about 30 percent of nonfarm incomes. Figure 22–1 presents the picture in more detail. The bottom line shows per capita incomes from farming. The middle line adds government subsidies and nonfarm income of farmers (dividends, interest, and so on), but even that brings farm incomes up to only about 75 percent of nonfarm. Farm incomes have risen dramatically in the last few years, and there are some very rich farmers. But most farmers are small and many are poor.

So, all things considered, how well would you say agriculture has responded to changing consumer demands?

AGRICULTURE'S CLAIMS TO SPECIAL AID

Do farmers have any claim to special aid from government or consumers? Consider a few of the arguments.

1. **Low-income status.** Low farm incomes are a major argument. Farmers want a reasonable living and a fair return for a hard day's work, just as much as anyone else. If you believe that everyone should have at least some minimum income, this plea is understandable. But while many farmers are in the lowest income groups, many others are not. Thus, helping all farmers is a shotgun approach that confuses personal needs with farming as an industry.

2. **Special susceptibility to business fluctuations.** Farmers are hard hit by depressions, but they also prosper in prosperities. Does agriculture have a special claim for help on this score, more than the steel industry? Surely the main approach must be through greater stability for the economy as a whole. This argument, you should note, is easy to confuse with the general

low-income argument above. Don't count the same thing twice.

3. **The weather.** The vagaries of nature may upset the best-laid farm plans. Droughts and floods come. There's nothing new about this problem, of course. Centuries ago the emperors of China sought to establish something surprisingly like the modern "ever-normal granary" storage plan, to save up surpluses in bumper years for the shortage years to come.

4. **Special aid to offset advantages of other groups.** Farmers claim that they are injured by special privileges for other groups, and hence that they deserve offsetting special assistance. For example, the American tariff on industrial products has long forced the farmer to pay higher domestic prices. Monopolistic conditions in business and labor have been tolerated by government officials in many industries. These raise the prices paid by farmers and restrict movement from farms to urban occupations.

5. **The need for soil conservation.** Most Americans believe it is desirable to conserve our natural resources. Often the advantage of conservation to society as a whole exceeds the dollars-and-cents return to the farmer in undertaking soil-conservation measures; this is a case where the social benefits exceed those to the individual producer. Thus, much of the farm-aid program has been justified as soil conservation (for example, conserving soil by not planting part of the land each year). In fact, however, much of the conservation talk has served to disguise programs whose main goal is to raise farm income. And for many years the

Technological progress has revolutionized farming. (Courtesy of Sperry New Holland.)

problem has seemed to be too much farmland rather than too little.

6. **Agriculture as a way of life.** Some people look on agriculture as a stable, sound way of life, harking back to the ways of our fathers—an anchor to windward in a hectic world of assembly lines, tenements, skyscrapers, and neuroses. The farmer is still an individual, not just a cog in a huge economic machine. This, they feel, is a way of life worth preserving.

But this case raises some economic dilemmas. The very traits of the farmer and his life that are admired most in this view are the ones associated with small-scale, often inefficient, family farming. Large-scale commercial farming that promises a higher farm standard of living compromises these very virtues.

A closely related argument hinges on large farm families. There is no provision in the price system, say some, for paying farmers for the outlays of money and effort they make in bearing, rearing, and educating a large number of children who later move into other economic areas. Economically, the argument runs, human beings are capital resources of the nation just as much as are buildings and machines.

But on closer examination, this, like the low-income argument, is logically a personal, not an industry, argument. If we want to encourage and pay for large families, all right. But if we do, the aid should be based on size of family, not on where they live.

All these claims face substantial counterarguments, as we shall see. But they have convinced enough congressmen to produce a large farm-aid program since the 1920's, and reaching back even further. Your economic tool kit can help you analyze these special aid programs for agriculture.

THE ECONOMICS OF FARM AID

There are four main paths by which the government has provided special aid to farmers:

1. Output restriction programs (sometimes ostensibly for soil conservation), aimed at raising farm prices and incomes.
2. Government crop purchase or loan programs, aimed at raising farm prices and incomes.
3. Direct income-support grants.
4. Programs to lower agricultural costs and promote efficiency.

Parity

Since the New Deal, "parity" between farm incomes and prices and those in the rest of the economy has been the foundation of the farm-aid program. To be fair, it is argued, farm prices and incomes should rise at least as fast as nonfarm.

As it was developed in the New Deal legislation, farm parity meant that prices paid and received by farmers should be in the same ratio as in the "normal" years 1909–14. If farm prices drop *relative to* other prices (or don't rise as fast as other prices), government action should push the farm prices back up to parity.

If you're a skeptic, you will recall that the period from 1909–14 was the golden age of agriculture. You may ask, why not a parity program for buggies and women's high-buttoned shoes, based on the years 1905–06, which saw the peak for the buggy and high-button shoe industries? But parity has been the foundation of our farm aid programs.

Output-Restriction Programs

One major approach to raising farm prices and incomes has been government restriction of farm output. Suppose that *SS* in Figure 22–2 is the supply curve and *DD* the demand curve for beans. Given these curves, the equilibrium price will clearly be twenty cents per pound with 20,000 bushels of beans produced each year. All farmers producing beans will be doing so at a cost of no more than twenty cents per pound, because at any lower price their incomes would not cover their costs. Everyone who is willing to pay twenty cents per pound for beans is getting all he wants to buy at that price.

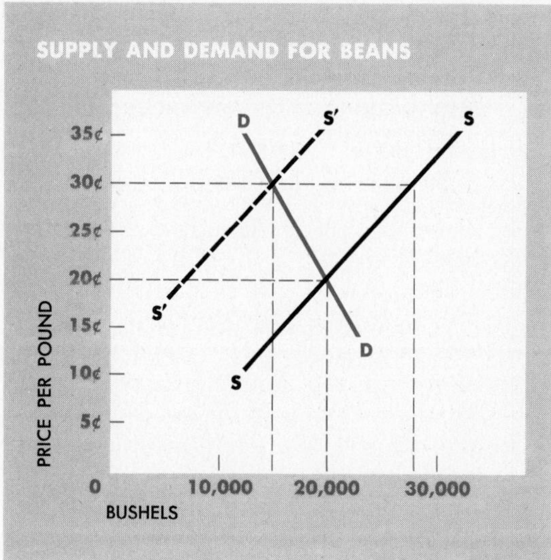

Figure 22–2

Market-clearing price for beans is twenty cents. If price is fixed at thirty cents, there are 13,000 pounds of unsold beans.

Suppose, however, that bean farmers protest that the price is too low, below parity, and they are not really making a decent living at that price. They lobby for a price-support program for beans, and they get it—at a price of thirty cents per pound, which they allege will give them a decent living standard. What is the result?

The first result is that there is a large excess supply in the market. At thirty cents per pound, roughly 28,000 bushels of beans will be produced, but buyers will only take about 15,000 bushels. Those farmers who sell at thirty cents per pound may be very happy, but there are a lot of farmers holding the unsold 13,000 bushels of beans.

The government, considerate of the bean farmers' plight, offers to pay them to cut back production to 15,000 bushels. It might, for example, provide a "soil conservation" payment of ten cents per bushel for beans to reduce bean acreage so that no more than 15,000 bushels are produced by the industry as a whole. This in effect, moves the supply curve back to the left so the total amount supplied at thirty cents per pound is just the 15,000 bushels that the private market will take. This movement of the supply curve is shown by S^1S^1.

How do the various parties fare? The bean farmers should be happy. They are getting thirty cents a pound for their beans and they are permitted to either produce, or be paid for not producing, a total of 28,000 bushels. But taxpayers end up spending ten cents per pound on subsidies for 13,000 bushels of beans not produced under the output-restriction plan. And consumers must pay thirty cents per pound for beans, getting only 15,000 bushels at that price—they are now paying more for 15,000 bushels than they were for 20,000 bushels before the farm-aid program, since demand is inelastic. Clearly, there are too many bean farms and farmers in the industry, but they are paid to stay there by the "soil conservation" subsidy paid by the government to reduce supply.

Government Purchase or Loan Programs

Alternatively, the government can maintain the bean price at thirty cents by buying up the excess supply (13,000 bushels) left by private buyers at that price. This moves the total private-plus-government demand curve to the right by 13,000 bushels at the thirty cent price on Figure 22–2, just clearing the market and assuring bean farmers their desired prices and incomes. This is fine for bean producers, but bad for consumers who are again paying more for fewer beans, and for taxpayers who have to pick up the bill for the 13,000 bushels of beans. The government cannot sell the beans on the open market, because to do so would undercut the price it is trying to support. Thus, in all probability it will store them—or perhaps find a way to give them away to hungry people, here or in other parts of the world.

Sometimes the government, instead of buying up the overhang, merely lends the farmers the parity price on the excess crops, with the beans as security—say thirty cents a pound on unsold beans. Then the farmer can pay off the loan and sell the beans if the price later rises above thirty cents, or default on the loan and turn the beans over to the government if the price stays below thirty cents. It's a heads-I-win–tails-you-lose deal for the farmer, much like the outright purchase plan for consumers and taxpayers.

If the government ends up with lots of beans in storage, which it can't sell here without depressing the market price, it can recoup part of its investment by selling them abroad at the competitive world-market price, well below the thirty-cent-supported domestic price. But if it does so, it will encounter cries of "dumping" by foreign bean producers who will find themselves in competition with a government-subsidized price from the United States. If the government can't sell the beans abroad, perhaps it can at least give them away to hungry countries or to the hungry poor at home. This will make the cost of the gifts quite clear, and the full amount of the subsidy will be seen as a loss to the government. But don't forget that even then domestic consumers are only getting 15,000 bushels in the market and have to pay thirty cents per pound for them.

Direct Income-Support Subsidies

Secretaries of Agriculture Brannan (under Truman) and Benson (under Eisenhower), frustrated by all this, proposed another modification that finally became the basis for the nation's farm-aid program in 1974. They said, if we want to guarantee farmers the thirty-cent price to keep their incomes up, let market forces determine the market price and let farmers produce what they will at that price (20,000 bushels at twenty cents in Figure 22–2). Then simply give each farmer a money subsidy of ten cents for each pound of beans sold to make up the desired thirty-cent price. This will at least avoid paying for nonproduction and piling up government surpluses in storage, and it will give the full output of beans to consumers at a free-market price. The taxpayers will still pay a big subsidy to farmers if the market price falls below the "target" price (the new name, replacing "parity"). Indeed, the taxpayer cost will be higher than under the previous crop-purchase plans *if* demand is inelastic, but consumers are clearly better off under the new guaranteed-income-support approach enacted by Congress for the years 1974–77.

The new farm legislation can be viewed as a major advance or as a sellout to the farm bloc. It was enacted in 1973, in the midst of the greatest farm boom in U.S. history—in the first U.S. peacetime "food shortage" in living memory. Worldwide crop failures in 1971 and 1972; record prosperity in the industrial nations which led to big increases in food demands (especially for meats); massive U.S. grain sales to Russia, Western Europe, and other nations; nationwide food hoarding by U.S. consumers as a near-panic developed when farmers temporarily held back meat from the market when the Nixon Administration temporarily froze meat prices; and international speculation in grains—all combined to shoot grain and meat prices temporarily up to unprecedented levels. Wheat, which for years had averaged below $2 a bushel, soared to over $5 a bushel. Soybeans rose even more. Beef and pork prices doubled.

Faced with soaring prices and domestic shortages of meat, President Nixon removed all planting restrictions on wheat for 1974, and proposed a return to a free market in farm products. But Congress passed the new target-price farm bill, which will avoid restricting supply as had previously been done, but retained farm subsidies. Even in the face of the highest farm prices in history and soaring farm incomes, Congress inserted the minimum price guarantee that would give unlimited subsidies to farmers, should basic farm products fall below their target prices. And target prices, while well below then-prevailing record market levels, were set well above previous market and parity levels. If run-away inflation and record farm prosperity continues, taxpayers will have low bills for farm subsidies. But if farm prices return to anything like what earlier history would predict, farmers will have an unlimited claim on the federal treasury for cash subsidies to keep incomes up to the target-price levels set. And, as in the past, the income subsidies will go mainly to big, already prosperous farmers, since they will be paid in proportion to the crops each farmer has to sell. The little, low-income farmers will receive only small cash subsidies.

The Farm-Aid Program in Action

The core of the farm-aid program over the past half century has been the effort to keep up prices and incomes by preventing crop "surpluses" or buying them up if they occur. The resulting pile-up of government-held surpluses is shown in Figure 22-3. Figure 22-4 shows the percentage of the annual crop bought up or loaned by the government each year since 1950 for wheat, cotton, and corn. Some twenty crops were covered by the price support program in 1973.[1]

[1]The others were barley, beans, butter, cheese, dried milk, honey, peanuts, flaxseed, sorghum, oats, rice, rye, soybeans, tung oil, tobacco, wool, and mohair. Surpluses were sold mainly abroad (where the world price was under the U.S. support price) and at low prices domestically when deterioration threatened. The average loss has been about 25 percent of the C.C.C. (government) investment.

Table 22-2 summarizes the cost of these farm-aid programs to the government over the past decade, and the beneficiaries; note that this does not include the costs to consumers in the form of higher prices.

What the table does not convey is the concentration of federal aid payments to a relatively small number of large farmers. For example, in one recent year one farm in Kern County, California, received a federal farm-subsidy payment of $4.4 million for not growing cotton; this reflected crop-reduction payments on a farm covering 83,000 acres. In four San Joaquin Valley counties in California, 2,300 cotton farms received a total of $65.4 million in federal farm subsidies. Although these are extreme cases, most poor small farmers, who need help most, get tiny subsidy payments because "conservation" payments are based on the acreage or crop cut back, usually some proportion of previous output lev-

Figure 22-3

This chart shows the amount of government funds tied up in farm crop loans and surplus stocks each year. Tobacco and soybeans account for most "Other" in recent years. (Source: Commodity Credit Corporation; 1972 figures are preliminary.)

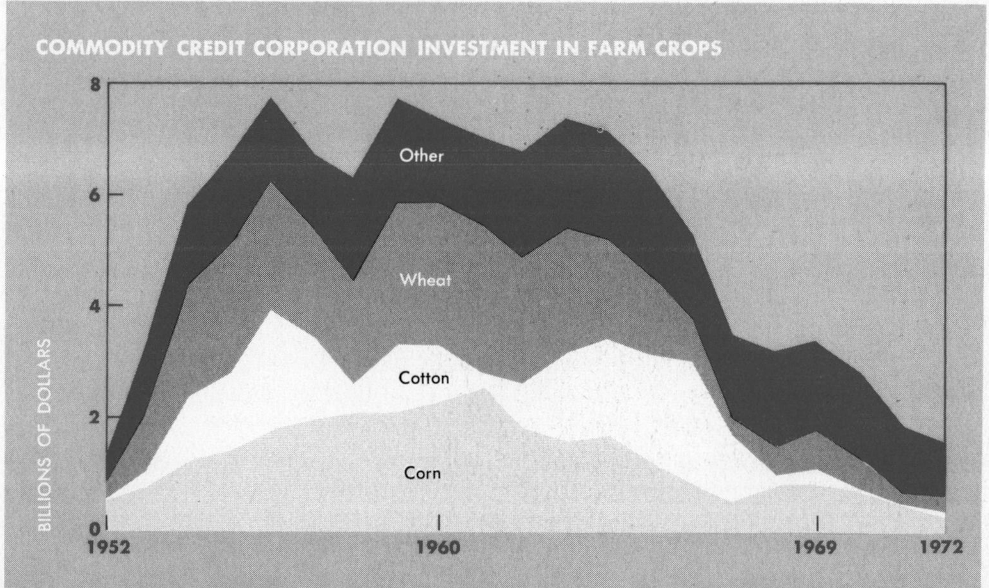

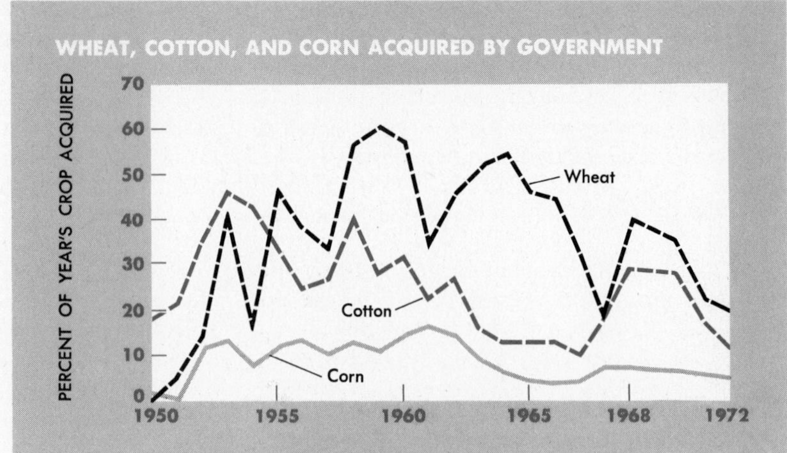

Figure 22–4

A big proportion of the cotton, wheat, and corn crops has been bought up or loaned on by the government in many years. (Source: U.S. Department of Agriculture. 1972 figures are preliminary.)

els. In 1970, the smallest 50 percent of all farms received only 9 percent of total government benefits; the smallest 40 percent (with annual sales under $2,500) only 5 percent, averaging less than $400 per farm. In 1970, Congress limited payments per crop to each farm to $55,000 and in 1973 to $20,000, but many large farmers have avoided this limit by breaking up farms into smaller legal units and by diversifying crops.

As was noted above, the new target-price farm program has important advantages over the old crop-restriction approach. At least as long as farm prosperity based on high market prices lasts, the cost to taxpayers will be cut sharply and market supplies will be expanded. But there is little reason to suppose the basic farm developments summarized in Table 22–1 have suddenly vanished. And if they return, the American taxpayer will be back paying large subsidies to farmers to stay in farming when the market tells them to go elsewhere—and the biggest subsidies will go to the biggest farmers.

TABLE 22–2

Federal Government Aid to Agriculture

	FEDERAL AID (IN BILLIONS)	PERCENT OF TOTAL FEDERAL BUDGET	FARM POPULATION (IN MILLIONS)
1961	$3.3	3.4%	14.8
1963	5.1	4.6	13.3
1965	4.8	4.1	12.4
1967	4.4	2.8	10.9
1969	6.2	3.4	10.3
1971	5.4	2.7	9.4
1973	6.1	2.4	8.7
1974	5.6	2.1	8.4

Source: Data from U.S. Budget for Fiscal 1974 and from *Economic Report of the President*. Figures are for fiscal years.

Programs to Promote Agricultural Efficiency

Long before the government set out to raise farm incomes by restricting production, the Department of Agriculture was busy telling farmers how to *increase* production. A broad program of scientific research, on-the-ground help for farmers through nationwide agricultural experiment stations, advice on soil-conservation practices, and a variety of other measures have played a major role in raising the efficiency of American agriculture to a level unparalleled in most other nations.

But by carrying out this eminently sensible program, the Department of Agriculture has been sabotaging its own crop-restriction programs. The American farmer is nobody's fool, and he has taken full advantage of modern methods to increase yields even while he is cutting back acreage under the income-support programs. Would you do differently if you were a farmer?

Effects

The effects of nearly a half century of price support and production-control plans are hard to assess precisely. Presumably, farm prices have been higher than they otherwise would have been, although it is not clear that total farm production has been reduced since farmers substitute another product when one is cut back. Billions after billions of dollars have gone into supporting farm prices and into paying farmers not to produce, mainly through withholding land from the production of particular crops. In 1973, $5 billion was budgeted for price and income supports. These plans have consistently provided large benefits to the big farmers (with large crops to sell and large acreage to cut back) and little help for the little farmers who need it most.

But two results are crystal clear. First, over the past ten years federal agricultural expenditures, mainly through price- and income-support programs, amounted to more than the entire increase in farm income over the period, though even this support was insufficient to raise average farm incomes relative to nonfarm ones.

Second, the huge farm surpluses piled up by the government have been mute, if expensive, evidence of the difficulties of trying to maintain prices above market levels through government action, even when billions were spent paying farmers not to produce. To the man from Mars, the American farm program would be a strange phenomenon. It would be hard to explain to him why we should pay people not to produce food and buy up available food to hold prices at levels where people won't consume it.

The new 1974 program would be easier to explain—we want to provide a general taxpayer subsidy to farmers if their prices fall. But why the biggest subsidies should go to the biggest farmers might well still seem strange.

U.S. AGRICULTURE AND THE WORLD FOOD PROBLEM

U.S. farm policy has seemed especially anomalous in view of the total world food situation. Over two billion of the world's people live in countries where malnutrition and undernourishment are widespread. And actual starvation is never far away. Why should the United States not produce all the food it can and sell the "surplus" above our needs to the hungry less-developed nations? A thorough analysis must wait for Parts Six and Seven, on the international economy. But the main answer is that the less-developed nations can't afford to pay for it at anything like world prices. In fact, the United States has given away every year during the past two decades a large amount of "surplus" food, accumulated under the U.S. farm-price-support program. During the 1960s, for example, food aid to the less-developed nations averaged between $1.0 billion and $1.5 billion annually.[2] More re-

[2]Much of this food aid was provided under "Public Law 480," which, in essence, permits the United States to sell surplus food to less-developed countries and accept payment in local currency, which the U.S. government promises not

cently, the total has declined gradually, reflecting partly reduced congressional willingness to provide foreign aid, and partly the smaller surpluses being accumulated by the U.S. farm program. Presumably the government will accumulate no more huge surpluses under the new target-price program, and we will have to buy food outright if we want to give it to the less-developed nations. What this will mean to the level of U.S. foreign aid remains to be seen.

AGRICULTURE IN THE POLITICAL ECONOMY

In fiscal 1973, the federal government spent nearly $7 billion on aid for agriculture. In the same year, total farm income from farming (excluding income from investments and other nonfarm sources) was about $19 billion. Thus, nearly 40 percent of total income from farming was accounted for by federal-government aid. Yet in 1973 there were fewer than three million farm families in the United States, out of a total of over sixty million family units.

In perspective, three big facts stand out about the farm legislation of the past half century: One is the farmers' success in getting what they want. As one Washington correspondent put it, "As long as they act together the farmers can get anything out of the government short of good growing weather—and Washington is working on that through cloud seeding." Some observers believe the political force of agriculture is weakening, and small reductions in annual farm-aid budgets give some support to this analysis. But this doesn't change the general picture painted above.

Second, forty years of massive federal aid haven't solved "the farm problem." As in past prosperities, the worldwide boom of the early 1970s has swept farm prices upward and U.S. farm incomes have risen rapidly, reflecting the highly unusual set of circumstances outlined above. But even then, with wild international speculation in grain prices and meat shelves temporarily bare in some U.S. supermarkets, small farmers' incomes remained at poverty levels. It was the big, efficient farmers who prospered. Moreover, the productive capacity of U.S. agriculture, once unleashed from government production restrictions, is huge indeed, and there is little reason to suppose that the farm dilemmas of the past half century have vanished permanently. There is an enormous need for food and fibres in the less-developed countries where poverty is rampant, but alas, they are unable to buy the food they so badly need now at market prices any better than they could yesterday. Indeed, the very high prices that bring farmers prosperity act to shut the poor out of the market for U.S. farm products.

Third, there has been widespread failure to distinguish between the economic problem of efficiency in resource allocation and the ethical problem of assuring minimum income levels. Fundamentally, the American farm problem is rural poverty. The underlying purpose of farm-aid programs is not higher farm prices per se, but higher farm incomes. Yet farm-aid legislation has by and large required farmers to stay in farming as a condition of receiving aid. They have been paid for not raising crops and have been guaranteed prices that include government subsidies. If they leave agriculture, they lose the subsidies.

Thus, tying benefit payments to products, not to people, has failed to channel aid to poor families, and it has produced an inefficient allocation of resources. By raising farm prices, the program has given the biggest benefits to the biggest farmers, because they have the most to sell. By paying farmers for cutting back production in proportion to acres farmed, the program

---

to take out of the country by converting it into dollars. Thus, for example, huge stocks of wheat have been provided to India for many years in exchange for "payment" in rupees. But since the United States has accumulated vastly more rupees than there is any likelihood it will be able to spend in India for the foreseeable future, the food is close to a gift. Part of U.S. government expenses overseas have been met by P.L.480 funds; "Fulbright aid" to American students and teachers to spend time in the countries involved is a well-known example in university circles. Recently the United States has made substantial direct dollar loans to less-developed countries to permit them to buy U.S. food in world markets.

has handed the biggest benefit checks to the highest income farmers, now including many huge corporate farms. This adds up to the anomalous result of passing out benefits in inverse relation to need. And in doing so it has kept surplus people and other resources tied to farming, counter to consumer votes that they should move elsewhere. Farmers may have some valid claims to special aid, but surely not to be comfortably supported indefinitely in agriculture by consumer and taxpayer subsidies, any more than had the buggy and bloomer industries when consumer demand passed them by. Our massive farm-aid program has failed to achieve either its economic or its ethical objectives, by failing to keep the two clearly separate.

REVIEW

For Analysis and Discussion

1. Why hasn't pure competition in agriculture worked as Chapter 21 says it should?
2. In a competitive economy, resources are supposed to move where consumer demand is strongest, as individuals seek higher incomes. In the light of the comparative incomes shown by Figure 22–1, how do you explain the fact that so many families stay in agriculture?
3. In agriculture, output per man has recently grown at the rate of 6 percent per annum, twice that for the rest of the economy. Since we apparently face a situation of continuing farm "surpluses," would decreased productivity in agriculture be a desirable solution to the farm problem?
4. Are there too many farmers?
5. Who has gained and who has lost the most from Congress' shift to the new target-price, direct-subsidy farm aid program?
6. There are fewer than three million farm families in the United States. Yet Congress has repeatedly voted to grant huge subsidies to agriculture. How do you explain this fact?
7. If you were a congressman, what legislation would you support on the "farm problem"?

Monopoly and Public Utilities

CHAPTER PREVIEW

CHAPTER TWENTY-THREE

Monopoly is something like sin. Everyone says he's against it, but a lot of people aren't very clear just what it is they're against. Like sin, monopoly has to be defined before one can talk much sense about it, or decide what, if anything, ought to be done about it.

The Spectrum from Competition to Monopoly

Monopoly is generally defined as a market in which there is only one seller—as the Greek derivation of the word suggests. But this is deceptively simple. There is no commodity that doesn't have some substitute, more or less close, and we have no sharp criterion of how close the substitute can be before we no longer have a monopoly. The Aluminum Company of America, until World War II, was often called a monopoly in this sense: There was no other American producer of basic aluminum. But steel, wood, copper, and other materials are possible substitutes for aluminum, if the price of aluminum gets too high. Thus, Alcoa had a monopoly in producing aluminum, but certainly not in producing metals. Or consider General Motors: It has a monopoly in producing Chevrolets, but there is Ford next door producing close substitutes. In one sense, every producer who isn't in a purely competitive market has a monopoly in selling his own product. But the closer the substitutes produced by others, the less his "monopoly" matters as a practical matter.

Pure Monopoly

In spite of these problems, economists have defined a situation they call "pure" monopoly. Consider the local power company in a small town as an example. It is the only producer of electricity in the town, it has an exclusive franchise from the city government, and the substitution of candles, oil lamps, or gas lighting by consumers who rebel at high prices is not a very serious likelihood. Clearly, Alcoa wasn't in as strong a position as is a public-utility company, but both approach the pure-monopoly classification, which is characterized by:

1. Only one seller of the good or service.
2. Rivalry from producers of substitutes so remote as to be insignificant.

Under these circumstances, the pure monopolist can set the market price himself, and customers don't have close substitutes to turn to. He is a "price maker," unlike the wheat farmer who is a "price taker." But even the monopolist has to face up to the realities of elasticity of demand. He can put his price where he wishes. But unless demand is perfectly inelastic, the higher he puts his price the less he will sell. Partly, the elasticity of demand for any product reflects the presence of potential substitutes, and there is no monopoly so pure that it can escape completely the possibility of partial substitutes. Thus, pure monopoly is never quite found in the real world, and pure monopoly shades, albeit imperceptibly, into monopolistic competition, just as pure competition shades into lesser degrees of competition.[1]

[1]The analogy to pure monopoly on the buyer's side is sometimes called "pure monopsony," which means one buyer. This case might prevail where there is only one buyer for labor services—say the mill in an isolated mill town. But like pure monopoly, pure monopsony is hard to find. For instance, workers are free to move to another town if the monopsonist exploits his position too much.

Monopolistic Competition and Oligopoly

There is a spectrum from pure competition to pure monopoly. Where there are many sellers of only slightly differentiated products, but not enough to make the market perfectly competitive, we call the situation "monopolistic competition." There may be a dozen or a hundred sellers of substantially identical products. But the products vary somewhat. For example, breakfast-food manufacturers don't make just breakfast food. They make Wheaties, Cheerios, and all the rest. Even corn flakes aren't just corn flakes; Post and Kellogg put them in differently colored boxes under different names, and to the buyer they are at least somewhat differentiated. Or stores may provide different services with the same product—say, free delivery. The degree of "product differentiation" gets to be more substantial for, say, television sets. Philco, RCA, and Sylvania may all show the same picture on the same-sized tube when tuned to Channel 4, but neither the makers nor the customers believe the sets are identical.

Where there are only a few competing producers and each producer must take into account what each other producer does, we call the situation "oligopoly," which means few sellers. In the auto industry, with only a few big producers, obviously General Motors, Chrysler, and Ford have to pay a lot of attention to each other's policies in setting prices, even though their products are all somewhat differentiated. Firms in oligopolistic industries may compete actively, or they may get together ("collude") formally or informally to agree on prices and on sharing the market.

Most of the American economic system lies in between pure competition and pure monopoly. Each industry seems to be a little different. Yet we need to classify this huge "in-between" area into some major groups if we are to make any headway in analyzing how it operates. In looking at the world of monopolistic competition and oligopoly, economists often emphasize the number of sellers, the closeness of substitutes, and the degree of price and nonprice competition among the sellers. For example, the monopolistic-competition group is usually subdivided into cases where competition is primarily on prices, and those where it primarily takes the form of nonprice and advertising competition. Oligopolies seem to fall into three groups depending on whether they collude on prices and output (in which case they are often called "cartels"), follow a "leader" on price setting, or compete actively.

We come out with a division like this:

I. **Pure competition**—many sellers of an identical product (wheat).

II. **Monopolistic competition**—a substantial number of sellers of closely substitutable products.
   a. Price competition (vegetables in local grocery stores).
   b. Nonprice competition and "demand creation" (beer, men's suits).

III. **Oligopoly**—a few sellers of closely substitutable products.[2]
   a. Competition—on prices and through nonprice competition and demand creation (television, autos).
   b. Collaboration.
      1. Formal collusion on prices and on output—"cartels" (nickel, internationally).[3]
      2. Price leadership or informal price stabilization (steel, gasoline).

IV. **Pure monopoly**—one seller of a product without close substitutes (local water company).

The examples are intended merely to provide some concrete impressions to go with the analytical categories. Few real-world cases fit neatly and exclusively into any one of the intermediate categories. For example, there is some demand creation, and quality competition as well as price competition, in groceries (case IIa). Broadly, most of the "service" industries (retail trade, legal services, banking, and so on) fall in the monopolistic competition category, as do a good many manufacturing firms. Much of manufacturing (probably over half) falls under the oligopoly head. Only public utilities provide major examples of "pure monopoly."

[2]Where there are only two sellers, another Greek word, "duopoly," is used. This is a special case of oligopoly.

[3]Formal collusion in setting prices or dividing up markets is illegal under the Sherman Act, as we shall see in Chapter 26.

THE BASES OF MONOPOLY

The basic test of an effective monopoly is its power to exclude competitors from the market. If a firm can keep out potential competitors, it can raise prices with relative impunity. The nearer the substitutes that competitors can put on the market, the weaker is the firm's monopoly position. The ideal monopoly (from the monopolist's viewpoint) would cover an absolutely essential product with no substitutes.

Government Action as a Basis for Monopoly

The strongest monopolies are the public utilities. An exclusive government franchise is about as airtight protection as any monopoly can hope for. This arrangement is found in most localities for water, electricity, gas, and telephone companies. Having granted this enviable monopoly position, however, governments invariably regulate the prices the monopoly can charge. Otherwise, the stockholders of the local water or gas company would be in a happy position indeed.

Governments intervene in other ways to provide partial bases for monopolies. The farm-aid programs of the past three decades have supported prices and induced farmers to behave like a cartel in restricting output. Local building codes, which specify particular types of construction and particular materials, are manifestly intended to protect the public against unsafe construction and poor work, but in fact provide a basis for monopolistic practices by building suppliers and building-trade unions.

The entire federal patent system, discussed below, protects the monopoly position of the inventor. Federal legislation establishes the right of workers to combine in unions that in essence act as monopolies in selling their labor to employers.

Patents and Research

The patent law gives the inventor exclusive control over his invention for seventeen years, to stimulate and reward inventions. Key patents underlie the industrial position of many major American concerns. Research has become part of the American industrial scene, and the "blue chips" of American industry come automatically to mind when we think of technological advance—IBM, General Electric, DuPont. These firms maintain their leading positions in oligopolistic industries in no small part by being first with the best in research. Over the past twenty years almost two-thirds of all patents have gone to corporations. General Electric alone, for example, received about 13,000; AT&T about 10,000. Research is an expensive and cumulative process. It's hard for the little firm to compete, quite aside from the patent laws.

Control of Raw Materials

If you can get exclusive control over the raw materials needed to make your product, you're sitting pretty—at least until someone figures out a substitute material. For example, the International Nickel Company of Canada for years owned more than nine-tenths of the world's known reserve of nickel, and produced more than 90 percent of the world's output of nickel.

Financial Resources and the Capital Market

The money needed to set up an efficient firm in many industries today is tens and even hundreds of millions of dollars. Not very many people have this much money, and it's hard to borrow ten million dollars unless you're already a very well established person or firm, no matter how engaging a picture you paint of your prospects.

In a "perfect" capital market, funds would be available whenever the prospective borrower was willing and able to pay the going rate of interest on loans of comparable risk. In fact, however, it is hard for newcomers to raise funds in the market. Lenders are skeptical of unknown faces. Moreover, borrowing is more expensive for small, new borrowers, even when they can get the funds. These facts give an important protection to established monopolists.

Advertising

Advertising by itself would have a hard time establishing or even maintaining a monopoly on any product. But the entrenched positions of names like Westinghouse and RCA in the mind of the American consumer are a cause of dismay to prospective competitors. Modern advertising has become increasingly "institutionalized." That is, ads aim primarily at building up the company's name and prestige, rather than at selling a particular product. Large-scale prestige advertising (for example, national TV advertising) costs big money, and only big and successful companies can afford it.

Unfair Competition

Running the little fellow out of business by unfair price cutting is one of the charges commonly brought against big business. If Safeway prices groceries very low, it is accused of a devious intent to run the independents out and then to boost its own prices when competition is gone. The old Standard Oil Company of the 1800s provided some spectacular cases of such behavior—and with great success.

Such unfair price competition is now illegal. But the line between legitimate price cutting and unfair price cutting merely to eliminate competition is hard to draw in many cases. The more efficient producers always tend to eliminate the inefficient.

Large-Scale Production and Decreasing Costs

Low-cost mass production is the pride of American industry. In many industries (steel, electrical equipment, autos, chemicals, and so on), maximum efficiency can be obtained only by large firms, each producing a substantial share of the total amount that can be sold on the market. In local areas, taking advantage of the economies of large-scale production may mean one or a few monopolistic firms—for example, the one grocery store a small town can reasonably support. In such cases, until a firm reaches this optimal scale it is operating in its range of "decreasing costs." That is, by increasing output it can cut its cost per unit produced.

Figure 23–1 represents such an industry. The *TUC* curves are simply total-unit-cost curves for different scales of enterprise for a firm in the industry, say a local gas company. Scale TUC^3 is the most efficient scale in this case; its least-cost point is the lowest of any possible scale of enterprise. Each cost curve is drawn in a heavy line through the range in which it is lower than any other. The heavy scalloped line is therefore a curve that indicates the total unit cost at which each output can be produced as the size of the firm increases. This will be a decreasing-cost industry if demand is small relative to the scale of enterprise TUC^3—for example, if demand is D^1D^1 or D^2D^2. It is a "decreasing-cost" industry because the economies of scale within the single firm have not yet been fully exploited at any output less than *OM*, the least-cost point on TUC^3.

The social advantage of limiting such an industry to one firm is obvious; this is the basis for most exclusive public-utility franchises. To insist on several firms would obviously mean higher costs and higher prices. But it would be equally foolish to expect the one firm not to exploit its monopoly position to obtain high profits unless it is regulated.

Figure 23–1

This industry has decreasing unit costs up to output M. For any demand short of that amount, competition is unlikely to work effectively.

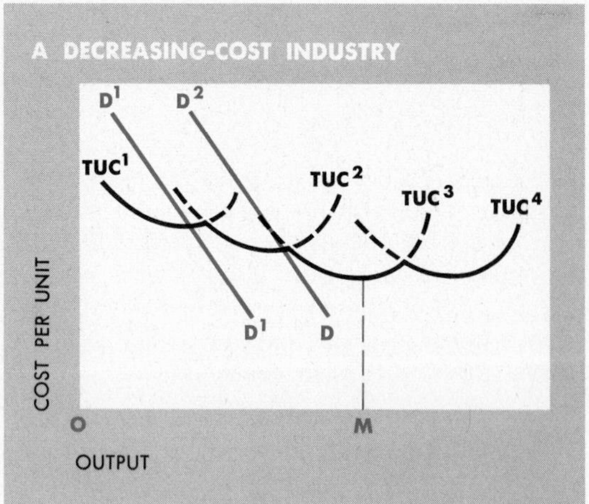

PURE MONOPOLY[4]

In the American economy, except in the public utilities, we seldom find only one firm, no available substitutes for the commodity produced, and no possibility that other firms may invade the market. Yet looking at such an extreme case is useful, because it gives some insight into what the world might be like if pure monopolies were tolerated without regulation. It suggests rules for controlling public utilities. And it may be a quite realistic description of the temporary monopoly position in which firms find themselves because of special advantages of location, development of new products ahead of competitors, or other such circumstances.

Imagine a single electric-power company in

[4]This section rests directly on the marginal-cost–marginal-revenue analysis of Chapter 20.

TABLE 23–1
Hometown Electric Company—Customer Demand Schedule

KILOWATTS (1)	PRICE (2)	TOTAL REVENUE (3)	MARGINAL REVENUE PER 100,000 KILOWATTS (4)	MARGINAL REVENUE PER KILOWATT (5)
1,000,000	8.0¢	$80,000		
			$3,600	3.6¢
1,100,000	7.6	83,600		
			3,400	3.4
1,200,000	7.25	87,000		
			2,700	2.7
1,300,000	6.9	89,700		
			1,300	1.3
1,400,000	6.5	91,000		
			500	.5
1,500,000	6.1	91,500		
			−300	−.3
1,600,000	5.7	91,200		

an isolated community, free to charge whatever rates it pleases. Suppose you are the owner-manager of this hypothetical concern. You are a price maker; you can set your price where you wish. Waiving the fear that the local government will begin to regulate your rates, how would you maximize your profits?

Total and Marginal Revenue

Suppose your market research people estimate demand as shown in columns 1 and 2 of Table 23–1. Column 3 shows the total revenue obtained at different prices. But as a monopolist, you need to face a new fact. You are a price maker, and you can sell more electricity only by lowering your price, unlike the to-him-infinitely-large (perfectly elastic) demand faced by the stereo manufacturer under pure competition. Under pure competition, price and marginal revenue were identical; if you sold one more stereo set for $1,000 you increased your total revenue by $1,000. But not here.

Now you face a downward sloping demand curve. To sell more you must cut price, not only on the extra sales but on all the electricity you sell.[5] **For the monopolist, marginal revenue is always less than price. This is because he must lower his price to sell more units, and he must lower it not just on the marginal unit but on all units sold.**

For example, Table 23–1 says you can sell 1,000,000 kilowatts at 8 cents per kilowatt. (To simplify the language, we will use the word kilowatt for kilowatt hours.) To increase sales to 1,100,000 you must reduce the price to 7.6 cents on all 1,100,000 kilowatts. Thus, your marginal revenue is your income from selling the extra 100,000 kilowatts (100,000 times 7.6 cents = $7,600) *minus* the .4 cent loss on each of the other 1,000,000 kilowatts (1,000,000 times .4 cents = $4,000). The marginal revenue from the extra 100,000 kilowatts is thus only $3,600 (not $7,600), as shown by column 4. To convert to marginal revenue per kilowatt, we simply divide the figures by 100,000, getting a marginal revenue per additional kilowatt of 3.6 cents (in column 5). And so it is all along the demand schedule. Marginal revenue is always less than price, and it even becomes negative when you must cut price to 5.7 cents in order to increase sales to 1,600,000 kilowatts.[6]

[5]This assumes that you sell at the same price to everyone, not discriminating between residential and commercial users, or others.

[6]Marginal revenue is always zero when elasticity of demand is unity, positive when demand is elastic, and negative when demand is inelastic. Why? From this proposition it obviously follows that no perceptive monopolist will ever increase his output into the range where demand is inelastic, because in this range cutting price to increase output would *reduce* his total revenue from sales.

This relationship between price and marginal revenue is fundamental for every seller who is not in a perfectly competitive market. Whenever he faces a downward sloping demand curve, to sell more he must cut price both for the extra units he hopes to sell and for the units he could otherwise sell at a higher price. **His gain from cutting prices is never as big as it appears at first glance.**

Maximizing Monopoly Profits

Suppose your costs are as shown in Table 23–2; total cost for the outputs shown is in column 2 and marginal costs, converted to a per kilowatt basis, in column 5. What price should you set to maximize your profits?

One answer is: Compare total cost and total revenue at each different level of output to find where the difference is biggest. As columns 2, 4, and 7 show, you should set price at 6.9 cents per kilowatt, which gives the maximum profit of $32,500.

Another way of calculating your maximum profit position is by comparing marginal costs and marginal revenues. This comparison is made in columns 5 and 6. As long as the marginal revenue from selling an additional unit of output is greater than the marginal cost of producing the unit, obviously profit is increased by producing the extra unit. This gain is clear when you increase output from 1,000,000 to 1,100,000 units, on up to 1,200,000 units, and then to 1,300,000 units. But if you try 1,400,000 units, the marginal cost is 3 cents per unit and the marginal revenue only 1.3 cents. This is a profit-reducing move, since it adds more to cost than to revenue—even though total profit would still be substantial at 1,400,000. The marginal approach gives the same answer as the total-cost–total-revenue comparison. The two are simply alternative ways of getting the same profit-maximizing answer. Still a third way would be by comparing marginal cost and marginal revenue per 100,000 units, instead of on a per kilowatt basis.

Which way is better? Take your pick. They give the same result.

Graphical Analysis of Profit Maximization

The same calculation can be shown graphically. Figure 23–2 plots the relevant per-unit data. *DD* is the estimated market-demand curve. *MR* is the associated marginal-revenue-per-unit curve. *TUC* is the estimated total-unit-cost curve. And *MC* is the associated marginal-unit-cost curve. The solid part of each curve repre-

TABLE 23–2
Hometown Electric Company—Profit Calculations

KILOWATTS (1)	TOTAL COST (2)	PRICE (3)	TOTAL REVENUE (4)	MARGINAL UNIT COST (5)	MARGINAL UNIT REVENUE (6)	TOTAL PROFIT (7)
1,000,000	$50,000	8.0¢	$80,000			$30,000
				2.8¢	3.6¢	
1,100,000	52,800	7.6	83,600			30,800
				2.4	3.4	
1,200,000	55,200	7.25	87,000			31,800
				2.0	2.7	
1,300,000	57,200	6.9	89,700			32,500[a]
				3.0	1.3	
1,400,000	60,200	6.5	91,000			30,800
				4.3	.5	
1,500,000	64,500	6.1	91,500			27,000
				5.9	−.3	
1,600,000	70,400	5.7	91,200			20,800

[a] Maximum total profit.

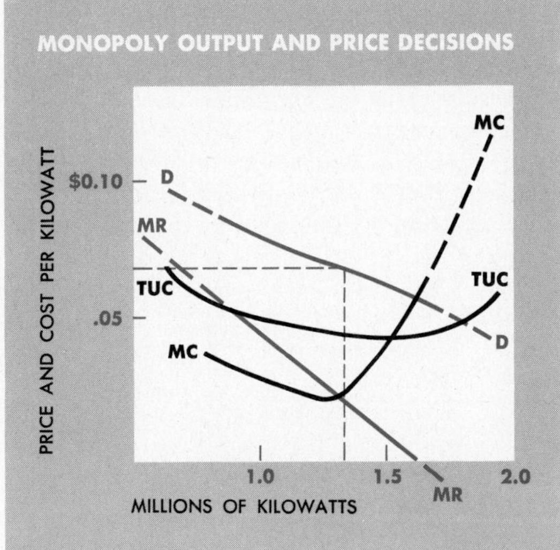

Figure 23–2

The monopolist maximizes profit by equating marginal cost and marginal revenue—here at an output of about 1.32 million kilowatts to be sold at a price just under seven cents.

sents the data from Table 23–2; the dotted lines extend the curves hypothetically beyond the range of data we have.

Be sure you know how to read the various curves. Reading from the graph, for example, at 1,200,000 units output the total cost per unit is about 4.6 cents. *DD* shows that this output can be sold at a price of about 7.25 cents per kilowatt. Obviously this is a profitable level of output—the demand curve is above the total-unit-cost curve. The marginal-cost curve shows that to increase output by 1 kilowatt—to 1,200,001 kilowatts—would add about 2.4 cents to total cost. And the *MR* curve shows that this additional unit would add about 3.4 cents to total revenue. Thus, we can readily see from the graph: (1) that an output of 1,200,000 kilowatts is profitable, and (2) that a larger output would be still more profitable, since at the 1,200,000-kilowatt level marginal cost is still below marginal revenue.

Going on, you can easily determine the maximum-profit position. It will be the output at which marginal cost just equals marginal revenue. This is a little above 1,300,000 kilowatts, which you could sell at a price of about 6.8 cents, reading off the demand curve at that output. If you want to compute your total profit from this graph, first take the distance between the selling price and the *TUC* curve, and then multiply this profit per unit by the total number of units sold. This would give a profit of about $33,000 at the best level—roughly 2.5 cents per kilowatt on 1,320,000 kilowatts.

Note that this is a slightly higher profit than the maximum shown by Table 23–2. The graph, which gives you data for all levels of output rather than just one estimate each 100,000 kilowatts, tells you to produce an extra 20,000 kilowatts beyond the prescription of the table. The continuous curves on the graph give you a quick guide to the maximum-profit level of output and prices, which is more detailed than the table.

PURE MONOPOLY—EVALUATION

Monopoly leads to an inefficient allocation of resources from the consumers' point of view. If the monopolist restricts output and raises price to maximize his profits, he will be holding price above marginal cost. But Chapter 21 told us that $MC =$ price is the condition for achieving the most efficient allocation of productive resources to satisfy consumers' demands. Thus, monopoly price is too high and too few resources are hired into the monopolized industry. Consumers get too little of the monopolized product. Conversely, too many resources are used in other sectors of the economy. Resources shut out from the monopolized industry must seek employment elsewhere; prices are too low and output too large elsewhere, as judged by the test of consumer demands.[7]

[7]The difficulty in making a precise comparison with competitive price and output in such a case should be clear. Because the market is unlikely to be large enough to support a large number of producers, each with a least-cost point as low as the large monopolist's, we cannot demonstrate rigorously that monopoly price is higher than competitive price would be.

Monopolies are also likely to be inefficient and slow to introduce technological change. Pure competition forces each firm to be efficient or perish. If new production techniques are developed, the laggard who fails to keep up with the leaders soon loses out in the market. Under monopoly, these pressures are weak. It does not necessarily follow that monopolies are inefficient or uninterested in progress. But many observers feel that the absence of strong competitive pressures does often lead to inefficiency and lessened interest in meeting consumer needs. In any event, note that absence of large profits does not prove monopolies are doing no market harm; low profits may reflect inefficiently high costs, protected from the pressures of competition.

REVIEW

Concepts to Remember

Most of the major concepts used in this chapter were introduced in earlier chapters. But there are a few important new ones:

pure (simple) monopoly	**oligopoly**
monopolistic competition	**decreasing-cost industry**
price makers	

For Analysis and Discussion

1. Why do economists say that the basic *economic* criticism of monopolies is that they hold price above marginal cost?
2. If a monopoly is not making excessive (above-normal) profits, it is doing no serious harm to the public. True or false? Explain.
3. Why do many Americans distrust both monopolies and big business? Is there any significant economic distinction between the two?
4. The post office and your local water company are cases that are close to pure monopolies. How would you go about deciding whether they are doing an efficient job of serving the consumer at reasonable prices? Do you have a better way of evaluating the performance of such big partial monopolies as General Motors and Alcoa?
5. Chicago's George Stigler has argued that without government support, there would be few serious monopoly problems in America today. He cites public utilities, government support of unions, government-sponsored cartelization in agriculture, and "fair-trade" laws that hold up prices in retailing. How sound is this argument? Can you cite counterexamples?

CASE 12

How to Regulate Public Utilities

Almost everyone complains that the prices charged by the big public utilities are too high—for electricity, telephone service, gas, air travel. Suppose you are on your state regulatory commission and you must decide the right price for the Hometown Electric Company of this chapter to charge its customers. To make it easy, suppose you know that demand and costs are as shown in Table 23-2. What price would you decree?[8]

[8]This case is, in effect, an extension of the analysis in the chapter. Most students will need to use the suggestions at the end of the book to work out the analysis.

Monopolistic Competition and Advertising

CHAPTER TWENTY-FOUR

Almost no one has a pure monopoly. But many firms have partial monopolies. The corner druggist has a partial monopoly in his neighborhood. He can charge several cents more a quart for ice cream than the big dairy stores downtown. And he can get it—because he is so conveniently located for people in neighborhood.

Coca-Cola has a partial monopoly. No one else can make a drink exactly like Coca-Cola without infringing the law, and for years "a Coke" has been the habitual mid-morning and mid-afternoon drink of millions. But Pepsi-Cola, Royal Crown Cola, and a good many others look and taste enough like Coca-Cola to shrink Coca-Cola's share of the soft-drink market greatly in the last two decades. The Coca-Cola people will tell you they're in a highly competitive field.

A large part of the American economy is in the range between competition and monopoly—partly protected from competitors by trade names, location, tradition, and product quality, but far from perfectly protected; exposed to new competitors, but much less exposed than the wheat farmer. This is the area of "monopolistic competition." In it, each firm's product is "differentiated" from its competitors', but not enough to forestall active competition—on prices, selling costs, quality, or all three.

How much of the economy is in the monopolistic-competition category? The lines are hazy, but a fair, though very crude, answer would be, perhaps half the private sector. This would include nearly all of wholesale and retail trade, finance, real estate, and personal services (legal, medical, and the like); a substantial sector of manufacturing (for example, apparel, lumber, and printing); and most of construction and trucking. By contrast, a large part of manufacturing (autos, steel, heavy electrical equipment, glass, and tobacco products) is oligopolistic; railroads, airlines, and all public utilities are regulated by government; and agriculture is a special case of nondifferentiated products with prices substantially influenced by government policies. It's a complex world, but "monopolistically competitive" describes a big part of it.

PRICES AND OUTPUT UNDER MONOPOLISTIC COMPETITION

The Bases for Product Differentiation

The essence of monopolistic competition is that each firm's product is a little different from those of its competitors, but not very different. Each producer tries to differentiate his product and to increase the demand for it. To the extent he succeeds, he can get away with charging a little more for his product.

Sometimes product differentiation involves actual physical differentiation. For example, Schlitz beer tastes different than Pabst; a Frigidaire is different than a GE refrigerator. But often the differentiation hinges on the things that go along with the product—convenience of location, thick carpets on the floors, well-groomed waitresses, easy-credit terms. Sometimes the differentiation is largely illusory—it exists in the mind of the customer but not in fact. Most smokers can't tell one standard cigarette brand from another when they are blindfolded. If you can really tell the difference between the various high-test gasolines in your car on the road, you're better than most of the experts. Often when you think you're getting special easy-credit terms you're paying just what is normal in the trade.

Whatever the reason, whenever one seller is differentiated from others in the customer's mind, that seller is able to charge a price higher than his competitors without losing all his market. His demand curve slopes downward; it is not horizontal as under perfect competition.

Short-Run Output and Prices

The monopolistic competitor's problem is to set his price to maximize his profits. He has some freedom to raise price above what his competitors charge for similar products, but if he goes too far his share of the market will drop sharply. The more successful he is in differentiating his product, the less elastic his demand curve will be. With an inelastic demand curve, he can boost his price without a corresponding drop in sales. But it's hard to convince customers that no substitute will do.

The firm's optimal price-output decision in the short run is hard to specify under these conditions. What any one firm's demand curve looks like is hard to estimate. For it depends both on what this firm does through advertising to change consumer demand and on what competitors do that also affects the demand for our firm's product. The demand curve we face will depend on consumers' total demand for the whole group of slightly differentiated products, and on our firm's share of the total. Palmolive can increase and steepen the consumer demand curve for its soap either by getting customers away from Lux, Sweetheart, and the rest, or by somehow increasing total consumer demand for soap. If Palmolive succeeds in convincing people they should wash their faces more often, this may increase the demand for other soaps as much as for Palmolive. The trick is to be sure you get the big share of the benefit if you go in for this kind of advertising. Conversely, increased advertising by Lux may leave Palmolive with a lower, flatter demand curve, even though Palmolive soap is just as good as before. And if Palmolive's advertising steals Lux's customers, retaliation is almost certain. Thus, it should be clear that under monopolistic competition (and oligopoly), the level and elasticity of any firm's demand curve depend both on what it does and on what the other firms in the industry do as well. It is not possible to draw a stable, unambiguous demand curve for the individual firm's product.[1]

Presumably any monopolistic competitor will increase his expenditures on advertising and other demand-creating activities as long as he estimates that this will add more to his income than to his costs. But under monopolistic competition, uncertainty about what competitors will do makes short-run output and price behavior very hard to predict. Thus, as with pure competition, we are on much safer ground when we look at long-run adjustments than when we try to predict short-run behavior.

Long-Run Adjustments under Monopolistic Competition

In the long run, new firms enter industries and old firms leave. The search for profits goes on, with productive resources freely transferrable throughout the economy. Monopolistic competition is like pure competition in that new firms can enter the industry. It is different in that new firms cannot exactly duplicate the product of existing firms. A new drugstore across the street from an established one might provide very close substitutes. But a new women's wear store that sets up in competition with Saks Fifth Avenue will have a tougher time. For one thing, drugs, candy, and ice cream are relatively standardized as compared with women's clothes. For another, few drugstores have the prestige and location of Saks.

But even though newcomers face problems, high profits in any monopolistically competitive field will draw new competitors. As more firms enter, the total market is divided up more ways. The demand curve for each established firm is moved downward (to the left). Profits per firm are reduced by this sharing of the market. Gradually, as more firms enter, profits tend to be eliminated, just as under pure competition. A new (unstable) equilibrium with excess profits eliminated may be achieved.

This sounds just like pure competition. But in this temporary equilibrium, under monopolistic competition each firm is restricting output a little to take advantage of its product differentiation. Marginal cost is less than price, and the demand curve is tangent to the cost curve to the left of the minimum point. Each firm is thus operating below its optimal capacity and producing at a cost above the least-cost point on its optimal-cost curve. From a social point of view, too little of the product is being produced and sold, since price is being held above marginal cost.

This is illustrated in Figure 24–1. Case *A* pictures a typical firm making a good profit. Its demand curve is above its total-unit-cost curve over a substantial range. The demand curve is downward sloping, because this product is differentiated from its competitors.

What will happen? Competition will pick up. As new firms enter the market, the demand curve for each old firm moves downward as its share of the market falls. Eventually, the demand curve for a typical firm will be pushed down far enough to be just tangent to the cost

[1] *Given* the firm's cost and demand curves, the technical conditions for maximizing profit in the short run are identical with those for the monopolist described above. Thus, in the adjoining figure, to maximize profits the firm will set price and output where marginal cost equals marginal

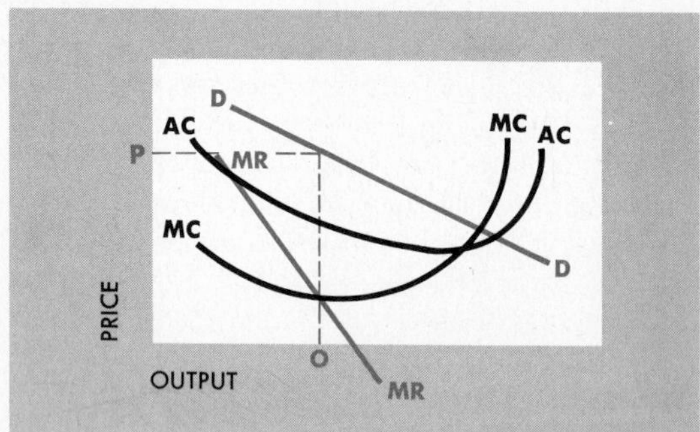

revenue. This gives output *O* to be sold at price *P* as the optimal position. But when we say *given* the demand curve, we are assuming away a big piece of the problem, as is explained in the text.

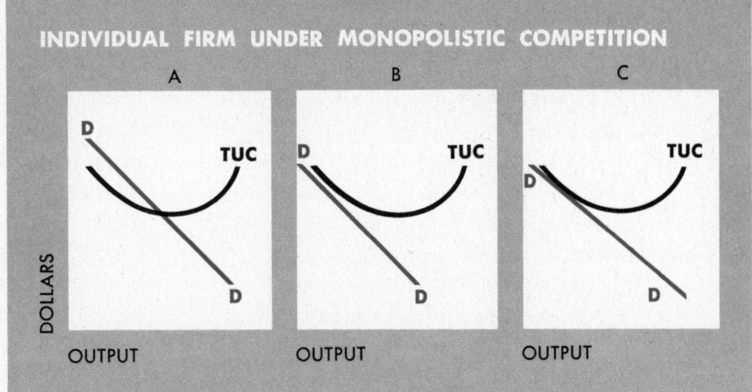

Figure 24–1

This figure shows a firm making money on left, losing money in middle, and in no-profit, temporary equilibrium on right.

curve. All profit will be eliminated, and there will be no further incentive for new firms and new resources to enter the industry. Neither will there be any incentive for existing firms to leave, unless some especially attractive opportunity opens up elsewhere in the economy. This is case *C* in Figure 24–1.

Case *B* shows firms making losses. Here firms will gradually drop out of the industry and the demand for the products of each remaining firm will gradually rise. This process will continue until a no-loss situation has been reached, when there is no further incentive for resources to move out of the industry. The firm will then be in a case *C* equilibrium position.

Unstable Equilibrium under Competitive Demand Creation

But this is not the end of the story; the equilibrium is almost surely unstable. If you were running a drugstore and were in position *C* in Figure 24–1, what would you do? Maybe you'd just sit, but probably you'd try to figure a way to get more business. You might try improving your service to customers. Or putting in air conditioning. Or advertising more. All these attempts would cost you money. They might bring you more customers—that is, they might raise your demand curve—probably by drawing customers away from competitors. And they would upset the equilibrium situation shown in *C*. Such attempts to increase demand for products are apparent everywhere, keeping equilibrium (with the demand curve tangent to the cost curve) from being achieved or maintained.

Imagine a monopolistically competitive milk industry in a large city, with fifteen milk companies of about equal size and no advertising. Company *A* begins an advertising campaign. It gets more customers by luring a few away from each competitor. *A*'s costs are now higher, but its profits are up because of increased volume.

It doesn't take a business genius to predict the reaction of the other companies. After spending a few well-chosen words on the manager of Company *A*, they will get busy on their own advertising campaigns, designed to get their customers back and (hopefully) to lure new customers into the fold. If every company just matched *A*'s advertising, we might think of a new equilibrium situation, with each producer having back just his original customers, but with every company's cost higher by the amount of the advertising and with price correspondingly higher to the consumer.

But having tasted success, *A* is unlikely to sit quietly at the restored higher-price equilibrium. Nor are *B*, *C*, *D*, and all the others. Each will be busy contriving a new and better advertising campaign. If another round of advertising expenditures starts, or trading stamps with each gallon of milk are introduced, the result is likely to be similar. **Everybody's costs go up. Nobody** ends up with many more customers, or with any more profits. And consumers end up with higher prices. Now they're buying advertising and trading stamps along with their milk—without having anything to say about whether they really want to buy them or not. And nobody can tell where the whole process will stop.

Even in the happy event that the advertising campaign increases total spending on milk, a similar problem remains. Where do these additional funds for milk come from? Maybe the milk advertising stimulates total spending and raises the level of total spending and GNP, but as we saw in Part Two this is unlikely. If total spending is unchanged, more spending on milk must mean less spending on something else. Producers in these other industries will fight back to regain sales. This will cause another reshuffling of demand, with still other industries (possibly including milk) losing customers to the newest advertisers.

QUALITY COMPETITION

Every housewife knows about quality competition. She knows which stores have the freshest vegetables, and where there are enough clerks to provide quick service. When you buy a suit, you go to a store you know will stand behind it if something goes wrong. These are examples of quality competition, just as much as the more obvious cases of using better materials and better workmanship in the physical construction of products.

Alert businessmen are very much interested in knowing how much quality consumers want. They spend thousands of dollars on market research to find out whether consumers want softer seats in autos, cellophane around fresh vegetables, more carbonation in ginger ale, a new look on auto models each year. A shrewd businessman will improve the quality of his product whenever he believes customers will want the improvement enough to pay the extra cost—and a little bit more. He will reduce product quality—for example, by putting his store on a cash-and-carry basis—whenever he believes that most customers would prefer to pay less and go without delivery service.

Some observers believe that quality competition is the pervasive form of competition in modern America, and that price competition is of secondary importance. There is much evidence to support this point of view. Filling stations long ago learned that a clean rest room is more important to a touring family than a half cent off the price of gas. The first air-conditioned movie had an enormous quality advantage; now they're all air-conditioned.

Such is often the case in quality competition. Once one firm pioneers, others feel they must follow—or risk losing their customers as a consequence of holding out. If GM comes out with new auto models each year, Ford and Chrysler can't stick with last year's look without losing their share of the market. The result is higher "quality" all around, and higher prices to cover the higher costs involved in providing it, whether or not all consumers want to pay for the changes. Then every manager starts scratching his head to figure out a new change that will give him at least a temporary jump on the field again.

Quality competition can be a perfectly valid type of competition, just as much as price competition. Sometimes people don't want the extra "quality" built into new products. But if there is active competition, there's always a competitor to provide a cheaper, "lower-quality" product—witness the success of discount stores and of compact cars. On the other hand, without competitors ready to try "lower-quality" products, competitive quality competition can seriously reduce the options open to consumers.

ADVERTISING

Recently social critics have levelled their big guns on advertising as big business' and Madison Avenue's main device for manipulating consumer demand. Certainly advertising plays a major role in many monopolistically competitive industries, and it deserves a further look.

In 1972, American business spent about $22 billion on advertising, and the total has risen steadily over the last two decades. In 1940, it was only $2 billion. Figure 24–2 summarizes these facts, and shows the composition of the total each year.

Twenty-two billion dollars is a lot of money, and it represents a lot of persuasion. It would have bought a lot of other goods and services had consumers had the cash to spend instead. On the other hand, it was only about 2 percent of the total gross national product in most recent years.

Who were the big advertisers? Table 24–1 shows the top seven for 1971, plus a few others that may be of special interest. Strikingly, it was not the big-ticket companies like autos and appliances that spent a large proportion of their sales dollars on advertising; autos averaged only .7 of 1 percent. Drugs, cosmetics, soap, packaged foods, and other such small consumer items spent the highest percentages; drugs and cosmetics averaged nearly 20 percent. P.&G. is by far the world's largest advertiser; AT&T, Exxon, and General Motors, the world's largest companies, lag far behind in their use of the sales dollar to persuade customers away from their competitors.

Figure 24–2

Advertising has grown persistently over the past decade, though more slowly in recession years. Newspapers get most of the advertising dollars.

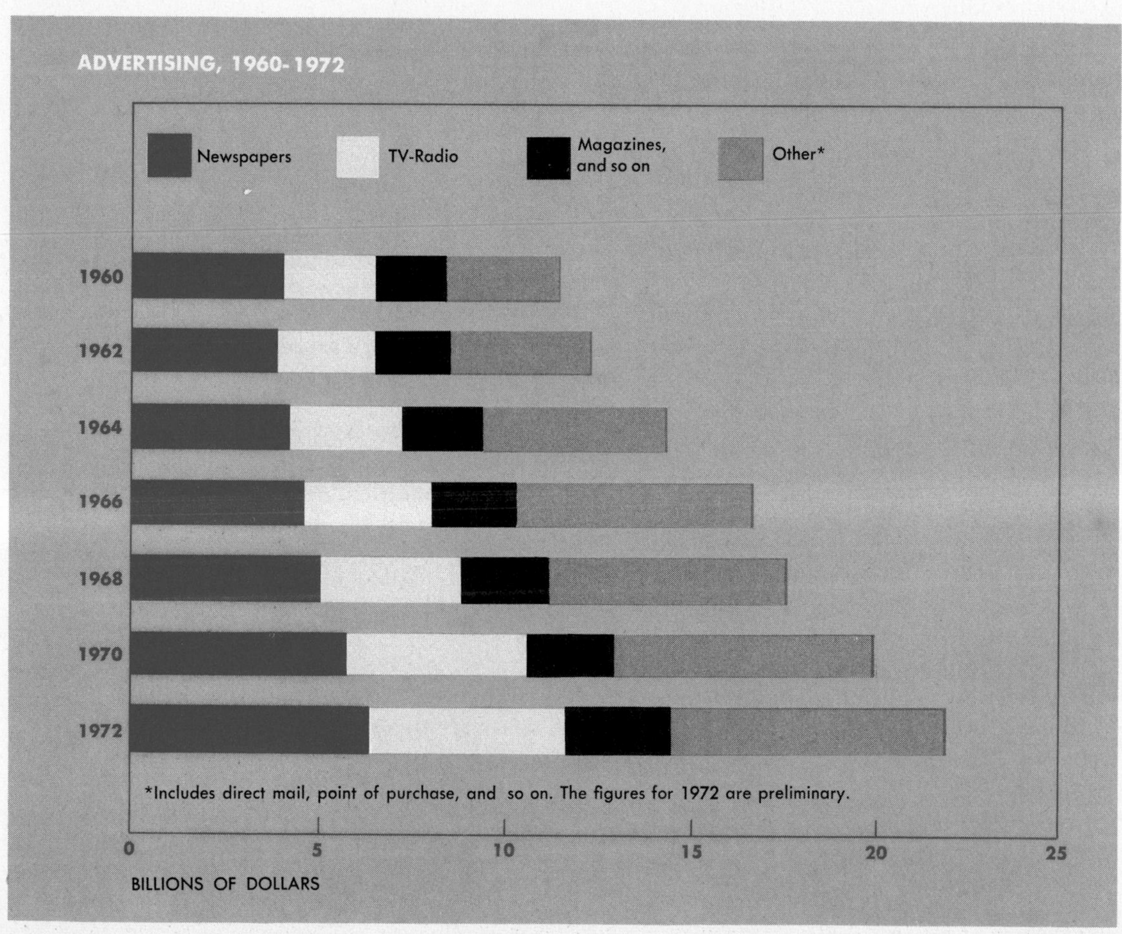

TABLE 24–1
Advertising Expenditures, 1971

RANK	COMPANY AND PRODUCTS	AMOUNT (IN MILLIONS)	PERCENT OF SALES
1	Proctor & Gamble (soaps, etc.)	$275	7.8
2	Sears Roebuck (general retail)	200	2.0
3	General Foods (packaged foods)	160	7.8
4	General Motors (autos)	140	0.4
5	Warner Lambert (drugs & cosmetics)	128	15.1
6	Bristol Myers (drugs & cosmetics)	110	12.6
7	Colgate, Palmolive (cosmetics)	110	20.0
10	AT&T (communications)	84	0.5
13	General Electric (electrical products)	76	0.5
27	Alberto-Culver (drugs & cosmetics)	55	32.0
63	Exxon (oil products)	29	0.1
96	United Air Lines (air travel)	17	1.0

Source: *Advertising Age*, August 1972.

The Use of Resources in "Demand Creation"

As the preceding pages have emphasized, in a substantially fully-employed economy, we must choose between alternative uses of resources. For our advertising dollar (paid in the price of the product) we get information on products, TV movies, sport events, billboards, the Metropolitan Opera, and a wide variety of other services, the worth of some of which might be disputed vigorously. Advertising expenditures make possible ten-cent daily papers, and a fifty-cent *Newsweek* magazine. But by financing these services through advertising, little effective choice is left to the consumer as to how much of each he buys. The beer drinker pays for TV westerns even though he never watches TV. Still, almost everyone buys many advertised products and enjoys some of the fruits of advertising. Most people benefit from cheap newspapers and other news sources largely financed by advertising. Perhaps aside from cases of misleading advertising, everything pretty much evens out and consumers get just about the information and "entertainment" they would have bought anyway with their advertising dollars. But you may understandably have your doubts.

How much does advertising actually increase demand for advertised products? As was emphasized above, a large part of the total is counteradvertising, where the companies involved largely just offset each other's advertising. When TWA takes full-page newspaper ads to extoll the virtues of its new 747 coach lounges, it is trying to increase the demand for its product by convincing (a) more people to fly, and (b) those who do fly to fly TWA instead of United or American. But United's and American's full-page ads about their 747s appear in the same papers. A 747 is pretty much the same airplane, whichever of the three big companies flies it. It gets there as fast with one as the other; prices are the same, set by government regulation; and it's hard to make your coach lounge much plusher than your competitors'. Demand may not be changed much, but in the long run air fares have to be enough higher to pay for the advertising. Do the ads increase total air travel? Possibly so, especially if they provide useful information on fares and service to possible customers. But then there's the question of counteradvertising to lure people's dollars into other industries.

Lastly, may advertising help everyone by increasing *total* spending and thereby providing more jobs and more total gross national product? The answer, if the economy's resources are already fully employed, is obviously no. If there are unemployed resources (for example, in a recession), more advertising might increase demand and consequently the amount of goods produced. But even if it could, monetary and fiscal policy, as you saw in Part Two, are more powerful ways to increase demand and they do not use up resources in the process.[2]

What Do We Get for Our Money?

The most important positive product of advertising is information. Each household maximizes its utility from the income it receives when it allocates that income among all the things it buys so as to equate the utility received from the last dollar spent on each good and service. To make this allocation most effectively, the household needs the best possible information on the alternatives available to it. Thus, insofar as advertising provides information on the alternative goods and services available (as to price, quality, or other relevant characteristics), it helps buyers maximize the utility obtainable from their incomes. In a rapidly changing world, it may be especially useful in providing information on new products; how else can consumers learn of them? Insofar as advertising provides erroneous information, of course, it has the opposite effect. If advertising simply alters consumer wants, rather than providing better information by which an optimum allocation of income can be made, it is hard to say whether that advertising increases or decreases consumer satisfaction. This is a tough ethical question.

The information content of advertising varies widely. Many advertisers are more concerned with attracting consumers away from competitors and with building a "corporate image" than with providing information on which consumers can make more intelligent choices. Watch TV a whole evening and record all the information you get that is of value in helping you decide among the products advertised. Read a copy of one of the big-selling magazines. Try the morning newspaper.

Figure 24–2 showed the relative importance of different kinds of advertising. Newspaper advertising, which generally contains useful information (grocery and clothing ads, want ads, and so on) makes up about one-third of the total. TV and magazine advertising, which are more commonly aimed at brand emphasis and prestige building, account for another third. The remainder is a wide variety of types, some of which (trade magazines, and in-store advertising) include significant customer information, while others (for example, direct mail) tend to have limited informational value.

Do Advertisers Manipulate Consumer Wants?

Radical critics of today's scene, and some not so radical, argue that the American consumer has no real freedom of choice—that his "wants" are created and manipulated by big business and Madison Avenue, mainly through advertising. Businesses decide what will make the largest profits, and convince consumers to "want" that. To some extent, the problem is dishonest and misleading advertising. But more fundamentally, advertising directly and TV indirectly mold our very style of life—we learn to want what the TV dangles before us. Perhaps the best-known critic along these lines is Harvard's J.K. Galbraith, in his best-selling *The New Industrial State*.

This attack challenges the very foundation of private-enterprise economics. If consumers merely respond to what businesses tell them to want, the whole intellectual case for an individualistic consumer-directed economy falls.

Stated in the extreme form above, this argument is obviously unacceptable. Something under 2 percent of the total gross national product hardly seems adequate to govern the entire pattern of "wants" of every consumer in America. Moreover, there is a long history of business firms gone broke trying to convince consumers through advertising and other selling campaigns

[2]It is doubtful that advertising has much influence on total consumer spending in the economy, but the evidence is not conclusive.

to buy products that consumers stubbornly refuse to purchase. The classic case is Ford's Edsel in the 1950s, which flopped colossally in spite of an enormous advertising campaign. Less than a dozen of the fifty best-known automobile brands of the past half century are still with us, in spite of the best advertising assistance Detroit and Madison Avenue have been able to provide over the years. The history of American business is littered with well-advertised products that just didn't sell.

On the other hand, it would be ridiculous to argue that advertising has no effect on how consumers spend their incomes. TV is indeed pervasive in American life, and it is full of "beautiful people" and beautiful things to want. Just how far advertising goes to influence the expenditures of the American public is a much argued issue. Alas, there is no evidence that can give a simple, clear-cut answer. Look back at Table 5–1, which summarized what consumers buy, and make your own judgment on how much of it is dominated by the kinds of advertising you see around you.

Conclusion

With advertising, as with almost everything else, the principle of marginalism applies. It would be surprising indeed if we were to come to the conclusion that advertising is all bad or all good, that we should completely eliminate advertising or increase it to some very large amount. From a social point of view, the decision as to whether we want more or less advertising is a marginal one. We need to weigh the gains from the last dollar spent on advertising against alternative possibilities for that dollar devoted to other uses. Clearly, some advertising has high social value—for example, if it tells consumers about a new, highly desirable product. Conversely, misleading or dishonest advertising has a negative marginal value. And the marginal value of the last dollar spent on some types of advertising may seem to you very low, particularly when the effect is simply to offset someone else's advertising. As to how much advertising we ought to have in our society, marginalism is the principle to follow.

REVIEW

Concepts to Remember

Many of the major concepts used in this chapter were introduced in earlier chapters. But there are important new ones too:

product differentiation
quality competition
demand creation
unstable equilibrium

For Analysis and Discussion

1. Explain why equilibrium in a monopolistically-competitive industry is likely to be unstable.
2. Is the absence of high profits in an industry satisfactory evidence that monopolistic competition is not injuring consumers of the product concerned? Explain your answer to a noneconomist.

3. "As long as there is relatively free entry to an industry, I can't get worried about the dangers of monopoly in that industry." Do you agree or disagree? Explain.
4. Some critics argue that we now have "producers' sovereignty" rather than "consumer sovereignty," because advertising determines what we think we want. Marshal the evidence for and against this argument.
5. "If we had adequate 'Truth-in-Advertising' legislation, I wouldn't worry about excessive advertising or manipulation of consumer wants by Madison Avenue." Do you agree or disagree?
6. As a consumer, would you like to see aggressive price competition among sellers of all the products you buy? Under such competition, would you get the same breadth of display, return privileges, and charge-account arrangements now provided by major department stores?
7. Do you get your money's worth out of the advertising for which you pay? If not, what specific steps would you propose to improve the situation?

CASE 13

Advertising and Consumerism

A consumer protection group recently proposed that Congress and/or all state legislatures pass legislation providing that:

1. No advertising be permitted that does not provide information useful to consumers.
2. No firm be permitted to spend on advertising more than 10 percent of its income from sales in the preceding year.
3. No firm be permitted to engage in dishonest or misleading advertising, and that any firm doing so be liable to triple damages to all injured consumers through class action suits brought by either consumers or the government.
4. The Federal Trade Commission, or appropriate state agencies, be empowered to enforce the above rules.

Would you recommend that your representatives vote for the proposed legislation?

Oligopoly, Collusion, and the Mixed Economy

CHAPTER PREVIEW

CHAPTER TWENTY-FIVE

Three companies—General Motors, Ford, and Chrysler—make nearly all the automobiles produced in the United States. The top four companies account for over 90 percent of all flat glass and electric light bulbs produced. In dozens of major industries, from half to three-fourths of the total business is done by fewer than ten firms. These are the oligopolies—industries in which a few firms dominate, though there may be many small firms that generally follow the leaders, or take what is left over. Figure 25-1 summarizes the market domination by the leading four firms in a number of major industries.

These examples are on a national scale. The number of oligopolists in local markets is far larger. Building materials (such as cement and bricks) are produced by hundreds of different firms scattered all over the country. But in any one local market, production is usually concentrated in one or a few firms. The more important transportation costs are and the harder it is for customers to shop around, the more likely local oligopolies are to be found.

Economists consider "concentration ratios" (the percentage of total sales concentrated in the largest four, or sometimes eight, firms) an important indication of likely market performance. But it is important to recognize that this is only one rough measure of the degree of monopoly power held by the leading firms. Probable price-output behavior may be quite different, for ex-

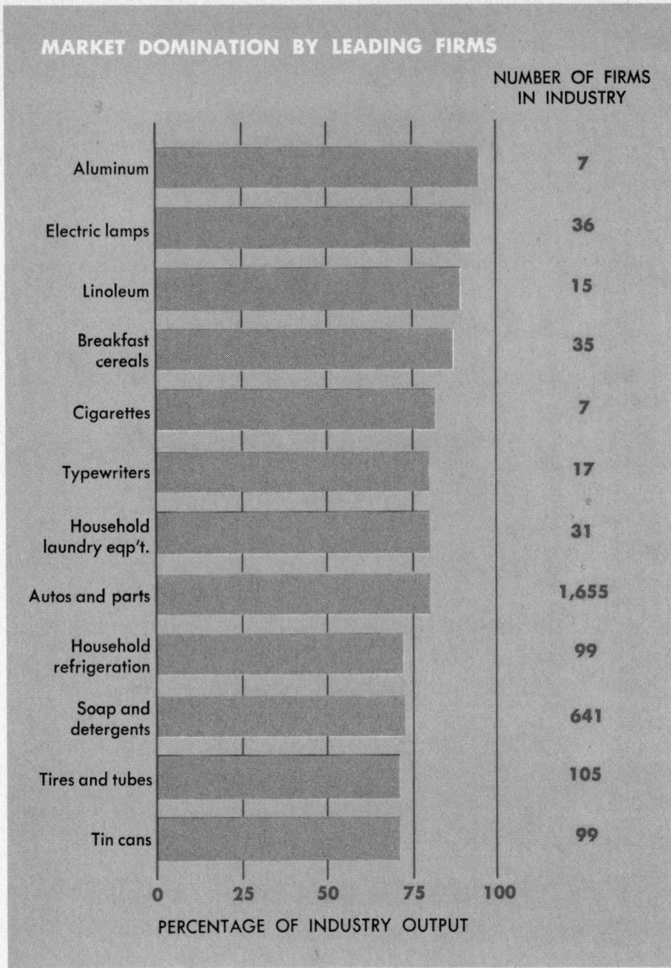

Figure 25–1

The largest four firms dominate the industry's output in leading U.S. industries. The total number of firms varies greatly from industry to industry. (Source: U.S. Department of Commerce; data are for value of shipments in 1966; number of firms data are for 1963.)

ample, in two industries with the same concentration ratio of 80 percent, if in one case the biggest firm has 60 percent of the market while in the other it has only 25. Similarly, the total number of firms in the industry outside the leaders may make a difference. The soap and match industries have similar four-firm concentration ratios, with the additional industry characteristics shown in the following table. Which would you say is more concentrated? In general, economists suspect that monopoly-like results are more likely in highly concentrated than in less concentrated industries. But this measure provides only a rough first presumption.

	SOAP	MATCHES
Total number of firms	267	14
Percentage of total industry sales by:		
Largest 4 firms	85	74
Largest 8 firms	89	93
Largest 20 firms	95	100

The degree of concentration in different industries has varied substantially over the years. But some industries, with the characteristics noted below, have been dominated persistently by a few large firms, and overall data on concentration show a surprisingly stable pattern for a dynamically changing economy.

International data on concentration are also

illuminating. Table 25–1 compares concentration ratios for leading industries in five industrialized nations. Over all, concentration patterns are strikingly similar, which suggests common underlying factors in the industries concerned. But here again, there are numerous cases that don't fit the general pattern.

THE FOUNDATIONS OF OLIGOPOLY

At bottom, most oligopolies rest on one or both of two factors: (1) the necessity of large-scale production (relative to the size of the market) for low-cost output, and (2) barriers against the entry of new firms into the industry.

If total market demand will support only a few firms of optimum size, clearly the competitive struggle will tend to make a few big firms the winners. This situation rests fundamentally on the economies of large-scale production. In each of the industries in Figure 25–1, large-scale production is essential to obtain low unit costs.

How do these big firms maintain their positions, once attained? As we shall see presently, aggressive price competition is unlikely. Instead, the oligopolist often tries to increase his market share and his profits by improving his product, by demand-creating activities, and by setting up barriers against the intrusion of new competitors. Patents, an established marketing organization, or control over raw materials may be of key importance in keeping out newcomers. The bases for oligopoly power are similar to those for other monopolies indicated in Chapter 23. But dominant firms in an oligopoly are seldom safe from potential competition. It is the rare oligopoly that escapes for long the pressures of competition from new firms and new products. Even patents, large size, and technological dominance provide only partial and temporary insulation.

OLIGOPOLY PRICES, OUTPUT, AND PROFITS

Analytically, the crucial thing about an oligopoly is the small number of sellers, which makes it imperative for each to weigh carefully the

TABLE 25–1
Concentration Ratios in Five Nations[a]

	U.S.	U.K.	CANADA	FRANCE	JAPAN
Primary aluminum	100	43	100	100	100
Autos	98	74	100	79	76
Cigarettes	82	74	85	100	
Trucks	77	86	100	78	
Matches	74	86	98	100	74
Steel ingots	64	32	81	40	52
Flour	40	46	35	12	53
Petroleum refining	32	93	79	72	41
Beer	27	11	49	25	98
Cement	31	89	100	52	48
Cotton textiles	18	4	60		7

[a]Ratios are for four firms in the United States, three firms in other nations. Figures show percent of total sales accounted for by leading firms. Data vary between 1950 and 1960 for different nations.

Source: J. Bain, *International Differences in Industrial Structure* (New Haven: Yale University Press, 1966), pp. 67–106.

reactions of the others to his own price, production, and sales policy. Given the wide range of possible reactions of different sellers in most oligopolistic markets, it is difficult to predict precisely what these reactions will be, and therefore difficult for the oligopolist to determine what price-production levels will give him the largest profits. We have, therefore, no simple oligopoly theory to tell us reliably just what the price-output equilibrium condition will be. The outcome will be different depending on the assessments each businessman makes of the likely reactions of his competitors to his own policies.

While many reaction patterns are possible, history suggests some central tendencies in oligopoly price-production decisions. In oligopoly, one attractive alternative for the rivals is collectively to establish the profit-maximizing price for the industry as a whole, and then divide up the market and profits among themselves. The law prohibits open collusion of this sort, so oligopolists must make secret agreements or rely on the willingness of all to "go along" with avoiding price competition. But in such a situation, it will also generally be to the self-interest of each individual producer to get a bigger share of the market for himself, which he might hope to do by cutting prices and luring away some of his competitors' customers. On the other hand, if he cuts price, there is always the danger that competitors will meet the price cut, and the only result will be a lower price and lower profits for all the oligopolists.

Oligopoly Theory: Avoidance of Aggressive Price Competition

Suppose that you are the manager of a local brick factory, and that you have two competitors in the area. You are making a reasonable profit, and so are your competitors. Each of you sets the price at which he sells. You are price makers. Each of you knows he could make a larger profit if he could manage to increase his share of the market, because each of you is operating below capacity. Will you cut your price to get customers away from your competition?

Maybe you will. But you'd better think twice before you try it. Your competitors will almost surely retaliate by meeting your price cut. Maybe they'll undercut you if you stir them up by disturbing the stability of the market. Your price advantage can't last more than a day or two before they know about it, and you can't get very rich in that length of time. Heaven only knows just what will happen if you start a local price war, but three things look reasonably sure: All three of you will end up with lower prices; none of you will have lured many customers away from the others; and everyone's profits will have taken a beating. In the end, you might just glower at each other in the local Rotary Club meetings, but you'd probably get together and agree to put prices back to some reasonable level near where you started.

This is only a small-scale, hypothetical example. But the questions are the same ones that the presidents of huge corporations ask when they consider cutting prices in oligopolistic markets, in steel, automobiles, cigarettes. With only a few firms in the industry, the forces toward letting well enough alone are strong. Price reductions are likely to come only to meet a competitor's cut or under severe pressures—in recessions, for example. When firms do cut, they usually do so in the expectation that their cut will be met by rivals. Thus, the cut is made with the intention of moving the whole industry price scale to a lower level, in the hope of stimulating overall demand for the industry's product. In many cases, one major firm in an oligopolistic industry acts as a "price leader" in this way, although there may be no formal agreement.

Such a "live-and-let-live" policy makes sense to most producers. It leaves room for each firm to try quality and advertising competition to increase its share of the market. It leaves room for some price shading and juggling when times are hard or when one firm is losing out badly in the market. But aggressive price competition will probably blow the situation wide open. Cigarettes are a good example: The leading firms almost never compete on prices, but spend huge sums on advertising and other demand-creating activities.

Oligopoly Theory: The Kinked Demand Curve

Economic theory helps present the price problem that faces the oligopolist. Go back to the brickworks case above. The current price is twenty cents a brick, and you are selling 10,000 bricks per week. As you sit in your office, you try to imagine what your demand curve looks like, as a basis for deciding whether to change your price. Chances are you will come out with something like Figure 25–2, a "kinked" demand curve.

It says that if you raise your price and the others don't follow, your sales will fall off sharply because your customers will desert you; your demand curve looks highly elastic if you raise price above twenty cents. On the other hand, if you cut the price, you can be almost sure your rivals will follow to avoid losing customers to you. Thus, a lower price may increase sales a little, because the market will take some more bricks at a lower price; but there's little reason to suppose you'll get a bigger share of the market away from your competitors. Your demand curve looks very inelastic if you cut price below twenty cents. This situation obviously puts a high premium on keeping the price where it is, just as the common-sense reasoning above suggested.

Figure 25–2

Kinked demand curve suggests that you will lose total revenue if you either raise or lower price. Demand is elastic above twenty cents, inelastic below it.

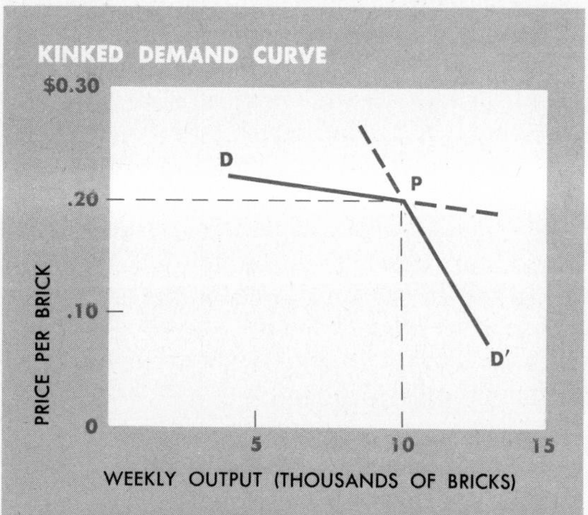

Note now the critical assumptions. The first is that if you **raise** price, your rivals **will not** follow. It is this assumption that underlies the highly elastic curve to the left of the "corner" *P*. If, by contrast, you are a price leader and your rivals will follow your increase, the *DP* section of the curve will be much less elastic and will probably just extend directly on up from *D′P*, as in the dashed line. This is because you won't lose a share of the market to the others; the only loss in sales volume comes from the market as a whole, because fewer bricks will be bought at the higher price.

The second crucial assumption is that if you **cut** price, the others **will** also cut. If they do not, than *D′P* of your demand curve will probably be highly elastic, as your rivals' customers switch to you. Then the "corner" in the demand curve would again vanish and your demand curve will just be an extension of *DP*. This would be a wonderful situation for you, but it is not very likely unless you can hide your price cuts from your rivals. And that's difficult in an oligopoly.

In summary, then, the kinked demand curve exists because you assume a **different** reaction from your competitors when you raise than when you lower your price. If you are the recognized price leader, there will be no kink, and you are merely moving price up or down along the demand curve for the whole industry. If you are so little that nobody reacts to your price changes, there is also no kink—but this case is really a violation of the oligopoly situation, because the essence of oligopoly is the existence of so few competitors that each must be concerned with the others' reactions. Lastly, your freedom to move price without immediately risking rivals' reactions is larger the more differentiated your product is.[1]

[1]Where the demand curve is kinked, the corresponding marginal-revenue curve has a break, or discontinuity. The following graph shows the demand and marginal-revenue curves from Figure 25–2. Note that given this marginal-

Oligopoly and "Game Theory"

Another approach to understanding oligopoly behavior is through "game theory." This likens competing oligopolists to participants in a game—a contest for market share and profits. In an oligopoly of, say five leading firms, there are many possibilities of partial collusion and different forms of competition. If you change your price, will all the others react together? May they "gang up" on you? If you have been the price leader, will they follow you this time? How shall you play the game to avoid having newcomers break into your profitable circle of five?

Game theory systematically explores the outcomes of different strategies and coalitions. It suggests the outcome of different policies, but the combinations and permutations of different assumptions mount rapidly, and the theory becomes very complex. Thus, unfortunately, game theory gives no simple predictions of what profit-seeking oligopolists will do, although it helps to suggest some likely limiting cases.

Oligopoly Theory: Price-Fixing and Market-Sharing Agreements (Cartels with Free Entry)

Presumably, oligopolists would like to maximize profits for the industry as a whole, thereby obtaining the largest profit pie to divide by sharing the market. Such a price-fixing market-sharing arrangement is often called a "cartel."

This practice is illegal. But analyzing a formal cartel can suggest the consequences of today's informal cartel-like price-stabilization arrangements. And the line between not competing aggressively and agreeing to stabilize price is nebulous. In the brickworks example above, there was no open collusion on prices, though the result was much the same as if there had been. Moreover, formal cartels are a dominant form of market organization in many European countries.

Assume a hypothetical furnace industry, in which there are only ten firms. What are the long-run results of a cartel in the industry, if the ten firms agree to "stabilize" prices and to share the market equally?

In effect, the firms will act like one pure monopoly in setting price and then divide up the business and profits.[3] Assume that the competitive price for furnaces would be \$400, the lowest point on the total-unit-cost curve of each producer. At \$400, consumers would buy 30,000 furnaces monthly. But by restricting output, the ten firms can make substantial profits. So they agree to raise the price to \$500, at which level 20,000 furnaces can be sold monthly, this price being estimated to maximize profits for the group as a whole. Then each firm sells only 2,000 furnaces monthly, but at the higher price it reaps a profit of about \$75 per furnace (the

---

revenue curve, a marginal-cost curve (*MC*) could move up or down considerably without logically leading the firm to change its price. This fact may further explain the observed oligopoly tendency toward price stability, even when costs change substantially. (The lower half of the *MR* curve need not be negative, though of course it will be if *D'P* shows inelastic demand.)

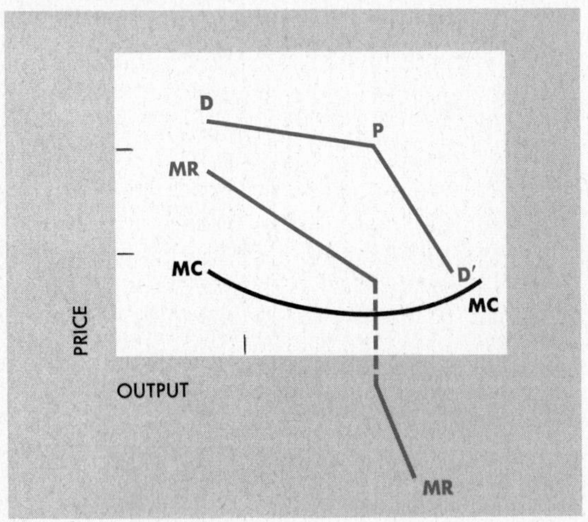

[3]Logically, the cartel would maximize its profits by setting price and output where marginal cost equals marginal revenue for the industry as a whole. See Figure 23–2.

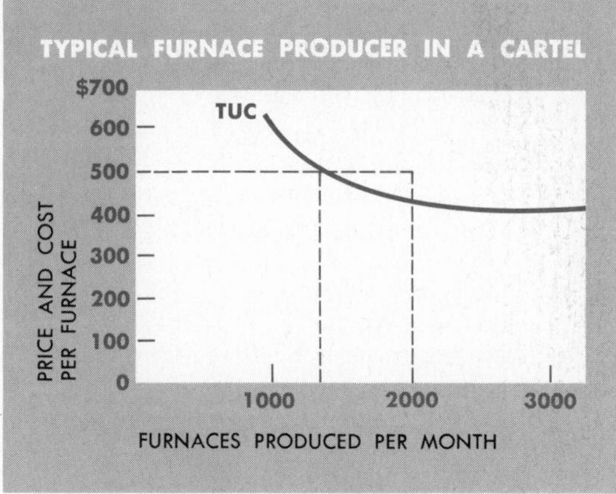

Figure 25–3

At the cartel price of $500, a firm first makes $75 profit per furnace. As more firms enter, each firm's market share and profit diminish.

difference between the $500 price and the $425 total unit cost at the 2,000 output level). The situation is pictured in Figure 25–3.

Price is now higher than the competitive level; output is lower; employment of labor and raw materials is lower; and production is less "efficient." Consumers take a beating; price is well above marginal cost. If the furnace makers can keep new competitors out, they're sitting pretty.

But suppose new firms can't be kept out. Oligopoly profits lure them in. The entry of new firms will divide up the same total sales among more and more firms. With, say, twelve firms, monthly sales per firm would be only 1,667 (assuming each firm gets the same share of the market). Thus, profits are eliminated as new firms enter, not by price reduction but by rising unit costs as each firm reduces output to a less and less efficient level. New firms will continue to enter, cutting down the market available to each, until finally the cost per unit has risen to equal the cartel price of $500 at an output of 1,333 for each of fifteen firms.

Consider Figure 25–3, which shows the total-unit-cost curve of a typical producer. The original cartel members agreed to stabilize the price at $500, so each producer could sell 2,000 furnaces monthly and make $75 per furnace. But as more firms enter, building similar plants, the sales allotted to each producer fall until with fifteen producers each can sell only 1,333 furnaces monthly and rising costs have eliminated profits.

Now look at the results. Producers are no better off than under competition; consumers suffer all the results of monopoly with price still up at $500 and total output restricted to 20,000 furnaces; and society bears the loss of extensive "overinvestment" in the industry, because far more productive facilities have been built than are required. **Such a cartel arrangement with free entry, it might thus be argued, is not a halfway point between competition and monopoly, but rather an arrangement that combines the worst characteristics of each and the benefits of neither.**

Obviously, this fifteen-firm "equilibrium" would be highly unstable. Each producer sees a big potential gain from cutting his price, and he has little inducement to remain in the agreement since profits have been eliminated. Formal cartels without effective restrictions on entry seldom last long.

Oligopoly Theory: Restrictions on Entry

The preceding section points up the importance of restrictions on entry of new firms in determining the price-output performance of an oligopolistic industry. If the furnace producers above had had some effective way of keeping new firms out of the industry, their original cartel would have worked out very nicely for them in terms of continuing profits—though there would always be the danger that one firm would become dissatisfied and cut prices to increase its share of market and profits. But once outsiders are free to enter, profits are eroded for everyone as more firms enter, and the incentive to fight back becomes almost irresistible.

Thus, oligopolists try hard to insulate themselves against new competitors, by product differentiation, by patents, by developing secret

DO PARTIAL MONOPOLISTS MAXIMIZE PROFITS?

Do partial monopolists, operating with various degrees of protection from market competition under monopolistic competition and oligopoly, produce efficiently and maximize their profits? If businessmen in highly competitive industries don't make a fairly good stab at this behavior, competition will remove them from the scene in due time. With the monopolist and partial monopolist, we can't count so fully on competition to exert this pressure.

There are several reasons why a businessman may not be maximizing profits at any time:

1. It's the long run that matters, and he may be willing to absorb a short-run loss for long-run gain.
2. It takes time to adjust to changes in demand, costs, and the like.
3. Businessmen never know what costs and demand in the future will be. They can only estimate, and often they're wrong.
4. Sometimes managers just aren't very efficient. They don't do a very good job of either minimizing costs or increasing revenues.
5. Unusually large profits may be an invitation to new competitors, lured by the hope of winning some customers away. Thus, the partial monopolist may think twice before reaching for more profits that may invite more competition.
6. Unusually large profits may bring unwanted scrutiny from the government's antitrust officials.
7. Historians point to many firms that have grown big as a result of the promoters' and managers' desire for bigness per se. They focus on growth in total sales and share of market, rather than on profits per se.
8. Some managements engage in "business statesmanship." They concentrate on improving the community and on social responsibilities. These things cost money and may or may not help long-run profits.
9. Lastly, the modern hired manager (as distinct from the owner-operator) may have important objectives in addition to profits—the desire to get along well with others in the company; to avoid ulcer-producing arguments with the union; to avoid looking foolish by being wrong when he takes risks. Management has more freedom to follow these other motives if it is sheltered from vigorous competition. (There is some evidence that owner-controlled firms do achieve a higher rate of return on investment than do similar management-controlled firms. Between 1952 and 1963, owner-controlled firms earned a 12.3 percent rate of return on investment as against 7.3 percent for management-controlled firms.)[2]

There are clearly wide differences among firms on all these scores. We assume in this chapter that, by and large, making profits is a dominant goal for partial monopolists. But in using profit-maximizing models, don't forget these other possible motives and problems.

[2] R.J. Monsen, J. Chin, and D. Cooley, "The Effect of Separation of Ownership and Control on the Performance of Large Firms," *Quarterly Journal of Economics,* August 1968, p. 441. See also page 336.

production know-how, by bringing out new products that are hard to reproduce. And in many cases they are helped by modern technology and the high cost of entering such businesses. Where large-scale investment and production are required for efficient output, it's hard for newcomers to break in.

Recent research suggests that barriers to entry are effective ways of protecting above-average profits, at least temporarily. Table 25–2 classifies major oligopolistic industries by the apparent barriers they have against new entrants, and shows the average rate of return on owners' investment in each for the years 1950–66. Those with the highest entry barriers generally showed the highest profit rates, though the experts disa-

TABLE 25-2
Rate of Return on Owners' Investment in Oligopolies, 1950–66

VERY HIGH BARRIERS TO ENTRY:	AVERAGE PROFIT RATE (PERCENTAGE)	
Nickel	18.0	
Sulphur	17.6	
Ethical drugs	17.4	
Flat glass	16.4	
Automobiles	15.7	
Cigarettes	11.9	
Liquor	8.4	
Class average		15.0
SUBSTANTIAL BARRIERS TO ENTRY:		
Soap	13.3	
Cement	13.2	
Biscuits	10.9	
Copper	10.9	
Steel	9.7	
Farm machinery	8.4	
Sugar refining	8.4	
Shoe machinery	6.6	
Floor coverings	5.9	
Class average		10.4
MODERATE-TO-LOW BARRIERS TO ENTRY:		
Gypsum products	12.6	
Glass containers	12.5	
Tires and tubes	12.0	
Metal containers	9.9	
Shoes	9.6	
Meatpacking	5.3	
Class average		11.8

Source: Data from H.M. Mann, "Barriers to Entry and Long-Run Profitability," *The Antitrust Bulletin,* Winter 1969. He also found that profit rates vary directly with the share of market held by the largest eight producers in thirty major oligopolistic industries. But some economists dispute his findings.

gree over the effectiveness of barriers in some industries.[4]

[4]For a more detailed account, see J. Bain, *Barriers to New Competition* (Cambridge: Harvard University Press, 1956).

Try one last check on oligopoly theory. Suppose the ten barbers in Hometown are pricing haircuts at $2.50 and making what seems to them a very bad living. So they get together and agree to raise the price of haircuts to $3.50. Predict the results of this cartel-type agreement —for barbers and for customers. Hints: What is the elasticity of demand for haircuts? What will happen to the number of barbers in Hometown?

RESEARCH, DEVELOPMENT, AND INNOVATION

Oligopoly gets dubious marks on the criterion of efficiency in the allocation of resources. But there is another important kind of efficiency—efficiency in using resources to promote economic progress. How does oligopoly score on that test?

The general presumption of static economic theory is against monopoly on this score as well. The pressure of competition is the greatest prod to progress, Adam Smith and his successors tell us. The more protected from competition any businessman is, the less likely he is to work hard at producing new and better products.

But there is another side to the issue. Progress in the modern economy depends heavily on research and development spending. And only big firms have the resources to afford large R&D expenditures. Thus, as a practical matter, only with oligopolistic market structures are we likely to get the heavy R&D spending on which modern industrial progress depends.

What do the facts show? Table 25–3 details R&D done in industry in 1970, financed by both federal and industrial funds. Out of industrial R&D expenditures, less than 5 percent was in industries dominated by small firms—for example, textiles and construction. Conversely, the great bulk of R&D is done by big firms, and by the same token in oligopolistic industries—for example, aerospace, chemicals, and electrical equipment, though much of this research is ultimately financed by government funds. Only in

SOME PRACTICAL ASPECTS OF BUSINESS PRICING

Businessmen frequently have inadequate information on future costs and revenues. Yet decisions have to be made, day in and day out. Many managers thus look for some reasonable rules of thumb to avoid the necessity of starting from scratch on each price problem.

Standard Costing

Cost per unit of output varies at different output levels. Yet you can't quote everybody a different price and be jiggling your price up and down all the time. So a lot of businessmen ask their accountants and engineers to estimate the total cost of one unit of output at near-capacity operations. They call this estimate the "standard cost," and use it for price setting, even though actual output may vary markedly from day to day.

"Standard costing" may not be very precise, and many economists explain that it may lead the firm to less than maximum profits on some orders. But standard costing is a rule-of-thumb shortcut for getting the day's business done when there are thousands of different customers and orders. The alternative might well be utter confusion rather than a more perfect approach to profit maximization.

Cost-Plus Pricing

Using standard costs as a basis, many firms engage in "cost-plus," or "full-cost," or "markup" pricing. They price their product by taking their standard-cost estimate and adding on some standard markup—10, 50, or 100 percent—to provide a reasonable profit. They are likely to use this same markup to quote prices on all orders, regardless of substantial variations in the actual cost of filling the orders. This approach leads to reasonable simplicity in business operations, but it is easy to see how it may also lead to less-than-maximum profits on individual orders.

Actually, businessmen are often better economists than this would suggest. When standard-cost pricing gets them too far out of line with the results they would get through using an actual cost calculation, they often modify their standard-cost pricing. For example, in booming markets where standard-cost pricing clearly undershoots what the market will bear, larger markups are common. In depression, price cutting under "full-cost" prices is widespread. And big buyers often get price concessions on large orders.

Return on Investment

Increasingly in recent years, big corporations use some "target" return on capital investment as a rough guide to pricing policy (and to capital investment in new ventures as well). General Motors, for example, shoots for 20 percent on invested capital after taxes. This, of course, doesn't give any automatic guide to setting prices, but it provides some guidelines. Thus, current pricing and plans for expansion are all wrapped up in the same general process, in which the test of effective performance is whether it meets this profit-rate standard.

Why does GM choose 20 percent as the target rate? U.S. Steel is reported to use 8 percent after taxes, Alcoa 20 percent before taxes. Maybe each is out to maximize profits, and their target rates are merely about the peak they think they can earn. Certainly we need to know more about how the targets are set to evaluate their impact on pricing. But for better or worse, lots of big businesses use this approach as one major guide in pricing and investment planning.[5]

[5]There is a large literature on business pricing practices. For easy-to-read accounts, see A.D.H. Kaplan, J. Dirlam, and R.F. Lanzillotti, *Pricing in Big Business* (Washington, D.C.: The Brookings Institution, 1958), and G. Burck, "The Realities of Corporate Pricing," *Fortune,* April 1972.

agriculture among the industries approaching pure competition is there large R&D spending, and this is financed almost entirely by the government and conducted largely in the universities, not shown in Table 25–3.

But the picture is more complex. Among the large firms that do have research and development organizations, the medium-large ones spend as large a fraction of their sales dollars on research as do the huge ones. Although modern industrial research is heavily concentrated in oligopolistic industries, increasing firm size above a certain level doesn't seem to increase the relative stress on research.

Whose research contributes the most to innovation and economic progress? We have few clear measures of success. Researchers have looked especially at three measures—patents received, important innovations achieved, and the rate of increase in productivity.

A few giants dominate the total number of patents awarded (Bell Labs, GE, and DuPont), but in general big firms receive patents only in proportion to their larger expenditures on research. If anything, the middle-sized firms appear to have done a shade better in relation to their research spending, except for the few research giants.

A more important, but more difficult, measure is the number of important innovations actually produced by different-sized companies. Here Penn's Edwin Mansfield has studied three major industries intensively. He finds that in petroleum refining and coal mining, the larger firms have produced a larger proportion of the important innovations than their share in industry sales. But in steel, the reverse was true. He speculates on the basis of his evidence that large, but not giant-sized, companies are the most promising sources of R&D innovations—though this statement must be recognized as only a very tentative judgment. Many of the major advances have originated outside the big business labs, in universities and small research ventures.

Which industries show the highest rates of growth in productivity? Broadly speaking, those with the highest growth rates tend to be the oligopolies—chemicals, aerospace, and commu-

TABLE 25–3

Research and Development Spending, 1970[a]

INDUSTRY	R&D SPENDING (IN BILLIONS)	PERCENTAGE OF ALL R&D	FEDERAL FUNDS AS PERCENTAGE OF TOTAL
Aircraft and missiles	$ 5.2	28.9%	78.2%
Electrical equipment	4.3	23.6	52.6
Chemicals	1.8	10.1	10.4
Machinery	1.7	9.4	16.6
Autos, transport equipment	1.5	8.4	16.2
Instruments	.7	4.0	26.6
Petroleum and extraction	.6	3.4	7.1
Food products	.2	1.1	1.0
Rubber products	.2	1.1	20.0
All other[b]	1.7	9.4	41.2
Total	$17.9	100.0%	43.6%

[a]Estimates by National Science Foundation. This series excludes certain commercial-product-development activities sometimes included in R&D estimates.

[b]Includes mining, construction, transportation, public utilities, agriculture, and others.

nications. Productivity has grown more slowly in industries dominated by small firms—the services, construction, and textiles. Agriculture is a strong counterexample, with a very high growth rate in productivity, but its research is almost entirely financed by the government and disseminated through state agricultural extension services.

How about the influence of entry barriers on the rate of innovation? As was indicated above, profits on invested capital tend to be higher where barriers to entry are high, which might suggest that oligopolists have been progressive in reducing costs. However, numerous cases can be cited in which well-protected oligopolists have failed to introduce major innovations until the way has been charted by others. Examples are the early introduction of radio outside GE and Bell Telephone, the dominant communication firms; and the development of jet engines outside the established aircraft engine manufacturers. But there are numerous counterexamples. Pending more conclusive research, we are left with only a general theoretical presumption that pressures to innovate will be strongest where firms are not protected against the threat of new entrants.

What is the conclusion on oligopoly and economic progress? Clearly firms of substantial size are needed in most industries to undertake substantial R&D activities, if we expect the research to be done by private firms.[6] But just how big firms should be for optimal progress remains an unsettled issue.[7]

The Dynamics of Oligopoly

Many rapidly growing industries are dominated (led) by one or a few firms. Rapid growth tends to come with the introduction of new products or new methods, and understandably the firms that innovate achieve a leadership position. Figure 25–4 shows a typical life-cycle curve for a new product. After introduction, sales grow slowly as it becomes better known on the market. Then, as it catches on, it grows

[6] Some observers suggest introduction of government-financed research and dissemination for the business sector, to parallel the arrangements that have worked so well in the small-firm agricultural sector.

[7] For a survey of the evidence, generally unfriendly to big business, see J. Blair, *Economic Concentration* (New York: Harcourt, Brace Jovanovich, 1972), Chaps. 9 and 10.

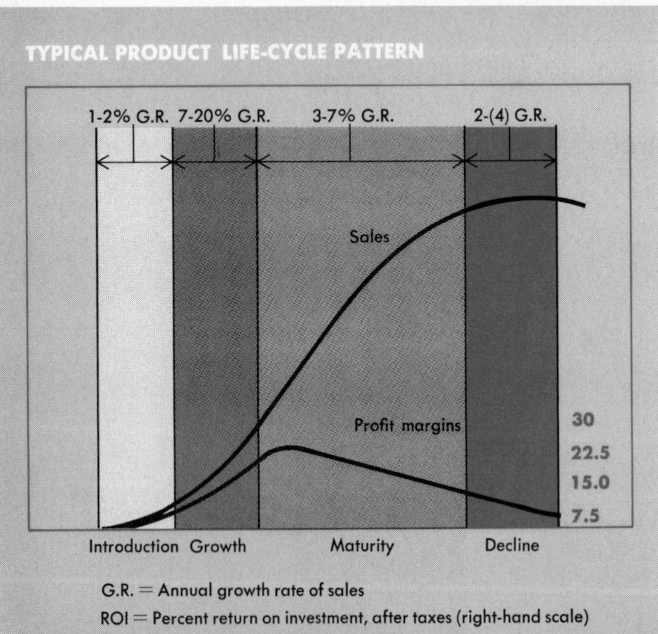

Figure 25–4

Typically, sales of successful products grow rapidly at first, then gradually level off, and ultimately turn down. Profits peak earlier. (Source: Economic Concentration, Hearings before the Senate Subcommittee on Antitrust and Monopoly, 1964, p. 138.)

TABLE 25–4
Growth Rates of Innovative Industries, 1945–70

COMPANY	PRODUCT LINE	AVERAGE ANNUAL GROWTH RATE SALES	JOBS
Texas Instruments	Transistors, integrated circuits	29 %	11 %
Xerox	Photocopiers	28	19
IBM	Computers, office systems	18	13
3M	Tapes	15	8
Polaroid	Instant photography	15	8
Total economy		2.5 (GNP)	1.4

Source: U.S. Department of Commerce, *Technological Innovation: Its Environment and Management* (1967), p. 5; and *Fortune*.

rapidly, often reaching rates of 10–30 percent per year; in extreme cases, growth rates are even higher. Profits soar, both because new products are often priced to "skim the cream" off the market and because of the rapidly rising sales volume.

As the product matures and other producers come into the market, the growth rate tends to slow. Profit margins for the innovating firm tend to level off. As the product reaches "maturity," the sales growth rate slows and finally turns down, as new products and new methods tend to replace this one.

Figure 25–4 is, of course, only illustrative. Many products never catch on in the market at all; others have short lives and are soon outpaced by competitive products. But the success stories usually look something like Figure 25–4, and in such cases one or a few firms very often dominate the market.

Table 25–4 shows some of the great success stories of modern times. These are companies that pioneered new product lines, and then stayed ahead of competitors during the rapid growth of their industries. Each firm was dominant in its industry during this rapid growth period.

The fact that each industry grew around one pioneering firm is not a coincidence. Competition has developed only as the successes became apparent. Oligopoly thus often comes with rapid growth, but oligopolies, of course, do not necessarily produce rapid growth.

One last observation on the dynamics of oligopoly. Alert firms know that spectacular growth rates for individual products must end. Thus, most large firms try to diversify with several or many products. They always try to have a new growth product in the wings as established lines reach maturity. Otherwise, they may fade as new competitive products make them obsolete. The most successful oligopolists are those that manage to keep a step ahead of their competition with new products and new production methods.[8]

[8]This suggests that oligopolists often make their biggest profits on new products, and they do. During the rapid growth period, price may be set far above marginal cost to "skim the cream" of market demand, and the wide profit spread continues as costs fall with production experience and rising volume. As the product reaches maturity and competition intensifies, profit spreads narrow. Then the innovative firm may be willing to accept small profits or even losses, continuing production from its fixed plant as long as price exceeds variable cost. The overall profits of multi-product firms may thus reflect a combination of large and small profits, and even losses, on different product lines in any given year.

OLIGOPOLY IN THE AMERICAN ECONOMY

Big business has been the favorite target of radical critics of the American economy in recent years, and of some not so radical. High prices, pollution, poor products, misleading advertising, dehumanization of work, manipulation of consumer demand, international imperialism—big business is said to be the devil in the piece for all. And when such critics say big business, they generally mean the big oligopolies in the industries we've been talking about. We shall examine some of these wide-ranging charges further in the following chapters. Here a concluding note merely on the *market* powers of oligopolies in America.

High-fixed-cost oligopolies have filled the American economic history books. The railroads between New York and Chicago before rates were regulated by the federal government are an interesting example. There were four main routes. Each had an enormous fixed investment in right-of-way, stations, rolling stock, and so forth. Variable costs associated with adding a few more cars to any given train, or even adding whole trains, were inconsequential compared with the fixed costs. The *TUC* curve for each (for ton-miles of freight or for passengers) was downward sloping far beyond the traffic level any one of them could realize. Thus, marginal costs were low and the incentive was great to cut prices in order to get more of the available traffic. The New York Central could boost its profits spectacularly if it could get traffic away from the Pennsylvania, and vice versa. Cutthroat competition, not surprisingly, therefore broke out intermittently.[9]

You might suppose that after about the third price war the railroads would get together and agree on a market-sharing, price-stabilization policy. And they did periodically. But the lure of profits was great, and those were the days of the swaggering industrial tycoon. It was not until the government stepped in with the Interstate Commerce Commission to regulate rates that the price wars were ended and price discrimination against short-haul shippers was eliminated.

Most of the industries listed in the tables and charts of this chapter face similar cost and demand situations. The cost of a modern steel mill, for example, has to be spread over an enormous tonnage to keep the cost per ton down to a reasonable figure. Steel demand is highly sensitive to business fluctuations and only in good times do the steel companies run near capacity. Thus, much of the time each company can increase its profits markedly by increasing volume, since its *TUC* curve is downward sloping and marginal cost is low until reasonably high-level operation is reached. The pressure to shade prices is great, and few firms resist it when demand is weak.

Some oligopolies have managed to avoid open price competition for many years without illegal collusion; cigarettes are an example, with lots of "quality" competition and advertising. But the pressures toward illegal collusion are great. A spectacular case was the heavy electrical equipment industry in the 1950s, where executives of GE, Westinghouse, Allis Chalmers, and others were found guilty of elaborate price fixing and market-sharing arrangements.[10] But as we shall see in Chapter 26, antitrust enforcement has now made formal collusion a dangerous and little-used policy for oligopolies. Price leadership, go-along attitudes, and heavy demand creation outlays are the rule of the day in most modern oligopolies—with more price competition than many of them like. Even in oligopoly, the pressures of competition are never very far away.

[9]Throughout, the railroads kept up their short-haul rates to shippers who were served by only one of the four roads and who therefore had no alternatives. In many cases, it cost more to ship freight a few hundred miles between intermediate points than to ship the same freight all the way from Chicago to New York.

[10]For a vivid account, see "The Incredible Electrical Conspiracy," *Fortune,* April and May 1961.

REVIEW

Concepts to Remember

This chapter reuses most of the analytical concepts introduced throughout Part Three. Beyond these, be sure you understand the following new ones:

administered prices	price leadership
cartel	price stabilization
concentration ratio	kinked demand curve
standard costs	cost-plus pricing

For Analysis and Discussion

1. "The big oligopolies like General Motors, General Electric, and Alcoa have been primarily responsible for making better goods available to consumers. Breaking them up into smaller units to obtain more active price competition would be counterproductive." Do you agree or disagree? Support your position against a critic.
2. Is the rate of profit earned on invested capital a good indication of whether an oligopoly is abusing its position?
3. Suppose you were manager of one of the furnace firms originally forming the cartel described in Chapter 25. What policies would you follow to promote your own best interests as additional new firms entered the industry?
4. What are the main forces that determine whether there will be few or many firms in any given industry?
5. In many of the major oligopolistic industries, entry is difficult for new firms because of both the technical know-how and the large financial investment required for effective competition. Can you suggest desirable ways to overcome these difficulties?
6. Suppose that you are president of the largest firm in an industry in which the great bulk of the business is done by the largest five firms. As the industry leader, your firm ordinarily initiates any price changes in the industry.
   a. How would you go about deciding what price to charge for your product?
   b. Is there a conflict or community between your interests and those of the other four firms in the industry?
   c. Would consumers be better off, by and large, if active price competition were enforced rather than price leadership in the industry?

CASE 14

The Battle of the Supermarkets

In early 1972, there were 288,000 retail food stores in the United States, down from 313,000 five years earlier. In 1971, sales of the top four supermarket chains totalled about $17 billion, somewhat under 20 percent of total retail food sales (excluding tobacco and liquor) of about $90 billion. A total of fourteen supermarket chains reported sales of over a billion dollars each and their combined sales of about $30 billion were about one-third of total national sales.

	SALES (IN BILLIONS)
A&P	$ 5.5
Safeway	5.4
Krogers	3.7
Food Fair	2.1
	$16.7

Very small stores have accounted for almost all the dropouts from the industry; some have merged together.

At the national level, food retailing was thus a highly competitive industry as measured by the number of firms, but in some areas a few big supermarkets dominate, with local oligopolies. As judged by profits as a percentage of sales, the industry is highly competitive. Average profit per dollar of sales has recently been less than one percent.

For half a century, The Great Atlantic and Pacific Tea Company (A&P) has been the world's largest food retailer. But late in 1971, culminating a long, rapid growth, Safeway edged past A&P in total sales. A&P, which markets largely in the eastern half of the country, had steadily slipped in market share and profitability over the preceding decade, while its chief competitors, marketing more heavily in the west and south, gained. Some of the regional chains (Albertsons, Jewel, Winn-Dixie, and Safeway itself) have done especially well, though, as the table shows, none except Safeway and Kroger's approach A&P in total size.

In 1971, the A&P management took a dramatic step. In what some competitors labelled a desperate move to regain market leadership, they converted most of their stores to a new "Where Economy Originates" (WEO) "discount store" format. Prices were slashed by 10–20 percent on thousands of products to lure the customers back.

The results were dramatic. By 1972 A&P sales had jumped 15 percent, but profits nosedived. The company lost $41 million during the first half of 1972. Between 1968 and 1972, the price of A&P stock fell from 40 to 15. With the market leader cutting prices, smaller stores had to cut too or lose customers, and most cut. Customers smiled happily at the price cuts in the middle of inflation, but in October 1972 the *New York Times* reported:

> Five of the 10 largest supermarket chains in the country are in "bad financial shape" while half a dozen food chains in the metropolitan New York area are on the brink of insolvency, Clarence Adamy, president of the National Association of Food Chains, declared yesterday. He attributed the situation to:
>
> One of the most dramatic and widespread price competitions that we have had in the retail food field since the 1930s. . . .
>
> Inflation, which is particularly difficult for such a tightly-competitive industry. Stores are being forced to absorb rising costs. . . .
>
> Earnings in the supermarket industry will probably fall to less than 0.50 percent of sales by the year's end, he added, down from 0.86 percent during the summer and 1.41 percent in 1965.

As the price war spread in 1972 with more stores converting to "discount" pricing, profits turned to losses for many of the leading supermarket chains—and apparently for many small retail stores, though accurate published data are not available for such small retailers. Nearly all supermarket stocks nosedived on the security markets. Accusations and counteraccusations of unfair price cutting filled the air. Joseph Binder, president of Bohack, a large New York supermarket chain, charged: "The truth of the matter is this: The Great Atlantic and Pacific Tea Co. didn't know how to run its own business, so it decided to run everybody else out of business." But A&P shrugged off the complaints. William Kane, A&P's chairman, said the charges levelled by competitors "seem a little strange in an economic system that prides itself on being based on competition."

1. Why did cutthroat competition break out in this oligopolized industry in a period of generally rising prices and inflation?

2. Did A&P management act wisely in its own self-interest in adopting its new policy?

3. If you were head of one of the competing supermarkets, would you meet the A&P price cuts?

4. If you ran a small corner grocery near a supermarket, what would you do?

5. How long would you expect this war of the supermarkets to last, and how would you expect it to end?

6. If you were a supermarket chain head, what would you do to restore reasonable stability and profits to your firm? To the industry?

7. Are customers (at A&P and elsewhere) likely to be better, or worse, off as a result of A&P's policy change? In the short run? In the long run?

8. If price cutting continues, would you expect more or less investment in food retail stores in the future?

9. What, if anything, should the government do?

CASE 15

Some Managerial Applications[11]

Elasticity of Demand and Product Pricing. Demand is often elastic. And when it is, a price policy that doesn't recognize this fact can mean disaster. But a price policy founded on full knowledge of demand elasticity can make life pleasant for the stockholders, and unpleasant for competitors.

The record industry is a classic case. For decades classical records were high-priced luxury items, aimed at a small market. In 1938, Columbia broke the oligopoly price pattern, cutting the price per record (on the old shellac 78-rpm records) from $2 to $1. The response was overwhelming. Total expenditure on classical records, to the amazement of almost everyone else, rose drastically. Demand turned out to be highly elastic, and the competition was left behind. Soon RCA and other companies had to meet the cut.

About the same time, the railroads, desperate for revenue, raised their fares. The result was equally impressive. The customers switched to cars and buses, or just stayed home in droves; total revenue dropped as the railroads learned about elastic demand the hard way.

Of course, individual product demand is sometimes inelastic. But over and over again, businessmen have underestimated the gain to be had from reducing prices and expanding markets in which elastic demand prevails. Economists sometimes describe this as "elasticity pessimism." Mass markets based on low costs and low prices have been the foundation of the growing American economy.

[11]For more detailed analyses of the use of economic analysis in managerial decision making, see M. Spencer and L. Siegelman, *Managerial Economics* (Homewood, Ill.: Richard D. Irwin, Inc., 1968); and D.S. Watson, *Price Theory in Action* (New York: Houghton Mifflin Company, 1972).

New-Product Decisions—Marginal Cost versus Average Cost. Suppose you manage a filling station. You have handled only gasoline, oil, and a few miscellaneous supplies like auto polish, windshield-wiper blades, and so on. The local wholesaler approaches you to put in a line of batteries and tires. He argues there will be very little extra expense because you're not pressed for space, and that you have a small but ready-made market in your regular customers who don't want to go to the inconvenience of shopping around for these items.

You've had a course in economics and you know about costs. So you calculate carefully what the marginal (extra) cost of putting in these lines would be compared to the likely increase in revenue. The answer looks good. The only marginal cost you can see is the money tied up in keeping an inventory on hand, and it looks as if you might sell $200 to $300 a month worth of tires and batteries. At a markup over wholesale that will keep the final price roughly competitive with other retailers, this should yield an extra $50 to $75 a month even after allowing for interest cost on the money tied up in inventory. On the other hand, if you allocate against the tires and batteries their proportionate share of other costs (space, your time and that of the help, taxes, electricity, and so on), the line would probably show a small loss. **Should you put in the tires and batteries?**

The answer clearly hinges on whether you use marginal or average costs, assuming your estimates are reasonable. Adding the line will clearly increase revenue more than cost for the enterprise as a whole, unless you've overlooked some new costs associated with the tires and batteries. Following the principles of Chapter 20, you'll increase your total profit by expanding, even though when you compare the "total" cost of the batteries and tires against their selling prices they wouldn't appear to provide a profit. If it's total profit that matters to you, the comparison based on marginal cost will point to the best answer.

But this is a rule to be used with care. It depends on being sure of what is truly marginal and what is not. Suppose you add the tires and they seem a great success, selling more than you'd expected and taking up more and more space and time. You have to add a new man and expand your building. Where do you allocate the cost—to the gasoline, the tires, where? You can look at any one part of your output first, and then the rest looks marginal.

Many businessmen use the above kind of marginal (or incremental) analysis in adding products, but only when the addition is small relative to their total activity, and understandably so. When any product line becomes relatively large, they expect it over the long pull to carry its regular share of the "overhead," or the "burden," as indirect costs of running the business are sometimes called. In principle, comparing marginal cost with marginal revenue always gives the right answer in deciding whether or not to take on a new product or to expand output. The trick lies in applying the principle carefully, and being sure which costs are really marginal in the short run and in the long run. Remember Continental Airlines in Case 11.

Sunk Costs and Operating Decisions. Try another case—similar but different. You manufacture men's suits. Your costs fall roughly into two groups—variable (mainly labor and materials), and fixed (rent, management salaries, and so on). You know that for the range of output in which you usually operate, you must add about 30 percent to your variable costs to get a price that permits you to break even; you normally price by adding 40 percent to variable costs, with the prices of individual suits varying largely with differences in cloth and the amount of hand labor.

This season, demand has been slow and you are operating well under your normal rate. It has been a bad year, and you probably will not even break even. You have a chance to make 1,000 suits on a special order from a wholesaler who is not a regular customer. However, he will only pay a price that would cover variable costs plus 20 percent. **Should you take the order?**

Your fixed costs are "sunk." That is, they go on and must be paid, at least for the short run, whether you operate or not. Because they are sunk, economic analysis says they should have no effect on your decision to accept or reject the order. By taking the order you will cover all your variable costs and will have the 20 percent addition to apply on your fixed costs. You may not make a profit on your total operations, but your loss will be smaller than without the order, as was explained in Chapter 20.

The logic is right. But many businessmen would think a long time before taking the order. They worry about the long run, and properly so. Suppose you cut the price on this order and your regular customers hear about it. Might this break your whole price line, with dire results for profits over the longer run? Or might it lead your competitors to cut their prices? If the answer is "yes," looking only at the particular gain from taking this order would be wearing blinders to the long-run result. *In the short run* you may minimize losses by taking orders at less than total cost, but both economic analysis and managerial common sense say that *in the long run* your price has to cover all costs or you'll end up in bankruptcy.

The Nature of Costs: Depreciation. You operate a fleet of taxicabs. With the hard use the cabs receive you estimate that after three years they will have depreciated to the point where it is no longer economical to operate them. At that time you anticipate you will be able to sell or trade them for about 10 percent of the original cost of $3,000 each. Thus, you account as a cost an annual depreciation charge of 30 percent ($900) each per cab, in addition to regular operating and maintenance costs.

At the end of three years you have fully depreciated the cabs, except for the small turn-in value. Yet they seem to be still in reasonably good condition. Should you turn them in on new cabs, using the accumulated depreciation reserve to finance the new cabs, or continue to use the old ones?

The forward-looking nature of economics, and the principle above that "sunk costs are sunk," suggest the answer. The fact that you estimated a three-year life and have now accumulated a 90 percent depreciation reserve does not give you an answer to when you should replace these particular cabs. Don't be overimpressed by the bookkeeping. The optimal choice depends on analyzing the cost and performance of new cabs against the cost and performance of continued use of the old cabs. If the total profit by continuing to use the old cabs exceeds the profit with new cabs,[12] then keep the old ones. If not, buy new ones. The crucial point is the importance of the forward-looking decision, not the fact that three years is the end of your estimated depreciation period. If you made a mistake in estimating the cabs' useful life, it may pay you to replace long before the cabs are fully depreciated or to wait until long after. Depreciation charges represent only an estimate of the proper cost to be currently charged for the use of durable assets, not a determinant of when assets should be replaced.[13]

[12] Remembering possible consumer preferences for new models and all such relevant considerations, and recognizing that the money can temporarily be used another way if it is not used to buy new cabs.

[13] For a precise analysis of how to decide the best time to replace durable plant and equipment, a more advanced text is needed. See, for example, E.L. Grant and W. Ireson, *Principles of Engineering Economy* (New York: Ronald Press, 1960), Chaps. 10 and 16.

Government, Business, and the Public Interest

CHAPTER PREVIEW

CHAPTER TWENTY-SIX

Business, especially big business, is a favorite target of critics of American capitalism. Radical critics blame just about everything on big corporations and corporate executives—high prices, pollution, concentration of economic power, poor products, manipulation of consumers, racism, sexism, dehumanization of workers, international imperialism—and their solution is often to abolish business completely and turn to a communist state. Others, less radical, see much virtue in the American economic system, but still raise serious questions about big business' power and the need for more effective government regulation. Still others argue that individual self-interest is the most powerful incentive of all—the driving force that has made the American standard of living the highest in the world—and that more regulations risk killing the goose that lays the golden eggs.

Turning to communism or to massive government responsibility for producing the goods we want would mean a revolution indeed that few Americans seem to want—and it is convenient to postpone analysis of this alternative until we have a more complete picture of how the present American economy works. And some of the critics' specific charges (for example, on pollution and international economic imperialism) have to be postponed until more analytical tools are developed in later chapters. But what, if anything, ought to be done to make business serve us better in the marketplace deserves careful attention here.

BIGNESS, MONOPOLY, AND PUBLIC OPINION

Why should government intervene at all in business affairs? Adam Smith had one answer: Because self-seeking can be channeled to the common good only if *competition* prevails. Seldom do merchants gather together, he wrote, that their talk does not turn to means of obtaining higher prices for their produce. It is the job of government, representing all the people, to see to it that competition prevails.

Everyone agrees, moreover, that in an individualistic society there have to be some rules of fair play in economic life, just as in personal behavior. Without common consent to eliminate fraud, to respect property ownership, and to honor legal contracts, business dealings would be carried on under a great handicap. By general agreement, it is the job of the government to establish and enforce these basic rules to enable men to work effectively together. Among Adam Smith's nineteenth-century followers, "laissez faire" never meant that the government should do nothing, but rather that it should leave economic affairs alone *within* a framework of basic moral and governmental rules of the game.

But economic theory gives no clear answer as to just how much competition is optimal—just how the public interest is best served where Adam Smith's pure competition is not feasible. Moreover, the issue of monopoly power shades almost imperceptibly into the problems of bigness and power per se. Consider the following comparison between General Electric and an isolated country grocery.

In 1972, the General Electric Company had assets of $7 billion, and reported profits before taxes of $530 million on sales of $10 billion. It had about 370,000 employees. Although no exact figures are available, GE apparently accounted for nearly half the total sales in the country of heavy electrical machinery, light bulbs, and other major categories of electrical equipment. It was rivaled only by Westinghouse, another giant about half the size of GE. Big companies like Allis Chalmers in heavy equipment and Sylvania in bulbs and lighter equipment absorbed another sizable chunk of the market, but they were far short of the two leaders in overall size and market power. Does GE have too much monopoly power? Should it be broken up into several smaller concerns in the public interest?

Now consider Jones' Grocery Store, at the crossroads corner of an isolated village in northern Minnesota—population 150. Jones' total sales in 1972 were about $12,000, on which he realized a return after paying all costs (except his own salary) of about $4,000, as near as he could figure it. Jones had one employee—himself. His service was so-so. There is no other grocery store within thirty-five miles. Is Jones' Grocery Store a monopoly? Should it be broken up into several smaller concerns in the public interest?

No reasonable person would answer that Jones' store ought to be broken up to provide more competition in the village. The market can't support one respectable grocery, let alone two or three. Yet Jones' monopoly power over the customers in that village may far exceed GE's power over its customers. If Jones takes advantage of Widow Smith down the street and slips in a bad potato with every peck, she's pretty much out of luck. Let GE treat one of its customers that way, and Westinghouse will get a phone call the next day from the outraged purchasing agent.

How about GE? If you think the Antitrust Division ought to look into GE, why? Because GE clearly has a dominant position in its different products, with around half the market for many of them? Or just because GE seems too big—because you feel that no one business ought to control so much wealth, with the far-reaching economic and political power that goes with it?

Analytically, it is important to distinguish

between these two reasons, even though they are closely intertwined. The degree of monopoly power depends largely on the size of the seller *relative* to the market in which he sells. Broader economic and political power depends more on *absolute size,* which bears no necessary relationship to the degree of monopoly the firm possesses. Jones' Grocery has a pretty effective monopoly in its market, according to the economist's definition, but it's a tiny concern. GE clearly holds some monopoly powers too—it's an oligopolist. But the striking difference is GE's absolute size. The company affects immediately millions of consumers, employees, and stockholders by its economic actions. Its managers exert economic power—the power of $7 billion—over the lives of nearly 400,000 workers, over the communities in which they live, and over the consumers who buy electrical products. And, some would add, great political power over what happens in Washington and in state capitals.

It may be that you can't get very excited about GE one way or the other, if you're like a lot of other Americans today. GE is indeed a huge business, and you may sympathize with the workers when they strike for higher pay. But you know that GE has long been a pioneer in research and development of new and better products for consumers. It makes lots of money, but it turns out high-quality, reliable products, and you have at least a sneaking suspicion that it got that big by being better than its competitors. You know, too, that for every GE product you buy, you can find competing ones from Westinghouse and a bevy of other companies, depending on the item. And you're really not much interested in 10,000-horsepower turbines. GE is certainly an oligopolist, but it seems to be doing a pretty good job of serving the American consumer—and of providing a lot of stable, well-paying jobs in the process.

But if you're a student activist critic of the capitalist establishment, it looks different. GE is part of a greedy military-industrial complex that bleeds powerless workers, manipulates consumers to buy what will produce the largest GE profits, and produces shoddy products. It connives with other big businesses and politicians to avoid pollution controls and paying its fair share of taxes.

Elmo Roper and Lou Harris, the public-opinion pollsters, have repeatedly sampled the man-in-the-street's feelings about big business. Although individual views vary widely, for years they have gotten surprisingly consistent answers: (1) Americans on the whole believe that big business is good for the economy, and that on balance it does a good job of turning out good-quality products. (2) The American public doesn't trust big business, and feels that we need a government that keeps an eagle eye on the big businessman to see that he doesn't abuse his enormous potential power over consumers, workers, and smaller competitors; businessmen are greedy although they do many socially useful things outside their main goal of making profits. The last few years have seen an upswing in criticism of big businesses, especially on university campuses, but the basic Roper-Harris conclusions apparently haven't changed fundamentally.

IS ECONOMIC CONCENTRATION GROWING?

Is monopoly growing? Are big firms dominating the economy more and more? The answer is mixed, and it's easy to cite figures that seem to prove the answer either way.

If we look at the manufacturing sector above, the answer seems to be yes. Table 26–1 shows that the market share of the biggest firms has risen substantially since 1948, though most of the increase occurred early in the period and shares haven't changed much in the last two decades. If we use sales instead of assets, the picture is similar.[1]

[1]Concentration statistics are tricky, and it is possible to convey significantly different pictures by changing the groupings of products and measures used (assets, sales, value-added, and so on). When reading such statistics, it is generally wise to probe for possible biases of the writer.

TABLE 26–1
Concentration in Manufacturing

	SHARE OF TOTAL ASSETS IN:	
	1948	1971
largest 5 firms	10%	13%
largest 20 firms	21	27
largest 100 firms	39	49
largest 200 firms	48	63

Source: Federal Trade Commission and *Fortune*.

However, even in manufacturing, the picture is complicated. Although the share of the top 200 or 500 firms in manufacturing has been increasing, the share of the very biggest firms in that total has been falling—in 1954 the top ten held 27 percent of the assets of the top 500 firms, but by 1971 it was down to 22 percent; and the profit share of the giants has fallen relative to the rest of the top 500, though the 500 have increased their share of total manufacturing profits. Moreover, the top is a slippery pinnacle. Table 26–2 shows the largest ten industrial firms in 1909, and what happened to them by 1971. Only one was still in the top ten, and six had vanished from the list of the largest one-hundred firms. General Motors, Ford, and IBM, three of the top five now, didn't even exist in 1909.

One other warning: Most of the giants now produce many products, not just one. Thus, the firm concentration figures don't necessarily tell us the degree of monopoly exercised by that firm in the different industries in which it competes. GM, for example, has over half the automobile market, but it is far behind GE in home appliances, which it also produces. Exxon is the leading petroleum refiner but lags far behind several of the chemical firms in chemical sales, which also make up a substantial part of its business. The big "conglomerates," like ITT and Ling-Temco-Vought, operate in dozens of different industries.

If we look at the whole economy, not just manufacturing, there is little evidence of increasing market concentration. In the rapidly growing services area, markets are widely divided among large and small sellers. Construction continues to be dominated by relatively small firms. There are still millions of farmers, though the market share of big commercial farms has been rising steadily. But the biggest development has been the explosive growth of the government (see Part Five) and nonprofit sectors, especially in the service areas—hospitals and Blue Cross, private education, research institutes, and the like. The share of the national income produced by profit-seeking corporations apparently reached a peak of 55 percent in the mid-1950s. By 1968 it was back down to 53 percent, its level of twenty years earlier. The problem of growing economic concentration, if we eliminate the already-highly-regulated public utilities, appears to be centered in the manufacturing sector, if it exists anywhere.

Mergers to form huge conglomerates, some-

TABLE 26–2
Largest Ten Industrial Firms, 1909–71

RANK		
1909	1971	
1	11	U.S. Steel Corporation
2	1	Standard Oil Co. (New Jersey) (now Exxon)
3	[a]	American Tobacco Co.
4	[a]	International Mercantile Marine Company
5	73	Anaconda Co.
6	35	International Harvester Co.
7	[a]	Central Leather Company
8	[a]	Pullman Inc.
9	[a]	Armour & Co.
10	[a]	American Sugar Refining Co.

[a]No longer in top one-hundred firms.
Source: A.D.H. Kaplan, *Big Enterprise in a Competitive System* (Washington, D.C.: The Brookings Institution, 1964) and *Fortune*. Rankings based on total assets.

times called mega-corps, were the big news of the 1960s. From only 219 in 1960, corporate mergers rose to nearly 2,500 in 1969, when assets of the acquired companies totalled $13 billion. But the glamor of such mergers faded as many of the new conglomerates showed low profits or losses, and as the Antitrust Division challenged the legality of several. Mergers have continued, but at a far slower pace over the last few years—back down to about 1,000 annually in 1971 and 1972.[2]

THE LAW AND COMPETITION

The law is what is written down in the statute books, and more. It is what the courts say it is, what the long rows of past court decisions suggest, altered as the judge thinks proper in any particular case. It is what the Justice Department thinks it is; most law is enforced without ever coming near a courtroom. It is what the president and his advisers think it is, through the way they instruct the government's law-enforcement branches. Above all, it is what the people will obey and support. In our democratic system, no law that does not command widespread public support can long be enforced. Sometimes the law is changed when it loses support, but equally often its enforcement varies to mirror the times.

This description is especially accurate in the field of government-business relations. Here much of the law is in the mass of court decisions, and in the policies of the government's administrative agencies. Both reflect (with lags) what the public wants—often more accurately than we realize. Our antitrust laws seldom change by formal congressional action. But in fact they alter constantly—with changing congressional appropriations for enforcement, changing personnel in the antitrust agencies, and changing judicial attitudes.

[2]See "What We Learned from the Great Merger Frenzy," *Fortune,* April 1973.

The Common Law

Until 1890, there was no federal legislation that declared monopoly illegal. Nor did the states have any antimonopoly laws of consequence. Under the common (unwritten) law inherited from England, contracts to restrain trade unreasonably or to raise prices were unenforceable. But the common law did not hold monopoly practices to be criminal, nor did it even provide for damages to those harmed by the restraint of trade. The contracts were merely unenforceable. Thus, the common law provided little protection to the consumer or to the little competitor who got squeezed out by combinations in restraint of trade.

Legislation

The last half of the nineteenth century saw the development of the great trusts. Standard Oil, American Sugar, American Tobacco, and dozens of others amassed huge empires that held almost complete monopolies over the products concerned. Standard Oil at its peak controlled over 90 percent of the country's oil-refining capacity, and the bulk of the pipelines. American Sugar controlled 98 percent of the country's sugar-refining capacity. American Tobacco had virtually complete control of tobacco manufacturing.

Moreover, the means used to build up these monopolies aroused widespread ire and fear. Standard Oil, for example, apparently drove small competitors to the wall by cutthroat competition, bought them up cheap, and then raised prices. Competitors who resisted found themselves up against ruthless force.

THE SHERMAN AND INTERSTATE COMMERCE ACTS. With half a hundred trust giants on the American scene, popular resentment was reflected in two major acts—the Interstate Commerce Commission Act (1887) and the Sherman Antitrust Act (1890). The Interstate Commerce Act established federal control over railroad rates and services for the first time, eliminating the rampant competition and rate discrimination that had long characterized this industry. The Sherman Antitrust Act was aimed at industrial monopoly. It declared illegal every contract or combination in restraint of interstate trade—to protect both small competitors and consumers. It is the foundation for our treatment of public utilities.

The Interstate Commerce Act takes the alternative of strict, comprehensive government regulation of an industry that cannot operate satisfactorily on a competitive basis. By the late 1800s, it was abundantly clear that regulation of interstate railway rates and service through market competition was impracticable. Most markets were simply not big enough to support several railway systems, each operating near its minimum-cost level.

Under such circumstances, there was little point in trying to enforce competition. Instead, the I.C.C. Act made the railroads regulated public utilities. General operating responsibility is left with the management elected by the private stockholders, but prices and the amount and quality of service must be approved by the I.C.C. to protect the public interest. Under this approach, the railroads are guaranteed monopoly positions, but how they use their monopoly powers is carefully regulated.[3]

The Sherman Act was aimed at the other part of the economy, where competition could reasonably be expected to do a good job of regulating prices, output, and quality for the public good. Here the approach was exactly the opposite of that in the I.C.C. legislation. In order to enforce active competition, the Sherman Act outlawed restraints of trade and attempts to monopolize, as follows:

> Section 1. Every contract, combination in the form of a trust or otherwise, or conspiracy, in restraint of trade or commerce among the several states, or with foreign nations, is hereby declared to be illegal. . . .

[3]With modern truck, bus, pipeline, and airline competition, many economists now suggest that the day has come to try freer competition again, on the argument that competition provides more stimulus to efficiency and good service than does government regulation.

> Section 2. Every person who shall monopolize, or attempt to monopolize, or combine or conspire with any other person or persons to monopolize any part of the trade or commerce among the several states, or with foreign nations, shall be deemed guilty of a misdemeanor. . . .

This was broad and sweeping language. Inevitably, a wide range of questions arose over the years as to just what was actually outlawed. As with all such legislation, such questions have been answered primarily through a long series of court rulings interpreting the law. No legislation regulating the complex modern economy can hope to specify in detail every case and situation that is to be covered.

The Clayton and Federal Trade Commission Acts. In 1914 two new acts were passed—the Clayton Act and the Federal Trade Commission Act—to clarify the Sherman Act by specifically prohibiting certain practices, regardless of the group or individual engaging in them, and by setting up new enforcement procedures.

The Clayton Act listed specifically as illegal (1) discriminatory price cutting; (2) tying contracts, which require buyers to purchase other items as a condition of getting one item; (3) acquisition of stock in competing companies to obtain monopoly powers; and (4) interlocking directorates in competing corporations. But each of these was prohibited only "where the effect may be to substantially lessen competition or tend to create a monopoly. . . ." Thus, the Clayton Act cleared the picture by defining some illegal acts. But it still left open the basic problem of interpretation for the courts in many individual cases.

The Federal Trade Commission Act created a commission to act as a watchdog against unfair competitive practices aimed at creating monopoly or injuring competitors. The commission was given power to hold hearings and to issue "cease and desist" orders that require offending firms to discontinue illegal practices. When the first major appeal from a Commission ruling reached the Supreme Court in 1919, however, the Court held that it is for the courts, not for the F.T.C., to make the ultimate decisions in interpreting the law. The F.T.C., nevertheless, plays an important role in policing cases of seller misrepresentation (for instance, artificial silk as silk, domestic lace as Irish lace), and in arranging voluntary agreements among business competitors on fair-trade practices.

New Deal Legislation of the 1930s. During the Great Depression of the 1930s, the New Deal was mainly concerned with recovery, greater economic security, and helping the little fellow. It sought to halt falling prices and cutthroat competition. The National Recovery Act (N.R.A.) led businessmen to band together in formal cartels, aimed at raising prices. In agriculture, the Agricultural Adjustment Administration (A.A.A.) had a similar purpose—to raise farm prices and incomes by government-sponsored cartel-like agreements to restrict production. The Bituminous Coal Act did the same thing for soft coal. In labor markets, the Wagner Act threw the full force of the government behind workers' right to unionize and bargain collectively, thus lessening the cutthroat price competition among workers for scarce jobs. Both N.R.A. and A.A.A. were later declared unconstitutional, but the powerful competition-restricting effects of the agricultural and labor programs have become central parts of our governmental policy on market structure and performance.

This desire to help the small competitor and avoid "destructive" competition was reflected in two other new pieces of legislation. The Robinson-Patman Act of 1936 strengthened the prohibition against price discrimination that might help such large buyers as chain stores to undersell small retailers. In 1937, the Miller-Tydings Act guaranteed protection from Sherman Act prosecution to manufacturers and retailers who participated in "fair-trading" arrangements, whereby the manufacturer specifies that no retailer may sell his product below a specified price. Too much competition was feared more than too little.

The Celler Antimerger Act of 1950. After World War II, many corporations found that acquiring other companies outright was a profitable way to expand. Such extension of market power through merger was not limited by earlier antitrust legislation. To close this loophole, in 1950 the Celler Antimerger Act was passed forbidding the acquisition of, or merger with, other companies where the effect "may be substantially to lessen competition, or tend to create a monopoly."

The Law in Operation

Antitrust law is what its administrators and the courts make it. And its administrators and the courts by and large make it what the public wants, albeit often very roughly and with a considerable lag. The first big enforcement campaign under the Sherman Act was President Teddy Roosevelt's, conducted with a total staff of seven lawyers and four stenographers. With this tiny staff, but with the big stick of aroused public opinion, the government tackled the biggest trusts. In 1911, the Supreme Court required both Standard Oil and American Tobacco to divest themselves of a large share of their holdings and to desist from numerous specific unfair competitive practices. But there, too, for the first time, the Court enunciated the now-famous "rule of reason." Only trusts that "unreasonably" restrained trade were illegal. In a series of earlier cases, the Court had given a broad interpretation to the interstate-commerce clause, permitting federal regulation to apply to all firms that had any direct dealing across state lines or (later) in products or materials crossing state lines; this interpretation brought most big businesses within the purview of federal antitrust legislation.

By 1920, the attitude toward big business had altered, with the checking of the flagrant abuses of the 1800s. In the *U.S. Steel* case of 1920, the Supreme Court refused to dissolve the company. It held that neither mere bigness nor unexerted monopoly power was illegal as such; that actual unreasonable restraint of trade must be proved under the Sherman Act. The tenor of the 1920s was one of prosperity and "leave well enough alone." The total budget allocated the Antitrust

Division averaged only $250,000 annually for the decade. Big business was popular during the twenties.

With the strong antibusiness sweep of the New Deal, the last major change in the application and interpretation of the antitrust laws began in the late 1930s. Under Thurman Arnold, Antitrust began an aggressive drive in the late 1930s against several of the industrial giants. Antitrust's budget was upped to $1 million (to police the entire economy). The Eisenhower, Kennedy, Johnson, and Nixon administrations have continued active prosecution under antitrust legislation. Appropriations to both the Federal Trade Commission and the Antitrust Division of the Department of Justice have been greatly increased. The Antimerger Act has become a powerful barrier to business growth through acquisition of competitors. The government does not win all the antitrust cases it initiates, but over the last decade it has won most of them.

Not all economists, understanding the theoretical presumption against monopoly, agree that antitrust always serves the public interest. Some economists, for example, argue that the courts' strong interpretation of the Antimerger Act can give topsy-turvy results. To prevent mergers among relatively small firms may hinder useful, cost-saving combinations and protect small inefficient competitors more than it protects consumers. In the 1966 *Von's Groceries* case the court forbad a merger between two Los Angeles grocery chains, which together held less than 8 percent of the Los Angeles market. (See Case 16 at the end of this chapter.)

Where does antitrust law stand now, as a practical matter? First, all price-fixing agreements are illegal per se. Second, oligopolies in which a few firms dominate the market are probably legal so long as no leading firm tries to expand its market share by merger or by aggressive competition that endangers small firms.[4] Third, growth through merger in the same industry is virtually forbidden, except among very small firms—although growth without merger is generally permissible. The IBM case now in the courts raises this issue squarely. How far the law prohibits conglomerate mergers remains to be determined by the courts, or possi-

[4]J.K. Galbraith has argued vigorously that the effect of present antitrust is to let the big, established oligopolies go untouched while applying the Antimerger Act to smaller firms trying to grow through mergers.

"It so happens, Gregory, that your Grandfather Sloan was detained by an agency of our government over an honest misunderstanding concerning certain antitrust matters! He was not 'busted by the Feds'!" (Drawing by W. Miller; © 1971. The New Yorker Magazine, Inc.)

bly through new legislation. Fourth, many specific practices (price discrimination, tying clauses in contracts, and the like) are illegal when they may tend to create a monopoly or significantly reduce competition. Fifth, retail price-fixing under "fair-trade" agreements is legal in many states, but fair-trading is of limited importance because retail competition has generally broken out in spite of the price floors set by manufacturers.

Why has Antitrust again become a potent force since the 1930s? First, the budget given the Antitrust Division by Congress is now about $13 million, larger than ever before; Antitrust now has some 300 lawyers to police the economy. Looked at another way, however, this is still a tiny sum compared with the vast resources of the billion-dollar corporations it has to police. The budget reflects America's ambivalent attitude toward Antitrust. We admire and want big business, but we also want the government watching closely to be sure that big business doesn't abuse its powers. And the Supreme Court has generally supported the government's accusations in recent years.

One last point on the law in action: The main impact of the antitrust law is preventive, not punitive. Since 1890, only about 1,600 suits have been brought under the Sherman Act. Of these, the government has won about three-fourths, with a large proportion settled out of court through "consent decrees." Total fines paid by defendants over the eight decades were only $30 million dollars—very little compared to the billions of dollars of assets in the companies concerned. But a company convicted of antitrust violation is also liable for triple damages if customers or competitors can show they were injured by the illegal acts. GE and Westinghouse were sued for hundreds of millions of dollars by customers after they were found guilty of price fixing in 1961. Moreover, no business likes to be called criminal. It does not like to have its affairs dragged into open court, even though it thinks it may win out in the end. Most observers agree that Antitrust has been a powerful force on the American business scene, even though some would like to see more aggressive enforcement.

WHERE TO FROM HERE?

Where to from here? Nobody thinks the modern American economy can look like the economist's perfectly competitive model. It never has, even back in the pre-Civil War days, and it certainly doesn't now. We're in for a mixed economy of some sort. How shall we assure that business performance is efficient and in the public interest?

Antitrust and Economic Efficiency

Would stronger antitrust action really produce a more "efficient" economy, in the sense of giving consumers the largest possible amount of what they want at the lowest feasible prices? More firms create a general presumption of more active competition. But no magic number of firms is needed to assure effective competition. Sometimes (for example, in the auto industry) there is aggressive competition with only three or four big firms. But most observers agree that more firms generally increase the likelihood of strong price and quality competition.

If more firms are generally good for competition, we need to face the issue of whether this is consistent with having firms big enough to be efficient, low-cost producers. Clearly, business has to be big for efficiency in many industries. But it's also true that business can get too big from the cost standpoint. Various studies have indicated that in many industries middle-sized to large companies have lower costs than gigantic ones. But not always.

It is important to remember that most technological economies of scale come at the *plant* level, so no more production efficiency is gained by combining similar-sized plants in one *firm*. Some critics argue that U.S. Steel, for example, is little more than a number of Inland Steels put together in one firm, although Inland is big enough to be technologically efficient. But bigger firms may yield marketing, financial, and managerial efficiencies. Nothing but a detailed analysis of each industry is likely to provide clear answers on such issues.

Professors George Stigler and Thomas Saving suggest that the market will settle the issue for us if we just let firms battle it out.[5] They postulate that by and large the most efficient sizes of plant and firm will win out in the competitive race. During the postwar period, medium-sized plants (relative to their total markets) have survived most effectively in most industries. This test therefore suggests that in most industries plants small enough to permit effective competition can produce efficiently. But in some industries, for example, computers, the biggest firm is clearly the most efficient by this test.

In some industries (for example, autos, cigarettes, oil refining, and steel) the cost of an efficient plant is so high that there is little point pretending that competition can be readily open to new producers. Look back at Table 25–2, which groups industries by overall ease of entry, taking into account minimum efficient scale of plant, capital requirements, distribution facilities needed, and other barriers to entry. A lot of major products fall into the "very difficult" and "moderately difficult" entry classes. This means that relying on competition to regulate output and prices in these industries is risky, but that government action to break up the oligopolies would also risk insisting on inefficiently small firms.

Many economists are critical of the Robinson-Patman and Miller-Tydings acts. Both were designed primarily to protect small competitors against large ones, and they often do so even when the large competitors are more efficient in satisfying consumer needs. Recent Supreme Court decisions applying the Antimerger Act are open to the same criticism. They tend to protect small **competitors,** not **competition.** From the economist's and the consumer's point of view, it's not clear why price cutting isn't just what competition is supposed to produce, so long as it isn't used as a device for driving out competitors by temporarily selling below cost just to gain a monopoly position.

[5]See, for example, T.R. Saving, "Estimation of Optimum Size of Plant by the Survivor Technique," *Quarterly Journal of Economics,* November 1961.

Antitrust and Economic Progress

The other big question about monopoly and partial monopoly is what they do to the rate of economic progress—whether they contribute to, or impede, a dynamically growing economy. The issues and some of the facts were presented in the concluding sections of Chapter 25. Broadly speaking, those industries with the highest growth rates tend to be oligopolies—big firms with large R&D expenditures. Most research and development spending is done by large and medium-sized firms. Productivity has grown more slowly in industries dominated by small firms (except agriculture, with its government financing and distribution of research). But the picture is far from uniform; there are numerous exceptions, and industries protected against entry by new competitors clearly have the power to suppress innovations that might otherwise have been forced by competition.

What is the implication for Antitrust? Not clear. It seems certain that we can generally not expect much R&D spending from tiny firms in industries that approach perfect competition, however aggressively they may compete for the consumer's favor. If we want R&D in such industries, the pattern of government financing and dissemination of results in agriculture may be the best way. But remember that firms far short of giant size can spend heavily on research and obtain results that compete with the giants' in many industries. Even on the score of economic progress, few industries require such large firms for efficient R&D that they cannot support numerous sellers and effective price competition.

Bigness and the Concentration of Economic Power

Can Antitrust do anything about the problem of the sheer power of bigness? This is the most basic question of all for some people. Political power, economic power, power over other people's lives, just the power that goes with a billion dollars—these are the things that worry many people most about big business.

The power of big business seems especially alarming to some observers because in many firms "inside management" has a substantially free hand. Although stockholders theoretically direct the management, as a practical matter few stockholders know much about the details of management or have any interest in interfering in it. To whom is big management really responsible in the exercise of its economic power?

A.A. Berle, a long-time observer of the business corporation, has pointed up this problem. Only 500 corporations control approaching two-thirds of the entire manufacturing sector of the American economy, he writes, and within each of those 500 a relatively small group holds the ultimate decision-making power. "Since the United States carries on not quite half of the manufacturing production of the entire world today, these 500 groupings—each with its own little dominating pyramid within it—represent a concentration of power over economies which makes the medieval feudal system look like a Sunday School party. In sheer economic power this has gone far beyond anything we have yet seen." Berle's solution: More effective antitrust action.[6]

J.K. Galbraith, in his best-selling *Economics and the Public Purpose* argues even more—that big-business planning and parallel government planning are replacing market competition in modern America. He updates Berle's data on the role of the largest corporations in manufacturing, and points to a growing tendency of self-perpetuating management in the big oligopolies toward long-range planning for efficiency, for avoidance of vigorous price competition, and for stabler relations with organized labor. Solid, prosperous growth is the keynote, without undue, disruptive, old-style competition. With these policies, the big quietly grow bigger and more powerful. In essence, government protects and approves this secure, stable world for the giants, unless they abuse the mores unduly or openly try to aggrandize their positions by acquiring or squeezing out smaller firms. Antitrust acts mainly to prevent open collusion and mergers among the smaller competitors, which, as a practical matter, are probably their only way of challenging the concentrated power of the giants.

Galbraith's solution? Not to break up the giants, for that would waste the economic benefits of modern technology that underlie the success of big firms. Rather he says that the answer is increasing government participation to provide the good life—more and better public services in the modern affluent society. Parks, modern housing, better education, state-supported symphonies and drama—through a bigger public sector with more taxes and more government spending we can improve the quality of modern life, not merely the quantity of GNP.

Most economists believe that Berle and Galbraith have overdrawn their case. Competition in most markets is far too pervasive to permit the comfortable life for the giants that Galbraith paints, except in a few industries. Manufacturing now accounts for only about a quarter of total GNP and 22 percent of all jobs; and big firms are far less dominant in the nonmanufacturing sectors of the economy. The turnover in firms at the top is too fast and the number of failures too large to support Galbraith's picture of comfortable security.

Yet Galbraith has touched a sensitive nerve. Many Americans are uneasy about the concentration of economic power in the big corporations, even though their achievements and their well-paid top managers are widely admired. More on this broad issue of economic and political power in the next chapter.

The Dilemma of Modern Antitrust Policy

The dilemma of antitrust policy in the modern economy is a painful one. How can we have both the efficiencies of size and the benefits of active competition among many sellers? Recent antitrust enforcement has generally sought a compromise, but one leaning toward more firms and more competition. Business claims of

[6] *Economic Power and the Free Society* (New York: Fund for the Republic, 1958), p. 14.

cost economies from large scale production have been ruled inadmissible as protection against application of the antitrust laws.

By contrast, *Fortune* magazine has recently urged a major revolution in our antitrust laws and philosophy, as follows:[7]

> Congress should amend the antitrust statutes to make it clear that the national policy is to foster competition by punishing restraints of trade, including conspiracies to fix prices, limit production, allocate markets, and suppress innovation; but that it is not the national policy to prefer any particular size, shape, or number of firms to any other size, shape or number; and that mergers—horizontal, vertical, or conglomerate—are entirely legal unless they spring from a manifest attempt to restrain trade.

Would this be a good substitute for our present antitrust policy? How is the public interest best served? The man in the street is certainly concerned about undue concentration of power in big business, big labor, and big government. But it is far from clear that the public really wants an economy of rampant competition—neither farmers, labor, businessmen, nor consumers. Most people appear to be interested not so much in a perpetual competitive struggle as in a steady job at good pay, good profits, good-quality products, and predictable, stable times economically. But they don't want someone else to hold unchecked power over their lives. And it's not clear that they trust the government much more than they trust big business.

BUSINESS AND GOVERNMENT IN THE NEW CAPITALISM

Government regulation of business goes far beyond antitrust. The Federal Trade Commission regulates the kind of advertising business may do. The Securities and Exchange Commission regulates its practices in issuing securities. The Federal Reserve controls the terms on which it can borrow money from the banks. Federal law sets the minimum wage it must pay its workers, and prescribes that it must deal with them in unions when they choose. Through its income tax, government takes about half of all business profits. On the vast amount of government contracts issued to business (over $100 billion in 1972), it sets elaborate standards of performance; specifies that business cannot discriminate among employees on the basis of race, creed, or color; and often reserves the right to renegotiate prices downward retroactively if business profits are excessive by government standards.

When labor disputes threaten to disrupt the economy, government brings pressure to settle on terms it prefers. If the business is an airline, it is regulated in detail by the Civil Aeronautics Authority and the Civil Aeronautics Board as to where it can fly, how much it can charge, the kinds of equipment it can use, and the safety standards it must meet. At the local level, government tells business for what purpose land can be used, and the taxes it must pay to help support schools and roads. Beyond all this, government constantly hovers in the background, ready to impose new restrictions or bring new pressures to bear.

Some businessmen strongly oppose this government interference with the freedom of managers to manage as they please. They argue that overregulation reduces efficiency and saps the private initiative and judgment on which private enterprise depends.

Others argue that increasing government intervention reflects a gradual change in the role of business toward greater responsibility to the general public—a change that has modified the nature of "capitalism" but has not fundamentally altered the basic forces of the profit motive, self-interest, and private ownership of property. The old automobile has had its face lifted; horsepower has been stepped up and gas consumption along with it; a governor and safety padding are compulsory; power steering has become standard equipment. Sometimes the machine works better as a result of this tinkering, sometimes worse. But on the whole, they

[7] Max Ways, "Antitrust in an Era of Radical Change," *Fortune,* March 1966.

argue, it is now a better automobile. And above all, the gasoline that makes it go is still the same—self-interest and the profit motive. Writers sometimes speak of "the new capitalism." Sometimes government and business interests become almost inseparable—for example, when the private firm's main business is on government contracts. Chapter 27 examines this problem—"the military-industrial complex"—in detail.

REVIEW

For Analysis and Discussion

1. Does big business have too much power? (Define "power" carefully in your answer.) If so, who should do something about it, and what should they do?
2. How should we decide whether it is in the public interest for any industry to consist of a large or a small number of firms?
3. Does big business, through advertising, effectively control what consumers want? How about products like the Edsel, Corvair, Packard, and Hudson in the auto industry, that have vanished through lack of consumer acceptance in spite of massive advertising?
4. Many businessmen argue that vigorous government prosecution under the antitrust laws is a sign of government antagonism toward business and profits. Is this a proper criticism? If you think it isn't, how would you convince such a critic?
5. Critics of big business often argue that the majority of large modern corporations could be broken up into several competing units without loss of productive efficiency because as a rule they control many different plants, each of which could just as well operate as a separate, competitive business. Is this argument a sound one? If so, how should we go about implementing the proposal?
6. Should conglomerate mergers be challenged under the antitrust laws, even though the merging firms handle noncompeting products?
7. Would you favor direct government conduct or support of all basic research with the results freely available to all? List the advantages and disadvantages? Who should pay for the research?
8. Trucks, buses, pipelines, and airlines now are at least as important as railroads in freight and passenger transportation in most areas. Has the time come to abolish the Interstate Commerce Commission and turn the transportation field back to open competition, to provide more effective incentives to efficiency and progress?
9. Would you favor tripling the congressional appropriation to the Department of Justice for antitrust enforcement?

CASE 16

U.S. versus Von's Groceries[8]

In 1966, the Supreme Court, by a 6–2 decision, found that a merger of Von's Grocery Company and Shopping Bag Food Stores in Los Angeles violated Section 7 of the Clayton Act (often called the Celler Anti-merger Act). The following extended excerpts summarize the majority and minority decisions. Which do you think was right? (See the questions at the end of the case.)

The Majority Decision. On March 25, 1960, the United States brought this action charging that the acquisition by Von's Grocery Company of its direct competitor Shopping Food Stores, both large retail grocery companies in Los Angeles, California, violated #7 of the Clayton Act which, as amended in 1950 by the Celler-Kefauver Anti-Merger Bill, provides:

> No corporation engaged in commerce shall acquire the whole or any part of the assets of another corporation engaged also in commerce, where in any line of commerce in any section of the country the effect of such acquisition may be substantially to lessen competition or to create a monopoly.

The market involved here is the retail grocery market in the Los Angeles area. In 1958 Von's retail sales ranked third in the area and Shopping Bag's ranked sixth. In 1960 their sales together were 7.5 percent of the total two and one half billion dollars of retail groceries sold in the Los Angeles market each year. For many years before the merger both companies had enjoyed great success as rapidly growing companies. From 1948 to 1958 the number of Von's stores in the Los Angeles area practically doubled from 14 to 27, while at the same time the number of Shopping Bag's stores jumped from 15 to 34. During that same decade, Von's sales increased fourfold and its share of the market almost doubled while Shopping Bag's sales multiplied seven times and its share of the market tripled. The merger of these two highly successful, expanding and aggressive competitors created the second largest grocery chain in Los Angeles with sales of almost $172,488,000 annually.

In addition the findings of the District Court show that the number of owners operating a single store in the Los Angeles retail grocery market decreased from 5,365 in 1950 to 3,818 in 1961. By 1963, three years after the merger, the number of single-store owners had dropped still further to 3,590. During roughly the same period from 1953 to 1962 the number of chains with two or more grocery stores increased from 96 to 1950. While the grocery business was being concentrated into the hands of fewer and fewer owners, the small companies were continually being absorbed by the larger firms through mergers. According to an exhibit prepared by one of the Government's expert witnesses, in the period from 1949 to 1958 nine of the top 20 chains acquired 126 stores from their smaller competitors. . . . These facts alone are enough to cause us to conclude contrary to the District Court that the Von's Shopping Bag merger did violate #7. . . .

From this country's beginning there has been an abiding and widespread fear of the evils which flow from monopoly—that is the concentration of economic power in the hands of the few. On the basis of this fear, in 1890, when many of the Nation's industries were already concentrated into what Congress deemed too few hands, it passed the Sherman Act in an attempt to prevent further concentration and to preserve competition among a large number of sellers. . . .

Like the Sherman Act in 1890 and the Clayton Act in 1914, the basic purpose of the 1950 Celler-Kefauver Bill was to prevent economic concentration in the American economy by keeping a large number of small competitors in business. In stating the purpose of the bill, both of its sponsors, Representative Celler and Senator Kefauver, emphasized their fear, widely shared by other members of Congress, that this concentration was rapidly driving the small businessman out of the market. As we said in Brown Shoe Co. versus United States, 370 U.S. 294,315, "The dominant theme pervading congressional consideration of the 1950 amendments was a fear of what was considered to be a rising tide of economic concentration in the American economy." By using terms in #7 which look not merely to the actual present effect of a merger but instead to its effect

[8]384 U.S. 270.

upon future competition, Congress sought to preserve competition among many small businesses by arresting a trend toward concentration in its incipiency before that trend developed to the point that a market was left in the grip of a few big companies. Thus, where concentration is gaining momentum in a market, we must be alert to carry out Congress' intent to protect competition against ever-increasing concentration through mergers.

The facts of this case present exactly the threatening trend toward concentration which Congress wanted to halt. The number of small grocery companies in the Los Angeles retail grocery market had been declining rapidly before the merger and continued to decline rapidly afterwards. This rapid decline in the number of grocery store owners moved hand in hand with a large number of significant absorptions of the small companies by the larger ones. In the midst of this steadfast trend toward concentration, Von's and Shopping Bag, two of the most successful and largest companies in the area, jointly owning 66 grocery stores merged to become the second largest chain in Los Angeles.

Appellee's primary argument is that the merger between Von's and Shopping Bag is not prohibited by #7 because the Los Angeles grocery market was competitive before the merger, has been since, and may continue to be in the future. Even so, #7 "requires not merely an appraisal of the immediate impact of the merger upon competition, but a prediction of its impact upon competitive conditions in the future; this is what is meant when it is said that the amended #7 was intended to arrest anticompetitive tendencies in their 'incipiency.'" (United States v. Philadelphia Nat. Bank, 374 U.S., p. 362.) It is enough for us that Congress feared that a market marked at the same time by both a continuous decline in the number of small businesses and a large number of mergers would, slowly but inevitably gravitate from a market of many small competitors to one dominated by one or a few giants, and competition would thereby be destroyed. . . .

The Minority Dissent. First, the standards of #7 require that every corporate acquisition be judged in the light of the contemporary economic context of its industry. Second, the purpose of #7 is to protect competition, not to protect competitors, and every #7 case must be decided in the light of that clear statutory purpose. Today the Court turns its back on these two basic principles and on all the decisions that have followed them.

The Court makes no effort to appraise the competitive effects of this acquisition in terms of the contemporary economy of the retail food industry in the Los Angeles area. Instead, through a simple exercise in sums, it finds that the number of individual competitors in the market has decreased over the years, and, apparently on the theory that the degree of competition is invariably proportional to the number of competitors, it holds that this historic reduction in the number of competing units is enough under #7 to invalidate a merger within the market, with no need to examine the economic concentration of the market, the level of competition in the market, or the potential adverse effect of the merger on that competition. This startling per se rule is contrary not only to our previous decisions, but contrary to the language of #7, contrary to the legislative history of the 1950 amendment, and contrary to economic reality.

The concept of arresting restraints of trade in their "incipiency" was not an innovation of the 1950 amendment. The notion of incipiency was part of the report on the original Clayton Act by the Senate Committee on the Judiciary in 1914, and it was reiterated in the Senate report in 1950. That notion was not left undefined. The legislative history leaves no doubt that the applicable standard for measuring the substantiality of the effect of a merger on competition was that of a "reasonable probability" of lessening competition. The standard was thus more stringent than that of a "mere possibility" on the one hand and more lenient than that of a "certainty" on the other. I cannot agree that the retail grocery business in Los Angeles is in an incipient or any other stage of a trend toward lessening of competition, or that the effective level of concentration in the industry has increased. Moreover, there is no indication that the present merger, or the trend in this industry as a whole, augurs any danger whatsoever for the small businessman. The Court has substituted bare conjecture for the statutory standard of a reasonable probability that competition may be lessened.

I believe that even the most superficial analysis of the record makes plain the fallacy of the Court's syllogism that competition is necessarily reduced when the bare number of competitors has declined. In any meaningful sense, the structure of the Los Angeles grocery market remains unthreatened by concentration. Local competition is vigorous to a fault, not only among chain stores themselves but also between chain stores and single-store operators. . . . The record simply cries out that the numerical decline in the number of single-store owners is the result of transcending social and technological changes that positively preclude the inference that competition has suffered because of the attrition of competitors.

Section 7 was never intended by Congress for use by the Court as a charter to roll back the supermarket revolution. Yet the Court's opinion is hardly more than a requiem for the so-called "Mom and Pop" grocery stores—the bakery and butcher shops, the vegetable and fish markets—that are now economically and technologically obsolete in many parts of the country. No action by this Court can restore the old single-line Los Angeles food stores that have been run over by the automobile or obliterated by the freeway. The transformation of American society since the Second World War has not completely shelved these specialty stores, but it has relegated them to a much less central role in our food economy. Today's dominant enterprise in food retailing is the supermarket. Accessible to the housewife's automobile from a wide radius, it houses under a single roof the entire food requirements of the family. Only through the sort of reactionary philosophy that this Court long ago rejected in the Due Process Clause area can the Court read into the legislative history of #7 its attempt to make the automobile stand still, to mold the food economy of today into the market pattern of another era.

The District Court found that Von's stores were located in the southern and western portions of the Los Angeles metropolitan area, and that the Shopping Bag stores were located in the northern and eastern portions. In each of the areas in which Von's and Shopping Bag stores competed directly, there were also at least six other chain stores and several smaller stores competing for the patronage of customers. . . . The actual market share foreclosed by the elimination of Shopping Bag as an independent competitor was thus slightly less than 1 percent of the total grocery store sales in the area. . . .

Moreover, it is clear that there are no substantial barriers to market entry. . . .

In your judgment, should this merger have been allowed—under Section 7 of the Clayton Act? Was forbidding the merger in the public interest, whatever you think about its legality?

The Military-Industrial Complex: A Case Study

CHAPTER PREVIEW

CHAPTER TWENTY-SEVEN

Over the past decade, criticism of a "military-industrial complex" has mounted. Analysis of these criticisms can provide an interesting case study of one set of government–business relationships that many radicals, and some not so radical, believe demonstrates the excessive power of big business and the way it connives with a powerful military bureaucracy to dominate national policy.

WHAT IS IT?

"The military-industrial complex" means different things to different people. To radical critics of the American system, it means a pervasive conspiracy of big business, defense contractors, the Pentagon, and "bought" congressmen, to maintain military domination of society, to swell arms makers' profits at the expense of the working poor, and to promote American imperialism abroad.

Among moderates, President Eisenhower's valedictory statement is widely quoted:

> This conjunction of an immense military establishment and a large arms industry is new in the American experience. . . . In the councils of government we must guard against the acquisition of unwarranted influence, whether sought or unsought, by the military-industrial complex.

Two other influential statements can help define the problem. Senator George McGovern, a leading critic of the military-industrial complex, writes:

> It includes all groups and individuals that have an interest in more arms spending. Defense contractors press for more business. Communities in which they exist or where defense installations are located seek to preserve and expand the local economic stimulus of arms dollars. Workers want job security. The scientists and technicians who work in the research phases have a built-in interest in seeing their work bear fruit. Politicians list, among their accomplishments, their successes in bringing military business to their districts. The military establishment headquartered in the Pentagon—in economic terms a bigger enterprise than all but seven other *countries* in the world—is at the center . . . . Trade and professional military organizations keep their members informed about arguments for new weapons.[1]

Professor Galbraith, whose *The New Industrial State* has been influential in challenging the role of the large corporation in modern society, has spelled out his picture of the "military-industrial complex" at some length:

> It is an organization or a complex of organizations and not a conspiracy . . . . In the conspiratorial view, the military power is a collation of generals and conniving industrialists. The goal is mutual enrichment; they arrange elaborately to feather each others' nests. The industrialists are the *deus ex machina*; their agents make their way around Washington arranging the payoff . . . .
>
> There is some enrichment and some graft. Insiders do well . . . . Nonetheless, the notion of a conspiracy to enrich the corrupt is gravely damaging to an understanding of military power . . . .
>
> The reality is far less dramatic and far more difficult of solution. The reality is a complex of organizations pursuing their sometimes diverse but generally common goals. The participants in these organizations are mostly honest men . . . . They live on their military pay or their salaries as engineers, scientists, or managers, or their pay and profits as executives, and would not dream of offering or accepting a bribe . . . .
>
> The men who comprise these organizations call each other on the phone, meet at committee hearings, serve together on teams of task forces, work in neighboring offices in Washington or San Diego . . . . The problem is not conspiracy or corruption, but unchecked rule. And being unchecked, this rule reflects not the national need but the bureaucratic need—not what is best for the United States, but what the Air Force, Army, Navy, General Dynamics, North American Rockwell, Gruman Aircraft, State Department representatives, intelligence officers, and Mendel Rivers and Richard Russell believe to be best.[2]

But lastly, many other observers believe the military-industrial complex is a fantasy of the alarmists. No one denies that a great deal of money is spent on arms, but the leap from that fact to the proposition that the military-industrial complex dominates our lives, or even the military budget, seems to them a large leap indeed.

THE FACTS

What are some of the major facts on the link between the military budget and America's corporate structure?

During the late 1960s, peak years for military spending—the total defense budget ran between $70 billion and $80 billion, perhaps 8–10 percent of the total GNP. In fiscal 1968, a typical peak spending year, defense contracts let by the Department of Defense (D.O.D.) totaled $39 billion. Of this total, the largest one-hundred companies in the United States and their subsidiaries received about two-thirds, or $27 billion—roughly 10 percent of their total 1968 sales.

Table 27–1 provides a more detailed picture. Two big companies (General Dynamics and Lockheed) depended heavily (over 80 percent) on D.O.D. contracts. United Aircraft is the only other with D.O.D. contracts exceeding 50 percent of sales. Only General Electric, of the real

[1] *Christian Science Monitor,* July 12, 1969.

[2] J.K. Galbraith, *How To Control the Military* (New York: Signet Books, 1969), pp. 23–31.

TABLE 27–1
Defense Contracts[a]

COMPANY	(IN BILLIONS)	PERCENT OF TOTAL CONTRACTS	PERCENT OF COMPANY SALES
Total D.O.D. Contracts	$38.8	100.0	–
Top 100 Companies	26.1	67.4%	10.0%
1. General Dynamics	2.2	5.8	84.3
2. Lockheed Aircraft	1.9	4.8	86.2
3. General Electric	1.5	3.8	17.7
4. United Aircraft	1.3	3.4	54.1
5. McDonnell-Douglas	1.1	2.8	30.5
6. AT&T	.8	2.0	5.4
7. Boeing	.8	2.0	20.3
8. Ling-Temco-Vought	.8	2.0	27.4
9. North American Rockwell	.7	1.7	24.9
10. General Motors	.6	1.6	2.7
15. Raytheon	.5	1.2	37.5
20. Honeywell	.4	.9	28.6
25. Standard Oil (New Jersey)	.3	.7	1.9
30. IBM	.2	.6	3.1

[a]Contracts let by D.O.D. in fiscal year 1968. Company sales data are for calendar year 1968.
Source: *Congressional Quarterly*, November 1968, and *Fortune*, August 1969.

corporate giants, appeared near the top of this list, with D.O.D. contracts totaling 18 percent of sales. The other two giants on the top ten list are AT&T (with D.O.D. contracts equal to 5 percent of sales) and General Motors (with D.O.D. contracts equal to 3 percent of sales). Standard Oil (New Jersey) was twenty-fifth on the list with $300 million in contracts, but this represented less than 2 percent of sales. IBM was thirtieth, with $200 million in contracts that accounted for only 3 percent of sales.

The top ten companies on this list are certainly not industrial pygmies; however, they do not include most of the real giants (by size) of American industry. Medium-sized corporations receive the largest share of Defense Department orders, and they depend most heavily on D.O.D. business. Without military business, their sales would slip heavily. But the widespread notion that the biggest American corporations depend primarily on military contracts for their business and profits is clearly incorrect. The top ten corporations in the United States, by size, depend on military contracts for less than 5 percent of their sales.[3]

Where was the work actually done on military contracts? Prime contractors subcontract a large portion of the work on their projects. It has been estimated that between 20,000 and 40,000 different U.S. firms are involved to some extent in the production of military-contract items. Defense Department business is very important to the American industrial scene. But perspective is needed too. Military business does not dominate the business of large or small companies to the extent often claimed by critics of the military-industrial establishment.

[3]Addition of the space contracts (NASA) would increase the total volume by 12 percent and would change somewhat the rank ordering of the big companies; but it would not significantly change the overall picture presented in Table 27–1.

CONSEQUENCES

Clearly a lot of companies have enough military business to make it of real concern to them, though only a handful sell predominantly to the military. It is not surprising that these companies, their communities, the people who work for them, and their congressmen try to increase the economic benefits they gain from D.O.D. business. And their combined political-economic interactions with the military clearly give them leverage on the size and composition of the military budget. What are the main consequences?

1. The military-industrial complex probably increases the allocation of resources to the military budget, away from civilian use. The political process is an imperfect mechanism for allocating resources most efficiently to supplying public wants. Pressure groups play a significant role in congressional and administration budget decisions.

It is far from clear how important these pressures are in explaining the total military budget. Hardly anyone believes that the military-industrial complex has no influence in maintaining a large military establishment. But quite aside from any military-industrial complex, the American people have long been willing to allocate vast sums of money to national defense; the votes in Congress have seldom been close on huge defense budgets, in times of war or peace. National defense is one public good where we have no reasonable way of comparing what the private marketplace would do to meet the same social needs. We shall look in more detail at the problem of achieving the optimal level of resources to producing such "public goods" in Part Five.

2. Critics argue that profits are excessive on military contracts. Measurement of profits and their relationship to capital investment is a complex issue. A variety of studies have been conducted; some find profits "excessive," others "inadequate." Professor Murray Weidenbaum of Washington University conducted a widely noted study of the mid-1960s that showed that profits as percent of sales were only about half as large on military contracts as on nonmilitary business, but that profits as a percent of the owners' investment were larger on defense than on nonmilitary contracts. This difference results from the fact that the government provides part of the working capital and plant for many military contractors, so that the actual private investment was smaller relative to final sales than in many nonmilitary businesses.[4]

A larger study, breaking down the profits of different companies between their defense and nondefense business, is reported in Figure 27–1, covering the ten years from 1958 to 68. Profits as a percent of sales on military contracts were consistently only about half as high as those on nonmilitary business. Profits on military and

[4]M.L. Weidenbaum, *The Modern Public Sector* (New York: Basic Books, Inc., 1969), p. 56.

Figure 27–1

Defense profits as a percentage of sales were consistently only about half those on nondefense business during the 1960s. As a percentage of owners' equity capital invested, defense and nondefense profits have varied; recently those on defense business have been substantially lower. (Source: Fortune, August 1969.)

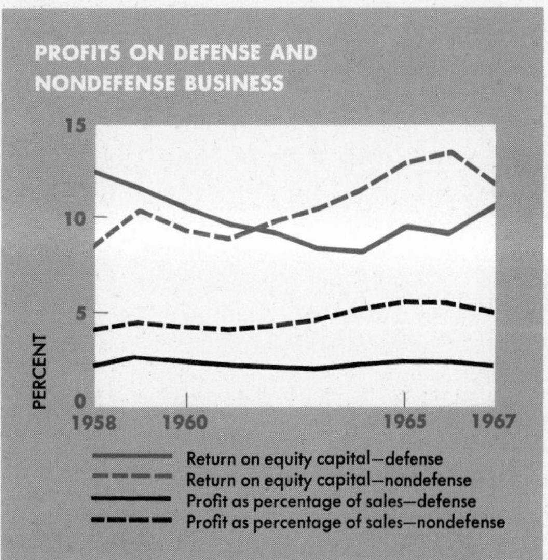

civilian business as a percent of private equity capital invested varied substantially over the decade. On the average they were not far apart, but from 1961 to 68 profits as a percent of owners' investment were appreciably lower on defense than on general manufacturing business.

Substantially the same conclusions were reached by the government's General Accounting Office for D.O.D. contracts during the four years ending in 1970. Profits before taxes were 4.3 percent of sales on defense contracts, compared to 9.9 percent on nondefense business by the same corporations. Profits as a percent of stockholders own investments were substantially identical on defense and nondefense business—about 22 percent before taxes on both.[5]

Private investors in the stock market clearly consider military less attractive than civilian business. The market places relatively low values on the shares of the primary military suppliers, despite their good earnings on major contracts; that is, price-earnings ratios on D.O.D.-oriented companies are substantially lower than for civilian-oriented companies. Defense is often a feast-or-famine business for individual companies. In the eyes of investors, the returns on military contracts are not high enough to make the major defense-oriented companies attractive investments compared to civilian companies.

3. Those who have worked most closely with military spending, both in the government and outside, agree that the huge volume of D.O.D. expenditures reflects primarily the huge military commitments the United States has undertaken, more than inefficient use of federal dollars in buying national defense. Repeated congressional investigations have turned up waste in military spending, and this needs to be prevented. But when the "wasteful" items are totaled up, they still amount to only a small share of the total military budget. The painful fact is that if we want the huge military establishment we now have, it is going to cost a fantastically large amount. No doubt substantial further savings can be made, and billions of dollars of cost overruns on military contracts have periodically shocked congressmen and the general public. More modern management methods beginning in the 1960s have improved efficiency substantially. But missile systems, modern aircraft, and the maintenance of a large U.S. armed force cost a huge amount, no matter how efficiently defense procurement is carried out. It is important to remember, moreover, that well under 50 percent of the total military budget goes into "hardware," so that savings vis-à-vis the "industrial complex" can operate on only a fraction of the total military budget.[6]

[5] General Accounting Office release on Defense Industry Profit Study, March 17, 1971 (release B-159896).

ECONOMICS AND POLITICS

Clearly, national defense is a "public good." The optimal amount of national defense certainly must be set through the political process, not through the marketplace. The central economic issue is whether the political process allocates the right amount of productive resources to military activity (as judged by the true desires of the people) and uses those resources efficiently. Nowhere is the interlinkage between economic and political processes more apparent.

Two separable issues are involved in the allocation of economic resources to defense. First, how much national defense do we "need"—that is, are we willing to pay for? Second, given that amount of national defense, are we producing it with the smallest possible use of productive resources, that is, most efficiently? Economic analysis can help to answer both questions. Comments by three distinguished economists throw light on these interlinked issues.

(1) Charles Schultze of The Brookings Institution, Director of the Budget for President Johnson, writes:

[6] Beyond these economic issues, it is a plausible inference that pressures by the military-industrial complex to maintain or increase military spending contribute to the long-run likelihood of war. On the other hand, some argue that a strong U.S. defense is the best deterrent to war in the future. This is clearly a question that the economist, as such, has no special ability to answer.

> The uniformed armed services and large defense contracts clearly exist. . . . Yet I do not believe that the "problem" of military budgets is primarily attributable to the complex. If defense contractors were always as disinterested in enlarging sales as are local transit magnates, if retired military officers all went to selling soap and TV sets instead of missiles, if the Washington offices of defense contractors were all moved to the West Coast, if all this happened and nothing else, then I do not believe that the military budget would be sharply lower than it now is. Primarily we have large military budgets because the American people, in the cold-war environment of the 1950s and 1960s, have pretty much been willing to buy anything carrying the label "National Security Necessity."[7]

(2) Weidenbaum suggests that the close and continuing relationship between the Department of Defense and its major suppliers is resulting in a convergence between them, which is blurring the distinction between public and private activities in that portion of the economy. Government participation in private-business decision making is great: D.O.D. virtually determines the choice of products a defense firm produces, strongly influences the source of capital funds that it uses, and closely supervises the firm's internal operations. Weidenbaum argues that this attempt to peer closely over the shoulders of defense contractors every step of the way is likely to cost the taxpayers more, not less, in the end. Elaborate procurement procedures regulate the awarding of defense contracts. The D.O.D. reviews, and may veto, company decisions as to which activities to perform directly and which to subcontract, which firms to use as subcontractors, which products to buy domestically rather than to import, what wage rates to pay, how much overtime work to authorize.

Weidenbaum concludes that contracting processes that would give contractors stronger economic incentives and the freedom to reduce costs would lead to more efficient production on these contracts. Profit is a powerful incentive. The great fear that the government may be fleeced on defense contracts has probably increased the average cost of the items procured. He concludes:

> In some ways, the federal government is taking on the traditional role of the private entrepreneur, while the companies are behaving less like other corporations and more like government agencies or arsenals. Certainly, the detailed day-to-day government surveillance of internal company operations which is now so characteristic in the military market is a poor precedent to follow in establishing the future roles of industry and government in the public sector areas, both military and civilian.[8]

(3) Galbraith sees the military-industrial complex as a part of the general domination of economic-political life by the modern corporation and the technostructure of which it is a central part. His "solution" is essentially political.

> The primary goal is to get the military power under firm political control. This means electing a president on this issue next time. . . . The Armed Services and Appropriations committees of the House and Senate must obviously be the object of special effort. . . . The goal of the campaign is not to make the military power more efficient or more righteously honest. It is to get it under control. These are very different objectives. The first seeks out excessive profits, poor technical performance, favoritism, delay, or the other abuses of power. The second is concerned with the power itself and the spending on which that power depends.[9]

Galbraith proposes a special body of highly qualified scientists and citizens, a "military audit commission," to oversee the military establishment. The military-industrial complex is a reflection of the increased bureaucratization of modern society, based as it is on vast economic and technological complexities in our system.

[7] C.L. Schultze, "Reexamining the Military Budget," *The Public Interest,* Winter 1970, pp. 20–21. For a more detailed analysis, see Schultze et al, *Setting National Priorities: The 1973 Budget* (Washington, D.C.: The Brookings Institution, 1972), pp. 24–174.

[8] M.L. Weidenbaum, "The Military-Industrial Complex," *Vital Speeches,* June 15, 1969, pp. 523–28.

[9] J.K. Galbraith, *How To Control the Military,* pp. 72–75.

We need to substitute new national priorities, he argues, and to override the natural biases of the military-industrial complex.

CONCLUSION

What does all this add up to? Economics tells us that more resources should be allocated where the marginal return is higher than the marginal cost. American political processes are by no means a surefire way of achieving this allocation. The military-industrial complex no doubt exerts significant influence in increasing the flow of resources into the military establishment. But the biggest questions about defense spending have less to do with the much-discussed military-industrial complex than with the need for a hard reappraisal of U.S. strategic assumptions and potential enemy strength. If the military-industrial complex is indeed a threat to the U.S. economy, it is mainly because it exercises inordinate influence through the political process and thereby helps to overallocate resources to defense. More on this in Part Five.

Economic analysis suggests, too, that detailed government bureaucratic oversight of military spending may well be counterproductive. The record of competition in the private marketplace has been impressive over the years in driving down costs and providing efficient production. Substitution of economic incentive plans in government contracting, rather than increasingly detailed government surveillance of operations, is likely to provide more defense output for the dollar. The convergence of D.O.D. and corporate roles that Weidenbaum stresses raises serious problems. The basic goal for the nation is the provision of needed national defense with a minimum use of economic resources, not the minimization of defense contractors' profits.

Lastly, the Lockheed case at the end of this chapter illustrates how intricately the government can become enmeshed with private suppliers under present arrangements. But the military-industrial complex doesn't always win out. After years of controversy and enormous pressure from aerospace lobbyists, voters, workers, stockholders, and congressmen, Congress finally voted down in 1971 further government money for a U.S. supersonic transport.

REVIEW

For Analysis and Discussion

1. Is there a military-industrial complex? If your answer is yes, define precisely what you understand by it.
2. What specifically should we do about the military-industrial complex, if you believe there is one?
3. Is there an education–Department of Health, Education, and Welfare complex? A medical care–National Institutes of Health complex? How do these interest groups inside and outside government compare with the military-industrial complex?
4. How should we decide how much to spend each year on national defense and who should get the defense contracts? How about education? How about medical care and research?
5. Suppose a company like Lockheed or General Dynamics is faced with failure if government cuts its military-space spending next year. What, if any, responsibility does the government have to the workers and stockholders involved? Should it keep the company in existence to meet future military-space needs?

The Lockheed Aircraft Corporation

Over the past decade, Lockheed Aircraft Corporation has been the nation's largest defense contractor, with annual sales averaging over $2 billion of which nearly 90 percent were military. The C-5A (the world's largest airplane), the Cheyenne helicopter, and the Polaris and the Poseidon missiles accounted for a large part of the total. In 1964, Lockheed's bid of $1.8 billion won the C-5A airframe contract, with delivery scheduled to begin in 1970. By 1969, the C-5A had become a major national issue. Although it exceeded performance specifications, costs had soared to $4 billion (including about $1.5 billion of unforeseen inflation), and Lockheed calculated it had already lost $400 million on the contract, even after passing on many of the increased costs to the government. (This 35 percent cost overrun, after allowing for inflation, was less than those on numerous other developmental military contracts.)

Such huge defense contracts are complex and many of the figures were disputed, but in 1969 Lockheed informed the government that it could proceed only with a revised contract that would at least hold losses to about that level; otherwise it faced bankruptcy. After much hard bargaining and numerous Congressional inquiries, a settlement was reached that brought Lockheed's loss (before taxes) on the C-5A and other disputed contracts to $480 million, but permitted Lockheed to proceed with the D.O.D. absorbing the further additional costs. Lockheed's average profit on all sales for the decade was about 2 percent, with losses totalling over $100 million in 1969–70. Between 1966 and 1970, the price of Lockheed stock fell from 70 to 7.

At the same time Lockheed was trying to lessen its reliance on military business by developing and selling a new commercial transport, the Tristar or L-1011, and appeared to be on the way to a profitable venture if it could get over its financial crisis arising from heavy military losses. It finally, in 1970, obtained a $400 million loan from twenty-six large banks. But immediately thereafter, without notice, Britain's Rolls Royce Ltd., supplier of the engines for the L-1011, went bankrupt and announced it could not furnish engines without financial advances and large price increases.

Facing this crisis, Lockheed could obtain no further loans from its banks, and potential buyers of the L-1011 understandably began to talk of switching their orders to other companies. Lockheed informed the D.O.D. and other government agencies of its plight. If it closed down completely, vast military projects under way would be endangered and the D.O.D.'s largest supplier would vanish. More than 30,000 workers would lose their jobs in the already-depressed aerospace industry. Unemployment was 6 percent nationally, and much higher in aerospace-dominated areas, especially in California. Hundreds of subcontractors would be endangered. Leading banks might have to absorb huge losses. Lockheed urged a government guarantee on $250 billion of additional loans to tide it over, because the banks would lend more only with a firm government guarantee.

After vitriolic debates in and out of Congress, the Nixon Administration recommended and Congress approved the quarter-billion-dollar loan guarantee—with provisoes for complete government surveillance of Lockheed's affairs while the loan was outstanding and priority for the government-guaranteed loan over other creditors.

If you had been a senator in 1971, would you have voted for or against the Lockheed loan guarantee?

APPENDIX TO PART THREE

Current Research

As with the Appendix to Part Two, the purpose here is to suggest a sample of recent research in economics that may be of interest to students who want to know more of what economists do, and especially of the excitement that goes with research—the search for new knowledge and new understanding. Here again the items listed are merely a sample. They are not necessarily the best, nor even a cross section, of current research in the area. They are chosen because I hope some of them may be intriguing to you and may make you want to look further. They vary widely in approach, substance, and difficulty.

The most controversial and lively study of modern business is J.K. Galbraith's best-selling *The New Industrial State* (New York: Houghton Mifflin Company, 1967). For equally lively antidotes, see the review of Galbraith's book in *Fortune,* July 1967 (pp. 90ff.) and the amusing but penetrating exchange on the analysis by R. Solow, R. Maris, and Galbraith in *The Public Interest,* Fall 1967 and Spring 1968. In 1973, Galbraith published an equally controversial follow-up book, *Economics and the Public Purpose* (Houghton Mifflin Co.), which argues that the federal government should buy out owners of the big industrial corporations.

For different, broad looks at the issues involved, try Edward Mason's "Introduction" to his *The Corporation in Modern Society* (Cambridge: Harvard University Press, 1959); Chapter 8 of Milton Friedman's *Capitalism and Freedom* (University of Chicago Press, 1962); and Neil Jacoby, *Corporate Power and Social Responsibility* (New York: The Macmillan Company, 1973).

Industry and Market Studies. You can find a research study on just about every major industry. Brief studies of all the major industries, with a bibliography on each, are collected in Walter Adams, ed., *The Structure of American Industry* (Macmillan, 1971). Two more extended analyses are L.J. White's *The Automobile Industry Since 1945* (Harvard University Press, 1972), and M.A. Adelman's *A&P: A Study in Price-Cost Behavior and Public Policy* (Harvard University Press, 1959). For a very different industry (music, the theatre, and ballet), see W. Baumol and W. Bowen, *Performing Arts—The Economic Dilemma* (Twentieth Century Fund, 1966). Broader coverage is given in *Pricing in Big Business: A Case Approach,* by A.D. Kaplan, J. Dirlam, and R. Lanzilotti (The Brookings Institution, 1958); and Kaplan's *Big Enterprise in a Competitive System* (The Brookings Institution, 1964) provides a further readable overview.

Antitrust Policy and Mergers. A sample of leading economists' analyses of antitrust policy is provided by J.F. Weston and S. Peltzman, eds., *Public Policy Toward Mergers* (Pacific Palisades, Calif.: Goodyear Publishing Co., Inc., 1969); and by Edwin Mansfield, ed., *Monopoly Power and Economic Performance* (New York: W.W. Norton & Company, Inc., 1968). For more detailed analyses of the conglomerate merger problem, which is a central issue of modern antitrust policy, see *Economic Report on Corporate Mergers,* by the Staff of the Federal Trade Commission (1969), which is generally antimerger; J.S. McGee's *In Defense of Industrial Concentration* (New York: Praeger Publishers, Inc., 1971); and *Conglomerate Merger Performance: An Empirical Analysis of Nine Corporations,* a further report by the FTC Staff, (November 1972), which finds that the major conglomerate mergers of recent years have had little or no anticompetitive effects.

Public utilities and other "natural monopolies" are customarily governed by government regulatory commissions. Paul MacAvoy's *The Crisis of the Regulatory Commissions* (W.W. Norton, 1970) collects recent research studies and policy statements on this approach to market regulation. At the competition end of the spectrum, Charles Schultze analyzes *The Distribution of Farm Subsidies: Who Gets the Benefits?* (The Brookings Institution, 1971) when a different approach is taken to markets that don't function satisfactorily on their own.

Economic Theory and Human Behavior. You can always start a lively dispute in economics by asking how well generally accepted economic theory corresponds to actual human behavior. One persistent question is how closely consumer spending actually mirrors consumers' free choices, and how well the market responds, therefore, to consumers' desires. See the symposium on "The Doctrine of Consumer Sovereignty," especially the paper by Tibor Scitovsky, (*American Economic Review,* May 1962). Then look at "The Costs of Automobile Model Changes Since 1949," by F. Fisher, Z. Griliches, and C. Kaysen, (*Journal of Political Economy,* April 1962). On the behavior of businessmen, see R.A. Gordon's classic *Business Leadership in the Large Corporation* (University of California Press, 1966). James Earley comes to the defense of marginalism in "Marginal Policies of 'Excellently Managed' Companies" (*American Economic Review,* March 1956). J. Monsen and others argue in "The Effect of Separation of Ownership and Control," (*Quarterly Journal of Economics,* August 1968), that owner-managers make larger profits than comparable hired managers.

INCOMES, ECONOMIC POWER, AND PUBLIC POLICY

PART FOUR

Incomes: The Pricing of Productive Services

CHAPTER PREVIEW

CHAPTER TWENTY-EIGHT

One of the hottest issues in economics has long been the distribution of the national income—between wages and profits, rich and poor, farmer and industrial worker, the "haves" and the "have-nots." Governments have risen and fallen on the struggle for income shares. The revolutionary doctrines of Karl Marx centered around the "exploitation of the worker" by the "rich and greedy capitalist." In a different setting, this same struggle over income shares is the issue when the United Steelworkers fight the steel companies for wage increases. It is the issue behind the race riots in the cities, as well as when Congress votes government support for "parity prices" on farm products. History tells a recurrent story of the "have-nots" fighting for more and the "haves" struggling to protect and to increase their share.

Thoughtful observers of the private-enterprise economy point out that we're all in the same boat. If everyone pulls together—labor, capital, management—total output will grow and everyone can have more. No one who understands the basic interdependence inherent in the modern economy would deny this. There is an enormous community of interest in making the private-enterprise economy work effectively, and the spectacular growth of U.S. total output, with rising income for every group, is the great success story of economic history.

But part and parcel of that community of interest is a basic conflict, rooted deep in our ethics and traditions of self-interest and competition. This is the struggle of each individual to get more for himself and his family. It is the struggle over who gets how much of the economic pie—at the level of the individual worker, his union, and his boss, and at the level of national policy. However rich the nation is, we're all interested in our own shares—relative and absolute. Nothing is gained by refusing to face this fact.

This chapter has two major sections. First, the facts—who gets how much income in the United States today? Second, the theory of income distribution—why do people receive the incomes they do? Then the following chapters apply this theory to explaining wages and salaries, rents and interest, and profits, with a close look at the problems of poverty and inequality.

WHO GETS HOW MUCH?

The Income Revolution

American incomes have risen persistently and rapidly for over two centuries, and nearly every group has participated. Our standard of living is the highest in the world.

Table 28–1 summarizes the facts since World War II. Total real national income (that is, the sum of all incomes adjusted to eliminate rises due only to higher prices) has nearly tripled—from $375 billion to $930 billion (in 1972 prices). In 1947, median family income was about $5,700 in 1972 dollars; in 1972, it was $11,100.[1] In 1972, 56 percent of all families earned over $10,000, compared to only 15 percent twenty-five years earlier. The other big element of the U.S. income revolution was the rise of the huge middle class. In 1972, about 60 percent of all families received incomes between $7,000 and $20,000. But the extremes are interesting, too, as Table 28–2 will show.

Figure 28–1 poses an interesting question about the distribution of incomes in America. The regular, bell-shaped curve shows what statisticians call a "normal" distribution. Intelligence, physical traits, and many other phenomena seem to approximate closely this type of normal distribution, when large numbers are considered. More people are at the midpoint of the curve than at any other level, and those above and below the average shade off about equally either way.

[1]The median is the figure that divides the total number of families in half. Thus, in 1972 half of all families received more than $11,100, half less.

TABLE 28–1
Family Incomes in 1947 and 1972

ANNUAL INCOME (In 1972 dollars)	PERCENT OF FAMILIES 1947	PERCENT OF FAMILIES 1972
Under $3,000	24	7
3,000–5,000	25	9
5,000–10,000	36	28
Over $10,000	15	56
Median family income	$5,700	$11,100
Total income—all families	$375 billion	$930 billion

Source: U.S. Census Bureau. Preliminary estimates for 1972.

TABLE 28–2
Family Income Shares, 1929–70

	PERCENT OF TOTAL INCOME RECEIVED			
	1929	1950	1960	1970
Bottom fifth	3.5	4.5	4.8	5.8
Second fifth	9.0	12.0	11.7	12.5
Middle fifth	13.8	17.4	17.4	17.8
Fourth fifth	19.3	23.5	23.6	23.4
Top fifth	54.4	42.6	42.6	40.5
All families	100.0	100.0	100.0	100.0
Top 5 percent	30.0	17.0	16.8	14.5

Source: U.S. Census Bureau.

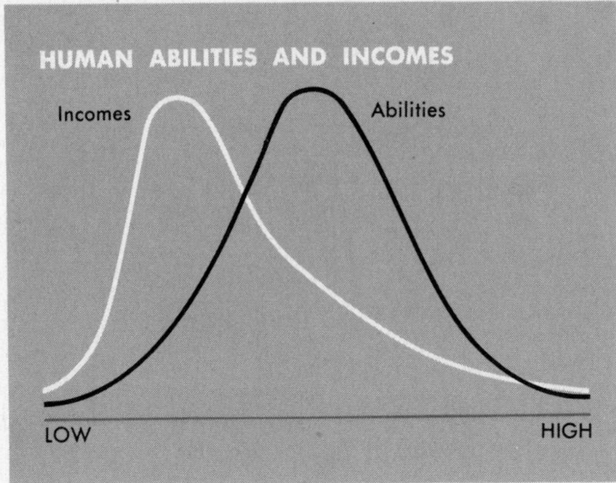

Figure 28–1

Ability and most other human characteristics seem to be "normally" distributed through the population, as shown by the black curve. Incomes are much more unequally distributed. Why?

We might assume that general ability is normally distributed among the total population. But incomes received, shown by the white line, are "skewed." That is, there are many more relatively poor than rich individuals. These account for the big hump in the curve toward the lower-income end of the scale. There are a few very rich, who give the curve a long "tail" out to the right. Why are incomes less "normally" distributed than human abilities?

Is income becoming more or less equally distributed? Since the 1920s, more equally. (Before that, the data are highly unreliable, although apparently the same conclusion would apply.) The facts are shown in Table 28–2.

Another way of measuring changes in income distribution is shown by the "Lorenz curve" in Figure 28–2. The income of all families is cumulated along the horizontal axis, beginning with the lowest-income family; the percentage of total income received by those families is cumulated along the vertical axis. For example, in 1929, the bottom 40 percent of all families received about 12 percent of the total national income, the lowest 90 percent received about 60 percent. By comparison, in 1972, the bottom 40 percent of families received about 18 percent, and the bottom 90 percent received about 75 percent.

Obviously, if all family incomes were equal, the points plotted would all fall on the diagonal. That is, the lowest 10 percent would receive 10 percent of the total income, and so on up the

Figure 28–2

Incomes are somewhat more equally distributed now than in 1929 or 1935–36. The more bowed the curve is, the less equal the distribution of income was in that year. (Source: U.S. Census Bureau.)

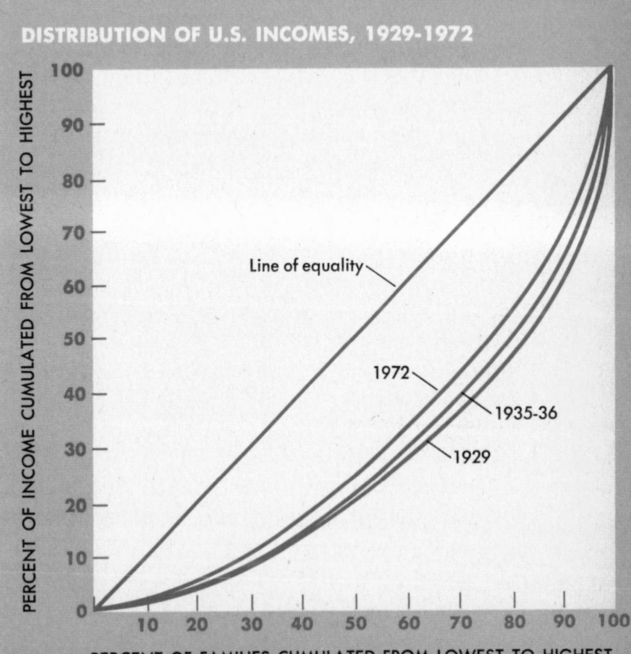

line. Thus, the more bowed out the Lorenz curve is, the *more unequal* the distribution of income is; the nearer it is to the diagonal, the *more equally* incomes are distributed.

Figure 28–2 thus shows that incomes are somewhat more equally distributed now than either in 1929 (the peak of the boom) or in 1935–36, the Great Depression years. It also shows that the distribution has changed only moderately over that tumultuous period.

One last historical observation: Are the very rich—the millionaires—being squeezed out by high-income- and inheritance-tax rates? Apparently not. Invested capital continues to be the main source of most very high incomes. In 1962 (the last reliable study), the bottom 80 percent of all families held only 22 percent of the wealth. In 1970, there were some 50,000 millionaires in the nation in terms of wealth; compared to only a few hundred in the 1920s; and in 1970, about 1,000 people had annual incomes exceeding $1 million. But the share of total wealth held by the top 1 percent of all families was estimated at under 30 percent in the 1960s, down from 36 percent in 1929.

TABLE 28–3
Median Incomes in Different Occupations, 1971[a]

Occupation	Median income
Physicians and surgeons	$40,500
Dentists	22,500
Lawyers	22,200
Engineers	16,700
Managers and proprietors	11,900
Accountants	11,400
Foremen	11,200
Teachers—grade and high school	9,900
Manufacturing operatives	8,100
Secretaries	6,800
Unskilled workers—nonfarm	6,700
Unskilled workers—farm	3,600

[a]Some figures are averages of very diverse groups (for example, managers and proprietors) and should be viewed as only rough approximations. Figures do not include "fringe benefits." Incomes of part-time workers are typically much lower in the same occupations.

Source: Preliminary estimates based on U.S. Census Bureau and Department of Labor data; median incomes for full-time workers.

Occupational and Educational Differences

What jobs provide the best incomes? Table 28–3 gives part of the answer. It shows median incomes for a sample of occupations in 1971.

The table speaks for itself, but there are some surprises. Physicians, surgeons, lawyers, and other highly trained professionals top the list. The median figures for managers and proprietors don't look like the huge salaries you've heard about for corporation presidents. Answer: there are some huge salaries, but many middle-level managers earn lots less. Nor does the figure for self-employed proprietors look as if many people in business for themselves get rich quick; some succeed, many don't. At the bottom of the list, it's clear that unskilled laborers in industry or agriculture don't do very well.

Table 28–4 presents a more detailed breakdown for a sample of occupations. The figures are estimates of lifetime (age eighteen to sixty-

TABLE 28–4
Estimated Lifetime Earnings in Different Occupations

Occupation	Lifetime earnings
Physicians and surgeons	$983,000
Lawyers	848,000
Managers and proprietors	810,000
Dentists	805,000
Economists	596,000
Aeronautical engineers	540,000
Accountants	428,000
High-school teachers	360,000
Electricians	343,000
Plumbers	323,000
TV mechanics	250,000
Clergymen	239,000

Source: Herman Miller, *Rich Man, Poor Man* (New York: Thomas Crowell, 1964). Adjusted to 1972 prices. More recent data would raise the relative position of physicians substantially.

four) earnings in 1972 dollars, based on Census Bureau data for the mid-1960s. Note the high correlation between the amount of education and probable lifetime earnings, even when the long years of no-income schooling for professionals are figured in. The education figures show up directly, apart from the occupational break. In 1972, for example, the median income for all heads of families with an eighth-grade education or less was $6,300. That for college-educated family heads was $18,300, and the figure rises steadily with the number of years of schooling.

Regional income differences also reflect these occupational and educational facts. The high incomes are concentrated in urban areas, where high-paying occupations are centered. Incomes are generally low in the South, especially in rural areas. Per capita incomes in the Deep South are still around the New York levels of a half century ago. But the South is pulling up. New England, the traditional high-income area, is slipping relatively. And the West Coast is rising rapidly.

Women and Minority Groups

The average income of working women is less than two-thirds that of working men. In 1972, the median income for men working full time was $10,500, for women, $6,100. Women generally get paid less than men do for similar jobs. But more than that the difference reflects the heavy concentration of women in low-paying jobs—especially clerical and service work, and unskilled labor. Women are now increasingly showing up in higher-paid occupations—the professions, skilled labor, and middle management. But there are still relatively few in peak-income jobs.

Similar income differentials prevail for minority groups, of which blacks are the largest. The median black family income in 1972 was only $6,900, compared to $11,500 for white families. Only 14 percent of all black families had incomes over $15,000, compared to 32 percent for whites. Conversely, 14 percent of all black families had incomes under $3,000, while only 4 percent of whites had incomes below this figure. Apparently similar or even greater income gaps prevail for other minority groups, such as Spanish-speaking Americans and American Indians, for whom we have less detailed information.

But the income status of minority groups has improved markedly. In 1947 the median black family income was only 51 percent of that for whites; by 1972, it was 60 percent. Much of this rise was related to a massive move of blacks from the South to the North, where higher wages prevail. The overall figures mask dramatic differential movements for men and women. Since 1939, black male full-time earnings rose from 45 to 60 percent of their white counterparts, mainly during the tight labor market of World War II; but black full-time female workers' incomes rose from 38 to 82 percent of their white counterparts over the same period, including a big advance in the 1960s.

Why do all these differences exist and why are they changing? To answer these questions we need a theory of income distribution, to which the last half of this chapter is largely devoted.

WAGES AND PROFITS—FUNCTIONAL SHARES

Most very rich people get a big part of their incomes from invested capital—from interest and profits. Most low- and middle-income families receive almost nothing from such investments, except for the use of the houses some own. Yet the American economy today doesn't look much like Karl Marx's picture of capitalism in its death throes, with the workers poised to seize ownership of the means of production. American labor and management do exchange some violent words, and strikes are sometimes long and bitter. But in the showdown, management and labor get together; production goes on with the worker's rights still intact and the capitalist's control over his investment substantially maintained. When the workers go to the polls, they vote Republican or Democratic, not communist. The radicals who want to destroy the capitalist system have usually been students and other revolutionaries, who have found themselves lined up against management and workers defending the economic system.

But within this framework, labor and management wrestle constantly over the division of the consumer's dollar between wages and profits. Figure 28–3 gives an overall picture of the outcome of this wage-profit bargaining during the last four decades. The left-hand part plots the actual dollar shares of national income that go to wages and salaries, corporate profits, unincorporated business incomes (a mixture of salaries and profits), rents, and interest, all before payment of income taxes. The right-hand portion shows the percentage shares that go to these various groups.

The first lesson comes from the left-hand chart. Everyone's income has grown rapidly, but in a serious depression we're very much all in the same boat—everyone takes a beating. The second lesson, from the right-hand chart, is the surprising general stability in the major income shares, except during big business fluctuations. The wage and salary share persistently hovered in the 60–70 percent range, with a gradual upward trend. Partly, the rising wage share reflects the steady population shift from farms to urban jobs, but beyond this there has apparently been some tendency for the profit-plus-interest share to be squeezed.

A rather different picture of the outcome of the labor-capital struggle for income shares is given if we compare the return *per unit* of labor and capital used in the economy. Real wages per hour are four times as high as they were in 1900, while the real long-term interest rate (a crude measure of the return per dollar of capital invested in the economy) is still about the same. The profit rate appears to be about the same as a half-century ago, or somewhat lower. Looked at this way, it appears that virtually all the fruits of increased output have gone to labor and virtually none to capital.

How are these different ways of looking at the same world to be reconciled? The answer is given in detail in Chapter 43, on economic growth. (1) The total capital stock has grown

Figure 28–3

Everyone's income has grown since 1929, but wages and salaries by far the biggest amount. They have also gradually increased their share of the total. Note that profits vanished in the great depression. (Source: U.S. Department of Commerce.)

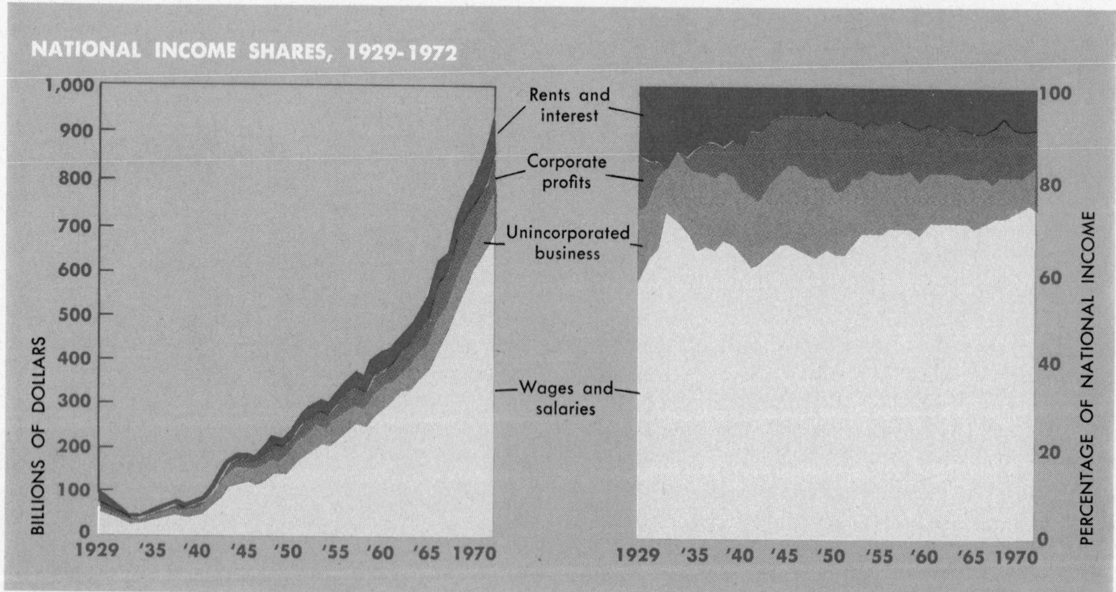

much faster than the labor force. Thus, the law of diminishing returns has acted to diminish the return per unit of capital relative to that per unit of labor (see the appendix to Chapter 19). (2) But improving technology has helped increase total output faster than the combined inputs of labor and capital, so diminishing returns have not reduced the return per unit of

INEQUALITY, OPPORTUNITY, AND UPWARD MOBILITY

Have industrialization, big business, and modern technology increased economic, and social stratification in modern America? Does today's inequality of income and wealth mean that only the children of the rich have a chance to become rich and powerful in their generations?

These answers are complex and the evidence on them is mixed. Clearly the poor face a tough path in trying to rise from poverty. Each year over 70 percent of the poor were poor the year before. Education seems increasingly the requisite for economic and social advancement, especially to society's top positions, and prestige education is still dominantly the property of the middle- and upper-income classes. But it has always been tough to rise from the lower-income classes, and today's concentration of income and wealth is clearly less than it was a century ago. Overall the evidence suggests that economic stratification is less rigid today than it was fifty or a hundred years ago.

A recent *Scientific American* study of the sources of top business executives found that:

> Only 10.5 percent of the current generation of big business executives . . . (are) sons of wealthy families; as recently as 1950 the corresponding figure was 36.1 percent, and at the turn of the century, 45.6 percent. . . . Two thirds of the 1900 generation had fathers who were heads of the same corporations or who were independent businessmen; less than half of the current generation had fathers so placed in American society. On the other hand, less than 10 percent of the 1900 generation had fathers who were employees; by 1964 this percentage had increased to nearly 30 percent.[2]

The post-World War II period brought the greatest increase in the proportion of those from economically poor backgrounds (from 12.1 percent in 1950 to 23.3 percent in 1964) who entered the top echelons of American business; and there was a corresponding decline in the percentage from wealthy families. The replacement of family-owned enterprise by the public corporation, the bureaucratization of American corporate life, the recruitment of management personnel from the ranks of college graduates, and the awarding of higher posts on the basis of a competitive promotion process were all important factors. Because of the spread of higher education to the children of the working classes (almost one-third now attend college), the ladder of bureaucratic success is increasingly open to those from poorer circumstances. Business and professional families are still by far the largest sources of business leaders. Privileged family and class backgrounds continue to be enormous advantages in the quest for corporate success, but training and talent can increasingly make up for their lack.

Other recent sociological studies reach the same conclusion, though with some vigorous dissenters from the communist-socialist wing. But to say that apparently more opportunity now exists for upward mobility than a half century ago is not enough. Particularly, members of minority groups, such as blacks, Spanish-speaking Americans, and American Indians, have made very little progress in reaching top economic positions, even though their incomes have risen relative to whites.

[2]See S.M. Lipset, "Social Mobility and Equal Opportunity," *The Public Interest,* Fall 1972, for a summary and references to a number of studies.

capital, but merely kept it from rising with technological advance. (3) The relatively stable total shares of labor and capital in GNP thus reflect the rapid growth in income per unit of labor, and a correspondingly faster growth in the capital stock than in the labor force, with the two factors just about offsetting each other to keep the total labor and capital shares in GNP roughly unchanged. Figure 43–2 provides the data.

THE THEORY OF INCOME DISTRIBUTION

Why do people receive the incomes they do—some large, some small, some stable, some insecure? The answer is complex, as with most other important issues in economics, and there is still much debate on the finer points. But the core of the answer is summarized in the remainder of this chapter; then it is applied specifically to wages, interest, rent, and profits in the following chapters. You will find that you already have the central analysis from Part Three.

The income you get (leaving aside gifts, social security benefits, and such transfer payments) depends on the productive services you have to sell—your labor and your capital, if you have any. Most people get virtually all their income as wages or salaries, but owners of capital also get income from rent, interest, and profits.

The price of each productive service (for example, the wage of a worker) is set through supply and demand, roughly equal to the marginal productivity of that productive resource—that is, equal to the contribution that that worker makes toward producing what consumers demand. Whenever the price of, say, labor is below its marginal product (what one more worker would add to the firm's salable output), businessmen can increase their profits by hiring more labor. Competition among businesses for workers will bid up the wage rate toward the marginal productivity of that type of labor. Conversely, if the wage rate is more than labor's marginal product, it will pay businessmen to hire fewer workers, and the wage rate will fall. Only when the wage rate just equals labor's marginal product will business firms and the labor market be in equilibrium.

Each person's earned income, therefore, will depend on his marginal productivity and on how much he works, plus the marginal productivity of capital multiplied by the amount of capital he owns. His education and training, his IQ, his family background, how hard he works, his race and sex, the match of his interests with what consumers will buy, and luck—all these and more will determine his wage or salary. Add how wealthy his parents were, how much he saves, his skill in investing or in running a business, and again luck, for his income from capital. Some of these factors are clearly under the individual's own control; others he can't do much about. In the simplest language, he has to have something to sell that consumers (or businesses catering to consumers) want to buy.

"Distribution theory," explaining why different productive resources earn the incomes they do, is thus merely price theory from Part Three, viewed from the reverse side. There we focused on the pricing of final products, like autos; here we focus on the pricing of productive services, like labor and capital used to produce autos. Obviously, when the businessman decides to produce 10,000 autos this week, he is, ipso facto, deciding to hire the labor and to rent or buy the machines he needs to do the job. When we compare this demand with the supply of labor or machines offered, we can determine the prices set for productive services through the same supply-and-demand mechanism as in Part Three. Obviously, the degree of competition or monopoly in the market will affect the outcome for both productive services and final products.

The Supply Side

To determine the price of any productive service, first we need a supply curve, or schedule. Consider the supply of some type of labor in your town, say carpenters, as an example. The supply this month may be highly inelastic—fixed by the number of carpenters there and by their preference to work about forty hours a week. Or the supply may be elastic, if carpenters can readily be drawn in from neighboring areas. Or overtime work may be feasible. All these things together produce a labor-supply curve for the market for the time period under study, probably an upward-sloping supply curve indicating that more labor hours will be supplied at higher than at lower wage rates.

Labor supply conditions vary widely for different jobs, and over different periods of time. The supply of neurosurgeons is highly inelastic in the short run and only moderately elastic in the long run; that of waitresses or store clerks is highly elastic, because their jobs require little training and workers can be drawn quickly from other jobs by higher pay. In general, the elasticity of supply goes up as a longer time is allowed for training, education, and movement of workers from other areas.

The supply of labor for any occupation can be increased by investment in "human capital" through education and training, just as the supply of machinery, factories, and other forms of nonhuman capital can be increased by investment. Thus, as we shall see in Chapter 29, the value of an individual's services over his lifetime will reflect how much investment he has made in himself through education, experience, and the like, to prepare for the jobs he seeks.

The Demand Side[3]

The demand for productive services is primarily a derived demand. The local drugstore hires clerks because customers want to be waited on—not because the druggist wants clerks in the same way that he wants consumer goods and services. Businesses' demands for productive services thus reflect ultimate consumer demands. If consumers want lots of prescriptions filled, the demand for prescription clerks will be strong. But if the customers stay away, the druggist doesn't need many clerks.

How many workers (or other productive resources) will a firm demand at any given wage rate? The familiar marginal-cost-equals-marginal-revenue rule gives the answer. **If it is to maximize profits, the firm will hire additional workers as long as each additional worker adds more to the firm's income (marginal revenue) than he adds to its costs (marginal cost). If the wage of another worker is more than that worker adds to revenue, to hire him would lower the firm's profits. If the wage is less than the worker's marginal product, hiring him will increase profits. Profits will be maximized by hiring additional productive resources until the marginal cost just equals marginal revenue.**

The marginal revenue obtained from hiring productive resources is often called "marginal revenue product," or "marginal value product," to differentiate it from marginal revenue per unit of output as the term was used in Part Three. To understand the determinants of marginal revenue product of any productive resource (and hence business firms' demand for it), we need to separate two components. Additional *physical* output ("marginal physical product") is what the worker adds to total output. But from management's point of view it is the increase in sales dollars that matters most; hence, it is the marginal *revenue* product in which we are most interested, so multiply the marginal physical product by its price. It is the marginal revenue product that the businessman compares with the marginal cost incurred by hiring another worker in deciding how many workers to hire to maximize his profits.[4]

Be sure you understand that this is merely a repetition of the central profit-maximizing propositions from Part Three. There we thought of the firm's planning in terms of units of out-

[3]The appendix to Chapter 19, Physical Production Relationships Underlying Cost Curves, provides a rigorous logical foundation for this section. If you studied that appendix it may be useful to review it before proceeding. The "marginal product" of that appendix is identical with the "marginal physical product" of this chapter.

[4]The existence of monopoly raises some special problems, which will be considered in the next chapter.

put; here the firm plans in terms of units of inputs of productive services used. But the $MC = MR$ to obtain maximum profit rule applies either way, and the equilibrium position is the same either way you go at it.[5]

The Interaction of Supply and Demand

We now have the broad outlines of the market for productive services—a supply curve and a demand curve for each type of productive service in each market area, local or national. Employers will compete for more workers as long as their wage is below their marginal revenue product, but no employer will pay more than labor's marginal revenue product. **Thus, competition will bid wages up to about the level of labor's marginal productivity, and no higher. And so the wage will be set.**

Figure 28–4 pictures a simple supply-and-demand market equilibrium for one type of labor (say electrical engineers) in a local market this year. The supply curve is inelastic; in this period not many more labor hours will be supplied at moderately higher wage rates. The demand curve slopes down for the reasons suggested above. A weekly wage of $200 just clears the market, at 400 engineers per week demanded and supplied. At a higher wage more would be supplied but less demanded; at a lower wage, the reverse.

Give your theory a workout to explore some implications of this analysis. Suppose Figure 28–4 pictured the market for heart surgeons. The total supply is highly inelastic (substantially fixed in amount) in the short run, a bit more elastic to any given community. Now suppose Congress greatly increases appropriations to support research in this area and to finance heart operations for needy patients. What will happen to the incomes of heart surgeons in the short and in the long runs? (Hint: The median income of physicians in 1970 was $41,000, up from $24,000 in 1960; total expenditures on health services rose from $13 billion to about $70 billion over the decade while the number of physicians per 100,000 population remained roughly constant.)

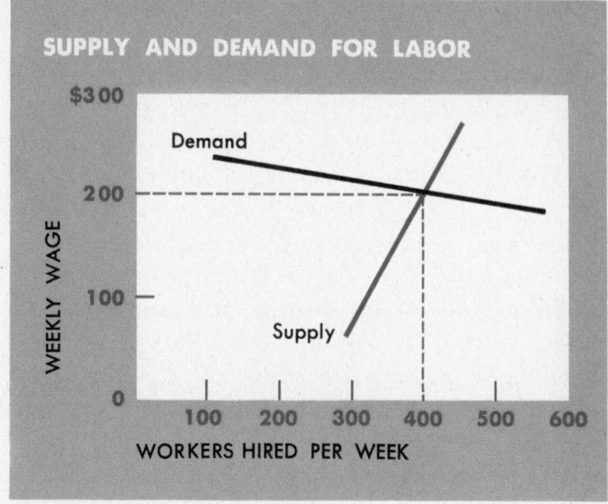

Figure 28–4

Wages, like other prices, are determined by supply and demand forces. Here the equilibrium wage is $200 per week, with 400 workers hired.

THE INTEGRATION OF PRICE AND DISTRIBUTION THEORY

The preceding section emphasized that price theory and distribution theory (Parts Three and Four) are substantially the same. They both look at the pricing process and at the allocation of resources in response to consumer demands.

To see how the total general equilibrium system fits together, go back and reread the section "General Equilibrium of a Competitive Economy" on pages 285–287 in Chapter 21. They are the analytical core of this section as well. The pricing of productive services is part

[5] Although the above statements indicate only how much of a single resource it will pay the business to hire, this approach can readily be generalized to cover all the productive resources the firm hires. It will pay to hire more of *each* resource as long as its marginal cost is less than its marginal revenue product. In equilibrium, therefore, each resource will be hired up to the point where its marginal cost just equals its marginal revenue product, which is the same as saying that marginal cost equals marginal revenue for the firm as a whole, the profit-maximizing condition stated in Chapter 20. (For a more complete statement, see the appendix to this chapter.)

and parcel of the general equilibrium pricing process. The costs paid out by business firms are the incomes received by the factors of production. Thus, the profit-maximizing decisions of businessmen simultaneously provide the goods most desired by consumers at the lowest feasible prices and provide to resource owners the largest incomes that are consistent with their abilities and willingness to contribute to producing what consumers demand. The whole system relies on each individual (worker, consumer, businessman, capitalist) to look out for his own self-interest; it relies on competition to see that the end result is in the best interest of all.

Wages, Rents, Profits, and Prices Simultaneously Determined

Wages, rents, profits, and product prices are all *simultaneously* determined in the competitive market system. In Figure 28–5, let *DD* be the downward sloping marginal-revenue-product curve of labor. It shows how much labor will be hired by businesses at different wage rates—less at higher wage rates, more at lower.

Figure 28–5

Marginal productivity determines return to both labor and capital, although each can be considered a residual after the other is determined.

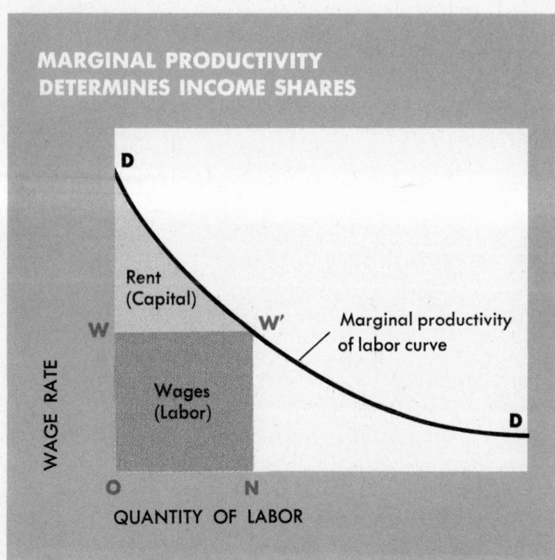

Suppose the wage rate is *W*. At that wage rate, all workers willing to work at *W* are hired, a total of *N* workers. Total wages paid will thus be the rectangle *OWW′N*.

But total output is the entire area under the marginal-productivity curve, *ODW′N*. Who gets the rest of the product? The answer is capitalists—for simplicity assume they are all land- and machinery owners. They get the triangle *DWW′*, labelled rent, as earnings on their capital. In competitive equilibrium all economic profits are eliminated. Rent is what is left over after wages have been paid.

Suppose now we had begun with the marginal-productivity curve of capital instead of labor. Although the shape of the curve might be different, the total area under it is the same as in Figure 28–5, because both show the possible total output of the economy using all its capital and labor. If we now compute the total rent paid to capitalists, what is left over will be wages for labor, just the inverse of the calculation in Figure 28–5. Each factor of production will get a share of the total product (income) dependent on its own contribution interacting with other factors of production and consumer demands for final products. Product prices and factors are all determined simultaneously.[6]

Economists are fond of quoting the following little rhyme by H.J. Davenport, a famous economist, to point up the interdependent determination of all product and factor prices:

The price of pig is something big;
Because its corn, you'll understand,
Is high-priced, too; because it grew
Upon the high-priced farming land.

If you'd know why that land is high,
Consider this: Its price is big
Because it pays thereon to raise
The costly corn, the high-priced pig.

[6] The appendix to this chapter provides a more rigorous statement of the marginal-productivity relationships involved. Mathematically inclined readers are referred to Mathematical Appendix IV at the end of the book, where the preceding theory of income distribution (factor pricing) is stated rigorously and some of its interconnections with the macro explanations of relative income shares are explored.

Consider the jingle. It tells an important truth.

Wages, Profits, and Short-run Dynamics

The preceding analysis is largely in terms of short- and long-run equilibrium—what wages and returns to capital will be in equilibrium. In competitive long-run equilibrium all economic profits are eliminated—though remember that a "normal" profit, or interest on total investment, is considered an economic cost, so accounting profits would continue even in equilibrium. But the real world is always changing, never staying in equilibrium for long—if it ever gets there at all. The profit squeeze of 1965–70, for example, which saw profits decline drastically as a share of national income and as a percentage of sales, was clearly not an equilibrium situation for many companies. Over half of all corporations reported losses on their tax forms in 1970, and the facts and controversies in the news mainly reflect the short-run dynamics of adjusting to change. Without basic equilibrium analysis we would be at a loss as to the basic forces determining why people get the incomes they do. But to assume that actual results will quickly, or in some cases ever, necessarily just match equilibrium predictions is naïve indeed, as with equilibrium analysis in other cases.

REVIEW

Concepts to Remember

Check your understanding of the following new concepts introduced in this chapter. You ought to be able to relate them directly back to Part Three, especially to the various cost and demand concepts developed there.

derived demand	distribution theory
marginal physical product	Lorenz curve
marginal revenue product	short-run dynamics

For Analysis and Discussion

1. Are most people's incomes a good measure of what they are worth?
2. The two biggest shares of the national income are wages and profits. Are the basic interests of wage earners and of their employers competitive or complementary?
3. Explain carefully how incomes are distributed in a highly competitive, market-type economy.
4. Would a distribution of income based purely on marginal productivity give everyone about what he is worth? Explain. If you don't think the market properly measures people's worth, how would you measure it?
5. Would the equalization of incomes in the United States, as is proposed by some socialists, solve the problem of poverty? Use the figures on national income (in Chapter 8) and those on income distribution (in this chapter), insofar as you think they are relevant, to support your answer.

6. According to Table 28–3, farmers and unskilled laborers have made substantially lower incomes than the other groups shown. If this is so, why do people continue to become farmers and unskilled laborers?
7. "The distribution of incomes to factors of production is no problem to one who has studied the behavior of business firms. In determining what prices to charge and what output to produce, the firm simultaneously determines how many workers to hire and what wages to pay out, what rents and interest charges to incur, and so on for the other income shares." Can you show how your analysis of Part Three has in effect explained the distribution of incomes?

APPENDIX

Production Theory, Price Theory, and Distribution Theory

This optional appendix provides (for those who studied Chapter 20) a more rigorous statement of what economists call the theory of production and the way in which it underlies price theory and distribution theory.

THE THEORY OF PRODUCTION. The theory of production is concerned with the physical relationship between the factors of production used (input) and the product produced (output). The central principle is the law of diminishing returns, or of variable proportions. This law states (appendix to Chapter 19) that as the proportion of one input to other inputs rises, the additional units of output per unit of that input may rise at first, but will sooner or later begin to fall, and fall persistently thereafter (other things, such as technology, being unchanged).[7]

Because the law of diminishing returns applies to each productive factor as more of it is used relative to others, it constitutes a powerful analytical tool for deciding the optimal proportions among factors of production if we want to obtain the most efficient, or least-cost, production of any commodity. As more of each factor is added relative to the others, its marginal physical product will decline. To obtain the minimum cost of production for any given output, we should add more of each productive factor until the last (marginal) dollar spent on each provides the same addition to total output—that is, the same marginal physical product. This is so because under any other condition more physical product could be obtained for the same cost by switching a dollar from a lesser-contributing factor of production to a higher contributing factor. Thus, in equilibrium:

$$\frac{\text{Marginal physical product of } A}{\text{Price of } A} = \frac{\text{Marginal physical product of } B}{\text{Price of } B}, \text{ etc.}$$

Another (equivalent) way of saying the same thing is that in the least-cost condition the marginal physical products of the factors of production must be proportional to their prices. That is:

$$\frac{\text{Marginal physical product of } A}{\text{Marginal physical product of } B} = \frac{\text{Price of } A}{\text{Price of } B}, \text{ etc.}$$

This proposition implicitly underlies the discussion of the unit-cost curves in Chapters 19 and 20. The U-shape of the firm's cost curve derives in part from the physical relationships described by the law of variable proportions. Most important, assuming the prices of factors of production to be given, the minimum-cost point on the firm's unit-cost curve can be achieved only when the factors of production are used in the proportions indicated above.

[7] A more complete analysis of these relationships may be found in most economic theory textbooks. See, for example, M.J. Bowman and G.L. Bach, *Economic Analysis and Public Policy* (Englewood Cliffs, N.J.: Prentice-Hall, Inc., 1949), Chaps. 18 and 19.

This theory of production also provides the answer to how a change in the price of any factor will affect its use. If the price of one resource (say, labor) falls, its use will be increased until its marginal physical product falls to the same proportion with other marginal physical products as the new proportion among the factor prices concerned. In other words, more labor will be hired until the marginal dollar spent on labor again produces the same marginal product as when spent on any other factor of production. Hiring more labor becomes desirable even though this reduces labor's marginal physical product under the law of diminishing returns.

Maximum-Profit Positions in Price Theory and Distribution Theory. The statement of the least-cost conditions above does not necessarily specify the maximum-profit position of the firm. It only specifies the conditions for obtaining the least-cost production for any given production level. The condition for maximum-profit (or minimum-loss) production is to increase production as long as marginal cost is less than marginal revenue (up to $MC = MR$). This is identical with the proposition that maximum profit (or minimum loss) will be obtained by adding units of each factor of production as long as its marginal cost (price, under competitive conditions) is less than its marginal revenue product. The statement in terms of individual factors of production merely specifies in more detail the mix of productive factors that must be used in arriving at the maximum-profit position. The $MC = MR$ proposition of earlier chapters is silent on the optimal factor combination; it implicitly takes the optimal combination for granted. We can now add the proposition that for maximum profit the marginal cost of each factor used must be equal to its marginal revenue product and that the marginal costs of all the factors used must be proportional to their marginal revenue products:

$$\frac{\text{Marginal cost of factor } A}{\text{Marginal cost of factor } B} = \frac{\text{Marginal revenue productivity of } A}{\text{Marginal revenue productivity of } B}.$$

Or, to put it another way, that:

$$\frac{\text{Marginal cost of } A}{\text{Marginal revenue productivity of } A} = \frac{\text{Marginal cost of } B}{\text{Marginal revenue productivity of } B}.$$

Wages and Salaries: Applying the Theory

CHAPTER PREVIEW

CHAPTER TWENTY-NINE

Wages and salaries account for over two-thirds of the total national income, and for nearly all of most people's incomes. By the same token, they constitute about two-thirds of total business costs. So it is not surprising that people, ever since they began to write about economics, have been spinning out theories to explain why wages are what they are.

Economists' theories mirror the times in which they live, and several different theories have been widely accepted over the last two centuries. Today, we do not yet have a fully satisfactory theory of wages. Yet most economists agree that the simple marginal-productivity, supply-and-demand theory stated in the last half of Chapter 28 provides a fruitful way to examine why individual wages are what they are. **This chapter is primarily an application of that theory—to explain why different people get the wages and salaries they do.**

Some Dubious Theories

But first let us turn briefly to three theories of wages that attained widespread acceptance during the last century, and that still have considerable influence in day-to-day thinking, even though economists consider them largely fallacious, or at least of dubious value.

The Subsistence Theory. Nearly two centuries ago, Thomas Malthus argued that wages would never long remain above the subsistence level for the masses—the so-called "Iron Law of Wages." Malthus said that population will tend to grow geometrically—2, 4, 8, 16. . .—while the food it can produce is limited. Thus, the growing supply of labor will always tend to force wages down toward the subsistence level. Wages cannot permanently stay below the subsistence level, for obvious reasons. But they will not for long stay above it in the absence of artificial means to limit the rate of population growth. Marx accepted much of the theory and predicted the downfall of capitalism, as workers become increasingly unwilling to accept their menial existence while capitalists appropriate the "surplus value" created by the workers whose wages fall increasingly short of the total value they create.

But history has shown an escape from this bitter prospect. In most Western industrialized nations, technological advance and capital accumulation have saved us from Malthus and Marx. In fact, real wages have risen rapidly and (except for cyclical fluctuations) steadily over the past century. Moreover, in the nations with the highest living standards, birthrates have fallen far below the rates in less-advanced countries.

But don't write off Malthus too fast. Even with modern technology and capital accumulation in the West, for well over half the world's population in the less-developed nations, Malthus' predictions on wages look perilously close to right. Total output has grown in most nations, but for over half the world's population little faster than the number of mouths to feed, and starvation looms on the horizon each bad crop year.

The Lump-of-Labor Theory. Another widely held, but almost completely fallacious, theory is that there is some fixed amount of work to be done in the short run, so more people seeking work will merely bid wages down and steal jobs from those already at work. This theory, often unarticulated, lies behind widespread opposition to letting new workers into the labor market—foreigners, women, apprentices, and so on. It lies behind union restrictions on entry to many occupations, and behind widespread resistance to "automation"—to the introduction of machines that appear to replace human beings.

What is the fallacy in this lump-of-labor theory? A big part of the answer was given in Part Two. We can always—through governmental monetary and fiscal policy—assure enough demand to provide jobs for as many workers as enter the labor market. At the level of the individual industry, the demand for labor is a function of the marginal productivity of that labor. Workers willing to work for a wage at or below their marginal productivity can always be employed profitably if we assure the right amount of total national demand. The total amount of labor that will be hired is thus a function of both ultimate demand and the price (wage) of the labor. There is no fixed amount of work to be divided up; the number of jobs depends on aggregate demand and the real wage that workers demand.

The Bargaining Theory. A third theory, with an important element of truth, is that wages depend on the relative bargaining power of employers and employees. Clearly, relative bargaining strength does matter sometimes, for example, when the United Auto Workers sit down to bargain with General Motors. But the bargaining theory leaves one big question unanswered: What are the limits within which the bargaining can vary the wage, and what sets those limits? If the union is very strong, does that mean there is no upper limit as to how high it can push its members' wages? Obviously not. At some level, the employer would have an economic incentive to substitute nonunion labor or machinery for the high-cost union members, or eventually go broke. If there is no union, does that mean the employer can drive down the wage virtually to zero? Obviously not. If his wages go far below prevailing levels, his employees will look for jobs elsewhere. Thus, to say that wages depend on relative bargaining strength is an obvious half-truth. The following pages should go a long way toward defining the limits within which bargaining power may dominate under different conditions.

But to point out the inadequacies of these theories does not provide a satisfactory explanation of what does set wages. We need a theory that will encompass the cases where Malthus appears to be right, where "automation" occurs, where bargaining power varies, and where new workers enter the labor market.

WAGES IN COMPETITIVE MARKETS

Supply and demand for labor, with marginal productivity determining the demand, goes a long way toward explaining all the cases in market type economies. The wage earned by each class of labor will tend to equal its marginal revenue productivity, for the reasons outlined in Chapter 28.

Figure 29–1 shows the close correspondence between average output per man-hour and real wages in the American economy since 1900. **Although this doesn't show the path of marginal productivity, it does suggest a basic fact: It is rising productivity that has made possible the steadily rising wages of American workers. Even though there are many more workers seeking jobs now than in 1900, their average productivity is so much higher that businesses demand the larger number, and at higher wages as well.**

But before we look at the application of our theory in more detail, two preliminary warnings. First, there are about ninety million people in the American labor force, and in some respects, every one of them is unique. No two people are exactly alike. Thus, it is meaningless to talk of "labor" and "wages" as if they were homogeneous. We need to look separately at many different types of labor, at people with different capacities, different education and training, different attitudes, living in different places. On the other hand, unless we lump individuals into different types of labor in different market areas, we're left with the job of looking separately at ninety million individuals. So we do group workers together where they are similar and in the same area.

Second, we shall be looking at the determinants of individual wages, or wages of particular groups of workers, in contrast to the "macro" issues of wage-profit shares in the total national income. **Thus, this is a chapter mainly at the "micro" level. It takes the levels of aggregate spending (total money gross national product) as given, determined by the forces described in Part Two.**

Begin with a relatively simple case. What determines the wage received by William Welder, a hypothetical laborer who works for the

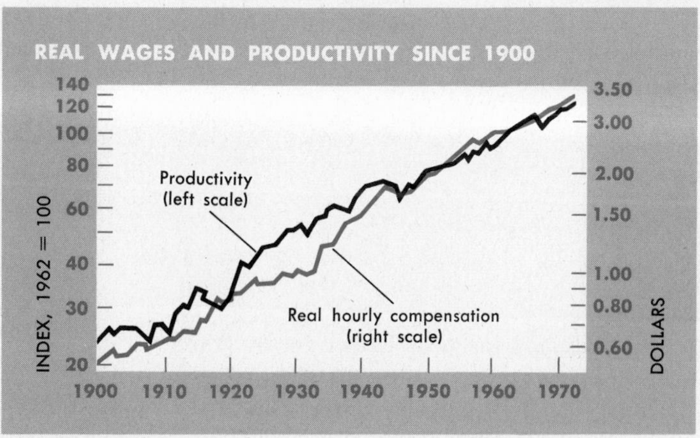

Figure 29–1

Rising productivity has made possible the steadily rising real wages of American workers. (Source: Council of Economic Advisers.)

Acme Plumbing Company, a small plumbing-fixtures manufacturer. There is no welders' union in the area. Will's abilities are substantially undifferentiated from those of other welders. There are many businesses and construction contractors in the area who hire welders. And there are many plumbing-supplies manufacturers in the United States who compete actively with each other in the product market. So there is active competition at three levels—among welders for jobs, among businesses for the services of welders, and among businesses for the consumer's sales dollar.

What determines Will's wage? He gets the going hourly rate for welders—say, $6 an hour. Acme Plumbing doesn't haggle over wage rates with each man it hires. It pays the going rate.

Something beyond Acme determines the "going rate" for welders in the area. By now, the answer "supply and demand" ought to come easily to you as the framework for looking at this price—the price of labor.

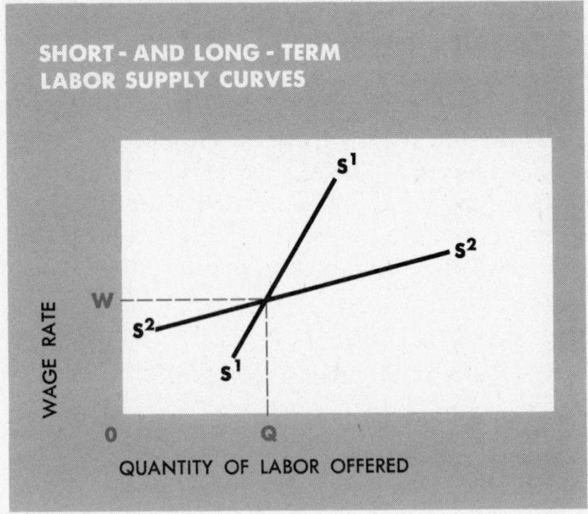

Figure 29–2

The short-run supply curve for labor is typically much less elastic than the long-run curve. If OQ labor is offered now at wage OW, a higher wage will increase labor offered only slightly in the short run, much more in the long run.

The Supply Side

What determines the supply of welders in the area? In any real-world case we could write a book on the subject, but the essential points would probably boil down to the following:

In the short run, it depends largely on the number of welders in the area, the availability of additional welders from nearby areas, and the willingness of welders to work longer hours. In the long run, supply will be more elastic. Welders may be drawn from long distances; workers may shift from other occupations; new labor-force entrants may learn welding. Plumbing manufacturers, the government, or workers themselves may invest in human capital by training nonwelders to become welders.

Figure 29–2 pictures the general relationship between short-run and long-run labor supply curves. In any particular market, the short-run supply is usually inelastic. Except for overtime and the possibility of getting workers away from other areas or occupations, higher wages won't greatly increase the amount of labor offered. See curve S^1S^1. But in the long run, there are many new sources of supply; the curve is more likely to look like S^2S^2.

Everywhere, long-run supply elasticity is greater than short-run. But the facts vary greatly among different occupations. Training a new welder is easy—the dollar investment is small, the time is short. But producing a new corporation lawyer, doctor, or manager takes a huge investment—years of time in school, practical experience, thousands of dollars. Even long-run supply may be relatively inelastic in such cases. And just who should, or will, make the investment is not clear in many cases, a problem we shall examine presently.

The Demand Side

The demand for welders' services is a derived demand—derived from the ultimate consumer demand for the plumbing fixtures Acme produces. Acme (and other businesses) will demand more welders whenever they have unfulfilled demand for their product at profitable prices. More precisely, Acme will demand more welders as long as the wage is below welders' marginal revenue productivity. Other firms will do likewise. By aggregating the demands of all firms, we could draw a demand curve for welders' services. The market will demand more welders, the lower is their wage (marginal cost).

If the marginal revenue productivity of welders underlies employers' demand for welders, we need to look at the underlying determinants of marginal revenue productivity. Remember, MRP is compounded of marginal physical productivity and a product price factor, though they may be hard to separate in some cases—for example, in engineering and selling.

Will Welder's marginal *physical* product is the additional physical product Acme Plumbing turns out by having Will on the job, compared with the output without him, all other productive factors being identical. This marginal physical product depends on Will's own mental and physical abilities, training, morale, and so on. It also depends, probably even more, on the other productive agents with which he works. With an old-fashioned welding torch and poor working conditions, he will have a low marginal physical product. If he is well equipped and works on a well-designed, balanced production line, his marginal physical product will be higher.[1]

The production manager is mainly interested in the sinks turned out per day. But the president and the stockholders are more interested in profit figures—in dollars and cents rather than in numbers of sinks and faucets. For them, productivity figures have to be converted into **marginal revenue (sales dollar) terms.**

Will's marginal revenue productivity is the additional sales dollars brought in by employing him. If his marginal physical product is two sinks per day, and the wholesale price of sinks is $30, then Will's marginal revenue productivity at Acme Plumbing is $60. Marginal revenue productivity is found by multiplying the marginal physical product by marginal revenue (price under pure competition). Consumer demand for the ultimate product is just as important as the worker's physical output in determining his value to the business.

The marginal revenue productivity of welders will eventually decrease as more welders are put to work producing sinks—because of the law of diminishing returns, and because as more sinks are produced by this and competing firms, their price will fall, consumer demand remaining unchanged, although Acme alone is too small to influence market price. Thus, the demand curve for workers will generally be downward sloping, as in Figure 29–3. Starting from any equilibrium

Figure 29–3

The competitive firm's demand curve for labor is downward sloping. The demand curve is labor's marginal-revenue product in the firm, since it will pay to hire more workers as long as marginal-revenue product is more than wage.

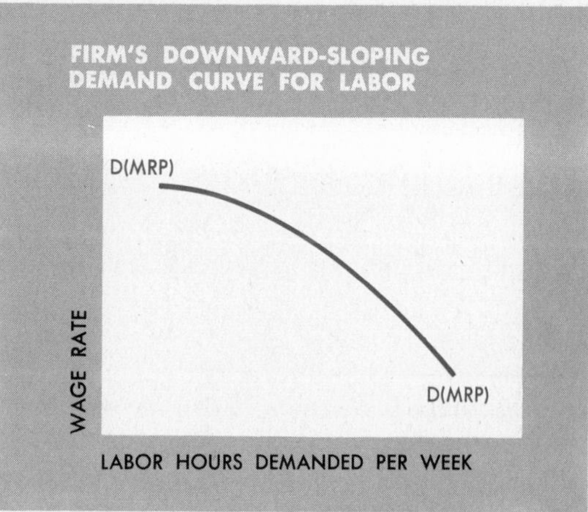

[1]A worker's marginal physical product depends on the *proportion* of workers to other productive agents, as well as on the quality of the machinery and tools he works with. For example, if welding is one operation on a metal-sink production line, the addition of the first welder to that line means a big increase in the firm's output. But once the line is roughly balanced between welders and other workmen, adding more welders may increase output somewhat, but the additional (marginal) product is much lower than it was when the first few welders were added. This is the law of diminishing returns again.

Generations of economists have worried about all the angles. Suppose we have five ditchdiggers and five shovels. What is the marginal product of a sixth shovel? Answer: Small, but positive. It has some value as a spare. How about a sixth ditchdigger with only five shovels? Same answer. He can fill in during rest periods, or he can go for beer.

DOES DEMAND REALLY DEPEND ON MARGINAL REVENUE PRODUCTIVITY?

In a purely competitive labor market, the individual employer is a wage taker, not a wage maker. He has to pay the going wage; his problem is how many men to hire at that wage. This depends on the marginal product an additional worker will provide. But how can businessmen estimate anything as complex as a worker's marginal revenue productivity?

In a small firm like Acme Plumbing, with only a few employees, the boss will have a good idea of how much his daily output will go up if he puts on an extra man. And he knows the price of sinks. This was the kind of situation economists had in mind when they developed the marginal-productivity approach to explaining the demand for labor.

But what about the marginal revenue productivity of a welder at U.S. Steel? It has nearly 300,000 employees scattered over the United States, with hundreds of welders among them. Welders work on jobs many steps removed from the ultimate steel products sold to customers. For example, one welder may do repair work on the company's railway cars that shuttle materials around the mills. What is his marginal productivity?

Obviously, no one knows precisely. It would be impossible to isolate the effect on the ultimate production of steel of laying off that one welder. And there are millions of workers in American industry who present similar problems in estimating marginal productivity.

Still, U.S. Steel has to decide how many welders it will hire. Company officials might tell you it's simple. They hire enough welders to get the steel produced for which they have orders. But this answer, which is probably quite correct, drives us back to the question of the price at which U.S. Steel will book orders. Clearly, this decision depends in large part on the costs estimated by the steel people for producing steel sheets. All these interrelated variables have to be put together, and somehow the hiring officials at the plant level have to decide when it will pay to hire another welder.

Where does all this leave us on the demand for labor? First, it's clear that no very precise estimate of marginal productivity is possible in many cases. Second, hard as the estimating job is, businessmen have to make some such calculation (consciously or subconsciously) in their hiring and pricing decisions if they are intelligently trying to maximize profits. Third, often several types of labor must be hired as a group to operate as a production unit. You either have the people it takes to run a modern assembly line, or you just shut the line down. In such cases, it is very difficult to separate out the marginal physical product of each kind of laborer.

Out of all this emerges a rough notion that businessmen are willing to pay workers only what they are "worth," sometimes viewing them as individuals but often as groups required for an integrated operation. What workers are worth logically boils down to a notion of marginal revenue productivity. Although this figure can't be estimated precisely in most cases, many businesses use their cost-accounting systems to get working ideas of when it pays to take new orders and to hire more workers. Behind these money-cost estimates are time-and-motion studies of how much labor time should turn out how much product. Using such studies the businessman can get a rough estimate of the "productivity" of different types of workers.

position, firms will hire more labor only as wage rates fall, given an unchanged demand for sinks. The marginal-revenue-product curve for welders in the firm is that particular firm's demand curve for welders.[2]

[2] Note that if firms are prepared to increase the amount of other resources with which welders work (for example, the scale of plant), the effect of diminishing physical productivity can be avoided. But the declining-price effect will nevertheless pull down marginal value productivity.

SUPPLY, DEMAND, AND PURELY COMPETITIVE WAGES

To demonstrate rigorously that the wage will equal marginal productivity, assume (1) that welders are all identical, (2) that employment conditions are similar at different plants in the area, and (3) that information on wages at different plants is circulated freely. Then all plants will have to pay about the same wage to get welders, just as there tends to be a single price for any identical commodity within any given market area.

Suppose that the going wage for welders is \$50 a day, but that Acme Plumbing and other plants figure that welders' marginal productivity is around \$60 per eight-hour day. What will happen? Those firms will try to hire more welders. When they do (1) the wage rate will be bid up and (2) the value (marginal revenue productivity) of welders in these plants will fall as more welders are added because of the law of diminishing returns and a lower price for sinks. Each firm will bid for additional welders as long as the rising wage is lower than what it estimates welders' marginal product to be. At some rate between \$50 and \$60 (say \$55) a new equilibrium wage will be established, with market supply and demand in balance at that new wage.

The right-hand portion of Figure 29–4 shows that Acme hires ten welders when the daily wage is set by the market at \$55; remember that Acme simply pays the going wage rate to get the welders it needs. The left-hand portion of the chart shows the equilibrium for the entire labor market; this is a summation of all the firms demanding welders as against the total supply of welders in the area.

In this equilibrium situation, we would expect to find the following:

1. The wage rate is equal to welders' marginal revenue productivity in the plants where they are hired.
2. Welders' wages are identical at all plants in the area.
3. Each firm is hiring as many welders as it "can afford" at that wage, because each firm continues to hire welders as long as the wage is lower than welders' marginal revenue productivity.
4. All welders in the area who are seeking work at that wage are employed. If any were still looking for work at that wage or less, the market wage rate would be bid down, since employers could hire unemployed workers at less than they were paying employed welders.

Thus, each worker earns what his labor is "worth," as measured by its marginal contribution to producing the goods and services consumers demand. But remember: Each individual's marginal revenue productivity, and hence his wage, depends on a lot of forces completely outside his own control—on shifts in consumer

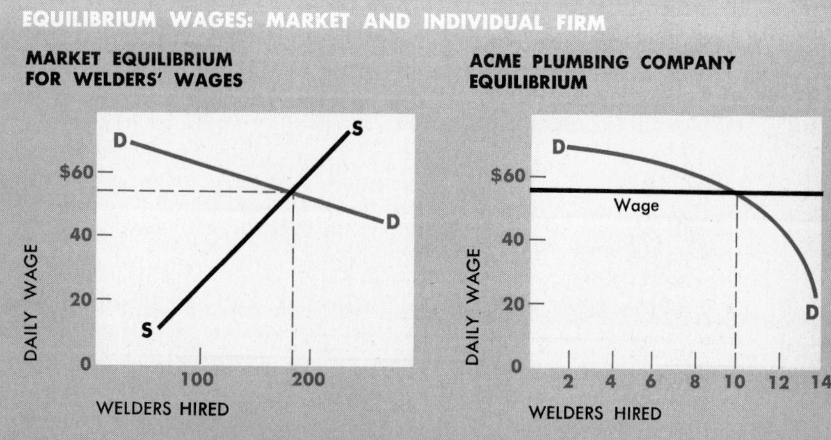

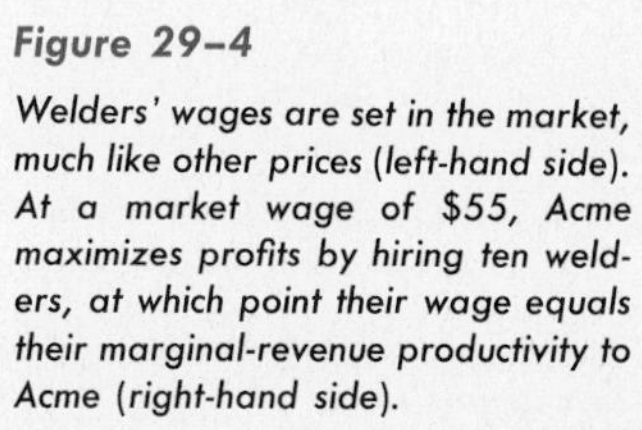

Figure 29–4

Welders' wages are set in the market, much like other prices (left-hand side). At a market wage of \$55, Acme maximizes profits by hiring ten welders, at which point their wage equals their marginal-revenue productivity to Acme (right-hand side).

demand, changing technology, the efficiency of management, the state of the business cycle.

Now try applying the same analysis to a related question. What will *your* starting salary be when you graduate from college? Five years later?

WAGE DETERMINATION IN MONOPOLIZED INDUSTRIES

What difference does it make if the plumbing-supplies industry is monopolized by one or a few major producers? Continue the assumptions that each firm does the best it can to maximize profits, and that firms in this and other industries actively compete for welders.

As under competition, each firm will continue to hire more welders as long as the wage is lower than welders' estimated marginal worth to the concern. But the total number of welders hired in this industry will be lower than under competition, because the monopolist restricts output to get higher prices and higher profits.

Thus, fewer welders will have jobs making plumbing supplies. If welders could work only there, clearly wages would be forced down by their competition for the reduced number of jobs. But since (we assume) welders are mobile, those unemployed will compete for jobs elsewhere, forcing down welders' wages there. Welders' wages will again be identical everywhere in the new equilibrium, but at a lower level than without the monopoly. **By restricting output below the competitive "ideal," the monopolist forces an inefficient allocation of labor, and this produces a lower wage for welders than under competition, both in the plumbing-supplies industry and elsewhere. Too few workers are employed in making plumbing supplies, too many in the rest of the economy. They are not efficiently allocated.**[3]

WAGE DETERMINATION UNDER EMPLOYER MONOPSONY

Now assume a different situation, where there is no competition among employers for labor. An example might be an isolated company mining town, where there is no significant alternative to working in the mine. The mine operator has a substantially complete "monopsony"—that is, a monopoly in hiring workers. Such a business is a wage maker, not a wage taker. There is no reason to suppose that it will pay a wage as high as the workers' marginal revenue productivity. If the workers are immobile, the manager may "exploit" them—that is, he may pay them a wage below their marginal revenue productivity to him.

How much can the monopsonist exploit his workers? It depends mainly on their mobility. If his wages get too far below rates elsewhere, workers may move away to other areas where they can earn more. If he has to go outside his monopsony area to hire more workers, competition with other employers is likely to eliminate his ability to exploit the workers.

Economists define **exploitation** as a wage below a worker's marginal revenue productivity. Although such cases may seem unethical or improper to you, "exploitation" in economics is an analytical, not a moral, term. Willie Mays or a corporate executive may be exploited in this sense, just as may a secretary or an itinerant fruit picker. (Note that this is quite different from Marx's definition of the term.)

To hear workers tell it, monopsony is a common case, often because employers agree not to compete for labor. Thus, the worker needs a union to protect himself against exploitation. According to employers this is a rare case. The evidence suggests a mixed world. But everywhere the strength of monopsony positions di-

[3] The argument can be stated rigorously, as follows. Since the monopolist always faces a downward-sloping demand curve, marginal revenue is always less than price. The marginal revenue product obtained by hiring more labor is therefore always less than marginal physical product times the product price; instead, it is marginal physical product times marginal revenue. Since the marginal-revenue-product curve is the firm's demand-for-labor curve, the firm's demand for labor under monopoly will always be less than in a comparable competitive case.

minishes as job-information channels improve, and as workers' mobility increases. For example, even though waitresses' wages are low in most cities, it is very difficult for employers to exploit them. There are hundreds of restaurants, so collusion is difficult, and any waitress will soon move elsewhere if her boss pays wages below the going competitive rate.

WAGE DETERMINATION UNDER BILATERAL MONOPOLY AND OLIGOPOLY

The next model is one that comes close to real-world conditions in some of the current big-union–big-business areas. "Bilateral monopoly" is the case where employers with monopsony power bargain with unions with monopoly power in selling labor. A simple case would be the mining-town example above, after the workers formed a union to represent them as exclusive bargaining agent. A more realistic example, a case of bilateral oligopoly, is wage bargaining in the steel industry, where the United Steelworkers represent most of the workers and the major firms in the industry in effect act together in bargaining for new contracts.

Under bilateral monopoly or bilateral oligopoly the wage outcome is logically uncertain. The employer will be unwilling to pay more than the labor's marginal revenue productivity without cutting back the number employed; he will pay less if he can get the labor he needs at a lower wage, and without a union he can exploit the workers to some extent in this way. The union, with a monopoly in the sale of its members' services, pushes up wages as far as it can. If the wage is pushed above labor's marginal value product at the present employment level, fewer men will be hired. But the exact wage level is indeterminate between this marginal-value-product ceiling and a wage floor above which the employer could (without a union) get all the labor he needs. The outcome will depend on the relative bargaining strength of union and employer, on how badly the employer wants to avoid a strike, on the size of the union's strike fund.[4]

WAGE AND SALARY DIFFERENTIALS—THE RICH AND THE POOR

Now turn to another application of the marginal productivity theory—the explanation of wage and salary differentials. Why should TV stars, corporation presidents, and home-run hitters get over $100,000 a year when most of us have to be content with a small fraction of that? And especially, why should they get it when their work by and large looks so pleasant compared with ditchdigging or typing, which pay only a couple of dollars an hour? We shall see that marginal productivity again provides the biggest part of the answer.

Even within the range of occupations that seem reasonably likely for most of us, the differentials are big. Look again at Table 28-4. In lifetime earnings, the expectations of a doctor in 1972 were $983,000, of an engineer $540,000, of a high-school teacher $360,000, of a plumber $323,000.

Supply and Demand Again

The most fundamental things about wage and salary differentials can be seen by using the same supply-and-demand, marginal-productivity model again. Give your theory a workout.

Salaries are extremely high where the supply is tiny and the demand is large. Wages are low where there are lots of workers relative to the demand. How "hard," how unpleasant, how tedious the job is—such considerations aren't very important except as they influence either the supply or the demand side of the picture.

Why has Jack Nicklaus collected over a million dollars just for playing golf on warm summer afternoons? Mainly because he is better at

[4] A new analytical approach from mathematics—"game theory"—presents some interesting insights into alternative outcomes under different types of bargaining strategies.

playing golf than anyone else; and we Americans lay our dollars on the line with enthusiasm to watch good golf players in person and on TV.[5] How can a surgeon get away with charging hundreds of dollars an hour? Because his skills are very scarce, and the demand for them is very strong. His marginal productivity is very high. In contrast, it's easy to be a delivery boy or a retail clerk, and lots of people try these jobs. Their marginal productivity is low.

The biggest factor accounting for wage differentials thus lies in the ability of the individual to do something that few others can do—something that is demanded by consumers with money to pay for it. There are big differences in the capabilities of different people, some reflecting innate physical and mental differences, others the amount of investment in human capital through education, training, and experience. Some of these differences we can't do much about. Joe Louis's split-second timing was largely born, not made, in spite of the years of training that went into it. Psychologists tell us that our basic intelligence apparently changes little over the years, no matter how hard we study. But our capabilities also depend on family environments, the amount and quality of education, hard work, and other things that are, to at least some extent, controllable. To understand the incomes different people earn, we therefore need to analyze both their basic abilities, how these abilities have been modified by environment, education, and training, and the markets for the particular workers.

Psychologists dispute bitterly over the relative importance of heredity and environment in making people what they are. Here we can look only at the economic factors involved in determining marginal productivities.

[5] Anomalously, athletic stars like Willie Mays and Babe Ruth may have been more susceptible to wage exploitation than most common laborers. This is because there was little active competition for their services to force the Giants and the Yankees to pay them their full marginal product. Under organized baseball's "reserve clause," other clubs couldn't hire Mays or Ruth away; they would have had to "buy" them from the Giants or Yankees. But Mays and Ruth each obviously had a monopoly in selling his own services. Thus, each situation was one of bilateral monopoly.

Clearly, most of the highest paying occupations have high educational requirements. Look back at Table 28–3. Nine of the ten best-paid occupations are professional or managerial, averaging over sixteen years of schooling. Salary studies consistently show a high rate of return on investment in education—over 10 percent in nearly all cases. In other words, every year of additional schooling beyond the eighth grade seems to be worth an extra $500 or so a year over one's working lifetime; college may be worth $100,000 or so in extra earnings, a tidy return. (There is some trickery in these figures, of course, since we know that those who go on to college are generally more able and would presumably earn above average salaries without the extra schooling. But even making a rough allowance to eliminate that factor, higher education pays well on the average.)

Table 29–1 shows the relationship between education and earning power in more detail. There is a consistent rise in income with increased education, for whites and nonwhites. While there is a lot of individual variation, low-education families are concentrated at the lower-income levels; very few ever reach the higher levels. Just the reverse is true for highly educated groups. Interestingly, although nonwhites show a substantially identical pattern, their average incomes are lower for each level of education but the gap between white and nonwhite decreases at high-education levels.

Don't fall into the trap, however, of thinking that formal education is the only important form of investment in human capital, or that education determines the incomes people receive. On the contrary, we learn basic habits and skills in everyday life, at home and on the job, and recent sociological studies suggest that for most people, especially in the below-median-income groups, nonschool forces dominate the learning process. Moreover, most highly-skilled jobs (medicine, law, management, engineering, and so forth) require continued learning after formal education has been completed. Some of this further investment in human capital is

TABLE 29–1
Education Level and Family Income, 1970

	PERCENTAGE RECEIVING INCOMES:						
YEARS OF SCHOOL	UNDER $3,000	$3,000–4,999	$5,000–6,999	$7,000–9,999	$10,000–14,999	$15,000 AND OVER	MEDIAN INCOME
WHITE FAMILIES	7.7	9.3	11.1	21.4	28.8	21.9	$10,300
Less than 8 years	23.1	20.0	16.2	19.1	15.1	6.5	5,799
8 years	12.3	17.2	15.1	23.5	22.0	9.8	7,651
Completed high school	4.2	6.0	10.6	24.4	34.1	20.7	10,563
Completed college	2.3	2.7	4.1	12.9	30.0	48.1	14,685
OTHER FAMILIES	19.5	18.9	17.3	19.7	15.9	9.0	$ 6,540
Less than 8 years	32.1	24.6	16.9	14.5	8.5	3.5	4,351
8 years	20.3	20.1	20.6	20.5	14.2	4.4	5,927
Completed high school	9.9	13.6	19.2	23.2	23.7	10.6	7,875
Completed college	2.1	7.4	5.9	15.6	24.5	44.4	13,682

Source: Department of Commerce, Bureau of the Census. Education level is for head of family.

financed by employers; a lot is the result of drive and hard work by those who win out in the highly competitive race for the best-paying jobs. The importance of continued investment in human capital is confirmed by the lifetime earnings patterns of different occupations. The annual earnings of doctors, lawyers, managers, and others with extensive education and continued learning by experience peak in their fifties and sixties, while the annual earnings of low-education, unskilled workers who depend largely on simple physical labor peak in their twenties or thirties and slide downhill thereafter.

Four concluding questions for discussion: (1) How much education should each individual invest in, assuming he wants to maximize his lifetime income (remember that education has costs as well as benefits)? (2) If education pays off so well, should we count on people to finance their own education, by borrowing if need be? (3) How much should the government spend on education, who should get the subsidized education, and who should pay the bill? We shall return to these questions in Part Five on government policy and the provision of public services. (4) Do existing differentials (for TV stars, surgeons, corporation presidents, school teachers, nurses, factory workers, farm laborers) reward most highly those who make the greatest contribution to human welfare? If your answer is no, how do you explain why we pay the overly-large incomes to the people who receive them?

Discrimination and Inequality

Table 29–1 suggested the magnitude of discrimination against nonwhites in America today. Table 29–2 reemphasizes this discrimination and adds women to the picture.

For economic analysis, we need to define discrimination precisely. If an employer can hire a black or a woman for wage W, but he in fact acts as if the effective wage were $W + D$, then D can be called a coefficient or measure of discrimination. For an employer who completely refused to hire blacks at any wage, however low, D would be infinitely large. If the employer

TABLE 29–2
Estimated Hourly Earnings of Adult Hourly Employees by Age, Sex, and Race, 1967[a]

	MALE		FEMALE	
AGE	WHITE	BLACK	WHITE	BLACK
20–24	$2.43	$2.24	$2.07	$1.90
25–34	3.16	2.45	2.27	2.03
35–44	3.56	2.64	2.33	2.06
45–54	3.72	2.65	2.35	2.01
55–64	3.65	2.40	2.31	1.83
65 and over	2.93	2.22	1.86	1.66

[a]Data for twelve large cities.

discriminates in favor of blacks or women, his D is negative.

Let us analyze the *economic* effects of discrimination. Discrimination clearly harms the group discriminated against, say black workers. They are partly or completely shut out of some jobs, which means they are forced to compete for less-attractive jobs, forcing down the wage for those jobs. White workers in the jobs from which blacks are excluded clearly gain, since fewer workers compete for the jobs and white wages are therefore higher. But discriminating employers lose, rather than gain, economically from their discrimination. They presumably feel better by not having blacks in the jobs, but they are foregoing profits by not hiring blacks up to the point where their wages are equal to their marginal products. They are paying higher wages to the whites than they could have paid blacks for the same work. This conclusion is in striking contradiction to the standard Marxist argument that employers discriminate in order to increase their profits.

In effect, discrimination shutting minority workers out of some jobs sets up "dual labor markets"—with the best jobs reserved for whites. Then each market must be analyzed separately, though there is clearly some spillover between them. Note, for example, that any white workers who must compete for jobs in the lower (minority) job areas will suffer from the antiminority discrimination because wages are forced down in those areas.

Employers may discriminate not because of their own prejudices, but because they believe customers or other workers would object to being served by, or working with, minority groups or women. If this belief is correct, it is less clear that discriminating employers forego maximum profits by discriminating; the result then depends on the particular circumstances, mainly on how strong the prejudices of customers or other workers are.

Discrimination in the United States now seldom takes the form of paying lower wages to minority groups or women than to white males for the same job in the same place, because this is a clear violation of the law. Instead, discrimination usually involves refusing to employ minorities or women in jobs for which they are qualified, or insisting on higher qualifications than for white males for the same job. But the overall economic result is similar in either case. Nor does the economic analysis of discrimination against women differ in essentials from that against minority groups.[6]

A substantial part of the lower earnings of minorities and women reflects not current discrimination but their lower productivity. Employers argue, often correctly, that few blacks and few women are currently qualified for many of the highest paying jobs. Exclusion of minorities and women from the best jobs thus often reflects past rather than present discrimination, in both education and on-the-job training. Differences in education are hard to measure, and they clearly do not account for all, or perhaps even most, of the relevant differences in productivity. But we know that minorities have substantially fewer years of education than whites on the average, and there is much evidence that the quality of their education is generally inferior. Minority groups are closing the education gap, but they are still far behind. In

[6]For an analysis of the consequences of "black separatism" in ghettos, either voluntary or involuntary, see Case 22, "Black Economic Development."

1970, 78 percent of all whites had completed high school, and 17 percent had completed college. The comparable figures for nonwhites were 58 and 10 percent, but in 1940, only 12 percent of nonwhites had completed high school, and 2 percent college. As Table 28–1 suggested, because of job discrimination the return on education for minorities is still lower than for whites. Moreover, minorities are generally less able to finance higher education, and they find it more difficult to borrow for this purpose. These facts partially explain the concentration of educated blacks, until very recently, in the lower and middle ranks of the civil service, elementary and secondary teaching, and the ministry.

All things considered, what is the economic cost of being black? Only the roughest estimates are possible. Some suggest that perhaps a third of the total shortfall of black income, equalizing for age, education, and location, is due to current discrimination. Another says that the annual income cost of being black averaged about $1,000 in the early 1960s, after adjustment to equalize age, education, and the like. But others deny that the cost is substantial. Obviously the estimated cost of discrimination can be raised or lowered substantially by attributing more or less of existing education and training differences to past discrimination.[7]

Unions and Barriers to Entry

Unions have some influence on wage differentials, as we shall see in Chapter 30. Where employer monopsony exists, clearly unions can improve workers' positions compared to nonunion shops. By shutting out nonmembers through restrictions on entry into particular occupations (for instance, the building trades), unions can clearly raise their members' wages in those occupations while lowering the wages of workers forced to compete in nonunionized areas.

Generally, only the craft unions have exercised effective barriers to entry. Many craft unions have traditionally excluded blacks, but most industrial unions (such as autos and steel) have open-door policies for minorities. Much evidence suggests (see Chapter 30) that unions have generally raised the wages of the unskilled relative to the skilled, so despite the discriminatory policies of many craft unions, unions on the whole have probably somewhat narrowed wage differentials by race.

AUTOMATION AND WAGES

Technological advance is a dominant force in the American economy, perhaps the single most important foundation of our rising standard of living. New methods, new machines, new products are the lifeblood of a dynamic, growing economy. Without the linotype we'd still be setting type by hand, and books and newspapers would still be for the elite few. Without the electric light bulb, we'd still be lighting our houses with candles, oil, and gas.

But "automation" (as technological advance is sometimes called when new automatic machines replace men) is often blamed for widespread unemployment. Computers replace thousands of clerks in processing checks and keeping records in banks and businesses. Modern chemical plants are almost fully automated. On a humbler level, spray guns and rollers get work done a lot faster than the old-fashioned paintbrush. Everywhere new factories produce more goods with fewer workers.

Technological progress increases output per unit of input—output per worker, output per unit of capital, or both, whichever way you wish to divide up total output. Thus we might expect it to raise both wages and the rate of return on capital—and so it generally will, other things equal. But how much of the gain goes to each under what circumstances is a more complex question.

[7] For more details see B. Schiller, *The Economics of Poverty and Discrimination* (Englewood Cliffs, N.J.: Prentice-Hall, Inc., 1972), Chaps. 9–10; L. Thurow, *Poverty and Discrimination* (Washington, D.C.: The Brookings Institution, 1969), Chaps. 7 and 9; and, for a sociological view, C. Jencks et al, *Inequality* (New York: Basic Books, 1972).

Some Facts

Figure 29–1 showed the steady parallel growth in output per man-hour and wages in the American economy. Moreover, the growth in total output has been much greater than the total input of labor and capital combined. Look ahead to Figure 43–2 for the facts. The total incomes of both capital and labor have risen greatly over the past century, but the return per unit of labor (the real wage rate) has gone up much more than the return per unit of capital (the real interest rate), as the bottom half of Figure 43–2 shows dramatically. The average real wage now is about 500 percent of what it was in 1900, while the real interest rate is substantially unchanged. Labor has apparently been the great gainer from technological advance as measured this way. However, as Figure 28–3 shows, the percentage shares of the total national income going to labor and capital have been relatively stable, because the quantity of capital has grown much faster than the quantity of labor.

Analysis

Against this factual backdrop, let us examine the impact of automation on wages in a particular industry and occupation. Look back at Will, the welder. Suppose a new machine is invented that stamps out metal sinks, eliminating the need for welding. Let us trace through the results, assuming that all markets are perfectly competitive and all prices flexible both upward and downward.

1. Sink producers will adopt the new method if it's cheaper per unit produced than the old one, and competition will force sink prices down to the lower cost level.
2. Welders will lose their jobs in plumbing-supply companies. Welders' wages will fall as they compete for jobs elsewhere.
3. Employment will increase in plants that manufacture the new stamping machine, in industries producing raw materials and parts, and in plumbing-supply companies that need men to install, service, and operate the new machines. Wages will rise for those workers.
4. At the lower price of sinks, more sinks will be produced and sold, and consumers will be better off, with more sinks and more other goods, since sinks are now cheaper (though note the importance of elasticity of demand). More goods in total can be produced because technical advance has made it possible to produce the same number of sinks with less resources, so some resources (welders) can make something else instead.

In all this, what has happened to the wages of different labor groups and to the wage share in the national income?

First, welders' wages drop. Welders thrown out of work look for other jobs. If they stay unemployed, average wages of all welders are clearly down. Even if they get jobs as welders elsewhere, welders' wage rates and incomes will be pulled down as more welders seek jobs there.

Second, the demand for other types of labor rises—for workers to make the new machines and to service and operate them. Wages will rise in those other industries and occupations.

Third, if we assume constant total expenditures in the economy, no long-run unemployment need result. Welders thrown out of jobs will get work elsewhere or at different jobs in the sink industry, as consumers buy more sinks and other products. Consumers will spend more on other products if they spend less on sinks, and more jobs will be available in other industries. This pleasant conclusion, however, depends on two critical assumptions: that workers are mobile in moving to new jobs, and that individual wages are flexible, so that the displaced workers can be absorbed elsewhere. Thus, it skips lightly over the big short-run retraining and readjustment problems facing individual workers. Probably the biggest help in assuring jobs and incomes elsewhere in the face of "automation" is government assurance of prosperity and continued high, total spending in the economy.

Fourth, what happens to the total wage share in the national income will depend largely on the elasticity of demand for the product concerned and on the ratio of labor to capital used

in the innovating industry, relative to the rest of the economy. This gets pretty complicated. But since labor clearly benefits along with all of us in its role as consumer, in the real world it's reasonably clear that labor's real aggregate income is raised by technological advance, whatever happens to its **relative** share of the national income. The real wage per worker has grown rapidly. And the gradually rising share of wages and salaries in the national income over many years of rapid technological advance suggests that both labor and nonlabor incomes share the benefits of technological progress, and that if anything, the labor portion has grown a little. There's no doubt that wage earners have benefited greatly from technological advance.

MARX AND THE RESERVE ARMY OF THE UNEMPLOYED

One last application of the theory: Marx put great emphasis on the "reserve army of the unemployed" as a force inevitably driving wages down to a minimum subsistence level—his "iron law of wages." The final result would be revolt and the overthrow of capitalism. How about it?

Suppose the demand for and supply of labor are as shown in Figure 29–5. Suppose the wage rate is W^1; then there is indeed unemployment (excess supply of labor), as shown on the chart. This unemployment, presuming competitive markets, will indeed push wages down, incidentally providing jobs for some of the unemployed workers at the lower wage rate. But will wages fall to W^3, assumed to be the minimum level of subsistence? Clearly not. They will fall to W^2, the level at which the amounts of labor demanded and supplied are just equal, but there is nothing to make them fall further. Quite possibly employers would like to pay still lower wages, but competition among them will prevent this outcome. Workers, on the other hand, might like to have wages higher than W^2, but at a higher wage fewer men will be hired and competition among the unemployed will push the wage rate back down to W^2.

Suppose, to examine a last possibility, wages were somehow depressed to W^3, the subsistence level. Would they stay there? They would not. At wage W^3 there would be a large employer excess demand for labor, and competition among employers would bid wages up. Only if competition among either employers or laborers is eliminated by collusion or government action can the wage rate stay far below or above W^2 in the economy shown in Figure 29–5. Is this conclusion contradicted by the minimum-subsistence wage levels found in some of the less-developed economies, such as India? No. The minimum-subsistence wage level is the equilibrium level there because productivity, given their populations, lack of education, and lack of capital, is at about that level. Marginal productivity is the fundamental determinant of the real wage level in both economies. The higher average wage in our Western economies reflects higher productivity; and given the productivity, the average real wage cannot be forced down to a minimum subsistence level by greedy capitalist employers as long as there is substantial competition for labor among them.

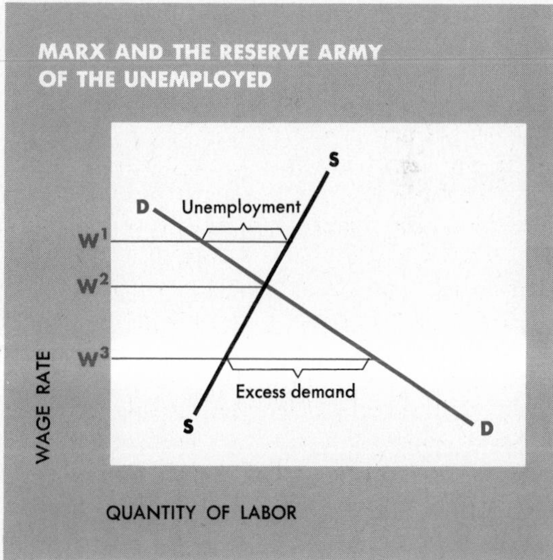

Figure 29–5

Marx argued that unemployment would always force wages down to the minimum subsistence level (W^3). But if we assume unemployment shown at some wage rate (W^1), competition for workers will keep wages from falling below W^2.

REVIEW

Concepts to Remember

Be sure you understand the following important concepts:

monopsony	discrimination
exploitation	dual labor markets
investment in human capital	"automation"
wage taker	wage maker

For Analysis and Discussion

1. Suppose you want to maximize your lifetime income. What factors should you take into account in selecting your occupation and in timing your entry into it? How much should you invest in your own human capital?
2. "Labor is just another commodity, and wages are its price. All we need to explain wages is a basic understanding of supply and demand." Do you agree with this quotation from an economics textbook? Is it immoral? Explain.
3. Wilt Chamberlain was reported to get over $300,000 annually for playing basketball for the Los Angeles Lakers. Can you explain this huge salary by the marginal productivity theory of Chapter 29?
4. Look at Table 29–1. Are the income differentials between whites and nonwhites shown there a measure of discrimination? What other factors may help explain the differences?
5. Is "automation" good or bad for workers in the industries in which it occurs? For workers elsewhere? For consumers? Explain.
6. Malthus argued that population would tend to outrun the world's food supply, and that wages would tend to be forced back down toward a bare subsistence level.
    a. Is this an acceptable theory of wages?
    b. How would you differentiate between its usefulness in explaining wages in America and in India?
7. One theory holds that wages are the result of bargaining between workers and employers, and that the only important determinant of the outcome is the relative bargaining power of the two parties. Is this theory correct?
8. Is inequality of economic opportunity a major factor in the present unequal distribution of personal incomes in the United States? If it is important, what, if anything, should be done to reduce such inequality of opportunity?
9. Define "exploitation" as it is used by economists. What are the factors that determine whether or not any worker is likely to be exploited?
10. Can you explain to a confirmed Marxist why greedy employers will not force workers' wages down to subsistence levels?

CASE 18

Economics of the Draft

Should we fill the needs of the armed services by a "draft" or by paying wages high enough to induce the required number of men to volunteer? The draft was highly unpopular during the Vietnam War. Yet shifting to a volunteer army also faced strong opposition. The issue is still in dispute.

The pro-draft forces argue that a draft, based entirely on chance, is the only fair way to decide who must serve in the armed forces. Moreover, it is the cheapest way of maintaining the national defense. One may argue about the proper size of the army and navy, but however big they must be, the draft is the way to fill them.

On the contrary, the antidraft forces argue that fully-volunteer armed forces are both more efficient and more equitable. The government would have to offer a salary big enough to get the troops needed, and every individual could decide for himself whether he prefers the armed services to other employment opportunities at going salary rates. But the pro-draft forces counter that this will produce an army of poor and minority youths who have few other employment opportunities, while well-to-do whites would not volunteer, even at higher military salaries.

Which is the economically preferable and more equitable way of maintaining the armed services? What should our national policy be? (Hint: Draw the demand and supply curves for the two alternatives and remember the importance of the concept of opportunity costs.)

Unions, Collective Bargaining, and Public Policy

CHAPTER PREVIEW

CHAPTER THIRTY

Labor unions loom large on the current American scene. On the economic front, they exercise great pressures on wages, hours, and working conditions. They are behind the worker in his differences with the foreman, the day-to-day arguments that seldom reach the public's eye. Politically, their voice is heard in the selection of candidates, and their votes are felt in elections—usually on the Democratic side. Their lobbyists are among the most effective in Washington and the state capitals, and it is a secure congressman indeed who can afford to disregard what organized labor thinks.

Important as unions are, don't overrate their importance. Unions do indeed influence wages and hours. But supply and demand still set a confining framework for labor-management negotiations. Although the combined AFL-CIO loosely joins many unions, the member unions are still separate, often disputing among themselves. Less than one-fourth of all workers are unionized, and union membership has grown little in recent years although the labor force has expanded steadily. Throughout the services, agriculture, and clerical and professional areas, unions have little hold. They have grown rapidly among government workers and teachers, but how powerful they will be in the public sector remains to be seen. Politically, the divisions within organized labor weaken the power it can exercise, and since World War II, labor has gone down to defeat on some of its most bitterly fought issues—notably the passage of the Taft-Hartley Act.

To understand organized labor's position, we must remember history. With today's big, powerful unions, it may be hard for you to realize that only forty years ago unions were hanging on by the skin of their teeth, with an active membership of only three million workers and little or no recognition in the great mass-production industries of the country; union leaders were tarred and feathered, heads were broken. But older union members and their leaders know it well. And that memory, though fading, still colors union behavior today.

HISTORY OF AMERICAN UNIONISM[1]

The foundations of labor unionism in America lay in the skilled crafts during the early 1800s. But it was not until the 1870s that the first loose nationwide labor association appeared. This was the Knights of Labor, founded as a secret society to avoid public antagonism and employer's reprisals against members. A decade later, the American Federation of Labor (AFL) became the first effective national union organization. Under the leadership (from 1886–1924) of Samuel Gompers, a remarkable figure in American labor history, the Federation became a significant force, with an outspoken philosophy of "practical" unionism. Gompers reflected the spirit of the times in organized labor—"Get more, now." Only this pragmatic, typically American, attitude began to win a little grudging acceptance for unionism from employers and the public at large.

But it was Franklin Roosevelt and the New Deal that gave unions their place in modern industrial society. Depression was everywhere—massive unemployment, low wages, low purchasing power. Higher wages and higher prices to promote recovery were cornerstones of the New Deal. The National Industrial Recovery Act for the first time gave workers the right to organize and bargain collectively with employers. Although NIRA was soon declared unconstitutional, the Wagner Act of 1935 was passed shortly thereafter, to become the foundation of modern union powers. It spelled out workers' rights vis-à-vis employers, put teeth in the unions' powers to bargain collectively, and forbade prevalent employer antiunion practices. Unions were guaranteed recognition if they won a majority vote among the workers.

The labor history of the middle 1930s was stormy. The newly formed Congress of Industrial Organizations, (CIO), with the fiery John L. Lewis as its first president, opened big organization drives—violent, spectacular, and successful. Open defiance of management rather than workers' traditional subservience was the tone. The famous sit-down strikes, when the unions seized possession of the major auto plants, rocked the companies and the public. But in the bloodshed and bitterness that ensued, the unions won recognition time after time—with the open support of the Roosevelt administration and local Democratic government officials. The Who's Who of American industry fell to CIO organizing drives one by one—U.S. and Bethlehem Steel, General Motors, General Electric, Goodyear, and so on down the list. By 1940, union membership had more than doubled, to about ten million. By 1945 it was nearly fifteen million, about one-third of the nonagricultural labor force.

Public sympathy during the 1930s was by and large prolabor, though many friends were lost by the violent sit-down strikes. But strong union wage demands during World War II, interunion jurisdictional quarrels and strikes, and open defiance of the federal government by a few leaders convinced the bulk of the public that organized labor's power had gone too far. In 1947 Congress passed the Taft-Hartley Act, restricting the powers of unions and restoring some rights that employers had lost during the preceding decade. And the years since World War II have seen a definite levelling of union power.

Figure 30–1 shows the picture. Union mem-

[1]For a good account, see U.S. Labor Department, *Brief History of the American Labor Department* (Washington, D.C.: U.S. Government Printing Office, 1964).

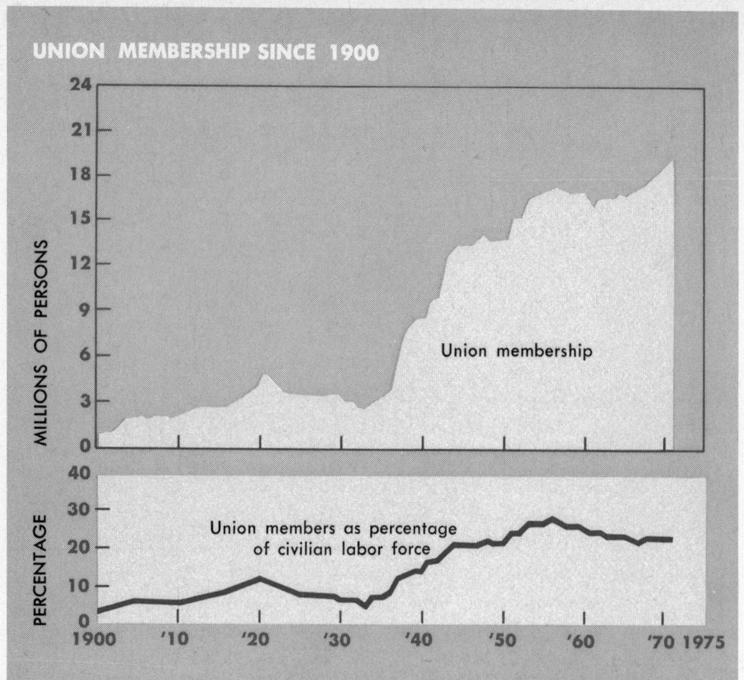

Figure 30–1

The big growth period for unions was during the 1930s and 1950s. Since then, union membership has declined somewhat as a percentage of the civilian labor force. (Sources: National Bureau of Economic Research and U.S. Department of Labor.)

bership (excluding Canada) rose above seventeen million in the mid-1950s, but then levelled. Unions have made slow headway with white-collar workers and employees of the rapidly growing service industries. The bottom half of the chart shows the union problem more strongly. Union membership as a percentage of the total civilian labor force hit a peak of 23 percent in 1963, and has declined since then. Union membership as a percentage of the non-agricultural labor force is somewhat higher—about 26 percent. Only in the public sector (government and education) has unionism made big gains in the last decade.

In 1955, the "merger" of the AFL and the CIO into one loose organization (the AFL-CIO) marked a major step toward a united labor movement. But interunion rivalries have kept the new organization from acting as an effective unit, economically or politically. Neither the United Auto Workers, the Teamsters, nor the United Mine Workers now participate. Jurisdictional disputes have been a persistent source of quarrels.

Moreover, the unions face a new problem. The average union member has a good job, and often a house in the suburbs. He belongs to the big middle-income class, well above the insecurity and poverty that threatened during the 1930s. He wants more pay, longer vacations, better fringe benefits. But the old class solidarity that once united workers against the capitalist employers is gone. There is an increasing gap between the goals of young union members and the militancy that motivated the now-aging leaders. Some describe the modern scene as "mail-order unionism." The members turn over their dues and want higher wages and other benefits delivered by union officials in exchange; otherwise, many younger members feel little tie to the union. And unions can hope for big gains only among white-collar workers in the services, education, government, and the like. Total employment in manufacturing has been slowly declining over the last decade.

UNION WAGE POLICY

From one point of view, a union is merely a monopoly that sells the labor services of its members. Neglecting for the moment all the other things that unions do, how effective are they in raising wages under different circumstances? And how does the public fare?

The analytical models of the last chapter provide a simple framework for examining the próblem. Let us first assume that the union is a completely effective organization in controlling its workers. It speaks for them all, and it need not worry about defections from the ranks. Assume also, for the moment, that aggregate spending in the economy is constant, unaffected by the behavior of individual unions and employers.

Competition

First, consider the case where employers are highly competitive with one another both in selling products and in hiring workers—for example, waitresses in a large city. Here, in the long run, all economic profits will tend to be eliminated. Price will be forced down to about the minimum average cost at which each product can be produced. From the labor side, wages will be roughly equal to the marginal revenue productivity of each class of labor hired.

Suppose now that a union comes in and organizes all waitresses in the area. It demands a wage increase and gets it. This raises costs, and forces up prices. At the higher prices, consumers will buy fewer restaurant meals (assuming that aggregate income and spending are constant). With less output, there are fewer jobs for waitresses; how many less will depend on the elasticity of demand for restaurant meals. With a higher wage but the same marginal product, it pays employers to hire fewer waitresses. Union wage demands lead to higher wages for members who keep their jobs, but fewer jobs. In a highly competitive industry, there isn't much unions can do to push up wages without reducing employment in the long run (unless aggregate spending is somehow increased). The workers who keep their jobs are better off, but those laid off bear the brunt. And it becomes harder for new job-seekers to find work as waitresses.

Monopoly and Partial Monopoly

Second, consider the case where there is monopoly or monopolistic competition in selling products, but still active competition among firms for workers. Suppose, for example, there are only a dozen or so restaurants or stores in the area, or at the extreme only one. Can the new union now force the stores to pay higher wages without reducing the number of jobs? Our theory tells us, probably not. If the firms are maximizing profits before the union, they will be hiring workers up to the point where the wage equals the workers' marginal product. If the union raises wages, it will, logically, pay employers to cut back on the number of workers hired and to raise prices; the new maximum-profit output will be smaller than before. Again, logically, the union can obtain higher wages only at the cost of less employment.

But partial monopolists—especially oligopolists—may not be maximizing profits in the precise sense above. Oligopoly is the world of live-and-let-live, of price leadership, of partially protected markets. Under these conditions, the effect of a wage increase on prices and employment is far harder to predict. If firms have a protected profit position, this special profit provides a melon over which the union and management can bargain, and higher wages need have no effect on either product price or output and employment. In oligopolies where firms behave as if they faced kinked demand curves, the union may have a considerable range over which it can force up wages without inducing higher prices and reduced employment. But wherever the union makes substantially the same bargain for all major firms in the industry, it faces much the same likely result on employment and prices as with a single monopoly firm; higher wages for union workers will generally mean fewer available jobs.

Monopsony and Bilateral Monopoly

Where workers are being exploited through a wage less than their marginal revenue productivity, a union can push the wage up without decreasing employment.[2] The employer is making a special profit by exploiting the workers and theoretically the union can grab this sum back for the workers. But the employer isn't going to be enthusiastic about turning his profits over to the workers. He'll fight to keep wages down. Where this struggle comes out is indeterminate so far as economic theory is concerned. To guess who will win, look at the relative bargaining power of employer and union. How big is the union strike fund? How adept are both parties around the bargaining table? How badly does the employer want to get his customers' orders out on time? This is a case of bilateral monopoly, where the union (a monopolist in selling labor) meets a single employer (a monopsonist in buying labor).

Impact of Unions on Nonunion Wages

If unions reduce the number of jobs in unionized industries, they force wages down elsewhere by increasing the number of workers who must seek work in nonunionized industries. A substantial part of union gains thus comes at the expense of nonunion workers. But in some cases unions may also indirectly raise nonunion wages. If nonunion employers want to keep unions out (perhaps to protect other managerial prerogatives), they may, and often do, raise their wages roughly apace with union increases. This is known as the "union-threat effect." It works most strongly where employers are exposed to possible union organizing drives, and in prosperity when labor is scarce.

[2]In fact, the union theoretically might *increase* employment by eliminating exploitation. Without the union, the employer bargains wages down and gets as many workers as possible at his low wage. With a union, he must pay the going wage and he can get as many workers as he wants at that wage. Thus he hires workers up to the point where the wage equals their marginal revenue productivity; there is no longer any incentive to restrict output and employment to get the advantage of low wages.

Union Wages and Capital Substitution

The short-run effect of union wage pressures on the number of jobs in an industry is often hard to predict accurately. But a longer-range effect is highly predictable. Higher labor costs will lead businessmen to invest in labor-saving machinery more rapidly than they otherwise would. It will pay to shift to coal-mining machinery to replace miners as hourly wages rise, to install mechanical dishwashers in restaurants, to replace farm laborers by automatic vegetable pickers. Higher union wages clearly speed "automation."

Do Unions Really Raise Wages?

This may sound like a silly question. Everyone has read of many cases where union demands for higher wages have finally been granted by employers. But such instances don't really answer the question. Maybe supply and demand would have produced the same raises in the market without any union. Don't forget the fallacy of *post hoc, propter hoc.*

Although any union man and most employers will tell you that of course unions raise wages, the dispassionate, objective evidence is less clear. One careful study estimates that unions raised the wages of their members by about 25 percent relative to nonunion workers in 1933 at the bottom of the depression (reflecting temporary union resistance to wage cuts), by about 5 percent in the inflationary boom of the late 1940s when all wages were bid up rapidly in tight labor markets, and by 10–15 percent during the 1950s.[3] Another concludes that in perhaps one-third of all cases, unions have raised wages by 15–20 percent; in another third by perhaps 5–10 percent; in the other third not at all.[4] The unions' effects are greatest during recessions when union contracts hold up wages, least in

[3]H.G. Lewis, *Unionism and Relative Wages in the United States* (Chicago: University of Chicago Press, 1963), p. 193.

[4]A. Rees, *Wage Inflation* (New York: National Industrial Conference Board, 1967), p. 27.

booms when strong employer demand bids up all wages rapidly. In the latter case, nonunion wages may actually rise faster, because union wage increases are often slowed by three-year contracts made earlier.

Union effects vary greatly from industry to industry. Most evidence suggests that over all they have raised unskilled wages relative to skilled wages. Economic theory doesn't explain this completely. In part, it seems to reflect industrial union pressures to raise low wages relative to high ones. They have also pressed to eliminate interfirm and regional differentials by levelling up the lower rates.

Note a commonly cited but unconvincing bit of evidence, that union wages are by and large higher than nonunion ones. This is true, but many unionized industries were high-wage industries before they were unionized—big companies with lots of highly skilled labor. One other interesting piece of evidence is that labor's share of the national income has increased somewhat since the 1920s, before the big modern union increase. But the shift is not enough to provide clear evidence that unions have raised the aggregate wage share.

COLLECTIVE BARGAINING AND LABOR-MANAGEMENT RELATIONS

The big wage negotiations and strikes always make the headlines. But the great bulk of union-management collective bargaining and negotiation goes on unheralded behind the scenes. After a union contract is signed, the day-to-day relations of the foreman and his workers take over. Wage rates have to be set for individual jobs; broad contract wage provisions must be translated into elaborate wage structures in large firms. Decisions must be made as to which jobs are on a flat hourly pay basis and which "on incentive," where the pay depends on the number of units turned out. Arrangements have to be agreed on for handling the introduction of new machinery and new methods. Wrangles between foremen and individual workers have to be adjudicated. A thousand and one problems arise in a big plant that involve disputes between labor and management.

In these disputes, the union steward is the worker's first-line negotiator, just as the foreman is management's. Good feelings and cooperation between foremen and stewards can do more for effective union-management relations than almost any amount of fine top-level policy making. Down in the plant is where the work gets done and where most of the disputes arise, except for the major wage and hour negotiations at contract-expiration dates.

Some union-management agreements provide elaborate machinery for handling worker-management disputes that can't be settled by the foreman and the worker. These often culminate in calling on an impartial arbitrator, paid jointly by union and management, whose decision is final on disputed issues under contract. Such agreements usually try to set up a body of rules under which workers and management can minimize friction and disagreement. The contract is something like the laws under which we operate our democratic system. This procedure has gone far toward creating stability and order in employee-management relations in thousands of industrial plants. But in industrial as in political democracy, the rules alone can't make the system work. They only provide a framework within which men of reasonable goodwill can work peaceably together.[5]

[5]One source of controversy between unions and management is the "union shop" and "right-to-work" laws. Under a union-shop agreement, everyone who works in the firm covered must join the union. The union's big argument for this arrangement is that if workers get all the benefits of union activities (higher wages, better working conditions, and so on), they should have to pay dues and bear their share of the union costs. Otherwise they get a "free ride," which makes no more sense than permitting a citizen to benefit from government but decide for himself that he won't pay taxes.

The counterargument says that union shops take away the individual worker's right to work without joining a union, and that this abrogates an important individual freedom. Make up your own mind. The union shop is legal under federal law but prohibited in a number of southern and western states which have enacted state "right-to-work" laws. Such right-to-work laws are fought bitterly by the unions.

Union and Management Motivation in Bargaining

You don't need a course in economics to tell you the main reason why unions fight for higher wages. They want more pay! But some other things aren't so easy to explain.

The thing that seems to amaze people most is that unions will strike for an extra few cents an hour pay, when third-grade arithmetic will show that it would take months or even years at the extra rate to make up for the pay lost in a long strike. Why are the union leaders willing to keep the men out over a few dollars? The same question can be asked the other way around, too. Why doesn't the company give in and end the divisive strike?

Try putting yourself in the workers' shoes. What would you think? You'd probably think: "That so-and-so who runs the company! He gets a big salary and has everything. His plushy stockholders are getting big dividends. Yet we have to scrape along on pay that just keeps the wolf away from the door. He won't even give us a few cents extra when he could save himself profits by doing it instead of trying to break this strike. We'll fight it out and lick him yet!"

Now turn around and see how you'd feel as the employer. You see the generous wages your company is already paying. You see the workers stubbornly holding out for unreasonable demands. You may see the union leaders as self-seeking hypocrites, out to protect their own jobs. The whole business is just one more step in the union's attempt to dictate to management. Would you give in if you were the employer?

Now put yourself in the union president's shoes. You know that your best bet in the long run lies in getting along with management. But you also know that there's never enough money to go around, and that you're going to have to push hard to get the wages to which your members are (in your eyes) honestly entitled. You know a strike is costly to everyone, but you know too that a threat often repeated but never carried out loses its force.

You know that unless you produce for your members, you're likely to be just another ex-president. If other unions have been getting twenty cents an hour plus fringe benefits, you'd better get that much too. You know that your chances of rising in the union ranks, say to a position in the international, depend in part on your success in getting more than other unions do. As you sit across the bargaining table from management, with tempers frayed by a long strike, would you give in?

The issues at stake in a labor negotiation are seldom simple. Human motives are strong and complex. The quarrel that the public sees in the newspapers is often only part of the real issue. The fine speeches made by both sides—about the need for wage increases to prevent recession and the like—sound good on the news broadcasts but often have little to do with settling the dispute at the bargaining table. To look at the issue in terms of a simple dollars-and-cents comparison is naïve. The issues are real, and no purpose is served by pretending that nothing but a common interest is involved. Unfortunately, there is seldom a clear, objective, right-or-wrong answer.

The Changing Role of Strikes

Collective bargaining is a process of challenge and response. For the most part it settles the disputes between employers and unions. But sometimes they can't, or won't, reach agreement. Tempers fray. Bitterness grows. Finally the union goes out on strike.

Strikes are rare events. With over 150,000 collective bargaining contracts in force, strikes over the last five years have caused a loss of less than one-fourth of 1 percent of the total working time involved. Table 30-1 shows the record since 1935. Time lost reached three-fourths of 1 percent in only one year—1947.[6]

Moreover, most of today's strikes are orderly and nonviolent, in sharp contrast to the bitter, bloody battles of thirty years ago. Strikes now arise largely over renewal of contracts and most

[6] A Department of Labor study shows that higher wages were the main issue behind 44 percent of all strikes between 1964 and 1970; work rules or conditions, 15 percent; union recognition or union shop, 13 percent; and union jurisdictional differences, 11 percent.

TABLE 30–1

Time Lost in Strikes, 1935–71

PERIOD	NUMBER OF STRIKES (ANNUAL AVERAGE)	WORKERS INVOLVED (ANNUAL AVERAGE) (IN THOUSANDS)	PERCENTAGE OF WORKING TIME LOST
1935–39	2,862	1,130	0.27
1940–44	3,754	1,386	.16
1945–50	4,210	2,940	.61
1951–55	4,540	2,510	.31
1956–60	3,602	1,620	.29
1961–65	3,560	1,365	.14
1966–70	5,032	2,653	.27
1971	5,135	3,263	.26

Source: U.S. Department of Labor.

often involve wage and work rule arguments, far less-explosive issues than the life-or-death organizing conflicts of the 1930s. Arbitration is now largely used to settle disputes that arise during the life of the contract. International officers generally try to help avoid or settle "wildcat" strikes, in which local unions strike in contravention of contract arrangements.

Thus, conflict resolution between labor and management has been moved increasingly to an orderly, peaceful procedural basis. But conflicts do persist, and the strike remains organized labor's weapon of last resort to enforce its views. Sometimes big strikes are enormously disruptive—for example, a long steel or public utility strike. But many labor observers feel that an occasional strike in most industries does no great harm and indeed may be a useful incident in the continuing bargaining relationship between labor and management. A strike is a device for letting off steam, for reasserting bargaining powers. It is not necessarily a symbol of the failure of collective bargaining. Thus, few labor experts favor laws to outlaw strikes, except possibly strikes that clearly threaten the public interest. For to outlaw strikes would not resolve conflicts but merely force them into other channels. But public tolerance of disruptive strikes has been strained in recent years, and better devices are needed to settle labor disputes within less costly, more orderly channels. (More on this subject in the next section.)

GOVERNMENT AND LABOR

Many labor-management disputes are now a test of strength between equals—sometimes equals of prodigious strength. When Leonard Woodcock sits down to bargain for the United Auto Workers, he speaks for a million men. Not millions, but billions, of dollars are at stake in these bargains; not only wages, but also the pensions of tomorrow's retired families, workers' health and disability insurance, their working hours, their vacations. In every election, the support of organized labor is eagerly sought. A nationwide Teamsters strike could bring the economy to a grinding halt in a matter of days. In local areas, small groups of union workers can achieve comparable results; a mere dozen bridge-tenders nearly shut down New York City in 1971.

Is union power excessive? Many say "yes"; they stress that there are no antitrust laws to limit union power. Most union members say "no." Do we need more stringent laws to limit union powers? Should government intervene when disruptive strikes occur, or when wage settlements threaten the government's antiinflation programs? Labor-management relations have many unanswered questions.

Major Legislation

The Norris-LaGuardia Act of 1932 was the first major national prolabor legislation. Employers had long been able to get court injunctions against labor groups to prohibit just about anything—for example, striking or picketing. Once the injunction was obtained, labor was the wrongdoer in the eyes of the law. Norris-LaGuardia outlawed the injunction in federal courts as an employer weapon against a wide variety of union activities—strikes, joining a union, peaceful picketing, or giving financial aid to unions. The intent of the law was clear. It was to give unions support in achieving a more equal bargaining status with employers, and to eliminate one of the most powerful employer weapons.

The New Deal, a year later, was frankly and aggressively prolabor. The Wagner Act of 1935 is the cornerstone of modern prolabor legislation. The Act:

1. Affirmed the legal right of employees to organize and bargain collectively, free from employer interference or coercion.
2. Required employers to bargain with unions of the workers' own free choosing.
3. Specifically prohibited a list of "unfair" employer practices.
4. Set up the National Labor Relations Board to provide a mechanism through which workers could gain recognition for unions of their own choosing, and to act as a quasi court to protect workers against unfair labor practices. (The NLRB does not act directly to mediate or settle labor-management disputes.) Employer intimidation, antiunion discrimination in hiring and firing, company attempts to influence union elections, and a variety of other practices were soon outlawed as unfair practices as NLRB and court decisions interpreted the new law.

By the early 1940s, the bitterest union organizing struggles were over, and industrial unionism in the mass-production industries was firmly entrenched. In the courts, labor also fared better. The Supreme Court, reflecting the changing temper of the times and the presence of several Roosevelt-appointed judges, in the *Apex* and *Hutcheson* cases (1940 and 1941) reversed a long line of judicial precedent and granted unions virtual immunity from the Sherman Act, though in the *Allen Bradley* case of 1945 an exception was made where they conspired with employers to fix prices or divide markets.

The federal *Fair Labor Standards Act of 1938* established minimum wages, maximum basic hours, and other fair-labor standards for all labor in interstate commerce. FLSA has been periodically amended since 1938, both to widen its coverage and to raise the minimum wage.

All through the 1930s and during World War II, labor rode high. But the pendulum had swung too far. More and more middle-of-the roaders began to feel that labor had overstepped its bounds; first in the sit-down strikes of the 1930s; then in the spreading jurisdictional disputes and strikes that the public and employers seemed powerless to halt; in its persistent wage demands during the World War II fight against inflation; and lastly, in its outright defiance of the federal government itself in disputes of critical importance to the national economy. The Taft-Hartley Act of 1947 was passed to redress the balance of power between management and labor.

Taft-Hartley defined unfair labor practices of unions to parallel those of employers. It clarified the powers of employers to speak against unions; it prohibited the closed shop; it contained provisions to protect the individual workers against the union; it empowered the president under conditions of national emergency to obtain an eighty-day cooling-off period, and required a secret union ballot on the latest company offer before the end of that period.

By 1950, labor racketeering had become a national scandal, and Congress passed the *Landrum-Griffin Act,* again over the violent objections of union leaders. Landrum-Griffin included a new "bill of rights" for individual union members, requirements for more detailed financial reporting by unions of all transactions with officials and members, and a requirement for secret-ballot elections and limitations on the terms of office of labor officials.[8]

Labor and the Antitrust Laws

Unions are substantially exempt from the antitrust laws, except as they may collude *with* employers to restrict output or to fix prices. The Wagner Act put the National Labor Relations Board in the position of granting official patents of monopoly to the unions it certified as exclusive bargaining agents. Most businessmen, and many economists who believe in the efficacy of competitive markets, believe that the antitrust laws should, at least in part, be applied to unions as well as businesses.

But unless a union has exclusive power to bargain for its members it has little market power. One proposal is to forbid industry-wide bargaining, just as firms may not collude to fix prices and output. Union supporters retort that this would *de facto* emasculate unions, moving back to the old relationships where all the power was on the employer's side. Another approach would forbid union pressures on employers to restrict output and union "featherbedding" (for example, by work rules that prohibit use of paint sprays in place of brushes). But such distinctions have proven very hard to enforce. Only legal reforms that command widespread public support have much chance of enactment and enforcement on such emotionally charged issues. And such widespread public support is hard to mobilize when the issue seems to be the working man against business, even where indirectly the ultimate consumer pays the bill.[9]

[8] For a fuller account of the changing legal foundations of unions and collective bargaining, see L.G. Reynolds, *Labor Economics and Labor Relations,* 6th ed. (Englewood Cliffs, N.J.: Prentice-Hall, Inc., 1974), Chap. 5.

[9] For an economic survey of the antitrust laws in relation to unions, see G. Hildebrand, "Collective Bargaining and the Antitrust Laws," in J. Shister, ed., *Public Policy and Collective Bargaining* (New York: Harper & Row, 1962).

The Government as Watchdog and Wage Setter

Congress has long been quick to investigate labor-management affairs. The biggest issues arise around disruptions of the national economy. Suppose a nationwide steel strike is in progress. The union, pointing to rising living costs, high profits, and increasing productivity, argues that fifty cents an hour more in pay and fringe benefits is the lowest raise it will even consider. Management in the steel industry's Big Six say they won't offer a penny more than twenty cents. They say that profits are down, that capacity is up enormously, that foreign competition is murderous, that steel wages have risen faster than prices, and that steelworkers are already among the best-paid in the nation. After long months of bickering with no progress, the union calls a strike. The strike has gone on now for two long months, and the steel shortage is shutting down not only civilian production but also arms production. If you were president, what would you do?

You might say, let the strike go on. It's none of the government's business. But with the economy grinding to a halt and with critical defense needs, you probably wouldn't.

You might invoke the national-emergency provision of the Taft-Hartley Act. This probably would get the union back to work and would give you eighty days to bring all the pressure you could on both sides to settle their differences. You'd focus as much public pressure as you could on the negotiators. If you felt strongly that right was mainly on one side or the other, you might tell the American people so and build up pressure on the other side to capitulate. But your position is especially tough if you're also worried about inflation, so you don't want to see a settlement that leads the companies to raise steel prices.

The power of the federal government is great, and this kind of pressure might well bring some kind of settlement, hopefully noninflationary. But, suppose neither the companies nor the union will give in. So the workers go out on strike again at the end of eighty days, more bitter than ever. What then?

UNIONS AND STRIKES IN THE PUBLIC SECTOR

Strikes have long been illegal in the public sector—at the federal level and in most states. Only recently has the right of public employees to join unions been widely recognized. Yet today, collective bargaining between public employees and governments (or quasi government agencies like school boards and transit authorities) poses the most difficult problems in labor relations.

A few public workers, for example postal employees, have long had unions. But membership in public service unions and "associations" (for example, the National Education Association of over one million teachers) has soared in recent years. Today, probably 40 percent of the nation's twelve million public employees belong to either unions or associations that are increasingly acting like unions in collective-bargaining relationships, and membership is growing faster than anywhere in the private sector. But public employee strikes are still illegal almost everywhere.

Until the 1950s, strikes by public employees were virtually unheard of. But as resort to power tactics spread in society, especially during the 1960s, public employees began increasingly to use strikes to achieve their goals, just like other unionized workers, albeit illegally. The New York subway workers, then bus drivers, airport traffic controllers, postmen, garbage collectors, teachers, and even firemen went out, and often achieved their demands when important services were crippled and public attitudes were divided. Antistrike laws were discreetly disregarded by public officials, or quickly amended in some cases. Although federal workers now are assured of the right to join unions, strikes are still illegal under the Taft-Hartley Act, and except for the postal workers have not yet been used on a significant level. Sometimes, nonstrike actions are used to get the same results. If airport traffic controllers just work "according to the rule book," the result can be to slow down air traffic dramatically without their violating any antistrike provision. If a lot of teachers report in sick, it is very difficult to teach the school children.

Should public employees have the same rights to strike and to bargain collectively as private workers have? Most people apparently still say "no," although attitudes toward public unions are far more permissive than two decades ago. Clearly, this issue goes far beyond economic analysis, into ethics and politics. Shutting down the schools, or air travel, or subway service, or fire protection imposes a cost many people are unwilling to tolerate. But if we deny these powers to public workers, how are they to be sure of getting a fair deal, comparable to private employees? Indeed, as a practical matter, how are we to keep them from striking, law or no law, if they just go ahead and strike? Bringing in the army to teach school, run the subways, or collect garbage is not a very attractive alternative.

The answers, if there are any, lie in considerable part outside economics. Some would tie public-employee salaries to comparable private salaries, but that leaves many other issues unsolved. Many urge arrangements for employees and public officials to "meet and confer in good faith" on disputed issues, followed by compulsory arbitration if disagreement persists (see the following section). Increasingly, when penalties are levied by the government they are in the form of heavy fines against unions, not widespread punishments against individual employees. Fining or firing several thousand individual public workers is generally neither realistic nor popular.

How do *you* believe we should handle the snowballing problem of public-employee demands and strikes? What should the law say? Perhaps even more important, what should the relevant public officials do if and when the public employees strike anyhow?[7]

[7]For a good survey of the issues, see J. Stieber, *Public Employee Unionism: Structure, Growth, Policy* (Washington, D.C.: The Brookings Institution, 1973); and *Collective Bargaining in American Government* (New York: The American Assembly, 1971).

Then is the tough time. By now tempers are really frayed. Labor and management have been over the issues *ad nauseam*. Each has been provoked into saying a lot of things better left unsaid. Everybody's dirty linen has been thoroughly aired before 200 million Americans.

You might decide to seize the steel industry and ask the workers to stay on the job. But this means seizing a vast, privately-owned industry, against all the traditions of American freedom and probably against the Constitution. Or you might order the workers to stay on the job, in the interests of the public welfare. But you know perfectly well you can't make men make steel, either under the law or any other way, if they just won't go back to work and do it.

Well, what would *you* do?

Compulsory Arbitration?

Often a skillful third party can soothe hot tempers and help get labor and management together when they are negotiating a contract or settling a grievance. The federal government and most state governments provide "mediators" and "conciliators" who serve as impartial go-betweens in trying to get disputes settled without resort to strikes. Sometimes these men enter at the request of labor and management; sometimes they are sent by public officials who want to avoid work stoppages. Their work is generally unheralded and unspectacular, but they are successful in a great number of cases.

With the exception of a few cases (for example, railway labor disputes) the government has no legal power to enforce a settlement on the parties. Many observers believe it should have some such power, or that Congress should prescribe "compulsory arbitration," at least in disputes vitally affecting the public interest. Under compulsory arbitration, both management and labor would be bound to accept the decision of a third party, the arbitrator, if they could not resolve their own differences. No strike or employer lockout would be permitted.

Most unions and many employers oppose such a law. They want to be left alone to settle their own disputes. But many people believe that society cannot afford the costly, disruptive strikes we now frequently face, or the inflationary wage settlements that often come out of long strikes during boom periods. These feelings are especially strong against public-sector strikes—by teachers, postmen, transit workers, and the like. But the case for compulsory arbitration is much weaker for smaller, run-of-the-mill labor disputes. How to define big disputes where the public interest would require compulsory arbitration is a tough problem, if you want to use compulsory arbitration only in those cases.

SHOULD THE GOVERNMENT GET OUT?

Ours is an economy of power groups. The unions and their leaders have great power. So do big employers. Wage setting has moved from the competitive marketplace to the industry-wide bargaining table in many leading industries. The wage bargains in steel, autos, electrical equipment, and coal go far to set a pattern for the rest of the economy. How can the government stand aside and see its antiinflation program split open, the operation of the whole economy periled by disputes in these industries? Less than 1 percent of the nation's labor force is employed in trucking. Yet that 1 percent could probably bring the economy almost to a dead stop in a few weeks.

But if it is drawn in, what can government really do? Many observers think that government intervention, especially when it becomes habitual, does more harm than good. They argue that when both sides know the government will eventually step in, there is little chance of settling the dispute beforehand. This is particularly true, they say, in inflationary periods when both labor and management know they will ultimately get much of what they want, and the main question is how much prices will be pushed up for the consumer. One side or the other will nearly always feel it can get a better bargain by waiting to get government involved in the settlement. Thus excessive government intervention in bargaining may hide the need for management and labor to accept basic responsibility in a free society, and may end up with more inflationary settlements too.

The American economy has come a long way from the highly competitive, individualistic system described by the classical economists. Concentrated economic power is here, like it or not. The problem is somehow to develop a framework within which economic power is responsibly channeled to the public good. The hard fact is that we cannot order huge groups of workers around in a democratic society. Wage setting must be by consensus when two powerful groups face each other across the bargaining table. And it must be by political as well as economic consensus once the government steps into the scene as a major participant in the process of wage setting.

REVIEW

Concepts to Remember

This is mainly an applications and policy chapter, using the concepts from earlier chapters. But be sure you have the following clearly in mind:

collective bargaining	compulsory arbitration
capital substitution	union shop
mediation	right-to-work laws

For Analysis and Discussion

1. If you were a factory worker and union members in the plant put pressure on you to join the union, would you join? Would you consider such pressures an infringement of your personal freedom of choice?
2. Should public service unions (for example, teachers, firemen, and postal workers) have the same rights to strike as other unions? If not, what rights do they have to enforce their demands?
3. "Unions are justified where employers would otherwise be able to exploit employees, but nowhere else." Do you agree? Explain.
4. Should production employees be put on regular annual salaries like those used for white-collar workers and middle management? Explain.
5. Would it be better to give employees the extra money rather than all the fringe benefits commonly included in union contracts, so that each person could decide for himself how to spend the money?
6. When the government intervenes in wage negotiations—for example, in autos or steel—what criteria should it use in deciding what wage settlement to urge?
7. Should compulsory arbitration be required by law to avoid strikes that involve government employees or otherwise affect the public interest? How would you define the public interest for this purpose?
8. Should labor unions be subject to the antitrust laws?
9. The Taft-Hartley Act requires unions and management to bargain "in good faith." Suppose an employer decides to make his best offer at the outset and thereafter refuses to improve the offer. Is he bargaining in good faith?

CASE 19

The Economics of Minimum-Wage Laws

In 1972, the federal government defined as in "poverty" any four-person urban family earning less than $4,300. By this test, over twenty million Americans were poor.

If we figure that a full-time job involves about 2000 hours of work a year, an hourly wage of $2.25 would just about provide the $4,300 poverty-level annual income, but most "poor" people earned substantially less. Many have proposed, therefore, that Congress raise the legal minimum wage to at least $2.25, or better $2.50, per hour to assure at least a bare minimum above-poverty income for all American workers. Less than that will clearly not provide a decent standard of living.

Do you favor this proposal? What would be the main effects of such legislation? Who would gain and who lose? (For simplicity, assume that total national expenditure is constant.)

Property Incomes: Rent, Interest, and Capital

CHAPTER PREVIEW

CHAPTER THIRTY-ONE

Most people obtain virtually all their income from wages or salaries. But nearly all the rich, and an increasing share of the moderately well-to-do, get a lot of income from rent, interest, and profits—from property they own. In 1972, wages and salaries were about $700 billion (75 percent) of the $925 billion total national income, while rents were $26 billion (3 percent), interest was $41 billion (4 percent) and corporation profits were $90 billion (10 percent).[1] The highest corporation salary reported was $800,000 (including bonuses) for the president of General Motors, but several hundred individuals reported taxable incomes over $1 million. The very rich get most of their income from capital.

Ours is a "capitalist" economy. One of its central tenets is the right of each individual to accumulate property (capital) of his own—a house, a factory, land, stocks, bonds. And most capital produces income for its owner—rent on land, interest on bonds, dividends on stocks. Some of the income may be consumed directly by the owner—housing services received by living in one's own house instead of renting. Thus, every homeowner is to that extent a capitalist, just as is a bondholder or stockholder. Indeed, if we think of ourselves as owning our own productive capacities (human capital) we are all capitalists, with our incomes depending substan-

[1]The rest of the national income goes to unincorporated businesses (farmers, lawyers, small shopkeepers, and the like) as a mixture of wages and profits.

tially on how much we have invested in human and nonhuman capital.

This chapter deals with two types of income from nonhuman capital (rent and interest), leaving profits until Chapter 32. Substantially the same marginal productivity, supply-and-demand theory explains the return on both human and nonhuman capital.

RENT

In everyday usage, "rent" is the price paid for the use of land, buildings, machinery, or other durable goods. This is the way we shall use the term, except in one later section where a special meaning is given to the term "economic rent."

What determines the rental income received by owners of land and other such durable productive resources? Although there are important institutional differences (we don't have a slave society in which we buy and sell human beings like we do land), the answer is much the same as what determines the wage income of labor—supply and demand, with demand based largely on the marginal productivity of the land or other asset in question. Whether the landlord is a greedy fellow or not is generally far less important than the impersonal forces of supply and demand.

The *supply* of nonhuman productive resources, and hence of their services, varies widely from case to case. At one extreme, the supply of land at the corner of Fifth Avenue and 50th Street in New York City, where Saks Fifth Avenue and Rockefeller Center sit, is completely inelastic—there's just so much and no more can be manufactured. At the other extreme, garden tools, a simple productive resource, can be reproduced readily, and their supply is highly elastic. Most cases lie somewhere in between. By and large, the supply of any productive resource is likely to be reasonably elastic *in the long run*—that is, given a long enough period for adjustment. Even farm land can readily be improved through the use of fertilizer, drainage, and so forth, if it pays to do so. For practical purposes, this is similar to making more land—you still have the same number of acres, but the acres have increased productivity.

The *demand* for the services of property depends basically on how much the service rendered is worth to the user. The property's marginal productivity underlies the business demand for its services, as for human labor. **Competitive bidding by businesses tends to draw each resource into its most productive use. Thus, each piece of land is rented to the highest bidder, and the high bidder must use the land where its marginal productivity is greatest to justify his paying the high rent. Under competition, the rent will just equal the marginal productivity of the land. As with labor, monopsony or monopoly may lead to "exploitation" of resource owners, to inefficient allocation of resources, or to unemployment of some of the resources.**

An Example

Take a simple example. What will the rent be on a ten-acre site on a highway near the outskirts of a city? Look at the demand side first. One demand may be for use in truck farming. How much renters will pay for this use will depend on the fertility of the soil, the water supply, and other such factors. Another demand may be for use as small individual business properties, such as restaurants, garden-supply stores, and so on. Here the amount of traffic passing by, the convenience of the location for potential customers, and other such factors will be especially important. Still another demand might be for use by a single supermarket, with surrounding parking area. Here again, traffic flows, convenience of location, availability of adequate parking space, and desirability of nearby neighbors might be especially important. Each potential renter would make some estimate of how much he could afford to pay in rent for the site—logically, up to its estimated marginal productivity for him.

Who will get the site, and at what rent? If there is active competition among the potential renters, the rent will be bid up until only the highest bidder is left. This will be the renter who estimates the marginal productivity of the site as being the highest. Thus, the site will be drawn into the use that promises the highest return to the renter, and through this mechanism into the use where consumers value it most highly. The rent will equal its marginal productivity in this most valuable use.

Can we be sure the rent will be bid up all the way to the estimated marginal productivity of the highest bidder? Not if the value to one user is substantially higher than to others. Suppose the site is ideal for a supermarket. Then the local Kroger's manager needs only to bid higher than the truck farmers and small shop operators, to whom the land is potentially worth less. Kroger's may get the site at a rent below its estimated marginal productivity as a supermarket site. But Kroger's won't if there's a local A&P or Safeway also in the market for sites.

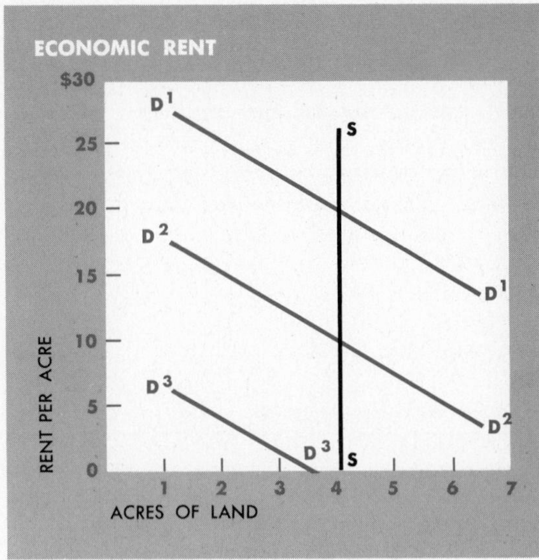

Figure 31–1

When the supply is a fixed amount, price (rent) is determined solely by demand.

"Economic Rent"—A Price-Determined Cost

Economists have one special definition of "rent" that differs from ordinary usage: **Economic rent is the payment for the use of a scarce, nonreproducible resource.** For example, the rent paid for one corner of Fifth Avenue and 50th Street in New York covers a mixture of "site value" and use of the building on the space, with all the improvements. If we isolate the site value of that corner—the land itself exclusive of any improvements on it—we have a resource that is scarce and completely fixed in supply; the supply is perfectly inelastic.

The rent on such nonreproducible productive agents is determined exclusively by the demand for them. The supply curve is a vertical line. If there is no demand, there is no rent; the rent rises directly as demand rises, without relation to the original costs of producing the resource. Figure 31–1 illustrates the point. Since the supply is a fixed amount, *SS* is a vertical line. If the demand is D^1D^1, the rent will be $20 an acre. If demand is D^2D^2, rent is only $10 an acre. If demand is only D^3D^3, the land commands no rent at all.[2]

Outside the site value of land, few cases of pure economic rent exist. But there are many cases with some element of economic rent, especially in the short run. For example, the great Wagnerian soprano, Brigit Nillson, is unique today, and nonreproducible in the short run. The high fees she charges the Met and other opera houses can be considered a partial economic rent for the use of her great voice. Similarly, if a firm patents a new productive process, for the life of the patent the process is much like the site value of land; it cannot be reproduced (except by consent of the patent holder). Indeed, if a firm has a temporarily protected monopoly position, part of the monopoly profits may better be considered a temporary economic rent on the monopoly position.[3]

[2] Years ago, Henry George argued that all rents should be confiscated through a "single tax," because they reflect a bonanza to landowners that arises as society's demand for the God-given, not man-made, land grows. Some cities, for example Pittsburgh, still tax land more heavily than buildings on the remnants of single-tax reasoning. A few disciples still advocate this as the basis for our entire tax system.

[3] Economists sometimes use the term "quasi rent" to describe the return on *temporarily* nonreproducible resources.

INTEREST

Most of us put our savings into financial assets, instead of buying real property directly. We buy bonds, or deposit the money in a bank or a savings and loan association. Our property is then a financial asset, and we collect the income from our capital in the form of interest. **Interest is the price paid for the use of money or credit, and indirectly for the capital or consumer goods that can be obtained with that money or credit.**

Why are interest rates what they are? Fundamentally, they depend on the marginal productivity of the real capital goods obtainable with the funds involved. (Temporarily, as we saw in Part Two, they may be heavily influenced by monetary policy and other special factors.) The same marginal-productivity, supply-and-demand framework is again the right one to use in answering the question.

Three special points about interest need to be made:

1. Interest is paid for the use of money, or credit, rather than directly for the use of productive resources. Money itself has no productivity. It doesn't build buildings or dig ditches. But money does give its owner purchasing power to obtain men and machines that will build buildings and dig ditches, and demand for loan funds traces back in considerable part to their power to buy or rent real productive resources. Thus, fundamentally the marginal productivity of real capital goods determines the interest rate, as it does rents.

2. Interest is stated as a *rate* of return (4 percent) rather than as an absolute sum. To say that the interest rate is 4 percent is merely to say that the borrower pays $4 interest per year for each $100 borrowed. The statement in percentage terms as a rate permits ready comparison between the payments of different amounts for widely differing resources. You can easily compare the return on money invested in an office building, in a turret lathe, and in your own education, by converting all three returns into a percentage on the funds invested. For example, if the office building cost $1 million and provides an annual net return of $50,000 after depreciation and other expenses, the rate is 5 percent. If the lathe cost $1,000 and provides an annual net return of $40, the rate is 4 percent. If a $1,000 investment in an electronics course will increase your annual income by $45, the rate of return is 4½ percent. According to these figures, funds invested in the office building provide a better return than funds invested in turret lathes or the electronics course.

3. There are hundreds of different interest rates. In 1972, for example, the government paid about 5¾ percent on long-term bonds. Short-term bank loans ranged from about 6 percent for well-established business concerns to 8 percent on mortgage loans to buy houses, and as much as 18 percent on small loans to individual borrowers. Some consumer loan agencies charged up to 40 percent per annum. You got no interest on demand deposits, but most banks and savings and loan institutions paid 4–6 percent on savings deposits. These different rates reflect differences in risk, locality, length of loan, cost of handling the loan, and a variety of other factors, as well as the "pure" interest rate that is included in each. To simplify matters, economists often talk about "the" interest rate. They mean the interest rate on a long-term, essentially riskless loan. The rate on long-term U.S. government bonds is often considered a close approximation. At mid-1972, therefore, we might have said "the interest rate" was about 5¾ percent. But don't make the mistake of assuming you could borrow money at this rate.

Nominal and Real Rates of Interest in Inflation

During inflation, the nominal (market) rate of interest exceeds the "real" rate. If you borrow $100 for one year at 6 percent and prices rise by 4 percent, in real purchasing power you pay only 2 percent interest because the money you pay back will buy 4 percent less than when you borrowed it. Thus, economists say the nominal interest rate is 6 percent but the real rate is only 2 percent. Conversely, if prices should fall, the real rate will be higher than the money rate.

Presumably, if borrowers and lenders correctly anticipate inflation (say 4 percent per annum), they will both take this into account in making their contracts. If the real productivity of capital is 3 percent, they will add on the 4 percent inflation allowance, making a 7 percent market rate. If their anticipation of inflation is perfect, the 7 percent nominal rate will be just high enough to produce the 3 percent real rate justified by the real productivity of capital. But we can never foresee inflation accurately, and the inflation allowance between market and real rates is correspondingly imperfect. Nonetheless, it is important to think always of the real rate of interest if we want to make correct analyses of saving and investment decisions.

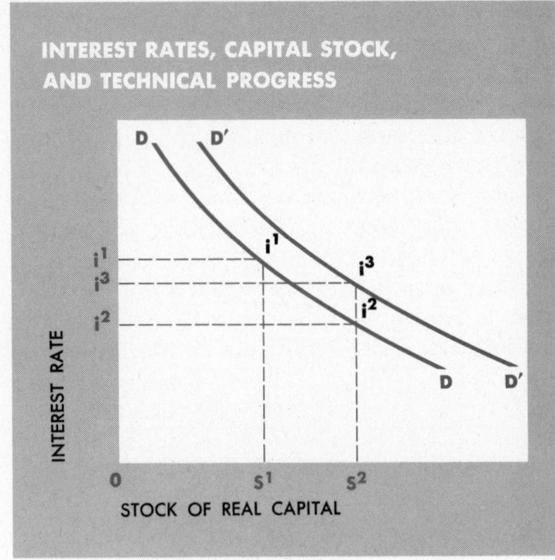

Figure 31–2

Given some level of technology and demand for capital DD, growth in the capital stock will reduce the interest rate from i^1 to i^2. Advancing technology partially offsets the growth in capital stock by increasing the demand for capital, and resulting interest rate in second year is i^3.

Interest and the Stock of Real Capital

Fundamentally, interest is paid for the use (productivity) of real capital—machinery, factories, airplanes, houses. Assume for the moment there is no technical advance to increase the productivity of capital; growth in the capital stock means merely adding more units of the same capital goods, say through saving and investing in more factories. Thus, in Figure 31–2, S^1 is the stock of capital now, S^2 next year. *DD* is the demand for real capital, dependent on its marginal productivity. Thus, as the capital stock grows we would expect the interest rate to fall from i^1 to i^2, other things being equal.

Figure 31–2 can also show the effect of technical advance. Suppose that inventions occur that increase the productivity of capital—say, a new computer or improved programs (software) for computer use. With higher marginal productivity, more capital will be demanded than before at the same price (interest rate). The *DD* curve will move to the right, say to *D'D'*. Thus, with both more capital and technical progress, the interest rate here falls slightly, to i^3, but much less than without technical progress. Of course, if the technical progress is very large, it may completely dominate the growth in capital stock, so that the interest rate would rise in spite of the increased stock of capital. In fact (look ahead to Figure 43–2) over the past century the two effects have been roughly offsetting; the real interest rate has fluctuated cyclically but without any clear long-term trend.

The Interest Rate, Resource Allocation, and Capital Accumulation

The interest rate helps potential business and individual investors allocate their funds among the millions of potential investment opportunities in the economy. When credit is allocated where the expected rate of return is highest, risk and other factors taken into account, it is optimally allocated from the consumer's viewpoint as well as from the investor's, because the highest returns will be found where consumer demand is relatively strongest. Unless an investment promises a return high enough to pay the going rate of interest under a private-enterprise economy, it does not justify exploitation, by the test of the market. Money capital is the fluid embodiment of real productive resources. Thus, the credit market, by channeling funds into those investments where the potential return exceeds the interest rate, provides a most valuable service to private investors and to society as a whole.

The interest rate plays another, more subtle, role. It provides a rough measure of the relative advantages of current consumption and saving—of the present against the future. By saving, the individual or business can get a continuing return of, say, 6 percent annually. If that return is enough to justify foregoing consumption now, it is advantageous to save. Without the interest rate to indicate the return on saved funds, savers would have no standard by which to measure the relative advantages of current consumption and saving.

Similarly, the interest rate helps businessmen and government planners decide among projects of different capital intensity. Suppose we can produce product *A* either with lots of labor and a simple plant, or with little labor working with long-lived, expensive machinery. Which is better? Only by calculating the "capital cost" (the interest rate times the dollar investment discounted back to the present—see the following section) of each and comparing the expected total labor-plus-capital cost of the two alternatives can we accurately choose between the two methods.

Perhaps most important of all, the interest rate exerts a powerful influence on the rate of economic growth in a capitalist economy like ours. A low interest rate encourages investment and faster growth, because it is cheap for businessmen to borrow to expand their productive capacity. A high interest rate has the opposite effect.

Interest as the Price of Credit

Interest as you know it in everyday life is the price of money, or of credit. Like any other price, it is determined by supply-and-demand factors in the market.

The private *demand* for credit comes from business firms and households. Businesses borrow when they think they'll make money by doing so—when the expected rate of return on their use of the money exceeds the interest rate they have to pay for it, as was explained in Chapter 11. You can readily see that each firm's demand for credit will directly reflect the marginal productivity of the borrowed capital in that firm. The other big, private demand for credit comes from individual households. In 1972, total consumer credit outstanding reached $150 billion, and over half of all department-store sales were made on charge accounts or installment plans. Most house purchases involve borrowing part of the price; in 1972, total mortgage debt on houses reached $340 billion, and was rising by over $25 billion annually.

The third major demand for credit is from governments—federal, state, and local. State and local governments borrow mainly to finance long-term capital improvements—highways, schools, waterworks. The federal government borrows to finance capital improvements, to pay for other government expenditures when taxes don't cover expenditures, and sometimes to finance deficits intentionally generated to combat depression.

The *supply* of credit depends on how much households and businesses save and lend, on the behavior of financial institutions like banks, and on government policy that can lead banks to lend more or less and to raise or lower the interest rates they pay and charge. Table 31–1 summarizes the complex of credit demanders (top half) and suppliers (bottom half) in 1966 and 1971. It thus shows the match between those who borrowed and lent.[4]

[4] Advanced texts in economic theory explain that in equilibrium the interest rate must be equal to the marginal productivity of real capital, must equilibrate the loanable funds market, and must equilibrate the market for money (currency and deposits) so that everyone is just willing to continue holding the existing amount of money rather than spending it on goods and services or securities; and that it will simultaneously do all three.

TABLE 31–1

Credit Borrowed and Supplied in Credit Markets

FUNDS BORROWED BY:	1966	1971
	(IN BILLIONS)	
Private Domestic:	$65.0	$130.8
Households	23.2	41.6
Businesses	34.1	63.0
State and local government	6.4	20.6
Financial institutions	11.5	9.6
Federal government	3.6	25.5
	$80.2	$156.3
FUNDS SUPPLIED BY:		
Private Domestic Nonfinancial:	$17.9	−$1.0
Households	16.4	−16.8
Businesses	−0.6	8.0
State and local government	2.3	7.7
Financial institutions (incl. Fed. Reserve)	59.2	136.5
Rest of the world (net)	0.8	21.7
	$80.2	$160.4

Source: Federal Reserve Flow-of-Funds data. Parts do not add to totals because of rounding, errors, and omissions. Table does not include common stocks.

Government Policy and Interest Rates

Since the 1930s, the federal government has exerted substantial influence on interest rates, through both Treasury borrowing and Federal Reserve monetary policy. As Part Two emphasized, the monetary authorities influence interest rates directly through purchase and sale of government securities, and indirectly through regulating bank reserves.

Remember from Chapter 13 that Federal Reserve activities influence *money,* or nominal, interest rates more than *real* rates. Real interest rates are determined by the demand for and supply of real capital. If the Fed increases M but there is no change in the real forces at work, the result is likely to be inflation. Temporarily, more M will reduce short-term interest rates. But if substantial inflation develops, borrowers and lenders are likely to agree on adding an inflation allowance to the real interest rate. Nominal interest rates will then rise by the inflation allowance but real rates are unchanged. In the early 1970s, for example, the long-term nominal interest rate was about 8 percent on industrial bonds, but with 4–5 percent annual inflation the real rate stayed near its long-term historical level of 3–4 percent.

VALUATION OF INCOME-PRODUCING PROPERTY

Income distribution is primarily concerned with the pricing of productive *services*, not with the prices of the productive agents themselves—land, machinery, buildings, and the stocks and bonds representing their ownership. But income-producing assets are bought and sold daily in our economy, and the interest rate plays an important part in setting the prices at which they sell.

To estimate the price of an income-producing asset, we need to know (1) its net annual return, and (2) the going rate of interest.

Valuation of Perpetual Fixed Income ("Capitalization")

Take a simple hypothetical case. Suppose we have a mine that will *forever* produce ore worth $100 annually, net after all expenses are met. Suppose further that the going rate of interest on substantially riskless investments is 4 percent. What will the mine be worth?

To get the answer, we simply "capitalize" $100 at 4 percent. That is, we find that sum on which 4 percent interest would amount to $100 annually. The arithmetic is simple. Four percent of x (the unknown value) is $100. In equation form, this is: $.04 \cdot x = 100$. Dividing the .04 into 100, we get $2,500 as the present value of the mine. Put another way the formula is:

$$PV = \frac{\$ \text{ Return}}{\text{Interest rate}}$$

Can we be sure the mine will really sell for $2,500? No, but we can be sure it will sell for something near that. No one will be willing to pay a much higher price, because by investing $2,500 anywhere else at equal risk he can get $100 annually. On the other hand, if the mine's price is much less than $2,500, people will find it a very attractive investment and the price will be bid up toward $2,500.

Valuation of Machinery

The principle involved in valuing non-perpetual assets is the same. Consider a machine that will last twenty years and whose marginal revenue productivity (rent) per year is $60. The going rate of interest on comparable investments is 6 percent. Using the same approach as before, we might capitalize $60 at 6 percent, and find that $60 is 6 percent on $1,000.

But there's a catch. The $60 annual income only lasts for twenty years, because the machine wears out. Our problem then is: What is the present, or capitalized, value of an income stream of $60 at 6 percent over twenty years, rather than in perpetuity? Mathematicians and industrial engineers have worked out a series of tables giving the answers for all combinations of interest rates and time periods for such problems. The answer here is $688.

The basic reasoning runs like this: At the end of the first year, we get $60. At the end of the second year we get another $60. And so on for the twenty years. Sixty dollars today is obviously worth $60, but $60 to be received, say, one year from today is clearly worth less than $60 today, since we do not have the use of it until a year hence. How much money today is equivalent to $60 a year from today? If the interest rate is 6 percent, $56.60 invested today at 6 percent will amount to just $60 a year from now. And we can make a similar calculation to get the amount equal to $60 two years hence, and so on up to twenty years. If now we add together all these "present values" of $60 to be received at the end of each of the next twenty years, we will get how much we ought to be willing to pay now for the series of twenty annual $60 net returns anticipated from the machine. Adding these twenty present values together gives the $688 above, the present value of the income stream promised if we buy the machine.

So you'd better not pay more than about $688 for the machine if you don't want to get stung. It's easy to see why this amount is less than the $1,000 the machine would be worth if it provided the $60 annually in perpetuity. If you have to pay more than about $688, you could earn more on your money by investing it elsewhere at 6 percent for the twenty years.

One other point is needed to complete this example. Unless this is a patented machine, others like it can be produced. If the current cost of producing such machines, for example, is only $500, you can be pretty sure that even the $688 price won't last. At a price of $688, it will pay to produce more machines like this one. As more are produced, the price will gradually fall. Not until the price falls to $500 will a new equilibrium be established. With a lot more machines, the marginal revenue productivity of each will be lower, both because of the law of diminishing returns and because the product of the machine will have fallen in price, so that the net annual yield per machine will no longer be $60.

To summarize: (1) At any time, the capitalized present value of an income-producing asset will be based on its net yield and on the going rate of interest on investments of comparable risk. (2) In the long run, the value of any asset will tend to be equal to its cost of reproduction, although it may vary widely from this figure at any given time.

Valuation of Corporate Stocks: The Stock Market

The same general principle holds in valuing corporate stocks and bonds, which represent claims on income earned by the issuing companies. But don't take your nest egg and rush for the stock market with this new knowledge. Corporate securities are interesting illustrations of the capitalization principle especially because they point up so many of the pitfalls. So far, we've assumed that we knew the yield of each asset, its life, and the appropriate going rate of interest. But in the real world all three of these are usually uncertain, especially on corporate stocks. The yield on most stocks fluctuates from year to year. There is no sure way of telling what it will be for any extended period in the future. Moreover, what rate of interest should we use in capitalizing? The appropriate one is the rate that prevails on other investments of comparable risk and other characteristics. But you pick it out.

Last, and most important, the market price of stocks is determined by thousands of other people who are all guessing at the same imponderables as you. Many of them are in the market as speculators, looking for a quick dollar on the price rise rather than for a long-pull investment. There is no reproduction cost to set a fairly stable base level that anyone can count on. The actual market price will reflect what all those people think is going to happen. So you're betting on what other people will bet on, and they in turn are betting on what you and others will bet on. Stock market investors talk about the "price-earnings ratio" for different stocks—the number of times the stock's price exceeds its annual earnings. For example, in late 1972 the price-earnings ratio on Westinghouse was 19 to 1. It took an investment of $19 to buy $1 of annual earnings. The higher the price-earnings ratio, the lower is the implicit interest rate used in capitalizing the company's earnings.

The stock market is no place for neophytes. The capitalization principle can give you a rough steer and it can help you in comparing different securities. But the much-quoted statement of Bernard Baruch is relevant here:

> If you are ready to give up everything else—to study the whole history and background of the market and all the principal companies whose stocks are on the board as carefully as a medical student studies anatomy. If you can do all that, and, in addition, you have the cool nerves of a great gambler, the sixth sense of a kind of clairvoyant, and the courage of a lion, you have a ghost of a chance.

The point of this section is not to warn you against investing in common stocks. On the contrary, over all, stocks have been a good investment over the long pull. Rather, the point is to stress the wide range of special factors at work in determining the actual market price of different income-producing assets. The analytical framework outlined in the simple cases above can help in most instances, but like all analytical models it provides only a framework for analyzing any particular situation.

REVIEW

Concepts to Remember

This is a difficult chapter. Recheck your understanding of the following concepts:

- rent
- economic rent
- quasi rent
- interest
- "the interest rate"
- "real" and "nominal" interest rates
- rate of return
- capitalization
- "present value" of an income stream

For Analysis and Discussion

1. How would you compare the rate of return on investment in yourself (human capital) through going to graduate school with the rate on investment in stocks or bonds (nonhuman capital)?
2. "Rent and wages are determined by substantially the same set of supply-and-demand forces, even though people are human and land is not." Do you agree? If not, what are the main differences?
3. "Rent is an unearned increment for any landowner, since he does not have to do any work for the rent he receives. Therefore the government should confiscate rents through special taxes." Do you agree? Why or why not?
4. "The profits made by a company on the basis of an exclusive patent are essentially rents, not profits." Do you agree or disagree?
5. Some economists predict persistent inflation over the years ahead. If they are correct, how would you expect this inflation to affect money and real rates of interest? Explain.
6. Other things equal, would you expect rapid technological advance to raise or lower the long-term rate of interest? Why?
7. Suppose the Federal Reserve tightens bank reserves and raises interest rates. Would this increase or decrease real investment, other things equal?
8. Find out the "carrying charge" on some article you are considering buying. Then calculate the interest rate you would be paying on the funds you in effect borrow from the seller. Would you be better off to borrow the money at a bank and pay cash? (See Case 20.)
9. Suppose you inherit an eighty-acre tract of farmland. You are uncertain whether to sell it or to retain it and rent it out. How would you go about comparing the advantages of the two courses of action?

Nominal and Actual Interest Rates[5]

Interest rates aren't always what they seem to be. The following three cases may help you to protect yourself against some common mistakes, by looking at some situations that frequently arise in everyday life.

Installment Charges. You buy a $120 rug at the local furniture store. The store offers to let you pay over a full year, at $10 per month plus $1 per month additional carrying charge. (1) What is the actual interest rate the store is charging on the money it lends you over the year? (2) A local finance company will lend you the money at 15 percent on your unsecured note. Should you borrow from them and pay cash for the rug, or buy on the installment plan?

ANALYSIS. The store's offer looks like a 10 percent interest rate, a reasonable rate for such a loan, especially since it has to include something extra for the nuisance of keeping the books and maybe having to dun you for the money. But look again. The actual rate is far higher. You pay a dollar carrying charge each month, but the total amount you have on loan from the store goes down $10 each month. The last month you owe them only $10; yet you are still paying interest at the rate of $1 a month, or $12 per year. The actual rate on your unpaid balance during the last month is 120 percent per annum. The average for the year is about 20 percent, twice the apparent rate, because the average loan to you is about half the purchase price of the rug. The actual rate for each month is calculated in the accompanying table. If you want to pay the smallest amount of interest, in this case go to the finance company at 15 percent.

General lesson: Compare carefully the actual interest rate included in installment carrying charges with what the money would cost you if you borrowed it directly elsewhere. This is not to suggest that installment sellers are crooked; they have to cover their costs of foregoing interest on the money they lend you, plus their operating expenses. But actual interest rates are often higher than they seem.

[5] Because some of the necessary analysis is not included in this chapter, the suggestions for analysis are included here.

	UNPAID BALANCE	INTEREST ($1 MONTHLY; $12 PER YEAR)	INTEREST RATE ON UNPAID BALANCE
1st month	$120	$12	10.0%
2nd month	110	12	10.9
3rd month	100	12	12.0
4th month	90	12	13.3
5th month	80	12	15.0
6th month	70	12	17.1
7th month	60	12	20.0
8th month	50	12	24.0
9th month	40	12	30.0
10th month	30	12	40.0
11th month	20	12	60.0
12th month	10	12	120.0

Bond Yields. You have about $1,000 to invest. You are considering an 8 percent corporation bond. It is a $1,000 face value bond, so the annual interest is $80. Its current market price is $1,100, and it is due in ten years. Your main alternative is putting the money into U.S. government bonds, which pay 6 percent, can be bought at face value ($1,000), and are also due in ten years. Assume that the two investments are equally safe and attractive on all other grounds. Which one should you choose?

ANALYSIS. At first glance, the corporate bond seems to win hands down. But look again. You pay $1,100 for the bond, but you'll only get back $1,000 at the end of ten years. To get the true net yield, you need to "write off" $10 of the value of the bond each of the ten years, so your actual net annual yield would be only $70, rather than $80. Now you can calculate the exact yield on the corporate bond. It's $70 per year on $1,100 invested. This figures out to about 6.4 percent per annum, barely above the 6 percent offered on the government bond. If the risk on the two bonds is really identical, the corporate bond is the better buy. But if (as is likely in the real world) the corporate bond is riskier, the choice is not clear. Which you should prefer will depend on your attitude toward risk.

Inflation, Risk, and Growth. Suppose again that you have $1,000 to invest. You can put it in a bank or a savings and loan account at 5 percent, buy 6 percent government bonds due in ten years, or buy Sears Roebuck common stock at 100 to yield about 1.6 percent in dividends (4 percent in total earnings, including those plowed back into the company; the price-earnings ratio is 25 to 1). Of course you are not sure, but you judge that we face inflation of about 3 percent annually over the decade ahead. Which investment should you make?

Analysis. This a trickier problem still, because it involves not only your risk aversion (as in the preceding case), but also probable inflation and the historically persistent growth in Sears profitability. Inflation first: If prices rise 3 percent per year, the real rate of interest on the bank account is only 2 percent, on the government bond 3 percent, and the Sears dividend doesn't even cover the inflation loss. Better face it that your real return will be a good deal less than the nominal rates. Second, risk: There is virtually none on the bank or savings and loan account; their deposits are government-insured up to $20,000 per person, and you can withdraw your money whenever you want. On the government bond, there's no risk on repayment when the bond comes due, but the price may fluctuate in the meantime, so you might have to sell at a loss if you want your money before ten years. Of course there's also a possibility the bond's price will rise in the meantime (for example, if market interest rates on comparable bonds fall—work out the capitalization for yourself), in which case you'd make a gain on your sale. On Sears, there's real risk. You have no guarantee at all that Sears will keep on paying its present dividend, or that the price-earnings ratio will stay as high as it is now. Everyone knows that Sears' earnings and dividends have risen persistently over the last three decades, and investors' present willingness to pay so much for a currently small dividend reflects their belief that Sears' earnings, dividends, and stock price will continue to grow in the future. Moreover, many investors figure that if inflation comes Sears can pass along rising costs through higher prices, so money earnings will rise with the inflation rather than be eroded. If investors' expectations turn out to be seriously wrong on any of these points, Sears' high price-earnings multiple of about 25 to 1 is likely to fall, and you'll find that you can only sell your stock at a loss. But if the optimistic forecasts turn out to be right, Sears' earnings, dividends, and stock price will rise substantially.

What should you do with your money? Economic analysis can point up the issues and some consequences of various possible developments. But the best investment for you will depend on your assessment of the probability of these various developments and your attitude toward risk—and note that risk here is a far more complicated issue than just whether you will receive some stated number of dollars at a given time.

Profits: Theory, Facts, and Fantasy

CHAPTER PREVIEW

CHAPTER THIRTY-TWO

In 1970–72, corporation profits before taxes averaged $84 billion annually, about 8 percent of the nation's GNP. After payment of corporation income taxes, the comparable figures were $47 billion and 4.4 percent. If we add in unincorporated businesses (farmers, lawyers, doctors, small shopkeepers, and the like), the pretax profit figure is probably increased by $10–20 billion; the amount can only be estimated roughly because we have no clear separation between profits on the one hand, and implicit wages, interest and rent on the unincorporated businessmen's own labor and investments on the other. Indeed, a substantial part of reported corporate profits is also actually implicit interest on invested capital owned by the stockholders. Implicit interest is probably between a quarter and a half of total corporation pretax profits. Thus pure economic profits, after taxes and allowance for implicit interest, were probably small, or possibly even nonexistent.

Nearly $100 billion in reported pretax profits is enough to provide a lot of income to stockholders and unincorporated businessmen, especially well-to-do ones, but obviously it's only a small fraction of the total income received by the public. Whether profits are too big—an unconscionable exploitation of the workers, as the Marxists and modern radicals claim—or too low—an inadequate return to induce capital and risk takers to perform their proper social functions—is one of today's, and everyday's, hottest issues.

Our look at the market system thus far has stressed two big roles for profits. They're the incentive to produce what consumers demand—the carrot that entices businessmen to perform their social function. And they're a major source of funds for the investment that makes the economy grow by the construction of new plant and equipment. Now it's time for a summary look at profits in their own right.

PROFITS ON THE MODERN SCENE

Potential profit indicates where society wants more resources used. Thus, the individual businessman who predicts most successfully what the consumer will want, who meets consumer demand most effectively, who handles his production most efficiently, and who buys his labor and materials most adroitly, will end up with the biggest profit. The inefficient producer who fails to respond to consumers' demands is likely to end up with red ink on his books. If a seller has a partial or complete monopoly, he may be able to maintain positive economic profits over a substantial period without innovations, real productive efficiency, or close adaptation to consumer demands. But wherever other firms are free to enter the market, competition will tend to bid prices down and costs up, eliminating economic profits.[1] The pursuit of profits plays a central organizing role for the entire economy.

If you ask the man in the street, he probably won't be very sure just what profit does mean, but he'll almost certainly have an antagonistic attitude. Public-opinion polls show this time after time; most people think profits are too big. And it's highly likely he will have only a vague idea about how big profits actually are. So a further look at the facts may be in order.

The Facts

Figure 32–1 summarizes the course of *corporate* profits before and after income taxes, since 1929. About half the total now goes to the government in corporation income taxes, before payment of dividends or reinvestment in the firm. Clearly, the size of profits looks a lot different before and after taxes. Remember too that two-thirds of the huge growth since 1929 is inflation—prices have nearly tripled.

The aggregate dollar figures alone don't have much meaning, even when corrected for infla-

[1] Remember that elimination of *economic* profits by competition does not eliminate all accounting profits, since a substantial share of reported accounting profits is implicit interest on stockholders' investment in the firm.

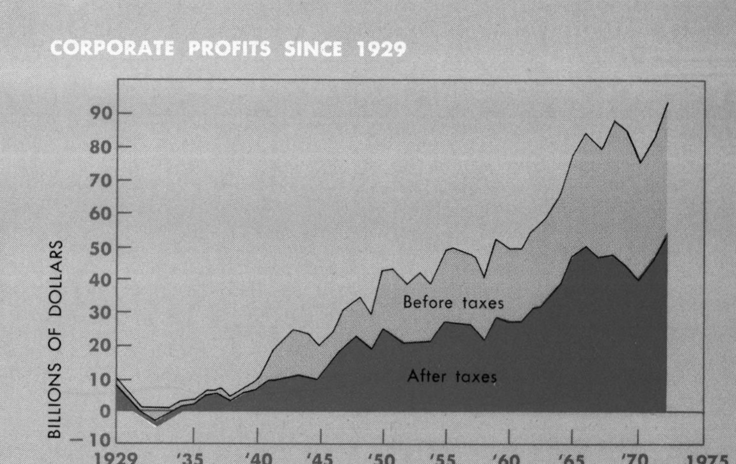

Figure 32–1

Corporate profits, in current dollars, have risen sharply but irregularly since 1929. Corporate income taxes now take somewhat less than half the total. (Source: U.S. Department of Commerce.)

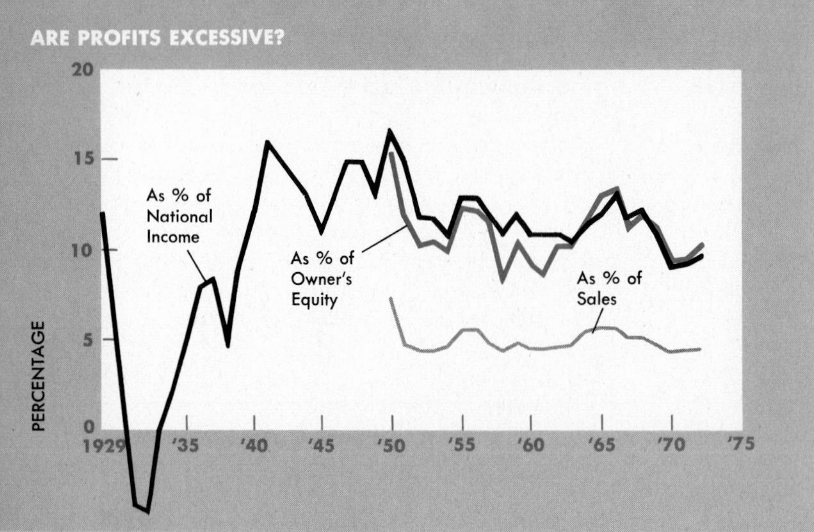

Figure 32–2

Corporate profits reached peaks during and after World War II. Since then they have fluctuated at somewhat lower levels relative to national income, sales, and owners' equity, declining since the mid-1960s. (Source: U.S. Department of Commerce. Profits as percentage of national income are before taxes for all corporations; other comparisons are profits after taxes for manufacturing corporations.)

tion. Everything in the economy has grown immensely since 1929. Have profits risen or fallen compared to other income shares? Are businesses making more or less profit these days per dollar of sales, or per dollar of investment? Figure 32–2 gives some of the answers.

It's clear that the profit share in the gross national product (based on reported corporate profits) has jumped all over the place in business cycles. Corporate profits were actually negative in the years 1931–32 (negative by a far larger amount if we consider *economic* profits), and hit a peak of 15 percent of GNP in the boom year of 1950. Since the mid-1960s, profits have declined substantially, as a percentage of both GNP and corporate sales. Lesson in statistics: Note how you can make the profit share look sharply rising or sharply falling, depending on whether you take the 1930s or 1940s as your starting point.[2]

[2] No official long-period series is available showing profits as a rate of return on invested capital. A private series (First National City Bank of New York) shows profits after taxes for a large sample of manufacturing corporations as 10 percent on net worth in 1929, about zero in 1932, a peak of 14 percent in 1948. The official government series then shows them as fluctuating between 9 and 15 percent for the years 1950 to 1966, and gradually declining since the mid-1960s to about 9–10 percent in 1970–72.

Public opinion surveys have repeatedly shown that the public holds wildly erroneous ideas about the size of corporate profits. Public estimates of after-tax profits as a proportion of sales have ranged all over the map, but have generally concentrated in the 25–35 percent range. This is some five to eight times the actual return of 4–5 percent in 1970–72. If actual profit margins on sales had reached publicly-guessed levels, total corporate profits before taxes in 1972 would have been over a half-trillion dollars, or nearly half the total GNP. Little wonder that many people believe that corporate profits could absorb the cost of almost any social reforms if only corporations were less greedy! And equally little wonder that many corporate executives are severely frustrated at how little the public understands business.

Last, a fact we wish we knew, but don't. Total reported corporate profits are a combination of implicit rent and interest on stockholders' investment, monopoly or quasi-monopoly profits, and economic profits arising largely out of dynamic change in the economy. Presumably our attitude toward these three parts would be different if we could separate them. Types one and three look socially legitimate and useful, but it's hard to justify type two. But alas, we have nothing more than the crudest guesses at such a division.

THE TWO ROLES OF PROFITS

The preceding chapters have stressed profits as the carrot that lures businessmen and investors into meeting consumer demands, reducing costs, and innovating with new products. And losses are the stick that beats those who fail in their attempts. Part Two stressed profits as a major source of financing new investment and growth for individual businesses and the economy. Let us now look more intensively at these critical roles of profits in our society, and at the theory of profits, preparatory to asking the final question: How big *should* profits be in the modern American economy?

Profits as an Incentive

The primary social function of profits is to give businessmen an incentive to produce what consumers want, when and where they want it, at the lowest feasible cost. This includes innovation of new products and new methods. The profit motive is at the center of a private-enterprise economy.

But a lot of questions are raised about just how the profit motive does, and should, work as a practical matter. For example, most after-tax profits go to stockholders who have little to do with managing the businesses they own. Clearly profits give them an incentive to invest, but professional managers (rather than owner-operators) now run most big businesses. Thus, some critics ask whether profit is still the most effective incentive to innovation and efficiency. The modern corporation president gets a salary plus a bonus dependent on profits, but as president he gets only a small fraction of 1 percent of the company's total profits. We rely on top management's urge to excel and to make large profits for the stockholders to produce the desired results, as well as on their personal enrichment from profits. We rely heavily on profits per se to draw investors' funds into the businesses where profit prospects are highest. The functions of management, entrepreneurship, and providing capital are thoroughly entangled in today's big businesses.

Second, remember that it's the *expectation* of profits that must be there to make the system tick, not the achievement of profits. Never forget that this is a *profit-and-loss,* not just a profit, system. Every year the big stick of losses pounds a large number of businesses that don't succeed in meeting the test of the market. Many a firm has gone broke.

In 1970, half of all corporations reported losses on their income-tax returns. During prosperous 1972, failures (bankruptcies) of incorporated businesses averaged nearly 1,000 per month. Total liabilities of these failures were $2 billion. Fewer than 25 percent of the businesses established during the immediate postwar years were still operating a decade later. Yet each year new thousands rush in, confident that they have the knack to succeed where others have failed. Big-business failures are less common than failures among small firms. People who have $50 million or $100 million to venture are rare, and profitability calculations on such investments are made with a great deal of care. And failing big firms are often merged into other firms to avoid massive disasters. But even for big business the story is far from one of unbroken success. Think of the auto industry, with its spectacular growth over the present century. The Oakland, Stanley Steamer, Maxwell, Hupmobile, and dozens of others were once as much household words as Ford and Pontiac are today. Yet only a few decades later they are as extinct as the dodo. More recently, Douglas Aircraft, a multi-billion-dollar giant, was saved only by merger with McDonnell Aircraft; Lockheed Aircraft had to be bailed out by a quarter-billion dollar government loan guarantee.

Hope springs eternal in American businessmen's and investors' breasts. Their mistakes lead to a good deal of waste in resources devoted to ventures that don't succeed. But their optimism gives the American economy much of the dynamic vigor that has pushed the American standard of living well above its nearest competitor. It is doubtful that dynamic progress in a private-enterprise system is possible without widespread losses from bad business guesses as well as widespread profits from good ones. But without the *expectation* of profits, the system will grind to a halt.

Profits as a Source of Investment and Growth

Profits have a second major social function. Undistributed corporate profits (profits not paid out as dividends) are one important source of funds for business investment. In 1972, for example, they totalled $25 billion, and almost all were plowed back into new plant, equipment, and other such business uses. Corporation depreciation allowances are also considered by most businessmen as sources of funds for business investments (though remember that a depreciation allowance is merely a bookkeeping charge, not actual money set aside). Because businesses seldom replace worn-out assets with identical assets, it is often hard to identify what is replacement and what net new investment. Thus, business investment is often viewed gross (including replacement), as in the gross national product accounts. In 1972, depreciation charges totalled $68 billion, so net "internal" sources for investment spending totalled about $93 billion.

THE THEORY OF PROFITS

Profits in a Static Economy

In a *static* economy, without technological advance, population change, capital accumulation, and changing consumer wants, only monopoly profits would continue in long-run equilibrium. Competition would gradually eliminate all other *economic* profits as resources were shifted into high-profit industries. Capitalization would bid up the prices and rents of especially productive resources. Throughout the economy, economic (though not accounting) profits would be eliminated when equilibrium was achieved, except for those industries where new businesses were prevented from entering. There, and there only, monopoly and oligopoly profits would continue indefinitely. In effect, monopoly and oligopoly profits would then be a kind of rent on exclusive monopoly position.

Profits in a Dynamic Economy

But continuous, unpredictable change is the dominant characteristic of the real world. Uncertainty confronts the entrepreneur or manager daily. He must somehow "guesstimate" the future demand for his product, his future costs, future changes in technology, future behavior of his competitors. Then he must keep an eagle eye out for how the government is going to behave —on taxes, spending, antitrust policy, labor relations, and international affairs. In the midst of all this, he needs to worry about keeping his costs below those of competitors, keeping the union at least tolerably happy, being sure that his sales organization is on its toes, and so on.

If he does all these things better than his competitors, and especially if he has a partial monopoly position to help him, he'll end up with a good profit. If he misses on many of the important decisions, the red ink will appear. The biggest job of the modern entrepreneur is to live with and to make the best of uncertainty. If he doesn't thrive on this kind of life, he'd better save himself a big doctor bill for ulcers and go to work for someone else.

Insurable Risk, Uncertainty, and Dynamic Change. Many kinds of risk can be insured against. In this way, the uncertainty can be eliminated by incurring a known dollar cost. The best-known example is the risk of loss from fire or theft. Without insurance, this uncertainty would be a major problem for any business concern. But the likelihood of fire loss is reasonably predictable for a large number of buildings of any given type, even though it is unpredictable for any given building. By pooling together the moderate insurance premiums on a large number of buildings, the insurance company has enough funds to pay off the fire losses on those few buildings that do burn each year. Long experience has reduced the likelihood of such occurrences to a scientific, statistical basis. Businesses can now convert this type of uncertainty into a known cost through insurance.[3]

Professor Frank H. Knight has pointed out that insurable risks are thus really only another business cost to be included with other business costs, and that economic profits arise only from bona-fide cases of uninsurable uncertainty. Alas, the businessman can't go to his insurance agent and say: "I'm bringing out a new-style dishwasher; insure me against its being a flop." Economic profits beyond profits on monopoly positions, Knight argues, are thus analytically linked solely to a world of dynamic change and uninsurable uncertainty.

Since profits arise largely out of dynamic change and uncertainty, much of what happens to profits is outside the control of any individual manager or entrepreneur. The biggest profits arise in booms, the biggest losses in depressions. "Windfall profits" are widespread in a lusty boom; in a bad depression, the best management in the world has a tough time making ends meet. The manager who can foresee business fluctuations and adjust successfully to them is worth his weight in gold.

Shifting consumer demand for individual products is a second big area of change largely outside the control of the individual businessman. Even General Motors is going to have a tough time making profits on automobiles if consumers decide to ride in helicopters instead. But the alert entrepreneur is far from helpless. He can change his product to keep in step with the times, and through his advertising he can influence what consumers want to buy.

Changes in costs are a third big area of uncontrollable uncertainty. What happens to the price of steel is outside the control of Westinghouse; yet steel represents one of the major costs in making Westinghouse refrigerators. The same thing is true of many other costs. The businessman can bargain with his local union, but he isn't going to get far with a wage rate much below the rates that prevail elsewhere for similar work, any more than he can buy steel below prevailing market prices. Technological changes continually change costs.

Basically, it's the manager who does a good job of prediction under conditions of dynamic uncertainty, and who adjusts effectively to unforeseen conditions, who is likely to turn in good profits.

The Profits of Innovation. One noted economist, Joseph Schumpeter, has argued that profits boil down largely to payments for keeping a jump ahead of your competitors through innovation. The big profits come from big, successful innovations—the motor car, color TV, and so on.

Unfortunately, no one has yet figured out a sure way of telling in advance whether a new mousetrap or a new auto engine will prove a success. First, there is the technological problem of developing the idea into a usable process or product. When this is licked, there is still that capricious monarch of all the surveys—the consumer. Business history tells a fascinating story of the sure things that flopped, and also of the thousand-to-one shots that have become the industrial giants of today.

Successful innovation in effect gives a temporary monopoly to the innovator, and often big profits. Like other monopoly profits, the economic profits of innovation persist only until competitors catch up and bring profits in the industry down to competitive levels. But innovations are often protected by seventeen-year patents. And a running start on your competitor is often more important than the legal protection of patents. The firm with the know-how and experience that go with a new product or new method is likely to have a new innovation at hand by the time competitors catch up on the last one. The continuing success of the industrial giants of today—General Electric, IBM, DuPont—rests as much on this kind of continuing innovation as on any other single factor.

[3]Very large firms may "self-insure." If a firm has hundreds of buildings itself, it may figure that the predictable likelihood of fire loss in any given year is less than the cost of buying commercial insurance on them.

HOW BIG SHOULD PROFITS BE?

Are profits too big? Is business too concerned with making profits, and not enough with social responsibilities, as a large majority of college students reported in a recent survey? How big do profits need to be to give the incentives they need to managers and investors to provide a dynamic, progressive, basically private-enterprise economy?

In principle, the answer is clear. Profits are big enough when businessmen and investors act as if they were big enough—when we get a satisfactory response to consumer demands in a dynamic economy, and the rate of economic growth we want. This answer puts the focus on the social functions of profits, not on the equity of the incomes received by profit makers, in contrast to much popular discussion about whether coupon clippers and dividend receivers are too rich.

The facts on profits were summarized above. In the past five years, corporate profits after taxes averaged about $45 billion, or about 4 percent of GNP. This is the amount society might consider taking away from profit receivers, if it considers profits too big. To judge the effects of such a profit transfer, we need first to remember, from above, that the total is made up of three quite different parts: (1) monopoly and quasi-monopoly profits, (2) returns (implicit interest) on stockholders' investments, and (3) true economic profits in a dynamic economy. Few economists would defend the first, but most evidence suggests it comprises a relatively small part of the total. If we oppose the second, we are essentially saying that savers should receive no interest on their investments. This is a position Marxists and many radicals hold and that we shall examine in the appendix; this opposition would presumably apply equally to interest on bonds, bank deposits, and other savings. If we reduce the third part of profits, we question the need for profits as an incentive to businesses in both meeting consumer demands and investing for economic growth and higher living standards.

To assess these issues we need to ask, who gets the profits? Whose incentives are the crucial ones? The $10–15 billion of profits in unincorporated businesses go to millions of individuals—doctors, lawyers, small shopkeepers, some poor, some rich. These are not the profits most critics challenge. Corporate profits go to some thirty million stockholders. On these, first remember that nearly half of those profits are plowed back into the business involved, and hence do not show up in the current income of stockholders. Dividends actually paid out to stockholders averaged about $25 billion annually over the past five years—just over 2 percent of GNP. Second, while there are over thirty million stockholders, most own only small amounts of stock and their dividend incomes are a tiny proportion of their wages and salaries. In 1970, 20–30 percent of all wealth was held by the top 1 percent of families, and stockholdings of individuals were probably at least comparably concentrated. Third, a large and growing proportion of all stock is held by financial institutions (trust companies, banks, insurance companies, and pension funds), which in turn reflect the investments of millions of people, rich and poor. Fourth, the big incomes of corporate executives are primarily salaries, not profits, though many also receive bonuses based on the profits earned and own stock on which they receive dividends.

How big profits must be to get these diverse groups and individuals to perform their social functions of investing and entrepreneurship is obviously a complex question. Traditional Marxist doctrine and some modern radicals say the answer is easy. Profits and interest serve no social function; they should be zero. All property, except personal belongings, should be owned by the state, and state planners should decide what is to be produced, and how much of it. Only labor is productive, and there should be no return to property.

This answer obviously looks to a communist system completely different from ours, and one with which few Americans agree. (We shall look at it briefly in the following appendix and in detail in the final chapter.) Thus it doesn't help

CASE 21

Profits for the Picking?

In 1972, corporate profits after taxes were about $53 billion, dividends about $25 billion. This total demonstrated to many the ability of corporations to absorb the costs of producing better products, providing better services, and paying higher wages without raising prices to consumers. Suppose we agree (though many stockholders would not) that profits are bigger than they need be, and we propose to make corporations more responsive to consumer and social needs, which we argue they can perfectly well afford to be with their huge profits. Using the theory of the preceding chapters, analyze the likely consequences of the following.

Consumerism—Who Pays? Ralph Nader recently released a study showing that aerosol cans (of shaving cream, bug and hair sprays, deodorants, and the like) can be dangerous bombs if they are punctured or get too hot, with potential loss of eyesight and other injuries from flying metal. Admittedly, such explosions are very rare, but the danger could be further reduced by making the cans of heavier metal or other material of greater strength. Nader said consumers have a right to safer products.

Should we apply consumer pressure, or pass a new law, to force manufacturers to use only heavy steel containers for such aerosol sprays? It looks like a good idea—safer products for consumers, and the manufacturer can well afford to do it out of those big profits. So we pass the law. Your economic theory should suggest what happens next; manufacturers raise prices and consumers have to pay more for the aerosol sprays. Maybe businesses *should* absorb the higher costs out of profits, but it's unlikely that they will. They feel they need all the profits they are making, whether or not you agree, and if costs go up for everyone in industries using aerosol sprays, you can be pretty sure prices will too. Consumers get safer sprays, and pay for them. Whether they're better or worse off as a result depends on how much you think that extra safety is worth.

But suppose consumers are outraged at the greed of businesses in raising prices for such an obviously needed piece of consumer safety, and get Congress to pass a law forbidding aerosol-spray manufacturers to raise prices on the new product. Assuming the law is strictly enforced, what does your economic theory tell you will happen then? Right! Manufacturers will stop making aerosol sprays, on which they will now make a loss or smaller profit than on other products. Maybe they'll keep on for a while, but in the long run capital will be transferred to other products where the potential profit rate is positive. If consumers want completely safe spray cans they can get them, but in the long run only by paying their higher costs.

Consider another case. Recently courts and juries have been holding sellers strictly responsible for damages to consumers from products that are in any way faulty. Juries have awarded large settlements to individuals injured in accidents presumably due to product defects. A Wisconsin man recently received $500,000 for the loss of a leg when a safety guard on a chain saw slipped after he thought he had fastened it firmly. The average award rose from $12,000 to $67,000 over the past five years in such seller-liability household chemical cases, from $38,000 to $78,000 in automobile cases. And the total number of such cases litigated rose from about 100,000 to 500,000 annually over the same period.

Fair enough! you may say. Consumers deserve safe, reliable products, and if businesses don't make them, let them pay. But get out your economic theory again. Where is all that money coming from? If the culprit is just one firm in an industry, its profits may indeed have to absorb the costs of coming up to industry standards. But if what consumers demand is higher safety and reliability standards for all, the result is probably higher costs, and if so almost certainly they'll be passed along in higher prices, in the long if not the short run. Same reasoning as with the aerosol cans above.

Some consumers say the insurance companies will have to pay the damages, so businesses won't have to charge consumers more. But that again is probably short sighted. Insurance companies must also cover their costs to stay in business, and they push up rates quickly for any class of customers who show unusually large claims. Unless you can find an industry with a protected monopoly profit pool, it's unlikely that consumerism will get its better products and big consumer awards out of profits for very long; they'll be paid for in prices that cover full costs in the long run.

Now try the same reasoning on auto safety (where new legislation will add about $300 per car (about $3 billion total costs for the industry) annually by 1975—and on "Clean Air" and "Clean Water" legislation to force businesses to reduce pollution.

Wages and the Profit Pool. Similar reasoning throws a sobering light on the perhaps-ethically-justifiable claim that workers getting very low wages should have more and wealthy dividend receivers less. Why not form a union or pass a law to raise their wages and let profits be squeezed? Go back to Chapters 29 and 30 for the answers. If profits rest on exploitation of workers, unions or minimum-wage laws can shift income from profits to wages. And in high-profit oligopoly industries perhaps some profits-to-wages shift may work. But wherever competitive pressures are strong, well-meaning attempts to get higher wages for workers out of profits will not succeed in the long run. Higher wage rates will mean not lower profits but higher prices and fewer jobs in the industry concerned.

All this does not mean that consumers shouldn't insist on safer, better products, or that workers shouldn't press for higher wages. Both may be worth what they cost. But economic analysis should help you avoid using fantasy rather than fact on how far society can solve its problems by drawing on a huge pool of profits just waiting to be tapped, however strongly you may feel that profits *should* bear the cost.

Note that this problem parallels closely the corporate "social responsibility" arguments that businesses should reduce pollution, hire hard core unemployed workers, and the like, instead of just trying to make profits. Should corporations concentrate on doing social good instead of meeting consumer demands? If one company spends heavily on "social responsibilities" while others don't, what happens to its competitive position? If we pass a law requiring all companies to reduce pollution or help clean up the slums, who will pay? (More on these issues in the following chapters.)

---

much as a practical matter in answering our question on how big profits should be. The operationally important questions in America are whether we should tax away more corporation profits to provide money grants or subsidized services to lower-income groups, and whether we should attempt to make stockholders pay out of profits for social improvements like cleaner air and water, jobs for the hard-core unemployed, and the like.

One may argue that investors would still invest as much if profit rates were lower; what else can they do with their money? Moreover, ethically the cost of abstaining from consumption to save is said to be very low for rich investors; they have all they want and deserve no substantial reward for saving. Similarly, actual corporation decisions in responding to consumer demands are made by paid managers, whose incomes are mainly salaries, not profits; they would do just as well if profits were lower.

These arguments seem plausible to some, but experience suggests that they should be viewed skeptically. Even if you believe profit receivers *should* be content with less, the case, "Profits for the Picking?", suggests that making profits pay for good causes may be much harder than it seems. And whether the system would function as well with substantially lower profits is far from clear. Investors certainly do have other places to put their savings than in corporate equities; savers have a long history of searching out the investments that provide the best returns for them, shifting frequently from one to another as relative rates of return change. Perhaps they will feel they should readily give up part of their dividends to others less fortunate, without lessening their enthusiasm for risky, uncertain investments—but the stock market hasn't looked that way. Perhaps managers would do as well without a strong profit incentive, and certainly they have important other motives as well, but the drive for profits still looks like a powerful spur to getting goods and services produced efficiently in response to consumer dollars laid on the counter.

All this doesn't say that the present level of profits is just right. No one knows what is just right. But both the critics who are ready to throw out the profit incentive and the conservatives who say the American system is sinking because profits are too low, have a lot of history to explain away, here and in other nations. By most tests, the U.S. economy, relying heavily on profits as the carrot and losses as the stick, has been phenomenally successful in giving the masses the goods and services they want—the world's highest standard of living. Every high-per-capita-income nation in the world relies heavily on the profit motive in a market system. In this country, real wages have grown spectacularly while profit rates have been roughly unchanged for a century, and there is little evidence that the dynamic impetus is gone from the American economy.

Human motivation is a complex affair, and it varies widely from person to person. There are many incentives to fine management and pioneering entrepreneurship. Pride in achievement, the social acclaim for success, traditions of sound management, the development of professional standards, the pure joy of risk taking—all these incentives and others like them may be powerful supplements to the monetary incentive of profits. The long hours of unpaid toil that millions put in each year for causes they consider worthwhile are impressive evidence that money is far from everything. And the billions of dollars we spend each year on gambling devices we know are loaded against us provide impressive evidence of our love for risk taking. With business innovation there is no reason to suppose that the dice are loaded against entrepreneurs in the aggregate. Indeed, the long record of rapid growth in the economy points strongly the other way. Profits are just big enough when they induce entrepreneurs and investors to provide the social functions we want from them.

REVIEW

For Analysis and Discussion

1. Are current profits excessive? (See Figure 32-2.) What are the best criteria to judge whether profits are too large or too small?
2. What are the main functions of profits in the modern American economy? Should businessmen be proud, rather than apologetic, when they make record profits?
3. "By and large, continuing profits for any firm demonstrate it is doing a good job in satisfying consumer demand." Do you agree or disagree? Explain.
4. Go back to Case 1, on page 24. Suppose that you and other consumer advocates want to be sure the cost of new auto safety features is borne by the manufacturers and not passed on to consumers. How would you accomplish this?
5. "So long as we let businessmen think they have a chance to make profits, it doesn't matter whether they actually make any profits or not." Is this a sound analysis of the incentive role of business profits?
6. Who actually gets the profits made by the American corporations? (Refer back to Chapter 4 for some of the relevant information.) If it is not primarily managers, how do profits serve their presumed incentive function?

7. Many economists say that Marxist criticism of capitalist profits as creating big incomes for stockholders is misplaced—that the main function of profits is as an incentive to get businesses to do what we (the consumers) want done, and that we should expect successful businesses to earn substantial profits for serving this social function. Who is right?
8. How much should a business firm spend on "social responsibilities" like reducing pollution, supporting universities, and hiring hard core unemployed workers, rather than concentrating on maximizing profits? Who will ultimately pay for such corporate activities—stockholders or customers?

APPENDIX

Marx, "Radical Economics," Interest, and Profits

Karl Marx, writing a century ago, developed an elaborate theory about the workings and ultimate downfall of capitalism. The central points were the following:

1. All history can be interpreted primarily in terms of economic issues and conflicts.
2. Value is created only by labor, and the labor time socially necessary for the production of any commodity will determine its value (price).
3. Capitalists (employers) do not pay workers the full value of the goods they produce. They take the "surplus value" above what they pay workers for themselves as profits and interest on their capital, using this surplus to support their own rich living and further accumulation of capital. Indeed, the dominant capitalist class will force the wages of the working class down to a subsistence level.
4. The operations of any economy can be understood best in terms of a class struggle between capitalists and workers, oppressors and oppressed, the rich and the poor. The capitalists also dominate governments. "The State," Marx wrote, "is nothing but the organized collective power of the possessing classes."
5. Out of this class struggle will emerge, eventually, the end of capitalism and the beginning of a communist society. The class struggle will develop "contradictions" in the capitalist system. Most important, unemployment and human misery will increase as the capitalists seize more and more surplus value and accumulate more capital, while the poor are increasingly unable to purchase the growing production of the capitalist society. Capital will be increasingly monopolized by a few huge firms, which imperialistically reach abroad for new opportunities to oppress workers in other nations and to further expand their own capital hoards. But in the end, the oppressed workers will rise in revolt, overthrow the capitalists, and establish a socialist or communist system.

Modern Marxists and radicals make many modifications on the argument, but this is the core.

PROFITS, INTEREST, AND WAGES. Marx declared profits and interest to be immoral—without social function and obtained entirely by expropriating the surplus value produced by the workers. But modern economists point to crucial flaws in his "labor theory of value" on which the argument rests. The labor theory of value says that only labor is productive and that all prices will be proportional to labor inputs. Clearly this is wrong; prices are basically determined by the forces of supply and demand in markets, as was explained in the preceding chapters. How will the labor theory of value explain the high price of a perfect pearl picked up with little labor by a passing beach walker? The argument that capital is not itself productive is equally fallacious, or a play on words. Without the capital they work with, total output with the same workers would clearly be less.

Similarly, most modern economists, including many in the USSR and Eastern Europe, agree that without the interest rate to help guide the choice between more-and-less-roundabout means of production (for example, how much expensive machinery to use compared to labor-intensive production), it is impossible to plan efficiently. For this reason, until recently communist planners made major errors in production processes. Similarly, without profits as a guide and an incentive to efficient production, the communist nations have faced increasingly serious difficulties in getting central plans carried out. Recently both interest and profits have been openly introduced into the USSR and other communist countries' economic planning.

MARX AND HISTORY. Marxists have for a century persistently proclaimed the death throes of capitalism. Capitalism has been uncooperative. Indeed, income and growth statistics (see Table 2–1) show the Western, capitalist economies dominating the list, with the USSR the only communist nation in the top twenty countries. In the capitalist nations the poor have not become poorer and more numerous; on the contrary, the bottom-quarter income recipients in the Western capitalist nations are notably better off economically than even the middle classes in the communist nations. Capitalist economies' income distributions have remained remarkably stable. Property income, depending on precisely how it is defined, has hovered around 25 percent of GNP in the United States (see Figure 28–3), and not far from that in other major Western capitalist nations. Profits have not eroded from lack of mass purchasing power and overaccumulation of capital. Neither have they ballooned to sweep control over spendable income into capitalist hands. Aided by persistent technical progress, they have remained roughly constant as a rate of return on investment.

Modern monetary and fiscal policy appears to have tamed the worst excesses of the business cycle with its massive depressions. Wealth is certainly concentrated in the Western, democratic, capitalist nations, but the concentration is gradually diminishing. Although monopoly is a serious problem for many capitalist countries, it is not clear in America, for example, that the degree of monopoly has changed significantly in this century. The great middle classes look more and more stable and conservative, not increasingly ground down into an ever-hungrier proletariat. "The people" persistently refuse to vote to tax either profits and interest, or the rich per se, out of existence; the Nixon-McGovern election of 1972 provided a recent test of these attitudes. But neither have governments turned out to be merely agents of the rich; the income tax and the "welfare state" have proved more attractive to the masses than has the sword in dealing with the rich.

What went wrong with the Marxist predictions? Today, many Marxists and other radicals say, "Just wait!" They say that capitalist statistics mask a growing sickness and economic instability, that modern capitalism with its profit motive is only temporarily shored up by wars and imperialism through which we live off the poor in other nations and at home.[4]

No one can know the future, but the Marxist arguments find limited support thus far in the data of history. Marx flatly denied any useful role for profits or interest in the operations of an economic system. But, as was indicated above, both have recently been introduced into Soviet economic planning and management of the economy.[5] Strikingly, most modern "radicals" indicate little interest in the problem of economic incentives. To many of them, the problem is easily manageable. If everyone, especially the rich, would only be less greedy and share what they produced, economists' persistent concern with "scarcity" and more efficient use of resources would be seen to be fatuous. In any event, others say, government planning can do whatever needs to be done.

Not surprisingly, most economists and many others in both the Western and the less-developed economies disagree. Good will and all-powerful government planning have yet to demonstrate their superiority over profits and individual initiative. The optimal mix of planning and private economic incentives remains unsettled. But in a world with wants far in excess of the resources available to meet them, economic incentives lie inescapably at the heart of the problems faced by every society.[6]

[4]For some data on the "imperialism" issue, see Chapter 44.

[5]Although Marx was quite explicit about the death throes of capitalism, his writings are devoid of any picture of how he would see a true "Marxist" economy functioning after the revolution. Thus, it is hard to compare actual capitalist and communist developments with what Marx might have considered optimal. He predicted the gradual withering away of government after the workers' revolt, but failed to specify who would then run what parts of the economy and how. Clearly, the USSR, Communist China, and Cuba today are far from the government-less economy Marx forecast.

[6]For a lively, authoritative, modern Marxist statement, see P. Baran and P. Sweezy, *Monopoly Capital* (New York: Modern Reader Paperbacks, 1966).

Poverty and Inequality

CHAPTER PREVIEW

CHAPTER THIRTY-THREE

Poverty and inequality are as old as history. America is rich, and by the standards of most of the world poverty has been virtually eliminated here. Most of our "poor" in New York live as well as the average worker in Leningrad or Mexico City. The visitor from India or the Congo sees nothing that even approaches the poverty that the mass of his people take for granted. Even by our own standards, less than 12 percent of our people live in poverty. But even in the affluent society of modern America there is an economic underworld of poverty.

Poverty and inequality provide an excellent opportunity for you to apply both the micro- and the macroeconomic theory you have learned. Thus, this chapter is written in the form of a case. The first section (to page 447) presents the problem: What is poverty? What are the facts? Who are the poor? Then you should stop and ask yourself—why are the poor poor, and what, if anything, should we do about the poverty problem and the inequality it reflects?

The remainder of the chapter goes on to suggest an analysis—hopefully not to be read until after you have thought through the problem for yourself. Economic theory provides some powerful tools for understanding poverty, but you will find that even those tools cannot provide "the answer" to the complex problem of what, if anything, to do about poverty. For the poverty problem is a mix of economic, social, and political issues, where each person will have his own value judgments as to which goals should dominate and which give way when different desired ends conflict.

POVERTY—THE PROBLEM

Perhaps the most widely used definition of poverty is that suggested by the Social Security Administration and used by government agencies in compiling their statistics. This definition says that, as of 1972, any urban four-person family receiving less than $4,275 was considered poor. For rural families, this figure is reduced by 30 percent. For larger or smaller families, the figure is adjusted appropriately; for individuals living alone, the poverty line was about $2,300. Note that under this definition, the "poverty" level will change each year if the cost of purchasing the prescribed market basket of food and other goods and services changes. Thus, since the early 1960s there has been substantial inflation, and the poverty income level for urban families has risen from about $3,200 to $4,300.

These poverty-line figures were based on an extensive analysis of the living standards of people under different circumstances in the United States during the 1960s. The figure for each year is arrived at by finding the cost of a very modest diet, and multiplying this amount by 3; this ratio is based on analysis of a large number of low-income family budgets. Obviously, this approach is arbitrary, and the figures arrived at each year provide nothing more than a working definition of poverty. Moreover, it is important to remember that these figures include only *money* income; many poor receive substantial income in kind (food stamps, subsidized housing, and so forth) in addition to their money incomes, so they are better off than the money income figures suggest, and many experts argue for a poverty definition based on a broader definition of income to include all income.[1]

[1]For a full description of Social Security Administration procedures and historical data, see U.S. Department of Commerce, *Poverty in the United States* (Current Population Reports, Series P-60), December 31,1969.

Another definition of "poor" is anyone whose income is below half the median income. As of 1972, this would have put the poverty line at about $5,600, and the level would rise as the median income rises. This definition emphasizes that poverty is a relative matter; the bottom part of the income structure will always seem poor, however rich the society becomes in absolute terms. But critics argue that this is just a liberal-do-gooder definition, designed so that there will always seem to be a case for the government's taking money away from upper- and giving it to lower-income families.

What is considered poverty changes with the times. Only twenty-five years ago, over a third of all families would have fallen below the poverty level that we use now (in constant prices). Economic growth has steadily pushed most families above the minimum levels that seemed reasonable a generation or two ago. But our aspirations have risen with our rising incomes. Figure 33–1 shows what has happened to the number of poor in the United States since 1947, using the Social Security Administration definition.

What are the detailed facts about poverty now? In 1972, the median family income in the United States was $11,120, and the poverty line was $4,275. In that year, 5.1 million families, (just 10 percent of the total) had money incomes of less than $4,275; their average income was $3,800, and over 1 million of the families were raising four or more children on that income. Another 5 million people living alone had incomes below $2,300. Together, these two groups included about 24.5 million Americans, 11.9 percent of the population. These were the poor.

Who Are the Poor?

In 1962, Michael Harrington wrote a book, *The Other America,* which touched the conscience of many Americans. The other America, Harrington wrote, is the world of the poor in the midst of plenty—a world of desolation, of hopelessness, of bitterness and resentment, of slums, of discrimination. It is the world of blacks, Puerto Ricans, and Mexican-Americans living in

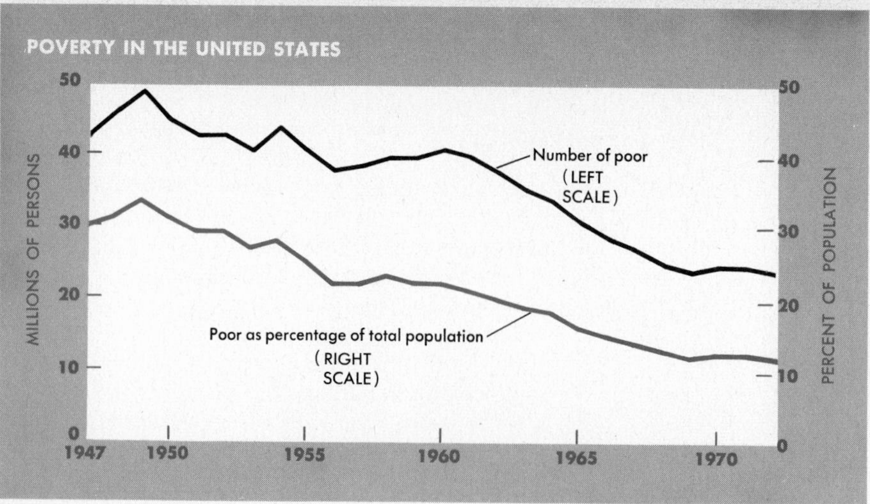

Figure 33–1

Rapid economic growth has persistently reduced the number of poor people in the United States during the post-World War II years. (Source: Council of Economic Advisers and the Census Bureau.)

the great city slums; of old men and women living alone in rented tenement rooms; of poor southern farmers living in ramshackle huts without plumbing; of fatherless families whose mothers struggle to support their children; of failures and rejects for a dozen other reasons.

To understand poverty, Harrington argued, we must add sociology to economics. The poor, he wrote, live in a subculture of their own. Most of them feel—with apathy or resentment—that no one cares. It is a world whose inhabitants are isolated from the mainstream of American life and alienated from its values. It is a world whose occupants are literally concerned with day-to-day survival, where minor illness is a major tragedy, where fatback and cheap greens are a standard diet. Lastly, it is a world turned in on itself in its values and its habits, a world in which the poverty of the parents is visited upon the children.

Each year, many families move up from the ranks of the poor, and some families slide down below the imaginary line. But the great bulk of the poor stay poor; over 70 percent of the poor this year will be poor next year.

To understand the problem of poverty, you must recognize that the poor differ widely. Five groups loom large.

Blacks. About two-thirds of all poor are white; one-third are members of minority groups, mainly blacks. About one-third of all blacks are poor, compared to only 9 percent of whites. Over eight million of the twenty-five million poor persons in 1972 were minorities. Many poor black families live in the rural South; 43 percent of black farmers are in the poverty group. But increasingly, blacks have moved to the northern cities. In the city slums, over half the black youths are high-school dropouts. The breakdown of the black family in the city slums is a critical part of the problem of black poverty. Nearly three-fifths of poor blacks live in family units headed by females.

Farmers. The rate of farm poverty is higher than in towns and cities. Rural poverty is concentrated in the South. A substantial portion of poor southern farmers are the blacks mentioned above. Government aids to agriculture provide virtually no help to the poor farmers; the money goes largely to the big, well-capitalized farmers. Look back at Chapter 22 for more complete data on farm incomes.

Old People. Old age often brings poverty. Nearly one million families where the hus-

The poor live in dismal environments in both city and rural areas.

Harlem slums. (K. Thomas—Photo Researchers, Inc.)

Rural poverty: Jonesboro, Louisiana. (Ann Meuer—Photo Researchers, Inc.)

band is over sixty-five are poor; this is about 12 percent of all such families. In addition, 37 percent of all old people living alone were poor in 1972. Social security helps some. But the average benefit it provides is only a little over $1,500 a year, and only half of the nation's poor receive such payments. However, social security benefits have been raised dramatically for the future, coverage has been extended, and a new federal Supplemental Security Income Program guarantees a minimum annual income of $1,560 for all elderly and disabled individuals and $2,340 for couples, effective with 1974.

Fatherless Families. Nearly 40 percent of the families headed by women left alone to provide for their children are poor. For nonwhites the figure is nearly 60 percent. Looked at another way, 64 percent of all poor black families are headed by women. The woman who has to earn her family's living must either leave her children alone (which she often does in the poverty groups) or find someone to look after them. She faces many lost workdays and consequently job instability. The breakdown of the family is near the core of the black poverty problem in the city slums. Probably not one out of three black children in poor families who now reaches age eighteen has lived all his life with both his parents. Nationwide, the number of children on public "welfare" has risen from less than one million to eight million since 1950, with most of the increase during the 1960s, a decade of growing prosperity. In New York City alone, over one million mothers and children were on welfare in 1972, out of a total population of under eight million.

Others. About one-third of all poor families don't fit into any of the groups above. They live in depressed areas; they have poor motivation; they have low intelligence; most have had little education; they have chosen occupations that demand has passed by. By the test of the market they are failures, the rejects of our modern economy.

One generalization applies to all these groups. Most come from poor families and have been poor all their lives.

The above picture is substantially accurate, but statistics can be misleading. Some observers argue that using money income as a test overstates the magnitude of the problem. The poor southern farmer with an annual income of $2,000 and six children eats better off the land than arithmetic would suggest. Some poor families, especially the elderly, have accumulated assets, and draw on them to supplement their current incomes. Thus, their actual consumption is well above the incomes they report. As a college student, you may well be another example of someone technically poor who lives reasonably well, and almost certainly your poverty is temporary. In many ways, consumption would be a better measure of poverty than is current money income, and such a measure might show an appreciable number of the poor families better off than they seem. Clearly, families whose incomes drop temporarily may appear very poor by the income test, but they may maintain their consumption standards while waiting for a return to normal incomes. But with all these reservations, most of those who are poor by the income test above *are* poor by modern American standards.

Now, before you read further, stop and ask yourself—and argue out with others—these questions. Why are the poor poor? Who, if anyone, should do anything to alleviate poverty? What policies, if any, would you favor to deal with the poverty problem?

In answering the questions, the central concepts and models of the preceding chapters should help. Remember especially aggregate demand, economic growth, scarcity and the need to economize, economic incentives, marginal productivity, economic efficiency in the allocation of resources, consumer welfare and freedom in spending incomes, market imperfections and barriers to efficient allocation of resources, and equity and efficiency as different social goals, as key concepts for this problem. The following sections use these concepts in suggesting ways of analyzing the poverty problem and proposals for eliminating poverty.

WHY ARE THE POOR POOR?

There are many reasons why the poor are poor. In a brief analysis, we must simplify drastically. But you have the theory and concepts to get the most important parts of the answer.

Inadequate Aggregate Demand. In recessions, unemployment raises the proportion of the population below the poverty line. Conversely, prosperity brings more jobs, especially for marginal members of the labor force who are the last to be taken on. A major depression is a catastrophe for the poor.

But only a small fraction of the poor in most years are unemployed, as measured by the unemployment statistics. In 1972, only 6 percent of all poor families were headed by an unemployed person. Two of every three poor individuals are simply out of the labor market. Children were 10 million of the 24 million poor. Another 3.7 million were elderly people, past their working years. Many in the slums, especially minorities, had given up looking for work. Others were not in the labor force for a variety of other reasons. Rising aggregate demand and falling unemployment help to lessen poverty, but they give jobs and higher incomes only to those who have a service to sell. The best estimates suggest that reduction of the overall unemployment rate from 4 to 3 percent would reduce the population below the poverty line by only 1 percentage point.

But the indirect effects of a prosperous economy are more important than this figure suggests in lessening barriers against minority groups as labor markets tighten, in providing more on-the-job training for marginal workers, in providing partial employment for the elderly, and in other indirect ways.

Low Productivity. The message of Chapters 28 and 29 was that individual incomes generally depend, to a *rough* first approximation, on the marginal productivity of the individuals concerned. If this is correct, given a reasonable level of aggregate demand, poor people in the labor market are by and large poor because their marginal productivity is low. They are poor because they are not worth more to employers in a profit-motivated economy. Or, if they are elderly, they are poor now because they did not adequately plan ahead or because they did not have high enough lifetime incomes to provide a reasonable retirement income through their savings.

This is a harsh conclusion, and, as we shall see, one that is only partially correct. But it has a strong core of truth. Over 40 percent of all poor families are headed by an individual with an eighth-grade education or less; only 25 percent by individuals who completed high school. Many old people, even though seeking work, can offer only limited services in the market. Women attempting to support their children inescapably lose more time than others. Many of the adult poor have no skills, or obsolete ones.

Discrimination and Other Market Imperfections. A basic cause of nonwhite poverty is discrimination—in education, jobs, access to medical care, on nearly every score. Nonwhite incomes are 35–40 percent lower than those for whites with the same years of education, area of residence, and sex, and this overall spread has decreased only moderately. Just how much of nonwhite poverty is accounted for by discrimination is sharply debated by the experts. Look back at pages 397–399 for the analysis and some facts. Some estimates suggest the total discrimination reduction may be about $15 billion, but this is only a very rough approximation.[2]

But minorities have made substantial progress. Over a third of all black families received over $10,000 in 1972, compared to 17 percent in 1960 (in constant 1972 dollars). The biggest gains were made by black women, whose incomes are now almost equal to those of white women, whereas they were only about half as

[2] See, for example, J. Kain, *Race and Poverty* (Englewood Cliffs, N.J.: Prentice-Hall, Inc., 1969); B. Schiller, *The Economics of Poverty and Discrimination* (Englewood Cliffs, N.J.: Prentice-Hall, Inc., 1972); and L. Thurow, *Poverty and Discrimination* (Washington, D.C.: The Brookings Institution, 1969), especially Chaps. 7 and 9.

large twenty-five years ago. For black families headed by a male between twenty-five and thirty-four, incomes in 1972 were about 90 percent those of comparable whites, but older and younger black males showed little relative improvement. The black unemployment rate declined sharply over the past decade, though it remains roughly twice that for whites. The number of black "professional and technical" employees more than doubled during the 1960s, compared to a 40 percent increase for whites. Progress in reducing economic discrimination against nonwhites has been substantial. But the problem is still a massive one.[3]

Apart from the special problems of market discrimination against nonwhites, immobility, apathy, and ignorance of job openings are generally characteristic of the poor. Poor southern farmers, both black and white, appear to be highly immobile, except for the young. In Appalachia, there has been a massive exodus of population, but again almost entirely of young people. Thus, the poor of middle age and beyond tend neither to know about alternative job opportunities nor to be willing or able to move to them if the information is available. To move is expensive and uncertain. The subculture of the poor has little contact with the formal processes of employment exchanges and the information and mobility devices available to the middle classes. Even in the cities, the poor have little contact with the job markets of the middle classes.

Absence from the Labor Force. Two-thirds of all poor people are not in the labor force. Many are elderly people and children, but many others are discouraged youths and mothers of fatherless families who have given up looking for work. Thus, the problems of poverty, family instability, and insecurity in old age are inseparably intertwined. Others are out of the labor force for a variety of reasons—because of ill health, lack of motivation, or family circumstances. In some states, welfare payments plus other special aids for the poor are large enough to induce some persons to prefer them to work, especially when the effective marginal tax rate on earnings approaches 100 percent in actual taxes plus poverty benefits foregone (see Chapter 18 and the next section). Unless rising aggregate demand, lessened discrimination, improved aid practices, or improved information and mobility pull some of these individuals back into the labor force, no improvement in economic conditions or in the workings of the market can help alleviate their poverty.

Beyond these four economic causes, most observers add a socioeconomic analysis. Poverty breeds poverty—a vicious circle. A poor individual or family has a high probability of staying poor. The poor live largely in slums or in backward rural areas. Their children do not learn to read, to write, even to speak well. They grow up to apathy or resentment, and they go to poor schools with other poor children. They lag far behind children in middle-class schools, and their dropout rate is high—not surprisingly, for there is little in their culture to make them care about education. When the poor are sick they stay sick longer because they have inadequate medical care. Thus they find it harder to keep jobs. Broken homes are common. Often there is little motivation or hope to rise from the vicious circle of poverty, for either the young or the adults.

POLICIES AGAINST POVERTY

What can we do to reduce or eliminate poverty? The above analysis, together with the macro and micro theory of earlier chapters, should suggest some broad lines of attack.

Maintain High Employment

Macroeconomics tells us that maintaining high employment, a labor market with strong

[3]For interesting analyses, see D. Moynihan, "The Schism in Black America," *The Public Interest,* Spring 1972, and R. Freeman, "Changes in the Labor Market for Black Americans, 1948–1972," *Brookings Papers on Economic Activity* (1973:1).

aggregate demand, should be a powerful force reducing poverty. Against poverty, as against many of our other problems, a combined attack on the macro and micro levels makes sense. To try to eradicate poverty without strong aggregate demand and general prosperity offers little hope of success. The basic case for high employment is further strengthened by the special need to alleviate poverty.

Accelerate Economic Growth

Over the long run, faster growth in output per capita provides a fundamental approach to eroding poverty. This is shown dramatically by Figure 33–1. Over the past two decades, economic growth has reduced poverty by somewhat over 1 percent per year. If the rate of the 1960s could be maintained (remember that the decade included an upswing from a slack economy in the early 1960s), poverty would be virtually eliminated in another ten years. But important as rapid growth is, the nearer poverty approaches zero the harder it will be to make further gains. The remaining poor will increasingly be those insulated from labor markets—the aged, the disabled, what some have called the "hard-core poor."

Improve the Productivity of the Poor

Probably the most basic reason for low incomes is the low productivity of the poor. By and large, investment in human beings increases their productivity, just as does investment in nonhuman wealth. For many reasons, society's investment in the poor falls far short of its investment in most individuals who rise above poverty. The poor live in slums, in squalor. They receive short and poor educations. They get little job training in schools or on the job, since they so often find no employment. They receive inadequate medical care. If we wish to raise the productivity of many of the poor, larger investment to develop their productive capacity is the first prescription that arises from standard economic analysis.

Lessen Discrimination

For nonwhites, lessening of discrimination is essential to long-run economic progress. Barriers to current jobs must be reduced. Better educational opportunities can improve minority groups' chances to break out of the vicious circle of poverty.

Debate over steps to eliminate racial discrimination far transcends issues of how best to reduce poverty. The answers are at least as much political and social as they are economic. The economic magnitude of the problem is mapped out above, and some of its elements are examined in detail in Case 22, at the end of this chapter. Both government and private steps have made some headway in recent years, but it is only a beginning. The public sector has a better record than the private one; the ratio of blacks to total government employees far exceeds the comparable ratio in private business. Discrimination in education and housing poses even deeper problems, which are probably basic to the meaningful establishment of economic equality of opportunity. Reduction of discrimination makes economic sense; it would raise the real income of both whites and blacks. But economic measures alone will fall far short of solving the problem.

Improve Labor Markets

Many of the poor are effectively isolated from jobs by lack of information, immobility, and inertia, in addition to discrimination. This is especially true in the rural South. But it is also true in the slums of the great cities, where for thousands of unskilled and poorly educated teenagers and adults there is no practical channel into the jobs that are opening up elsewhere in the economy, even in the same city. To say that individuals with proper motivation would seek out the jobs that may be open elsewhere is a very partial answer for the Puerto Rican or black teenager in Harlem or in the backwoods of Alabama.

Better job-training programs, employment exchanges, guidance and counseling services, and the like could help those who suffer merely from inadequate information or are immobile because of financial difficulties. Better information, education, and training programs make sense both to fight poverty and on their own merits to improve the efficiency of our economic system. More subsidized day-care nurseries for poor, working mothers could both improve their *de facto* economic productivity and get underprivileged youngsters off to a better educational start.

Many economists blame unions and the government itself for important job barriers. Many craft unions still have *de facto* barriers against nonwhites for apprenticeships and union membership and limit memberships for whites as well, thus in effect blocking them from higher-paying jobs. And the federal minimum-wage law, however admirable its purpose, surely shuts many low-productivity workers out of jobs that might be there at lower wage rates.

Direct Money Grants—"Welfare"

The simplest way to raise the incomes of the poor would be to give them money—direct money transfers from the nonpoor to the poor. In 1972, direct grants of $12 billion (about $500 per poor person) would have been enough to bring every poor person up to the poverty cutoff level—assuming that they continued to receive all the other income they get now.

In fact, we already make a large volume of such income transfers—in the form of welfare payments and other such government grants financed by taxes. In 1972, the poor received about half their total money income as direct money grants from federal, state, and local governments—about $11 billion of their total income of $22 billion. If we add in other government aid to the poor (medicaid, food stamps, subsidized public housing, and the like), the total actually exceeds the poor's reported money income. (See Figure 34–5 for the data.)

Some economists urge that direct money transfers are the simplest and most efficient way of erasing poverty. They add that it would have the advantage of permitting the poor to spend their incomes on what they want most, presumably maximizing their own utility from the income and minimizing government administrative intervention. But there are serious problems, and most observers agree that the present welfare system is a mess.

First, direct money grants would not raise total income; they would merely redistribute what we now produce without using the productive potential of many poor. Second, and more important, universal welfare payments to bring everyone's income above the poverty level could readily *reduce* society's real output because people now working might prefer a monthly welfare check to working to earn the same amount. Indeed, even the present less-generous welfare system has major negative incentive effects. If someone on welfare takes a job, in most states he will find his welfare payments reduced by sixty-seven cents for each dollar he earns. Moreover, if his income goes above welfare standards, he may lose all his welfare benefits, plus his eligibility for food stamps, medicaid, and public housing subsidies. The more children he has, the bigger will be this loss, because part of welfare is specifically paid as children's benefits. Numerous recent studies have found that the implied marginal tax rate (in the form of actual taxes plus welfare benefits given up) on dollars earned when one is on welfare may run as high as 85 percent.[4] Little wonder that some people on welfare have little incentive to take a job unless it pays well above welfare-benefit levels. This is not to say that all welfare recipients prefer loafing on the public purse to working; on the contrary, there is much evidence that many do not. But the present welfare system surely has the wrong built-in incentives. And these anti-work incentives could readily raise the effective cost of lifting everyone above the poverty level to twice the $12 billion shortfall, or even more than that.

[4] See Joint Economic Committee, U.S. Congress, *Studies in Public Welfare,* especially Papers No. 1 (April 10,1972) and No. 6 (March 26,1973).

The "Negative Income Tax"

In the 1960s, a somewhat startling proposal to reform the welfare system was advanced simultaneously by two such different economists as Chicago's Milton Friedman, an advisor to Barry Goldwater and President Nixon, and Yale's James Tobin, economic adviser to President Kennedy. It is to substitute a "negative income tax" for part or all of the present welfare system—to combine compassion with incentives by guaranteeing everyone a basic minimum income and permitting him to keep, say, half of what he earns in addition—up to some moderate income level, when he would slide over to regular taxpayer status.

The recent welfare system has had four big deficiencies: (1) It excludes a lot of poor people, mainly because most states give no welfare benefits to families headed by an adult male able to work, even though he earns nothing or less than the welfare level. This means that less than two-thirds of all poor families receive cash welfare payments. And it creates a strong pressure toward breaking up families—if the husband moves out, the family becomes eligible for welfare. (2) The system imposes a very high marginal tax rate on any welfare-family earnings, as was just noted. (3) Benefits are largely set by the individual states, and they vary widely. The family that received $5,900 in New York City would get only half that amount in Atlanta, and still less in other southern states. (4) Administration of the present complex welfare system is inefficient, cumbersome, costly, and very confusing to the poor.

The negative income tax (NIT) proposal has many variations but two essential elements to correct these welfare-system weaknesses. First, it would guarantee some minimum income to everyone, say $3,000 to a four-person urban family. Everyone would file a simple tax form and the government would pay low-income people rather than collect taxes from them. Second, this negative tax (subsidy) would decline if poor people earned in addition, but it would decline by only a moderate fraction (say, half) of those earnings, so the poor family would always have more after-tax income by working than by merely staying idle on government aid. Table 33-1 shows how it might work, assuming a guaranteed minimum income of $3,200 for a family of four and a marginal negative income tax rate of 50 percent, combined with the regular 1972 federal income tax.

If a family has no private income, it would receive from the government a $3,200 annual income (negative income tax), possibly in weekly or monthly checks—see columns 4 and 5. If the family earns $1,000, it keeps the $1,000, but its payment from the government drops by half that amount. Net result: Its after-tax income is $3,700, up $500. Since each family can keep 50 percent of all earned income, its dollar aid from the government will not fall to zero until its earned income is $6,400. Moreover, since its marginal tax rate is not to exceed 50 percent, exact after-tax equality with the present tax system would not be reached until an income of $7,920, when it is back on the regular tax system, with a tax of $760.

The NIT offers some impressive advantages. It would assure *everyone* the minimum benefit, removing the discrimination against those who work and reducing the present state inequalities. It would greatly reduce the disincentive effects of the present welfare system. It would cut the administrative red tape that now produces great inequities and uses a big part of the poverty budget for the administrators rather than the poor.

How much would it cost? The minimum cost of the plan in Table 33-1 would be around $8 billion annually, assuming that no one stopped working because of the new NIT benefits. Probably some who now work would work less, and estimates double the $8 billion look more realistic to many experts. Note that if we want the maximum work-incentive effect from the NIT, the government out-of-pocket cost will be still higher, since the marginal tax rate on earned income must be reduced for both the poor and the large numbers just above the poverty line. If we reduce the marginal tax rate to 25 percent (remember it is a tax on the poor), the total cost skyrockets—probably to $30 billion or more

TABLE 33–1

Negative Income Tax Example[a] (Family of Four)

	UNDER 1972 TAX LAW		WITH NIT ADDED	
PRIVATE INCOME	TAX (−)	AFTER-TAX INCOME	NET BENEFIT (+) OR TAX (−)	INCOME AFTER NIT AND TAX
$ 0	$ 0	$ 0	$+3,200	$3,200
1,000	0	1,000	+2,700	3,700
2,000	0	2,000	+2,200	4,200
3,000	0	3,000	+1,700	4,700
4,000	−140	3,860	+1,200	5,200
5,000	−290	4,710	+ 700	5,700
6,000	−450	5,550	+ 200	6,200
6,400[b]	−511	5,889	0	6,400
7,000	−603	6,397	− 300	6,700
7,920[c]	−760	7,160	− 760	7,160
8,000	−772	7,228	− 772	7,228

[a]On the assumption that the government would provide a minimum family income of $3,200, with a marginal income tax rate of 50 percent to supplement the regular tax system.
[b]End of government direct subsidy.
[c]Point of after-tax equality with 1972 tax system.

annually for the Table 33–1 plan. Obviously, the cost would also vary greatly for different minimum income levels.

In 1969 and again in 1971, President Nixon submitted a modified negative income tax plan (called "Family Assistance Plan") to Congress, with base income levels of $1,600 and $2,400, respectively. It was shot down both times in the Senate by a coalition of conservatives (who said it did too much) and liberals (who said it didn't do enough). One thing became clear in the controversy: Congress was in no mood to provide aid to able adults without some requirement that they work if jobs are available, and Nixon incorporated this requirement into his plans. Advocates of a pure NIT plan object. First they say, a decent income is a right, not a privilege; free men and women should not be subjected to the indignity of being "investigated" by government agents as a condition of receiving this right. Second, even if you don't accept the preceding argument, trying to check up on the relatively small number of slackers just isn't worth it. The administrative morass of the present system suggests the problems such checkups involve. But these arguments haven't convinced either Congress or the American public.[5]

Direct Aid In Kind

One objection to all money-aid programs is that the poor may not spend the money wisely. Welfare mothers may buy TVs and new clothes for themselves instead of nourishing food and medicine for their children. Under NIT, beneficiaries might buy booze, drugs, and expensive automobiles.

Some observers say that each man is the best judge of what he wants and needs, and that he should be free to spend as he wishes. But most societies agree only in part. We provide direct free education for all children to be sure they

[5]Several government-financed experimental NIT projects are now under way. Preliminary results suggest that NIT recipients work at least as much to obtain private incomes as do a comparable "control" group of families without NIT.

get it. We guarantee health services for the elderly poor. We provide food stamps so the poor must use their aid to buy food, and we subsidize public housing. It's easy to see that the aid-in-kind principle could be extended to the entire welfare program, though with substantial administrative problems as the "in-kind" list lengthened. Here's an issue where the consumer freedom analysis of Chapter 5 and your own ethics may come in conflict; look back at Case 2 on page 63.

The Government as Residual Employer

Following the destructive city riots of the 1960s, another dramatic proposal was advanced by some observers. The government should step in as residual employer for the poor—it should guarantee jobs for all who want them. It could employ the jobless in city cleanup work, in providing more mail deliveries, or in other jobs useful to the public. Jobs, incomes, and a feeling of personal usefulness, these observers argued, are essential if we are to break the syndrome of poverty, especially in the city ghettos. Another million jobs for the currently unemployed, especially young people, could make the difference between constructive forward movement and increasing social disintegration, riots, and blight in the central cities. The expense, they argue, while immediately large, would be small compared to the enormous social and economic costs of inaction.

TOTAL GOVERNMENT INCOME SECURITY PROGRAMS

In 1964, President Johnson declared all-out war on poverty, and each president since has echoed this call. But the government's concern for the income security of its people has been far broader than just for the poor. Table 33–2 summarizes the $116 billion of federal expenditures in fiscal 1974 for income security programs, including social security and other retirement programs for all workers, rich and poor; welfare; unemployment insurance benefits; in-kind grants such as food stamps and subsidized health care and housing; special tax benefits for particular groups such as the poor, aged, and veterans. Federal income security spending has skyrocketed in recent years. Five years ago the total was only $58 billion. National defense no longer dominates the federal budget. Its $80 billion total in 1974 was far short of income security expenditures.

Not antipoverty measures but social security and related retirement benefits clearly dominate the picture in Table 33–2, accounting for nearly $70 billion. The middle section lists major federal programs providing in-kind aid, primarily

TABLE 33–2

Federal Income Security Benefits, 1974

	(IN BILLIONS)
Federal cash benefits:	
Social security (OASDI)	$ 53.2
Federal employee benefits	10.7
Veterans benefits	6.3
Public assistance	6.9
Unemployment insurance	4.6
Railroad retirement	2.5
Other programs	1.1
Subtotal, cash benefits	$ 85.3
Federal outlays for in-kind benefits:	
Food and nutrition	3.9
Health care	16.7
Housing	2.0
Subtotal, in-kind benefits	$ 22.6
Special tax benefits:	
To the aged	5.6
To veterans	.5
To welfare recipients and working mothers	.3
To disabled	1.4
Subtotal, tax benefits	$ 7.8
Total benefits	$115.7

Source: *Special Analyses, Budget of the U.S. for Fiscal Year 1974.*

to the needy and other special groups. The bottom section lists special tax benefits for the groups shown—for example, double personal deductions for the elderly on the federal income tax. Clearly, the line is an arbitrary one as to which tax loopholes should be listed here under income security; oil depletion allowances help to provide income security for owners of oil companies, though they're not listed.

Figure 33–2 picks out some major categories and adds estimates of the number of beneficiaries in each category, including state and local welfare and related programs. Again, the programs included are only those categorized by the government as having income security as their major goal.

What portion of this huge expenditure goes to the poor? We have no precise figures, but the government provided estimates for fiscal 1973, shown in Table 33–3. Presumably the figures for 1974 were somewhat larger because the total income security budget rose by $10 billion. Note that these benefits exceed the total money income of the poor by some 40 percent, because they include benefits in kind and other benefits like medicaid not included in money income.

TABLE 33–3

Federal Aid to the Poor

	(IN BILLIONS)
Cash payments (welfare, etc.)	$ 5.6
Benefits in kind	3.6
Health (mainly medicaid)	6.0
Education	1.7
Manpower training, etc.	2.6
Other	2.0
Total	$31.5

Source: *Special Analyses, U.S. Budget for Fiscal Year 1973.*

With over one hundred million Americans now covered by some part of the government's social security system, it is no wonder that Congress and the president have pushed up benefits far faster than aid to poor families. Social security benefits have been increased four times in the last five years, one form of income that has definitely risen faster than the cost of living. But social security, as we shall see in Part Five, is a two-edged sword. Although it is commonly

Figure 33–2

Retirement benefits for the elderly dominate the government's income security picture, but benefits for the poor and health services also run into the billions. Figures include state and local governments. (Source: Special Analyses, U.S. Budget for Fiscal 1974.*)*

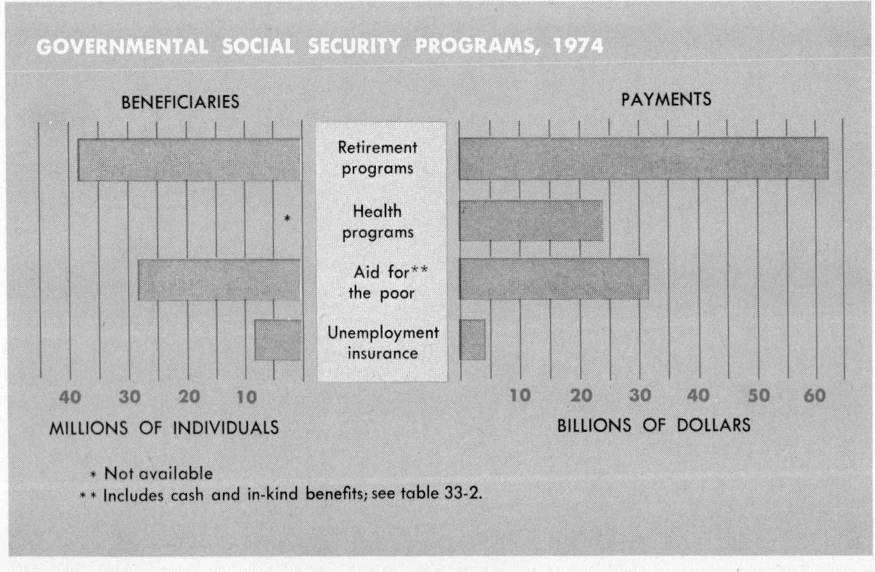

thought of as insurance, its benefits bear no direct relationship to the contributions made by each individual. Instead, it is a massive income-transfer program, not from the rich to the poor, but basically from the young who work to the elderly who do not. Fundamentally, payments each year are financed by the social security (payroll) tax collected that year from virtually all workers. Those retiring now collect much larger benefits than they have "bought"—benefits provided by today's workers, who must hope that tomorrow's workers will be equally generous in providing for them. Moreover, many experts protest that the plan is inequitable. Every worker (as of 1974) pays the payroll tax of about 6 percent on the first $12,600 of his income, and the employer pays a comparable tax, making a total of about 12 percent. Thus, the poor worker pays 6 percent on his entire income, while the wealthy man pays only a small part of his income. In addition, the part of the tax levied on employers is almost certainly passed on to the workers, which doubles the tax burden. Thus, the social security tax is both large and regressive; it takes a larger proportion of low than of high incomes.

REVIEW

For Analysis and Discussion

1. How unequal should incomes be?
2. Should the government do something about the poverty problem? If so, what criteria should we use to decide who deserves help?
3. Should government aid to the poor be primarily in money or in kind? Is your answer consistent with the analysis of individual utility maximization in Chapter 5?
4. "The simplest and cheapest approach to eliminating poverty would be simply to give a tax-financed cash subsidy to each poor individual big enough to raise his income above the poverty level, perhaps through the negative income tax. This would avoid the waste and misdirection of elaborate programs and would give each individual freedom to spend his income as he pleases." Do you agree? Why or why not?
5. Would you favor government action to raise the legal minimum wage to $3 per hour to eliminate poverty? Explain.
6. "A strong aggregate demand policy to assure high employment would solve the poverty problem and eliminate the need for the hodgepodge of government measures adopted over recent years." Do you agree?
7. How good a living can the current workers in our society afford to provide for nonworkers, such as children, the aged, and unemployed? What criteria do you use in answering?
8. What is your program to reduce or eliminate poverty in the United States?

CASE 22

Black Economic Development

Many blacks who live in urban slums, or ghettos, are understandably bitter, especially when most of the businesses and housing seem to be owned by absentee whites. Although blacks comprise over 10 percent of the population, only about 2 percent of all businesses are owned by blacks. They own 7.2 percent of personal service businesses (barbershops, dry cleaners, and the like), but only 0.8 percent of manufacturing businesses, 1.5 percent of construction businesses, 1.5 percent of wholesale trade firms, and 3.2 percent of retail trade establishments. Youth unemployment in the ghettos is often over 25 percent.

Some blacks demand an active policy of dispersal, opening up the suburbs to blacks and helping them to find jobs and housing there. Others say the answer is development of the ghetto into a viable economy and a decent place for blacks to live—black economic development.

Enrichment of the ghetto has become a highly controversial issue, both as to its desirability and how it should be accomplished. One approach is separatist—to make the ghetto a separate black economic entity, controlled by and operated for the benefit of blacks. The other stresses breaking down the barriers to movement of people and capital in and out of the ghetto—integration with the white economy. The following quotations from two black leaders and an influential white observer summarize the arguments.

First, a statement by Malcolm X:

> Our economic philosophy of Black Nationalism means that instead of our spending the rest of our lives begging the white man for a job, our people should be reeducated to the science of economics and the part that it plays in our community. We should be taught just the basic fundamentals: that whenever you take money out of the neighborhood and spend it in another neighborhood, the neighborhood in which you spend it gets richer and richer, and the neighborhood from which you take it gets poorer and poorer. This creates a ghetto, as now exists in every so-called Negro community in this country. If the Negro isn't spending his money downtown with what we call "the man," "the man" is himself right in the Negro community. All the stores are run by the white man, who takes the money out of the community as soon as the sun sets. We have to teach our people the importance of where to spend their dollars and the importance of establishing and owning businesses. Thereby we can create employment for ourselves, instead of having to wait to boycott your stores and businesses to demand that you give us a job.[6]

Roy Innes, national director of the Congress of Racial Equality, has put the argument this way:

> Black people must seek liberation from the dominance and control of white society. . . . We black nationalists must speak of separating ourselves. We live in a setting where one group—not our own—controls the institutions, and a flow of goods and services. We can change our position by liberating ourselves and placing the vital instruments of social and economic change in our own hands. This is what we mean by separation. . . .
>
> Black people are not talking about black capitalism, black people are talking about economic development. We are talking about the creation and acquisition of capital instruments by means of which we can maximize our own economic interests. . . . The question of autonomy is critical. . . . Extensive areas like Harlem in New York, Roxbury in Boston, Watts in Los Angeles . . . exist as colonial appendages of the urban center. . . . The urban centers are managed by political and institutional barons who include our piece of "turf" in their domain. . . . Whenever we make any attempt to change that relationship—political, social, or economic—we meet the massive resistance of these barons. . . .
>
> There is a very striking similarity between the so-called underdeveloped countries and our underdeveloped black communities. Both have always been oppressed; almost always there is an un-

[6] *The Speeches of Malcom X at Harvard,* A. Epps, ed. (New York: William Morrow & Co., Inc., 1968), pp. 141–42.

favorable balance of trade with the oppressors or exploiters; both suffer from high unemployment, low income, scarce capital, and we can point to a number of other similarities.[7]

The argument against black separatism is that, like it or not, whites own most of the capital in our society and without capital no economy, or sub-economy, can support high output and living standards; and that blacks will thus often be able to earn higher incomes working for whites than by staying in a separate black economy with white capital excluded. Moreover, separatist steps are likely merely to make the ghetto less attractive to white capital and a still more depressed area. One sympathetic observer has stressed this danger, describing the black ghetto today as an "underdeveloped, decadent economy":

> Economic anarchy is most visible in the important matter of jobs and employment. . . . The ghetto core do not respond to the simple opportunity of a job. . . . The militant and status-conscious young man in East Harlem calls his neighbor an "Uncle Tom" if he takes a job, especially a menial one. He doesn't line up at the employment gate, because he believes it is a waste of time and he won't be hired. He is certain that, for blacks, all jobs are deadend jobs. . . .
>
> In the slum economy, many commonplace events interfere with a man's ability to get or hold a job. Ghetto residents are constantly fighting off finance companies and arguing with the car dealers who have cheated them. Their cars break down and are towed off the street. These conditions not only interfere with an employee's on-the-job reliability, but they also build more theft, crime, inability to meet rent payments, evictions, and bad credit—the very obstacles that prevent people from getting and holding jobs. Plainly, the system of anarchy is self-perpetuating. . . .
>
> Businessmen framing programs for new industry in ghetto areas are frequently bewildered by another unpredictable aspect of the slum economy—the implacable and illogical Negro opposition to programs for enrichment of the slums. When a major Wall Street firm announced in July, 1968 that it had signed a ten-year, half-million dollar lease for space in a Harlem furniture store to operate a branch brokerage office. . . .and had committed 7.5 percent of the slum's branch's gross commissions to a foundation organized to provide capital for ghetto businesses and new job opportunities, the company was denounced by blacks as "A conspiracy by state, municipal, and Wall Street interests to take over Harlem. White power sees Harlem as the potentially most valuable piece of real estate in New York City. . . . Harlem is too valuable to leave in black hands. . . ."
>
> The Negro economy is not simply underdeveloped; it is determinedly so and hostile to efforts to change it. . . . Meetings of black militants teach the advantages and techniques of bankruptcy.[8]

He continues that credit is available to ghetto enterprises only at high rates. The risks of establishing a business in the slums are so great that stockholders or bank examiners cannot ignore the probable erosion of capital. But if the banker or merchant sets a price on his production or his capital high enough to cover the extra risks, ghetto residents understandably complain of white discrimination. Bankers are reluctant to make high-risk loans because foreclosure will predictably bring a charge of white discrimination against blacks.

Economically, who is right—the black separatists or the economic integrationists? Suppose you have black friends in the ghetto, who, knowing you are taking a course in economics, ask your advice. What would you tell them? (Remember that you are asked for advice *only* on the economics of the issue. However important you may think the political and social aspects of black independence and separatism are, disregard them for purposes of this analysis.)

---

[7]Roy Innes, "Separatist Economics: A New Social Contract," in *Black Economic Development,* W.H. Haddad and G.D. Pugh, eds. (Englewood Cliffs, N.J.: Prentice-Hall, Inc., 1969), pp. 51–53.

[8]T.L. Cross, *Black Capitalism* (New York: Athenum Publishers, 1969), pp. 22–25.

APPENDIX TO PART FOUR

Current Research

Wages, Unions, and Collective Bargaining. Chicago's H.G. Lewis summarizes the quantitative impact of unions on wages in "The Relative Employment effects of Unions" (*American Economic Review,* May 1964). A controversial analysis, *Collective Bargaining in the Steel Industry,* by Harvard's R. Livernash, looks closely at one leading industry. A lively collection of analyses is assembled in *Unions, Management, and the Public,* E. Bakke, C. Kerr, and C. Anrod, eds. (New York: Harcourt Brace Jovanovich, Inc., 1967). Albert Rees' and George Shultz' *Workers and Wages in an Urban Labor Market* (University of Chicago Press, 1971) illustrates a modern approach to labor-market analysis.

There is vast literature describing unions and the attitudes and behavior of organized labor groups. M. Perlman's *The Machinists* (Harvard University Press, 1962) is a good example. A collection of leading studies focused on union attitudes and behavior is assembled in *Labor and Trade Unionism,* edited by California's W. Galenson and S. Lipset. Interesting studies of grass roots union politics and policies are presented by L. Sayles and G. Strauss, *The Local Union* (New York: Harper & Row, Publishers, 1961). The hottest collective bargaining issue of this decade lies in the public sector. For a summary of several studies (on teachers, postal workers, and nurses), see R.L. Rowan, ed., *Readings in Labor Economies and Industrial Relations* (Homewood, Ill.: Richard D. Irwin, Inc., 1972), pp. 363–416; and J. Stieber, *Public Employee Unionism* (The Brookings Institution, 1973).

Automation. Chapters 1 and 2 of H.A. Simon's *The Shape of Automation* (Harper & Row, 1965) provide a good introductory overview of the impact of "automation," with special emphasis on the likely role of the computer; reversing the order of the chapters may make them easier reading. C. Silberman's *Myths of Automation* (Harper & Row, 1966) brings the arguments to bear on current issues. Paul Hartman, in *Collective Bargaining and Productivity* (University of California Press, 1969), analyzes experience with the West Coast longshoremen's pioneering plan to eliminate resistance to technical change in return for a share of the savings.

Poverty. For historical perspective, see the studies by Friedman, Solow, Goldsmith, and Lampman in E.C. Budd, ed., *Inequality and Poverty* (W.W. Norton, 1967). H.P. Miller, ed., *Poverty: American Style* (Belmont, Calif.: Wadsworth Publishing Co. Inc., 1968), provides another collection of analyses. Bruno Stein's *The Economies of Poverty and Public Welfare* (New York: Basic Books, Inc., 1971) is a more unified analysis. Another lively volume is P. Moynihan, ed., *On Understanding Poverty* (Basic Books, 1969).

On antipoverty policy, James Tobin, one of the chief authors of the "negative income tax," analyzes the entire issue in "Raising the Incomes of the Poor," *Agenda for the Nation,* Kermit Gordon, ed. (The Brookings Institution, 1968). The "welfare problem" has been examined in detail by Congressional Committees. See especially *Studies in Public Welfare,* Papers No. 1 and 6, prepared for the Joint Economic Committee (April 1972 and March 1973), which stress the disincentive effects against working built into the present system and the very uneven distribution of benefits. Leonard Goodwin's *Do the Poor Want to Work?* (The Brookings Institution, 1972) reports extensive field studies on the problem. A series of case studies is presented in P. Doeringer, *Programs to Employ the Disadvantaged* (Prentice-Hall, 1969).

At the other end of the income structure, R. Barlow, H. Brazer, and J. Morgan of the University of Michigan have studied the richest families in *Economic Behavior of the Affluent* (The Brookings Institution, 1966).

Discrimination and Black Economic Development. A factual introduction to problems of blacks in getting jobs is provided by H. Northrup and others in *Negro Employment in Basic Industry* (Philadelphia, Pa.: University of Pennsylvania Press, 1970), and a parallel series of studies of individual industries. Estimates of the economic effects of racial discrimination abound. Both Richard Freeman, in *Brookings Papers in Economic Activity* (1973:1), and James Gwartney, "Changes in the Nonwhite/White Income Ratio," (*American Economic Review,* December 1970) find substantial black economic progress. Lester Thurow's *Poverty and Discrimination* (The Brookings Institution,

1969) reaches less optimistic conclusions. Broader analyses of the problems of "black capitalism" and "black economic development" are presented by A. and R. Wohlstetter, "Third Worlds Abroad and At Home," and J. Kain and J. Persky, "Alternatives to Gilding the Ghetto," (both in *The Public Interest,* Winter 1969). See also *Black Economic Development* (Prentice-Hall, Spectrum Books, 1969), especially Chapters 3, 4 and 7; and T. Cross, *Black Capitalism* (New York: Atheneum Publishers, 1969).

Research on economic discrimination against women is just beginning, mainly on the factors that influence women's entry into different job markets. See *Economic Report of the President,* January 1973, Chapter 4, and the colloquium on "What Economic Equality for Women Requires," (*American Economic Review,* May 1972, pp. 157–76).

One of the few intensive studies of the poverty problem among American Indians is Alan Sorkin's *American Indians and Federal Aid* (The Brookings Institution, 1971), among Chicanos Vernon Briggs' *Chicanos and Rural Poverty* (Baltimore, Md.: The Johns Hopkins University Press, 1972).

PUBLIC GOODS, EXTERNALITIES, AND THE PUBLIC SECTOR

PART FIVE

The Public Sector

CHAPTER PREVIEW

CHAPTER THIRTY-FOUR

What should the government do in economic affairs? How much should it tax and how much should it spend? The influential nineteenth-century English liberals argued that the primary function of the state was merely to set up and enforce certain "rules of the game" under which private enterprise could then be counted on to get goods efficiently produced and distributed. At the other extreme, the communists argue that all productive resources should be owned by the state, and that production and distribution should be directed in detail by the government.

The present attitude in America is somewhere in between, but much closer to the private-enterprise position. Most Americans believe strongly in capitalism and the virtues of a free, individual-initiative economy. Yet government action has grown far beyond the minimal regulatory duties prescribed by the laissez-faire advocates.

THE FOUR BIG FUNCTIONS OF GOVERNMENT

Modern government has four big economic functions. People may disagree widely on how far government should go on each front, but nearly everyone agrees that government needs to play all four roles.

Government as Stabilizer: Stably Growing Aggregate Demand

Two centuries ago Adam Smith didn't worry about booms and depressions, because they didn't exist. But with the emergence of our modern industrial society, economic instability became a major problem. There is no reason why aggregate spending (consumer plus business plus government) will automatically just match the growing output potential of the system at stable prices. Clearly, no private agency can assure the needed stable growth in aggregate demand. Government has to help, through monetary and fiscal policy, if we are to avoid the massive depressions and inflations that have marred the past. This was the topic of Part Two.

Government as Policeman: The Rules of the Game

Even Adam Smith said that government has to act as policeman—to spell out some rules of the economic game and to see that people obey them. To live effectively together in a complex economic world, we have to agree that contracts will be respected. Equally important, competition must prevail in the marketplace to assure the benefits of private enterprise, and only government can undertake this kind of regulation. The role of government in setting up and enforcing the rules of the competitive game was a main theme of Parts Three and Four. It's a vital role if a system like ours is to work effectively.

As indicated earlier, it's a complex question as to just how far government rules should go. Some, for ethical as well as economic reasons, would regulate minimum wages and working hours, the fares airlines can charge, wage bargains between unions and business, and many other economic actions. Others demur. But nearly everyone agrees that where externalities bulk large, the marketplace will fail to produce the optimal output. If a paper mill produces dirty water and an objectionable odor as well as paper, government action is needed to see that paper buyers, in addition to paying the private costs of producing paper, pay for keeping the water and air clean. One way of doing this is for the government to forbid the pollution of water and air. Then the manufacturer's total cost will include pollution-control measures as well as labor, raw materials, and the like. Another approach is to impose a special tax on polluters and to use the funds to clean up the water or air. Either way, government action is needed. The line between simple government regulation and active intervention is often very fuzzy.

Government as Provider of Services: The Public Sector

There are some things a private-enterprise, profit-motivated system clearly will not provide adequately—national defense, education, highways, moon shots, police protection. Partly, these are instances of large externalities—social costs or benefits larger than private costs or benefits. At the extreme are pure "public goods," such as the court system, where we clearly want the "product" but where there is no practical way of producing and selling it through the market. The critical point in such cases is the inability to withhold the benefits of the expenditure from anyone who wouldn't pay for them voluntarily.

In such cases, the government needs to act as a public store, providing the public good and collecting for it through taxes. Instead of relying on the private store to produce everything we want, we thus set up a public store alongside to handle what the private store can't or won't stock under the profit incentive. The public store is the "public sector," where we rely on political votes rather than the market to decide what to produce. The public sector allocates over 20 percent of all resources in the United States today, through taxes and government purchase of goods and services, although most of the actual production (say, of highways) is contracted out to the private sector. The taxes are the price we agree, through the political process, to pay.

Government as Income Redistributor: Transfer Payments

The fourth major economic function of government is to redistribute income—mainly by taxing some persons and making transfer payments to others. The aged, the poor, farmers, the unemployed, and the vast middle-income classes—all receive government transfer payments financed mainly by taxes on others, and these money transfers provide a corresponding shift in control over resources. Because the payments go mainly to middle-and lower-income groups, and our tax system is "progressive" (that is, the rich pay a higher percentage of their incomes than the poor), this redistribution shifts income from upper- to lower-income groups. But, contrary to common belief, the great bulk of the redistribution is within the middle-income classes, who comprise the bulk of the population. They pay most of the taxes, and they get most of the government transfer payments—social security, housing subsidies, and the like. Government redistribution of money income is the second big activity of the public sector. It currently shifts about 12 percent of the total national income. Thus, the public store and direct income transfers together account for nearly a third of total economic activity. The public sector is a big part of the modern American economy.

THE PUBLIC SECTOR TODAY

First, a look at the facts. In 1973, federal, state, and local governments spent over $400 billion, and their expenditures are rising every year. These expenditures have been roughly matched by growing tax collections. Thus, taxes, including social-security payroll taxes, are now approaching $2,500 a year for every man, woman, and child in the United States. Excluding military personnel, some fourteen million workers—nearly one out of every six—are on government payrolls. You may not like having government so big, but there it is.

The Growing Role of Government

It is useful to begin with some historical perspective. Look at Figure 34–1.

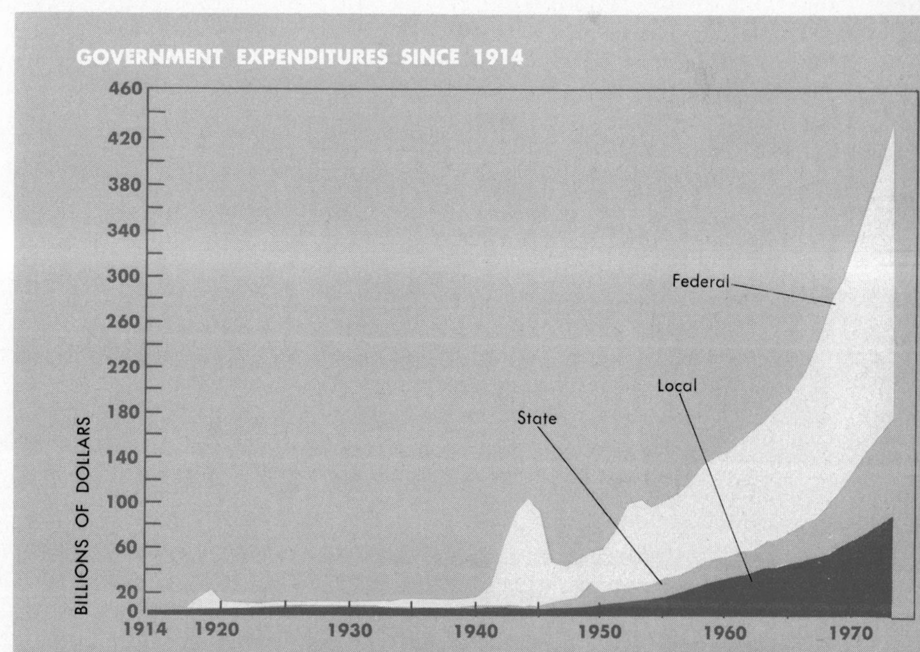

Figure 34–1

Federal spending has shot up during wars and again in recent peacetime years. State and local spending has grown rapidly since World War II. (Source: U.S. Treasury Department. Figures include social security.)

1. One major reason for the growth is war—past, present, and future. War is fabulously expensive. Today, over $100 billion (more than one-third of the annual federal budget) is directly or indirectly attributable to past and future wars (including veteran's benefits, interest on the national debt, and so on), although direct national defense costs fell from 44 percent of the federal budget in 1968 to 30 percent in 1973.

2. Partly, the increase is due to more people and higher prices. Since 1914, population has more than doubled and prices have quadrupled, so real government spending per capita has risen only about twenty-fold, rather than the astronomical increase suggested by Figure 34–1—but twenty-fold is a lot.

3. The biggest reason by far for the increase is that we have wanted our governments to do more for us—education, highways and streets, social security, welfare, sewers, moonshots,

Figure 34–2

Federal, state, and local governments collected about $390 billion in taxes and spent about $440 billion (including intergovernmental grants) in 1973, including social security programs. Chart does not include government-operated businesses, such as public utilities, but it does overstate net government outlays by including state–local spending of federal grants totalling $43 billion. (Source: U.S. Budget and Department of Commerce; preliminary estimates.)

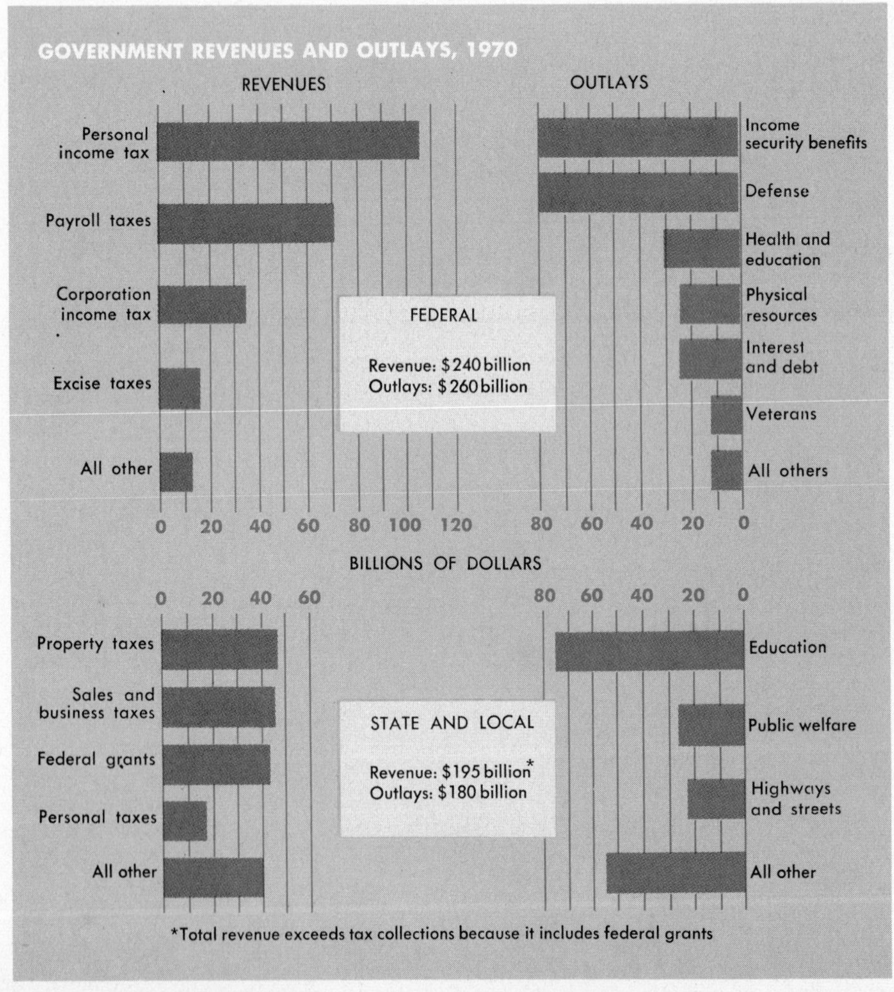

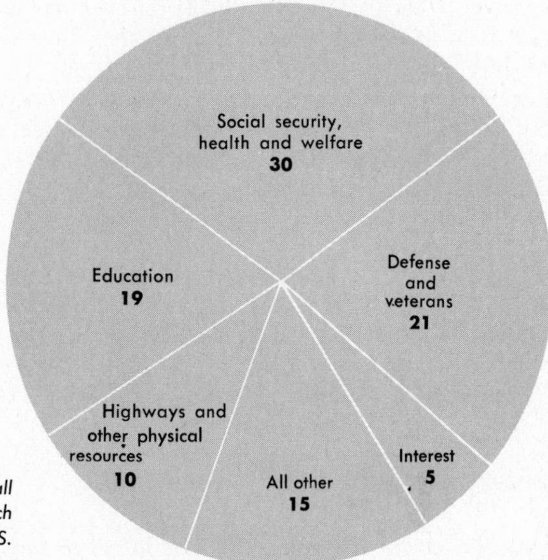

Figure 34–3

Personal income security and education account for about half of all government expenditures, now far exceeding national defense, which used to dominate the picture but is now only 21 percent. (Source: U.S. Treasury and Commerce Departments; preliminary estimates.)

health. The nation's shift from a rural to an urban economy accounts for a big share of the state–local increase. The desperate plight of the big cities, with snowballing needs for welfare, education, police protection, and slum renewal, may soon become the nation's number one public finance problem. But there's a lot more than just the cities involved. Now we want six-lane highways instead of dirt roads. Universal education and modern medical care are enormously expensive. Social security, which didn't exist fifty years ago, has become a bigger part of the government budget than national defense.

Figure 34–2 summarizes what governments spent in 1973 and the taxes they collected to pay the bills. The length of each bar shows the size of the tax or expenditure involved. Although Figure 34–2 speaks for itself, $400 billion deserves a closer look.

Government Expenditures

Figure 34–2 pictured government expenditures and taxes in 1973, showing the different levels of government separately. Now, Figure 34–3 combines government spending at all levels and lumps the spending into a few big categories, to give an overview of total spending in the public sector. Chapter 35 will look at government spending in more detail, but two big developments emerge from this initial overview.

1. First is the enormous growth in spending on "human resources"—social security, health, welfare, and education—in the last decade. In every earlier edition of this book, national defense was by far the largest single item in the federal budget, and it dominated the total government spending picture. But no more! In 1973, federal income security payments alone (mainly federal social security) passed national defense, and when other human resources spending is lumped in, the human resources total is more than double that for national defense. Moreover, human resources spending is growing rapidly, while national defense spending has been essentially stable in dollar terms since the late 1960s and has fallen steadily as a percentage of GNP and government spending. Improvements in social security benefits already

built into the law will push benefits over $100 billion annually before 1980. By the time you retire at sixty-five, under the present law you and your spouse will collect a retirement benefit of $3,150 per month—that's *per month*—assuming only a modest price inflation of 2.5 percent annually. Health costs have soared astronomically. So have those for education and other nondefense goods and services.

Moreover, although national defense spending has been falling as a percent of total government spending, it too still takes huge numbers of tax dollars. One B-1 bomber now costs $56 million, compared to only $700,000 for a World War II B-29. A new nuclear-powered aircraft carrier in 1973 was estimated to cost nearly $1 billion. Partly, all this reflects inflation, but it also reflects the increasingly complex nature of modern war and defense.

2. The second big development of recent years has been the rapid growth of state and local governments. Between 1960 and 1973, state and local spending rose from 10 to 15 percent of GNP, while federal spending rose only from 18 to 20 percent. Today, state and local governments spend more on goods and services than the federal government; excluding national defense, they spent over $150 billion in 1972, compared to only $30 billion by the federal government. About 11 million people now work for state and local governments, only 2.6 million for the federal government. This distribution reflects the fact that the bulk of federal spending is on transfer payments like social security (which require relatively few employees) and on goods and services contracted out to private industries (highways, aircraft, and so on), whereas state and local governments primarily provide services themselves (education, police protection, and the like).

Perhaps the biggest unsolved government finance problem today is the desperate plight of the central cities, which face spiralling costs of providing vital services (education, law and order, welfare, sanitation, and the like) at the same time as the well-to-do business and individual taxpayers are moving to the suburbs, leaving a population that needs increasingly costly services but has little ability to pay taxes.

3. It is important to recognize the distinction just indicated between real (or "exhaustive") expenditures on currently produced goods and services, and transfer payments. Real expenditures use up goods and services—for example, buying aircraft or hiring teachers. Transfer payments are merely monetary shifts—for example, old-age pension payments and interest on the national debt. Obviously, the immediate effect on the economy is different in the two cases. Although transfer payments redistribute purchasing power, they do not *directly* reallocate, or use up, productive resources. In 1973, government real expenditures were about $250 billion, transfer payments about $190 billion.[1]

Taxes

Figure 34–4 shows what taxes provided the revenue in 1973, combining federal, state, and local governments. Ours is increasingly a personal tax system. Over half of all taxes are raised that way—32 percent through personal-income taxes alone. At the federal level, personal income and payroll taxes now bring in three-fourths of all revenue. Corporate-income, sales, excise, and property taxes account for most of the rest; property taxes still bring in nearly all local government revenue. If you feel you're taxed wherever you turn, you're right. We can't collect nearly a half trillion dollars annually to finance the services we want our governments to provide without making nearly everyone pay.

Who pays this $400 billion of taxes? Chapter 37 is devoted to this question, but Figure 34–5 provides some preliminary, *very rough*, estimates of the burden of different taxes by income levels. Other estimates, as we shall see, vary, and suggest a lower percentage burden for the very poor,

[1]This distinction between real and transfer payments corresponds to that used in the GNP accounts; real government expenditures are those on currently produced goods and services. The distinction is not, of course, the same as that between real and money GNP when we compare GNP in current prices with that in constant prices.

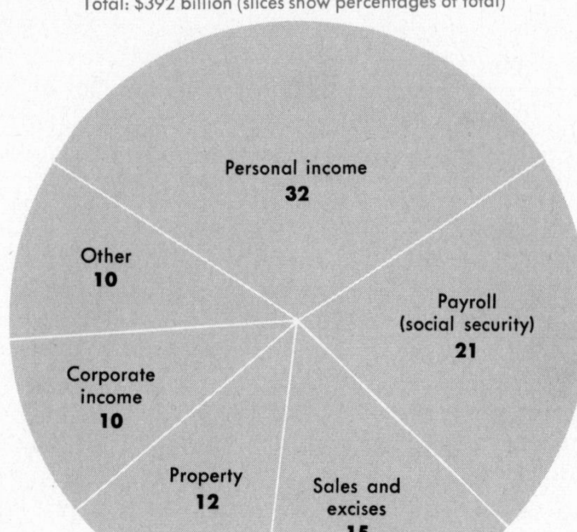

Figure 34–4

Personal income and payroll taxes produce over half the nation's tax revenues, sales and property taxes most of the rest. (Sources: U.S. Treasury and Commerce Departments; preliminary estimates.)

Figure 34–5

Federal personal and corporation income taxes account for most of the progression in the total tax system. The property and social security (payroll) taxes account for most of the regression. Estimates are subject to substantial disagreement, especially on the degree of regression in state–local property taxes. (Source: H. Miller and R. Herriot, "The Taxes We Pay," Conference Board Record, May 1971.)

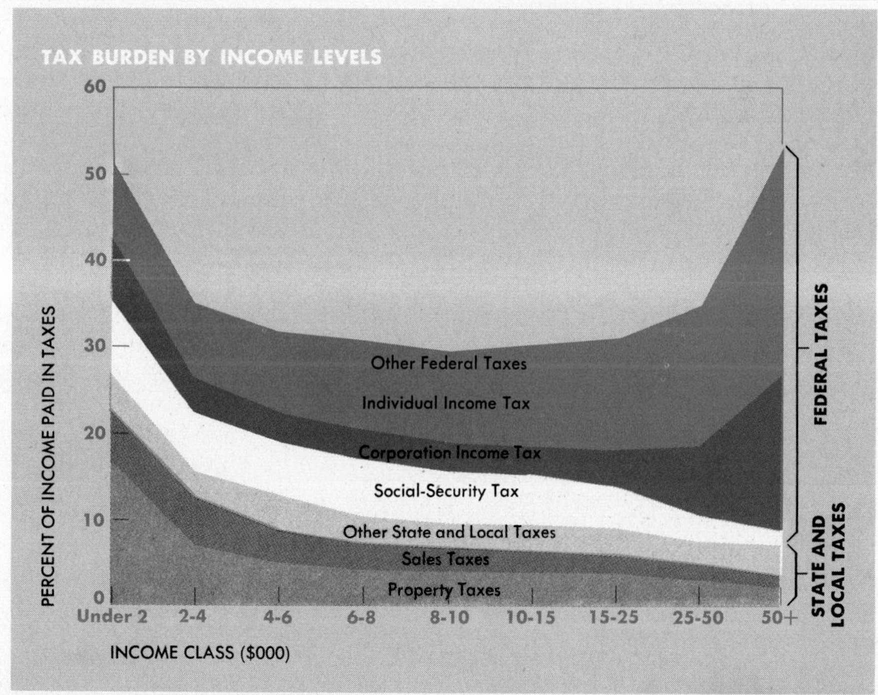

but they agree on the general shape of the burden shown by Figure 34–5.

It is important to recognize, in reading this chart, that the burdens shown are for those who ultimately paid the taxes (for example, consumers when the cigarette tax or sales tax is passed on to them by retailers), rather than the person who turns the money over to the government. For several taxes we can only roughly estimate who bears the final burden. It is also important to recognize that the tax burdens are percentages of money income only; the poor, especially, get substantial additional transfer income in kind, for example food stamps, subsidized housing, and the like, so the net real burden of their taxes is less heavy than the picture suggests.

Overall, according to these estimates, taxes take a very high percentage of the money income of the very poor, then fall to around 30 percent for the great bulk of the population (families earning from $4,000 to $20,000 per year), and then rise rapidly for the rich above that level. The details are as interesting as the big picture. State and local taxes (at the bottom of the chart) obviously account for a big part of the tax system's "regression"—the fact that it takes a higher percentage of low than of middle and upper incomes.[2] Conversely, the federal personal and corporate income taxes account for most of the system's "progression"—the fact that it takes a higher percentage of high than of lower incomes. They account for 80 percent of the taxes paid by families with incomes above $50,000. One other tax deserves special attention because it is growing so rapidly and is now our second biggest source of revenue—the payroll tax used to finance social security. This is a highly regressive tax, taking between 5 and 10 percent of low and middle incomes but only a tiny fraction of very large ones.

[2] As Figure 34–5 shows, this regressivity is primarily due to the property tax, which is assumed to be largely shifted to renters. This analysis is debatable. Other economists argue that property owners cannot shift the tax, and that the tax burden on low-income families is much lighter than Figure 34–5 suggests.

REDISTRIBUTION OF INCOME THROUGH THE PUBLIC SECTOR

What is the net redistributional effect of these massive tax collections and public expenditures? Figure 34–6 provides a *very rough* set of estimates. The light bars show the benefits received at different income levels, and the dark bars the taxes paid. While the tax system is regressive at the bottom and becomes sharply progressive only for high incomes, government benefits are a large percent of income for the poor but only a small percent for the rich. Thus, overall, the government redistributes income substantially from the rich to the poor. But the great mass of both tax payments and benefits are transfers within the big middle-income classes, as will be explained more fully in Chapter 35. The big redistribution is not from rich to poor, but from politically-less-effective to more-effective middle-income groups.

It is important to recognize just what these rough estimates show. The tax burden estimates are similar to those in Figure 34–5, but note that Figure 34–6 shows no separate estimates for families above $15,000 income, so it doesn't show the sharp tax increases for high incomes or the more dramatic rich-to-poor shift when those families are shown separately. The benefit estimates are even rougher than those for tax burdens. They attempt to measure who gets the ultimate benefit from each government expenditure, including transfer payments. (That, incidentally, explains how benefits can be more than total income for the poor, since the annual family income data exclude substantial nonmoney benefits included in the benefits estimates.) Estimating the final beneficiaries of old-age pensions, for example, is relatively easy. But for services such as national defense, education, police protection, and the like, only an arbitrary allocation is possible. The general picture shown by Figure 34–6 is almost certainly correct (remembering that all families over $15,000 are lumped together here), but don't take the details too seriously.

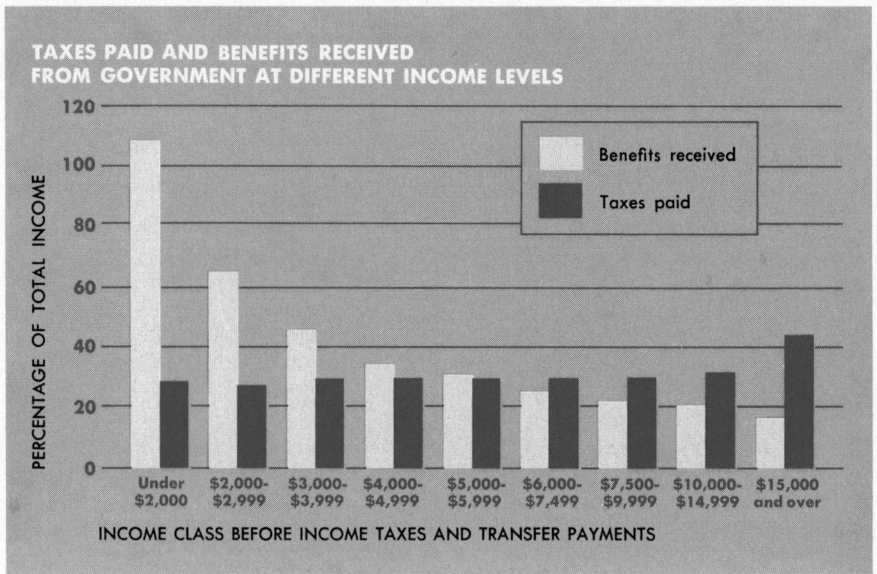

Figure 34–6

Low-income groups receive much more from government in services and payments than they pay in taxes. The reverse is true for high-income groups. Estimates, for 1965, are rough. (Source: Tax Foundation.)

THE PUBLIC SECTOR IN THE UNITED STATES AND ABROAD

How big is the public sector in the United States compared to other leading Western nations? Table 34–1 answers the question, and includes a few less-developed nations for comparative purposes. These figures show tax collections as a percentage of GNP in 1971, including taxes used to finance both real and transfer expenditures.

Taxes may seem heavy in the United States, but we are one of the lightest-taxed of the major developed nations. This reflects especially the broader range of social services provided by most West European governments. Note also the low figure for Japan, which maintains virtually no military establishment. Governments of poor, less-developed countries nearly all have relatively low taxes and expenditures.

TABLE 34–1

The Public Sector in Different Nations

COUNTRY	TAXES AS A PERCENTAGE OF GNP
Sweden	43
Netherlands	40
United Kingdom	37
France	36
West Germany	34
Italy	30
Canada	30
United States	29
Japan	19
India	12
Mexico	10

Source: Data for 1971 from Organization for Economic Cooperation and Development, except for India and Mexico.

FEDERAL AID TO STATES AND LOCALITIES

Franklin Roosevelt's New Deal began a long expansion of federal government participation in economic life. Local government spending, mainly on education, streets, and general government, which had exceeded federal activity, faded into relative insignificance. But after World War II, state–local spending, especially on education, began to grow steadily, and then shot up in the late 1960s as welfare, community development, transportation, and other expenditures were piled on top of skyrocketing educational costs. The plight of the central cities, with soaring expenses and racial crises, became the number one problem of government finance. Clearly, poor local areas, especially in the central cities and the South, could not themselves pay for welfare, education, and health programs that would meet the standards many Americans consider minimal.

Federal income and payroll taxes are the big revenue providers of the national tax system, accounting for \$210 billion of the \$390 billion of taxes collected in 1973. Local governments rely almost entirely on property taxes, and homeowners in the 1960s increasingly protested their heavy tax burdens, as tax rates soared to provide the revenues needed. Thus, increasingly over the past decade, federal aid to state and local governments has been expanded, almost entirely to support specific programs such as welfare, health, manpower training, and the like. Figure 34–7 shows this growth and the purposes of federal aid.

In the 1970s, the Nixon Administration moved strongly to slow the growth of the federal bureaucracy, returning the implementation of important federal programs to the states and localities. Nixon proposed large-scale general revenue sharing, that would return a set percentage of federal tax collections to the states and localities for their unrestricted use. He further proposed substituting a few big block grants to state and local governments for broad purposes like poverty alleviation, education, and community development, in lieu of the detailed federal grants developed during the 1960s—on the argument that the state and local governments are closer to the people and should be able to do a better job of administering such programs. Not surprisingly, the Nixon proposals faced widespread opposition from those who feel that federal planning and administration, with uniform high national standards, are the preferable way of making rapid progress toward the nation's big social goals. Just which state and local governments or groups should receive the federal funds became a source of widespread dissension.

Control over the spending of billions of dollars annually is a major economic and political issue. Figure 34–7 shows the beginning of general federal revenue-sharing grants. But how far the nation will go in turning over billions of federal tax dollars to the states and localities without substantial federal control remains to be seen.

Figure 34–7

Federal aid to state and local governments has soared during the last decade. (Source: U.S. Budget Bureau. Data are for fiscal years.)

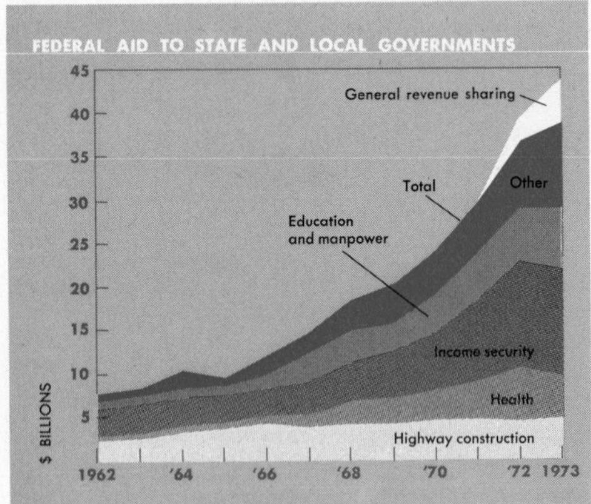

REVIEW

Concepts to Remember

Some new analytical concepts are introduced in this chapter, and important old ones are reused. Be sure you understand the following:

the public sector
real (or exhaustive) expenditures
transfer (or nonexhaustive) expenditures
progressive and regressive taxes

For Analysis and Discussion

1. What are the main economic functions of government?
2. Does government spend too much? What are your criteria for deciding?
3. If a copy is available (for instance, in the *New York Times* about the third week of each January, or in *The Federal Budget in Brief*), read the President's most recent budget message to Congress. What are the major increases and decreases proposed from the preceding year? Do these changes seem desirable to you? What criteria have you used, implicitly or explicitly, in making these judgments?
4. Should the government do more to equalize the distribution of income? If you say yes, how do you justify your position to a doctor or businessman who is earning a large income and says he doesn't see why he should work hard to support others?
5. Locate your family income level on Figure 34–6. Assuming that these data are roughly accurate, do you feel that your income level is being treated fairly in the government's overall redistribution of income? Should you be taxed more heavily?
6. Recently, much concern has been expressed that in many areas our educational facilities are inadequate, especially in the rural South. Should the federal government spend more money to improve these educational facilities, say, by building new schoolhouses or making grants to raise teachers' salaries? If your answer is yes, who should pay? How much would you be willing to see your taxes raised to help pay for such new expenditures?

Public Goods, Externalities, and the Public Sector

CHAPTER PREVIEW

CHAPTER THIRTY-FIVE

What should the public sector do? How can government best serve the public interest? Who should get the benefits and who should pay the taxes? To answer these questions, we need a theory of the public sector—a theory that will tell us when to turn to the public sector rather than relying on the private marketplace. This chapter provides such a theory: Where important externalities or public goods are involved, or where we want to alter the distribution of income, we should turn to the public sector. Lastly, the chapter examines some of the practical problems of using the public sector to so serve the public interest, for as a practical matter there are important "public sector failures," just as we saw important "market failures" in the private sector.

WHAT SHOULD THE PUBLIC SECTOR DO?

In the United States, we have a strong tradition of trying private enterprise first and calling on government only when private enterprise would clearly fall short. Partly, this rests on the pragmatic view that the country has done very well under the private-enterprise system—partly, on the theoretical case for an individual-initiative, market-directed economy spelled out in parts Three and Four. As long as trades take place voluntarily between two parties, a buyer and a seller, and affect only those two, we can be sure that their satisfactions and the general welfare are increased by each trade. Both buyer and seller must believe they are better off from the trade; otherwise, they would not have traded. And no one else is harmed, so total satisfaction must be increased. This is summarized by Adam Smith's famous argument that it is not from his benevolence that we get our meat from the butcher, but out of his regard for his own self-interest. He buys beef and cuts it to sell to you because he feels he will be better off by doing this. You buy the meat because you would rather have the steak than the money you give him in exchange.

Unless you believe that super-wisdom resides in dictators or elected leaders, it is hard to imagine a system that will guard the interests of both you and the butcher better, though it is important to remember that competition must prevail in the markets concerned. One of the system's most important advantages is the freedom it provides for individual choices, and its minimization of others' power over you and other individuals.

Externalities and Public Goods

However, when the world becomes complex and your bargain affects the interests of others, the answer is less clear. If I sell you cement made in a plant that pollutes the air for miles around, we can be reasonably sure that you and I both gain from the trade; otherwise we would not have traded. But our transaction, in effect, worsens the lot of people who live near the cement mill, and they have had no say in our transaction. Thus, we can no longer be sure that the general welfare is increased by the transaction. This is the case of "externalities," noted in Part Three as an important market failure. An external effect, or externality, occurs when your behavior affects the well-being of someone else without his explicit agreement. Externalities can be either positive or negative; your action can either improve or worsen the lot of others without their assent. The cement case produces negative external effects; but if I hire a landscaper to beautify my lot, this produces positive external effects for my neighbors.

A favorite example of economists, reaching back to the days of Adam Smith and David Hume, is that of a commonly-owned village meadow, surrounded by the homes of many villagers. To be useful for grazing, picnics, and other advantageous activities, the meadow needs draining. Suppose that the cost of draining the land would be $10,000 and the combined benefit to all the families clearly exceeds this cost. Yet there is no surety that the meadow will be drained. Although a contractor is ready to undertake the task, it is not to the advantage of any single villager to pay the $10,000. If he did so, there would be obvious large positive externalities for all the others, but unless he is a philanthropist, the meadow will stay wet and unused.

But won't it pay someone to organize a company to make a profit selling shares in the to-be-improved meadow? Couldn't he sell shares in the drained meadow's use for more than $10,000, making a profit for himself and promoting the village welfare as well, as the private-enterprise system suggests? The answer is no, because the meadow is commonly owned and he would have no right to exclude some of the villagers from the newly-drained meadow. Why would any villager pay for the meadow-dredging project, when he could equally well sit it out and benefit from the expenditures of others? He could, in essence, be a "free rider." Without some form of nonmarket collective action, the meadow will stay wet, in spite of the obvious collective advantage in having it drained.

What are the crucial variables in the problem? First, this is a case of complex exchange, with more than the interests of a single buyer and a single seller at stake. There are externalities. Second, one of the important resources is not privately owned; private rights to the use of the meadow are ill-defined. Without both these elements, the dilemma would not ordinarily be a serious one. Note that if the meadow were owned by one villager, or even a small part of it owned by each villager, the private-enterprise solution would, in principle, work. It would pay a private owner to drain the land for $10,000 and rent out its use for more than that if he owned it all, excluding those villagers who did not pay. Or it would pay an entrepreneur to buy rights to use the land from the multiple owners and then rent out the drained meadow in the multiple-ownership case, though the complexities of getting land-use rights assembled might complicate the project in the second case. Such complexities are called "transaction costs," and they may bulk large enough to block socially desirable results, even where private-property rights are clearly defined. If very few parties are involved (for example, if there were only four villagers) transaction costs may be small and private bargaining may settle the problem.

Given common ownership of (ill-defined private property rights in) the meadow, some form of collective (government) action seems essential to obtain efficient use of the available resources. By agreeing to government control of the meadow, with power to compel adherence to the vote of the majority, a tax can be levied on everyone to finance the drainage and rules can be established to govern use of the meadow.

This same combination of important externalities, many parties involved so as to make private arrangements difficult, and ill-defined private-property rights, is frequently present in the modern world. Consider the cement plant polluting the surrounding air. Production of cement imposes heavy negative externalities on nearby residents. There are too many parties affected to permit easy negotiation of a private solution. And rights to use (pollute) the air over nearby homes are ill-defined. Note that if the homeowners had clear property rights to the air above them, they could charge the cement plant for the right to pollute that air, thus returning the problem to a private-sector solution—though the situation is complex enough to pose large transactions costs in reaching a socially-optimal solution. But in the actual case, government action is clearly required to protect the nearby homeowners.

The extreme case is that of pure "public goods," as they are called by economists. National defense and the judicial system are examples. Nearly everyone agrees that we need both. Yet it is obviously impractical to rely on the private market to provide them, because it is impossible to exclude any nonpayers from the benefits. With millions of people involved and no possibility of exclusion, the free-rider problem would be insuperable. Only by turning to collective action through government, with compulsory taxes to pay the bills, can we obtain the national defense and court system we collectively want. A lighthouse is another favorite economists' example. Once in place, the lighthouse's rays are visible to all, and there is no way of keeping free riders from benefitting. Domestic police protection is similar, but not quite a pure public good, because direct policy protection could, in principle, be denied those who do not help pay the costs, though the general benefits of a safer society could not. Education is another quasi-public good. While we could shut out from schools people who do not help pay for them, we could not keep everyone from reaping part of the benefits of a better educated general population, whether or not they help pay.

How should the government deal with externalities and public goods when it does intervene? Externalities are the sole topic of the next chapter, and how to deal with public and quasi-public goods is examined in detail in a later section. But looking ahead, in those cases where externalities are a relatively minor part of the total situation, most economists advocate retaining private enterprise but "internalizing" the externalities—that is, levying a tax on each negative externality that will become part of the costs of production of the product involved and hence raise its price and restrict its output and consumption. For example, in the cement plant case, the government could levy a tax per unit of pollution from the plant, just high enough to cover the full cost of paying for the pollution damage depending on how much it wanted to reduce the pollution. The tax would raise the factory's costs and make its cement more expensive, thereby reducing production and consumption of cement (at the limit, driving the plant out of business). Consumers of cement would thus end up paying the *full* cost of producing the cement they buy. Alternatively, the government might simply pass a law limiting the amount of dust each factory can exude per day, although, as we shall see, this approach has serious disadvantages.

For pure public goods and quasi-public goods where the product is very important and the externalities are both widespread and important, the common solution is for the government to take over production and distribution—national defense, education, streets, and space exploration are examples. Such services are generally financed by taxes and provided free (though not always—remember toll bridges, city transit systems, and partial tuition at state universities).[1] But how much the government should spend on education or public parks is less clear. In principle, government ought to increase production of each good up to the point where full marginal cost just equals full marginal benefit to society; but alas, there is no simple way of measuring either marginal cost or marginal benefits. Another alternative is simply to rely on a majority vote of the electorate, but as a practical matter this is seldom feasible and it would give dubious results even if it were feasible. What actually happens in most cases, as we shall see presently, is a decision in the push and pull of practical politics as the chief executive proposes a budget and the legislature approves, modifies, or disapproves. We shall presently compare decision making in the private and public sectors more systematically.

Redistribution of Income

The second big activity of the public sector is redistributing income, through money transfer payments and through transfers of real goods and services. Many observers believe that the distribution of income produced by our largely individualistic, market-directed economy is too unequal. Even though the market may produce the most efficient use of our resources and the maximum total output consistent with our social and economic mores, the income-distribution result is ethically unacceptable. The spread between rich and poor is too wide.

This proposition is an ethical, or value, judgment, not one that follows from economic reasoning. But if one accepts it, direct government redistribution of money income from rich to poor is the simplest and most efficient way of attaining the ethically desired result. Then all individuals can be left free to spend their after-tax and after-transfer-payment incomes as they wish, with markets responding to these expenditures. Welfare payments to the poor, financed by taxes on higher income groups, are an example of such an income transfer. Alternatively, government may intervene more directly with real transfers, especially where some additional ethical standard is involved. For example, we aid the poor partly in the form of food stamps and cheap public housing, presumably because we want to be sure they use their aid for these purposes rather than for automobiles, liquor, or other presumably less acceptable purposes. Figure 34–6 showed the substantial government redistribution of income from the rich to the poor.

But the most striking thing about government redistribution of income is that it is not primarily from the rich to the poor, but from some groups to others within the great mass of middle-income families—those in roughly the $5,000–20,000 range, which includes most American families. Figure 34–6 suggests this fact. The federal government alone now lists its income security expenditures at nearly $100 billion annually, enough to give the bottom fifth of the income distribution $10,000 per family, even if they received no other income. Obviously, most of that money doesn't go to the poor. The big middle-income classes pay most of the taxes and receive most of the benefits from the government expenditures. Social security and related income security transfers are mainly from some middle-income groups to other middle-income groups, basically from workers to the elderly and other nonworkers. Federal government housing subsidies mainly benefit middle-income home buyers and homeowners. Actual government redistribution of income as

[1]For a pure public good, the answer is given unambiguously by the analysis of Part Three. Since the marginal cost of adding another user for national defense or our lighthouse is zero, the price should be set at zero; to exclude any users would be wasteful.

a practical matter is far from the common statement that we tax the rich to help the poor. Why, we shall explore in the following section on the public sector in action.

Actually, income distribution and resource allocation goals are often combined in the same government programs. Poverty and education provide two examples. Income transfers to reduce poverty presumably rest largely on ethical grounds; yet improving the lot of the poor can provide substantial positive externalities to the more fortunate, through higher future productivity, a more stable society, and the like. General free education is provided by government largely because education is considered a quasi-public good with large, widespread externalities. But it also involves a substantial element of income redistribution. We want to be sure poor children get a good education even though their families are unable to pay for it.

THE PUBLIC SECTOR AND THE POLITICAL PROCESS

Government expenditure in a fully employed economy means a reallocation of resources or incomes—from taxpayers to recipients of government funds or services. The fundamental problem here as in the private sector is to use our limited resources most effectively to satisfy our wants.

Balancing Costs and Benefits in the Public Economy

In deciding how much the government should spend, the principle of maximizing utility by equating returns at the margin suggests a rough guide to how big the public sector should be. Government expenditures should be increased up to the point where the marginal loss in giving up resources in the private sector just equals the marginal benefit from public expenditures. As long as the marginal gain is greater than the marginal loss, there is a net gain in overall welfare.

If society were a single unity, and *if* government were the all-comprehending brain of that unity, application of this principle would be feasible. The government could then weigh satisfactions lost against those gained. But in fact there is no such all-comprehending brain. At best, we can make only the roughest sort of approximation. Yet, however rough its application, the marginal principle of economizing the use of scarce resources poses the question to ask in thinking about the right size for the public sector. And some progress has been made toward making such comparisons (see box).

Note that the chances of getting good government decision making on such issues go up as the size of the government unit goes down. At the local level there is some chance that voters can weigh tax costs of proposed projects directly against potential benefits. In a few cases, citizens actually vote simultaneously on authorizing a new local expenditure (a new school or street improvement project) and the increase in taxes needed to finance it. Even where the required taxes are not formally tied to the expenditure, citizens' votes for local expenditures may not unreasonably be considered evidence that they're willing to pay the bills. And locally there is a much better chance than at state and national levels that legislators and administrators will be responsive to citizens' preferences.

Consumers' Sovereignty and Citizens' Sovereignty

Does the political process or the market process do a better job of meeting people's desires on how our productive resources should be used? Allocation of resources through the private economy occurs primarily in response to consumers' money demands for goods and services. This is "consumers' sovereignty." In the public sector, we as citizens express our preferences for roads, rockets, and zoos by voting for representatives, who in turn will, we hope, levy taxes and provide the government services we want. Thus, in the public sector there is a "citizens' sovereignty," somewhat analogous to consumers'

COST-BENEFIT ANALYSIS: PLANNING-PROGRAMMING-BUDGETING

In recent years, economists have begun to tackle the problem of public-sector costs and benefits empirically through "cost-benefit analysis," an approach pioneered under Defense Secretary Robert McNamara in the 1960s but now applied widely. Should the government build a series of dams in the High Sierras to provide water for the cities and farms of California? To make a sound economic judgment, costs of alternative dams and water distribution systems must be calculated, including possible ecological damage. Benefits must be estimated—for irrigation, for industrial use, for household use in cities, for electricity generated at the dam. For a multi-billion dollar water system, the job of fully estimating the complex intermesh of costs and benefits is a difficult one. Massive changes in property values will result and the calculations must cover many decades ahead. Effective cost-benefit analysis is one of the most difficult, but also potentially most valuable, branches of modern economics.

To extend cost-benefit analysis of proposed government programs, President Johnson instructed the Budget Bureau in the mid-1960s to push the spread of "Planning-Programming-Budgeting" (PPB) through the civilian agencies of the federal government. Should the post office automate its handling of mail? Should the Antipoverty Program spend more on retraining programs for the poor? PPB, utilizing cost-benefit analysis to help make government program decisions, is, in principle, the right move. But getting it used effectively in the political bureaucracy has proved a difficult undertaking.

At least, this kind of marginal cost-benefit analysis helps to avoid the nonsense often heard in public discussion of such issues. (1) For example, the assertion is often made that we "need" more police protection, or more classrooms; hence we should spend more for them. But such statements give no basis for intelligent economic judgement about whether the government should meet these "needs." To make that decision, the additional costs must be compared with the anticipated benefits. (2) Equally foolish is the common assertion that "we can afford" better schools and urban renewal; therefore we should have them. There are many things we "can afford." Their limit is set by our total productive resources. What and how resources should be used in the public sector can be decided rationally only by comparing expected marginal costs on each venture with expected marginal benefits.

sovereignty in the private economy. But there are some very significant differences. Four, especially, deserve attention.

1. In the marketplace, voting for resource allocation is on a *one-dollar–one-vote* basis. In the public sector, in a democratic country, it is on a *one-person–one-vote* basis. Thus, in the private sector the rich man has many more votes than the poor man. In the public sector a democratic system attempts, though not always successfully, to give each citizen equal voting power, regardless of whether he is rich or poor. Which way provides the better machinery for determining what to produce with our productive resources is a very fundamental question.

2. In the public sector, it is difficult for individuals to weigh specific benefits and costs, as we do daily in the private economy. In private life, Mr. X can consider carefully whether he prefers to spend $20 on football tickets, an electric razor, a new pair of shoes, or nothing at all. But when X votes to elect his representative, he has little opportunity to distinguish in detail between the things of which he approves and of those he disapproves—he votes for one complex, ill-defined combination against another when he chooses among candidates. And once he has voted, he has to take the package of virtues and failings rolled up in his representative—and to pay the taxes levied whether he thinks he gets his money's worth or not. Only

when a specific decision is put to the voters is there an exception—for example, when a special bond issue to finance a new school must be approved by the voters. And even then the individual has to accept the majority verdict. Consumers' sovereignty clearly gives him greater power both to decide specifically what he wants for his dollars, and to get it.

3. The public sector thus involves a big element of compulsion. Even with democratic processes, once our elected representatives decide we're going to put a man on Mars, you and I must pay the taxes to support the project, however foolish we may think it is. Not so in the private sector. There I'm not forced to pay for something I don't want.

Admirers of the market process thus stress the ability of the market to give effective representation to majority votes while adequately protecting minority interests. The market has a built-in protection for every interest. The rich man gets the most votes, but the little fellow has his say too, in proportion to the dollars he has to spend. One dollar counts one vote, and no man needs to spend a dollar on any product unless he personally decides it's worth a dollar to him.

4. As a practical matter, even in a democratic government like ours, few issues are decided on a simple town-meeting, majority-rule basis. As we shall see, properly reflecting many diverse voter's interests is very difficult even in theory, and in operating politics the legislative and administrative processes of government favor some groups over others. Our governments are more responsive to the folks back home than we often given them credit for. At both state and national levels, representatives are elected from fairly small areas, which gives local minorities a chance to be heard. In legislatures, business is largely done by committees and in informal discussion, which work out compromises on important issues that can command majorities among legislators representing widely diverse interests. The groups that are well organized, generally fare well. The "little man," the consumer, the great unorganized masses, often get the short end of the stick.

And without the test of the market there is no assurance that any public service will actually render benefits greater than its cost. But here again the case can be overstated. At least in the federal government, a new budget is enacted each year, with widespread publicity about major issues. The arguments aren't all on the side of either the private or the public sector.[2]

Often advocates of bigger government stress how an ideal democracy would reflect the wishes of the people, in comparison with all the practical shortcomings of the market system. Conversely, private-sector enthusiasts often compare an ideal, perfectly competitive economy with the painful shortcomings of practical politics in action. Clearly, we ought to compare ideal with ideal, or the two sectors in practical operation, to make a meaningful judgment as to which will serve us better under what circumstances. Parts Three and Four stressed a number of important "market failures." Will the public sector, as a practical matter, serve the public interest better than the private sector does?

Private Preferences and Collective Decisions

Consider a publicly-owned, polluted lake surrounded by homes, similar to the village meadow above. The cost of cleaning up the lake is $10,000, and the potential benefit in improved fishing, swimming, and boating is $1,500 for each of the surrounding ten families. Clearly, collective action to eliminate the pollution is in the public interest. Perhaps informal negotiation will do the job, but the free-rider problem is likely to rear its ugly head. Certainly, with a larger number of families formal government action is likely to be the only feasible way of achieving the obviously desirable social action. Presumably, in a town meeting of the lakeside

[2] See, for example, *Economic Analysis and the Efficiency of Government,* Report of the Joint Economic Committee, U.S. Congress, 1970.

residents a motion to levy an equally-distributed tax of $1,000 per family to finance the cleanup would pass unanimously. Democratic government action looks impressive in solving the problem.

But now assume, probably more realistically, that different families attach different values to a cleaner lake, as in Table 35–1. Should the local government take on the job of cleaning the lake?

If we look only at the aggregate benefit, the government clearly ought to levy the tax and clean up the lake. And it is easy to predict that the vote will be 6 to 4 in favor of precisely that action. Has democratic government produced an efficient allocation of the community's resources? Maybe, but not from the viewpoint of families 7 through 10.

Now consider a more complex case. The cost of cleaning up the lake is the same, but the benefits are shown in Table 35–2. Here the net village benefit is negative. Yet a clear majority stands to gain from the action. Should the lakeside government levy the tax and clean up the lake? Will it? How would you vote if you were family 1?

If you believe in simple majority-rule democracy (or perhaps if you're an ardent ecologist), you will approve of the proposed government action here. But if you worry about protecting the "rights" of minorities, you will be uncomfortable. **In a real sense, the majorities in both Tables 35–1 and 35–2 are imposing externalities on their neighbors just as much as the cement factory did back in the earlier section. They are doing it through a "political failure" of the democratic process; the cement baron did it through a "market failure."**

Now consider a case that will, at least at first, seem simpler. A chemical plant pollutes the air in a city, to the disadvantage of the residents. The air could be cleaned up to a level acceptable to 70 percent of the residents by plant changes costing $1,000,000. But the other 30 percent demand still cleaner air, which can be achieved only at a cost of $2,000,000. There are 10,000 families, so the cost of the first improvement would be $100 per family, that of the second $200 per family. A benefit table like the preceding ones would show that virtually every family thinks it would be worth over $100 to get rid of the worst of the pollution, though only 30 percent think it would be worth over $200. Should the government levy the $1,000,000 tax and subsidize the chemical company to clean up to at least the minimum standards?

Absolutely not! you probably reply. Pass a law and make the factory clean up itself. That bloated capitalist has no right to pollute the clean air. Make the company pay for it out of profits, or pass the added costs along to its cus-

TABLE 35–1

FAMILY	TAX COST	BENEFIT	NET GAIN
1	$ 1,000	$ 2,000	$1,000
2	1,000	2,000	1,000
3	1,000	2,000	1,000
4	1,000	2,000	1,000
5	1,000	2,000	1,000
6	1,000	2,000	1,000
7	1,000	500	−500
8	1,000	500	−500
9	1,000	500	−500
10	1,000	500	−500
	$10,000	$14,000	$4,000

TABLE 35–2

FAMILY	TAX COST	BENEFIT	NET GAIN
1	$ 1,000	$1,100	$ 100
2	1,000	1,100	100
3	1,000	1,100	100
4	1,000	1,100	100
5	1,000	1,100	100
6	1,000	1,100	100
7	1,000	500	−500
8	1,000	400	−600
9	1,000	300	−700
10	1,000	200	−800
	$10,000	$8,000	−$2,000

tomers in higher prices. So you urge the city council to pass the antipollution measure without delay. Here is a case where you can righteously insist that someone else pay the whole cost.

All of Chapter 36 is devoted to the pollution problem and alternative ways to deal with it; here we are concerned only with how well the political process functions to reflect the preferences of the citizens. Clearly, a majority will want to impose some kind of antipollution restriction on the chemical plant, from the evidence given. Will the Council act? Not clear, is the answer. For the chemical company will surely point out that the higher costs will mean higher prices, less sales, fewer jobs for the town's citizens. They may even shut the plant down, throwing everyone out of work, reducing sales of the city's merchants, and so on. The company will argue that it cannot compete against other companies that do not face such stringent clean-air laws. If the plant makes fertilizer that many of the citizens buy, their interests as consumers will also enter into the picture. Besides, the company may argue, the plant was there before most of the residents in the city, who thus knew about the bad-smelling air when they moved there. What do you predict the Council will do? What is the "right" answer for the political process to give? Should the consumers of the chemical plant's products have a right to vote on the new law since they are affected by it—another case of externalities? Suddenly, what is the public interest is not so clear.

As a practical matter, democratic governments seem highly responsive to pressure groups, often little concerned with the "public interest"—the welfare of the mass of the taxpaying voters. This is easy to explain in self-interest terms. Suppose a case like our polluted lake problem above, where a few people have a very large financial interest (worth, say, $10,000) in having government take a particular action, while the other 10,000 taxpaying residents of the area have little interest in the matter. We can be sure the special interest group will bring all possible pressure to bear on the city council to obtain their $10,000 subsidy. But most other voters, to whom the cost will be only $1 each if the measure passes, will pay little attention. For $1 it would be scarcely worth the cost of digging out information on the matter and taking time to urge council members to vote against it. (This is sometimes called the "rational ignorance effect.") Thus, it is not surprising that the council may vote the subsidy to the special interest group, even though it may be unjustifiable on grounds of the "public interest."

Last, turn to the question of how effectively collective action meets the wishes of the public in redistributing income. As we saw above, government does redistribute income from the rich to the poor, but only to a modest extent. The bulk of income transfers are from more- to less-politically effective middle-class groups. Here we have no objective test of market efficiency, as with Pareto optimality; the issue of what is the "right" distribution of income is essentially an ethical one.

One theory is that the well-to-do use the state as a mechanism for making gifts to the poor. A second is that in a democracy the poor are able to use their votes to get income transferred from the rich. Neither of these explains the modest rich-to-poor transfers, compared to those among the middle classes. An alternative, self-interest theory is often advanced by those who face the facts as to what transfers actually occur through government; most people look out for their own interests, some more effectively than others.

The simplest view is that the many poor outvote the few rich to transfer income from rich to poor. The bottom 51 percent can use their majority to take income away from the top 49 percent. But it is far from clear that the bottom 51 percent of the population works together in any such coalition; the top of that group are not poor by far, and their interests diverge substantially. The really poor are only 10 percent of the population, or 20 percent of the votes in the bottom-half coalition. Clearly, such a small minority cannot dominate the political coalition. Thus, who in the bottom 51 percent is going to get how much of the income taken from the upper half is likely to be a crucial issue in forming and maintaining a political coalition. Indeed, the upper-income 49 percent could become the majority merely by wooing over the top 2 percent of the lower coalition. Thus, not the poor, but the large lower-to middle-income group in the lower-half coalition is likely to end up as dominant in any bargaining process. Unless the ethical values of the rich lead them to coalesce with the poor, the resulting income transfers may well be from the well-to-do but primarily to the middle classes, which is roughly what we observe.[3]

So far, we have assumed that government programs are made simply to accomplish transfers among income groups per se. But realistically, organized groups in the political process are usually centered differently—they are farmers, the elderly, homeowners, college students, owners of oil wells, and the like. The poor are not only relatively small in number but also generally not well-organized politically. Collective action tends to shift income toward organized groups, mainly comprised of the middle classes, although often the stated rationale is to help the poor. And the taxes must come largely from those same middle classes, because that is where the bulk of the taxable income is. Social security, farmers' aid, housing subsidies, and higher education in state universities are all examples. In each case, tax funds are used to provide benefits primarily to the middle classes. Social security benefits go to those who have a record of past earnings; farm aid is paid largely in relation to the size of the farmer's output; government housing subsidies are largely to those who can afford to buy their own homes; students at subsidized state universities come heavily from middle- and upper-income families.

Thus, as a practical matter, democratic government operates to a considerable extent through coalitions and organized interest groups. Only on major national issues does anything approaching a simple majority view of the public dominate. The same is true to a lesser extent at state and local levels. Ours is a pluralistic society, and nowhere is this evidenced more clearly than in the political process. In a huge complex society it is difficult to see how anything like the old New England town-meeting ideal of democracy can operate. Add to this the realistic fact of large bureaucracies as a way of running big government, and political failures in the public sector look as pervasive as market failures in the private sector.

[3] Bargaining theory provides a formal analysis of the way such coalitions form and the conditions under which various bargainers will gain or lose.

Social Choice: The Problem of Social Balance

One last look at the central issue of consumers' versus citizens' sovereignty from another angle may be helpful. Those who say the public sector is too big have a basic presumption that individual freedom to spend in the marketplace should guide the allocation of resources; any other allocation of resources is presumptively inferior. But Professor Galbraith has made a forceful counterargument in his bestseller, *The Affluent Society*. He argues that such general distrust of the government process has led to a serious underallocation of resources to the public sector (leaving national defense aside). In the world's richest economy, we allocate only about 20 percent of GNP to satisfying all nondefense collective wants through public goods and services.

Galbraith argues that our economy is so rich we can readily afford more and better public services, that we need them badly, and that the alternative is generally wasteful civilian consumption just to keep our economic machinery going. Yearly model changes on automobiles, plush night clubs, and mink coats are symbols of conspicuous consumption, meeting demands developed by pervasive advertising. Yet our public services are barely adequate. Our cities are marred by slums. Our streets are jammed. Our air and streams are polluted. Our police forces and local governments are often peopled by incompetents, so poorly paid as to be constant targets for graft. Few of our symphonies

THE VOUCHER EDUCATION PLAN— COMBINING THE PUBLIC AND PRIVATE SECTORS

Nearly everyone agrees on the importance of assuring all youngsters a good education, at least through the high school level. But many parents, and professional educators too, are dissatisfied with the educations provided by our public schools, which all children must attend unless they happen to have rich parents who can afford a private school.

The "voucher education plan," with both conservative and liberal supporters, has gained considerable attention in recent years as a possible means of improving the situation. Its most extreme form shows the central issues most clearly, although less drastic alternatives are also feasible. Let each state or community take the same amount it is now spending on public education, determined in the usual democratic political fashion. Instead of spending this sum on public schools, let it divide the total up and give a voucher of equal value (say $1,000 annually) to the parents of each child, this voucher to be spent on education at any school of the parent's choice, so long as the school meets minimum state standards.

A wide range of private, profit-seeking schools would spring up, seeking to obtain the business of different parents with different educational objectives for their children. While state standards would presumably require subjects like reading and arithmetic for all beginners, high school curricula might range widely from college preparatory to vocational focus. Instead of being faced with a monopoly school as now, consumers would be free to buy the education they want where they think they get the most for their voucher. Just as government decides how much national defense and highways we should have, but contracts out laying the concrete and building the bombers on a competitive basis, so it would count on private enterprise to provide more varied, responsive education for children in response to the vouchers given to all parents.

This plan attempts to combine the best of the public and the private sectors. Only the public sector can assure that every child gets his minimum guaranteed level of education; this is essential on grounds of equity and attaining the positive externalities from widespread education. But most evidence suggests that profit-seeking competitors (the private sector) do the best job of actually producing what consumers want to buy; so why shouldn't we take advantage of this fact in education, one of the most important services we buy? Who, the private enterprise advocates ask, will try harder to educate our youngsters better—the local public school principal and teachers who are responsible only to the school board, or their counterparts who must satisfy you to get the dollars to stay in business?

Does the voucher-education plan offer the best of both the public and private sectors? At first, the idea of turning education over to profit-seeking business may shock you, but the plan has won many advocates and modified experiments are being conducted in several states under the auspices of the U.S. Office of Education. As you can guess, opponents point to potential dangers, notably three. First, they say most parents aren't really competent to decide what is the best schooling for their youngsters, and they would be easy picking for unscrupulous businesses selling poor education. Second, the plan could be used to finance church schools, violating the constitutional separation of church and state. And third, it might permit development of racially segregated schools. Voucher supporters answer that they'd rather trust parents who can judge directly what they're getting for their money than the present unresponsive political school system, and that safeguards can, and should, be built in to forbid both religious and racial misuse of the plan, by refusing to certify such schools under the voucher plan. Indeed, they argue, the proposed voucher plan should speed integration by breaking present ties between the school attended and residential location.

and art museums receive adequate public support. The scientist who invents a new gadget is greeted with public acclaim, but the politician who suggests a new public service is deemed a wastrel. All this, Galbraith argues, reflects a basic social unbalance in the affluent American economy. Somehow, we have no effective machinery to translate the obvious need for greater public services into reality.

Why do we so often assume that a dollar spent on taxes is wasted, while a dollar spent in the market provides a valuable return? Galbraith suggests that as taxpayers each of us sees the cost of public services to himself, but the benefits are so widespread and generalized that it is hard for the individual to value them.

America can clearly "afford" more public services and the end to such negative externalities as pollution if we want them. The test of Galbraith's position lies in whether we collectively want them badly enough to pay for them, and by that test it is far from clear that government should be bigger. Social cost-benefit analysis, program by program, is the basic foundation for rational decision making in the public, as in the private, sector.[4]

SUMMARY— WHAT IS THE PUBLIC INTEREST?

Fundamentally, in our individualistic society the public interest is what 200 million Americans say it is. But how best to get their diverse preferences registered and compromised is a very difficult problem. By and large, the private sector does an impressive job of efficiently producing the different goods and services millions of different consumers want. But it has important shortcomings, and to overcome some of these, we clearly must turn to collective action. As a practical matter, only government can produce public goods, insist on due attention to externalities, and redistribute incomes as the public wishes. Yet government too has serious shortcomings in meeting the public's wishes. Clearly, simple cliches that more, or less, government is needed, deserve distrust. Which sector serves us best depends on the particular circumstances of each case, and especially on the sort of government (collective decision making and action) that is the operational alternative to the marketplace.

[4]For an excellent summary of these issues, see Peter Steiner, "The Public Sector and the Public Interest," in *The Analysis and Evaluation of Public Expenditures* (Joint Economic Committee of Congress, 1969), Vol. 1.

REVIEW

Concepts to Remember

This chapter presents the basic theory of the public sector and introduces important new concepts. Be sure you understand the following:

externalities	citizens' sovereignty
public goods	balancing alternatives at the margin
free riders	cost-benefit analysis
private property rights	"political failures."

For Analysis and Discussion

1. Does consumers' sovereignty or citizens' sovereignty provide a better process for allocating society's productive resources?
2. As a practical matter, are the "market failures" of the private economy or the "political failures" of the public economy more serious barriers to having individuals' preferences carried out effectively?
3. Chapter 35 suggests that we should rely on the public sector only where important externalities or public goods are involved, or where we want to alter the distribution of income. Is this the proper guiding principle? Can you list cases where it should not be followed?
4. Many argue that our national priorities should place a higher value on better public services—education, slum clearance, public health, and so on—than on more consumer goods. Analyze this argument.
5. What are externalities? Give three examples of cases in which probable externalities provide a basis for government intervention in the private market.
6. What is cost-benefit analysis? How can it help in deciding what projects government should undertake?
7. a. Many people believe that there is always a presumption in favor of reducing government expenditures. Do you agree?
   b. Why, if at all, is the above presumption more defensible than a presumption that government spending to provide public services should be increased?

CASE 23

The Urban Crisis

The problems of the modern public sector are nowhere more vividly apparent than in the urban crisis—the plight of the great cities that already, with their sprawling appendages, include two-thirds of our population and may encompass 80 percent or more by the year 2000. Consider New York, the largest metropolis of all, with the biggest problems of all. The following paragraphs summarize briefly some of the major problem areas. For students who want to make this a major research case, additional references are listed at the end.

Housing and the Environment. New York has nearly a million run-down housing units, in effect, slums. In some areas, literally blocks of slums stand empty, with broken windows, stolen plumbing and wiring, littered streets—buildings abandoned by their owners who could not get enough from them to cover operating costs and taxes, and abandoned by even the poorest tenants who could not stay without lights, heat, or working plumbing. Residents of these areas tend to be members of minority groups, especially blacks and Puerto Ricans. Nonsubsidized private construction of low- and middle-cost housing in the central city has been at a virtual standstill for nearly a decade; it simply isn't profitable without subsidies to build such new housing, given building costs, land costs, taxes, and skyrocketing operating expenses. Worse, it doesn't pay to keep much of the existing slum-area housing stock in repair. Landlords, given existing conditions, are often better off to let their apartments deteriorate, collecting rents as long as they can and then just abandoning the property as the neighborhood deteriorates. Rents are high nonetheless, reflecting the mass of low-income families and the stable or declining supply of housing. Nearly all old housing (almost 1.5 million units) is still under legal rent ceilings, continued from World War II days with intermittent increases.

Crime. Crime rates are high in the central city, especially in slum areas. Muggings and vandalism are commonplace, and violent crime spills over into the higher-income neighborhoods. Drug addiction and pushing seems to be everywhere.

Poverty and Racial Problems. For all of American history, the cities have been magnets for the poor and the uneducated, from abroad and from the rural areas. Since World War II, blacks and Puerto Ricans have poured into New York, partly in search of one of the nation's highest welfare payments. Today over a million persons are on welfare in New York City, one person of every seven who lives there. Poverty rates are highest among minority groups, and the bulk of welfare recipients are in families headed by women. Social conditions mirror the broken families and poverty-stricken, deteriorating neighborhoods in which many mothers and children live. Slum schools sometimes resemble minor battlefields more than educational establishments. Racial groups quarrel incessantly over control of their schools. Harlem and Bedford-Stuyvesant bubble with racial tensions.

Transportation. Transportation threatens a gigantic breakdown as the ratio of autos to space soars, and auto exhausts pollute the atmosphere. Parking in midtown is over $5 a day; yet the number of cars entering Manhattan continues to rise. Insurance costs, with the city's high theft and accident rates, equal the value of a car in two or three years. Public transportation, although plentiful compared to many cities, is noisy, dirty, and increasingly expensive, though it already operates with a large public subsidy.

Taxes and Public Outlays. City taxes are so high they drive investments and households away. Yet city services are clearly inadequate. Crime and dirt seem to be everywhere. Salaries of city employees have tripled in the past decade, and strong unions are pushing them higher. The average city employee now earns more than the average taxpayer, and one out of every three employees in the city now works for some branch of government. The city seems to hang on the brink of bankruptcy, in continual conflict with the state and federal governments in pursuit of larger grants to help meet the ever-mounting bills.

The City and the Suburbs. The postwar period has seen a continuous exodus of upper- and middle-class households, business firms, and jobs from the central city to the suburbs. These income groups live elsewhere in more pleasant surroundings, where they send their children to school, pay their property taxes, and from whence they commute daily, complaining loudly about the bad transport facilities, dirty city air, and the like. New York City is becoming increasingly a commercial and financial city, inhabited by the rich who live well and the poor who live badly, but not the middle classes. Thus, the households with high taxpaying ability leave, while the poor who need welfare and other city services stay. The number of manufacturing jobs in the city has fallen steadily since World War II; yet such jobs were traditionally the livelihood of unskilled labor from the rural areas. The surrounding metropolitan area is a mass of hundreds of overlapping towns, counties, school districts, water districts, local authorities, and the like. Each is concerned to maintain its own tax base, and to maximize the services it obtains while minimizing the costs to its own members. The suburbs contribute as little as possible to the finance of the central city. Understandably, there is little coordinated metropolitan-area planning.

The list could go on. New York City is the nation's urban crisis on display, and this only suggests the total problem. Clearly, the urban crisis is not one crisis, but a mass of interlinked economic, social, and political problems, far beyond our ability to deal with here. But consider what your elementary economic analysis can tell you as to who should do what about slum housing. Among the steps proposed are:

1. Stricter rent controls to reduce rents.
2. Abolish rent controls to encourage new construction.
3. Government-financed public housing, renovation of existing buildings, or rent subsidies to low-income families.
4. Private renovation of deteriorating buildings.
5. Develop new low-cost methods of building mass housing.
6. Reduce construction union wages.
7. Encourage poor families to move to the suburbs.
8. Punish greedy landlords.
9. Negative income tax to help the poor, but let them get their own housing.

Which, if any, of these do you advocate? Is saving the central cities a problem for public or private sector action, or for neither?

For those who wish to make this into a larger scale case, the following series of articles in *The Public Interest* provides more detailed background material and analyses of proposed remedies:

"New York's Housing Problem: A Study in Immobilisme" (Summer 1969)

"Alternatives to the Gilded Ghetto" (Winter 1969)

"Where Shall They Live?" (Winter 1970)

"Why We Have Not Built More Houses" (Spring 1970)

"The City as Sandbox" (Fall 1971)

"Woodlawn: The Zone of Destruction" (Winter 1973)

Pollution and the Environment

CHAPTER PREVIEW

CHAPTER THIRTY-SIX

National concern for the deteriorating quality of the environment has snowballed in recent years. Concern for economic growth has been supplanted by the question, growth for what? Air and water pollution are pervasive by-products (externalities) of modern industrial society. On every side there are cries for the government to "do something" to halt pollution. Some examples:

1. **Water.** In 1969, the oily, chocolate-brown Cuyahoga River, which runs through Cleveland into Lake Erie, burst into flames. The Cuyahoga is so laden with industrial and municipal waste that not even the leeches and sludge worms that thrive in many badly polluted rivers are found in it. By 1970, along the entire southern shore of Lake Erie there were virtually no fish left and most other forms of marine life had vanished. Once called "the beautiful river," the Ohio is now perhaps the most contaminated of all our rivers, the receptacle for thousands of tons of pollutants from plants and cities along its valley. Swimming, even boating, in many of our inland waterways has become too dangerous to risk.

Although the nation has invested about $20 billion since 1952 in the construction of thousands of municipal sewage-treatment plants, sewers, industrial-pollution control, and related facilities, 40 percent of the nation's sewage is dumped, raw and untreated, into the streams and water resources of the nation. Only about

25 percent of the total receives what sanitary engineers call "two-stage treatment"—which may, under ideal conditions, satisfy 90 percent of the biochemical oxygen demand before the sewage is released into the streams of natural water. The remaining 30–35 percent of communities have "one-stage" treatment, which merely takes out the solids from the raw sewage. In the great majority of sewage systems, the same facilities are used for rain runoff and industrial and household sewage, so when heavy rainstorms exceed the capacity of sewage-treatment plants, the city's raw sewage bypasses the sewage plant with the street-water runoff and is washed directly into the waterways without treatment.

2. **Air.** Each year, America's industries, homes, and cars spew over 200 million tons of smoke and fumes into the air. Autos account for about half of this total, and in some areas, particularly Los Angeles, for nearly all of it. As long ago as 1952, four thousand deaths were recorded in London in one period of massive smog, when air conditions held all the pollutants being poured out by furnaces, fireplaces, industrial plants, and autos down close to the earth. The famous New York Thanksgiving Day smog of 1966 reached almost the same danger level, as air inversion held the smog motionless over the metropolitan area. Scientists warn that Los Angeles hovers on the brink of a similar danger. Air pollution is not new, nor peculiar to the United States. Ancient Romans complained of the smoke that enveloped their city. But the magnitude of the problem has increased vastly in recent decades.

3. **Solid waste.** As a result of America's massive production of goods and services that make up our incredible GNP, every year we junk 7 million cars, 50 million tires, 20 million tons of paper, 28 billion bottles, and 48 billion cans. Just to collect the nation's garbage costs nearly $3 billion a year. Graveyards of junked cars are the most visible symptom of our massive waste-disposal problem. But the problem is even worse than it seems, for increasingly packaging materials (cans and the like) have been shifted to a "no-return" basis and to materials that are virtually indestructible (for example, plastics and aluminum instead of steel). Every major city

Industrial pollution: Darkness at noon. (Richard Frieman—Photo Researchers, Inc.)

faces a crisis on the disposal of its massive wastes already, or in the years ahead.

4. **Noise.** Especially in the cities, noise is approaching the level of persistent intensity that threatens both the mental and physical well-being of the inhabitants. According to a widely cited standard, 85 decibels represents the level above which continuous noise can cause deafness. A typical subway train produces 95 decibels, a power mower 110 decibels, and a jet aircraft at takeoff 150 decibels. Electronically magnified rock and roll reaches well above 100 decibels. Noise at a level of 165 decibels can kill animals such as rats and cats. Experts warn that it can damage human ears, nerves, and general bodily functioning.

5. **The ecological system.** Ecologists, who study the interactions of entire systems of living things, go far beyond the above problems. They suggest that population growth and modern technology have gone so far so fast that they threaten man's very existence on this globe. Partly, they point to the rapid using-up of natural resources. More fundamentally, they argue that our throwoffs of all forms of waste are interacting to make the planet uninhabitable. For example, chemical fertilizers and pesticides used in farming are only partly absorbed by growing plants; many of them wash into the streams and oceans where they may seriously affect both marine life and those who consume the water. Thus, attempts to increase the output of agricultural land through the use of such modern methods may boomerang. The pollution of Lake Erie is due more to the washoff of agricultural chemicals than to industrial wastes. The natural balance of living things is said to be a delicate one, and man's incredibly rapid development over the past century threatens to disturb these fundamental balances with disastrous results.

Deterioration in the quality of the environment is not confined to the United States, although our massive increases in real GNP and modern technology make the problem especially vivid for us. Nor is the problem confined to capitalist systems. Soviet newspapers complain of the same conditions in the USSR, and Soviet cartoonists are equally caustic in their drawings of pollution as it envelopes the Russian man-in-the-street. Their rivers vie with ours for the title of dirtiest.[1] Japan's environmental problems may already be worse than ours. The Rhine, fabled in song and verse, is possibly the dirtiest of the world's major rivers. Moreover, pollution is far from new. Early Roman writers complained of filthy drinking water. Early Spanish explorers noted that campfire smoke hung thick and low in what is now the Los Angeles basin.

Highways in California. (Robert Perron—Photo Researchers, Inc.)

[1]For example, see K. Iosifob, "The Vokhna River Flows," and O. Volkov, "A Writer's Notes: A Trip to Baikal," reprinted in M. Goldman, ed., *Controlling Pollution* (Englewood Cliffs, N.J.: Prentice-Hall, Inc., Spectrum Books, 1967).

Open sewers and polluted water are daily threats to health and life itself in the world's less-developed nations, many of which are neither rich nor capitalist.

THE PROBLEM

Pollution in the United States is largely a problem of externalities. In responding to market demands, businessmen do not charge the full social cost of their operations in their prices to consumers. The result is that the price of industry's products is too low, consumers buy too much paper and steel produced by the polluting plants. In effect, we make those harmed by pollution subsidize users of steel and paper. In the same way, the price of autos does not reflect their full cost to society; car users do not have to pay for the air pollution they create.

Put another way, manufacturers and auto drivers treat clean water, clean air, and quiet as if they were free goods, when in fact they are increasingly scarce and are overconsumed at a price of zero. We should be able to charge users of clean air and clean water for the privilege of making them dirty, but we don't. So far we have not developed effective ways of recognizing air, water, and quiet as property, and of charging a price for their use. If General Motors owned the Ohio River, we can be sure it would charge for dumping sewage and industrial wastes into it, and the externalities created by riverside factories would be internalized into their costs. But most water, air, and quiet are publicly owned, if they are owned by anyone.

In principle, to provide an optimal allocation of society's resources in response to the public's wishes, costs should include both private and by-product social costs. If the price system doesn't do the job, we must turn to collective action.[2]

In considerable part, environmental deterioration reflects our rapidly growing population, rapid movement toward high-technology production, and above all, the enormous demand of American citizens for a bigger and better life—bigger and better cars, bigger and better airplanes, bigger and better household appliances, more electricity and man-made energy, redder apples, greener beans. The villain of the piece is not some profit-hungry industrialist who can be fined into submission, nor some lax public official who can be replaced. The villains are the failure of free markets to take into account full social costs, and consumers themselves who demand new, bigger, cheaper things without counting the cost in the dirtier environment that results as a by-product. The quips of critics are often telling. Smog, they say, is the Air Apparent. Paraphrasing Perry's famous battle report from Lake Erie, they quip "We have met the enemy, and he is us." Ours is an effluent, as well as an affluent, society.

Physically, much of the pollution problem traces to a simple proposition: You can't get rid of matter. We can change the form of matter, in the earth, on it, and in its atmosphere, but we can't do more than transform it. Thus, we can change coal into heat and pollutants such as fly ash, gases, and soot, but the same amount of matter remains in a different form. This is most obvious in the form of solid wastes, but it is equally important in pollution of the air and the water, which are the recipients of some of the by-products in transforming materials. We live on "spaceship earth," and it is up to us to keep our self-contained ecological system a viable one.

POLLUTION POLICY

Pollution, Population, and Economic Growth

Pollution, population growth, and economic growth are intimately related. But this does not mean that the way to reduce pollution is to stop economic growth. Economic growth means growth in total economic output per

[2] Although governments themselves are often major polluters, especially through inadequate sewer systems.

capita—it is growth in generalized productive capacity. We may use the increased capacity to produce things that pollute (for example, leaded gasoline), things that involve no pollution (art museums), or things that reduce pollution (smoke filters on chimneys). Though output of some goods inescapably involves pollution (solid waste from many products), in general we can use our productive capacity to produce the combination of goods, services, and cleanliness we want and are willing to pay for. The choice of more clean air will mean less steel and auto transportation from the resources available, but more steel and autos need not mean dirtier air if we are willing to pay for "clean" methods of production. GNP in total and per capita will not then be as large as with pollution, because cleaner air (less pollution) doesn't get included as we compute GNP; but this does not change the fact that we can allocate our productive resources as we wish to maximize our satisfaction from them. Indeed, the more we grow (increase productive capacity), the greater will be our ability to have *both* cleaner air and water *and* more of the other goods and services we want. To oppose economic growth because that seems the only way to lessen pollution is shortsighted indeed. (More details in Chapter 43.)

Population growth is different. More population, other things equal, means *less* output *per capita*—a lower standard of living. It also inescapably means more crowding of the environment, because the total amount of space to be shared is substantially fixed.

As a practical matter, combined population and economic growth have brought a devastating amount of environmental pollution over the last half century. But this does not mean that zero economic growth (ZEG), or even zero population growth (ZPG), is the best way to clean up the environment. On the contrary, we need to be careful not to throw the baby out with the bathwater.

Controlling Water Pollution—An Example

There are, broadly, three approaches to pollution control—voluntary action, direct government regulation, and effluent charges. Let us consider briefly how each would work in controlling water pollution.

Voluntary Action. To many environmentalists, pollution is a moral issue. Those who pollute are immoral, especially if they are large corporations. They ought to stop. Economics cannot pass judgment on people's moral and ethical values. But it must warn such moralists that their approach is not likely to get very far in cleaning up the nation's lakes and streams. First, the notion that big corporations are the devil in the piece is a half-truth. Much of the worst water pollution comes from public sewer systems, from private homes. Much comes from use of chemical fertilizers, pesticides, and the like on farms, large and small, without which, incidentally, our food would be substantially more expensive. And much comes from little firms as well as large ones, though a lot does come from big corporations. Second, and still more important, elimination of pollution from industrial and agricultural production will be very expensive for many firms and farms. Thus, if only one paper mill along a river, voluntarily or under social pressure from its critics, spends the money to treat or recycle its effluents that have been polluting the river, it will find its costs higher than its competitors, and that it is pricing itself out of the market. Alone, it can do little good in reducing the overall level of water pollution, and it is likely to go broke trying. Only if other paper mills are required to meet similar effluent standards is any one firm economically safe in spending the money to reduce its pollution.[3]

To rely on voluntary action by businessmen to eliminate pollution, therefore, is to misconstrue the nature of the competitive process.

[3] Similarly, it would be unreasonable to expect the individual consumer to invest voluntarily in an expensive smog-control device for his car when other car users were not required to do so. Alone, he could do no measurable good in reducing smog. Only if all, or most, car users are required to add smog-control devices can the individual feel he is paying his part of the price of clean air with assurance that others are doing the same and that cleaner air will in fact result.

Effective action to alleviate pollution (to internalize the externality) must, in most cases, be collective action, however cooperative individual businessmen may be. Only government can assure compliance and uniformity for antipollution policies. Moral pressure and persuasion may help, but by themselves they are unlikely to produce major changes against the pressures of market competition.

Direct Regulation. To reduce water pollution, the government may simply order all industries to reduce the amount of effluents they discharge into the lakes and rivers concerned. First, it must decide how clean it wants the lake or river to be, say, 90 percent cleaner than now. Then it orders each firm to reduce its untreated discharges by 90 percent. This would appear to be the simplest approach.

In fact, direct regulation faces many problems, even if a law is passed ordering a cleanup of the waterways. Under the 1956 and 1965 Amendments to the Water Pollution Control Act, first, the government was to determine the standard of cleanliness needed in each lake or stream to meet the overall goal; then it was to determine how much each polluter contributed to the excess pollution, and order each to cut back its pollution to meet the prescribed standard. But there are some 40,000 individual industrial sources of water pollution. Some firms have previously dumped few effluents, some many. The former understandably argue that they pollute little, that they should not have to reduce their effluents by a further 90 percent, and are likely to go to court against the Environmental Pollution Agency if it applies the 90 percent rule to them. Moreover, it is obvious that the most efficient way to achieve the 90 percent overall reduction goal would be to concentrate cleanup action where the costs of doing so are the least, not across-the-board. The total cost of achieving the new standard may be far higher across-the-board than in the concentrated approach. But either way, individual firms will protest that they are not in fact responsible for the pollution observed and long court battles have ensued over the reasonableness of the regulatory actions.

The regulatory approach faces further problems. As noted above, a substantial proportion of total water pollution comes from untreated or inadequately treated city sewage, where the culprit is the local government. A federal or state regulatory agency faces heavy going in imposing and enforcing absolute standards against other governments—and indeed the federal approach has been large cash grants to improve local sewage treatment facilities to parallel higher antipollution standards. Second, agricultural pollution from chemical fertilizers, animal wastes, and the like poses very difficult problems of setting standards and enforcing them. Chemical fertilizer residues may end up polluting streams or lakes many miles away. To demonstrate that Farmer *A* is responsible for pollution of Lake *B* fifty miles away is just about impossible, though it may be clear that all farmers together in the area are responsible.

Effluent Charges. Increasingly, economists and conservationists favor special taxes, or effluent charges, per unit of effluent discharged, to limit water and air pollution. As with direct regulation, the first step is to decide how much pollution is to be reduced, say, by 90 percent. Then an across-the-board tax per unit of effluent discharged is levied (for example, two cents per pound of solid waste dumped into the stream). The level of the tax is set to reduce pollution to the desired level; by reducing their effluents, firms can avoid the tax. If a higher degree of cleanliness is desired, raise the effluent tax.

Unlike direct regulation, this approach gives each polluter a continuing incentive to reduce his effluents. It has three big advantages over direct regulation. (1) It avoids the necessity of making a special administrative decision as to the limit to be placed on each separate firm; each firm pays the tax in proportion to its own polluting. (2) It achieves the desired reduction in total pollution at a lower cost. The incentive to reduce effluents will be greatest for those who can reduce their pollution at the lowest cost; those firms that face a very high cost of producing without pollution will prefer to pay the tax,

"Now *maybe they'll be moved to do something about water pollution!"*
(Drawing by Chas. Addams; © *1969. The New Yorker Magazine, Inc.)*

though since all firms face rising costs per unit as they eliminate more and more pollution, we can be sure that the effluent charge will lead virtually all polluters to reduce their effluents to some extent. The result will be that the cost (price) of goods produced by the polluters will rise as little as is consistent with reducing pollution to the desired level. (3) With direct regulation, once a firm meets the legal standard it has no incentive to reduce pollution further. But with an effluent charge, it always has an incentive to reduce pollution further—for example, if technological advance reduces the cost of cutting back on effluents, it will pay the firm to reduce its pollution further to reduce its effluent tax. Conversely, with direct regulation the firm has no incentive to reduce effluents further, even if it becomes cheaper to do so; on the contrary, it has an incentive not to do so, because going beyond the regulatory limit would increase costs and reduce profits.

Some critics have called effluent charges "licenses to pollute," because a firm may choose to pay the tax and continue polluting. But the same charge can be levied against a regulatory limit; then all firms have a free license to pollute up to that limit. Precisely the same pollution reduction can be obtained under either approach, but more cheaply with effluent charges. Effluent charges can be set high enough to discourage any amount of pollution we want to eliminate. The only way to eliminate completely any license to pollute would be to forbid pollution completely, by either regulation or a prohibitively high effluent tax.

Marginalism—How Clean is Clean?

It should be clear by now that the cost of clean water depends substantially on how clean we want the water to be. If we want all our streams and lakes to meet distilled water standards, the cost will be astronomical. If the standards are more modest, so will be the cost.

Urban sewage disposal, an unglamorous but central part of the water-pollution problem, illustrates this point. As was indicated at the beginning of this chapter, in many American communities raw sewage is dumped directly into flowing streams. In about 35 percent of the cases, sewage is passed through a one-stage treatment, in another 25 percent through a two-stage treatment, which removes perhaps 90 percent of the pollutant qualities of the sewage before it is dumped into streams. In virtually all cases, common sewers are used for rainwater runoff and sewage waste. Thus, heavy rainstorms may produce such flooding that the combined sewage plus rain runoff must be bypassed around the treatment plants, pouring directly into flowing streams or lakes without any sewage treatment at all.

Use of sewers for both waste and rain runoff works well most of the time; both sewage and rainwater are funneled through the sewage-treatment plants. To protect against infrequent overloads would require either a vastly larger sewer system or new sewage-treatment plants so large that they would handle even the massive runoffs in large storms. These would be extremely expensive. For industrial wastes, costs soar similarly as firms try to clean up their effluents to higher and higher standards of cleanliness. Cost estimates vary, but a total additional annual cost of $25–30 billion would possibly suffice to provide two-stage sewage treatment for all major municipalities. This would of course, fall substantially short of 100 percent water purification for the nation. To move the standard up to 95 percent cleanliness with three-stage treatment would probably increase the additional cost to $60–70 billion annually. In virtually all cases, the cost of additional cleanliness rises far more than proportionately as absolute cleanliness is approached.

How clean is clean? Clean water is not an all-or-nothing proposition. As almost everywhere in economics, the question is one of degree, a tradeoff between cleaner water and higher costs. Sensible policy involves comparing the marginal cost of each additional unit of cleanliness against the marginal benefits of that unit. And, to repeat, in most cases marginal costs rise sharply as cleanliness standards go up.

A simple example may emphasize this point. Johnny's mother tells him to wash his hands before he comes to dinner. When she sees the result, she says he has not *really* washed his hands. Johnny protests that he has; he has passed his hands through a stream of cold water before coming to the table. His mother sends him back, to use hot water, soap, and a towel, and then his hands pass inspection. Yet Johnny's hands, even after a two-stage treatment, are far from clean enough to meet a surgeon's hospital operating room standards. He would demand a third-stage process. Johnny measures cleanliness by the fact of washing his hands. His mother's measure is a visual one—how much dirt she can see. The surgeon is interested in bacterial count. To insist on the surgeon's third level of cleanliness in day-to-day life for most of us would be incredibly expensive in terms of time, energy, and money—and pointless. So it may be with many pollution issues.

THE ECONOMICS AND POLITICS OF POLLUTION

Reducing pollution, we have learned painfully over the past few years, is a complex, expensive job. The economic analysis involved is simple in principle, but complicated in its application to individual situations. Much of the difficulty arises from the fundamental fact of conflicts of interest that can be compromised only through the political process.

The last decade has seen a vast surge of concern for the environment. In 1956 and 1965, Congress passed the first major clean water acts. In 1969, it established the Council on Environmental Quality (CEQ), parallel in many respects to the Council of Economic Advisers. In 1970, President Nixon submitted a broad program of environmental restoration, stressing major steps toward both water- and air-pollution control, including radically stiffer antipollution requirements for autos and a $10 billion, five-year sewage improvement program for municipalities, heavily subsidized by the federal government. Between the 1950s and 1970, federal spending to reduce water pollution rose from $1 million to $300 million annually; the 1974 budget carried $2.1 billion for pollution control.

Yet progress has seemed painfully slow to many environmentalists. In its 1972 report, the Council on Environmental Quality said, quoting figures on cleaner air, that "we are winning the battle against air pollution," but that progress on the water-pollution front is mixed. The sewage and industrial effluents situation is clearly improving, but pollution from agricultural fertilizers and other chemicals is worsening. In 1972, business firms invested $5 billion in pollution-control equipment, about 5 percent of their total investment. The CEQ estimated that during the seventies, the nation, mainly private firms, will need to spend $287 billion to meet 1972 legal standards for cleaner air and water, assuming no further inflation. The Council emphasized that, though this is a huge sum, it would represent only about 2 percent of total GNP over the decade, and well under half of the growth in GNP over the period. But it might also equal a quarter of business' total net investment for the decade.

In 1973, Congress passed a new Water Pollution Act, over President Nixon's veto, further tightening the standards to be met. This reflected disenchantment with progress under the 1956 and 1965 regulatory approach; the job of dealing individually with over 40,000 industrial firms seemed insuperable as a practical matter. Congress decreed that by 1977 all companies must install the "best practicable" pollution control technology, by 1983 the "best available" technology, and by 1985 have reached "zero discharge," complete elimination of water pollution—with heavy fines for violators. What this new legislation will mean as a practical matter remains to be seen. Although most environmentalists and many economists agreed on the need for a change, many doubt that the new bill will prove workable—and Congress registered its own doubts by simultaneously establishing a new National Study Commission to investigate the "total economic, social, and environmental effects" of meeting these standards. Experts question whether the new legislation will get around the problem of dealing individually with standards for many different firms and industries (what does "best practicable" mean in any particular case?), point out that "zero discharge" may be more than we will really want to pay for, and reemphasize the advantages of a flexible effluent-charge approach.[4]

[4]Effluent-charge systems have proved workable in action. For example, water pollution in the Ruhr River valley in Germany, one of the world's most concentrated industrial complexes, has for over forty years been controlled by such a set of charges—and very effectively, in the eyes of most observers. For a brief description, see L.E. Ruff, "The Economic Common Sense of Pollution," *The Public Interest*, Spring 1970, pp. 84–85. Excellent, more detailed treatments of the pollution problem are presented in E.G. Dolan, *TANSTAAFL* ("There Ain't No Such Thing As a Free Lunch") (New York: Holt, Rinehart and Winston Inc., 1971), and Chap. 11, "The Environment," in C. Schultze et al, *Setting National Priorities: The 1973 Budget* (Washington, D.C.: The Brookings Institution, 1972).

REVIEW

For Analysis and Discussion

1. Explain why you would expect "market failure" in cases of large externalities?
2. Devise a workable program to eliminate water pollution in your own community, including an acceptable means of financing your program.
3. Should the Ohio River be cleaned up so that it is again attractive for swimming, boating, and fishing? If so, how, and who should pay for the reclamation?
4. Many critics argue that the auto manufacturers are responsible for smog and air pollution in the cities. They argue that the auto companies should be required to bear the cost of eliminating the auto-exhaust contribution to smog.
   a. Is this a correct analysis of responsibility?
   b. If you believe the cost of eliminating auto air pollution should be placed on the auto manufacturers, how would you accomplish this? (Remember your price theory from Part Three and Case 21 in Chapter 32.)
5. Your city has an air-pollution problem, primarily from autos, private furnaces, and industry. Devise an acceptable program to clean up the air to acceptable standards. Will direct effluent limits or effluent charges work better?
6. Should the federal government pay for upgrading the sewage systems of cities that do not meet the new federal water cleanliness standards? Why?
7. Should the federal government spend more to improve the environment? How do you decide how much is the right amount (remember that Congress must decide), and who should pay?
8. Should students picket corporations that cause air or water pollution?

The $66 Billion Mistake

On February 21,1973, the Mobil Oil Company placed the following full-page advertisement in major newspapers throughout the country.

In 1970, Congress passed a series of amendments to the Clean Air Act. One of them said that all cars sold in the United States after 1974 must be near-zero polluters.

It sounded fine. Near-perfect emission control seemed not only desirable, but imperative. At that time, people widely assumed that the air was getting steadily dirtier because of the automobile. Most people also assumed that industry could solve any technical problems that might be encountered—and at a reasonable cost.

The goal has proved elusive. Despite the expenditure of hundreds of millions of dollars and uncounted hours of research and development time, no control system that meets all the requirements of the federal standards has yet been proved.

Bad news? Not necessarily. Today both industry and government have the benefit of research results and other information that were simply not available when Congress passed its amendment in 1970. Today we know that:

• Total air pollution from cars has already been rolled back to the level of about 1960, and is continuing to drop.

• Cars that met the federal standards would probably be poor performers and gasoline-guzzlers. They also could need costlier maintenance than today's cars.

• A less restrictive level of controls on automotive emissions would do very nearly as much for air quality as the federal standards would.

• Meeting the federal standards could cost $100 billion over ten years starting in 1976; meeting the less-restrictive standards could cost $34 billion. The difference could be a $66 billion mistake.

If Not Perfection, What? The only way to completely eliminate auto pollution would be to do away with the auto itself. Since this would be neither practical nor desirable, what percentage reduction of emissions should we aim at? By what date? And at what cost?

The goal should be to make the auto as small a contributor to air pollution as technology allows—but without incurring exorbitant costs for dubious results. Since technology does not stand still, this would be a moving goal. Today's impractical dream often can be tomorrow's reality.

Today's reality in automotive-pollution control is, in fact, yesterday's dream: As Chart 1 indicates, emissions of hydrocarbons, carbon monoxide, and nitrogen oxides have been drastically reduced from the days (not long ago) when exhaust emissions were uncontrolled. Changes in engine design plus pollution-control devices have reduced emissions by 1973-model cars an average of 66 percent.

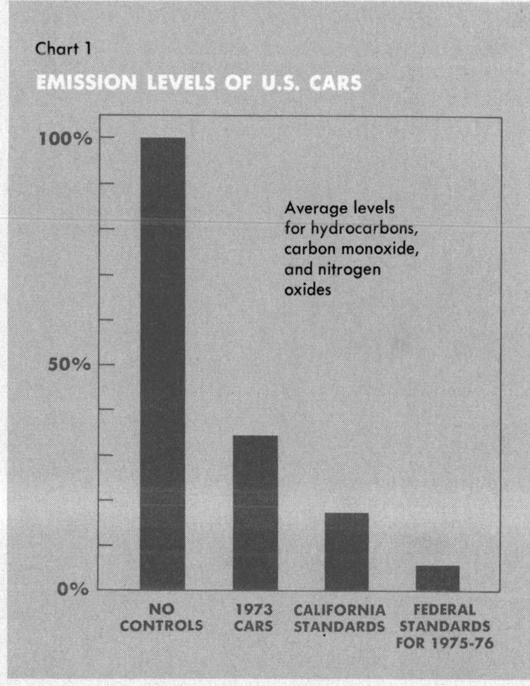

This is quite an achievement. And as a result, total air pollution from automobiles has been declining in the United States since 1968, and is now down to the levels of about 1960. It would continue to decline for several more years even if no further controls were imposed, as old cars with few if any controls are scrapped.

So, how much further should we go? And by when?

California Has a Better Way. The Air Resources Board of the State of California has proposed automotive emission-control levels based on air-quality standards calculated to restore the atmosphere of Los Angeles to its quality of the early 1940s. California proposes to cut the three principal auto emissions by an average of 83 percent. . . .

The California standards are similar to those proposed by the federal government's own Department of Health, Education, and Welfare in 1970.

The HEW standards were not accepted. Instead, Congress voted for the last bar on Chart 1. The Clean Air Act now mandates that the three emissions be reduced by 97, 96, and 93 percent—for an average of 95 percent. These levels must be reached by 1975 for hydrocarbons and carbon monoxide, and by 1976 for oxides of nitrogen, unless the federal government grants an extension.

A 95 percent reduction in emissions may not seem much more difficult to achieve than an 83 percent reduction. But did you ever try to wring the last drop of water out of a wet towel? One good twist and most of the water flows out. Another hard twist and a little more dribbles out. But now the law of diminishing returns sets in. It's just plain impossible to wring the towel dry, and not worth the effort.

Auto Emission Reductions Below Pre-Control Levels

	HYDRO-CARBONS	CARBON MONOXIDE	OXIDES OF NITROGEN
1973 Cars	80%	69%	50%
California	94	81	75
Federal	97	96	93

Similarly, the last few percentage points of automotive emission control are far costlier and far more difficult to achieve than the first 80 to 85 points.

Mobil sells gasoline, but we have no desire to see our products wasted. Cars built to the federal standards could consume as much as 15 percent more gasoline per mile than cars built to the California standards. That 15 percent would require refining an extra 30 million barrels of crude oil in 1976, and an extra 150 million barrels a year by 1980. All that crude oil would have to be imported, with a substantial—and necessary—drain on our country's balance of payments.

Up the Matterhorn. Which brings us to Chart 2. The one with a curve that looks like the southeastern slope of the Matterhorn.

Control equipment to meet the 1973 standards adds about $65 to $100 to the cost of a new car. Not excessive, considering how far the cars have come in reducing harmful emission.

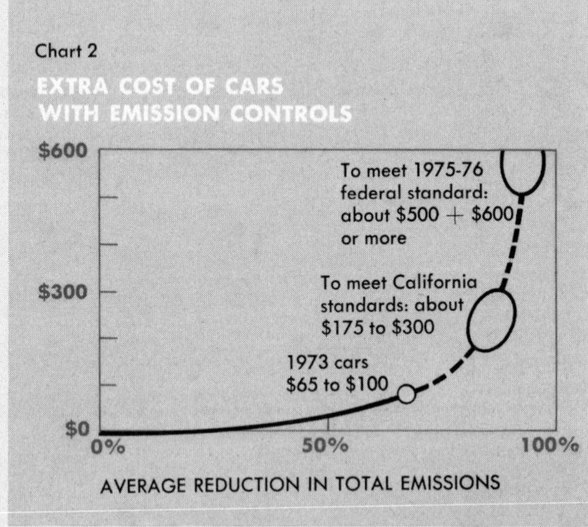

The price curve turns up to meet the California standards—to a range of $175 to $300 per car for the control equipment. Perhaps still not too expensive, considering the extra gains in pollution reduction. But to reach the federal standards that are now the law for 1975 and 1976 models, the cost curve heads almost straight up. These systems could cost $500 to $600 a car—and maybe more. We can't determine the exact cost, since systems to meet the 1976 standards have not been proved.

These are just the initial costs of the emission-control systems. Add the extra maintenance, and throw in the additional gasoline, and the grand total for meeting the federal standards comes to $100 billion over the decade starting in 1976.

What Would $66,000,000,000 Buy?

The program Mobil outlines in this report could save the American consumer $66 billion over ten years. . . . Here are a few things $66 billion could do:

- Build the water-treatment plants needed for all the country's household, municipal, and industrial sewage and waste water—and maintain those facilities for more than five years.
- Nearly pay the annual U.S. expenditures for all health and medical care ($67 billion in 1970).
- More than finance all new private and public housing construction in this country for two years (1970 total: $30 billion).
- Almost pay the total cost of all types of education in the United States, at all levels, for a year (1970 total: $67 billion).
- Buy various combinations of subways, BART systems, commuter trains, longer-haul railroads, and express lanes for buses on freeways.

Add the same expenses for the California standards, and the grand total is $34 billion. (All these figures are Mobil engineers' estimates, expressed in today's dollars.)

Our calculations do not include a cost for the special kind of gasoline that would be needed to meet the federal standards.

Clean Air and Public Transportation. Is there a better way to spend all or part of $66 billion to reduce total automotive air pollution?

There is indeed. Public transportation. Public transportation clean enough, safe enough, fast enough, and priced attractively enough to induce Americans to use their automobiles less and public transportation more.

More and better public transportation can go a long way toward several desirable objectives: Less air pollution. Less waste of gasoline. Less pressure on the U.S. balance of payments as our imports of oil inevitably rise. And maybe less emotional strain on motorists and fewer accidents.

Under such a program, motorists could drive better-performing, less expensive, and safer cars. A substantial drain on the U.S. balance of payments, for crude oil and platinum, would be avoided. A vital and scarce natural resource—petroleum—would be conserved. And the advance of technology would enable automakers to meet even stricter control standards—if they were found necessary at some future date—with durable, trouble-free, and reasonably economic systems.

Not to mention avoiding a $66 billion mistake.

Do you agree with Mobil's recommendations? If not, what is your program for handling the auto's air-pollution problem? Under Mobil's proposal and yours, who are the main beneficiaries, and who would pay most of the costs of cleaner air?

Taxes and Tax Reform

CHAPTER THIRTY-SEVEN

Everyone complains about high taxes. But if we want public goods and services, we must get resources transferred from private to public use. If we assume full employment, taxes are the most straightforward way to get the necessary funds, since they take private incomes that would otherwise bid for the resources. With full employment, more government spending without more taxes means increased total spending and inflation; then resources are taken away from those whose incomes fall behind during inflation.

With government spending at nearly a half trillion dollars annually and headed higher, a sound and equitable tax system is very important. The multi-billion dollar federal budget may not mean much to you—the figures are too big. But the fact that when you leave college with an average, middle-class income of perhaps $10,000, you will start turning over to Uncle Sam and to state and local government units over $2,500 each year puts the dollars and cents in more meaningful terms.

GOOD AND BAD TAXES

Few subjects generate as much heat in popular discussion as taxes. But all too often the heat is unaccompanied by light. You can't judge intelligently what are good and what are bad taxes until you've clarified the criteria by which you're judging. Since many people don't bother to clarify, it is little wonder that they often disagree violently on what taxes should be.

The same broad social objectives we've used before can be pointed up conveniently in three questions in analyzing the tax system:

1. **Progress.** Does the tax encourage or hinder investment, employment, and stable economic growth?
2. **Freedom and Individual Choice.** Does the tax hinder or aid the allocation of resources in accordance with consumer preferences? Does it interfere with the free choices of individuals and businesses in earning and spending?
3. **Equity.** How equitably is the tax burden distributed? Government taxing and spending significantly affect the distribution of income. Unless government tax collections exactly equal the benefits provided to each family, the issue is not *whether* the government will redistribute income, but *how*.

Progress: Stable Economic Growth

Economic growth depends on an intricate complex of factors, but especially on technological advance, on saving and investment, on education, and on hard work by the labor force. (See Chapters 42 and 43.) Any tax is a drain on someone's income from work or investment, and in general taxes will deter economic growth (although the related government expenditure may have an offsetting effect). One tax **structure** may be less restrictive on (more conducive to) rapid growth than another.

Theory tells us that taxes that bear on profits and other returns from investment will discourage **growth** compared to taxes that fall on personal income and consumption. Similarly, taxes that give special advantages to expenditures on investment, research and development, and education, are an incentive to faster growth. We have learned over the past decade how to provide such incentives—the special "investment tax credit" of 1962, and more generous depreciation guidelines for plant and equipment are examples.

Tax contribution to **stability** is equally important. We want taxes that tend to keep after-tax incomes growing at a reasonably stable rate, not fluctuating sharply. Individual and corporate income taxes, for example, provide such "built-in tax flexibility." When national income rises, these tax liabilities rise even more rapidly, because individual income-tax rates are progressive and because corporate profits subject to taxes rise sharply in business expansion. The opposite is true when national income falls. This built-in flexibility tends to damp the swings in private incomes and spending. By contrast, a tax that is insensitive to income changes (for example, the property tax) makes no contribution to stabilizing private spending.

Noninterference with Free Choices

If we want free private choices to determine the allocation of resources and the distribution of income, a "good" tax system should be neutral in the sense that it does not affect these results. But a tax system as pervasive as ours cannot be truly neutral. In a few cases—for example, taxes on tobacco and liquor—we consciously discourage the use of particular products through taxation. In these cases the tax is used to bring resource allocation into line with our social preferences.

But in most cases, the distortions produced by taxes on individual commodities (excise taxes) are unfortunate. These distortions occur because higher taxes on particular commodities lead people to buy less of that commodity than they otherwise would, relative to other commodities. Or they lead people to work less in particular occupations than they would otherwise choose. By distorting resource use this way, a tax may produce a "deadweight" loss to the economy—a cost against which there is no offsetting gain. Such a cost is in excess of the resources given up by the private sector through taxation to finance public expenditures. The economy is misled into producing the wrong combination of goods.

To minimize this deadweight loss while raising any given amount of revenue, we should use taxes that produce the smallest changes in private production and consumption behavior (excluding cases with externalities). A "head" tax (a lump-sum tax on each person regardless of income or expenditure) would rate high on this criterion. Because no one could avoid it, it would not affect his economic behavior much, if at all. Taxes on commodities with highly inelastic demand (for example, a salt tax) are similar, since people buy about as much of the product at the higher (taxed) price as before. Conversely, excise taxes on commodities with elastic demand are apt to be highly distorting in their effects.[1]

"Equity" in Taxation

A tax system should be equitable as well as nondistorting and conducive to stable growth. Three tests of equity are often advanced. One is to levy taxes on the people who get the benefits. Another is to levy taxes according to ability to pay. The third stresses equal treatment of taxpayers equally situated. Equity means different things to different people, and economics cannot say which is right. It can only clarify the effects of different taxes so that you can judge for yourself which result is most "equitable." Figure 34–5 showed what income groups pay which taxes in the United States.

The "Benefit" Principle. It seems fair to a lot of people that those who benefit from government services should pay for them. Would this be a good general rule?

One obvious problem is how the principle could be applied practically. If a city is putting in a new sewer, it's easy to see who the primary beneficiaries will be and to assess the cost against these property owners through a "special assessment." But how can the benefits derived from national defense, or the judicial system, be divided up among the citizens?

[1]By this same criterion, to avoid distorting effects, marginal tax rates should be low relative to average rates; on this score, our progressive personal income tax rates low.

An even more fundamental question: Would we really want the benefit principle applied? Look at education, for example. Now we have free public schools for everyone. But suppose we put all education on a benefit-tax basis. Then each parent would have to pay a special school tax depending on how many children he had in school—for example, $1,000 per child. This policy might work out fine for the local banker and doctor. But how about the poor family on the other side of the tracks, with eight school-age children? The well-to-do could continue sending their youngsters to school (and more cheaply than now), but millions of poor children would be priced out of the market. Government activities like welfare, would be completely ruled out by the benefit principle, since there would be little point in imposing special taxes on the poor just to return the funds to them.

Broad use of the benefit principle would thus be far more revolutionary than it sounds at first. It would mean, in effect, direct sale of government services to the user, and would preclude any redistribution of income through the public economy.

The "Ability-To-Pay" Principle. Taxation according to ability to pay is widely favored. But how should we measure ability to pay? Net money income received in the current year is a widely accepted criterion, though this is a more complex problem than it seems, as we shall see presently.

Even if we agree on net income as the best measure of ability to pay, there is still the problem of the rate at which different incomes should be taxed. Some argue that the rate should be *proportional*—that is, the same percentage of each person's income. For example, the tax rate might be 1 percent, giving a $10 tax on $1,000; $100 on $10,000; $1,000 on $100,000. More argue that rates should be *progressive*—that is, a higher percentage tax on high incomes than on low (for example, $5 on $1,000; $100 on $10,000; $2,000 on $100,000). All ability-to-pay advocates argue against *regressive* taxation, in which a larger percentage of income is taken from the lower-income groups.

It is important to see that ability-to-pay as a base for taxation has no exactness or "absolute" validity. There is no objective way of deciding whether rates should be proportional or progressive, or, if progressive, how steeply progressive. The "ability" phrase is, however, convenient for working purposes, since in America we generally agree that progressive taxation of income and inheritances represents the primary application of the ability-to-pay principle. When the term is used in this book, therefore, it will mean progressively higher tax rates as net income rises, without specifying any particular rate of progression. In the last analysis, the issue of how much progression is "equitable" is an ethical one. It boils down to the question of who should get how much of the national-income pie—a fundamental and explosive question. This issue of relative tax burdens at different income levels is often called the issue of "vertical" equity. Look back at Figure 34–5 and you will see that the federal tax system is strongly progressive, while state–local taxes are regressive, if those estimates are correct.

"Equal Treatment of Those Equally Situated." A third principle of equity states that persons equally situated should be taxed equally. This is a powerful guide to tax policy, and one that is accepted by most observers. But what is "equally situated"? Are two people with the same income always equally situated? For example, is a disabled, retired man with an annual pension income of $5,000 equally situated with a healthy young man with the same income? Are both equally situated with the $5,000-a-year laborer who has a wife and ten children to support? Does it matter where the income comes from? For example, is a factory superintendent who earns $15,000 a year equally situated with someone who gains $15,000 on General Motors stock that has gone up in price between his buying and selling it? Our tax laws treat the first two identically, but apply a much lower tax rate to the "capital gain" on the GM stock than to earned income. Should they? This is the issue of "horizontal" equity.

SHIFTING AND INCIDENCE OF TAXATION

Often the person who hands the funds over to the government does not actually bear the burden of the tax. The federal tax on liquor, for example, is paid to the government by distillers. But it is largely "shifted" forward to consumers through higher prices. The final "incidence" of a tax may be far from the man who turns the money over to the government.

It is safe to assume that a taxpayer will shift a tax whenever he can. The question generally is, therefore, **when can a tax be shifted?** A tax can be shifted only when, as a result of the tax, the taxpayer is able to obtain a higher price for something he sells or to pay a lower price for something he buys. A price transaction of some sort is essential if shifting is to occur.

Generally, taxes do nothing to increase demand for taxed commodities (remember that we are examining the impact of the tax alone, apart from what is done with the money collected). But many taxes do raise costs and prices. If, as a result of a tax (for example, on cigarettes), the price is higher than it otherwise would have been, the tax has been shifted to that extent.

Because tax shifting depends on the prices charged and paid, it is largely an application of the general supply-and-demand analysis of Part Three. But a warning is necessary. A rise in price following the imposition of a tax in the real world is not necessarily proof that the tax has been shifted. The price rise may have come from some other cause. (Remember the fallacy of post hoc, propter hoc.) Empirical verification of tax shifting is very difficult, since it is hard to isolate one cause and its effects in the multitude of forces simultaneously at work in economic life. Analytically, however, we can trace through the effects of any tax assuming "*other things equal*"—that is, assuming the tax to be the only new element in the situation. Tax incidence analysis is simply an application of the price theory you learned in Part Three.

Three Examples

Personal Income Tax. The personal income tax, which accounts for about a third of all tax revenues, is an example of a nonshiftable tax. The tax does not affect the demand for the services of the people taxed, nor does it decrease the supply of labor. (The latter statement is not quite accurate; some people may work less because their earnings are taxed, but there is little evidence that this effect is large in America. Even though the government takes some of your earnings, you still have more left when you work than when you don't, and for many people keeping ahead of their neighbors is as important as absolute after-tax income level.) Thus, there is no way the taxed individual can raise his price to shift the tax forward, and there is no one onto whom he can shift it backward.

You may ask: How about unions? Won't they ask for bigger wage increases if their taxes are raised? They may ask, but nothing has increased the demand for their labor to permit them to get a bigger wage increase. If they get more money after the tax, we must ask, why didn't they get it before?

Payroll Taxes. Payroll taxes, levied on both workers and employers to finance social security benefits, are the second biggest tax, totalling $71 billion in 1973. The portion levied on the worker is like the income tax; it can't be shifted, for substantially the same reasons. But the part levied on the employer generally is shifted—back onto the worker. Consider the reasoning. The tax on the employer increases the effective wage cost of the employee. Since cost per unit of output is now higher, unless the employer can reduce the wage rate he pays he will have to raise prices, which will reduce output, and will substitute machinery for labor, in order to keep maximizing his profits. If wage rates are flexible, wages will fall as the demand for labor falls. If wage rates are inflexible downward, some workers will be laid off. Either way, the burden is largely shifted onto the workers, though some of it may be shifted forward to consumers through higher prices.

A simple diagram makes clear that the incidence of both halves of the payroll tax is on the worker. In Figure 37–1, let D^L be the demand for labor and S^L its supply, fixed in amount. Part *A* shows that the wage will be W^1 without any tax. Now suppose a payroll tax is imposed on all workers, which they must pay to the government. Neither demand nor supply is changed, so the wage paid by employers is unchanged. Unhappily, workers' wages *after taxes* are only W^2, lower by the amount of the tax they must pay.

Figure 37–1

Payroll taxes are generally borne by workers, whether they are imposed on workers or employers.

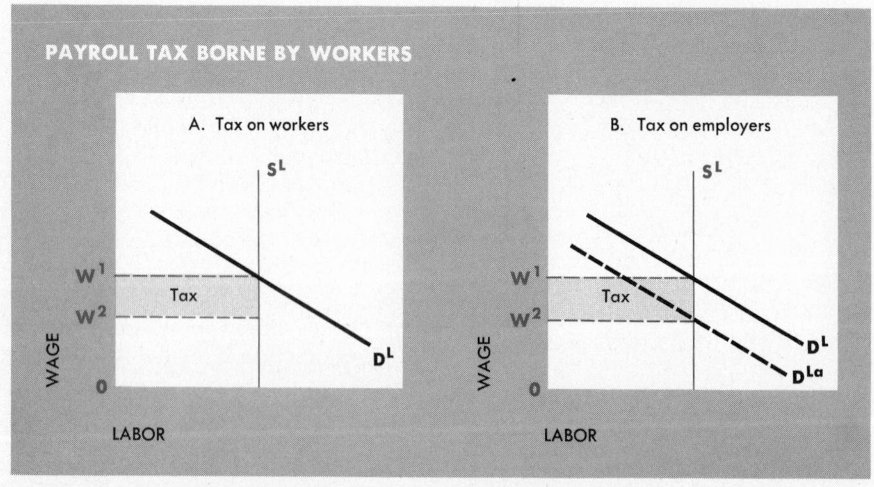

Part B starts with the same S^L and D^L curves, and the same wage, W^1. Now the government imposes the same wage tax *on employers*. Workers are worth no more than before to employers, so the employers' demand curve shifts down at all outputs by the amount of the tax, to D^{La}. If employers must pay the tax on all employees, their wage without tax will again fall to W^2, just as in Part A. In both cases, employment stays constant and the wage after tax is reduced just by the amount of the tax. It should be easy to see that the critical factor underlying the full incidence on workers is the fixed stock of labor, the perfectly inelastic labor-supply curve. The same result would follow for a tax imposed on the wage (or rent) of any other fixed resource. (If the wage rate is fixed at W^1, say by union rules, work out for yourself what will happen to employment.)

If we want workers to bear the cost of old-age insurance and unemployment, payroll taxes may be a good means of financing social security. But putting half of the tax on the employer, even though you *want* him to pay, doesn't necessarily mean that he *will* pay it.

The incidence of other taxes can be analyzed in the same way. Look back at Figure 6–9, for example, for the incidence of excise taxes (on cigarettes, liquor, gasoline, and the like) under different demand conditions.

Property Taxes. Property taxes, the third most important revenue source, are levied mainly on residential and business property. They are generally considered highly regressive (see Figure 34–5), but a reasonable counterargument can be made that they fall largely on capital and hence are not regressive, certainly not as regressive as Figure 34–5 shows. Consider separately the main parts of the tax.

The part of the tax that falls on land mainly stays there—on the land owner. Note that the supply of land is fixed. The first effect of the tax is to reduce the net after-tax yield on the land. Thus future buyers will be willing to pay less for the land after the tax. Since the capital value of the land has been reduced by the tax, we say the tax has been "capitalized." No future buyer of the land will invest unless the price falls enough to provide a net return *after taxes* equal to that obtainable on other comparable investments. The burden of the new tax is placed permanently on the owner at the time of first taxation; he has no way to shift it by transferring his investment and reducing the supply. Future owners buy free of the special land tax.

The part of the tax on residences is probably partly shifted, partly borne by capital. The tax will be gradually shifted to renters if the tax drives investment out of housing into other areas where taxes are lower, thereby reducing the supply and raising the rents on taxed buildings. This effect is plainly visible in big-city slums, where effective property tax rates rise as buildings age but assessments are not reduced. Property owners just let their buildings depreciate and transfer their investment elsewhere. But insofar as alternative investment opportunities are also taxed so homeowners have no real alternative to keeping their investment in housing, they are stuck with the tax; it cannot be shifted.

One last point on the incidence of real property taxes: Low-priced buildings are widely overassessed relative to high-priced ones; assessment practices are regressive. Thus, the actual incidence depends on a combination of basic tax and administrative factors.

Taxes on business property like inventories and machinery are business costs, quite similar to excise taxes on business products. They are usually shifted, but sometimes partly borne by owners of the business.

Put all these factors together and it is clear that the incidence of the property tax is complex. Most economists rate it on balance regressive, though less so than Figure 34–5 shows, and modern analysis is moving toward allotting more of the burden to capital.

TAX REFORM

Recent years have produced many complaints about the inequity of the present tax system. These charges have been levelled mainly against loopholes and special privileges allegedly enjoyed by the rich and powerful, and against the heavy tax burdens borne by the poor and middle classes.

As Figure 34–5 showed, the heaviest relative tax burdens are borne by the very rich and the very poor, with the latter due largely to state and local taxes. It is the great middle classes, which include most of the votes and most of the income, that bear the lightest tax burdens relative to their incomes. But, though their tax *rates* are lowest, it is they in the aggregate who pay the bulk of the taxes, because that's where the bulk of the income is. The cry of the radicals that we should make the rich pay the taxes and lift the burden from the back of the common man makes fine rhetoric, but it runs up against the fact that even a confiscatory 100 percent tax on all income over $1 million per family would yield less than an additional $5 billion, compared to total federal tax collections of nearly $300 billion. A 100 percent tax on all incomes over $50,000 would add less than $20 billion to federal taxes, even including capital gains in the concept of taxable income. Thomas Jefferson's ideal of "a country made a paradise by the contribution of the rich alone" won't work any more—the country's too big and the rich don't have enough income. If the government needs big increases in tax revenue, they will have to come from the general public, not just a super-rich few. But that doesn't say we may not want tax reform to close some loopholes that especially help the rich.

Loopholes and "Tax Expenditures"

Oil depletion allowances, cattle ranches, and tax-exempt bonds make the headlines as tax loopholes. The federal Internal Revenue Code is full of special deductions, exemptions, and provisions that permit some citizens and businesses to pay less than others. For example, interest on state and municipal bonds is exempt from federal taxes. Capital gains are taxed at lower rates than regular income. Interest on mortgages and other borrowed money, losses on personal businesses, like farming, and taxes paid to states and localities can be deducted from taxable income. Nearly all transfer payments, such as social security and workmen's benefits, are exempt. The aged and the blind are given other special exemptions. Poor families get a complete exemption if their income is under about $4,000 for a family of four.

These legal loopholes can be looked at as much the same thing as federal government subsidies to the affected taxpayers. They are sometimes called "tax expenditures." Table 37–1 shows the magnitude of these federal tax expenditures, or loopholes. They totalled about $52 billion in 1971, according to rough Treasury estimates. This table does not include the additional personal deductions available to all taxpayers ($750 exemption for each individual), omission of imputed rent on owner-occupied homes, and the like. Addition of these general concessions would add another $25–30 billion to the tax expenditures. Put in other terms, elimination of all special exemptions would have raised total taxable income in 1972 from $478 billion to $644 billion.

While tax loopholes are of greatest benefit to the well-to-do, Table 37–1 shows clearly the wide range of benefits received. The biggest tax expenditures are items that help us all when we fill out our tax forms—deduction of state and local taxes paid, interest payments, charitable contributions, and the like. Some primarily benefit the rich, notably the lower tax rate on capital gains. Others are aimed to help special groups, like the aged and the blind. The table shows separately each tax expenditure estimated by the Treasury at over $1 billion. The much-discussed oil depletion allowance is striking by its absence; its cost was estimated at only $980 million in 1971. Most super-rich families that paid low taxes had heavy investments in tax-exempt state and municipal bonds, offsetting losses in other years, big interest payments, or large capital gains partly offset by capital losses. A few manage to escape taxation entirely each year, mainly by holding tax-exempt bonds, having large interest payments on money borrowed for personal business purposes (like cattle-

TABLE 37–1

Tax Loopholes, or Tax Expenditures, 1971

LOOPHOLE	TAX LOSS TO TREASURY (IN BILLIONS)
Deduction of state–local taxes	$ 8.3
Lower rate on capital gains	5.6
Exemption of social security, unemployment, benefits, etc.	4.6
Deduction of interest payments	4.2
Tax postponement on employee pension plans	3.9
Deduction of medical expenses	3.9
Deduction of charitable contributions	3.5
Exemption of interest on state–local bonds	2.6
Business investment tax credit	1.8
All other	13.3
	$51.7

Source: Estimates by U.S. Treasury Department.

feeding), and by having large losses carried over from earlier years. But these are less than 1 percent of all high-income taxpayers, and to make them pay more will do more to assuage our feelings of inequity than to raise more money.

Many Americans are outraged by such legal tax avoidance by the very rich, and clearly rich families gain most from the intricate loopholes in the tax law. But big revenue gains from plugging loopholes will have to come from steps that affect a lot of taxpayers. The super-rich just don't have enough total income to pay a lot more of the total tax bill, even if their loopholes were closed. It is no accident that Congress shows little enthusiasm for closing the big loopholes, in spite of the vivid rhetoric about their injustice to the common man. Most of the exemptions were put in to help special groups or causes—tax-exempt interest to help municipal governments, charitable deductions to help charities, schools, and so on, the social security exemption to help the elderly—and the beneficiaries are understandably unenthusiastic about losing them. But it seems unlikely that Congress or the public would support annual cash subsidies of these amounts to the groups concerned if they were openly visible.[2]

Just about everyone agrees that the federal income tax code has become such a thicket of special provisions, understandable only to tax lawyers and accountants, that sweeping reform is necessary. Some observers propose eliminating all exemptions, and then applying a flat tax rate to all income, from whatever source received. Calculations vary, but with such a reform a flat tax rate of about 18 percent would produce as much revenue as the present tax with its rates

[2]One special capital-gains loophole, which helps mainly the very rich, seems especially difficult to justify. Property held till death can be transferred to heirs free of all capital gains tax, however large the capital gain may be. For example, if you fortunately invested $1,000 in IBM stock fifty years ago, you are a millionaire now. If you die, leaving the stock to your children, they get it without paying any capital gains tax on the million-dollar appreciation, either now or when they sell the stock (though of course you must pay regular estate taxes). By holding the asset to death, you completely escape taxes on the capital gains, and a similar avoidance is possible if you give the stock away prior to death. Many tax experts, even those who favor special lower rates on capital gains and permitting the owner to postpone taxes on capital gains until they are realized, favor making the estate recipients pay a capital gains tax in such cases.

ascending to 70 percent. Few Americans would advocate a flat federal tax rate for all income levels, but the example highlights the position in which we have gotten ourselves through the increasing complexity of the tax code.

Shifting the Mix of Taxes

Figures 34–2 and 34–5 provided an overview of the taxes that now comprise our total tax system and how their burden falls on different income groups. Should we change the mix of taxes we use?

Federal personal and corporation income taxes are progressive in their impact. The personal tax now provides a $750 exemption per person plus exemptions for working expenses, charitable contributions, most taxes and interest paid, and a variety of other special causes. The result is that all income below roughly the poverty level is tax-free. Moreover, tax rates rise rapidly from a 14 percent minimum on income above exemptions to 70 percent on taxable income over $200,000, although beginning in 1972 there is a 50 percent ceiling on *earned* income; the higher rates apply to other income from dividends, interest and the like. Although most wealthy families hold down their effective average rates well below these peaks by use of legal loopholes, the overall impact is still markedly progressive.[3] The incidence of the corporation income tax is less certain, but most of it is probably borne by capital (stockholders), so it too is generally progressive because most stock is held by wealthy owners. The corporate tax rate is 48 percent on all corporate profits over $25,000, 22 percent on profits below that level to provide a lower rate for small businesses.

But the other big federal tax—the payroll tax to finance social security—is regressive. All workers pay it, including the employer portion, however low their income may be. Moreover, the tax (now about 6 percent each on employers and employees) applies only to the first $12,000 of wages. Thus, the total paid is a smaller proportion of incomes above $12,000. Because the payroll tax burden is rising rapidly under the expanding social security system (remember Chapter 33), many critics argue that reform of the payroll tax is the biggest need in the whole tax system if we want to make its overall impact more progressive. Either the payroll tax should be replaced as the major means of financing social security, they argue, or low incomes should be partially exempted to eliminate the worst regression.

Property and sales taxes are the two big state–local revenue sources. Sales taxes are largely shifted to consumers. Even when they exempt food and clothing, they fall most heavily on lower incomes, because poor families spend nearly all their incomes on taxed commodities while wealthier families save a larger portion of their incomes. Property taxes, as was explained above, are probably (on balance) regressive, though a substantial part of the burden falls on capital. As Figure 34–5 showed, these state and local taxes account for most of the serious regressivity of the tax system at very low-income levels, though the extreme impact of the property tax shown there is open to debate.

These considerations lead many observers to favor heavier reliance on income taxes and reduced roles for payroll, property, and sales taxes, in order to make the system more progressive. They argue that income taxes are also superior on grounds of minimal interference with the spending and earning behavior of individuals (you have to pay your tax, but you can spend what's left as you please), in contrast with government distortion of individual prices through other taxes. And income taxes are tops for built-in economic stabilization. Their tax take rises rapidly as national income rises to damp the upswing, and falls sharply when national income declines. Conversely, sales and excise taxes raise some prices relative to others, thereby distorting the resource allocation that would come from free consumer spending. And neither property nor sales taxes have built-in stabilization

[3]Taxes will always be a lower percentage of total income than the peak marginal rates that apply to a family. Though marginal rates reach 50 percent at the $44,000 income level, the actual average amount paid by families above that level was less than 35 percent in 1970.

effects comparable to income taxes; property taxes in particular are sluggish when national income rises, further intensifying the already difficult fiscal plight of many local governments.

Together with reform of the individual tax loopholes noted in the preceding section, shifting the makeup of the tax system is the most direct path to improving its equity and effectiveness. But many people oppose the shifts suggested in the preceding paragraphs. They think the system is already too progressive, and that present peak income-tax rates are confiscatory as well as serious deterrents to work and risky investments. They argue that corporate profits are already doubletaxed—as profits to the corporation and again as income when stockholders receive them as dividends. If we assume that all of the corporation income tax and half of the property tax is borne by capital, in 1972 this $60 billion total alone took 40 percent of all returns to capital. If you want to encourage *investment and growth,* we should lower taxes on capital, profits and high incomes, not increase them. Tax reform is a complex and controversial issue.[4]

Revenue Sharing— Allocation of the Tax Base

Since World War II, state–local government spending has risen rapidly. Localities, including the great cities, depend heavily on property taxes, and these taxes have risen spectacularly. The anguished cries of homeowners and other property owners have been heard ever more loudly, and in some areas taxpayers' rebellions have occurred. Many local school bond issues have been voted down. At the same time, middle- and upper-income families have increasingly deserted the central cities for the suburbs, leaving the cities with declining tax bases just when education, welfare, police, and other expenses are soaring for the masses of low-income families left behind.

State and local governments complain that the best revenue sources have been preempted by the federal government. Personal and corporate tax yields grow automatically with the economy; each year these taxes produce a federal "fiscal dividend" of $10 billion or more, without any increase in tax rates. And over the past decade Congress has steadily increased federal aid to states and localities—look back at Figure 34–7 for the evidence. Federal aid was over $40 billion in 1973. Since 1970, President Nixon has pushed for general revenue sharing, whereby the states and localities would automatically get some percent of total federal income-tax collections, to do with as they wish, in place of specific aid grants that prescribe in detail how the money can be spent. As Chapter 34 pointed out, opposition to such revenue sharing has been strong, and recently the move has been toward block grants to the states and localities, with considerable flexibility as to how the money is spent within some broadly-defined purpose.

Basic issues of equity as well as billions of dollars are at stake. When the federal government subsidizes state and local spending on welfare or education, it is generally transferring funds from upper- to lower-income groups, because the federal tax structure is relatively progressive. It also tends to subsidize the poor states at the expense of wealthy ones, because federal taxes come heavily from income taxes. Broadly speaking, the transfer is from the wealthy Northern and Western states to those in the South. Finally, such federal grants are a way of taxing the wealthy in the suburbs and countryside for the benefit of the poor, crowded central cities, many of which face fiscal crises. Those who favor equal standards of education, welfare, and the like across the nation clearly must favor federal revenue sharing of some sort; the poor states and cities simply can't and won't levy taxes heavy enough to provide services comparable to those provided in high-income areas.

But there are plenty of exceptions to these generalizations. If federal tax funds are used to replace local property taxes and if the property taxes fall heavily on capital, it's not clear that

[4]A more thorough analysis of the issues is provided by J. Pechman in *Federal Tax Policy* (Washington, D.C., The Brookings Institution, 1971).

the net result is a more progressive tax system. If federal funds from middle-income Northern families are used by poor Southern states to benefit their well-to-do rather than their poor, the result may be less, rather than more, progression. Thus, the political and ethical problems of revenue sharing are obvious: Who should have control over the funds transferred to localities, the federal or local governments? How should minimum standards for beneficiaries and administration be set for federal aid? Should new groups be established to oversee the use of federal aid, or the funds be given outright to local political authorities? Federal aid and revenue sharing will predictably be major fiscal issues over the decade ahead.

How Much Taxation Can We Stand?

Hardly a day goes by but someone complains that we've reached the limit of our ability to pay taxes. Is there some definite limit to how much taxation the country can stand? Are we approaching it?

The general answer to both questions is "no." But to answer more fully, we have to ask: What is the meaning of "what we can stand"? The usual connotation is that with more taxes the system's growth would slow, people would stop working, there'd be no incentive for businessmen to invest. Faced with predictions of such a debacle, the economist asks, how will it come about, and why?

Economic analysis suggests that if more taxes are going to bring disaster, it will probably be through one or more of the following effects:

1. **Heavier taxes may reduce the incentive to work.** If the government takes too big a share of the income you earn, you may just quit working—or at least work less. But as long as something remains after taxes and most people still have much less than they want, the incentive to earn is a powerful one, even when earnings must be shared with the government. Still, for well-to-do people who feel less income pressure, the amount of work *may* fall off as tax rates rise. And this holds even for middle-income people, when it's a question of overtime work or a second job. The evidence we have doesn't settle the question. Most formal studies find little evidence that higher income taxes seriously reduce the work at any income level. But this runs contrary to many people's intuitive notions.

2. **Heavier taxes may reduce the incentive to invest,** especially if the taxes fall heavily on profits. If taxes fall differentially on one type of investment, investors will flee from it in droves. But taxation on all corporate income leaves few alternatives to which investors can escape. They may turn to partnerships or individual enterprises, or to tax-exempt state and municipal bonds. But corporations are the only practical form of organization for most big businesses, and government bonds have limited appeal to profit-seeking investors. There's little evidence that wealthy individuals just consume more instead of investing. More likely, they complain bitterly about the low return on investment, and go on investing—*if* profits are good (which is the more fundamental stimulus to investment).

3. **Heavier taxes may lead to legal tax "avoidance."** The law provides many loopholes for people who feel taxes heavily enough to hire a good tax lawyer. At last count, the Treasury listed about 100,000 tax counselors and tax lawyers whose business was to help on income tax returns. And the effort pays off. In spite of the 70 percent peak rate on incomes over $200,000, Treasury statistics show that less than 35 percent of all income above that level is collected in personal income taxes. What is worse, desire to avoid high tax rates often leads to distortions in investment and diversion of earning activities into special channels (like oil drilling) that permit wealthy people to avoid peak tax rates under the law.

4. **Heavier taxes may lead to illegal tax "evasion."** The case of France is often cited, where for years the government has been able to collect only a modest fraction of the taxes due because of the expense and energy required to run down the individuals who just don't pay.

By and large, we Americans report and pay our taxes without being pursued. But a recent National Bureau of Economic Research estimate suggested that 5 percent of all wages, and 30 percent of unincorporated business incomes (farmers, doctors, lawyers, and so on) went unreported. How much harder it would become to collect taxes at higher rates nobody knows. Introduction of widespread employer reporting and computerized checking of all tax returns has made tax evasion increasingly difficult for most people, and most dividend and interest income is probably now caught.

5. **Higher taxes may lead to inflation.** This seems a perverted argument, since modern fiscal policy rests on the premise that higher taxes check inflation. This argument is that if taxes get too high everyone will raise his asking price to offset them—unions, businessmen, lawyers, farmers, everyone. Careful thought will show that this behavior can result in continuing inflation only if the government helpfully puts in more money to support total purchasing power at the higher prices. But there are great pressures on government to do just that, if the price of inaction or restraint is unemployment and recession.

What do all these points add up to? Not a conclusion that we can't stand any more taxation. Clearly we can, and a lot more if we want more public goods urgently enough. Our standard of living is so high we could divert far more resources to the public sector and still have the highest private-consumption standard in the world. But they do point to some real dangers as the level of taxation climbs relative to the national income.

A "MODEL" TAX SYSTEM

What would a model tax system look like? What changes would you make in our tax system? As a citizen, this is one issue on which you will repeatedly get a chance to say your piece. At federal, state, and local levels, tax changes are continually being made.

It's clear that different taxes look good on different criteria. Recognizing that what is considered a "good" tax system must depend heavily on each individual's weighting of different objectives, some economists have proposed a "model" tax system along the following lines. It would make some drastic changes in the present system, and it is presented only to stimulate you to think through your own views on what an ideal tax system would be.

This "model" tax system would have four major taxes:

1. A progressive personal income tax would account for at least two-thirds of all tax revenue. This would mean more than doubling present income-tax revenues. Much higher rates would reach down through the middle-income groups, and the bulk of the income-tax yield would necessarily come from these groups. This tax places the burden directly on individuals where it ultimately must rest, and it makes clear who is paying how much. The exact rate structure would depend on our collective judgments on equity, together with recognition of the importance of adequate income incentives. The tax would be supplemented by progressive death and gift taxes. To encourage incentives and economic growth and to improve equitable treatment of similarly situated people, the present punitively high peak rates of the federal tax would be lowered to about 50 percent, but at the same time the sieve of avoidance loopholes for high-income taxpayers would be closed.

State income taxes would be added to the federal income tax, with the funds returned to the states concerned, in order to simplify tax reporting and collection procedures. Thus, the personal income tax base would be shared by federal and state governments, and there would be federal revenue sharing with local governments.

2. Both to stimulate economic growth and to improve equity by switching to the personal income tax, present corporation income tax rates

would be lowered substantially. The new tax would fall on all businesses, not merely corporations. Undistributed profits above generous reinvestment levels would be prorated out to stockholders for taxation, to avoid use of corporations as tax-avoidance devices.[5]

3. Taxes on real property would be continued at roughly present levels, not so much because the property tax is a good tax as because it is a major revenue source for local governments to which economic life has become well-adjusted, and because its removal would mean a large subsidy to present real-property owners.

4. There would be special "user charge" taxes that are clearly justifiable either to correct externalities or on the benefit principle. In this group would be: (a) special assessments; (b) highway taxes (on fuel and on vehicles), with the revenue to be spent on highways and streets; and (c) payroll taxes on the worker (not the employer) to finance social security benefits. All three have strong claim to use as benefit levies.

[5]Some would substitute a value-added tax for the business-income tax. The value-added tax (VAT) is similar to a general sales tax, but is partially collected at each stage of manufacture instead of all from the final consumer.

Could such a tax system yield adequate revenue to pay the governments' bills? The answer is clearly "yes," because personal income-tax rates could be set to produce any desired yield. Could it yield the revenue without impairing the incentive to work and earn? This is a big question raised by critics of the income tax, which in this system would supplant hidden excise and sales taxes, plus part of present corporation taxes. One way of putting the question is: Do we really want as many government services when we recognize individually what we have to pay for them?

Taxes are going to take over a quarter of the income you earn during the rest of your life, if something like present conditions continue. So stop and ask yourself: What does *your* model tax system look like?

REVIEW

Concepts to Remember

Public finance mainly involves the application of analytical concepts already learned in the preceding chapters. But it has some concepts and terms of its own that you need to have firmly installed in your economic tool kit:

benefit principle
ability-to-pay principle
progressive taxation
regressive taxation
"deadweight loss"
incidence
tax shifting
vertical equity
horizontal equity
incentive effects
"tax expenditures"
capital gain
tax capitalization

For Analysis and Discussion

1. Are taxes too high? What is your criterion?
2. Can you suggest ways of minimizing the negative incentive effects of rising taxes as government expenditures grow?
3. Some tax experts argue that taxes should be highly visible (like the personal income tax) in order to make citizens keenly aware of the taxes they are paying. Others argue that indirect and hidden taxes (for example, excise and sales taxes) are better because taxpayers don't feel the burden so strongly and are less unhappy about the costs of government services. Analyze these arguments. What are the main issues, and where do you stand on them?
4. What are tax loopholes? Should all tax loopholes be closed by Congress? (See Table 37–1 in answering.)
5. Suppose a new excise tax were imposed on the following products, at the producer's level:
    a. Steel (where there is mixed price leadership and competition, plus strong labor unions).
    b. Potatoes (where the market is highly competitive and little unionized labor is involved).
    c. Ladies' garments (where the market is highly competitive and there is a strong labor union).
    d. Refined oil and gasoline (where the market is oligopolistic and little strongly unionized labor is involved).

    Explain in each case whether you would expect the incidence of the tax to be on the consumer, labor in the industry, the producing firm, or some combination. (Remember your price theory from Chapters 22–25.)
6. Assume a period of strong inflationary pressures as a result of government arms spending. Which of these alternatives would you consider the more equitable, and why?
    a. A general sales tax to balance the budget.
    b. Inflation.
7. Given a full-employment situation and the need for more taxes to finance increased government spending, what tax program would you propose to raise an additional $10 billion? Defend your program against likely criticism from those who would bear the major burden.
8. What is your model tax system?

APPENDIX TO PART FIVE

Current Research

Research on the fiscal policy aspects of public finance was included in the Appendix to Part Two. Here we concentrate on the allocative and distributional effects of government taxes and expenditures. As awareness has spread that the public sector accounts for between a fourth and a third of all economic activity, economic research on public sector problems has burgeoned in recent years.

GOVERNMENT EXPENDITURES. An excellent annual analysis of the main components of each year's federal budget is provided by Charles Schultze and his Brookings colleagues in *Setting National Priorities: The 1974 Budget,* and other years (The Brookings Institution); sample any major area, such as national defense. Murray Weidenbaum's *The Modern Public Sector* (Basic Books, 1969) and J. Burkhead and J. Miner's, *Public Expenditures* (Chicago, Ill.: Aldine-Atherton, Inc., 1971) provide good, more traditional introductions to the whole area of public expenditures and public goods. *The Economics of Defense in a Nuclear Age,* by Charles Hitch and Roland McKean (Harvard University Press, 1960), remains the best economic analysis of promoting efficiency in public expenditures, but there are many good studies of different aspects of the problem. On cost-benefit analysis, Stephen Enke's "Government-Industry Development of a Commercial Supersonic Transport" (*American Economic Review,* May 1967) provides an accessible introduction; and the following articles on water resources and the federal antipoverty program in the same volume are examples of other applications. More advanced analyses are presented in the Joint Economic Committee's *The Analysis and Evaluation of Public Expenditures: The PPB System,* (1969) Vol. 1, especially the articles by Steiner, Davis and Kamien, and Bonnen.

Government transfer payments presumably to help the lower income groups are not always what they seem. See Henry Aaron's *Shelters and Subsidies: Who Benefits from Federal Housing Policies?* (The Brookings Institution, 1972); Charles Schultze's *The Distribution of Farm Subsidies: Who Gets the Benefits?* (The Brookings Institution, 1971); and J. Pechman, H. Aaron, and M. Taussig, *Social Security: Perspectives for Reform* (The Brookings Institution, 1970). The Joint Economic Committee studies of the "welfare" problem cited in the Appendix to Part Four are equally relevant here, as are another series of JEC papers and hearings on "The Economics of Federal Subsidy Programs," and federal subsidies in all major areas (housing, health, education, and the like), running through 1972 and 1973. For a broader examination of the issue of who really gives and who gets in income transfers, see Gordon Tullock, "The Charity of the Uncharitable," (*Western Economic Review,* December 1971).

POLLUTION AND EXTERNALITIES. A. Kneese's and R. d'Arge's "Pervasive External Costs and the Response of Society," in the Joint Economic Committee volume cited under Government Expenditures above, is a penetrating analysis of externalities. L.E. Ruff's "The Economic Common Sense of Pollution," (*The Public Interest,* Spring 1970), applies the principles understandably, as will the current edition of Schultze's *Setting National Priorities,* described at the beginning of the Government Expenditure section above. From the flood of recent books on pollution, E.G. Dolan's *TANSTAAFL* ("There Ain't No Such Thing as a Free Lunch") (Holt, Rinehart and Winston, 1971), and Marshall Goldman's *Ecology and Economics: Controlling Pollution in the 1970s* (Prentice-Hall, 1972) are among the best.

URBAN PROBLEMS. The cities' problems reach far beyond economics, but economic issues are near the center of the problems. *The Metropolitan Enigma,* J.Q. Wilson, ed., offers a readable introduction; see especially the pieces by Meyer and Netzer. And the entire set of readings suggested in Case 23 is lively and readable. Beyond those, R.E. Grieson, *Urban Economics: Readings and Analysis* (Boston, Mass.: Little, Brown and Company, 1973), and *The Quality of the Urban Environment,* H. Perloff, ed. (Resources for the Future, 1969) collect the analyses of a number of leading economists on different aspects of the urban dilemma. The National Commission on Urban Problems' *Building the American City* (U.S. Government Printing Office, 1968) provides the commission's recommendations.

Taxes. Joseph Pechman's *Federal Tax Policy* (The Brookings Institution, 1971) is a standard reference on the federal tax system. L.C. Thurow's analysis in *The Impact of Taxes on the American Economy* (Praeger Publishers, 1971) is more controversial. The Joint Economic Committee's *Hearings on Tax Subsidies and Tax Reform* (July 19–21, 1972) focus on some lively current issues. *Federal Tax Policy for Economic Growth and Stability,* a volume of papers prepared by seventy-five leading tax experts for the Joint Economic Committee in 1955, but still timely, provides a detailed cross section of research in the field of taxation. For a beginning, try R.A. Musgrave's "Incidence of the Tax Structure and Its Effects on Consumption," or Keith Butters's "Effects of Taxation on the Investment Capacities and Policies of Individuals." J. Pechman's "The Rich, the Poor, and the Taxes They Pay" (*The Public Interest,* Fall 1969) updates incidence analysis and argues for greater progression. The Tax Institute's *Tax Incentives* (Lexington, Mass.: D.C. Heath & Co., 1971) collects several leading analyses of this tricky problem, including the "loopholes" issue. California's George Break looks further at the alleged deterrent effect of high personal income taxes on work, without finding much evidence of it, in "Income Taxes and Incentives to Work" (*American Economic Review,* September 1967). H. Grubel and D. Edwards report a study of Stanford student's behavior in "Personal Income Taxes and Choice of Professions" (*Quarterly Journal of Economics,* February 1964). For the revenue-sharing issue and state-local problems, see L. Ecker-Racz, *The Politics and Economics of State-Local Finance* (Prentice-Hall, 1970).

THE INTERNATIONAL ECONOMY

PART SIX

International Trade and Lending

CHAPTER THIRTY-EIGHT

In the "one world" of today, the close interdependence among nations is painfully obvious. The big economic issues fill the newspapers. Should we raise or lower our tariffs? Do low foreign wages threaten our standard of living? Is the dollar weak or strong?

Since prewar days, our sales of goods and services abroad have soared—from $4 billion in 1939 to $60 billion in 1972. Our imports from abroad have grown even faster, to $66 billion in 1972. The best estimates indicate that perhaps four to five million American workers owe their jobs directly to export sales, and exports come from every state in the union. Our exports of goods and services total only about 6 percent of GNP, but to many industries foreign trade is the blood of life—we export half of our cotton crop and import almost all the tin and nickel we use. To most of the world, foreign trade is more urgent than it is to us. England must import most of her food or starve, and she can pay for these imports only by selling her exports abroad. And so it is with other nations—their living standards depend heavily on foreign trade.

In spite of the importance of foreign trade, governments have long followed policies that restrict rather than encourage such trade—tariffs, quotas, exchange controls. Prima facie, the case for international division of labor and

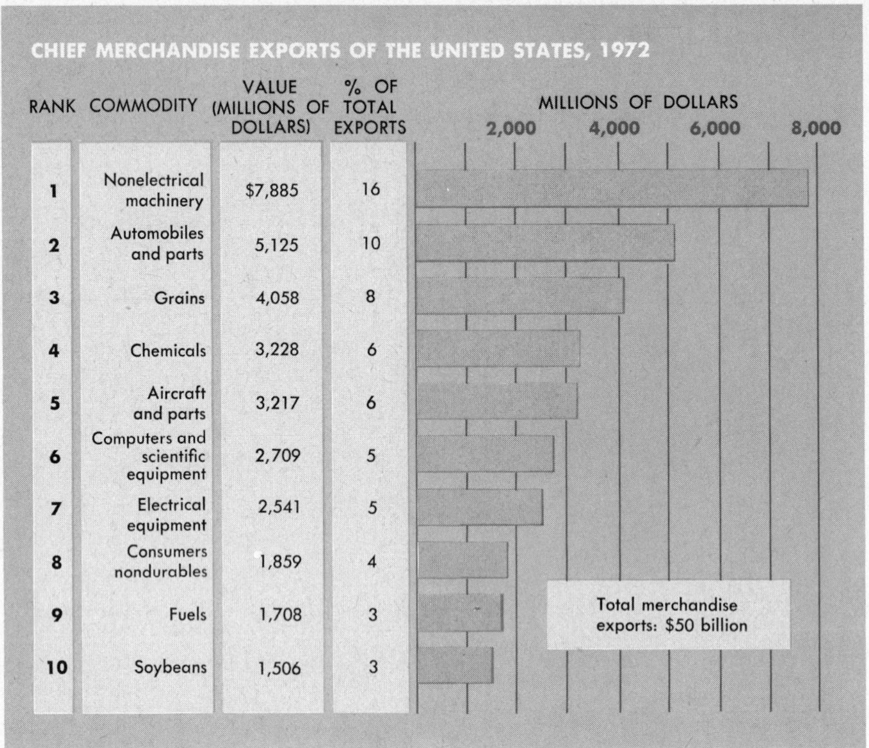
CHIEF MERCHANDISE EXPORTS OF THE UNITED STATES, 1972

RANK	COMMODITY	VALUE (MILLIONS OF DOLLARS)	% OF TOTAL EXPORTS
1	Nonelectrical machinery	$7,885	16
2	Automobiles and parts	5,125	10
3	Grains	4,058	8
4	Chemicals	3,228	6
5	Aircraft and parts	3,217	6
6	Computers and scientific equipment	2,709	5
7	Electrical equipment	2,541	5
8	Consumers nondurables	1,859	4
9	Fuels	1,708	3
10	Soybeans	1,506	3

Figure 38–1

High-technology manufactures (machinery, autos, chemicals, and aircraft) plus grains dominate our exports. (Source: U.S. Department of Commerce. Excludes government military aid.)

exchange is as clear as it is in domestic affairs. On the surface, there would appear to be no reason to suppose that human welfare could be improved by obstructing the processes of specialization and exchange. Why, then, have laymen and lawmakers so often distrusted foreign trade and favored the tariff? Why have nations so often flown in the face of apparent economic reason? Nowhere in economics is there a better opportunity to apply relatively simple economic analysis to popular fallacies.

THE BALANCE OF TRADE

First consider our exports and imports of commodities. Figure 38–1 summarizes the goods we exported in 1972. The figures speak for themselves. They show the huge sales abroad by many of our basic industries, especially high-technology manufactured goods and farm products. It's easy to see why a lot of American businessmen, workers, and farmers are in favor of foreign trade. Figure 38–2 presents the other side of the picture—the goods we imported in 1972. From this, it's easy to see why some businessmen and workers are opposed to foreign trade, which competes directly with them.

Figure 38–3 throws more light on this comparison. It shows exports and imports of goods and services as a percentage of GNP. During the prosperous 1920s, about 7 percent of all goods and services produced in the United States were exported. During the depression, this figure fell off to around 4 percent. After World War II, the ratio rose sharply, then fell back and has since crept up again.

In recent years, the pattern of U.S. foreign trade has changed significantly. Overall, the

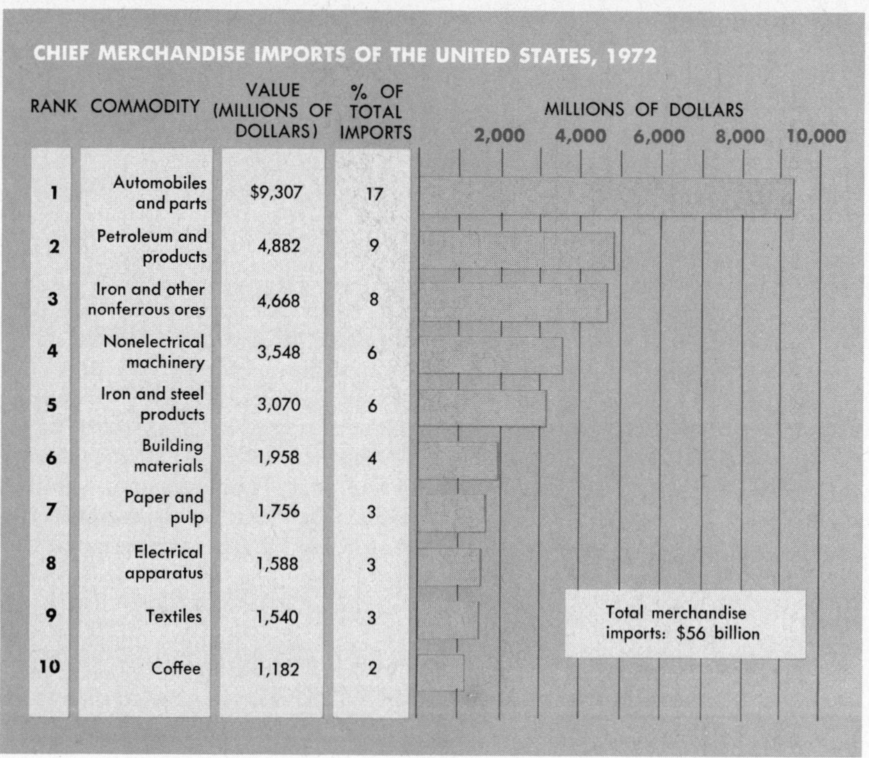

CHIEF MERCHANDISE IMPORTS OF THE UNITED STATES, 1972

RANK	COMMODITY	VALUE (MILLIONS OF DOLLARS)	% OF TOTAL IMPORTS
1	Automobiles and parts	$9,307	17
2	Petroleum and products	4,882	9
3	Iron and other nonferrous ores	4,668	8
4	Nonelectrical machinery	3,548	6
5	Iron and steel products	3,070	6
6	Building materials	1,958	4
7	Paper and pulp	1,756	3
8	Electrical apparatus	1,588	3
9	Textiles	1,540	3
10	Coffee	1,182	2

Figure 38-2

Manufactures also dominate our imports, though raw materials (especially petroleum and mineral ores) are also important. (Source: U.S. Department of Commerce.)

Figure 38-3

U.S. exports of goods and services have exceeded imports, with rare exceptions. During the last decade, both have varied in the range of 4–7 percent of GNP. (Source: U.S. Department of Commerce.)

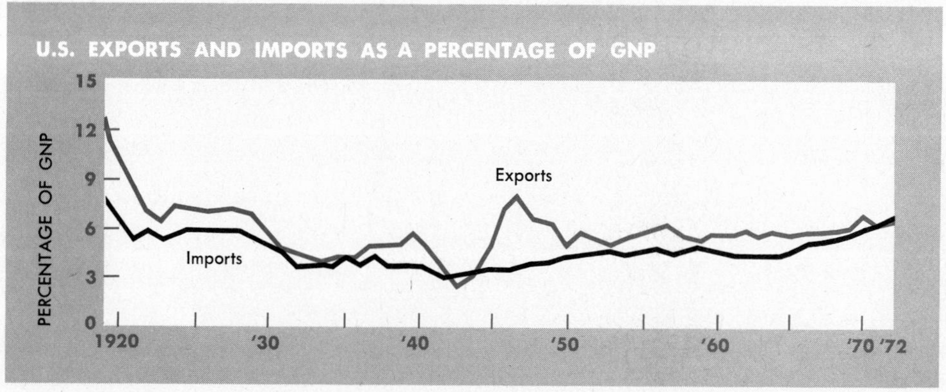

U.S. share has declined from about 20 to 13 percent of total world exports. Our exports have been increasingly concentrated in high-technology manufactured products (computers, automatic machine tools, aircraft, and the like) and in farm products (where we also use the most advanced technology). Markets for lower-technology manufactures (textiles, iron and steel, and consumer durables), have been increasingly usurped by other nations with lower labor costs than ours.

There is still another interesting way of looking at our foreign-trade picture: Who are our main customers and suppliers? Figure 38–4 provides the answer. Canada leads the list by far, and all Western Hemisphere nations combined constitute over 40 percent of our customers. But Western Europe is nearly as important and Japan has been coming up fast. "Developed" countries account for about three-fourths of our exports and imports, "developing" countries for only about one-fourth.

The commodities we buy and sell abroad are the most visible part of our foreign trade, and the part most directly related to American jobs. But in Figures 38–3 and 38–4, $23 billion of sales of American services abroad (shipping, banking, and the like, plus returns on U.S. investments abroad) were added to the $50 billion of merchandise exports. To get a complete picture of the international "balance of payments," we will need to add "capital movements" (the transfer of short- and long-term monetary investments). But first, let us consider the basic analytical case for free international trade and lending.

Figure 38–4

Canada is by far our best customer, followed by Japan. Western Hemisphere and Western European nations together each account for about 40 percent of our total exports. "Developed" countries account for about three-fourths of both exports and imports, "developing" countries for about one-fourth of each. (Source: U.S. Department of Commerce.)

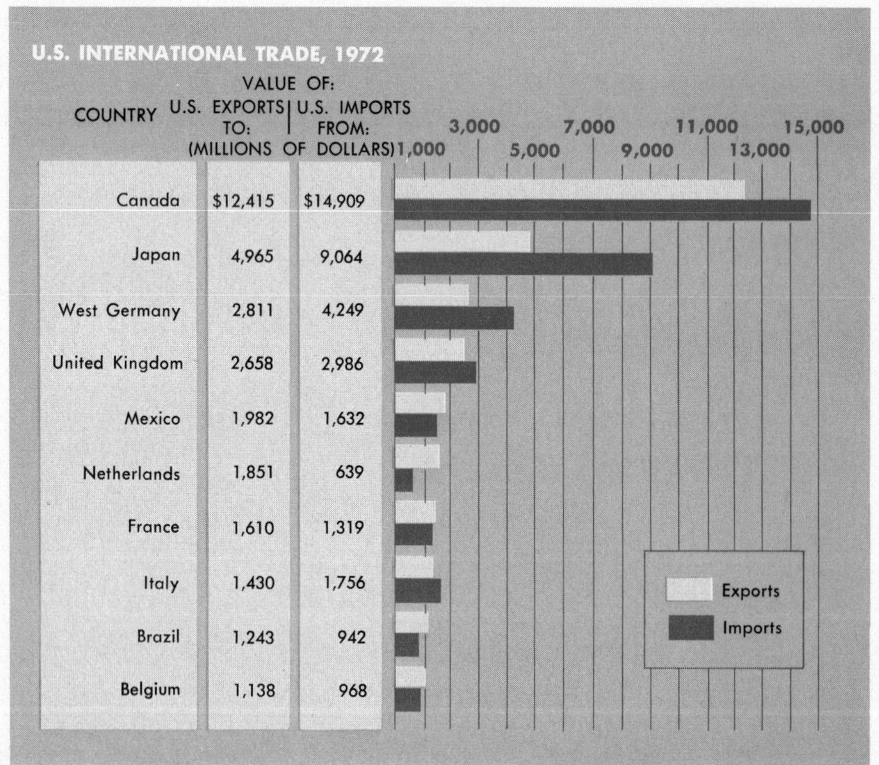

COUNTRY	VALUE OF: U.S. EXPORTS TO: (MILLIONS OF DOLLARS)	U.S. IMPORTS FROM:
Canada	$12,415	$14,909
Japan	4,965	9,064
West Germany	2,811	4,249
United Kingdom	2,658	2,986
Mexico	1,982	1,632
Netherlands	1,851	639
France	1,610	1,319
Italy	1,430	1,756
Brazil	1,243	942
Belgium	1,138	968

THE CASE FOR INTERNATIONAL TRADE

Florida produces oranges; Iowa produces corn and hogs; Pittsburgh produces steel. Each sells its products to the others. When each specializes on what it does best, we produce more in total and we all have more to consume than if we each tried to be self-sufficient. In the same way, Brazil sells coffee to us, we sell computers to England, England sells cloth to Brazil. When each nation specializes on what it does best and then exchanges with others, we produce more in total and we all end up consuming more than if we each tried to be self-sufficient.

The advantages to all in the first case—to Florida, Iowa, and Pittsburgh—are obvious. No one would question them. For each area to try to live alone, barring trade with the others, would be foolish. The advantages to nations from specialization and exchange are identical; more is produced for all to consume. The case for free international trade is that simple and that powerful. By using our total resources most efficiently through specialization and exchange, the world can move all the way out to its combined production-possibilities frontier. But it seems very hard for voters and legislators to see and to remember this simple truth.

Interregional and International Trade

Nations (like regions within a nation) vary greatly in efficiency in producing different goods, differences that persist largely because of international immobility of resources. These differences arise largely out of five considerations:

1. Over the face of the earth climatic and geographical conditions vary widely. Brazil is admirably suited for raising coffee, the lower Nile valley for cotton production. Texas and Oklahoma are great oil-producing centers. Chile has rich nitrate deposits. Such geographical and climatic differences alone would justify world-wide specialization.

2. Human capacities vary over the globe. Some groups are large and strong, suited for physical labor. Others excel at dexterity and manual skills. Still others stand out in enterprise and organizational ability. These differences may be due to long-standing racial characteristics, or to the varying political, social, and economic environment. Whatever the causes, they constitute a reason why international specialization and trade will be beneficial.

3. The accumulated supply of capital goods as well as the kinds of capital, vary greatly from nation to nation. In some countries, centuries of accumulation have produced large supplies of capital—railroads, buildings, machinery, and so forth. Examples are the United States and England, which specialize in industrial products. In other countries—for example, Greece and Nigeria—capital is scarce; they specialize in farming and simple production that requires little elaborate equipment.

4. The **proportions** among different resources vary widely among nations. Australia has vast plains but relatively few people and capital goods. Therefore, she specializes in farm products that require a high proportion of natural resources to labor and capital goods. In England, land is scarce relative to human beings and capital. Therefore, she is best fitted for manufacturing and industry, even though her soil may be as good as Australia's for wheat growing.

5. In addition to these "economic" considerations, great differences exist in the political and social climate in different countries. In countries with stable government, vast industrial organizations requiring large long-period capital commitments are likely to grow. In less-developed, badly-governed areas, conditions virtually prohibit mass-production industry. A hustling, mechanical-minded nation like the United States could hardly be expected to be satisfied again with a small-unit, predominantly rural economy, any more than we would expect the South Sea islanders to be efficient auto makers.

The Principle of Comparative Advantage

Given these differences among nations, it is clear that some international trade will be advantageous. But how far each nation should specialize and how much international trade is to its advantage is not so obvious. Disregard costs of transport between nations for the moment in answering that question.

The greatest possible advantage for all from trade will be obtained if each nation specializes in what it can do relatively most cheaply. In the simple case of Iowa and Florida, where the cost advantage of each in its representative products is clear and large, and with only two products, Iowa should raise all the corn, Florida all the oranges. The greatest total of corn plus oranges will be obtained in that way. But such money-cost comparisons don't provide much guidance when it comes to comparing costs between different nations with different monetary units, different proportions of the factors of production, different qualities of labor, and different productive techniques. Perhaps as between coffee and computers, Brazil has an "absolute" advantage in the former, the United States in the latter. But even in such an extreme case, it is hard to be precise on just why these absolute advantages exist and what they mean. When less-striking differences are considered, such as textiles in the United States and in England, the difficulty of such comparisons becomes insurmountable. Monetary comparisons mean little, because different monetary units are used in the two countries.

But fortunately, as David Ricardo demonstrated a century-and-a-half ago, the advantages of international trade don't depend on such absolute cost calculations at all. Even if one nation were more efficient than another in the production of **everything**, it would still be to the advantage of both to specialize and engage in international trade. **Each, and both combined, will gain most when each specializes in producing those commodities for which its comparative, or relative, costs of production are lowest.**

Let us first illustrate this "principle of comparative advantage" with a case involving only two countries and two commodities—the United States and France producing wheat and cloth. To simplify, let us assume that labor is the only factor of production (or that a day of labor is a shorthand measure of a bundle of land, labor, and capital used in producing things). Assume further that in the United States one man-day can produce one bushel of wheat or one yard of cloth. Thus, in the United States we can obtain one bushel of wheat by giving up the production of one yard of cloth, and vice versa.[1]

TABLE 38–1
Comparative Costs of Production, in Man-Days

	U.S.	FRANCE
Wheat (1 bushel)	1	1
Cloth (1 yard)	1	2

Assume that in France one day of labor also produces one bushel of wheat, but only a half yard of cloth. In this sense, American labor is more productive than French labor, but, as we shall see, this is not the critical factor. The critical factor is that in France two bushels of wheat must be given up to produce one more yard of cloth. This situation is shown in Table 38–1.

First suppose that there is no trade between France and the United States; each country produces all its own wheat and cloth. Will it pay them to begin specializing and trading? The answer is "yes." In the United States, we can obtain **one** more bushel of wheat by giving up one yard of cloth. But in France they can obtain **two** more bushels of wheat by giving up one yard of cloth. **Therefore, there will be an increase in total world output if the United States uses more of her labor to produce cloth while resources in France are shifted to raising wheat.**

[1]Temporarily assume that wheat and cloth are industries of constant costs both here and abroad. That is, unit costs of production do not increase or decrease as output in the country changes. This is sometimes called the assumption of constant returns to scale.

By transferring labor from cloth to wheat in France, Frenchmen produce two additional bushels of wheat for each yard of cloth they forego; by transferring labor from wheat to cloth, Americans produce an extra yard of cloth for each bushel of wheat we forego. Obviously, we should shift more of our resources to producing cloth, France should shift more of hers to wheat. Then by exchanging we can both live better.

A simple example may help demonstrate this point. Assume that there are one hundred workers each in the United States and France. At the beginning, in each country half are producing wheat and half cloth. Total world output is one hundred bushels of wheat and seventy-five yards of cloth, as in Table 38–2.

TABLE 38–2
World Output Before Specialization

U.S.
50 workers on wheat = 50 bushels
50 workers on cloth = 50 yards
FRANCE
50 workers on wheat = 50 bushels
50 workers on cloth = 25 yards

Now suppose that we specialize completely on cloth and France specializes completely on wheat, as the principle suggests. As Table 38–3 shows, the result is one hundred bushels of wheat and one hundred yards of cloth, an increase of twenty-five yards of cloth to divide between us.

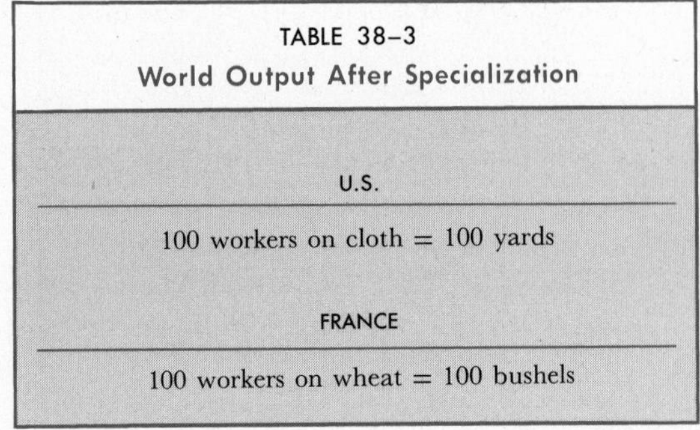
TABLE 38–3
World Output After Specialization

U.S.
100 workers on cloth = 100 yards
FRANCE
100 workers on wheat = 100 bushels

It might appear from these tables that the United States has an **absolute** advantage in efficiency over France, since in France it takes two man-days to produce a yard of cloth, whereas here it takes only one. But it is easy to show that these absolute differences are not the critical point at all. Suppose, instead, that we had begun with the assumption that French labor was the more efficient—that one man-day in France would produce two bushels of wheat or one yard of cloth. Total world output can be larger because of the higher productivity of French labor. But work out the new example, and you will see that it pays each country to specialize where its comparative advantage is higher, just as before, and then to exchange part of its production.

The principle is that gain in total world output is possible from specialization and trade if the cost ratios of producing two commodities are different in different countries. This same principle would have applied in the above example had the cost ratios for producing wheat and cloth been 3 to 2 in the United States and 5 to 1 in France, or any other set of differing ratios. To repeat, absolute costs in the two countries are not relevant. It would make no difference, for example, if U.S. labor were vastly more efficient than French. Total output could be increased by further U.S. specialization on cloth, because our **comparative** advantage is greater in producing cloth. **This is the principle of comparative advantage: Total output will be maximized when each nation specializes in the lines where it has the greatest comparative advantage or the least comparative disadvantage.**[2]

[2]Note that we use this principle all the time in our domestic economic life. Suppose that in a business firm the president is better at typing than any of the secretaries. Should he do his own typing? Obviously not. He should specialize where his comparative advantage is greatest, in managing the firm, leaving the typing to his secretary even though she types slower than he does. Or suppose a fine surgeon is also the best driver in the community. Should he drive the hospital ambulance instead of spending all his available time in the hospital operating room?

From this statement we can also tell how far it is advantageous to carry specialization and trade. Gain from trade is possible until the cost ratios of producing the two commodities are the same in both the United States and France. With constant costs complete specialization would occur; the cost ratios never become equal, because they are fixed by the constant-cost assumption. But now, realistically, drop the assumption of constant costs. As production of cloth increases in the United States, and that of wheat increases in France, the cost ratios will move together. Here the cost of producing cloth will rise relative to that of producing wheat as more cloth is produced. In France, the cost of producing wheat will rise relative to that of producing cloth. Finally, at some levels of output the cost ratios will become identical. Thereafter, there is no advantage in further specialization and exchange, since no further increases in total output can be obtained. (Realistically, we should introduce transport costs between nations, which would correspondingly reduce the potential gains from international exchange.)

When the law of comparative advantage is generalized to many countries and thousands of products, no new principles are introduced, but the picture becomes more complex. Gain will still be maximized if each country specializes in those goods and services where its comparative advantage is greatest or its comparative disadvantage least, and if this specialization is carried to the point where the cost ratios involved are equal to those of other countries producing the same products. In any given country, production of many products will never take place, because the country's comparative disadvantage in their production is so great and because of international transportation costs. Most nations will find it advantageous to produce a variety of products.[3]

[3] If this were an advanced treatise, we would introduce the fact that different industries in different countries may use differing ratios of labor to capital, and note that this raises interesting, intricate problems of exactly how far each country should go toward specialization in different industries. But these complications do not change the general principle of comparative advantage, and we need not become involved in them here.

You may have noted that thus far we have said nothing about the division of the gains from international trade. For example, in the case of Table 38–3, will France or the United States get the extra twenty-five yards of cloth obtained by specialization, or will they be divided between the two nations? In most cases, the gain will be divided, based on a complex set of considerations, mainly the relative cost structures of the countries involved. In extreme cases, it is possible to demonstrate logically that all the gain would accrue to one country, but this requires some highly unlikely assumptions.

The Law of Comparative Advantage, Free Trade, and the Price System

In world markets, the search for profits and the price system tend to bring about this international specialization and optimal allocation of resources in each country automatically. If we are relatively inefficient in producing coffee but very efficient in producing computers, American producers are going to have a tough time competing with Brazil in the world's coffee markets, but we'll beat out other computer manufacturers in the marketplace. Under an international free-trade system, in each country the greatest profits can be obtained by producing those commodities most desired by consumers at home and abroad. If our comparative advantage is great in producing computers, this fact will be reflected in high returns to resources in the computer industry. If our comparative advantage is low in producing spices, American spice producers will be unable to pay wages high enough to bid resources away from the more efficient computer industry, since world prices for spices are set by relatively efficient East Indian production. Thus, under free trade, the resources of each nation would tend to be drawn into its most efficient industries. No one would manage or direct international trade. Each producer would simply try to maximize profits and each buyer would simply buy where the price was lowest. The central mechanism is the same as domestically with Adam Smith's invisible hand.

Worldwide Multilateral Trade

To provide the full advantages of international specialization and exchange, trade must be multinational, or "multilateral." That is, goods and services must move freely among all nations. This eliminates the necessity that the exports and imports between any two nations must be in balance, which would severely restrict the degree of international specialization. Vis-à-vis all other countries combined, a nation's exports and imports must roughly balance (omitting capital movements), but with multinational trade this balance may result from a combination of export and import imbalances with different individual nations, depending on the individual-country comparative advantages involved.

This fact is illustrated by Figure 38–5, which shows the pattern of multinational trade among major areas of the world. The United States, for example, exports more to Europe, Canada, and nontropical Latin America than it imports from them. But our imports from the tropical nations exceed our exports to them. Our international trade is multinational, in fact much more complex than the patterns of exchange shown in Figure 38–5.

THE CASE FOR INTERNATIONAL LENDING

Society benefits when individuals and institutions save and invest, because useful capital goods are thereby accumulated. The saver gains individually from the return on his investment, and society gains from the increased efficiency of round-about, mechanized production. Both the saver and society gain most when savings are invested where their productivity is highest.

In the domestic economy, we mainly trust the price system to allocate savings to the most desirable investments. Those who save invest their funds (either directly or through such institutions as banks) where the combination of safety, liquidity, and rate of return seems most attractive. Because the rate of return tends to be highest where investments fulfill the strongest consumer demands, savings are drawn into those industries where consumers most want output increased. Consumer choices direct the allocation of savings among investments.

Internationally, as domestically, society is generally best off if savings are allocated where their marginal productivity is greatest. International loans are "better" than domestic loans

THE COMPLEX PATTERN OF MULTILATERAL WORLD TRADE

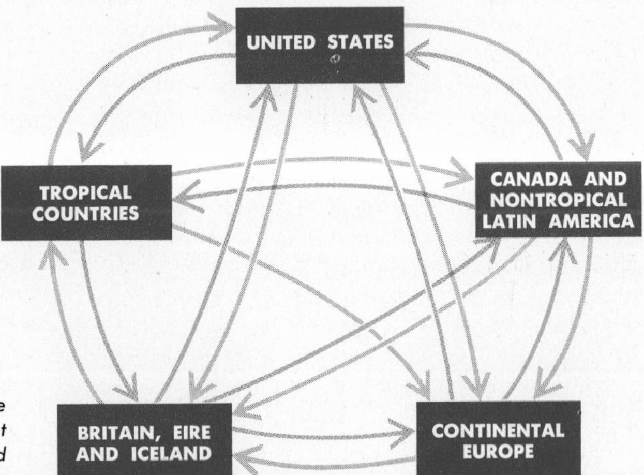

Figure 38–5

The grey arrows show the directions of flow of exports where they exceed imports, while the blue arrows represent the net imports moving in the opposite directions. (Source: United Nations.)

when the anticipated rate of return on them (including liquidity and risk allowance) is greater. For decades, both England and the New World gained from heavy loans by Britishers to the rapidly developing Western Hemisphere. British lenders gained by receiving good returns on their investments; U.S. borrowers gained by getting capital to combine with the plentiful natural resources of the New World. The overall result was a faster growth in world output, divided between the United States and Britain. Today the United States is the big international lender, but the general result is similar. Internationally, as domestically, lending may be unwise if the loan is unsafe, or undesirably illiquid, and the risk is often greater on international investments. But here again national political boundaries do not invalidate basic economic principles: We gain as individuals and as nations from having savings invested where their marginal productivity is highest.

THE FOREIGN-TRADE MULTIPLIER AND DOMESTIC EMPLOYMENT

Thus far we have implicitly assumed that full employment prevails, and that the problem is to allocate our fully-employed resources most efficiently. But in the real world of intermittent underemployment and inflation, international trade can affect the level of domestic employment and output as well.

Export sales provide jobs, just as domestic sales do. Conversely, imports replace domestic jobs. Thus, the net excess of exports over imports ("net exports" in the GNP accounts) is one component of aggregate demand that calls forth production and employment. And like any other autonomous expenditure, such as private investment, it may have a multiplier effect on GNP. Thus the net export balance produces jobs in its own right and also has a further multiplier effect tending to create additional jobs.

But this "foreign-trade multiplier" is smaller than the regular domestic-investment multiplier, because our increased exports, by increasing domestic income, will indirectly induce more imports into the United States. We import more when our incomes rise and the foreign-trade multiplier is reduced by the extent to which induced imports offset the original export balance.

This reasoning makes it easy to see why nations with unemployment want to increase their net export balances, by increasing exports and/or reducing imports. Either way the result will be more jobs at home. Creation of a net export surplus is a way of exporting unemployment to the nation that buys more U.S. goods or has its exports to the United States cut. For this reason, it is often called a "beggar-my-neighbor" policy for increasing domestic employment.

But if any nation tries to export its unemployment in a world of widespread unemployment (as in the 1930s), say by raising its tariffs to shut out imports, it's easy to predict the result. Rather than importing unemployment, other nations will retaliate by raising their tariffs too. Obviously it is not possible for all nations to increase their exports and none to increase their imports, for each export is someone else's import. Thus the main result of import restrictions aimed at exporting unemployment is likely to be retaliation abroad and a shrinkage in the total volume of international trade with no more than transient gains to any nation. This was exactly the result in the 1930s, when snowballing trade restrictions cut world trade to a small fraction of its level during the 1920s.

THE BALANCE OF PAYMENTS

Table 38–4 summarizes the complete U.S. balance of payments in 1972, including foreign investments and government foreign aid, as well as exports and imports of private goods and services. Basically, the table shows what we paid to foreigners and what they paid to us. The minus items are payments from the United States to foreigners; the other items payments from foreigners to us. The four lines in the white background are the major balances. III shows

TABLE 38–4

U.S. Balance of International Payments, 1972[a]

		(IN BILLIONS)	
I. U.S. Exports (payments due United States):[b]			
Merchandise	$50.0		
Services	9.7		
Income from investments abroad	13.8		
Total exports		$73.5	
II. U.S. imports (payments due to foreigners):[b]			
Merchandise	−60.4		
Services and U.S. travel abroad	−5.9		
Income on foreign investments here	−11.5		
Total imports		−77.8	
III. Balance on goods and services			−$4.2
IV. Private foreign investment in United States (long term)		0.3	
V. U.S. government grants[b]		−2.2	
VI. U.S. private long-term investment and private remittance abroad		−4.9	
VII. Balance on current account and long-term capital			−9.2
VIII. Nonliquid short-term private capital, net		−1.6	
IX. Allocation of SDRs		.7	
X. Errors and unrecorded transactions		−3.8	
XI. Net liquidity balance			−14.0
XII. Foreign short-term dollar balances, net		3.7	
XIII. Official settlements balance			−10.3

[a] Some minor items are omitted and data are rounded to nearest $100 million, so figures may not add or subtract exactly. − shows payment from the United States.
[b] Excludes direct military aid; but includes military sales and purchases.
Source: U.S. Department of Commerce.

that we imported $4.2 billion more goods and services than we exported. VII shows that when net U.S. capital movements to other nations are added, our net deficit rose to $9.2 billion. If we then add outflows of special short-term funds and errors and omissions (probably mainly unreported short-term capital outflows), our total **liquidity deficit** for 1972 was $14 billion. Our payments to foreigners exceeded their payments to us by that amount.

In other words, foreigners accumulated $14 billion of dollar balances during 1972; $3.7 billion of these were held by private individuals or organizations at year-end, while the other $10.3 billion were held by foreign central banks. Thus our **official settlements deficit** was $10.3 billion; we owed that much more to foreign central banks at year-end than a year earlier. Both private and official foreign holders kept most of these additional dollars in U.S. Treasury bills or U.S. bank accounts. This is what is meant when we say that foreigners accumulated dollar balances during the year because of the U.S. balance of payments deficit.

You may be struck by the fact that gold does not appear on the table. Before 1972, foreigners might have chosen to convert part or all of their dollar balances into gold at the U.S. Treasury, but in 1971 the U.S. government announced it would (at least temporarily) no longer freely convert dollars into gold. Thus, the government now simply holds its $10 billion gold stock as part of its monetary reserves. More on the rapidly changing role of gold in Chapter 41.

The Balance of Payments and the Balance of Trade

Table 38–4 points up the importance of being clear about the difference between the "balance of payments" and the "balance of trade." The balance of payments includes all payments between the countries concerned (all of Table 38–4). The balance of trade includes only trade in goods and services (I and II of the table).[4] Popular discussion, which generally runs in terms of the balance of trade, is often confused because of the failure to consider the entire balance of payments. Capital flows (short- and long-term investments overseas) have been huge since World War II, and even on a net basis have frequently exceeded the balance of trade in accounting for U.S. payments surpluses or deficits.

Recently the newspapers have been full of talk about America's huge balance-of-trade deficit. This is a very recent phenomenon; 1971 was the first year this century in which U.S. merchandise imports exceeded merchandise exports. Before then, our exports of goods and services consistently exceeded imports. But the total balance-of-payments picture has varied widely. During the 1920s and 1930s, we generally accumulated gold and short-term balances abroad, because payments were due us on balance. Since about 1950, by contrast, we have run a persistent balance-of-payments deficit. Thus, foreigners have steadily accumulated gold and dollar balances (U.S. bank deposits and short-term investments) here, as we have made large investments abroad and have annually given foreign nations a large amount of economic and military aid.

[4]It is the difference between these two (III in Table 38–4) that is the "net exports" figure shown separately in the GNP accounts. When not shown separately, it is usually included as part of gross private investment.

Since 1950, foreigners have taken about $16 billion in gold and increased their "dollar balances" by about $80 billion. As we shall see in Chapter 41, our persistent balance-of-payments deficit has become a serious problem in the past few years. But it should be clear that international payments imbalances are settled in large part in foreign currency balances, only in small part or not at all by gold transfers.

INTERNATIONAL COMMUNITY AND CONFLICT OF INTERESTS

Free international trade and lending are in the interest of the world as a whole. This is the big lesson to be learned. Since World War II the Western noncommunist world has moved persistently toward freer trade, with the United States a leader. And the results have been satisfying. Since 1950, world trade has more than tripled, from less than $60 billion to nearly $400 billion in 1973. This is a substantially faster growth rate than in the domestic production of most of the individual countries.

For the most part, freer trade and lending also benefit each of the individual countries concerned while world output increases. But not always. It is possible, though unlikely, that an individual nation may temporarily increase its domestic employment by shutting out competing foreign goods and exporting its unemployment. But, even assuming full employment, some other possible conflicts of interest deserve attention, as qualifications to the general argument.

1. **Personal Migration.** If the "economic welfare" of the world as a whole is our aim, then international migration probably should occur whenever real wages obtainable in one country are higher than in another. But for workers in high-wage countries, immigration of workers from low-wage countries might prove a major blow. Assume such an influx into the United States, and assume that the immigrants are substitutable for American workers. Work out the supply-and-demand analysis yourself.

Average real wages for workers throughout the world would rise, but the influx of foreign workers would surely lower the incomes of present American workers. Given the international distribution of resources, the law of comparative advantage applies. But the law does not say that each nation must gain from an international shift of resources, even when the shift raises the world's average standard of living.

2. **Monopoly-Type Action by One Country.** Just as a domestic monopolist can benefit himself by restricting output, so a country may be able to benefit itself by restricting trade. But the attempt may not always work. For one thing, the international monopolist must always face the potential competition of other countries. More important, any country's restrictions on imports are likely to provoke retaliatory restrictions by other countries, and then both are worse off.

The extreme cases of nations acting as monopolists are those where foreign trade is centralized under government control—Russia, for example. But to a smaller extent, other countries have also centralized their foreign-trade activities. Brazilian coffee is an example.

3. **Growth of Less-Developed Areas.** When a rich country lends to less-developed areas, the lender *may* find itself worse off because of the loans. This result may occur if the new areas develop industries that compete with the lender's. More often, however, the new industries are not directly competitive. In any case, as the developing country sells abroad it can begin to buy abroad, and the law of comparative advantage ultimately applies. Three-fourths of U.S. trade is with other highly industrialized nations.

4. **War.** The most important potential conflict goes beyond economics. It centers around war and preparation for war. No nation wants to depend on potential enemies for vital raw materials and finished goods, or to help build up the strength of potential enemies. With this major exception, however, economic and political considerations point in the same direction. Wide-ranging international trade and finance are probably the soundest bases for lasting peace.

THE GREAT AMERICAN RESPONSIBILITY

In the century before World War I, England was the world's great creditor nation and the financial center of the world. This was an era of free international trade. Trade was multilateral—based on an intricate web of exchanges in which no two countries balanced out directly with each other. The gold standard assured stable exchange rates among the world's currencies, to facilitate foreign trade. The British pound provided a standard currency and, along with gold, comprised the basic monetary reserves of most leading nations. London was the financial center of world trade, the banker to the world. The system was complex, but it operated, like the free-price system, in a mainly automatic fashion—through the multitude of buying and selling activities of individuals around the world.

The day of British leadership has passed. On the United States falls much of the responsibility for providing leadership in today's world economy. The dollar, even with its recent troubles and devaluations, is still the major international currency of the free world. Our task is incomparably more difficult than was Britain's in the nineteenth and early twentieth centuries. Nations no longer accept unquestioningly the "discipline" of international gold flows in regulating their domestic money supplies. "Planned" domestic economies have replaced free private enterprise in many countries. Maintenance of domestic high employment has become the first objective of most nations' economic policies. Many nations have come to look upon the United States as a continuing source of military and economic aid.

The United States does not dominate the world economy as it did two decades ago. Nonetheless, it has been widely suggested that we must do four things:

1. Maintain a stable, prosperous U.S. economy as

a foundation for international economic prosperity.

2. Maintain a strong, stable dollar internationally, as the world's major transactions currency.
3. Continue to lead in reducing trade barriers.
4. Support international institutions to aid international monetary stability and investment in less-developed countries.

REVIEW

Concepts to Remember

International economics is essentially fundamental economics applied to international economic activity. But it has some new terms and concepts that you need to understand to be able to operate effectively on international problems:

law of comparative advantage
comparative costs
balance of payments
balance of trade
liquidity deficit
official-settlements deficit
foreign-trade multiplier
multilateral trade
capital movements
beggar-my-neighbor-policies

For Analysis and Discussion

1. State the basic case for specialization, division of labor, and free exchange. Are there reasons why this case applies differently within a nation and across national boundaries?
2. What industries in your area are most affected by international trade? (See Tables 38–1 and 38–2.) How important is such trade to your immediate area?
3. Suppose U.S. imports were reduced by half due to new tariffs or import quotas. What effect would this probably have on jobs in export industries in your area? (See Table 38–1).
4. Explain the difference between the balance of payments and the balance of trade. On which do the data in Figures 38–1 through 38–4 throw the most light?
5. "Anyone who believes in free trade ought to believe in free international migration of labor, unrestricted by immigration barriers." Do you agree? Why or why not?
6. What is the principle of comparative advantage?
7. Canada and China both have large land masses, but China has a larger work force. Explain why you would expect Canada to export wheat to China, not vice versa.
8. Why is multilateral trade more advantageous than bilateral trade?
9. If you were wealthy, would you invest any of your money abroad? Why or why not?
10. Why is the foreign-trade multiplier ordinarily smaller than the domestic-investment multiplier?

Tariffs, Quotas, and Free Trade

CHAPTER PREVIEW

CHAPTER THIRTY-NINE

Adam Smith's *Wealth of Nations* in 1776 was a major attack on barriers to free international trade. The case for free trade internationally is the same as the case for free trade domestically, Smith argued. It is that specialization and division of labor with free exchange of the resulting products that makes possible a higher standard of living for everyone. Tariffs, import quotas, or other barriers to free international trade impede such mutually advantageous specialization and exchange and reduce living standards throughout the world, just as would barriers to free trade within a nation.

Yet from Smith's day to this, many have remained unconvinced. Support for tariffs and import quotas to "protect the American standard of living and the high wages of American workers" is still widespread. Why?

THE TARIFF

A tariff is a tax on imports; whoe major goal is to restrict imports. Figure 39–1 shows average U.S. tariff rates on dutiable imports since 1820. It shows clearly the peaks of restrictionism and the major attempts to whittle away barriers to free international trade. From peak rates of about 60 percent under the Tariff Act of 1833 and the Smoot-Hawley Tariff of 1930, average tariff rates on covered products have been cut to below 10 percent in the last two decades, including a last downward push by the "Kennedy round" in the 1960s. These figures understate the real restrictive effect of the tariff, because some products are shut out completely by the tariff, and they don't show up in Figure

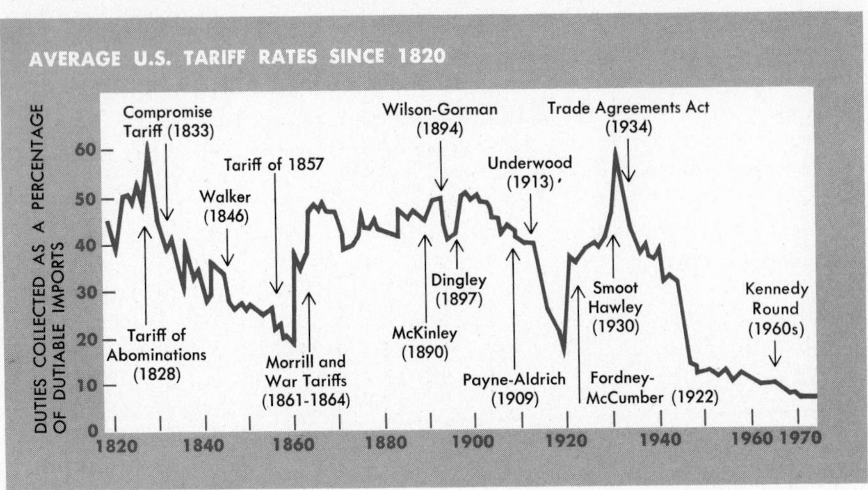

Figure 39–1

U.S. tariff rates have fluctuated with changing times and attitudes. Since 1934 they have been reduced sharply to the lowest levels in our history. (Source: U.S. Department of Commerce.)

39–1. But any way you look at it, major progress has been made in reducing U.S. tariff barriers since the early 1930s. The United States, after a spotty history of restrictionism, has been a leader in a worldwide push toward freer trade.

The history books are full of accounts of the tariff acts battled through Congress over nearly two centuries, and of the regional and political issues underlying them. Our job is to look objectively at the economics of tariffs—to apply the economic analysis of the preceding chapters to the major arguments advanced in support of tariffs. And the central principle to use is the law of comparative advantage.

Some Partially Valid Arguments

The Infant-Industry Argument. A protective tariff may help "infant industries" until they are able to stand on their own. This was the most stylish argument for tariffs in the early 1800s. For example, the newly formed iron industry found it difficult to get established in the face of strong competition from British iron makers. If foreign competition were shut out for a few years, it was argued, the American iron industry could soon not only meet, but outstrip, foreign competition.

There is some validity to the "infant-industry" argument. It is hard for a new industry to establish itself in the face of vigorous competition from older competitors, even though the new industry once established may compete effectively with the old.

But a tariff once on the books is hard to get off. For example, the steel industry, still protected today, a century and a half later, is a very mature infant.

The National-Self-Sufficiency Argument. In a world of international tension, every nation wants to be as nearly self-sufficient as possible in the event of war. The desire for economic self-sufficiency may overbalance all other considerations, regardless of the costs.

The economist cannot say whether a nation should try to become self-sufficient in the face of such considerations. But he can point out what self-sufficiency costs in terms of a lowered standard of living so that this factor will be weighed with others in deciding whether or not we will seek more self-sufficiency. And the cost for most nations would be great.

The Diversified-Economy Argument. When a nation specializes in producing one or a few major products, its economy may be highly vulnerable to variations in foreign demand. Brazil's coffee economy is an example; usually such one-product nations export a foodstuff or raw material. If foreign markets weaken, the result is domestic disaster. For such nations, greater economic diversification may be desirable, even though the new industries are comparatively inefficient. Tariffs may be used to shelter them in a diversification program. But for widely diversified countries like the United States, this argument has little relevance.

Over the last century in the United States these partially valid arguments have carried little weight in tariff controversies. Let us now turn to the arguments that have been the important ones in support of the tariff. As we shall see, they turn out to be largely fallacious.

The Favorable-Balance-of-Trade Argument

Most naïve of all the tariff arguments is the desire for a "favorable balance of trade" for its own sake. It goes back to the old mercantilist desire to gain more gold and silver as national treasure. Two major fallacies are involved.

First, there is nothing generally favorable about a "favorable" balance of trade. A continued "favorable" balance means that we continually give foreigners more goods and services than they give us; we receive in exchange gold (often to be held idle at considerable storage expense) or investments abroad. Thus, it means a reduced standard of living for the country sending away goods and services, certainly in the short run, and indefinitely if the "favorable" balance of trade continues without willingness to accept goods from abroad. We don't eat gold. Our standard of living is made up of the goods and services we obtain.

Second, a favorable balance of trade is impossible as a continuing policy, if we consider only the goods-and-services portion of the balance of payments. Foreigners can't buy from us unless they get dollars to pay for our products. The way they get dollars is by selling us their goods and services. It is only by buying from foreigners that we can expect to sell to them.

There is no point more fundamental than this: We can sell abroad only if we buy abroad. It is basic to understanding the fallacy in nearly every argument for protective tariffs and other trade-restriction policies. Figure 39–2 shows where other countries obtained the dollars to buy our exports from 1929–72 (U.S. exports are indicated by the heavy black line). Private investments abroad and government aid helped foreigners finance their purchases from us. But our purchases of foreign goods and services have always been the big source of dollars with which foreigners bought our exports. To sell abroad we must buy abroad. We cannot shut out foreign imports and continue to export.

The Protect-Home-Industry Argument

Perhaps the most popular argument for the tariff is that we need it to protect American industry against low-cost foreign competition.

A domestic industry asking for tariff protection argues that without protection its market will be lost to foreign competitors. This will force the domestic industry out of business, throwing workers out of jobs. Suppose that the industry is right; if it does not receive protection it will lose its market to foreign competitors. What are the effects of giving the tariff protection the industry wants?[1]

The first effect is that domestic consumers must pay more for the protected product than if it had come in free. If sugar comes in over

[1]Often industries seeking protective tariffs would be able to retain their markets without tariffs; tariffs enable them to raise domestic prices with lessened fear of foreign competition. Indeed, the tariff has been called "the mother of monopolies," because it helps domestic monopolies to exist without foreign competition.

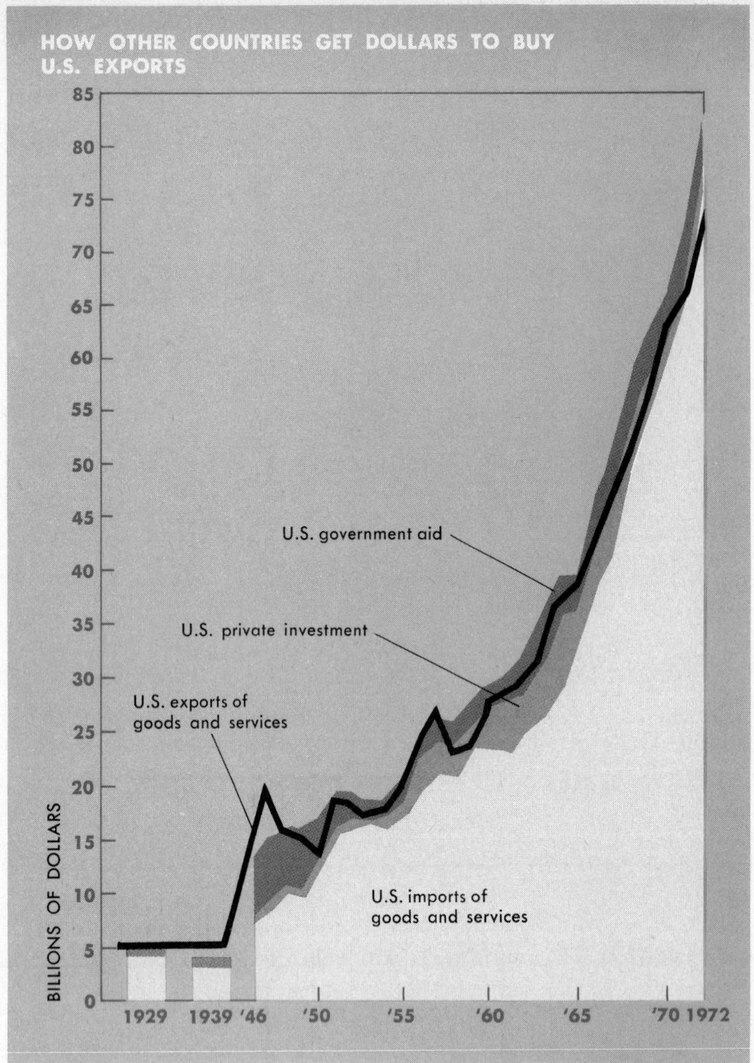

Figure 39–2

Other countries get dollars to buy U.S. exports mainly through our payments for imports. But net U.S. investments abroad and government foreign aid also provide a good many dollars. (Source: U.S. Department of Commerce. Military aid and exports excluded.)

the tariff, consumers must pay the regular price of the foreign sugar plus the tariff duty. If the tariff shuts out foreign sugar, domestic consumers must pay a higher price for domestic sugar. We know it's higher because domestic producers cannot, without a tariff, produce and sell at a price low enough to meet foreign competition. If they could, they wouldn't need the tariff.

Second, domestic sugar producers are subsidized by the tariff; they are enabled to charge higher prices than would have been possible if foreign competition had not been shut out. It's clear that domestic producers are the great gainers from a tariff on their product.

In effect, therefore, a tariff is a subsidy to domestic producers, financed by consumers through higher prices for the protected product. Moreover, the more inefficient domestic producers are, the higher tariff they need to protect them against foreign competition and the larger subsidy they receive.

Indeed, industry's argument for a tariff is often for a "scientific" tariff that would just "equalize domestic and foreign costs of production." A suggestion in Congress that special taxes be levied on consumers to finance subsidies to producers, each subsidy to be based on the producer's inefficiency, would horrify everyone. Yet this is substantially the result of a "scientific" protective tariff designed to equalize foreign and domestic costs of production.

A noted economist, Frederick Bastiat, put the free-trade case against protection tellingly over a century ago in his satirical "Petition of the Candlemakers." We need protection, said the candlemakers of Paris in their petition. Foreign competitors are bad enough, but it is the sun that is the most unfair competitor of all. Each day it shines and throws light over all, at no cost at all. If you only shut out the sun, pleaded the candlemakers, we can have a magnificent candle industry, giving jobs to untold numbers of workers.

Should we protect American domestic industry against cheap foreign competition today, using the same arguments as Bastiat's candlemakers a century ago?

The Protect-Our-High-Wages Argument

American wages are the highest in the world. Therefore, it is argued, unless we have a protective tariff, competition from low-wage nations will pull down high American wages to the level of wages abroad.

The "Petition of the Candlemakers" should suggest a fallacy here. Would the real wages of French workers have been raised by shutting out the sun? Would the French people have been better off? Look at the argument in detail.

First, why are wages now higher in the United States than in other countries? Fundamentally, because of the high productivity of American workers. Anything that raises their productivity makes it possible for them to receive higher real wages. And each worker can receive his highest possible wage when he works where his marginal productivity is highest.

What happens when a tariff is passed to "protect" high American wages? The tariff shuts out foreign products and permits relatively inefficient American industries to grow up where they otherwise could not have existed, giving new jobs to American workers. But, as a result, American exports will fall off because foreign countries cannot buy from us unless we buy from them. (Remember Figure 39–2.) Therefore, fewer workers are employed in the export industries. **The net result is a shift of workers from relatively efficient export industries (where they would be situated under free trade) into less-efficient protected industries. As workers move to lower-marginal-productivity positions in protected industries, the wages they can receive in the new jobs are necessarily lower than they could have been before the shift. The long-run result of a protective tariff is to lower real wages, not to raise them. People earn the most when they work where they are most efficient.**[2]

To be sure you understand this point, consider an extreme example cited by proponents of a tariff to protect American wages. Suppose that Japanese labor is paid only one-third as much as U.S. workers and we remove all tariffs on Japanese imports. Won't American workers be forced to take much lower wages to compete?

In analyzing this case, we first need to recognize that even though Japanese daily wages are much lower, it is not necessarily true that the labor costs of Japanese producers are correspondingly lower. The Japanese worker gets lower wages, but he also produces less in a day. Therefore, the labor cost per unit of output may be as much, or more, for the Japanese producer as for the American. For example, suppose the average hourly wage of Japanese industrial workers is about $1.40, that in America about $4.00. But suppose, for example, in the chinaware industry, that the hourly output per worker in Japan is 35 plates; then the labor cost per plate is 4 cents. If the hourly output per American worker is 100 plates, the labor cost per plate would be only 4 cents too. Wage cost per plate (per unit of output) is the one that counts.

The evidence is clear that although wages are lower everywhere else, U.S. unit costs are highly competitive in many industries. Our $50 billion

[2] This is not to deny that a protective tariff on a particular product may raise the real wages of workers *in that industry* by increasing the demand for labor there, so long as there are immobilities in the domestic labor market that keep other workers from moving in to take advantage of the higher labor demand provided there by protection.

"Don't be childish, man! Kicking Toyotas is no answer to our balance-of-trade gap." (Drawing by Donald Reilly; © 1971. The New Yorker Magazine, Inc.)

of annual merchandise exports are impressive evidence. American wages are by far the highest, but so is American output per man-hour.

Because wages are the biggest cost element in many industries, changes in relative unit-labor-costs are an important determinant of each nation's success in world markets. From 1960–65, for example, U.S. hourly wages advanced slower than in many competing nations while output per man-hour rose faster. U.S. unit-labor-costs actually fell slightly over the period while they rose from 2 to 5 percent annually in the United Kingdom, West Germany, France, and Japan. The United States showed a large trade surplus. But during 1965–70, U.S. wages soared in inflation and productivity growth slowed. U.S. unit-labor-costs soared over 20 percent during these five years, and our trade surplus eroded rapidly, leading to our first trade deficit of the century in 1971. What happens to unit-labor-costs is thus a function of both the rate of increase in wage rates and changes in labor productivity.

Suppose, to continue the hypothetical example, that even when productivity differences are taken into account Japan can far undersell us on china plates, and that we remove the tariff on china. This move, of course, would throw workers in the American chinaware industry out of jobs. But since Japan would then be selling more to us, she could now buy more from us. She would buy from us those goods that we are able to produce most efficiently—say, computers. Workers thrown out of jobs in making china would gradually be drawn into the computer industry. But since the United States is, by assumption, comparatively more efficient in producing computers than china, workers can receive higher wages in the computer industry. Workers in the china industry would surely be temporarily unemployed and, if personally unadaptable, might never be reemployed. But the general public would gain by obtaining cheaper china, and more workers would be drawn into the high-productivity industries where wages are highest. Removal of an existing tariff may ruin protected producer groups; yet in the long run average wages and the standard of living for the economy as a whole will be raised.[3]

This reasoning, however, rides easily over some tough short-run adjustment problems. Higher average wages for the economy don't help the fifty-year-old china maker thrown out of work by the new imports. Where will he get another equally good job, or even one at all?

[3]This argument applies strictly only if labor costs are the same proportion of total costs in the two industries concerned. In most real-world cases in the United States, this approximation is close enough to permit the above example to apply in substance.

The offsetting new jobs producing for export may not come immediately. The Japanese may temporarily accumulate dollars, or spend them elsewhere. Sooner or later, our expanded imports will mean new export markets. But with these uncertainties and the pain felt in the displaced industries, it's easy to understand why some labor opposition to tariff cuts is bitter. Nor does the higher national standard of living help those china-company stockholders whose investment is destroyed by the cheap imports. The opposition comes from investors and businessmen as well as from workers.

The Increased-Employment Argument

In the long run, it should be clear by now, a protective tariff neither increases nor decreases employment, but merely shifts resources from more-efficient to less-efficient industries. However, the short-run adjustments in moving toward the new long-run equilibrium may be slow and painful (as with any shift in demand). Removing an existing tariff may result in temporary unemployment—unemployment that may persist stubbornly if aggregate demand is weak.

But the protectionist argument claims more. It says that, at least in the short run, raising tariffs will create **more** jobs as domestic firms begin selling to the customers who previously bought imported goods. And the foreign-trade multiplier will amplify the creation of domestic jobs. Even though in the long run this may not increase total employment, temporarily the new tariff will raise exports relative to imports and create jobs.

But this is a short-sighted argument. Suppose America puts on a tariff to shut out foreign goods and to export our unemployment. What would you do if you were Belgium, or England, or France? You'd come right back with higher tariffs or quotas against American exports. And that's just what they did during the 1930s. If we can increase our exports relative to imports in a period of unemployment, this may temporarily raise employment and real GNP. But it's unlikely that higher tariffs will do the job, and likely that the main result will just be less trade for everyone.

Summary

From this analysis, we can draw a broad summary of the economic effects of tariffs. **In the long run,** a protective tariff lowers real wages and the standard of living. It diverts resources from self-sustaining export industries to less-efficient, protected domestic-consumption industries; and it forces consumers to pay higher prices. **In the short run,** advantages may be gained from imposing new tariffs to aid infant industries or to reduce unemployment. However, new tariffs will increase domestic employment only if almost inevitable retaliatory steps are not taken by other nations.[4]

Tariff Making in the United States

If the protective tariff is open to such serious criticism, and if it benefits only particular groups at the cost of the rest of society, why have we had high protective tariffs so long? There are two chief answers.

First, public opinion on the tariff has been greatly influenced by self-seeking propaganda, and many citizens are uninformed on the nature of international trade. Groups seeking protection have presented their case effectively in Congress and to the general public, and the appeal to nationalism against foreigners is a potent rallying cry.

Second, the benefits of freer trade are widespread—lower prices, and more jobs in export industries tomorrow. But the costs are concentrated and direct—on the businessmen and workers who lose out to cheaper foreign imports. The threatened interests are alarmed, organized,

[4]Though as a practical matter U.S. tariff reductions are usually advocated on the presumption of reciprocal reductions by other nations, the logic of comparative advantage shows that under most circumstances even unilateral tariff reductions will benefit the country making them.

and vocal. Consumers as a whole are not organized to speak effectively. Congress passes acts covering thousands of products, and most of the actual decisions are made by small subcommittees in the House and Senate. Each congressman is pressed by his constituents to vote for protection for the goods that they produce. Thus, the congressman from one state will agree to vote for a tariff on shoes if his colleague from another state will vote for one on sugar. The tariff is the classic example of congressional logrolling. (Remember the "political failures" of Chapter 35.)

Thus, the big tariff reductions since 1930 have come through congressional delegation of tariff-cutting authority to the president. Under the Reciprocal Trade Agreements Act of 1934 and the Kennedy Trade Expansion Act of 1962, the president was authorized to bargain down U.S. tariffs in return for similar reductions by other nations. The results are shown in Figure 39–1. Similar reductions have been made since the 1930s by most other major Western nations with whom we trade heavily.

In 1973, President Nixon asked Congress for renewed powers to negotiate tariff and import quota reductions, but he added powers to raise as well as lower individual rates, and improved financial aids for U.S. workers and businesses injured by tariff reductions. He emphasized the need for a strong U.S. bargaining stance vis-á-vis other nations to assure larger U.S. exports and an improved balance of payments position. In this respect, his request differed from those of Presidents Roosevelt and Kennedy, who had stressed reciprocal tariff reductions.

IMPORT QUOTAS AND EXPORT SUBSIDIES

The United States and most other major nations now use import quotas as well as tariffs to protect domestic producers. In 1972, the United States had import quotas for sixty-seven major product categories, ranging from oil, steel, and textiles to minor consumer items like brooms. Japan and most European nations had roughly similar import quota structures.

Import quotas are more disruptive to free trade than tariffs. With a quota, additional foreign goods cannot enter, no matter how much more efficient foreign producers may be. With a tariff, at least foreign goods may enter if their cost advantage is large enough to overcome the tariff barrier.

Bargaining on import quotas has become a more important means of adjusting competitive trade positions than tariff negotiations. U.S. unions and businessmen in areas exposed to foreign competition have become strong advocates of tougher U.S. quotas, and have pressed for Japanese and West European agreements to limit exports to the United States. Large U.S. trade deficits in the early 1970s strengthened their position, and there is clearly some danger that the United States will retreat from its position of world leadership in reducing trade barriers. The Nixon request to strengthen aid to injured U.S. workers and businesses was a move to buy off some opposition to freer trade, a move clearly justified to avoid imposing the full cost of socially desirable changes on a small sector of the economy. Moreover, national fears of an energy shortage and sharply rising food prices in 1973 led Nixon to remove all quota restrictions, at least temporarily, on oil and meat imports.

Export subsidies are another device widely used to provide domestic producers a special advantage over foreign competitors in world markets. U.S. farm price-support programs are considered by many foreigners to provide, in effect, a large export subsidy to U.S. farm exporters. U.S. legislation also permits the use of "countervailing duties" against such subsidies given by foreign nations that sell in this country. Such countervailing duties have recently been levied on a variety of food imports from Europe. Moreover, the United States calculates its tariff duties on major chemical imports by pricing them at U.S. market levels, in effect, imposing a higher tariff barrier; this is the controversial so-called "American selling price" provision. Conversely, some nations (especially Japan and many developing economies) use foreign-exchange controls to limit the purchase of particular products from foreigners.

Nontariff barriers to trade constitute the major current threat to continued progress toward free world trade. Unfortunately, countries often find it easier to retaliate against such barriers by imposing similar restrictions than to negotiate them down. Rising nontariff barriers dot the international scene.

THE EUROPEAN COMMON MARKET

After World War II the spirit of internationalism was strong. All the victorious nations except the USSR moved to extend their wartime collaboration into economic cooperation that would reverse the restrictionist wave of the 1930s. Within the framework of the United Nations, the General Agreement on Tariffs and Trade (GATT) was created. It provides for regular discussion of means to reduce international trade barriers among members, and each member nation agrees to work toward freer trade practices, insofar as these practices are not in conflict with the country's national legislation.

But the biggest postwar move toward international economic cooperation is the European Common Market, and a major move it is. After earlier cooperation on coal, iron, and atomic energy, in 1958 six European nations—Belgium, France, Italy, Luxembourg, the Netherlands, and West Germany—banded together in the European Economic Community (EEC), generally called the Common Market. This precedent-shattering agreement has eliminated all tariff and similar trade barriers against one another and has gradually equalized all their restrictions on trade with nations outside the six, so they present a common tariff to the outside world. Barriers against internal movement of capital and labor are being abolished. Other economic policies will be "harmonized." A common antitrust policy is provided to eliminate long-time restrictions on competition, though here considerable freedom is left for national differences. In essence, the Common Market is a new, massive, free-trade area.

In 1973, Denmark, Ireland, and the United Kingdom joined the Common Market. "The Nine" now have a total population of 255 million, larger than either the United States or the USSR. Their combined GNP was about $750 billion in 1972, more than the USSR's and nearly two-thirds that of the United States. Combined, The Nine are by far the largest exporter and importer in the world; their 1972 exports and imports (including intercountry trade) were about $150 billion each, more than double those of the United States. Their combined international monetary reserves were $55 billion, far in excess of ours. The EEC is a huge economic bloc.

While the Common Market has been a powerful force toward free trade among its member countries, whether it will push equally for freer world trade remains to be seen. The Nine agree to have a common external tariff against other countries, including the United States, but the agreement says nothing about the level of that external tariff. This situation confronts American business firms and American trade policy with a new challenge. American export markets inside the Common Market are in serious danger, because our products must pay the common external tariff while competitive products made within the Common Market pay no tariff. Intra-Common-Market trade is booming and entire new patterns of trade are developing. Paris department-store counters are loaded with Italian fashions and shoes, German leather goods and housewares, Dutch clothing and pottery. The same is true in other cities throughout the Common Market. Thanks to reduced internal tariffs, prices on many basic items are dramatically lower throughout the Common Market area. A revolution of consumer buying habits is under way. The comparison is widely drawn with the mass consumer market that is the foundation of the American economy. We negotiate with the EEC on roughly equal terms.

America's response thus far has been a combination of private and public action. Many American companies have established plants or subsidiaries inside the Common Market, thus escaping the external tariff. Indeed, American investment by large multinational firms has grown so large that some European nations, especially France, have increasingly restricted U.S. investment there. The other U.S. response has been governmental—to bargain with the Common Market countries for lower tariffs against U.S. commodities (especially farm products) in exchange for larger European exports to the United States. Part of the fate of these negotiations will depend on Congress' response to the Nixon Administration's proposed Trade Reform Act of 1973, mentioned above. It is still too early to tell what the outcome will be. U.S. trade expansion with Western Europe is interlinked with questions of international monetary reform (discussed in the following chapters) and political-military relationships.

REVIEW

For Analysis and Discussion

1. Recently, when France raised her import barriers against some U.S. farm products, the United States raised its tariff on French brandy. Who gained and who lost by these actions? Are such retaliatory tariff increases good for the country making them?
2. What is the fallacy in the "Petition of the Candlemakers" for protection against the sun? Is the same fallacy present in other arguments for protective tariffs?
3. List the factors that explain the high wages received by American workers in the steel and chemical industries. Which, if any, would be affected and in which direction, if American tariffs were raised on steel and chemicals?
4. Presidents Kennedy and Nixon both urged that workers and firms presently protected by tariffs receive government subsidies for retraining and compensation for loss of markets when U.S. tariffs are reduced? Do you agree? Why?
5. Are there any industries in the United States today that seem clearly to deserve tariff protection as "infant industries"?
6. One leading economist has argued: "Removal of tariffs is clearly desirable, but the associated transition effects would be tolerable only in times of prosperity and in the absence of monopolistic restrictions in the more efficient American industries." Can you explain this apparently paradoxical statement?
8. Can you suggest any ways whereby, in a period of depression, the United States could raise its tariffs against foreign goods and avoid probable retaliation?

CASE 25

Imports: Bane or Boon?

The following are excerpts from a statement of I.W. Abel, President, United Steelworkers and Industrial Union Department, AFL-CIO, in *Tariff and Trade Proposals,* Hearings before the House Ways and Means Committee, on May 22, 1970, (pp. 1776–1781):

"We are here today because many of our members have already been hurt by imports, and many more live in apprehension, with the fear that in the not too distant future they too will be elbowed out of a job by the growing flood of foreign imports. We are here to voice these deep-rooted concerns.

"The world has changed. . . .

"First, there has been a dramatic revival of the war-devastated economies, a revival which we helped. Japan is a most remarkable example of this recovery. . . . The Japanese expect—in five years—to be producing more steel than the United States. . . .

"Another change is that technology has become international. It has become international because of improved communications and a sharp rise in United States investment in foreign countries—investment not only of money but of American technology.

"Another startling new phenomenon on the world scene is the multinational corporation. . . .

"As Fortune magazine has pointed out, these multinational firms like to buy cheap and sell dear—producing where costs are lowest and selling where prices are highest. The operations of American firms on the Mexican side of the border are another example of the problem of the multinational corporation. . . . They take advantage of Mexican law for its border area, U.S. tariff regulations, and low-wage Mexican labor, then ship the goods back to the United States, and sell them at U.S. prices. . . .

"To put it bluntly, these American corporations which use components and complete units made overseas—at sweatshop wages—and sold here with no reduction in price—commit a kind of fraud against the American consumer.

"In some circles, efforts are made to perpetuate the myth that American consumers benefit from such arrangements. But the truth is that in most cases, American consumers pay American prices. . . .

"Delegate after delegate at our (last) convention arose to describe the impact of these new world trade conditions upon his members. . . .

"In the textile industry, for example, we learned that imports more than doubled between 1964 and 1968. Today, the textile industry is up against the wall because of imports. The glass workers, too, are seriously concerned about imports. In one Pennsylvania county alone imports have caused the loss of 1,500 jobs in the county's glass industry. . . .

"Also in the electronics field, some 60 percent of black and white TV sets, and 17 percent of the color TV sets last year were made in foreign countries, and virtually all transistors are now made overseas. . . .

"The shoe workers, like the textile workers, are living in a nightmare of an increasing flood of imports that is washing out factories and jobs. Since 1955, the number of foreign-made shoes imported in 1969 were equivalent to the exportation and the loss of 65,000 job opportunities. . . .

"Some will make the charge that we are putting on the cloak of protectionism. Those who do so fail to recognize that old concepts and labels of "free trade" and "protectionism" have become obsolete. They have been outdated in this new world of managed national economies, international technocracy, multinational corporations and record U.S. investment overseas.

"I would also say to those who charge us with seizing the banner of protectionism: we still believe in a healthy expansion of trade with other nations. But our support for the balanced expansion of trade does not mean we believe in the promotion of private greed at public expense. It does not mean that such expansion of trade should undercut unfairly the wages and working standards of Americans. . . .

"That international trade is a two-way street is a truism which has long been neglected. The very countries, like Japan, which most strongly criticize our movement toward import restrictions, themselves are among the most protectionist in the world. That is, we open our markets to them while they close their markets to us.

"Here are a few suggestions:

1. Industries, large and small, which have been seriously hurt by unrestricted tides of foreign imports include: textiles, including man-made fibers and rugs; autos, radios, TVs, and other consumer electronic products; shoes, sheet glass, furniture, pianos,

apparel, ceramics, stainless steel flatware, and so forth. The list is by no means complete, and it is growing.

We believe these industries to be of basic importance to the American economy. We believe our more seriously affected industries must be assured of at least a modest share in the total economy's growth. This means that future import increases in such industries must be regulated and that their import growth, whether from foreign firms or from U.S.-owned offshore production facilities, must be proportionate to the total growth of the domestic market. . . .

Sound policy also means we must adopt measures to limit and tax the export of capital which finances the establishment, acquisition or expansion of U.S.-owned manufacturing facilities abroad.

2. Truth-in-import labeling legislation to identify the manufacturer and nation of origin of all imported products would serve an important purpose.

3. It is important that there be a clearly defined international crash program to quickly raise substandard wage levels to acceptable minimums, together with a longer range program to raise such wages closer to our own domestic legal minimums within prescribed periods of time. There is a clear need for the creation of international fair labor standards, and the U.S. Government should take aggressive leadership in such efforts. . . .

4. There should be more effective adjustment assistance for all workers displaced by a rise in imports, where it is a major or significantly contributing cause of such displacement. . . ."

Your congressman is a member of the House Ways and Means Committee. Do you advise him to accept or reject Mr. Abels's analysis and recommendations. Write him a letter explaining why. If you favor any of the recommendations, indicate what specific steps you believe Congress should take.

International Adjustments and the Balance of Payments

CHAPTER PREVIEW

CHAPTER FORTY

Domestic and international trade are essentially similar, but in foreign trade two different currencies are involved. This chapter explains first how international transactions are financed, and then how international economic adjustments occur under different international monetary systems.

FINANCING FOREIGN TRANSACTIONS

If you buy woolens from England, the English seller wants British pounds, not American dollars. You need to convert your dollars into pounds if you're going to buy his cloth. What do you do?

There is a continuous demand for this sort of currency conversion, and many big city banks stand ready to sell you pounds, or almost any other foreign currency, for dollars. If you go to your local bank to buy pounds, it will simply pass the transaction along to a big bank in the foreign-exchange business.

Suppose that you want to pay a Britisher £1,000 in British money for the woolen goods. You go to a bank, say the Chase Manhattan in New York, to buy 1,000 British pounds. The Chase Manhattan is a regular dealer in foreign currencies. It sells you the pounds at the going rate—assume it's £1 for $3. You pay the Chase Manhattan Bank $3,000 and get a special check, made out to the bearer, for £1,000. This special type of check is called "foreign exchange."

Then you send the check over to the British manufacturer. He takes it to his bank in London and gets his £1,000. His bank presents the check to the Chase Manhattan's London branch for payment, and the transaction is completed (except that we have omitted the small commission charged you by the Chase Manhattan on the deal). You have paid $3,000. The seller has received £1,000.[1]

The rate at which you can buy British pounds with American dollars is called the "exchange rate." When you buy pounds with dollars, you are purchasing foreign exchange. Foreign exchange is merely a claim on some foreign currency, and the rate of exchange is the number of units of one currency it takes to purchase one unit of another currency. If the franc–dollar exchange rate is 5 to 1, for example, then it takes five francs to buy one dollar; the price of one franc is twenty cents.

Like other prices, exchange rates are determined by supply and demand. Suppose American importers need large numbers of pounds to pay British manufacturers. When they try to buy these pounds with dollars, the increased demand will force up the price of pounds, say to $4 for £1. Conversely, when Britishers want to make heavy payments here, they buy dollars. This bids up the price of dollars, and the exchange rate moves toward $2 to £1.

This situation can readily be represented by a simple supply-and-demand diagram, as in Figure 40–1. With the solid supply and demand curves, the price of pounds is $3. If demand increases to *D′D′* (when Americans need more pounds to pay for their imports), the price of pounds goes up to $4, given the supply of pounds shown. Try for yourself to show the effect of an increased British demand for dollars to pay for movies imported from America.

There are always Americans buying British pounds with dollars, and Britishers buying dollars with pounds, which keeps things reasonably well in balance on both sides of the Atlantic.

[1]This example is not exactly accurate. However, the actual procedure, though sometimes more complicated, follows the same general principle.

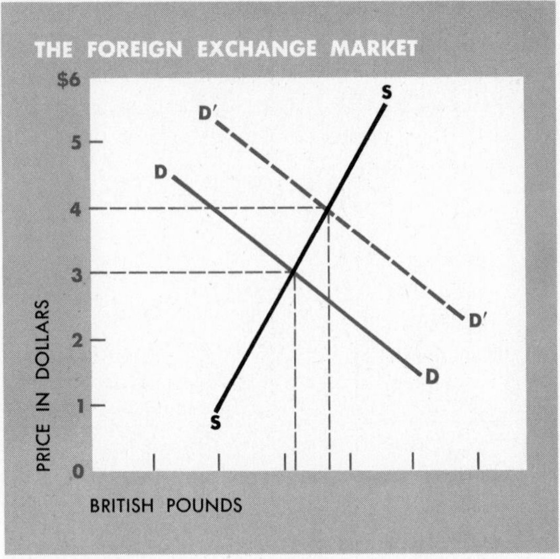

Figure 40–1

The supply and demand for British pounds looks just like the supply and demand for a commodity.

In both London and New York there are regular foreign-exchange markets, in which foreign-exchange dealers buy and sell foreign currencies. As long as the total demand for pounds in New York equals the total demand for dollars in London, all transactions can be settled without any change in the exchange rate or any shipment of gold. Here again the marketplace does the complex job more or less automatically.

EXCHANGE RATES

Freely Fluctuating Exchange Rates

Exchange rates are set by the demand for, and the supply of, the currencies in question, **except** where rates are somehow fixed by government decree. In a completely "free" exchange market, exchange rates would fluctuate freely ("float") in response to varying demands for the different currencies. With fluctuating demands for currencies, swings in foreign-exchange rates could be expected—remember that capital movements affect exchange rates just as do merchandise exports and imports. But as long as supply and demand for the various currencies remained in balance, stable exchange rates would prevail.

Exchange Rates under the Gold Standard

For many years before World War I and again during the 1920s, most important countries were "on the gold standard." During these periods, no direct control was exercised over exchange rates by governments, but through the gold standard exchange fluctuations were held within narrow bounds.

Under the gold standard, each monetary unit "contained" (was convertible into) a fixed number of grains of gold. For example, the prewar dollar was 23.22 grains and the prewar British pound 113 grains of fine gold. Thus, the pound had 4.86 times as much gold as the dollar, a relationship that established a par of exchange between the currencies. And remember, from Chapter 16, that domestically the money supply varied roughly in proportion to changes in each nation's gold stock.

Under these circumstances, suppose there was an increased demand for dollars, which sent the price of dollars up so that £1 would buy less than $4.86 (say the exchange rate moved to 1 to 4.80). Then, instead of buying dollars and getting only $4.80 for £1, Britishers could simply convert their pounds into gold, send the gold to America, and there get $4.86 for the 113 grains of fine gold in each pound. Obviously, therefore, the exchange rate could not vary far from 4.86 to 1 or gold would be shipped instead of foreign exchange being used at all. Actually, shipping costs and interest losses in transit made it unprofitable to ship gold unless the exchange rate varied more than three cents either way from the 4.86 to 1 ratio. Hence, exchange rates could fluctuate within these "gold points" of 4.89 and 4.83, but no farther.

This stability of exchange rates was a great boon to international traders. They always knew just what foreign currencies would cost to make payments abroad and just what price they could get for foreign currencies received. Such stable exchanges may prevail without the gold standard, but as soon as one country is off the gold standard the guarantee of stable rates vanishes.

The International Gold-Reserve Standard

In the Great Depression of the 1930s, every major nation went off the gold standard. Facing massive unemployment, each chose to go its own way, refusing to be bound by international gold flows. Exchange rates fluctuated. Country after country imposed controls on capital outflows to conserve its scarce gold. Together with widespread tariff increases designed to stimulate domestic employment, these capital controls increasingly stifled international trade and lending, without, in retrospect, significantly helping any of the nations participating in the economic warfare.

Following World War II, everyone agreed that the folly of the 1930s must not be repeated. International cooperation, beginning with the Bretton Woods Conference of 1944, reintroduced stable exchange rates among the major currencies and gradually reduced restrictions on capital outflows. Finally in 1958, substantially free convertibility of currencies at fixed exchange rates was restored among the major nations of the "free world." Some controls over capital movements still existed, and no major nation restored the prewar gold standard with its rigid linkage of the domestic money supply and economic conditions to international gold flows. But most major currencies were made freely convertible into gold at fixed prices, and rates of exchange among major free-world countries were fixed by international agreements, based on the dollar as the key currency. Gold was exchanged freely among central banks in settlement of international balances.

But for numerous reasons (to be explored in Chapter 41), some nations ran persistent deficits and others persistent surpluses. During the 1960s, large U.S. deficits piled up gold and dollars in Western Europe and Japan. Thus, in 1968, the leading central banks modified this arrangement by agreeing they would neither buy nor sell gold to private holders or producers. This substantially fixed the amount of *monetary* gold in the Western world and shut off private speculation in gold vis-à-vis the central banks, but retained free exchange of gold among central banks and fixed exchange rates among those currencies. The move was coupled with an important parallel agreement to supplement gold with a new international reserve (Special Drawing Rights) created cooperatively by international agreement, much as new domestic reserves are created by the Federal Reserve in the United States.

This arrangement was called an "international gold-reserve standard." Gold served as an international reserve for each country, which could use it to meet its international payments. Exchange rates were fixed by international agreement and the various currencies were convertible into gold at fixed prices for official settlements, as under the old gold standard. But nations did not necessarily tie their domestic monetary policies to gold flows, nor did central banks guarantee to buy gold from or sell it to private individuals and businesses.

But U.S. deficits continued, and speculators transferred large amounts of dollars to Europe and Japan, expecting the value of the dollar to fall vis-à-vis other currencies. As foreign nations accumulated some $80 billion and the U.S. gold stock fell to $10 billion, in 1973 the United States declared it would no longer convert those dollars into gold, even for foreign central banks. At least until the international monetary system is further reformed, the dollar is not now convertible into gold and most major foreign currencies are free to float vis-à-vis the dollar. More details in Chapter 41.

INTERNATIONAL ECONOMIC ADJUSTMENTS

International trade and capital flows link the economies of the world together. It is important to understand these linkages in the modern world. For they have a major impact on most economies, and play an important role in the United States, even though foreign trade totals only about 6 percent of our GNP. Consider first the international adjustment process in a simple case involving only commodity trade, initially under the gold standard and then under floating exchanges; and finally introduce international capital movements and the entire balance of payments.

Under the Gold Standard

The full gold standard provided a more or less automatic procedure for keeping different countries "in balance" with one another. Suppose the United States begins to buy more goods and services from France without a corresponding increase in exports to France, both countries being on the gold standard. The United States will need an increasing number of francs to pay for its imports, and francs will become more expensive in terms of dollars. But as soon as the dollar-franc rate moves to the gold point, U.S. importers will begin to ship gold rather than francs to pay for their additional imports from France.

What happens when gold moves from America to France? In America there is less gold backing for the money supply; currency and credit are contracted. In the absence of offsetting action, this movement will mean depressed prices, costs, and incomes here. In France, the reverse effect occurs. The new gold provides more bank deposits and more excess reserves. Currency and credit expand, with rising incomes, costs, and prices.

As these effects proceed, it will become harder for U.S. importers to buy from France, and easier for the French to buy here. Frenchmen have larger incomes to spend on U.S. goods, and prices of U.S. goods are falling. Conversely, we have lower incomes to spend on French goods and French prices are rising. This combination gradually shuts off the excess of U.S. imports from France, pulling the exports and imports of the two countries back into balance. When exports and imports are restored to balance, the gold flow ceases and equilibrium has been restored in both American and French balances of payments.

But remember that gold flows tend to bring equilibrium only if they are permitted to affect prices, costs, and incomes in the countries involved. If central banks offset these gold flows their equilibrating effects are negated.

Under Fluctuating ("Floating") Exchanges

How do international adjustments take place when exchange rates are free to fluctuate? Assume the same United States–France situation as before, with an American trade deficit. As before, Americans will buy francs to pay for their imports, and will thereby drive up the exchange rate—that is, the cost of francs in terms of dollars. French goods become more expensive to us, and our goods become cheaper to France. French incomes rise because of their increased exports, without any such corresponding increase in America. These circumstances will gradually cut down on U.S. purchases from France, and will increase French purchases from us, until finally exports and imports between the two countries are restored to balance. As under the gold standard, there is an automatic tendency for the payments between the two countries to be brought back into equilibrium.

But the adjustment process is restricted to a smaller segment of each economy in the flexible-exchange case. The rising price of francs effectively raises the price of French exports to us, but it does so without raising French domestic prices generally in terms of dollars, as a gold inflow would have done by expanding the French money supply under the gold standard. Similarly, the falling dollar-exchange rate effectively lowers the price of U.S. exports to French buyers, but it does so without imposing deflationary pressure on the whole U.S. economy, as a gold outflow from the United States would have done.

All this makes a floating exchange standard sound very attractive. But it has one very important drawback. International traders and investors have to live in a world of uncertainty about the rates at which they convert their foreign receipts into domestic currency. More on this problem in Chapter 41.

Under the International Gold-Reserve Standard

How do adjustments to eliminate disequilibrium occur under the international gold-reserve standard? The answer is not simple, and we shall mainly postpone it until the next chapter that deals with current balance-of-payments problems. But the central points can be outlined here.

Suppose the same U.S.–French case, with U.S. imports exceeding exports. The deficit in the U.S. balance of payments will again lead to gold being transferred to France. But now the United States need not accept a deflationary contraction of her money supply, nor France an inflationary expansion of hers unless each country feels this would fit in with its domestic stabilization goals. Each nation attempts to balance its international and domestic goals.

A big country like the United States, if its gold reserves are large and its international trade is a small part of GNP, can afford to give dominant weight to domestic goals for a long time in the face of a balance-of-payments deficit and gold outflows. Smaller countries that depend heavily on foreign trade have little option; their prices and costs must be closely in line with balance-of-payments needs or they will quickly exhaust their gold reserves and be unable to pay their bills. But either way the international adjustment process is less direct and predictable than under either the gold standard or fluctuating exchange rates. The pressures for international adjustment build up on any country that continually runs a balance-of-payments deficit, and the nation may eventually run out of reserves to pay its international bills, as the United States nearly did in the early 1970s. But it is vital to recognize that any nation may postpone adjustment to international pressures as long as its reserves hold out, in order to pursue its own domestic policies.

CAPITAL MOVEMENTS, RESERVES, AND THE ADJUSTMENT PROCESS

Now introduce capital movements into the picture. U.S. investment abroad involves foreign payments, just as when we buy goods abroad. If Westinghouse decides to build a plant in the Netherlands, for example, it must have the Dutch guilders to pay its bills there. It uses dollars to buy guilders. If an individual American buys Royal Dutch Shell stock on the Dutch stock exchange, the same is true. In both cases the Dutch end up with more dollars.

Long-term capital investment tends to move in response to long-run profit prospects. In the postwar world, such capital flows have been enormous. U.S. long-term investment abroad totalled $120 billion in 1972, most of it made since World War II. Such capital transfers do not fluctuate sharply. However, individuals, businesses and banks also shift *short-term* funds from nation to nation in search of the highest interest rates, and these shifts are often both huge and unpredictable. A big corporation or bank may have hundreds of millions of dollars in cash, and the interest gain from a difference of only a fraction of a percent for a few days is large. Some estimates place the total amount of such "hot money" in the modern world at over $200 billion, vastly more than the international reserves of any nation.

A rumor that a currency is "weak" (likely to depreciate vis-à-vis other currencies), or rising interest rates elsewhere, may thus trigger large short-term capital outflows. If the country has large reserves, it may simply pay out the gold or other currencies involved in the transfer. But few countries have large enough reserves to meet such hot money drains. Thus the result is likely to be either a suspension of gold payments (if the country is on the gold standard), or a sharp fall in the nation's currency vis-à-vis others.

Day-to-day transactions in exchange markets push the prices of different currencies up and down vis-à-vis one another. Under fixed-exchange-rate systems, it is the job of each central bank to intervene if the price of its currency deviates very far from parity. This it does by buying or selling its own currency or other currencies it holds as part of its international reserves.

For example, suppose there is a heavy demand for dollars by pound-holders in London, and the price of pounds vis-à-vis dollars falls below its parity of $2.40, say to $2.38. Then the Bank of England would "protect" the pound by buying pounds with dollars it holds as part of its international reserves. Conversely, if the pound were to rise above parity in the open market, the Bank of England would sell pounds, accumulating dollars or some other foreign currency.

In order to protect its currency in a fixed-rate system, each central bank must have a big enough international reserve in other currencies, gold, or SDRs, to be able to buy its own currency and maintain its price at parity if need be. If a nation's balance of payments is near equilibrium, normally market forces will keep its currency near parity; private purchases and sales will roughly balance off. But if its balance of payments is in persistent deficit, a nation's currency will "weaken"—that is, its price will tend to fall. Thus, its central bank will need substantial reserves to keep the currency at parity. If a nation runs out of reserves and other nations are unwilling to accumulate more of its currency, it can no longer keep its currency at par, and must either borrow reserves temporarily or "devalue" (that is, let the price of its currency fall). Of course, if the nation's currency is freely floating, market forces are permitted to determine its exchange value, and the central bank does not intervene.

THE UNITED STATES—WORLD CREDITOR

Growing nations tend to pass through four stages of economic development. Each produces a different payments position for temporary balance-of-payments equilibrium.

1. **Early Borrower.** A less-developed country often borrows heavily abroad to obtain the capital goods it needs to develop its natural resources. For example, until about 1873 the United States apparently was a substantial capital importer from Europe. Imports of supplies, machinery, and consumption goods exceeded exports. In this stage, the trade balance must be "unfavorable" (imports must exceed exports) if the needed goods and supplies are to be obtained, and this "unfavorable" balance is covered by borrowing.

2. **Mature Debtor.** After the 1870s, debt repayment by the United States began to exceed new borrowing, though we were still a heavy debtor. In this stage, exports tend to exceed imports—the trade balance is "favorable." Our net export balance transferred the real goods to other nations as we paid off our debts. As in stage 1, money transfers are only the first step. It is the real transfer of goods and services that counts.

3. **Early Creditor.** Stage 3 is entered when the nation shifts over to a net creditor basis—when total investments abroad exceed foreign investments here. World War I and the 1920s thrust the United States abruptly into this stage, as we made heavy loans to our European allies. Government and private lending during and after World War II repeated the World War I experience with billions upon billions of dollars. Today, the United States is the great creditor nation of the world. In this stage, a continued export surplus is to be expected. This surplus transfers abroad in real form the loans we make as we increase our creditor position.

4. **Mature Creditor.** In stage 4, the creditor nation's outstanding loans are so great that current income on foreign investments more than offsets the net new loans being made abroad. In this stage, the trade balance must shift to an import surplus in order to transfer to the mature creditor nation the excess of its current return on investment over new loans being made abroad. England was a mature creditor early in this century; whether the United States is now on the edge of that stage is debated by the experts. Our flow of interest and profits from overseas investments is growing rapidly, but so are our new investments abroad. Also, foreigners are investing large amounts in the United States, partially offsetting U.S. investments abroad. Only the years ahead will tell.

As a nation passes through these four stages, a changing trade balance is normal and essential. Whether a "favorable" balance of *trade* is in fact favorable depends basically on how well it fits in with the country's overall balance-of-payments position. Severe disequilibrium will result if the trade balance is maintained (by tariffs or other controls) in a position unsympathetic to general balance-of-payments equilibrium requirements.

REVIEW

Concepts to Remember

This chapter adds a few more important concepts to the list at the end of Chapter 38.

- foreign exchange
- exchange rate
- flexible ("floating") exchange rates
- devaluation
- international gold reserve standard
- controlled exchange rates
- balance-of payments equilibrium

For Analysis and Discussion

1. Explain how balance-of-payments disequilibrium tended to be eliminated under the gold standard, with fixed exchange rates. How is disequilibrium eliminated in a system of flexible exchange rates?
2. Using Figure 40–1, trace through the effects of the following, beginning from the equilibrium shown by *DD* and *SS:*
   a. General Motors decides to buy a British automobile plant to get production facilities there.
   b. British students come to study in America.
   c. British citizens decide to buy General Electric stock in America at the same time as American imports from England decline.
3. Suppose that you and many others decide to travel to France next summer. Trace through carefully the effect your trip might have on dollar–franc rates, gold flows, and prices in each country under:
   a. An international gold standard.
   b. A flexible exchange-rate system.
4. Domestically, free-price movements serve to equilibrate supply and demand in the markets concerned. Since foreign exchange rates are substantially frozen under the gold standard, how can the gold standard be said to be an international equilibrating system?
5. The U.S. official international reserves of gold and foreign currencies in 1973 were about $13 billion. Yet potential "hot money" dollar balances were said to be many times that amount. How does this help explain the U.S. move to floating rates in 1973?

Current Balance-of-Payments Problems

CHAPTER PREVIEW

CHAPTER FORTY-ONE

In recent years, the "weak" dollar and the U.S. balance-of-payments deficit have been front-page news. Are the predictions of impending disaster overdone? How worried, if at all, should we be? Above all, what should we do about it?

One of the first things to recognize is that economic problems change rapidly. Two decades ago, the big international problem was the "dollar shortage" and too much of the world's gold accumulated in the United States. As this is written, it is the U.S. payments deficit and the sagging dollar. By the time you read this, the problem may have changed again. A brief look at history, therefore, is a useful background for understanding the problems we face today.

THE DOWNFALL OF THE GOLD STANDARD

Before 1914, the international gold standard ruled the international monetary scene. It was, in theory and to a substantial degree in practice, an "automatic" system. Central banks "managed" the money supply to a limited extent, but gold was the center of a "religion" of money. It was accepted by most economists and the public alike as an ultimate repository of value. In the rapidly-expanding, reasonably-flexible pre-1914 world, this gold standard supplied an important element of international-exchange stability, and the requisite domestic price and income adjustments were generally accomplished without excessively painful consequences.

The monetary disruptions of World War I were extreme. Wild inflations occurred in several European nations, serious inflation in all. Reestablishment of the international gold standard in the 1920s was thus fraught with difficulties. What should exchange rates be? Finally, new gold contents were prescribed for currencies in an endeavor to place these currencies in "equilibrium" balance-of-payments positions vis-à-vis the rest of the world. The Western world went back "on gold."

But the depression of the 1930s dealt the deathblow to the prewar gold standard. Losing gold in a period of growing unemployment meant even further deflationary contraction of national money supplies. First England in 1931, then most other major nations, decided this price was too high to pay. They "went off gold," devaluing their currencies relative to gold and to other currencies in order to avoid the domestic deflation implicit in adherence to the gold standard, and to encourage foreign purchases of their domestic products. The American dollar was devalued in 1934 to 59 percent of its earlier gold content. Eventually every major currency was devalued, exchange and capital movement controls were established, and domestic currencies were cut loose from gold flows.

In retrospect, three major factors led to the downfall of the gold standard:

1. The Great Depression of the 1930s made the domestic price of gold-standard orthodoxy too high to pay.

2. Downward cost-price rigidities served to aggravate the impact of price and income deflation, and to thwart the equilibrating forces previously at work under the gold-standard system. Unions, industrial monopolies, agricultural groups—all contributed to holding up prices when incomes fell in the depression.

3. With waning faith in the gold-standard religion, and with growing political instability, capital flights to "safer" countries became common. Huge "hot-money" drains were more than any nation could stand. The religion of gold worked admirably so long as no infidels entered the temple to whisper misgivings. Once doubt spread, however, capital flights never envisaged in a stable, well-behaved international system spelled doom to the gold standard in a rigid, depression-conscious world.

EXCHANGE DEPRECIATION AND EXCHANGE CONTROLS

Widespread desertion of the gold standard and currency devaluations failed to bring the results expected. One country acting alone could expand its exports by depreciation. But when everyone's currency was depreciated, the actions just offset one another.

In retrospect, thus, the main result of the competitive depreciation race of the 1930s was disruption of international trade and investment, widespread friction and ill will, and few important gains to any of the competitors. As with tariff increases, exchange depreciation was a "beggar-my-neighbor" attempt to shift unemployment to other nations. And it was doomed to defeat by the virtual certainty of retaliation.

As exchange depreciation failed to eliminate the unemployment that plagued the Western world, crosscurrents of conflict and cooperation were everywhere apparent in international economic relations. New types of exchange controls proliferated. Nations set their exchange rates at varying levels, searching for the one to maximize their gain from foreign trade. Many countries, especially Nazi Germany, "blocked" the use of foreign exchange received from their foreign sales, and rationed the foreign exchange received to control its expenditure. Nearly every major nation introduced controls over capital exports.

THE INTERNATIONAL MONETARY FUND

To the nations mapping peacetime reconstruction at the end of World War II, the international monetary disruption and conflict of the 1930s were bitter memories. There was little sentiment for restoring the old gold standard. But there was widespread agreement on the need for reasonable exchange stability and for reduced restrictions on international trade and capital movements.

In 1945, some forty nations established the International Monetary Fund to help attain these goals; the total membership is now over a hundred.[1] The Fund consists of about $30 billion of gold and member-country currencies made available for stabilization activities in accordance with the Fund's charter. Each country's contribution was based on its national income; the United States put up about one-third of the total. As world trade has grown, the size of the fund has been increased three times. Voting control over the fund is roughly in proportion to contributions to its capital.

The primary operating purposes of the Fund were to help member nations reestablish free convertibility among their currencies, and to maintain exchange-rate stability, coupled with reasonable flexibility to make any necessary long-run adjustments. In this respect, the philosophy of the fund differs substantially from that of the old gold standard, whose keynote was exchange stability at all costs.

The Fund is intended to help member countries meet temporary exchange deficits only—to give them time to correct balance-of-payments maladjustments without being forced to adopt repressive measures under exceptional strains. The Fund can thus lend foreign currencies to a country that is caught temporarily short of exchange. Whereas previously the only likely alternative would have been devaluation or imposition of exchange controls, with the Fund's assistance such acts may be avoided. The Fund stands ready to lend to any member country up to one-fourth of its quota in any year, if the proposed use of the exchange is in keeping with the Fund's stated objectives.

If any country faces a lasting disequilibrium in its balance of payments, the Fund tries to play a different role, helping to arrange consultations among the major countries concerned, looking toward more fundamental adjustments.

The Fund does not prohibit member-country controls over capital movements. Most participants agreed that hot-money movements may be too disruptive to tolerate, and retained their freedom to control them individually.

The Fund appears to be a useful step toward international monetary collaboration after the disastrous decade of the 1930s. It has repeatedly helped to tide member countries over temporary balance-of-payments pressures that otherwise might have generated major international financial crises or disruptive domestic deflations. But it can work satisfactorily only in a relatively stable world, where cases of "fundamental disequilibrium" are rare. Indeed, member countries have already defied the Fund's regulations, devaluing their own currencies when they thought it essential, without the Fund's approval. Domestic economic goals have dominated nations' commitments to international monetary cooperation in such cases.[2]

[1] After participating in the planning, the Soviet-bloc countries did not join.

[2] Parallel to the International Monetary Fund, the same forty countries also established the $8 billion International Bank for Reconstruction and Development. It was set up to facilitate foreign lending for postwar reconstruction and for development of less-developed areas. The organization and management of the bank closely parallel those of the fund. The bank's operating head is from this country, in recognition of the United States' large contribution to the bank's capital and the dominant demand for dollar loans. There are now seventy member nations, and total capital is about $20 billion. In 1971, new loans to the less-developed economies totaled $1.8 billion.

Although the IBRD may lend out its own capital, it operates primarily through two other channels—attaching its guarantee to private loans, and borrowing funds in the various member countries to finance its loans. For example, if Peru wants a loan to develop its industries and plans to spend most of the loan in the United States, the bank will either try to arrange a direct loan for Peru from American lenders, attaching its own guarantee to the loan, or it will float a bond issue in the American market to obtain funds for the Peruvian loan. In either case, the U.S. representative on the bank's board would have to approve, because every loan must be approved by the major country in which the loan is to be raised and spent, as well as by the bank's officers.

Special Drawing Rights

During the 1960s, the need for some collective means to increase international monetary reserves became increasingly clear. Newly mined gold became available erratically, and reliance on the U.S. balance-of-payments deficit was an obviously unsatisfactory way of obtaining reserves for other countries, as will be explained presently. Thus, in 1968, the leading free-world nations agreed to give the IMF power to create "Special Drawing Rights"—in essence, new international reserves (often called "paper gold") created outright, much as new money might be printed. Member countries can then draw their shares of these new reserves as needed. New SDRs can be created only by an 85 percent vote of the fund's shareholders, which gives both the United States and the Common Market countries (if they vote together) a veto over new issues. Countries' quotas correspond roughly to the general fund borrowing quotas (the United States' is now about 25 percent of the total). But SDRs, unlike regular loans, need not be repaid to the fund. About $3 billion of SDRs were issued in each of the first three years, beginning in 1970, with the expectation that more would be approved as needed. But no SDRs need be created if reserves are adequate.

U.S. FOREIGN LENDING

A major development of the postwar financial world has been the massive growth of U.S. lending abroad. Our large postwar payments deficits have been attributable mainly to our heavy private foreign investments and to government loans and foreign-aid programs (including military aid) since we have had an export surplus on trade and services consistently until 1972. U.S. investors have acquired ownership of a huge volume of assets abroad—factories, oil refineries, assembly plants. Thus, it is important to look carefully at international capital movements if we are to understand recent international economic events.

Figure 41–1 shows how U.S. investment abroad has burgeoned since 1929. The three lower areas in each bar are direct American investments. The area at the top is investment in foreign securities, including short-term investments. Even allowing for inflation, the rise has been phenomenal.

Figure 41–2 shows the picture in terms of annual new U.S. investment abroad and annual earnings on our investments abroad. The earnings bars show that our earnings each year on investments abroad now about equal our new investments abroad. Foreign investments are profitable business. As with domestic firms, a big part of new U.S. investment abroad each year consists of plowing back earnings on the investments already there. About three-fourths of U.S. private investment since World War II has been in the developed nations (mainly Canada and Western Europe), about one-fourth in the less-developed economies.

Figure 41–2 also suggests a central fact about foreign lending. To collect earnings and amortization on loans and investments abroad, we must either accept payment through importing goods and services or be prepared continually to reinvest the principal and earnings abroad. (Remember the early and mature creditor positions from Chapter 40.) Government and private lending abroad has been a major factor in permitting us to continue our traditional export surplus of goods and services. If we ever stop our annual net lending abroad, we will be able to collect our earnings and repayments on principal only by running a net import surplus of goods and services.

RECENT INTERNATIONAL MONETARY DEVELOPMENTS

What kind of international monetary system has evolved out of these circumstances, and what is the role of the dollar in it? To answer, we need to review one more piece of history, the period since World War II, with particular focus on the dollar and the U.S. balance of payments.

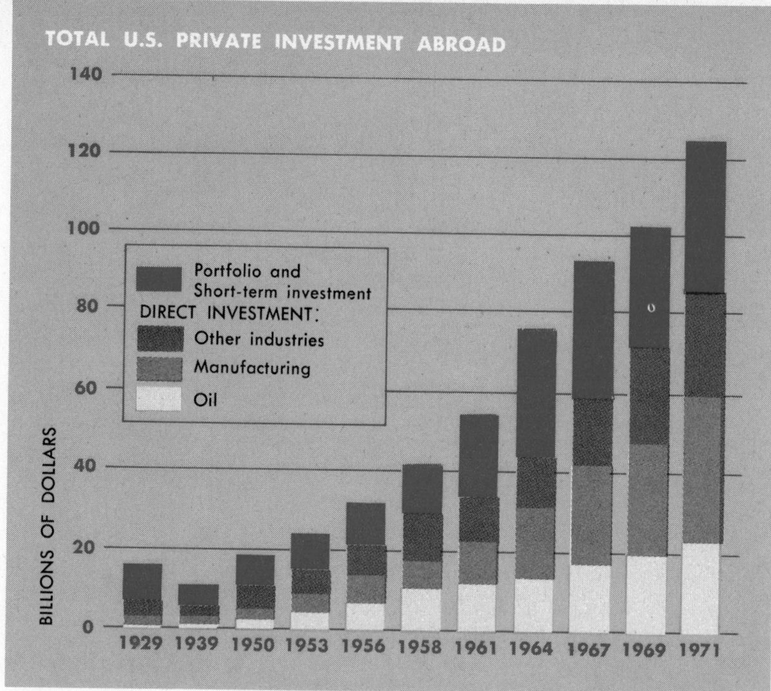

Figure 41–1

Since the 1930s, U.S. private investment abroad has soared. Manufacturing and petroleum are the biggest industry groups, but investments have been widely diversified. (Source: U.S. Department of Commerce.)

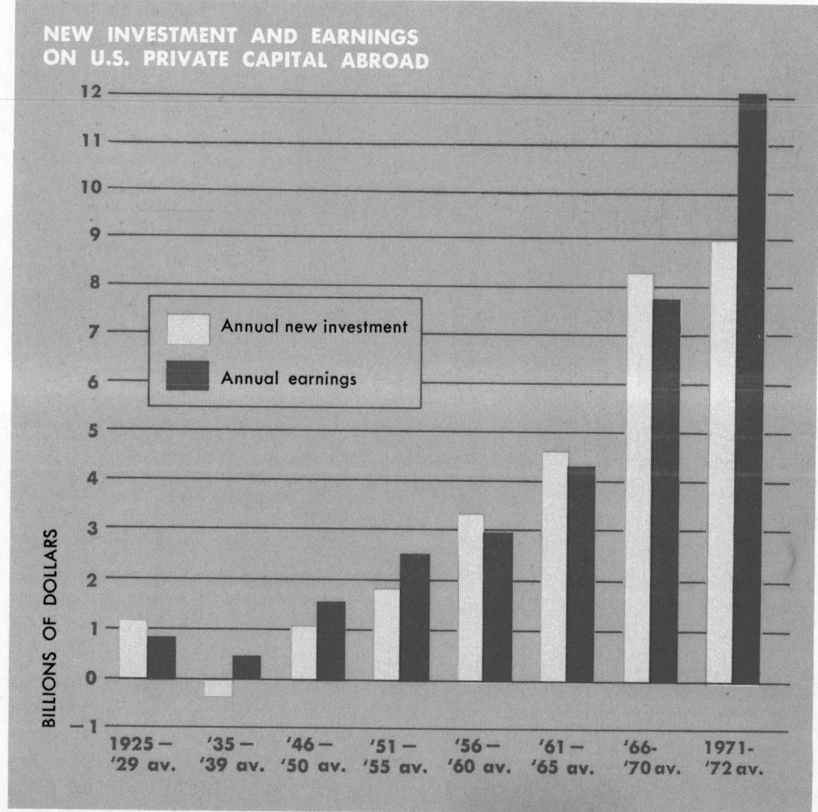

Figure 41–2

Annual new U.S. private investment abroad has grown rapidly, but returns on such investments abroad have grown even faster in recent years. (Source: U.S. Department of Commerce.)

The Post-World War II "Dollar Shortage"

Western Europe, Russia, and Japan emerged from World War II tired, physically devastated, with their foreign assets depleted, and heavily in debt. The United States emerged powerful, prosperous, unbombed, and a massive international creditor. Our real GNP more than doubled under the pressures of war from the depression of the late 1930s, so that we not only provided a large portion of the war material for our allies but simultaneously substantially raised the American standard of living in terms of consumer goods between 1940 and 1946. Until our allies used up their ability to pay, we sold war material and civilian supplies to them, and later provided many of them on loans and "lend-lease," rather than as gifts or our contributions to the common war. Thus, they ended the war heavily in debt to us.

In 1946 the reconstruction needs of Europe, Russia, and Japan were enormous. The unscathed American economy offered vast productive power to meet these needs. The resulting "dollar shortage" dominated the international scene. No nation seemed to have enough dollars to pay for the goods and services it needed from America. The Marshall Plan, under which we extended billions in reconstruction aid to allied nations, was one major answer to helping foreign nations rebuild and to alleviating this dollar shortage during the postwar years. Our exports of goods and services soared. But our total balance of payments was persistently in deficit, reflecting our large investments and government aid abroad.

Thus, each year foreign nations received more payments from the United States than they made to us. With the option of taking gold or accumulating dollar balances, they mainly chose dollars through the 1950s. The dollar was better than gold. It could be freely exchanged for gold at $35 an ounce; one could earn interest on dollar balances held in New York banks or invested in short-term U.S. securities; much of what nations wanted to buy was available in the United States and dollars were needed to pay; and throughout the free world dollars were as acceptable as gold.

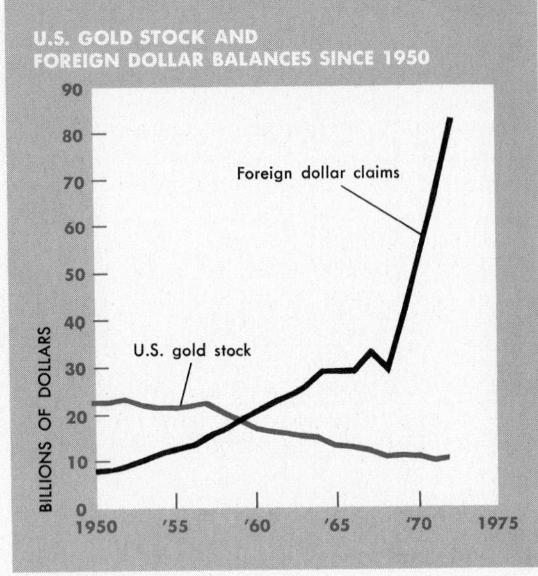

Figure 41–3

Since 1950, foreigners and foreign governments have accumulated huge holdings of U.S. dollars and short-term claims on dollars. They have also taken much of our World War II gold stock. (Source: Federal Reserve Board.)

Figure 41–3 shows the steady accumulation of short-term dollar balances by foreign nations after 1950 and the gradual decline in the U.S. gold stock as foreign nations took some payments in gold.

Dollar Shortage to Dollar Glut

By the mid-1950s, the rehabilitation of Europe and Japan was substantially complete, and their economies were booming. But the U.S. payments deficit continued. Foreign nations, with their own international-reserve balances substantially rebuilt, continued to hold growing dollar balances, but they also began to take increasing amounts of gold. Although the

United States was still carrying the major burden of defense spending for the free world and of providing economic aid to the less-developed nations, increasing concern was voiced abroad over our continuing large payments deficit. International bankers and conservatives at home warned of dire dangers to the dollar and that we must "put our house in order" if we were to maintain confidence in the dollar and avoid a crisis in our international situation. Specifically, they urged tighter money and fiscal restraint in spite of intermittent slack in the U.S. economy.

Since 1960, the dollar has been subject to growing criticism at home and abroad, as U.S. payments deficits continued and the stock of dollars held abroad grew steadily. Our gold stock eroded to about $10 billion by the end of the decade, and Figure 43–3 shows the enormous increase in dollar balances held by foreigners during the late 1960s and early 1970s. The dollar shortage of a decade earlier had become a dollar glut. Foreign central banks, which had long sought more dollars as the world's "key" currency, now had more than they wanted.

The International Gold-and-Dollar-Reserve Standard

Under the international monetary system that evolved during the 1950s and 1960s (the international gold-and-dollar-reserve standard), most nations held both gold and dollars as their basic international reserves, with the two freely convertible into one another. The international reserves for the world were thus supplied by gold and by short-term dollar balances, the latter produced, in effect, by U.S. international payments deficits. The very U.S. international deficits that were so often criticized were thus the source of about one-third of the Western world's entire basic international monetary reserves.

The United States thus, without conscious planning, became the banker to the free world. The dollar became the "key," or "reserve," currency of that world. It was critical to this arrangement that dollars be freely convertible into gold by official holders, even though in the United States and some other nations gold was not available domestically in exchange for currency. In many nations—for example, France and Switzerland—any large holder who had dollars could convert them into gold—by first converting the dollars into (say) francs at the fixed exchange rate and then buying gold with his francs. This would in turn, reduce the Bank of France's gold stock and build up its supply of dollars, so that the Bank of France was likely to exchange some of its increased dollars for gold from the United States. Thus, in essence, under the gold-dollar reserve system of the 1960s, foreign dollar-holders could demand gold in exchange on short notice. Figure 41–3 shows how far our short-term dollar liabilities exceeded our gold holdings. To many, it seemed that we were at the mercy of foreign dollar-holders.

The Two-Tier Gold System and SDRs

In 1968, two major modifications to the international gold-and-dollar reserve standard were agreed on by the major Western nations. First, SDRs were adopted to provide for rational, managed growth in international reserves, as was noted above. Second, repeated speculative runs on the dollar (conversions of dollar balances into gold) emphasized the basic instability of the prevailing system, and the leading nations agreed to stop buying and selling gold to private holders and miners. This meant that private speculators could no longer count on getting gold for their dollars or other major currencies, but gold was continued as an official international reserve, freely exchanged by the major central banks to settle international balances at the established price of $35 per ounce. The amount of official monetary gold was thus substantially fixed at the amount held by the central banks, with additions to reserves to be provided mainly by SDRs, once the dollar deficit was eliminated.

This was called a "two-tier" gold system, be-

"Then it's agreed. Until the dollar firms up, we let the clamshell float." (*Drawing by Ed Fisher; © 1971. The New Yorker Magazine, Inc.*)

cause gold held by the central banks was fixed in amount and price ($35 per ounce), while all other gold became in effect just another commodity, to bring whatever price market supply and demand might set.

Dollar Devaluation, Inconvertibility, and Floats

While the two-tier gold system worked well in insulating central banks from the whims of private gold speculators, the U.S. payments deficit rose, not fell, following 1968. Conversely, other nations (especially West Germany and Japan) ran large surpluses. Rumors of dollar devaluation and of mark and yen upward revaluation spread. There were repeated speculative "runs" on the dollar, in which private dollar-holders converted their funds into other currencies (especially German marks and Japanese yen) that were expected to be valued upward relative to the dollar. These speculators included large corporations, banks, and wealthy individuals in the United States and abroad, as well as Middle-Eastern oil-rich governments and sheiks. In 1971, the German central bank had to buy up over $5 billion in only three days to keep the mark from rising above its agreed parity with the dollar, and in 1973 even larger sums were shifted into marks and yen in speculation that the dollar would be devalued again.

Under these pressures, the leading Western nations twice agreed, in 1971 and 1973, to President Nixon's proposals that the dollar in fact be devalued, relative to other leading currencies and to gold, in order to halt speculative runs on the dollar, to check the unwanted flow of dollars into Germany and Japan, and to reduce the U.S. balance-of-payments deficit. In terms of gold, the dollar was devalued in total about 20 percent; that is, the official price of gold was raised from $35 to $42.22 an ounce, though this was a largely formal act, because in 1973 the

United States also announced that it would no longer convert dollars into gold even for other central banks. But the devaluation of the dollar vis-à-vis other leading currencies was real, increasing their buying power over U.S. exports and making their goods more expensive to us. Thus, although devaluation used to be defined primarily in terms of a currency's relationship to gold, this is no longer so; the more meaningful view of devaluation is directly in terms of other currencies. Note that devaluation of the second sort can occur, quite irrespective of what is done about the official price of gold.

Last, as part of the revolutionary responses to the speculative currency runs of early 1973, most of the major Western trading nations agreed to let their currencies float, at least temporarily, against the dollar. Even the two dollar devaluations were not adequate to stop speculative shifts from dollars to other "strong" currencies, and foreign governments decided they were simply unwilling to continue buying such vast amounts of dollars to support agreed-on exchange parities. Their central banks no longer promised to maintain any set exchange parities against the dollar, and the dollar fell still further against strong currencies in Western Europe, especially the German mark.

Advocates of freely-floating exchanges viewed this as a great step forward. But most governments and their central banks were unwilling to go all the way to freely-floating rates. Though they were not obliged to do so, most continued to intervene in exchange markets to some extent to keep rates from fluctuating too widely. The price of a nation's currency seems too important to most nations, controlling as it does the nation's ability to export and import, to be left solely to private market forces. Thus, the floats following the 1973 announcements were mostly "dirty" floats, with some central bank intervention, not "clean" ones with rates left completely to market forces.[3]

[3]Over the postwar period, numerous runs developed against other currencies, especially the British pound and the French franc, sometimes ending in devaluations. But these speculations were less disruptive to the whole system than were attacks on the key currency, the dollar.

The international monetary system today is clearly in a state of transition—a system with the dollar incovertible and linked to other major currencies through a series of dirty floats, with the determinants of the total supply of international reserves uncertain, with exchange relationships among most major currencies also uncertain, and with the future role of gold to be decided. Clearly, both short-run stabilization and long-run reform are needed for the international monetary system.

THE U.S. PAYMENTS PROBLEM

The Chronic U.S. Payments Deficit

The chronic U.S. payments deficit during the 1960s and 1970s has clearly been one fundamental cause of the world's international monetary troubles. Why has this imbalance been so large and so persistent? There is no one simple answer, but a brief summary might look like this:

1. **U.S. Foreign Aid and Government Loans.** Since World War II, we have provided government direct aid and loans totaling over $140 billion to the rest of the world. Table 41–1 tells the story. This aid has had military, economic, and humanitarian goals, widely approved

TABLE 41–1
U.S. Government Foreign Aid, 1945–72

	(IN BILLIONS)
Nonmilitary aid	$ 56.4
Loans	32.3
Military aid	52.4
	$141.1

Source: U.S. Department of Commerce. Excludes IMF and World Bank operations.

by the American people. But the net result has been a vast outflow of dollars.

2. **U.S. Inflation.** Since World War II, U.S. inflation has pushed up prices and costs here, in some years rapidly. Such inflation, other things equal, of course worsens a nation's international competitive position. But over the period since 1950 our inflation has, on average, been less than in most European countries and in Japan. Thus, inflation here may have hurt our international position some, but it has not been the major factor.

3. **U.S. Private Investment Abroad.** The largest single private element contributing to our payments deficit has been the enormous outflow of private capital seeking profitable investment in Western Europe, the Americas, and Japan. These private investments obviously seemed economically sound to the investors, else they would not have been made. And in the long run, they produce a large countervailing flow of interest and dividends. But in the short run, their net effect is to increase the size of the U.S. payments deficit.

4. **Slower Productivity Growth Here Than Abroad.** Since World War II, productivity has grown at a spectacular rate in Japan, and rapidly in Western Europe. Our production technology over all is still ahead of theirs. But starting from a postwar low, their heavy new investment and rapid technological advance have rapidly reduced this gap, even though U.S. productivity has continued to grow at somewhat above its long-run rate. Thus, our overall international competitive position deteriorated, price- and cost-wise, especially in 1965–72. But remember that, even so, we had a substantial trade surplus every year until 1971.

5. **Lack of Confidence in the U.S. Economy and the Dollar.** Foreign capital will not be invested in the United States, either at long or short term, if foreigners do not have confidence in the American economy and the stability of the dollar. Over the postwar period as a whole, both the dollar and the American economy have been widely agreed to be the soundest in the world. But as our efforts to reduce our payments deficit fell short in the 1960s, criticism was widespread, and speculation against the dollar has clearly accounted for massive short-run capital outflows.

6. **An Overvalued Dollar.** Looking at all these factors and at the continuing U.S. payments deficit, in retrospect the U.S. dollar was clearly "overvalued" during the 1960s and early 1970s. That is, exchange rates between the dollar and other major currencies made it too hard for foreigners to buy American products and too easy for us to buy foreign products and to obtain foreign currencies for investment abroad. Whether the devaluations in 1971 and 1973 were enough, or too much, is debatable. The history of the next few years will tell.

The Total U.S. International Position

All this may lead you to suspect that the U.S. is internationally bankrupt and the dollar of dubious value. Far from it! The dollar is backed fundamentally by the powerful U.S. economy, the most efficient and productive in the world. And our total foreign assets, once we add in our vast long-term investments overseas, far exceed our total liabilities, as is shown by Table 41–2.

The United States is in much the position of any other banker. Though our basic position is excellent, our short-term liabilities substantially exceed our reserves and other short-term assets. Widespread confidence makes such systems work well. But we are a banker without deposit insurance. Internationally there is no FDIC to insure deposits or Federal Reserve to assure liquidity to temporarily frozen assets in case a confidence crisis develops, although the IMF helps.

Conflict and Compromise between Foreign and Domestic Goals

Domestically, we want a high-employment, stably-growing economy. Internationally, we want balance-of-payments equilibrium and a stable dollar as a foundation for a stable international payments system. Often these domestic

TABLE 41–2
Total Foreign Assets and Liabilities of the United States, January 1, 1972

		(IN BILLIONS)
Assets:		
Gold and foreign currency	$ 16	
U.S. short-term private investments abroad	19	
U.S. long-term private investments abroad	116	
U.S. government claims abroad	34	
Total assets abroad plus gold		$181
Liabilities:		
Short-term dollar balances of official organizations	53	
Short-term private dollar balances	20	
Long-term foreign investments here	49	
Total liabilities to foreigners		122
Excess of assets over liabilities		$ 59

Source: Department of Commerce and Federal Reserve Board, Preliminary data.

and international goals are consistent, and the policy prescription is clear. But sometimes these goals conflict.

Suppose we have a slack economy, with 6 percent unemployment. But simultaneously, for some or all of the reasons listed above, we also have a substantial balance of payments deficit. This was essentially the situation in 1960–65 and in 1970–71. To stimulate the domestic economy, easy money and a budget deficit is the prescription. But to reverse the international payments deficit, it is just the reverse—monetary and fiscal restraint to reduce our demand for imports, reduce our costs, and lure capital here through higher interest rates.

Which is the right policy? There is no simple answer; then we face a real conflict of domestic and international goals. Most economists, and most politicians as well, say, give top priority to restoring prosperity at home. That's most important for American citizens, and they're our first priority. Continued unemployment means wasted resources and output, while the real costs of continuing an international payments deficit are less. Moreover, they argue, higher U.S. interest rates in such a case might make the balance of payments worse rather than better. By deepening depression and reducing U.S. profits, they might reduce foreign capital flows to the United States, rather than increase them, since foreign capital is attracted by profit potential as well as higher interest rates.

Some economists would advocate a mixed strategy—raise interest rates to check the capital outflow, but increase the federal budget deficit to stimulate domestic production and employment. This would use each macro-policy instrument to achieve the separate objective for which it is best suited. The economic analysis sounds good; but whether we could manage such a complex, coordinated policy mix between the Administration, Congress, and the Fed is uncertain. Not only the timing, but also the amounts of monetary restraint and fiscal stimulus, would have to be just right to work successfully.

Still others would advocate direct controls over our international transactions to reduce the payments deficit while leaving monetary-fiscal policy free to fight the recession at home. They propose higher tariffs, import quotas, export subsidies, and regulation of U.S. capital exports.

In fact, the United States adopted extensive capital controls during the 1960s, both through absolute limitations on U.S. loans and investments abroad and through special taxes on U.S. investments overseas. Many economists doubt that such interventions are either effective or desirable; they run counter to the basic objective of stimulating foreign trade and investment.

Last, advocates of freely floating exchange rates point out that the dilemma largely vanishes under their plan. Tend to the domestic economy, and let the dollar depreciate against other currencies if we have a large payments deficit, is their solution. The drop in the dollar's value will directly act to reduce our imports and stimulate our exports, correcting our payments deficit without forcing unwanted general deflation on the domestic economy.

How Shall We Restore Payments Equilibrium?

Temporarily putting aside questions of long-run reform, what should the United States do to eliminate our chronic balance-of-payments deficit? Nearly everyone agrees that this is a vital step. Clearly, there are a variety of possible steps. Let us first list some of the ones on which most economists would agree, and then note some more dubious possibilities.

1. Lower American costs by increasing U.S. labor productivity and speeding technological progress, to improve the competitive position of American exports. Speeches and exhortation don't help much; the problem is to improve both labor and management performance and to spend more on research and development.
2. Hold down American inflation. The critical question here is not the absolute level of U.S. inflation, but its speed compared to inflation in countries with whose products we compete.
3. Improve American selling practices in international markets.
4. Get our trading partners to recognize that surplus as well as deficit countries have responsibilities. We cannot reduce our international deficit unless other countries correspondingly reduce their surpluses. This means that countries now boasting comfortable surpluses must be prepared to take more imports from America. Often such countries have been better at complaining about the U.S. deficit than at reducing their barriers against U.S. imports.
5. Get other nations, now prosperous, to carry a larger share of the burden of international defense and aid to developing nations.
6. Induce foreigners to invest more in the United States.

Now some measures that some economists consider more dubious, but others support:

7. Further depreciate the dollar against other major currencies. This has various drawbacks, including the danger of retaliation and the possibility that the depreciations of 1971 and 1973 have already eliminated the overvaluation of the dollar, given time for foreign trade to adjust.
8. Use repressive monetary and fiscal policy at home to depress the American economy, in order to reduce U.S. imports, stimulate exports, and pull capital toward higher U.S. interest rates. While there is little support for this general policy, note that one of the widely-approved policies above is to slow the American inflation, which may require a less buoyant economy.
9. Put further restrictions on the export of American capital, by reducing the loans and investments American banks and businesses can make abroad, or by putting larger special taxes on U.S. purchases of foreign securities.
10. Extend American import quotas against foreign products and increase U.S. export subsidies.

To this list, some economists would add: Do nothing—follow a policy of benign neglect. If foreigners want to continue sending more goods and services to us than we send to them, and letting us buy up their industries without spending the dollars they receive to buy more American goods, why should we object. Other countries have an easy way to eliminate the U.S. payments deficit any time—just start buying more American goods and services with all those dollars they have accumulated.

LONG-RANGE REFORM

Even if U.S. payments equilibrium were reestablished tomorrow, the international payments system would still be in need of basic, long-range reform. Most experts agree that we need to focus on three big problems which have plagued the system since World War II.

The Liquidity Problem

World trade increased from $50 billion to over $200 billion between 1950 and 1970, requiring more reserves. International lending grew even faster. Yet the world's monetary gold stock grew only from $36 billion to $41 billion. Gold production has increased irregularly, at only about 2 percent annually, compared to nearly 8 percent annually for world trade, and much of the new gold is needed for jewelry, industry, or other nonmonetary uses. Clearly, we cannot count on gold production to provide just the needed amount of new international monetary reserves each year. Nor is it reasonable to count on the U.S. payments deficit to provide the needed growth in international reserves, for all the reasons noted above.

Adoption of the SDR plan in 1968 was a major step toward a more rational collective action to gradually increase international monetary reserves. The plan is new and remains to be tested. The experts do not agree on just how fast reserves should be increased or how large they should be. Some argue that a generous supply is the best protection against confidence crises for individual currencies and against undesirably drastic pressures on deficit countries to restore balance through precipitous action. Others argue that generous liquidity makes it too easy for deficit countries to avoid painful steps needed to put their houses in order. But nearly everyone agrees that the SDRs are a sensible step in the direction of rational, managed growth of international reserves.

The Confidence Problem

When holders of any currency expect its value to fall in terms of other currencies, they tend to sell the currency in which they have lost confidence. In early 1973, for example, widespread suspicion that the dollar would be devalued against at least the mark and the yen led to massive conversion of dollars into those two currencies. To maintain existing exchange rates, the German and Japanese authorities bought huge quantities of dollars—some $6 billion in three days. But they did not want such huge quantities of dollars, and monetary officials of the leading nations agreed that the only short-run solution to the confidence crisis was a devaluation of the dollar, or, what is substantially the same thing, an upward valuation of the mark, yen, and other strong currencies. Such negotiations are highly complex because of the infighting over the exact relationships to be established among the currencies involved (exchange rates go far to determine nations' international competitive positions); and as part of the bargain the United States agreed to devalue the dollar by 10 percent against gold as well (raising the official price of gold to $42.22 an ounce). We shall look separately at the gold issue in a later section.

In a fixed-exchange-rate system, major confidence crises are highly disruptive. No one knows, for example, how many dollars are held around the world that might be converted into other currencies if another dollar confidence crisis should develop. Some estimates put the total at over $200 billion, held by banks, international businesses, wealthy individuals, Middle-Eastern governments, and others. Whatever the exact figure, the total is so large that no central bank could hope to maintain the exchange rate between the dollar and its own currency if a substantial part of the dollars were sold against another currency en masse. This is the confidence problem, sometimes called the "hot money" problem.

No one has found an adequate solution to this problem, unless it is those floating-rate advocates who are willing to see exchange rates fluctuate as widely and rapidly as market forces decree. They argue that if speculators knew that rates might fluctuate widely, the wide fluctuations would in fact seldom occur because the falling value of the attacked currency would soon eliminate the incentive to speculate against it. Certainly, this effect would tend to occur, but critics argue that rates might swing widely and disruptively before the self-correcting market forces checked them, and that this danger would seriously deter international traders and investors who need to know what they can count on when they buy and sell abroad.

Rejecting the freely-floating-rate "solution," most governments during the 1960s turned to cooperation among central banks and legal controls over capital flows. The major central banks frequently cooperated to make huge loans to protect currencies under attack, and these sometimes did the job. Reluctantly, many countries adopted capital controls against the inflow of unwanted hot money. But the confidence problem is still a major unresolved problem for the international monetary system, although the floating rates established in 1973 seem to some the most promising step toward solution.

The Adjustment Problem

The present mixed international monetary system, combining (as of 1973) substantial national independence of action, dirty floats, and partial inconvertibility of major currencies, provides an uncertain mechanism for bringing about international adjustments. Sooner or later, nations running large deficits must face up to restoring equilibrium, though this day may be long-postponed if they hold large reserves or, like the United States, are a reserve-currency country. Under the present system, there is little pressure on surplus countries to help restore general equilibrium except their possible unwillingness to continue to accumulate reserves. Nearly everyone agrees that a better adjustment mechanism is needed, but they don't agree on what. Two basic approaches, each with many variants, have received the most support.

Flexible (Floating) Exchange Rates. Freely fluctuating (floating) exchange rates would automatically reflect excess demand or supply of any currency. As the price of that currency moved up or down, it would discourage or stimulate imports into the country, and conversely exports—thus directly pulling the country's balance of payments back into equilibrium. Moreover, the floating exchange rate would *directly* affect the prices of the nation's exports and imports. No central bank or treasury needs to intervene to help achieve equilibrium; freely fluctuating exchange rates do the job automatically. Here again, the marketplace will do the job if we free it from restrictions.

Men of affairs generally reject this solution. Floating rates would impose major barriers to international trade and lending, they say, because creditors would never know what their future receipts would be in terms of their own currency. Importers, lenders, and borrowers alike would face serious uncertainties on all except the shortest-term transactions. While floating rates might make overall international adjustments easier, as a practical matter they'd kill the goose that lays the golden eggs—trade and lending itself.

Economists have an answer. Just as in the markets for wheat and copper, organized "futures" markets in different currencies would develop in which importers and exporters could buy and sell currencies for delivery at the future date needed, thus eliminating the uncertainty produced by possibly fluctuating rates. They could "hedge" against the possibility of higher or lower prices for the foreign currency involved.

But there is a counteranswer. Businessmen and bankers doubt that effective forward markets would actually develop in all major currencies, especially for long-term commitments. And both they and some economists fear that speculation on such forward markets might be destabilizing instead of stabilizing to rates themselves. With commodities, the cost of production provides a central level around which prices tend to move. With foreign exchange rates, there is no cost of production to serve as a stabilizing force. Instead, if the dollar weakened, speculators might lose confidence in it and all decide to sell dollars at once, driving the dollar rate far down.

Only experience will settle the controversy. The Canadian dollar has floated for some years, but the Canadian economy is so tied to the United States' that the experience cannot be generalized. Widespread floats of different currencies against the dollar in 1973 will provide some evidence, though many were "dirty" rather than "clean" floats, and the picture will be complicated by the fact that all Common Market currencies are presumably moving toward fixed links within the EEC. Early experience with the floats produced fewer problems for businessmen and investors than many critics anticipated.

The "Sliding Peg." It seems doubtful that most governments will long accept floating rates with no intervention. Thus, many economists, and recently government officials as well, favor a compromise—the "sliding, or crawling, peg." This policy would recognize the need to keep exchange rates reasonably stable as a foundation for foreign trade and lending. But it would deviate from fixed exchanges in two ways. First, it would permit exchange rates to fluctuate moderately (say by 2 to 5 percent on each side of parity) under market pressures, so they could do part of the equilibrating job. Second, if a currency consistently moved above or below par vis-à-vis other currencies, the par (peg) itself would automatically be adjusted gradually, say by ½ or 1 percent a quarter or half year. This sliding peg would be responsive to the fact that costs and prices do move differently in different nations, for example reflecting different rates of technological progress. But the changes would be gradual enough to retain most of the benefits from fixed rates.

The sliding peg doesn't solve the basic dilemma if one nation gets badly out of international equilibrium—say, because its technical progress is very slow or because it tries to live beyond its international means by importing much more than it exports. But it does offer a more flexible system than the present one, without running the risks some see in a more drastic shift to a floating-rate system.

The painful fact is that no one has discovered a surefire system for assuring basic balance-of-payments adjustments without unwanted pressure on domestic economies. Assurance of adequate international liquidity, to avoid crises while adjustments are taking place, can help. And we must recognize that under the present system international adjustments to eliminate payments disequilibriums may be slow, compared to earlier expectations. If we want the system to work, we must learn to suppress alarm and disruptive speculation merely because deficits are not eliminated overnight. But the present system seems fully satisfactory to scarcely anyone, and there is little doubt that the search for more effective arrangements will be active over the years ahead.

THE ROLE OF GOLD

What is the future role of gold in the world's international monetary system? To answer, one needs a crystal ball, especially because so much of gold's present role depends on centuries-old tradition and "psychology." Given the mixture of myth and reality that surrounds gold, the following seem probable.

1. Gold has declined greatly in monetary importance since the 1920s. Still, it remains a widely acceptable means of international payments. Central banks now hold over $40 billion of gold reserves, and most adhere to the two-tier system. On the other hand, nations seem highly unlikely to return gold to its former position of control over their domestic monetary policies. It makes little sense to tie a nation's money stock to the vagaries of the mining industry in two nations (South Africa and the USSR) and of private speculators' wishes to hold gold. Nor is there an obvious reason why we should pay

South African miners to dig up gold at increasing expense so we can rebury it in Fort Knox, Kentucky.

2. Gold is likely, together with key currencies and SDRs, to continue to serve as international monetary reserves in many nations, given their existing gold stocks, but with a relatively declining role for gold. Different countries will prefer different mixes of gold and other reserves, depending on their individual trade and financial relationships.

3. What about the possibility that the world's central banks may simply demonetize gold, selling off their present holdings to the free market and using SDRs, or some other new international asset, plus other currencies as reserves? Many economists favor such a change, but fewer believe it is in the cards for the near future. The mystique of gold is still strong. But advocates say it is foolish to hold tons of gold in carefully-guarded vaults. At present free-market prices, the United States' $10 billion of gold would bring about $30 billion, a nice tax saving that would be appreciated by taxpayers; perhaps the price would fall if we began to dump our stock, but some tax relief is better than none, and at least we would save safe-keeping expenses, they say. Understandably, South Africa and the USSR, the two major gold producers, oppose any such move, as do the many speculators who have bought gold in the hope that its price will rise even higher. But what, ask the economists, is the function now served by the United States' large gold hoard, which we will (at least as of 1973) neither sell nor give to other governments in payment of our international obligations? Why not sell it?

4. Last, how about the other extreme—raise the official price of gold to provide a large stock of international reserves for central banks and reestablish gold as *the* major international reserve. Advocates (a few economists, French government officials, and some financiers) suggest doubling or tripling the official gold price—to perhaps $80 or $120 an ounce—providing a huge profit for gold-holding central banks and private gold speculators, and providing enough international reserves for decades to come. Understandably, South Africa, the USSR, and governments like France that have accumulated gold, like such proposals, as do private gold-holders who fear that the free-market price will tumble if governments don't resume buying gold. But would the world be well served by reestablishing gold as the foundation of its monetary system? Most economists say no, and add that the huge increase in monetary reserves envisioned in the gold price increase could well lead to more of the inflation that has plagued the world in recent years.

REVIEW

Concepts to Remember

This chapter reuses the central concepts of both domestic macroeconomics and Chapters 38–40 and adds the following important concepts and institutions:

devaluation
International Monetary Fund
special drawing rights (SDRs)
two-tier gold system
clean and dirty floats
sliding, or crawling, peg
liquidity problem
confidence problem
adjustment problem

For Analysis and Discussion

1. Explain what it means to say the dollar is "weak", or "strong."
2. What does it matter to the typical U.S. resident whether the dollar is weak or strong internationally?
3. Should the United States be concerned about its continuing balance-of-payments deficit, or treat it with "benign neglect"? If we should be concerned, what should we do about it?
4. How much gold do we really need for domestic and international reserves? Explain.
5. Describe the two-tier gold system of 1968. What are its presumed advantages? Was it fair to private holders of dollars abroad?
6. How could we have a continuing balance-of-payments deficit during the 1960s when our exports exceeded our imports by a wide margin?
7. "Our continued balance-of-payments deficits clearly say that we are not competitive enough abroad and that restrictive monetary and fiscal policy is needed to restrain American prices and wages so we can become more competitive." Do you agree? What would be the likely consequences of such a policy?
8. What are SDRs? Are they "as good as gold" to the countries that get them through the IMF?

Up or Out for Gold?

In May, 1973, substantially the following story appeared in several major newspapers:

The powerful Committee of Twenty meets today to continue its search for an acceptable plan to reform the international monetary system. The Twenty are high Treasury and central-bank officials of the free world's major nations.

Although all sessions are secret, it was reported that the United States will continue to push the plan earlier advanced by Treasury Secretary Shultz. This stresses greater flexibility of exchange rates, use of warning and "trigger" points in each nation's reserves to require consultations when disequilibria occur, increased use of SDRs, and gradual phasing out of gold. The United States will not now redeem its dollars in gold, even for other central banks.

Major opposition is expected to come from the French delegation. France has long felt that the international role of the dollar should be decreased, and that gold should be restored to a more important reserve role. In the past, French officials have frequently criticized American inflation and U.S. balance-of-payments deficits, and argued that American companies are buying up French firms with dollars which are irredeemable promises to pay.

President DeGaulle repeatedly advocated restoration of the gold standard, whereby each nation would have to pay its international debts in gold if called on to do so. He and his advisers also are understood to have argued for raising the price of gold, perhaps to twice its present official price. This would eliminate international reserve shortages and help substitute gold for dollars as the major international reserve held by central banks. While France has recently been less outspoken in favor of these gold steps, many observers believe that is still their preferred plan. The French government now holds about $4 billion in gold, and large, but unknown, amounts of gold are held by private individuals in France. Gold is a favorite form of hoarding by French peasants, who traditionally distrust paper money, including that issued by their own government. The French franc has been devalued several times since the 1920s.

France is thought to have only limited support for a return to a bigger role for gold, or for further increases in the official price of gold at this time. However, yesterday the free market price of gold touched $120 an ounce in Paris and London. This is nearly three times the official price of $42.22 an ounce used by central banks in their gold transactions with each other.

---

1. Why should France favor a return to a larger international role for gold, and replacement of dollars by gold as the major international reserve held by central banks?

2. Are French officials right, that in effect U.S. investors are able under present arrangements to buy up French firms with irredeemable dollars? Irredeemable in what—gold, other currencies, or goods and services?

3. Do you favor the plan to raise the price of gold and make gold a much larger part of international monetary reserves? Would you if you were French? Who would be the major gainers and losers?

4. Can the official price of gold stay at $42.22 an ounce when the free market price is three times as high?

5. If you were an American Treasury official, how would you reply to the French criticisms?

APPENDIX TO PART SIX

Current Research

Research in the area of international economic affairs has snowballed since World War II. The U.S. balance-of-payments deficit, attacks on the dollar, and the price of gold have been front-page news. Leaving aside our problems vis-à-vis the less-developed countries (covered in Part Seven), the following sample may provide some impression of the lively probing into international economics in recent years.

GOLD AND THE BALANCE OF PAYMENTS. A useful, relatively simple beginning is provided by the *Economic Report of the President,* January, 1973, Chapter 5; and by R. Aliber's *The International Money Game* (Basic Books, 1973). Then try Milton Friedman, "The Advantages of Flexible Exchange Rates," and Henry Wallich, "In Defense of Fixed Exchange Rates," before the Joint Economic Committee, *Hearings on the U.S. Balance of Payments* (1963), pp. 451–59 and 495–99. Gold is the focus of M.A. Kriz's interesting *Gold: Barbarous Relic or Useful Instrument* (Princeton International Finance Section, 1967). A recent look at the role of gold is given by the Joint Economic Committee Hearings, *Gold and the Central Bank Swap Network* (Sept. 11–15, 1972); see especially the conflicting statements by Edward Bernstein and Jacques Rueff.

A useful description and analysis of "Eurodollars" is provided by the Federal Reserve Bank of Cleveland's *Economic Review,* for March, April, and May, 1970.

U.S. TRADE POLICIES AND THE WORLD. The Joint Economic Committee's report, *A New Initiative to Liberalize International Trade* (March 8, 1973), though a policy statement rather than research, is a good introduction. The research and policy statements underlying it are available in numerous Committee Hearings, for example, *The Balance of Payments Mess* (June 16–23, 1971). L. Krause's *European Economic Integration and the United States* (The Brookings Institution, 1968) is an authoritative look at U.S. trade vis-à-vis the "Common Market." A broad and still up-to-date picture of research on U.S. tariff policy is provided by *Foreign Trade Policy,* a compendium for the Foreign Trade Policy Subcommittee of the House Committee on Ways and Means (1958). Many of the papers are partisan pleas by industry representatives, but the papers by Piquet, Salant, and Kravis are readable, analytical research pieces.

Both the United States and other nations continue to impose barriers to free trade, in order to help their own economies. Charles Kindleberger's *The Politics of International Economics and the Economics of International Politics* (Basic Books, 1971), and M.A. Adelman's *The World Petroleum Market* (Johns Hopkins University Press, 1973) look at some of the hot international political-economic issues of the decade. How the Japanese Mount That Export Blitz," (*Fortune,* September 1970), explains some of the devices used by Japan in obtaining a bigger share of total markets. R. Baldwin's *Nontariff Distortions of International Trade* (The Brookings Institution, 1970) assesses the impact of these measures.

THE MULTINATIONAL CORPORATION. One of the most controversial issues of modern international trade and investment is the role of huge multinational corporations. See Raymond Vernon, *Sovereignty At Bay: The Multinational Spread of the U.S. Corporations* (Basic Books, 1971); S. Rolfe and W. Damon, *The Multinational Corporation in the World Economy* (Praeger Publishers, 1972); C. Kindleberger, *American Business Abroad* (New Haven, Conn.: Yale University Press, 1969); and, for an interesting case study, T. Geiger, *The General Electric Company in Brazil* (National Planning Association, 1961). A highly critical, socialist view of the whole process is presented by Harry Magdoff in *The Age of Imperialism* (Monthly Review Press, 1969).

ECONOMIC GROWTH

PART SEVEN

The Theory of Economic Growth

CHAPTER PREVIEW

CHAPTER FORTY-TWO

For over half the world's population, the number one economic problem is getting enough to eat. By our standards, they are desperately poor. For them, economic growth—more output per capita—offers the only real hope of rising above a bare subsistence level of food and shelter.

Even in the United States there are millions of poor, miles of squalid slums—and few in our population of over 200 million do not continually hope for more income, for the better things in life. Thus, here too economic growth is a central issue, though a far less pressing need than for the world's less-developed, poverty-stricken nations.

Today many people, especially the young, argue that concern for the "quality of life" should replace our traditional stress on the quantity of GNP. Some advocate zero economic growth (ZEG). Extremists allege that technology has taken over society, and that man is now a mere slave to machines; their solution is often vague—to somehow slow technology and return to a simpler life. Others claim that mass starvation is just around the corner because population is growing too fast.

This chapter begins with some facts on economic growth, but it is mainly concerned with the theory of growth. Why do economies grow as fast or as slowly as they do? Chapter 43 then uses this theoretical framework to explain growth in today's American economy; and Chapter 44 turns to the policy issues we face—should we grow faster or slower, and how? Chapter 45 does the same for the less-developed economies, which contain the great bulk of the world's people.

SOME FACTS ON GROWTH

Economic Growth Defined

Economic growth means growth in the amount of goods and services produced—in total, or per capita. For some purposes, growth in total output is most important—for example, in assessing a nation's economic potential for war. But for most purposes we are more interested in output per capita (or per family)—that is, growth in the ratio: $\frac{\text{total output}}{\text{population}}$. For output per capita provides a rough measure of the average standard of living of individuals in the economy. You will find "economic growth" used widely in both senses, but here economic growth will mean growth in output per capita unless growth in total output is specified.

The two definitions can color the facts quite differently. If total output grows but population grows even faster, the standard of living of the typical individual falls. In this country, total output has risen on the average about 3.5 percent annually over the last century, while output per capita has risen only about 2.5 percent per annum as population grew about 1 percent per annum. In India, total output has recently grown too, at a rate not far behind ours, but population has grown nearly as fast as output. Hence there has been little change in output per capita, and the Indian standard of living today is little higher than it was a century ago.

Economic Growth in Perspective

Look back at Table 2–1 and then ahead to Table 45–1 to get a first picture of the results of such widely varying economic growth rates in the world today. The United States stands at the top, well ahead of the nearest challengers—even though we are a new nation compared to most of the other leaders. The success story of the American economy is written in these figures on our spectacular economic growth over a mere two or three centuries of world history.

What about comparative growth rates for major industrialized countries over the last century? Table 42–1 tells the story. Growth rates have varied widely even among these industrialized nations. Although some rates are surprisingly close (for example, those of the United States and Sweden), don't forget the enormous difference that even a fraction of 1 percent annually can make when compounded over an entire century. A dollar invested at 1.5 percent per annum grows to $4.43 in 100 years; at 2 percent to $7.25; and at 3 percent to $19.22.

Try matching up these rates with the present standings shown in Table 2–1. When, for exam-

TABLE 42–1
Long-Term Growth Rates in Output per Capita[a]

	ANNUAL PERCENTAGE INCREASE
Japan	3.0
Sweden	2.2
United States	2.1
USSR	2.0
Canada	1.8
Denmark	1.7
France	1.6
Germany	1.6
United Kingdom	1.2
Italy	1.2

[a] Based on data for approximately 100 years. Exact beginning date varies slightly; for example, U.S. data begin in 1871 to avoid Civil War period.

Sources: D.C. Paige, "Economic Growth: The Last Hundred Years," *National Institute Economic Review,* July 1961; Simon Kuznets, "The Pattern of U.S. Economic Growth," *The Nation's Economic Objectives,* E. Edwards, ed. (Chicago: University of Chicago Press, 1964); and United Nations. Inclusion of recent years would raise most of the figures shown appreciably, especially those for Japan.

TABLE 42-2
Comparative Annual Growth Rates, 1950–72[a]

	GNP PER CAPITA	GNP
Japan	9.8	10.8
West Germany	4.9	6.1
Italy	4.4	5.2
Sweden	3.9	4.6
USSR	3.7	5.3
France	3.5	4.8
United States	3.2	4.5
Canada	3.0	4.5
United Kingdom	2.3	2.9

[a]Estimates based on United Nations and International Monetary Fund data; in real terms.

ple, did the United States gain its present big advantage over Japan, Sweden, and the USSR? How about Japan, which began to industrialize very late? She now has the world's third largest GNP, behind only the United States and the USSR, and is growing far faster than either. When will she falter? Tables like these show why economic historians and economic theorists have a fascinating time explaining the facts.

One last introductory look at the facts. What about recent comparative growth rates? Table 42–2 provides the answer. Since World War II we have grown nearly 50 percent faster than over the previous century. But a number of other nations have done still better, especially Japan and West Germany. And the order is very different from those of Tables 2–1 and 42–1.

A word of warning is needed here, however. Growth figures for any short period are tricky, and the years in Table 42–2 reflect partly special circumstances growing out of World War II.

The Difference between Growth and Cycle Upswings

It is important to distinguish between long-run growth rates and short-run swings reflecting business-cycle fluctuations. For example, output per capita usually rises rapidly as an economy moves from depression to high employment. But this is clearly a temporary factor, and should not be extrapolated out as a long-run growth rate. Thus, most economists look upon the long-run growth rate as something to be measured only over extended periods that cover at least the years from one cycle peak to another, and preferably several cycles. Alternatively, they look at the growth in the "full-employment capacity" of the economy—that is, its growing capacity to produce at "full employment" of men and machines.

THE THEORY OF ECONOMIC GROWTH

Why have some nations grown so fast and others not at all? Alas, there is no one simple theory that seems to explain everything. But there is growing consensus on some central factors in the growth process and it is on these that we shall concentrate.

Supply and Demand Factors in Economic Growth

The classical economists had a simple answer to questions about economic growth. The basic productive factors were land, labor, and capital. Growth in total output depended on the combined expansion of these productive factors, reflecting especially enterprise, hard work, and thrift. And the growth in output per capita depended largely on the growth in population relative to the growth in land and capital available for production. They stressed the *supply* factors—the ones that move out the nation's production-possibilities curve.

Nearly two centuries later the classical economists still look basically right. It is the "real" (supply) factors that matter most in economic growth—the accumulation of capital goods; growth in the size and efficiency of the labor force; the natural resources ("land") that a nation has; and its research, education, and technical advance which permit it to produce more with any given amount of capital, labor, and natural resources.

Beyond land, labor, capital, and technology, many historians and economists point to other, more tenuous factors—the energy and "drive" of a nation's people, the social and economic mobility of its classes, its economic institutions, its governmental and political stability. Although we set most of these forces aside for the moment, it is important not to forget them.

These "supply" factors matter most, but in a private-enterprise economy money *demand* matters too. Unless aggregate demand is adequate to take goods off the market, they will not be produced for long. And unless prospective money demand promises reasonable returns on new investments, savings will not be invested and the new capital goods and research necessary for economic growth will not be forthcoming.

Summary: On the supply side, the problem of economic growth is to increase productive capacity—basically through diverting resources from current consumption to investment in capital goods, research, education, and other activities that increase future productive capacity; through increasing the size and quality of the labor force; and through improving the economic and social-political organization of the society. **On the demand side,** the first problem is to be sure that there is always adequate total demand to induce high-level utilization of productive capacity. The second problem is to channel spending from consumption into saving and investment so that society's stock of capital goods and human resources will be built up to increase future output.

Adam Smith— Progress through Enterprise and Thrift

How is it that in the last 200 years, only in a few now-industrialized nations of the Western world, has man managed to rise rapidly from poverty to our present comfortable way of living? In 1776, Adam Smith, in his *Wealth of Nations* first saw the central rationale of an individual-self-interest, market-directed economy. Would these forces of self-interest lead man to economic progress and an ever better life? His answer was "yes"—because self-interest would produce not only hard work and enterprise, but also thrift and accumulation. As man saved part of what he produced, the savings of many individuals could mean new factories, new machines, better houses. Thus, thrift and accumulation, savings from the fruits of hard labor, were the foundations of economic growth—of progress toward a better life.

To be sure, more machinery and more capital would mean a larger demand for workers, and this in turn would lead to higher wages, so that profits—the special source of, and stimulus to, accumulation—would tend to be eaten away. But Smith saw no crisis in this process. He observed that higher wages and more food would lead to more people, and thus to more workers. This in turn would tend to push wages back down, lowering the costs to businessmen as it lowered the real wages of the worker. And so profits and accumulation would again become possible, with further progress.

Smith's was an optimistic world, of self-interest and of order. It was a world of progress for those who worked hard and saved, and for societies made up of such men. And Smith's analysis still has fundamental lessons to teach us today.

Malthus, Ricardo, and Marx— Strife and Diminishing Returns

Two Englishmen, writing shortly after Smith, saw instead a gloomy world of conflict and strife—of workers, capitalists, and landlords climbing on each others' backs, each trying to increase his own share of the sustenance produced by society. T.R. Malthus and David Ricardo, two other great founders of modern economics, challenged the orderly world of Smith with disturbing predictions that still have a modern look, nearly two centuries later.

Malthus and the Specter of Famine. More people mean more productive power and more output. But more people also mean more mouths to feed, more backs to clothe. In 1798, Malthus, a young British minister, wrote his now famous *Essay on the Principle of Population.* He gloomily predicted that population would rise far faster than the productive power associated with more people. Looking at rising birthrates, Malthus pointed out that the population could double every generation if each woman had only four surviving children, half of them girls who would produce more children in the next generation. Malthus felt that this might well give a geometrical population increase—2, 4, 8, 16, 32, 64, and so on—with a doubling each generation.

But the world's land could not possibly increase its food output at this rate over the long run, Malthus argued. Thus, unless population growth was checked by moral restraint, or by such disasters as war or disease, it must ultimately be checked by recurrent famines as the population outran the food supply. The British standard of living was hardly above the subsistence level for much of the population; unless steps were taken to control population growth, the outlook for growth in output per capita and for a better life was bleak.

Ricardo and the "Law of Diminishing Returns." David Ricardo, another famous British economist, provided a further intellectual justification for Malthus's fears. Ricardo first stated the law of diminishing returns. If the number of workers applied to any fixed supply of land is increased, the crops obtained from the land will increase, but output will increase at a slower rate than the rate at which workers are added.

The implications of this "law" for the standard of living of a growing population seemed clear. Given the world's supply of arable land, sooner or later food output per worker would fall when the point of diminishing returns was passed. And as population grew thereafter, food output per capita (more accurately, per worker) would decline steadily, even though total food output might continue to grow.

But at the same time as diminishing returns pressed down on the food available for individual workers, it would enrich the landlords. For as more and more workers sought sustenance from the land, the price of each piece of land (in sale or in rent) would rise. Ricardo, the economic theorist par excellence, explained through the law of diminishing returns precisely how fast rents would rise and wage rates fall as more workers were applied to the increasingly scarce land. Each factor of production would earn essentially its marginal contribution to total productivity—what we called in Part Four its marginal productivity.

But what of capital accumulation, the path to progress in Smith's system? Ricardo saw the importance of thrift and accumulation in man's attempt to improve his lot. But here again, Ricardo wrote, the fact of diminishing returns rears its ugly head. As more and more capital is accumulated relative to scarce land, the return on capital (interest or profits) will be squeezed down more and more. In the end it is the landlords who will wax ever richer, while both workers and capitalists find their individual returns (in the form of wages and of profits) squeezed to the barest minimum.

Were Malthus and Ricardo right? If history has proved them wrong in the nations of the Western world, where did they go astray? Have they been proved right in China and India, where starvation is an ever present threat for over a billion people? As with Smith, Malthus and Ricardo have lessons for today. Their arguments will reappear in the modern analysis of growth.

Marx and the Collapse of Capitalism. Fifty years later came Karl Marx, the gloomy prophet of the downfall of the capitalist system. Like his classical predecessors, Marx was interested in the grand dynamics—the progress of society or its road to collapse. But he saw no progress. Instead, he foresaw collapse, as capitalists seized ever larger incomes while forcing the workers into degradation and eventually to revolt which would overthrow the capitalist system.

Marx built an elaborate theoretical structure on the fallacy that labor is the source of **all** value. He said that any return to another productive resource, such as capital or land, is merely a misappropriation of the "surplus value" produced by labor. But we need not be concerned with the details of this argument.[1] To Marx, capital accumulation was again at the center of things. The desire for profit leads men to accumulate capital and to wring every ounce of effort out of the workers who must labor for their bread. Because capitalists are powerful and rich, whereas laborers are poor and divided, capitalists can push down the real wages of their workers to the point where workers can barely subsist. The higher profits lead to more and more capital accumulation, as Smith and Ricardo had predicted before him.

But to Marx the end result of all this was quite different, though it had been hinted in the worryings of Parson Malthus. Capitalism will develop increasing crises, Marx wrote. Too much of society's income will go to the rich capitalists. Too little will be paid to the masses to permit them to buy the output of the new factories and machines. Thus capitalism will face declining profit rates and increasingly severe crises and depressions, with resulting unemployment and chaos. Finally, the hungry workers, long ground under the heel of wealthy capitalists, will rise in revolt and overthrow the capitalist system. So, wrote Marx, will come the downfall of capitalism, brought on by the very process of capital accumulation that the classical economists had praised as the foundation of economic growth.

Clearly, Marx has been wrong in the Western world. Real wages have not been ground down over the long run. Both they and profits have risen rapidly in total, and real wages per worker are vastly higher now than one hundred years ago. Interestingly, the real rate of return per dollar of capital invested (loosely, the profit rate or the interest rate) has apparently been about constant, though of course the total return to capital has grown enormously with the vast accumulation of capital. And apparently modern monetary-fiscal policy has brought great depressions under control.

Let us now examine more rigorously some of the issues exposed by Smith, Malthus, Ricardo, and Marx.

The Deepening of Capital and Diminishing Returns. It is relatively easy to explain the growth in total output of an economy as capital and labor grow. The production-possibilities curve moves out. Unless unbalanced "excessive" capital accumulation brings on the crises suggested by Malthus and Marx, an increase in any or all of the factors of production will raise total output. Thus, more workers, more capital goods, or more natural resources will increase total production. (Note that increased natural resources are a real possibility in new nations; for example, until almost 1900 the United States had continuous access to more land through the open frontier westward.) But how to increase output **per capita** is a much more difficult problem. For more workers, given the law of diminishing returns, will produce more total output, but output per worker will fall, assuming that the stock of capital and land remain constant.

Disregard for a moment the supply of land (natural resources) as of decreasing importance in the advanced economies. Then, if the number of workers increases, at least a parallel increase in the stock of capital would appear to be the only hope for avoiding declining real wages as a result of the law of diminishing returns. The stock of capital must rise faster than population grows, if output per worker is to rise.

This is what economists call the "deepening" of capital—more capital per unit of labor. **It is this deepening of capital, the analysis of the preceding paragraphs suggests, that is the fundamental hope for progress.**

Let us now reconsider, more analytically, the effects of capital deepening in a simple system. To take the simplest case, assume there is no land, but merely labor and capital as productive factors. Suppose capital grows faster than the labor supply. What then happens to per capita output? The answer is given by Ricardo's law of diminishing returns. Total output will grow,

[1]See the Appendix to Chapter 32.

but not in proportion to the growth in the capital stock. Thus, the return per unit of capital (the interest rate or profit rate) will fall as capital deepens. Here labor is the relatively fixed factor (just as was land in Ricardo's case). Thus, the wage rate (the return to labor) will be bid up as labor becomes ever scarcer relative to capital; labor replaces the "greedy landlord" of Ricardo's system. But last, note that higher wage rates and lower interest rates in the system do not necessarily imply a higher percentage share of the total national output for labor. This is because there are more units of capital being used. The increased number of units may offset the lower return per unit of capital and may thus keep the aggregate share of capital in the national output from falling absolutely, or even relative to the share of labor.

It is important to be clear about the reasoning of the preceding paragraph. It is the foundation for much of the modern theory of growth, and for moving on to a new factor—technological progress.

The New Look—Technical Advance and Innovation

Why have Malthus, Ricardo, and Marx proved wrong in nearly all the nations of the Western world, although they may be discomfortingly right for two billion people in the less-developed nations? Is the answer a simple one—that Adam Smith was basically right in his optimistic prediction of growth in private-enterprise economies, but that the less-developed nations have not yet heeded his advice?

Most modern economists say that Smith deserves credit for a powerful analysis of some of the basic forces. But something else has been added to give the victory to Smith's optimism over Malthus's and Ricardo's gloom. This is technical advance and its partner, innovation. **The revolution of science, technology, and education has saved us from diminishing returns!**

The basic fact is that total output has grown much faster than the combined inputs of the factors of production. Only part of the growth in total U.S. output since 1900 can be explained by the growth in capital and labor inputs, disregarding land as substantially fixed in quantity. Similar patterns apparently prevail in other advanced industrial nations. And, modern economics says, the main reason is technical progress and innovation. New machines, better management methods, computers to do the work of adding machines, new fertilizers to double the output of farms, new management techniques—these have more than offset the once-feared law of diminishing returns.

It is important to remember that technical change shows up in higher skills and better education for workers, scientists, and managers, as well as in new machines and methods. Modern computers drastically reduce business costs and make possible fantastic new scientific developments. Is the technical advance in the computers, or is it in the skills of the scientists who designed the computers and the programmers who apply them to new problems? Both, is the answer. Thus technical advance is introduced through education and training (investment in human beings) as well as through new capital goods and techniques (investment in research and development and in new capital).

Technical progress has made Adam Smith right. It has gone far to prove that the pessimists were wrong, mainly because they overlooked the vast power of modern technical change. Joseph Schumpeter, a famous economist writing early in this century, first stressed innovation (in productive techniques and in new products) as the mainspring of economic growth. History appears to be bearing Schumpeter out.

GROWTH IN THE DEVELOPED ECONOMIES

A satisfactory modern theory of growth for the developed Western economies like the United States must explain at least the following facts:

1. The strong, upward movement in real wages in the face of a rapidly growing popula-

tion and labor force. (In the United States, population has tripled since 1900, while real wages have risen more than fivefold.)

2. A still more rapid increase in capital stock with a resultant deepening of capital, but (disregarding business-cycle fluctuations) with a roughly stable long-term real interest rate, contrary to the falling expectation given by the law of diminishing returns.

3. A slightly falling ratio of capital to total output for the economy in the face of the rapid deepening of capital, where the law of diminishing returns would lead us to suppose that the capital-output ratio would rise.

4. A surprisingly stable division of the total national product between wages and salaries on the one hand and returns to property (profits, interest, and rent) on the other—with a gradual increase in the labor share in recent decades.

Supply Factors: Capital, Labor, and Technology

Modern growth theory stresses the fact that total output grows when capital and labor grow and technology improves, disregarding land as a relatively minor factor in highly-developed countries.[2] In general, then, output *per capita* will grow only when capital grows faster than labor or when there is technical advance, or both. When capital is deepened, unless there is technical change the law of diminishing returns will reduce the rate of return on capital and increase the real wage of labor. But with technical advance, the rate of return on capital need not fall; it may be stable or even rise while the real wage rises even more rapidly. What happens to the relative shares of capital and labor in the total national income depends on the relative rates of growth of the two.

[2] Some economists like to summarize this relationship in a simple "production function" for the entire economy:

$$\text{Output} = a(A \cdot K \cdot L)$$

where K is the stock of capital, L is the stock of labor, and A is technical progress. Thus, output depends on the combined effect of all three. For a more complete discussion, see the appendix to this chapter.

Saving and investment (diversion of real resources from consumption to increase investment) is thus central to the growth process. For investment is required both for capital deepening and research and, in most instances, to incorporate technical advance. The larger the portion of its current output that a society devotes to investment, the faster capital will deepen and the faster output per capita will rise. Moreover, the more of its resources it devotes to investment in research and development and to education, the faster technical progress will occur.

Demand Factors

Malthus and Marx warned of breakdowns in the growth process because aggregate demand might fall short of buying all the goods that could be produced as the stock of capital grows. This was a valid warning. We now recognize that aggregate demand must grow roughly apace with the productive capacity of the economy if unemployment and inflation are to be avoided. It is clear, further, that when aggregate demand does fall short and depression occurs, the ratio of investment to GNP, and therefore the rate of economic growth, declines.

Equally important, decisions on money spending or saving within the total are vital to a stable growth process. This is because they largely control the division of the national output between consumption on the one hand and saving-investment on the other. For a brainteaser on the saving-investment rate needed to just maintain stable growth in GNP, see the appendix to this chapter.

Growth and Fluctuations

Schumpeter stressed the intimate relationship between growth and economic fluctuations. As we saw in Chapter 14, the bunching of real investment is the essence of a boom and of rapid growth. But this very process usually involves overshooting the amount of real productive capacity needed to meet consumer demands. When the overshoot becomes obvious, private investment is cut back and a recession occurs until a better balance between capacity and growing consumption is restored. Excessive expansion of credit helps to speed investment booms, supplementing the intended savings of the public and thus intensifying real overinvestment beyond a sustainable growth rate. On both real and monetary scores, the theory of growth and the theory of fluctuations are inseparable.

The Eclectic Consensus

Most modern economists thus look at the stock of capital, the stock of labor, and technical advance as a framework for analyzing growth in total output. The law of diminishing returns, partially or completely offset by technical advance and innovation, provides a powerful tool for understanding what happens to output per capita, and to the relative shares of capital and labor, in the growth process. The extent to which any growth is sustainable, rather than leading to overinvestment through excessive capital accumulation, depends partially on monetary-fiscal factors and partially on the bunching of real investment in the process. Throughout, there must be adequate demand to buy the growing full-employment output. This general theory helps to explain the basic facts on growth listed at the beginning of this section. It is a modern eclectic consensus, that provides the foundation for the following chapters.

Other Factors

One last preliminary word is needed. Many economists believe that this framework is too narrow to explain the basic forces of economic growth, in either the United States or less-developed nations. They say that private initiative and our free-enterprise economic institutions have played a major role in explaining our rapid growth. Our success breeds further success, since our markets are now so big that we can take full advantage of the economies of mass production, an important factor in making effective use of our resources. The *noneconomic* factors mentioned at the outset—the initiative of the people and their "drive," social and economic mobility in the system, the flexibility of economic and social institutions, religious traditions and ethical mores, and particularly the political stability of a nation—may be as important as the purely *economic* factors stressed in the preceding pages. Certainly absence of these factors has seriously deterred growth in many of the less-developed nations.

REVIEW

Concepts to Remember

Be sure you understand the following basic concepts introduced in this chapter. They are reused repeatedly in the following chapters.

economic growth
growth versus cycle upswings
supply (real) factors in growth
demand (money) factors in growth
technical advance
capital deepening

For Analysis and Discussion

1. Does Adam Smith or Malthus–Ricardo provide a better explanation of economic growth over the past century in the United States? In India and the less-developed nations? If your answers are different, why?
2. Suppose you want to explain Japan's rapid economic growth. At what factors does the theory of Chapter 42 suggest you should look?
3. Can you explain why capital deepening is so important to economic progress?
4. "Increased aggregate demand is a first-rate answer to the depression problem, but it can't help much to speed up long-term growth." Do you agree? Why or why not?
5. Suppose you want to speed up the rate of economic growth in the United States. What does the theory of Chapter 42 suggest as promising measures?
6. Explain the relationship between business cycles and economic growth.
7. In what sense, if any, has modern technological advance repealed Ricardo's law of diminishing returns?
8. If the rate of population growth speeds up relative to the rate of capital accumulation, what effect, if any, would you predict on the shares of labor and capital in the national income?

APPENDIX

Some Special Points on Economic Growth

Growth theory raises a host of interesting problems. This appendix is intended for students who want to look a little further into the intricacies of the subject.

A SIMPLE GROWTH MODEL. Shortly after World War II, Oxford's Sir Roy Harrod and MIT's Evsey Domar simultaneously developed a simple growth model that has since been widely used. It builds on the fact that investment (increase in the capital stock) is a prime cause of economic growth, and assumes for simplicity that the capital-output ratio is constant. Note that a constant capital-output ratio assumes away the existence of diminishing returns.

Let Y = output, K = capital stock, and designate changes in any variable by Δ. Suppose the constant capital-output ratio is β—for example, 3—so that 3 of additional capital means 1 of additional output. Suppose further that savings (S) are a constant proportion of income (Y). Let that proportion be σ. Lastly, let us assume full employment, that is, we are concerned with the growth in full-employment potential output for the economy.

Since β is fixed, we know how much Y will increase for any increase in K:

$$\Delta K = \beta\,\Delta Y$$

But ΔK in any year is simply net investment in that year, and we know that saving equals investment in any year. Thus:

$$\Delta K = I = S = \sigma Y$$

Now combine the equations, substituting σY for ΔK. Then:

$$\beta\,\Delta Y = \sigma Y, \text{ so}$$

$$\frac{\beta\,\Delta Y}{Y} = \sigma, \text{ or}$$

$$\frac{\Delta Y}{Y} = \frac{\sigma}{\beta}$$

Since $(\Delta Y/Y)$ is the growth rate, the full-employment growth rate for the economy is given by $\frac{\sigma}{\beta}$. Thus, if β is 3 and σ is 15 percent, the economy will grow at 5 percent per year $\left(\frac{.15}{3} = .05\right)$.

This model stresses some important relationships. But remember the simplified assumptions before you conclude that it will tell you just how much saving your favorite economy needs to grow at 5 percent annually. In the real world, we often don't know what the capital-output ratio for new capital will be, and the savings-income ratio also has a slippery way of sliding around. Moreover, we've abstracted from a lot of real-world factors, such as business savings, taxes, and the like.

HOW TO MAINTAIN STABLE GROWTH. A difficult brainteaser: Is there some rate of saving and investment out of total output that is necessary for "balanced" or "sustainable" growth, avoiding too rapid or too slow an increase of capital that might lead to an "oversupply" or "undersupply" of productive capacity? If there is a constant capital-output ratio given by technology, then we can show that there is indeed such a required rate. Suppose labor grows at 1 percent annually and technological advance at 2 percent, so the basic capacity of the system to produce grows at 3 percent. Suppose further that the fixed capital-output ratio is 3:1. That is, $3 of additional capital will produce $1 of additional output.

Then, using the highly simplified Harrod-Domar model above, we can show that the economy must save and invest just 9 percent of its output to grow stably. Why? Begin with a total output of 100. The extra 9 units of capital ($\sigma = 9$ percent) will produce just the 3 additional units of output that match the 3 percent growth in potential output from more labor and technical change ($\beta = 3$). Less saving and investment would provide inadequate capital to produce the possible 3 percent annual growth in output, given the 3:1 capital-output ratio. Larger saving and investment would pile up more capital than could be used in producing the 3 percent growth in output. In this model, a knife-edge saving rate is required for stable economic growth. But remember that this is only one model, based on extremely limited assumptions, so the conclusion may not directly apply to the real world.

IS TECHNICAL PROGRESS "NEUTRAL"? Does technical progress tend to increase the share of Y going to labor or to capital, or is it "neutral" as between the two shares? Obviously, technical progress might be "labor saving" or "capital saving." That is, it might reduce or increase the relative amount of labor or capital needed to produce a given output. If the technical advance is labor saving, so that less labor is now needed for a given output, we might predict that the labor share of Y would fall.

In fact, we observe in the real world that the labor and capital shares of national income have been surprisingly constant (abstracting from cyclical fluctuations), with a small tendency for the labor share to rise. Can we infer that technical progress has been "neutral" in the above sense? Consider two possible explanations.

First, it is possible that in the absence of technical change the elasticity of substitution between K and L is 1. That is, if the wage rate falls relative to the cost of capital, businessmen will hire just enough more labor to offset the lower wage rate, and just enough less capital to offset the higher price per unit. Then the relative income shares of capital and labor will remain unchanged. We can write an aggregate "production function" to show this case as follows:

$$\text{Output} = A(L^{a} \cdot K^{1-a}),$$

where A is technical progress, L is the stock of labor, and K is the stock of capital. If this is the economy's production function, constant relative shares of total output for labor and capital are shown by the coefficients a and $1 - a$; a is the fraction of total output earned by labor, and $1 - a$ is the corresponding fraction for capital. This is sometimes called a Cobb-Douglas production function, after the economists who developed it, to explain the apparent stability of relative income shares. If the elasticity of substitution between capital and labor is 1, the a and $1 - a$ will be constant shares of total output going to labor and capital, and A is "neutral" with respect to the relative shares going to labor and capital.[3]

Alternatively, it may be that without technical change the elasticity of substitution is not 1. Then if investment produces a relatively faster growth in capital (as in the U.S. economy), the interest rate might fall enough and the wage rate might rise enough for the income share of capital to fall, that of labor to rise. Indeed, there seems little a priori reason to suppose the elasticity of substitution between K and L is just 1. But if so, how shall we explain the surprising relative stability of income shares? The answer, some modern economists argue, is that technical progress is not neutral, but instead it provides a built-in mechanism for keeping income shares roughly constant. If, for example, this second case occurs, businessmen will be induced by the profit motive to shift their technical change (innovations) toward the labor-saving type. They do so because labor is becoming relatively more expensive, capital relatively cheaper. Moreover, it is argued, this inducement will be roughly enough to offset any tendency for the relative shares of capital and labor to shift.

Is this induced-innovation theory of stable income shares right? Or is innovation generally "neutral," so that the observed rough stability in income shares comes from an elasticity of substitution between K and L of about 1? We don't know. This is the kind of research project on which modern economists work—both because it is intellectually challenging and because the conclusions may throw light on fundamental social issues.

[3] For a more complete account of the forces determining the incomes received by labor and capital see Part Four, and Mathematical Appendix IV which provides a rigorous analysis of the Cobb-Douglas production function.

Economic Growth in the United States

CHAPTER PREVIEW

CHAPTER FORTY-THREE

We think of ourselves as the richest and most productive nation in the world. We have a right to. Starting from nowhere only two centuries ago, the U.S. economy has produced results that are spectacular by any standards. Our 1973 GNP of $1.3 trillion was nearly one-third of the world's total, yet we have only 6 percent of the world's population. How have we done so well? And why have we fallen behind some other nations in the recent growth race?

THE U.S. RECORD

Figure 43–1 shows the record. Over the past century total U.S. real GNP has risen fiftyfold. Over the same period per capita GNP (in 1964 prices) rose from about $450 to $4,200, or nearly tenfold. Total output has grown at a rate of about 3.4 percent and per capita output at about 2.2 percent annually.

The historical record raises some intriguing problems. Table 42–1 showed our long-term growth rate compared to those of other leading countries over the past century. How shall we explain the wide lead of present U.S. output per capita over that of other nations such as Germany, Japan, and the USSR? A plausible inference from the estimates would be that somehow the United States grew very fast during the first century of its existence, so that we had already established a substantial lead over the other nations by the middle of the nineteenth

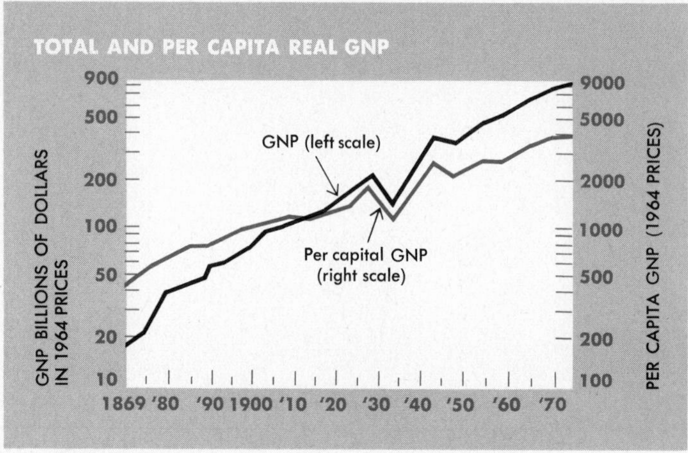

Figure 43–1

Both total and per capita real GNP have risen persistently over the past century, faltering seriously only during the 1930s. Data are plotted only at five-year intervals to show the main growth trends. (Source: U.S. Department of Commerce.)

century. But many historians reject this explanation, arguing that the U.S. growth rate began to pick up with the Industrial Revolution here in the middle 1800s. Whatever the answer, don't forget one impressive fact: Only a fraction of a percentage point difference in annual growth rate can accumulate to enormous totals over a century or more.

To fill in the factual background, let us take a closer look at the anatomy of U.S. economic growth since 1900. Figure 43–2 shows the major variables in the growth process that were stressed in the theory of Chapter 42. Note that all curves are plotted on a ratio scale, so the slopes of the lines show comparative growth rates.

What can we see here? A rapid but jagged rate of growth in real GNP, reflecting a roughly similar rate of growth in the capital stock and a much slower growth in population. The theory of Chapter 42 would suggest rising real wages relative to the return on capital, and this is indeed what we see in the lower part of the chart. Further, the theory would predict that without technical progress the rate of return on capital would fall absolutely. But, interestingly, the return on capital (the interest rate), though fluctuating widely in the Great Depression, is roughly flat in trend. (Much of the recent rise is merely inflation.) Something, presumably technical advance, has buoyed up **both** real wages and the return to capital, as the theory suggests. Our growth theory from Chapter 42, with technical advance included, is confirmed by the evidence.

EXPLAINING U.S. GROWTH TO DATE

The Sources of Growth

What have been the main sources of economic growth in the United States? Table 43–1 gives one courageous expert's estimates of the quantitative importance of the big forces at work during this century. Although he doesn't pretend that these are more than crude approximations, they provide an interesting introduction to the rest of this chapter.

Note the significant differences between the pre- and post-1929 periods. The increasing **quantity** of labor and capital goods dominates the pre-1929 picture. But since 1929, improvements in the **quality** of labor and capital (technical advance incorporated in both real capital and human beings) have accounted for half of our total growth, according to these estimates. And if we eliminate growth in the labor force (population) because it doesn't significantly raise output *per capita,* improvements in quality accounted for two-thirds of the total increase.

These allocations are in dispute among research workers. Harvard's Zvi Griliches and Dale Jorgenson, using different methods, conclude that increased inputs account for more of the growth in output, leaving a smaller role for technical advance as a separate factor. Distinguishing between the contribution of more capital and improved technology is extremely difficult, because with advancing technology new machines almost always have higher productivity than their predecessors. How much of the increased output shall we attribute to *more* capital, how much to *improved* capital? There is no undisputed way to draw the line. But almost all research experts agree that Denison's factors are the right ones to look at.[1]

[1]Denison has lumped together all "advances of knowledge" in a more recent study of growth in nine Western nations and has somewhat reduced the importance allocated to it in the United States since 1955. *Why Growth Rates Differ* (Washington, D.C.: The Brookings Institution, 1967), p. 299.

Figure 43-2

Since 1900 the capital stock has grown much faster than the labor force, and GNP has grown faster than have the combined inputs of labor and capital. Real wages and interest rates have moved about as would be expected from our theory of growth, recognizing the big role played by technological advance. Note that interest rates are not adjusted for price changes; real interest rates were much higher in recent inflation years. (Source: Long Term Economic Growth, 1860–1965, U.S. Department of Commerce, 1966. This volume summarizes much of the available statistical data on U.S. growth.)

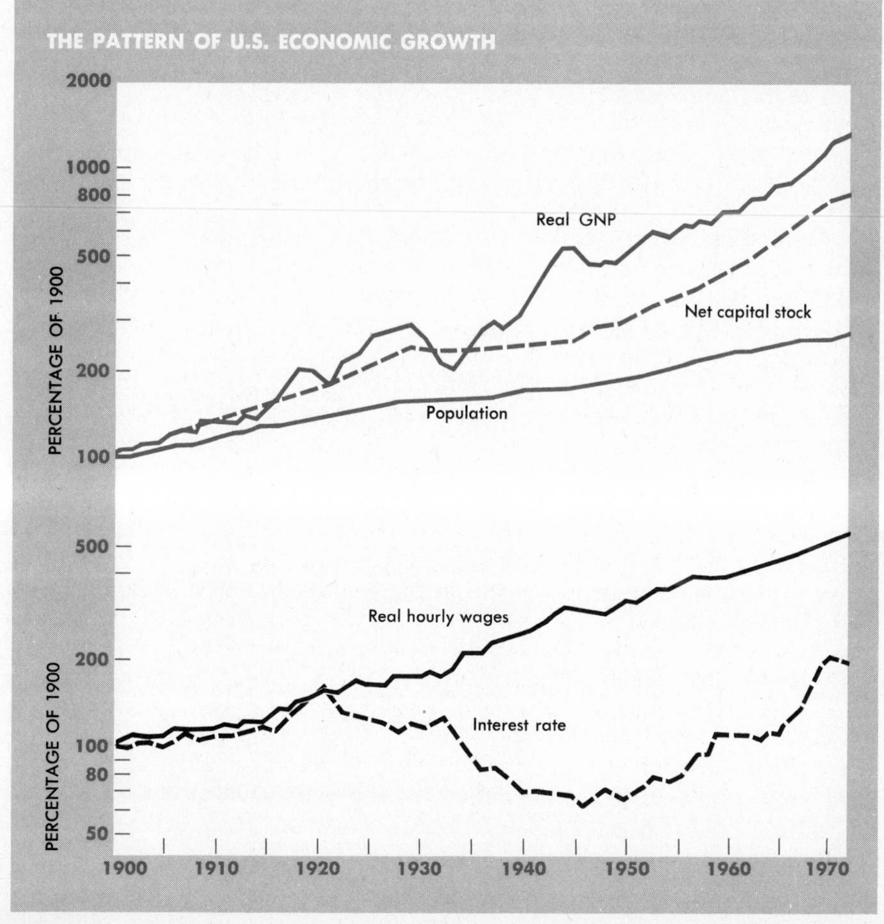

TABLE 43–1
Sources of U.S. Economic Growth, 1909–57

SOURCE	PERCENTAGE OF TOTAL GROWTH 1909–29	1929–57
Total growth in national real income	100	100
Increase in labor force[a]	35	27
Improved education and training	13	27
Increased stock of capital goods	23	15
Improved technology	19	22
Economies of scale[b]	10	9

[a] Adjusted for decreasing number of working hours per year.

[b] Economies of large-scale production with growing total size of the market.

Source: Edward Denison, *The Sources of Economic Growth in the United States* (Committee for Economic Development, 1962).

To fill in this framework completely as an explanation of U.S. economic growth would require a separate book. The charts on pages 592–97 summarize some of the main factors at work. They need only brief comments.

Natural Resources

The United States has been rich in natural resources, and they help explain our record growth. But the most striking fact has been our success in substituting new resources for old as technology advances. In 1850, 65 percent of all energy came from animal and human power, only 35 percent from inanimate sources (water, petroleum, and so on). Today only 1 percent of all power is furnished by humans and animals, 99 percent by inanimate sources.

Recently, there have been widespread fears that we will soon run out of natural resources, especially energy sources. We shall look at this issue carefully in Chapter 44. Figure 43–3 shows the rapidly changing sources of energy used over the past half century. Atomic energy is developing rapidly as a new source. Will solar energy be next?

Capital Goods and Capital Accumulation

History suggests that the long-term economic growth rates of the major countries correspond roughly to the proportion of their total outputs that they save and invest. When we recognize that most technical advance also requires investment (in research and development,

Figure 43–3

Petroleum and natural gas have increased as major sources of energy for the modern economy. Will nuclear and solar power soon take over? (Source: National Industrial Conference Board.)

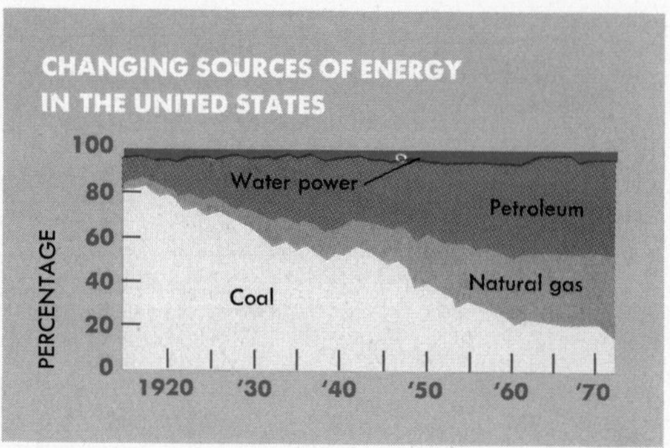

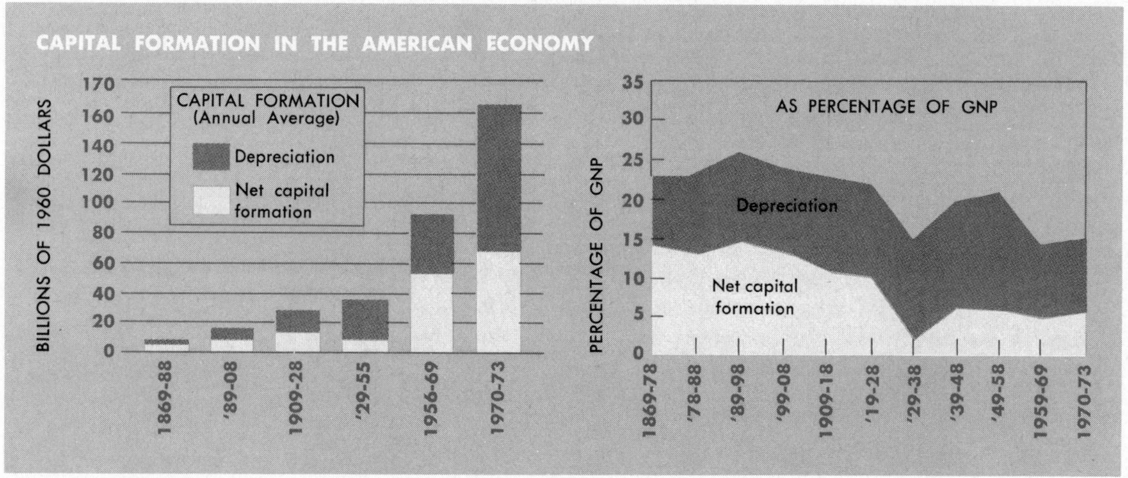

Figure 43–4

Gross capital formation has risen enormously over the past century, but recently both gross and new capital formation have been much smaller percentages of GNP than in earlier decades. (Sources: S. Kuznets, Capital in the American Economy, Princeton Univ. Press, 1961; and Council of Economic Advisers.)

in human beings, and as a vehicle for introducing technical changes), the need to save and invest for economic growth becomes doubly obvious.

Throughout the nineteenth century, the United States was a high-saving and high-investment economy. It paced the world in economic growth. During the present century, though we have invested huge sums, the proportion of our national product devoted to investment has dropped substantially—especially during the Great Depression of the 1930s and again since World War II.[2]

Figure 43–4 tells the story. During the past decade we have invested over $100 billion annually (in current dollars), a total exceeding the entire GNP of all except a half dozen nations. The result is an enormous productive machine underlying our trillion dollar GNP. Investment per employee in manufacturing is over $20,000. Our capital stock has grown sixfold since 1900.

Yet, as the right-hand part of Figure 43–4 shows, investment has trended down as a percentage of GNP. This country is no longer a high-saving economy, and it is perhaps not surprising that our growth rate recently has been well under those of such high-savings nations as Japan and West Germany.

Technical Change

Modern technology and innovation have long been the trademarks of American business. Behind this advance have been both a spirit of American entrepreneurship and an enormous increase in spending on research and development. Figure 43–5 tells the story. From only $1 billion annually in 1941, R&D spending has soared to nearly $30 billion annually, three-fourths the amount of total net private business expenditures on plant and equipment. But R&D, like investment spending on plant and equipment, has been falling in recent years as a percentage of GNP. Some experts predict that this will slow our high rate of technological advance and growth over the decades ahead

[2]This is much less striking if we include consumers' durables as investment.

unless we again step up our rate of R&D spending. Strikingly, about two-thirds of R&D is paid for by the federal government; over 90 percent of *basic* research is government-financed. Since 1940, the federal government has spent over $150 billion on R&D, though most of the work has been done in private industry, universities, and private research organizations.

Half of all the measured research in our history has occurred in the last fifteen years. But the growth in federal financing of research slowed in the late 1960s; the flattening of the government portion of the total is clear in Figure 43–5. And when we allow for inflation, *real* government spending on research has dropped absolutely in recent years—reflecting mainly cutbacks in military and space programs. Private industry has concentrated largely on developing the basic research of others into commercially profitable applications. Digital computers, many drugs, atomic energy, communications satellites, and modern aircraft are notable examples of major innovations originally financed by government research funds.

Population and the Labor Force

Denison allocates about a third of all growth in output to growth in the labor force. Figure 43–6 shows this persistent growth since 1900. Except for bulges during major wars, the growth has been a steady one, reflecting a combination of growing population and a gradual increase in the percentage of the population in the labor force. Figure 43–7 shows the persistent decline in the growth rate of population in the United States; while population is still growing by about two million annually, the present birthrate has dropped to roughly a zero-population-growth rate. However, even if this rate continues, it will take until about the year 2000 before we reach stability at around 250 million people because of the large number of young people who have yet to pass through their child-bearing periods.

We have steadily increased the years of schooling before our youth enter the job market, and now most people retire earlier. Offsetting this drain, the proportion of women working has

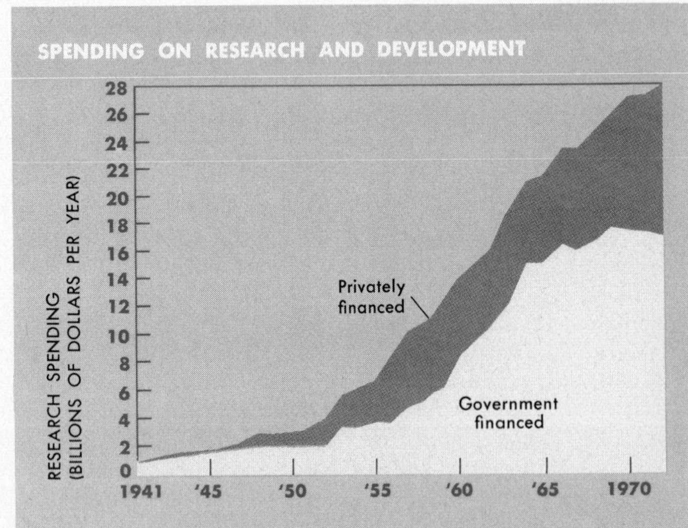

Figure 43–5

Research is the newest major industry in the United States. It has developed largely since World War II, and is about two-thirds government financed. Most is applied and developmental, only a little basic, research. (Source: National Science Foundation.)

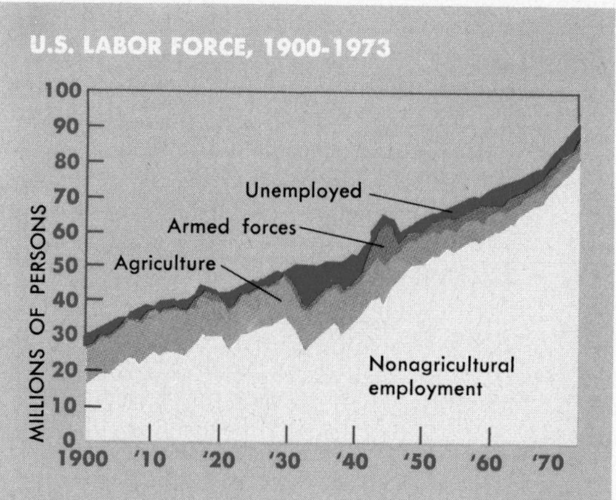

Figure 43–6

The U.S. labor force has grown steadily, with bulges during major wars. Most have taken nonagricultural jobs. Note the big unemployment pocket during the 1930s. (Source: U.S. Department of Labor.)

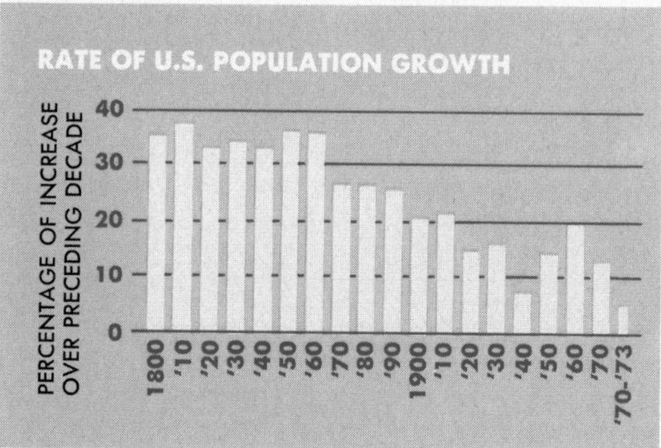

Figure 43–7

The postwar baby boom produced a big increase in our population growth rate. But the rate has fallen dramatically since then. Each bar shows the percentage increase over the preceding decade. (Source: U.S. Census Bureau.)

risen rapidly in recent decades. A century ago, few women worked at paid jobs. Once married, a girl retired sedately to her new home to keep the furniture dusted, get the meals ready on time, and raise a family. Today 45 percent of all women of working age and 42 percent of all such married women have paid jobs, and women comprise 40 percent of the labor force.

A century ago, the average factory worker in the United States put in seventy-five to eighty hours a week—generally ten hours or more a day including Sundays. Today he works only around forty hours. Over the decades America has faced a continual choice between work and leisure. We have chosen a slow but steady increase in the amount of leisure. Short hours and long vacations may produce fewer cars and houses, but leisure, though not sold in the marketplace or counted in GNP, has a real value for the persons enjoying it.

Investment in Human Capital

The growth of education in America has been phenomenal. In colonial days, few people received any formal education beyond elementary reading and writing. By 1870, only one in fifteen persons of high-school age was attending school. Today this figure is over 95 percent, with fourteen million students in some 25,000 high schools. The proportion of illiterates in the population is below 3 percent. Nearly half of all high-school graduates now go on to college, while only a generation ago a college education was a special privilege available only to the well-to-do.

Figure 43–8 shows the rapid growth in spending on education since 1900. During the first three decades of the century, the rate of growth in investment in human resources was more than twice that in nonhuman capital; the upward slope of the education line on the ratio chart is roughly twice that of the top line showing investment in capital goods. (Query: How long is the time lag between more education and a resulting increase in output per capita?)

Figure 43–8 indicates three other interesting facts: (1) The growth in spending on education has been much more stable than on private investment in capital goods. (2) Since World War II, the rates of growth in investment in human and nonhuman resources have been roughly comparable, unlike the 1900–30 period.

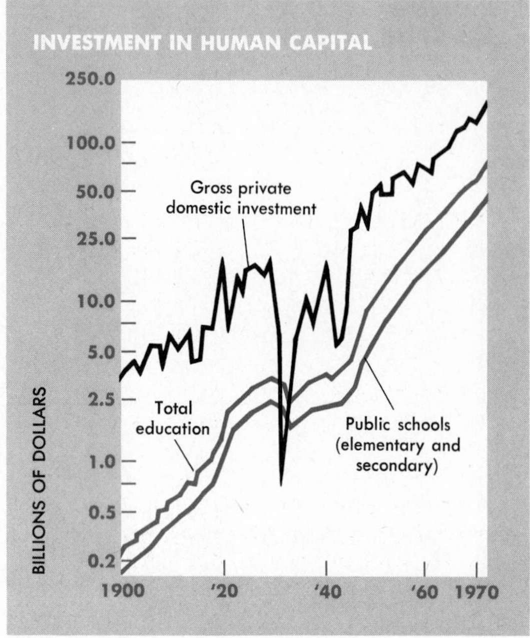

Figure 43–8

Investment in education has grown faster than private investment in capital goods since 1900, and at a much more stable rate. (Sources: U.S. Department of Commerce, and Health, Education, and Welfare.)

Figure 43–9

The average annual gain in productivity has fluctuated, but the trend has been upward. (Data are for output per man-hour in the private sector.)

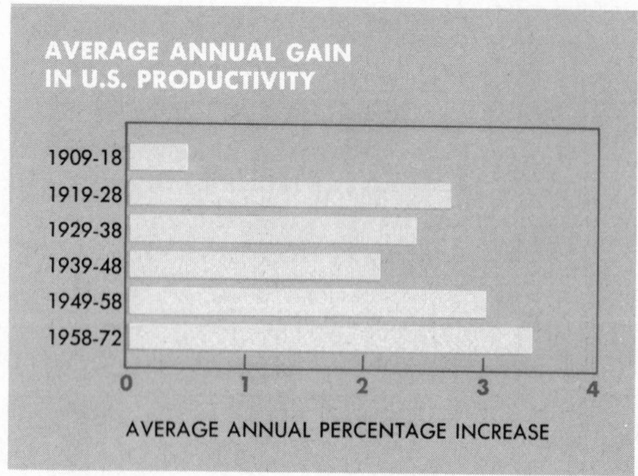

(3) The overwhelming bulk of our expenditure on education goes into elementary and secondary schools. Even with our recent big increase in college education, it still accounts for only a minor portion of our total investment in human capital.

Productivity

Average hourly or annual output per worker is often called worker "productivity." Thus, total output can be viewed as the number of workers times the average output per worker. But don't let the common practice of using "productivity" to mean output per man mislead you into attributing all the increased output to workers. We could equally well do a productivity calculation showing output per unit of capital, by dividing total output by the number of units of capital employed.

Figure 43–9 points up the wide fluctuations in productivity from decade to decade—and also its growth trend. Annual increases vary from as high as 12 percent (1919) to minus 8 percent (1917), though few years show a negative figure.

Moreover, the economy-wide figures cover up wide differences among industries. Figure 43–10 shows the widely differing increases in various sectors of the economy. Separate data on individual firms within industries would show an even more dramatic spread.

Figure 43–10 also suggests that occupational shifts may significantly affect the national average growth rate. The persistent shift of manpower out of agriculture, for example, has recently meant a move of workers from lower- to higher-productivity industries, and has thus raised the national growth rate. (This shift was a major factor in the high growth rates in Western Europe following World War II. Without this shift, their total measured growth rates would have been little higher than ours.)

Scale of Market

Mass production is obviously more efficient than small-scale output in many industries.

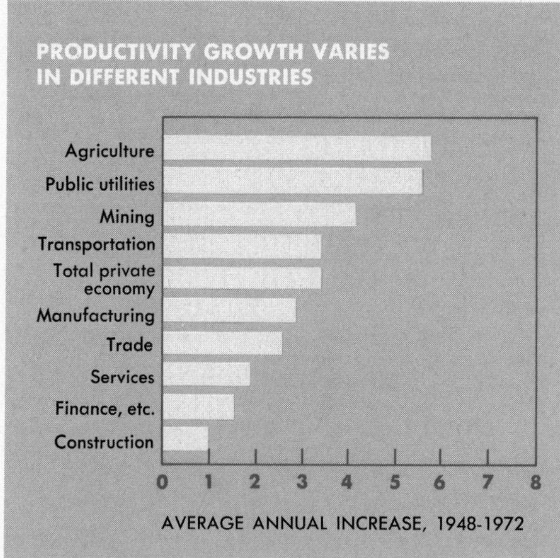

Figure 43–10

Since World War II, output per man-hour has increased at widely differing rates in different sectors of the economy. (Source: U.S. Department of Labor.)

Steel, aluminum, automobiles, glass, and dozens of other major products must be produced on a massive scale to permit use of the expensive capital equipment and sophisticated techniques that characterize modern mass production and underlie low prices. Thus, an economy must have large markets if it is to take advantage of the economies of mass production.

Table 43–1 allocates 10 percent of our total growth this century to economies of scale. Other economists have come up with even larger estimates. The very fact that the American economy grew so fast and became so large gave it an edge for still faster growth, compared to the smaller economies of the world. Chalk up economies of scale as an important factor, and one on which the United States has had a big advantage.

Economic Organization and Social-Political Environment

How much of our economic growth is due to our individual-initiative, basically-private-enterprise, free society? America's economic, political, and religious atmosphere has been peculiarly favorable to individual initiative, hard work, and the pursuit of material rewards. Success in business has been a mark of distinction. The "protestant ethic," which looks upon work as good in itself, has been an important part of our mores. And the basic tradition of "each man for himself" has provided an inviting setting for individual attempts to move up the economic ladder. America's risk-taking entrepreneurs have clearly played a central role in our rapid growth. Experts trying to help the less-developed countries are increasingly impressed with the value of such traditions as a foundation for economic growth.

American economic institutions have shown unusual flexibility in adjusting to the needs of the growing economy. Banking and financial institutions developed rapidly in response to the need to accumulate savings for investment. Development of the modern corporation facilitated the accumulation of capital for business ventures without undue risk for nonmanagerial investors.

Reflecting this climate, government has been generally friendly to vigorous, open competition. Preservation of peace and order, protection of property rights, and provision of necessary government services all provided a strong foundation for economic activity.

How much credit should Denison have given these factors back in Table 43–1? He couldn't measure them, so he didn't put them in. Yet many observers feel they deserve much of the credit for our spectacular performance.

Aggregate Demand

The preceding "real" factors fundamentally determine how fast an economy can grow. But aggregate demand to generate full employment without inflationary booms is also important in a market-directed economy.

Today we recognize that government monetary-fiscal policy can go a long way toward assuring roughly the right rate of growth in aggregate demand. Through most of our history, however, this was not true, and it is only since the 1930s that monetary-fiscal policy has been seriously mobilized to maintain a stably growing level of aggregate demand. The growth in the money stock and aggregate demand since 1900, shown back in Figure 12–1, came primarily from private financial behavior, not from government stabilization policy.

Whether the growth in the money stock has been mainly cause or effect of the growth in real output, the end result has been somewhat faster growth in aggregate demand than in real output, with a resulting gradual inflationary trend. Except during the long depression of the 1930s, deficient aggregate demand apparently has not seriously held back our rate of economic growth.

Some observers point to our repeated booms and depressions as evidence that misbehavior of aggregate demand has indeed slowed growth. One test would be the average level of unemployment of men and machines over the long pull. Here the decade of the 1930s was our big failure; on the average we have had about 5 percent of our labor force unemployed over the past century—not a great success story but not enough to seriously retard the nation's growth rate.

CONCLUSION

In retrospect, does the theory of Chapter 42 do a good job of explaining U.S. economic growth? The answer appears to be "yes." Growth in the United States has been a complex, shifting process. But this basic analytical framework can go a long way in pointing up the main forces, and in keeping you from getting bogged down in details.

REVIEW

For Analysis and Discussion

1. Has the U.S. record on economic growth been satisfactory over the period since World War II? What criteria do you use in making your judgment?
2. Make a list of the major factors likely to increase the labor force over the next twenty years, and those likely to decrease it. Which are likely to dominate?
3. How long should the workweek be? What are the major considerations in answering this question?
4. Suppose today's college generation decides that it prefers the "simple life" to working for business firms. What would be the effect on the standard of living of (a) this college generation over the next decade? (b) the rest of the American public?
5. "Rising productivity (output per man-hour) is obviously the key to American growth. Thus, it is clear that the American worker deserves the big credit for our rapidly rising living standards." Do you agree with this statement by a labor leader? Explain.
6. Is Denison right (Table 43–1) in giving no weight to natural resources in explaining the causes of U.S. economic growth since 1909? Explain.
7. Most Americans feel that private initiative and our market system deserve great

credit for our high standard of living compared to other nations. Suppose you meet a foreigner who disagrees. What arguments can you advance to convince him?

8. Critics of the law of diminishing returns argue that the law must be unimportant or invalid in the United States because the U.S. population has grown enormously over the past century while the stock of natural resources has been fixed, yet output of food per capita has risen greatly. Are the critics right?
9. "More rapid growth of population in the United States would mean a decline in our standard of living." Do you agree? Explain.

Growth Policy

CHAPTER PREVIEW

CHAPTER FORTY-FOUR

Now, a look to the future. How fast *should* the American economy grow? Most living things—trees, animals, people—grow more slowly as they mature. Is this true of economies too? If so, should we expect our growth rate to slow down, or is the United States still a healthy, growing youngster?

The optimal rate of growth has become a controversial issue. Most Americans want a higher standard of living—more income and the things that income can buy. They want better houses, automatic washers and dryers, better education for their children, better highways, and to get rid of the slums and poverty that mar American life. We must produce more if we are to have more. But Zero Economic Growth (ZEG) has become a rallying cry of those who argue that modern technology and the economic growth it helps generate are dehumanizing society and destroying the environment. Our social values are perverted, the critics say. Not more GNP, but a higher quality of life should be our major goal.

Before examining the great growth controversy, it is important to distinguish between economic growth and population growth. Economic growth is growth in output, or output per capita. Population growth means more people—more mouths to feed—but not necessarily any more output. Thus, other things equal, economic growth means a higher standard of living, population growth a lower one.

Although as a practical matter economic and population growth often come together, it is important to separate them analytically. This chapter is primarily concerned with economic growth and with growth policy in industrially-developed countries like the United States. Population growth typically slows as income per capita rises, and indeed the American birthrate has recently fallen below a long-run ZPG level—about 2.1 children per family. Thus, fears of a "population bomb" now appear to have little force for the economically developed nations. But they are very real indeed for many of the less-developed nations, where population is growing rapidly and living standards are very low; these nations are the subject of Chapter 45.

THE GREAT GROWTH CONTROVERSY

The Benefits of Growth

The growth rate of the American economy will largely determine your standard of living during the rest of your life. Consider Table 44–1, which shows U.S. real GNP in 1980 and 2000, for growth rates of 3, 4, or 5 percent for the rest of this century.

Put simply, if we grow at 3 percent per annum, the average family's *real* income, as measured by real GNP per family, will be about twice as high by the year 2000 as it is now—about $20,000 compared to $11,000 in 1973. If we grow at 5 percent, this average family-income figure would soar to over $35,000 (in 1973 prices). Five percent would be very high by historical standards, but it is the goal set by most West European nations in their recent planning. Even 4 percent, about our post-World War II rate, would yield an extra trillion dollars of real GNP annually by the year 2000, as compared to 3 percent. This difference is nearly as much as our total GNP in 1973. The stakes in the growth game are huge!

TABLE 44–1
U.S. Real GNP For Alternative Growth Rates
(In trillions, 1973 prices)

	1973	1980	2000
With 3 percent annual growth	$1.3	$1.5	$2.8
With 4 percent annual growth	1.3	1.7	3.7
With 5 percent growth	1.3	1.9	5.0

These figures are so large as to be almost beyond comprehension. The benefits of growth as a practical matter can be illustrated by looking back at the growth in American living standards since 1900, when the economy's GNP has grown at about 3.5 percent annually.

The most obvious change is the dramatic reduction in hard, back-breaking, physical labor, on the job, in housekeeping, and on the farm. In 1900, such labor was commonplace, today very little remains. The average factory workweek has fallen from fifty-five to less than forty hours. In 1900, the typical housewife cooked on a wood or coal kitchen stove, which she fired several times a day. To do the weekly wash, she carried a huge tub of water to boil on top of the stove. Today, 99 percent of all families have refrigerators, 92 percent automatic washers, 41 percent automatic clothes dryers, 39 percent air conditioners. Today's family eats better (more meats, fruits, and dairy products), lives more comfortably, has hot running water and indoor plumbing, is healthier, and lives longer. Life expectancy today is seventy years, up from fifty.

The list could go on indefinitely. Today's average American goes more places and sees more things in a year than his 1900 counterpart did in a lifetime. Today's family has vastly more freedom for the amusement, travel, and other leisure activities it enjoys. With a four-times-higher real income, its economic security is far greater. Its life insurance today totals nine times as much as in 1900, in real terms. All these facts are commonplace to us. But they are the envy of poorer nations, and they would have been utterly unbelievable to students in 1900.

Some argue that the United States is indeed

now so affluent that we no longer need to increase total output—that we have enough economic goods and services. But it is striking that this cry for ZEG should come just when the nation appears to be establishing a new set of enormously expensive "national priorities." Chapter 2 listed some of these. To raze and rebuild the nation's city slums would cost, it has been estimated, at least a quarter to a half trillion dollars. Twenty-five million Americans are still officially classified as poor—families receiving less than $4,200 annually. To reduce existing air and water pollution to 1972 legal standards will cost over a quarter trillion dollars during the 1970s, and most environmentalists consider these standards too low. Add better housing for those outside the slums, higher education standards, improved mass transportation, and so on, to say nothing of more private goods and services for most families, and it becomes painfully clear that, instead of a surplus of economic productive capacity, we face a massive resource crunch if we hope to make significant headway on our new national priorities and meet the personal aspirations of most people. Our aspirations have risen as fast as our ability to produce. Nor do they show any sign of slowing down.

If we then add the vast needs for aid to the less-developed nations (with over 2 billion people living barely above the subsistence level), the need for economic growth seems overwhelming. Even dramatic steps to redistribute current U.S. incomes *equally among all* (leaving aside the probably large drop of total output with complete elimination of individual economic incentives to produce) would leave most American families below their aspirations—below about $11,000 annually, with nothing to meet the new national priorities. Spreading the U.S. income equally over the world's 3.8 billion people would raise their average income by only about $25 annually. It is no accident that neither the lower-income groups, the less-developed nations, nor economists are prominent in the ZEG movement. **The main hope for a better life lies in more output, not in redistributing what there is now.**

The Costs of Growth

Offset against these potential benefits of growth are two major types of costs. First, we can have more tomorrow only by consuming less today. Second, and more central to modern radical criticism, growth may involve undesirable side effects—air and water pollution, exhaustion of natural resources, overcrowded cities (caused by economic or population growth?), large organizations that dehumanize work and alienate people from "the system." Consider the costs in that order.

Less Today for More Tomorrow

Given full employment of resources, we can grow faster only by working harder or accepting less leisure and lower consumption now than we could otherwise have had. Rapid technical advance can help, but remember that R&D takes resources too. Economists often say, "There's no such thing as a free lunch," to emphasize the fundamental economic problem.

Your inclination may be to say, "Of course we should save more today for a better tomorrow. We should sacrifice more for the benefit of our children and grandchildren." But don't be too quick. Even with the present growth rate, the average per capita income of your children a generation hence will be more than 50 percent higher than yours is today; that of your grandchildren two generations hence will be far more than double the present level. Given these facts, some observers don't find the case for paying the cost of faster growth very impressive. Why, they ask, should we squeeze down on consumption now to make the future even richer? It's a good question.

Undesirable Side Effects of Growth

Destruction of the environment, deterioration of the quality of life, and exhaustion of scarce natural resources are the major charges widely levelled against economic growth. It is clear that economic growth in the United States has helped produce the pollution of air, water, and quiet that plagues the land. Smog, dirty water, noise, and dirt are *real* and *objectionable.* Highways and streets are cluttered with unsightly neon signs, wires, and hot dog stands; parks are full of autos and empty beer cans. The facts are well known; there is little need to repeat them.

But as Chapter 36 pointed out, anger at pollution should not be permitted to confuse our analysis of what to do about it. While growth is responsible for some of today's pollution, to stop growth in order to stop pollution would be short-sighted, inefficient, and unnecessarily costly—cutting off our noses to spite our faces. For growth in total economic capacity can be used to produce what we want most. If it is cleaner air and water, we can readily produce more sewage disposal plants, quieter trucks, cleaner cars. We can do this and have capacity left to produce more of the other things we want—better houses, health, education, comfortable living. Even if we spend the $287 billion estimated by the Council on Environmental Quality to clean up the environment over the 1970s, this will be less than half the total growth in GNP during the decade. To give up the half trillion dollars of GNP to avoid the pollution it might create would be foolish. We would end up with no reduction in the present level of pollution and we would have thrown away additional vast improvement in our economic living standards. Sensible pollution policy certainly is to enforce pollution reduction through government policy while encouraging the national growth that will permit us to pay for it without reducing our national standard of living to do so.

Other costs of growth—crowding as we move into cities, the rush of modern urban life, alienation of workers from their jobs, and the like—are harder to deal with through economic analysis alone. But economics can help. Look back at Table 8-6, which presented the estimates of Professors Tobin and Nordhaus of what has happened to total economic welfare as the economy has grown since 1929. Although the estimates are rough, Tobin and Nordhaus conclude that even when full account is taken of "undesirables" (like spending needed just to cope with the complexities of modern life) and "disamenities" (like the noise and dirt found in modern cities), net economic welfare roughly doubled between 1929 and 1965, while GNP was tripling. Thus, the costs of growth are real, but they far from use up the total productive capacity associated with growth. **If we manage our affairs sensibly, we can have both a better, cleaner environment and the additional real benefits available from growth.**[1]

The allegation that growth dehumanizes work and alienates workers from their jobs obviously reaches beyond economics into psychology and sociology. But many of the alleged facts warrant a closer look. First, although some high-skill jobs have been eliminated by modern technology, there has been relatively little change in the overall skill-requirements pattern of the national job market. The modern computer, for example, has displaced mainly routine, low-skilled clerical jobs in banks and insurance companies. It has created mainly high-skill jobs in manufacturing, programming, and servicing computers. Perhaps the biggest modern job shift has been from manufacturing to services—store clerks, airline employees, beauty parlor operators. There have been enormous changes in jobs since frontier days, but whether today's jobs are less difficult, less interesting, and less challenging is far from clear. Similarly, it is far from clear whether big business necessarily leads to alienation and unhappiness. There is little doubt that some people find the modern corporation an oppressive, dull master. Others find it a comfortable, if unexciting, place to earn a good living. Still others find it an exciting, challenging environment where first-rate ability and hard work can bring big salaries and satisfying success. Unhappy workers didn't arrive with economic growth and the

[1]Since Professor Tobin is widely acclaimed as one of the leading liberal economists of the day, there is little reason to suppose that these estimates may be slanted in favor of "the conservatives." He was one of President Kennedy's chief economic advisers.

modern corporation. Moreover, don't forget that only about a quarter of all Americans work for the big corporations that are often alleged to dominate the American economy. (See Chapter 25.)

Exhaustion of Natural Resources. Both population and economic growth use up natural resources. The American economy chews up an enormous volume of raw materials, and conservationists have long predicted dire consequences from our "extravagant" use of raw materials and energy reserves. But so far new reserves and, more important, substitute materials and energy sources have been discovered as fast as our uses have grown. Oil and natural gas, nuclear and solar energy, are examples. The massive substitution of artificial for natural rubber and of nylon and other man-made fibers for silk are other examples. Clearly, natural resources are not limitless, but technical ingenuity has more than overcome the major shortages to date. Most experts appear to take a middle position. We do indeed face problems ahead on some resources, but most doomsday predictions are overdone.

Nonetheless, fear is widespread that America will soon run out of natural resources, especially energy sources. (See the box on "The Energy Crisis.") No one can be sure of the future, but both history and economic theory can help assess the danger.

First, what are the facts? U.S. per capita consumption of natural resources has grown steadily, with our rising standard of living. Over the past half century, growth in per capita consumption of all natural resources has been less than 1 percent per year while per capita real income has grown at over 2 percent; remember the large shift from manufactured goods to services. Consumption of minerals has grown substantially faster, perhaps 1.5 percent per year since World War II. Only for forest products has per capita consumption fallen, reflecting the growing scarcity of wood resources and a corresponding increase in their relative prices. Second, if natural resources were becoming relatively scarce, one would expect their prices to rise relative to the prices of other things. In general, again with the exception of forest products, the *relative* prices of natural resources (minerals, agricultural products, and the like) have *fallen* up to 1973—though if the much-discussed energy crisis materializes, we can expect energy prices (of oil, gas, and the like) to rise rapidly. Third, if we were suffering from natural-resource shortages, one would expect a rise in the proportion of raw materials and food imported from abroad. There has recently been some increase, but relatively little change over all. The share of our oil imported is rising substantially. But all imports total less than 10 percent of total consumption over the past century—less than 5 percent if we include agricultural products.

These facts do not support the doomsday predictions about natural resource exhaustion that are so frequently made today. And the ratio of population to land and other natural resources is still low in the United States—although that ratio has not proven a very useful predictor of relative living standards in recent centuries. Switzerland, Sweden, Norway, and Denmark, for example, have high per capita incomes with limited natural resources. Just the reverse is true in China. But the ratio of rhetoric to reason is unfortunately high on questions of natural resources in the future of America. It is easy to overstress the likelihood that exhaustion of natural resources will seriously limit American growth in the foreseeable future. But it is easy, too, to be short-sighted about the fact that our demands for many minerals and energy sources are now growing very fast relative to known reserves. Clearly, America will have to find substitutes or new sources on a large scale if we are to avoid serious shortages, and most of these new sources will need to be outside the United States.[2]

[2] For a thorough, official study that recognizes both the problem and alternative solutions to it, see D.A. Brobst and W.T. Pratt, *U.S. Mineral Resources* (U.S. Geological Survey, 1973). See also the series of reports, *Toward a National Materials Policy,* by the National Commission on Materials Policy (U.S. Government Printing Office, 1972).

The Energy Crisis

In 1965 a massive blackout shut down the entire northeast, when a major generator failed during a heat wave that had pushed the electrical generating facilities of the entire area to their limit. Smaller brownouts hit other sections in following years. Scattered fuel oil and gasoline rationing were necessary as supplies ran short during the early 1970s. Today, fear of a national energy crisis during the decades ahead has come front and center in the nation's news media and in Congress. Our modern economy runs on energy, and our energy use is doubling every twenty years.

Table 44–2 provides rough estimates of U.S. domestic energy reserves in 1973 and how long they are likely to last at presently-forecasted use rates. To assess their importance, look back at Figure 43–3, which shows the shifting importance of different energy sources. Although our coal resources are almost unlimited, domestic oil and gas, the two most important current energy sources, may be exhausted in only ten years or so at currently expected use rates, assuming no further supplies are found. Little wonder that concern over a possible energy crisis has hit the headlines. Obviously, some big changes have to be made fast, or we will become heavily reliant on foreign sources for much of our energy.

TABLE 44–2

U.S. Energy Reserves, 1973

	ESTIMATED RESERVES	YEARS' SUPPLY
Oil (billion barrels)	52	10
Natural gas (trillion cu. ft.)	3,000	11
Uranium (tons)	450,000	13
Shale oil (billion barrels)[a]	160–600	35–120
Coal (trillion tons)	1.5	500

[a]Recoverable only if crude oil prices are at least 2.5 to 3 times present levels.

Source: U.S. Geological Service; estimates are for "proven" reserves.

Whether we in fact face an energy crisis depends on both technological developments and the policies we adopt. Nearly everyone involved assumes that the scientists will come up with major developments over the decade ahead, especially in nuclear energy using "fast breeder" technology that, amazingly, produces more fuel (plutonium) than it burns. Such advances should revolutionize power production by the year 2000, hopefully as soon as 1985. Solar power and other far-out developments may materialize. But between now and 1985, the nation faces some painful alternatives.

There is no world shortage of energy sources, and removing import quotas against foreign oil is obviously sensible if we fear domestic shortages. But if we let ourselves become too heavily dependent on the Middle East for our oil, we open ourselves to economic and political pressures, even blackmail, from those countries. The producing countries have already escalated oil prices over the past few years. Some estimates suggest that we could develop a $20 billion (or even larger) annual balance-of-payments deficit vis-á-vis these countries by 1985. Indeed, the greatest danger of a major oil crisis in the next decade lies in the possibility that the Arab Mid-Eastern oil-producing nations might reduce supplies to us for political reasons.

At home, we have plenty of coal, but most of it (except for some western deposits) is high-sulfur coal, which causes substantial pollution; moreover, to obtain it would involve massive strip mining, which elicits further environmentalist cries of opposition. We have substantial undeveloped oil reserves, but many of them are offshore where drilling would risk oil spills, again drawing bitter environmentalist objection. Other big reserves lie in northern Alaska, but environmentalists for years successfully blocked construction of the Alaskan pipeline. Retreat from new antipollution rules for autos could reduce auto use of gasolines by perhaps 10 percent, but with substantial environmental costs. Exploitation of our huge shale oil reserves will be profitable only at oil prices perhaps triple their present levels.

The government could also stimulate increased deep drilling for natural gas by raising the prices gas companies are permitted to charge, where such drilling is not now economically profitable, but this would bring widespread charges of a government sellout to the big gas companies. The price of natural gas has long been held down by the Federal Power Commission; this has, of course, encouraged its use and discouraged drilling for new sources. Raising the tax depletion allowances on gas and oil would have the same effect, but the cries for tax reform propose reducing this special tax incentive, not raising it. Nuclear power and development of fast-breeder technology are considered by most experts to be the most promising solution for the next two decades, but environmentalists block construction of new nuclear plants on grounds of both inadequate safety provisions and environmental effect. A different approach would involve persuading Americans not to use so much energy—to drive less, give up air conditioning, turn off their lights, and the like. But this does not seem very promising as a practical matter, unless we impose highly objectionable government regulations or permit sharply higher prices for energy. The mere thought of continuing peacetime national gas rationing for autos, for example, sends shivers up the back of every government administrator, as well it should.

Just about everyone agrees that we need a unified national energy policy to replace our present hodgepodge of regulations. The problem is enormously complex, and any successful policy will surely have many facets. But two fundamental approaches dominate the discussion. One is increased use of government intervention and regulation—government controls over what forms of energy to produce where, how the energy should be distributed, and who should get it and for what purposes. The other is increased use of built-in individual incentives—letting the price system do a big part of the job. This would involve letting energy prices rise sharply as demand grows relative to supply—in order to stimulate production and to reduce use of increasingly expensive fuels for less essential purposes. Under our public utility regulation, Americans have long had the cheapest gas and electricity in the world—little wonder we use lots and face dwindling supplies relative to demand. Either approach might be combined with international policies to minimize our exposure to exploitation by Mid-Eastern oil nations. What is your program to solve America's approaching energy crisis?[3]

[3]See suggestions for analysis at end of the book.

GROWTH POLICY— INCREASING POTENTIAL SUPPLY

Suppose we want to grow faster. Leaving aside questions of how increased capacity should be allocated among different private and social priorities, how can we increase the growth rate of total output? Many experts look at this question in two parts—first, how can we increase the amount of labor, and second, how can we increase the rate of growth in that labor's productivity? Since World War II, total man-hours of labor have grown at about 1.4 percent per annum, while productivity has grown at about 3 percent for the total public-plus-private economy.

A Menu for Economic Growth

Edward Denison, who made the estimates in Table 43–1, has also provided a menu for economic growth—a list of ten steps, which combined might raise the nation's annual growth in total output by 1 percentage point (for instance, from 4 to 5 percent per annum) over the next two decades. Each of the steps might account for .1 percent increase in the average growth rate. Remember that these estimates omit short-term business cycle movements, and concern only the long-term growth in real productive capacity of the economy. Note also that an increase of 1 percentage point in the annual growth rate would be a big increase, of about 25 percent in the existing rate.

More Work

Half of Denison's major proposals involve steps to increase the amount of work done by the working-age population. They are:

1. **Double the rate of immigration of working-age adults.** (Note that this would not correspondingly increase per capita output.)
2. **Draw into the labor force one-tenth of all able-bodied adults (mainly women and young people) who would not otherwise be working.**
3. **Increase the average workweek for all workers by one hour.**
4. **Cut in half the time lost from work because of sickness and accidents.**

Most experts expect a gradual increase in labor-force participation by women to be roughly offset by a shorter workweek, longer education for young people before they enter the labor force, and earlier retirement. The U.S. Department of Labor estimates that over the present decade our labor force will grow at a high 1.6 percent annually, compared to only 1.3 percent over the preceding fifteen years, but that total annual working hours per working-age person will grow at only about 1.4 percent.

Ours is a free society. We believe that a housewife and her husband, not the government, should decide whether she stays home or looks for a job. How many hours a week you work is largely up to you, your employer, and your union. The government may plead and explain the facts of economic growth. But short of national emergencies like war, there is little it can do to change the long-term trends of labor-force participation and the gradually lessening workweek. Indeed, government's main intervention has been through encouraging earlier retirement through social security, a shorter workweek through overtime rules, and low labor-force participation rates through free or cheap education. What would you suggest to accomplish proposals 2, 3 and 4?

5. **Reduce the average unemployment rate in the economy by 2 percentage points.** You should have your own menu of proposals on how to accomplish this after completing Part Two above. Note that the one-year increase in output from reducing unemployment (say from 5 to 3 percent) would mean a big increase in that year's growth, but once having been achieved, it would add little further to the growth rate over the next two decades, except through the higher investment rates that typically characterize high-employment periods.

Denison's other proposals involve ways to increase the annual growth in productivity (output per worker).

Saving and Investment

6. **Increase the rate of net private saving and investment by about 25 percent.** This would mean an increase of some $30–40 billion annually in gross private investment. While the United States saves and invests a huge amount annually, our private saving and investment as a percentage of GNP is one of the lowest of all major nations. Table 44–3 tells the story.
7. **Increase government investment in productive assets by 50 percent annually.**

How could we induce such a large increase in private-plus-public investment relative to GNP? The main ways would be through monetary and fiscal policy. Lower interest rates would lead to more investment. Tax reform to shift the burden from high incomes and corporate profits onto lower incomes would reduce consumption and stimulate saving and investment. Government investment of funds obtained through taxation could raise the investment rate at least temporarily. But even if we were to adopt these monetary and fiscal policies, it is not clear how big a difference they would make. Private saving and investment rates appear to be persistent. Even though tax increases and public investment were to reduce consumption relative to saving, households could offset this effect by reducing their after-tax savings and investments. The end result might well then be merely a substitution of public for private investment.

Communist nations, like the USSR and China, directly allocate resources to investment through central planning and control. The central planners decree that resources shall be allo-

TABLE 44–3

Private Investment Rates and Productivity in Major Nations

	INVESTMENT AS PERCENT OF GNP	AVERAGE ANNUAL INCREASE IN PRODUCTIVITY
Japan	38	13.1
France	26	6.8
West Germany	25	5.3
United Kingdom	19	3.6
United States	18	3.4

Source: Organization for Economic Cooperation and Development; data for 1966–71. The position of the United States would be above the United Kingdom in productivity if more recent years were included. Investment is gross private investment; productivity is for the private manufacturing sector.

cated to investment, and consumption is held down by simply not producing consumption goods. The communist leaders say that the masses really want such investment in future growth, but such dictatorial methods would be highly objectionable in a free society like ours.

Technical Advance—Research and Development

8. Increase by 10–15 percent the rate of technical advance.

9. Shorten by three years the lag between technical advances and their actual use in production.

The importance of increasing the rate of growth in productivity is suggested by Table 44–3. Although the United States was long a leader in innovation and technical advance, the final column shows that our growth rate in productivity is now slower than that in most other countries. By contrast, the extraordinary Japanese performance is largely attributable to their spectacular growth in productivity.

Although productivity reflects all the factors determining a nation's output except growth in the labor force, research and development spending and the effectiveness with which new knowledge is put to use are central forces determining the growth in total output. Following World War II, U.S. spending on R&D soared as a percentage of GNP (see Figure 43–5), with most of the spending financed by the federal government. Recently, this growth rate has slowed appreciably. No one knows just how long the lag is between R&D and its application, but clearly more spending on R&D would speed technical advance.

Private industry can probably be counted on to finance most developmental and applied research leading directly to salable products. There is no obvious way to increase such private spending on R&D, short of providing a government subsidy. Firms can already charge off most research expenses as direct costs and hence as full tax deductions. But the case for direct government support of *basic* research is strong. The results of truly basic research are unpredictable; and they seldom have direct commercial profitability. Even more important, if a company does make a major basic breakthrough, it is seldom able to protect its discovery for long from use by others. Thus, it is hard to see why many firms will spend much money on such basic research. But history records that it is the basic-research breakthroughs that have provided the foundation for the great scientific and practical benefits of our times.

Government support for the rapid dissemination of new knowledge and techniques also makes sense, on the same grounds. This is especially true for the outpouring of information from the government's own vast R&D spending on defense, space, and health projects. The agricultural experiment stations and extension services established at state universities throughout the nation a century ago have played a major role in speeding innovation in American agriculture. Similar aid in manufacturing, services, and other areas might produce similar results.

Investment in Human Capital

10. **Increase by one and one half years the average amount of education for all school-age members of the population, or improve the average quality of education by a corresponding amount.** Human beings are capital to a society, just as buildings and machines are. Modern research suggests that the return on investment in human capital (through formal education, training, and the like) is higher than the return on investment in capital goods. If this is true, both individuals and society would gain economically by spending more on education. In addition, we would get the large but immeasurable benefits of a better-educated population for a stable social-political system. The external economies again make a strong case for government action.

If education is such a good investment, why don't private individuals make the investment voluntarily? Many do. Beyond free education for all through high school, about half of all youths go on to college. Anyone who has done the arithmetic knows that a good education for his son is likely to be a better investment than buying stocks and bonds.

Nevertheless, either most of the population hasn't done the arithmetic or doesn't believe it. Most families and teenagers seem reluctant to borrow to make this investment in human capital, even though it is clearly profitable in the long run. Moreover, our society frowns on slavery; thus there is no sure way a capitalist with spare funds can get back a big return if he wants to invest in John Jones' education, instead of in a business venture. More publicly-financed education would probably speed economic growth. Another approach would be to make adequate loan funds for education available to all, especially to low-income levels.

Many modern researchers argue that on-the-job training is the highest-return form of investment in human capital, although Denison does not stress it. Such training has a sure, quick payoff, unlike academic education that may or may not be put to immediate practical use. Some propose subsidies to businesses to provide such training for potential employees, but such subsidies raise serious questions of equity among employers and workers. Others argue that the best inducement is merely to assure prosperous times, and businesses will increase such training as they seek more workers in their own self-interest. Still others stress eliminating barriers to such private training—for example, the high legal minimum wage required for inexperienced young workers that makes it unprofitable for employers to invest in on-the-job training for them.

Improved Economic Efficiency

The preceding list includes the main possibilities Denison suggests for raising the nation's growth rate. Strikingly, it omits a number of measures often proposed—for example, changes in the tax structure, elimination of discrimination, and improvements in the efficiency of markets. The potential of tax structure reform he lists at only .02 percentage points, elimination of discrimination at .04. All potential improvements in the efficiency of labor and product markets combined might total over .1 percentage point, but none alone seems to Denison to have major potential. Other economists place more emphasis on elimination of monopoly restrictions by both unions and businesses, and on steps to improve information and mobility in labor markets, but quantification of that potential is extremely difficult.

The Economic Climate—Initiative and Enterprise

Denison warns that he has omitted some factors that may be important, because they are so hard to quantify. Individual initiative, the spirit of enterprise, open markets with active competition, economic and social mobility, and a generally favorable economic-social-political climate clearly deserve much credit for America's growth over the past two centuries. But how to make them contribute *more* to growth in the future is less clear.

On the contrary, many observers believe they see a recent lessening of the contribution of these factors to American growth, especially beginning with the "liberal" social reforms and increased government intervention of the New Deal. They point to the spectacular productivity increases in postwar Germany and Japan as evidence that hard work, high saving and investment, and relatively low government expenditures for social overhead still are the main roads to rapid economic growth. By contrast, they see the modern American economy as increasingly comfortable, affluent, security-conscious, and critical of traditional American individualism and hard work.

Denison's refusal to estimate the quantitative importance of these factors is understandable. Economic historians suspect that they—the economic and social mores of a nation—play a vital role indeed. But important or not, they are obviously difficult factors to change significantly through government growth policy.

GROWTH POLICY—THE DEMAND SIDE

Increasing our productive capacity (moving out the production-possibilities frontier) is the main requisite for faster economic growth. But in a largely private-enterprise economy, the demand side matters too. For businessmen will not long produce goods they cannot sell at a profit. On the other hand, excess aggregate demand will produce inflation and instability. What level of aggregate demand should monetary and fiscal policy encourage to assure stable economic growth, avoiding both depressions and inflations?

What Aggregate Demand is Needed for Stable Economic Growth?

Assume that national productive capacity is growing 4 percent annually because of population growth, capital investment, and technological advance. Then aggregate demand should rise at about 4 percent a year (the same rate as productive capacity), and the division between consumption and investment spending should match the division between consumption and saving decisions (omitting government taxes and spending). More total spending will mean inflation. Less will mean underemployment and waste. A malallocation of spending between consumption and investment is likely to generate short-run fluctuations that may become serious booms or depressions.

If we start, for example, with a trillion-dollar GNP, aggregate demand should increase about $40 billion next year to produce stable, high-employment growth without inflation. But note that in the following year, aggregate demand must grow by more—by $44 billion, or 4 percent of the new $1,040 billion GNP. And if the ratios of saving and government spending to GNP remain stable, private investment must also grow at 4 percent annually to assure a stable growth.

In principle, there is no reason why we need to have a stable price level to achieve stable, full-employment growth. If, for example, total spending rises only 2 percent while capacity grows by 4 percent, full-employment output can still be achieved if the price level falls 2 percent. Conversely, if total spending rises 6 percent, full-employment output can be maintained with a 2 percent increase in average prices.

As a practical matter, however, as we saw in Part Two, substantial economy-wide price reductions without unemployment are unlikely in the modern American economy. With downward inflexibility of costs and prices, inadequate total spending means unemployment of men and machines. Thus, few economists now believe that aggregate demand can safely grow less than roughly in proportion to total capacity, and many believe it should grow faster because of basic inflationary pressures.

A look ahead to 1980 will illustrate some of the magnitudes involved in such growth. Assume stable prices at 1973 levels and roughly constant proportions between consumption, saving-investment, and government taxes-spending. Then a 4 percent growth rate gives a 1980 GNP of about $2 trillion, divided roughly as follows:

	IN BILLIONS
Total GNP	$2,000
Consumption	1,240
Investment and saving	280
Government taxes and spending	480

Will Private Decisions Provide the Right Amount of Aggregate Demand?

Will private consumption and investment spending decisions provide just the right amount of aggregate demand year after year? Will private banks' lending decisions provide just the right growth in the money stock to support the needed growth in aggregate demand? Part Two provided the answer loud and clear: It would be an economic miracle if millions of independent private spending and banking decisions produced just the right aggregate demand. The case for conscious stabilizing monetary and fiscal policies to keep aggregate demand growing on track is clear, although it is a far from simple job to carry them out successfully.

Capital and Labor Shares in Stable Growth

Even if aggregate demand grows stably, may not the investment-consumption balance get out of kilter? And a closely related question: What balance between wages and profits is required for stable, sustained growth?

The answer depends partly on how fast we want to grow. Fast growth requires a high-profit, high-investment economy. Wages and consumption shouldn't rise too fast.

But if profits and investment get *too* large relative to wages and consumption spending, excess capacity will develop and the boom will collapse. Indeed, when it comes to maintaining high-level employment, union leaders hammer away at one proposition: Wages are the biggest, single source of buying power in our economy, and too-low wages are the major cause of depression. But don't be trapped by the obvious fallacy that business profits necessarily represent savings withdrawn from the income stream. Many business profits flow directly into investment spending, and there is no necessary reason to classify big profits as a deflationary force. What matters for economic health is total spending on consumption plus investment, not just consumption. Wages are purchasing power, but so are profits.

The investment-consumption-balance issue is a thorny one. Economists have a variety of "growth models" that illustrate the relative paths of investment and consumption needed to assure stable, sustainable growth under different conditions—different propensities to consume, different capital-output ratios, different rates of technical progress, and the like. One such simple model was represented in the appendix to Chapter 42. Nearly all these models, and historical experience, tell us that growth must be reasonably balanced if it is to be stable. Consumption and investment must be kept growing at *roughly* the same rates. If either investment or consumption gets too far out of line with the other, we're in for trouble. And although profits and wages are by no means identical with investment and consumption spending, *very roughly* the same balanced growth proposition holds for them.

A CONCLUDING NOTE

An interesting and provocative concluding note on national growth policy has been provided by Herbert Stein, a distinguished conservative economist:

We have had a good deal of talk about the desirability of economic growth. There have been national policies which contributed to growth but also many which retarded it. There has been no national determination of a desirable rate of growth, no effort to formulate a comprehensive program to achieve any specified rate of growth, and few policy decisions that were dominated by growth considerations. Growth in America has been the outcome of the efforts of millions of families to improve their own conditions and the conditions of their children, rather than the outcome of a national policy. The picture of a government of tyrannical Philistines forcing economic growth upon a citizenry of Henry David Thoreaus is fantasy. The spontaneous and decentralized origins of the growth suggests how difficult it would be to influence its rate very much, in either direction, by national policy.[4]

[4] From "An Economist Looks at the 1970s," speech at Rider College, Trenton, New Jersey, May 15, 1970, pp. 5–6. At the time, Stein was a member of President Nixon's Council of Economic Advisers.

REVIEW

For Analysis and Discussion

1. How fast should the American economy grow over the decade ahead? What measures would you propose to achieve your desired growth rate?
2. How much of your personal income are you willing to use over the next decade to build up the economic capacity of the nation for future production? Does the government have a right to dictate to you a rate different from the one you prefer?
3. Can you see how we can have continued economic growth and also a cleaner, more attractive environment? Explain.
4. Are economic growth and a better "quality of life" competitive or complementary? Explain.
5. Why do many economists who favor slower *population* growth simultaneously support faster *economic* growth?
6. Only about 3 percent of GNP is devoted to research and development. Would it be sound policy to double this amount? Who should decide? If the amount should be doubled, who should pay for it?
7. Can you suggest ways of increasing the nation's rate of saving and capital formation that do not impinge on the freedom of individuals and businesses to spend or to save their incomes as they please?
8. By 1983, the population of the United States may be 230 million. Assume that the same proportion (about 40 percent) of the population is in the labor force as in 1973, that the average propensity to consume out of GNP remains at about two-thirds; that output per worker rises about 2 percent per annum; and that the price level remains constant:
   a. What level of gross national expenditure will be required in 1983 to assure full employment? Explain.
   b. What level of private investment will be required, assuming government expenditures on goods and services remain at their 1973 level of about $275 billion?
   c. Suppose that only 35 percent of the population is in the 1983 labor force. How would your answers to (a) and (b) change?

d. Suppose now that the average workweek is reduced from forty to thirty hours. How would per capita real output compare with 1973, when population was 210 million?

9. Is Stein right in his last sentence, at the end of the text above?

APPENDIX

The Limits to Growth—Doomsday Models

In 1798, Malthus gloomily predicted recurrent famines for mankind, as population growth outran the ability of land to produce food. Every generation since then has had its prophets of doom, but recent years have seen a new brand of doomsday models, more persuasive to some because they are cast in mathematical form and spun out of computers. The best known of these is a recent model by a group of MIT engineers and scientists who, using a highly simplified computer model of world growth, find that growth must end soon, probably by the middle of the next century, and that our growth joyride will end with a bang, not a whimper.[5]

The authors pick up Malthus' stress on the tendency of population to outrun food supplies, and modernize it by adding two further propositions from ecology. First, we will soon exhaust the world's natural resources through the rapid growth of industrial production, and second, the same industrial production will strangle us in pollution. Using the trends of 1900–70 world experience, they combine these relationships in a simple computer model, and the resulting printouts tell us the limits to economic growth. The results follow directly from the assumptions that arable land and other natural resources are substantially fixed while population and industrial production tend to grow exponentially. Given these assumptions and no extenuating conditions, it is clear that growth in population and industrial output will run up against limits, and do so with force as exponential growth picks up speed. As the authors point out, any series that grows exponentially can become very big, very fast.[6]

The core of the Meadows analysis is summarized in Figure 44–1. The picture is self-explanatory. If population and industrial output continue to grow at exponential rates in the absence of checks, the world will rapidly exhaust its natural resources, including arable land, and pollution will rapidly become intolerable. Although industrial output and food will grow rapidly for a few more years, both will soon reach their peaks, probably around the end of this century. Growing hunger, shortages of raw materials, and pollution will soon thereafter combine to bring growth to a screeching halt, with widespread famine and strangulation from pollution, probably by the middle of the next century.

Meadows examines a variety of alternative assumptions. For example, doubling the stock of natural resources (except arable land) only postpones the debacle a decade or so, because of the enormous increases in demands for food and industrial output produced by the exponential growth assumptions; pollution and famine soon overtake us. Drastic steps to control pollution plus technological advance to extend the use of our natural resources could post-

[5] D. Meadows et al, *The Limits to Growth* (New York: Universe Books, 1972). Strikingly, the authors excluded all economists and other social scientists from their team. The foundations of the analysis lie in J. Forrester, *World Dynamics* (Cambridge: Wright-Allen Press, 1971). Forrester is a well-known computer expert.

[6] They cite the old fable of the poor gypsy who saved the king's life, and when offered his choice of fabulous rewards, asked only for wheat from the king's granary to cover his chessboard—one grain on the first square, two on the second, four on the third, eight on the fourth, and so on. The king, no mathematician, was delighted to grant such a modest request. Do the arithmetic. The fifth square gets 16 grains, but as the doubling continues, the fortieth square requires one trillion grains—with twenty-four more squares to go on the chessboard.

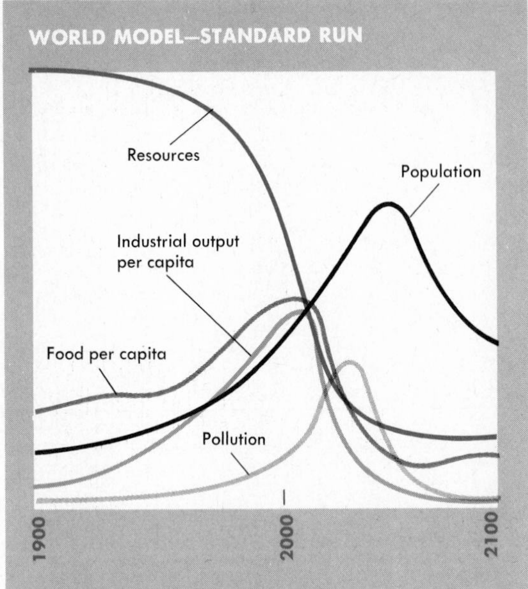

Figure 44–1

If recent trends continue, this model predicts massive starvation and deaths from pollution after about the middle of the twenty-first century. Living standards will also fall dramatically as resources are rapidly exhausted. (Adapted from D. Meadows et al, The Limits to Growth, New York: Universe Books, 1972, p. 124.)

pone doomsday, but the former would slow the growth in industrial output per capita and we would not escape the famine problem. Figure 44–2 summarizes Meadows' results on what he presents as his optimistic assumptions—"unlimited" natural resources (except arable land) and "successful" drastic pollution controls. This permits a huge increase in industrial output with only a moderate increase in pollution, and it postpones the downturn in food output per capita. But Malthus is still there; famine eventually checks population and industrial output per capita falls since it is possible to extend our stock of natural resources only at rising real costs.

Although the Meadows-Forrester book received widespread acclaim by environmentalists, most economists expressed serious reservations. Why?

(1) The price system appears nowhere in the entire Meadows analysis. Yet history demonstrates that when something becomes scarce, its relative price rises, reducing consumption of the scarce good and stimulating a search for substitutes and new modes of production. This has been the history of the industrial and technological revolutions. This is not to deny that supplies of existing natural resources may be exhausted, but to suggest that this very process will produce substitutes and means of extending supplies. (Actually, in spite of the doomsday prospects, the prices of most natural resources have thus far risen little, relative to other goods and services—see "The Energy Crisis" above.)

(2) Meadows allows for no further technical advance that may radically increase food output per acre of arable land; his "unlimited natural resources" assumption excludes arable land. Here is modern Malthus. If history tells us anything, it is that technical advance can help expand food production on existing land, as well as to expand other output. Note the productivity of American agriculture.

Figure 44–2

This model assumes that resources (except arable land) do not run out and that effective pollution controls are developed. Food and industrial output per capita nevertheless turn down early next century, and starvation limits population soon thereafter. This version might be termed the modern Malthus. (Adapted from D. Meadows et al, The Limits to Growth, New York: Universe Books, 1972, p. 136.)

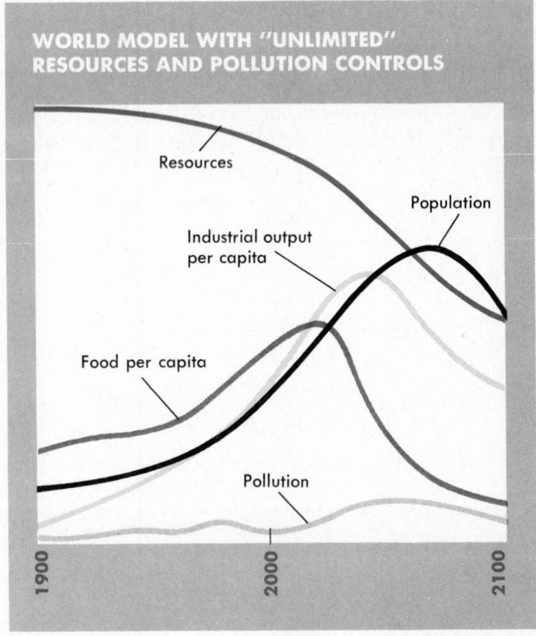

(3) Meadows' analysis assumes a blind continuation of population growth until it is checked by famine, even if world living standards rise dramatically. Again, history shows convincingly that population growth slows with affluence and rising living standards. Even Malthus recognized that voluntary restriction of births might occur to avoid famine, and modern birth-control methods are making this far easier. The extremity of Meadows' population assumption is indicated by the fact that beginning with two people, his system would blow up from overpopulation within 500 years. As one critic put it, apart from putting the Garden of Eden in the fifteenth century, what's new?

All this is not to deny that the Meadows study raises serious problems deserving careful study. A sustained per capita growth rate of 3 percent per annum would imply an average income 150 years hence about 100 times as large as today's, and 8,000 times as large 300 years from now. Such figures seem highly improbable. In the meantime, hunger, pollution, and proper use of our natural resources deserve our most careful attention and considered action. But sweeping doomsday conclusions drawn from simplistic assumptions and models, though they may help focus attention on important problems, should be taken as provocative speculations, not demonstrated conclusions. The conclusions are no better than the underlying assumptions on which they rest, and sweeping, generalized worry about the "predicament of mankind" should not divert us from concern with the smaller, practical steps that can reduce pollution and lessen hunger today.[7]

[7] For lively discussions of the growth issues, see "The No-Growth Society" (*Daedalus,* Fall, 1973); and A. Weintraub et al., eds. *The Economic Growth Controversy* (White Plains: International Arts and Sciences Press, 1973), especially the paper by Robert Solow, which is reproduced as selection 56 in M. Joseph, N. Seeber, and G.L. Bach, *Economic Analysis and Policy* 4th ed., (Englewood Cliffs: Prentice Hall, Inc., 1974).

Growth in the Less-Developed Countries

CHAPTER PREVIEW

CHAPTER FORTY-FIVE

In the United States, economic growth is the road to raising further our already high standard of living. But for over two billion people who live in the economically less-developed countries (LDCs), economic growth is a necessity if they are to escape from the bitter poverty that has been their lot through history. Per capita GNP in the United States in 1972 was about $5,500. In the less-developed countries (sometimes called the "Third World") it averaged about $150, and perhaps 30–40 percent of these people were living on less than $50 a year.

Table 45–1 classifies the nations of the world into three groups, depending on their per capita annual GNPs. *Highly-developed* countries are those with per capita GNPs above $1,000. The *intermediate* group are countries where the figure was between $500 and $1,000. The *less-developed* nations are those with per capita GNPs below $500.

The figures in Table 45–1 are very rough. They probably substantially underestimate income levels in the poorer nations on two counts. First, incomes there may be relatively underestimated because so much home-produced food and clothing does not go through the market. Second, prices of the staples that form the standard of living of the masses there are generally very cheap compared to items bought by higher-income families; thus, conversion of, say, Indian rupee incomes into U.S. dollars at the official exchange rate that is based on prices of

TABLE 45–1

Countries Grouped by 1971 per Capita GNP—In U.S. Dollars[a]

HIGHLY DEVELOPED COUNTRIES (ABOUT 800 MILLION PEOPLE)
(OVER $1,000 PER CAPITA)

In the Americas:		*In Europe (cont'd)*	
United States	$5,000	Switzerland	$3,200
Canada	3,850	Denmark	3,200
Puerto Rico	1,550	West Germany	3,000
Argentina	1,050	France	2,850
		Norway	2,800
In Oceania and Asia:		Belgium	2,700
Australia	2,900	Netherlands	2,450
New Zealand	2,150	United Kingdom	2,300
Japan	1,900	USSR	1,800
		Finland	1,700
In Africa and Middle East:		Austria	1,600
Kuwait	4,600	Italy	1,600
Israel	1,850	Czechoslovakia	1,450
Libya	1,650	East Germany	1,450
		Ireland	1,400
In Europe:		Hungary	1,100
Sweden	4,100	Poland	1,100

INTERMEDIATE COUNTRIES (ABOUT 500 MILLION PEOPLE)
($500–1,000 PER CAPITA)

In Africa:			
Union of South Africa	$800		
Gabon	750		
In the Americas:		*In Europe:*	
Venezuela	$950	Greece	$1,000
Uruguay	850	Spain	1,000
Chile	700	Bulgaria	900
Cuba	700	Rumania	800
Mexico	700	Portugal	700
Panama	700		

LESS-DEVELOPED COUNTRIES (OVER 2 BILLION PEOPLE)
(LESS THAN $500 PER CAPITA)

All of Africa except countries listed above	about $150	Southeast Europe	$500
All of the Americas except countries listed above	about 350	Communist China	150
Middle East	about 300	India	100
		All of Asia except countries listed above	about 100

[a]Remember the text warning that data are very rough for the less-developed nations, and that figures for such nations are probably substantially understated by using official exchange rates—perhaps by as much as 100 percent. Estimates for communist-bloc countries are rougher than for others. Subsequent alterations in exchange rates have changed relative positions substantially for some countries. In particular, incomes in Western Europe and Japan have increased substantially relative to the United States. Several smaller nations are omitted.

Figures are estimated 1971 gross domestic product for each nation (rounded to nearest $50), converted to 1971 U.S. dollars at official exchange rates and divided by population. Estimates are based on United Nations data and E.E. Hagen and O. Hawrylshyn, "Analysis of World Income and Growth," *Economic Development and Cultural Change,* October 1969.

a wide range of commodities will tend to give a misleading picture of actual comparative living standards. But even if the per capita incomes in the poor nations were doubled to adjust for these possible underestimates, the less-developed nations would still appear desperately poor. For most of the world, poverty is far and away the number one economic problem.[1]

Worse, this huge gap between rich and poor nations is widening rapidly, not closing. Table 45–2 tells the story for the United States and India since 1960. Although it shows the extremes, it suggests the rapid rate at which the Western industrial nations are pulling away from the less-developed world. A 2 percent annual increase on the U.S. base of $5,500 means a $110 increase in one year, more than the *entire* per capita GNP in India. In India, the same 2 percent increase, if it could be achieved, would be only $2 per capita.[2]

Why do these vast differences in standards of living exist? Why is the gap between the rich and the poor widening even further? The theory of economic growth presented in Chapter 42 can help answer these questions, and most of this chapter is devoted to applying that theory to the LDCs.

Development of these economically less-developed countries has become the most explosive socioeconomic problem of our times. Poverty is a source of acute discontent for hundreds of millions of people, aroused by their leaders. In China and India alone there are nearly 1.5 billion people—two huge nations awakening to the fact that poverty and misery may not be the inescapable lot of their masses. A great change is moving Asia, Africa, and Latin America, a change compounded of growing nationalism and a desire for economic progress and power. A revolution of rising expectations—of economic progress, individual status, and national prestige and power—is sweeping the less-developed nations.

[1]The country comparisons of Table 45–1 are also very sensitive to the exchange rates used to convert local currencies to dollars. As Part Six explains, the "official" exchange rates sometimes vary substantially from free-market rates, and substantial rate changes occurred in 1972 and 1973 that would raise the level of most other countries (especially Japan and Western Europe) relative to the United States. See Table 2–1 for some 1972 estimates.

[2]Two good general references on the less-developed areas and their problems are J. Bhagwati, *Economics of the Underdeveloped Countries* (New York: McGraw-Hill Book Company, 1966), and Charles Kindleberger, *Economic Development* (New York: McGraw-Hill Book Company, 1965).

TABLE 45–2

Per Capita Real GNP in the United States and India[a]

	1960	1972
United States	$3,250	$5,500
India	90	100

[a]Data in 1972 U.S. dollars. Figures for India are probably understated relative to United States but the 1960–72 change is roughly accurate.

THE ANATOMY OF UNDERDEVELOPMENT

Poverty is the central economic fact of the less-developed areas. But there are many differences among them. Some are primitive; others, like India and China, boast civilizations that are far older than those of the Western world. Some have generous natural resources; others are bitterly poor in the endowments of nature. Some have a high ratio of population to land; others have vast open spaces. The poverty of a beggar on the streets of Calcutta is different from that of the Bushman of South Africa, or the desert nomad of the Middle East. But in spite of these differences, there are some strong resemblances. And the theory from Chapter 42 provides a useful framework for analyzing them.

Patterns of Economic Activity

First, a brief look at the economies of the less-developed nations as a backdrop for analysis

Farming in Indochina. (Wide World Photos.)

of why they are poor, and of what can be done to raise their production.

Poverty and the Dominance of Low-Productivity Agriculture. In the less-developed countries, food is the main item of production and consumption. It has to be, for starvation hovers uncomfortably near. For the entire group of LDCs, about 70 percent of all production is food. In the United States, the comparable figure is below 20 percent. Although diets in most nations are adequate to preserve life, they are often inadequate to fend off disease or, even allowing for the small bodily stature of many peoples, to provide enough energy for continued hard work.

A mud or thatched hut and some simple clothing make up most of the rest of the consumption pattern. Remember that only around $50 per year per capita is left to cover everything except food. Hospitals, plumbing, highways, and other services that we take for granted have no place in such standards of living. The masses in these nations save little or nothing at all. In Calcutta, a teeming city, between a quarter- and a half-million people have no homes or jobs so they simply wander the streets.

Because human labor is very cheap and capital scarce, hard work and laborious details are done by hand. Tractors and other mechanized farm equipment are scarce, and would often be unusable even if available, because of lack of fuel, maintenance facilities, and sufficient education to use them. Figure 45–1 shows vividly how little the poor nations rely on nonhuman energy (electricity, water, and minerals) compared to the developed nations. (In this and the following figures, income per capita is always shown on the vertical axis. Both income and energy use are plotted on ratio, or logarithmic, scales to make relative comparisons easy.)

The nonagricultural population is crowded into a few large cities, where small-scale industry, services for the wealthy, and government employment provide most of the jobs. Simple textiles are important in many less-developed economies; the cloth is used for clothing and home furnishings. In the more developed countries, modern large-scale industry (steel, chemicals, fertilizers, and the like) has begun to appear in the major cities.

Dual Economies: Limited Development of Markets. Thus, many nations are, in essence, "dual economies." One part is a money, market-oriented economy centered in a few large cities, with modern industry mixed with crowded slums. The other part is a subsistence-level, rural, barter-type economy of hand labor and primitive superstitions, comprising 75 percent or so of the population, substantially isolated from the markets and industry of the cities. To go from one to the other is to go from one world to another, from the dark ages to the present.

Transportation is crude. The highways of the cities rapidly dwindle to dirt roads and to mere paths a hundred miles away. Religious and cultural barriers fragment the nation. One can scarcely call them "economies"—for economic

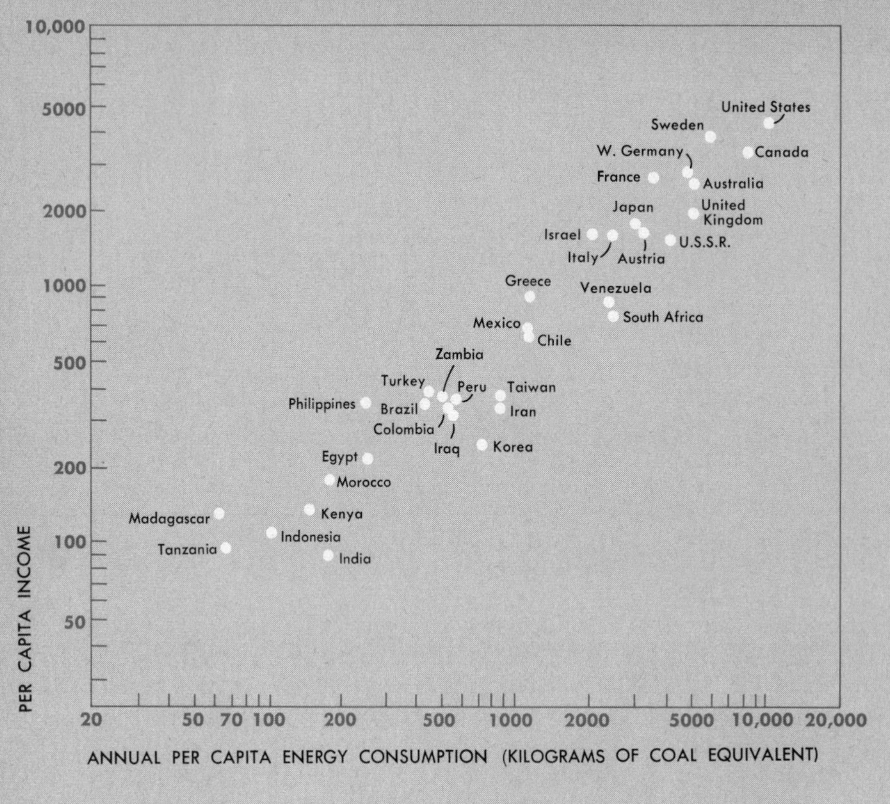

Figure 45–1

Energy consumption per capita is closely correlated with the degree of economic development. (Source: United Nations. Data are for 1970.)

life as we know it exists only around the cities and towns. Without roads and communication, there is little chance for a market economy to develop.

In some nations, one-product export economies have developed—copper in Chile, oil in Saudi Arabia. Much of the investment to develop these export enclaves is foreign, and resentment against foreign ownership and operation is common. Often it leads to nationalization, whether or not there is a native competence to operate the industry.

Unequal Distribution of Income. In most less-developed countries, income is very unequally distributed—far more unequally than in the highly-developed, capitalist economies. There are often a few rich landholders, sometimes a few industrialists. The masses are dismally poor, mainly living just above the subsistence level on farms or in villages, often as tenant farmers who keep little of what they raise. There is often no "middle class" of shopkeepers, professional men, and skilled workers, which is a major portion of Western populations.

Weak Governments. A few less-developed nations have well-established democratic institutions, but they are the exception. Governments are typically unstable, revolutions are commonplace. There can be little long-range planning of basic government services such as schools, highways, and the like. Equally important, there is no basis for long-run planning by investors and businessmen. Often governments are dominated by the entrenched "haves," who block any social and political change that might endanger them.

Governments, which must provide leadership in development, are usually weakly staffed, reflecting the newness of the nations and the lack of education and traditions of honest civil service. Government jobs are often political perquisites, which mainly provide an accepted position for corruption. All too often, confusion, red tape, and bungling characterize government "programs." There is little chance for such governments to establish and administer effective tax systems to collect the funds needed to provide schools, highways, and sanitation.

So much for a general, if discouraging, overview. Now let us look more analytically at the problem, using the theory from Chapter 42. The theory predicts that low per capita output in the less-developed nations will reflect a high ratio of population to natural resources and to capital, a slow rate of capital accumulation and technical advance, an uneducated, low-productivity labor force, and a general environment unconducive to initiative, enterprise, and organized economic activity. And in fact, this is a reasonable description of most of the LDCs. Look now at these factors one at a time.

Natural Resources

Lack of natural resources explains little of the plight of the less-developed nations. Switzerland has one of the world's highest per capita incomes on virtually no natural resources; Africa and Asia have some of the lowest on vast natural resources. The ratios of population to arable land for Switzerland, Belgium, and the Netherlands are about the same as those for Bolivia, Peru, and Egypt.

Nonetheless, plentiful natural resources can certainly help. The United States, Canada, and Australia all have rich resources and low ratios of population to land. Surely the vast western frontier helped to speed our early growth. Many poor nations would be much worse off without generous resources—the copper and nitrates of Chile, the oil of the Middle East. Perhaps climate, rather than natural resources in the usual sense, is critical. Most of the world's well-to-do nations lie in the temperate zone; none of them in the tropics. But within the temperate zone there are wide variations in economic development. Nor does primary reliance on agriculture necessarily characterize the poor nations. Denmark and New Zealand demonstrate that agricultural countries need not be poor. The poor nations are poor not because they are agricultural, but because productivity in their agriculture is so low.

Shortage of Capital and Primitive Technology

The stock of capital explains much more. No less-developed country has a large stock of capital goods per capita; every well-to-do nation does. Modern factories, machinery and equipment, highways, hospitals—all are scarce in the LDCs. Without them, high output per capita is very difficult.

The reason is easy to see. When nations are poor, they find it hard to save. Saving in India or Tanganyika means cutting back an already pitifully low standard of living. Saving in America is easy. Yet without capital goods the poor nation can never hope to raise the standard of living of the masses very much.

Capital investment of over $20,000 per factory worker in America was cited above. In the poorest nations, the comparable figure is only a few dollars. Gross capital formation is only 5–10 percent of gross national product in such poor nations as Paraguay and Nigeria. In the well-to-do nations it runs 15–20 percent, and in the very rapidly growing nations, like Japan, up to 30–40 percent. It is easy for the rich to become richer. The poor, like the queen in *Through the Looking Glass,* must run as fast as they can merely to stay in the same place, as population grows constantly.

Closely related, most less-developed countries have little modern technology. Human beings and beasts do virtually all the work in agriculture. Handicraft methods dominate in small-scale industry in the towns and cities. To the illiterate native of Tanzania or Yemen, Detroit's mass-production methods have little relevance. Where economic development is beginning, sometimes wild contrasts exist in the dual economies. In the cities of India and Venezuela, some of the world's most modern oil refineries and chemical plants loom against the sky. Fifty miles away there is the most primitive agriculture, unchanged for a thousand years.

Overpopulation and the Labor Force

In one fundamental sense, overpopulation is the crux of the less-developed economies' problem. The population is so large that, given the natural resources and capital available, there is barely enough output per person to maintain life. And when total output increases because of improved technology or capital accumulation, population increases nearly as fast, so there is little improvement in the average standard of living. This is not the picture in all the less-developed economies, but it is in most.

In recent years, total production has risen at substantial rates in many LDCs, 4–6 percent per annum in Latin America, Africa, and southeast Asia. This is near the growth rate of total output in the industrialized countries. But population has grown nearly as fast as output.

What are the facts about population? In most less-developed economies, the annual birthrate is between thirty and fifty per thousand people; in the United States and Western Europe, the comparable rate has generally declined to around fifteen to twenty per thousand. But in the less-developed economies, until recently,

Hong Kong. (United Nations.)

death rates typically ran from twenty-five to thirty-five per thousand, compared to ten or below in the Western world. Thus, population growth rates in the two types of economies were roughly similar, running around ten to fifteen per thousand (1–1.5 percent per year).

Since World War II, this picture has changed dramatically. Western methods of disease prevention have drastically reduced the death rate in many LDCs, especially the rate of infant mortality. DDT alone is estimated to have saved 50 million lives through checking the spread of infectious disease. During the 1950s, the death rate declined by 46 percent in Puerto Rico, 43 percent in Formosa, 23 percent in Jamaica. The result is a population explosion. In Latin America and West Africa, population is doubling every twenty years, on the Asian mainland every twenty-five years. China's growth rate is nearly 2.5 percent. Her population of 800 million is growing by 20 million every year, and at the present rate may reach 1 billion before 1980.

Figure 45–2 shows this contrast dramatically. Note the high birthrates in most less-developed countries, and their rapid rates of population growth implied by the big spread between their birth and death rates.

The world population problem is thus centered in the less-developed countries. In the developed nations of the Western world, population is generally growing only 1 percent or less per year. But given the explosive growth rates in the rest of the world, total world population may nearly double—from about 3.6 to 6.5 billion—in the next twenty-five years, while the last doubling took forty-five years, and the one before that eighty years. If that high rate should continue, it would imply a world population of thirty billion a century from now.

Such a population would make the earth into a human anthill, but we will not reach

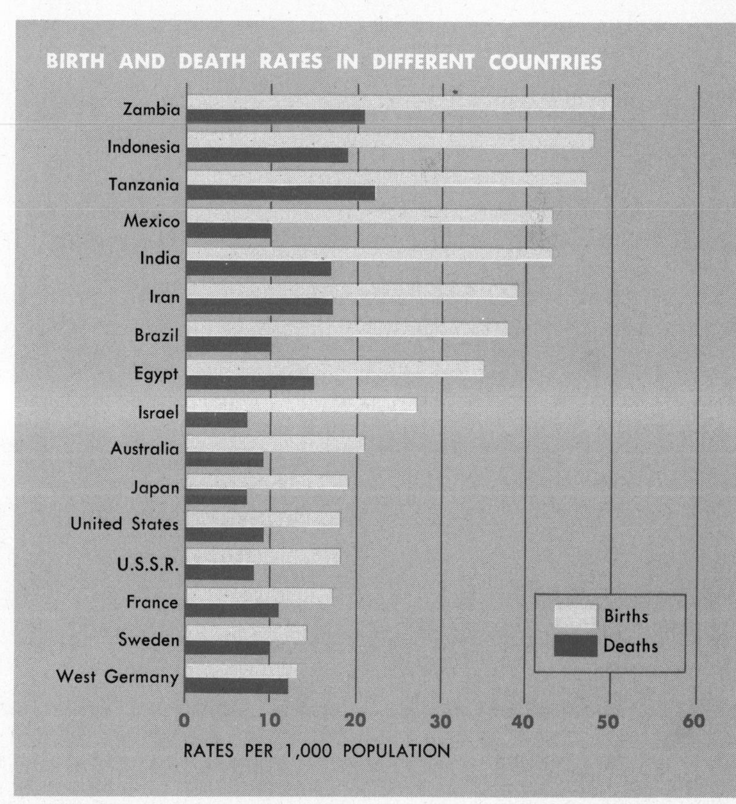

Figure 45–2

The less-developed nations have the fastest growing populations. For the whole world, the birthrate is about 34 per thousand and the death rate about 11. (Source: United Nations. Figures for 1970.)

it or anything like it. Famine would check the growth long before then, if nothing else did. Although food production has been rising rapidly, and there are still periodic food surpluses in many developed nations that call for government action to support prices and restrict output, over half the world's population has less than what most experts consider an "adequate" diet.

Table 45–3 shows average daily consumption of calories for some regions. Experts do not agree on the precise calorie level needed for maintenance of health, but they do agree that diets below 2,000 calories per day are surely close to the minimum level for reasonable nutrition, while 2,400 calories a day or thereabouts may be needed to provide the basis for good health and energy.

Calories alone are an inadequate measure of nutrition. Protein and fat consumption provide other measures that supplement the calorie figures. Data on per capita protein and fat consumption do not substantially change the order of ranking of the countries and areas indicated, but they widen the spread between them. For example, protein consumption in India and Communist Asia averaged about 50 grams per person per day, while that in the United States and Canada was nearly double this figure. Fat consumption in grams per day ranges from about 20 in Communist Asia to about 145 per day in the United States. Cereals and other starchy foods make up more than 80 percent of the calories in many LDC diets, a level far too high for good health.

TABLE 45–3
World Food Consumption

COUNTRY	CALORIE CONSUMPTION PER DAY
Australia-New Zealand	3,260
United States	3,190
Northern Europe	3,060
USSR	3,040
Southern Europe	2,720
Central and Eastern Africa	2,410
South and Central America	2,250
India and China	1,900
World	2,360

Source: *The World Food Budget, 1970* (U.S. Department of Agriculture), p. 25.

The population bomb is thus a real threat, not in the developed Western nations, but in the vast less-developed areas with 2–2.5 billion people. Unless food production rises faster than in the past, many of their people will be hungry and undernourished if present population growth rates continue. Technical advance—the much-discussed "green revolution"—promises dramatically higher crop yields in some areas, but these results are still far from certain, and some combination of population control and increased food production is essential if many of the less-developed nations are to avoid disaster.[3]

The population problem is all the more serious because in many less-developed nations, much of the population is illiterate. New methods that involve even the simplest changes often meet barriers of superstition and inadequate understanding—for example, use of chemical fertilizers and crop rotation. In Africa, only about 25 percent of all children between five and eighteen go to school, about 40 percent in Asia. In the United States, the figure is over 95 percent. Figure 45–3 shows the strong correlation between literacy and living standards.

Environment and Initiative

Rapid economic growth has occurred mainly in the Western world where the social and economic groundwork was laid centuries ago. Nowhere has there been rapid, continuing growth without reasonably stable government

[3] For authoritative analyses of the population and world food problems, see P. Hauser, ed., *The Population Dilemma* (Englewood Cliffs, N.J.: Prentice-Hall, Inc., Spectrum Books, 1963); and W.W. Cochrane, *The World Food Problem* (New York: Crowell Collier and Macmillan, Inc., 1969), which draw heavily on United Nations studies.

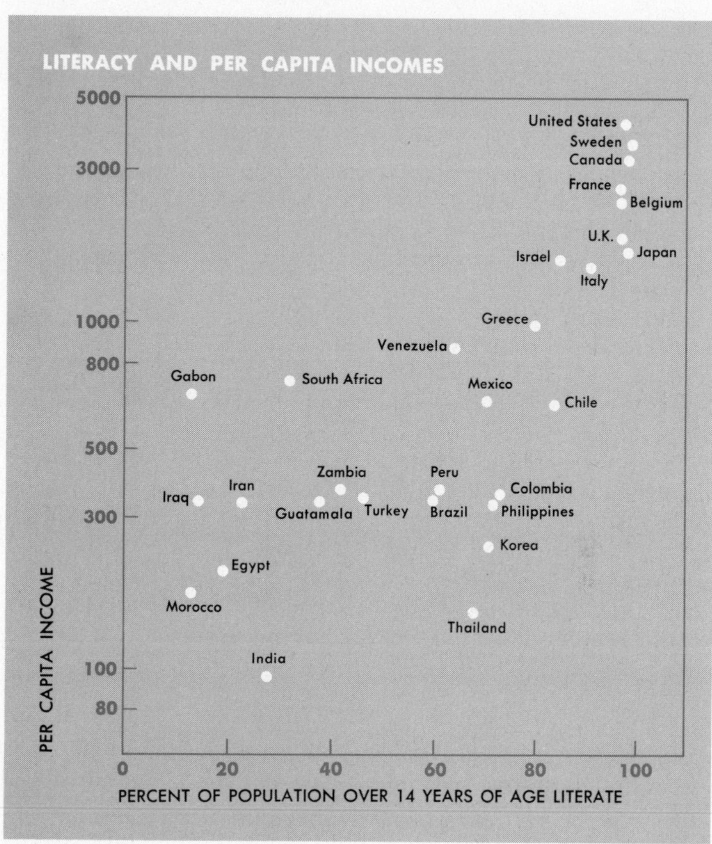

Figure 45-3

The degree of literacy is strongly correlated with the extent of economic development, as both cause and effect. (Source: UNESCO. Income data for 1970; literacy data for various dates in the 1960s.)

and financial and economic institutions. In all the countries of the highly-developed group of Table 45-1 except the USSR, the profit motive and individual initiative have played a central role.

On these scores, the problems faced by the less-developed economies are enormous. Apathy and ignorance characterize the great mass of their populations. Except for government leaders and small educated groups, there is often little effective impetus for economic development; and all too often even the leaders appear more concerned with their own positions than with economic progress for the masses. In central Africa, the medicine man is still the most influential member of many tribes. In some nations, manual labor is considered beneath the dignity of a man, certainly of an educated man, and is left entirely to women. In most LDCs, few of the peasants own much, if any, land. They see little reason to work harder to produce more when most of it must be given up to the absentee landlord.

Thus, it is not surprising that the LDCs lack entrepreneurs—individuals with imagination and initiative to seize economic opportunities and to develop them. In the traditional societies, such attitudes and activities are often frowned upon. Caste systems bar occupational changes, and class hierarchies prevent vertical mobility. Things have been done the same way since time immemorial.

Nor can such nations expect to surge upward without what economists call an "infrastructure" of "social overhead capital"—highways, schools, communications, hospitals, sanitation. These all require capital and planning—and their benefits to the entire economy far exceed the individual benefits that individual investors might see. Enforced saving through government tax collections is the only practical way to finance them. Thus stable, established governments, capable of collecting taxes and spending efficiently, are essential—but rare.

Absence of stable governments and well-established tax systems leads to persistent government deficits and to inflation. There are vast needs. But subsistence living standards make taxes very difficult to collect. The predictable result is government spending without corresponding taxes, and inflation in the market sector of their economies.

The resulting inflations are bad partly because of the inequities they wreak on the masses, who have no way to protect themselves from the higher prices of essentials. Inflation thus becomes a kind of "forced saving" that substitutes for tax collections. But worse, inflation and financial instability repel foreign investors, whose capital is so desperately needed, and make foreign purchases difficult. And inflation makes it more difficult to sell exports in world markets.

The Vicious Circle of Poverty

The less-developed nations vary widely. But in most, the problem seems to be a vicious circle of poverty. Incomes and living standards are so low that productivity is low and saving is impossible for the mass of the population. Without more capital goods, highways, and education, output per capita cannot be increased. If total output increases, population grows nearly as fast.

Throughout the less-developed economies, a significant part of the farm population is "surplus" in the sense that it could be removed from the farms of the countries concerned without any reduction in *total* farm output. But to move this surplus population to productive employment seems impossible. What will keep them from starving until they become established in industrial jobs? How can uneducated people be made into effective industrial workers? Where will the industrial jobs come from? Who will provide the tools for new factory workers, capital for factory equipment, and the enterprise to establish new concerns? How could the newly-made industrial goods be sold either domestically or abroad without an established market and without adequate transportation and commercial facilities?

Lastly, government planning and taxation are required to enforce saving and to channel investment into socially desirable uses; yet governments are weak, inefficient, unstable. Inefficient bureaucracies bungle rules and frustrate businessmen with red tape. Inflations and financial instability are commonplace. It seems that everywhere they turn, the LDCs face insoluble dilemmas. Their leaders may know the prescriptions of the theory of Chapter 42, but what shall they do?

POLICY FOR ECONOMIC DEVELOPMENT

How can the LDCs break out of the vicious circle of poverty and take off into self-sustaining growth? There is no simple answer. Indeed, there may be no answer at all for some of them. The main approaches suggested by the experts follow the lines of the theory suggested above.

Environment and Institutions for Economic Development

It is striking that everyone of the top ten countries in the highly-developed group of Table 45–1 is either in Western Europe or has inherited much of Western European culture and traditions. Max Weber, a famous sociologist, in his *The Protestant Ethic and the Spirit of Capitalism,* argued that the rapid economic development of Western Europe was linked intimately with what he called the "Protestant ethic"—the belief that work is good for its own sake and that the individual should be free to seek after his own welfare through work.

Weber emphasized the institutions of capitalistic society that have accompanied rapid economic development in the West: (1) private ownership and control of the means of production; (2) freedom of the market from such restrictions as guild monopolies, social-class barriers, and government price fixing; (3) the reign of calculable law, enabling people to know in advance what rules they operate under in economic life; (4) freedom of individuals to work for wages; (5) "commercialism" of economic life through a market system of wages and prices to mobilize and allocate productive resources; and (6) speculation and risk taking (which had been largely prevented in the preceding feudal and guild societies).

Were the Protestant ethic and the institutions of capitalism essential to the rapid economic growth of today's richest countries? The facts fit Weber's description reasonably well, but there are important exceptions.

Everyone agrees that sustained rapid economic growth is extremely unlikely without a stable government, law, and order. Without such stability, neither domestic nor foreign investors are willing to risk their funds, the essential economic infrastructure of highways, communications, and other public utilities is unlikely to come. But revolution and instability have been common in the LDCs. Struggles for power by competing factions have been common. Illiterate, superstitious people find it hard to make democracy work effectively after they wrest power from rich dictators or foreign rulers. But difficult as it may be, establishment of stable government appears to be a *sine qua non* for the takeoff into economic growth.

Development of individual initiative and an entrepreneurial class, plus acceptance of a market economy, also seems vital. There must be individuals who take leadership, who see potential gains in taking risks, who manage to mobilize capital, who have the drive to push ahead through difficulties and to organize the work of others. Often immigrants from a different culture, who are materialistic, experimental, frugal, industrious, and ambitious for their families have provided entrepreneurial leadership.

Equally important, and perhaps most difficult, a spirit of greater initiative must be instilled in the masses. Apathy and ignorance lead to acceptance of poverty and the status quo—to acceptance of the life of one's parents and their parents before them. No other problem seems more frustrating to the planners trying to pull economies up from poverty.

How initiative, a market, and an entrepreneurial class develop in traditional tribal or village societies is far from clear. Sociologists, economists, and anthropologists have studied dozens of cases and find no single explanation. In some instances (Japan, for example), an entrepreneurial class seems to develop from pressures of social and cultural change. Dissatisfied groups outside the ruling elite see trading and business as a way to rise to higher status. In other cases (Egypt, for example), the spirit of entrepreneurship is imported through colonial rule, which is later thrown off. Increasing awareness of the outside world seems everywhere to be important. In many cases, the development of an entrepreneurial class has been a revolt against prevailing tribal or village mores, a social as well as an economic revolution.[4]

Capital Accumulation and Industrialization

As our theory would lead us to expect, substantial capital accumulation has marked every major case of rapid economic development. To rise from poverty, every nation faces the central problem of increasing saving and investment as a share of total output. Figure 45–4 shows the wide variation among countries in the ratio of gross investment to GNP. Although a few nations with very high investment ratios have relatively low per capita incomes (for

[4]E.E. Hagan has spelled out an entire theory of economic growth centering around these socioeconomic interactions, which also uses modern psychological analysis of personal behavior patterns in the emerging societies (*On the Theory of Social Change,* Homewood, Illinois: Dorsey Press, 1962).

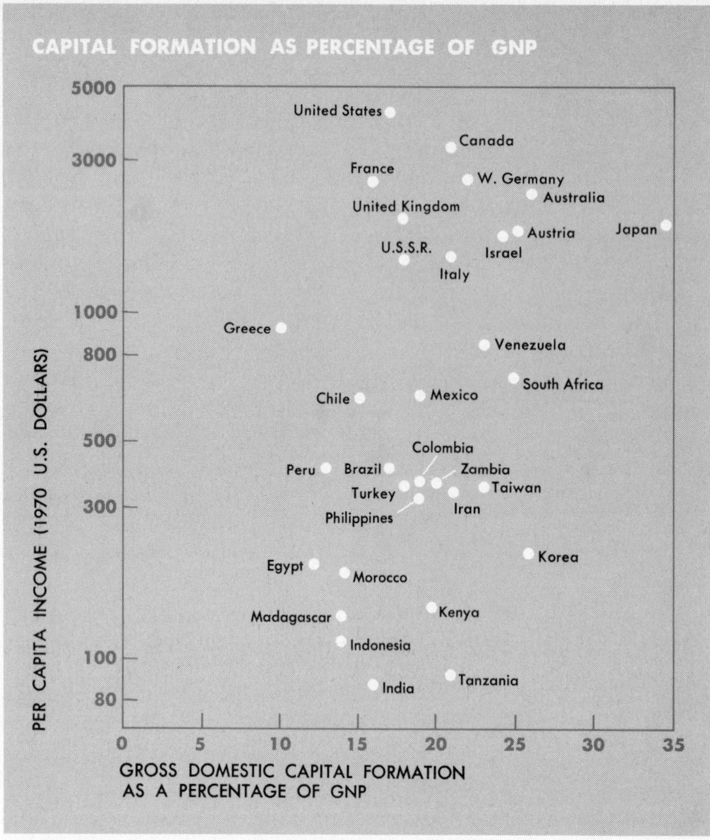

Figure 45–4

High per capita incomes and high rates of capital formation generally go together, as interacting cause and effect. But there are exceptions; note Japan. (Source: United Nations. Data for 1970.)

example, Yugoslavia), they are now growing rapidly. The United States, with the highest per capita income, has a moderate savings-investment ratio but also a relatively slow rate of growth over recent years; we had a high savings ratio during the nineteenth century.

There is some evidence that it takes about \$3–4 of new capital goods to increase current income by \$1 annually in these countries (a "capital-output ratio" of 3 or 4:1). With a 4:1 marginal capital-output ratio, an economy that saves 4 percent of its income to accumulate capital will, other things equal, increase its national income by 1 percent annually. Then, if population grows at about 1 percent annually, per capita income is just held constant. To raise its living standard the economy must either save more or slow its population growth. Any saving rate below 4 percent of income will mean decreasing per capita incomes.

This relationship between the capital-output ratio and the rate of saving is illustrated by Table 45–4. If 4 percent of total income is saved, there will be a 1.33 percent annual increase in output in case the capital-output ratio is 3:1, but only a 1 percent increase with a 4:1

TABLE 45–4
Capital-Output and Savings Ratios

	ANNUAL INCREASE IN OUTPUT (PERCENTAGE) WITH:	
SAVINGS-INCOME RATIO	CAPITAL-OUTPUT RATIO = 3:1	CAPITAL-OUTPUT RATIO = 4:1
.04	1.33	1.0
.05	1.67	1.25
.10	3.33	2.5
.15	5.0	3.75

capital-output ratio. Obviously both higher saving ratios and lower capital-output ratios are good for economic growth. A few countries have apparently managed a capital output ratio of 2:1, which has permitted them to expand output rapidly with modest saving ratios.

Many LDCs have turned to government tax and investment programs to force more saving and investment, especially in economic infrastructures—roads, schools, and dams that aid development throughout the nation. When the mass of the population is barely above subsistence level, to obtain more voluntary saving is very difficult. Recent research emphasizes the importance of developing financial institutions to gather together small savings and channel them to useful investments.

Foreign Investment and Imperialism

Some nations, for example India, have obtained substantial portions of their growth capital from abroad, through both private investment and government aid. The United Nations estimates that the provision of capital by the developed to the less-developed nations rose from $2 billion in 1950 to $15 billion in 1970. About half was loans or grants from other nations or international agencies, and half was private investment from the developed nations. Just under half came from the United States.

Poor nations desperately need capital from abroad. Economic analysis says that there will be benefit to both borrower and foreign lender if the expected rate of return on the capital in the developing nation exceeds that which the lender can obtain elsewhere. Nonetheless, many developing nations have invited foreign private investment only with stringent restrictions. With burgeoning national pride they want no part of foreign control, and they distrust foreign investors who may try to exploit them. The memories of many decades of colonialism are still strong. Thus, as badly as they need foreign capital, many of the poor nations have hedged foreign capital and companies around with restrictive controls reaching into day-to-day operations.

Are these fears of foreign imperialism irrational? There is little doubt that over the past century, foreign investors have often exploited native resources and workers, making large profits with little concern for the welfare of the less-developed nations. This economic domination was often paralleled by ruthless political and social repression of native populations. Although native living standards may well have been higher than they would have been with no foreign capital at all, bitter resentment was a predictable consequence.

Since the emergence of national independence for nearly all people since World War II, the pendulum has swung. Foreign companies (for example, in petroleum) that formerly paid only 25 percent of their profits to local nations for the privilege of extracting natural resources have seen their shares fall to 50 percent, and even lower. Restrictions on foreign operations have been steadily tightened. Outright expropriation has become more common. Prospective foreign businesses have often been turned away because offers were considered inadequate, sometimes with the result that nothing happens—no foreign capital, no jobs for native people.

Socialist doctrine says that foreign "imperialist" investment will bleed the less-developed economy by withdrawing the profits it extorts from the native population. But, although this may sometimes occur, two counterarguments are important. First, at least in the last two decades when reliable figures have become available, only a moderate share of profits has actually been withdrawn, and these withdrawals have been vastly overbalanced by new foreign investments. Thus, there has been a continuous large net inflow of private foreign capital from developed to less-developed nations—note the $7 billion figure above for 1970.

Second, even if all profits were withdrawn by the foreign investor, the developing nation might well gain from the investment. Remember the desperate need for capital to raise output and provide jobs for the surplus native population. If native workers take jobs voluntarily in the foreign business, they presumably prefer that to their other alternatives. If local customers voluntarily buy the foreign product, they presumably prefer it to other alternatives, even though its price may have yielded a large profit to the foreign company. Hard-boiled realism would ask—whether I like the foreigner or not, am I better off with his capital invested here, or without it? Clearly, the developing nation would be still better off if part or all of the profits were reinvested there, as occurs in the great bulk of the cases. But what if the alternative is no foreign investment at all?[5]

Most of the developing nations have attempted to compromise this dilemma. They seek foreign capital, but on terms they dictate. Some compromises have been effective in attracting foreign capital; others have not. To the outsider, restrictions that lead foreign investors to turn away may seem shortsighted, for the less-developed nation ends up with its restrictions and no capital for development. But simple economic analysis is not always clear when emotions run strong. And fear of foreign exploitation is understandably strong indeed in many of the less-developed nations.

Technical Advance and Education

Technological advance and development of an educated, skilled labor force have played a central role in the development of the Western economies. How can the poor nations achieve such technical advance?

Their problem may look easy—just borrow the technology of more advanced nations. The USSR after World War II adopted industrial methods and techniques wholesale from the West. Japan has adopted foreign technology even more effectively. But such importation often requires heavy capital investment; skilled laborers, technicians, and managers; and mass markets to justify many modern methods—conditions not met in many poor nations.

Think, for example, how you would go about introducing modern technology into Somalia, an emerging African nation of about two million people, most of them illiterate nomads. Literacy: perhaps 10 percent. Total college graduates in the country: about one hundred. Per capita income: about $75 a year. Politics: longstanding bitter rivalry among tribal groups.

In fact, the biggest promise for technical change probably lies in agriculture rather than in industry. Primitive, low-productivity agriculture is the greatest millstone around the necks of the poor economies. Improving productivity in agriculture has led the way in nearly every case of growth. Here technology can be introduced in small stages, and with more modest capital costs—simple tools, fertilizers, improved irrigation.

Technological advance requires an educated labor force and willingness to accept change. Thus, mass education and development of a core of skilled technicians and teachers are goals of virtually every LDC. Investment in education may not pay a fast return. But Figure 45-3 speaks for itself. The long-run payoff is big, in economic terms and in laying a foundation for a better life for all.

Steps toward mass education in the less-developed economies have been spectacular since World War II. But schools are expensive and teachers are very scarce. Thus, educational efforts have been concentrated on the young. It will be generations before half the population in many of the less-developed nations is even literate. For example, Indonesia, with 110 million people, has only two universities.

Population Policy

Until the LDCs slow their rates of population growth, they are unlikely to escape far from Malthus's dire predictions. Even high growth rates in aggregate output cannot outdistance high rates of population growth.

Thus, governments of some LDCs, notably India, have given high priority to birth control and family planning programs. But the problem of providing effective bases for family planning

[5] For a more complete analysis, see Charles Kindleberger, *American Business Abroad* (New Haven, Conn.: Yale University Press, 1969), Chap. 5.

among hundreds of millions of illiterate, widely scattered people is great. Religious barriers appear to be less formidable than was previously believed. The family is the main economic and social unit, and parents must look to their children for support in old age. Once people in the poor nations recognize that with modern death rates they need not have seven or eight children to be reasonably sure three or four will survive, perhaps birth control will be more readily accepted. But progress is far from certain.

Balanced versus Unbalanced Growth

In the less-developed nations and among the experts, the debate rages as to whether poor nations can grow faster by concentrating on the development of either industry or agriculture alone, or by striving to develop both sectors in balance.

Sooner or later, industrialization is necessary for full economic development. Every high-income nation in Table 45-1 has a major industrial and commercial sector. Transport and steel play prominent roles in industrialization. Adequate transport facilities and communication permit specialization and underly mass production and mass markets. Steel is used in nearly every facet of modern industrial activity. Figure 45-5 shows the close correlation between per capita steel consumption and per capita incomes. Every growing nation longs for its own modern steel mill, as a symbol of national pride.

Figure 45-5

The highly developed nations use much more steel per capita than do the LDCs. (Source: United Nations. Data for 1970.)

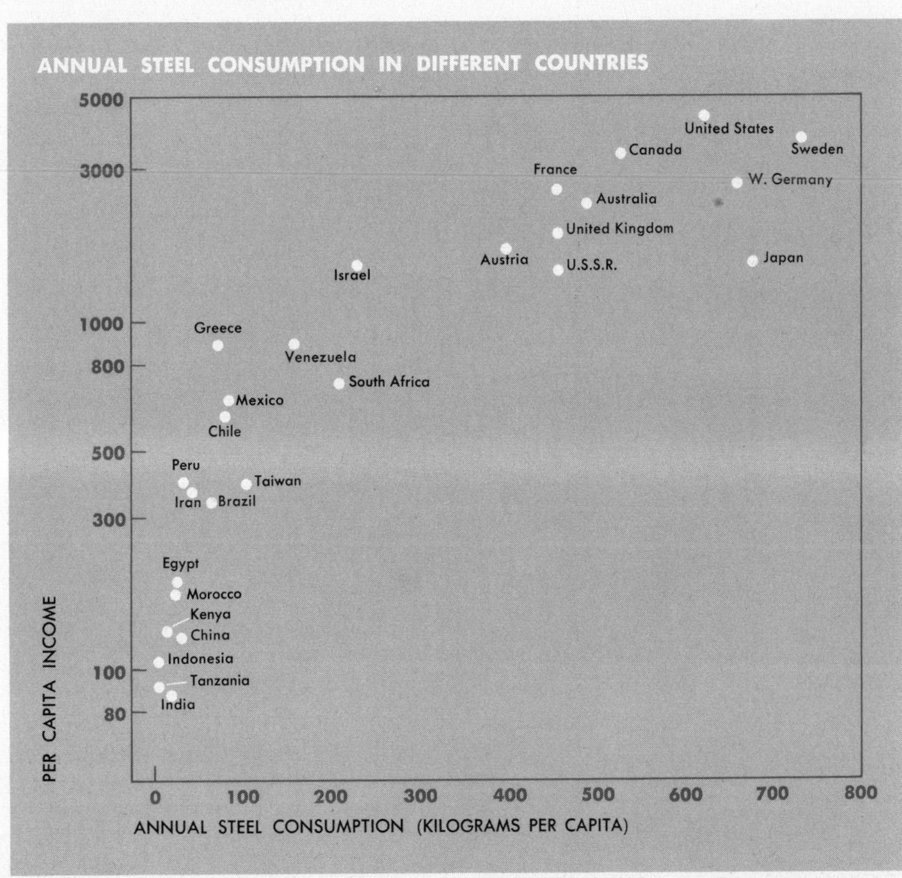

Moreover, if a nation can develop its own industry, it can then substitute domestic products for expensive imported goods, for which there is never enough foreign exchange. Thus, "import substitution" is always an alluring goal for the developing nations.

However, large industrial plants in the developing nations have often proved costly and inefficient, with their products costing far more than the imports for which they are supposed to substitute. Thus, they generally require heavy subsidies and tariff or import protection to get started. Often little foreign exchange is saved.

Thus, mounting experience suggests that improving agricultural productivity is the first need if LDCs are to break out of their vicious circle. With 70–80 percent of the population in agriculture, that's where the first problem is. A more efficient agriculture could produce more food for domestic use and export. More workers would be freed for gradual transfer to other jobs.

Some simple arithmetic dramatizes the importance of improving farm productivity. Suppose a nation wants to increase total output 5 percent annually but finds it impossible to raise agricultural productivity. If the "modern," nonagricultural sector produces 20 percent of total output, *its* productivity would have to increase 25 percent a year in order to provide the desired overall 5 percent increase. Such a spectacular performance is hardly likely.

Thus, allocation of scarce capital to raising agricultural output makes sense. Improving agricultural efficiency through fertilizer, simple tools, and improved methods requires little capital compared to mass industrialization. It requires less social disruption, less transfer of people, less infrastructure than does movement to a modern industrial sector.

Economic Planning or the Price System?

Many Americans, seeing the success of our essentially private-enterprise, market-directed economy, argue that the LDCs should rely on private initiative and let the marketplace decide what should be produced and who should produce it. But this view has found little sympathy in the LDCs. There is too much to be done and too little evidence that individual initiative and the marketplace will bring the desired changes fast enough—if at all. These nations do not trust the unseen hand of Adam Smith to guide the complex process of growth, to assess the long-range importance of alternative uses of resources. They want roads, schools, fertilizers, and industrial plants now. Thus, government intervention on a wide scale is the active agent in less-developed nations. The main issue is whether it shall involve complete government control over economic life (as in Communist China) or merely government direction of broad lines of activity with wide scope left to private initiative (as in India).

Nearly everywhere it is agreed that government must provide infrastructure. Even where most of the economy stays private, basic investment priorities have become the province of the government. Nearly everywhere, foreign exchange is under government control, so that scarce foreign currencies are used for high-priority imports rather than for private luxuries.

But in recent years, the experts have turned back to the crucial importance of individual initiative, and the role of self-interest in providing that initiative. There is disenchantment with government planning to solve all the problems. Many government planners and native bureaucrats have proved incompetent; corruption is commonplace. Some LDCs now try to regulate the behavior of individuals to a degree unknown in the Western world since mercantilism. All foreign trade and use of foreign exchange is regulated in detail; new businesses require government licenses. Rents, wages and basic commodity prices are controlled; internal shipments of grains and other basic commodities require government permits. The amount of red tape horrifies both native entrepreneurs and foreign businessmen. With the best of intentions, such complex regulations plus widespread incompetence in their administration can stifle business rather than speed the development.[6] Many

[6] See P.T. Bauer, *United States AID and Indian Economic Development* (American Enterprise Foundation, 1969), for Indian examples.

countries are learning that government control *per se* is no answer to the real problems of development, even though government planning is needed to supplement markets and individual initiative. Only Communist China and Cuba have adhered rigidly to a communist complete planning approach, even they make some use of the markets.

Monetary-Fiscal Policy and Economic Growth

Part Two stressed aggregate demand and expansionary monetary-fiscal policy to eliminate underemployment and to stimulate investment. Why don't the governments of the poor nations use deficit-financed spending to set up factories and lure the surplus farm population away from disguised unemployment into useful work, thereby increasing output and improving everyone's welfare?

The answer is that the main result would be inflation rather than increased output. As in the United States, raising the long-term growth rate is basically a *real* "supply" problem, not one of inadequate demand.

Suppose the government of Peru or Afghanistan prints money to lure workers into industry. There are no idle factories where output can be increased by calling the unemployed back to work. The critical shortage is real capital, not aggregate money demand. The situation is very different from the depression period in advanced countries, with vast unused productive capacity.

With this barrier to increasing real output, government spending without corresponding tax collections is likely to lead mainly to inflation as spending rises and output does not. Rapid inflation may endanger the stability of the government. Sound government finances are the first thing outside investors look for. And the higher domestic costs and prices make it harder to sell in world markets, a major blow when foreign exchange is badly needed to finance imports. **To repeat, the problems of the less-developed economies are basically "real" problems.**

Two Important Cases: India and China[7]

One third of all the people in the world live in two countries: India (575 million) and China (825 million). And these countries exemplify dramatically different approaches to economic development.

In many respects, India and China face similar problems. They are both vast land masses, heavily populated in many areas but with great reaches of mountains and wasteland. Both, in 1950, had per capita incomes around $85 in present U.S. prices. In both, around 80 percent of the total population is engaged in agriculture. And both, since World War II, have undertaken vigorous planned programs of economic development.

INDIA. In her first five "five-year plans," covering 1951 to 1979, India has chosen an essentially democratic approach. This has left considerable freedom to private enterprise under government planning, while using government projects in such major areas as irrigation, transportation, and education. Over one-third of total investment has been private. Taxes were raised only a little, and in spite of India's claim to be a "socialist" state the great bulk of her economic activity remains in private hands. Government taxes and spending remain only about half as large a percentage of GNP as in the United States and Western European nations. The plans pushed both industrialization and agricultural productivity—primarily the former at first, with more stress on agriculture recently. Industrial investment concentrated on both small-scale industry, such as textiles, and on larger projects, such as power development, fertilizers, coal, and heavy manufacturing. The plans called for increased capital accumulation in both agriculture and industry, plus added government services.

[7] Interesting overviews of the two economies in action are provided by John Lewis, *Quiet Crisis in India* (Washington, D.C.: The Brookings Institution, 1962), and *People's Republic of China* (Joint Economic Committee of Congress, 1972). A more informal picture by a distinguished American economist is James Tobin's "The Economy of China: A Tourist's View," *Challenge,* March 1973.

Results of the first four plans were mildly encouraging, but far from spectacular. Real national income rose 3–4 percent per annum and population about 2.5 percent, giving perhaps a 1 percent annual increase in per capita income—a pitifully small $1 a year. It is not clear that the living standard of the typical Indian peasant is much higher than it was a thousand years ago. Industrial improvement is more promising. Industrial production has quadrupled since 1950, and the 1979 goal in the fifth plan is another 50 percent increase. Net investment rose from about 5 to 10 percent of net national product, and saving is apparently rising.

But the achievements have fallen far short of India's optimistic goals. Moreover, unemployment has risen from probably ten–twenty million people in the cities, perhaps many more; no one has reliable statistics. Agriculture has been the great problem sector. And all the plans would have foundered had not large-scale foreign aid, mainly from America, eased India's desperate foreign-exchange shortages as she tried to finance the imports required for food and capital investment. Heavy military expenditures, reflecting concern over Indian relations with both China and Pakistan, have cut the supply of civilian-type goods.

The fifth five-year plan, ending in 1979, calls for a 5.5 percent annual growth in output and a large increase in both public and private investment. This plan emphasizes manufacturing, energy sources, and agriculture plus agricultural-support products such as fertilizers. It also calls for a massive population-control program.

India has wavered uncertainly as to the amount of government control she wants. In the second and third plans, governmental regulation of investment, foreign trade, and other aspects of economic activity became more and more detailed. Complaints of bureaucratic red tape and corruption multiplied, from Indians, foreign businesses in India, and potential investors. The major shortfalls of the third plan were attributed by many to this increasing bureaucracy and government inefficiency. The public sector and detailed government planning are thus less prominent in the later plans. Detailed industry targets have been replaced by planning estimates, except for a few key industries. Inducements to private investments are up. More stress is placed on encouraging initiative of individual farmers.

The hopeful view is that India is on the verge of her takeoff into self-sustaining growth. But her successes have been modest. Many Western observers, while admiring the humanistic, individualistic attitudes of India's leaders, believe she must have both more firm, effective governmental leadership and more freedom for private initiative to make real progress in economic development. Bureaucracy, indecision, and red tape frustrate foreign visitors who try to help the Indians. Today, India remains a restless giant, unsure of the success of her individualistic, humanistic program of mixed public-private enterprise.

China. China's first five-year plan, covering 1952–57, called for drastic increases in industrialization, collectivization of agriculture, and ruthless suppression of consumption to obtain the resources required for capital accumulation. The plan centralized economic control in the communist government. It called for rapid increases in agricultural output and mass transfer of agricultural population into industry. High government taxes on the masses and "profits" on government-monopolized necessities were used to seize a larger portion of total income for government investment, and large-scale external aid was received from the USSR. Hard work and long hours were forced on the Chinese people. The result was a substantial pickup in the rate of economic growth, which had been zero or negative during the preceding war decade.

The second five-year plan called for a further "great leap forward" with the primary focus on heavy industry, although food targets were also upped substantially. In 1958, government seizure of huge land masses and forced concentration of millions of agricultural families in huge "communes" virtually abolished individual family units. Women were pressed into all areas of work, and children were placed in state nurseries. Communist dictation of thought patterns made George Orwell's *1984* seem very real indeed.

But Mao's great leap forward turned out to be China's great failure. After an initial surge, industrial output collapsed. In the years 1959–61 both industrial and agricultural output fell radically—food production apparently by nearly one-half, as bad weather compounded the troubles. The strains of the previous decade's massive conversion to industry and of the communists' ruthless abolition of traditional family values apparently forced a massive retreat from the "communes" policy that had seized all private land and forced families into closely regulated agricultural communes. Some land was returned to individual family ownership, and some degree of family life was restored. More stress was placed on food production, and industrialization plans were revised downward radically.

Since the failure of the great leap forward, China has followed a more moderate development policy. The 1960s were devoted to restoring more orderly growth, and it was not until the mid-1960s that food and industrial production again reached the levels of a decade earlier. China's forward progress was again interrupted by the "cultural revolution" of 1967–69, which involved a massive social and political revolution to assure the dominance of Maoist thought. By 1970, more regular economic planning was again restored, and apparently industrial output has grown rapidly since then. Over the entire 1952–72 period, GNP has apparently grown at an average of about 4 percent annually, with large swings above and below that figure.

Today, China is the world's most completely planned communist nation—a rapidly growing, dual economy with substantially more progress in the industrial than the agricultural sector. The impressive growth in industrial output is shown in Table 45–5. Visitors are impressed by the hard work of the Chinese people, by the clean cities, and by their obviously improving standard of living. China has launched space satellites, built atomic bombs, and mounted a major military force. She is clearly no longer a typical less-developed nation.

But the differences between the cities and agriculture are great. Eighty percent of all Chinese live on the land, and most still spend their lives at backbreaking labor, with little help from modern machinery, or even animals. As in most LDCs, farm incomes are apparently only about one-third to one-half those in the cities. The

TABLE 45–5
Economic Growth in India and China

	INDIA		CHINA	
	1950	1971	1950	1971
GNP (in 1971 U.S. dollars)	24	56	45	125
GNP per capita (in 1971 U.S. dollars)	85	100	85	145
Industrial production (1950 = 100)	100	390	100	480
Electric power (million kilowatt hrs.)	4	64	5	62
Cement (million tons)	1	15	1	14
Steel (million tons)	1	7	1	18
Cotton cloth (billion meters)	1	4	2	8
Grain (million tons)	55	85	135	240
Fertilizers (million tons)	.1	12	.1	8

Source: United Nations. Data are based on reports by Indian and Chinese governments. Figures are rough estimates and may be overstated in some cases.

farm sector is organized into peoples' communes, which are both local government subdivisions and economic units for production, including some nonagricultural output. The communes vary in size from 5,000 to 40,000 people. They are in turn divided into production brigades of about 1,000 members, and these into production teams of 150–200. The team is responsible for cultivating its assigned land, and for carrying out all the associated activities. Part of the output is allocated to local public and social services, and taxes are paid to the central government. Each team is given delivery goals for sales to the state at state-established prices. So long as it meets these goals, it is apparently free to consume what it wants of what more it produces. Peasants are allowed small plots for their own cultivation, and there are small private markets for this output, as in most other communist economies, reflecting what are termed "spontaneous forces" of the rural economy.

Although communism stresses equality of incomes, there are substantial income differentials. In textile factories, for example, the average wage is about sixty yuan per month, while a beginning, low-output worker gets about half that amount. (A yuan equals about forty-five cents in U.S. money.) High-skilled workers get about 100 yuan, while engineers and technicians earn up to 130–140 yuan. Some physicians and surgeons apparently earn 200–300 yuan. Thus, incomes are considerably more equal than in the Western capitalist societies, because there are no high incomes from capital, but high-skilled experts may still earn ten times what common workers do, and perhaps twenty times as much as farm workers. The Chinese apparently find that monetary rewards are important, as have the Russians and other communist societies.

All universities were closed for three years during the "cultural revolution," and they are still only partially reopened. Students are chosen from the workers apparently without regard to intellectual achievement, highly educated individuals are periodically sent off to work in the fields, and production decisions are presumably made collectively in the communes and factories—though always within the central plan. How many skilled scientists, engineers, doctors, and the like will be developed in the future remains to be seen. There is some evidence that the central leadership has carefully protected a few intellectual leaders (for example in the fields of physics and computer science) to assure continued rapid progress in those fields.

Table 45–5 sums up the growth race between India and China. Today, China is clearly ahead, though her living standards are low compared to other successfully-developing, market-oriented nations like Japan, Taiwan, and Korea. Many Western observers question whether China's economic progress is worth the loss of individual freedom and the thought control it imposes on the Chinese people; and they question whether such conformist behavior is consistent with continuing economic and intellectual vitality. But communist supporters counter that results are what count, and that it is entirely proper for everyone to be governed by Maoist doctrine.

The Future of the Less-Developed Nations

Clearly, many of the less-developed nations are economies in motion. During the 1960s, labelled by the U.N. as the "decade of development," GNP for all developing countries combined grew at a surprising 5.6 percent per annum. Some countries—Lybia (oil), Greece, Taiwan, Israel, Iran (oil), Korea, and Brazil—averaged 7 percent or better. While special factors, like oil, explain some of the spectacular success stories, the overall picture is reasonably encouraging.

Most nations are learning from experience. A leading American economist has summarized the lessons of development policy over the past two decades:

> Both the practical and theoretical emphasis is now more on agriculture and less exclusively on industry, more on human and relatively less on physical capital investment, more on private enterprise and less on state industries, more on reducing birthrates and less on increasing national output, and

> more on cultural and technological change instead of making foreign loans and grants called "capital." The lack of real managers and technical specialists is seen as especially acute in the recently decolonized nations. The importance of efficient and honest government is becoming more appreciated.[8]

There is no chance the LDCs will catch up with developed-nation per capita incomes in the foreseeable future. Even on the most optimistic assumptions of annual growth rates in the LDCs, the absolute gap between rich and poor nations is widening at a breakneck pace. A 2 percent annual increase on $6,000 (roughly the present U.S. per capita figure) is $120, roughly the total present annual per capita income in India and China. Even if the Indian-Chinese growth rates were to be double ours (say 4 percent per capita as against 2 percent)—a most unlikely situation—by the end of the century U.S. per capita income would still be nearly $9,000, Indian-Chinese about $500. Clearly the less-developed nations can raise their living standards greatly. But even if success surpasses their wildest dreams, the absolute gap between the "haves" and "have-nots" in our ever smaller world seems certain to widen spectacularly over the years ahead.

What would you advise Mme. Gandhi, Prime Minister of India, to do to raise the standard of living of the Indian people?

U.S. POLICY

Mankind is passing through the most pervasive revolution it has ever known—the revolt of two-thirds of the world's people against the poverty, misery, and degradation of their present conditions of life, and against the domination of the industrialized, wealthy, Western powers. The speed and force of this revolution are hard to perceive, sitting in the comfort of an American home or classroom. But they may well do more than any other force to determine the kind of world in which we will live a half century hence.

[8] Stephen Enke, "Economists and Development," *Journal of Economic Literature,* December 1969, p. 1135.

What should American policy be? As the world's richest nation, and the proud leader of a democratic, humanitarian tradition, what should we do? What interests do we have in the less-developed nations, many of whose names we scarcely recognize?

First, an unhappy, resentful world of LDCs will be politically unstable. Rising living standards can give hope to the world's undernourished billions, though they certainly can not guarantee friendship or quiesence.

Second, we have economic interests. But it would be foolish to overstress this element. Trade with *all* the LDCs amounts to only about 2 percent of U.S. GNP. Except for foodstuffs and raw materials, there is relatively little direct competition in world markets between the developing economies and American exports. International exchange with such areas thus looks favorable for both us and the LDCs. We provide the largest foreign market for many of their raw material exports.

Third and perhaps most important, many Americans feel that we have a humanitarian interest in the relief of starvation, the lessening of disease and misery, and the improvement of education and living standards of the billions of people in the less-developed areas. There but for the grace of God go I, they say. We are very rich and they are very poor, and they need our help. Others disagree, especially when the time comes to pay the taxes to finance help to the LDC. Here obviously is a moral issue on which you must make up your own mind.

Channels of American Aid

If we want to help, for political, economic, or humanitarian reasons, we should first ask the question: Can we really make any difference? The task of helping one or two billion people to a better life is a huge one. And the preceding pages surely show that the task is not simply one of providing more dollars of foreign aid.

Yet we should remember some facts. The total income of all the billion people in the noncommunist less-developed nations in 1970 was less than $250 billion. The GNP of the United States was about $1 trillion. In 1970 we spent over $70 billion on military purposes. Total arms spending in the world was perhaps $150 billion. Elimination of these war expenditures could have raised by over 50 percent the living standard of each of the billion people.

The United States has the economic ability to help significantly. What have we done? What should we do?

Total Aid and Private Investment. In 1970, total government loans, grants, and private investments from the developed countries to the LDCs totalled about $14 billion, about half of it from the United States. About half was private long-term investment, presumably made in search of profits. The rest was government aid, either bilaterally or through international organizations. The U.S. $6 billion was $3.5 billion government aid, including "Food for Peace," with the remainder private investment, mainly in Latin America and the Middle East. These totals do not include military aid. Although the United States dominated total grants and investments, our $6 billion was only about .6 percent of our GNP, below the .75 percent for all other developed nations. The paragraphs below summarize what the United States has done.

Capacity of Less-Developed Nations to Absorb Aid. Obviously, the LDCs have a vast need for assistance. But, as a practical matter, how much aid in the form of foreign capital could they currently absorb effectively? The experts have come up with widely varying answers. But most estimates range between $15–25 billion a year. These estimates reflect the fact that development in most of the poor nations is held back by many other factors as well as capital—by lack of education, skilled workers, and managers; by unstable governments; by absence of initiative, and the like. It is clear that on these grounds some LDCs are more "ready" to absorb foreign aid than others, and some experts advocate concentrating aid on these nations.

1. Government Loans and Gifts. Since World War II, U.S. government loans and gifts to other nations have totaled over $100 billion, first to Europe through the Marshall Plan and since then mainly to the LDCs. About two-thirds of this has been nonmilitary aid. Since the 1950s, U.S. nonmilitary aid has averaged between $3–4 billion annually, with the biggest shares to India, Korea, and Latin America. But Congressional enthusiasm for the program has waned, reflecting growing discouragement over the results of such aid, and in 1971 Congress abolished the U.S. A.I.D. program. Ad hoc aid grants have been continued, but at a reduced level. In 1973, exhaustion of U.S. surplus food stocks (which had been used in the "Food for Peace" program) further undercut the aid program, and total U.S. aid fell to about $2 billion. This steady reduction in U.S. aid runs counter to the recommendation of international organizations that all developed nations provide aid (including private investment) equal to at least 1 percent of GNP.

2. Private U.S. Capital Investment. The large growth potential of the less-developed economies might seem attractive to American capital seeking investment at good rates of return. But risks are high, and many of the LDCs distrust foreign investment as threatening foreign intervention and control. Thus, they place elaborate regulations, special taxes, and restrictions on withdrawal of profits on foreign investments. Moreover, many governments are unstable, and the next regime may decide to seize foreign property.

Nevertheless, potential profits are high, and over the past decade private U.S. net investments in the LDCs have averaged over $2 billion annually, with nearly two-thirds of the total going into Latin America. Total accumulated U.S. private investments in the less-developed areas by 1972 were about $27 billion, nearly all of them made during the postwar period.

Private direct investments in less-developed nations can hardly be considered U.S. aid, since they are presumably made as voluntary profit-seeking business ventures. However, they do represent a major source of capital for the LDCs.

3. **Technical Assistance.** After the post-war burst of enthusiasm for aid to the less-developed economies came the sobering recognition that many of the crucial problems were internal ones. "Technical assistance" programs to help local governments and local peoples help themselves thus have grown during recent years, partly because they seem to work well, partly because they are far cheaper than mass capital-investment grants. Assistance in establishing better schools, efficient local government administration, sanitation and public health projects, better farming techniques are examples.

United States and multinational technical-assistance programs stress training natives to take over essential jobs themselves at the earliest possible moment. In most cases, U.S. technical assistance has been provided on a matching basis, with half the cost of the joint programs being borne by local governments. Technical assistance is a bright spot in our foreign-aid program.

4. **Lowering of International Trade Barriers and Purchase of Local Products.** In order to grow, most LDCs must sell basic products abroad if they are to secure foreign exchange with which to finance needed imports. Many of their economies are centered around one or two basic products—oil, rubber, nitrates, coffee, tin. Trade barriers that shut these products out of American markets strike a serious blow to the economies concerned. Contrary to the "imperialism" argument that we are bleeding the LDCs of their natural resources, those nations bitterly resent any barriers to their sales in U.S. markets. We have led the way in reducing tariff barriers and in helping to provide stable international markets for such basic commodities, but many less-developed nations think we should do still more.

Perspective on U.S. Policy

How successful has American aid to LDCs been? If the test of success is maintenance of political and military alliances with America or neutrality vis-à-vis the communist bloc, the verdict is favorable in some cases, but not in others. If the test is friendliness and gratitude for American generosity, the verdict is at best mixed. Few people like to think they are objects of charity, and we probably make a great mistake to expect thankfulness in return. If the test is economic improvement and the lessening of human misery abroad, the verdict is, some progress.

To expect fast results from our foreign aid is unreasonable. Economic growth is a slow process, even when the conditions are favorable. It is instructive to remember that the United States, with extremely favorable conditions for development, relied heavily on capital from abroad for nearly a century. At most, foreign aid can only help. The real force for development must come from within the LDCs themselves.

Lastly, recognition of the powerful force of growing nationalism and the desire for status and respect in every less-developed nation must be the cornerstone of successful aid, whatever our basic motives are. Increasingly, American experts urge that all American foreign aid except technical assistance be channeled through international organizations, to remove any implication of political pressure or domination by the United States. Those who want to use foreign aid as a political weapon or who want direct recognition understandably oppose such proposals.

Economic analysis can tell you a lot about the problem of raising living standards for the world's impoverished billions. It can give some guidance on how our help can do the most lasting good. But the problem of U.S. aid is moral and political as much as economic. It is one of the biggest issues on which this nation must take a stand over the decades ahead. Should we continue our recent gradual reduction of foreign aid, or reverse the trend?

REVIEW

For Analysis and Discussion

1. How well do the theories of Adam Smith and Malthus explain the plight of the less-developed nations? Has modern growth theory (from Chapter 42) added much to their analyses?
2. To develop rapidly, a nation must save and invest a substantial portion of its income. What steps would you advise the Indian government to take to increase India's saving rate when the majority of the population is on the brink of starvation?
3. Suppose the U.S. government sends you to a less-developed nation to assess its development prospects over the next decade. What would be the key information you would seek for your report?
4. Nearly everyone agrees that slower population growth is essential to reducing poverty in the LDCs. Suppose you were prime minister of India or Colombia; how would you bring this about?
5. Development of an entrepreneurial class seems critical for nations trying to break out of the vicious circle of poverty. If you were a government official in Peru or Zaire, what would you do about this problem?
6. "Modern economics tells us to pump in purchasing power in order to eliminate unemployment when depression occurs in the Western world; but this approach has no relevance for the less-developed nations, where a shortage of real capital is the basic problem." Is this statement correct? Explain your answer.
7. The United States has spent over $70 billion annually for defense expenditures in recent years. Yet it has spent only about $2–3 billion annually on direct aid to the less-developed economies. Should we divert $10 billion annually from the military budget to an all-out effort to speed economic development and to win friends among the less-developed nations?
8. Will the gap between U.S. and underdeveloped nations' living standards narrow or widen over the next quarter century?
9. Are large-scale U.S. purchases of raw materials from the LDCs a sign of U.S. exploitation at work or a major aid to development through providing badly-needed foreign exchange?

APPENDIX TO PART SEVEN

Current Research

GROWTH IN THE DEVELOPED NATIONS. Yale's James Tobin examines the case for faster growth as a major goal of national policy in "Economic Growth as an Objective of Government Policy," (*American Economic Review,* May 1964); look also at Herbert Stein's rejoinder (both in the JSB Readings). For perspective on growth in the long sweep of the history of the world, try Simon Kuznets's fascinating "Notes on the Pattern of U.S. Economic Growth," in *The Nation's Economic Objectives* (University of Chicago Press, 1964). A quite different view of growth is given by A.D. Chandler's *Ford, G.M., and the Automobile Industry* (Harcourt, Brace Jovanovich, 1965), a case study of one major industry; and by Chapter 6 of W. Baumol's provocative little book, *Business Behavior, Value and Growth* (Macmillan, 1967). Lastly, the role of technology in growth is thoroughly assessed by R.R. Nelson, M.J. Peck, and E. Kalachek in *Technology, Economic Growth, and Public Policy* (The Brookings Institution, 1967); and by Edwin Mansfield in *Technological Change* (W.W. Norton, 1971).

THE GREAT GROWTH CONTROVERSY. The controversy over growth, technology, and the quality of life has spawned a large literature. The attempt by Tobin and W. Nordham to measure net economic welfare, noted in Chapter 8 of the text, is one of the most imaginative pieces of recent research (*Economic Growth,* National Bureau of Economic Research, 1972). Another pioneering study is Kenneth Boulding's *Beyond Economics* (Ann Arbor, Mich.: University of Michigan Press, 1968). "The No-Growth Society" (*Daedalus,* Fall, 1973) assembles the views of experts on several elements of the issue. The direct attack on growth is led by E.J. Mishan in *Growth: The Costs We Pay* (London: Staples, 1969); for a counterattack see P. Passell and L. Ross, *The Retreat from Riches* (New York: The Viking Press, Inc., 1973). If you want to look at the basic research model underlying the Meadows doomsday predictions for economic growth, described in the Appendix to Chapter 44, see Jay Forrester, *World Dynamics* (Wright-Allen Press, 1971).

THE LESS-DEVELOPED ECONOMIES. There is a flood of research on the less-developed economies, why they are less-developed, and how they might grow faster. For a starter, try two classics: Albert Hirschman's *Journeys Toward Progress* (Garden City, N.Y.: Doubleday & Company, Inc., 1963), on Latin America; or Gunnar Myrdahl's *Asian Drama* (1 vol. ed.) (Twentieth Century Fund, 1971). Derek Healey sums up recent experience in "Development Policy: New Thinking About an Interpretation," (*Journal of Economic Literature,* September 1972). On Communist China, see *People's Republic of China: An Economic Assessment,* a compendium of papers prepared for the Joint Economic Committee (1972), and the *Hearings* on the volume (June 13–15, 1972). See also "Plans and their Implementation in the People's Republic of China," by D.H. Perkins, (*American Economic Review,* May 1973); and N.R. Chen and W. Galenson, *The Chinese Economy under Communism* (Aldine-Atherton, 1969). A recent look at India is Wilfred Malenbaum's *Modern India's Economy* (University of Pennsylvania Press, 1971). Lastly, on the controversial issue of whether the LDCs face an imminent starvation threat, balanced analyses are presented by W. Cochrane's, *The World Food Problem* (New York: Thomas Y. Crowell Co., 1969), and P. Hauser (ed.), *The Population Dilemma* (Prentice-Hall, 1969).

THE CHANGING ECONOMIC WORLD

PART EIGHT

Comparative Economic Systems: United States, USSR, and Japan

CHAPTER PREVIEW

CHAPTER FORTY-SIX

What type of economic system serves man best? On the evidence of Tables 1–1 and 45–1, it is private-enterprise, market-directed capitalism. Of the top ten nations in real income per capita, every one has basically this type of economy. But nearly all have recently mixed in a liberal dose of government planning and regulation. Moreover, one-third of the world's people live in communist nations (mainly China and the USSR,) and Soviet Russia is the world's second great industrial and military power. Many of the smaller nations are still hovering as to the type of economy they prefer.

At the end of a long book, devoted mainly to our type of largely private-enterprise system, it is well to look briefly at how other types of economic systems work. Russia is perhaps the most interesting comparison, because it is the world's second most powerful economy and because it exemplifies modern socialism in action in a developed, industrial economy, the main alternative to our type of economic organization. But a briefer look at Japan is also appropriate, because it has been the world's great economic success story since World War II and because it exemplifies a more heavily planned capitalist economy than the United States. Add to these China, India, and the other LDCs from Chapter 45 and you have the spectrum of economic systems currently on trial, though there are many variations among the other nations.

CAPITALISM AND COMMUNISM[1]

Communism today has heavy political as well as economic overtones. To look at the economic side of any "ism" alone is to miss its essence. Communism has become inseparably associated with political and economic dictatorship because we see them together in Russia and Communist China, today's predominant communist countries. Yet in its original form, Marxian socialism was highly democratic in spirit. Karl Marx's famous *Das Kapital,* the foundation of modern communism, provided a detailed critique of capitalism, but he was conveniently vague when it came to blueprinting the communist economy. Still, one thing is sure. Marx wasn't looking for any political or economic dictatorship except the dictatorship of the proletariat—of the whole working class.

From an economic viewpoint, there are two big differences between capitalism and communism. **Under private-enterprise capitalism as we know it, most productive resources are privately owned, and economic activity is largely directed by the interaction of supply and demand in the market. Under communism, conversely, most productive resources are publicly owned, and economic activity is directed largely by central planning; this type of economy is often called a "command economy."** The two critical questions, then, are: (1) Are productive resources privately or publicly owned, and (2) is economic activity directed by individual choice and the price system or by government planning?

Obviously, both are matters of degree. Not all productive resources are privately owned under American capitalism—governments own land, highways, dams, buildings, and so on. Nor are all resources publicly owned in Russia. Also, an economy can have private ownership of resources and nevertheless be centrally planned. The American economy during World War II was a partial example. Hitler's fascism in Germany was a more complete example. India makes substantial use of central planning today, with primarily private ownership of resources.

Thus, economic systems fall along a spectrum on both these conditions, something like the arrangement shown in the diagram above. The location of the countries is only approximate, but it is intended to suggest the variation on the two scores. The American and Russian systems differ widely on both. They are thus especially worth careful comparison. But don't forget that

Private ownership {Japan, U.S. ——— India ——— USSR — China Public ownership

Price-directed U.S. ——— Japan ——— India ——— USSR ——— China Centrally planned

most of the world's economies lie in between, on one or both of the spectrums shown. Nor is Russia at the extreme of communism; today China is a purer example.

The following pages are mainly an analysis of how the Soviet economy operates, and an evaluation of how well it does its job. But throughout there's a running comparison with the way the American economy accomplishes the same tasks. And at the end there's a final comparative look at Japan and Yugoslavia as in-between economies. A major purpose is to help you to focus your own understanding and evaluation of the American economy.

HOW DOES THE SOVIET ECONOMY WORK?

Objectives

The modern Soviet economy rests on the doctrines of Marx. "From each according to his abilities, to each according to his needs," was

[1]There are many volumes on comparative economic systems and on the "isms." Three readable ones are G. Grossman, *Economic Systems* 2nd ed. (Englewood Cliffs, N.J.: Prentice-Hall, Inc. 1974); W. Ebenstein, *Today's Isms* (Englewood Cliffs, N.J.: Prentice-Hall, Inc. 1970), which stresses the political-economic mix; and P.J. Wiles' *The Political Economy of Communism* (Cambridge: Harvard University Press, 1961).

Marx's foundation for communist society. The rule of the masses, with productive resources owned by the state and used for the common benefit of all, remains, on paper, the foundation of the modern communist economies—of China as well as the USSR.

The goals stressed by modern communist leaders look very much like those stated by Americans—improved living standards, economic growth, more leisure, freedom, security, elimination of poverty. From the words, it is hard to distinguish Russia from the Western democratic societies.

In fact, the USSR appears to most outsiders to be a "command" economy, with the big commands issued by a small group of communist officials over whom the people have little control. Centralization of political power in Russia is especially significant for our economic survey, because all basic economic plans and policies are made by the controlling political group. Even after recent steps to decentralize planning and control, among the major nations the Soviet economy is still the most highly planned and controlled, save that of Communist China. In America, we leave everyone relatively free to use his private property and his income as he wishes within the law, and we accept the outcome as being by and large the best one for the public welfare. The Russian leaders decide what they want to happen economically, and they use a comprehensive system of plans and controls to make it happen.

So much for Russia's stated objectives and approach. How do the Soviets go about solving the four big problems that all economies face?

(1) Deciding What To Produce and (2) Getting It Produced[2]

In the USSR, the central planners decide what is to be produced. After the Russian revolution of 1917–18, the communists made an almost fatal mistake. They assumed that central economic control was easy—that all they had to do was to confiscate private productive resources, tell people what to produce, and everything would go along nicely. It didn't! Russian total output in 1919–20 dropped back to near the 1890 level. The Russian peasants didn't see why they should produce just to have their crops taken away and given to someone else. There was virtually no modern industrial capacity. The economy was thrown into chaos.

The central planners made many mistakes, but they learned. After years of experimentation and a series of "five-year plans" for economic development since 1928, the Soviets have developed this general pattern:

First, the basic policy decisions are made by the central communist authorities—which industries to develop, which to let lag, how much to allocate for consumption, how much for industrial expansion, how much for the military. Then the lower-level planners map out detailed directions for units in the economy to follow in implementing these decisions. Lastly, these plans have to be carried out by millions of officials, managers, and workers throughout Russia.

This process has been modified many times. In recent decades, the communists have become increasingly aware of the problems of centrally planning and controlling a vast economy, and since Stalin's death in 1952 controls have been substantially liberalized. Especially since 1965, the Soviets have admitted having serious problems with their top-heavy planning mechanism, and they have both substantially decentralized authority to plant and industry managers and placed more reliance on market prices and consumer demands to guide production. But the big decisions are still made by the central planners.

Making the Plan

The broad goals for the economy are set by the Praesidium and the Central Committee of the Communist Party. Since 1928, the goals have been contained in a series of comprehensive five-year plans. The ninth plan, for 1971–75, calls for an annual growth rate of 7 percent in industrial production and 6 percent in national income. While early plans concentrated on military output and investment, recently more

[2]Two good studies of the Russian economy are Robert Campbell, *Soviet Economic Power* (Boston: Houghton Mifflin Co., 1973); and Alex Nove, *The Soviet Economy* (New York: Praeger Publishers, Inc., 1968).

weight has been given to satisfying consumer wants, especially in the eighth plan. The present plan continues the increase in consumer goods output, but returns somewhat to the earlier stress on industrial growth. It calls for steel, oil, and electrical energy output surpassing the United States by 1975, with increases in each of about 50 percent over the five-year period. But, as we shall see, the Soviets have often fallen short of achieving their goals, and they are having serious trouble with the ninth plan.

Within these broad objectives, the plan for each year is developed by the Gosplan (State Planning Commission), working with a huge Central Statistical Administration which provides data on available resources and productive capacities. Their job is immense. Suppose you had to plan only aircraft. How would you plan production of all the hundreds of thousands of components that go into a modern airplane, scheduling each to be on hand when it was needed? Now back up and decide how you would plan the production of all the subcomponents to produce the parts you need for the airplanes. By now you'll be up in the millions of individual decisions, just for one major product. And the complexities multiply geometrically when you add other products, because of all the interlinkages between materials, labor, and manufacturing facilities needed. It's this vast complex of decisions that we leave to supply and demand in the marketplace in our private-enterprise economy. And this complexity has led the Soviets into more and more trouble as their economy has grown. How do they do it now?

First, they don't start from scratch each year. They use last year as a bench mark, which greatly simplifies the task. Second, the Gosplan apparently focuses each year primarily on some fifty basic products and industries that are of critical importance in attaining the prime goals of the overall plan.[3] They apparently then construct for some 1,500 major commodities (industries) a materials balance, a labor balance, and a geographical balance. These show the materials, labor, and other resources needed to produce the desired output throughout the economy, and the net output required to add to present inventories in order to meet the plan goals. By combining these balances for all major products, they have a reasonably complete picture of the overall materials, labor, facilities, and regional balances for the entire economy. From this "input-output" model, they can see roughly where there are likely to be material shortages, where labor surpluses, and so on, and they can then adjust accordingly.

Once the broad outline of an annual plan is completed, it is sent to regional and industry councils throughout the economy. They check their quotas against the productive capacities in their region or industry to see whether the plan appears feasible. If they think the quotas are too high, or if they believe their tentative allocations of materials and equipment would be inadequate to meet them, they have the right to protest—and they do! Local plant managers often argue that the goals are too high and that inadequate raw materials and machinery are being allocated to meet them. The local workers may protest that they are already speeded up to the limit of their capacity. Then it's a subject for negotiation with the regional and industry-level planners, and after that between them and the national planners at the Gosplan. The Soviet planning process involves a lot of talk. Some observers have called it the most gigantic collective-bargaining process in history.

Finally, all this information gets reflected back to Moscow, where the Gosplan must settle on the final plan so that everything balances out for the whole economy. The planners do the best they can, using some modern mathematical and electronic computer techniques, and making adjustments in minor industries to accommodate the major goals.

The final stage, after the plan has been approved by top communist officials, is to send it back down to the regional and industry councils for implementation.

We know the planners make mistakes. Plans are continuously adjusted. If the small-machinery plan runs into labor shortages while

[3]During World War II, when the U.S. industrial economy was extensively but by no means completely planned, the whole planning process hinged largely on allocation of three major materials—steel, copper, and aluminum.

that for electric light globes turns up a surplus, the planners don't wait until next year to make an adjustment. This doesn't make for a quiet life among Gosplan employees or for managers throughout the economy, and the number of adjustments has apparently snowballed in recent years as the Russian economy has grown in complexity. Complaints from below have become increasingly bitter. Industry plans are changed dozens of times a year. These crises have led the pragmatic rulers in the Kremlin to consider delegating more responsibility and freedom to local managers in carrying out the broad goals handed down from above.

Carrying Out the Plan

The annual plan is a *physical* blueprint for the use of productive resources and the production of intermediate and final goods for the year. How do the Soviets get their plans carried out? In essence, by telling people what to do and by paying them for doing it.

Managerial Incentives. Under the early plans, each plant manager received a production *quota,* together with detailed information on the supply of materials he would receive, the equipment that would be allocated to him, the labor he was to use, and so on. Then it was up to him to get the final product out. His job was to meet the quota, not to question why. If he exceeded his quota, he was praised by the party and received substantial economic rewards, including money, better housing, a car, paid vacations, and other benefits not available except through the official reward system. These are powerful incentives in a low-consumption society. On the other hand, if his plant ended the year below quota, or if he required more labor and materials than were allocated to him, the rewards went the other way.

The Soviets are thoroughly aware of the importance of good managers to the success of their plans. Managers are among the highest paid. They receive medals and public commendation for exceeding quotas. The Soviets are also harsh critics when managerial performance falls short. Good managers are very important under communism, the Soviets have found, just as they are under capitalism.

But the Soviets have had major problems on managerial incentives. Because rewards have depended mainly on meeting physical output quotas, managers have concealed production possibilities in order to get lower quotas, hoarded materials, and avoided doing too well lest quotas be raised for next year. There has been no penalty for wasteful use of materials or manpower so long as it doesn't violate the plan.

"Blat" (using influence with higher-ups in industry) and "tolkachi" (special purchasing agents from plants who go around buying up scarce materials and parts outside the plan) are well-known, if technically illegal, parts of the Russian industrial scene. Russian managers have learned to make their own performances look good by hoarding labor and materials, bootlegging scarce materials outside the plan, and even fudging the basic performance reports on which they are judged. This is not utterly different from the American case, where local managers sometimes try to make their own units look good by devices that reduce rather than increase total corporate profits. Either way, it's tough to make middle managers stick to top-level plans. But in America the dollars and cents on the income statement at year-end, the percentage return on investment, and the per share earnings for the stockholders provide visible measures that facilitate evaluation of management performance.

Innovation has been another special managerial problem. New ideas involve risks, and the Soviet system has lacked effective rewards for risk taking. In the Soviet climate, doing reasonably well is more conducive to the manager's peace of mind than taking a chance on a new idea that may flop. There's nothing like the American private-enterprise entrepreneur out to make a million (or go broke) in a gamble on a new product or new method. Soviet criticism of managers for lack of imaginative innovation has been bitter.[4]

[4]For a lively, still relevant comparison of Soviet and American managers, see D. Granick, *The Red Executive* (Garden City, N.Y.: Doubleday & Company, Inc., 1960).

"Profits" and the New Look in Soviet Planning. As the central planning process increasingly bogged down and as inefficiences piled up at the local level, in the 1960s the Soviets began to question whether more reliance on a kind of "profit motive" for individual managers couldn't help the planners to avoid the local wastes of physical planning and increase total output. In 1965 the communists announced an experiment that freed managers in the shoe and food-processing industries from planned quotas, and directed them to maximize their profits, much as in America, with their own bonuses based on the profits they make. Each manager was substantially free to set the price of his product and the wages he paid, and to choose his own production methods. The profits themselves, above the special awards to the successful manager, of course revert to the state. In the following years, apparently about one-third of all consumer goods production was shifted to such a plan.

But the new look inevitably raised basic issues. Local managers free to bid resources away from others came into conflict with central plan goals, and the ties on local managers were again tightened in such cases. Thus in 1973 another major reform was announced. Recognizing that dispersion of authority to 50,000 local managers didn't work satisfactorily under the general planning process, the Soviets combined much of the economy into intermediate-level industry corporations, or production associations for major industries. Managers of these industry production centers are apparently to have some freedom to attempt to maximize "profits" for their industries, and they will assume much of the planning function for their industries. Most individual plants will become, in effect, operating divisions of the new corporations, with the decision-making powers granted to factory managers in 1965 now given to the corporations. The central planning ministries will merely set basic goals for these industries, determine investment and technological improvements, and establish overall policies.

The problem of how much decentralization of decision making and operating authority is optimal remains unsettled in the USSR. The parallel to the problem faced by a large American corporation like GM is substantial. In America, decentralized decisionmaking and authority, under only broad rules from headquarters, have been widely accepted as the best way of maintaining local managerial initiative and of coupling the advantages of central planning with local, firsthand management. But in the USSR, Gosplan still makes the basic plans and the blueprints for carrying them out for most of the economy.

Labor Incentives and Labor Unions. How do the Soviets get the workers to carry out their plans? Just as in the United States, money is the big incentive, but it is supplemented by continuous emphasis on national pride and party loyalty for members.

The planners decide how much should be paid for each type of work, and they do it so as to get the plan carried out effectively. The biggest pay goes to scientists, artists, inventors, and managers who overproduce their quotas. About 75 percent of all industrial workers are on "piece rates," whereby each worker gets paid according to how much he turns out. This is a much higher percentage than in the United States. Money wages thus play much the same role in pulling labor into jobs and stimulating good performance as they do in America, except that in Russia they are set by the planners to channel workers where the planners want them, rather than freely by market supply and demand. It is striking that money incentives—differential pay for workers turning out more output—are used more strongly than in such capitalist countries as the United States. And resulting pay differentials for workers are considerably wider in the USSR than here, where union pressures have tended to lessen them.

Table 46–1 shows incomes received by various Soviet groups. It is useful mainly to suggest relative incomes for different jobs. Since the figures shown are for the early 1960s, they should probably be increased by 50–75 percent for 1970 incomes in 1970 U.S. dollars. The Soviet authorities have stated that average Soviet

TABLE 46–1

Soviet Incomes[a]

	MONTHLY EARNINGS IN RUBLES
Leading scientist	800–1500
Senior government official	700
Opera or ballet star	500[b]
Professor (science or medicine)	400–1000
Plant manager	300–1000
Engineer	100–300
Worker (skilled)	100–250
Physician	85–180
High-school teacher	85–100
Worker (semiskilled)	60–90
Worker (unskilled)	27–50

[a]One ruble equals $1.11 at the official exchange rate; this exchange rate understates the real buying power of Russian incomes in our money. Figures do not include extra perquisites such as special housing, cars, and the like, or social services such as free vacations, health services, and subsidized housing for all.

[b]Plus outside earnings to 2,000 rubles.

Source: U.S. Department of Labor. Data are for early 1960s; see text.

monthly wages and salaries for 1970 were 125 rubles (about $140 at the official exchange rate).

How free are Soviet workers to work where they wish? Substantially free, given the immobility inevitably associated with low incomes and limited geographical mobility—except for farm workers who are not free to move to industrial jobs because of the major Soviet problem in raising farm output, and workers who have been "recruited" for special projects or have received special training or education at state expense. The complaints of managers about labor turnover suggest that labor moves from job to job with considerable freedom; labor turnover was reported at 20 percent in the early 1970s. The main coercion used to hold workers in particular jobs is preference on desirable housing, which may be lost if the worker leaves. With a nationwide housing shortage, this is a powerful incentive.

Most Soviet workers belong to unions. But they are quite different from unions in America. Soviet unions have nothing to do with setting wages; wages are established by the central planners. The unions are worker organizations that are expected to help in implementing government plans. As such, they apparently have a substantial role in urging workers to meet quotas and in channeling labor from surplus to shortage occupations. But they are more like workmen's clubs than like the unions we know. Make your own comparison with the role of unions in America, where there is far more union power—and far more conflict.

Checking on Performance: The Gosbank and the State Control Commission. Basic planning is done in physical terms. But the Gosplan also makes up a complete set of "value" (or financial) plans to parallel the basic physical plans. Using these financial plans, the Gosbank (state banking system) provides money to managers to pay for labor and materials to carry out the production plans. For example, if the annual plan calls for ten million pairs of shoes, the Gosbank provides shoe-plant managers just enough rubles to pay for the labor, leather, and so on, allocated to the production of those shoes. It does the same for all other products. And managers must deposit their receipts in the Gosbank, except for cash payments made to workers. Except for wages and citizens' purchases of consumer goods, transactions in Russia are made by check through the Gosbank.

The Gosbank plays two significant roles. First, it provides a financial control over managers. If they run out of money, this is a sign they are buying more than the inputs allocated to them under the physical plan. And because they can get materials and labor only by paying for them, the control is close and effective. When the manager deposits his receipts in the Gosbank, this provides an automatic check on whether he has produced the amount specified in the plan. How much this financial control will be relaxed under the 1973 reforms remains to be seen. Second, the Gosbank provides a regular banking function, transferring funds, advancing working capital, and creating money for the economy.

In some respects, the Gosbank with its local branches is like banks in the United States. It advances working capital to carry out productive processes, transfers funds, and creates money for the economy. But it is strictly government-operated, and its main goal is to help implement the physical plan. It advances new checking accounts (creates money) when they are needed to facilitate production, and it reduces funds to industries that have been absorbing too much labor or material.

How does this checking on performance compare with the private-enterprise process? In America, too, the availability of funds to carry out any economic service exercises a basic control over what is done and who does it. In America, the firm continuously gets funds from selling its product; thus consumers (rather than the government) exercise a continuous check on whether any firm is doing its job effectively. If a firm wants to expand, it must either have stored up its own profits or it must go to the competitive capital market for funds. There its project is evaluated by bankers, private investors, and other lenders against other alternative demanders of funds. If the firm's prospects look good, it will get loans; if they look bad, it will have trouble raising funds. The capital market controls who can expand and who cannot.

Which process is more effective? It obviously depends on your point of view. Who should check on whom? The Soviet procedure gives direct control to the planners through the Gosbank and the control commission. In America, we place most of our faith in the impersonal market, where lenders and business firms are counted on to look out for their own capital and incomes and thereby to get resources allocated most effectively. Here the Socialists criticize the American economy vigorously. They say that under capitalism, capital is rationed out by monopolistic lenders to big, favored borrowers in a way that makes it hard for new, smaller firms to compete effectively with the established giants. But even fewer officials decide who gets the capital to expand in the USSR. Think back to the chapters on monopoly and competition and on the American banking system to decide how much weight to give this criticism.

The Recalcitrant Problem of Agriculture. Agriculture has been the communists' knottiest problem. Their early attempts to collectivize Russian agriculture, carried through by bloody force during the 1920s and 1930s, met bitter and sullen resistance. Forced to work on collective farms, farmers produced less than before and kept crops and animals for themselves rather than turning them over to the authorities for export to the cities. Frustrated communist planners tried one tack, then another—but with little success in meeting expanded food goals for the rapidly growing industrial population or in freeing farm labor for industrial jobs.

In theory, a collective farm is a cooperative, democratic association of farmers who have pooled their land, tools, and labor to make a large farm, which they operate in common. Proceeds are shared in proportion to the quantity and quality of work they do. Large-scale operation produces the economies of large-scale mechanized farming, eliminating the waste and inefficiency that for centuries have characterized Russian agriculture.

It sounds fine, but not to the peasants. Soviet planners found crops vanishing into farm consumption and total production declining. Bloody reprisals brought only temporary compliance and smoldering resentment. Over millions of acres and widely scattered farmers, effective control was impossible.

There are now some 100,000 collective and state farms, compared to perhaps 25 million small peasant farms four decades ago. About 5,000 of these are huge state farms of many thousand acres, operated outright as "business" firms by the Ministry of Agriculture in much the same pattern as prevails for industrial production. The rest are collective farms, ranging from a few "communes" (which involve complete sharing of property, labor, and results) to many cases where the collective farm is scarcely more than a sharing of major machinery and some exchange of labor. In most cases, part of the land is farmed collectively but each family retains a small plot for its own individual operation. These private plots make up only 5–10 percent of the total land under cultivation, but they apparently produce nearly one-third of total farm output of vegetables, eggs, meat, milk, and other products that are suited to labor-intensive production and that can be sold in small lots in markets.

Payments to farmers are calculated on a complicated basis. For work on collective farms they receive partly payment in kind and partly money income that varies above a guaranteed minimum depending on how much they produce. Apparently about a third of total output is delivered directly to the state, about a third is used on the farms for further output (seed, feed for animals, and so on), and about a third is given to the farmers themselves. A substantial portion of the latter finds its way onto the free market for food consumption in the cities. This supply is augmented by products from the millions of small family holdings, as indicated above. Private initiative is far from dead in Russian agriculture.

In any case, agricultural output has persistently lagged far behind the plan goals, in spite of one reform after another. The 1970s farm output goals in the plans are viewed by most outsiders as unrealistic. Most outsiders estimate that since 1950 Soviet farm output has grown no more than 2 or 3 percent a year, if that much. Several times Russia, historically a large wheat exporter, had to import large quantities of wheat for food. Food output per capita has barely held stable over the last decade.

The importance of agriculture in Russia is great. A third of the Russian labor force is in agriculture—nearly forty million workers, compared to four million in the United States. Yet U.S. total farm output exceeds Russia's. One American farmer can feed forty-eight people, one Russian farmer only seven. Low productivity in agriculture is the communists' number-one production problem.

(3) Deciding How Income Is To Be Distributed

Marxist doctrine says: To each according to his need. The Soviet leaders today season this liberally with: To each according to how hard he works and how much he contributes. Incomes are more equally distributed than in the United States, because in Russia income **from property** is very limited, whereas many of the highest American incomes are from dividends, interest, and capital gains on private property. There are no millionaires in modern Russia. But money incomes derived **from work** are about as unequally distributed in Russia as in America. This inequality reflects the strong use of incentive payments to achieve the central planners' goals.

Table 46–1 tells the story. Artists, scientists, professors, managers, and government officials receive the highest incomes, including special supplements in premium housing, use of government autos, paid vacations, and so on. As in America, common labor is at the bottom of the totem pole—except for farmers, many of whom take much of their incomes in kind from their farms. Within the ranks of factory workers and comparable laborers, apparently the spread between the lowest and highest monthly incomes is nearly one to eight, far *wider* than in America.

The Soviets adjust wage rates up and down frequently for different occupations and industries, to help implement the overall plan. The planners may be good Marxists on paper, but their behavior on wages suggests that they have learned a good deal about the power of monetary incentives.

Government Services and Income Redistribution. Although it uses money incentives freely to stimulate production and to allocate resources, the state provides widespread free social services to help the masses. Soviet authorities claim that one-third of the income of low-income groups is provided by free government services. Nearly all housing is government-owned, and rents are extremely low; on the average, Soviet citizens apparently pay only about 2–3 percent of their income for housing, far under the 15–25 percent common in America. A Moscow two-bedroom apartment rents for $20–30 a month—if you can find one. Russian housing is generally bad, but it's very cheap. Paid vacations, government nurseries, special grants to large families, free education, and extensive health services all supplement money incomes.

But to evaluate these government services we have to ask, who pays for them? A general sales (turnover) tax accounts for over half of all government income. Profits on state enterprises provide most of the rest. Direct personal taxes (mainly an income tax) take only 8 percent of personal income. All told, government collections and expenditures comparable to our combined federal-state-local government taxes and expenditures are apparently about 35–40 percent of GNP, though estimates vary substantially.

Because the turnover tax varies widely from product to product and from year to year, estimation of its incidence by income levels is extremely difficult. Increases and decreases in the tax are used to adjust the prices of individual products up and down to discourage or to stimulate consumption. This way the planners make consumer demand match the goods produced, somewhat as free market prices provide this adjustment in the United States. This tax, therefore, substantially offsets the apparent big government supplement to low incomes.

On the other hand, the Soviets use especially low prices on some major commodities in addition to housing to subsidize low-income consumers. This means that such goods are sold below "cost." Prices are set very high on such luxuries as autos. Here again, pricing is used to promote the goals that seem important to the planners.

(4) Deciding Between Current Consumption and Economic Growth

In America the choice between current consumption and economic growth depends on consumer and business saving, business investment decisions, private educational and research decisions, and government tax and investment behavior. In Russia, the decision is made and implemented by the central planners. And their choice has been in favor of rapid industrialization and growth, at the expense of current consumption.

Since the early 1920s, Russia's GNP has grown at about 4 percent annually, about the same as the U.S. rate. Soviet growth during the 1950s was spectacular—about double that rate—but it has slowed down substantially since about 1960. To press its postwar growth, the USSR allocated an extraordinarily large portion of its output to capital formation. Until recently private consumption was held below 50 percent of GNP and nonmilitary investment apparently was 20–25 percent. Soviet consumption was so repressed that per capita real consumption was no higher in 1958 than it had been in 1928; only since about 1960 has the average Russian benefited much through higher consumption from the last half century of economic growth. But this Soviet policy produced an average annual increase of 10 percent in the Russian capital stock, which went far to account for rapid Soviet growth—aided by her ability to borrow a large amount of technology from the West, and a rapid growth in the labor force.

The decline in Russian growth since 1960 has reflected in substantial part a decline in the capital accumulation rate, as more was allocated to satisfying consumer wants. Even with central planning and control rather than individual choice and the price system, Russia faces the same fundamental problem in growth as does any other economy—she must divert scarce resources from consumption to investment, improve her technology, and step up the ability and performance of her labor force. There is no other way, for either communism or capitalism. As post-Stalin liberalization has opened up the Soviet economy to Western standards and Western ideas, the pressure has intensified on communist leaders for more consumption goods.[5]

[5] Under Marxist doctrine, only labor is truly productive. Thus, interest on money or real capital plays no role in communist doctrine. Western economists properly point out that this position, if followed, will lead Soviet planners to improper decisions in allocating resources. Some methods involve a heavy use of productive resources per unit of output, others a low investment. Only by taking these differences into account can optimal decisions be made as to what capital goods should be produced. And the interest rate, as was pointed out in Chapter 31, is the price system's tool in making such comparisons among such alternatives. Interestingly, the pragmatic Soviet planners (who are smart fellows too) are now slipping the interest rate into their calculations through the backdoor.

How fast the Russian economy grows depends on the decisions of the central planners, but it also depends on fundamental political forces—on how long the population will be content to see most of the increased output go into capital expansion and military products. In the American economy, the public speaks on this division continuously, through its own savings-spending behavior and through its directions to congressmen on government spending and taxes. Under the Soviet system there is little evidence that the man in the street has much voice in the decisions. Yet the Soviet leaders constantly face the need to keep the masses reasonably content if they are to stay in power. Recent increases in consumption-goods output attest to this concern.

No reliable estimates of total Soviet expenditure on research are available, but apparently, with a national income about half ours, Russia spends about as much as we do on basic research.

Government Monetary and Fiscal Policy and Economic Stabilization

The Soviet central planners do not program men or machines into unemployment. If there is unemployment, it is because planning has gone awry or because someone is not behaving according to plan. And there has been very little official unemployment in the USSR. But there is still the problem of keeping total spending power roughly equal to goods available for purchase. If buying power gets too large, inflationary pressures will mount. If buying power is too low, prices must be cut or unsold inventories will pile up.

The Soviets manage this balance largely through the turnover tax (fiscal policy) and the Gosbank (monetary policy), the same two tools we use. In Russia, most of the burden falls on the turnover tax. If total demand is excessive, the turnover tax is raised all along the line, or on those products where demand seems most excessive, raising prices and siphoning off income to the government. If total demand is inadequate, turnover taxes are lowered. In a real sense, the Russians have adopted "functional finance" as the core of their stabilization and allocation mechanism.

In spite of this plan, inflation has been a persistent problem for the Soviets. The Russians are human beings too, and when there isn't enough to go around they apparently tend to plan a little more resources for all the demands than there are to parcel out. The result is a demand pressure that tends to bid up prices all along the line as shortages occur; black markets spring up everywhere. Twice since World War II, the Soviets have virtually repudiated their national debt, thereby wiping out bondholders' accumulated savings. The basic pressures that make for inflation—shortage of goods relative to the purchasing power provided by incomes paid out—are the same in communist and capitalist societies.

COMMUNISM AND CAPITALISM IN PERSPECTIVE

How well have communism and capitalism done in the USSR and the United States? To answer, we must specify criteria for judgment. It may be convenient to use the five suggested in Chapter 2, but if you prefer others, use your own.

Progress—Rising Living Standards

Which economic system has provided the highest standard of living for its people? However you measure, the United States is far out in front. In 1972, the U.S. GNP was $1.2 trillion. The USSR's, with a vastly larger area and forty million more people, was only about half as large. Per capita GNP, a more significant measure of individual economic well-being, was $5,500 in the United States, $1,900 in the USSR. Such comparisons may be substantially off because of measurement problems and currency conversion difficulties. Some observers put Russian per capita incomes as high as half ours, but not more.

The Soviets have made impressive economic headway since they took over in the 1920s. Yet housing, especially outside the major cities, is appallingly poor. Nearly 40 percent of city families still live in a single room, sharing a kitchen and bath with others. Food for the masses is no more than adequate, with little variety. Consumer "hard goods" are scarce. Only the very powerful have private autos—one auto per hundred people compared to one for every two people here. Less than 20 percent of all Russian families have their own refrigerators and washing machines, compared to over 90 percent in the United States. Russia has four vacuum cleaners per hundred people, the United States, twenty-nine. For TV sets, the comparable figures are sixteen and forty-eight; for sewing machines, sixteen and fourteen. Life in the USSR is repeatedly described as drab.

The Soviet economic growth rate substantially surpassed ours from the 1920s to the 1960s, omitting the World War II period. While the American economy sagged during the depression of the 1930s, Soviet output grew steadily at 5 percent or more. Again after World War II, the Soviets set industrial growth goals of 7–8 percent per annum, and often met them, though agriculture lagged far behind, holding down the economy's overall growth performance. But beginning around the mid-60s, Soviet growth slowed perceptively, and during the 1970s it has persistently fallen short of even reduced planning goals, to a rate roughly comparable to that in the United States.

In perspective, the rapid communist growth of the 1950s reflected very high investment while consumption was ruthlessly suppressed; massive increases in the industrial labor force as workers shifted from low-productivity agriculture and most women entered the labor force; and wide-

Russian women in line to buy bread at Moscow's Gum Department Store. (Luis Villota—Photo Researchers Inc.)

spread borrowing of technology from the Western economies. But post-Stalin liberalization and a more open society have recently led to more consumers goods. By the 1960s, over 90 percent of the able-bodied population, including women, was either in the labor force or going to school; the labor force grew from 97 million in 1950 to 125 million in 1970, but further increases will be more difficult. As Soviet industry caught up in technology with other nations, this source of growth also faded. Explanation of the high Soviet growth rate in past years thus appears to be much like that for high-growth capitalist countries, and the reasons for the recent Soviet slowdown also look much like those found in maturing capitalist nations. Productivity (output per man-year) has slowed in recent years, though apparently it is still growing around 4–5 percent annually in industry, faster than in the United States.

One last comparison. Some critics argue that GNP per capita is an inadequate measure of economic well-being. They are right. GNP doesn't take into account leisure, such real costs as pollution, and a variety of other factors, noted in Chapter 8. But as best we can tell, the USSR is no better off than we are on these unmeasured factors. Their press and their officials complain about water, air, and noise pollution, much as we do. Inclusion of leisure in GNP would clearly *worsen* Russia's relative position. Although the industrial workweek is about the same in both countries, a much larger proportion of the total population works in Russia. In particular, nearly all wives have jobs there, compared to less than half in the United States. No other non-GNP factor would appear to change the relative standard of living comparison much; if we could construct a Russian measure of net economic welfare, it would probably relate to GNP about the way ours does.

Consumer Control—Dispersion of Economic Power

Clearly the American economy produces the biggest economic pie for consumers and for growth. How does it rate in giving the individual citizen control over what is produced, over the allocation of productive resources? In Russia, the communist central planners, not the consumers, decide what is to be produced. Consumers have substantially free choice in spending their money—but they can spend it only on goods available and at the prices set by the planners.

Does the American system do a better job of producing the goods and services consumers want? The answer is "yes" *if* we take "one dollar, one vote" as our criterion. About three-fourths of our GNP is allocated through the private economy, pretty much in response to consumers' dollar demands. The way our market system responds to consumer demands is far from perfect. Varying degrees of monopoly and monopsony throughout the economy impede allocation of resources in accord with the purely competitive "ideal" of consumers' sovereignty. To some extent businesses dictate what consumers "want" through advertising and other selling techniques. Social costs and social benefits not mirrored in prices and costs distort resource allocation. But overall, consumer choice is *the* powerful director of economic production in our basically market-directed, unplanned economy.

Lastly, how about the quarter of the GNP channeled through the public sector? The Russian political process governs almost the entire allocation of resources there. Surely our democracy is far from perfect in meeting the one-man-one-vote ideal, but it surely comes closer than the Soviets to democratic control over resources allocation through the public sector.

Equity

Which system does a better job in slicing up the national economic pie fairly among competing claimants? By substantially eliminating incomes from property, the communists have eliminated most of the very high incomes of capitalist systems. *Worker* money incomes, on the other hand, are more unequally distributed than in the United States, but then somewhat equalized by subsidized government services and pricing policies. This fact reflects the heavy emphasis placed on monetary work incentives by the communists.

How about American capitalism? Our incomes are unequally distributed, before and after taxes. But the emergence of the huge, reasonably well-to-do middle class is the most striking development of recent American economic history. And the past half century has seen a tendency toward greater income equality.

How equal should incomes be? Partly, this is an ethical issue; make up your own mind. Partly, it is an economic issue. If we want to live comfortably, we need to retain effective incentives to work and invest. Remember the Russian experience that individual money rewards seem to be a more powerful economic incentive than the communists used to admit. Any income redistribution that reduces total output is very hard to defend. Table 45–1 showed how the spectacular growth of the Western market-directed economies has dominated all distributional issues. Even the poor at the bottom of the income scale in the wealthy Western economies have higher incomes than the middle-income citizens in the command-type economies. Individual initiative based on individual reward has been the foundation of most successful economic growth in the nineteenth and twentieth century world.

Individual Freedom

The American economy provides almost complete freedom on where to work, where to live, how to spend your money, and other economic choices. The freedom to go into business for yourself is completely unmatched in the Soviet system. American unions are a powerful device for equalizing the economic power of employers and employees. Government taxes are heavy and to this extent economic freedom may be said to be curtailed—though less so than in Russia.

How much "economic freedom" the Soviet economy provides for the individual depends on what you mean by the phrase. Today, the Soviet citizen has considerable freedom to move to another job and to spend his income on whatever he can find to buy. But the meaning of this freedom is subject to dispute, since the government determines what goods will be available for purchases and indirectly tells him where he should work. America has nothing like the Soviet insistence that workers stay on farms in spite of incomes there well below those available in the cities—because the plan calls for raising farm output. Further, Russian unions have no voice in determining the wages at which the citizens will work. Nor have the Soviets shown concern for their minorities and dissenters that compares favorably with the American record. Concern for human rights goes far beyond economics, but the economic component is an important one.

It seems obvious to us that our individual economic freedom surpasses that available in Russia. But the then-premier, Nikita Khrushchev, made it sound different:

> Indeed, there is freedom in the capitalist countries, but for whom? Of course, not for the working people, who are forced to hire themselves out to capitalists on any conditions to avoid finding themselves in the huge army of people who are unemployed. Neither is there freedom for the peasants, who are constantly threatened by "liberation" from their holdings as a result of bankruptcy. Nor is there freedom for the intelligentsia, whose creative activity is in the grip of material dependence on the moneybag. . . . Freedom in the capitalist countries exists only for those who possess money and who consequently hold power.[7]

Security

What is economic security? Is it freedom from the fear of unemployment? Of arbitrary discharge? Of poverty and disaster in old age or ill health? Is economic security separable from political security?

How economic security is defined will partly determine the rating of the American and Soviet

[7] Speech before twenty-first Party Congress in Moscow, January 31, 1959.

systems on this score. By one test, the Soviet citizen is secure economically. He is assured of a minimum of public services and of a job if he works reasonably hard and conforms to the rules of the leaders in power. In a planned economy, workers aren't planned into unemployment. Probably the Soviet leaders believe their system provides more economic security than does capitalism, where (to them) the worker lives in constant fear of discharge by the all-powerful capitalist and of unemployment in periodic depressions.

The United States has moved a long way toward similar security (see Chapter 33). Our social security system, including Medicare and Medicaid, now offers protection against most types of economic insecurity likely to strike older individuals. And private pension plans are now widespread. But beyond these, the great protection to economic security in the American system are the jobs and high per capita incomes that make it possible for workers to look out for themselves. Still, the capitalist system has some unwanted insecurity that will persist until we learn to eliminate recessions and inflations, a problem not unique to America.

How much security *should* an economic system provide? Many Americans believe the system ought to deal out big rewards to those who work hard and "produce", and that those who don't produce have no right to guaranteed economic security. This is the incentive that has made the American economic system a success, they argue, and to substitute guaranteed economic security would undermine the very foundation of the system. But most voters disagree, arguing that elimination of unnecessary insecurity will make our system work better—and even if it didn't, we can now well afford the cost of reasonable economic security.

PLANNING WITH PRIVATE ENTERPRISE: THE NEW LOOK?

Most of the world's economies lie somewhere between America's private enterprise and Russia's communism. Some, like Japan, are basically private enterprise but with extensive government-industry cooperation and joint planning. Others, like Yugoslavia, are near the communist end of the spectrum, but with a new twist that allows widespread individual initiative and market guidance, with collective ownership of productive resources. Still others, like France, are basically private-initiative, market-directed economies that are experimenting with limited joint government-private planning. Most of the world's economies can only be classified as mixed. Japan is worth special attention, because of her spectacular rise to third place among the world's economies during the postwar years.

JAPAN

Japan is the economic success story of the postwar world. Her growth rate since World War II has been a spectacular 10 percent, and she grew at a rapid, though slower, rate over the preceding century. Before the Meiji era, beginning in 1868, Japan was an isolated, backward, feudal economy. To analyze the Japanese growth performance since would take a book itself. Here we are primarily interested in the role played by Japan's economic organization—a type of mixed economy that is uniquely Japanese.

Growth experts suggest that Japan's recent performance reflects an unusual set of forces, woven together in a carefully planned national growth policy. (1) Her postwar saving-investment rate has averaged a huge 30–35 percent of GNP, producing an annual growth of 12 percent in the capital stock, while consumption grew relatively slowly. (2) There was a massive shift of labor from low-productivity agriculture to industry, producing a nearly 4 percent annual growth in the nonagricultural labor force. (3) Japan was extraordinarily effective in adapting new technology from the United States and West European economies. (4) She devoted virtually no resources to national defense. (5) She began from a very low post-World War II level. (6) Both laborers and management demonstrated an extraordinarily high level of hard work and skill development. (7) Business-government joint efforts proved especially effective in selling Japanese exports. (8) An unusual program of joint government-industry planning and operations facilitated growth as the nation's number one economic objective. It is on this peculiarly Japanese combined growth effort that we want to focus.

National Commitment to Growth

Japan (government officials, industrialists, bankers, workers, just about everyone) is committed to rapid growth as a keystone of national economic policy. Just how this commitment was achieved is unclear to most westerners, but it provides the framework for the entire interlinked, coordinated Japanese growth effort. Many outsiders have reported the Japanese extraordinary commitment to common goals, their hard work, and their focus on achieving the goals they set. Private goals are important; the national goal of growth seems even more so.

Government-Business Relations

The relations between big business and government are very close, peculiarly Japanese, and difficult to describe in Western terms. The giant industrial combines that dominate the economy (zaibatzu) both compete vigorously and work together and with the government on plans for domestic and (especially) foreign markets. Japanese profit rates have been high. Direct government intervention in day-to-day business activities is moderate, probably less than in the United States, though the Japanese government does operate the railroads, the major airline, telecommunications, and the cigarette and salt monopolies. But the government ministries and the Bank of Japan on the one hand and the major business groups on the other comprise an intricate planning net, which interacts closely and continuously on major economic decisions for the economy.

Broad economic plans are developed by the Economic Planning Agency, working with business organizations. Some 300 consultative committees of government and trade association officials work out detailed implementation of these plans. All Japanese industry is organized into trade associations, which in turn combine into a prestigious federation of economic organizations, which represents all industry. Neither government nor business is monolithic. Different government ministries and different industries have different needs and approaches. Yet, as compared to all Western economies, Japanese business and government plan and operate very closely together; some American businessmen call the result "Japan, Inc.," as if the nation were one big integrated economic firm.

Japan's spectacular success in world markets shows this cooperation most clearly. The Japanese export offensive produced a 15 percent annual increase in exports during the 1960s. The Japanese Supreme Trade Council is headed by the premier himself; top business executives and government officials personally set export goals. The government backs corporations with special tax incentives and credit facilities. Cartels of Japanese exporters are encouraged to fix prices and make collaborative plans for invading foreign markets. Giant trading companies market Japanese products throughout the world, often at prices that are substantially below Japanese domestic prices. At the same time, the government has imposed import quotas on a wide range of products and limits foreign investment in Japan in many industries to protect Japanese firms. Little wonder that businessmen in the United States and Europe complain that competing with Japanese exports seems almost impossible, and that they in turn need government help to let them compete on even terms.

Monetary-Financial Policies for Growth

Adequate financing is a first requirement for capital investment. Japanese firms finance most (up to 85 percent) of their investment through bank loans, an extraordinarily high figure. This heavy debt ratio leaves them badly exposed in case the banks ever run short of funds and call their loans. The banks in turn operate with nearly 100 percent of their deposits offset by loans. How can the economy operate so precariously? The answer is that the Bank of Japan (fundamentally, the Japanese government) stands firmly committed to financing rapid growth and to providing the reserves needed to support it through bank loans. This financing system works especially well for the giant zaibatzu. Each industrial group is tied closely to a major bank or financial group, which is directly responsible for assuring finance to the wide-ranging industrial activities of the group, and which also helps to see that financial resources within the zaibatzu are channeled to those activities that promise the highest yield. Because only a few zaibatzu dominate much of Japanese industry, it is easy for them and the big banks to work directly with the government and the Bank of Japan in making their plans for expansion and national economic growth. The monetary support for rapid growth has produced persistent inflation, but it is a cornerstone of the Japanese growth policy.

Employment Practices and Work Habits

Japan is the only non-Western economy to industrialize successfully, but in the process she has become only partly westernized. When the typical Japanese factory worker, clerk, or minor manager is employed, it is for life. His salary depends almost entirely on age, education, and seniority, not on his job or productivity. In effect, he becomes a member of that business family for the rest of his life, with both benefits and responsibilities. Strikingly, the system produces high labor productivity. Workers identify closely with their companies, and the Japanese tradition of hard, careful work is strong. Although union membership is about as widespread as in the United States and union leaders are often left wing, strikes are rare and generally mild. Since pay and status do not depend on job assignments, managers have great freedom in moving workers among jobs, and employment flexibility is high, in spite of the apparent rigidity of the traditional arrangement. Union work rules and "featherbedding" are almost unknown. Clearly, this employment system can work only with continuing high-level employment; firms would go bankrupt rapidly if they had to keep on paying workers when markets vanished. Again, the system depends on the government's commitment to maintain high employment and to sustain rapid growth, and the commitment is a firm one on which the business firms rely.

The Future of Japanese Growth

Has Japan found the key to success through its own brand of mixed economy? The record is impressive, but there are problems and most experts predict that Japanese growth will slow substantially over the decades ahead. Inflation has proved a persistent problem to the Japanese as they operate their high-pressure economy. Consumers appear increasingly anxious to get a bigger share of the growing national output for higher living standards, and the savings rate is falling. Workers are becoming less content to follow traditional patterns of work, promotion, and pay. Large supplies of excess farm labor are no longer available. Technology can no longer be borrowed wholesale from the West. Pollution and urban crowding will require investment resources, as in the United States. Stronger retaliation by other nations in foreign markets seems likely. A few Westerners predict a popular uprising against big business-government domination of economic life, but even Japanese left-wingers challenge only particular parts of the highly successful Japan, Inc.—not the system itself. Japanese nationalism is an important part of the mix that has produced her postwar economic growth. Japanese growth will almost certainly slow well before she overtakes the United States in total and per capita output, as some journalists now predict by extrapolating recent growth rates, but she is still growing lustily.[8]

YUGOSLAVIA

Yugoslavia provides an example of a communist economy adopting substantial parts of the capitalist system. In 1948, under Tito she broke with the Stalin regime. She was unconvinced of the value of strict central control over all economic activity, she could ill afford the inefficiencies apparent in Soviet industry and agriculture; nor did she have an educated and trained elite of central planners. Since then she has pragmatically evolved a different and successful mixed system, in which most productive resources are state-owned and there is some overall state planning (especially of investment and growth), but in which most production is worker-managed and market-oriented and most incomes are heavily dependent on the individual's own performance.

Central Planning

The central authorities today retain control over about two-thirds of all investment—both overall level and allocation among old and new industries. Investment funds are obtained largely from taxes levied on business profits and individuals throughout the economy. Investment control is exercised mainly by spending investment funds in expanding old companies or establishing new ones, which then operate as independent enterprises. Public services are extensive, but less so than in the USSR. The central planners use control over the banking system both to enforce investment allocations and to maintain overall balance between aggregate demand and supply.

[8] Lively, popular accounts of the modern Japanese system are provided by J.C. Abegglen, "The Economic Growth of Japan," *Scientific American,* March 1970; and "How the Japanese Mount that Export Blitz," *Fortune,* September 1970. For more scholarly and complete treatments, see A. Maddison, *Economic Growth in Japan and the USSR* (London: George Allen and Unwin, 1969), and H. Rosovsky and K. Ohkawa, *Japanese Economic Growth* (Stanford: Stanford University Press, 1973).

Agriculture

At first, the Yugoslavs followed the Russian pattern of collectivizing farms, but like the Russians, they met widespread hostility and sullen resistance. Farm output fell. Rather than use force, the Yugoslavs in 1953 abruptly reversed their stand, returning most land to private ownership and operation, and shifting the remaining publicly owned land to cooperative (rather than state-directed) operations. The result has been moderately successful. Yugoslavia has avoided the persistent problems faced by the Soviets, and farm output has grown around 5 percent annually—more than in the USSR, but less than in the leading Western economies.

Industry—Workers' Management

At first, the Yugoslavs also tried central government control over production and distribution. But they rapidly moved toward decentralized management of individual enterprises and substantial reliance on the market system to mirror consumers' preferences and to allocate finished products. This reflected a pragmatic recognition of the independence of the people, widespread inefficiencies in trying to make central planning work, and inadequate expertise to carry out the elaborate central functions needed to run a command economy.

Today, most production and distribution is done by worker-managed individual enterprises that try to make as large profits as they can. The workers collectively own the enterprise and collectively select and oversee the manager. Broadly, the manager's job is to maximize profits, but also to keep the workers reasonably satisfied. The firm must pay substantial taxes to the national government, but thereafter it can either distribute its profits to the workers or reinvest them in the enterprise. Each worker receives (under state rule) a minimum income, but above that his income depends on the success of the enterprise. Officially there are no "wages," only profit-sharing, since the enterprise belongs to the workers. But in essence the guaranteed minimum is close to a minimum standard wage.

What has been the result? Most observers agree the system has worked well. From a backward, agrarian Balkan economy with a very low standard of living, Yugoslavia (according to official statistics) grew at over 8 percent annually after World War II. The system provides effective incentives for most individuals, it appears to stimulate workers' morale, and it avoids the enormous administrative burden involved in planning and controlling an economy on a centralized basis. Since the Yugoslav economy is a relatively simple one, conflicts between the investment priorities of the central planners and the operating activities of individual enterprises have so far been manageable without extending central controls.

Some problems have developed. Some of the worker-managed firms have become excellent profit maximizers and have seen advantages in growing larger to obtain monopoly powers and profits. There has been inadequate incentive to organize new firms, with the result that the central planners have had to assume primary responsibility for finding and developing new products. Lastly, with reliance on the market enterprise managers have made mistakes, and unemployment has intermittently appeared, much as it would in a capitalist society.

CONVERGENCE OF ECONOMIC SYSTEMS?

Other nations have tried their own approaches to economic "rationalization" over the postwar period. Britain has moved toward a pervasive government-sponsored "incomes policy" prescribing growth rates for wages and profits in a stably growing economy, though without detailed government planning. Even West Germany, commonly considered far over on the private-enterprise side, does a lot of behind-the-scenes planning. During two postwar decades, 56 percent of Germany's net investment was financed by the government—directly, or indirectly through government loans and special tax privileges to industries that followed policies consistent with the plans for German growth. Many other countries have tried their own public-private mixes.

Some observers say that these experiments are the new look for the democratic societies—planning combined with private enterprise. But others take a dimmer view. They question whether such planning may not be an entering wedge for more government control over the private economy. At first the plan is voluntary. But after a while, when some private firms or unions decide not to play the roles assigned them under the plan, it is a short step for the government to exert pressure, or even to shift the plan to a compulsory basis through legislation.

American observers raise another question: What about antitrust laws? In Japan and several European nations, cartelization rests on a long history of firms working together in the major industries. In the United States, not only is that tradition lacking but collusive price-and-output planning by competing firms is strictly illegal. Should we abrogate our antitrust laws for planning?

Lastly, informal planning sooner or later requires agreement on an "incomes policy," which specifies the shares of the growing GNP that should go to labor and to profits. Cooperative planning has repeatedly collapsed when unions refuse to accept the wage holddowns provided in the official plans.

Economists debate whether capitalist and communist economies are converging on a middle ground. No one argues that all nations will soon have identical mixed economies. It is unlikely that Russia, Yugoslavia, Japan, and the United States will soon look the same. But after a survey of European economies, Stanford's J.E. Howell and UCLA's Neil Jacoby advance the following two hypotheses:[9]

1. Optimum performance by advanced economies requires a judicious and probably changing

[9] *European Economics: East and West* (New York: World Publishing Company, 1967).

blend of central economic management and decentralized competitive market direction.

2. There is an increasing appearance of convergence among the economic management systems of advanced countries.

Time will tell whether Howell and Jacoby are right. Do their hypotheses point the optimal path for the United States?

CONCLUSION

Since the beginning of recorded history, men have sought the perfect society. In the books that fill the libraries, many of these utopias promise peace and plenty for all. But it is a long step from dream to reality. In the real world, the utopias that look best in the writing sometimes turn sour for quite unforeseen reasons.

Over the years, some economists have worked out the details of an "ideal" democratic economy. In it, resources would be allocated in accordance with consumer market demands, individuals would be free to work and spend as they wish, state-owned capital resources would be devoted to producing what consumers want, and the proceeds from state enterprises would be distributed among the people to provide as much income equality as the public desired. This is much like the utopia of the early socialists, with state ownership of resources and operation of enterprise, with political democracy, and with economic implementation through the price system. Its advocates claim it combines the best features of private enterprise and of socialism.

But in the real world, are centralized economic control and democratic freedom in fact compatible? The Russian official blueprint looks surprisingly like this model, but in operation it looks different. Wise observers have often noted that dispersion of economic and political power are usually handmaidens to each other—that centralized economic power and political democracy seldom live long together. If this is true, the attempt to plan and centrally control economic activity toward the goals we want may be a false dream, likely to lead to political and economic slavery rather than to organized plenty.

The economic system must be our servant, not our master, in an effective society. If the society has fundamentally democratic, individualistic ideals, most people must be at heart satisfied with the way the system works—not in detail and all the time, buy by and large. Lewis Carroll, in *Alice in Wonderland*, puts his finger tellingly on the basic problem:

> The Dodo suddenly called out, "The race is over!" and they all crowded round, panting, and asking, "But who has won?"
>
> This question the Dodo could not answer without a great deal of thought, and it sat for a long time with one finger pressed upon its forehead, while the rest waited in silence. At last the Dodo said, "Everybody has won, and all must have prizes."

In a working, democratic society most must win, and most must have prizes. What shall the prizes be, and how can the economic system keep everyone satisfied with his reward? The American economy provides prizes in abundance, compared with all the other nations of the world. And its ability to adapt, without revolution, to the changing demands of the people has been one of its most impressive qualities. Any reasonable evaluation must count it highly successful. But to be pleased should not make us smug. The American economic system is far from perfect. And it will change further over the years ahead, as it adapts to shifting demands and objectives.

You should now be able to do a good share of your own thinking on how the American economy should steer over the years ahead. Economic analysis alone cannot give you answers to the hard problems we face. But it can help greatly to illuminate the way in a changing world.

REVIEW

For Analysis and Discussion

1. In light of your study of the American economic system and alternative systems, make a careful list of the major defects, if any, you see in the American system. What, if any, reforms do you think are needed, and how feasible do you think each of your reforms is?
2. During the past half century, the economic climate of the world has shifted toward central economic planning. What factors do you think have been most important in bringing about this change?
3. Recently the USSR has apparently moved toward a limited profit motive for managers in some consumer-goods industries. If this experiment is broadened, do you think it will be compatible with basic planning for the rest of the economy? Explain your answer.
4. Since World War II, four of the nations showing the highest growth rates are Russia (a communist state), West Germany (a basically private-enterprise economy), Japan (a mixed capitalist economy with extensive government intervention), and Yugoslavia (a modified socialist country). How do you account for this fact? Does it indicate that the two types of economic organization are equally fitted for producing continued, rapid growth? Or that other factors are the important ones in determining growth rates? Is there another explanation?
5. In Russia, wages are set by the central planners to keep total purchasing power about in line with the supply of goods to be bought. Would some variant of this plan be a good approach to our problem of avoiding creeping, wage-push inflation? If you think so, defend your answer against the likely attack of a union member.
6. Make a list of those attributes of present-day communist Russia that seem most objectionable to you. How many of these attributes are economic, how many social, how many political?
7. Do you believe the United States should adopt some of the cooperative government-business planning approaches of Japan? What are the main advantages and disadvantages?
8. What does your economic utopia look like?

APPENDIX TO PART EIGHT

Current Research

THE USSR. Two good accounts of Soviet economic planning and performance are N. Spulber, *The Soviet Economy* (W.W. Norton & Company, Inc., 1969) and Harry Schwartz, *An Introduction to the Soviet Economy* (Columbus, Ohio: Charles E. Merrill Publishing Company, 1968), though both may need updating for the 1973 economic reforms. Marshall Goldman writes of a problem we share with the Soviets, in *The Spoils of Progress: Environmental Pollution in the Soviet Union* (MIT Press, 1973); and a noted Soviet economist, T.S. Khachatourov, explains their approach to planning in "Long-Term Planning and Forecasting in the USSR," (*American Economic Review,* May 1972). Marshall Goldman looks ahead in "The Reluctant Consumer and Economic Fluctuations in the Soviet Union" (*Journal of Political Economy,* August 1965), which predicts that the Soviets may soon face problems of unemployment and business fluctuations Western style. At a more advanced level, A. Bergson's *Economics of Soviet Planning* (Yale University Press, 1964) provides an authoritative analysis of the entire planning process; and R. Powell's "Economic Growth in the USSR," (*Scientific American,* December 1968), illustrates how skilled researchers probe such a difficult area.

COMPARISONS AMONG COMMUNIST SYSTEMS. Peter Wiles edits an interesting symposium on the outlook for different national adaptations of communist planning, in *The Prediction of Communist Economic Performance* (New York: Cambridge University Press, 1971). N. Spulber, *The Economics of Socialism* (Bloomington, Ind.: Indiana University Press, 1971), puts more stress on ideological differences in comparing different communist countries. For more detailed studies of individual countries, see C. Mesa-Logo, ed., *Revolutionary Change in Cuba* (Pittsburgh, Pa.: University of Pittsburgh Press, 1971), a volume of somewhat uneven studies on an economy for which we have little reliable information; and D.D. Milenkovitch, *Plan and Market in Yugoslav Economic Thought* (Yale University Press, 1971).

Cutting across the Soviet and Western "mixed" economies, two studies, *The Red Executive* and *The European Executive* (Doubleday & Company, 1959 and 1963) by Wisconsin's David Granick, draw an intriguing parallel between managerial problems and behavior in the two types of economies.

Lastly, though to us many of its articles smack more of propaganda than of research, sample the publication, *Problems of Economics,* if your library has it. This is a monthly translation into English of current papers by leading Soviet economists on all phases of Russian economics and the performance of the Soviet economy.

JAPAN. Three good studies of the Japanese "economic miracle," in roughly increasing order of completeness and difficulty, are A. Maddison, *Economic Growth in Japan and the USSR* (W.W. Norton, 1969); H. Rosovsky and K. Ikhawa, *Japanese Economic Growth* (Stanford University Press, 1973); and L. Klein and K. Okhawa, *Economic Growth: The Japanese Experience Since the Meiji Era* (Irwin, 1968). See also Martin Bronfenbrenner, "Japan's Galbraithian Economy," (*The Public Interest,* Fall 1970), for a lively look at the peculiarly Japanese way the Japanese get things done.

Mathematical Appendixes[1]

In economics, as in many other disciplines, mathematics has important uses. Mathematics provides a convenient, concise language for stating complicated ideas and relationships. It facilitates the analysis of complicated interrelationships and helps in reaching "correct" conclusions from sets of assumptions or premises. It provides a language for stating "models" or theories in a precise way that makes them testable by rigorous statistical analysis of empirical data ("econometrics").

Since an increasing number of college students know some mathematics, these brief appendixes use mathematics (through elementary calculus) to state precisely and rigorously some of the concepts and arguments developed verbally or graphically in the text. Each appendix relates directly to the chapter or section of the text indicated. If you know some mathematics and especially if you find the language of mathematics a helpful one, the following appendixes may prove a useful supplement to the verbal and graphical exposition of the same ideas in the relevant chapters.

The appendixes show, in very elementary form, how mathematical language and mathematical reasoning can simplify and illuminate the (sometimes complex) interrelationships with which economic analysis must deal. Although a half century ago there were virtually no economists interested in applying mathematical analysis to economic problems, today use of mathematics in economics has become commonplace; and, as the appendix to Chapter 10 indi-

[1]Prepared in collaboration with Professor Michael Lovell of Wesleyan University.

cates, *econometrics* (the use of mathematically stated models as the basis for quantitative measurement in analysis of economic variables) has become the fastest growing branch of modern economics. The following appendixes give a small indication of how mathematics can help in stating clearly and precisely some of the important concepts and relationships in economics.[2]

[2] If you find these appendixes interesting and want to investigate mathematical economics a bit further, R.G.D. Allen, *Mathematical Economics* (New York: The Macmillan Company, 1956) provides an excellent introduction for students who know calculus. Lawrence Klein's *Introduction to Econometrics* (Englewood Cliffs, N.J.: Prentice-Hall, Inc., 1974) is a comparable introduction to the field of econometrics, though it is designed primarily for readers who have also had a course in elementary statistics.

APPENDIX I (to Chapter 5)

DEMAND FUNCTIONS AND ELASTICITY OF DEMAND

The demand curve for any commodity shows how many units will be bought at each price. Looked at another way, it represents the function indicating how price responds to changes in the quantity of a commodity offered for sale, given buyer preferences and incomes, and may be denoted as $p(q)$. [This function might also be denoted by p, or by $f(q)$.] It will be assumed that this function is differentiable.

As is explained in Chapter 5, demand curves are ordinarily negatively sloped; that is, $dp/dq < 0$. This information does not tell precisely how the total revenue obtained by the sellers will respond to changes in price and quantity sold, but simple analysis of the demand function can provide an answer to this important question.

Total revenue, denoted by $r(q)$, is simply price times quantity.

$$r(q) = p(q)q \tag{I.1}$$

Differentiating with respect to quantity yields

$$\frac{dr}{dq} = p(q) + \frac{dp}{dq}q \tag{I.2}$$

This derivative, which economists call **marginal revenue**, may be either positive or negative (remember, $dp/dq < 0$). Selling more at a lower price will reduce total revenue if the fall in price is not offset by the increase in the quantity of the commodity purchased; that is, if the demand is inelastic. (Note that this is the same as saying that a reduction in price will increase the number of units sold less than proportionately.)

What level of output with its resulting price would maximize **total revenue** (but not necessarily profits)? We can tell by examining the demand function with the aid of a few rules of elementary calculus. Remember that a necessary condition for a maximum is that the first derivative of revenue with respect to quantity be zero.

$$\frac{dr}{dq} = p(q) + \frac{dp}{dq}q = 0 \tag{I.3}$$

This maximum can be defined in terms of the elasticity of the demand function. Economists, following the reasoning on elasticity in Chapter 5, customarily denote elasticity more precisely as[3]

$$\eta = -\frac{dq}{dp}\cdot\frac{p}{q} \tag{I.4}$$

Thus, when elasticity of demand is unity, revenue is maximized.

If demand is inelastic ($\eta < 1$), note that a reduction in the quantity of the commodity offered on the market would increase total revenue. Thus, a businessman with control over his selling price and output would be foolish to produce at a point where the demand for his commodity is inelastic, for then he could obtain more revenue by producing and selling less!

It is easy to determine graphically the elasticity of demand. Consider the demand curve q^*p^*, first graph below. To find the elasticity of demand at any point a (corresponding to price p and quantity q) we note that $-dq/dp = (q^* - q)/p$; hence

[3] If, as for the individual seller under perfect competition $\frac{dq}{dp} = \infty$, then we say elasticity is infinite.

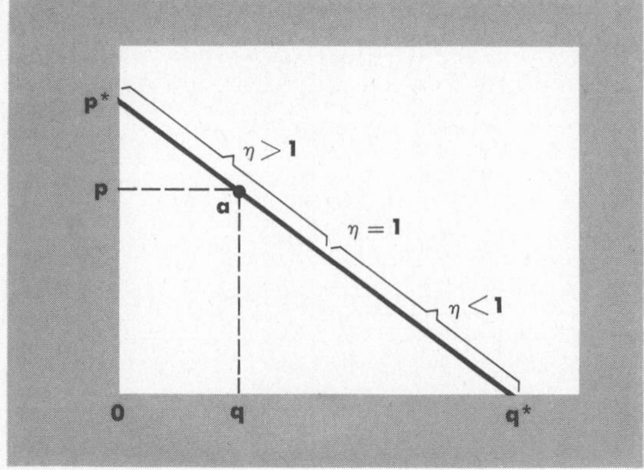

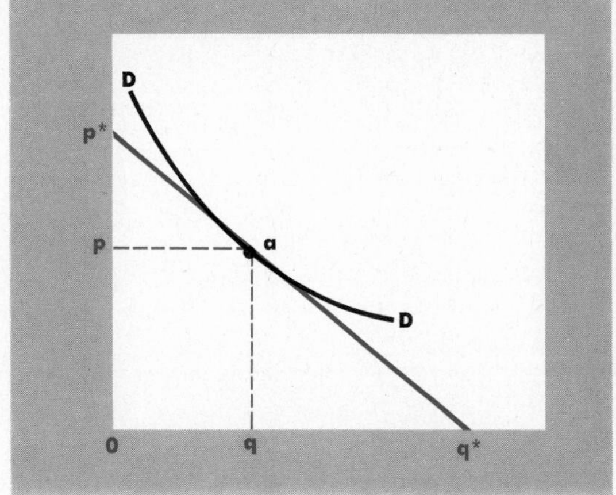

$$\eta = -\frac{dq}{dp} \cdot \frac{p}{q} = \left(\frac{q^* - q}{p}\right)\frac{p}{q} = \frac{q^* - q}{q} \quad \text{(I.5)}$$

From the last equality we see that for a linear demand curve, the elasticity of demand is simply the ratio of the excess of the quantity that could have been sold at a zero price over actual sales [i.e., $(q^* - q)$, divided by quantity sold (q)]. Note that, although this demand curve has a constant slope, it is not characterized by a constant elasticity. The elasticity changes along the curve. If q^* units were sold at zero price, the elasticity of demand would be zero; for higher prices, less is sold and elasticity increases without bound as the price approaches p^*.

To determine the elasticity of demand at some point on a nonlinear demand curve, such as point a on curve DD on the second graph, draw a straight line tangent to the demand curve at that point, and from it determine the location of point q^*. Since at point a the demand curve and the tangent line have the same slope, as well as the same p and q values, they also have the same elasticity at that point; hence formula I.5 again applies.

$$\eta = \frac{q^* - q}{q}$$

Is it possible for a demand curve to have constant elasticity throughout its entire length? Yes. Suppose that $q = \alpha p^\beta$, $\beta < 0$;

then

$$dq/dp = (\beta\, \alpha p^{\beta - 1}) = \beta \frac{q}{p}$$

and

$$\eta = -\left(\beta \frac{q}{p}\right)\frac{p}{q} = -\beta.$$

That is, the parameter $-\beta$ of the demand curve is the elasticity of demand. For example, a rectangular hyperbola has a constant elasticity equal to 1.

APPENDIX II (to Chapter 10)
GNP DETERMINATION AND THE MULTIPLIER

Chapter 10 presents a simple algebraic model showing how, in an economy assuming no government or foreign trade, private investment and the marginal propensity to consume interact to determine the level of GNP. This appendix first states the model quite generally in mathematical terms, and then develops more rigorously "the multiplier" and the way in which it helps explain the impact of changes in investment on GNP. This is the reasoning from the text put in mathematical language.

A. The Income-Determination Model. In Chapter 10 two consumption functions were presented. In one, consumption (C) was simply a fixed proportion of GNP, (Y). In the other, a somewhat more general form was used:[4]

$$C = a + bY \qquad \text{(II.1)}$$

(Of course, if $a = 0$, then this reduces to the simpler consumption function.) As in Chapter 10, since all of GNP is either consumed or invested, (I)

$$Y = C + I \qquad \text{(II.2)}$$

Now substitute the consumption function into this last equation in order to obtain

$$Y = a + bY + I \qquad \text{(II.3)}$$

Next, subtract bY from both sides.

$$Y - bY = (1 - b)Y = a + I \qquad \text{(II.4)}$$

Dividing both sides by the marginal propensity to save, $1 - b$, gives us

$$Y = \left(\frac{1}{1 - b}\right)(a + I) \qquad \text{(II.5)}$$

as the equilibrium level of GNP, in which consumption is at the level prescribed by the consumption function (equation II.1) for the given level of I and the resulting level of Y. In particular, if $a = 40$, $b = .6$, and $I = 100$ (as in Chapter 10), this last equation reveals that gross national product must be 350.

$$\left(\frac{1}{1 - .6}\right)(40 + 100) = 350$$

B. The Multiplier. The multiplier tells us what happens as a result of a rise in investment to a new level (I^*). Clearly GNP will rise, and as people receive more income, consumption will rise as well. Let Y^* denote the new equilibrium level of income and C^* the new equilibrium level of consumption, when the increase in I has exercised its full effect.

Since these new equilibrium values, Y^* and C^*, must satisfy both equations II.1 and II.5, the same line of reasoning as before implies that

$$Y^* = \left(\frac{1}{1 - b}\right)(a + I^*) \qquad \text{(II.5*)}$$

Subtracting equation II.5 from this last expression yields

$$Y^* - Y = \left(\frac{1}{1 - b}\right)(I^* - I) \qquad \text{(II.6)}$$

The expression in large parentheses, the reciprocal of the marginal propensity to save, is the multiplier. It tells us by how much the change in investment ($I^* - I$) must be multiplied in order to determine the change that it will induce in GNP.

C. Addition of Government Spending and Taxes. Government spending and taxes can readily be introduced into this multiplier analysis. Government spending, G, then represents purchases of one part of the current GNP. Consequently, we must rewrite equation II.2 to read

$$Y = C + I + G \qquad \text{(II.7)}$$

In addition, we must now recognize a distinction between gross national product and disposable income. Specifically, let T denote tax revenue, and suppose that consumption depends on disposable (after-tax) income, so that $C = a + b(Y - T)$. Then

$$Y = a + b(Y - T) + G + I \qquad \text{(II.8)}$$

Proceeding as before, we obtain

$$Y = \left(\frac{1}{1 - b}\right)(a - bT + G + I)$$

as the equation explaining the equilibrium level of GNP as determined by private investment, consumption behavior, government expenditure, and taxes. Note that for any given tax take, government spending and investment both have the same multiplier. On the other hand, the effect of an increase in taxes is to change GNP by a negative "tax multiplier" of $-b/(1 - b)$. Thus, if government expenditure and taxes both increase by \$3 billion, we would have

$$Y^* = \left(\frac{1}{1 - b}\right)[a - b(T + 3) + (G + 3) + I] = Y + 3$$

That is, income increases by the same amount as taxes and government spending, which in Chapters 10 and 15 is called the "balanced-budget multiplier."

[4] You will remember from the text discussion that

$$0 < b < 1$$

D. Dynamics of the Multiplier. This exercise tells us nothing about the nature of the adjustment process. Let us now consider the dynamic process by which Y rises as a result of the increase in I. This corresponds to the discussion of successive rounds of consumption spending out of rising income in Chapter 10. Let time be measured in discrete units, say months, and suppose that the level of consumption during the current month depends upon the income earned in the immediately preceding month. Thus

$$C_t = a + bY_{t-1} \tag{II.9}$$

where the subscripts serve to indicate the time period.

Now let us suppose that the marginal propensity to consume, b, is .75; that $a = 20$: and that initially, at time zero, investment is 67.5, $G = T = 0$, and income $Y_0 = 350$. From equation II.9 we find that, in period one, consumption will be

$$C_1 = 20 + .75 \cdot 350 = 282.5$$

If investment were to remain constant at 67.5, there would be no tendency for GNP to change from 350. (Check that $C_1 + I_1 = Y_1 = 350$). This is the sense in which the economy is said to be in **equilibrium.** But suppose that instead investment increases by 10, to 77.5. Our initial equilibrium is disturbed, and the economy will gradually adjust to the disturbance. The nature of the adjustment process is suggested by the following:

PERIOD	$I_t - I_0$	$C_t - C_0$	$Y_t - Y_0$
1	10		10
2	10	7.5	17.5
3	10	13.1	23.1
4	10	17.3	27.3
⋮	⋮	⋮	⋮
∞	10	30	40

Each increase in income induces additional consumption in the next period, which constitutes additional income to the seller of goods or services, and so on ad infinitum. Will the process stop? The total increase in income is

$$10 + 7.5 + 5.6 + 4.2 + \cdots$$

But this is readily seen to be a sum of an infinite number of terms. More generally, of course, for any arbitrary marginal propensity to consume, the change in income resulting from a change in investment will be

$$\Delta I + b\Delta I + b^2\Delta I + b^3\Delta I + \cdots = \Delta I(1 + b + b^2 + b^3 + \cdots) \tag{II.10}$$

The conditions under which such a sum will be finite can be determined if we recall the procedure for deriving the sum of a geometric series. Let S_n be the first n terms in such a series,

$$S_n = 1 + b + b^2 + \cdots + b^n \tag{II.11}$$

Multiplying by b gives

$$bS_n = b + b^2 + \cdots + b^{n+1} \tag{II.12}$$

Subtracting equation II.12 from II.11 yields

$$S_n - bS_n = (1 - b)S_n = 1 - b^{n+1}$$

Consequently,

$$S_n = \frac{1 - b^{n+1}}{1 - b} \tag{II.13}$$

It is now obvious that

$$\lim_{n \to \infty} S_n = \frac{1}{1 - b} \tag{II.14}$$

if and only if the marginal propensity to consume is less than unity. This limiting expression is, of course, the multiplier of equation II.6. If the marginal propensity to consume were greater than unity, something that is conceivable but not likely except in temporary special cases, GNP would increase without bounds in response to an increase in private investment spending, at least under the simple assumptions used here.[5]

More advanced analysis would recognize that rising GNP and business sales might well induce a

[5] Readers interested in the complexities of dynamic analysis will note that equation II.6 correctly tells us that equilibrium GNP will decrease as a result of an increase in investment spending if the marginal propensity to consume is greater than unity; that is, if, somehow, GNP did decline to the level suggested by that equation it would remain there indefinitely. But if $b \leq 1$ this equilibrium is *unstable,* and with the passage of time GNP will diverge further and further from its equilibrium as a result of the increased consumption induced by the augmented level of investment spending. This, however, while it is analytically interesting, is extremely unlikely, since empirical studies show that the marginal propensity to consume is less than unity except under very special circumstances.

further rise in investment spending, and thus increase the stimulative effect of any of the above assumed increases in I or G. Such further "induced" investment is often called the "accelerator" effect, and is considered more completely in Chapter 14. See especially the second appendix to that chapter for a simple mathematical model incorporating both multiplier and accelerator effects.

APPENDIX III (to Chapters 19–20)

COST CURVES AND PROFIT MAXIMIZATION

To determine what level of output will maximize profits, production costs in relation to demand considerations must be analyzed. This appendix mathematically analyzes this interrelationship.

A. Key Cost Concepts. In Chapter 19 the dependence of production costs upon the level of output was examined in detail, and a number of basic concepts were explained. Table 19–1 reported hypothetical cost figures for a firm producing a single commodity. In such cases, the total cost function, $c(q)$, reveals how the total costs incurred by the firm depend on the level of output; we assume that the function is differentiable. Other cost concepts discussed in the text may be expressed in terms of $c(q)$, as shown in the following list.

Fixed costs:	$c(0)$
Variable costs:	$c(q) - c(0)$
Total unit cost:	$c(q)/q$
Variable unit cost:	$[c(q) - c(0)]/q$
Fixed unit cost:	$c(0)/q$
Marginal cost:	$\dfrac{dc(q)}{dq}$

B. Maximizing Profits. Profit, at any level of output, $\pi(q)$, is simply the excess of total revenue over total cost,

$$\pi(q) = r(q) - c(q) \qquad \text{(III.1)}$$

where $r(q)$ is the total revenue function discussed in Mathematical Appendix I: the three curves are plotted in Figure 20–1 on page 270. From elementary calculus we know that if profits are maximized at some level of output $q > 0$, it is necessary that

$$\frac{\partial \pi(q)}{\partial q} = \frac{\partial r(q)}{\partial q} - \frac{\partial c(q)}{\partial q} = 0 \qquad \text{(III.2)}$$

Equation III.2 implies

$$\frac{\partial r(q)}{\partial q} = \frac{\partial c(q)}{\partial q} = 0 \qquad \text{(III.3)}$$

This mathematically states the fundamental proposition that a necessary condition for profit maximization at $q > 0$ is that marginal cost equ s marginal revenue.

It is essential to note that condition III.2 does not necessarily yield a level of output, q, at which profits will be positive. In the short run, before the firm can liquidate its fixed investment, it may be worthwhile to operate at a loss rather than shut down. Remember that zero output involves fixed cost, $c(0)$, in the short run. Would a zero output minimize losses (negative profits) when there are fixed costs? Not if

$$\pi(q) = r(q) - c(q) > \pi(0) = -c(0) \qquad \text{(III.4)}$$

or equivalently:

$$r(q) - [c(q) - c(0)] > 0 \qquad \text{(III.5)}$$

In other words, the firm will produce a positive output at a loss if revenue exceeds total variable costs. Dividing both sides of III.5 by q yields, since $r(q)/q = p$, an equivalent condition:

$$p - [c(q) - c(0)]/\text{q} > 0 \qquad \text{(III.6)}$$

This is the condition (on page 273) that the firm will minimize losses by shutting down altogether only if there is no positive level of output where price would exceed average variable cost.

C. Some Observations on Competitive Equilibrium. Under competitive conditions, the output of the individual firm constitutes an insignificant contribution to the total market sales of the commodity. Consequently, the price the firm receives for its output is unaffected by variation in the quantity it offers for sale; its demand curve is horizontal ($dp/dq = 0$), and from equation I.2 we have marginal revenue equal to price ($dr/dq = p$). Hence, equation III.3 implies that if firms maximize profits under competitive conditions, they produce at the point where marginal cost equals price.

This constitutes a basic proposition of economic theory that explains the general presumption of economists in favor of competition: When firms maximize profits under competitive conditions, the increment to total cost incurred in producing the last unit sold is exactly equal to the price, which is precisely as it should be. For the price reflects the consumer's evaluation of the benefits he will obtain from the purchase of that last unit; if the benefits were less he wouldn't buy the unit, and if they were greater he would buy more units.

Chapter 21 points out that in long-run competitive equilibrium price is equal to the minimum point on the total-unit-cost curve. This must be the case, for a higher price would encourage new firms to enter the industry in search of profits, while a lower price would yield continued losses and induce firms to leave the industry. But if price is to be equal to the minimum point on the total-unit-cost curve, can we be sure it also equals marginal cost, as required under competition (condition III.3, with $dr/dq = p$)? It is easy to show that the answer is, necessarily, yes. If output is at the minimum total-unit-cost level, then marginal cost will be equal to total unit cost. To establish this proposition, we note that the condition that output be at the minimum total-unit-cost level implies:

$$\frac{d\left[\frac{c(q)}{q}\right]}{dq} = \frac{\frac{dc(q)}{dq}}{q} - \frac{c(q)}{q^2} = 0$$

Multiplying through by q yields:

$$\frac{dc(q)}{dq} = \frac{c(q)}{q}$$

Thus, marginal cost is equal to average cost if output is at the firm's lowest average-unit-cost point. The marginal-cost curve cuts the average-cost curve at the latter's minimum point.

APPENDIX IV (to Chapters 28–29)
PRODUCTION FUNCTIONS AND THE DISTRIBUTION OF INCOME

Most firms have alternative ways to produce any given output. Thus, within limits, the services of machinery may be substituted for labor in the production of steel, or vice versa. A "production function," that states the relationship between various combinations of inputs and the resulting outputs (products), can be a helpful concept for exploring the way in which technological considerations influence the distribution of income among different factors of production (labor, capital, and so on).

A. Simple Production Functions. For simplicity, suppose that only two factors of production, labor (L) and machinery (M), are used in producing a commodity. The output (q) produced each period depends on the quantity of labor and machinery services employed. We assume that this production function can be described by a differentiable function of the two inputs:

$$q = f(L, M) \qquad \text{(IV.1)}$$

Such functions can be estimated empirically from business and engineering production data or derived from engineering or physical principles.

We wish to determine the optimal (highest profit) mix of labor and machinery to produce any output. We will maximize profits (π) by maximizing the excess of revenue over cost. If we assume that labor and machinery services are purchased on competitive markets at prices w and p_m we have:

$$\pi = r(q) - wL - p_m M \qquad \text{(IV.2)}$$

or, substituting from IV.1,

$$\pi(L, M) = r[f(L, M)] - wL - p_m M \qquad \text{(IV.3)}$$

If the optimal quantity of labor is indeed being employed, it must be impossible to increase profits by either increasing or decreasing the amount of labor used. Consequently, a necessary condition for profit maximization is that

$$\frac{\partial \pi(L,m)}{\partial L} = \frac{dr}{dq} \cdot \frac{\partial q}{\partial L} - w = 0 \qquad \text{(IV.4)}$$

Similarly, if the optimal quantity of machinery services is being employed,

$$\frac{\partial \pi(L,m)}{\partial M} = \frac{dr}{dq} \cdot \frac{\partial q}{\partial m} - p_m = 0 \qquad \text{(IV.5)}$$

As Chapters 28 and 29 indicate, economists call

$$\frac{\partial r}{\partial q} \cdot \frac{\partial q}{\partial L}$$

the marginal-revenue product of labor. Thus, equation IV.4 shows that to maximize profits, a firm hiring on a competitive market must hire additional workers just to the point where the marginal-revenue product of labor equals the wage rate (pages 393–94).

It follows from IV.4 and IV.5 that

$$\frac{\frac{\partial q}{\partial m}}{p_m} = \frac{\frac{\partial q}{\partial L}}{w} \qquad \text{(IV.6)}$$

The economist calls

$$\frac{\partial q}{\partial L}$$

the marginal productivity of labor; similarly,

$$\frac{\partial q}{\partial m}$$

is the marginal productivity of machinery services. Equation IV.6 thus shows that under profit-maximizing equilibrium conditions in competitive markets, each factor of production is rewarded in proportion to its marginal productivity (pages 381–84).

B. The Cobb-Douglas Production Function: An Example. As an illustration, let us consider a much discussed conjecture of Professors C.W. Cobb and Paul H. Douglas (later U.S. senator) that the total industrial output of the American economy may be described by a simple production function of the form:

$$q(L, M) = aL^{\lambda}M^{1-\lambda} \qquad \text{(IV.7)}$$

Statistical investigations have disclosed that a function of this form fits the historical data quite closely when $\lambda = .75$. Note that this function is characterized by constant returns to scale; that is, if the initial inputs are all multiplied by some scale factor, $\rho > 0$, then output will also increase by ρ; more precisely:

$$q(\rho L, \rho M) = \rho q(L, M) \text{ for all } \rho \geqslant 0 \qquad \text{(IV.8)}$$

What are the implications of the Cobb-Douglas analysis for the shares of labor and machinery (capital) in the national income? Not only did Cobb-Douglas find that equation IV.7 provides a reasonable explanation of how capital and labor contribute to the generation of industrial output. They also found that this function, in conjunction with equation IV.4, embodying the assumption of competition, helps to explain an important observed fact—that labor income (wages and salaries) has been a roughly stable percentage of total income over many decades.

Their explanation of the rough constancy of labor's share can be appreciated if we first observe that the marginal productivity of labor is

$$\frac{\partial q}{\partial L} = \lambda a L^{\lambda-1} M^{1-\lambda} = \lambda \frac{Q}{L} \qquad \text{(IV.9)}$$

Similarly, the marginal productivity of capital services is

$$\frac{\partial q}{\partial M} = (1 - \lambda)\, aL^{\lambda} M^{-\lambda} = (1 - \lambda) \frac{Q}{M} \qquad \text{(IV.10)}$$

If output is sold on a competitive market at price p (so that $dr/dq = p$), then condition IV.4 implies

$$p\lambda \frac{Q}{L} = w \qquad \text{(IV.11)}$$

Hence

$$\frac{Lw}{Qp} = \lambda \qquad \text{(IV.12)}$$

Now remember that Lw is labor income while Qp is the value of total output; consequently equation IV.12 implies that the ratio of labor income to total income, labor's share, is equal to the parameter λ of the Cobb-Douglas production function.

Suggestions for Analysis of Cases

This section includes suggestions to help you with the analysis of each case in the book. The cases are primarily designed to get you to use the concepts and principles in the chapter that each case follows. You will generally benefit the most if you work each case through for yourself, or in discussion with others, before you check against these suggestions.

In some cases, especially the earlier ones, the suggestions are quite explicit and detailed. In others, especially the later ones, they are brief, often consisting more of questions you should be asking yourself than of specific suggestions on how to proceed and what principles to use. Even in the former, you will seldom find simple "answers" to the cases. The purpose is to get you to think through your own answers, and many of the cases are designed so that there is no one "right" answer that is unambiguously superior to all others. In many cases, you will have to combine your value judgments with economic analysis. (Case 1 is a good example.) Especially on such cases, though on the others as well, you will usually gain by discussing the problem and your answer with other students, in or out of class. One of the tricks in thinking through such real-world cases is to be sure that you see the problem from different points of view, and your friends are almost certain to see some of the cases from different angles than they appear to you. But never forget that a major goal is to practice your economic analysis. Though your value judgments differ, you should be able to agree on the relevant economic concepts and principles, and on the economic analysis involved.

Case 1: How Much for Auto Safety? Auto passenger safety legislation sharply poses the issue of priorities and resource allocation by individual choice through the market as against collective action through the political process. Supporters of the legislation say that everyone "should" be protected against death or serious injury in case of accident; obviously, the protection is worth far more than a hundred dollars in case of a serious accident. But opponents counter that each individual should be free to decide for himself how much the protection is worth to him. They point out that this case is quite different from other auto safety legislation that is designed to protect people against injury by others, such as speed laws, requirements for operating head- and taillights, and so on. Everyone agrees that laws are needed to protect society against injury by others, but seat belts and air bags protect only their users. They do nothing to lessen the risk of injury for others. And car owners could buy a lot of other things with the $1 billion they are required to spend on seat belts, air bags, and other safety features—things they might value more highly, such as ski trips to Squaw Valley, new clothes, T-bone steaks, health insurance, or any of thousands of other goods and services available on the market.

Thinking through this controversy should help you sort out the issues on the conditions under which individual free choice should control our priorities, as against "collective" action that is binding on everyone. In the process, consider the following two related questions: (1) Should Congress pass a law requiring everyone who goes out in below-freezing weather to wear warm clothing? (2) Should Congress pass a law requiring steel mills to reduce the amount of smoke and dirt they emit? How, if at all, do these two cases differ from each other and from the auto passenger safety case?

Case 2: Cash or Food Stamps for the Poor? The main economic issue here is which form of aid is more efficient? That is, which increases the well-being of the poor more, $106 of food stamps or $106 in cash? Economic analysis cannot decide the issue of whether the poor should be given aid or whether those giving the aid should have the right to determine in which form the aid should be given.

If a family is given cash, we can assume it will spend the money along with its other income to maximize its satisfaction by allocating its income so that the last dollar spent on each good yields about the same marginal utility. If, instead, the family receives food stamps, its freedom to allocate its income is restricted. If the amount of the food stamps is less than the amount that would have been spent on food anyhow, the food stamps would be equivalent to cash because the household would be able to spend the money saved on food for anything it wanted (including more food). But if the food stamps are more than the family would otherwise have spent on food, the family consumes more food than it prefers relative to other goods; it is forced to take a lower total satisfaction than it could have obtained from an all-cash income. On the grounds of economic efficiency, cash aid is likely to be better than food stamps.

But many people do not believe that economic efficiency is the most important consideration in this case. They believe that Congress does know better than the poor what is best for them; or they simply are not interested in maximizing the satisfaction of the poor, but just want to assure a minimum diet; or they doubt that many recipients will resist the temptation to waste the money on nonessentials, instead of adequately feeding their youngsters. These are matters of ethics, however, not economics. Chapter 5 does not have much to say about ethics, but it is important to separate clearly the ethical from the economic arguments. You should also recognize that in making the actual decision, Congress must decide on both types of issues.

Make up your own mind. Then ask yourself whether your arguments hold equally for cash aid versus subsidized public education, public housing, and public health services.

Case 3: Consumer Credit and Usury Laws. Simple supply and demand analysis can help on this problem. The new laws are fixing a price ceiling (interest rate) on loans, below the free market price. Suppose the supply and demand curves for consumer credit in your state are as on the following chart. Then the free market interest rate would be 20 percent per year, and $300 million would be offered and borrowed per month. The supply curve says that lenders would offer more at higher interest rates, less at lower ones. Why? Because at higher interest rates on consumer loans, it will pay to divert more credit from other potential borrowers, and because at higher rates it will pay to lend to higher-risk borrowers. The demand curve says that more will be borrowed at lower than at higher rates. Obviously the "finance charge" (of which the interest rate is a big part) helps determine whether or not people can afford a new refrigerator or a new car. The lower the interest rate, the lower the monthly payments and the effective

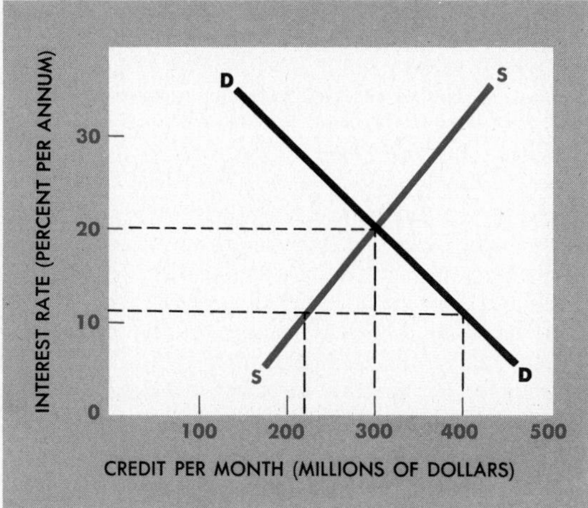

price of the product to people who buy on credit rather than paying cash.

Suppose, now, the state legislature decrees that no lender shall charge consumers more than 1 percent monthly—12 percent per year. At that rate, lenders will lend only $225 million monthly, but consumers will want to borrow $400 million. Clearly, there is a large excess demand—$175 million of unsatisfied consumer wants for credit. The first effect of the new law is that some consumers get cheaper credit, but some who were previously borrowing at 20 percent now get nothing. Seventy-five million dollars less is lent and an additional $100 million of demand goes unsatisfied. We can be sure there are going to be a lot of angry consumers who get a friendly but firm "no" from auto dealers, banks, finance companies, department stores, and credit card companies. And the lenders are not going to be very happy about alienating their present and potential customers.

But the law is the law. Who gets the limited supply of consumer credit at 1 percent a month? Probably the well-established, low-risk customers of the lenders. But pity the consumer who applies for a new credit card, or charge account, or finance company loan in your state, especially if his income is low and he does not look like a top-notch credit risk. If you were a lender, you would stick with your established, sure-pay customers for what credit you have to lend—and that is just what lenders did in Arkansas, Minnesota, Washington, and Wisconsin. If the free price system does not decide who gets the available credit, lenders will have to ration it out on some other basis—unhappy customers or not.

What other effects would you expect? Rejected borrowers who live near the state boundary can reasonably be expected to take their business next door where credit is available. This is not calculated to make your home-state merchants very happy. Some borrowers and lenders may cheat a little—some of those rejected potential borrowers may offer to slip the finance man, auto dealer, or credit card manager a little something on the side to get credit, or a new credit card. "Black markets" can develop in credit just as they did in butter and gasoline, which were price-fixed and rationed in World War II. For sure, angry consumers turned away will complain bitterly to their legislators that they are being treated unfairly—they were supposed to get cheaper credit, but in fact they are getting none. It is those greedy moneylenders trying to gouge them again, especially the poor, minority groups, and others who need the credit most if they are to buy.

Last, and a bit outside our assumptions, the whole supply curve (*SS*) is likely to move to the left—because big consumer lenders, like the nation-wide finance companies, may essentially drop out of business in your state. Why suffer the criticisms and take the lower interest rates there if they can make more money with happier customer relationships in other states? Move the *SS* curve to the left and see what that does to the problem.

Who has gained and who has lost from the new law? Should your state legislature be next to put a 1 percent monthly ceiling on customer credit rates?

Case 4: Should GNP Measure Economic Welfare? There are no suggestions for analysis on this case, because Dr. Okun's statement effectively lays out the arguments on both sides of the issue. But be sure you look back at the Tobin-Nordhaus analysis, in the latter part of the chapter, as you think through this issue.

Case 5: Does Capitalism Need War for Prosperity? Scarcity, aggregate demand, and government fiscal policy are the keys to the answer. First, resources are scarce relative to human wants. The huge amounts of manpower, steel, electronics, and other resources now used for defense could, if freed, help provide better housing, education, civilian goods, and health services for the nation. Even $40 billion would fall far short of meeting our new national priorities. To continue to waste the resources on unneeded national defense would be stupid indeed when there are so many other unfilled human wants.

But wouldn't the cutback merely throw millions

into unemployment? Not if the government uses fiscal policy effectively. The first lesson of macroeconomics is that in the short run aggregate output and employment are determined basically by the level of aggregate demand. If we cut aggregate demand drastically, we can certainly expect employment to fall. A $40 billion cut in government spending would directly cut aggregate demand by about 3 percent (GNP is about $1.2 trillion), but if the multiplier is, say, 2, the total drop in aggregate demand would be closer to $80 billion. This would be enough to raise unemployment by five to six million people, including those discharged from the armed services; the unemployment rate would soar from 5 to 10 percent.

But it would be a shortsighted government indeed that permitted this shrinkage of aggregate demand. One obvious alternative is to increase nondefense spending by $40 billion, thereby keeping the government's contribution to aggregate demand unchanged, and using the resources to meet the new much-discussed national priorities, such as health, the environment, urban reconstruction, and education. The negative multiplier is thereby avoided, and no new unemployment is engendered.

Another alternative, more attractive if you want to keep government small and let people spend their incomes as they wish, is to cut taxes. Suppose we cut taxes by $40 billion. This gives the public $40 billion of additional disposable income. But note that it will probably not fully offset the cut in government spending, because the public's marginal propensity to consume will be less than 1; they will probably save some of the additional disposable income. To assure $40 billion of induced consumer spending to offset the government cut, the government will need to reduce taxes by more than $40 billion. Precisely how much more will depend on the public's marginal propensity to consume. Put in other words, to reduce both government spending and taxes by $40 billion would probably produce a negative balanced budget multiplier of 1, or thereabouts.

Are tax cuts or increased government nonmilitary spending better means of avoiding unemployment? Either can do the job, as indicated above. Your preference will presumably depend on how highly you value dollars spent by the government on the new social priorities, as compared with letting people make their own individual decisions as to how to spend their incomes in the market. If you like allocating resources primarily through the marketplace, advise your congressmen to cut taxes. If you believe we need a bigger public sector, with more spending on highways, environmental control, public health, and the like, advise him to vote for more spending on those projects.

Two warnings on this simple exercise in fiscal policy analysis: First, we have entirely disregarded the transitional problems of getting all the people who are thrown out of defense jobs shifted to civilian jobs, either in the industries where government civilian spending rises or where consumers decide to spend their new disposable income.

Second, we have completely neglected the monetary factors at work, as we did in the preceding chapter. As we shall see in Chapters 16 and 17, the government has another powerful approach to controlling aggregate demand—monetary policy, which it exercises by changing the amount of money in the economic system. Without considering monetary factors, we are seeing only part of the picture, and with money in, the problem becomes more complex. Remember that we've temporarily made the problem too simple by focusing only on fiscal policy.

Case 6: Interest Rates, Investment, and Inflation. Chairman Patman is right that interest is a cost that must be covered by the price charged by businesses for their products. It comprises a small fraction of the cost of most products, though it is a substantial part in a few cases. And he is of course right that the interest cost on any given amount of federal debt would be lower if interest rates had been kept lower.

The opposing economists are right that interest is a peculiarly important price (cost), in that it helps regulate the amount of investment businesses make, and investment plays an especially important role (directly and through the multiplier) in determining the level of aggregate demand and inflation.

The truth is thus not entirely on either side, but Congressman Patman finds little support among economists of either political persuasion for his extreme position favoring low interest rates even in inflationary periods. The case for low interest rates is strong on both scores when there is widespread unemployment and little danger of inflation. But when there is substantially full employment, the small direct effect of higher interest rates in raising costs and prices is far more than overcome by high interest rates' strong deterrent effect on new business investment, as spelled out in Chapter 11. The higher interest rates would also deter consumer borrowing to buy durables, though many economists consider this a weaker restraint on total spending. In high-employment periods, the small interest cost saving to the government through holding interest rates down by creating more money is quickly overcome by the higher prices it must pay on its huge purchases of goods and services, to say nothing of the higher costs to the general public as the price level is bid up through excess aggregate demand. Thus, in such periods the government is likely to have to borrow more if interest rates are held down, and more inflation results, leading to a larger, not a smaller, national debt.

("Monetarists", whose position is presented in the following two chapters, would take an even stronger anti-Patman position, because they believe the impact of more money on aggregate demand is even more direct and powerful than the income-expenditure theory of Chapters 10 and 11 suggests.)

Case 7: How To Fight Unemployment? This case raises a number of problems. First, do you prefer fiscal or monetary policy, or some combination of both? If you choose fiscal policy, note the problem you will face unless *M* is simultaneously increased. Without more *M,* interest rates will rise because the government has to borrow $20 billion to finance the deficit and because people will demand more money to hold as their incomes rise. Fiscal action with no increase in *M* seems unlikely to produce the full desired multiplier effect.

On the other hand, if you choose monetary policy alone, how will you get the money to the public so that it will increase their spending as desired? Merely to buy up government bonds with the new money will increase neither the public's wealth nor its disposable income. Although the bond buying would reduce interest rates and perhaps thus indirectly stimulate investment, this result looks uncertain when businessmen are facing a depressed economy. But if you want to pay out the money directly to increase the public's wealth and disposable income, say by unemployment relief or other direct gifts, this implies using fiscal policy—having the government spend the money, running a deficit and financing it with the newly created money. Clearly, you're likely to need more new *M* to increase GNP by $40 billion if you buy up bonds than if you pay the new money out through fiscal policy as new wealth to the public.

If you choose fiscal policy, say with a supporting increase in *M,* should it be increased expenditures or tax cuts? Here the answer will depend heavily on your personal values—whether you prefer having individual spending in the marketplace decide what is produced, or government action to produce things that the free market doesn't seem to provide. (Part Five provides a detailed analysis of this issue.) But either way, here you should recognize that to get the desired increase in aggregate demand, a dollar of government spending and a dollar of tax cuts are not identical. In technical terms, the expenditure and tax multipliers are different. Go back to Chapter 10 for the explanation. Basically, it is because the government expenditure directly increases GNP while the tax cut merely increases disposable income, out of which a part will presumably be saved. Either way, past experience suggests a lot of uncertainty about the public's short-run marginal propensity to consume. Although the average propensity to consume out of disposable income has been quite stable at reasonably high income levels, MPC has varied widely over periods of several quarters, especially when the public thinks the income increase may be only temporary.

Conclusion: There's no simple "right" answer. Make your own judgment. Most economists would opt for a combined strategy, using both fiscal and monetary policy, but just how much of each is a matter for expert professional judgment, on which your congressman is unlikely to get complete agreement. (More details to come in Chapters 15–18.)

Case 8: Are We Going Broke? The TV commentator's argument runs head-on into much of the analysis in the preceding pages. To point up the issues, ask yourself the following questions. (Your answers ought to help you decide how convincing the arguments are.)

1. Is the public debt just like private debt? Is the nation one big family so that what is true for one family is equally true for the nation as a whole? (The fallacy of composition?)
2. Are the reasons governments run deficits the same as why families go into debt?
3. When the government runs a deficit, are we "going on a binge" now that we will have to pay for in the future? Who pays for the binge in the future if the debt is continuously refunded?
4. What is the best measure of how well-off the nation is economically? Is the size of the public debt part of this measure?
5. Are you carrying a $10,000 bag of stones on your back?
6. Is it bad for individuals and businesses to go into debt? (Note Figure 15–6.)
7. What does the commentator really want the

government to do? Pay off the debt by running big budget surpluses? If not, what? Would you advise your congressman to follow his advice?

8. What criteria would you use in deciding when the public debt is too big, and when it should be reduced by running a current budget surplus to be used for debt retirement?

Case 9: The Lessons of Monetary Experience. This is a series of real-world policy cases, or situations, faced by the Federal Reserve authorities over the past half century. Each one is different, and to provide detailed suggestions for the analysis of each would be to rewrite the chapter. You're on your own! Each situation presents some fascinating policy dilemmas involving both economic analysis (straight out of the preceding chapters), and value judgments. The life of an economics student. . .!

Case 10: Stabilization Policymaking. This case is a tough one. It requires you to use your whole tool kit of macroeconomic theory. It also asks you to combine your value judgments on social goals with economic analysis to reach conclusions on practical economic policy in the complex real world. Not only the life of a central banker is not easy! Consider the following questions in your analysis:

1. How fast should aggregate demand rise in the year ahead to achieve your goals for the economy? (Remember the long-run growth in the economy's productive capacity as well as the unemployment and inflation problems. Where are we now in the business cycle?)
2. How much would a faster growth in aggregate demand reduce unemployment in 1973, and how much would it just induce a higher rate of inflation and new inflationary expectations?
3. What combination of monetary and fiscal policy will best produce the desired growth in aggregate demand? (Remember the inside and outside lags in using both kinds of policy. How fast can the President actually influence aggregate demand through either channel?)
4. Can aggregate demand policy do the job, or do we need supplementary policies? What are the administrative and political problems of using such supplementary policies?
5. Underlying all the above questions, what are the relative social and individual costs of inflation and unemployment? What should our tradeoff function be between the two in the year ahead?

Case 11: Airline Takes the Marginal Route. The main lesson is pointed up in the box on page 276. As long as the marginal cost is below marginal revenue, it pays Continental Airlines to increase its output (add more flights), even though the extra income (marginal revenue) may not cover the full average cost of production. Continental's total profit is larger with the flights in question than without them. Mr. Whelan gets an *A* in Economics I.

But there is a second lesson, too, which Mr. Whelan recognizes in the tenth paragraph. Some flights can add to total profits even though they do not cover *full* costs, but clearly for all flights together income must cover full costs if the firm is to make a profit and to stay in business. Those marginal Continental flights are good business because the company has the planes, airport docks, reservation clerks, and other needed facilities on hand anyway. For purposes of this analysis, these are *fixed* costs; they go on whether or not Continental adds the marginal flights in question. As Whelan says, the out-of-pocket (marginal) approach comes into play only after the airline's basic schedule has been set—but income from some flights obviously has to cover all those costs if the company is to make a profit.

Case 12: How to Regulate Public Utilities. This is a tough problem, with which public utility commissions and economists have been unhappily wrestling for a long time. First, an unsatisfactory alternative: If we just let Hometown Electric set the price it wants, that will be about 6.9 cents, and Hometown will make a juicy profit of about $33,000 monthly. But marginal cost is only about 2.5 cents at that output, so price would be far above marginal cost, the condition for a socially optimum allocation of resources. Thus consumers would be getting too little electricity and paying too much for it.

How about following the social optimum rule of price = marginal cost and setting price at 5.5 cents (where *MC* intersects the demand curve on Figure 23–2)? At that price consumers would buy over 1,600,000 kilowatts, and the company would make a profit of about $20,000. Looks reasonable, but there may be a problem. Does the $20,000 provide the company with a fair rate of return on its investment, so that it will keep its capital invested in producing electricity here, and expand if demand rises? We can't tell from the limited data here, but if the price doesn't provide a fair rate of return we can expect resources to be pulled out and future shortages of electricity in Hometown.

Suppose the $20,000 *is* below the normal rate of return on Hometown's investment. How can we get the socially optimum price and output without a long-run outflow of resources because of inadequate profits? One answer is, have the government (all consumers) pay a lump-sum benefit to Hometown to bring its rate of return up to the market rate. This would be ideal economics, but no government unit has yet faced up to the political problems of explaining to the voters and the taxpayers the case for such a tax-financed subsidy to public utilities, especially when the underlying consumer demand data would only be roughly estimated.

As a practical matter, most regulatory commissions have substituted a second-best rule. They say to the utility: We'll give you an exclusive franchise; you produce as efficiently as possible, and charge the lowest price that will give you a fair return on your investment. Of course, this price may or may not be near marginal cost; in industries where demand is small relative to the most efficient scales of production, price may be far above *MC* although only approximately the same as *TUC* for that output. Moreover, this approach runs into two knotty problems: How shall we measure the company's investment, and what is a "fair" rate of return? As we shall see later, the investment figure varies greatly during inflations depending on whether we use the original cost of investment less depreciation or the higher replacement cost (because of the inflation). On rate of return, commissions and courts vary, often arbitrarily setting 6, 7, or 8 percent. Many lawyers and economists make a living arguing the proper rate in these cases.

Last, none of these plans offer anything about how to keep the company efficient and on its toes, to minimize costs without the pressure of competition.

What is your answer—both as to the optimum price and how to assure efficient operation and a continued adequate supply of electricity in Hometown?

Case 13: Advertising and Consumerism. The concepts and analysis of the preceding chapters should help you decide on the proposed legislation. Try answering the following questions:

1. Who would gain? What would be the benefits to them?
2. Who would lose? What would the costs be to them? (Look at different groups of consumers and businesses.)
3. Would paragraphs (1) and (2) infringe the freedom of speech or freedom of individuals to seek profits so long as they do no harm to others?
4. How should the FTC decide what advertising is "useful" to consumers? What advertising is "misleading"? (If you don't think these terms are sufficiently clear, can you suggest better ones?)
5. Would you be concerned about concentration of power in the hands of the FTC?
6. Would consumers have more or less influence over what businesses produce?
7. Would you expect the price of newspapers and magazines to change if the legislation passed? How?
8. Would you expect TV programing and financing arrangements to change? How?
9. If triple damage suits under paragraph (3) involved large settlements, who would you expect to bear the cost? In the short run? In the long run?
10. If you see problems with this proposal, can you suggest an alternative that you think the country needs?

Case 14: Battle of the Supermarkets. This case illustrates both the managerial and the social problems of oligopoly. The questions at the end of the case point up some of the main issues. Questions 1–6 focus on management problems in this oligopoly; so viewed, this case is much like the ones you will face if you go on to a graduate school of business. Questions 7–9 focus on the social issues; who will gain and who will lose, what is the public interest here, and what, if any, government intervention seems called for?

A&P's situation is a classic example of the problem faced by an oligopolistic market leader who is losing his share of the market. The A&P management surely knew that its price cutting would bring retaliation; presumably they decided that, nonetheless, this was their best chance of retaining their market share without such a serious price war that profits would be more than temporarily eroded. Possibly they were surprised at the vigor of the price war they started; many have criticized their managerial strategy. Another hypothesis is that they were really more interested in sales volume and growth than in profits per se. It's not clear what other steps they could have taken to improve their deteriorating position; they had tried the obvious measures such as more advertising, improved service, and the like.

The problem of the competitive chains is equally easy to understand, but no easier to solve. If they didn't meet the cuts, they would almost surely lose business to A&P, which would thus achieve its goal, at least in part. But meeting the cuts would clearly produce a price war, which would help no one's profits and would probably be hard to stop—which is precisely what happened. One approach would have been to fight back through advertising and other sales techniques, instead of cutting prices. And advertising budgets did rise. But this raises costs, and there's no guarantee that you can convince housewives to buy your products if they can get substantially the same thing cheaper down the street. Or you might just sit it out in the hope that A&P will soon see the costs of cutting its own prices and profits. Do you have a better alternative?

Note, too, the strong market pressures in such a case toward open (illegal) or covert collusion. If there were now some way to stop the price war, all firms would clearly be better off, especially some of the weaker ones that face extinction if their losses continue for long. But the law against price collusion is clear, and who dares risk being the leader in putting his prices back up to a profitable level and leaving them there to establish a new pattern without some assurance the others will go along? Only a strong, acknowledged price leader would dare to do so, and it's not obvious just which firm that is in this complex case. All things considered, from a managerial point of view, the case provides strong support for a price policy of leaving well enough alone in an oligopoly, as the text suggests is common practice in such markets.

Turning to the social issues, consumers seem to be the big gainers from the price war. But if the war ends up bankrupting many smaller, weaker firms, the long-run result is less clear. (Remember that's what some smaller firms say A&P is trying to do.) With fewer firms there's less certainty of effective competition to hold down prices in the future. Moreover, after taking a "bath" like this, you can be sure that every firm is going to think a long time before it risks starting another price war. And new investment in the industry is going to be unattractive unless there are both reasonably stable competitive relationships and reasonable returns on investment. The demand for food is growing steadily; unless investment in food retailing continues to grow, services to consumers will deteriorate.

Lastly, investors are part of society too. Price wars that benefit consumers can also bankrupt investors. Remembering that, what is "the public interest" in this case?

Case 15: Some Managerial Applications. These little cases are designed to illustrate the application of economic concepts and principles in relatively simple business situations. Because each example includes an explanation of the principles and concepts involved and how they apply, no further suggestions for analysis are needed.

Case 16: U.S. versus Von's Groceries. Just how many firms are needed to assure the benefits of competition under different conditions is a complex issue. The purpose of this case is to pose this problem in a particular situation, and to let you see how the Supreme Court goes about analyzing such cases when it must decide them under the law. Although it is important to understand something of how the Court applies the broadly stated law to particular cases, the main purpose is to induce you to think through for yourself what would best serve the public interest here, using your economic analysis to do so.

In arriving at your answer, consider the following questions:

1. What do we want competition to accomplish for us?
2. How many grocery firms does it take in the Los Angeles market to assure the benefits of competition? (Note both the total number of firms in the Los Angeles market, the share of market covered by the merger, and the small overlap in the markets served by Von's and Shopping Bag.)
3. How shall we balance the lower costs of supermarkets against the potentially greater competition among more small, but higher-cost, stores?
4. Should the purpose of antitrust be to protect competition or small competitors?

Case 17: Lockheed Aircraft Corporation. This case illustrates the problems that arise when big business and the military establishment become, perhaps inescapably, closely interlinked. Simple economic analysis suggests that by the dictates of the market and the profit-and-loss system, Lockheed should have had to take its lumps. Since it couldn't produce the aircraft at the committed price and still make a profit, it had failed and deserved to take the loss, possibly going bankrupt in the process. Ours is a profit-*and-loss* system; not everyone makes a profit all the time.

But the world of the military-industrial complex is not quite so simple. In the first place, Lockheed is dealing with the world's most powerful monopsonist, the U.S. government, and it's not clear whether the original contract price was a fair one, arrived at in fair bargaining as one would expect in a competitive market. Second, both Lockheed and the government know that there is a long history of renegotiated contracts where original bids have turned out to be too low to cover actual costs of production, and the government has the right to renegotiate if profits turn out to be "excessive," even if the main reason is the firm's efficiency. Third, the government needed Lockheed nearly as much as Lockheed needed the government, at least in the short run. For Lockheed to shut down would have been enormously costly to the military effort, and would have caused civilian unemployment and related disruption as well. If the government lost Lockheed, it would have to find someone else, probably a firm of similar size and capacities, to take its place. It's not clear that starting all over with someone else would have been cheaper.

But none of this changes the fact that the government (the taxpayer) took an awful beating on the original C-5A contract, and that we normally expect a producer to live up to his contracts and to swallow his losses if he's not efficient enough to cover his costs. In principle, the government ought to buy on competitive bids and insist that the winning bidder live up to his commitments. Huge cost overruns have been alarmingly common on military contracts, and it's hard to escape the impression that producers without normal market competition often aren't as efficient as they ought to be.

All things considered, complex negotiated contract prices and settlements when the original contract is clearly far off are probably inescapable on major military contracts for new, untried products. The best minds in both government and industry have worked on the problem for a long time and no one has come up with a foolproof answer yet. Many economists consider the Lockheed precedent a mistake, and they argue that we should move further toward a free competitive market for all government purchases. But buying a billion-dollar nuclear aircraft carrier or a billion-dollar fleet of radically-new bombers is a long way from ordering a few dozen shirts or even a thousand tons of cold-rolled steel. The military-industrial complex problem is indeed a complex one.

Case 18: The Economics of the Draft. Supply and demand, marginal productivity, and opportunity cost are the basic economic concepts we need to analyze the two approaches to the draft. The figure shows the economics of the draft, using rough illustrative figures for supply and demand curves. The left-hand portion shows the draft. Military pay is plotted on the vertical axis, the number of servicemen in the army on the horizontal axis. Since both are set by law, the equilibrium point (E) shows 2.5 million men in the army at an average rate of $5,000 per year. The supply curve is vertical, indicating that the required number of men will be forthcoming at whatever wage the army offers to pay, in this case $5,000;

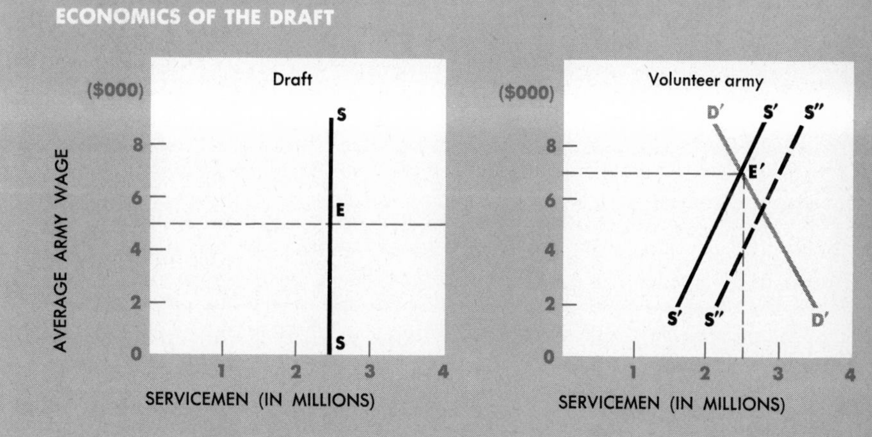

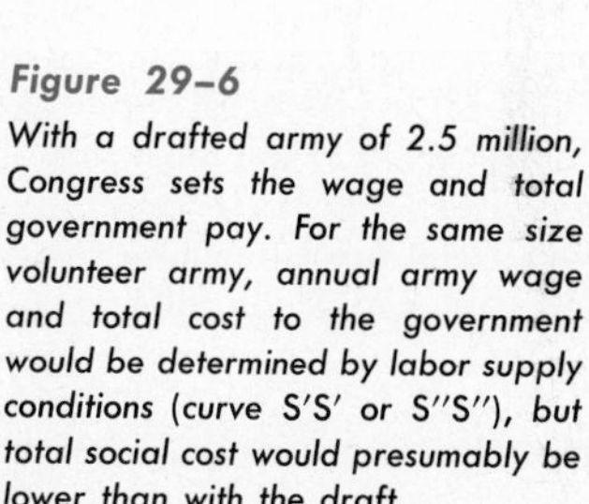
Figure 29–6

With a drafted army of 2.5 million, Congress sets the wage and total government pay. For the same size volunteer army, annual army wage and total cost to the government would be determined by labor supply conditions (curve S′S′ or S″S″), but total social cost would presumably be lower than with the draft.

the supply is perfectly inelastic. If Congress raises the average salary to $6,000, or lowers it to $4,000, the number of men in the army remains unchanged, while the tax bill for financing the army is increased or lowered correspondingly.

The right-hand portion of the figure shows the supply and demand situation if we had an army in which men volunteered in response to the wage offered, just as they do for other jobs. Thus, the supply curve ($S'S'$) slopes upward to the right, indicating that more men would volunteer at a higher wage than at a lower one. In the same way, the demand for servicemen ($D'D'$) slopes downward to the right, indicating that with high servicemen's pay, it would pay the army to use civilians for many posts that servicemen might fill under a draft; conversely it would pay the army to use more servicemen relative to civilians at a lower service wage.

Given the army's demand curve in the figure, it would hire 2.5 million men at an average wage of $7,000. It could get more by raising the offered wage; if it wished to get along with less, it could get them at a lower wage. The equilibrium E' at $7,000 is a $2,000 higher annual wage than E in the left-hand portion, indicating that in the draft many men are required to enter the armed services who would not do so voluntarily at that wage.

Note that the supply curve ($S'S'$) will presumably shift with economic conditions. If a depression comes with widespread civilian unemployment, more men will volunteer for military service at the same wage rates. For example, $S''S''$ might be the new supply curve, and the army could get its 2.5 million men for a $5,000 average wage.

Which is the economically cheaper way? Given the facts shown, with volunteer supply curve $S'S'$, clearly total army wages, and hence the nation's tax bill, are less in the draft case. With the draft, the total wage bill for 2.5 million men is $12.5 billion; with the volunteer army it is $17.5 billion. But from society's viewpoint the *real* cost of the army is the opportunity cost of the civilian goods foregone by having 2.5 million men in the army—and that opportunity cost will partly depend on who the men in the army are.

The amount each individual could earn in the private marketplace (his marginal revenue product) is a measure of the civilian output society foregoes if he serves in the army instead. Suppose a star athlete, like Kareem Abdul-Jabbar (formerly Lew Alcindor) is drafted. He would have earned, say, $200,000 in professional basketball, and that (not his army pay of $5,000) is the opportunity cost of his army service. Similarly, for every soldier drafted involuntarily at the army's going wage, the opportunity cost is presumably higher than his army wage. Clearly, to allocate these men to the army through the draft is to allocate them inefficiently in economic terms.

But if we don't draft Jabbar and others, the army still needs men. Would a volunteer army be cheaper in *real* (opportunity cost) terms. The answer is, "yes". $S'S'$ in the figure tells us that 2.5 million men would volunteer for army duty at a $7,000 wage. We can safely presume that these are people who would have made less, or certainly not very much more, in civilian life. Thus, the total civilian output foregone by having the men in the army is $7,000 per man per year, or less. In terms of overall economic efficiency, resources are best allocated by the voluntary service plan, leaving the choice up to each individual as to whether he prefers a $7,000 job in the army to what he can earn in civilian life. We can safely assume that Jabbar and other high civilian marginal product men will not volunteer for the army. Those whose marginal product is higher in the army go there, those with a higher civilian marginal product take civilian jobs.

There are two further efficiency arguments in favor of the volunteer army. When men are drafted, they seldom stay in the army more than the required two years. If the army were on a volunteer basis with higher pay, we can safely presume that more men would decide to undertake military careers, so the turnover in the armed services would be lower than it is with the draft. This would cut down the training costs involved. Second, with a volunteer army there would be a lower degree of uncertainty for everyone otherwise potentially subject to the draft. He would go into the army if he wished and the government would have to pay a high enough wage to be sure to obtain the number of men in the army they need at that wage.

Economics and Ethics. While a volunteer army would clearly be cheaper in terms of opportunity costs, that does not prove it would necessarily be better. Consider the ethical issues involved.

Presumably the major equity of the draft is that everyone has an equal chance of being chosen in a lottery system. But note the related inequities. If Jabbar is drafted at $5,000 away from a $200,000 civilian job, the implied tax rate he pays to support the defense effort is 97.5 percent. By comparison, a draftee with no civilian alternative above $5,000 pays no special tax at all, merely his regular income tax of a few percent of his income. Equitable? With a volunteer army, general taxpayers would pay what it takes to fill the armed services, not the luckless young men who happen to be drafted.

But opponents of the volunteer system reply that as a practical matter, a volunteer army would end up with mainly low-income men, including a heavy representation of blacks and other minorities who have limited civilian employment opportunities. To be sure, they might be making more in the army than they could in civilian life—but why should they be the cannon fodder while higher-income whites remain civilians?

It is far from obvious which arrangement is more equitable, even if the volunteer army is clearly more efficient economically. Probably a lot depends on whether army service involves any serious danger of wartime death or injury. In a war, especially an unpopular one, the fundamental argument that everyone should have to face an equal chance of death in battle appears to dominate, and indeed it is not clear that any army wage would fill a volunteer army during a major war. But during peacetime, the case for a volunteer army, on both equity and economic grounds, looks strong to most observers.

A concluding question to focus the issues: If we use a military draft, should we use a similar draft to preempt men for police, postal, and all other public-service duties, at a wage equal to that paid in the armed forces draft? Or, at a more extreme level, should we preempt workers through a draft-like plan to make steel and to mine coal, rather than leaving it up to the private economy where firms clearly have to pay more than army draft wage rates? A volunteer army would determine who serves by the same method that laborers are normally allocated to different industries in the United States.

Case 19: The Economics of Minimum Wage Laws. 1. Assume that a $2.50 minimum wage is passed by Congress. This is above the existing wage rate for many workers, and economic theory says that it will now pay employers to hire fewer workers, if they are profit-maximizers. Workers whose marginal productivity is less than $2.50 will lose their jobs, although those who keep their jobs will get at least the $2.50 minimum rate. The new jobless may stay unemployed or they may go to work elsewhere in jobs not covered by the minimum-wage law. If they do the latter, the uncovered substandard wages are forced even lower as the labor supply there rises without any increase in demand. One net result is to injure many of the lowest-wage, lowest-income workers whom the law was designed to help, and especially unskilled young people, because they are the ones with the lowest marginal productivities.[1]

2. If employers were "exploiting" labor before the law by paying wages below labor's marginal productivity, the minimum-wage law might simply boost wages without reducing employment. Wages would then get more of the consumer's dollar, profits less. This is the situation implicitly assumed in most of the ardent arguments for minimum-wage legislation.

3. Even if there is no exploitation of labor, the law's upward pressure on wage rates may drive employers to more efficient methods, thereby absorbing the higher wages without reducing employment. This, too, is a favorite argument of minimum-wage advocates. How often it works this way is not clear from the evidence. A lot depends on how effective businessmen have been at running their businesses without the pressures of the minimum-wage laws. If they were maximizing profits before, the results are as described in the first paragraph above.

4. Minimum-wage laws tend to redistribute incomes—from employers to labor, and mainly from workers who get pushed out to those who keep their jobs at higher pay. What happens to the total labor share in the national income depends basically on the elasticity of demand for labor. If employers' aggregate demand for labor is inelastic, the law will mean higher total wage payments. Unfortunately, we don't know what the general elasticity of demand for labor is, though we do know that higher wages induce the substitution of capital for labor over extended periods. It's much easier to estimate what the elasticity may be in particular industries at particular times. The impact of a minimum-wage law is uneven, operating mainly against low-productivity workers wherever they are.

5. While the above analysis is correct, as a practical matter the minimum-wage law probably hasn't had much effect thus far on the American economy. It has been repealed by inflation. By the time the act originally went into effect, minimum wages in most covered industries had already risen above the specified level. Wages in some industries, especially in the South, lagged behind the minimum figures, but these were mainly industries not covered by the law—agriculture, services, local shops, and so on. Further inflation and rising wages robbed first

[1]Note that the effect here and in the following points is substantially the same as if an economy-wide union was enforcing the minimum wage.

a new $.75, then a $1.00, a $1.25, a $1.40, and a $1.60 legal minimum of much of their intended impact. If inflation continues, it would again tend to erode the effect of the new $2.50 minimum—although even then the $2.50 floor would affect low-wage pockets throughout the economy, and such special low-productivity groups as uneducated workers and teen-agers. Recent legislation has broadened the coverage to include most occupations.

Given this analysis, what is your answer on the proposed $2.50 minimum wage? Clearly, it is likely to have conflicting results. Where you come out will depend largely on which effects you think would predominate, and how you weight the welfare of different groups in the economy.

Case 20: Actual and Nominal Interest Rates. Suggestions for analysis are given with the case at the end of Chapter 31.

Case 21: Profits for the Picking? Suggestions for analysis are given with the case in Chapter 32.

Case 22: Black Economic Development. Economically, the integrationists clearly have the better advice to offer. Consider the basic concepts and principles from Parts Three and Four, and look at the black ghetto resident as worker and as consumer.

Productivity and Wages. Most ghetto residents get all their income (except for welfare and other such transfer payments and for income from crime, such as dope pushing and "numbers") from wages and salaries. The analysis of Chapters 28 and 29 tells us that higher real wages depend fundamentally on higher productivity. Low black ghetto incomes reflect a multitude of causes, but most of these can be summed up in low productivity of workers and scarcity of capital in the ghetto, plus discrimination. The fundamental road to more income for ghetto families lies in higher productivity of their breadwinners. It lies in improving worker skills by education and training, and in harder, more reliable work. At least equally, it lies in more capital to work with, regardless of the source, because most rising worker incomes reflect increasing amounts of capital per worker. It thus lies in facilitating the movement of both capital and labor to those markets where their marginal productivity is highest.

Discrimination. Clearly, black wages would be higher if discrimination were reduced. But alas, what ghetto blacks themselves can do to reduce discrimination is limited, at least through direct economic action. Blacks may boycott white firms that discriminate against them. But this is a costly policy for poor blacks if, as is often true, prices are higher in black- than in white-owned stores, frequently because local black stores are too small to gain the economies of large-scale production and because their other costs are higher. Blacks' most promising weapons against discrimination are probably political and moral. Your basic economics can show you the costs of discrimination (see Chapter 29), but it doesn't show how to alter people's ethical, economic, and political standards.

Maximizing Consumer Satisfaction. Given their incomes, black consumers get the most for their money by buying where prices are lowest for the goods and services they want. (The formal analysis is in Chapter 5.) Perhaps the black consumer gets special satisfaction from buying from other blacks (that is, from discriminating against white sellers). If so, he will maximize his utility by buying from blacks even at higher prices, but he will not maximize his real income. And, as was noted in the preceding paragraph, most studies show consumer goods' prices higher in black ghetto stores than in white stores, especially those outside the ghetto. Ghetto prices are higher, whether in white- or black-owned stores, because ghetto costs are higher. Blacks (and other low-income consumers as well) are often cheated through unscrupulous sales agreements and hidden charges on durables, but this treatment is not confined to white sellers. More protection of low-income consumers is needed in the ghetto and out, but the proposition remains that the ghetto black will maximize his real income by buying where he gets the best bargain, whether from white or black, in the ghetto or out.

Specialization, Exchange, and Comparative Advantage. Both economic analysis and history warn against black economic separatism as the approach to raising ghetto incomes. The ghetto is poor mainly because its workers' productivities are low and because its inhabitants own little capital of their own. To shut off economic flows between the ghetto and the rest of the economy will not raise ghetto productivities; indeed, it will lower them insofar as it limits both the movement of ghetto residents to jobs outside the ghetto and the flow of capital into the ghetto. To build an economic wall around the ghetto is to guarantee its continued poverty.

The economic fallacy that regions or nations can improve their economic lot by "keeping the money at home" is an old one. Many observers, but few economists, argue that the ghetto is poor merely because it is bled by white capitalists, who withdraw their ill-gotten gains. Undoubtedly, many slum landlords behave this way. But in fact the rate of return on business investment in the ghetto is generally below that on nonghetto investment in spite of what seem to be discriminatorily high prices. And profits comprise only a small part of most sales' dollars. To require that all profits made in the ghetto be reinvested there would only reduce further the attractiveness of the ghetto as an area for outside investment, which is so desperately needed.

Suppose, ghetto residents spent their money only within the ghetto, shutting off the flow of funds between the ghetto and the rest of the economy. This would merely further impoverish the ghetto. For example, Harlem would soon be very hungry indeed if it were to shut off all outpayments from local grocery stores for food products. To raise its own wheat, grind its own flour, and bake its own bread would mainly raise the price of bread to very high levels, even if it were feasible to raise the wheat in Harlem. So it is with other production. The cheapest food is that produced where it can be raised most efficiently. Ghetto residents, like other individuals, regions, and nations, will generally obtain the highest real incomes by specializing on the work they do best, in or out of the ghetto, and using their earnings to buy goods and services most efficiently produced by others. This principle of comparative advantage was a central principle in Parts Three and Four, and is again the center of attention in Part Six.

It is important to reemphasize that this has been a purely *economic* analysis. Psychologically and politically, black economic independence may be so important as to overcome the economic advantages of interdependence with the white economy. If so, it should be so recognized on its own merits, with recognition of the economic costs involved. *Economic* progress for most blacks in the ghettos will depend heavily on their effective interaction with the total economy. [A useful reference is Carolyn S. Bell's *The Economics of the Ghetto* (New York: Pegasus Books, 1970).]

Note also that the question in the case is narrowly confined to the issue of black separatism versus economic integration. There are many other issues involved in the problem of minority ghettos in the large cities. Many other measures may be useful in raising ghetto incomes, improving the ghetto economic and social environment, and, perhaps most fundamentally, dispersing existing big-city ghettos by opening up both jobs and better housing in the now-largely-white suburbs. (See Case 23, The Urban Crisis, at the end of Chapter 35 and the references there, most of which are equally applicable here.) Last, your macroeconomics will remind you that prosperous times can do much to help ghetto residents; conversely in recession ghetto workers are often the first to be laid off. But there is little that separatism can do to assure prosperity, even in the ghetto. Residents there, like others, must rely heavily on government monetary and fiscal policy to help assure a stably growing, prosperous economy.

More Jobs by Keeping the Money at Home. All this has skipped the argument that jobs for unemployed ghetto blacks would be created by blacks' spending their money only in the ghetto, not elsewhere. The high economic cost to consumers (everyone) of doing so was indicated above. But would it, nevertheless, create jobs for the ghetto unemployed?

There is an obvious parallel to the problem faced by poor, less-developed countries internationally. Would Nigeria create jobs for poor Nigerians by shutting out all imports and requiring Nigerians to buy only home-produced products? Some new jobs might well be produced, making goods that were formerly imported; but if Nigeria stops buying foreigners' products, how long will they keep buying Nigeria's exports? Unless we assume that the outside world will continue to buy from Nigeria without selling to her, an unlikely event, the gain in new import-substitution jobs will soon be offset by the loss of jobs in the export industries. (The reasoning is spelled out in more detail in Chapters 38 and 39.)

Try applying the reasoning yourself to the ghetto.

Case 23: The Urban Crisis. 1. The most striking fact about the urban crisis is that it is a mass of externalities. If one landlord lets his property run down, this reduces the value of nearby properties. If crime and drugs infest one block, housing values drop and middle-income families move out. When they move, values fall and deterioration spreads to the next blocks. If higher taxes are required to pay the police and sanitation workers in poor areas, all of New York becomes less attractive to new investment. It is doubtful that private initiative will solve the problem of urban slum decay under these conditions. Collective action seems essential, and action reaching beyond housing per se. Expensive public housing units have deteriorated rapidly in city slums, as they are engulfed by poverty, social decay, and vandalism.

2. Economic analysis warns that, although

rent ceilings may temporarily hold down rents, enforcement will be difficult and the long-run effect will be to reduce the supply of housing and to raise rents. This result is clear in New York. Landlords have little incentive to build new apartments, or even to maintain old ones, unless they produce income exceeding costs. It is evident from the absence of new, private, low-cost housing that it is simply not profitable to build. Removing rent ceilings would lead to higher rents in the short run, but would open the way to more construction, renovation, and maintenance of existing housing over the longer run.

3. Even without rent ceilings, it is not clear that the stock of low-income housing would be increased in the central city. Land is expensive; construction costs, taxes, and operating costs have risen astronomically; risks are high in low-income neighborhoods; and the ability of low- and middle-income families to pay is limited. Most building cost studies suggest that there no longer can be unsubsidized new low-cost housing in cities like New York. Costs simply place any new housing out of reach of low-income families' ability to pay. This suggests that programs to maintain and renovate existing housing, even though the results are still old housing, offer the only hope of success without massive government subsidies. Whether private maintenance and renovation will occur without subsidy depends on the costs of individual projects compared to expected returns; the outlook is not promising for city slum areas.

4. Suggestions 5 and 6 sound nice, but economics warns you not to hope for much. If entrepreneurs could figure out ways of constructing mass housing cheaply, we can be reasonably sure they'd be doing it already. The potential returns are enormous. Similarly, consider the incentives of construction unions to take lower wages. From their viewpoint, why should they? Again, if we want these changes, government action is probably essential—to subsidize housing construction research and legislation to reduce union restrictions on entry—but how much even these steps would stimulate low-rent housing is uncertain.

5. The long-run future of the central city is a complex economic, social, and political question. Many economists, but by no means all, believe that in the long run low-income families must move or be moved out of the central cities to the suburbs, where the jobs increasingly are and where lower housing costs are feasible. The central city may have a viable future only as a location for commercial and financial enterprises, cultural activities, and living quarters for the well-to-do who prefer city life. Costs are simply too high for low-income families and many businesses that don't need the city environment.

This analysis can lead to two different conclusions. One is government measures to help pull or push poor central city families to the suburbs as rapidly as possible, including measures to open up the suburbs to them. The other is, no government action at all—just let the forces of the market work. The central city slums will worsen and gradually people will emigrate from the cities, in their own self-interest. Self-interest here, as in the past, is the only reliable and workable way of accomplishing massive economic changes, according to this reasoning. Government actions to "gild the ghetto" will not only cost huge sums of money and fail, but will also counteract the basic economic forces at work to make both city and suburbs serve their economic functions. Many economists have considerable sympathy with this analysis, however painful it may seem, but they are unwilling to pay the human costs involved in letting market forces do the whole job. Instead, they favor a composite strategy of helping to improve the lot of the poor in the central cities but simultaneously pushing measures to get them to the suburbs as rapidly as possible.

6. For many, the greedy landlord is the devil in the slum housing piece. While some slumlords have no doubt made large profits, your economics should warn you of two major difficulties faced by this theory. First, the evidence of landlords abandoning their properties outright is simply inconsistent with the presumption that they are making handsome profits on them. Second, even if we feel that landlords *should* be content with lower returns on their capital, how can we force them to keep investing in low-income housing when they find the profit prospects unattractive? Rent ceilings are one approach to putting on pressure. Strict enforcement of city code standards on plumbing, heat, sanitation, and the like to provide better housing for tenants is another. Both may temporarily help low-income tenants, but over time, both will decrease the stock of available, low-rent housing, desirable though they may be.

7. The huge expenditure of government funds on public and subsidized private housing for the poor over the past decades, with little apparent success, has driven many observers to reconsider the entire approach. Believers in private enterprise increasingly urge that the government's most useful approach is to assure a decent minimum income to all (perhaps through a negative income tax), and

then let the recipients spend what and where they will on housing, leaving the private market free to respond to these housing expenditures. If you want better housing for the poor, but believe in the ability of the individual to judge best how to maximize his own satisfaction and in the market to respond to consumer dollars, this may seem an attractive alternative. But before you jump on the bandwagon, don't forget those externalities back in the first paragraph. Trying to prescribe for the urban housing crisis is a sobering experience, for experienced economists as well as for beginners.

Case 24: The $66 Billion Mistake. If you are an ardent environmentalist, you may be understandably wary of a proposal on auto pollution control by one of the major oil companies. Clearly, you have no basis for judging the accuracy of Mobil's $66 billion estimate, and that is not the main point of the case. The $66 billion has been disputed, as has been the exact nature of the rising cost curve in Chart 2. If you prefer, assume that the $66 billion extra cost is only $33 billion and that the Chart 2 curve only rises half as fast between the California and national standards, figures that even Mobil critics would agree are reasonable. In analyzing the proposals, it may be useful to focus on the three broad questions (using whichever cost figure you prefer).

1. How clean is clean enough? Is meeting the 1976 clean air standards for auto emissions worth $66 (or $33) billion over the next ten years? Note that economics can give no one "right" answer to this question; each person must decide for himself whether having air that is clean is worth the alternatives foregone. Marginalism and alternative cost are the key concepts here. Mobil is right in stressing the other things we could get with our $66 billion if we settle for the California standards on air cleanliness. But be careful about the figures; Mobil's $66 billion extra cost is spread over ten years, while most of the alternatives given are for one year.

2. Accepting the need for government controls, should the direct regulation approach be used, as Mobil suggests, or would we be better served by an effluent-charge approach (for example, a special charge per unit of emission from each car, perhaps based on the type of car and mileage driven annually, or a special tax on gasoline)? Should every car owner pay the same amount (by buying an emission-control system for his car), regardless of how much, and where, he drives? Regulation versus stress on individual incentives is a big issue here.

3. If Congress accepts the Mobil proposal for large, modern, mass transit systems, who should pay the bill—the general taxpayer (as Mobil suggests), car drivers, mass transit riders, local taxpayers in the areas served? What principle do you use in deciding who should pay?

Case 25: Imports: Bane or Boon? This case requires no extended suggestions for analysis. For the most part, Mr. Abel's statement is in head-on opposition to the reasoning supporting freer trade in Chapter 39, with one important exception. Abel argues that the presumed advantages of free trade are not obtained when multinational corporations use cheap labor to manufacture abroad and then sell here because they retain all the lower-cost advantages for themselves as profits. Consumers, he argues, do not benefit.

If Abel is right, clearly the presumed consumer gain from free international trade would be short-circuited. How would you check up on his allegation? Note that there are two ways. One would be to look at profits of multinational firms compared to others; this would not be definitive, because many other factors also influence company profits. The other is to use your theory, which tells you to ask whether substantial competition exists in the areas discussed by Abel. If there is competition, and other firms selling in the United States are free to duplicate low-cost production overseas, we can be reasonably sure the multinational firms won't be able to hold onto their excess profits because competition will force prices down toward costs of production.

On the basis of Abel's statement, under what conditions do you believe he would favor free trade? What steps do you believe the U.S. government might take to "raise substandard wage levels abroad to acceptable minimums," so that there would be "fair competition" between U.S. and overseas workers?

Case 26: Up or Out for Gold? This case raises complex issues. It is useful to separate the major questions.

1. On the central issue of whether the world should return to the international gold standard, economists heavily vote no. The reasons are indicated in the closing section of Chapter 41, and in the earlier discussions of the reasons for the downfall of the gold standard.

2. If we want to eliminate gold gradually from the international monetary scene, it makes little sense to emphasize its role by raising its price and expanding its role in international reserves. Even if

we continue, as now, to use gold as one part of international reserves, raising the official price would be a dubious step. (a) First, under the two-tier system, central banks do not buy or sell gold, except among themselves. To raise the official price would inevitably encourage expectations of a revived role for gold in monetary systems and would stimulate further speculation on further gold price increases (currency devaluations). Note that there is no necessary connection between the official and free-market gold prices if central banks stick to the two-tier system. Soaring free-market gold prices make big headlines, but no necessary problems for central banks and monetary policy. In the free market, gold is just another commodity. (b) Raising the official price would increase the danger of more worldwide inflation by increasing most nations' international reserves. (c) It would give special profits to South Africa, the USSR, and those governments and individuals who have speculated against the major currencies by hoarding gold, not a list of those who most deserve special advantage. (d) It would stimulate the use of further resources to dig gold out of the ground, assuming that central banks would buy gold at the new higher price. Counterbalancing advantages: Aside from the special profits for goldholders, the big increase in world reserves would be the major gain, and it's far from clear that the world now needs increased inflationary potential.

3. The case illustrates the sharply differing national interests involved in many international monetary issues. It's not hard to understand why the French and Americans differ here.

4. The French position highlights a basic weakness of the international gold-plus-dollars system of the past two decades. The United States has been able to run continuous deficits while the Western European nations and Japan have, as a practical matter, been unable to convert their growing stock of excess dollars into gold or other currencies without destroying the set of stable exchange parities they were committed to maintain. While the French and other nations could use their excess dollars to buy more American goods and services, to do so would destroy their payments surpluses and threaten the jobs of their domestic workers. It is easy to understand why other nations should resent America's continuing huge deficits under these circumstances, even though their refusal to buy more American goods was partly responsible. But the solution seems to most economists to lie more along the lines of reforms outlined in Chapter 41 and suggested by the American position in the second paragraph of the case, than in moving back toward the international gold standard.

Case 27: The Energy Crisis. In considering the two major alternative approaches to the energy crisis, be concrete as to what would be done under each. Specifically, what new government regulations would you suggest to increase energy production without permitting drastically higher prices, or large direct subsidies to producers that amount to much the same thing since we are nearly all both taxpayers and energy buyers. How would you make gas and oil companies drill more domestic wells if you hold prices below profitable levels and raise costs by antipollution regulations? How would you induce power companies to build the new nuclear plants you need where you want them? How would you reduce the pollution from autos without sharply higher prices or rationing of fuel?

If you chose the individual-incentive (price system) route, would you free energy prices from all government controls? (Remember that electricity and gas are widely considered public utilities.) Whichever approach you favor, how would you deal with the ever-present tradeoff between energy and ecology?

Nowhere is the fundamental economic problem of tradeoffs more central than here. The tradeoffs that face us are all too painfully evident. We can have cleaner air and water *if* we accept less energy or more expensive energy. We can have wanted energy *if* we pay more for it and *if* we will forego some of our environmental goals. How much dirtier air should we accept to keep down the prices of gas, oil, and electricity—for example, by using more coal with modified clean-air standards? There's no such thing as a free lunch, is the number one lesson of economics. In thinking through your solution, you should find the following concepts from earlier chapters useful:

Alternative cost—tradeoffs.

Marginalism—comparison of alternatives at the margin, rather than on an all-or-nothing basis.

Rising marginal costs—the more energy we want, the more it will cost to find and produce each additional unit; similarly with rising standards for cleanliness and the environment. How clean is clean enough when the cost in terms of energy prices rises rapidly?

Importance of economic incentives—how can we make individuals and businesses act "in the public interest" if the action is not in their own self-interests? (For example, how shall we convince consumers to economize on natural gas, and gas companies to drill for more, if the price of natural gas is held down?)

Importance of technical advance

Interdependence—any move on one part of the energy problem is likely to affect other parts. If we raise the price of natural gas, users will shift to oil and create an oil "shortage," which in turn will create tanker and dock "shortages" and probable price increases by foreign oil producers. Refusal to build the Alaskan pipeline would increase demand for parts for atomic reactors and raise their prices. In the energy problem, interdependence is inescapable.

INDEXES

Subject Index

D

E

F

I

Q

R

Name Index

C

D

E

F

G

H

I

J

K

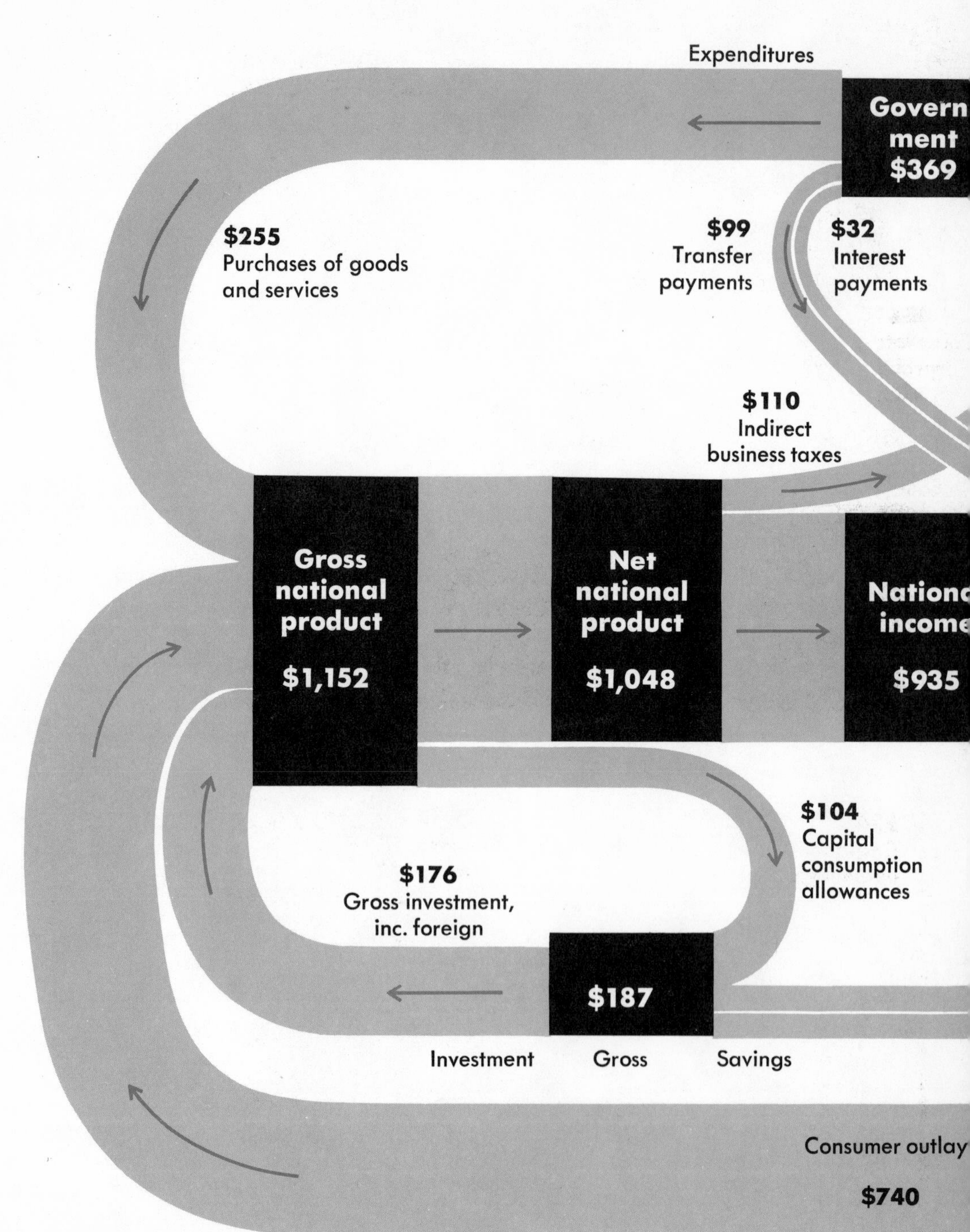

Expenditures
Govern
ment
$369
$255
Purchases of goods
and services
$99
Transfer
payments
$32
Interest
payments
$110
Indirect
business taxes
Gross
national
product
$1,152
Net
national
product
$1,048
Nationa
income
$935
$104
Capital
consumption
allowances
$176
Gross investment,
inc. foreign
$187
Investment
Gross
Savings
Consumer outlay
$740